CONSTITUTIONAL LAW
IN AMERICAN POLITICS

☆   ☆   ☆   ☆   ☆

CONSTITUTIONAL LAW IN AMERICAN POLITICS

John R. Schmidhauser
University of Southern California

Brooks/Cole Publishing Company
Monterey, California

Brooks/Cole Publishing Company
A Division of Wadsworth, Inc.

Printed in the United States of America

10 9 8 7 6 5 4 3 2 1

LIBRARY OF CONGRESS CATALOGING IN PUBLICATION DATA
Schmidhauser, John R. (John Richard), [date]
    Constitutional law in American politics.

    Includes index.
    1. United States—Constitutional law—Interpretation
and construction—History. 2. United States. Supreme
Court—History. 3. Political questions and judicial
power—United States—History. I. Title.
KF4550.S25 1984   342.73′02   83-25210

ISBN 0-534-03244-3   347.3022

Sponsoring Editor: Marquita Flemming
Production Editor: Gay L. Orr
Manuscript Editor: Carol L. King
Permissions Editor: Carline Haga
Interior and Cover Design: Stanley Rice
Interior Illustration: Kathie and Ralph
Typesetting: Omegatype Typography, Inc.
Printing and Binding: The Maple Press Company

Preface

The constitutional decisions of the United States Supreme Court have an enduring impact upon the American citizenry and the American political system, and the Court's subtle but often direct power and influence as a political institution are important matters for study and analysis. This book is organized to explore the Supreme Court's development as both a judicial and a political institution.

Many students entering a liberal arts or pre-law program are aware that the Supreme Court has stimulated tremendous changes in public education. Some may be personally aware of decisions of a more specialized nature: Students from the Pacific Northwest who enjoy sports fishing, for example, may be keenly aware of the Court's action upholding certain native American fishing rights safeguarded in 19th-century treaties. However, the significance of many important Supreme Court decisions is often not recognized or is only remotely perceived by students. This text is designed to inform interested students and enable them to independently explore and evaluate the Court's major constitutional decisions.

For several academic generations it has been asserted, as if it were a novel discovery, that the Supreme Court of the United States is a political institution, or that it is a judicial institution that engages in activities that classify it as political. Most contemporary students would not be surprised by these characterizations. Since it is obvious that the Court utilizes judicial procedures in the exercise of considerable political power and influence, it is appropriate to explore what kind of a political institution it really is. Does it allocate constitutional power and dispense influence in the same manner as chief executives and legislators? Or is the role of the justices fundamentally different, as is often argued? Is that role influenced primarily by internal institutional procedures and traditions such as *stare decisis* (the adherence to precedent) and an aloofness from the day-to-day conflicts and compromises of external politics? The limitations imposed by the judicial role require considerable attention. Finally, does the Supreme Court of the United States respond to the needs or requirements of significant economic and political developments? And if so, how? These basic questions serve to emphasize the important and diverse dimensions of the political role of the Supreme Court.

Some Comments and Recommendations for Teachers

The work of Christopher Columbus Langdell, the major developer of the case method, and subsequent conventional law school emphasis upon a particular, rather formalistic perspective for the organization of constitutional law textbooks have been the dominant influences in political science law textbooks since the 19th century. The fundamentals of such a perspective consist of basic commitments to a number of subject matter categories of cases, and emphasis upon form, and, often, a tendency to eschew political analysis or explanation. The subject matter categories have been retained as a basic organizing concept for most case books that are politically oriented: Categories such as the contract clause, separation of powers, or civil liberties are generally employed. Political analysis usually consists of attached commentary or an occasional article reproduced from a political science or public affairs journal. Even when an historical arrangement of cases and subject matter categories is employed (such as by sequential chief justices), the underlying organizing principle is *doctrinal* rather than *political* change. In short, the political analysis ordinarily has been a secondary consideration as an organizing principle. This book differs from both the traditional law school-oriented model and the "politics is secondary" model, and emphasizes the primacy of politics.

Doctrinal developments are not, of course, omitted. They are an integral part of the examination of the social and political role of the Supreme Court. The relationship of important doctrinal developments and innovative judicial approaches to major political transformations are explored in the textual discussions of the substantive chapters. The clash of different political generations in American constitutional development was made virtually inevitable by the constitutional guarantee for life tenure, on good behavior, for justices and judges, a matter fully discussed in subsequent chapters. In addition to this chapter by chapter examination, the interrelationship of judicial doctrine and political change is summarized comparatively in historical sequences in the Table of Comparisons provided immediately after the table of Contents.

The three introductory tables

In order to provide flexibility in the organization and presentation of the textual analysis and the Supreme Court decisions, three introductory tables have been provided. The first is a standard table of contents arranged in accordance with the major political transformations; a number of subheadings in each chapter provide comfortable access to the major portions of each. The second, as mentioned earlier, is a table of comparisons that references each major topical doctrinal development in comparison with the salient political changes of each historical era. Third, a complete table of cases is included. Titles of principal cases, which are reproduced in whole or in part in the text, are in *italics*; all other cases are referenced in roman type.

The use of chapter 11

Chapter 11 may be employed flexibly. It is designed to fulfill two related purposes. First, it provides a chronological account of the significant changes in Supreme Court membership and ideological positions in the context of each critical election and other less dramatic electoral changes. Thus, students may occasionally refer to the portion of this chapter that is related to the textual exposition of Court decisions. Second, after most or all of the textual material in Chapters 1 through 10 has been completed by the class, Chapter 11 read in its entirety provides a comprehensive appraisal of the total relationship of critical elections to personnel changes and doctrinal transformation on the Supreme Court throughout its entire history.

ACKNOWLEDGEMENTS

This book owes a great deal to the foundation in American constitutional law and history that was the basis for the graduate program at the University of Virginia in the 1950s. I am especially grateful for the training and inspiration of two excellent professors at Charlottesville, James Hart and George W. Spicer.

A number of reviewers read *Constitutional Law in American Politics* in manuscript and made valuable suggestions. I would like to thank Michael McCann, University of Washington; Robert J. Steamer, University of Massachusetts; Burton Atkins, Florida State University; Thomas G. Walker, Emory University; Albert Melone, University of Southern Illinois at Carbondale; Justin Green, Virginia Polytechnic Institute and State University; Jerry Goldman, Northwestern University; Austin Sarat, Amherst College; and George Cole, University of Connecticut.

Editor Marquita Flemming, Production Editor Gay Orr, and the entire editorial staff at Brooks/Cole Publishing Company were very helpful. Stan Rice designed the book. Patricia Johnson, Kay Neves, Jody Battles, and Candace Chronister provided expert manuscript typing.

And finally, at home, Thelma, Sara, and Susan were supportive and understanding.

John R. Schmidhauser

Contents

7 The Supreme Court and the Critical Election of 1896: The Triumph of Conservative Principles and the Decline of Public Participation and Confidence 255

8 The New Deal and the Supreme Court Crisis: Its Dimensions and Its Aftermath   352

9 The Transformation of Judicial Values in the 1950s and 1960s: A Judicial Revolution without a Critical Election   429

Table of Comparisons:
The Relationship of Doctrinal Change to Major Political Transformations

Table of Comparisons: The Relationship of Doctrinal Change to Major Political Transformations

Major political transformations

- The American Revolution (1776)
- The adoption of the Constitution (1789)
- The critical election of 1800
- The critical election of 1828
- The critical election of 1860 and the South's revolt against the Union in 1861
- The critical election of 1896
- The critical election of 1932
- The aftermath of the New Deal (1945)
- The Nixon era and its successors (1968)

Judicial review and the scope and limitations of judicial power

- *Marbury* v. *Madison* (1803)
- *Stuart* v. *Laird* (1803)
- *United States* v. *Judge Peters* (1809) [Also listed under Federalism]
- *Martin* v. *Hunter's Lessee* (1816)
- *Cohens* v. *Virginia* (1821)
- *Eakin* v. *Raub* (1825)
- *Prigg* v. *Pennsylvania* (1842)
- *Luther* v. *Borden* (1849)
- *Dred Scott* v. *Sanford* (1857)
- *Ableman* v. *Booth* (1859)
- *Ex Parte McCardle* (1869)
- *Baker* v. *Carr* (1962)
- *Wesberry* v. *Sanders* (1964)

Federalism

- *Chisholm* v. *Georgia* (1793)
- *Ware* v. *Hylton* (1796)
- *Calder* v. *Bull* (1798)
- *United States* v. *Judge Peters* (1809) [Also listed under judicial power]
- *McCulloch* v. *Maryland* (1819)
- *Barron* v. *Baltimore* (1833)
- *Bank of Augusta* v. *Earle* (1839)
- *Texas* v. *White* (1869)
- *The Slaughterhouse Cases* (1872)
- *Kansas* v. *Colorado* (1907)
- *Coyle* v. *Smith* (1911)
- *Missouri* v. *Holland* (1920)
- *Pennsylvania* v. *Nelson* (1956)
- *Cooper* v. *Aaron* (1958)

Commerce clause

- *Gibbons* v. *Ogden* (1824)
- *Willson* v. *Blackbird Creek Marsh Company* (1829)
- *New York* v. *Miln* (1837)
- *The Passenger Cases* (1849)
- *Cooley* v. *Board of Wardens of the Port of Philadelphia* (1851)
- *Wabash, St. Louis, and Pacific Railway Company* v. *Illinois* (1886)
- *United States* v. *E.C. Knight Company* (1895)
- *In Re Debs* (1895)
- *Interstate Commerce Commission* v. *Cincinnati, New Orleans, and Texas Pacific Railway Company* (1897)
- *Champion* v. *Ames* (1903)
- *Northern Securities Company* v. *United States* (1904)
- *Swift and Company* v. *United States* (1905)
- *Adair* v. *United States* (1908) [Also listed under Fifth Amendment due process clause]
- *Loewe* v. *Lawlor* (1908)
- *Standard Oil Company of New Jersey* v. *United States* (1911)

...Railway Company v. United States (1914)
- Hammer v. Dagenhart (1918)
- Schechter Poultry Corporation v. United States (1935)
- National Labor Relations Board v. Jones and Laughlin Steel Corporation (1937)
- United States v. Darby Lumber Company (1941)
- Wickard v. Filburn (1942)
- Heart of Atlanta Motel, Inc. v. United States (1964)
- Katzenbach v. McClung (1964)
- National League of Cities v. Usery (1977)

Contract clause
- Van Horne's Lessee v. Dorrance (1795)
- Fletcher v. Peck (1810)
- New Jersey v. Wilson (1812)
- Dartmouth College v. Woodward (1819)
- Proprietors of Charles River Bridge v. Proprietors of Warren Bridge (1837)
- Home Building and Loan Association v. Blaisdell (1934)

Economic applications of the Due Process Clauses of the Fifth and Fourteenth Amendments
- Munn v. Illinois (1877)
- Chicago, Milwaukee, and St. Paul Railway Company v. Minnesota (1890)
- Smythe v. Ames (1898)
- Lochner v. New York (1905)
- Muller v. Oregon (1908)
- Adair v. United States (1908)
- Bunting v. Oregon (1917)
- Truax v. Corrigan (1921)
- Adkins v. Children's Hospital (1923)
- Wolff Packing Company v. Court of Industrial Relations (1923)
- Nebbia v. New York (1934)
- West Coast Hotel v. Parrish (1937)

First Amendment freedoms: Speech, press, religion
- Schenck v. United States (1919)
- Gitlow v. New York (1925)
- Near v. Minnesota (1933)
- DeJonge v. Oregon (1937)
- West Virginia State Board of Education v. Barnette (1943)
- New York Times Company v. Sullivan (1964)
- New York Times Company v. United States (1971)
- Miller v. California (1973)
- Buckley v. Valeo (1976)
- First National Bank of Boston v. Bellotti (1978) [Also listed under corp. as citizen and person]

Executive authority
- Kendall v. United States (1839)
- The Prize Cases (1863)
- Ex Parte Milligan (1866)
- Mississippi v. Johnson (1867)

Major political transformations

Timeline column headers:

- The American Revolution (1776)
- The adoption of the Constitution (1789)
- The critical election of 1800
- The critical election of 1828
- The critical election of 1860 and the South's revolt against the Union in 1861
- The critical election of 1896
- The critical election of 1932
- The aftermath of the New Deal (1945)
- The Nixon era and its successors (1968)

Executive authority cont.
- In Re Neagle (1889)
- Myers v. United States (1926)
- Humphrey's Executor (Rathbun) v. United States (1935)
- United States v. Curtiss-Wright Export Corporation (1936)
- United States v. Belmont (1937)
- Korematsu v. United States (1944)
- Youngstown Sheet and Tube Company v. Sawyer (1952)
- United States v. District Court for the Eastern District of Michigan (1972)
- United States v. Nixon (1974)
- Immigration and Naturalization Service v. Jagdish Rai Chadha (1983)

Bankruptcy and currency
- Sturgis v. Crowinshield (1819)
- Ogden v. Saunders (1827)
- Hepburn v. Griswold (1870)
- The Legal Tender Cases (1871)

Intergovernmental tax immunity
- Collector v. Day (1870)
- South Carolina v. United States (1905)
- Metcalf and Eddy v. Mitchell (1926)

Prohibitions of test oaths
- Cummings v. Missouri (1867)

Fifteenth Amendment
- United States v. Reese (1879)
- South Carolina v. Katzenbach, Attorney General (1966)

The corporation as citizen and person
- Louisville, Cincinnati, and Charleston Railroad Company v. Letson (1844)
- Santa Clara County v. Southern Pacific Railroad Company (1886)
- Connecticut General Life Insurance Company v. Johnson (1938)
- First National Bank of Boston v. Bellotti (1978) [Also listed under Freedom of Speech]

Citizenship and the Fourteenth Amendment
- Dred Scott v. Sanford (1857) [Also listed under judicial review]
- United States v. Wong Kim Ark (1895)

The Equal Protection Clause
- Hall v. De Cuir (1878)
- Virginia v. Rives (1880)
- The Civil Rights Cases (1883)
- Yick Wo v. Hopkins (1886)
- Plessy v. Ferguson (1896)
- Smith v. Allwright (1944)
- Brown v. Board of Education 1 & 2 (1954 and 1955)
- Reynolds v. Sims (1964)
- Moose Lodge No. 107 v. Irvis (1972)
- San Antonio v. Rodriguez (1973)
- Regents of the University of California v. Bakke (1978)
- Reed v. Reed (1971)
- Orr v. Orr (1979)

The Fourteenth Amendment and the Bill of Rights and defendants
- Hurtado v. California (1884)
- Powell v. Alabama (1932)
- Palko v. Connecticut (1937)
- Mapp v. Ohio (1961)
- Gideon v. Wainwright (1963)
- Miranda v. Arizona (1966)
- Harris v. New York (1971)

The taxing power
- Hylton v. United States (1796)
- Pollack v. Farmer's Loan and Trust Company (1895)
- McCray v. United States (1904)
- United States v. Doremus (1910)
- Bailey v. Drexel Furniture Company (1922)
- United States v. Butler (1936)
- Carter v. Carter Coal Company (1936)
- Steward Machine Company v. Davis (1937)

Congress, its members, investigations and the other branches
- McGrain v. Daugherty (1927)
- Selective Draft Law Cases (1918)
- Dennis v. United States (1951)
- Yates v. United States (1957)
- Watkins v. United States (1957)
- Barenblatt v. United States (1959)
- Powell v. McCormack (1969)

Due process and the right to privacy
- Griswold v. Connecticut (1965)
- Roe v. Wade (1973)

Table of Cases*

*Cases in italics are quoted in the text.

CONSTITUTIONAL LAW
IN AMERICAN POLITICS

CHAPTER
1

Introduction

The hallmark of the 1980s has been a consistent and unrelenting attack upon the Supreme Court by a gradually growing group of members of Congress and by a number of single-issue organizations reacting to decisions as wide ranging as abortion, salmon-fishing, crime, and legislative reapportionment. The attacks of the 1980s have lacked the spectacular public impact of the political conflict over the Court Packing Plan of the 1930s, but what the attackers of the '80s lack in drama they have compensated for in dogged persistence and ideological fervor. As has been true in past controversies about the nature and scope of judicial authority, the legitimacy of the Supreme Court's public policy role is once again directly challenged.

During such a debate, it is inevitable and quite appropriate to raise fundamental questions about the origin and nature of the power of the Supreme Court and the federal judiciary. How did the Supreme Court emerge in a tripartite division of national governmental powers in 1789? What were the expectations of its creators and the fears of its detractors? How did this novel institution fit into the existing pattern of American political institutions? What is its relationship to salient political principles and institutions such as democracy or political parties?

The origin and development of the Supreme Court of the United States is intimately related to fundamental political change in the nation itself. Paradoxically, at different times and under different circumstances, the Supreme Court has been supported by those who desired significant transformations in values and public policies, such as modern advocates of civil rights and liberties, and by those who preferred stability and resisted change, such as 19th century defenders of property rights under the contract clause. These situations appear less paradoxical and less perplexing when the role of the Court in the political life of the nation is examined closely.

Today the Supreme Court, the entire structure of the federal judiciary, the court systems of the fifty states, and, indeed, the continuously expanding legal profession all appear to be so powerful and politically and socially significant that it is difficult to imagine that any of these elements in the American legal culture

once were weak and seriously threatened. The historical evidence indicates that
all were indeed weak and some have been threatened by wide public disapproval
and occasional political limitations. The relative successes of all of these elements
were determined during the 19th century by a variety of political and social
factors that are basic to the modern American political system.

The Court and political change

Significant political change has frequently been identified by the degree to which
societies were drastically, and often permanently, altered in a fundamental reordering of political power. Eisenstadt, like several other scholars of fundamental
social, economic, and political change, attempted to categorize such changes. In his
seminal *Revolution and the Transformation of Societies: A Comparative Study of Civilizations*,
he emphasized the consequences of such transformations—the alteration of the
composition of political elites, of political power distributions, and of the relationships between groups in a particular society.[1] Many scholars have concentrated
on the most drastic kind of political transformation, the violent revolution. But in
societies that have maintained a high degree of stability, such as the United
States, other indices must be included to measure change.

Drastic political changes are defined in a descending order of intensity. In U. S.
political experience, the most drastic and most far-reaching of these changes are,
as expected, violent revolutions, notably the American Revolution of 1776 and the
Southern Confederacy's rebellion against the Union in 1861. There have been
regional outbreaks such as Shay's Rebellion, but the revolts of 1776 and 1861
were nationwide rather than regional. Second, less drastic political transformations
have occurred as a result of peaceful but fundamental constitutional changes. The
transition from the Articles of Confederation to the new Constitution of 1789 is
the most important change in this category. Third, certain kinds of elections have
been important indicators of major political changes. Modern analysts, such as
V. O. Key and Walter Dean Burnham, have categorized these as *critical elections* to
distinguish them from less significant contests.[2]

Three categories of elections are generally identified in the electoral experience
of the American people since 1789. The most commonplace and most stable is a
maintaining election. In such elections, the presidential candidate of the majority
party is elected and the contemporary pattern of party alignment and strength is
continued virtually unchanged. A second category is a *deviating election*. In these
contests, the minority party registers some gains including election of its presidential candidate, but the basic alignment of the two political parties remains
intact. The third category, *realigning* or *critical elections*, represents a fundamental
and enduring shift in party alignment with a minority party becoming the majority
party for a number of decades. The first critical election in the United States did
not occur until 1800. It was repeated in 1828, 1860, 1896, and 1932. These major
categories of political change in the United States—revolution, constitutional
alteration, and critical election—provide the fundamental framework within which
the Supreme Court emerged and performed its institutional and political roles
from its inception in 1789 through the 1980s. The categories are summarized
chronologically in Table 1-1.

TABLE 1-1   Periods of significant political change

Events and dates of change	Periods immediately following basic changes[3]
1. The American Revolution (1776)	(1777–1788)
2. The adoption of the Constitution (1789)	(1789–1800)
3. The critical election of 1800	(1801–1810)
4. The critical election of 1828	(1829–1838)
5. The critical election of 1860 and the South's revolt against the Union in 1861	(1861–1870)
6. The critical election of 1896	(1897–1906)
7. The critical election of 1932	(1933–1942)
8. The aftermath of the New Deal	(1945–1968)
9. The Nixon era and its successors	(1969–present)

Historians and political scientists agree about the inclusion of the American Revolution and the rebellion of the Southern Confederacy. Similarly, there is general agreement on the critical election category, although it should be noted that the critical election of 1860 immediately preceded and, in certain respects, precipitated the violent revolution of the Southern Confederacy. There have been some arguments for the inclusion of 1968 and 1980 as critical elections, but the former lacked the major-party realignment associated with bona fide critical elections, and the claim for 1980 is generally viewed as a premature partisan hope rather than an empirically verified electoral political transformation. One additional type of major political change involves periods of partisan realignment that extend for quite a few years without the intervention of a single, dramatic critical election. The periods between the critical elections of 1860 and 1896, between the critical elections of 1896 and 1932, and the long period without a bona fide critical election after 1932 are illustrative. In such intervening periods, great shifts in public values and attitudes took place, often with serious repercussions in the relative influence and power of political parties and with correspondingly controversial changes in the relationship of the Supreme Court and emergent victorious political coalitions.

Changes in the characteristics of U.S. national executive, judicial, and legislative elites often have been related to changes in political ideology and policy.[4] Thus, conflicts in political ideology and policy often have been related to differential recruiting and tenure patterns, which are formally accentuated by changes in the occupational career patterns of national executives, jurists, and legislators.[5] The relationships among presidents, members of the Congress, and justices of the Supreme Court have provided the basis for a number of investigations of judicial activism or restraint and legislative reactions to the federal judiciary. Because members of the Supreme Court generally serve for considerably longer periods of time than either members of Congress or presidents, the possibility for serious differences of opinion always exists. Such potential for conflict is especially important after major shifts such as critical elections or major realignments between critical elections.

Since most members of the Supreme Court remain in office far longer than do presidents and members of Congress, when there is a substantial shift in political attitudes resulting in a sweeping change in political control of the presidency and Congress, the Supreme Court is ordinarily not affected immediately. But if the members of the Court persist in handing down decisions considered out of step with the ideas of the new political majority, conflict is inevitable. In technical terms often used in political science, the conflicts result from differential recruitment patterns. Differential recruitment is generally attributed to the structural effect of the constitutional guarantee for life tenure on good behavior for justices of the Supreme Court and the contrasting provisions for periodic renewal of the entire House of Representatives and of one-third of the Senate every two years. Policy differences between the Court and the Congress have been identified as conflicts between political generations during lag periods, which are defined as the time between a new political coalition's assumption of executive and legislative control and the time when a new president has appointed enough justices to control the Supreme Court. Although conflicts between justices and congressmen have been described either as generally temporary or seriously disruptive of the urgently needed programs of a new political regime, there is general agreement that policy differences are more numerous and more intense during periods of significant political change, notably critical elections periods. The major sources for these findings are summarized in chronological order in Table 1-2.

Students of legislative recruitment and policymaking have indicated that the election of "a new cohort" in a significant number of congressional districts and "legislative policy shifts in new directions" are typical of critical election periods. The characteristics that studies of period effects generally have in common are the use of periods of significant political change, the political variables associated with such periods, and their effects upon judicial activism or restraint. All studies have dealt with some aspects of congressional-Supreme Court relations and some have included presidential-Supreme Court relations as well. Understandably, they emphasize recruitment, tenure, and policy differences and explicitly or implicitly are largely limited to the analysis of political rather than economic or social factors.

Although Robert Dahl's 1957 article on the Supreme Court as national policymaker is generally cited as the work stimulating scholarly discussion of the significance of differential recruitment, Robert Jackson, Franklin Roosevelt's attorney general (and later associate justice), preceded Dahl in writing about the impact of tenure on good behavior as the "check of a preceding generation on the present one." Dahl, who tended to minimize such influence, asserted that "the policy views dominant on the Court are never for long out of line with the policy views dominant among the lawmaking majorities of the United States." Dahl attributed this result to a kind of political generational tempo by which presidents averaged a new Supreme Court appointment every 22 months. Presumably, when enough justices of the new political generation have been chosen, the Supreme Court will alter its position to conform to the views of the new dominant coalition.

The factual bases for Dahl's assertion were entirely limited to the exercise of judicial review,[18] the power of the courts to determine the constitutionality of executive or legislative actions. His descriptive empirical measures were criticized in turn by Jonathan Casper because they were limited to national judicial review.[19] David Adamany and Richard Funston both, with different emphases, linked changes in Supreme Court decision-making with critical elections.[20] The portion of Funston's study that develops this linkage is reproduced below.

THE SUPREME COURT AND CRITICAL ELECTIONS[21]*

Richard Funston

. . . If we take the preferences of the law-making majority to represent the will of the national majority, and if we take as our operational definition of the preferences of the law-making majority federal legislation passed by majorities in the House and Senate and signed by the president, then we may conclude that the Supreme Court is out of line with the majority will when it holds congressional statutes unconstitutional. We may then examine over time the behavior of the Court in exercising its power to declare congressional statutes unconstitutional in order to determine if this behavior occurs randomly, as the traditional conception of the Court's function would suggest, or if it tends to occur at given, identifiable intervals, as Dahl's thesis implies.

To examine the hypothesis that the Supreme Court follows the election returns, the first thing to which we should turn are the election returns. Were American national elections, especially presidential elections, mere popularity contests, there would be a considerable degree of electoral flux or instability in American political history. If a party's victory in a presidential election depended upon nothing more than the personal attractiveness of its candidate, each party would win in random fashion, unless one wishes to assume that one party would have a monopoly on all of the attractive candidates. Examining American political history, however, one does not find that such behavior has been the case. Instead, as Dahl pointed out, Americans' electoral behavior has been quite stable, with one party or another dominating national politics for long periods of time. How to explain such behavior?

The Survey Research Center, of course, explains it by emphasizing the influence of party identity upon a voter's choice between presidential candidates. Elections, according to this view, are essentially reaffirmations of party allegiance. The outcome of any given election may be seen as the result of short-term forces acting upon the underlying distribution of party loyalties within the electorate. The study of electoral behavior, then, becomes the study of the flow of partisan allegiances rather than the study of single elections.

To facilitate such study, the S.R.C. has, of course, formulated an electoral classification scheme characterizing each presidential election as (1) maintaining, (2) deviating, or (3) realigning, depending upon whether the movement of the vote results in the election of the candidate of the majority or minority party and upon whether the movement of the vote is associated with transient, short-term forces or with a basic shift in long-term partisan loyalties. In a maintaining election, the current pattern of party differences is maintained, and the candidate of the majority party is elected. In a deviating election, the net short-term forces are both to the advantage of the minority party and strong enough to influence the election of its presidential candidate, but the electorate's underlying pattern or distribution of partisan loyalties is unaffected. In a realigning election, however, popular political feeling is so intense that the basic underlying patterns of the electorate's party identifications are changed, and a new party balance is created which endures over several decades. Such fundamental shifts in national political alignments, usually associated with national crises,

*Reprinted by permission of the author and *American Political Science Review*.

TABLE 1-2 The correlates or determinants of judicial activism

Source	Independent variable(s)	Dependent variable(s)	Key indicator(s)
Jackson (1941)[6]	(a) Tenure on good behavior, (b) party influence in judicial appointments	(a) "Check of a preceding generation on the present one"; (b) "check of a conservative legal philosophy on a dynamic people"; and (c) "check of a rejected regime on one in being"	Judicial review
Dahl (1957)[7]	(a) Presence or absence of "weak" lawmaking majorities in Congress, (b) lag periods	Supreme Court policymaking	Exercises of judicial review within four years of legislative enactment
Mendelson (1959)[8]	(a) "Periods of unusual weakness in our party system," (b) differential recruitment	"Court intrusion upon national policy"	Judicial review
Roche (1961)[9]	(a) "Absence [or presence] of a disciplined, internally cohesive national two-party system	Judicial public policymaking	Judicial review
Schmidhauser (1961)[10]	(a) Party affiliation, (b) region, (c) age and era of appointment, (d) other socioeconomic variables	Propensity to support or oppose slavery, broad Congressional authority over interstate commerce, and expansion of private corporate power	Judicial decisions on slavery, commerce power, and status and power of private corporations
Nagel (1969)[11]	(a) Degree of party difference between Congress and the Court, (b) nature of party in the national government, and (c) party affiliations of individual justices	Judicial policymaking	Judicial review
Goldman and Jahnige (1971)[12]	Presence of (a) critical election, (b) major Congressional Court-curbing attempts, and (c) strong presidential criticism of Supreme Court	Judicial policymaking or "outputs"	Judicial review and other exercises of judicial authority
Adamany (1973)[13]	(a) Presence of "new party coalition"; (b) "Court used its checking power to thwart significantly" new coalition policies; (c) on eve of or after realigning elections	"Justices check and delegitimize popular government and constitute a force for instability"	Judicial review and other exercises of judicial authority

TABLE 1-2 (continued)

Source	Independent variable(s)	Dependent variable(s)	Key indicator(s)
Funston (1975)[14]	Presence or absence of "realignment phases or, . . . critical periods . . ."	Greater tendency to declare federal legislation unconstitutional	Judicial review
Canon and Ulmer (1976)[15]	Presence or absence of "lag" periods (time between new coalition's assumption of executive and legislative control and time when new president appoints enough justices to control the Supreme Court)	Greater tendency to hold federal legislation unconstitutional	Judicial review
Handberg and Hill (1980)[16]	Presence or absence of "periods of political discontinuity"; periods in which "the political universe has changed while the court's membership has not"	Does the Supreme Court respond to changes in congressional attitudes?	Judicial review and selected categories of statutory interpretation
Caldeira and McCrone (1982)[17]	Partisan realignment is perhaps a sufficient, but not a necessary condition for a period of judicial activism toward Congress	The number of assertions of the Court's power to declare [federal] laws unconstitutional	Judicial review

are not, of course, actually accomplished in a single election. One, instead, must speak of realignment phases or of a realigning electoral era. For example, the partisan realignment which produced New Deal Democracy was begun by Al Smith in 1928, when he changed the image of the Democratic party from that which William Jennings Bryan had given it and captured small pluralities in the populous, Catholic, urban Northeast; it was completed by Roosevelt's sweep in 1936. Naturally enough, there have been very few realigning phases in American political history.

But what has this to do with the Supreme Court? Simply this—this conceptual framework allows us to gauge voter preference over time, and, it will be recalled, we are using voter preference as an indicator of the majority will. If we construct a simple, chronological chart of the ebb and flow of electoral patterns and compare it with the behavior of the Court in exercising its power of judicial review, we shall then be able to test the Dahl-Dooley thesis that the Court is never long out of line with the dominant political coalition, except during transitional periods, which we shall identify as realignment phases.

First, however, an intermediate step may be taken. It may be useful to determine for whom and for what the electorate voted, since our operational definition of the majority will is not simply the electoral preference but rather the action of the law-making majority.

The test of Supreme Court responses to electoral patterns chosen by Funston was the exercise of the power of judicial review, as was true in most earlier investigations. Unfortunately, this factor can at best provide only a partial analysis of the linkage between electoral change and decision-making behavior. A more comprehensive test incorporating all of the issues salient to fundamental political change is needed. Consequently, for each era of basic political transformation— the American Revolution, the adoption of the Constitution of 1787, the Civil War, the critical elections of 1800, 1828, 1860, 1896, and 1932, and the occasional periods of realignment between critical elections—all major issues directly related to each of these periods of basic change are used, including judicial review, statutory interpretation, or state authority. The central concern is the political significance of these issues in the context of major party transformations. The first two of these eras could not illustrate the relationship between Supreme Court decision-making and electoral or legislative actions because the Supreme Court did not yet exist. But the major developments in the American Revolution and the subsequent constitution-building period affecting the creation and strengthening of judicial institutions and the Supreme Court are essential elements in the total evolution of the role of the Supreme Court in U. S. political life.

In order to determine the relative significance of the issues in presidential and congressional elections accurately, a two-fold assessment of such issue saliency is utilized in this book. First, the issue selections of leading historians for each era are examined. And second, issues deemed most politically divisive in successive Congresses are selected. These issues are then compared to the issues that were most divisive in the decisions of the Supreme Court in each identical era. Consequently, it can be determined whether the Supreme Court divided politically in a manner similar to the Congress. Since the Congress presumably responds with great sensitivity to electoral change, its reactions to major issues provide a fairly reliable indicator of the fundamental bases for issue and value transformation in the society.

Most perspectives that have been developed to map the purposes and characteristics of judicial systems and legal professions are based upon the fundamental assumption that these institutions evolved or were created in order to institutionalize conflict resolution based upon fair and objective procedure. Indeed, this assumption is an integral part of the "received tradition" in most law school training in the United States. Conversely, in most revolutionary situations, an existing judicial system or legal profession is characterized as an instrumentality of the regime that must be overthrown and replaced. It is viewed as unfair, corrupt, or despotic and a cause of social, economic, and political conflict. The contradiction inherent in these two characterizations of the attributes and nature of judicial systems and legal professions deserves serious consideration and critical analysis. The contrast between these two frames of reference is especially important to the study of the Supreme Court of the United States because many of the distinctive characteristics of that institution, including its significant grants of jurisdictional authority, were initially the result of policy choices influenced importantly by America's own revolutionary experience. In the context of its times, the American Revolution was, indeed, a colonial war for independence.[22]

Key objectives of this book

The analysis of the relationship of Supreme Court doctrinal change and political change is the central purpose of this book. The first step in the fulfillment of this goal is the examination of the constitutional and political bases for the power and influence of the Court in Chapter 2.

North American judiciaries and the legal profession were the products of the British legal experience during the colonial period. That experience, however, did not always support either the mother country or the judicial institutions and the profession. What was the nature of and status of such institutions and of lawyers during the period of British colonial domination? How did this colonial experience contribute to the development of judicial institutions, the legal profession, and, ultimately, the Supreme Court of the United States?

REFERENCES

1. S. N. Eisenstadt, *Revolution and the Transformation of Societies: A Comparative Study of Civilizations* (New York: Free Press, 1978).
2. *See, for example,* Walter Dean Burnham, *Critical Elections and the Main Springs of American Politics* (New York: W. W. Norton, 1970).
3. Paul Allen Beck, "Critical Elections and the Supreme Court: Putting the Cart after the Horse," *American Political Science Review* 70 (September 1976): 930–932.
4. *See, for example,* Kenneth Prewitt and William McAllister, "Changes in the American Executive Elite, 1930–1970," and Michael R. King and Lester G. Seligman, "Critical Elections, Congressional Recruitment and Public Policy," in *Elite Recruitment in Democratic Politics: Comparative Studies Across Nations,* ed. Heinz Eulau and Moshe M. Czudnowski (New York: John Wiley, 1976).
5. Ibid.
6. Robert Jackson, *The Struggle for Judicial Supremacy* (New York: Alfred Knopf, 1941).
7. Robert A. Dahl, "Decision-Making in a Democracy: The Supreme Court as a National Policy-Maker," *Journal of Public Law* 6 (1957), pp. 192–286.
8. Wallace Mendelson, "Judicial Review and Party Politics," *Vanderbilt Law Review* 12 (1959): 447.
9. John Roche, *Courts and Rights: The American Judiciary in Action* (New York: Random House, 1961).

10. John R. Schmidhauser, "Judicial Behavior and the Sectional Crisis of 1837–1860," *Journal of Politics* 23 (1961): 615.

11. Stuart S. Nagel, "Curbing the Court: The Politics of Congressional Reaction" and "Curbing the Court: The Politics of Judicial Review," in *The Legal Process from a Behavioral Perspective,* ed. Stuart S. Nagel (Homewood, Ill.: Dorsey Press, 1969), pp. 245–279.

12. Sheldon Goldman and Thomas Jahnige, *The Federal Courts as a Political System* (New York: Harper and Row, 1971), pp. 261–268.

13. David Adamany, "Legitimacy, Realigning Elections, and the Supreme Court," *1973 Wisconsin Law Review* (1973): 790 ff.

14. Richard Funston, "The Supreme Court and Critical Elections," *American Political Science Review* 69 (1975): 795–811.

15. Bradley Canon and Sidney Ulmer, "The Supreme Court and Critical Elections: A Dissent," *American Political Science Review* 70 (1976): 1215–1218.

16. Roger Handberg and Harold F. Hill, Jr., "Court Curbing, Court Reversals, and Judicial Review: The Supreme Court v. Congress," *Law and Society Review* 14 (1980): 309–322.

17. Gregory A. Caldeira and Donald J. McCrone, "Of Time and Judicial Activism: A Study of the U.S. Supreme Court, 1800–1973," in *Supreme Court Activism and Restraint,* ed. Stephen Halpern and Charles Lamb (Lexington, Mass.: D. C. Heath, 1982).

18. Jackson, op. cit., p. 315, and Dahl, op. cit., p. 279.

19. Jonathan D. Casper, "The Supreme Court and National Policy-Making," *American Political Science Review* 70 (March 1976): 50–63.

20. Adamany, op. cit., pp. 790–846, and Funston, op. cit., pp. 795–811.

21. Funston, op. cit., pp. 795–811.

22. Thomas C. Barrow, "The American Revolution as a Colonial War for Independence," *William and Mary Quarterly* 25 (1968): pp. 452–464.

2

The Emergence of the Supreme Court in the Seminal Period of American Political Development

The experiences of the American colonists with the colonial court systems were often difficult. Ultimately, British colonial judicial policies and practices contributed to the development of first a critical and finally a rebellious spirit in America. Conflicts over colonial policies often centered upon issues and institutions that became identified with British abuse of executive power. The colonial judicial system, through its institutional organization and often corrupt appointment practices, also was identified with British abuse of power. In the decades immediately preceding the revolution, political corruption in the American colonies was defined in part as the granting of public appointments ascriptively—to individuals lacking competence and merit. Many American political leaders and legal professionals bitterly resented the arrogance and venality of most British appointees and opposed, in the description of one critic, the "multiplication of officers to strengthen the court (i.e., monarchical) interest; . . . advancing to the most eminent stations men without education, and of dissolute manners, . . . sporting with our persons and estates, by filling the highest seats of justice with bankrupts, bullies, and blockheads . . ."[1] British domination of appointments to judgeships and other public professional offices became an important factor in the alienation of American colonial lawyers. John Jay, for example, seriously objected to the advancement of "needy and ignorant dependents on great men . . . to the seats of justice, and to other places of trust and importance . . ." Similarly, it was argued that with independence, "no longer would a distinguished public office, like that of Chief Justice in South Carolina, be filled through the influence of some English lord's mistress . . ."[2]

In the era before the American Revolution, the colonial legislatures persistently tried to curtail or take over the patronage powers of royal governors and to limit such gubernatorial power over colonial courts and judges. These colonial legislatures viewed themselves as a sort of medieval court in the tradition of the House of Commons, making private legal judgments as well as public law. Courts themselves were frequently involved in general governmental and administrative affairs during this era. "Both the county sessions courts in Massachusetts and the county courts in Virginia before and after the Revolution remained crucially important governing bodies, assessing taxes, directing expenditures on local projects, issuing licenses, and in general monitoring the counties over which they presided." Gordon Wood indicated that "in the judicial area the [state] constitutions and the chaotic conditions of war had the effect of reversing the growing mid-eighteenth-century distinction between legislative and judicial responsibilities, leading during the 1770s and eighties to a heightened involvement of the legislatures in controlling the courts and in deciding the personal affairs of their constituents in private law judgments." This endorsement of legislative supremacy and encroachment into traditionally executive and judicial functions occurred despite emphatic declarations, as in the Virginia Constitution, asserting that "the legislative, executive and judiciary departments shall be separate and distinct, so that neither exercises the powers belonging to the other." Thus, historians believe that the Americans in their 1776 state constitutions meant by "separation of powers" nothing more than a prohibition of plural office holding. The sentence following the declaration of separation of powers in the Virginia Constitution concluded, "nor shall any person exercise the powers of more than one of them at the same time."[3]

Colonial legislatures often identified colonial judges as serving the interests of the British monarchy, a conclusion that was not surprising in the aftermath of many questionable British judicial appointments. Wood summed up the situation accurately as follows: "In the tenure of their offices during the eighteenth century, the colonial judges had also seemed to be much more the creatures of the Crown than the English judges." The latter had tenure on good behavior (since the Glorious Revolution), but American colonial judges sat at the pleasure of the Crown (generally meaning the royal governor). In 1776 these "governors surrendered to the legislatures the traditional magisterial prerogative of appointing judges." Consequently some colonial legislatures—after 1776 notably Rhode Island, Connecticut, Vermont, New Jersey, and Pennsylvania—limited judges' terms to specific years.[4] Ultimately, the immediate revolutionary situation produced a weakening of executive authority, a reorganization of the judicial systems reflecting popular distrust of colonial judges selected by the Crown, and legislative preeminence.

The emergence of separation of powers

Despite this immediate revolutionary reaction to Crown-dominated courts, the distrust of courts tended to diminish after the Crown no longer controlled judicial selection. When state legislatures occasionally sought to dominate all branches of the new state governments, a reaction to legislative supremacy began to set in. Among the experiments designed to control legislative usurpation or error were proposals for or utilization of councils of revision (New York's was the most notable) to combine executive and judicial power to veto "unwise and unjust measures" of the legislatures.

Between 1776 and 1787 attitudes toward courts changed considerably. James Wilson, later Associate Justice of the U. S. Supreme Court, summed up this change in his "Lectures on Law." He acknowledged that Americans distrusted governors and judges in 1776 because of the roles such officials played under the British Crown. The legislators had been more popular because of their activities against British oppression. Wilson then argued that "it is high time that we chastise our prejudices . . . . The executive and judicial powers are now drawn from the same source, are now animated by the same principles, and are now directed to the same ends, with the legislative authority: they who execute and they who administer the laws, are so much the servants, and therefore as much the friends of the people, as those who make them."[5]

In short, the progress from 1776 to 1787 toward a new national constitution embodied the notion that under such a new charter of government, all three of the branches became representative of the people through the great act of ratifying a new constitution. As John Jay put it in *Federalist* no. 64,

> All constitutional acts of power, whether in the executive or in the judicial department, have as much legal validity and obligation as if they proceeded from the legislature.

Within the state constitutional systems, there was considerable movement toward some form of implementation of the concept of separation of powers. Wood indicated, "The department of government which benefited most from this new, enlarged definition of separation of powers was the judiciary. At the time of Independence, with the constitution-makers establishing legislative supremacy, the judiciary had been virtually ignored or considered to be but an adjunct of feared executive power. Only the experience of the following years gave the judicial department the position of respect and independence as one of 'the three capital powers of Government' that is so characteristic of later American constitutionalism." Institutionally, several significant changes in the position of judges were adopted in a number of states. "Judges were no longer to be elected but were to hold office during good behavior and were to have fixed salaries, since the liberties of the state are evidently connected with their independence."[6]

These institutional developments represented a remarkable and rapid transition in the status and role of the state judicial systems. Because one significant complaint against the Crown's selection of judges had been the lack of professional attainment of many of the patronage choices, some states, after independence, stressed training and experience in the selection of judges. Thus, in Massachusetts, one very significant development during the revolutionary era was the professionalization of the judiciary. This trend was formalized in 1782 by the act establishing the Massachusetts Supreme Judicial Court, which required that the justices be trained lawyers.[7]

Another important development in the revolutionary and immediate post revolutionary era concerned the scope of the authority of judiciaries in relation to executive or legislative authority, especially with relation to judicial review.

The views on the English Constitution of Sir Edward Coke, a noted 17th century British jurist, were often cited or utilized as a basis for American colonial or early postcolonial conceptions of limited government and the scope of judicial authority. Coke's *Institutes* and his *Commentaries on the Common Law* were frequently utilized by American lawyers. The few Americans trained in the British legal training centers, the Inns of Court in London, were also strongly influenced by his contributions because the Inns continued to accept his views even though they were generally rejected in England after the end of the 17th century. The *Institutes* of Coke contained his conception that Magna Charta's major guarantees were manifestations of basic principles of right and justice and that such principles of natural law were applied in contemporary affairs by applications of the common law. In 1610, Coke, as Chief Justice of the King's Bench, handed down an opinion in Dr. Bonham's Case, a matter involving a physician who practiced without acquiring a license from the London College of Physicians as required by an act of Parliament. Chief Justice Coke held for Bonham on the ground that the statute was void. In so ruling Coke contended that,

> . . . the common law will control acts of Parliament, and sometimes adjudge them to be utterly void; for when an act of Parliament is against common right and reason, or repugnant, or impossible to be performed, the common law will control it and adjudge such act to be void.

Coke's ruling has sometimes been cited as an unusually early application of the doctrine of judicial review, and undoubtedly did provide a basis for the subsequent development and application of the doctrine in U. S. constitutional law after 1789. But in the context of early 17th century England, Chief Justice Coke's opinion did not deal with the question of the power of a court to hold unconstitutional and void an act of a coequal branch of government, a legislature, which is basically the essence of modern judicial review. Instead Parliament was both legislature and High Court. Coke's ruling clearly invoked natural law and equally clearly contributed to the concept of limited government. But he, in essence, asserted the power of a common law court to challenge the authority of another court, the High Court of Parliament.

In 18th century colonial America as in 17th century England, the concept of separation of powers was not widely applied, although legislative and executive authority often shared judicial power in a number of jurisdictions and by means of a variety of institutional arrangements, as in the county courts of Virginia and later in the Council of Revision of New York.

On virtually the eve of the American Revolution, an American colonial lawyer in Massachusetts, James Otis, cited and applied Coke's works and his opinion in the Bonham Case in a politically significant controversy over writs of assistance issued in the name of King George III. A writ of assistance was, in effect, a blanket search warrant permitting English officials to search virtually any home, warehouse, or ship at will. Because England had recently attempted to stiffen enforcement of onerous commercial regulations on the North American colonies, colonial merchants attempted to resist application of the writs of assistance. In Boston a number of merchants retained Otis to challenge the writs in the Superior Court of that city. Otis lost. But the argument that the Act of Parliament conflicted with the common law because it contravened "reason and the constitution" and was therefore void was invoked by Otis again at the beginning of the crisis of the Revolution three years later in his critique of the Sugar Act. These arguments and others invoking such principles became crucial elements of the arguments for independence. Consequently, although colonial lawyers divided over the question of revolution and independence, pro-revolutionary lawyers such as Otis, John and Samuel Adams, and Thomas Jefferson were in the forefront of the movement, thus enhancing the profession among the American public.

On the meaning of Otis' argument in relation to judicial review, the evidence is less clear. In 1761, James Otis had taken the position that the writs of assistance were contrary to "the fundamental principles of law," arguing that any parliamentary act "against the Constitution is void: an Act against natural Equity is void, and courts must pass such Acts into disuse." Often cited as an early confirmation of revolutionary acceptance of judicial review, Otis' position, like that of many others, was rather ambiguous about the role and power of the judiciary. Indeed the principle of legislative supremacy was generally advocated. For example, Jefferson felt strongly: "Relieve the judges from the rigorous *text,* and permit them with pretorian discretion, to wander into its equity, and the whole system becomes incertain."[8]

The advantageous changes in the status of both the legal profession and judicial institutions within the states after 1776 were truly remarkable transformations. In a number of significant ways, these changes set the stage for a similarly significant change in the national government. Under the Articles of Confederation there was, in effect, no national judicial branch, unless one accepted the Court of Appeals in Cases of Capture, a highly specialized and jurisdictionally limited court whose rulings were not always honored by the states comprising the Confederation. States' rights was a doctrine of determinative influence under the Articles of Confederation. The relationship of the concept of a national judicial system to that of states' rights was, from the very beginning of the new constitutional system debated in 1787 and adopted in 1788, a matter of fundamental controversy.

The origin of the Supreme Court's power as arbiter in federal-state relations[9]

The conception of a powerful judicial body maintaining a division of powers between a government of a whole nation and governments of its parts or sections did not appear miraculously to the Justices of the Supreme Court after the adoption of the Constitution. It was clearly understood and partially applied during the period when America was a colony of Great Britain and under the old Articles of Confederation.

The British Empire maintained the fiction that it was a unitary system until after the American Revolution, but the Empire's relationships with the thirteen colonies had, in reality, become essentially federal. The government of the whole Empire, that of Great Britain, had been forced by the pressure of European wars and great distances to leave most problems of domestic legislation and administration to the governments of the "parts" of the Empire, notably the American colonial governments. Naturally enough, the development of local autonomy in the colonies led to conflicts of authority between the mother country and the colonies as well as among the colonies themselves. It was a quasi-judicial institution of the British Empire, the Committee on Trade and Plantations of the British Privy Council, which resolved such conflicts.

After the American colonies broke with Great Britain a new problem arose, that of balancing the powers of the states and the new central government in North America. A temporary solution was found in the creation of a confederate system. The old Articles of Confederation established a very limited form of judicial arbitration in two narrow fields: the settlement of disputes between the states and the settlement of disputes between the Confederation Congress and the states concerning cases of capture at sea.

The first category of disputes was to be settled in accordance with the ninth article of the Articles of Confederation. This provided that "the united states in Congress assembled shall also be the last resort on appeal in all disputes and differences now subsisting or that hereafter may arise between two or more states concerning boundary, jurisdiction or any other cause whatever. . . ." The parties to a dispute could be directed by Congress "to appoint by joint consent, commissioners or judges to constitute a court for hearing and determining the matter in question." Or if the disputing parties could not agree Congress could itself make the appointments. The article further provided that "the judgment and sentence of the court . . . shall be final and conclusive." A serious land dispute was peacefully resolved under this article in 1782. Yet such a court of arbitration lacked permanence. Consequently, it was probably the second judicial institution created under the Confederation which was more influential in the evolution of the judicial arbiter concept in American federalism. For the Court of Appeals in Cases of Capture was a permanent judicial body which heard 118 cases before the Articles of Confederation were replaced by the new Federal Constitution. A member of this court, Judge John Lowell, made the experiences of this judicial body available to the constitutional framers in 1787 and to the Senate in 1789, sketching a plan for a federal judiciary in a letter to some of the framers and later, in 1789, giving his counsel and advice to the Senate Judiciary Committee.

During the waning years of the Confederation itself, serious attention was given to various proposals to establish a more powerful central judiciary capable of putting an end to state encroachments on or defiance of the authority of the Confederation government. Although these proposals never were adopted by the Confederation, they do provide unmistakable evidence that political leaders of this era were fully aware of the potentialities of a judicial arbiter in confederate or federal governmental systems. A Confederation Congress committee report, submitted in 1786 by Charles Pinckney, contained, in essence, a complete arrangement for creation of a federal court capable of umpiring federal-state disputes. Pinckney's committee suggested that the Confederation Congress be authorized

> . . . to institute a federal judicial court for trying and punishing all officers appointed by congress for all crimes, offenses, and misbehavior in their offices, and to which court an appeal shall be allowed from the judicial courts of the several states in all causes wherein any question shall arise on the meaning and construction of treaties entered into by the United States with any foreign power, or on any law of nations, or wherein any question shall arise respecting any regulations that may hereafter be

made by congress relative to trade and commerce, or the collection of federal revenues pursuant to powers that shall be vested in that body, or wherein questions of
importance may arise, and the United States shall be a party . . .

Similar ideas for strengthening the Confederation government through creation
of some sort of federal judicial arbiter were formulated or discussed by Rufus
King, James Madison, and Nathan Dane. Just prior to the Philadelphia Convention
of 1787, however, a significantly different argument was discussed widely. Instead
of viewing a federal judicial arbiter as primarily a defender of the central government, a broadly circulated pamphlet proposed:

> In order to prevent an oppressive exercise of powers deposited with Congress, a
> jurisdiction should be established to interpose and determine between the individual
> States and the Federal body upon all disputed points, and being stiled The Equalizing
> Court, should be constituted and conducted in the following manner . . .

This proposal appeared in the *Pennsylvania Gazette* in Philadelphia on June 6, 1787
and was republished in the leading newspapers during the early days of the Convention. Thus, while supporters of the idea of a strong national government had
begun to favor the judicial arbiter concept as a means of restraining the states,
those who feared the encroachments of a strong national government had begun
to look upon a strong judicial system as a protector of individual and states' rights.
Recognition of this development makes more understandable the absence of states'
rights or anti–Federalist opposition to most of the proposals made in the Convention which strengthened the federal judiciary.

One of the major reasons for holding the Philadelphia Convention had been
the necessity to find a remedy for the evils arising from state legislation which
hurt or interfered with the interests of other states, infringed treaties made by
the Confederation Congress, oppressed individuals, or invaded the sphere of authority of the Confederation government. The convention delegates were faced
with the task of finding suitable means of restraining such state legislation or
action. Despite the fact that the idea of a judicial arbiter was understood and
widely discussed before the opening of the Convention, the creation of a high
federal court to solve this problem was by no means a foregone conclusion. Years
after the close of the Convention, James Madison referred to the situation in the
following manner: "[T]he obvious necessity of a control of the laws of the States
so far as they might violate the Constitution and laws of the United States left no
option, but as to mode . . . ," noting as the three possible choices "a veto (executive)
on the passage of the State laws, a Congressional repeal of them, a judicial annulment of them."

Analysis of the record of the Philadelphia Convention underscores the fact that
the granting of power to the Federal Supreme Court to arbitrate finally in federal-
state relations came about through a complex series of developments. Basically
they represented a compromise between the strong nationalists who originally
wanted a veto over the states vested in the new national legislature or executive
and the states' righters who either opposed such supervision of the states or
preferred that such power be vested in what they considered a weaker and more
impartial agency, notably the supreme federal court suggested in the original
Paterson Plan.

Among the more important of these developments were (a) the repudiation of coercion of the states by force and the adoption of coercion of individuals by law, (b) the readiness of every major bloc in the Convention to set up a federal judiciary, (c) the demands of one powerful group for a system of inferior federal tribunals, (d) the defeat of the congressional negative proposals and the substitution by Luther Martin of a supremacy clause, and (e) the tendency to look upon a federal judiciary as a protector of individual and states' rights which was reflected in the proposals for a Council of Revision. Very often these developments seemed totally unrelated, but their cumulative effect was the granting of final interpretive powers in federal-state relations to a supreme federal tribunal.

A provision for a congressional veto of state laws was prominent among the resolutions for the Union presented by Edmund Randolph at the opening session of the Convention. It provided "that the national legislature ought to be empowered . . . to negative all laws, passed by the several States, contravening, in the opinion of the national legislature, the articles of union." Later, on May 31, the Convention, in committee of the whole house, amended it by addition of the phrase "or any treaties subsisting under the authority of the Union." The entire resolution was agreed to by the committee without debate or dissent. However, when this resolution was reported from the committee to the Convention on July 17, it met with violent opposition. Gouverneur Morris thought such power "likely to be terrible to the States"; Luther Martin considered it improper; and Sherman believed that since the state courts would hold invalid any laws contravening the authority of the Union, such a veto would be unnecessary. Madison and Charles Pinckney did not share Sherman's confidence in the state courts, however, and held that the congressional means of preserving the harmony of the system was necessary. In spite of Madison's appeal, the Convention defeated the proposal for a congressional negative on state laws by a vote of seven to three.

Even before the rejection of the congressional negative by the Convention on July 17, there was clear-cut evidence that the advocates of a strong central government were prepared to limit the congressional negative by providing for final appeal to a national judiciary. As early as July 10, Randolph had sent Madison a list of concessions to be used "as an accommodating proposition to small states" which then were bitterly opposed to the principle of representation based upon population. In terms of the judicial arbiter concept, the fourth and fifth of Randolph's proposals were particularly significant, because they clearly anticipated the Supreme Court's modern role as both a federal umpire and as a defender of individual rights against state infringement. His suggestions provided:

IV. That although every negative given to the law of a particular state shall prevent its operation, any state may appeal to the national judiciary against a negative, and that such negative if adjudged to be contrary to the powers granted by the articles of the Union, shall be void.

V. That any individual, conceiving himself injured or oppressed by the partiality or injustice of a law of any particular state, may resort to the national judiciary, who may adjudge such a law to be void, if found contrary to the principles of equity and justice.

Randolph was prepared to offer these conciliatory proposals to the Convention on July 16, but did not do so because of the victory of the small states, on that day, in securing equal voting rights in the Senate.

Throughout the course of the Philadelphia Convention the major discussions of the federal judicial arbiter were generally related to the nationalists' attempts to gain approval for the congressional negative of state laws. However, other discussions in the Convention also contributed to the evolution of the supreme federal tribunal. The proposals for a council of revision, composed of the chief executive and judges of the highest national court, while eventually defeated, stimulated discussion of the power of judicial review. Rejection by the Convention of the proposals to coerce the states by force, contained in both the Randolph and Paterson Plans, were followed by adoption of the principle of direct coercion of individuals by the national government itself. This solution reflected the recognition by Convention leaders of the need to discover a peaceful mode of limiting state interference with national authority. The initiative in finding such a solution was now taken by the leaders of the small states bloc in the Convention, many of whom were of states' rights persuasion.

Using as their starting point a clause from the Paterson Plan guaranteeing the supremacy of the national government within the sphere of its legitimate authority, states' rights supporters attempted to placate the nationalists who were bitterly disappointed by the defeat of the congressional negative proposal on July 17. Luther Martin submitted what he undoubtedly considered a mild substitute for such a negative. His original proposal stated:

> . . . [T]hat the Legislative acts of the United States made by virtue and in pursuance of the Articles of Union, and all treaties made and ratified under the authority of the United States shall be the supreme law of the respective States, as far as those acts or treaties shall relate to the said states, or their citizens and inhabitants—and that the Judiciaries of the several States shall be bound thereby in their decision, anything in the respective laws of the individual States to the contrary notwithstanding.

Later, the nationalists in the Convention changed this relatively mild resolution in several important respects. These amendments were made in the closing days of the Convention in August and September. On August 5, 1787, the Convention's committee on detail had compressed Martin's resolution and made two significant changes—federal laws were declared supreme over state constitutions as well as state laws, and the duty to uphold the supreme law was imposed on "the Judges in the several States" instead of on "the Judiciaries of the respective states." On August 23, John Rutledge proposed the following important addition: "This Constitution and the laws of the United States made in pursuance thereof . . . shall be the supreme law of the several states." Thus the Constitution was made judicially enforceable law. The Convention adopted his proposal without debate. Finally, on September 12, the committee on style completed the final draft of the Constitution. Luther Martin's resolution had become a part of Article VI. From the point of view of federal-state relations this was the crucial provision in the fundamental document. Section three of that article read:

This Constitution, and the laws of the United States which shall be made in pursuance thereof; and all treaties made, or which shall be made, under the authority of
the United States, shall be the supreme law of the land; and the judges in every state
shall be bound thereby, anything in the Constitution or laws of any state to the
contrary notwithstanding.

Defeat of the congressional negative plan left the Convention with two institutional alternatives for the enforcement of national supremacy. The first was an
ultranationalistic suggestion put forth by Alexander Hamilton in his plan for union.
Section ten of the plan provided that "all laws of the particular States contrary to
the Constitution or laws of the United States to be utterly void; and the better to
prevent such laws being passed, the Governour or president of each state shall be
appointed by the General Government and shall have a negative upon the laws
about to be passed in the state of which he is Governour or President." Hamilton's
alternative was not even seriously considered by the Convention. The second was
the judicial arbiter which had been an integral part of the original Paterson Plan.
Section five had provided "that a federal judiciary be established to consist of a
supreme tribunal the judges of which to be appointed by the Executive . . ." Section two of the same plan proposed that violations of acts of the federal congress
be tried in the first instance in "the superior Common Law Judiciary" of the state
concerned, "subject . . . for the correction of all errors, both in law and fact . . . ,
to an appeal to the Judiciary of the United States."

Actually, every major plan for union—Randolph's, Hamilton's, and Paterson's—
had provided for a national judicial system. The essential difference between the
nationalistic plans for Randolph and Hamilton and the states' rights plan of Paterson is that the latter failed to provide a system of inferior federal courts. The
nationalists did not actually oppose the adoption of a judicial arbiter, but merely
felt, as James Wilson later indicated, that a judicial check on the states would not
be sufficient to maintain a strong central government. On August 10, 1787,
Charles Pinckney grudgingly admitted that the federal judges "will even be the
Umpires between the United States and individual states as well as between one
State and another." However, a few days later, on August 23, he tenaciously
sought to reinstate the congressional negative, but was defeated by a six to five
vote. In urging support for Pinckney's motion, Wilson recognized impliedly that
in the absence of a congressional negative, the national judiciary would seek to
maintain the supremacy of the national government. This he felt was not enough
because "the firmness of Judges is not of itself sufficient. Something further is
requisite—it will be better to prevent the passage of an improper law, than to
declare it void when passed."

A letter exchange between Thomas Jefferson and James Madison concerning
the relative merits of the congressional negative and the judicial arbiter illustrates
clearly the contrasting positions of the states' righters and the nationalists. Although he did not attend the Convention, Jefferson was representative of those
who, while they feared establishment of a national government in which all
authority would be centralized, realized quite clearly that some degree of centralized control was necessary to bring stability to the then chaotic thirteen states.

In his reply to Madison's inquiry concerning a congressional negative on state laws, Jefferson presented a viewpoint which might be taken as indicative of the attitude of other advocates of strictly limited government. He wrote:

The negative proposed to be given them on all the acts of the several Legislatures is now for the first time suggested to my mind. Prima Facie I do not like it. It fails in an essential character, that the hole and the patch should be commensurate; but this proposed to mend a small hole by covering the whole garment . . . Would not an appeal from the state judicatures to a federal court in all cases where the act of Confederation controlled the question, be as effectual a remedy, and exactly commensurate to the defect?

On the other hand, the advocates of a strong central government, while favoring the granting of broad judicial powers, had realized that judicial nullification of state laws was possible only when federal questions arose in bona fide cases before the new Supreme Court. Madison's letter to Jefferson after the close of the Convention indicated the lack of assurance he shared with other strong government advocates. He wrote:

It may be said that the Judicial authority under our new system will keep the states within their proper limits and supply the place of a negative on their laws. The answer is that it is more convenient to prevent the passage of a law than to declare it void, after it is passed; that this will be particularly the case, where the law aggrieves individuals who may be unable to support an appeal against a state to the Supreme Judiciary, that a state which would violate the legislative rights of the Union would not be very ready to obey a Judicial decree in support of them, and that a recurrence to force, which in the event of disobedience would be necessary, is an evil which the new Constitution meant to exclude as far as possible. A Constitutional negative on the laws of the states seems equally necessary to secure individuals against encroachments on their rights. The mutability of the laws of the States is found to be a serious evil.

After the final defeat of the congressional negative in the Convention on August 23, the nationalists determined to make the best of an unhappy situation by strengthening the federal arbiter by means of grants of broad constitutional jurisdiction and through institution of a complete system of inferior federal courts. The extension of the Supreme Court's jurisdiction to all cases, state and federal, arising under the Constitution was made without states' rights argument. But the attempt at creation of a system of inferior federal courts aroused such fierce opposition that the nationalists were compelled to accept a compromise by which the establishment of such courts was left to the discretion of the new Congress.

Nationalist bitterness at the substitution of a judicial arbiter for their cherished congressional negative persisted to the end of the Convention. For example, on September 12, James Madison supported a motion by Mason which provided that the clause relating to export duties be amended to allow the states to lay such duties for "the sole purpose of defraying the charges of inspecting, packing, storing and indemnifying the loses in keeping the commodities in the care of public officers before exportation." Gorham and Langdon had asked: "How was redress to be obtained in case duties should be laid beyond the purpose expressed?" Madison coldly replied that "[t]here will be the same security as in other cases—the jurisdiction of the Supreme Court must be the source of redress. So far only had provision been made by the plan against injurious acts of the States. His own opinion was, that this was insufficient—a negative on the State laws alone could meet all the shapes which these could assume. But this had been overruled."

The Philadelphia Convention record indicates unmistakably that the new Supreme Court had been clearly designated the final judicial arbiter in federal-state relations and that it was primarily the states' righters in the Convention who had brought this to pass. The nationalists had not opposed the creation of the judicial arbiter, but had felt strongly that a national judiciary would not, by itself, be strong enough to cope with state encroachments on national authority.

In spite of their misgivings, the advocates of strong central government did not let lack of confidence in a federal judiciary weaken their efforts to secure ratification of the Constitution. Two of the contributions to the *Federalist* by Madison and Hamilton were devoted to an examination of the proposed judicial arbiter, its purposes and its impartial character. Within the state ratifying conventions, the nationalists frequently found themselves the staunchest defenders of the same judicial arbiter for which they had indicated only lukewarm enthusiasm during the Philadelphia Convention; for serious states' rights objections were raised to certain provisions of the judicial clauses in the new Constitution, notably those concerning the possible establishment of a system of inferior federal courts and those extending federal jurisdiction to suits between a state and individuals. In five of the more important of the state ratifying conventions—Connecticut, North Carolina, Virginia, Pennsylvania, and South Carolina—the new Supreme Court's function of resolving state and federal conflicts was discussed clearly and ultimately was accepted. In virtually all of the ratifying conventions some jurisdictional grants to the new federal court system were subjected to severe criticism. Out and out opponents of the Constitution, such as Robert Yates of New York, recognized the scope of the Supreme Court's power and made the judicial grants a major point for attack on the proposed new system of government. Under the pseudonym of "Brutus," Yates wrote that "the opinions of the Supreme Court . . . will have the force of law; because there is no power provided in the Constitution that can correct their errors or control their jurisdiction. From this court there is no appeal." But in the end, the nationalists managed to secure early ratification in all of the most important states.

These facts stand out as a result of this analysis of the Philadelphia Convention and the state ratifying conventions. Both the nationalists and the states' righters were in substantial agreement on the need for a supreme judicial arbiter in federal-state relations. By 1789 it was clearly understood that the Supreme Court of the United States was to fulfill that role. Naturally enough, the nationalists tended to emphasize the aspect of judicial arbitership concerned with the protection of national supremacy against state encroachments. However, both nationalists and states' righters explicitly recognized that the Supreme Court's role was that of an impartial arbiter. Thus, it was also anticipated that federal laws violative of states' rights were to be declared unconstitutional. The prevailing contemporary conception of the new Supreme Court's role is best illustrated by Oliver Ellsworth's description in the Connecticut Ratifying Convention of January, 1788:

> This Constitution defines the extent of the powers of the general government. If the general legislature should at any time overlap their limits, the judicial department is a constititutional check. If the United States go beyond their powers, if they make a law which the Constitution does not authorize, it is void; and the judicial power, the national judges, who, to secure their impartiality, are to be made independent, will declare it to be void. On the other hand, if the states go beyond their limits, if they make a law which is a usurpation upon the general government, the law is void; and upright, independent judges will declare it so.

On March 4, 1789, the wheels of the new central government began to turn; but for eleven months after the United States came into existence, it lacked a judicial branch of government. Although the first judiciary bill was introduced the very next day after the new Senate was organized, it was six months before the bill became law and before President Washington could appoint members to the first Supreme Court.

While the constitutional framers had drawn the broad outlines of the judicial power, they had left to congressional discretion the composition of the federal courts, the extent of the appellate jurisdiction of the Supreme Court, the existence or non-existence of any inferior federal courts and the extent of their jurisdiction. Consequently, the manner in which the first Congress dealt with these problems in the Judiciary Act of September 24, 1789, set the pattern for subsequent development of the federal judicial system. This act was especially important because without broad grants of appellate jurisdiction to the Supreme Court by Congress, the entire judicial arbiter plan would have fallen into abeyance for lack of implementation.

The first judiciary act was largely the product of the Senate Judiciary Committee, and within the committee, Oliver Ellsworth and William Paterson took leading roles in drafting the bill. In the early stages of this drafting, Ellsworth sought to establish a complete network of inferior federal courts and to extend their jurisdiction to the limits set by the Constitution. However, to secure the concurrence of Richard Henry Lee, Ellsworth apparently had to accept a more limited inferior federal court system. This setback was mitigated by inclusion of a provision which allowed a defendant sued in a state court in a case involving a federal question to remove the case to a federal circuit court, or to appeal to the Supreme Court, by writ of error, after trial in the highest court of law or equity in a state in which a decision in the suit could be had.

When debate on the draft bill began in the Senate in committee of the whole, on June 22, the issue centered around the question whether there should be any district courts at all or whether the functions of executing federal laws should be left in the first instance to the state courts. Ellsworth had been opposed to giving the state courts such power on the grounds discussed in a letter he wrote later on the subject. He felt that to annex to State Courts jurisdiction which they had not before, as of admiralty cases, and perhaps, of offenses against the United States, would be constituting the Judges of them, *pro tanto*, Federal Judges, and of course they would continue such during good behavior, and on fixed salaries, which in many cases, would illy comport with their present tenure of office. Besides, if the State Courts, as such, could take cognizance of those offenses, it might not be safe for the General Government to put the trial and punishment of them entirely out of its own hands."

Debate over the various proposals in the bill raged for three months in the Senate and the House. The crucial issues were whether there should be any inferior federal courts, and, if there were to be any such courts, whether the Constitution required that they be vested with the full jurisdiction which the Constitution permitted. In its final form the bill was a compromise. The nationalists were forced to abandon their contention that the federal courts be granted the broadest jurisdiction possible under the Constitution, while the states' righters were unable to confine federal cases to state courts, subject only to final appeal to the new federal Supreme Court. Section twenty-five, which became the very cornerstone of federal judicial supremacy, established the appellate jurisdiction of the Supreme Court over state courts where such courts decided against a claimed federal right. Significantly, the states' righters in Congress actually advocated this crucial grant of jurisdiction in 1789.

In sum, the modern states' rights charges of federal "judicial usurpation" of power to arbitrate in federal-state relations may be viewed as a particularly persistent bit of political mythology. For examination of the Philadelphia Convention, the state ratifying conventions, and the legislative history of the first judiciary act indicates unmistakably that the framers clearly intended that the Supreme Court be given responsibility for umpiring the federal system, that the federal judicial arbiter was understood and accepted by the more important of the state ratifying conventions, and that appellate jurisdiction necessary for the fulfillment of its responsibilities was granted the Supreme Court by the first Congress.

Ironically, it was the states' righters of that era—the anti-Federalists—who were largely responsible for the acceptance of the judicial arbiter in the Philadelphia Convention. Similarly, they strongly supported its implementation in the first Congress. Later their basic assumption, gloomily shared by many nationalists, that the federal judicial arbiter would be a rather mild check on state authority, proved to be false. And later, the confidence of the states' righters in the impartiality of the Supreme Court was shaken, particularly during the tenure of Chief Justice John Marshall. But during the formative period, 1786–1789, both the states' righters and the nationalists, the former with confidence, the latter with grave misgivings, had accepted the new Supreme Court as the arbiter in federal-state relations.*

---

*"The Origin of the Supreme Court's Power as Arbiter in Federal-State Relations" is reprinted (footnotes omitted) with permission of the publisher. Copyright 1958 by the *Wayne State University Law Review*.

Conclusion

The period of British colonial authority, from its rudimentary origins in the 16th century to its violent revolutionary end in the 18th century, had stimulated a great deal of adverse American reaction regarding law and judges. To be sure, the basic framework of law in the newly independent states in 1776 was British in origin. But American resentment of nepotism, political corruption, and economic exploitation altered the colonists' views of how courts and judicial personnel should be organized or chosen. Thus, when independence had been achieved, a significant transformation in the organization and political status of both courts and the legal profession began. The violent revolution for independence from Great Britain was followed by a peaceful but profound and thorough constitutional revision culminating in 1789.

Measured by the criteria which Eisenstadt chose in estimating the outcomes of significant political transformations, the results were profound and fundamental for the courts, state and federal, of sweeping consequence for the concept of a national judiciary, and of great encouragement for the legal profession. First, the composition of political elites in the United States not only changed from British or British-oriented executive, legislative, and judicial leadership to American (a result that is not surprising considering the outcome of the Revolution). Second, independence brought a startling change in the fortunes of the legal profession. Judicial selection at most court levels became a virtually permanent monopoly of lawyers, and after 1789, lawyers predominated in legislative and executive posts. Prior to the Revolution of 1776 and the major constitutional change of 1789, lawyers had held an insignificant number of posts in all three substantive branches. In the alteration of the relationship between groups in society, lawyers and judges enjoyed enhanced prestige and influence—although it is not likely that they achieved the status of the true "Aristocracy in America" accorded them by Alexis de Tocqueville in the 1830s. Finally, in the redistribution of political power, judicial institutions at both the state and federal levels of government were for the first time accorded equal status with the legislative and executive branches of government under the constitutional doctrine of separation of powers.

REFERENCES

1. Cited in Gordon Wood, *The Creation of the American Republic, 1776–1787* (New York: W. W. Norton, 1969), pp. 78, 145.
2. For a full account of the selection of the last colonial chief justice of South Carolina *see* Richard Barry, *Mr. Rutledge of South Carolina* (New York: Duell, Sloan, and Pearce, 1942).
3. Wood, op. cit., pp. 154–155; *see also* "Judicial Action by the Provincial Legislature of Massachusetts," *Harvard Law Review* 15 (1901–02): 1–5.
4. Pennsylvania and New Jersey adopted seven-year terms; Georgia elected the chief justice annually, while the other judges and justices of the peace served at the pleasure of the legislature; Vermont, Connecticut, and Rhode Island provided legislative election of judges annually. Wood, op. cit., pp. 160–61.
5. Wood, op. cit., pp. 454–55.
6. Wood, op. cit., p. 602.

7. Wood, op. cit., pp. 439 and 453; and Gerald Gawalt, *The Promise of Power* (Westport, Conn.: Greenwood Press, 1979), p. 236.

8. Alfred H. Kelley and Winfred A. Harbison, *The American Constitution: Its Origins and Development* (New York: W. W. Norton, 1976), pp. 44–46, 63–64; and Wood, op. cit., p. 262, note 75.

9. John R. Schmidhauser, "'States' Rights' and the Origin of the Supreme Court's Power as Arbiter in Federal-State Relations," *Wayne State University Law Review* 4 (Spring, 1958): 101–14.

3

The New Constitution and Its Implementation

The Beginning of the Supreme Court

The adoption of the Constitution of 1788 represented a very important accomplishment, particularly because it incorporated a significant shift of power and authority from the individual states to the national government. But a careful examination of the controversies over ratification, the exchanges of ideas by political leaders, some of whom did not attend the Philadelphia Convention of 1787, and the fierce congressional fights over the implementation of the Constitution indicate that many issues related to federal-state relations as well as other matters were not fully resolved in Philadelphia. The judiciary was often the focus of such controversy. For example, while many of the advocates of strictly limited government in the Federal Convention had felt that a strong federal judiciary would provide protection for the rights of individuals and states and be a bulwark of the general government, none of them had recognized that a bill of rights incorporated in the Constitution could serve as a basis for the protection of human rights by the Supreme Court. Jefferson, however, after studying the original text of the Constitution while in Paris, recognized this possibility. In a letter to Madison, he wrote:

> In the arguments in favor of a declaration of rights, you omit one which has great weight with me; the legal check which it puts in the hands of the judiciary. This is a body, which, if rendered independent and kept strictly to their own department, merits great confidence for their learning and integrity.[1]

The Court and ratification

In spite of their misgivings, the advocates of strong government did not let lack of confidence in a strong judiciary weaken their efforts to secure ratification of the Constitution. Although Madison had felt little confidence in the federal judiciary as a stabilizing force when he wrote to Jefferson in October 1787, he appears to have experienced fresh hope a few months later. In *The Federalist* 39 he wrote

> that in controversies relating to the boundary between the two jurisdictions (*i.e.,* state and national), the tribunal which is ultimately to decide, is to be established under the general government. . . . The decision is to be impartially made, according to the rules of the Constitution; and all the usual and most effectual precautions are taken to secure this impartiality. Some such tribunal is clearly essential to prevent an appeal to the sword and a dissolution of the compact.[2]

In *The Federalist* 80, Hamilton wrote as follows:

> What, for instance, would avail restrictions on the authority of the state legislatures, without some constitutional mode of enforcing the observance of them? The States, by the plan of the Convention, are prohibited from doing a variety of things, some of which are incompatible with the interests of the Union, and others with the principles of good government. The imposition of duties on imported articles, and the emission of paper money, are specimens of each kind. No man of sense will believe, that such prohibitions would be scrupulously regarded, without some effectual power in the government to restrain or correct infractions of them. This power must either be a direct negative on the State laws, or an authority in the Federal courts to overrule such as might be in manifest contravention of the articles of Union. . . . The latter appears to have been thought by the Convention preferable to the former, and, I presume, will be most agreeable to the States.[3]

Although the states' rights advocates in the Philadelphia Convention of 1787 had contributed a great deal to the development of the concept of a strong, independent Supreme Court, not all of them were comfortable with this development. Those in disagreement opposed what they described as strong centralization of power in the national government. They became the leaders in the first emergent opposition party, the anti–Federalists. One of the clearest expressions of such anti–Federalist disagreement was penned by Robert Yates of New York. Yates, who had refused to approve the Constitution in the Philadelphia Convention, wrote a series of letters which, in accordance with the custom of the era, were identified with the name of an opponent of tyranny, in this instance, the Roman Brutus. The Brutus letters were printed in the *New York Journal and Weekly Register* in 1788. Letters numbered 11, 12, and 15 contain the most searching, critical analysis of the proposed judicial institution to appear in that era. For modern advocates of a states' rights position, Yates' letters are prophetic. The arguments against ratification of the Constitution by Yates and other anti–Federalists stimulated letters by the advocates of ratification. The most famous of these is the series of letters by Alexander Hamilton, John Jay, and James Madison known as the *Federalist Papers*. Number 78 by Alexander Hamilton addressed the precise concerns expressed by Yates. Reprinted here are the contrasting arguments, which opened a debate about the powers and limitations of the Supreme Court that has never been fully resolved.

ROBERT YATES IN *THE LETTERS OF BRUTUS*[4]

*Brutus, No. 11, January 1788**

. . . Much has been said and written upon the subject of this new system on both sides, but I have not met with any writer who has discussed the judicial powers with any degree of accuracy. And yet it is obvious, that we can form but very imperfect ideas of the manner in which this government will work, or the effect it will have in changing the internal police and mode of distributing justice at present subsisting in the respective states, without a thorough investigation of the powers of the judiciary and of the manner in which they will operate. This government is a complete system, not only for making, but for executing laws. And the courts of law, which will be constituted by it, are not only to decide upon the constitution and the laws made in pursuance of it, but by officers subordinate to them to execute all their decisions. The real effect of this system of government will therefore be brought home to the feeling of the people through the medium of the judicial power. It is, moreover, of great importance, to examine with care the nature and extent of the judicial power, because those who are to be vested with it, are to be placed in a situation alto-gether unprecedented in a free country. They are to be rendered totally independent, both of the people and the legislature, both with respect to their offices and salaries. No errors they may commit can be corrected by any power above them, if any such power there be, nor can they be removed from office for making ever so many erroneous adjudications.

The only causes for which they can be displaced, are, conviction of treason, bribery, and high crimes and misdemeanors.

This part of the plan is so modelled, as to authorize the courts, not only to carry into execution the powers expressly given, but where these are wanting or ambigu-ously expressed, to supply what is wanting by their own decisions. . . .

They [the courts] will give the sense of every article of the constitution, that may from time to time come before them. And in their decisions they will not confine themselves to any fixed or established rules, but will determine, according to what appears to them, the reason and spirit of the constitution. The opinions of the supreme court, whatever they may be, will have the force of law, because there is no power provided in the constitution, that can correct their errors, or controul their adjudications. From this court there is no appeal. And I conceive the legislature themselves, cannot set aside a judgment of this court, because they are authorized by the constitution to decide in the last resort. The legislature must be controuled by the constitution, and not the constitution by them. They have therefore no more right to set aside any judgment pronounced upon the construction of the constitu-tion, than they have to take from the president, the chief command of the army and navy, and commit it to some other person. The reason is plain; the judicial and execu-tive derive their authority from the same source, that the legislature do theirs; and therefore in all cases, where the constitution does not make the one responsible to, or controulable by the other, they are altogether independent of each other.

The judicial power will operate to effect, in the most certain, but yet silent and imperceptible manner, what is evidently the tendency of the constitution:—I mean, an entire subversion of the legislative, executive and judicial powers of the individual states. Every adjudication of the supreme court, on any question that may arise upon

*The *Letters of Brutus* reproduced with permission of Princeton University Press.

the nature and extent of the general government, will affect the limits of the state jurisdiction. In proportion as the former enlarge the exercise of their powers, will that of the latter be restricted.

That the judicial power of the United States, will lean strongly in favour of the general government, and will give such an explanation to the constitution, as will favour an extension of its jurisdiction, is very evident from a variety of considerations.

1st. The constitution itself strongly countenances such a mode of construction. Most of the articles in this system, which convey powers of any considerable importance, are conceived in general and indefinite terms, which are either equivocal, ambiguous, or which require long definitions to unfold the extent of their meaning. The two most important powers committed to any government, those of raising money, and of raising and keeping up troops, have already been considered, and shewn to be unlimited by anything but the discretion of the legislature. The clause which vests the power to pass all laws which are proper and necessary, to carry the powers given into execution, it has been shewn, leaves the legislature at liberty to do every thing, which in their judgment is best. It is said, I know, that this clause confers no power on the legislature, which they would not have had without it—though I believe this is not the fact, yet, admitting it to be, it implies that the constitution is not to receive an explanation strictly, according to its letter, but more power is implied than is expressed. And this clause, if it is to be considered, as explanatory of the extent of the powers given, rather than giving a new power, is to be understood as declaring, that in construing any of the articles conveying power, the spirit, intent and design of the clause, should be attended to, as well as the words in their common acceptation.

This constitution gives sufficient colour for adopting an equitable construction, if we consider the great end and design it professedly has in view—this appears from the preamble to be, "to form a more perfect union, establish justice, insure domestic tranquility, provide for the common defense, promote the general welfare, and secure the blessings of liberty to ourselves and posterity. . . ."

2d. Not only will the constitution justify the courts in inclining to this mode of explaining it, but they will be interested in using this latitude of interpretation. Every body of men invested with office are tenacious of power; they feel interested, and hence it has become a kind of maxim, to hand down their offices, with all its rights and privileges, unimpaired to their successors; the same principle will influence them to extend their power, and increase their rights; this of itself will operate strongly upon the courts to give such a meaning to the constitution in all cases where it can possibly be done, as will enlarge the sphere of their own authority. Every extension of the power of the general legislature, as well as of the judicial powers, will increase the power of the courts; and the dignity and importance of the judges, will be in proportion to the extent and magnitude of the powers they exercise. I add, it is highly probable that emolument of the judges will be increased, with the increase of the business they will have to transact and its importance. From these considerations the judges will be interested to extend the powers of the courts, and to construe the constitution as much as possible, in such a way as to favour it; and that they will do it, appears probable.

3d. Because they will have precedent to plead, to justify them in it. It is well known, that the courts of England, have by their own authority, extended their jurisdiction far beyond the limits set them in their original institution, and by the laws of the land. . . .

When the courts will have a [precedent] before them of a court which extended its jurisdiction in opposition to an act of the legislature, is it not to be expected that they will extend theirs, especially when there is nothing in the constitution expressly against it? and they are authorized to construct its meaning, and are not under any control?

This power in the judicial, will enable them to mould the government, into almost any shape they please.—The manner in which this may be affected we will hereafter examine.

Brutus, No. 15, March 1788

I said in my last number, that the supreme court under this constitution would be exalted above all other powers in the government, and subject to no control. The business of this paper will be to illustrate this, and to shew the danger that will result from it. I question whether the world ever saw, in any period of it, a court of justice invested with such immense powers, and yet placed in a situation so little responsible. . . .

The framers of this constitution appear to have followed that of the British, in rendering the judges independent, by granting them their offices during good behavior, without following the constitution of England, in instituting a tribunal in which their errors may be corrected; and without adverting to this, that the judicial under this system have a power which is above the legislative, and which indeed transcends any power before given to a judicial by any free government under heaven.

I do not object to the judges holding their commissions during good behaviour. I suppose it is a proper provision provided they were made properly responsible. But I say, this system has followed the English government in this, while it has departed from almost every other principle of their jurisprudence, under the idea, of rendering the judges independent; which, in the British constitution, means no more than that they hold their places during good behaviour, and have fixed salaries, they have made the judges *independent*, in the fullest sense of the word. There is no power above them, to controul any of their decisions. There is no authority that can remove them, and they cannot be controuled by the laws of the legislature. In short, they are independent of the people, of the legislature, and of every power under heaven. Men placed in this situation will generally soon feel themselves independent of heaven itself. . . .

The supreme court then have a right, independent of the legislature, to give a construction of the constitution and every part of it, and there is no power provided in this system to correct their construction or do it away. If, therefore, the legislature pass any laws, inconsistent with the sense the judges put upon the constitution, they will declare it void; and therefore in this respect their power is superior to that of the legislature. . . .

I have, in the course of my observation on this constitution, affirmed and endeavored to shew, that it was calculated to abolish entirely the state governments, and to melt down the states into one entire government, for every purpose as well internal and local, as external and national. . . .

ALEXANDER HAMILTON, *THE FEDERALIST*, NO. 78[5]

We proceed now to an examination of the judiciary department of the proposed government. . . .

Whoever attentively considers the different departments of power must perceive that, in a government in which they are separated from each other, the judiciary, from the nature of its functions, will always be the least dangerous to the political rights of the Constitution; because it will be least in a capacity to annoy or injure them. . . . The judiciary . . . has no influence over either the sword or the purse; no direction either of the strength or of the wealth of the society; and can take no active resolution whatever. It may truly be said to have neither FORCE nor WILL, but merely judgment; and must ultimately depend upon the aid of the executive arm even for the efficacy of its judgments.

This simple view of the matter suggests several important consequences. It proves incontestably, that the judiciary is beyond comparison the weakest of the three departments of power; that it can never attack with success either of the other two; and that all possible care is requisite to enable it to defend itself against their attacks. It equally proves, that though individual oppression may now and then proceed from the courts of justice, the general liberty of the people can never be endangered from that quarter; I mean so long as the judiciary remains truly distinct from both the legislature and the Executive.

Some perplexity respecting the rights of courts to pronounce legislative acts void, because contrary to the Constitution, has arisen from an imagination that the doctrine would imply a superiority of the judiciary to the legislative power. It is urged that the authority which can declare the acts of another void, must necessarily be superior to the one whose acts may be declared void. As this doctrine is of great importance in all the American constitutions, a brief discussion of the ground on which it rests cannot be unacceptable.

There is no position which depends on clearer principles, than that every act of a delegated authority, contrary to the tenor of the commission under which it is exercised, is void. No legislative act, therefore, contrary to the Constitution, can be valid. To deny this, would be to affirm, that the deputy is greater than his principal; that the servant is above his master; that the representatives of the people are superior to the people themselves; that men acting by virtue of powers, may do not only what their powers do not authorize, but what they forbid.

If it be said that the legislative body are themselves the constitutional judges of their own powers, and that the construction they put upon them is conclusive upon the other departments, it may be answered, that this cannot be the natural presumption, where it is not to be collected from any particular Constitution. It is not otherwise to be supposed, that the Constitution could intend to enable the representatives of the people to substitute their will to that of their constituents. It is far more rational to suppose, that the courts were designed to be an intermediate body between the people and the legislature, in order, among other things, to keep the latter within the limits assigned to their authority. The interpretation of the laws is the proper and peculiar province of the courts. A constitution is, in fact, and must be regarded by the judges, as a fundamental law. It therefore belongs to them to ascertain its meaning, as well as the meaning of any particular act proceeding from the legislative body. If there should happen to be an irreconcilable variance between the two, that which has the superior obligation and validity ought, of course, to be preferred; or, in other words, the Constitution ought to be preferred to the statute, the intention of the people to the intention of their agents.

Nor does this conclusion by any means suppose a superiority of the judicial to the legislative power. It only supposes that the power of the people is superior to both; and that where the will of the legislature, declared in its statutes, stands in opposition to that of the people, declared in the Constitution, the judges ought to be governed by the latter rather than the former. They ought to regulate their decisions by the fundamental laws, rather than by those which are not fundamental. . . .

If, then, the courts of justice are to be considered as the bulwarks of a limited Constitution against legislative encroachments, this consideration will afford a strong argument for the permanent tenure of judicial offices, since nothing will contribute so much as this to that independent spirit in the judges which must be essential to the faithful performance of so arduous a duty.

This independence of the judges is equally requisite to guard the Constitution and the rights of individuals from the effects of those ill humors, which the arts of designing men, or the influence of particular conjunctures, sometimes disseminate among the people themselves, and which, though they speedily give place to better information, and more deliberate reflection, have a tendency, in the meantime, to occasion dangerous innovations in the government, and serious oppressions of the minor party in the community. Though I trust the friends of the proposed Constitution will never concur with its enemies, in questioning that fundamental principle of republican government, which admits the right of the people to alter or abolish the established Constitution, whenever they find it inconsistent with their happiness, yet it is not to be inferred from this principle, that the representatives of the people, whenever a momentary inclination happens to lay hold of a majority of their constituents, incompatible with the provisions in the existing Constitution, would, on that account, be justifiable in a violation of those provisions; or that the courts would be under a greater obligation to connive at infractions in this shape, than when they had proceeded wholly from the cabals of the representative body. Until the people have, by some solemn and authoritative act, annulled or changed the established form, it is binding upon themselves collectively, as well as individually and no presumption, or even knowledge, of their sentiments, can warrant their representatives in a departure from it, prior to such an act. But it is easy to see, that it could require an uncommon portion of fortitude in the judges to do their duty as faithful guardians of the Constitution, where legislative invasions of it had been instigated by the major voice of the community.

But it is not with a view to infractions of the Constitution only, that the independence of the judges may be an essential safeguard against the effects of occasional ill humors in the society. These sometimes extend no farther than to the injury of the private rights of particular classes of citizens, by unjust and partial laws. Here also the firmness of the judicial magistracy is of vast importance in mitigating the severity and confining the operation of such laws. . . .

The objections and concerns of Yates were raised not only in the ratifying convention of his own state, New York, but in many others as well. The complaint of Elbridge Gerry of Massachusetts indicates the typical anti–Federalist fear:

My principle objections to the plan are . . . that the judicial department will be oppressive. . . . There are no well-defined limits of the Judiciary powers, they seem to be left as a boundless ocean. . . . It would be a Herculean labor to attempt to describe the dangers with which they are replete.[6]

Sixteen of the seventy-nine amendments suggested by the ratifying conventions of Massachusetts, New Hampshire, Virginia, New York, and North Carolina were proposals for changes in the judiciary article.[7] In a complete review of all the debates, Willoughby found that the major objections in the ratifying conventions were that state judiciaries would be interfered with and oppressed and that the states would be held liable by federal courts to suits by individuals.[8] In the Virginia convention, the latter charge was emphatically denied by Madison and Marshall, both stating that "it is not in the power of individuals to call a state into court."[9]

Although they faced strong opposition in a number of the ratifying conventions, the supporters of the Constitution stated concisely the role of the Supreme Court in the new system of government and ably defended the judicial arbiter concept. The clearest statements of the power of the Supreme Court to act as final interpreter in conflicts arising between the three branches of the federal government and between the states and the federal government were given in a South Carolina legislative debate and in the constitutional ratifying conventions of Connecticut, North Carolina, and Virginia.

In the debates in the South Carolina legislature on the question of calling a constitution ratifying convention, Charles Pinckney unequivocally stated this doctrine:

> That a supreme federal jurisdiction was indispensible cannot be denied. It is equally true, that in order to insure the administration of justice, it was necessary to give all the powers, original as well as appellate, the constitution has enumerated. Without it we could not expect a due observance of treaties, that the state judiciaries would confine themselves within their proper sphere; or that a general sense of justice would pervade the Union. . . . That to insure these, extensive authorities were necessary; particularly so were they in a tribunal, constituted as this is, whose duty it would be, not only to decide all national questions, which should arise within the Union; but to control and keep the state judiciaries within their proper limits, whenever they should attempt to interfere with the power.[10]

In January 1788, in the Connecticut ratifying convention, Oliver Ellsworth gave his conception of the role envisaged by the constitutional framers for the Supreme Court:

> This Constitution defines the extent of the powers of the general government. If the general legislature should at any time overleap their limits, the judicial department is a constitutional check. If the United States go beyond their powers, if they make a law which the Constitution does not authorize, it is void; and the judicial power, the national judges, who, to secure their impartiality, are to be made independent, will declare it to be void. On the other hand, if the states go beyond their limits, if they make a law which is a usurpation upon the general government, the law is void; and upright, independent judges will declare it so.[11]

William R. Davie in the North Carolina ratifying convention stated:

> The Constitution might be violated with impunity by particular states—if there were no power in the general government to correct and counteract such laws. This great object can only be safely and completely obtained by the instrumentality of the federal judiciary.[12]

In June of the same year, Madison held, in the Virginia ratifying convention, that:

> It may be a misfortune that, in organizing any government, the explication of its authority should be left to any of its coordinate branches. There is no example in any country where it is otherwise. There is new policy in submitting it to the judiciary of the United States. That causes of a Federal nature will arise, will be obvious

to every gentleman who will recollect that the states are laid under restrictions, and that the rights of the Union are secured by these restrictions. They may involve equitable as well as legal controversies. With respect to the laws of the Union, it is so necessary and expedient that the judicial power should correspond with the legislative, that it has not been objected to. With respect to treaties, there is a peculiar propriety in the judiciary's expounding them.

These may involve us in controversies with foreign nations. It is necessary, therefore, that they should be determined in the courts of the general government. There are strong reasons why there should be a Supreme Court to decide such disputes. If in any case, uniformity be necessary, it must be in the exposition of treaties. The establishment of one revisionary superintending power can alone secure such uniformity.[13]

On the basis of these and other discussions in the constitution ratifying conventions, it is apparent that the role of the Supreme Court as final arbiter in federal-state relations was clearly understood and generally accepted.

In most of the convention battles the Federalists successfully, but sometimes by only the slimmest of margins, managed to secure ratification by promising to introduce amendments at the first session of Congress.[14] It was not until June 21, 1788 that the ninth state ratified the Constitution.

The first judiciary act

On March 4, 1789, the wheels of government began to turn; but for eleven months after the United States came into existence, it lacked a judicial branch of government. Although the judiciary bill was introduced the very next day after the new Senate was organized with a quorum present, six months passed before the bill became law and President Washington could appoint members to the first Supreme Court.[15]

While the constitutional framers had drawn the broad outlines of the judicial power, they had left to congressional discretion the composition of the federal courts, the extent of the appellate jurisdiction of the Supreme Court, the existence or nonexistence of any inferior federal courts, and the extent of their jurisdiction. Thus, while in form the Federal Judiciary Act of September 24, 1789 was an ordinary legislative act, in substance it was of broad constitutional significance.[16]

Oliver Ellsworth and William Paterson took leading roles in drafting the bill in committee. In the early stages of this drafting, Ellsworth sought to establish a complete network of inferior federal courts and to extend their jurisdiction to the limits set by the Constitution.[17] To secure the concurrence of Richard Henry Lee, however, Ellsworth apparently had to accept a greatly limited inferior federal court system. This setback was mitigated by inclusion of an additional provision that allowed a defendant sued in a state court in a case involving a federal question to remove the case to a federal circuit court or to appeal to the Supreme Court by writ of error after trial "in the highest court of law or equity of a State in which a decision in the suit could be had."[18]

When debate on the bill began in the committee of the whole on June 22, the issue centered around the question whether there should be any district courts at all or whether the function of executing federal laws should be left in the first instance to the state courts. Ellsworth was opposed to giving the state courts such power.[19]

Debate over the various proposals in the bill raged for three months in the Senate and the House. The crucial issues were whether there should be any inferior federal courts, and, if there were to be any such courts, whether they would be vested with the full jurisdiction that the Constitution permitted.[20]

The bill in its final form was a compromise. The Federalists were forced to abandon their contention that the federal courts must be granted the fullest jurisdiction possible under the Constitution, while the anti-Federalists were unable to confine federal cases to the state courts, subject to appeal, and were compelled to accept federal courts possessing a very limited jurisdiction. The bill apparently pleased the anti–Federalists more than it did the Federalists.[21]

Section 25, which became the very cornerstone of federal judiciary supremacy, had been adopted by the Senate substantially as drafted. The establishment of the appellate jurisdiction of the Supreme Court over state courts where such courts decided against a claimed federal right did not arouse any serious opposition and was readily agreed to by the anti–Federalists.[22] It is noteworthy that this party, which later bitterly opposed appeals from state courts to the Supreme Court, in 1789 actually advocated such jurisdiction.

The relationship of Section 25 to the supremacy clause of the Constitution and the theory upon which these provisions and the federal judicial system were founded were best stated by Madison in a letter on nullification many years later:

> A political system which does not contain an effective provision for a peaceable decision of all controversies arising within itself would be government in name only. Such a provision is obviously essential, and it is equally obvious that it cannot be either peaceable or effective by making every part an authoritative empire. The final appeal in such cases must be to the authority of the whole, not to that of the parts separately or independently. This was the view taken of the subject while the Constitution was under consideration of the people. It was this view of it which dictated the clause declaring that the Constitution and laws of the United States should be the supreme law of the land, anything in the constitution or laws of the states to the contrary notwithstanding. It was the same view which specially prohibited certain powers and acts to the states, among them any laws violating the obligation of contracts, and which dictated the appellate provision in the judicial act passed by the first Congress under the Constitution.[23]

In the provisions of Section 25, the First Congress completed the task begun by the convention and made the Supreme Court the final arbiter in federal-state relations. How the federal judges and justices utilized the powers conferred by convention and Congress in 1787 and 1789 to assert and maintain the supremacy of the national government was destined to become a central issue in virtually every significant electoral contest for the next six decades. The newly created federal judiciary became involved in every important political issue arising in the first decade of its existence.

The extension of the Supreme Court's jurisdiction to all cases in law and equity arising under the Constitution and the laws of the United States, and the granting by the first Congress of final appellate power to the Court had made that organ the ultimate stabilizing organ in the political system. In setting up a permanent judicial tribunal with compulsory jurisdiction over states, the federal convention and the first Congress had contributed an entirely novel institution to the American political system. The powers of this new institution were broad and untested; its jurisdiction overlapped areas in which older, entrenched institutions, particularly the state courts, had reigned supreme. The career of Gideon Olmstead, a seaman, provides a dramatic illustration of the practical impact of such institutional changes.

Gideon Olmstead tests the new federal judiciary

Although the states had banded together for certain purposes during the American Revolution, the concept of national authority, as indicated in Olmstead's problem, was often strongly resisted by individual states. In 1778 Gideon Olmstead and three other citizens of Connecticut were captured by the British, carried to Jamaica, and put on board the sloop *Active* to assist as mariners in navigating the sloop to New York, which at that time was in British possession. During the voyage, Olmstead and the others overcame the British crew and attempted to reach Egg Harbor, New Jersey. However, they were overtaken and captured by the brig *Convention*, a privateer authorized by the state of Pennsylvania. The *Convention's* captain claimed the sloop *Active* as a prize in Philadelphia. Olmstead and his companions, on the other hand, claimed the *Active* as their exclusive prize. A state court of admiralty awarded Olmstead and his fellow claimants only one fourth of the prize, dividing the rest between the state of Pennsylvania and the privateers.

Olmstead appealed to the Confederation Congress' court of commissioners, a national prize court that Congress had established to meet the needs of a disorganized period. The tremendous increase in privateering during the American Revolution made necessary the setting up of prize courts to replace the old vice-admiralty tribunals that had existed under the royal governors. Privateers were commissioned not only by the states but by the Continental Congress as well. In 1779, Gideon Olmstead was awarded the proceeds of the sale of the sloop, but Judge Ross of the state court refused to carry out this decree. He placed the disputed prize money in the care of the state treasurer, David Rittenhouse.[24]

The Confederation Congress then investigated the affair. Its committee reported that the congressional prize court had the authority to review the state court's decision, and resolved that "no act of any state can, or ought to, destroy the right of appeal to Congress." The legislature of Pennsylvania thereupon ordered the state admiralty court to ignore the congressional committee resolution. The Confederation Congress did not take any further action, and Olmstead again resorted to the state courts. This time he obtained a judgment by default in a county court, but lost again when the case was taken on appeal to the Supreme Court of Pennsylvania. Chief Justice McKean declared that "the decree of the Committee of appeals [is] contrary to the provisions of the act of Congress, and of the general assembly, extra-judicial, erroneous and void."[25] After this judicial defeat, Olmstead made no attempt to contest the validity of the state court decision until 1803. He resurrected his claim that year because the Supreme Court of the United States, in *Penhallow* v. *Doane*,[26] a case unrelated to prize money issues, held that federal district courts had authority to execute the decrees of the old Confederation court of appeals in cases of capture.

Olmstead took the issue to a federal district court. In January 1803, Judge Peters upheld Olmstead's claims and, under the Penhallow doctrine, decreed that the prize money be paid to Olmstead. The Pennsylvania legislature immediately passed a law defying the federal district court's ruling as a usurpation of jurisdiction. The statute directed the governor "to protect the just rights of the state from any process issued out of any federal court." Finally, after five years, this direct challenge to the federal judiciary was reviewed by the Supreme Court. In 1808, Olmstead, now eighty-two years old, applied to the highest national tribunal for issuance of a *mandamus* to Judge Peters to compel him to enforce obedience to his district court decision of 1803. Such a mandamus was issued directing Peters to exercise the sentence pronounced by him in *Gideon Olmstead and others* v. *Rittenhouse's Executrices* or show cause for not so doing. Judge Peters answered that "from prudential, more than other motives, I deemed it best to avoid embroiling the government of the United States and that of Pennsylvania (if the latter government should choose to do so), on a question which has rested on my single opinion."[27]

In 1809, in *United States* v. *Judge Peters*, Chief Justice John Marshall pointed out that it was with "great attention, and with serious concern" that the Supreme Court had considered "the return of Judge Peters to the *mandamus*." Marshall stated:

> If the legislatures of the several states may, at will, annul the judgments of the courts of the United States, and destroy the rights acquired under those judgments, the constitution itself becomes a solemn mockery; and the nation is deprived of the means of enforcing its laws by the instrumentality of its own tribunals. So fatal a result must be deprecated by all; and the people of Pennsylvania, not less than the citizens of every other state, must feel a deep interest in resisting principles so destructive of the Union, and in averting consequences so fatal to themselves.[28]

Marshall held that "the ultimate right to determine the jurisdiction of the courts of the Union" necessarily resides in "the supreme judicial tribunal of the nation," not the state legislatures. After briefly reviewing and upholding the lower federal court decision, Marshall "with extreme regret" awarded a preemptory *mandamus*.

Governor Snyder of Pennsylvania immediately sent a message to the state legislature informing the representatives that he intended to call out the militia to prevent enforcement of the decree. On March 24, Judge Peters issued process against the holders of the contested prize money, Mrs. Sergeant and Mrs. Waters, executrices of the deceased state treasurer, David Rittenhouse. When the United States marshal attempted to serve process, he met with the resistance of a body of state militia commanded by General Bright. He then summoned a *posse comitatus* of two thousand men. For a time bloodshed seemed imminent. On April 3, the Pennsylvania legislature adopted resolutions denying that the Supreme Court had the power "to decide on State rights." But by April 6, the Pennsylvania authorities had begun to weaken.[29] As one discerning newspaper correspondent observed,

It had been supposed that the marshall [sic], good, easy man, would make but a faint attempt to enforce the service of the process. The active attempt made by him has awakened the most serious apprehensions . . . it is understood that measures will be taken to compromise matters with the much injured, old veteran.[30]

On April 6, Governor Snyder wrote to the President, James Madison, expressing the hope that the latter would "justly discriminate between opposition to the Constitution and laws of the United States and that of resisting the decree of a Judge founded . . . on a usurpation of power." The newly elected President replied as follows:

The Executive is not only unauthorized to prevent the execution of a decree sanctioned by the Supreme Court of the United States, but is expressly enjoined, by statute, to carry into effect any such decree, where opposition may be made to it.[31]

The Pennsylvania legislature ordered removal of the state militia from the Rittenhouse residence and began consideration of a bill to appropriate enough money to restore the contested prize fund. Mrs. Sergeant, now under arrest for refusal to obey the federal court order, applied for a writ of *habeas corpus* to Chief Justice Tilghman of the Pennsylvania Supreme Court. He dismissed her petition, holding that she was properly in federal custody.[32] By April 26, the state had made the payment required by the federal court. Relieved, President Madison wrote to Attorney General Rodney: "The affair of Olmstead has passed off without the threatened collision of force."

The final humiliation for the state of Pennsylvania came when General Bright was tried and convicted before Justice Bushrod Washington in federal circuit court. For forcibly resisting a federal marshal, Bright and his associates were sentenced to fine and imprisonment. President Madison pardoned them, however, on the ground that "they had acted under a mistaken sense of duty."[33]

At the very height of the controversy, the Pennsylvania legislature had stated, in resolutions that were submitted to the legislatures of the other states, its own version of the doctrine of state sentinelship. It acknowledged the supremacy of "the General Government," but while it submitted to the latter's authority when such authority was:

. . . exercised within Constitutional limits, they [the state legislature] trust they will not be considered as acting hostile to the General Government, when, as guardians of the State rights, they cannot permit an infringement of those rights, by an unconstitutional exercise of power in the United States Courts. . . . To suffer the United States' courts to decide on state rights will, from a bias in favor of power, necessarily destroy the Federal part of our government.[34]

The Pennsylvania resolutions were answered by resolutions of disapproval by the legislatures of Tennessee, Kentucky, New Jersey, Maryland, Ohio, Georgia, North Carolina, Virginia, New Hampshire, and Vermont.[35] In reply to the Pennsylvania proposal that the "sister states" support it in endeavoring to get a constitutional amendment establishing an "impartial tribunal to determine disputes between the General and State Governments," the Virginia legislature resolved that,

. . . a tribunal is already provided by the Constitution of the United States; to wit: the Supreme Court, more eminently qualified from their habits and duties, from the mode of their selection, and from the tenure of their offices, to decide the disputes aforesaid in an enlightened and impartial manner, than any other tribunal that could be erected.[36]

The conflicts between levels of government overshadowed the persistent old seaman. Yet Gideon Olmstead's ability to pursue his litigatory interests to the very apex of the legal system demonstrated a unique characteristic of the American legal system. Although it was not easy, nor commonplace, this new legal system created in Philadelphia in 1787 and implemented by the first Congress in 1789 made it possible for an ordinary citizen in pursuit of his rights or claims to invoke the full authority of the highest judicial institution in the nation. If his claim tested the limits of authority of the various levels of government involved, such testing was deemed a necessary part of a system in which the individual could invoke the law in his own behalf. Olmstead's legal efforts spanned three decades from the American Revolution to the post-constitutional adoption period in U. S. history and the presidencies of George Washington, John Adams, Thomas Jefferson, and the beginning of James Madison's. The conflicts of national and state authority that his litigation stimulated were the central issues of these periods in American political development. The manner in which the Supreme Court and the circuit and district courts comprising the federal judiciary handled these issues was determined in part by the choice of judicial personnel made from the very beginning of the new system in 1789.

Federalist justices and early judicial politics

President George Washington selected John Jay, strong Federalist advocate of the new Constitution, as chief justice. He chose John Rutledge, James Wilson, James Iredell, John Blair, and William Cushing as associate justices. All were strong Federalists who had taken important roles in either development or ratification of the new Constitution. Rutledge resigned without actually sitting on the bench. His successor Thomas Johnson, also a Federalist, served from 1791 to 1793, when he was succeeded by William Paterson.

President Washington carefully divided the appointments between North and South. The new appointees were chosen from among the wealthy mercantile and business elite of the northern or middle Atlantic states or the plantation economy of the south. Jay, Cushing, and Wilson were from New York, Massachusetts, and Pennsylvania respectively, while Rutledge, Blair, and Iredell hailed from South Carolina, Virginia, and North Carolina. All of the appointees favored a strong central government and had played important political roles in establishing one.

For the first two years, the Supreme Court did not have a single case before it, but during this period the justices were able to acquaint the people with the new judicial institution in the federal circuit courts. In a number of extremely hard-fought legislative actions, the first Congress had succeeded in establishing a complete federal judiciary composed of (1) trial courts—the district courts, (2) intermediate appellate courts—the circuit courts, and (3) the highest appellate court

—the Supreme Court of the United States. Originally, however, the Judiciary Act did not provide for separate circuit judges. Instead, the federal district judges and the Supreme Court justices were assigned to specific circuits where they served together as circuit judges for certain designated periods during the year. For virtually the first hundred years of its existence, the Supreme Court was intimately linked to the rest of the federal judiciary. Indeed, the work of most individual justices was divided rather evenly between circuit and high tribunal.

At the beginning of the system individual justices utilized the opportunities afforded in their roles as circuit judges to make statements supporting the political position of the Federalist party. The charges to the grand jury made in these courts are significant because they indicate the justices' attitudes toward the new government and their opinions concerning the role of its judicial system.

Chief Justice Jay's charge at the circuit court in New York City on April 4, 1790 illustrates the scope and emphasis given a strong Federalist position tempered with caution:

> We had become a Nation. As such we were responsible to others for the observance of the Laws of Nations; and as our National concerns were to be regulated by National laws, National tribunals became necessary for the interpretation of them. No tribunals of the like kind and extent had heretofore existed in this country. From such therefore, no light of experience, no facilities of usage and habit were to be derived. Our jurisprudence varied in almost every state, and was accommodated to local, not general convenience, to partial, not National policy. This convenience and this policy were nevertheless to be regarded and tenderly treated. A judicial controul, general and final, was indispensible. The manner of establishing it with powers neither too extensive nor too limited rendering it properly independent and yet properly amenable involved questions of no little intricacy. The expedience of carrying justice, as it were, to every man's door was obvious; but how to do it in an expedient manner was far from being apparent. To provide against discord between National and State jurisdiction, to render them auxiliary instead of hostile to each other, and so to connect both as to leave each sufficiently independent and yet sufficiently combined was and *will be* arduous. Institutions formed under such circumstances should therefore be received with candor and tried with temper and prudence.[37]

A number of circuit court cases concerned the validity of state statutes, and the most important of these was *Van Horne's Lessee* v. *Dorrance*.[38] Before the signing of the Constitution, a territorial controversy between Connecticut and Pennsylvania had raged for a number of years. Connecticut had claimed a large portion of northeastern Pennsylvania and had sent settlers into the area to bolster her claim. For a time armed conflict between opposing bands of settlers appeared imminent. The controversy between the two states was not settled until after the signing of the Articles of Confederation.[39] It was from this background of conflicting claims that the case arose.

In the April term of 1795, Justice Paterson and District Judge Peters took the Dorrance case under consideration. After a lengthy investigation of the conflicting land claims, Justice Paterson held that a Pennsylvania statute that gave state commissioners the power to vest in Connecticut settlers the estates of Pennsylvania claimants was void because it impaired the obligation of a contract.[40] Aside from its importance as an example of federal circuit court invalidation of a state law, *Van Horne's Lessee* v. *Dorrance* provides a clear statement of the doctrine of judicial review and the nature of a written constitution. Eight years before *Marbury* v. *Madison*, Justice Paterson clearly distinguished the difference between Great Britain's system of parliamentary supremacy and the new system of constitutional limitations adopted in the United States in 1789, asserted the power of judicial review, and invoked the contract clause of the Constitution to invalidate the state law in question.

VAN HORNE'S LESSEE v. DORRANCE
2 Dallas 304 (1795)

I. The constitutionality of the conforming act; or, in other words, whether the legislature had authority to make that act?

Legislation is the exercise of sovereign authority. High and important powers are necessarily vested in the Legislative body: whose acts, under some forms of government, are irresistible and subject to no control. In England, from whence most of our legal principles and legislative notions are derived, the authority of the Parliament is transcendant, and has no bounds. . . .

Some of the judges in England, have had the boldness to assert, that an act of parliament, made against natural equity, is void; but this opinion contravenes the general position, that the validity of an act of parliament cannot be drawn into question by the judicial department: It cannot be disputed, and must be obeyed. The power of parliament is absolute and transcendant; it is omnipotent in the scale of political existence. Besides, in England there is no written constitution, no fundamental law, nothing visible, nothing real, nothing certain, by which a statute can be tested. In America the case is widely different: Every state in the union has its constitution reduced to written exactitude and precision.

What is a constitution? It is the form of government, delineated by the mighty hand of the people, in which certain first principles of fundamental laws are established. The constitution is certain and fixed; it contains the permanent will of the people, and is the supreme law of the land; it is paramount to the power of the legislature, and can be revoked or altered only by the authority that made it.

The life-giving principle and the death-doing stroke must proceed from the same hand. What are legislatures? Creatures of the constitution; they owe their existence to the constitution; they derive their powers from the constitution; it is their commission; and, therefore, all their acts must be conformable to it, or else they will be void. The constitution is the work or will of the people themselves, in their original, sovereign, and unlimited capacity. Law is the work or will of the legislature in their derivative and subordinate capacity. The one is the work of the Creator, and the other of the creature. The constitution fixes limits to the exercise of legislative authority, and prescribes the orbit within which it must move. In short, gentlemen, the constitution is the sun of the political system, around which all legislative, executive and judicial bodies must revolve. Whatever may be the case in other countries, yet in this, there can be no doubt, that every act of the legislature, repugnant to the constitution, is absolutely void. . . .

The constitution of a state is stable and permanent, not to be worked upon by the temper of the times nor to rise and fall with the tide of events: notwithstanding the competition of opposing interests, and the violence of contending parties, it remains firm and immovable, as a mountain amidst the strife of storms, or a rock in the ocean amidst the raging of the waves. I take it to be a clear position: that if a legislative act oppugns a constitutional principle the former must give way, and be rejected on the score of repugnance. I hold it to a position equally clear and sound, that, in such case, it will be the duty of the court to adhere to the constitution, and to declare the act null and void. The constitution is the basis of legislative authority; it lies at the foundation of all law, and is a rule and commission by which both legislators and judges are to proceed. It is an important principle, which in the discussion of questions of the present kind, ought never to be lost sight of, that the judiciary in this country is not a subordinate, but co-ordinate branch of the government. . . .

In the course of argument, the counsel . . . relied upon certain parts of the late bill of rights and constitution of Pennsylvania . . . [relevant to these issues].

From these passages it is evident; that the right of acquiring and possessing property and having it protected, is one of the natural inherent and unalienable rights of man. Men have a sense of property: Property is necessary to their subsistence, and correspondent to their natural wants and desires; its security was one of the objects, that induced them to unite in society. No man would become a member of a community, in which he could not enjoy the fruits of his honest labor and industry. The preservation of property then is a primary object of the social compact, and, by the late constitution of Pennsylvania, was made a fundamental law. Every person ought to contribute his proportion for public purposes and public exigencies; but no one can be called upon to surrender or sacrifice his whole property, real and personal, for the good of the community, without receiving a recompence in value. This would be laying a burden upon an individual, which ought to be sustained by the society at large. The English history does not furnish an instance of the kind; the parliament with all their boasted omnipotence, never committed such an outrage on private property; and if they had it would have served only to display the dangerous nature of unlimited authority; it would have been an exercise of power and not of right. Such an act would be a monster in legislation, and shock all mankind. The legislature, therefore, had no authority to make an act divesting one citizen of his freehold, and vesting it in another, without a just compensation. It is inconsistent with the principles of reason, justice, and moral rectitude; it is incompatible with the comfort, peace, and happiness of mankind; it is contrary to the principles of social alliance in every free government; and lastly, it is contrary both to letter and spirit of the constitution. In short, it is what every one would think unreasonable and unjust in his own case. The next step in the line of progression is, whether the legislature had authority to make an act, divesting one citizen of his freehold and vesting it in another, even with compensation. That the Legislature on certain emergencies, had authority to exercise this high power, has been urged from the nature of the social compact, and from the words of [the] constitution, which says, that the house of representatives shall have all other powers necessary for the legislature of a free state or commonwealth; but they shall have no power to add to, alter, abolish, or infringe any part of this constitution. The course of reasoning, on the part of the defendant, may be compromised in a few words. The despotic power, as it is aptly called by some writers, of taking private property, when state necessity requires, exists in every government; the existence of such power is necessary; government could not subsist without it; and if this is the case, it cannot be lodged any where with so much safety as with the legislature. The presumption is, that they will not call it into exercise except in urgent cases, or cases of the first neces-

sity. There is force in this reasoning. It is, however, difficult to form a case, in which the necessity of a state can be of such a nature, as to authorize or excuse the seizing of landed property belonging to one citizen and giving it to another citizen. It is immaterial to the state, in which of its citizens, the land is vested; but it is of primary importance, that, when vested it should be secured, and the proprietor protected in the enjoyment of it. The constitution encircles, and renders it an holy thing. We must, gentlemen, bear constantly in mind, that the present is a case of landed property; vested by law in one set of citizens, attempted to be divested, for the purpose of vesting the same property in another set of citizens. It cannot be assimilated to the case of personal property taken or used in time of war and famine, or other extreme necessity; it cannot be assimilated to the temporary possession of land itself, on a pressing public emergency, or the spur of the occasion. In the latter case there is no change of property, no divestment of right; the title remains, and the proprietor, though out of possession for a while is still proprietor and lord of the soil. The possession grew out of occasion and ceases with it. Then the right of necessity is satisfied and at an end; it does not affect the title, is temporary in its nature, and cannot exist forever. The constitution expressly declares, that the right of acquiring, possessing, and protecting property is natural, inherent, and unalienable. It is a right not *ex gratia* from the legislature, but *ex debito* from the constitution. It is sacred; for, it is further declared, that the legislature shall have no power to add to, alter, abolish, or infringe any part of the constitution. The constitution is the origin and measure of legislative authority. It says to legislators, thus far ye shall go and no further. . . .

After the opinion delivered on the preceeding questions, it is not necessary to determine upon the validity of the repealing law. But it being my intention in this charge to decide upon all the material points in the cause, in order that the whole may, at once, be carried before the supreme judicature for revision, I shall detain you, gentlemen, a few minutes only, while I just touch upon the constitutionality of the repealing act. . . .

This act was made after the adoption of the Constitution of the United States, and the argument is, that it is contrary to it.

1. Because it is an *ex post facto* law.

2. Because it is a law impairing the obligation of a contract.

1. That it is an *ex post facto* law. But what is the fact? If making a law be a fact within the words of the constitution, then no law, when once made, can ever be

repealed. Some of the Connecticut settlers presented their claims to the commissioners, who received and entered them. These are facts. But are they facts of any avail? Did they give any right or vest any estate? No—whether done or not done, they leave the parties just where they were. They create no interest, affect no title, change no property, when done they are useless and of no efficacy. Other acts were necessary to be performed, but before the performance of them, the law was suspended and then repealed.

2. It impairs the obligation of a contract, and is therefore void. If the property to the lands in question had been vested in the state of Pennsylvania, then the legislature would have had the liberty and right of disposing or granting them to whom they pleased, at any time, and in any manner. Over public property they have a disposing and controlling power, over private property they have none, except, perhaps, in certain cases, and those under restrictions, and except also, what may arise from the enactment and operation of general laws respecting property, which will affect themselves as well as their constituents. But if the confirming act be a contract between the legislature of Pennsylvania and the Connecticut settlers, it must be regulated by the rules and principles, which pervade and govern all cases of contracts; and if so, it is clearly void, because it tends, in its operation and consequences, to defraud the Pennsylvania claimants, who are third persons, of their just rights; rights ascertained, protected, and secured by the constitution and known laws of the land. The plaintiff's title to the land in question, is legally derived from Pennsylvania; how then, on the principles of contract, could Pennsylvania lawfully dispose of it to another? . . .

Justice Paterson's interpretation and the rigor of his espousal of the concept of vested property rights reflected the strong concern of the Federalists of that era for the sanctity of property rights. His judicial interpretation was especially important for those concerned about the actual intention of the framers of the Constitution. Paterson had played a key role in every crucial stage in the development and implementation of the Constitution. He was a member of the Philadelphia Convention of 1787 that drafted the document, was a member of the state ratifying convention of New Jersey that accepted it, and one of the key senators who, as members of the Senate judiciary committee, created the entire inferior federal judicial system of which the circuit court was a part.

The doctrine of judicial review also was asserted by implication against the national Congress in the 1790s. By the Act of March 23, 1792, Congress had provided that the circuit courts should pass upon certain claims of disabled Revolutionary War pensioners. The justices and district judges were to make administrative rulings. Justices Wilson and Blair had refused to consider the claim of an invalid named Hayburn. Although they considered the act an unconstitutional violation of separation of powers, they simply filed an order that "it is considered by the Court that the same be not proceeded upon."

When Hayburn presented a memorial to Congress asking for relief, the following statement was made in the House of Representatives: "It appeared that the Court thought the examination of invalids was a very extraordinary duty to be imposed on the Judges—and looked on the law that imposed that duty as an unconstitutional one."[41] Although the matter was settled undramatically, the Congress became more sensitive to the matter of separation of powers.

The early federal circuit court decisions were of particular importance because they were the first means of acquainting the country at large with the new judicial institution and because they served to pave the way for the broad exercise of judicial powers by the Supreme Court itself. While the circuit courts were able to nullify state laws without arousing serious opposition, however, a number of suits arising in Georgia, Maryland, and Virginia brought the Supreme Court into a head-on clash with the states.[42]

Can a state be sued?

The issue facing the Supreme Court in all these suits was whether a state could be sued by a citizen or corporation of another state or nation. Article III, Section 2, of the Constitution extended the judicial power of the United States to controversies "between a state and citizens of another state." In a number of state ratifying conventions, this provision had aroused anti–Federalist fears concerning this very question of the suability of a state. A number of the leading Federalist political leaders had faced the challenge squarely by stating unequivocally that this constitutional provision would never be construed in such a manner.[43]

Consequently, when these suits arose before the Supreme Court, the anti-Federalists became alarmed, and public interest in the controversies became aroused to a much greater extent than had been the case when state laws were being considered in the federal circuit courts.

The question whether or not a state could be sued by citizens of another state came before the Supreme Court in the August term of 1792. The two executors of the British creditor, Farquhar, who brought suit were citizens of South Carolina.[44] The defendant, the state of Georgia, was given ample "time to deliberate on the measures she ought to adopt"; thus the case was postponed until the February term of 1793.[45] Although the question of the suability of a state was in itself of far-reaching importance, *Chisholm* v. *Georgia*[46] is of particular significance because it is the first of the great determinative cases decided by the Supreme Court, and because it represents the first attempt by this Court to deal with the delicate problem of the nature of the Union. When the February term of the Supreme Court began, Georgia refused to appear. Instead, Dallas and Ingersoll, two able Pennsylvania lawyers, presented a written remonstrance in her behalf. In it Georgia denied that the Court had jurisdiction because a sovereign state could not be sued without its consent. This contention posed the crucial question concerning the nature of the Union.

In this formative decade, the Supreme Court followed the practice of having each justice file an individual opinion, called a *seriatim* opinion. Consequently, while Iredell was the only justice denying the Court's jurisdiction in the suit, the diverse approaches to the problem by the other justices robbed the decision of some of its impact. Iredell held that the action asked for by Attorney Edmund Randolph representing the private citizens could not lie against a state because the states, as inheritors of British sovereignty, were not open to suits under common law.[47]

Justice Blair stood with the majority, which held that once a state has adopted the Constitution, she is subject to the judicial power of the United States and in this respect gives up her right of sovereignty. However, he went on to suggest delay in rendering a judgment by default because such an action would be "too precipitate . . . and too incompatible with the dignity of a state."

Justice Wilson wrote a particularly forceful opinion. In his opening paragraph, he went directly to the heart of the matter, asking the question ". . . do the people of the United States form a nation?" He investigated at great length the question of sovereignty, and determined that sovereign power resided in the "people of the United States" and "as to the purposes of the Union, . . . Georgia is not a sovereign State."

Justice Cushing's opinion anticipated the great judicial pronouncements of John Marshall in one important respect. In dealing with the question of the suability of a state, Cushing chose to disregard the investigations into British history made by his fellow jurists, and instead treated the issue in terms of the federal Constitution. His second paragraph indicates that he considered the Constitution the formal source of all judicial power within our legal system:

> The point turns not upon the law or practice of England, . . . nor upon the law of any other country whatever, but upon the Constitution established by the people of the United States.

Like Wilson, Cushing held that Article III, Section 2, of the Constitution, by declaring that the judicial power extended to suits between a state and citizens of another state, provided the basis for the Supreme Court's action.[48]

Chief Justice John Jay's opinion, reproduced below, provided the most extensive analysis of the issue. Chief Justice Jay stated that:

CHISHOLM v. GEORGIA
2 Dallas 419 (1793)

The question we are now to decide has been accurately stated. Namely, is a State suable by individual citizens of another State?

It is said that Georgia refuses to appear and answer to the plaintiff in this action, because she is a sovereign State, and therefore not liable to such actions. . . .

[A]ny one State in the Union may sue another State in this court, that is, all the people of one State may sue all the people of another State. It is plain, then, that a State may be sued, and hence it plainly follows that suability and state sovereignty are not incompatible. As one State may sue another State in this court, it is plain that no degradation to a State is thought to accompany her appearance in this court. It is not, therefore, to an appearance in this court that the objection points. To what does it point? It points to an appearance at the suit of one or more citizens. But why it should be more incompatible that all the people of a State should be sued by one citizen, than by one hundred thousand, I cannot perceive, the process in both cases being alike, and the consequences of a judgment alike. Nor can I observe any greater inconveniences in the one case than in the other, except what may arise from the feelings of those who may regard a lesser number in an inferior light. But if any reliance be made on this inferiority, as an objection, at least one half of its force is done away by this fact, namely, that it is conceded that a State may appear in this court as plaintiff against a single citizen as defendant; and the truth is that the State of Georgia is at this moment prosecuting an action in this court against two citizens of South Carolina.

The only remnant of objection therefore that remains is, that the State is not bound to appear and answer as a defendant at the suit of an individual. . . . This inquiry naturally leads our attention, 1st. To the design of the constitution. 2d. To the letter and express declaration in it.

Prior to the date of the constitution, the people had not any national tribunal to which they could resort for justice; the distribution of justice was then confined to State judicatories, in whose institution and organization the people of the other States had no participation, and over whom they had not the least control. There was then no general court of appellate jurisdiction by whom the errors of State courts, affecting either the nation at large or the citizens of any other State, could be revised and corrected. Each State was obliged to acquiesce in the measure of justice which another State might yield to her or to her citizens; and that even in cases where State considerations were not always favorable to the most exact measure. There was danger that from this source animosities would in time result; and as the transition from animosities to hostilities was frequent in the history of independent States, a common tribunal for the termination of controversies became desirable, from motives both of justice and of policy.

Prior also to that period the United States had, by taking a place among the nations of the earth, become amenable to the laws of nations, and it was their interest as well as their duty to provide that those laws should be respected and obeyed; in their national character and capacity the United States were responsible to foreign nations for the conduct of each State, relative to the laws of nations, and the performance of treaties; and there the inexpediency of referring all such questions to State courts, and particularly to the courts of delinquent States, became apparent. While all the States were bound to protect each, and the citizens of each, it was highly proper and reasonable that they should be in a capacity not only to cause justice to be done to each, and the citizens of each, but also to cause justice to be done by each, and the citizens of each; and that, not by violence and force, but in a stable, sedate, and regular course of judicial procedure.

These were among the evils against which it was proper for the nation, that is the people of all the United States, to provide by a national judiciary, to be instituted by the whole nation, and to be responsible to the whole nation.

Let us now turn to the constitution. The people therein declare that their design in establishing it comprehended six objects. 1st. To form a more perfect union. 2d. To establish justice. 3d. To insure domestic tranquillity. 4th. To provide for the common defence. 5th. To promote the general welfare. 6th. To secure the blessings of liberty to themselves and their posterity. . . .

The question now before us renders it necessary to pay particular attention to that part of the second section which extends the judicial power "to controversies between a State and citizens of another State." It is contended that this ought to be construed to reach none of these controversies, excepting those in which a State may be plaintiff. The ordinary rules for construction will easily decide whether those words are to be understood in that limited sense.

This extension of power is remedial, because it is to settle controversies. It is, therefore, to be construed liberally. It is politic, wise, and good, that not only the controversies in which a State is plaintiff, but also those in which a State is defendant, should be settled; both cases, therefore, are within the reason of the remedy; and ought to be so adjudged, unless the obvious, plain, and literal sense of the words forbid it. If we attend to the words we find them to be express, positive, free from ambiguity, and without room for such implied expressions: "The judicial power of the United States shall extend to controversies between a State and citizens of another State." If the constitution really meant to extend these powers only to those controversies in which a State might be plaintiff, to the

exclusion of those in which citizens had demands against a State, it is inconceivable that it should have attempted to convey that meaning in words not only so incompetent, but also repugnant to it; if it meant to exclude a certain class of these controversies, why were they not expressly excepted; on the contrary, not even an intimation of such intention appears in any part of the constitution. It cannot be pretended that where citizens urge and insist upon demands against a State, which the State refuses to admit and comply with, that there is no controversy between them. If it is a controversy between them, then it clearly falls not only within the spirit, but the very words of the constitution. What is it to the cause of justice, and how can it affect the definition of the word controversy, whether the demands which cause the dispute are made by a State against citizens of another State, or by the latter against the former? When power is thus extended to a controversy, it necessarily, as to all judicial purposes, is also extended to those between whom it subsists.

The exception contended for would contradict and do violence to the great and leading principles of a free and equal national government, one of the great objects of which is to insure justice to all. To the few against the many, as well as to the many against the few. It would be strange, indeed, that the joint and equal sovereigns of this country should, in the very constitution by which they professed to establish justice, so far deviate from the plain path of equality and impartiality, as to give to the collective citizens of one State a right of suing individual citizens of another State, and yet deny to those citizens a right of suing them. . . .

For the reasons before given, I am clearly of opinion that a State is suable by citizens of another State; but lest I should be understood in a latitude beyond my meaning, I think it necessary to subjoin this caution, namely, that such suability may nevertheless not extend to all the demands, and to every kind of action, there may be exceptions. For instance, I am far from being prepared to say that an individual may sue a State on bills of credit issued before the constitution was established, and which were issued and received on the faith of the State, and at a time when no ideas or expectations of judicial interposition were entertained or contemplated. . . .

Chief Justice Jay's position was that the suability of a state was not forbidden by the Constitution and was not incompatible with the residuary sovereignty of the states. Because of the earlier assurances of Federalist leaders that the judicial power would never be used in such a manner, the Chisholm decision produced surprise and dismay throughout the country. Newspaper attacks on the decision were numerous and bitter,[49] and though much was written about the annihilation of state sovereignty, the very serious economic consequences for all the states also were discussed. The states feared the "numerous prosecutions" that would "immediately issue from the various claims of refugees, Tories, etc.," claims that would "introduce such a series of litigation" as would "throw every State in the Union into the greatest confusion."[50] And immediately after the decision, suits of this nature were actually instituted in South Carolina, Georgia, Virginia, and Massachusetts.

A number of state legislatures denounced the decision, and Massachusetts, through her senators and representatives, initiated a resolution in Congress for a constitutional amendment. Two days after the Court's decision, a resolution was introduced in the U.S. Senate and within a year the following amendment was submitted to the states:

> The judicial power of the United States shall not be construed to extend to any suit in law or equity, commenced or prosecuted against one of the United States by citizens of another State, or by citizens or subjects of any foreign State.

By January 8, 1798, the necessary number of states had ratified it, and President John Adams announced that the Eleventh Amendment had become part of the Constitution.[51]

As the decade of the 1790s developed, the Supreme Court members became more intensively involved in the partisan controversies between Federalists and anti-Federalists. The passage of the Eleventh Amendment was viewed by many as a serious Federalist setback. The Chief Justice, John Jay, had served as chief negotiator of the treaty of peace with Great Britain, a highly unpopular treaty, which intensified anti-Federalist opposition. Jay then resigned in order to run as the Federalist candidate for governor of New York. After this resignation in 1795, President Washington appointed John Rutledge as his successor, and Rutledge journeyed to Philadelphia and assumed his seat on the Court during the short August term. Before accepting the appointment, however, he had made a speech in Charleston attacking the Jay treaty.[52] For this act of political heresy, his nomination was rejected by the Federalist-dominated Senate by a vote of fourteen to ten.[53] Jefferson's reaction to this rejection harbingered growing Republican opposition to the largely Federalist government. He observed:

> . . . they [the Senate] cannot pretend any objection to him but his disapprobation of the treaty. It is, of course, a declaration that they will receive none but Tories hereafter in any department of the government.[54]

After the rejection of Rutledge, President Washington offered the Chief Justiceship to Patrick Henry and Justice Cushing, but both declined. Washington then appointed Oliver Ellsworth of Connecticut. Ellsworth, a wealthy landholder, successful lawyer, and staunch Federalist politician, had led the fight for ratification of the Connecticut convention and was, with Paterson, a principal architect of the Judiciary Act of 1789. In the same year that Ellsworth assumed the duties of Chief Justice, Blair of Virginia retired from the Court. As Blair's successor, President Washington chose Samuel Chase of Maryland, a very outspoken Federalist advocate.[55]

More tests of national authority

In the February term of 1796, the Supreme Court handed down the second of the great determinative decisions that set the stage for the critical election of 1800. Like the Chisholm decision, it aroused strong anti–Federalist opposition. The vital question before the Supreme Court was whether or not a state law that conflicted with the treaty of peace with Great Britain was valid. The decision of the Supreme Court in *Ware* v. *Hylton*[56] had serious and immediate economic and political consequences in many of the states as well as important constitutional implications.

During the Revolutionary War, the Virginia legislature passed a number of laws[57] that provided for sequestration and confiscation of the property of Loyalists and nullified debts of Virginia citizens that were due to British creditors. These laws conflicted with article four of the peace treaty, which expressly provided for the recovery by British creditors of the value "in sterling money" of debts contracted by American citizens before the treaty.

Four justices took part in the case, and, as was customary in the first decade of the Court, each wrote a separate opinion. Justice Chase's opinion, the fullest and most direct on the question of federal supremacy, is reproduced in full:

WARE v. HYLTON
3 Dallas 199 (1796)

The question . . . may be stated thus: Whether the 4th article of the said treaty nullifies the law of Virginia, passed on the 20th of October, 1777; destroys the payment made under it; and revives the debt and gives a right of recovery thereof against the original debtor?

It was doubted by one of the counsel for the defendants in error (Mr. Marshall) whether congress had a power to make a treaty that could operate to annul a legislative act of any of the States, and to destroy rights acquired by, or vested in individuals in virtue of such acts. Another of the defendant's counsel, (Mr. Campbell) expressly, and with great zeal, denied that congress possessed such power.

But a few remarks will be necessary to show the inadmissibility of this objection to the power of congress.

1st. The legislatures of all the States have often exercised the power of taking the property of its citizens for the use of the public, but they uniformly compensated the proprietors. The principle to maintain this right is for the public good, and to that the interest of individuals must yield. The instances are many; and among them are lands taken for forts, magazines, or arsenals, or for public roads, or canals, or to erect towns.

2d. The legislatures of all the States have often exercised the power of devesting rights vested, and even of impairing, and in some instances, of almost annihilating the obligation of contracts, as by tender laws, which made an offer to pay, and a refusal to receive paper money for a specie debt, an extinguishment to the amount tendered.

3d. If the legislature of Virginia could, by a law annul any former law, I apprehend that the effect would be to destroy all rights acquired under the law so nullified.

4th. If the legislature of Virginia could not by ordinary acts of legislation do these things, yet possessing the supreme sovereign power of the State, she certainly could do them by a treaty of peace, if she had not parted with the power of making such treaty. If Virginia had such power before she delegated it to congress, it follows that afterwards that body possessed it. Whether Virginia parted with the power of making treaties of peace, will be seen by a perusal of the ninth article of the confederation (ratified by all the States on the 1st of March, 1781), in which it was declared, "that the United States in congress assembled, shall have the sole and exclusive right and power of determining on peace or war, except in the two cases mentioned in the sixth article, and of entering into treaties and alliances, with a proviso, when made, respecting commerce." This grant has no restriction, nor is there any limitation on the power in any part of the confederation. A right to make peace necessarily includes the power of determining on what terms peace shall be made. A power to make treaties must of necessity imply a power to decide the terms on which they shall be made. A war between two nations can only be concluded by treaty.

Surely the sacrificing [of] public or private property to obtain peace cannot be the case in which a treaty would be void. . . . It seems to me that treaties made by congress, according to the confederation, were superior to the laws of the States, because the confederation made them obligatory on all the States. They were so declared by congress on the 13th of April, 1787; were so admitted by the legislatures and executives of most of the States; and were so decided by the judiciary of the general government, and by the judiciaries of some of the state governments.

If doubts could exist before the establishment of the present national government, they must be entirely removed by the sixth article of the constitution, which provides "that all treaties made, or which shall be made under the authority of the United States, shall be the supreme law of the land; and the judges in every State shall be bound thereby, any thing in the constitution or laws of any State to the contrary notwithstanding." There can be no limitation on the power of the people of the United States. By their authority the state constitutions were made, and by their authority the constitution of the United States was established; and they had the power to change or abolish the state constitutions, or to make them yield to the general government, and to treaties made by their authority. A treaty cannot be the supreme law of the land, that is, of all the United States, if any act of a state legislature can stand in its way. If the constitution of a State (which is the fundamental law of the State, and paramount to its legislature) must give way to a treaty, and fall before it, can it be questioned whether the less power, an act of the state legislature must not be prostrate? It is the declared will of the people of the United States that every treaty made by the authority of the United States, shall be superior to the constitution and laws of any individual State, and their will alone is to decide. If a law of a State, contrary to a treaty, is not void, but

voidable only by a repeal, or nullification by a state legislature, this certain consequence follows, that the will of a small part of the United States may control or defeat the will of the whole. The people of America have been pleased to declare that all treaties made before the establishment of the national constitution, or laws of any of the States, contrary to a treaty, shall be disregarded.

Four things are apparent on a view of this 6th article of the national constitution. 1st. That it is retrospective, and is to be considered in the same light as if the constitution had been established before the making of the treaty of 1783. 2d. That the constitution, or laws, of any of the States, so far as either of them shall be found contrary to that treaty, are, by force of the said article, prostrated before the treaty. 3d. That consequently the treaty of 1783 has superior power to the legislature of any State, because no legislature of any State has any kind of power over the constitution, which was its creator. 4th. That it is the declared duty of the state judges to determine any constitution, or laws of any State, contrary to that treaty, or any other, made under the authority of the United States, null and void. National or federal judges are bound by duty and oath to the same conduct.

The argument, that congress had not power to make the 4th article of the treaty of peace, if its intent and operation was to annul the laws of any of the States, and to destroy vested rights, which the plaintiff's counsel contended to be the object and effect of the 4th article, was unnecessary, but on the supposition that this court possess a power to decide whether this article of the treaty is within the authority delegated to that body, by the articles of confederation. Whether this court constitutionally possess such a power is not necessary now to determine, because I am fully satisfied that congress were invested with the authority to make the stipulation in the 4th article. . . .

Justices Paterson, Wilson, and Cushing also held the Virginia laws invalid. Although Wilson held that the treaty "annuls" the conflicting state laws, he did not point out the constitutional provision that established the superiority of the treaty. Paterson and Cushing were more explicit. Like Chase, they based their decisions on the supremacy clause of the Constitution. Referring to the primacy of the treaty over conflicting state laws, Cushing stated:

. . . there is no want of power, the treaty being sanctioned as the supreme law, by the Constitution of the United States, which nobody pretends to deny to be paramount and controlling, to all state laws, and even state constitutions, wheresoever they interfere or disagree.[58]

In *Ware* v. *Hylton*, the Supreme Court defeated decisively the challenges of the state legislatures to the treaty-making power of the national government. The doctrine that a valid treaty is superior to any state laws or state constitutional provisions that are in conflict with it became a fundamental one in American constitutional law. Politically and economically, the decision in *Ware* v. *Hylton* threatened the financial stability of some of the states as well as hundreds of American debtors. The anti–Federalists gained in political strength as many debtors flocked to the party that had opposed paying the British creditors.[59]

The Hayburn episode had all the earmarks of a direct Court confrontation with Congress, but because of the manner in which the Court handled the issue and the mild reaction in Congress, a major controversy was avoided. The subsequent issue of the validity of the 1794 federal tax on carriages provided the basis for a direct conflict. The case was *Hylton* v. *The United States*.[60] If the carriage tax was interpreted as a direct tax, the law would be held invalid. The three justices participating again wrote separate opinions. Justice Paterson's dealt with all of the significant issues:

HYLTON v. UNITED STATES
3 Dallas 171 (1796)

By the second section of the first article of the constitution of the United States, it is ordained that representatives and direct taxes shall be apportioned among the States, according to their respective numbers, which shall be determined by adding to the whole number of free persons, including those bound to service for a term of years, and excluding Indians not taxed, three fifths of all other persons.

The eighth section of the said article declares that congress shall have the power to lay and collect taxes, duties, imposts, and excises; but all duties, imposts and excises, shall be uniform throughout the United States.

The ninth section of the same article provides, that no capitation or other direct tax shall be laid, unless in proportion to the census or enumeration before directed to be taken. . . .

The question is, whether a tax upon carriages be a direct tax? If it be a direct tax, it is unconstitutional, because it has been laid pursuant to the rule of uniformity, and not to the rule of apportionment. . . .

What are direct taxes within the meaning of the constitution? The constitution declares that a capitation tax is a direct tax; and both in theory and practice, a tax on land is deemed to be a direct tax. In this way, the terms direct taxes, and capitation and other direct tax, are satisfied. It is not necessary to determine, whether a tax on the product of land be a direct or indirect tax. . . . Whether direct taxes, in the sense of the constitution, comprehend any other tax than a capitation tax and tax on land, is a questionable point.

. . . I never entertained a doubt that the principal, I will not say the only objects, that the framers of the constitution contemplated as falling within the rule of apportionment, were a capitation tax and a tax on land. Local considerations, and the particular circumstances and relative situation of the States, naturally lead to this view of the subject. The provision was made in favor of the southern States. They possessed a large number of slaves; they had extensive tracts of territory, thinly settled and not very productive. A majority of the states had but few slaves, and several of them a limited territory, well settled, and in a high state of cultivation. The Southern States, if no provision had been introduced in the constitution, would have been wholly at the mercy of the other States. Congress in such case, might tax slaves, at discretion or arbitrarily, and land in every part of the Union after the same rate of measure; so much a head in the first instance, and so much an acre in the second. To guard them against imposition, in these particulars, was the reason of introducing the clause in the constitution, which directs that representatives and direct taxes shall be apportioned among the States according to their respective numbers.

All taxes on expenses or consumption are indirect taxes. A tax on carriages is of this kind, and of course is not a direct tax. Indirect taxes are circuitous modes of reaching the revenue of individuals, who generally live according to their income. In many cases of this nature the individual may be said to tax himself. . . .

I am, therefore, of opinion that the judgment rendered in the circuit court of Virginia ought to be affirmed.

Like the issue of direct taxes, the meaning and scope of *ex post facto* legislation was of great interest after the adoption of the Constitution. The meaning of the provisions of the new Constitution was still undetermined. In 1798, the Supreme Court first interpreted the *ex post facto* clause in the case of *Calder* v. *Bull*.[61] Justice Chase's opinion is reproduced in part:

CALDER v. BULL
3 Dallas 386 (1798)

The effect of the resolution or law of Connecticut, above stated, is to revise a decision of one of its inferior courts, called the court of probate for Hartford, and to direct a new hearing of the case by the same court of probate, that passed the decree against the will of Norman Morrison. By the existing law of Connecticut a right to recover certain property had vested in Calder and wife (the appellants) in consequence of a decision of a court of justice, but, in virtue of a subsequent resolution or law, and the new hearing thereof, and the decision in consequence, this right to recover certain property was divested, and the right to the property declared to be in Bull and wife, the appellees. The sole enquiry is, whether this resolution or law of Connecticut, having such operation, is an ex post facto law, within the prohibition of the federal constitution?. . . .

All the restrictions contained in the constitution of the United States on the power of the state Legislatures, were provided in favor of the authority of the federal government. The prohibition against their making any ex post facto laws was introduced for greater caution, and very probably arose from the knowledge, that the Parliament of Great Britain claimed and exercised a power to pass such laws, under the denomination of bills of attainder, or bills of pains and penalties; the first inflicting capital, and the other less, punishment. These acts were legislative judgments; and an exercise of judicial power. . . . The ground for the exercise of such legislative power was this, that the safety of the kingdom depended on the death, or other punishment, of the offender; as if traitors, when discovered, could be so formidable, or the government so insecure! With very few exceptions, the advocates of such laws were stimulated by ambition, or personal resentment, and vindictive malice. To prevent such, and similar, acts of violence and injustice, I believe, the Federal and State Legislatures, were prohibited from passing any bill of attainder; or any ex post facto law. . . .

I shall endeavor to show what law is to be considered an ex post facto law, within the words and meaning of the prohibition in the Federal constitution. The prohibition, "that no state shall pass any ex post facto law,"

necessarily requires some explanation; for naked, and without explanation, it is unintelligible, and means nothing. Literally, it is only that a law shall not be passed concerning, and after the fact, or thing done, or action committed. I would ask, what fact; of what nature, or kind; and by whom done? That Charles 1st. king of England, was beheaded; that Oliver Cromwell was Protector of England, that Louis 16th, late king of France, was guillotined, are all facts, that have happened; but it would be nonsense to suppose, that the states were prohibited from making any law after either of these events, and with reference thereto. The prohibition, in the letter, is not to pass any law concerning and after the fact; but the plain and obvious meaning and intention of the prohibition is this; that the Legislatures of the several states shall not pass laws, after a fact done by a subject or citizen, which shall have relation to such fact, and shall punish him for having done it. The prohibition considered in this light, is an additional bulwark in favor of the personal security of the subject, to protect his person from punishment by legislative acts, having a retrospective operation. I do not think it was inserted to secure the citizen in his private rights, of either property, or contracts. The prohibition not to make anything but gold and silver coin a tender in payment of debts, and not to pass any law impairing the obligations of contracts, were inserted to secure private rights; but the restriction not to pass any ex post facto law, was to secure the person of the subject from injury, or punishment, in consequence of such law. If the prohibition against making ex post facto laws was intended to secure personal rights from being affected, or injured by such laws, and the prohibition is sufficiently extensive for that object, the other restraints I have enumerated, were unnecessary, and therefore improper; for both of them are retrospective.

I will state what laws I consider ex post facto laws, within the words and the intent of the prohibition. 1st. Every law that makes an action done before the passing of the law; and which was innocent when done, criminal; and punishes such action. 2d. Every law that aggravates a crime, or makes it greater than it was, when committed. 3d. Every law that changes the punishment, and inflicts a greater punishment, than the law annexed to the crime, when committed. 4th. Every law that alters the legal rules of evidence, and receives less, or different, testimony, than the law required at the time of the commission of the offense, in order to convict the offender. All these, and similar laws, are manifestly unjust and oppressive. In my opinion, the true distinction is between ex post facto laws, and retrospective laws. Every ex post facto law must necessarily be retrospective; but every retrospective law is not an ex post facto law: The former, only, are prohibited. Every law that takes away, or impairs, rights vested, agreeably to existing laws, is retrospective, and is generally unjust, and may be oppressive; and it is a good general rule, that a law should have no retrospect: but there are cases in which laws may justly, and for the benefit of the community, and also of individuals, relate to a time antecedent to their commencement; as statutes of oblivion, or of pardon. They are certainly retrospective, and literally both concerning, and after, the facts committed. But I do not consider any law ex post facto, within the prohibition, that mollifies the rigor of the criminal law; but only those that create, or aggravate, the crime; or increase the punishment, or change the rules of evidence, for the purpose of conviction. . . .

I am of the opinion that the decree of the Supreme Court of Errors of Connecticut be affirmed, with costs. Judgment affirmed.

Calder v. *Bull* did not stimulate adverse political reaction, but the hardening of political lines was accentuated by the strong Federalist positions taken by the justices on both the Supreme Court and the federal circuit courts. The original anti–Federalist opposition coalesced into an emergent full-blown political party under the leadership of Thomas Jefferson. This party, known as the Jeffersonian Republican (in contrast to the alleged monarchical tendencies of the party in power), became especially concerned over Federalist attempts at punishing what the Republicans considered legitimate political criticism. Several members of the Federalist Supreme Court became active in this effort. The Jeffersonians considered the judicial effort at establishing a federal common law jurisdiction, a very dangerous threat to the concept of a loyal opposition. Common law jurisdiction created punishable offenses by federal judicial doctrinal development rather than by statutory action by the Congress. Thus, as early as May 22, 1793, Chief Justice John Jay had stated the federal common law doctrine in the following terms in a charge to the grand jury in Richmond, Virginia:

> To oppose the operation of this Constitution and of the government established by it, would be to violate the sovereignty of the people, and would justly merit reprehension and punishment.[62]

Later, Justices Cushing, Iredell, Wilson, Washington, and Chief Justice Ellsworth all sustained indictments at common law. Only Justice Chase opposed the doctrine.[63] In 1799, Ellsworth, in a charge to the grand jury of the South Carolina Circuit Court, gave this statement of the doctrine:

> . . . an offense consists in transgressing the sovereign will, whether that will be expressed, or obviously implied. Conduct, therefore, clearly destructive of a government or its powers, which the people have ordained to exist, must be criminal.[64]

Of this assumption of common law criminal jurisdiction, Jefferson declared: "I consider all the encroachments made on that [the Constitution] heretofore as nothing, as mere retail stuff compared with . . . [this] whole sale doctrine." The Republicans recognized quite clearly that establishment of a federal common law criminal jurisdiction could lead to the complete submergence of states and individual rights. This attempted encroachment by the federal judiciary was irreconcilable with the theory that the national government is limited to the exercise of only those powers delegated to it by the people. A writer in the *Virginia Argus* pointed up the implications of the doctrine in this manner:

> . . . instead of the General Government being instituted for particular purposes, it embraces every subject to which government can apply . . .; the whole range of legislation and jurisprudence is within its omnipotent grasp.[65]

In engrafting a common law jurisdiction upon the American legal system, the members of the federal judiciary went beyond the bounds of the provisions of the Constitution. With the advent of the Federalist-sponsored Alien and Sedition Laws, the opposition party leaders formulated a constitutional theory that challenged the supremacy of the judicial branch of the national government in determining the limits of federal and state powers. When the Federalists passed a stringent naturalization law, an Alien Act, an Alien Enemies Act, and a Sedition Act, the Republicans became fully convinced that the new legislation was designed to destroy opposition to the administration in power, and eventually provide a legal facade for the institution of a monarchical form of government. These convictions became strengthened when the Federalist authorities systematically instituted proceedings against the leaders of the Republican press.[66]

Jefferson had originally had great confidence in the federal judiciary as a protector of individual rights,[67] but excessive judicial partisanship drove him to seek new means of declaring the obnoxious Alien and Sedition Laws unconstitutional. He and Madison collaborated in drawing up a set of resolutions, which were introduced in the legislatures of Kentucky and Virginia.[68] Although the resolutions were drafted primarily to influence voters in the coming political campaign, their chief importance lies in the constitutional theory embodied in them.

This theory posed a direct challenge to the exercise by the Supreme Court of power to arbitrate finally in disputes between the states and the federal government. The challenge in the Virginia Resolutions, which were drawn up by Madison and presented by John Taylor of Caroline, was worded as follows:

> In case of a deliberate, palpable, and dangerous exercise of other powers not granted by the said compact, the states, who are parties thereto, have the right and are in duty bound to interpose for arresting the progress of the evil, and for maintaining within their respective limits the authorities, rights and liberties appertaining to them.[69]

The Kentucky Resolutions were drafted by Jefferson and presented by Breckinridge. The challenge to the exclusive power of the federal judiciary in federal-state relations was a direct and unequivocal one:

> . . . the government created by this compact was not made the exclusive and final judge of the extent of the powers delegated to itself; since that would have made its discretion, and not the Constitution the measure of its powers; but . . . as in all other cases of compact among parties having no common judge, each party has an equal right to judge for itself, as well of infractions as of the mode and measure of redress.[70]

Copies of the Virginia and Kentucky Resolutions were sent to the "Co-States." Most of the states replied, but none adopted resolutions at this time approving the doctrine set forth in the Virginia and Kentucky documents. All rejected the contention that a state legislature could declare an act of the national government unconstitutional; Rhode Island, New Hampshire, and Vermont held that this power was vested exclusively in the federal judiciary.[71]

In a report to the Virginia legislature in 1800, Madison described declarations concerning the constitutionality of Congressional legislation by citizens or state legislatures as "expressions of opinion, unaccompanied with any other effect than what they might produce on opinion by exciting reflection."[72] However, the doctrine was circulated. The compact theory was later adopted and altered to suit the purposes of the Federalists of New England in the War of 1812, the nullifications of South Carolina in 1832, and finally the secessionists in 1861.

Conclusion

The role of the new Supreme Court had been determined, in a number of respects, by compromises developed and ultimately accepted by the nationalists and states' rights advocates in the Philadelphia Convention in 1787 and in the state ratifying conventions of 1788. In retrospect, the agreement by both contending groups that the Court become the final arbiter of constitutional issues of federalism made the political role of the Supreme Court inevitable.

Federalism was the central political issue of the latter part of the 18th century and of most of the 19th century. Cast as umpires of federalism, the justices of the Supreme Court could not escape political controversy unless they abdicated their constitutional responsibilities. In the context of the strong Federalist ideology of the 1790s, the Supreme Court appointees of Presidents George Washington and John Adams were not at all reluctant to assert doctrines of national supremacy, thus provoking strong partisan anti–Federalist reactions. Many things helped make the Supreme Court and the district and circuit courts targets of Jeffersonian Republican criticism and attack, including the federal judiciary's role in supporting pro-Federalist positions regarding federal supremacy, the suability of individual states by citizens of other states, the Jay Treaty of Peace with Great Britain, the strong enforcement of the Alien and Sedition Act, and the development and application of a federal common law jurisdiction.

Just as the constitutional grants of judicial authority as arbiter of federalism ensured a high degree of judicial involvement in the political conflicts over the relative power of the national and state governments, so too did other constitutional provisions ensure direct judicial conflict with the other major branches of government—the Presidency and the Congress. Conflicts of separation of powers involving the Supreme Court were most likely to occur when a significant political transformation took place. Guaranteed tenure for life unless impeached, justices of the Supreme Court could remain in office when members of their own party were swept out of the office of President and out of majority control in the House and Senate. When this occurred in a critical election, the stage was set for a potentially serious confrontation.

The critical election of 1800 proved to be one of the watershed contests that marked a fundamental and enduring shift in the political attachments of citizens. Its outcome brought about the defeat of President John Adams, and eliminated Federalist control of the House and Senate, but the immediate controversy over Aaron Burr's attempt to gain the presidency delayed Jeffersonian Republican consolidation of their victory. Burr was Jefferson's vice-presidential running mate, but because the Constitution originally did not distinguish between presidential and vice-presidential candidates, Burr, aided and abetted by Federalists, attempted unsuccessfully to gain the presidency. President Adams' successful effort in gaining passage from the lame-duck Federalist Congress in early 1801 for a new judiciary act creating a number of separate circuit judgeships (immediately filled with lame-duck Federalists) reduced the Supreme Court by one member after the next vacancy (to deny President Jefferson an appointment), set the stage for a violent Jeffersonian counterattack, and made the federal judiciary the very center of political combat. Jeffersonians controlled the Presidency and both houses of Congress. The Federalists totally controlled the Supreme Court. The first great institutional confrontation became the major political issue of the early 1800s.

REFERENCES

1. Jefferson's letter to Madison, March 15, 1789, quoted by Arthur Norman Holcombe, *Our More Perfect Union* (Cambridge: Harvard University Press), p. 287.
2. Madison's letter to *Independent Journal*, probably January 1788, quoted in Henry Cabot Lodge, ed., *The Federalist* (New York: G. P. Putnam's Sons, 1904), p. 238.
3. Hamilton in *The Federalist* 80, quoted by Lodge, ibid., pp. 494–495.
4. Robert Yates' letters to *The New York Journal and Weekly Register*, January 31 and March 20, 1788, reprinted in Edward S. Corwin, *Court over Constitution* (Princeton: Princeton University Press, 1938), pp. 231–233, 237–243, 251–253.
5. Lodge, op. cit., pp. 98–106.
6. Elbridge Gerry, quoted by Charles Warren, "New Light on the History of the Federal Judiciary Act of 1789," *Harvard Law Review* 37 (June 1940): 54–55.
7. Warren, "New Light," p. 55.
8. Westel W. Willoughby, *The Supreme Court of the United States, Its History and Influence in Our Constitutional System* (Baltimore: Johns Hopkins Press, 1890), pp. 20–21.
9. Jonathan Elliott, *Debates on the Adoption of the Federal Constitution*, vol. 3 (Philadelphia: J. B. Lippincott, 1901), pp. 530–539, 551–562.
10. Charles Pinckney, quoted by Joseph Story, *Commentaries on the Constitution of the United States*, vol. 1 (Boston: Little, Brown, 1858), p. 267.
11. Ibid., p. 196.
12. Elliott, op. cit., vol. 4, p. 155.
13. Elliott, op. cit., vol. 3, p. 532.
14. *See, for example,* the account of the astute political maneuvering necessary to achieve victory in the Virginia ratifying convention, in Albert J. Beveridge, *The Life of John Marshall*, vol. 1 (Boston and New York: Houghton Mifflin, 1916), pp. 357–480.
15. Charles Warren, "The First Decade of the Supreme Court," *University of Chicago Law Review* 7: 631.
16. This was the fourth of the great organic acts, *Laws of the United States* 2, 56 ff.
17. *See* letter of Ellsworth to Judge Richard Law, April 30, 1789; as quoted by Warren, "New Light," pp. 60–61.
18. *U.S. Statutes at Large,* vol. 1, p. 73 ff; Warren, ibid., p. 62.
19. Ellsworth's letter to Law, August 4, 1789; as quoted by Warren, "New Light," p. 66.
20. Warren, "First Decade," op. cit., p. 632.
21. Warren, "New Light," op. cit., p. 53.
22. Ibid., pp. 102–105.

23. Max Farrand, ed., *The Records of the Federal Convention of 1787*, vol. 3 (New Haven: Yale University Press, 1911), p. 537.

24. 5 Cranch 118–123 (1809).

25. Charles Grove Haines, *The Role of the Supreme Court in American Government and Politics, 1789–1835* (Berkeley: University of California Press, 1944), pp. 270–271.

26. *Penhallow* v. *Doane's Administrators*, 3 Dallas 54 (1795).

27. 5 Cranch 117.

28. Ibid., p. 115.

29. Allen Johnson, ed., *Readings in American Constitutional History, 1776–1876* (Boston: Houghton, Mifflin, 1912), pp. 254, 260–262.

30. *American Daily Advertiser*, March 29, 1809, as quoted by Charles Warren, *The Supreme Court in United States History*, vol. 1 (Boston: Little, Brown, 1937), pp. 381–382.

31. *Annals*, 11th Congress, 2nd session, pp. 2269–2290; cited in Warren, ibid., p. 382, note 2.

32. Warren, p. 384.

33. Johnson, op. cit., p. 254; *see also* Warren, *History*, vol. 1, pp. 385–387.

34. Warren, ibid., pp. 260–261.

35. Warren, *History*, vol. 1, p. 389.

36. Johnson, op. cit., p. 254.

37. Warren, *History*, vol. 1, p. 61.

38. Warren mentions cases involving the validity of Connecticut and Vermont statutes in 1793 and 1799 respectively. *History*, vol. 1, pp. 68–69.

39. Charles Warren, *The Supreme Court and Sovereign States* (Princeton: Princeton University Press, 1924), pp. 5–6, 13–14.

40. The Pennsylvania claimants had been granted land under an earlier state statute. 2 Dallas 319–320 (1793).

41. 1st Congress, 1st session, June 16–22, 1789; Warren, *History*, vol. 1, p. 84, note.

42. *Vanstophorst* v. *Maryland*, *Oswald* v. *New York*, *Indiana Company* v. *Virginia*, and *Chisholm* v. *Georgia*; cited in Warren, *History*, vol. 1, pp. 91–93.

43. Madison had stated in the Virginia convention: "It is not in the power of individuals to call any state into court," Beveridge, op. cit., p. 449; Marshall took a similar stand in the same Convention, ibid, p. 454; see also *The Federalist* (Ford, ed.), p. 545, for Hamilton's similar contention.

44. Warren, *History*, vol. 1, p. 93.

45. Herman V. Ames, ed., *State Documents on Federal Relations*, vol. 1 (1789–1809) (University of Pennsylvania, 1900), p. 7.

46. *Chisholm* v. *Georgia*, 2 Dallas 419 (1793).

47. Ibid., pp. 430–450; Edmund Randolph was attorney general of the United States. He served as a private attorney in the Chisholm case because he could not afford to serve as attorney general without also serving in private practice (which was then not prohibited!).

48. Blair's, Wilson's, and Cushing's positions are found in *Chisholm* v. *Georgia* (1793), ibid., pp. 450–453, 457, and 466, respectively.

49. Warren, *History*, vol. 1, pp. 96–98.

50. *Independent Chronicle*, July 25, 1793; quoted by Warren, *History*, vol. 1, p. 99.

51. Homer Carey Hockett, *The Constitutional History of the United States, 1776–1826*, vol. 1 (New York: Macmillan, 1939), p. 287.

52. For an account of this speech *see* Henry Flanders, *The Lives and Times of the Chief Justices*, vol. 1 (Philadelphia: J. B. Lippincott, 1858), pp. 633–636.

53. Haines, op. cit., p. 146.

54. As quoted in Haines, ibid.

55. Warren, *History*, vol. 1, pp. 124–144.

56. 3 Dallas 199 (1796).

57. Acts of October 20, 1777; May 3, 1779; May 1, 1780; May 6, 1782; October 20, 1783; and January 3, 1788; see 3 Dallas 204–208 (1797).

58. Paterson's, Wilson's, and Cushing's positions are found in the decision, *Ware* v. *Hylton* (1796), pp. 236–237 and 244–284.

59. Warren, *History*, vol. 1, p. 144.

60. 3 Dallas 171 (1796).

61. 3 Dallas 386 (1798).

62. Charge to the grand jury in Richmond; Francis Wharton, *State Trials,* pp. 49–56; as quoted by Haines, op. cit., p. 125.
63. *United States* v. *Worrall,* 2 Dallas 385 (1798); see Warren, *History,* vol. 1, p. 159, note 1.
64. As quoted by Warren, ibid., pp. 162–164.
65. Hockett, op. cit., pp. 267–269.
66. Frank Malory Anderson, "The Enforcement of the Alien and Sedition Laws," in *Annual Report of the American Historical Association, 1912,* p. 120.
67. Holcombe, op. cit., p. 287.
68. Irving Brant, *James Madison, Father of the Constitution, 1787–1800,* vol. 3, pp. 460–461; Hockett, op. cit., vol. 1, p. 289.
69. As quoted by Brant, ibid.
70. As quoted by Hockett, op. cit., vol. 1, p. 290.
71. Ames, op. cit., vol. 1, pp. 16–26.
72. Edward S. Corwin, "National Power and State Interposition," *Selected Essays in Constitutional Law* vol. 3 (Chicago: Foundation Press, 1938), p. 1181.

4

Jeffersonian Principles
and the Federalist Court

The Supreme Court and National Political Development

The transformations of political elites and political institutions that occurred in the colonies between 1760 and 1788 were dramatic and far reaching. Following political independence from Great Britain, law became an acceptable occupation and lawyers generally comprised the largest proportion of the elective and appointive political elites of the new states. And after the adoption of the new Constitution of 1789, lawyers extended that occupational influence to the executive, legislative, and judicial branches of the national government as well. Judiciaries emerged considerably more influential as political institutions because of widespread public distrust of executive authority. The Supreme Court of the United States was the unique institutional creation of this great transformation. These important changes were the accumulative results of violent revolution in 1776 and peaceful but fundamental and wide-ranging constitutional change in 1788.

The role of the Supreme Court and inferior federal judiciary in the first political party system[1] was one in which the Federalist justices and judges were often involved judicially in maintaining the ascendancy of their political party. For the first decade of the new political system, 1789–1799, there were no major political transformations in the form of realigning elections. But the stage was set.

What would happen to a Federalist-dominated Supreme Court and federal judiciary if the Federalist party lost control of the presidency and the Congress? As noted in Chapter 1, Robert Dahl had minimized the possibility of serious conflict, stating that "the policy views dominant on the Court are never for long out of line with the policy views dominant among the lawmaking majorities of the United States." Dahl attributed this result to the kind of political generational rhythm by which presidents averaged a new Supreme Court appointment every 22 months. Presumably, when enough justices of the new political generation had been chosen, the Court would alter its position to conform to the views of the new dominant political coalition. Dahl assumed considerable continuity, suggesting that, "national politics in the United States . . . is dominated by relatively cohesive alliances that endure for long periods of time."[2] Presented as a general overview of the first 160 years of national judicial relations with the presidency and the Congress, Dahl's appraisal has often been accepted as persuasive. His overview does not, however, deal with the wide variations in political circumstances that are seemingly subsumed in his generalized averaging of Supreme Court appointments every 22 months and his even broader generalization about long-enduring political alliances.

In the context of critical elections, a number of basic questions must be explored. In the period preceding each critical election, did the decisions of the Supreme Court deal with issues that were important in the subsequent critical election? Were the Court's positions on such issues contradictory to those taken by the party that took control of the executive and legislative branches as a result of a particular critical election? Or conversely, were the doctrinal positions of the Supreme Court preceding some critical elections largely irrelevant to these elections? Is there evidence in each critical election era that the "relatively cohesive alliances" referred to by Dahl have any significance for policy consistency? Can it be assumed that a massive electoral change characteristic of a critical election will invariably lead to policy differences between a Supreme Court majority selected in an earlier era and the newly elected president and Congress? In short, can electoral consistency be equated with policy consistency? Similarly, do presidents chosen in the massive tide of a critical election consistently nominate and appoint new justices for the purpose of creating a new doctrinal consensus on the Court? Do the presidents generally choose justices who reflect their own judicial policy preferences? Or, conversely, do presidents occasionally employ Supreme Court nominations and appointments for other purposes? Did members of the Supreme Court modify or abandon significant doctrinal positions because of the changes in political leadership and public policy positions brought about as a result of critical elections? Or, worded more directly, did the Supreme Court follow the election returns? Were internal procedural changes made within the Court as a result of such electoral changes? In a word, are the circumstances surrounding each critical election considerably more complex and variable than Dahl's overview suggested? The election of 1800 provided the first set of answers to these questions.

The election of 1800 and the Federalist Court's responses

The presidential election of 1800 was closely and bitterly fought. The Republicans, under the leadership of Jefferson and Madison, were solidly united in their opposition to the domestic and foreign policies of the Adams administration. The Federalists, on the other hand, were split asunder over foreign policy issues. The intrigues of the Hamilton faction fatally weakened the Federalist candidates.[3] President John Adams and the Federalist vice-presidential candidate, Charles Cotesworth Pinckney, received 65 and 64 electoral votes, respectively. John Jay received one electoral vote. However, Thomas Jefferson, the Republican presidential candidate, and Aaron Burr, his vice-presidential running mate, each received 73 electoral votes.[4] Until 1800 the candidate who received the most votes became president and the runner-up became vice-president.

Since Jefferson and Burr had tied, the election was thrown into the House of Representatives, which was constitutionally authorized to choose the president. Here the Federalists seized the opportunity to attempt either to elect Burr, or to create a deadlock and then choose a Federalist president. Not until the 36th ballot did Jefferson gain the necessary majority.[5] Thus, as Albert Beveridge put it, the Federalist party "went down forever in a welter of passion, tawdry politics, and disgraceful intrigue."[6]

In the latter part of 1800, Chief Justice Oliver Ellsworth had resigned. President Adams immediately nominated former Chief Justice John Jay as Ellsworth's successor. Adams' letter to Jay indicated the prevailing Federalist expectation that the federal judiciary would remain as a strong bulwark against Jefferson's Republicans. He wrote, "In the future administration of our country, the firmest security we can have against the effects of visionary schemes or fluctuating theories will be in a solid Judiciary."[7] Jay declined the nomination on the grounds of poor health and Congress' failure to relieve the Supreme Court justices from their onerous circuit court duties. President Adams then nominated his secretary of state, John Marshall. Interestingly enough, most Federalist leaders resented Marshall's appointment. Typical of Federalist sentiment was Senator Dayton's characterization of the appointment as "a wild freak" of President Adams. The Federalist-dominated Senate actually postponed voting on the Marshall nomination for a week, hoping to induce Adams to nominate Justice Paterson. Adams remained adamant, however, and the Senate reluctantly confirmed Marshall's nomination on January 27, 1801.[8] Marshall remained as Secretary of State until midnight, March 3, after assuming the chief justiceship immediately on February 4.

In December 1801, the lame-duck Federalist Congress began consideration of a circuit court bill. The Circuit Court Act was finally passed on February 13, 1801. It contained some substantial changes. The Supreme Court justices were relieved of circuit court duties. The number of district court districts was increased from 17 to 22, while the number of circuits was doubled, from three to six. Sixteen new circuit court judgeships were created. In addition, a new district attorney and a federal marshal were to be appointed to each of the five new districts.[9] In particular, the provision for reduction of the Supreme Court's membership after the next vacancy thoroughly aroused the Republicans. Not only did the Federalists seek to prevent a Republican appointment to the Supreme Court, but they also hastened to fill the new judicial vacancies with Federalist politicians. President Adams promoted six district judges to circuit judgeships. He then filled four of the district court vacancies with Federalist members of Congress. Thus, Senators Green, Paine, and Read, and Representative Hill were named as district judges for Rhode Island, Vermont, South Carolina, and North Carolina respectively. Federalist Representatives Otis and Kittera were appointed to replace two district attorneys promoted to judgeships.[10]

In a separate legislative action, the same lame-duck Federalist Congress that passed the Judiciary Act of 1801 also hurried through a bill providing for a rather large number of justices of the peace for the relatively sparsely populated counties comprising the District of Columbia, Washington, and Alexandria (the latter was destined to be returned to the jurisdiction of the state of Virginia before the Civil War). The Federalist Judiciary Act, passed on February 27, 1801, provided for presidential appointment of 42 justices of the peace for five-year terms (which would, of course, extend beyond the next presidential election). President Adams nominated all on March 2, and they were confirmed by the Senate on March 3. Similar to Adams' circuit court appointments, the commissions were to be delivered officially by the secretary of state before midnight on March 3.

John Marshall was still secretary of state despite the fact that he was also chief justice of the United States. Marshall had his brother, James, who had just been appointed a judge of the newly created circuit court for the District of Columbia, deliver the commissions to the potential justices of the peace. James failed to deliver several of them before midnight. One William Marbury was among those overlooked or omitted. After Jefferson took office on March 4, 1801, the incoming administration did not deliver the commissions, and the train of circumstances leading to the definitive decision in *Marbury* v. *Madison* was initiated. On January 31, 1803, just before the beginning of the February term of the United States Supreme Court, the Federalists in the U. S. Senate proposed a resolution directing the secretary of senate to give William Marbury, Robert T. Hooe, and Denis Ramsey an attested copy of the proceedings of March 2 and 3, 1801, relative to their appointment as justices of the peace in Washington and Alexandria in the District of Columbia. In the February term, the Court rendered its decision. Chief Justice John Marshall wrote the opinion of the Court:

MARBURY v. MADISON
1 Cranch 137 (1803)

. . . In the order in which the court has viewed this subject, the following questions have been considered and decided: 1st. Has the applicant a right to the commission he demands? 2nd. If he has a right, and that right has been violated, do the laws of this country afford him a remedy? 3rd. If they do afford him a remedy, is it a mandamus issuing from this court? . . . .
. . . It is . . . the opinion of the Court: 1st. That by signing the commission of Mr. Marbury, the President of the United States appointed him a justice of peace for the county of Washington, in the district of Columbia; and that the seal of the United States, affixed thereto by the Secretary of state, is conclusive testimony of the verity of the signature, and of the completion of the appointment; and that the appointment conferred on him a legal right to the office for the space of five years. 2d. That, having this legal title to the office, he has a consequent right to the commission; a refusal to deliver which is a plain violation of that right, for which the laws of his country afford him a remedy.

3. It remains to be inquired whether he is entitled to the remedy for which he applies? This depends on—
1st. The nature of the writ applied for; and 2d. The power of this court. . . .

This . . . is a plain case for a *mandamus*, either to deliver the commission, or a copy of it from the record; and it only remains to be inquired, whether it can issue from this court?

The act to establish the judicial courts of the United States authorizes the supreme court, "to issue writs of *mandamus*, in cases warranted by the principles and usages of law, to any courts appointed or persons holding office, under the authority of the United States." [Judiciary Act of 1789, Section 13.]. The secretary of state, being a person holding an office under the authority of the United States, is precisely within the letter of this description; and if this court is not authorized to issue a writ of *mandamus* to such an officer, it must be because the law is unconstitutional, and therefore, absolutely incapable of conferring the authority, and assigning the duties which its words purport to confer and assign.

The constitution vests the whole judicial power of the United States in one supreme court, and such inferior courts as congress shall, from time to time, ordain and establish. This power is expressly extended to all cases arising under the laws of the United States; and consequently, in some form, may be exercised over the present case; because the right claimed is given by a law of the United States.

In the distribution of this power, it is declared, that "the supreme court shall have original jurisdiction, in all cases affecting ambassadors, other public ministers and consuls, and those in which a state shall be a party. In all other cases, the supreme court shall have appellate jurisdiction." It has been insisted, at the bar, that as the original grant of jurisdiction to the supreme and inferior courts, is general, and the clause, assigning original jurisdiction to the supreme court, contains no negative or restrictive words, the power remains to the legislature, to assign original jurisdiction to that court, in other cases than those specified in the article which has been recited; provided those cases belong to the judicial power of the United States.

If it had been intended to leave it in the discretion of the legislature, to apportion the judicial power between the supreme and inferior courts, according to the will of that body, it would certainly have been useless to have proceeded further than to have defined the judicial power, and the tribunals in which it should be vested. The subsequent part of the section is mere surplusage—is entirely without meaning, if such is to be the construction. If congress remains at liberty to give this court appellate jurisdiction, where the constitution has declared their jurisdiction shall be original; and original jurisdiction where the constitution has declared it shall be appellate; the distribution of jurisdiction, made in the constitution, is form without substance. Affirmative words are often, in their operation, negative of other objects than those affirmed; and in this case, a negative or exclusive sense must be given to them, or they have no operation at all.

It cannot be presumed, that any clause in the constitution is intended to be without effect; and therefore, such a construction is inadmissible, unless the words require it. If the solicitude of the convention, respecting our peace with foreign powers, induced a provision that the supreme court should take original jurisdiction in cases which might be supposed to affect them; yet the clause would have proceeded no further than to provide for such cases, if no further restriction on the powers of congress had been intended. That they should have appellate jurisdiction in all other cases, with such exceptions as congress might make, is no restriction; unless the words be deemed exclusive of original jurisdiction.

When an instrument organizing, fundamentally, a judicial system, divides it into one supreme, and so many inferior courts as the legislature may ordain and establish; then enumerates its powers, and proceeds so far to distribute them, as to define the jurisdiction of the supreme court, by declaring the cases in which it shall take original jurisdiction, and that in others it shall take appellate jurisdiction, the plain import of the words seems to be, that in one class of cases, its jurisdiction is original, and not appellate; in the other, it is appellate, and not original. If any other construction would render the clause inoperative, that is an additional reason for rejecting such other construction, and for adhering to their obvious meaning. To enable this court, then, to issue a *mandamus,* it must be shown to be an exercise of appellate jurisdiction, or to be necessary to enable them to exercise appellate jurisdiction.

It has been stated at the bar, that the appellate jurisdiction may be exercised in a variety of forms, and that if it be the will of the legislature that a *mandamus* should be used for that purpose, that will must be obeyed. This is true, yet the jurisdiction must be appellate, not original. It is the essential criterion of appellate jurisdiction, that it revises and corrects the proceedings in a cause already instituted, and does not create that cause. Although, therefore, a *mandamus* may be directed to courts, yet to issue such a writ to an officer, for the delivery of a paper, is, in effect, the same as to sustain an original action for that paper, and therefore, seems not to belong to appellate, but to original jurisdiction. Neither is it necessary in such a case as this, to enable the court to exercise its appellate jurisdiction. The authority, therefore, given to the supreme court by the act establishing the judicial courts of the United States, to issue writs of *mandamus* to public officers, appears not to be warranted by the constitution; and it becomes necessary to inquire, whether a jurisdiction so conferred can be exercised.

The question, whether an act, repugnant to the constitution can become the law of the land, is a question deeply interesting to the United States; but, happily, not of an intricacy proportioned to its interest. It seems only necessary to recognise certain principles, supposed to have been long and well established, to decide it. That the people have an original right to establish, for their future government, such principles as, in their opinion, shall most conduce to their own happiness, is the basis on which the whole American fabric has been erected. The exercise of this original right is a very great exertion; nor can it, nor ought it, to be frequently repeated. The principles, therefore, so established, are deemed fundamental: and as the authority from which they proceed is supreme, and can seldom act, they are designed to be permanent.

This original and supreme will organizes the government, and assigns to different departments their respective powers. It may either stop here, or establish certain limits not to be transcended by those departments. The government of the United States is of the latter description. The powers of the legislature are defined and limited; and that those limits may not be mistaken or forgotten, the constitution is written. To what purpose are powers limited, and to what purpose is that limitation committed to writing, if these limits may, at any time, be passed by those intended to be restrained? The distinction between a government with limited and unlimited powers is abolished, if those limits do not confine the persons on whom they are imposed, and if acts prohibited and acts allowed, are of equal obligation. It is a proposition too plain to be contested, that the constitution controls any legislative act repugnant to it; or that the legislature may alter the constitution by an ordinary act.

Between these alternatives, there is no middle ground. The constitution is either a superior paramount law, unchangeable by ordinary means, or it is on a level with ordinary legislative acts, and, like other acts, is alterable when the legislature shall please to alter it. If the former part of the alternative be true, then a legislative act, contrary to the constitution, is not law: if the latter part be true, then written constitutions are absurd attempts, on the part of the people, to limit a power, in its own nature, illimitable.

Certainly, all those who have framed written constitutions contemplate them as forming the fundamental and paramount law of the nation, and consequently, the theory of every such government must be, that an act of the legislature, repugnant to the constitution, is void. This theory is essentially attached to a written constitution, and is , consequently, to be considered, by this court, as one of the fundamental principles of our society. It is not, therefore, to be lost sight of, in the further consideration of this subject.

If an act of the legislature, repugnant to the constitution, is void, does it, notwithstanding its invalidity, bind the courts, and oblige them to give it effect? Or, in other words, though it be not law, does it constitute a rule as operative as if it was a law? This would be to overthrow, in fact, what was established in theory; and would seem, at first view, an absurdity too gross to be insisted on. It shall, however, receive a more attentive consideration.

It is, emphatically, the province and duty of the judicial department, to say what the law is. Those who apply the rule to particular cases, must of necessity expound and interpret that rule. If two laws conflict with each other, the courts must decide on the operation of each. So, if a law be in opposition to the constitution; if both the law and the constitution apply to a particular case, so that the court must either decide that case, conformable to the law, disregarding the constitution; or conformable to the constitution, disregarding the law; the court must determine which of these conflicting rules governs the case: this is of the very essence of judicial duty. If then, the courts are to regard the constitution, and the constitution is superior to any ordinary act of the legislature, the constitution, and not such ordinary act, must govern the case to which they both apply.

Those, then, who controvert the principle, that the constitution is to be considered, in court, as a paramount law, are reduced to the necessity of maintaining that courts must close their eyes on the constitution, and see only the law. This doctrine would subvert the very foundation of all written constitutions. It would declare that an act which, according to the principles and theory of our government, is entirely void, is yet, in practice, completely obligatory. It would declare, that if the legislature shall do what is expressly forbidden, such act, notwithstanding the express prohibition, is in reality effectual. It would be giving to the legislature a practical and real omnipotence, with the same breath which professes to restrict their powers within narrow limits. It is prescribing limits, and declaring that those limits may be passed at pleasure. That it thus reduces to nothing, what we have deemed the greatest improvement on political institutions, a written constitution, would, of itself, be sufficient, in America, where written constitutions have been viewed with so much reverence, for rejecting the construction. But the peculiar expressions of the constitution of the United States furnish additional arguments in favor of its rejection. The judicial power of the United States is extended to all cases arising under the constitution. Could it be the intention of those who gave this power, to say, that in using it, the constitution should not be looked into? That a case arising under the constitution should be decided, without examining the instrument under which it arises? This is too extravagant to be maintained. In some cases, then, the constitution must be looked into by the judges. And if they can open it at all, what part of it are they forbidden to read or to obey?

There are many other parts of the constitution which serve to illustrate this subject. It is declared, that "no tax or duty shall be laid on articles exported from any state." Suppose, a duty on the export of cotton, of tobacco or of flour; and a suit instituted to recover it. Ought judgment to be rendered in such a case? Ought the judges to close their eyes on the constitution, and only see the law?

The constitution declares "that no bill of attainder or *ex post facto* law shall be passed." If, however, such a bill should be passed, and a person should be prosecuted under it; must the court condemn to death those victims whom the constitution endeavors to preserve?

"No person," says the constitution, "shall be convicted of treason, unless on the testimony of two witnesses to the same *overt* act, or on confession in open court." Here, the language of the constitution is addressed especially to the courts. It prescribes, directly for them, a rule of evidence not to be departed from. If the legislature should change that rule, and declare one witness, or a confession out of court, sufficient for conviction, must the constitutional principle yield to the legislative act?

From these, and many other selections which might be made, it is apparent, that the framers of the constitution contemplated that instrument as a rule for the government of courts, as well as of the legislature. Why otherwise does it direct the judges to take an oath to support it? This oath certainly applies in an especial manner, to their conduct in their official character. How immoral to impose it on them, if they were to be used as the instruments, and the knowing instruments, for violating what they swear to support!

The oath of office, too, imposed by the legislature, is completely demonstrative of the legislative opinion on this subject. It is in these words: "I do solemnly swear, that I will administer justice, without respect to persons, and do equal right to the poor and to the rich;

and that I will faithfully and impartially discharge all the duties incumbent on me as ＿＿＿, according to the best of my abilities and understanding, agreeably to the constitution and laws of the United States." Why does a judge swear to discharge his duties agreeably to the constitution of the United States, if that constitution forms no rule for his government? If it is closed upon him, and cannot be inspected by him? If such be the real state of things, this is worse than solemn mockery. To prescribe, or to take this oath, becomes equally a crime.

It is also not entirely unworthy of observation, that in declaring what shall be the supreme law of the land, the constitution itself is first mentioned; and not the laws of the United States generally, but those only which shall be made in pursuance of the constitution, have that rank.

Thus, the particular phraseology of the constitution of the United States confirms and strengthens the principle, supposed to be essential to all written constitutions, that a law repugnant to the constitution is void; and that courts, as well as other departments, are bound by that instrument.

The rule must be discharged.

The logic (or lack thereof) of the doctrine of judicial review in relation to the doctrine of separation of powers was not debated very thoroughly in the immediate political controversy over Marbury's commission, but was fully discussed in a dissenting opinion by Justice John B. Gibson of the Supreme Court of Pennsylvania more than 20 years later in the case of *Eakin* v. *Raub*:

EAKIN v. RAUB
12 Sergeant and Rawle (1825)

. . . I am aware, that a right to declare all unconstitutional acts void, without distinction as to either constitution, is generally held as a professional dogma; but, I apprehend, rather as a matter of faith than of reason. I admit that I once embraced the same doctrine, but without examination, and I shall therefore state the arguments that impelled me to abandon it, with great respect for those by whom it is still maintained. But I may premise, that it is not a little remarkable, that although the right in question has all along been claimed by the judiciary, no judge has ventured to discuss it, except Chief Justice Marshall, . . . and if the argument of a jurist so distinguished for the strength of his ratiocinative powers be found inconclusive, it may fairly be set down to the weakness of the position which he atttempts to defend. . . .

I begin, then, by observing that in this country, the powers of the judiciary are divisible into those that are

POLITICAL and those that are purely CIVIL. Every power by which one organ of the government is enabled to control another, or to exert an influence over its acts, is a political power. . . . [The judiciary's] civil, are its *ordinary* and *appropriate* powers; being part of its essence, and existing independently of any supposed grant in the constitution. But where the government exists by virtue of a *written* constitution, the judiciary does not necessarily derive from that circumstance, any other than its ordinary and appropriate powers. Our judiciary is constructed on the principles of the common law, which enters so essentially into the composition of our social institutions as to be inseparable from them, and to be, in fact, the basis of the whole scheme of our civil and political liberty. In adopting any organ or instrument of the common law, we take it with just such powers and capabilities as were incident to it as the common law, except where these are expressly, or by necessary implication, abridged or enlarged in the act of adoption; and, that such act is a written instrument, cannot vary its consequences or construction. . . . Now, what are the powers of the judiciary at the common law? They are those that necessarily arise out of its immediate business; and they are therefore commensurate only with the judicial execution of the municipal law, or, in other words, with the administration of distributive justice, without extending to anything of a political cast whatever. . . . With us, although the legislature be the depository of only so much of the sovereignty as the people have thought fit to impart, it is nevertheless sovereign within the limit of its powers, and may relatively claim the same pre-eminence here that it may claim elsewhere. It will be conceded, then, that the ordinary and essential powers of the judiciary do not extend to the annulling of an act of the legislature. . . .

The constitution of *Pennsylvania* contains no express grant of political powers to the judiciary. But, to establish a grant by implication, the constitution is said to be a law of superior obligation; and, consequently, that if it were to come into collision with an act of the legislature, the latter would have to give way. This is conceded. But it is a fallacy to support that they can come into collision *before the judiciary* . . .

The constitution and the right of the legislature to pass the act, may be in collision. But is that a legitimate subject for judicial determination? If it be, the judiciary must be a peculiar organ, to revise the proceedings of the legislature, and to correct its mistakes; and in what part of the constitution are we to look for this proud pre-eminence? Viewing the matter in the opposite direction, what would be thought of an act of assembly in which it should be declared that the supreme court had, in a particular case, put a wrong construction on the constitution of the United States, and that the judgment should therefore be reversed? It would doubtless be thought a usurpation of judicial power. But it is by no means clear, that to declare a law void which has been enacted according to the forms prescribed in the constitution, is not a usurpation of legislative power. . . .

But it has been said to be emphatically the business of the judiciary, to ascertain and pronounce what the law is; and that this necessarily involves a consideration of the constitution. It does so: but how far? If the judiciary will inquire into anything besides the form of enactment, where shall it stop? There must be some point of limitation to such an inquiry; for no one will pretend, that a judge would be justifiable in calling for the election returns, or scrutinizing the qualifications of those who composed the legislature. . . .

But, in theory, all the organs of the government are of equal capacity; or, if not equal, each must be supposed to have superior capacity only for those things which peculiarly belong to it; and as legislation peculiarly involves the consideration of those limitations which are put on the law-making power, and the interpretation of the laws when made, involves only the construction of the laws themselves, it follows that the construction of the constitution in this particular belong to the legislature, which ought therefore to be taken to have superior capacity to judge of the constitutionality of its own acts. But suppose all to be of equal capacity, in every respect, why should one exercise a controlling power over the rest? That the judiciary is of superior rank, has never been pretended, although it has been said to be co-ordinate. It is not easy, however, to comprehend how the power which gives law to all the rest, can be of no more than equal rank with one which receives it, and is answerable to the former for the observance of its statutes. Legislation is essentially an act of sovereign power; but the execution of the laws by instruments that are governed by prescribed rules, and exercise no power of volition, is essentially otherwise. . . . It may be said, the power of the legislature, also, is limited by prescribed rules: it is so. But it is, nevertheless, the power of the people, and sovereign as far as it extends. It cannot be said, that the judiciary is co-ordinate merely because it is established by the constitution: if that were sufficient, sheriffs, registers of wills, and recorders of deeds, would be so too. Within the pale of their authority, the acts of these officers will have the power of the people for their support; but no one will pretend, they are of equal dignity with the acts of the legislature. Inequality of rank arises not from the manner in which the organ has been constituted, but from its essence and the nature of its functions; and the legislative organ is superior to every other, inasmuch as the power to will and to command, is essentially superior to the power to act and to obey. . . .

[H]ad it been intended to interpose the judiciary as an additional barrier, the matter would surely not have been left in doubt. The judges would not have been left to stand on the insecure and evershifting ground of public opinion, as to constructive powers; they would have been placed on the impregnable ground of an express grant; they would not have been compelled to resort to the debates in the convention, or the opinion that was generally entertained at the time. . . . The grant of a power so extraordinary, ought to appear so plain, that he who should run might read. . . .

But what I have in view in this inquiry, is the supposed right of the judiciary to interfere, in cases where the constitution is to be carried into effect through the instrumentality of the legislature, and where that organ must necessarily first decide on the constitutionality of its own act. The oath to support the constitution is not peculiar to the judges, but is taken indiscriminately by every officer of the government, and is designed rather as a test of the political principles of the man, than to bind the officer in the discharge of his duty: otherwise it is difficult to determine what operation it is to have in the case of a recorder of deeds, for instance, who, in the execution of his office, has nothing to do with the constitution. But granting it to relate to the official conduct of the judge, as well as every other officer, and not to his political principles, still it must be understood in reference to supporting the constitution, *only as far as that may be involved in his official duty*; and, consequently, if his official duty does not comprehend an inquiry into the authority of the legislature, neither does his oath. . . .

But do not the judges do a positive act in violation of the constitution, when they give effect to an unconstitutional law? Not if the law has been passed according to the forms established in the constitution. The fallacy of the question is, in supposing that the judiciary adopts the acts of the legislature as its own; whereas the enactment of a law and the interpretation of it are not concurrent acts; and as the judiciary is not required to concur in the enactment, neither is it in the breach of the constitution which may be the consequence of the enactment. The fault is imputable to the legislature, and on it the responsibility exclusively rests. . . .

But it has been said, that this construction would deprive the citizens of the advantages which are peculiar to a written constitution, by at once declaring the power of the legislature in practice to be illimitable. . . . But there is no magic or inherent power in parchment and ink, to command respect and protect principles from violation. In the business of government a recurrence to first principles answers the end of an observation at sea with a view to correct the dead reckoning; and for this purpose, a written constitution is an instrument of inestimable value. It is of inestimable value, also, in rendering its first principles familiar to the mass of people; for, after all, there is no effectual guard against legislative usurpation but public opinion,

the force of which, in this country is inconceivably great. . . . Once let public opinion be so corrupt as to sanction every misconstruction of the constitution and abuse of power which the temptation of the moment may dictate, and the party which may happen to be predominant, will laugh at the puny efforts of a dependent power to arrest it in its course.

For these reasons, I am of opinion that it rests with the people, in whom full and absolute sovereign power resides, to correct abuses in legislation, by instructing their representatives to repeal the obnoxious act. . . . On the other hand, the judiciary is not infallible; and an effort by it would admit of no remedy but a more distinct expression of the public will, through the extraordinary medium of a convention; whereas, an error by the legislature admits of a remedy by an exertion of the same will, in the ordinary exercise of the right of suffrage,—a mode better calculated to attain the end, without popular excitement. . . .

But in regard to an act of [a state] assembly, which is found to be in collision with the constitution, laws, or treaties of the United States, I take the duty of the judiciary to be exactly the reverse. By becoming parties to the federal constitution, the states have agreed to several limitations of their individual sovereignty, to enforce which, it was thought to be absolutely necessary, to prevent them from giving effect to laws in violation of those limitations, through the instrumentality of their own judges. Accordingly, it is declared in the sixth article and second section of the federal constitution, that "This constitution, and the laws of the United States which shall be made in pursuance thereof, and all treaties made, or which shall be made under the authority of the United States, shall be the *supreme* law of the land; and the *judges* in every *state* shall be BOUND thereby; anything in the *laws* or *constitution* of any *state* to the contrary notwithstanding."

This is an express grant of a political power, and it is conclusive to show that no law of inferior obligation, as every state law must necessarily be, can be executed at the expense of the constitution, laws, or treaties of the United States. . . .

The long-term significance of *Marbury* v. *Madison* in establishing the power of judicial review was often lost upon early 19th century contemporaries because of the Republicans' immediate political and judicial successes in repealing the Federalist Judiciary Act of 1801 and establishing the constitutional validity of Congress' authority to alter and even abolish the inferior federal judiciary. One of the first actions of the incoming Jeffersonian Republicans was to introduce an act repealing the Federalist Judiciary Act of 1801.

When the Republicans succeeded in repealing it, their Federalist opponents made it evident that they would attempt to test the constitutionality of the repealing act in the courts. To prevent or postpone such a judicial test, the Republicans resorted to an unprecedented legislative maneuver. They speedily enacted a law abolishing the June and December terms of the Supreme Court and restoring the old February term, but not the old August term. By this device, the Supreme Court was forced to adjourn for fourteen months, from December 1801 to February 1803. Thus, this challenge was handled by the Court in the same term as *Marbury* v. *Madison.*

A number of leading Federalist politicians made two attempts to challenge the constitutionality of the repeal. A secret caucus of Federalists sought to persuade the members of the Supreme Court to refrain from participating in the circuit court system reinstated by the Jeffersonian Republicans in 1802.[11] They hoped for success because when Jefferson took office, the federal Supreme Court was completely dominated by staunch Federalists, the justices comprising William Cushing, William Paterson, Samuel Chase, Bushrod Washington, Alfred Moore, and Chief Justice John Marshall. However, the justices did not refuse to participate in circuit courts. The second attempt by Federalist political leaders forced the Federalist jurists to take a public stand. In a number of circuit courts, Federalists entered pleas or motions challenging the authority of the reinstated circuit courts. Federalist justices denied these motions. One of these motions was made by Federalist Charles Lee in the Fifth Circuit before Chief Justice Marshall in *Stuart* v. *Laird.* After Marshall dismissed Lee's arguments, Lee appealed to the Supreme Court on writ of error.[12] When the Supreme Court considered the issue, the oral argument for holding the repealing act void was again made by Lee, who had served as Federalist President Adams' attorney general. The argument and the Court's response are reproduced below:

STUART v. LAIRD
1 Cranch 299 (1803)

Oral argument of Charles Lee

The court of the fifth circuit ought not to have taken cognizance of the motion; because the court of the fourth circuit did exist, and not because it did not exist, as alleged in the plea.

If the acts of 8th March and 29th April, 1802, are constitutional, then it is admitted there is no error in the judgment; because, in that case, the courts ceased to exist, the judges were constitutionally removed, and the transfer from the one court to the other was legal. But if those acts are unconstitutional, then the court of the fourth circuit still exists, the judges were not removed, and the transfer of jurisdiction did not take place. The legislature did not intend to transfer causes from one existing court to another. If then the courts still exist, the causes, not being intended to be removed from existing courts, were not removed.

But we contend that those acts were unconstitutional so far as they apply to this cause.

1st. The first act (March 8, 1802) is unconstitutional in as much as it goes to deprive the courts of all their power and jurisdiction, and to displace judges who have been guilty of no misbehavior in their offices.

By the constitution the judges both of the supreme and the inferior courts are to hold their office during good behavior. So much has been recently said, and written and published upon this subject, that it is irksome to repeat arguments which are so familiar to everyone.

There is no difference between the tenure of office of a judge of the supreme court and that of a judge of an inferior court. The reason of that tenure, to wit, the independence of the judge, is the same in both cases; indeed the reason applies more strongly to the case of the inferior judges, because to them are exclusively assigned cases of life and death.

It is admitted that congress have the power to modify, increase or diminish the power of the courts and the judges. But that is a power totally different from the power to destroy the courts and to deprive them of all power and jurisdiction. The one is permitted by the constitution, the other is restrained by the regard which the constitution pays to the independence of the judges. They may modify the courts, but they cannot destroy them, if thereby they deprive a judge of his office. This provision of the constitution was intended to place the judges not only beyond the reach of executive power, of which the people are always jealous, but also to shield them from the attack of that party spirit which always predominates in popular assemblies. That this was the principle intended to be guarded by the constitution is evident from the contemporaneous exposition of that instrument, published under the title of *The Federalist*, and written, as we all know, by men high in the esteem of their country. . . .

Mr. Lee also cited and read the speeches of Mr. Madison in the convention of Virginia, . . . of Mr. Nicholas, . . . and of Mr. Marshall. . . .

The words *during good behavior* can not mean *during the will of congress*. The people have a right to the services of those judges who have been constitutionally appointed, and who have been unconstitutionally removed from office. It is the right of the people that their judges should be independent; that they should not stand in dread of any man, who, as Mr. Henry said in the Virginia convention, has the congress at his heels.

The Supreme Court's response to Lee's argument was presented by Justice Paterson. (Chief Justice Marshall took no part in the decision because he had presided over the circuit court from which the case arose.) Paterson rejected Lee's request for reversal in a manner fully cognizant of Congress' paramount authority. Justice Paterson stated that,

Congress have constitutional authority to establish from time to time such inferior tribunals as they may think proper; and to transfer a cause from one such tribunal to another. In this last particular, there are no words in the constitution to prohibit or restrain the exercise of legislative power.

The present is a case of this kind. It is nothing more than the removal of the suit brought by Stuart against Laird from the court of the fourth circuit to the court of the fifth circuit, which is authorized to proceed upon and carry it into full effect. This is apparent from the ninth section of the act entitled, "an act to amend the judicial system of the United States," passed the 29th of April, 1802. The forthcoming bond is an appendage to the cause, or rather a component part of the proceedings.

2d. Another reason for reversal is, that the judges of the Supreme Court have no right to sit as circuit judges, not being appointed as such, or in other words, that they ought to have distinct commission for that purpose. To this objection, which is of recent date, it is sufficient to observe, that practice and acquiescence under it for a period of several years, commencing with the organization of the judicial system, affords an irresistable answer, and has indeed fixed the construction. It is a contemporary interpretation of the most forcible nature. This practical exposition is too strong and obstinate to be shaken or controlled. Of course, the question is at rest, and ought not now to be disturbed.

Even before this rather concise Supreme Court rejection of the argument against the repealing act, Federalists in the House of Representatives attempted in two separate roll calls to defeat a Jeffersonian Republican resolution refusing a petition of the former circuit judges for their salaries. The Republican resolution finally passed by a vote of 61 to 37 on January 27, 1803, a few days before the beginning of the February term in which the Court decided both *Marbury v. Madison* and *Stuart v. Laird*. Similarly, the Senate produced two narrowly divided roll calls, one relative to *Marbury v. Madison*, and the second concerned with the repeal of President Adams' Circuit Court Act of 1801. On January 31, 1803, the Senate defeated, by a vote of 15 to 13, a resolution directing the Secretary of the Senate to give William Marbury, Robert T. Hooe, and Denis Ramsay (all parties to the court action in *Marbury v. Madison*) a copy of the Senate proceedings of March 2 and 3, 1801, relative to their appointment as justices of the peace. On February 3, 1803, the Senate again by an identical vote of 15 to 13 defeated a Federalist resolution requesting President Jefferson to cause a *quo warranto* proceeding to be filed by the attorney general against Richard Basset for the purpose of testing the validity of the act of March 8, 1802, which repealed the Federalist Judiciary Act of February 13, 1801.

The intensity of the partisan conflict over control of the federal judiciary is indicated by the persistence and magnitude of the division over the impeachment and conviction of federal district Judge John Pickering for intemperate and partisan behavior and the impeachment attempt on Associate Justice Samuel Chase. In the House of Representatives, divisions on 18 roll calls were recorded from the end of the Seventh Congress in 1803 through the end of the Eighth Congress in 1805. Some of these divisions included inquiries about the conduct of Federalist district Judge Richard Peters as well, but no recommendation for his impeachment was forthcoming. The partisan conflict in the Senate during the impeachment trials of Judge Pickering and Justice Chase was much more intense. There were 35 roll calls relating to these trials, which resulted in Pickering's conviction and Chase's successful defense. Issues involving the federal judiciary virtually overshadowed all others in the Seventh and Eighth Congresses.

The initial political conflicts between the Jeffersonian president and Congress versus the Federalist-dominated Court involved basic issues of political control of the system. It should be remembered that this system had never before experienced a peaceful, orderly transfer of political power from one political party to another. Many of these conflicts were directly related to this salient aspect of the first critical election in the United States. Thus, during President Thomas Jefferson's first term, strong Republican attacks were made upon the federal judiciary to stop or curtail what were perceived as attempts to limit or to interfere with the Jeffersonian presidency and Congress.

While the controversies between the Federalist judiciary and the Republican executive and legislative branches of the national government multiplied, Chief Justice John Marshall had quietly assumed leadership of the Supreme Court. During the August term of 1801, he ignored the earlier practice of the Court by which each justice delivered a separate opinion. Instead, he began delivering opinions for the whole Court, thus creating an impression of unity that the highest tribunal had hitherto lacked.

The major items of conflict between the Republicans and the Supreme Court during Jefferson's first administration were the attempt by Federalist judges to prosecute for libel the editor of a Republican newspaper, the refusal of a Connecticut (federal) circuit court to recognize as valid a presidential order, the repeal of the Federalist-sponsored Judiciary Act of 1801, the mandamus case, *Marbury* v. *Madison*, which asserted the right of the Supreme Court to declare acts of Congress unconstitutional, the impeachment of Judge Pickering, and the attempt to convict Justice Chase.

These issues, all manifestations of the stresses and strains of separation of powers, were in the forefront of the partisan divisions in Congress, but the deep-seated and enduring conflicts emerged as issues of federalism. Although Charles Grove Haines had argued that "Jefferson's election was rightfully looked upon as an endorsement of the states-rights interpretation of the 'federal compact,'" Jefferson himself did not indicate by action or utterance that he believed the election victory was a popular mandate for establishment of the doctrine of state interposition as a determinative constitutional principle. On the contrary, in his inaugural address, Jefferson stated that one of the guiding principles of his administration was "the preservation of the general government in its whole constitutional vigor." Nevertheless, federalism was destined to dominate political controversy throughout much of the 19th century and was inserted in the debates concerning the first great peaceful transition of power after a critical election. During the congressional debates on the repeal of the Judiciary Act of 1801, for example, Representative Giles of Virginia attacked the act on the ground that the new courts established under its provisions produced "a gradual demolition of state courts." And Senator Breckenridge of Kentucky was urged by one of his constituents to "go farther and make such a change in the Constitution as to limit the jurisdiction of the federal courts to cases of admiralty and cases arising under the constitution." However, the Republican leaders in Congress apparently had no intention of going "farther," and it seems there was little support at this time for the sort of legislation advocated by Breckenridge's correspondent.

The objections of Giles and Breckenridge to the expansion of judicial power under the act of 1801 were based on economic fears rather than upon adherence to the constitutional doctrine of state interposition. Landholders in Virginia and Kentucky believed that the federal courts would nullify the existing state land laws. If the Jeffersonian Republicans had really wished to implement the states' rights doctrine of state interposition that they had advocated in 1798-1800, they would have attempted to repeal the Judiciary Act of 1789 rather than that of 1801. For it was the former rather than the latter act that had established the Supreme Court as final arbiter in federal-state relations. However, in 1802 and 1803 as in 1787 and 1789 the anti-Federalists, now Republicans, did not consistently object to the exercise of such power by the Supreme Court.

Near the end of Jefferson's first administration, a case arose that contained a doctrine of far-reaching importance to the future expansion of national governmental power. In the February term of 1805, Chief Justice Marshall, in the case of *United States* v. *Fisher*,[13] repudiated by *dicta* the strict constructionist doctrine of constitutional power, and reasserted the supremacy of national legislation. (*Dicta* are opinions that are beyond the determination in the case and are thus extraneous.)

This case arose from a controversy concerning whether the United States "as holders of a protested bill of exchange . . . are entitled to be preferred to the general creditors, where the debtor becomes bankrupt." This claim for preference was based on the fifth section of a congressional act "to provide more effectually for the settlement of accounts between the United States and receivers of public money."[14]

Counsel for Fisher contended that "under a constitution conferring specific powers, the power (to grant the United States such a priority) must be granted, or it cannot be exercised." Chief Justice Marshall rejected this strict constructionist argument, stating that the Congress could grant such a priority under its authority "to make all laws which shall be necessary and proper to carry into execution the powers vested by the constitution in the government of the United States, or in any deparment or officer thereof." He then pointed out that

> In construing this clause, it would be incorrect, and would produce endless difficulties, if the opinion should be maintained, that no law was authorized which was not indispensably necessary to give effect to a specified power. Where various systems might be adopted for that purpose, it might be said, with respect to each, that it was not necessary, because the end might be obtained by other means. Congress must possess the choice of means, and must be empowered to use any means which are in fact conducive to the exercise of a power granted by the constitution.[15]

Counsel for Fisher had contended also that the claim of priority on the part of the United States would "interfere with the right of the state sovereignties . . ." and would "defeat the measures they have a right to adopt, to secure themselves against delinquencies on the part of their own revenue officers."

> But [answered Marshall] this is an objection to the constitution itself. The mischief suggested, so far as it can really happen, is the necessary consequence of the supremacy of the laws of the United States on all subjects to which the legislative power of congress extends.[16]

During the consideration of this case, attorney Harper had to cut short his argument in order to take part in the impeachment trial of Justice Chase.[17] However, although public attention was focused on the conflicts between the judiciary and the other two branches of the national government, Marshall's nationalistic judicial pronouncements were not entirely unnoticed. In the following year, Representative Clopton of Virginia introduced a constitutional amendment defining "necessary and proper" as including "only such laws as shall have a rational connection with and immediate relation to the powers enumerated." Clopton insisted that the trend toward the usurpation of powers by the federal government was weaving "the web of destruction" around state institutions.[18] Nevertheless, Clopton's challenge was relatively mild compared to the attacks made on the Court in the state of Pennsylvania during the last stages of the Gideon Olmstead litigation. The general Republican attitude, as expressed in the following letter, anticipated the strong criticism of the Supreme Court that greeted the decision in *United States* v. *Judge Peters* in 1809. As one Pennsylvania Republican wrote:

> The Federal Court prostrated the sovereignty of Pennsylvania at its feet by a sophistical construction of the Constitution. The State, disposed to assert its legitimate rights, protested against judicial usurpation. . . . The Constitution of the United States protects against the suability of States. By a hocus-pocus trick of a Federal Court, Pennsylvania is sued. She protests through her representatives the violation of her rights. Is there to be no remedy for a State against the unconstitutional exercise of power by a department of the General Government?[19]

In February 1804 the Republicans, in congressional caucus, had unanimously nominated Jefferson for re-election as president. The caucus had also nominated George Clinton of New York as candidate for vice-president. The Federalists chose Charles Cotesworth Pinckney and Rufus King as candidates for president and vice-president respectively. The election was a landslide for the Republicans. Jefferson won 162 electoral votes to Pinckney's 14, while the vice-presidential electoral votes were divided in the same manner.[20] The Federalist-dominated Supreme Court faced the prospect of another four years of strong executive and legislative opposition.

During Jefferson's second administration, the battle between the Federalist judiciary and the Republican executive and legislative branches of government continued unabated. In 1806 Representative John Randolph re-introduced his resolution for a constitutional amendment providing for removal of Supreme Court justices by the president on joint address of both houses of Congress;[21] in 1807 the conflict between chief justice and chief executive was joined in the famous Burr treason trial;[22] and in 1808 Republican Justice Johnson held invalid an executive order to port collectors, provoking vigorous administration criticism.[23]

These deep-seated conflicts over the substantive doctrines and institutional composition of the federal judiciary were significant parts of the most important of the critical elections experienced in United States politics. When Thomas Jefferson took the oath of office as president of the United States on March 4, 1801, twelve years of Federalist control of the presidency and Congress ended. The critical election of 1800 established the principle for the first time that the political power of the national government could be transferred from one political party to another peacefully,[24] but not without acrimony and deep party divisions. Federalist retention of control of the Supreme Court and President Adams' attempt at expanding the inferior federal judiciary (and with it more Federalist patronage) accentuated a problem that, by the nature of the constitutional requirements, was bound to occur after any major realignment of political parties. Because the justices and judges of the federal judiciary were insured tenure on good behavior, it could be expected that the judiciary would be composed largely of justices and judges whose political, social and economic attitudes and experiences were formed as part of a political generation different from that which took control of the presidency and Congress. The transformation of national political elites in the United States is thus always characterized by this constitutionally ordained factor of differential recruitment. This factor was important in the first era of significant political change.

Thomas Jefferson was elected to two four-year terms as president, but the Federalists did not lose control of the federal judiciary until years after Jefferson had left the presidency. During Jefferson's first term Justice Alfred Moore resigned. Jefferson chose as his successor a staunch Republican, William Johnson of South Carolina. In his second term, President Jefferson was able to fill two vacancies. He appointed Henry Brockholst Livingston of New York to the vacancy created by the death of Justice Paterson. By the Act of February 24, 1807, Congress created another associate justiceship in order to provide for the needs of the new Seventh Circuit, which comprised the states of Kentucky, Tennessee, and Ohio. Jefferson's choice for the new judicial post was Thomas Todd of Kentucky, a moderate Republican expert on regional land law.[25] After Jefferson's initial election in 1800, no Federalist ever served in the presidency again. But Federalists dominated the Supreme Court until well into 1812 through good health and longevity and a keen sense of the importance of their role. Even after 1812, the doctrinal defection of a nominal Republican, Joseph Story, weakened Republican control. The sequence of events and the attitudes of the key political participants indicated the political tensions of that era.

Even after the two administrations of Thomas Jefferson, the Federalists outnumbered the Republicans on the Supreme Court four to three. In Republican circles it was reported that the Federalists had prevailed upon the now senile Justice William Cushing "to retain his office . . . lest a Republican succeed him."[26] The election of James Madison in 1808, although characterized by a moderate increase in Federalist strength, was another Republican victory.[27] And after the adjournment of the Supreme Court in 1810, Justice Cushing, now 78 years old, died. Republican leaders, particularly Jefferson, were quite anxious to assure Republican ascendancy on the highest tribunal. In a letter to Gideon Granger, Jefferson wrote that he recommended

> the substituting in the place of Cushing, a firm unequivocal republican, whose principles are born with him, and not an occasional ingraftment, as necessary to compleat that great reformation in our government to which the Nation gave its fiat ten years ago.[28]

President Madison first chose Levi Lincoln, a staunch Republican, former attorney-general under Jefferson, to succeed Cushing. Lincoln declined the appointment because of poor health and failing eyesight. Madison then chose Alexander Wolcott, a mediocre lawyer and "party boss" of Connecticut. Wolcott was rejected by the Senate. Madison's third choice, John Quincy Adams, was immediately and unanimously confirmed by the Senate, but Adams would not accept the appointment. Finally in November 1811, Madison appointed, and the Senate confirmed, Joseph Story of Massachusetts, a young lawyer of 32. The Federalists were enraged at the appointment of "Joe Story, that country pettifogger," and even the Republicans were rather lukewarm. Jefferson considered Story a "pseudo-republican" and, prophetically, was apprehensive about Story's constitutional views.[29] As subsequent events were to prove, Story either was by inclination, or became by persuasion, as strong a nationalist as Chief Justice Marshall. In June 1811, Federalist Justice Samuel Chase died. President Madison nominated Gabriel Duval of Maryland as his successor. Duval's appointment was confirmed by the Senate, along with Story's, on November 15, 1811.[30]

These personnel changes did stimulate an institutional procedural change. For more than a decade, Chief Justice John Marshall had written nearly every decision of the Supreme Court. In 1812, however, the Republicans on the Court comprised a five to two majority, and beginning in that year the members of the Court took turns writing the majority opinions.[31]

During this period of exceedingly gradual transition in the membership of the Supreme Court, key issues of considerable importance to the stability of the national political system came before the Court. One was the conflict of federal authority with Pennsylvania in the case of Judge Peters resulting from Gideon Olmstead's long fight for his prize money.

In 1809 the United States Supreme Court invited the state to become a party to a suit to settle the conflicting claims. But the Pennsylvania legislature reacted violently, denying that the state had "surrendered to the General Government a power to defeat or destroy her right to enforce the collection of her own revenues." This act of defiance prompted Republican United States Attorney Dallas to write to Attorney General Caesar A. Rodney that "the conduct of our Legislature at Lancaster is very strange and may be very mischievous. They have prostrated the constitutional barrier between the Judicial and Legislative departments. The Legislature at Boston will probably attempt to prostrate the barrier between the State and Federal Governments. . . . The times are bad."[32]

Dallas' reference to "the Legislature at Boston" indicated the very real anxiety of the Republican administration concerning the strong states' rights tendencies in Federalist New England. For during this period, New England resentment to the Jeffersonian Embargo Acts had converted the formerly nationalistic Federalists into staunch advocates of state sovereignty. Jefferson's Louisiana Purchase had earlier infuriated the New England Federalists, and by 1809 separation from the Union and formation of a northern confederacy were being widely discussed by many embittered Federalist leaders.[33] Federalist Circuit Judge John Davis, in *United States* v. *Brigantine William*, upheld the administration's Embargo Act as a valid regulation of commerce, as a preparation for war under the congressional war powers, and as appropriate under the necessary and proper clause.[34] Successful defiance of the Supreme Court by any state would undoubtedly have encouraged the New England separatist movement, however, and would probably have weakened the authority of the federal government in the states outside that region.

Federalist economic conservatism on the Court

In this difficult situation, a conflict of state authority arose in regard to a statute of Georgia. The case of *Fletcher* v. *Peck*[35] arose from a controversy involving the infamous Yazoo land fraud. In a "saturnalia of corruption,"[36] the legislature of Georgia, during the winter session of 1794–1795, sold to four companies of land speculators more than 35 million acres of fertile land for $500,000, less than one and one-half cents an acre. When the people of Georgia had learned of the venality of their representatives, they elected new members to the legislature at the next election. Within a year the Yazoo land grants were declared void by the new legislature, but the Yazoo speculators had acted even more swiftly. They had disposed of most of their holdings to purportedly "innocent purchasers" throughout the United States.

When the Georgia rescinding law was published throughout the country, investors began to organize to protect their interests. Particularly in New England, where the original Yazoo speculators had reaped their biggest harvest, indignation and apprehension were great. A number of purchasers organized the New England Mississippi Company to contest the Georgia legislative reversal. Hamilton declared that the Georgia act violated the contract clause of the Constitution since "every grant . . . whether (from) . . . a state or an individual, is virtually a contract." He predicted that "the courts of the United States . . . will be likely to pronounce it" null and void.[37] For a number of years the controversy raged in the national Congress, and in a veritable barrage of pamphlets. The New England Mississippi Company carried on large-scale lobbying activities. However, a number of Congressmen, led by the fiery John Randolph, steadfastly defeated every attempt at congressional payment of the claims.[38] The lobbying was not limited to efforts convincing members of Congress, however. Joseph Story, a young National Republican lawyer at the time, was hired to lobby the Supreme Court and did meet with Chief Justice John Marshall for that purpose.[39]

In May 1803, Boston investors arranged a "friendly suit" in a federal district court. John Peck of Boston, a heavy dealer in Georgia lands, had sold 15,000 acres of Yazoo land to Robert Fletcher for $3,000. Fletcher had immediately filed suit against Peck for recovery of the purchase money. The case was "continued by consent" term after term from June 1803 to October 1806. In October 1807, Justice William Cushing, in circuit court, decided in Peck's favor. Fletcher brought the controversy to the Supreme Court on writ of error.[40]

Fletcher v. *Peck* was argued twice. In March 1809, the Supreme Court did not reach a decision but continued the cause for further consideration pending amendment of the pleadings.[41] In March 1810, Chief Justice Marshall finally delivered the opinion of the majority. Justice William Johnson wrote a concurring opinion. Marshall had delivered a brief opinion on March 11, 1809, requesting an amendment of the pleadings. This is omitted.

FLETCHER v. PECK
6 Cranch 87 (1810)

March 16, 1810, Marshall, C.J.,
delivered the opinion of the court as follows:

The pleadings being now amended, this cause comes on again to be heard on sundry demurrers, and on a special verdict.

This suit was instituted on several covenants contained in a deed made by John Peck, the defendant in error, conveying to Robert Fletcher, the plaintiff in error, certain lands which were part of a large purchase made by James Gunn and others, in the year 1795, from the State of Georgia, the contract for which was made in the form of a bill passed by the legislature of that State.

The first count in the declaration set forth a breach in the second covenant contained in the deed. The covenant is, "that the legislature of the State of Georgia, at the time of passing the act of sale aforesaid, had good right to sell and dispose of the same in manner pointed out by the said act." The breach assigned is, that the legislature had no power to sell.

The plea in bar sets forth the constitution of the State of Georgia, and avers that the lands sold by the defendant to the plaintiff, were within that State. It then sets forth the granting act, and avers the power of the legislature to sell and dispose of the premises as pointed out by the act.

To this plea the plaintiff below demurred, and the defendant joined in demurrer.

That the legislature of Georgia, unless restrained by its own constitution, possesses the power of disposing of the unappropriated lands within its own limits, in such manner as its own judgment shall dictate, is a proposition not to be controverted. The only question, then, presented by this demurrer, for the consideration of the court, is this, did the then constitution of the State of Georgia prohibit the legislature to dispose of the lands, which were the subject of this contract, in the manner stipulated by the contract?

The question, whether a law be void for its repugnancy to the constitution, is, at all times, a question of much delicacy, which ought seldom, if ever, to be decided in the affirmative, in a doubtful case. The court, when impelled by duty to render such a judgment, would be unworthy of its station, could it be unmindful of the solemn obligations which that station imposes. But it is not on slight implication and vague conjecture that the legislature is to be pronounced to have transcended its powers, and its acts to be considered as void. The opposition between the constitution and the law should be such that the judge feels a clear and strong conviction of their incompatibility with each other.

In this case the court can perceive no such opposition. In the constitution of Georgia, adopted in the year 1789, the court can perceive no restriction on the legislative power, which inhibits the passage of the act of 1795. They cannot say that, in passing that act, the legislature has transcended its powers, and violated the constitution.

In overruling the demurrer, therefore, to the first plea, the circuit court committed no error.

The 3d covenant is, that all the title which the State of Georgia ever had in the premises had been legally conveyed to John Peck, the grantor.

The 2d count assigns, in substance, as a breach of this covenant, that the original grantees from the State of Georgia promised and assured divers members of the legislature, then sitting in general assembly, that if the said members would assent to, and vote for, the passing of the act, and if the said bill should pass, such members should have a share of, and be interested in, all the lands purchased from the said State by virtue of such law. And that divers of the said members, to whom the said promises were made, were unduly influenced thereby, and, under such influence, did vote for the passing of the said bill; by reason whereof the said law was a nullity, &c., and so the title of the State of Georgia did not pass to the said Peck, &c.

The plea to this count, after protesting that the promises it alleges were not made, avers, that until the purchase made from the original grantees by James Greenleaf, under whom the said Peck claims, neither the said James Greenleaf, nor the said Peck, nor any of the mesne vendors between the said Greenleaf and Peck, had any notice or knowledge that any such promises or assurances were made by the said original grantees, or either of them, to any of the members of the legislature of the state of Georgia.

To this plea the plaintiff demurred generally, and the defendant joined in the demurrer.

That corruption should find its way into the governments of our infant republics, and contaminate the very source of legislation, or that impure motives should contribute to the passage of a law, or the formation of a legislative contract, are circumstances most deeply to be deplored. How far a court of justice would, in any case, be competent, on proceedings instituted by the State itself, to vacate a contract thus formed, and to annul rights acquired, under that contract, by third persons having no notice of the improper means by which it was obtained, is a question which the court would approach with much circumspection. It may well be doubted how far the validity of a law depends upon the motives of its framers, and how far the particular inducements, operating on members of the supreme sovereign power of a State, to the formation of a contract by that power, are examinable in a court of justice. If the principle be conceded, that an act of the supreme sovereign power might be declared null by a court, in consequence of the means which procured it, still would there be much difficulty in saying to what extent those means must be applied to produce this effect. Must it be direct corruption, or would interest or undue influence of any kind be sufficient? Must the vitiating cause operate on a majority, or on what number of the members? Would the act be null, whatever might be the wish of the nation, or would its obligation or nullity depend upon the public sentiment?

If the majority of the legislature be corrupted, it may well be doubted, whether it be within the province of the judiciary to control their conduct, and, if less than a majority act from impure motives, the principle by which judicial interference would be regulated is not clearly discerned.

Whatever difficulties this subject might present, when viewed under aspects of which it may be susceptible, this court can perceive none in the particular pleadings now under consideration.

This is not a bill brought by the State of Georgia, to annul the contract, nor does it appear to the court, by this count, that the State of Georgia is dissatisfied with the sale that has been made. The case, as made out in the pleadings, is simply this. One individual who holds lands in the State of Georgia, under a deed convenanting that the title of Georgia was in the grantor, brings an action of covenant upon this deed, and assigns, as a breach, that some of the members of the legislature were induced to vote in favor of the law, which constituted the contract, by being promised an interest in it, and that therefore the act is a mere nullity.

This solemn question cannot be brought thus collaterally and incidentally before the court. It would be indecent, in the extreme, upon a private contract between two individuals, to enter into an inquiry respecting the corruption of the sovereign power of a State. If the title be plainly deduced from a legislative act, which the legislature might constitutionally pass, if the act be clothed with all the requisite forms of a law, a court, sitting as a court of law, cannot sustain a suit brought by one individual against another founded on the allegation that the act is a nullity, in consequence of the impure motives which influences certain members of the legislature which passed the law.

The circuit court, therefore, did right in overruling this demurrer.

The 4th covenant in the deed is that the title to the premises has been, in no way, constitutionally or legally impaired by virtue of any subsequent act of any subsequent legislature of the State of Georgia.

The third count recites the undue means practised on certain members of the legislature, as stated in the second count, and then alleges that, in consequence of these practices and of other causes, a subsequent legislature passed an act annulling and rescinding the law under which the conveyance to the original grantees was made, declaring that conveyance void, and asserting the title of the State to the lands it contained. The count proceeds to recite at large, this rescinding act, and concludes with averring that, by reason of this act, the title of the said Peck in the premises was constitutionally and legally impaired, and rendered null and void.

After protesting, as before, that no such promises were made as stated in this count, the defendant again pleads that himself and the first purchaser under the original grantees, and all intermediate holders of the property, were purchasers without notice.

To this plea there is a demurrer and joinder.

The importance and the difficulty of the questions presented by these pleadings, are deeply felt by the court.

The lands in controversy vested absolutely in James Gunn and others, the original grantees, by the conveyance of the governor, made in pursuance of an act of assembly to which the legislature was fully competent. Being thus in full possession of the legal estate, they, for a valuable consideration, conveyed portions of the land to those who were willing to purchase. If the original transaction was infected with fraud, these purchasers did not participate in it, and had no notice of it. They were innocent. Yet the legislature of Georgia has involved them in the fate of the first parties to the transaction, and, if the act be valid, has annihilated their rights also.

The legislature of Georgia was a party to this transaction; and for a party to pronounce its own deed invalid, whatever cause may be assigned for its invalidity, must be considered as a mere act of power which must find its vindication in a train of reasoning not often heard in courts of justice.

But the real party, it is said, are the people, and when their agents are unfaithful, the acts of those agents cease to be obligatory.

It is, however, to be recollected that the people can act only by these agents, and that, while within the powers conferred on them, their acts must be considered as the acts of the people. If the agents be corrupt, others may be chosen, and if their contracts be examinable, the common sentiment, as well as common usage of mankind, points out a mode by which this examination may be made, and their validity determined.

If the legislature of Georgia was not bound to submit its pretensions to those tribunals which are established for the security of property, and to decide on human

rights, if it might claim to itself the power of judging in its own case, yet there are certain great principles of justice, whose authority is universally acknowledged, that ought not to be entirely disregarded.

If the legislature be its own judge in its own case, it would seem equitable that its decision should be regulated by those rules which would have regulated the decision of a judicial tribunal. The question was, in its nature, a question of title, and the tribunal which decided it was either acting in the character of a court of justice, and performing a duty usually assigned to a court, or it was exerting a mere act of power in which it was controlled only by its own will.

If a suit be brought to set aside a conveyance obtained by fraud, and the fraud be clearly proved, the conveyance will be set aside, as between the parties; but the rights of third persons, who are purchasers without notice, for a valuable consideration, cannot be disregarded. Titles, which, according to every legal test, are perfect, are acquired with that confidence which is inspired by the opinion that the purchaser is safe. If there be any concealed defect, arising from the conduct of those who had held the property long before he acquired it, of which he had no notice, that concealed defect cannot be set up against him. He has paid his money for a title good at law; he is innocent, whatever may be the guilt of others, and equity will not subject him to the penalties attached to that guilt. All titles would be insecure, and the intercourse between man and man would be very seriously obstructed, if this principle be overturned.

A court of chancery, therefore, had a bill been brought to set aside the conveyance made to James Gunn and others, as being obtained by improper practices with the legislature, whatever might have been its decision as respected the original grantees, would have been bound, by its own rules, and by the clearest principles of equity, to leave unmolested those who were purchasers, without notice, for a valuable consideration.

If the legislature felt itself absolved from those rules of property which are common to all the citizens of the United States, and from those principles of equity which are acknowledged in all our courts, its act is to be supported by its power alone, and the same power may divest any other individual of his lands, if it shall be the will of the legislature so to exert it.

It is not intended to speak with disrespect of the legislature of Georgia, or of its acts. Far from it. The question is a general question, and is treated as one. For although such powerful objections to a legislative grant, as are alleged against this, may not again exist, yet the principle, on which alone this rescinding act is to be supported, may be applied to every case to which it shall be the will of any legislature to apply it. The principle is this: That a legislature may, by its own act, devest the vested estate of any man whatever, for reasons which shall, by itself, be deemed sufficient.

In this case the legislature may have had ample proof that the original grant was obtained by practices which can never be too much reprobated, and which would have justified its abrogation so far as respected those to whom crime was imputable. But the grant, when issued, conveyed an estate in fee-simple to the grantee, clothed with all the solemnities which law can bestow. This estate was transferable; and those who purchased parts of it were not stained by that guilt which infected the original transaction. Their case is not distinguishable from the ordinary case of purchasers of a legal estate without knowledge of any secret fraud which might have led to the emanation of the original grant. According to the well-known course of equity, their rights could not be affected by such fraud. Their situation was the same, their title was the same, with that of every other member of the community who holds land by regular conveyances from the original patentee.

Is the power of the legislature competent to the annihilation of such title, and to a resumption of the property thus held?

The principle asserted is, that one legislature is competent to repeal any act which a former legislature was competent to pass; and that one legislature cannot abridge the powers of a succeeding legislature.

The correctness of this principle, so far as respects general legislation, can never be controverted. But if an act be done under a law a succeeding legislature cannot undo it. The past cannot be recalled by the most absolute power. Conveyances have been made, those conveyances have vested legal estates, and, if those estates may be seized by the sovereign authority, still, that they originally vested is a fact, and cannot cease to be a fact.

When, then, a law is in its nature a contract, when absolute rights have vested under that contract, a repeal of the law cannot devest those rights; and the act of annulling them, if legitimate, is rendered so by a power applicable to the case of every individual in the community.

It may well be doubted whether the nature of society and of government does not prescribe some limits to the legislative power; and if any be prescribed, where are they to be found, if the property of an individual, fairly and honestly acquired, may be seized without compensation.

To the legislature all legislative power is granted;

but the question, whether the act of transferring the property of an individual to the public, be in the nature of the legislative power, is well worthy of serious reflection.

It is the peculiar province of the legislature to prescribe general rules for the government of society; the application of those rules to individuals in society would seem to be the duty of other departments. How far the power of giving the law may involve every other power, in cases where the constitution is silent, never has been, and perhaps never can be, definitely stated.

The validity of this rescinding act, then, might well be doubted, were Georgia a single sovereign power. But Georgia cannot be viewed as a single, unconnected, sovereign power, on whose legislature no other restrictions are imposed than may be found in its own constitution. She is a part of a large empire; she is a member of the American Union and that union has a constitution in the supremacy of which all acknowledge, and which imposes limits to the legislatures of the several States, which none claim a right to pass. The constitution of the United States declares that no State shall pass any bill of attainder, ex post facto law, or law impairing the obligation of contracts.

Does the case now under consideration come within this prohibitory section of the constitution?

In considering this very interesting question, we immediately ask ourselves what is a contract? Is a grant a contract?

A contract is a compact between two or more parties, and is either executory or executed. An executory contract is one in which a party binds himself to do, or not to do, a particular thing; such was the law under which the conveyance was made by the governor. A contract executed is one in which the object of contract is performed; and this, says Blackstone, differs in nothing from a grant. The contract between Georgia and the purchasers was executed by the grant. A contract executed, as well as one which is executory, contains obligations binding on the parties. A grant, in its own nature, amounts to an extinguishment of the right of the grantor, and implies a contract not to reassert that right. A party is, therefore, always estopped by his own grant.

Since, then, in fact, a grant is a contract executed, the obligation of which still continues, and since the constitution uses the general term contract, without distinguishing between those which are executory and those which are executed, it must be construed to comprehend the latter as well as the former. A law annulling conveyances between individuals, and declaring that the grantors should stand seized on their former estates, notwithstanding those grants, would be as repugnant to the constitution as a law discharging the vendors of property from the obligation of executing their contracts by conveyances. It would be strange if a contract to convey was secured by the constitution, while an absolute conveyance remained unprotected.

If, under a fair construction of the constitution, grants are comprehended under the term contracts, is a grant from the State excluded from the operation of the provision? Is the clause to be considered as inhibiting the State from impairing the obligation of contracts between two individuals, but as excluding from that inhibition contracts made with itself?

The words themselves contain no such distinction. They are general, and are applicable to contracts of every description. If contracts made with the State are to be exempted from their operation, the exception must arise from the character of the contracting party, not from the words which are employed.

Whatever respect might have been felt for the state sovereignties, it is not to be disguised that the framers of the constitution viewed, with some apprehension, the violent acts which might grow out of the feelings of the moment; and that the people of the United States, in adopting that instrument, have manifested a determination to shield themselves and their property from the effects of those sudden and strong passions to which men are exposed. The restrictions on the legislative power of the States are obviously founded in this sentiment; and the Constitution of the United States contains what may be deemed a bill of rights for the people of each State.

No State shall pass any bill of attainder, ex post facto law, or law impairing the obligation of contracts.

A bill of attainder may affect the life of an individual, or may confiscate his property, or may do both.

In this form the power of the legislature over the lives and fortunes of individuals is expressly restrained. What motive, then, for implying in words which import a general prohibition to impair the obligation of contracts, an exception in favor of the right to impair the obligation of those contracts into which the State may enter?

The State legislatures can pass no ex post facto law. An ex post facto law is one which renders an act punishable in a manner in which it was not punishable when it was committed. Such a law may inflict penalties on the person, or may inflict pecuniary penalties which swell the public treasury. The legislature is then prohibited from passing a law by which a man's estate, or any part of it, shall be seized for a crime which was not declared, by some previous law, to render him liable to that punishment. Why, then, should violence be

done to the natural meaning of words for the purpose of leaving to the legislature the power of seizing, for public use, the estate of an individual in the form of a law annulling the title by which he holds that estate? The court can perceive no sufficient grounds for making that distinction. This rescinding act would have the effect of an ex post facto law. It forfeits the estate of Fletcher for a crime not committed by himself, but by those from whom he purchased. This cannot be effected in the form of an ex post facto law, or bill of attainder; why, then, is it allowable in the form of a law annulling the original grant?

The argument in favor of presuming an intention to except a case, not excepted by the words of the constitution, is susceptible of some illustration from a principle orginally ingrafted in that instrument, though no longer a part of it. The constitution, as passed, gave the courts of the United States jurisdiction in suits brought against individual States. A State, then, which violated its own contract, was suable in the courts of the United States for the violation. Would it have been a defence in such a suit to say that the State had passed a law absolving itself from the contract? It is scarcely to be conceived that such a defence could be set up. And yet, if a State is neither restrained by the general principles of our political institutions, nor by the words of the constitution, from impairing the obligation of its own contracts, such a defence would be a valid one. This feature is no longer found in the constitution; but it aids in the construction of those clauses with which it was originally associated.

It is, then, the unanimous opinion of the court, that, in this case, the estate having passed into the hands of a purchaser for a valuable consideration, without notice, the State of Georgia was restrained, either by general principles which are common to our free institutions, or by the particular provisions of the Constitution of the United States, from passing a law whereby the estate of the plaintiff in the premises so purchased could be constitutionally and legally impaired and rendered null and void.

Judgement affirmed, with costs.

*Johnson, J. In this case I entertain,
on two points, an opinion different from
that which has been delivered by the court:*

I do not hesitate to declare that a State does not possess the power of revoking its own grants. But I do it on a general principle, on the reason and nature of things: a principle which will impose laws even on the Deity . . .

The other point on which I dissent from the opinion of the court, is relative to the judgment which ought to be given on the first count. Upon that count we are called upon substantially to decide, "that the State of Georgia, at the time of passing the act of cession, was legally seized in fee of the soil, (then ceded,) subject only to the extinguishment of part of the Indian title." That is, that the State of Georgia, was seized of an estate in fee-simple in the lands in question, subject to another estate, we know not what, nor whether it may not swallow up the whole estate decided to exist in Georgia. It would seem that the mere vagueness and uncertainty of this covenant would be a sufficient objection to deciding in favor of it, but to me it appears that the facts in the case are sufficient to support the opinion that the State of Georgia had not a fee-simple in the land in question . . .

I have been very unwilling to proceed to the decision of this cause at all. It appears to me to bear strong evidence, upon the face of it, of being a mere feigned case. It is our duty to decide on the rights, but not on the speculations of parties. My confidence, however, in the respectable gentlemen who have been engaged for the parties, has induced me to abandon my scruples, in the belief that they would never consent to impose a mere feigned case upon this court.

More than 150 years later, the research of C. Peter Magrath established the fact that collusion did take place. Nevertheless, some of the "respectable gentlemen" went on to more exalted careers. One of the founding members of the Philadelphia Convention, Luther Martin, represented the plaintiff in 1809 and again in 1810. The defendant was represented by John Quincy Adams and Robert Goodloe Harper in 1809 and by Harper and Joseph Story in 1810. Adams became president of the United States in 1824 and Story became an associate justice of the Supreme Court in 1811. Harper served for several years as a Federalist U.S. Senator from South Carolina.

Marshall's interpretation of the contract clause had been made without reference to the intentions of the constitutional framers, and necessarily so. For as Professor Benjamin F. Wright pointed out, "If the broad interpretation of the contract clause enunciated by Chief Justice Marshall depended for its historical justification on the opinions expressed by the men who wrote and adopted the Constitution in 1787–1788, that justification would be indeed weak."[42] The framers had, with only two exceptions, apparently accepted a narrow definition of contract, limiting the application of the constitutional prohibition to private contracts rather than grants made by a state.[43] Regardless of the merits of Marshall's interpretation of the contract clause, his decision in *Fletcher* v. *Peck* was a particularly strong assertion of the power of the Supreme Court, a branch of the national government, to nullify a state statute that was inconsistent with a provision of the federal Constitution. Although state laws previously had been declared unconstitutional as violations of the contract clause by federal circuit courts, *Fletcher* v. *Peck* marks the first such invalidation by the Supreme Court.

On the day after the decision in *Fletcher* v. *Peck* was handed down, the Supreme Court, for the first time, considered a case involving Congress' power to govern a territory. After Jefferson's agents had purchased the Louisiana Territory, the president, motivated by constitutional scruples, debated with his advisors the feasibility of requesting a constitutional amendment. However, the treaty embodying the purchase terms was submitted to the Senate without such a request. After ratification, the Senate passed an act empowering the president to govern the territory until Congress should establish a government. The Federalists and some Republicans opposed such a grant of power, and Congress acted swiftly, in the same session, to establish a territorial government.[44]

In *Sere and Laralde* v. *Pitot*,[45] Chief Justice Marshall upheld the power of Congress to govern the territory of Orleans not only as a power expressly granted in Article IV, section 3, of the Constitution, but as a power implied from the right to acquire territory.[46]

A contract clause doctrine enunciated by Chief Justice Marshall in *New Jersey* v. *Wilson*[47] had serious implications for the continued existence of state governments. The case involved the constitutionality of a state rescinding law. In 1758 commissioners of the colonial legislature of New Jersey and a tribe of Delaware Indians had reached an agreement whereby the Delawares relinquished their claims to their lands in that colony in return for a particular tract of land that was to be purchased for them by the colonial legislature. In August 1758, the legislature had passed an act giving effect to this agreement. By this act, which authorized the purchase of a tract for the Delawares, the Indians were restrained from granting leases or making sales, while, on the other hand, the Indian lands were to be tax-exempt.

In 1801 the remnants of the Delawares requested and obtained from the legislature of the state of New Jersey permission to sell their land. This act contained no reference to the tax-exempt status of the land. In 1803, George Painter and others bought the Indian tract. In the following year the legislature of New Jersey passed an act rescinding the section of the old colonial legislative act of 1758 that exempted the land from taxation, whereupon the lands were assessed and taxes demanded of Painter and the other purchasers. The purchasers challenged the validity of the rescinding law in the state courts and brought the case to the Supreme Court on writ of error.

After referring to the doctrine laid down in *Fletcher* v. *Peck* that a grant by a state is a contract within the meaning of the Constitution, Chief Justice Marshall held that the original colonial law was a contract. Counsel for the state argued, with what appears to be historical plausibility, that the tax exemption was never distinct from Indian possession because the exemption had been granted to prevent seizure of the land for taxes. Marshall maintained, however, that the privilege of tax-exemption was annexed to the land, not to the Indians. According to Marshall, tax exemption was "annexed to the land, because in the event of a sale, on which alone the question could become material, the value would be enhanced by it." Here it might be noted that a companion provision in the original act was one forbidding the leasing or selling of the Indian lands![48] Although Chief Justice Marshall's primary interest in the contract clause opinions appears to have been the protection of the rights of private property and, very probably, the establishment of a doctrine of vested rights, *New Jersey* v. *Wilson*, like *Fletcher* v. *Peck* and the subsequent Dartmouth College case, deservedly ranks as a strong assertion of the power of the highest national tribunal to invalidate state statutes that conflict with the provisions of the federal Constitution.

In March 1813, the Supreme Court handed down a decision that had far-reaching consequences in terms of the Supreme Court's exercise of the power to arbitrate finally in federal-state relations. *Fairfax's Devisee* v. *Hunter's Lessee*[49] involved a controversy that had been argued in various Virginia court actions over a period of 22 years. The conflict involved the title to the rich timber and tobacco lands located on the Potomac River and known as the Northern Neck of Virginia. The Northern Neck belonged to Lord Fairfax. After his death in England in 1781, the tract was devised to his nephew, Denny Martin. However, the state of Virginia, holding that it had confiscated the estate in 1777 and that an alien did not have the right to inherit, granted a portion of the tract to David Hunter in 1789. In 1791 the first of the many court actions arose when Hunter brought a suit in ejectment against Martin in a Virginia county court.

The issue finally reached the Supreme Court on writ of error in 1796, but was never argued. Litigation was begun anew in the Virginia courts. Finally, another writ of error to the Virginia Court of Appeals brought the issue to the highest national tribunal in 1812. The Court took a year to consider the case and rendered an opinion in March 1813. Chief Justice Marshall and Justice Washington did not participate in the decision.[50] Since Justice Johnson dissented, the majority opinion was supported by only three justices.

Justice Story, writing the opinion, held that, in spite of the Virginia contention to the contrary, Lord Fairfax was the owner of the Northern Neck tract at the time of his death.[51] He further held that a Virginia law could not prevent an alien enemy from taking land by devise, because the alien's (Martin's) right to do so was protected by the treaty of peace with Great Britain, and, more particularly, the treaty of 1794. The latter treaty, "being the supreme law of the land, confirmed the title to (Martin), his heirs and assigns, and protected him from any forfeiture by reason of alienage."

In his dissent, Justice Johnson maintained that the treaty of 1794 did not cover this case because Martin's rights as a devisee did not exist at the date of the treaty. However, he expressly agreed with the majority that "whenever a case is brought up to this court, (under Section 25 of the Judiciary Act of 1789), the title of the parties litigant must necessarily be inquired into, and that such an inquiry must . . . precede the consideration how far the law, treaty, and so forth, is applicable to it; otherwise, an appeal to this court would be worse than nugatory." Within three years, the reversal by the Supreme Court of the Virginia Court of Appeals' latest Fairfax decision was to provoke the first of a series of large-scale assaults on the exercise of final determinative authority under Section 25 of the Judiciary Act of 1789.[52]

The federal Constitution provided for a division of governmental powers between the national and state governments. Article VI indicated that the national Constitution, laws, and treaties were to be supreme. The constitutional framers wished not only to maintain the supremacy of the national government, however, but also to preserve to the states their proper autonomy and independence of action. That conflicts would arise concerning the dividing line between national and states' rights and powers was recognized and provided for. The constitutional framers decided that the Supreme Court, a branch of the national government, should arbitrate any such conflicts that were justiciable. The choice of a branch of the national government followed from the nature of the Constitution itself, for if the states, who had been impliedly designated inferior political bodies by Article VI, were granted the power to determine the limits of national authority, the national government would have ceased to be the repository of supreme political authority (within the limits set by the Constitution) in the federal system. As Madison pointed out, the first Congress' granting to the Supreme Court of final appellate jurisdiction in cases involving federal rights was simply the final implementation of the desires of the constitutional framers.

The 25th section of the Judiciary Act of 1789 provided that final judgment in any suit in the highest court of law or equity of a state,

> . . . where is drawn in question the validity of a treaty or statute of, or an authority exercised under the United States, and the decision is against their validity, or where is drawn in question the validity of a statute of, or an authority exercised under any state, on the ground of their being repugnant to the Constitution, treaties or laws of the United States, and decision is in favor of their validity, or where is drawn in question the construction of any clause of the Constitution, or of a treaty, or statute of, or commission held under the United States, and the decision is against the title, right, privilege or exemption specially set up or claimed by either party, under such clause of the said Constitution, treaty, statute or commission may be re-examined and reversed or affirmed in the Supreme Court of the United States upon writ of error.

In 1789 both the nationalists and the anti-Federalists had approved the granting of such jurisdiction to the Supreme Court. The first major challenge to the exercise of final determinative authority by the Court had come in the form of the statement of the doctrine of state interposition in the Virginia and Kentucky Resolutions of 1798–1799 authored by Madison and Jefferson. These resolutions, however, had been drawn up to protest the failure of the Supreme Court to declare unconstitutional the Alien and Sedition Acts. Thus, this early challenge to the Court's power to arbitrate finally in conflicts involving federal-state relations was not aimed specifically at the Court's exercise of power under the 25th section of the Judiciary Act. Moreover, it appears that with the exception of the attacks of Pennsylvania, the Supreme Court was not seriously challenged in the exercise of such power for 26 years. By 1815, the Supreme Court had taken jurisdiction, without arousing serious opposition, of writs of error to state courts in 16 cases. In that year, however, the Court of Appeals of Virginia challenged for the first time the right of the Supreme Court to exercise that power. Virginia's attack marked the beginning of a new period in the Supreme Court's history—the advent of bitter attacks by a number of states upon the Court and the advent of a decade in which that tribunal was destined to make its greatest contributions toward the establishment of the supremacy of the national government.

When Justice Story reversed the judgment of the Virginia Court of Appeals in *Fairfax's Devisee* v. *Hunter's Lessee* in 1813, a mandate was sent to the Virginia court ordering it to execute the Supreme Court reversal decision. In 1814 the state court considered this mandate from the highest national tribunal. The Virginia Court of Appeals was not simply the highest judicial body in the state, but was "the controlling center of a dominant and self-perpetuating political party."[53] And in this period the chief justice of that state court was the most powerful politician in Virginia, Spencer Roane. Roane dominated the Virginia legislature, founded the *Richmond Enquirer*, and inherited the Virginia Republican party machine created by Jefferson and Madison, which he managed along with *Richmond Enquirer* editor

Thomas Ritchie and John Taylor of Caroline. It was reported in 1800 that Spencer Roane had been "slated" for the appointment as chief justice of the United States, but Ellsworth's timely resignation enabled John Adams to appoint John Marshall.[54] Whether because of personal animosity or constitutional scruples (or both), the members of the Virginia Court of Appeals refused to obey the Supreme Court's mandate.

Before rendering a decision, the Virginia tribunal consulted Jefferson, Monroe, and the leading members of the Virginia bar.[55] The crucial question for the state court was stated by Judge Cabell: Can Congress "confer on the Supreme Court of the United States, a power to re-examine, by way of appeal or writ of error, the decision of the state court" (when that decision involves the construction of a treaty), and affirm or reverse that decision, and "command the state court to enter and execute a judgment different from that which it had previously rendered?"[56]

The Virginia judges delivered *seriatim* opinions. Every judge denied that Congress had been empowered to grant the Supreme Court such jurisdiction. The opinions of Judges Cabell and Roane contained the best statements of the states' rights view. Judge Cabell held that

> . . . neither (Federal or state) government . . . can act *compulsively*, on the other or on any of its organs in their political or official capacities. . . . The Constitution of the United States contemplates the independence of both governments, and regards the *residuary* sovereignty of the states, as not less inviolable, than the delegated sovereignty of the United States. It must have been foreseen that controversies would sometimes arise as to the boundaries of the two jurisdictions. *Yet the Constitution has provided no umpire* . . . to give the general government or any of its departments a direct and controlling operation upon the state departments, as such, would be to change at once the whole character of our system.[57]

Similarly, Judge Roane denied that the Supreme Court had the authority to review and reverse the decision of the highest Virginia court. After an opinion that was perhaps more political than judicial, Roane concluded with the warning that "no calamity would be more to be deplored by the American people, than a vortex in the General Government, which should ingulph and sweep away every vestige in the State Constitutions."[58]

The Virginia judges then joined, in a unanimous opinion, in declaring that

> . . . the appellate power of the Supreme Court of the United States does not extend to this court, under a sound construction of the Constitution of the United States;— that so much of the 25th section of the act of Congress to establish the judicial courts of the United States, as extends the appellate jurisdiction of the Supreme Court to this Court, is not in pursuance of the Constitution of the United States; that the writ of error in this case was improvidently allowed under the authority of that act; that the proceedings thereon in the Supreme Court were *coram non judice* in relation to this court; and that obedience to its mandate be declined by this court.[59]

In *Martin* v. *Hunter's Lessee*, the Supreme Court, in an opinion by Justice Story, met this challenge to federal judicial power.

MARTIN v. HUNTER'S LESSEE
1 Wheaton 304 (1816)

The questions involved in this judgment are of great importance and delicacy . . .

The constitution, unavoidably, deals in general language. It did not suit the purposes of the people, in granting this great charter of our liberties, to provide for minute specifications of its powers, or to declare the means by which those powers should be carried into execution. It was foreseen that this would be a perilous and difficult, if not an impracticable, task. The instrument was not intended to provide merely for the exigencies of a few years, but was to endure through a long lapse of ages. . . .

The third article of the constitution is that which must principally attract our attention. . . .

Let this article be carefully weighed and considered. The language of the article throughout is manifestly designed to be mandatory upon the legislature. . . . The object of the constitution was to establish three great departments of government; the legislative, the executive, and the judicial departments. The first was to pass laws, the second to approve and execute them, and the third to expound and enforce them. Without the latter, it would be impossible to carry into effect some of the express provisions of the constitution. How, otherwise, could crimes against the United States be tried and punished? How could causes between two States be heard and determined? The judicial power must, therefore, be vested in some court, by congress; and to suppose that it was not an obligation binding on them, but might, at their pleasure, be omitted or declined, is to suppose that, under the sanction of the constitution, they might defeat the constitution itself. A construction which would lead to such a result cannot be sound. . . .

If, then, it is a duty of congress to vest the judicial power of the United States, it is a duty to vest the whole judicial power. The language, if imperative as to one part, is imperative as to all. If it were otherwise, this anomaly would exist, that congress might successively refuse to vest the jurisdiction in any one class of cases enumerated in the constitution, and thereby defeat the jurisdiction as to all; for the constitution has not singled out any class on which congress are bound to act in preference to others.

The next consideration is as to the courts in which the judicial power shall be vested. It is manifest that a supreme court must be established; but whether it be equally obligatory to establish inferior courts, is a question of some difficulty. If congress may lawfully omit to establish inferior courts, it might follow, that in some of the enumerated cases the judicial power could nowhere exist. . . .

But even admitting that the language of the constitution is not mandatory, and that congress may constitutionally omit to vest the judicial power in courts of the United States, it cannot be denied that when it is vested, it may be exercised to the utmost constitutional extent.

This leads us to the consideration of the great question as to the nature and extent of the appellate jurisdiction of the United States. . . .

As, then, by the terms of the constitution, the appellate jurisdiction is not limited as to the supreme court, and as to this court it may be exercised in all other cases than those of which it has original cognizance, what is there to restrain its exercise over state tribunals in the enumerated cases? The appellate power is not limited by the terms of the third article to any particular courts. The words are, "the judicial power (which includes appellate power) shall extend to all cases," &c., and "in all other cases before mentioned the supreme court shall have appellate jurisdiction." It is the case, then, and not the court, that gives the jurisdiction. . . .

But it is plain that the framers of the constitution did contemplate that cases within the judicial cognizance of the United States not only might but would arise in the state courts, in the exercise of their ordinary jurisdiction. With this view the sixth article declares, that "this constitution, and the laws of the United States which shall be made in pursuance thereof, and all treaties made, or which shall be made, under the authority of the United States, shall be the supreme law of the land, and the judges in every State shall be bound thereby, any thing in the constitution, or laws of any State to the contrary notwithstanding." It is obvious that this obligation is imperative upon the state judges in their official, and not merely in their private, capacities. From the very nature of their judicial duties they would be called upon to pronounce the law applicable to the case in judgment. . . .

A moment's consideration will show us the necessity and propriety, of this provision in cases where the jurisdiction of the state courts is unquestionable. . . . Suppose an indictment for a crime in a state court, and the defendant should allege in his defence that the crime was created by an ex post facto act of the State, must not the state court, in the exercise of a jurisdiction which has already rightfully attached, have a right to pronounce on the validity and sufficiency of the defence?

It must, therefore, be conceded that the constitution not only contemplated, but meant to provide for cases within the scope of the judicial power of the United States, which might yet depend before state tribunals. It was foreseen that in the exercise of their ordinary jurisdiction state courts would incidentally take cognizance of cases arising under the constitution, the laws, and treaties of the United States. Yet to all these cases the judicial power, by the very terms of the constitution, is to extend. It cannot extend by original jurisdiction if that was already rightfully and exclusively attached in the state courts, which (as has been already shown) may occur; it must therefore extend by appellate jurisdiction, or not at all. It would seem to follow that the appellate power of the United States must, in such cases, extend to state tribunals; and if in such cases, there is not reason why it should not equally attach upon all others within the purview of the constitution. . . .

Nor can such a right be deemed to impair the independence of state judges. It is assuming the very ground in controversy to assert that they possess an absolute independence of the United States. In respect to the powers granted to the United States, they are not independent; they are expressly bound to obedience by the letter of the constitution; and if they should unintentionally transcend their authority, or misconstrue the constitution, there is no more reason for giving their judgments an absolute and irresistible force, than for giving it to the acts of the other coordinate departments of state sovereignty.

The argument urged from the possibility of the abuse of the revising power, is equally unsatisfactory. It is always a doubtful course, to argue against the use or existence of a power, from the possibility of its abuse. . . . From the very nature of things, the absolute right of decision, in the last resort, must rest somewhere—wherever it may be vested it is susceptible of abuse. In all questions of jurisdiction the inferior, or appellate court must pronounce the final judgment; and common sense, as well as legal reasoning, has conferred it upon the latter. . . .

This is not all. A motive of another kind, perfectly compatible with the most sincere respect for state tribunals, might induce the grant of appellate power over their decisions. That motive is the importance, and even necessity of uniformity of decisions throughout the whole United States, upon all subjects within the purview of the constitution. Judges of equal learning and integrity, in different States, might differently interpret a statute, or a treaty of the United States, or even the constitution itself. If there were no revising authority to control these jarring and discordant judgments, and harmonize them into uniformity, the laws, the treaties, and the constitution of the United States would be different in different States, and might, perhaps, never have precisely the same construction, obligation, or efficacy, in any two States. . . .

There is an additional consideration, which is entitled to great weight. The constitution of the United States was designed for the common and equal benefit of all the people of the United States. The judicial power was granted for the same benign and salutary purposes. It was not to be exercised exclusively for the benefit of parties who might be plaintiffs, and would elect the national forum, but also for the protection of defendants who might be entitled to try their rights, or assert their privileges, before the same forum. Yet, if the construction contended for be correct, it will follow, that as the plaintiff may always elect the state court, the defendant may be deprived of all the security which the constitution intended in aid of his rights. Such a state of things can, in no respect, be considered as giving equal rights. To obviate this difficulty, we are referred to the power which it is admitted congress possess to remove suits from state courts to the national courts; and this forms the second ground upon which the argument we are considering has been attempted to be sustained.

This power of removal is not to be found in express terms in any part of the constitution; if it be given, it is only given by implication, as a power necessary and proper to carry into effect some express power. The power of removal is certainly not, in strictness of language; it presupposes an exercise of original jurisdiction to have attached elsewhere. . . . If, then, the right of removal be included in the appellate jurisdiction, it is only because it is one mode of exercising that power, and as congress is not limited by the constitution to any particular mode, or time of exercising it, it may authorize a removal either before or after judgment. The time, the process, and the manner, must be subject to its absolute legislative control. . . .

The remedy, too, of removal of suits would be utterly inadequate to the purposes of the constitution, if it could act only on the parties and not upon the state courts. . . .

On the whole, the court are of opinion, that the appellate power of the United States does extend to cases pending in the state courts; and that the 25th section of the Judiciary act, which authorizes the exercise of this jurisdiction in the specified cases, by a writ of error, is supported by the letter and spirit of the constitution. We find no clause in that instrument which limits this power; and we dare not interpose a limitation where the people have not been disposed to create one. . . .

John Marshall and the Supreme Court were subjected to increasingly intense attacks from Virginia states' rights leaders of whom Spencer Roane was the most persistent. In 1821 a case originating in a Norfolk, Virginia, hustings court provided Marshall an opportunity to reply. The case arose out of this situation: When the city of Washington, D.C., was incorporated by Congress in 1802, it was empowered to hold lotteries to raise money for civic improvements. In 1820 the Virginia legislature enacted a law forbidding, under penalty of fine, the drawing in the state of any lotteries other than those authorized by Virginia law. A few months after the passage of this state law, P. J. and M. J. Cohen violated this statute by selling national (Washington) lottery tickets in Norfolk. They were convicted and fined in the Norfolk Court of Hustings. The Cohens claimed that under the act of Congress they could sell lottery tickets anywhere in the United States. The Virginia Court of Appeals once more asserted that the state courts had possessed final authority to settle the issue. This claim was supported by a committee of House of Delegates, which drew up resolutions stating that

> . . . the Supreme Court of the United States have no rightful authority under the Constitution to examine and correct the judgment for which the commonwealth of Virginia has been "cited and admonished to be and appear at the Supreme Court of the United States."[60]

On February 9, 1821, the Virginia Senate passed a resolution instructing counsel engaged by the governor for the Cohens case to confine their arguments to the question of jurisdiction.[61] The Supreme Court took the case on writ of error.

In terms of its legal aspects, *Cohens* v. *Virginia* is identical in many respects with *Martin* v. *Hunter's Lessee*. Marshall not only reaffirmed that earlier decision of Justice Story, however, but also handed down an important interpretation of the scope of the Eleventh Amendment.

The fundamental questions to be answered in this decision were clearly stated by Chief Justice Marshall in his introductory paragraphs:

COHENS v. VIRGINIA
6 Wheaton 624 (1821)

The first question to be considered is, whether the jurisdiction of this court is excluded by the character of the parties, one of them being a State, and the other a citizen of that State?

The 2d section of the third article of the constitution defines the extent of the judicial power of the United States. Jurisdiction is given to the courts of the Union in two classes of cases. In the first, their jurisdiction depends on the character of the cause, whoever may be the parties. This class comprehends "all cases in law and equity arising under this constitution, the laws of the United States, and treaties made, or which shall be made, under their authority." This clause extends the jurisdiction of the court to all the cases described,

without making in its terms any exception whatever, and without any regard to the condition of the party. If there be any exception, it is to be implied against the express words of the article.

In the second class, the jurisdiction depends entirely on the character of the parties. In this are comprehended "controversies between two or more States, between a State and citizens of another State," "and between a State and foreign states, citizens, or subjects." If these be the parties, it is entirely unimportant what may be the subject of controversy. Be it what it may, these parties have a constitutional right to come into the courts of the Union. . . .

The jurisdiction of the court, then, being extended by the letter of the constitution to all cases arising under it, or under the laws of the United States, it follows that those who would withdraw any case of this description from that jurisdiction, must sustain the exemption they claim on the spirit and true meaning of the constitution, which spirit and true meaning must be so apparent as to overrule the words which its framers have employed.

The counsel for the defendant in error have undertaken to do this; and have laid down the general proposition, that a sovereign independent State is not suable, except by its own consent.

This general proposition will not be controverted. But its consent is not requisite in each particular case. It may be given in a general law. And if a State has surrendered any portion of its sovereignty, the question whether a liability to suit be a part of this portion, depends on the instrument by which the surrender is made. If upon a just construction of that instrument, it shall appear that the State has submitted to be sued, then it has parted with this sovereign right of judging in every case on the justice of its own pretensions, and has intrusted that power to a tribunal in whose impartiality it confides.

The American States, as well as the American people, have believed a close and firm Union to be essential to their liberty and to their happiness. They have been taught by experience, that this Union cannot exist without a government for the whole; and they have been taught by the same experience that this government would be a mere shadow, that must disappoint all their hopes, unless invested with large portions of that sovereignty which belongs to independent States. Under the influence of this opinion, and thus instructed by experience, the American people, in the conventions of their respective States, adopted the present constitution.

If it could be doubted whether, from its nature, it were not supreme in all cases where it is empowered to act, that doubt would be removed by the declaration that "this constitution, and the laws of the United States which shall be made in pursuance thereof, and all treaties made, or which shall be made, under the authority of the United States, shall be the supreme law of the land; and the judges in every State shall be bound thereby, any thing in the constitution or laws of any State to the contrary notwithstanding."

This is the authoritative language of the American people; and, if gentlemen please, of the American States. It marks with lines too strong to be mistaken, the characteristic distinction between the government of the Union and those of the States. The general government, though limited as to its objects, is supreme with respect to those objects. This principle is a part of the constitution; and if there be any who deny its necessity, none can deny its authority. . . .

With the ample powers confided to this supreme government, for these interesting purposes, are connected many express and important limitations on the sovereignty of the States, which are made for the same purposes. The powers of the Union, on the great subjects of war, peace, and commerce, and on many other, are in themselves limitations of the sovereignty of the States; but in addition to these, the sovereignty of the States is surrendered in many instances where the surrender can only operate to the benefit of the people, and where, perhaps, no other power is conferred on congress than a conservative power to maintain the principles established in the constitution. The maintenance of these principles in their purity, is certainly among the great duties of the government. One of the instruments by which this duty may be peaceably performed, is the judicial department. It is authorized to decide all cases, of every description, arising under the constitution or laws of the United States. From this general grant of jurisdiction, no exception is made of those cases in which a State may be a party. When we consider the situation of the government of the Union and of a State, in relation to each other; the nature of our constitution, the subordination of the state governments to that constitution; the great purpose for which jurisdiction over all cases arising under the constitution and laws of the United States, is confided to the judicial department, are we at liberty to insert in this general grant, an exception of those cases in which a State may be a party? Will the spirit of the constitution justify this attempt to control its words? We think a case arising under the constitution or laws of the United States, is cognizable in the courts of the Union, whoever may be the parties to that case. . . .

One of the express objects, then, for which the judicial department was established, is the decision of controversies between States, and between a State and individuals. The mere circumstance that a State is a party, gives jurisdiction to the court. How, then, can it be contended, that the very same instrument, in the very same section, should be so construed, as that this same circumstance should withdraw a case from the jurisdiction of the court, where the constitution or laws of the United States are supposed to have been violated? The constitution gave to every person having a claim upon a State, a right to submit his case to the court of the nation. However unimportant his claim might be, however little the community might be interested in its decision, the framers of our constitution thought it necessary for the purposes of justice, to provide a tribunal as superior to influence as possible, in which that claim might be decided. Can it be imagined, that the same persons considered a case involving the constitution of our country and the majesty of the laws, questions in which every American citizen must be deeply interested, as withdrawn from this tribunal, because a State is a party? . . .

The mischievous consequences of the construction contended for on the part of Virginia, are also entitled to great consideration. It would prostrate, it has been said, the government and its laws at the feet of every State in the Union. And would not this be its effect? What power of the government could be executed by its own means, in any State disposed to resist its execution by a course of legislation? The laws must be executed by individuals acting within the several States. If these individuals may be exposed to penalties, and if the courts of the Union cannot correct the judgments by which these penalties may be enforced, the course of the government may be, at any time, arrested by the will of one of its members. Each member will possess a veto on the will of the whole. . . .

These collisions may take place in times of no extraordinary commotion. But a constitution is framed for ages to come, and is designed to approach immortality as nearly as human institutions can approach it. Its course cannot always be tranquil. It is exposed to storms and tempests, and its framers must be unwise statesmen, indeed, if they have not provided it, as far as its nature will permit, with the means of self-preservation from the perils it may be destined to encounter. No government ought to be so defective in its organization, as not to contain within itself the means of securing the execution of its own laws against other dangers than those which occur every day. Courts of justice are the means most usually employed; and it is reasonable to expect that a government should repose on its own courts, rather than on others. There is certainly nothing in the circumstances under which our constitution was formed; nothing in the history of the times, which would justify the opinion that the confidence reposed in the States was so implicit as to leave in them and their tribunals the power of resisting or defeating, in the form of law, the legitimate measures of the Union. The requisitions of congress, under the confederation, were as constitutionally obligatory as the laws enacted by the present congress. That they were habitually disregarded, is a fact of universal notoriety. With the knowledge of this fact, and under its full pressure, a convention was assembled to change the system. Is it so improbable that they should confer on the judicial department the power of construing the constitution and laws of the Union in every case, in the last resort, and of preserv-

ing them from all violation from every quarter, so far as judicial decisions can preserve them, that this improbability should essentially affect the construction of the new system? We are told, and we are truly told, that the great change which is to give efficacy to the present system, is its ability to act on individuals directly, instead of acting through the instrumentality of state governments. But, ought not this ability, in reason and sound policy, to be applied directly to the protection of individuals employed in the execution of the laws, as well as to their coercion? Your laws reach the individual without the aid of any other power; why may they not protect him from punishment for performing his duty in executing them? . . .

It is very true that, whenever hostility to the existing system shall become universal, it will be also irresistible. The people made the constitution, and the people can unmake it. It is the creature of their will, and lives only by their will. But this supreme and irresistible power to make or to unmake resides only in the whole body of the people; not in any subdivision of them. The attempt of any of the parts to exercise it is usurpation, and ought to be repelled by those to whom the people have delegated their power of repelling it.

The acknowledged inability of the government, then, to sustain itself against the public will, and, by force or otherwise, to control the whole nation, is no sound argument in support of its constitutional inability to preserve itself against a section of the nation acting in opposition to the general will. . . .

It is true, that if all the States, or a majority of them, refuse to elect senators, the legislative powers of the Union will be suspended. But if any one State shall refuse to elect them, the senate will not, on that account, be the less capable of performing all its functions. The argument founded on this fact would seem rather to prove the subordination of the parts to the whole, than the complete independence of any one of them. The framers of the constitution were, indeed, unable to make any provisions which should protect that instrument against a general combination of the States, or of the people, for its destruction; and, conscious of this inability, they have not made the attempt. But they were able to provide against the operation of measures adopted in any one State, whose tendency might be to arrest the execution of the laws; and this it was the part of true wisdom to attempt. We think they have attempted it.

It has been also urged, as an additional objection to the jurisdiction of the court, that cases between a State and one of its own citizens, do not come within the general scope of the constitution; and were obviously never intended to be made cognizable in the federal courts. The state tribunals might be suspected of partiality in cases between itself or its citizens and aliens, or the citizens of another State, but not in proceedings by a state against its own citizens. That jealousy which might exist in the first case, could not exist in the last, and therefore the judicial power is not extended to the last. This is very true, so far as jurisdiction depends on the character of the parties; and the argument would have great force if urged to prove that this court could not establish the demand of a citizen upon his State, but is not entitled to the same force when urged to prove that this court cannot inquire whether the constitution or laws of the United States protect a citizen from a prosecution instituted against him by a State. If jurisdiction depended entirely on the character of the parties, and was not given where the parties have not an original right to come into court, that part of the 2d section of the third article, which extends the judicial power to all cases arising under the constitution and laws of the United States, would be mere surplusage. It is to give jurisdiction where the character of the parties would not give it, that this very important part of the clause was inserted. It may be true, that the partiality of the state tribunals, in ordinary controversies between a State and its citizens, was not apprehended, and therefore the judicial power of the Union was not extended to such cases; but this was not the sole nor the greatest object for which this department was created. A more important, a much more interesting object, was the preservation of the constitution and laws of the United States, so far as they can be preserved by judicial authority; and therefore the jurisdiction of the courts of the Union was expressly extended to all cases arising under that constitution and those laws. If the constitution or laws may be violated by proceedings instituted by a State against its own citizens, and if that violation may be such as essentially to affect the constitution and the laws, such as to arrest the progress of government in its constitutional course, why should these cases be excepted from that provision which expressly extends the judicial power of the Union to all cases arising under the constitution and laws? . . .

When, then, the constitution declares the jurisdiction, in cases where a State shall be a party, to be original, and in all cases arising under the constitution or a law, to be appellate—the conclusion seems irresistible, that its framers designed to include in the first class those cases in which jurisdiction is given, because

a State is a party; and to include in the second, those in which jurisdiction is given, because the case arises under the constitution or a law.

This reasonable construction is rendered necessary by other considerations.

That the constitution or a law of the United States is involved in a case, and makes a part of it, may appear in the progress of a cause, in which the courts of the Union, but for that circumstance, would have no jurisdiction, and which of consequence could not originate in the supreme court. In such a case the jurisdiction can be exercised only in its appellate form. To deny its exercise in this form, is to deny its existence, and would be to construe a clause dividing the power of the supreme court, in such manner as in a considerable degree to defeat the power itself. All must perceive that this construction can be justified only where it is absolutely necessary. We do not think the article under consideration presents that necessity. . . .

The constitution declares that in cases where a State is a party, the supreme court shall have original jurisdiction; but does not say that its appellate jurisdiction shall not be exercised in cases where, from their nature, appellate jurisdiction is given, whether a State be or be not a party. It may be conceded, that where the case is of such a nature as to admit of its originating in the supreme court, it ought to originate there; but where, from its nature, it cannot originate in that court, these words ought not to be so construed as to require it. There are many cases in which it would be found extremely difficult, and subversive of the spirit of the constitution, to maintain the construction that appellate jurisdiction cannot be exercised where one of the parties might sue or be sued in this court. . . .

It is most true that this court will not take jurisdiction if it should not; but it is equally true, that it must take jurisdiction if it should. The judiciary cannot, as the legislature may, avoid a measure because it approaches the confines of the constitution. We cannot pass it by because it is doubtful. With whatever doubts, with whatever difficulties, a case may be attended, we must decide it, if it be brought before us. We have no more right to decline the exercise of jurisdiction which is given, than to usurp that which is not given. The one or the other would be treason to the constitution. Questions may occur which we would gladly avoid; but we cannot avoid them. All we can do is, to exercise our best judgment, and conscientiously to perform our duty. In doing this on the present occasion, we find this tribunal invested with appellate jurisdiction in all cases arising under the constitution and laws of the

United States. We find no exception to this grant, and we cannot insert one. . . .

It is, then, the opinion of the court, that the defendant who removes a judgment rendered against him by a state court into this court, for the purpose of reëxamining the question whether that judgment be in violation of the constitution or laws of the United States, does not commence or prosecute a suit against the State, whatever may be its opinion where the effect of the writ may be to restore the party to the possession of a thing which he demands. . . .

The second objection to the jurisdiction of the court is, that its appellate power cannot be exercised, in any case, over the judgment of a state court.

This objection is sustained chiefly by arguments drawn from the supposed total separation of the judiciary of a State from that of the Union, and their entire independence of each other. The argument considers the federal judiciary as completely foreign to that of a State; and as being no more connected with it, in any respect whatever, than the court of a foreign state. If this hypothesis be just, the argument founded on it is equally so; but if the hypothesis be not supported by the constitution, the argument fails with it. . . .

That the United States form, for many, and for most important purposes, a single nation, has not yet been denied. In war, we are one people. In making peace, we are one people. In all commercial regulations, we are one and the same people. In many other respects, the American people are one; and the government which is alone capable of controlling and managing their interests, in all these respects, is the government of the Union. It is their government, and in that character they have no other. America has chosen to be, in many respects, and to many purposes, a nation; and for all these purposes her government is complete; to all these objects, it is competent. The people have declared, that in the exercise of all powers given for these objects, it is supreme. It can, then, in effecting these objects, legitimately control all individuals or governments within the American territory. The constitution and laws of a State, so far as they are repugnant to the constitution and laws of the United States, are absolutely void. These States are constituent parts of the United States. They are members of one great empire—for some purposes sovereign, for some purposes subordinate.

In a government so constituted, is it unreasonable that the judicial power should be competent to give efficacy to the constitutional laws of the legislature? That department can decide on the validity of the constitution or law of a State, if it be repugnant to the constitution or to a law of the United States. Is it unreasonable that it should also be empowered to decide on the judgment of a state tribunal enforcing such unconstitutional law? Is it so very unreasonable as to furnish a justification for controlling the words of the constitution?

We think it is not. We think that in a government acknowledgedly supreme, with respect to objects of vital interest to the nation, there is nothing inconsistent with sound reason, nothing incompatible with the nature of government, in making all its departments supreme, so far as respects those objects, and so far as is necessary to their attainment. The exercise of the appellate power over those judgments of the state tribunals which may contravene the constitution or laws of the United States, is, we believe, essential to the attainment of those objects.

The propriety of intrusting the construction of the constitution, and laws made in pursuance thereof, to the judiciary of the Union, has not, we believe, as yet, been drawn into question. It seems to be a corollary from this political axiom, that the federal courts should either possess exclusive jurisdiction in such cases, or a power to revise the judgment rendered in them by the state tribunals. If the federal and state courts have concurrent jurisdiction in all cases arising under the constitution, laws, and treaties of the United States; and if a case of this description brought in a state court cannot be removed before judgment, nor revised after judgment, then the construction of the constitution, laws, and treaties of the United States is not confided particularly to their judicial department, but is confided equally to that department and to the state courts, however they may be constituted. "Thirteen independent courts," says a very celebrated statesman, (and we have now more than twenty such courts,) "of final jurisdiction over the same causes, arising upon the same laws, is a hydra in government, from which nothing but contradiction and confusion can proceed."

Dismissing the unpleasant suggestion, that any motives which may not be fairly avowed, or which ought not to exist, can ever influence a State or its courts, the necessity of uniformity, as well as correctness in expounding the constitution and laws of the United States, would itself suggest the propriety of vesting in some single tribunal the power of deciding, in the last resort, all cases in which they are involved.

We are not restrained, then, by the political relations between the general and state governments, from construing the words of the constitution, defining the judicial power, in their true sense.

Banks, bankruptcy, and economic power

Although Chief Justice Spencer Roane of the Virginia Court of Appeals is correctly identified as a major intellectual contributor to states' rights doctrine, it would be a mistake to assume that his position on limiting federal judicial authority represented a consistent Jeffersonian Republican position by the late 1810s. The positions of some Republican leaders (such as Madison's) had changed or become more nationalistic over time. In fact, on some federal-state issues, the relative positions of the Republicans and the Federalists had shifted rather dramatically. During the war of 1812, for example, the Republicans, who were strongly anti–British, had become quite nationalistic, while the New England Federalists favored the interests of their section over those of the nation. Some of these Federalists had moved toward separatism. On the eve of the war, the Republican Congress had refused to recharter the first Bank of the United States, but the heavy financial demands of the war practically forced the Madison administration to request the re-establishment of a national bank "that the benefits of a uniform national currency should be restored."[62] In April 1816, Congress established the Second Bank of the United States.

The chartering of a national bank in 1816 came too late to put the nation's financial house in order, however. By 1819, the United States was in the throes of its first catastrophic financial depression. United States markets had been flooded with English manufactures after the war; overbuying had drained off American specie to English coffers. In the interim period before the chartering of the second United States bank, numerous state banks sprang up. By 1819, they were issuing paper money with reckless abandon. Land speculation in the South and West added to the economic turmoil. And to make matters worse, some of the transactions of the second national bank were fraudulent.[63]

During this period of economic chaos, Congress had failed to pass a national bankruptcy act, and the states had acted separately to relieve debtors. In 1819 a case involving a New York bankruptcy law came before the Supreme Court. *Sturgis v. Crowinshild*[64] was one of a trio of cases destined to make the 1819 term, in the estimation of Edward S. Corwin, "the greatest six weeks in the history of the Court."[65]

The New York bankruptcy law was challenged by Sturgis' counsel on two grounds: First, it was contended that since Article I, section 8, provides that "the congress shall have power . . . to establish a uniform rule of naturalization, and uniform laws on the subject of bankruptcies, throughout the United States," the states were prohibited from passing bankruptcy laws. Second, the New York statute was held to be an impairment of an obligation of contract.

In discussing the first contention, Chief Justice Marshall established the standard distinguishing the exclusive and concurrent powers of Congress:

When the American people created a national legislature, with certain enumerated powers, it was neither necessary nor proper to define the powers retained by the states. These powers proceed, not from the people of the United States, but from the people of the several states; and remain, after the adoption of the Constitution, what they were before, except so far as they may be abridged by that instrument. In some instances, as in making treaties, we find an express prohibition; and this shows the sense of the convention to have been that the mere grant of a power to Congress did not imply a prohibition on the states to exercise the same power. But it has never been supposed that this concurrent power of legislation extended to every possible case in which its exercise by the state has not been expressly prohibited. The confusion resulting from such a practice would be endless. The principle laid down by the counsel for the plaintiff, in this respect, is undoubtedly correct. Whenever, the terms in which a power is granted by Congress, or the nature of the power requires that it should be exercised exclusively by Congress, the subject is as completely taken from the state legislatures as if they had been expressly forbidden to act on it.

After stating that constitutional doctrine, Marshall declared that "until the power . . . be exercised by Congress, the states are not forbidden to pass a bankrupt law." He then held that

> The constitution does not grant to the states the power of passing bankrupt laws, or any other power; but finds them in possession of it, and may either prohibit its future exercise entirely, or restrain it so far as national policy may require. It has so far restrained it, as to prohibit the passage of any law impairing the obligation of contracts.[66]

On the day after the Sturgis decision, Chief Justice Marshall, in *McMillan* v. *McNeil*,[67] held a Louisiana bankruptcy law repugnant to the Constitution on the same ground as the New York statute that was considered in the Sturgis case.

The financial depression of 1819–1822, like subsequent cyclical crises, brought with it not only a general and drastic decline in property values but, as financial losses became heavier, an all-pervading pessimism. As in every situation characterized by great social and economic discontent, public opinion sought for the ultimate cause of public discomfort. With partial justification, many people blamed the Second Bank of the United States.

Although that bank had been established in 1816 to check inflation, by becoming the center of a large and spectacular speculation in its own stock, it had added to the inflationary tendencies. When, in 1818, the bank reversed its policies and contracted credit, it helped appreciably to precipitate the collapse of the unstable state banks and, ultimately, the whole financial structure. In addition, a Congressional investigating committee discovered evidence of mismanagement and dishonesty in some of the branch banks of the federal corporation. These disclosures and the hardships caused by foreclosures of property by the United States bank focused public attention and indignation upon this national institution.[68]

State legislators reflected the sentiments of their constituents, and many states attempted, by state constitutional provision or heavy taxation, to keep out the United States bank. Thus, the constitutions of Indiana and Illinois forbade a bank not chartered by the state legislature to do business in the state. And Maryland, Georgia, Tennessee, North Carolina, Kentucky and Ohio levied high taxes on the branches of the national bank.[69] Public temper was thoroughly aroused against the United States bank. The following statement of Senator Benton accurately reproduced the views of debtors and the financially embarrassed citizens throughout the nation:

I know towns, yea, cities . . . where this bank already appears as an engrossing proprietor. All the flourishing cities of the West are mortgaged to this money power . . . . They are in the jaws of the monster! A lump of butter in the mouth of a dog! One gulp, one swallow, and all is gone![70]

The intense dislike for the Second Bank of the United States had come largely as a result of the severe economic hardships suffered during the depression. The chief opponents of the bank however, generally chose to attack it on the ground that it was an unconstitutional usurpation of power rather than on grounds of economic or social policy. In 1814 President Madison had indicated that he considered the constitutional issue closed. The constitutional validity of a national bank had been established "by repeated recognitions . . . in acts of the legislative, executive, and judicial branches of the government, accompanied by indications in different modes, of a recurrence of the general will of the nation."[71] Despite Madison's stand on the subject, strict constructionists contended that the incorporation of the second bank, like that of its predecessor, was based on Hamilton's "unconstitutional" doctrine of implied powers. Senator Porter's admonition was a typical strict constructionist slogan: "Let the principle of constructive or implied powers once be established, and you will have planted in the bosom of the Constitution a viper, which, one day or another, will sting the liberties of this country to the heart."[72]

In *United States* v. *Fisher* in 1804, Chief Justice Marshall had announced and applied the broad constructionist doctrine of implied power without arousing widespread opposition. Now, in 1819, the situation had changed. Because of economic hardships, majority opinion opposed this doctrine, at least insofar as it applied to the second United States bank. The issue of broad versus strict construction was brought before the Supreme Court in a case involving a heavy tax by the state of Maryland upon a branch of the national bank.

The case was argued by six of the greatest lawyers of the era. Luther Martin, Joseph Hopkinson, and Walter Jones represented the state of Maryland, while William Pinkney, Daniel Webster, and William Wirt argued in behalf of the bank. Of the six, Pinkney gave an analysis of the constitutional status of nation and the states that is second only to the Court's opinion written by Chief Justice Marshall. Marshall's analysis follows:

McCULLOCH v. MARYLAND
4 Wheaton 316 (1819)

The first question made in the cause is—has congress power to incorporate a bank? It has been truly said, that this can scarcely be considered as an open question, entirely unprejudiced by the former proceedings of the nation respecting it. The principle now contested was introduced at a very early period of our history, has been recognised by many successive legislatures, and has been acted upon by the judicial department, in cases of particular delicacy, as a law of undoubted obligation. . . .

In discussing this question, the counsel for the state of Maryland have deemed it of some importance, in the construction of the constitution, to consider that instrument, not as emanating from the people, but as the act of sovereign and independent states. The powers of the general government, it has been said, are delegated by the states, who alone are truly sovereign; and must be exercised in subordination to the states, who alone possess supreme dominion. It would be difficult to sustain this proposition. The convention which framed the constitution was indeed elected by the state legislatures. But the instrument, when it came from their hands, was a mere proposal, without obligation,

or pretentions to it. It was reported to the then existing congress of the United States, with a request that
it might "be submitted to a convention of delegates,
chosen in each state by the people thereof, under the
recommendation of its legislature, for their assent and
ratification." This mode of proceeding was adopted:
and by the convention, by congress, and by the state
legislatures, the instrument was submitted to the *people*.
They acted upon it in the only manner in which they
can act safely, effectively and wisely, on such a subject,
by assembling in convention. It is true, they assembled
in their several states—and where else should they
have assembled? No political dreamer was ever wild
enough to think of breaking down the lines which
separate the states, and of compounding the American
people into one common mass. Of consequence, when
they act, they act in their states. But the measures they
adopt do not, on that account, cease to be the measures
of the people themselves, or become the measures of
the state governments.

From these conventions, the constitution derives its
whole authority. The government proceeds directly
from the people, is "ordained and established," in the
name of the people; and is declared to be ordained, "in
order to form a more perfect union, establish justice,
insure domestic tranquillity, and secure the blessings
of liberty to themselves and to their posterity." The
assent of the states, in their sovereign capacity, is implied, in calling a convention, and thus submitting that
instrument to the people. But the people were at perfect liberty to accept or reject it; and their act was final.
It required not the affirmance, and could not be negatived, by the state governments. The constitution,
when thus adopted, was of complete obligation, and
bound the state sovereignties. . . .

The government of the Union, then (whatever may
be the influence of this fact on the case), is emphatically
and truly, a government of the people. In form, and in
substance, it emanates from them. Its powers are
granted by them, and are to be exercised directly on
them, and for their benefit.

This government is acknowledged, by all, to be one
of enumerated powers. The principle, that it can exercise only the powers granted to it, would seem too
apparent, to have required to be enforced by all those
arguments, which its enlightened friends, while it was
depending before the people, found it necessary to
urge; that principle is now universally admitted. But
the question respecting the extent of the powers actually granted, is perpetually arising, and will probably
continue to arise, so long as our system shall exist. In
discussing these questions, the conflicting powers of
the general and state governments must be brought

into view, and the supremacy of their respective law,
when they are in opposition, must be settled.

If any one proposition could command the universal
assent of mankind, we might expect it would be this—
that the government of the Union, though limited in
its powers, is supreme within its sphere of action. This
would seem to result, necessarily, from its nature. It is
the government of all; its powers are delegated by all;
it represents all, and acts for all. Though any one state
may be willing to control its operations, no state is
willing to allow others to control them. The nation, on
those subjects on which it can act, must necessarily
bind its component parts. But this question is not left
to mere reason: the people have, in express terms decided it, by saying, "this constitution, and the laws of
the United States, which shall be made in pursuance
thereof," "shall be the supreme law of the land," and
by requiring that the members of the state legislatures,
and the officers of the executive and judicial departments of the states, shall take the oath of fidelity to it.
The government of the United States, then, though
limited in its powers, is supreme; and its laws, when
made in pursuance of the constitution, form the supreme law of the land, "anything in the constitution or
laws of any state to the contrary notwithstanding."

Among the enumerated powers, we do not find that
of establishing a bank or creating a corporation. But
there is no phrase in the instrument which, like the
articles of confederation, excludes incidental or implied
powers; and which requires that everything granted
shall be expressly and minutely described. Even the
10th amendment, which was framed for the purpose
of quieting the excessive jealousies which had been
excited, omits the word "expressly," and declares only,
that the powers "not delegated to the United States,
nor prohibited to the states, are reserved to the states
or to the people"; thus leaving the question, whether
the particular power which may become the subject of
contest, has been delegated to the one government, or
prohibited to the other, to depend on a fair construction of the whole instrument. The men who drew and
adopted this amendment had experienced the embarrassments resulting from the insertion of this word in
the articles of confederation, and probably omitted it,
to avoid those embarrassments. A constitution, to
contain an accurate detail of all the subdivisions of
which its great powers will admit, and of all the means
by which they may be carried into execution, would
partake of the prolixity of a legal code, and could
scarcely be embraced by the human mind. It would,
probably, never be understood by the public. Its nature,
therefore, requires, that only its great outlines should
be marked, its important objects designated, and the

minor ingredients which compose those objects, be deduced from the nature of the objects themselves. That this idea was entertained by the framers of the American constitution, is not only to be inferred from the nature of the instrument, but from the language. Why else were some of the limitations, found in the 9th section of the 1st article, introduced? It is also, in some degree, warranted, by their having omitted to use any restrictive term which might prevent its receiving a fair and just interpretation. In considering this question, then, we must never forget that it is a *constitution* we are expounding.

Although, among the enumerated powers of government we do not find the word "bank" or "incorporation," we find the great powers, to lay and collect taxes; to borrow money; to regulate commerce; to declare and conduct a war; and to raise and support armies and navies. The sword and the purse, all the external relations, and no inconsiderable portion of the industry of the nation, are intrusted to its government. It can never be pretended, that these vast powers draw after them others of inferior importance, merely because they are inferior. Such an idea can never be advanced. But it may with great reason be contended, that a government, intrusted with such ample powers, on the due execution of which the happiness and prosperity of the nation so vitally depends, must also be intrusted with ample means for their execution. The power being given, it is the interest of the nation to facilitate its execution. It can never be their interest, and cannot be presumed to have been their intention, to clog and embarrass its execution, by withholding the most appropriate means. Throughout this vast republic, from the St. Croix to the Gulf of Mexico, from the Atlantic to the Pacific, revenue is to be collected and expended, armies are to be marched and supported. The exigencies of the nation may require, that the treasure raised in the north should be transported to the south, that raised in the east, conveyed to the west, or that this order should be reversed. Is that construction of the constitution to be preferred, which would render these operations difficult, hazardous and expensive? Can we adopt that construction (unless the words imperiously require it), which would impute to the framers of that instrument, when granting these powers for the public good, the intention of impeding their exercise, by withholding a choice of means? If, indeed, such be the mandate of the constitution, we have only to obey; but that instrument does not profess to enumerate the means by which the powers it confers may be executed; nor does it prohibit the creation of a corporation, if the existence of such a being be essential, to the beneficial exercise of those powers.

It is, then, the subject of fair inquiry, how far such means may be employed.

It is not denied, that the powers given to the government imply the ordinary means of execution. That, for example, of raising revenue, and applying it to national purposes, is admitted to imply the power of conveying money from place to place, as the exigencies of the nation may require, and of employing the usual means of conveyance. But it is denied, that the government has its choice of means, or, that it may employ the convenient means, if, to employ them, it be necessary to erect a corporation. . . .

The government which has a right to do an act, and has imposed on it, the duty of performing that act, must, according to the dictates of reason, be allowed to select the means; and those who contend that it may not select any appropriate means, that one particular mode of effecting the object is excepted, take upon themselves the burden of establishing that exception.

The creation of a corporation, it is said, appertains to sovereignty. This is admitted. But to what portion of sovereignty does it appertain? Does it belong to one more than to another? In America, the powers of sovereignty are divided between the government of the union, and those of the states. They are each sovereign, with respect to the objects committed to it, and neither sovereign, with respect to the objects committed to the other. We cannot comprehend that train of reasoning, which would maintain, that the extent of power granted by the people is to be ascertained, not by the nature and terms of the grant, but by its date. Some state constitutions were formed before, some since that of the United States. We cannot believe, that their relation to each other is in any degree dependent upon this circumstance. Their respective powers must, we think, be precisely the same, as if they had been formed at the same time. Had they been formed at the same time, and had the people conferred on the general government the power contained in the constitution, and on the states the whole residuum of power, would it have been asserted, that the government of the Union was not sovereign, with respect to those objects which were intrusted to it, in relation to which its laws were declared to be supreme? If this could not have been asserted, we cannot well comprehend the process of reasoning which maintains, that a power appertaining to sovereignty cannot be connected with that vast portion of it which is granted to the general government, so far as it is calculated to subserve the legitimate objects of that government. The power of creating a corporation, though appertaining to sovereignty, is not, like the power of making war, or levying taxes, or of regulating commerce, a great substantive and independent power, which cannot be implied as incidental to other powers, or used as a means of executing them. It is never the end for which other powers are exercised, but a means by which other objects are accomplished. No contributions are made to charity, for the sake of an incorporation, but a corporation is created to administer the charity; no seminary of learning is instituted, in order to be incorporated, but the corporate character is conferred to subserve the purposes of education. No city was ever built, with the sole object of being incorporated, but is incorporated as affording the best means of being well governed. The power of creating a corporation is never used for its own sake, but for the purpose of effecting something else. No sufficient reason is, therefore, perceived, why it may not pass as incidental to those powers which are expressly given, if it be a direct mode of executing them.

But the constitution of the United States has not left the right of congress to employ the necessary means, for the execution of the powers conferred on the government, to general reasoning. To its enumeration of powers is added, that of making "all laws which shall be necessary and proper, for carrying into execution the foregoing powers, and all other powers vested by this constitution, in the government of the United States, or in any department thereof." The counsel for the state of Maryland have urged various arguments, to prove that this clause, though, in terms, a grant of power, is not so, in effect; but is really restrictive of the general right, which might otherwise be implied, of selecting means for executing the enumerated powers. . . .

But the argument on which most reliance is placed, is drawn from that peculiar language of this clause. Congress is not empowered by it to make all laws, which may have relation to the powers conferred on the government, but such only as may be *necessary and proper*" for carrying them into execution. The word *"necessary"* is considered as controlling the whole sentence, and as limiting the right to pass laws for the execution of the granted powers, to such as are indispensable, and without which the power would be nugatory. That it excludes the choice of means, and leaves to congress, in each case, that only which is most direct and simple.

Is it true, that this is the sense in which the word "necessary" is always used? Does it always import an absolute physical necessity, so strong, that one thing to which another may be termed necessary, cannot exist without that other? We think it does not. If reference be had to its use, in the common affairs of the world, or in approved authors, we find that it frequently imports no more than that one thing is conve-

nient, or useful, or essential to another. To employ the means necessary to an end, is generally understood as employing any means calculated to produce the end, and not as being confined to those single means, without which the end would be entirely unattainable. Such is the character of human language, that no word conveys to the mind, in all situations, one single definite idea; and nothing is more common than to use words in a figurative sense. Almost all compositions contain words, which, taken in their rigorous sense, would convey a meaning different from that which is obviously intended. It is essential to just construction, that many words which import something excessive, should be understood in a more mitigated sense—in that sense which common usage justifies. The word "necessary" is of this description. It has not a fixed character, peculiar to itself. It admits of all degrees of comparison, and is often connected with other words, which increase or diminish the impression the mind receives of the urgency it imports. A thing may be necessary, very necessary, absolutely or indispensably necessary. To no mind would the same idea be conveyed by these several phrases. . . . This word, then, like others, is used in various senses; and, in its construction, the subject, the context, the intention of the person using them, are all to be taken into view.

Let this be done in the case under consideration. The subject is the execution of those great powers on which the welfare of a nation essentially depends. It must have been the intention of those who gave these powers, to insure, so far as human prudence could insure, their beneficial execution. This could not be done, by confiding the choice of means to such narrow limits as not to leave it in the power of congress to adopt any which might be appropriate, and which were conducive to the end. This provision is made in a constitution, intended to endure for ages to come, and consequently, to be adapted to the various *crises* of human affairs. To have prescribed the means by which government should, in all future time, execute its powers, would have been to change, entirely, the character of the instrument, and give it the properties of a legal code. It would have been an unwise attempt to provide, by immutable rules, for exigencies which, if foreseen at all, must have been seen dimly, and which can be best provided for as they occur. To have declared, that the best means shall not be used, but those alone, without which the power given would be nugatory, would have been to deprive the legislature of the capacity to avail itself of experience, to exercise its reason, and to accommodate its legislation to circumstances. . . .

The result of the most careful and attentive consideration bestowed upon this clause is, that if it does not enlarge, it cannot be construed to restrain the powers of congress, or to impair the right of the legislature to exercise its best judgment in the selection of measures to carry into execution the constitutional powers of the government. If no other motive for its insertion can be suggested, a sufficient one is found in the desire to remove all doubts respecting the right to legislate on that vast mass of incidental powers which must be involved in the constitution, if that instrument be not a splendid bauble.

We admit, as all must admit, that the powers of the government are limited, and that its limits are not to be transcended. But we think the sound construction of the constitution must allow to the national legislature that discretion, with respect to the means by which the powers it confers are to be carried into execution, which will enable that body to perform the high duties assigned to it, in the manner most beneficial to the people. Let the end be legitimate, let it be within the scope of the constitution, and all means which are appropriate, which are plainly adapted to that end, which are not prohibited, but consist with the letter and spirit of the constitution, are constitutional. . . .

This clause, as construed by the state of Maryland, would abridge, and almost annihilate, this useful and necessary right of the legislature to select its means. That this could not be intended is, we should think, had it not been already controverted, too apparent for controversy. . . .

If a corporation may be employed, indiscriminately with other means, to carry into execution the powers of the government, no particular reason can be assigned for excluding the use of a bank, if required for its fiscal operations. To use one, must be within the discretion of congress, if it be an appropriate mode of executing the powers of government. That it is a convenient, a useful, and essential instrument in the prosecution of its fiscal operations, is not now a subject of controversy. . . .

But were its necessity less apparent, none can deny its being an appropriate measure; and if it is, the degree of its necessity, as has been very justly observed, is to be discussed in another place. Should congress, in the execution of its powers, adopt measures which are prohibited by the constitution; or should congress, under the pretext of executing its powers, pass laws for the accomplishment of objects not intrusted to the government; it would become the painful duty of this tribunal, should a case requiring such a decision come before it, to say that such an act was not the law of the land. But where the law is not prohibited, and is really

calculated to effect any of the objects intrusted to the government, to undertake here to inquire into the degree of its necessity, would be to pass the line which circumscribes the judicial department, and to tread on legislative ground. This court disclaims all pretensions to such a power. . . .

After the most deliberate consideration, it is the unanimous and decided opinion of this court, that the act to incorporate the Bank of the United States is a law made in pursuance of the constitution, and is a part of the supreme law of the land. . . .

It being the opinion of the court, that the act incorporating the bank is constitutional; and that the power of establishing a branch in the state of Maryland might be properly exercised by the bank itself, we proceed to inquire—

Whether the state of Maryland may, without violating the constitution, tax that branch? That the power of taxation is one of vital importance; that it is retained by the states; that it is not abridged by the grant of a similar power to the government of the Union; that it is to be concurrently exercised by the two governments—are truths which have never been denied. But such is the paramount character of the constitution, that its capacity to withdraw any subject from the action of even this power, is admitted. The states are expressly forbidden to lay any duties on imports or exports, except what may be absolutely necesary for executing their inspection laws. If the obligation of this prohibition must be conceded—if it may restrain a state from the exercise of its taxing power on imports and exports—the same paramount character would seem to restrain, as it certainly may restrain, a state from such other exercise of this power, as is in its nature incompatible with, and repugnant to, the constitutional laws of the Union. A law, absolutely repugnant to another, as entirely repeals that other as if express terms of repeal were used.

On this ground, the counsel for the bank place its claim to be exempted from the power of a state to tax its operations. There is no express provision for the case, but the claim has been sustained on a principle which so entirely pervades the constitution, is so intermixed with the materials which compose it, so interwoven with its web, so blended with its texture, as to be incapable of being separated from it, without rending it into shreds. This great principle is, that the constitution and the laws made in pursuance thereof are supreme; that they control the constitution and laws of the respective states, and cannot be controlled by them. From this, which may be almost termed an axiom, other propositions are deduced as corollaries, on the truth or error of which, and on their application to this case, the cause has been supposed to depend. These are, 1st. That a power to create implies a power to preserve: 2d. That a power to destroy, if wielded by a different hand, is hostile to, and incompatible with these powers to create and to preserve: 3d. That where this repugnancy exists, that authority which is supreme must control, not yield to that over which it is supreme. . . .

The power of congress to create, and of course, to continue, the bank, was the subject of the preceeding part of this opinion; and is no longer to be considered as questionable. That the power of taxing it by the states may be exercised so as to destroy it, is too obvious to be denied. But taxation is said to be an absolute power, which acknowledges no other limits than those expressly prescribed in the constitution, and like sovereign power of every other description, is intrusted to the discretion of those who use it. . . .

The argument on the part of the state of Maryland, is, not that the states may directly resist a law of congress, but that they may exercise their acknowledged powers upon it, and that the constitution leaves them this right, in the confidence that they will not abuse it. . . .

The the power to tax involves the power to destroy; that the power to destroy may defeat and render useless the power to create; that there is a plain repugnance in conferring on one government a power to control the constitutional measures of another, which other, with respect to those very measures, is declared to be supreme over that which exerts the control, are propositions not to be denied. But all inconsistencies are to be reconciled by the magic of the word *confidence.* Taxation, it is said, does not necessarily and unavoidably destroy. To carry it to the excess of destruction, would be an abuse, to presume which, would banish that confidence which is essential to all government. But is this a case of confidence? Would the people of any one state trust those of another with a power to control the most insignificant operations of their state government? We know they would not. Why, then, should we suppose, that the people of any one state should be willing to trust those of another with a power to control the operations of a government to which they have confided their most important and most valuable interests? In the legislature of the Union alone, are all represented. The legislature of the Union alone, therefore, can be trusted by the people with the power of controlling measures which concern all, in the confidence that it will not be abused. This, then, is not a case of confidence, and we must consider it is as it really is.

If we apply the principle for which the state of Maryland contends, to the constitution, generally, we shall find it capable of changing totally the character of that instrument. We shall find it capable of arresting all the measures of the government, and of prostrating it at the foot of the states. The American people have declared their constitution and the laws made in pursuance thereof, to be supreme; but this principle would transfer the supremacy, in fact, to the states. If the states may tax one instrument, employed by the government in the execution of its powers, they may tax any and every other instrument. They may tax the mail; they may tax the mint; they may tax patent-rights; they may tax the papers of the custom-house; they may tax judicial process; they may tax all the means employed by the government, to an excess which would defeat all the ends of government. This was not intended by the American people. They did not design to make their government dependent on the states. . . .

The question is, in truth, a question of supremacy; and if the right of the states to tax the means employed by the general government be conceded, the declaration that the constitution, and the laws made in pursuance thereof, shall be the supreme law of the land, is empty and unmeaning declamation. . . .

It has also been insisted, that, as the power of taxation in the general and state governments is acknowledged to be concurrent, every argument which would sustain the right of the general government to tax banks chartered by the states, will equally sustain the right of the states to tax banks chartered by the general government. But the two cases are not on the same reason. The people of all the states have created the general government, and have conferred upon it the general power of taxation. The people of all the states, and the states themselves, are represented in congress, and, by their representatives, exercise this power. When they tax the chartered institutions of the states, they tax their constituents; and these taxes must be uniform. But when a state taxes the operations of the government of the United States, it acts upon institutions created, not by their own constituents, but by people over whom they claim no control. It acts upon the measures of a government created by others as well as themselves, for the benefit of others in common with themselves. The difference is that which always exists, and always must exist, between the action of the whole on a part, and the action of a part on the whole—between the laws of a government declared to be supreme, and those of a government which, when in opposition to those laws, is not supreme. . . .

The court has bestowed on this subject its most deliberate consideration. The result is a conviction that the states have no power, by taxation or otherwise, to retard, impede, burden, or in any manner control, the operations of the constitutional laws enacted by congress to carry into execution the powers vested in the general government. This is, we think, the unavoidable consequence of that supremacy which the constitution has declared. We are unanimously of opinion, that the law passed by the legislature of Maryland, imposing a tax on the Bank of the United States, is unconstitutional and void. . . .

With *Sturgis* v. *Crowninshield* and *McCulloch* v. *Maryland*, the Dartmouth College case completed the trio of important cases in the 1819 term. In point of time, *Dartmouth College* v. *Woodward*[73] was decided before the other two, but was recorded by Supreme Court Reporter Henry Wheaton after the Sturgis and McCulloch decisions. In both the Sturgis and Dartmouth College cases, the Supreme Court applied the contract clause to declare state laws unconstitutional. The broad implications of the Sturgis case were limited by another decision[74] within eight years, but the doctrine enunciated in the Dartmouth College case was destined to determine the relation between government and economic life throughout most of the 19th century.[75]

In 1769 the royal governor of New Hampshire, John Wentworth, gave a charter to Eleazer Wheelock, in the name of George III. This royal charter established Dartmouth College, then a charity school for the education of Indians as well as whites. The charter provided that the college be governed by "one body corporate and politick . . . by the name of the Trustees of Dartmouth College." Wheelock was made president of the college and was given power to "appoint . . . by his last will" his successor.[76] When Eleazer Wheelock died in 1779, he had named his son, John, the new president.

By the provisions of the original charter the self-perpetuating trustees were empowered to remove the president. After 1793, a bitter feud between John Wheelock and the majority of the board developed. In 1815 the trustees removed President Wheelock and appointed Francis Brown as his successor. The controversy was further complicated by the active intervention of the two contending political parties of New Hampshire. The Federalists supported the trustees, and the Republicans backed the Wheelock faction. In 1816 the Republican-dominated legislature of New Hampshire intervened in the struggle by passing an act that changed the name of the school to Dartmouth University, increased the board of trustees from 12 to 21 members, vested appointment of new members in the governor and council, and empowered a board of overseers (appointed by the governor) to veto the acts of the board of trustees. The new members ousted the old trustees, reestablished Wheelock as president, and dismissed the faculty members who had supported Wheelock's opponents. The old "Trustees of Dartmouth College" countered by bringing suit against Woodward, the college secretary, for recovery of the charter, records, seal, and accounts.[77]

By consent of both parties the case was taken directly to the state court of appeals, where the old trustees were defeated. In answer to the contention that the contract clause forbade the action of the state legislature, Chief Justice Richardson had answered that the constitutional prohibition was "most manifestly intended to protect private rights only." Dartmouth College, he held, "is a publick corporation . . . the office of trustee of Dartmouth College is, in fact, a publick trust, as much so as the office of governor, or of judge of this court."[78]

The case was carried, by writ of error, to the Supreme Court. It was argued in the 1818 term, but because some justices were of "different opinions" and some "had not formed opinions . . . the cause" was continued. Marshall, Washington, and Story favored the old trustees; Duvall and Todd opposed them, and Livingston and Johnson had not yet decided.[79] Later, Livingston and Johnson conferred with Chancellor Kent of New York on the case and purportedly were influenced by him to vote with Marshall's supporters.[80]

On February 2, 1819, the Supreme Court decided the case. In the intervening year, the supporters of Woodward had hired William Pinkney, reputed to be the greatest lawyer of the times, to reargue the case. Chief Justice Marshall immediately launched into the decision, however, thus forestalling any requests for reargument.[81]

DARTMOUTH COLLEGE v. WOODWARD
4 Wheaton 518 (1819)

February 2d, 1819. The opinion of the court was delivered by Marshall, Ch. J.—This is an action of trover, brought by the Trustees of Dartmouth College against William H. Woodward, in the state court of New Hampshire, for the book of records, corporate seal, and other corporate property, to which the plaintiffs allege themselves to be entitled. A special verdict, after setting out the rights of the parties, finds for the defendant, if certain acts of the legislature of New Hampshire, passed on the 27th of June, and on the 18th of December 1816, be valid, and binding on the trustees, without their assent, and not repugnant to the constitution of the United States; otherwise, it finds for the plaintiffs. The superior court of judicature of New Hampshire rendered a judgment upon this verdict for the defendant, which judgment has been brought before this court by writ of error. The single question now to be considered is, do the acts to which the verdict refers violate the constitution of the United States?

This court can be insensible neither to the magnitude nor delicacy of this question. The validity of a legislative act is to be examined; and the opinion of the highest law tribunal of a state is to be revised—an opinion which carries with it intrinsic evidence of the diligence, of the ability, and the integrity, with which it was formed. On more than one occasion, this court has expressed the cautious-circumspection with which it approaches the consideration of such questions; and has declared, that in no doubtful case, would it pronounce a legislative act to be contrary to the constitution. But the American people have said, in the constitution of the United States, that "no state shall pass

any bill of attainder, *ex post facto* law, or law impairing the obligation of contracts." In the same instrument, they have also said, "that the judicial power shall extend to all cases in law and equity arising under the constitution." On the judges of this court, then, is imposed the high and solemn duty of protecting, from even legislative violation, those contracts which the constitution of our country has placed beyond legislative control; and, however irksome the task may be, this is a duty from which we dare not shrink.

The title of the plaintiffs originates in a charter dated the 13th day of December, in the year 1769, incorporating twelve persons therein mentioned, by the name of "The Trustees of Dartmouth College," granting to them and their successors the usual corporate privileges and powers, and authorizing the trustees, who are to govern the college, to fill up all vacancies which may be created in their own body.

The defendant claims under three acts of the legislature of New Hampshire, the most material of which was passed on the 27th of June 1816, and is entitled, "an act to amend the charter, and enlarge and improve the corporation of Dartmouth College." Among other alterations in the charter, this act increases the number of trustees to twenty-one, gives the appointment of the additional members to the executive of the state, and creates a board of overseers, with power to inspect and control the most important acts of the trustees. This board consists of twenty-five persons. The president of the senate, the speaker of the house of representatives, of New Hampshire, and the governor and lieutenant-governor of Vermont, for the time being, are to be members *ex officio*. The board is to be completed by the governor and council of New Hampshire, who are also empowered to fill all vacancies which may occur. The acts of the 18th and 26th of December are supplemental to that of the 27th of June, and are principally intended to carry that act into effect. The majority of the trustees of the college have refused to accept this amended charter, and have brought this suit for the corporate property, which is in possession of a person holding by virtue of the acts which have been stated.

It can require no argument to prove, that the circumstances of this case constitute a contract. An application is made to the crown for a charter to incorporate a religious and literary institution. In the application, it is stated, that large contributions have been made for the object, which will be conferred on the corporation, as soon as it shall be created. The charter is granted, and on its faith the property is conveyed . . .

The points for consideration are,

1. Is this contract protected by the constitution of the United States?

2. Is it impaired by the acts under which the defendant holds? . . .

That the framers of the constitution did not intend to restrain the States in the regulation of their civil institutions, adopted for internal government, and that the instrument they have given us is not to be so construed, may be admitted. The provision of the constitution never has been understood to embrace other contracts than those which respect property, or some object of value, and confer rights which may be asserted in a court of justice. It never has been understood to restrict the general right of the legislature to legislate on the subject of divorces. Those acts enable some tribunal, not to impair a marriage contract, but to liberate one of the parties because it has been broken by the other. When any State legislature shall pass an act annulling all marriage contracts, or allowing either party to annul it without consent of the other, it will be time enough to inquire whether such an act be constitutional.

The parties in this case differ less on general principles, less on the true construction of the constitution in the abstract, than on the application of those principles to this case, and on the true construction of the charter of 1769. This is the point on which the cause essentially depends. If the act of incorporation be a grant of political power, if it create a civil institution to be employed in the administration of the government, or if the funds of the college be public property, or if the State of New Hampshire, as a government, be alone interested in its transactions, the subject is one in which the legislature of the State may act according to its own judgment, unrestrained by any limitation of its power imposed by the constitution of the United States.

But if this be a private eleemosynary institution, endowed with a capacity to take property for objects unconnected with government, whose funds are bestowed by individuals on the faith of the charter; if the donors have stipulated for the future disposition and management of those funds in the manner prescribed by themselves; there may be more difficulty in the case, although neither the persons who have made these stipulations, nor those for whose benefit they were made, should be parties to the cause. . . .

Dartmouth College is really endowed by private individuals, who have bestowed their funds for the propagation of the Christian religion among the Indians, and for the promotion of piety and learning generally. From these funds the salaries of the tutors are drawn; and these salaries lessen the expense of education to the students. It is then an eleemosynary . . . and, as far as respects its funds, a private corporation.

Do its objects stamp on it a different character? Are the trustees and professors public officers, invested with any portion of political power, partaking in any degree in the administration of civil government, and performing duties which flow from the sovereign authority?

That education is an object of national concern, and a proper subject of legislation, all admit. That there may be an institution founded by government, and placed entirely under its immediate control, the officers of which would be public officers, amenable exclusively to government, none will deny. But is Dartmouth College such an institution? Is education altogether in the hands of the government? Does every teacher of youth become a public officer, and do donations for the purpose of education necessarily become public property, so far that the will of the legislature, not the will of the donor, becomes the law of the donation? These questions are of serious moment to society, and deserve to be well considered.

Doctor Wheelock, as the keeper of his charity school, instructing the Indians in the art of reading, and in our holy religion; sustaining them at his own expense, and on the voluntary contributions of the charitable, could scarcely be considered as a public officer, exercising any portion of those duties which belong to government; nor could the legislature have supposed, that his private funds, or those given by others, were subject to legislative management, because they were applied to the purposes of education. When afterwards, his school was enlarged, and the liberal contributions made in England and in America, enabled him to extend his cares to the education of the youth of his own country, no change was wrought in his own character, or in the nature of his duties. Had he employed assistant tutors with the funds contributed by others, or had the trustees in England established a school, with Dr. Wheelock at its head, and paid salaries to him and his assistants, they would still have been private tutors; and the fact that they were employed in the education of youth, could not have converted them into public officers, concerned in the administration of public duties, or have given the legislature a right to interfere in the management of the fund. The trustees, in whose care that fund was placed by the contributors, would have been permitted to execute their trust, uncontrolled by legislative authority.

Whence, then, can be derived the idea, that Dartmouth College has become a public institution, and its trustees public officers, exercising powers conferred by the public, for public objects? Not from the source whence its funds were drawn; for its foundation is purely private and eleemosynary. Not from the application of those funds; for money may be given for education, and the persons receiving it do not, by being employed in the education of youth, become members of the civil government. Is it from the act of incorporation? Let this subject be considered.

A corporation is an artificial being, invisible, intangible, and existing only in contemplation of law. Being the mere creature of law, it possesses only those properties which the charter of its creation confers upon it, either expressly, or as incidental to its very existence. These are such as are supposed best calculated to effect the object for which it was created. Among the most important are immortality, and, if the expression may be allowed, individuality; properties by which a perpetual succession of many persons are considered as the same, and may act as a single individual. They enable a corporation to manage its own affairs, and to hold property without the perplexing intricacies, the hazardous and endless necessity of perpetual conveyances, for the purpose of transmitting it from hand to hand. It is chiefly for the purpose of clothing bodies of men, in succession, with these qualities and capacities, that corporations were invented, and are in use. By these means a perpetual succession of individuals are capable of acting for the promotion of the particular object, like one immortal being. But this being does not share in the civil government of the country, unless that be the purpose for which it was created. Its immortality no more confers on it political power, or a political character, than immortality would confer such power or character on a natural person. It is no more a State instrument, than a natural person exercising the same powers would be. If, then, a natural person, employed by individuals in the education of youth, or for the government of a seminary in which youth is edu-

cated, would not become a public officer, or be considered as a member of the civil government, how is it that this artificial being, created by law, for the purpose of being employed by the same individuals for the same purposes, should become a part of the civil government of the country? Is it because its existence, its capacities, its powers, are given by law? Because the government has given it the power to take and to hold property in a particular form, and for particular purposes, has the government a consequent right substantially to change that form, or to vary the purposes to which the property is to be applied? This principle has never been asserted or recognized, and is supported by no authority. Can it derive aid from reason?

The objects for which a corporation is created are universally such as the government wishes to promote. They are deemed beneficial to the country; and this benefit constitutes the consideration, and, in most cases, the sole consideration, of the grant. In most eleemosynary institutions, the object would be difficult, perhaps unattainable, without the aid of a charter of incorporation. Charitable, or public spirited individuals, desirous of making permanent appropriations for charitable or other useful purposes, find it impossible to effect their design, securely and certainly, without an incorporating act. They apply to the government, state their beneficent object, and offer to advance the money necessary for its accomplishment, provided the government will confer on the instrument, which is to execute their designs, the capacity to execute them. The proposition is considered and approved. The benefit to the public is considered as an ample compensation for the faculty it confers, and the corporation is created. If the advantages to the public constitute a full compensation for the faculty it gives, there can be no reason for exacting a further compensation, by claiming a right to exercise over this artificial being a power which changes its nature, and touches the fund, for the security and application of which it was created. There can be no reason for implying in a charter, given for a valuable consideration, a power which is not only not expressed, but is in direct contradiction to its express stipulations.

From the fact, then, that a charter of incorporation has been granted, nothing can be inferred which changes the character of the institution, or transfers to the government any new power over it. The character of civil institutions does not grow out of their incorporation, but out of the manner in which they are formed, and the objects for which they are created. The right to change them is not founded on their being incorporated, but on their being the instruments of government, created for its purposes. The same institutions, created for the same objects, though not incorporated, would be public institutions, and, of course, be controllable by the legislature. The incorporating act neither gives nor prevents this control. Neither, in reason, can the incorporating act change the character of a private eleemosynary institution. . . .

[I]t appears, that Dartmouth College is an eleemosynary institution, incorporated for the purpose of perpetuating the application of the bounty of the donors, to the specified objects of that bounty; that its trustees or governors were originally named by the founder, and invested with the power of perpetuating themselves; that they are not public officers, nor is it a civil institution, participating in the administration of government; but a charity school, or a seminary of education, incorporated for the preservation of its property, and the perpetual application of that property to the objects of its creation. . . .

This is plainly a contract to which the donors, the trustees, and the crown (to whose rights and obligations New Hampshire succeeds) were the original parties. It is a contract made on a valuable consideration. It is a contract for the security and disposition of property. It is a contract, on the faith of which, real and personal estate has been conveyed to the corporation. It is then a contract within the letter of the constitution, and within its spirit also, unless the fact that the property is invested by the donors in trustees, for the promotion of religion and education, for the benefit of persons who are perpetually changing, though the objects remain the same, shall create a particular exception, taking this case out of the prohibition contained in the constitution.

It is more than possible that the preservation of rights of this description was not particularly in the view of the framers of the constitution, when the clause under consideration was introduced into that instrument. It is probable that interferences of more frequent recurrence, to which the temptation was stronger, and of which the mischief was more extensive, constituted the great motive for imposing this restriction on the State legislatures. But although a particular and a rare case may not, in itself, be of sufficient magnitude to induce a rule, yet it must be governed by the rule, when established, unless some plain and strong reason for excluding it can be given. It is not enough to say, that this particular case was not in the mind of the convention, when the article was framed, nor of the American people, when it was adopted. It is necessary to go further, and to say that, had this particular case been suggested, the language would have been so varied as to exclude it, or it would have been made a special exception. The case being

within the words of the rule, must be within its operation likewise, unless there be something in the literal construction so obviously absurd or mischievous, or repugnant to the general spirit of the instrument, as to justify those who expound the constitution in making it an exception. . . .

The opinion of the court, after mature deliberation, is, that this is a contract, the obligation of which cannot be impaired, without violating the constitution of the United States. This opinion appears to us to be equally supported by reason, and by the former decisions of this court.

We next proceed to the inquiry, whether its obligation has been impaired by those acts of the legislature of New Hampshire, to which the special verdict refers.

From the review of this charter, which has been taken, it appears that the whole power of governing the college, of appointing and removing tutors, of fixing their salaries, of directing the course of study to be pursued by the students, and of filling up vacancies created in their own body, was vested in the trustees. On the part of the crown, it was expressly stipulated that this corporation, thus constituted, should continue forever; and that the number of trustees should forever consist of twelve, and no more. By this contract, the crown was bound, and could have made no violent alteration in its essential terms, without impairing its obligation.

By the Revolution, the duties as well as the powers of government devolved on the people of New Hampshire. It is admitted, that among the latter was comprehended the transcendent power of parliament, as well as that of the executive department. It is too clear to require the support of argument, that all contracts and rights, respecting property, remained unchanged by the Revolution. The obligations, then, which were created by the charter to Dartmouth College, were the same in the new that they had been in the old government. The power of the government was also the same. A repeal of this charter at any time prior to the adoption of the present constitution of the United States, would have been an extraordinary and unprecedented act of power, but one which could have been contested only by the restrictions upon the legislature, to be found in the constitution of the State. But the constitution of the United States has imposed this additional limitation, that the legislature of a State shall pass no act "impairing the obligation of contracts."

It has been already stated, that the act "to amend the charter, and enlarge and improve the corporation of Dartmouth College," increases the number of trustees to twenty-one, gives the appointment of the additional members to the executive of the State, and creates a board of overseers, to consist of twenty-five persons, of whom twenty-one are also appointed by the executive of New Hampshire, who have power to inspect and control the most important acts of the trustees.

On the effect of this law, two opinions cannot be entertained. Between acting directly, and acting through the agency of trustees and overseers, no essential difference is perceived. The whole power of governing the college is transferred from trustees, appointed according to the will of the founder, expressed in the charter, to the executive of New Hampshire. The management and application of the funds of this eleemosynary institution, which are placed by the donors in the hands of trustees named in the charter, and empowered to perpetuate themselves, are placed by this act under the control of the government of the State. The will of the State is substituted for the will of the donors, in every essential operation of the college. This is not an immaterial change. The founders of the college contracted, not merely for the perpetual application of the funds which they gave, to the objects for which those funds were given; they contracted

also, to secure that application by the constitution of the corporation. They contracted for a system, which should, as far as human foresight can provide, retain forever the government of the literary institution they had formed, in the hands of persons approved by themselves. This system is totally changed. The charter of 1769 exists no longer. It is reorganized; and reorganized in such a manner, as to convert a literary institution, moulded according to the will of its founders, and placed under the control of private literary men, into a machine entirely subservient to the will of the government. This may be for the advantage of this college in particular, and may be for the advantage of literature in general; but it is not according to the will of the donors, and is subversive of that contract on the faith of which their property was given. . . .

It results from this opinion, that the acts of the legislature of New Hampshire, which are stated in the special verdict found in this cause, are repugnant to the constitution of the United States, and that the judgment on this special verdict ought to have been for the plaintiffs. The judgment of the state court must, therefore, be reversed.

> While Chief Justice Marshall carried a majority of the Court, Associate Justices Washington and Story wrote separate concurring opinions and Associate Justice Duvall dissented without opinion.
>
> A year after the Dartmouth decision, the *North American Review* commented: "Perhaps no judicial proceedings ever involved more important consequences . . ."[82] Important as were the implications of the Dartmouth College case in terms of limiting state control of private corporations, however, that decision received relatively little attention from contemporaries.[83] In contrast, the Supreme Court's decisions in *Sturgis* v. *Crowninshield* and *McCulloch* v. *Maryland* were printed in most of the leading newspapers. *Sturgis* v. *Crowninshield,* in the words of one Boston newspaper, "created much excitement and alarm in many states."[84] Because it was generally believed that the decision invalidated all state bankruptcy laws, demands for congressional legislation on the subject increased. But while public interest and debtor opposition was aroused because of the economic implications of the Sturgis decision, opposition of a different nature followed the widespread publication of the McCulloch decision.
>
> The general trend of anti–Supreme Court attacks was anticipated in the widely read *Weekly Register* of Hezekiah Niles. Wrote Niles, "A deadly blow has been struck at the *sovereignty of the states,* and from a quarter so far removed from the people as to be hardly accessible to public opinion . . ."[85] But the fiercest attacks were to come from Marshall's native Virginia. Chief Justice Marshall was aware of the coming attacks, for he wrote to Justice Story from Richmond on March 24, 1819, that
>
>> . . . Our opinion in the Bank case has aroused the sleeping spirit of Virginia, if indeed it ever sleeps. It will, I understand, be attacked in the papers with some asperity, and as those who favor it will never write for the publick it will remain undefended and of course be considered as damnably heretical.[86]

Six days later, Spencer Roane, writing under the pseudonym "Amphicton," opened the attack in the *Richmond Enquirer*.

The fundamental difference of opinion between Roane and Marshall concerned not economic policies, but theories of government. Roane based his arguments on the doctrines stated in the Kentucky and Virginia Resolutions of 1789–1799, and contended that should Marshall's decision stand, the "rights and freedom of the people of the states" would be lost. The Amphicton articles aroused so much excitement in Virginia and Kentucky[87] that by May of 1819, Marshall was seriously disturbed by the public reaction. On May 27, he wrote to Justice Story, "If the principles which have been advanced on this occasion were to prevail the constitution would be converted into the old confederation."[88] During the summer, Marshall wrote five articles in reply. However, the editor of the *Union of Philadelphia* condensed, or rather as Marshall put it "mangled,"[89] them into two articles. Writing under the pseudonym "A Friend of the Union," Marshall charged the author of the Amphicton articles with inflicting "deep wounds on the Constitution." He had seized upon the McCulloch decision, said Marshall, as an opportunity "for once more agitating the publick mind, and reviving those unfounded jealousies by whose blind aid ambition climbs the ladder of power."[90]

Roane then fired another broadside of four articles under the name "Hampden." The constitutional argument central to the Hampden articles was that the Constitution, like the old Articles of Confederation, set up a league, and was "a compact, to which the states are parties."[91] After the Hampden series, Virginia's politicians and newspapers turned their attention to another "usurper," General Jackson in Florida.[92] Marshall was destined to enjoy only a brief respite, however, for early in 1820, Roane, now "Publicola," again addressed the Virginia state legislators through the columns of the *Enquirer*. He contended that the Supreme Court was absolutely disqualified to "decide with impartiality upon controversies between the General and State Governments," and suggested that to "ensure unbiased" decisions, a new tribunal, consisting of members appointed partly by the states and partly by the national government, be established by constitutional amendment.[93]

During this period the proponents of states' rights were aroused not only over the bank issue, but also over the question of the admission of Missouri and over congressional approval of a protective tariff. Before 1820, opposition to the Supreme Court's assertions of national supremacy had been sporadic and divided. In the 1800–1820 period, nationalism generally had been stronger in the South than in any other part of the country. But the new issues brought about a realignment of the forces of nationalism. Keen observers recognized immediately the implications of the Missouri controversy. Prophetically, John Quincy Adams wrote that secession over the slavery issue would bring on war in a divided union; "its result must be the extirpation of slavery from this whole continent." Of the Missouri Compromise, Jefferson wrote:

This momentous question like a fire bell in the night, awakened and filled me with terror. I considered it at once as the knell of the Union. It is hushed, indeed, for the moment. But this is a reprieve only, not a final sentence. A geographical line, coinciding with a marked principle, moral and political, once conceived and held up to the

angry passions of men, will never be obliterated; and every new irritation will mark
it deeper and deeper.[94]

The beginning of the third decade of the 19th century marked the beginning of
a fundamental cleavage which, by 1860, was to rend the Union asunder. Roane's
attack on the McCulloch decision was only one of the symptoms. By 1821, the
Virginia legislature had adopted the Stevenson and Baldwin resolutions advocating
strong states' rights stands on the bank and Missouri questions respectively.[95]
Even before the Virginia action, Pennsylvania's legislature had proposed a constitutional amendment prohibiting the authorization by Congress of any bank outside the District of Columbia.[96] The Ohio legislature, which was aroused over the
long-smoldering Osborn bank issue, which directly affected the state,[97] condemned
the McCulloch decision and sent its resolution to the other states. The foremost
states' rights political theorist, John Taylor of Caroline, joined the fray with an
analytic attack on national governmental supremacy in general, and the Supreme
Court in particular, in his *Construction Construed, and Constitutions Vindicated.*[98]

Introducing Taylor's book to the public in an editorial in the *Richmond Enquirer,*
Thomas Ritchie wrote: "The crisis has come"—the Missouri, the bank, and the
tariff issues had aroused mighty states' rights opposition to national governmental
"usurpations."[99]

The Cohens decision also had raised a hornet's nest in Virginia. Governor
Thomas Randolph wrote, in his message to the Virginia legislature in December
1821, that

> The commonwealth has undergone the humiliation of having endeavored in vain to
> vindicate and assert her rights and her sovereignty at the bar of the Supreme
> Court of the United States, and now endures the mortification . . . of having
> altogether failed to procure a disavowal of the right, or the intention, to violate
> that sovereignty and those rights . . . It [the Supreme Court] arrogates to itself,
> always, the high authority to judge exclusively in the last resort how far the federal
> compact is violated. . . .[100]

Spencer Roane had opened the attack earlier, in May 1821. Writing now under
the name "Algernon Sidney," Roane poured forth five violent articles denouncing
the "artifices" of Chief Justice Marshall, the Republicans-turned-Nationalists on
the Court, and the "disastrous consequences" of the Supreme Court's decisions.[101]

The "Algernon Sidney" articles thoroughly aroused Marshall. On June 15, 1821,
he wrote to Story, "For coarseness and malignity of invention Algernon Sidney
surpasses all party writers who have made any pretentions to any decency of
character." And on September 18, 1821, Marshall, writing again to Story, referred
to his greatest Virginia opponent, Thomas Jefferson:

> . . . there is some reason to believe that the essays written against the Supreme
> Court were, in a degree, at least, stimulated by this gentleman, and that although
> the coarseness of the language belongs exclusively to the author, its acerbity has
> been increased by his communications with the great Lama of the mountains. . . . a
> deep design to convert our Government into a mere league of States has taken hold
> of a powerful and violent party in Virginia. The attack upon the judiciary is in fact
> an attack upon the Union. . . . An effort will certainly be made to repeal the 25th
> Section of the Judiciary Act.[102]

In February 1822, a resolution providing for presentation of a constitutional amendment depriving the Supreme Court of power to pass on the validity of state statutes failed to pass in the Virginia House of Delegates by a very small margin.[103] The attacks on the Supreme Court were not confined, however, to the state legislatures and courts and the newspaper columns. In December 1821, the first of a long series of national congressional attacks on the judicial powers was begun by Senator Richard M. Johnson of Kentucky. In December of that year, he introduced a constitutional amendment providing:

> In all cases where a State shall be a party, and in all controversies in which a state may desire to become a party in consequence of having the Constitution or laws of such a state questioned, the Senate of the United States shall have appellate jurisidiction.[104]

Johnson's motion was prompted by the economic as well as constitutional views of his constituents. He expressed concern over the "serious consequences which had lately taken place between several of the states and the Judiciary," and was particularly disturbed by the "disastrous" (first) decision in Green v. Biddle.[105]

Agitation for transference to the Senate of final appellate jurisdiction in cases involving federal-state relations continued for a number of years, even though Senator Johnson's amendment got little support in the Senate in 1821. One of the more temperate arguments in favor of his plan was given in Niles Register:

> . . . There is one very important effect that results from conflicting cases between the constitution and laws of the United States and of the several States. As yet, they have been decided, and settled by the Supreme Court, but its decisions, though acquiesced in, have not always satisfied what may be called State pride. This, however, is not the worst of it; for in the progress of time, the exposition of the Constitution of the United States may more depend on the opinions of the Supreme Court than on its own very carefully defined powers. It is not in human affairs to hope for perfection; and it is impossible to draw up any instrument such as the Constitution, without leaving some points that will bear different and opposing constructions; better that they should be established by the people through the representatives of the states in the Senate than be made to depend upon the opinions of a mere majority of the judges of the Supreme Court, who, however honorable and learned they may be, cannot be put down as infallible.[106]

This suggestion that final determinations in federal-state relations be made by a body more representative of local opinion got little support in Congress or in the nation. Opposition to the Supreme Court continued to be sporadic, cropping up in individual states whenever a particular piece of legislation or a particular sectional interest was touched upon by national judicial power. For example, Senator Johnson's amendment proposal failed to provoke congressional action in 1821, but later, in 1822, Virginia's Representative Stevenson introduced a resolution in the House Judiciary Committee calling for repeal of the 25th section of the Judiciary Act of 1789.

State and national legislative attacks on the federal judiciary in 1823 were just as uncoordinated as those of the two previous years. South Carolina's attack on the national judiciary arose from the combustible race question. Virginia and

South Carolina had passed laws forbidding the entrance of free Negroes into the states and providing for their detention in custody until the ship in which they arrived should leave port. The laws were passed to protect the states against Negro insurrections, in the belief that the presence of northern free Negroes would stir up the slave population.[107]

Significantly, Justice Johnson, a South Carolinian and a Republican, upheld national supremacy. In a circuit court decision,[108] he declared that the South Carolina statute was void because it contravened the commerce clause. Johnson held that the national government had a "paramount and exclusive right" to regulate commerce between the states. He then wrote:

> The plea of necessity is urged, and of the existence of that necessity, we are told, the State alone is to judge. Where is this to land us? It is not asserting the right of each State to throw off the Federal constitution at its will and pleasure? If it can be done as to any particular article, it can be done as to all; and like the old confederation, the Union becomes a mere rope of sand.

In 1824 the South Carolina legislature adopted resolutions, similar to those of Ohio in 1820 and Kentucky and Georgia in 1823, denying that the federal judiciary could constitutionally exercise jurisdiction in cases involving state legislation. The opposition again was sporadic and uncoordinated although in South Carolina it remained doggedly consistent.[109] One of the clearest examples of the uncoordinated and occasional nature of the opposition to the Supreme Court is provided by the experience of the state of Kentucky.

Of all the state opponents of the Supreme Court in this period of many controversies, the fiercest was Kentucky. The reasons for Kentucky's constant and increasing opposition to the Supreme Court's exercise of final appellate power in federal-state relations were many and complex. Four major sources of friction kept the state of Kentucky in turmoil for a period of approximately six years. First, federal courts had held that federal admiralty jurisdiction extended to Kentucky's rivers. Second, the federal judiciary invalidated the Kentucky land laws that protected settlers who had made improvements on disputed tracts. Third, the federal courts had refused to enforce Kentucky "stay" laws, which had delayed foreclosures for debt. And fourth, the federal courts sustained the rights of the hated Bank of the United States. Describing the "intense State sentiment" in Kentucky, judicial historian Charles Warren wrote that "nowhere in the United States had the feeling of hostility thus aroused been so generally entertained by the whole people of the State."[110]

The conflict over admiralty jurisdictions was ended by 1825. Before that date, the federal district courts had held that federal admiralty jurisdiction embraced inland waters such as Kentucky's rivers. Because trial by jury could be avoided, and because federal executions required payment in gold, cases involving seaman's wages and sales of river-boat supplies were brought to federal courts. This assumption of jurisdiction was attacked by Senator Johnson in Congress in 1821. Finally, in 1825 Justice Story removed this source of friction by holding, in *The Thomas Jefferson*,[111] that federal admiralty jurisdiction did not extend beyond the ebb and flow of the tide.[112]

The three other sources of conflict between Kentucky and federal judiciary, however, were not disposed of so easily. In 1821 the Kentucky legislature passed four acts to relieve debtors. One abolished imprisonment for debt. A second provided that a debtor's real estate could not be sold for execution for less than three quarters of the appraised value. Another incorporated a state bank that was empowered to issue notes not redeemable in specie. And a fourth prevented creditors from levying execution of a debt for a period of two years, unless the creditor was willing to accept state bank paper money in payment. When the state court of appeals declared these laws invalid under the contract clause, the irate Kentucky legislature abolished the court and set up a new one. The governor then appointed judges known to be supporters of the new debtor laws.

Acting under the Federal Process Act of 1792, the federal judges in Kentucky adopted rules providing that judgment in federal courts be discharged only by payments in specie. Nonresident creditors and the Bank of the United States were thus able to secure debt payments in Kentucky in gold or silver by bringing suit in federal courts.

Although the Supreme Court managed to avoid considering the constitutionality of these Kentucky laws in *Wayman* v. *Southard*,[113] *Bank of the United States* v. *Halstead*,[114] and *Bank of the United States* v. *January*,[115] it antagonized the debtors of Kentucky by refusing to enforce the Kentucky laws and by upholding the claims of the obnoxious United States bank. In *Wayman* v. *Southard*, Chief Justice Marshall established the doctrine that Congress has exclusive authority to regulate the proceedings of federal courts, and that the states have no authority to control those proceedings either directly or indirectly unless state process acts are adopted by Congress or by the federal courts under the authority of Congress. The Kentucky laws were held not binding in federal courts. Marshall then said: "If the laws do not apply to the federal courts, no question concerning their constitutionality can arise in those Courts." The twin Halstead and January decisions were given by Justice Thompson. He simply applied the doctrine stated in the Wayman decision to the Kentucky "stay" law. Kentucky debtor reaction to these decisions was faithfully mirrored by Senator Rowan in Congress when he charged that the federal judiciary had "turned Kentucky over, a prey to the Bank and the mercenary vultures that hovered round that institution."[116]

Irritating as were these conflicts with the judiciary, it was the Supreme Court's decision in *Green* v. *Biddle* that aroused the greatest opposition in Kentucky. As a result of innumerable and frequently overlapping land surveys and patents, the Kentucky state courts had for many years been faced with complicated land claim controversies. In order to mitigate the situation, the Kentucky legislature enacted laws providing that no land claimant would be awarded possession of land to which he proved title if he failed to compensate the occupier of the land for all improvements. Moreover, these laws provided that in default of payment for improvements, the title to the disputed land would rest with the occupier upon payment by him of the value of the land without improvements.

In 1819 the constitutionality of the Kentucky land claimant laws was attacked in a federal circuit court. Under the first interstate compact approved by Congress[117] all private rights and interests in Kentucky were to "remain valid and secure" and were to be determined according to the laws of Virginia existing in 1791. Opponents of the Kentucky land laws contended that the compact was a contract, the obligation of which was impaired by the Kentucky laws. When the case reached the Supreme Court in 1821, Justice Story held the compact unconstitutional.[118] Article 1, section 10, of the Constitution provides that "no State shall, without the consent of Congress . . . enter into any agreement or compact with another state." Congress had authorized the Virginia-Kentucky compact under this article. Bushrod Washington, in the second decision of *Green* v. *Biddle*, used the contract clause as the basis for his decision, and also referred to the congressional act, holding that "the terms compact and contract are synonymous."

After Story's first decision, the case had been reargued in 1822. And the final decision in *Green* v. *Biddle*,[119] like the first, held the Kentucky land-claimant laws unconstitutional. Although he was fully aware of the seriousness of the controversy, Justice Washington did not fail to assert the power of the federal judiciary to determine the case:

> . . . the duty, not less than the power of this court, as well as of every other court in the Union, to declare a law unconstitutional, which impairs the obligation of contracts, whoever may be the parties to them, is too clearly enjoyed [sic] by the constitution itself, and too firmly established by the decisions of this and other courts, to be now shaken. . . . Kentucky . . . being a party to the compact which guaranteed to claimants of land lying in that state, under titles derived from Virginia, their rights, as they existed under the laws of Virginia, was incompetent to violate that contract, by passing any law which rendered those rights less valid and secure.

After the decision in *Green* v. *Biddle* was published and commented upon in the newspapers, public opinion in Kentucky was further aroused by the report that the decision was rendered by only three justices. Johnson had dissented, and Marshall, Todd, and Livingston were sick when the decision was made. The Kentucky national congressmen protested the "minority opinion." Kentucky state courts refused to be bound by the Supreme Court's decision. In 1824 Kentucky Senator Isham Talbot and Representative Charles A. Wickliffe introduced resolutions that would have weakened or abolished the Supreme Court's appellate power under section 25 of the Judiciary Act of 1789. In December 1823, Senator Johnson, also of Kentucky, had proposed a bill requiring the concurrence of seven justices in opinions involving the validity of state statutes or acts of Congress. These proposed limitations of the federal judiciary failed to get widespread support.[120] Ironically, Virginia failed to support Kentucky, even though the latter state advanced the same arguments in 1823 and 1824 that Virginia had advanced after the Cohens decision in 1821. That the change in attitude stemmed from economic self-interest was angrily noted by Henry Clay. He wrote to a friend in Virginia, "When, in the case of *Cohens* v. *Virginia*, her authority [Virginia's] was alone concerned, she made the most strenuous efforts against the exercise of that power by the Supreme Court. But when the thunders of that Court were directed against poor Kentucky, in vain did she invoke Virginian aid. The Supreme Court, it was imagined, would decide on the side of the supposed interests of Virginia."[121] When the Kentucky legislature threatened to resist the *Green* v. *Biddle* decision by force, the *Richmond Enquirer*, trumpet of Spencer Roane, maintained that only "the most imperious necessity should justify such a resort!"[122]

The inconsistency of the positions of the Virginia Republican political leadership in relation to the Cohens decision and the subsequent Kentucky decision indicates a considerably more important generalization about the broad relationship of the Supreme Court and the Congress. By the mid–1820s, virtually the entire transformation that had begun with the first critical election of 1800 had been completed.

During this era of definitive decisions of the Supreme Court in federal-state relations and property rights protected by the contract clause, Jeffersonian Republican appointees now predominated on the federal courts. It might appropriately be assumed that the Republican majority would, after the considerable delay created by the ideological persistence and longevity of the old Federalist majority, realign the Supreme Court to conform to the positions of the Republicans who had dominated Congress and the presidency since 1800. This result would substantiate, albeit rather belatedly, the generally accepted position of Robert Dahl discussed in Chapter 1. The Jeffersonian Republicans certainly did demonstrate a high degree of electoral consistency. Their electoral alliances did, indeed, endure for a long time.

The Republicanism associated with Jefferson and his heirs lasted from 1800 until the critical election of 1828. But electoral consistency and policy consistency are often rather different because the constituent elements comprising a winning coalition may not combine in monolithic cohesion on most policy issues. By the latter part of the second decade of the 19th century, Jeffersonian Republicans divided on a number of issues, sometimes bitterly. These issues included internal improvements, the Yazoo land fraud, the sanctity of contracts, corporations, the status of lawyers and banks, to mention a few. Consequently, the relationship of the Supreme Court to the long-entrenched victors of the critical election of 1800 is considerably more complex than Dahl suggested. It was not simply a situation in which the policy positions of the Supreme Court conformed to those of the dominant majority in Congress and the presidency as soon as enough new judicial appointments had been made. The coalition that created that majority was not unified on many policy issues, and some elements of that coalition supported the same policy positions taken by Supreme Court majorities both before and after the Federalist judicial elite was largely replaced by a Republican judicial elite. To be sure, it has been argued significantly that the Republican judicial majority was influenced by Chief Justice John Marshall. But the fact that the dominant coalition was often divided is rather clearly substantiated in the journalistic and political opinions from contemporary accounts concerning reaction to the definitive federal-state authority and contract clause decisions.

A direct illustration of the persistence and long-term stability of Federalist and Whig doctrinal influence is provided by the relationship of successive judicial political generations of justices to each appointing president, and especially, to each critical election through that of 1860. There is a good deal of ideological and political continuity from Federalist to National Republican to Whig party affiliation. These relationships are summarized in Table 4-1.

TABLE 4-1   Judicial political generations and critical elections: The persistence of Federalist and Whig doctrinal influence, 1789-1869*

Appointing president and party	Chief Justice	Justices chosen in the Federalist-Whig eras							
George Washington Federalist 1789-1797	*J. Jay* 1789-1795 *J. Rutledge* 1795 *J. Ellsworth* 1796-1800	*J. Wilson* 1789-1798	*J. Blair* 1789-1796 *S. Chase* 1796-1811	*W. Cushing* 1789-1810	*J. Rutledge* 1789-1791 *T. Johnson* 1791-1793 *W. Paterson* 1793-1806	*J. Iredell* 1789-1799			
John Adams Federalist 1797-1801	*J. Marshall* 1801-1835	*B. Washington* 1798-1829				*A. Moore* 1799-1804			
Critical election of 1800: Jeffersonian Republicans take control of Congress and the presidency									
Thomas Jefferson Jeffersonian Republican 1801-1809				Vacant	*B. Livingston* 1806-1823	*W. Johnson* 1804-1834	*Court increased to 7 by act of Feb. 24, 1807* *T. Todd* 1807-1826,		
James Madison Jeffersonian Republican 1809-1817			G. Duval 1811-1835	*J. Story* 1811-1845, nominal Jeffersonian Republican at app't.			*nominal Jeffersonian Republican, doctrinal neo-Federalist*		
James Monroe Jeffersonian Republican 1817-1825				doctrinal neo-Federalist, became actual Whig	*S. Thompson* 1823-1843				
John Quincy Adams National Rep. 1825-1829							*R. Trimble* 1826-1828, Same as Todd Vacant		
Critical election of 1828: Jacksonian Democrats take control of Congress and the presidency									
Andrew Jackson Jacksonian Democrat 1829-1837	R. Taney 1836-1864	*H. Baldwin* 1830-1844, nominal Jacksonian Democrat, doctrinal Whig	P. Barbour 1836-1841			*J. W. Wayne* 1835-1867, nominal Jacksonian	*J. McLean* 1829-1861, actual Whig Republican (Lincoln)	*Court increased to 9 by act of March 3, 1837*	
Martin Van Buren Jacksonian Democrat 1837-1841			P. Daniel 1846-1860			Democrat, but doctrinal Whig		*J. Catron* 1837-1865	*J. McKinley* 1837-1852

*Justices of Federalist or Whig affiliation or doctrinal tendencies are in italics.

**TABLE 4-1 Judicial political generations and critical elections:
The persistence of Federalist and Whig doctrinal influence, 1789–1869* (continued)**

Appointing president and party	Chief Justice	Justices chosen in the Federalist–Whig eras						
William Henry Harrison Whig 1841								
John Tyler Whig-Jeffersonian Republican 1841–1845	Vacant 1844–1846			Vacant S. Nelson 1845–1872				
James K. Polk Jacksonian Democrat 1845–1849	R. Grier 1846–1870		*L. Woodbury 1846–1851*					
Zachary Taylor Whig 1849–1850								
Millard Fillmore Whig 1850–1853			*B. Curtis 1851–1857, Whig*					
Franklin Pierce Jacksonian Democrat 1853–1857								J. Campbell 1853–1861
James Buchanan Jacksonian Democrat 1857–1861		Vacant	N. Clifford 1858–1881					

*Justices of Federalist or Whig affiliation or doctrinal tendencies are in italics.

Conclusion

In the period preceding the first critical election, that of 1800, the Federalist judiciary supported doctrinal positions that directly contributed to the intense partisan conflict between Jeffersonian Republicans and Federalists. These doctrinal positions were often perceived by the Jeffersonians as partisan Federalist positions, either supportive of an encroaching national authority (*Chisholm* v. *Georgia*) or of a pro-British foreign policy (*Ware* v. *Hylton*), or destructive of two-party political competition (Federalist judicial attempts at establishing a federal common law jurisdiction). The Federalists, who completely dominated the Supreme Court at the time that Thomas Jefferson took office in 1801, were determined political partisans who not only resisted doctrinal change but, on occasion, sought to embarrass the new administration (as in *Marbury* v. *Madison*). These Federalists consolidated their control of the Court by centralizing decision-making in their new Chief Justice, John Marshall. Whereas during the first decade of the Court the justices had customarily written separate decisions, Chief Justice Marshall established the policy under which the Supreme Court usually decided cases by means of a unified majority opinion. In the context of the political conflicts of the early decades of the 19th century, the majority opinions were generally written by Chief Justice Marshall himself. One of President Thomas Jefferson's appointees, Associate Justice William Johnson of South Carolina, asserted and established the propriety of dissenting and concurring opinions. But the doctrinal influence of the Federalists, especially in areas such as federal supremacy and the sanctity of property rights, remained relatively undiminished, in part because of the longevity and doctrinal solidarity of the Federalist and neo-Federalist Justices and in part because Jeffersonian Republican judicial nominations were sometimes influenced by considerations other than ideological consistency.

The mid–1820s represented the beginning of the second critical election period. With what must have seemed to the Federalists to be terrible monotony, one Republican administration succeeded another. Jefferson served two terms as president, from 1801 to 1809. After two terms in office President Madison was succeeded by James Monroe, who was reelected in 1820 without even a contest. By that time the old Federalist party was extinct. Monroe received 231 electoral votes and John Quincy Adams one. Although Adams was not an opponent, a New Hampshire elector gave him a vote, not because the latter wanted no successor of Washington to share the honor of a unanimous election,[123] but rather "to prepare the public mind" for Adams' election "four years hence."[124] The election of 1824 was held in a transition period in which new party alignments were taking form. The successful candidate, John Quincy Adams, was a nationalist, but his election could not be accurately described as a clearcut vindication of nationalist principles because of the complex nature of his style of presidential leadership and the ascendancy of issues relating to the question of succession in 1828.

REFERENCES

1. Paul Goodman, "The First American Party System," in *The American Party Systems: Stages of Political Development*, ed. W. N. Chambers and W. D. Burnham (New York: Oxford University Press, 1975), pp. 56–89.
2. Dahl, op. cit., pp. 193, 285.
3. John Quincy Adams, *Parties in the United States*, pp. 24–32; Beveridge, *The Life of John Marshall*, vol. 2 (New York: Greenburg, 1941), pp. 514–519, 531, 532.
4. Edward Stanwood, *A History of Presidential Elections* (Boston: James R. Osgood and Company, 1884), p. 40.
5. Ibid., pp. 41–44.
6. Beveridge, *The Life of John Marshall*, vol. 2, p. 547.
7. Charles Warren, *The Supreme Court in United States History*, vol. 1, p. 172.
8. Ibid., pp. 172–178; cf. Beveridge, op. cit., pp. 553–558.
9. Max Farrand, "The Judiciary Act of 1801," *The American Historical Review* 5 (July 1900), pp. 682–685.
10. Ibid., p. 685, notes 7 and 8.

11. Richard E. Ellis, *The Jeffersonian Crisis: Courts and Politics in the Young Republic* (New York: Oxford University Press, 1971), pp. 59–65.
12. *Stuart v. Laird,* 1 Cranch 299 (1803).
13. 2 Cranch 358 (1805).
14. 1 U. S. Stat. 515; 2 Cranch 383.
15. 2 Cranch 395.
16. Ibid., pp. 396–397.
17. Ibid., p. 369, note a.
18. *Annals,* 9th Congress, 2nd session, (December 11, 1806), pp. 131–148; cited in Haines, op. cit., p. 268.
19. Letter to *Aurora,* October 6, 1808; cited in Haines, p. 370
20. Stanwood, op. cit., pp. 49–50.
21. Warren, *History,* vol. 1, pp. 295, 298–299.
22. Ibid., pp. 301–315; Beveridge, op. cit., pp. 274–545.
23. Warren, ibid., pp. 324–341.
24. Noble E. Cunningham, Jr., "The Election of 1800," in *The Coming to Power: Critical Presidential Elections in American History,* ed. Arthur M. Schlesinger, Jr. (New York: Chelsea House, 1971), pp. 64–66.
25. Warren, *History,* vol. 1, pp. 299–301.
26. Warren, *History,* vol. 1, p. 400, note 1.
27. Stanwood, op. cit., pp. 51–56.
28. Warren, *History,* vol. 1, p. 404, note 1.
29. Ibid., pp. 400–419.
30. Ibid., p. 423.
31. 7 Cranch 1, *passim;* see James B. Thayer, *John Marshall* (Boston and New York: Houghton Mifflin, 1901), pp. 55–56.
32. Ibid., pp. 373–374.
33. For example, as early as January 29, 1804, Pickering wrote to Cabot: "I do not believe in the practicality of a long continued Union. A Northern Conferderacy would unite congenial characters . . .;" Henry Adams, ed. *Documents Relating to New England Federalism* (Boston: Little, Brown and Company, 1877), p. 340, *passim;* see also Warren, *History,* vol. 1, pp. 321–324.
34. Warren, ibid., p. 345.
35. 6 Cranch 87 (1810).
36. Beveridge, op. cit., p. 548.
37. Quoted in Beveridge, ibid., p. 569.
38. This description of the Yazoo fraud controversy is drawn from the vivid account of Albert Beveridge, ibid., pp. 546–583.
39. C. Peter Magrath, *Yazoo: Law and Politics in the New Republic* (Providence, R. I.: Brown University Press, 1966), pp. 50–100.
40. Ibid., pp. 583–584.
41. 6 Cranch 124 (1810).
42. Benjamin F. Wright, *The Contract Clause of the Constitution* (Cambridge: Harvard University Press, 1938), p. 16.
43. Ibid., pp. 3–16.
44. Carl Brent Swisher, *American Constitutional Development* (New York: Houghton, Mifflin Company, 1943), pp. 123–124.
45. 6 Cranch 332 (1810).
46. Willoughby, *The Constitutional Law of the United States,* vol. 1 (New York: Baker, Voorhis and Company, 1929), p. 431.
47. 7 Cranch 164 (1812).
48. In *New Jersey v. Wilson,* Marshall did not face the problem created by his decision: whether a state legislature may permanently bargain away its virtually indispensable power to tax by entering into a contract; Wright, op. cit., pp. 26–61.
49. 7 Cranch 603 (1813).
50. Chief Justice Marshall disqualified himself apparently because of his financial interest in the outcome of the case.

51. Story based this part of the decision on the royal grants of Charles II and James II.
52. *Olney* v. *Arnold*, 3 Dallas 308 (1796); *Clerks* v. *Harwood*, 3 Dallas 342 (1797); *Calder* v. *Bull*, 3 Dallas 386 (1798); *Hallett* v. *Jenks*, 3 Cranch 210 (1805); *Sands* v. *Knox*, 3 Cranch 396 (1806); *Mathews* v. *Zane*, 4 Cranch 382 (1808); *Owings* v. *Norwood*, 5 Cranch 344 (1809); *Smith* v. *Maryland*, 6 Cranch 286 (1810); *New Jersey* v. *Wilson*, 7 Cranch 169 (1812); *Palmer* v. *Allen*, 7 Cranch 550 (1813); *Fairfax* v. *Hunter*, 7 Cranch 603 (1813); *Otis* v. *Bacon*, 7 Cranch 589 (1813); *Crowell* v. *McFadden*, 8 Cranch 94 (1814); *Prince* v. *Bartlett*, 8 Cranch 432 (1815); *Otis* v. *Watkins*, 9 Cranch 339 (1815); see Charles Warren, "Legislative and Judicial Attacks on the Supreme Court of the United States—a History of the 25th Section of the Judiciary Act," *American Law Review* 47 (1913): 5–6.
53. Beveridge, *The Life of John Marshall*, vol. 4, p. 147.
54. William E. Dodd, "Chief Justice Marshall and Virginia, 1813–1821," *The American Historical Review* 12 (July 1907): 776–777; and Beveridge, op. cit., vol. 4, pp. 146–147.
55. After reading what must have been an outline of Spencer Roane's reasoning on the constitutional question, Jefferson wrote that he could not see how the federal jurisdictional claims could be upheld; letter to Roane, October 12, 1815; Paul L. Ford (ed.), *Writings of Thomas Jefferson*, vol. 9 (New York: G. P. Putnam & Sons, 1898), p. 531.
56. Beveridge, ibid., pp. 158–159.
57. *Hunter* v. *Martin*, 4 Mumford 8–9 (1814); as quoted in Haines, *The Role of the Supreme Court in American Government and Politics*, 1789–1835, op. cit., p. 343.
58. Haines, ibid.
59. *Martin* v. *Hunter's Lessee*, 1 Wheaton 304 (1816).
60. *Journal of Virginia House of Delegates*, p. 108; cited in Haines, op. cit., p. 430.
61. Haines, op. cit., p. 431.
62. Madison; as quoted by Beveridge, op. cit., p. 180.
63. Beveridge, ibid., pp. 168–208; Hezekiah Niles, *Niles Weekly Register*, XIV–XVI, (1811), *passim*.
64. 4 Wheaton 122 (1819).
65. Edward Samuel Corwin, *John Marshall and the Constitution* (New Haven: Yale University Press, 1919), p. 124.
66. The New York bankruptcy law was held to impair the obligation of contracts made before the passage of the law.
67. 4 Wheaton 209 (1819).
68. Samuel Reznick, "The Depression of 1819–1822, a Social History," *The American Historical Review* 39 (October 1933): 28–29.
69. John Bach McMaster, *A History of the People of the United States*, vol. 6 (New York: D. Appleton and Company, 1904), p. 2.
70. As quoted in Reznick, op. cit., p. 33.
71. As quoted by Haines, op. cit., p. 352, note 61.
72. As quoted by Warren, *History*, vol. 1, p. 502.
73. 4 Wheaton 518 (1819).
74. *Ogden* v. *Saunders*, 12 Wheaton 213 (1827).
75. Wright, *The Contract Clause of the Constitution*, op. cit., p. 39.
76. Beveridge, op. cit., vol. 4, pp. 224–225.
77. Wright, op. cit., pp. 40–41; Beveridge, op. cit., vol. 4, pp. 223–234; Haines, op. cit., pp. 379–382.
78. *Dartmouth College* v. *Woodward*, 65 New Hampshire Reports 473 (1817); as quoted in Wright, ibid.
79. Beveridge, op. cit., vol. 4, p. 255.
80. Ibid., pp. 255–256.
81. Ibid., pp. 259–261.
82. As quoted in Beveridge, op. cit., p. 276.
83. Warren, *History*, vol. 1, pp. 487–488; Beveridge, op. cit., p. 276.
84. Warren, ibid., p. 495.
85. As quoted in Beveridge, op. cit., p. 309.
86. As reproduced in John E. Oster, *The Political and Economic Doctrines of John Marshall* (New York: Neale, 1914), p. 107.
87. Dodd, op. cit., pp. 780–781; Beveridge, op. cit., pp. 331–335.
88. Oster, op. cit., p. 108.

89. Ibid.
90. Beveridge, op. cit., pp. 318–319.
91. Roane also complained that "some of the judges had before been accounted republicans." Beveridge, ibid., pp. 315–318.
92. Dodd, op. cit., p. 781.
93. Beveridge, op. cit., p. 323.
94. As quoted by Haines, op. cit., p. 372.
95. Ibid., pp. 364–367.
96. Beveridge, op. cit., pp. 333–334.
97. Which did not reach the Supreme Court until three years later, in 1824.
98. Beveridge, ibid., p. 335; Haines, op. cit., pp. 444–458.
99. Beveridge, ibid.
100. Dodd, op. cit., p. 785.
101. Ibid., pp. 782–783; Beveridge, op. cit., pp. 358–359.
102. Oster, op. cit., pp. 113–115.
103. Charles Warren, "Legislative and Judicial Attacks on the Supreme Court," *American Law Review* 47 (1913): 19.
104. *Annals*, 17th Congress, 1st session, vol. 1, p. 23; Warren, op. cit., p. 26.
105. The first decision in *Green* v. *Biddle* was handed down in March 1821. The validity of Kentucky's "occupying claimant laws" came under consideration as appeal from a Federal circuit court. They were held unconstitutional.
106. *Niles Weekly Register*, XXVII, 1824–1825; Warren, "Legislative and Judicial Attacks," p. 20.
107. Warren, *History*, vol. 1, p. 623.
108. *Elkinson* v. *DeLiesseline*, Federal Cases No. 4366 (1823); cited in Warren, op. cit., p. 624.
109. Warren, "Legislative and Judicial Attacks," p. 20; Warren reported that the South Carolina courts continued to disregard Justice Johnson's decision for a quarter of a century.
110. Warren, *History*, vol. 1, pp. 633–644.
111. 10 Wheaton 428 (1825); the background material for this section is drawn largely from Warren's excellent chapter, "Kentucky Against the Court," *History*, vol. 1, 633–651.
112. Chief Justice Taney expressly overruled this decision in *The Genesee Chief*, 12 Howard 433 (1851).
113. 10 Wheaton 1 (1825).
114. Ibid., p. 51.
115. Ibid., p. 66.
116. As quoted in Warren, *History*, vol. 1, p. 647.
117. 1 Statutes at Large 189; Wright, *Contract Clause*, p. 47; the Congressional act admitted Kentucky into the Union.
118. Unfortunately, Story did not base his decision on the contract clause specifically but only by inference, stating that the Kentucky land laws violated the "compact" because "by the general principles of law, and from the necessity of the case, land titles can be determined only by the laws" of Virginia.
119. 8 Wheaton 1 (1823).
120. Warren, *History*, vol. 1, pp. 652–667.
121. As quoted by Warren, ibid., p. 642.
122. Ibid., note 1.
123. Stanwood, *A History of Presidential Elections*, p. 70.
124. William Plumer, letter to William Plumer, Jr., in *The Missouri Compromises and Presidential Politics, 1820–1825*, ed. Everett S. Brown (St. Louis: Missouri Historical Society, 1926).

The Jacksonian Era

Its Antecedents and Its
Implementation in Law and Politics

In 1824, when John Quincy Adams became president in spite of losing the election, the stage was set for the nation's second critical election, the election of 1828. Although Adams received fewer popular *and* electoral votes than Andrew Jackson, he was chosen in the House of Representatives with the crucial assistance of Henry Clay. Jackson's popular margin was 152,901 to Adam's 114,023, William Crawford's 46,979, and Henry Clay's 47,217. His electoral college margin was 99 to Adam's 84, Crawford's 41, and Clay's 37. When President Adams chose Clay as his secretary of state, Jackson resigned from the Senate, returned to Tennessee, and opened an attack on the "corrupt bargain" of Adams and Clay. The ensuing tempestuous four years would result in a sweeping victory for Jackson, the permanent elimination of the congressional caucus as a nominating institution, and a significant increase in citizen participation in electoral politics.[1]

The transformation in political elites was accompanied by concomitant changes in social and economic attitudes, which often were reflected in Supreme Court litigation involving commerce, the growth of national military authority, and, most important, commercial and banking power and influence. These developments, in turn, occasionally stimulated serious political attacks on the Court. But the relationship of the Supreme Court to the executive and legislative branches and to the political groups contending for power had changed considerably since 1800. Supreme Court decisions in the decade before 1828 were not closely related to issues important in the second critical election. Nor were its pre–1828 constitutional decisions immediately perceived as contrary to the early Jacksonian executive or legislative positions. But this absence of conflict changed within a few years.

Control of commerce, banking, and militia

The Supreme Court was often involved in political controversy in the pre–1828 era, but its decisions had little to do with the major issues of political control and participation that divided Adams and the Jacksonians. Instead, the controversy dealt with a great many issues crucial to the economy and political control of economic development.

In 1824, for example, the Court exercised its determinative power in federal-state relations in three important cases that stimulated strong political criticism. *Gibbons* v. *Ogden* was the Court's first interpretation of the important commerce clause. In handing down this decision, Chief Justice John Marshall stated a broad constructionist doctrine that not only ran counter to a powerful local interest group, the steamboat monopolists of New York, but also ran counter to the interpretation of the commerce clause given by the Republican administration of outgoing President James Monroe.[2] Only two years before the Steamboat Monopoly decision, President Monroe, in vetoing the Cumberland Road bill, had given the following narrow constructionist interpretation of the commerce clause:

> Commerce between independent powers or communities is universally regulated by duties and imposts. It was so regulated by the States before the adoption of the Constitution, equally in respect to each other and to foreign Powers. The goods and vessels employed in the trade are the only subjects of regulation. It can act on none other. A power, then, to impose such duties and imposts in regard to foreign nations and to prevent any on the trade between the states, was the only power granted.[3]

Monroe's position was directly contradictory to that of most of the delegates to the Philadelphia convention of 1787. In fact, one of the major reasons for calling the convention and creating and adopting a new constitution was commercial and mercantile concern about state trade barriers.

The positions taken by the Supreme Court justices in *Gibbons* were consistent with the views of most of the constitutional framers, rather than Monroe's. The background of *Gibbons* v. *Ogden* was as follows:

For more than a quarter of a century, Robert R. Livingston and Robert Fulton and their heirs and assigns had possessed the exclusive rights to operate steamboats in the waters of the state of New York.[4] When the grant of monopolistic rights had first been made by the New York legislature in 1798, the action met with derision rather than opposition. But after 1807, the success of Fulton's pioneering ventures attracted the attention of commercial leaders in other states. By 1822 the restrictive effect of the New York monopoly legislation had aroused great resentment. New Jersey, Connecticut, and Ohio had passed retaliatory legislation excluding boats "operated by fire or steam" under a New York license. The conflict began to resemble the interstate commercial warfare that had preceded and prompted the Philadelphia convention of 1787.

A case involving the validity of the controversial New York steamboat monopoly finally reached the Supreme Court in 1824.[5] Aaron Ogden of New Jersey had been enjoined by action brought by John R. Livingston from operating an independent steamboat line from Elizabethport, New Jersey, to New York. Ogden submitted and bought a license from the monopoly. However, Thomas Gibbons of Georgia, Ogden's former partner, started an opposition line in 1818 under congressional licensing authority. The New York courts upheld an injunction against Gibbons and the case finally reached the Supreme Court on appeal from New York's "Court for the Trial of Impeachments and Correction of Errors." On March 2, 1824, the decision was handed down.

GIBBONS v. OGDEN
9 Wheaton 1 (1824)

*Chief Justice Marshall delivered the opinion
of the Court, saying in part:*

The appellant contends that this decree is erroneous, because the laws which purport to give the exclusive privilege it sustains are repugnant to the constitution and laws of the United States.

They are said to be repugnant:

1st. To that clause in the constitution which authorizes Congress to regulate commerce.

2d. To that which authorizes Congress to promote the progress of science and useful arts. . . .

As preliminary to the very able discussions of the constitution which we have heard from the bar, and as having some influence on its construction, reference has been made to the political situation of these states, anterior to its formation. It has been said that they were sovereign, were completely independent, and were connected with each other only by a league. This is true. But when these allied sovereigns converted their league into a government, when they converted their congress of ambassadors, deputed to deliberate on their common concerns, and to recommend measures of general utility, into a legislature, empowered to enact laws on the most interesting subjects, the whole character in which the states appear, underwent a change, the extent of which must be determined by a fair consideration of the instrument by which that change was effected.

This instrument contains an enumeration of powers expressly granted by the people to their government. It has been said that these powers ought to be construed strictly. But why ought they to be so construed? Is there one sentence in the constitution which gives countenance to this rule? In the last of the enumerated powers, that which grants, expressly, the means for carrying all others into execution, Congress is authorized "to make all laws which shall be necessary and proper" for the purpose. But this limitation on the means which may be used, is not extended to the powers which are conferred; nor is there one sentence in the constitution, which has been pointed out by the gentlemen of the bar or which we have been able to discern, that prescribes this rule. We do not, therefore, think ourselves justified in adopting it. What do gentlemen mean by a strict construction? If they contend only against that enlarged construction which would extend words beyond their natural and obvious import, we might question the application of the term, but

should not controvert the principle. If they contend for that narrow construction which, in support of some theory not to be found in the constitution, would deny to the government those powers which the words of the grant, as usually understood, import, and which are consistent with the general views and objects of the instrument; for the narrow construction, which would cripple the government and render it unequal to the objects for which it is declared to be instituted, and to which the powers given, as fairly understood, render it competent; then we cannot perceive the propriety of this strict construction, nor adopt it as the rule by which the constitution is to be expounded. As men, whose intentions require no concealment, generally employ the words which most directly and aptly express the ideas they intend to convey, the enlightened patriots who formed our constitution, and the people who adopted it, must be understood to have employed words in their natural sense, and to have intended what they have said. If, from the imperfection of human language, there should be serious doubts respecting the extent of any given power, it is a well-settled rule that the objects for which it was given, especially when those objects are expressed in the instrument itself, should have great influence in the construction. We know of no reason for excluding this rule from the present case. The grant does not convey power which might be beneficial to the grantor, if retained by himself, or which can enure solely to the benefit of the grantee; but is an investment of power for the general advantage, in the hands of agents selected for that purpose; which power can never be exercised by the people themselves, but must be placed in the hands of agents or lie dormant. We know of no rule for construing the extent of such powers, other than is given by the language of the instrument which confers them, taken in connection with the purposes for which they were conferred.

The words are: "Congress shall have power to regulate commerce with foreign nations, and among the several states, and with the Indian tribes."

The subject to be regulated is commerce; and our constitution being, as was aptly said at the bar, one of enumeration, and not of definition, to ascertain the extent of the power it becomes necessary to settle the meaning of the word. Counsel for the appellee would limit it to traffic, to buying and selling, or the interchange of commodities, and do not admit that it comprehends navigation. This would restrict a general term, applicable to many objects, to one of its significations. Commerce, undoubtedly, is traffic, but it is something more; it is intercourse. It describes the commercial intercourse between nations, and parts of nations, in all its branches, and regulated by prescribing rules for carrying on that intercourse. The mind can scarcely conceive a system for regulating commerce between nations, which shall exclude all laws concerning navigation, which shall be silent on the admission of the vessels of the one nation into the ports of the other, and be confined to prescribing rules for the conduct of individuals, in the actual employment of buying and selling, or of barter.

If commerce does not include navigation, the government of the Union has no direct power over that subject, and can make no law prescribing what shall constitute American vessels, or requiring that they shall be navigated by American seamen. Yet this power has been exercised from the commencement of the government, has been exercised with the consent of all, and has been understood by all to be a commercial regulation. All America understands, and has uniformly understood, the word "commerce" to comprehend navigation. It was so understood, and must have been so understood, when the constitution was framed. The power over commerce, including navigation, was one of the primary objects for which the people of America adopted their government, and must have been contemplated in forming it. The convention must have used the word in that sense, because all have understood it in that sense, and the attempt to restrict it comes too late. . . .

The word used in the constitution, then, comprehends, and has been always understood to comprehend, navigation within its meaning; and a power to regulate navigation is as expressly granted as if that term had been added to the word "commerce."

To what commerce does this power extend? The constitution informs us, to commerce "with foreign nations, and among the several states, and with the Indian tribes."

It has, we believe, been universally admitted that these words comprehend every species of commercial intercourse between the United States and foreign nations. No sort of trade can be carried on between this country and any other to which this power does not extend. It has been truly said that commerce, as the word is used in the constitution, is a unit, every part of which is indicated by the term.

If this be the admitted meaning of the word, in its application to foreign nations, it must carry the same meaning throughout the sentence, and remain a unit, unless there be some plain intelligible cause which alters it.

The subject to which the power is next applied, is to commerce "among the several states." The word "among" means intermingled with. A thing which is among others is intermingled with them. Commerce among the states cannot stop at the external boundary line of each state, but may be introduced into the interior.

It is not intended to say that these words comprehend that commerce which is completely internal, which is carried on between man and man in a state, or between different parts of the same state, and which does not extend to or affect other states. Such a power would be inconvenient, and is certainly unnecessary.

Comprehensive as the word "among" is, it may very properly be restricted to the commerce which concerns more States than one. The phrase is not one which would probably have been selected to indicate the completely interior traffic of a State, because it is not an apt phrase for that purpose; and the enumeration of the particular classes of commerce to which the power was to be extended, would not have been made, had the intention been to extend the power to every description. The enumeration presupposes something not enumerated; and that something, if we regard the language, or the subject of the sentence, must be the exclusively internal commerce of a State. The genius and character of the whole government seem to be, that its action is to be applied to all the external concerns of the nation, and to those internal concerns which affect the States generally; but not to those which are completely within a particular State, which do not affect other States, and with which it is not necessary to interfere, for the purpose of executing some of the general powers of the government. The completely internal commerce of a State, then, may be considered as reserved for the State itself.

But, in regulating commerce with foreign nations, the power of Congress does not stop at the jurisdictional lines of the several states. It would be a very useless power if it could not pass those lines. The commerce of the United States with foreign nations, is that of the whole United States. Every district has a right to participate in it. The deep streams which penetrate our country in every direction, pass through the interior of almost every state in the Union, and furnish the means of exercising this right. If Congress has the power to regulate it, that power must be exercised whenever the subject exists. If it exists within the states, if a foreign voyage may commence or terminate at a port within a state, then the power of Congress may be exercised within a state.

This principle is, if possible, still more clear when applied to commerce "among the several states." They either join each other, in which case they are separated by a mathematical line, or they are remote from each other, in which case other states lie between them. What is commerce "among" them; and how is it to be conducted? Can a trading expedition between two adjoining states commence and terminate outside of each? And if the trading intercourse be between two states remote from each other, must it not commence in one, terminate in the other, and probably pass through a third? Commerce among the states must, of necessity, be commerce with the states. In the regulation of trade with the Indian tribes, the action of the law, especially when the constitution was made, was chiefly within a state. The power of Congress, then, whatever it may be, must be exercised within the territorial jurisdiction of the several states. . . .

We are now arrived at the inquiry, What is this power?

It is the power to regulate; that is, to prescribe the rule by which commerce is to be governed. This power, like all others vested in Congress, is complete in itself, may be exercised to its utmost extent, and acknowledges no limitations other than are prescribed in the constitution. These are expressed in plain terms, and do not affect the questions which arise in this case, or which have been discussed at the bar. . . .

The power of Congress, then, comprehends navigation within the limits of every state in the Union, so far as that navigation may be, in any manner, connected with "commerce with foreign nations, or among the several states, or with the Indian tribes." It may, of consequence, pass the jurisdictional line of New York, and act upon the very waters to which the prohibition now under consideration applies.

But it has been urged with great earnestness, that although the power of Congress to regulate commerce with foreign nations, and among the several states, be co-extensive with the subject itself, and have no other limits than are prescribed in the constitution, yet the states may severally exercise the same power within their respective jurisdictions. In support of this argument, it is said that they possessed it as an inseparable attribute of sovereignty before the formation of the constitution, and still retain it, except so far as they have surrendered it by that instrument; that this principle results from the nature of the government, and is secured by the tenth amendment; that an affirmative grant of power is not exclusive, unless in its own nature it be such that the continued exercise of it by the former possessor is inconsistent with the grant, and that this is not of that description.

The appellant, conceding these postulates, except the last, contends that full power to regulate a particular subject implies the whole power, and leaves no residuum; that a grant of the whole is incompatible

with the existence of a right in another to any part of it. . . .

In discussing the question, whether this power is still in the states, in the case under consideration, we may dismiss from it the inquiry, whether it is surrendered by the mere grant to Congress, or is retained until Congress shall exercise the power. We may dismiss that inquiry, because it has been exercised, and the regulations which Congress deemed it proper to make, are now in full operation. The sole question is, can a state regulate commerce with foreign nations and among the states, while Congress is regulating it? . . .

The act passed in 1803, prohibiting the importation of slaves into any state which shall itself prohibit their importation, implies, it is said, an admission that the states possessed the power to exclude or admit them; from which it is inferred that they possess the same power with respect to other articles.

If this inference were correct; if this power was exercised, not under any particular clause in the constitution, but in virtue of a general right over the subject of commerce, to exist as long as the constitution itself, it might now be exercised. Any state might now import African slaves into its own territory. But it is obvious that the power of the states over this subject, previous to the year 1808, constitutes an exception to the power of Congress to regulate commerce, and the exception is expressed in such words as to manifest clearly the intention to continue the pre-existing right of the states to admit or exclude for a limited period. The words are: "The migration or importation of such persons as any of the states, now existing, shall think proper to admit, shall not be prohibited by the Congress prior to the year 1808." The whole object of the exception is to preserve the power to those states which might be disposed to exercise it; and its language seems to the court to convey this idea unequivocally. The possession of this particular power, then, during the time limited in the constitution, cannot be admitted to prove the possession of any other similar power.

It has been said that the act of August 7th, 1789, acknowledges a concurrent power in the states to regulate the conduct of pilots, and hence is inferred an admission of their concurrent right with Congress to regulate commerce with foreign nations and amongst the states. But this inference is not, we think, justified by the fact.

Although Congress cannot enable a state to legislate, Congress may adopt the provisions of a state on any subject. When the government of the Union was brought into existence, it found a system for the regulation of its pilots in full force in every state. The act which has been mentioned adopts this system, and gives it the same validity as if its provisions had been specially made by Congress. But the act, it may be said, is prospective also, and the adoption of laws to be made in future presupposes the right in the maker to legislate on the subject.

The act unquestionably manifests an intention to leave this subject entirely to the states, until Congress should think proper to interpose; but the very enactment of such a law indicates an opinion that it was necessary; that the existing system would not be applicable to the new state of things, unless expressly applied to it by Congress. . . .

These acts were cited at the bar for the purpose of showing an opinion in Congress that the states possess, concurrently with the legislature of the Union, the power to regulate commerce with foreign nations and among the states. Upon reviewing them, we think they do not establish the proposition they were intended to prove. They show the opinion that the states retain powers enabling them to pass the laws to which allusion has been made, not that those laws proceed from the particular power which has been delegated to Congress.

It has been contended by the counsel for the appellant, that, as the word "to regulate" implies in its nature full power over the thing to be regulated, it excludes, necessarily, the action of all others that would perform the same operation on the same thing. That regulation is designed for the entire result, applying to those parts which remain as they were, as well as to those which are altered. It produces a uniform whole, which is as much disturbed and deranged by changing what the regulating power designs to leave untouched, as that on which it has operated.

There is great force in this argument, and the court is not satisfied that it has been refuted.

Since, however, in exercising the power of regulating their own purely internal affairs, whether of trading or police, the states may sometimes enact laws, the validity of which depends on their interfering with, and being contrary to, an act of Congress passed in pursuance of the constitution, the court will enter upon the inquiry, whether the laws of New York, as expounded by the highest tribunal of the state, have, in their application to this case, come into collison with an act of Congress, and deprived a citizen of a right to which that act entitles him. Should this collision exist, it will be immaterial whether those laws were passed in virtue of a concurrent power "to regulate commerce with foreign nations and among the several states," or in virtue of a power to regulate their domestic trade and police. In one case and the other, the acts of New

York must yield to the law of Congress; and the decision sustaining the privilege they confer, against a right given by a law of the Union, must be erroneous. . . .

The questions, then, whether the conveyance of passengers be a part of the coasting trade, and whether a vessel can be protected in that occupation by a coasting license, are not, and cannot be, raised in this case. The real and sole question seems to be, whether a steam machine, in actual use, deprives a vessel of the privileges conferred by a license.

In considering this question, the first idea which presents itself, is that the laws of Congress for the regulation of commerce, do not look to the principle by which vessels are moved. That subject is left entirely to individual discretion; and, in that vast and complex system of legislative enactment concerning it, which embraces everything that the legislature thought it necessary to notice, there is not, we believe, one word respecting the peculiar principle by which vessels are propelled through the water, except what may be found in a single act, granting a particular privilege to steamboats. With this exception, every act, either prescribing duties, or granting privileges, applies to every vessel, whether navigated by the instrumentality of wind or fire, of sails or machinery. The whole weight of proof, then, is thrown upon him who would introduce a distinction to which the words of the law give no countenance.

If a real difference could be admitted to exist between vessels carrying passengers and others, it has already been observed that there is no fact in this case which can bring up that question. And, if the occupation of steamboats be a matter of such general notoriety that the court may be presumed to know it, although not specially informed by the record, then we deny that the transportation of passengers is their exclusive occupation. It is a matter of general history, that, on our western waters, their principal employment is the transportation of merchandise; and all know, that in the waters of the Atlantic they are frequently so employed.

But all inquiry into this subject seems to the court to be put completely at rest by the act already mentioned, entitled, "An act for the enrolling and licensing of steamboats."

This act authorizes a steamboat employed, or intended to be employed, only in a river or bay of the United States, owned wholly or in part by an alien, resident within the United States, to be enrolled and licensed as if the same belonged to a citizen of the United States.

This act demonstrates the opinion of Congress, that steamboats may be enrolled and licensed, in common with vessels using sails. They are, of course, entitled to the same privileges, and can no more be restrained from navigating waters, and entering ports which are free to such vessels, than if they were wafted on their voyage by the winds, instead of being propelled by the agency of fire. The one element may be as legitimately used as the other, for every commercial purpose authorized by the laws of the Union; and the act of a state inhibiting the use of either to any vessel having a license under the act of Congress, comes, we think, in direct collision with that act.

As this decides the cause, it is unnecessary to enter in an examination of that part of the constitution which empowers Congress to promote the progress of science and the useful arts. . . .

The conclusion to which we have come depends on a chain of principles which it was necessary to preserve unbroken; and, although some of them were thought nearly self-evident, the magnitude of the question, the weight of character belonging to those from whose judgment we dissent, and the argument at the bar, demanded that we should assume nothing.

Powerful and ingenious minds, taking as postulates that the powers expressly granted to the government of the Union, are to be contracted by construction into the narrowest possible compass, and that the original powers of the States are retained, if any possible construction will retain them, may, by a course of well-digested but refined and metaphysical reasoning founded on these premises, explain away the constitution of our country, and leave it a magnificent structure, indeed, to look at, but totally unfit for use. They may so entangle and perplex the understanding, as to obscure principles which were before thought quite

plain, and induce doubts where, if the mind were to pursue its own course, none would be perceived. In such a case, it is peculiarly necessary to recur to safe and fundamental principles to sustain those principles, and, when sustained, to make them the tests of the arguments to be examined.

Republican Justice Johnson wrote a concurring opinion in which he unequivocally maintained that Congress' power of commerce was exclusive:

The law of nations, regarding man as a social animal, pronounces all commerce legitimate in a state of peace, until prohibited by positive laws. The power of a sovereign state over commerce, therefore, amounts to nothing more than a power to limit and restrain it at pleasure. And since the power to prescribe the limits to its freedom, necessarily implies the power to determine what shall remain unrestrained, it follows, that the power must be exclusive; it can reside but in one potentate; and hence, the grant of this power carries with it the whole subject, leaving nothing for the state to act upon.

Commerce means an exchange of goods; but in the advancement of society, labor, transportation, intelligence, care, and various mediums of exchange, become commodities, and enter into commerce; the subject, the vehicle, the agent, and their various operations, become the objects of commercial regulation. Shipbuilding, the carrying trade, and propagation of seamen, are such vital agents of commercial prosperity, that the nation which could not legislate over these subjects, would not possess power to regulate commerce.

In the same year that it handed down the Gibbons decision, the Supreme Court decided *Osborn* v. *The Bank of the United States.*[6] This case arose primarily from economic conditions, but the issues involved in it were of constitutional significance. In the 1811–1816 period, the number of banks chartered by the Ohio legislature increased from four to 21. Even before Congress chartered the second United States bank, "wild-cat" banks were flooding the state of Ohio with worthless paper money. Ten weeks before the establishment of the national bank, Ohio's legislature passed an act that imposed a fine of $1,000 on any agent of a bank of issue chartered by the laws of another state. The act also provided that the use of the courts and processes of justice be forbidden to such institutions. Somewhat earlier, in 1815, the Ohio legislature had also levied a tax of 4 percent on the dividends of any bank in the state.[7]

In March 1817, a branch office of the Second Bank of the United States was established in Cincinnati, and in October another branch was set up in Chillicothe. In 1818 the Ohio legislature voted to tax these branches. A House report on the measure held that "these branches must very seriously affect the operations of the state banks" and that "the capital introduced into the country through these branches, is directly calculated to wither our agriculture and cramp our manufactures."[8] Proceeding cautiously, the Ohio legislature asked for reports on the assets of the branches, but the branch bank officials refused to send the desired information. After the branches of the national bank had forced the suspension of many Ohio banks by demanding specie payments and calling for immediate payments of debts, Ohio's legislature retaliated by levying an annual tax of $50,000 on each branch office of the national bank. The state legislators claimed that the tax was constitutionally valid because the congressional act incorporating the Second Bank of the United States did not specifically exempt it from state taxation.

Although *McCulloch* v. *Maryland* had been decided in March 1819, Osborn, the Ohio state auditor, felt obliged to enforce the taxing law. In September 1819, Harper, Osborn's agent, went to the branch of the national bank at Chillicothe, and upon the refusal of the cashier to pay the state tax, jumped over the counter "and with force and violence . . . did take from the said office money and notes to the amount of upwards of one hundred and twenty thousand dollars."[9] A few days later, $20,000 was returned, $98,000 ws deposited in a state bank in the name of Ohio State Treasurer Curry, and $2,000 was retained by Harper as his fee. Later, Curry delivered the $98,000 to his successor, Sullivan. The day after Harper seized the funds, a federal circuit court had awarded the branch bank an injunction to prevent Osborn from enforcing the state tax law. After news of the seizure was received, the original bill in circuit court was amended, decreeing that Osborn and/or Harper, Curry, and Sullivan return the money to the Chillicothe branch. The circuit court also decreed that "the defendants . . . be perpetually enjoined" from collecting any tax levied under the Ohio statute of 1818.[10] Ohio appealed.

By December 1820, the Ohio legislature offered to compromise; if the national bank discontinued the suits and withdrew from Ohio, the tax money would be refunded. An act "to withdraw from the Bank of the United States the protection and aid of the laws of this state" was also passed. The latter act was not repealed until January 1826, but was never actually enforced.[11]

Chief Justice John Marshall handed down the Osborn decision on March 19, 1824. Counsel for Ohio challenged the Court's assumption of jurisdiction on several grounds. First, they contended that Congress could not empower the bank to sue in federal courts. In answer, Marshall announced the following broad interpretation of Congress' power to determine the jurisdiction of inferior federal courts:

This clause Article III enables the judicial department to receive jurisdiction to the full extent of the constitution, laws and treaties of the United States. . . . The Constitution establishes the Supreme Court, and defines its jurisdiction. It enumerates cases in which its jurisdiction is original and exclusive, and then defines that which is appellate, but does not insinuate, that in any such case, the power can not be exercised, in its original form, by courts of original jurisdiction. . . . We perceive . . . no ground on which the proposition can be maintained, that congress is incapable of giving the circuit court original jurisdiction, in any case to which the appellate jurisdiction extends.

The fact that the case involved several questions that were not connected with the construction of a federal law was held, by Marshall, to be no bar to the assumption of jurisdiction by the federal judiciary.

Counsel for Ohio also contended that the process of the federal circuit court, though not directed against the state by name, acted directly upon it by restraining its officers, thus violating the Eleventh Amendment. This argument Marshall also rejected, stating that if this objection to the exercise of federal judicial power was upheld,

> Every member of the Union is capable, at its will, of attacking the nation, of arresting its progress at every step, of acting vigorously and effectually in the execution of its designs, while the nation stands naked, stripped of its defensive armour, and laws, otherwise than by proceedings which are to take place after the mischief is perpetrated, and which must often be ineffectual, from the inability of the agents to make compensation. . . .
>   Consequently, the Eleventh Amendment . . . is, of necessity, limited to those suits in which a state is a party on the record.[12]

After dealing with the jurisdictional contentions of Ohio's counsel, Marshall reaffirmed the decision of the federal circuit court. The state law taxing the national bank was held unconstitutional under the McCulloch doctrine.

By the time the Osborn decision was announced, the depression of 1819 had to a great extent disappeared. Prices were rising, and public attention in Ohio was centered around the problems of education and canal and road-building. After the Supreme Court decision, no further efforts were made to contest the national bank in Ohio.[13]

The 1824 term brought a third and final clash between the Supreme Court and a state. Although the United States bank did not maintain a branch in Georgia, the banks of that state had for a number of years objected to the demands of the national bank for specie payments. The Georgia legislature passed laws in 1819 and 1821 forbidding the national bank's representatives' resort to Georgia's courts and prohibiting redemption in specie of state bank notes held by the United States bank. Acting under the state statutes, the largest state bank refused to cash in specie any of its notes presented by the national bank. Suit was brought in federal circuit court against the Planter's Bank of Georgia. Two important questions were raised by Georgia counsel which, if answered adversely to the national bank, would have effectively curtailed its activities in Georgia.[14]

In *Bank of the United States* v. *Planter's Bank of Georgia*,[15] Chief Justice Marshall upheld the national bank on both questions. Georgia counsel had argued that since the state had incorporated the Planter's Bank, it was a party to the suit. Such a suit was one directed against a state in violation of the Eleventh Amendment. Marshall maintained, however, that "when a government becomes a partner in any trading company, it divests itself, so far as concerns the transactions of that company, of its sovereign character." Thus, "a suit against the Planter's Bank of Georgia, is no more a suit against the state of Georgia, than against any other individual corporator."

To the contention that in the absence of diverse citizenship, the national bank could not sue in a federal court, Marshall answered that the bank was granted power to bring such suits in federal courts by its charter. "If the bank could not sue a person who was a citizen of the same state with any one of its members, in the Federal circuit court, this disability would defeat the power."

During the 1816–1825 period the Supreme Court successfully asserted federal judicial power in 18 cases of constitutional significance that involved federal-state relations. The Supreme Court's most controversial actions were the two assertions of final determinative authority in federal-state relations under Section 25 of the Judiciary Act of 1789, the judicial establishment of the doctrine of implied powers, and the statement of the broad constructionist interpretation of the commerce clause. During this decade the Court exercised its authority as final arbiter in the federal system in the face of opposition from Virginia,[16] New York,[17] Louisiana,[18] Maryland,[19] New Hampshire,[20] Pennsylvania,[21] Kentucky,[22] Vermont,[23] Ohio,[24] and Georgia.[25]

Between 1824 and 1826, the national Congress included a number of vocal opponents of the Supreme Court, but the efforts of men like Senators Johnson and Talbot of Kentucky and Representatives Charles A. Wickliffe of Virginia and John Forsyth of Georgia to weaken the Court were unavailing. In February 1825, the Kentucky senators criticized severely the McCulloch and Osborn decisions, but were answered by Senator Phillip P. Barbour of Virginia. In December of the same year, Wickliffe's resolution to repeal the important 25th section of the Judiciary Act of 1789 was not adopted.[26] During the debates concerning judiciary reform in 1826, several proposals were made in the national Congress to require the concurrence of a majority of all the justices in decisions invalidating state laws. These proposals were defeated.[27]

By 1827, only Chief Justice John Marshall and Justice Bushrod Washington remained of the old Federalist Court of 1800. Already some of the Republican appointees of Jefferson and Madison had died. In 1826 Justice Todd died and was replaced, as he had requested, by Robert Trimble of Kentucky.[28]

The 1826 term produced no significant cases involving judicial assertions of national supremacy, but the succeeding term brought two such cases. The first, *Martin* v. *Mott*,[29] settled decisively a question that had troubled the national executive for a number of years. During the War of 1812, General Dearborn, acting under the authority of the president of the United States, had attempted to requisition the militia of the New England states for coastal defense. Governor Strong of Massachusetts had refused to obey his order. The Massachusetts governor based his refusal on an advisory opinion of the Supreme Judicial Court of Massachusetts. The state judges had held that although the militia may be employed in the service of the United States to execute the laws of the Union, to suppress insurrections, and to repel invasions, the power to determine whether any of these exigencies existed was vested not in the president, but in the governors of the states.[30]

This constitutional issue did not reach the Supreme Court until 1827. *Martin* v. *Mott* arose from the failure of Jacob E. Mott, a former New York militiaman who had been court-martialed for failing to rendezvous with his federal commander during the war of 1812, to pay a fine imposed by federal court-martial. Determination of the case involved full consideration of the powers of Congress and the president over state militia. On February 2, 1827, Justice Story repudiated the

Massachusetts doctrine of state discretion in determining the existence of military exigencies. His decision was based on the constitutional grants to Congress of power "to provide for calling forth the militia, to execute the laws of the Union, suppress insurrections, and repel invasions" and "to provide for organizing, arming, and disciplining the militia, and for governing such part of them as may be employed in the service of the United States."[31] Story also relied on an act of Congress of 1795 that provided "that whenever the United States shall be invaded, or be in imminent danger of invasion from any foreign nation or Indian tribe, it shall be lawful for the president of the United States to call forth such number of the militia of the state or states most convenient to the place of danger or scene of action, as he may judge necessary to repel such invasion."[32]

Story's opinion clarified and defined the nature of the national government's power over the militia of the states. Of the congressional act of 1795, he wrote:

> It has not been denied here, that the act of 1795 is within the constitutional authority of Congress, or that Congress may not lawfully provide for cases of imminent danger of invasion, as well as for cases where an invasion has actually taken place. In our opinion there is no room for doubt on this point, even if it had been relied on, for the power to provide for repelling invasions includes the power to provide against the attempt and danger of invasion, as the necessary and proper means to effectuate the object.[33]

Story conceded that the power granted to the president was limited to cases of actual invasion or imminent danger of invasion. He then asked, "Is the president the sole and exclusive judge whether the exigency has arisen, or is it to be considered as an open question, upon which every officer to whom the orders of the president are addressed, may decide for himself . . . ?" Answering, he wrote:

> We are all of opinion, that the authority to decide whether the exigency has arisen, belongs exclusively to the president, and that his decision is conclusive upon all other persons. We think this construction necessarily results from the nature of the power itself, and from the manifest object contemplated by the act of congress. The power itself is to be exercised upon sudden emergencies, upon great occasions of state, and under circumstances which may be vital to the existence of the Union. A prompt and unhesitating obedience to orders is indispensible to the complete attainment of the object. The service is a military service, and the command, of a military nature; and in such cases, every delay, and every obstacle to an efficient and immediate compliance, necessarily tend to jeopardize the public interests.[34]

The president's power to determine the existence of an exigency necessitating federal control of state militia was held to be complete, exclusive, and not subject to appeal or review by subordinate officers. The Court then reversed the judgment of the New York Supreme Court, which had upheld Mott's claim that the president did not have the power to federalize state militia.

The year 1827 also marked the turning point in terms of contract clause decisions. Before the important decision in *Ogden* v. *Saunders*,[35] the Supreme Court had sustained only one state legislative act[36] that had been challenged as impairing the obligation of a contract. In the nine contract clause cases decided by the Marshall Court subsequent to 1827, the Court upheld every state act under consideration.[37]

The Sturgis case had involved a contract made before the enactment of a New York bankruptcy law. In *Ogden* v. *Saunders* the Court ruled, for the first time, on the validity of a New York insolvency law that had been enacted before the making of the contract it was alleged to violate.

For the first and only time in his years on the bench, Chief Justice Marshall found himself voting with the minority on a constitutional question. The majority, composed of Justices Washington, Johnson, Thompson, and Trimble, wrote separate opinions, but all agreed that a statute in effect at the time a contract is made is "a part of the contract" and thus cannot impair its obligation. Justice Washington's decision, which embodied most issues agreed upon by the majority, and Chief Justice Marshall's dissent are reproduced below.

OGDEN v. SAUNDERS
12 Wheaton 213 (1827)

*Justice Washington delivered
the opinion of the Court:*

The first and most important point to be decided in this cause, turns essentially upon the question, whether the obligation of a contract is impaired by a State bankrupt or insolvent law, which discharges the person and the future acquisitions of the debtor from his liability under a contract entered into in that State after the passage of the act. . . .

What is it . . . which constitutes the obligation of a contract? The answer is given by the chief justice, in the case of Sturges *v.* Crowninshield, to which I readily assent now, as I did then; it is the law which binds the parties to perform their agreement. The law, then, which has this binding obligation, must govern and control the contract in every shape in which it is intended to bear upon it, whether it affects its validity, construction, or discharge. . . .

The universal law of all civilized nations . . . is simply that all men are bound to perform their contracts. The injunction is as absolute as the contracts to which it applies. It admits of no qualification and no restraint, either as to its validity, construction, or discharge, further than may be necessary to develop the intention of the parties to the contract. And if it be true that this is exclusively the law to which the constitution refers us, it is very apparent that the sphere of state legislation upon subjects connected with the contracts of individuals, would be abridged beyond what it can for a moment be believed the sovereign States of this Union would have consented to; for it will be found, upon examination, that there are few laws which concern the general police of a State, or the government of its citizens, in their intercourse with each other or with strangers, which may not in some way or other affect the contracts which they have entered into, or may thereafter form. For what are laws of evidence, or which concern remedies—frauds and perjuries—laws of registration, and those which affect landlord and tenant, sales at auction, acts of limitation, and those which limit the fees of professional men, and the charges of tavern keepers, and a multitude of others which crowd the codes of every State, but laws which may affect the validity, construction, or duration, or discharge of contracts? Whilst I admit, then, that this common law of nations, which has been mentioned, may form in part the obligation of a contract, I must unhesitatingly insist that this law is to be taken in strict subordination to the municipal laws of the land where the contract is made, or is to be executed. The former can be satisfied by nothing short of performance; the latter may affect and control the validity, construction, evidence, remedy, performance, and discharge of the contract. The former is the common law of all civilized nations, and of each of them; the latter is the peculiar law of each, and is paramount to the former whenever they come in collision with each other.

It is, then, the municipal law of the State, whether that be written or unwritten, which is emphatically the law of the contract made within the State, and must govern it throughout, wherever its performance is sought to be enforced.

It forms, in my humble opinion, a part of the contract, and travels with it wherever the parties to it may be found. It is so regarded by all the civilized nations of the world, and is enforced by the tribunals of those nations according to its own forms, unless the parties to it have otherwise agreed, as where the contract is to be executed in, or refers to the laws of, some other country than that in which it is formed, or where it is of an immoral character, or contravenes the policy of the nation to whose tribunals the appeal is made; in which latter cases, the remedy which the comity of nations affords for enforcing the obligation of contracts wherever formed, is denied. Free from these objections, this law, which accompanies the contract as forming a part of it, is regarded and enforced everywhere, whether it affect the validity, construction, or discharge of the contract. It is upon this principle of universal law, that the discharge of the contract, or of one of the parties to it, by the bankrupt laws of the country where it was made, operates as a discharge everywhere. . . .

It is . . . most apparent that, which ever way we turn, whether to laws affecting the validity, construction, or discharges of contracts, or the evidence or remedy to be employed in enforcing them, we are met by this overruling and admitted distinction, between those which operate retrospectively, and those which operate prospectively. In all of them the law is pronounced to be void in the first class of cases, and not so in the second. . . .

To the decision of this court, made in the case of Sturges *v.* Crowninshield, and to the reasoning of the learned judge who delivered that opinion, I entirely submit; although I did not then, nor can I now bring my mind to concur in that part of it which admits the constitutional power of the state legislatures to pass bankrupt laws, by which I understand those laws which discharge the person and the future acquisitions of the bankrupt from his debts. I have always thought that the power to pass such a law was exclusively vested by the constitution in the legislature of the United States. But it becomes me to believe that this opinion was and is incorrect, since it stands condemned by the decision of a majority of this court, solemnly pronounced.

After making this acknowledgment, I refer again to the above decision with some degree of confidence in support of the opinion, to which I am now inclined to come, that a bankrupt law which operates prospectively, or in so far as it does so operate, does not violate the constitution of the United States. It is there stated "that, until the power to pass uniform laws on the subject of bankruptcies be exercised by congress, the States are not forbidden to pass a bankrupt law, provided it contain no principle which violates the 10th section of the 1st article of the constitution of the United States." The question in that case was, whether the law of New York, passed on the 3d of April, 1811, which liberates not only the person of the debtor, but discharges him from all liability for any debt contracted previous as well as subsequent to his discharge, on his surrendering his property for the use of his creditors, was a valid law under the constitution, in its application to a debt contracted prior to its passage. The court

decided that it was not, upon the single ground that it impaired the obligation of that contract. And if it be true that the States cannot pass a similar law to operate upon contracts subsequently entered into, it follows inevitably, either that they cannot pass such laws at all, contrary to the express declaration of the court, as before quoted, or that such laws do not impair the obligation of contracts subsequently entered into; in fine, it is a self-evident proposition that every contract that can be formed, must either precede or follow any law by which it may be affected. . . .

There is nothing unjust or tyrannical in punishing offences prohibited by law, and committed in violation of that law. Nor can it be unjust or oppressive, to declare by law that contracts subsequently entered into, may be discharged in a way different from that which the parties have provided, but which they know, or may know, are liable, under certain circumstances, to be discharged in a manner contrary to the provisions of their contract.

Thinking, as I have always done, that the power to pass bankrupt laws was intended by the authors of the constitution to be exclusive in congress, or, at least, that they expected the power vested in that body would be exercised, so as effectually to prevent its exercise by the States, it is the more probable that, in reference to all other interferences of the state legislatures upon the subject of contracts, retrospective laws were alone in the contemplation of the convention. . . .

But why, it has been asked, forbid the States to pass laws making any thing but gold and silver coin a tender in payment of debts contracted subsequent as well as prior to the law which authorizes it; and yet confine the prohibition to pass laws impairing the obligation of contracts to past contracts, or, in other words, to future bankrupt laws, when the consequence resulting from each is the same, the latter being considered by the counsel as being, in truth, nothing less than tender laws in disguise. . . .

[A]n answer . . . satisfactory to my mind, is this: tender laws . . . are always unjust; and, where there is an existing bankrupt law at the time the contract is made, they can seldom be useful to the honest debtor. They violate the agreement of the parties to it, without the semblance of an apology for the measure, since they operate to discharge the debtor from his undertaking, upon terms variant from those by which he bound himself, to the injury of the creditor, and unsupported, in many cases, by the plea of necessity. They extend relief to the opulent debtor, who does not stand in need of it; as well as to the one who is, by misfortunes, often unavoidable, reduced to poverty, and disabled from complying with his engagements. In relation to subsequent contracts, they are unjust when extended to the former class of debtors, and useless to the second, since they may be relieved by conforming to the requisitions of the state bankrupt law, where there is one. Being discharged by this law from all his antecedent debts, and having his future acquisitions secured to him, an opportunity is afforded him to become once more a useful member of society. . . .

Marshall wrote a dissenting opinion,
which was supported by Justices Story and Duvall:

That there is an essential difference in principle between laws which act on past and those which act on future contracts; that those of the first description can seldom be justified, while those of the last are proper subjects of ordinary legislative discretion, must be admitted. A constitutional restriction, therefore, on the power to pass laws of the one class, may very well consist with entire legislative freedom respecting those of the other. Yet, when we consider the nature of our Union, that it is intended to make us, in a great measure, one people, as to commercial objects; that, so far as respects the intercommunication of individuals, the lines of separation between States are, in many respects, obliterated; it would not be matter of surprise if, on the delicate subject of contracts once formed, the interference of state legislation should be greatly abridged or entirely forbidden. . . .

The first paragraph of the tenth section of the first article, which comprehends the provision under consideration, contains an enumeration of those cases in which the action of the state legislature is entirely prohibited. . . .

In all . . . cases, whether the thing prohibited be the exercise of mere political power, or legislative action on individuals, the prohibition is complete and total. There is no exception from it. Legislation of every description is comprehended within it. A State is as entirely forbidden to pass laws impairing the obligation of contracts, as to make treaties, or coin money. The question recurs, what is a law impairing the obligation of contracts?

In solving this question, all the acumen which controversy can give to the human mind, has been employed in scanning the whole sentence, and every word of it. Arguments have been drawn from the context, and from the particular terms in which the prohibition is expressed, for the purpose, on the one part, of showing its application to all laws which act upon contracts, whether prospectively or retrospectively; and, on the other, of limiting it to laws which act on contracts previously formed.

The first impression which the words make on the mind, would probably be that the prohibition was intended to be general. A contract is commonly understood to be the agreement of the parties; and, if it be not illegal, to bind them to the extent of their stipulations. It requires reflection, it requires some intellectual effort, to efface this impression, and to come to the conclusion that the words contract and obligation, as used in the constitution, are not used in this sense. . . .

So much of this prohibition as restrains the power of the States to punish offenders in criminal cases, the prohibition to pass bills of attainder and *ex post facto* laws, is, in its very terms, confined to preexisting cases. A bill of attainder can be only for crimes already committed; and a law is not *ex post facto,* unless it looks back to an act done before its passage. Language is incapable of expressing, in plainer terms, that the mind of the convention was directed to retroactive legislation. The thing forbidden is retroaction. But that part of the clause which relates to the civil transactions of individuals is expressed in more general terms; in terms which comprehend, in their ordinary signification, cases which occur after, as well as those which occur before, the passage of the act. It forbids a State to make any thing but gold and silver coin a tender in payment of debts, or to pass any law impairing the obligation of contracts. These prohibitions relate to kindred subjects. They contemplate legislative interference with private rights, and restrain that interference. In construing that part of the clause which respects tender laws, a distinction has never been attempted between debts existing at the time the law may be passed, and debts afterwards created. The prohibition has been considered as total; and yet the difference in principle between making property a tender in payment . . . or in discharge of the debt, is not clearly discernible. Nor is the difference in language so obvious, as to denote plainly a difference of intention in the framers of the instrument. "No State shall make any thing but gold and silver coin a tender in payment of debts." Does the word "debts" mean, generally, those due when the law applies to the case, or is it limited to debts due at the passage of the act? The same train of reasoning which would confine the subsequent words to contracts existing at the passage of the law, would go far in confining these words to debts existing at that time. Yet, this distinction has never, we believe, occurred to any person. How soon it may occur is not for us to determine. We think it would unquestionably defeat the object of the clause. . . .

The constitution, we are told, deals not with form, but with substance; and cannot be presumed, if it designed to protect the obligation of contracts from State legislation, to have left it thus obviously exposed to destruction.

The answer is, that if the law goes further, and annuls the obligation without affording the remedy which satisfies it, if its action on the remedy be such as palpably to impair the obligation of the contract, the very case arises which we suppose to be within the constitution. If it leaves the obligation untouched, but withholds the remedy, or affords one which is merely nominal, it is like all other cases of misgovernment, and leaves the debtor still liable to his creditor, should he be found, or should his property be found, where the laws afford a remedy. If that high sense of duty which men selected from the government of their fellow-citizens must be supposed to feel, furnishes no security against a course of legislation which must end in self-destruction; if the solemn oath taken by every member, to support the constitution of the United States, furnishes no security against intentional attempts to violate its spirit while evading its letter; the question how far the constitution interposes a shield for the protection of an injured individual, who demands from a court of justice that remedy which every government ought to afford, will depend on the law itself which shall be brought under consideration. The anticipation of such a case would be unnecessarily disrespectful, and an opinion on it would be, at least, premature. But, however the question might be decided, should it be even determined that such a law would be a successful evasion of the constitution, it does not follow, that an act which operates directly on the contract after it is made, is not within the restriction imposed on the States by that instrument. The validity of a law acting directly on the obligation, is not proved by showing that the constitution has provided no means for compelling the States to enforce it.

We perceive, then, no reason for the opinion that the prohibition "to pass any law impairing the obligations of contracts," is incompatible with the fair exercise of that discretion, which the State legislatures possess in common with all governments, to regulate the remedies afforded by their own courts. We think that obligation and remedy are distinguishable from each other. That the first is created by the act of the parties, the last is afforded by government. The words of the restriction we have been considering, countenance, we think, this idea. No State shall "pass any law impairing the obligation of contracts." These words seem to us to import that the obligation is intrinsic, that it is created by the contract itself, not that it is dependent on the laws made to enforce it. When we advert to the course of reading generally pursued by American statesmen in early life, we must suppose that the framers of our constitution were intimately acquainted with the writings of those wise and learned men, whose treatises on the laws of nature and nations have guided public opinion on the subjects of obligation and contract. If we turn to those treatises, we find them to concur in the declaration that contracts possess an original intrinsic obligation, derived from the acts of free agents, and not given by government. We must suppose that the framers of our constitution took the same view of the subject, and the language they have used confirms this opinion. . . .

We cannot look back to the history of the times when the august spectacle was exhibited of the assemblage of a whole people by their representatives in convention, in order to unite thirteen independent sovereignties under one government, so far as might be necessary for the purposes of union, without being sensible of the great importance which was at that time attached to the 10th section of the 1st article. The power of changing the relative situation of debtor and creditor, of interfering with contracts, a power which comes home to every man, touches the interest of all, and controls the conduct of every individual in those things which he supposes to be proper for his own exclusive management, had been used to such an excess by the state legislatures as to break in upon the ordinary intercourse of society, and destroy all confidence between man and man. The mischief had become so great, so alarming, as not only to impair commercial intercourse, and threaten the existence of credit, but to sap the morals of the people and destroy the sanctity of private faith. To guard against the continuance of the evil was an object of deep interest with all the truly wise as well as the virtuous of this great community, and was one of the important benefits expected from a reform of the government.

To impose restraints on state legislation, as respected this delicate and interesting subject, was thought necessary by all those patriots who could take an enlightened and comprehensive view of our situation; and the principle obtained an early admission into the various schemes of government which were submitted to the convention. In framing an instrument, which was intended to be perpetual, the presumption is strong that every important principle introduced into it is intended to be perpetual also; that a principle expressed in terms to operate in all future time, is intended so to operate. But if the construction, for which the plaintiff's counsel contend, be the true one, the constitution will have imposed a restriction in language, indicating perpetuity, which every State in the Union may elude at pleasure. The obligation of contracts in force, at any given time, is but of short duration; and, if the inhibition be of retrospective laws only, a very short lapse of time will remove every subject on which the act is forbidden to operate, and make this provision of the constitution so far useless. Instead of introducing a great principle, prohibiting all laws of this obnoxious character, the constitution will only suspend their operation for a moment, or except from it preexisting cases. The object would scarcely seem to be of sufficient importance to have found a place in that instrument. . . .

It is also worthy of consideration, that those laws which had effected all that mischief the constitution intended to prevent, were prospective as well as retrospective, in their operation. They embraced future contracts, as well as those previously formed. There is the less reason for imputing to the convention an intention, not manifested by their language, to confine a restriction intended to guard against the recurrence of those mischiefs, to retrospective legislation. . . .

As had the earlier Sturgis decision, *Ogden* v. *Saunders* produced widespread discontent, particularly among state legislators and among certain classes of debtors. Charles Warren believed that the Court would have contributed to economic stability if it had adopted a doctrine establishing the exclusiveness of congressional power over bankruptcy,[38] but it is doubtful whether public opinion in many of the states would have approved such a doctrine.

Incidentally, Marshall's dissent in *Ogden* v. *Saunders* offers a good illustration of his conservatism in economic matters. His contract clause decisions involved the protection of private property, and in these Marshall attempted in vain to establish a natural law doctrine of vested rights. Only in some of his contract clause decisions did Marshall attempt to base his decisions on something outside the constitution and laws of the United States. For example, while he referred to the contract clause in the Saunders case, he also based his dissenting opinion on natural law. Thus, the contract clause was described, in language reminiscent of the extremely conservative Federalists of New England, as "one on which the good and wise reposed confidently for securing the prosperity and harmony of our citizens."[39] But in the same dissent "individuals" were held as not deriving "from government their right to contract, but [instead] bring that right with them into society; that obligation is not conferred on contracts by positive law, but is intrinsic, and is conferred by the act of the parties."[40] Marshall had also based his decision in *Fletcher* v. *Peck* upon natural law as well as the contract clause, but, on the other hand, had based the important Dartmouth College decision on the constitutional provision alone.

Justice Story was perhaps an even stronger supporter of the doctrine that the right to contract is a natural right antecedent to the constitutional provision. His statement of the doctrine in *Terrett* v. *Taylor*[41] was reasserted in 1829 in *Wilkinson* v. *Leland*.[42] Here Story maintained that "the fundamental maxims of free government seem to require, that the rights of personal liberty and private property should be held sacred."[43]

The second strong assertion of national supremacy by the Supreme Court in 1827 was made in its decision in *Brown* v. *Maryland*.[44] In 1821, the Maryland legislature had enacted a law providing that

. . . all importers of foreign articles or commodities, of dry goods . . . or wines . . . and other persons selling the same by wholesale, bale or package . . . shall, before they are authorized to sell, take out a license . . . for which they shall pay fifty dollars. . . .

The act provided for fine and forfeiture as a penalty for neglect or refusal. Brown and others were indicted in a Maryland court for selling one package of foreign dry goods without a license. The case came on writ of error from the Maryland Court of Appeals to the Supreme Court.

Chief Justice Marshall wrote the majority opinion. The validity of the Maryland tax was considered in terms of two constitutional provisions—that "no state shall, without the consent of Congress, lay any imposts or duties on imports and exports, except what may be absolutely necessary for executing its inspection laws"[45] and that "Congress shall have power . . . to regulate commerce with foreign nations."[46]

Marshall pointed out that the prohibition against the states included in the first provision "would be as completely defeated by a power to tax the article in the hands of the importer the instant it was landed, as by a power to tax it while entering the port."[47] Where exclusive congressional power ends, held Marshall, is where the imported articles become part of the property of the country. The criterion he used to distinguish between the areas of federal and state control was described in the famous "original-package doctrine":

> . . . when the importer has so acted upon the thing imported, that it has become incorporated and mixed up with the mass of property in the country, it has, perhaps, lost its distinctive character as an import, and has become subject to the taxing power of the state; but while remaining the property of the importer in his warehouse, in the original form or package in which it was imported, a tax upon it is too plainly a duty on imports to escape the prohibition in the Constitution . . .[48]

In the Brown case, Marshall considered at length the power of the states to protect their citizens. He conceded that the original-package doctrine was not formulated to weaken this "police power" of the states.[49] He went on to point out, however, that "sale is the object of importation" and as an essential ingredient of commercial intercourse "must be considered a component part of the power to regulate commerce." Thus, "Congress has a right, not only to authorize importation, but to authorize the importer to sell." As a consequence, "any penalty inflicted on the importer, for selling the articles, in his character of importer, must be in opposition to the act of congress which authorizes importation."[50]

Here Marshall seized the opportunity for another statement of the supremacy of the national government:

> It has been observed, that the powers remaining with the states may be so exercised as to come in conflict with those vested in congress. When this happens that which is not supreme must yield to that which is supreme. This great and universal truth is inseparable from the nature of things, and the constitution has applied it to the often interfering powers of the general and state governments, as a vital principle of perpetual operation. It results, necessarily, from this principle that the taxing power of the states must have some limits. It cannot reach and restrain the national government within its proper sphere. It cannot reach the administration of justice in the courts of the Union, or the collection of the taxes of the United States, or restrain the operation of any law which congress may constitutionally pass.

The Maryland taxing statute was declared repugnant to the Constitution and void.

In 1828, in *American Insurance Company* v. *Canter*,[51] Chief Justice Marshall gave the definitive statement of Congress' power to acquire and govern territory. This power was implied from Congress' enumerated powers to make war and to make treaties. Congress' power to establish territorial courts was then implied not only from its power "to make all needful rules and regulations respecting the territory or other property of the United States," but also "in virtue of the general right of sovereignty which exists in the government."[52]

An era ended in 1828. During nearly three decades of Jeffersonian Republican political ascendancy, the Federalist Party had disappeared as a political party, but had retained a major forum for its property-oriented doctrines among some members of the federal judiciary, the most notable of which were Chief Justice Marshall and Chief Judge William Cranch of the federal circuit court for the District of Columbia.

The election of 1828 was as clear-cut and decisive as that of 1824 had been confused and indecisive. Four men had run for the presidency in 1824, but only two, Jackson and Adams, contested in 1828. Jackson won large majorities in popular and electoral votes, 647,276 to 508,064 and 178 to 83 respectively. His vice-presidential running mate, John C. Calhoun of South Carolina, won by a smaller margin.[53] In the autumn of the election year, September 1828, Justice Trimble died. President John Quincy Adams, defeated for reelection in the same autumn,[54] sought to replace Trimble. Adams nominated John J. Crittenden of Kentucky, but the Senate refused to take action on the nomination until after the inauguration of Jackson. Jackson's supporters claimed that the appointment should be left to the newly-elected president. After Jackson took office, he appointed John McLean of Ohio, postmaster-general in the administration of Jackson's political antagonist, John Quincy Adams. Carl Swisher held that Jackson had intended to retain McLean as postmaster-general because the latter had refused to campaign for Adams in the preceding election battle. When McLean refused to carry out the new policy of partisan removals in the postal system, however, Jackson gave him the associate justiceship instead.[55]

Charles Grove Haines contended that the Supreme Court manifested an "attitude of caution" after the election of President Jackson,[56] and cited as examples the decisions in *Willson* v. *Blackbird Creek Marsh Company*,[57] *Satterlee* v. *Matthewson*,[58] and *Wilkerson* v. *Leland*.[59] In the first decision, the Supreme Court narrowed the doctrine stated in *Gibbons* v. *Ogden*, intimating that the Delaware statute under consideration fell outside the ban of the commerce clause because it was an internal police regulation.[60]

WILLSON v. BLACKBIRD CREEK MARSH COMPANY
2 Peters 245 (1829)

Chief Justice Marshall delivered the opinion of the Court:

The jurisdiction of the court being established, the more doubtful question is to be considered, whether the act incorporating the Black Bird Creek Marsh Company is repugnant to the constitution, so far as it authorizes a dam across the creek. The plea states the creek to be navigable, in the nature of a highway, through which the tide ebbs and flows.

The act of assembly by which the plaintiffs were authorized to construct their dam, shows plainly that this is one of those many creeks, passing through a deep level marsh adjoining the Delaware, up which the tide flows for some distance. The value of the property on its banks must be enhanced by excluding the water from the marsh, and the health of the inhabitants probably improved. Measures calculated to produce these objects, provided they do not come into collision with the powers of the general government, are undoubtedly within those which are reserved to the States. But the measure authorized by this act stops a navigable creek, and must be supposed to abridge the rights of those who have been accustomed to use it. But this abridgment, unless it comes in conflict with the constitution or a law of the United States, is an affair between the government of Delaware and its citizens, of which this court can take no cognizance.

The counsel for the plaintiffs in error insist that it comes in conflict with the power of the United States "to regulate commerce with foreign nations and among the several States."

If congress had passed any act which bore upon the case; any act in execution of the power to regulate commerce, the object of which was to control state legislation over those small navigable creeks into which the tide flows, and which abound throughout the lower country of the middle and southern States; we should feel not much difficulty in saying that a state law coming in conflict with such act would be void. But congress has passed no such act. The repugnancy of the law of Delaware to the Constitution is placed entirely on its repugnancy to the power to regulate commerce with foreign nations and among the several States; a power which has not been so exercised as to affect the question.

We do not think that the act empowering the Blackbird Creek Marsh Company to place a dam across the creek, can, under all the circumstances of the case, be considered as repugnant to the power to regulate commerce in its dormant state, or as being in conflict with any law passed on the subject.

There is no error, and the judgment is affirmed.

Despite the modification of broad constructionist doctrine in *Blackbird*, the next important decision, that of *Weston* v. *City of Charleston*,[61] can hardly be characterized as a manifestation of an "attitude of caution." In February 1823, the city council of Charleston, South Carolina, passed "an ordinance to raise supplies for the use of the city." The ordinance provided for a tax of twenty-five cents per hundred dollars on stocks and bonds, including "six and seven per cent stock of the United States." Weston and a number of other holders of United States stock filed a "suggestion for a prohibition" in the Charleston common pleas court to prevent the city council from levying the tax on federal securities. The prohibition was granted but later reversed by the South Carolina Constitutional Court, the court of last resort in the state, from which the issue was brought before the Supreme Court on writ of error.[62]

In order to put the case in its true perspective as an issue between states' rights and national supremacy, Chief Justice Marshall pointed out that the Charleston city ordinance was the exercise of an "authority under the state of South Carolina." His strong assertion of the doctrine of national supremacy and his insistence upon the Supreme Court's capacity to act as umpire in disputes arising in the federal system seem inconsistent with any alleged uncertainty or hesitation:

> In a society like ours, with one supreme government for national purposes, and numerous state governments for other purposes; in many respects independent, and in the uncontrolled exercise of many important powers, occasional interferences ought not to surprise us. The power of taxation is one of the most essential to a state, and one of the most extensive in its operation. The attempt to maintain a rule which shall limit its exercise, is undoubtedly among the most delicate and difficult duties which can develop on those whose province it is to expound the supreme law of the land in its application to the cases of individuals. This duty has more than once devolved on this Court. In the performance of it we have considered it as a necessary consequence from the supremacy of the government of the whole, that its action in the exercise of its legitimate powers should be free and unembarrassed by

any conflicting powers in the possession of its parts; that the powers of a state cannot rightfully be so exercised as to impede and obstruct the free course of those measures which the government of states united may rightfully adopt.[63]

Congress was held to have the power to issue stocks under its borrowing power. A contract made by the national government in the exercise of this power was to be "independent of the will of any state in which the individual who lends may reside." Marshall reiterated the principles stated in *McCulloch* v. *Maryland* and held that United States stocks "ought . . . to be exempt from state taxation, and consequently from being taxed by corporations deriving their power from states." The Charleston city ordinance was declared repugnant to the Constitution, and the judgment of the South Carolina Constitutional Court was reversed.[64] Justices Johnson and Thompson filed separate dissents.

Delineating the boundaries of state and federal power

The Supreme Court's exercise of its power as a final arbiter in the federal system had aroused sporadic resistance for more than three decades. In 1828, however, John C. Calhoun repudiated his previous nationalistic attitude and began formulating a complete theory of government that was destined to unify opponents of national power in general and the Supreme Court in particular. Calhoun's first major attack on the Court came in the "South Carolina Exposition," which was presented as a committee report to the South Carolina legislature in December 1828.[65] His later "Discourse on the Constitution and Government of the United States" embodied essentially the same argument stated in the "South Carolina Exposition." Because he was vice-president of the United States, Calhoun's views were considered very seriously. Later, President Jackson would repudiate this interpretation and give full expression to his own strong nationalistic views on the subject.

In his "Discourse," Calhoun held that the relationship of the states and the national government was one of coordinates. In order to maintain that relationship, he realized, the Supreme Court's authority under the 25th section of the Judiciary Act of 1789 must be withdrawn. The effect of this act as interpreted in *Martin* v. *Hunter's Lessee* and *Cohens* v. *Virginia* wrote Calhoun, "is to make the government of the United States the sole judge, in the last resort, as to the extent of its powers, and to place the states and their separate governments and institutions at their mercy. It would be a waste of time to undertake to show that an assumption that would destroy the relation of coordinates between the government of the United States and those of the several states—which would enable the former, at pleaure, to absorb the reserved powers and to destroy the institutions, social and political, which the Constitution was ordained and established to protect is wholly inconsistent with the federal theory of government, though in perfect accordance with the national theory. Indeed, I would go further and assert that it is, of itself, all sufficient to convert it into a national, consolidated government."[66]

In January 1830, Robert Hayne restated Calhoun's nullification theory in the first of the famous Webster-Hayne debates on the nature of the Union. Webster's reply revealed the completeness of Marshall's contributions to nationalist political theory. The reiteration of nationalist principles by the Marshall Court for three decades had had such widespread ideological influence that the new generation of nationalist leaders, such as Webster and Clay, readily utilized the Court's views on the nature of the Union to refute the Southern nullificationists. As Professor Hockett pointed out, "Webster uttered no idea which Marshall and others had not held before his speech of January 1830," but whereas Marshall's nationalistic pronouncements had been generally limited to the courtroom audience,[67] Webster's speech was "broadcast . . . to the entire country."[68]

Only six weeks after Webster's strong defense of the Union and the federal judiciary, the Supreme Court heard the argument in *Craig* v. *Missouri*.[69] Senator Thomas Hart Benton argued the case for Missouri not as counsel, but as a "corps of observation" for the state. He protested that the language used by the Court in summoning the state was not "proper when addressed to a sovereign state." In closing his decision in the case, Chief Justice Marshall turned his attention to the arguments of Benton and Craig's counsel. His reference to their contentions may be viewed as an answer to the rising insistence upon states' rights in the Old South as well:

> In the argument, we have been reminded by one side of the dignity of a sovereign state; of the humiliation of her submitting herself to this tribunal; of the dangers which may result from inflicting a wound on that dignity; by the other, of the still superior dignity of the people of the United States, who have spoken their will, in terms which we cannot misunderstand.
>
> To these admonitions we can only answer: that if the exercise of that jurisdiction which has been imposed upon us by the constitution and laws of the United States, shall be calculated to bring on those dangers which have been indicated; or if it shall be indispensable to the preservation of the union, and consequently of the independence and liberty of these states; these are considerations which address themselves to those departments which with perfect propriety be influenced by them. This department can listen only to the mandates of the law, and can tread only the path which is marked out by duty.[70]

Craig v. *Missouri* involved the validity of an enactment of the Missouri legislature providing for the establishment of state loan offices that could issue "certificates." Although these certificates were not legal tender, they were to be used in Missouri to pay taxes, to discharge debts, and to pay state salaries. Marshall held that issuance of such a paper medium of exchange violated the constitutional provision forbidding the emission of "bills of credit" by the states. On that ground the Missouri law was held unconstitutional. Justices Johnson, Thompson, and McLean filed separate dissents.

The decision in *Craig* v. *Missouri* served to spur on opponents of the Supreme Court in the national Congress. In January 1831, a majority report of the House Judiciary Committee recommended the repeal of the vital 25th section of the Judiciary Act on the ground that the powers of the court had become so "vast and alarming that the constantly increasing evil of interference of federal with state authorities must be checked."[71] After bitter debates, a House bill embodying the committee's proposals was resoundingly defeated by a vote of 158 to 51. Significantly, most of the votes favoring repeal were cast by representatives from the southern states.[72]

The conflict between the state of Georgia and the Supreme Court began in 1830 and lasted until 1833. Because of the widespread rumors of President Jackson's alleged refusal to support the Court against what was in effect an act of nullification by the state of Georgia, Chief Justice Marshall was thrown into the depths of despair. Just before Jackson's reelection in 1832, Marshall wrote to Justice Story the following message:

> If the prospects of our country inspire you with gloom, how do you think a man must be affected who partakes of all your opinions and whose geographical position enables him to see a great deal that is concealed from you? I yield slowly and reluctantly to the conviction that our constitution cannot last. I had supposed that North of the Potomack a firm and solid government competent to the security of rational liberty might be preserved. Even that now seems doubtful. The case of the South seems to me to be desperate. Our opinions are incompatible with a united government even among ourselves. The Union has been prolonged thus far by miracles. I fear they cannot continue.[73]

The immediate cause for Marshall's lack of confidence was the apparent acquiescence of the chief executive in the nullifying actions of the state of Georgia.

The conflict with Georgia arose from the peculiar experiences of that state with the Indian tribes within its borders. Georgia had been the least populated of the original 13 states and, unlike the others, had not pushed out or conquered the Indians within its borders by the time the Constitution was adopted. The two tribes that inhabited most of western Georgia, the Creeks and the Cherokees, had by 1812 abandoned their habits as huntsmen and warriors and had become farmers and cattlemen in imitation of their white neighbors.[74] For their aid to the British in the war of 1812, many of the Creeks were driven out of Georgia, but the Cherokees stayed, multiplied, and prospered.

By the terms of an 1802 agreement between Georgia and the national government, the national government had promised to remove all Indians from within the state as soon as practicable.[75] By the 1820s many Georgians became impatient, but the national government refused to use force to drive out the Indians. By treaty, President John Quincy Adams' agents had persuaded the Creeks in Georgia to move west. Before the agreement went into effect, however, Governor Troup sent surveyors into Creek territory in defiance of the letter of the secretary of war forbidding such action. When President Adams threatened to use force against Georgia, Troup called out the state militia. When Adams called upon Congress to support him, he was humiliated to find it unwilling to do so. Adams then complied with Georgia's wishes and sent agents to induce the Creeks to surrender their lands.[76]

In a letter to Georgia's Congressmen written in February 1827, Governor Troup discussed Georgia's victory and gave the following challenge to the Supreme Court's exercise of final determinative authority in federal-state relations:

> I consider all questions of mere sovereignty as a matter for negotiation between the states and the United States, until the proper tribunal shall be assigned by the Constitution itself for the adjustment of them. . . . The states cannot consent to refer to the Supreme Court, as of right and obligation, questions of sovereignty between them and the United States, because that Court, being of exclusive appointment by the Government of the United States, will make the United States judge in its own cause.[77]

After the successful defiance of the chief executive in the Creek affair, it is not surprising that Georgia moved swiftly to remove the Cherokees also from within her borders.

The national government's efforts to move the Cherokees had been completely thwarted after 1823. In that year the council of Cherokee chiefs had announced to inquiring federal commissioners that "it is the fixed and unalterable determination of this nation never again to cede one foot more of our land."[78] The Cherokees had advanced far on the road of civilization. In 1825 Sequoyah had devised a Cherokee alphabet. In 1826 a printing press was set up in New Echota, the Cherokee nation's capital, to publish a newspaper, the *Cherokee Phoenix*. And in 1827, the Cherokees adopted a constitution providing for a system of representative government modeled on that of the United States.[79] Georgians were infuriated by these manifestations of Cherokee intentions to stay, and in December 1828 the state legislature passed a law providing that all Indians resident in Georgia were subject to Georgia law, and declaring null and void all laws of the Cherokee nation.

In 1829 matters were further complicated by the discovery of gold in Cherokee territory. Adventurers flocked to the Indian country in spite of the fact that such entry was forbidden by the laws of the three conflicting governments—the federal government, the state of Georgia, and the Cherokee nation itself. As a matter of policy, but not necessarily on constitutional grounds, President Jackson withdrew federal troops in 1830 and turned the Indian territory over to Georgia. When they realized that they could not count on the support of the chief executive, the Cherokee chiefs decided to make a final effort to save their lands by resorting to the federal judiciary.[80]

The Cherokees engaged William Wirt as counsel, and in 1830 Wirt introduced a motion before the Supreme Court for an injunction to restrain Georgia in the enforcement of her laws governing the Indian territory. Before this motion was argued, the Cherokees were afforded another opportunity to test the validity of the Georgia laws. George Tassel or Corn Tassel, a Cherokee, was convicted of murder and sentenced to death by a Georgia court. Upon writ of error to the Supreme Court, the state of Georgia, through its governor, was cited to appear and show cause why the writ should not be decided against the state.[81] Governor Gilmer of Georgia refused to honor the writ, and the Georgia general assembly supported him with a resolution providing

> . . . that the State of Georgia will never so far compromise her sovereignty as an independent state as to become a party to the case sought to be made before the Supreme Court of the United States by the writ in question. . . . The Governor was authorized and required, with all the force and means . . . at his command . . . to resist and repel any and every invasion from whatever quarter, upon the administration of the criminal laws of this state.[82]

Before the Supreme Court could take further action, George Tassel was hanged.

In March 1831 Chief Justice Marshall, in *Cherokee Nation* v. *Georgia*,[83] held that the Indian nation could not maintain the motion for an injunction. The Cherokee nation was held not to be an independent state within the meaning of the Constitution. Rather its status was that of a "domestic dependent" nation still "in a state of pupilage." Consequently, concluded Marshall, "if it be true that the Cherokee Nation have rights, this is not the tribunal in which those rights are to be asserted." "Interposition" by the Supreme Court would savor "too much of the exercise of political power." Accordingly, the motion for an injunction against Georgia was denied.

In order to prevent Cherokee defendants from carrying their cases to the Supreme Court, Georgia courts allowed the cases to drag as long as possible. Meanwhile, a friend of the Indians, a minister named Worchester, was convicted under Georgia's statute excluding unauthorized white men from Cherokee country. The case provided Counsel Wirt with the opportunity to test the validity of Georgia's laws. The minister had been appointed postmaster at New Echota by President John Quincy Adams. Later, after Worchester's arrest, Governor Gilmer of Georgia requested his removal, and President Jackson readily complied. The minister and a number of other missionaries were tried in a Georgia court for illegal residence and sentenced to four years' hard labor in the state penitentiary. The governor offered to pardon them if they left the state. Only Worchester and Elizur Butler refused, taking the state court decision to the Supreme Court.[84]

Worchester v. *Georgia*[85] was argued only by the counsel for the Cherokees, the Georgia governor and legislature having again angrily denied that the Supreme Court had the authority to issue the writ of error to a court of a sovereign state. Marshall, after an unusually long historical argument, declared that according to the treaty of Hopewell, "the Cherokees are under the protection of the United States." Through the operation of treaties and acts of Congress, the state of Georgia was barred from enforcing its laws in the territory of the Cherokee nation. "The whole intercourse," continued Marshall, "between the United States and this nation is by our Constitution and laws vested in the government of the United States."[86] The Georgia legislative acts that interfered "forcibly with the relations established between the United States and the Cherokee Nation" were declared repugnant to the Constitution, and hence Worchester's state court conviction was "reversed and annulled." A special mandate to that court was sent ordering the release of Worchester and Butler.

Georgia disregarded the Court's mandate, and in 1834 the state legislature authorized the distribution of Cherokee lands to Georgians by the land-lottery system. President Jackson also sent agents to persuade the Cherokees to move west.[87] That Jackson refused to carry out the Supreme Court's decision, however, is yet to be proven historically. Ever since the 1864 publication of Horace Greeley's *The American Conflict*, a number of historians have given credence to the report that President Jackson intimated, if he did not expressly state, that since Marshall had made his decision, he (Marshall) would have to enforce it.[88] Yet, Supreme Court Historian Charles Warren has pointed out that Jackson was never actually called upon to enforce the Court's mandate. In 1832 Jackson's political opponents accused him of refusing to aid the Court, but such charges were premature, for when the

Supreme Court adjourned in March 1832, it had not actually issued the mandate. No action could have been taken until the 1833 term. If the Court issued the mandate and it was disobeyed, the Court could then direct a United States marshal to summon a *posse comitatus* to execute its mandate. Presumably, if Georgia resisted successfully, the chief executive would have been called upon to set in motion the armed forces of the federal government.[89] But before any of these steps could be taken, President Jackson indicated in his powerful rejection of South Carolina's Nullification Ordinance of November 1832 that he would use the military forces of the whole nation to execute the laws of the Union.

President Jackson's action in the face of South Carolina's nullification threat was undoubtedly a factor in settling the Georgia issue. At President Jackson's request, Congress enacted the Force Bill. This act, among other things, enlarged the jurisdiction of the federal circuit courts, providing for removal to such courts of any suit commenced in a state court against a federal officer or against persons for acts done under the federal revenue laws. The act provided for *habeas corpus* in cases of prisoners in state jails held for acts done or omitted in pursuance of a federal law.[90] Within a few months of Jackson's show of force against South Carolina, Governor Lumpkin of Georgia pardoned Worchester and Butler, thus avoiding a real test of strength with the federal government.[91]

In his last years on the Court, Chief Justice Marshall saw the narrowing to some extent of his broad constructionist doctrines on commerce and the contract clause. For many years, Marshall had been out of step with the more liberal economic views of most of his fellow citizens. In his last year on the Court he probably realized that his many efforts to establish a doctrine of vested rights had failed.[92] Yet in 1833 he was able to view with satisfaction the adoption and application of his most cherished principle, that of national supremacy, by Andrew Jackson. Though he was a strict constructionist on the questions of the bank and internal improvements, in his Proclamation to South Carolina in 1832, President Jackson announced a doctrine reminiscent of the greatest of Marshall's nationalistic decisions:

> I consider the power to annul a law of the United States, assumed by one State, incompatible with the existence of the Union, contradicted expressly by the letter of the Constitution, unauthorized by its spirit, inconsistent with every principle on which it was founded, and destructive of the great object for which it was formed.

The identification of strong pro-nationalistic decision making has, quite appropriately, been associated with Chief Justice Marshall and the ideology of the Federalist Party and emergent political parties identified with its conservative tradition, notably the National Republicans, the Whigs, and the Republicans.[93] Not all of Marshall's decisions extended national authority, however, as the Blackbird Creek decision demonstrates. In Marshall's last major constitutional decision, he refrained quite clearly from extending the scope of a section of the Bill of Rights. The *Barron* v. *Baltimore* case arose out of a street paving project in the city of Baltimore, Maryland. The paving program accidentally resulted in the destruction of the business of the owner of Barron's Wharf in Baltimore harbor. Before the street paving, the wharf was adjacent to the deepest water in the harbor. But after the paving, the runoff of sand and gravel silted the harbor so that vessels could no longer dock at Barron's Wharf. Barron first took legal action against the city, but a lower court's verdict in his behalf for $4,500 compensation was reversed by the Maryland Court of Appeals. He then took his case to the Supreme Court of the United States via the writ of error, arguing that the paving project of the city of Baltimore violated the portion of the Fifth Amendment prohibiting the taking of private property for public purposes without just compensation. The decision is reproduced in full.

BARRON v. BALTIMORE
7 Peters 243 (1833)

The judgment brought up by this writ of error having been rendered by the court of a State, this tribunal can exercise no jurisdiction over it unless it be shown to come within the provisions of the twenty-fifth section of the Judicial Act.

The plaintiff in error contends that it comes within that clause in the fifth amendment to the Constitution which inhibits the taking of private property for public use without just compensation. He insists that this amendment, being in favor of the liberty of the citizen, ought to be so construed as to restrain the legislative power of a State, as well as that of the United States. If this proposition be untrue, the court can take no jurisdiction of the cause.

The question thus presented is, we think, of great importance, but not of much difficulty.

The Constitution was ordained and established by the people of the United States for themselves, for their own government, and not for the government of the individual States. Each State established a constitution for itself, and in that constitution provided such limitations and restrictions on the powers of its particular government as its judgment dictated. The people of the United States framed such a government for the United States as they supposed best adapted to their situation, and best calculated to promote their interests. The powers they conferred on this government were to be exercised by itself; and the limitations on power, if expressed in general terms, are naturally, and, we think, necessarily applicable to the government created by the instrument. They are limitations of power granted in the instrument itself; not of distinct governments, framed by different persons and for different purposes.

If these propositions be correct, the fifth amendment must be understood as restraining the power of the general government, not as applicable to the States. In their several constitutions they have imposed such restrictions on their respective governments as their own wisdom suggested; such as they deemed most proper for themselves. It is a subject on which they judge exclusively, and with which others interfere no farther than they are supposed to have a common interest.

The counsel for the plaintiff in error insists that the Constitution was intended to secure the people of the several States against the undue exercise of power by their respective State governments; as well as against that which might be attempted by their general government. In support of this argument he relies on the inhibitions contained in the tenth section of the first article.

We think that section affords a strong if not a conclusive argument in support of the opinion already indicated by the court.

The preceding section contains restrictions which are obviously intended for the exclusive purpose of restraining the exercise of power by the departments of the general government. Some of them use language applicable only to Congress; others are expressed in general terms. The third clause, for example, declares that "no bill of attainder or ex post facto law shall be passed." No language can be more general; yet the demonstration is complete that it applies solely to the government of the United States. In addition to the general arguments furnished by the instrument itself, some of which have been already suggested, the succeeding section, the avowed purpose of which is to restrain State legislation, contains in terms the very prohibition. It declares that "no State shall pass any bill of attainder or ex post facto law." This provision, then, of the ninth section, however comprehensive its language, contains no restriction on State legislation.

The ninth section having enumerated, in the nature of a bill of rights, the limitations intended to be imposed on the powers of the general government, the tenth proceeds to enumerate those which were to operate on the State legislatures. These restrictions are brought together in the same section, and are by express words applied to the States. "No State shall enter into any treaty," etc. Perceiving that in a constitution framed by the people of the United States for the government of all, no limitation of the action of government on the people would apply to the State government, unless expressed in terms; the restrictions contained in the tenth section are in direct words so applied to the States.

It is worthy of remark, too, that these inhibitions generally restrain State legislation on subjects intrusted to the general government, or in which the people of all the States feel an interest.

A State is forbidden to enter into any treaty, alliance or confederation. If these compacts are with foreign nations, they interfere with the treaty-making power which is conferred entirely on the general government; if with each other, for political purposes, they can scarcely fail to interfere with the general purpose and intent of the Constitution. To grant letters of marque and reprisal would lead directly to war, the power of declaring which is expressly given to Congress. To coin money is also the exercise of a power conferred on Congress. It would be tedious to recapitulate the several limitations on the powers of the States which are contained in this section. They will be found, generally, to restrain State legislation on subjects intrusted to the government of the Union, in which the citizens of all the States are interested. In these alone were the whole people concerned. The question of their application to States is not left to construction. It is averred in positive words.

If the original Constitution, in the ninth and tenth sections of the first article, draws this plain and marked line of discrimination between the limitations it imposes on the powers of the general government and on those of the States; if in every inhibition intended to act on State power, words are employed which directly express that intent, some strong reason must be assigned for departing from this safe and judicious course in framing the amendments, before that departure can be assumed.

We search in vain for that reason.

Had the people of the several States, or any of them, required changes in their constitutions; had they required additional safeguards to liberty from the apprehended encroachments of their particular governments, the remedy was in their own hands, and would have been applied by themselves. A convention would have been assembled by the discontented State, and the required improvements would have been made

by itself. The unwieldy and cumbrous machinery of procuring a recommendation from two-thirds of Congress, and the assent of three-fourths of their sister States, could never have occurred to any human being as a mode of doing that which might be effected by the State itself. Had the framers of these amendments intended them to be limitations on the powers of the State governments they would have imitated the framers of the original Constitution, and have expressed that intention. Had Congress engaged in the extraordinary occupation of improving the constitutions of the several States by affording the people additional protection from the exercise of power by their own governments in matters which concerned themselves alone, they would have declared this purpose in plain and intelligible language.

But it is universally understood, it is a part of the history of the day, that the great revolution which established the Constitution of the United States was not effected without immense opposition. Serious fears were extensively entertained that those powers which the patriot statesmen who then watched over the interests of our country, deemed essential to union, and to the attainment of those invaluable objects for which union was sought, might be exercised in a manner dangerous to liberty. In almost every convention by which the Constitution was adopted, amendments to guard against the abuse of power were recommended. These amendments demanded security against the apprehended encroachments of the general government—not against those of the local governments.

In compliance with a sentiment thus generally expressed, to quiet fears thus extensively entertained, amendments were proposed by the required majority of Congress, and adopted by the States. These amendments contain no expression indicating an intention to apply them to the State governments. This court cannot so apply them.

We are of opinion that the provision in the fifth amendment to the Constitution, declaring that private property shall not be taken for public use without just compensation, is intended solely as a limitation on the exercise of power by the government of the United States, and is not applicable to the legislation of the States. We are therefore of the opinion that there is no repugnancy between the several acts of the General Assembly of Maryland, given in evidence by the defendants at the trial of this cause in the court of that State, and the Constitution of the United States.

This court, therefore, has no jurisdiction of the cause, and [it] is dismissed.

The end of Chief Justice Marshall's tenure came relatively early in a long era largely dominated by the Jacksonian Democratic party. The judicial nationalism generally characteristic of the Supreme Court under Marshall's leadership did not end abruptly with his death in 1835. Nor did the harsh criticism of the Court by those who accused it of partiality in dealing with issues of federal-state relations. Perhaps of more seriousness than the charge of partiality was the charge of usurpation. As one might expect, its bluntest statement was made by John Caldwell Calhoun. His historical argument was in the form of an unequivocal denial that the constitutional framers chose the Supreme Court as final arbiter. Concerning the division of powers between the states and the federal government, Calhoun held that the court was not final arbiter, arguing that

> . . . the framers of the constitution contented themselves with drawing, as strongly as possible, the line of separation between the two powers—leaving it to time and experience to determine where the danger lay; to develop whatever remedy the system might furnish to guard against it—and if it furnished none, they left it to those who should come after them, to supply the defect.[94]

As recently as 1944 a book by Professor Charles Grove Haines was published that contained a somewhat softer version of the charge of usurpation. Haines admitted that the express provisions of the Constitution provided some basis for the Court's exercise of power over state legislation, but denied that the Court had been designated *final* arbiter in the system. Instead of stating harshly that the Court usurped much of its power in federal-state relations, Haines preferred to charge that much of that power was "progressively constructed through the judicial process of interpretation."[95] Until the 1830s, the consistency with which the Supreme Court asserted national supremacy evoked sporadic but generally inconsistent opposition. After 1800 the principle of national supremacy was no longer exclusively a principle of the Federalist Party. As John Quincy Adams, a long-time observer of, as well as participant in, the political affairs of the period pointed out,

> In this particular [that is, the question of national supremacy] there has been continual revolution of opinions between the Federal and Republican parties, and the practice of both has been in frequent and flagrant violation of their proposed principles.[96]

After the mid–1830s, the situation became considerably more complex. Slavery and slavery-related issues began to overshadow the issues that brought both the Jacksonian Democrats and their countervailing political opponents, the Whigs, into power. The major constitutional issues that divided the Court also divided the Congress, brought presidential administrations in and out of power, and eventually destroyed the Whig Party, seriously weakened the Jacksonian Democratic Party, and contributed significantly to the emergence of the Republican Party, which was destined to dominate national politics for many decades. But such a fundamental transition from economic to social issues did not take place rapidly. Indeed some of its major attributes and issues emerged gradually in the late 1830s and the 1840s, and came to the fore more rapidly and with greater controversy in the 1850s.

President Andrew Jackson and his immediate succesor, Martin Van Buren, were able to achieve a virtually complete transformation in the membership of the Supreme Court between Jackson's first victory in 1828 and Van Buren's defeat in 1840 and exit from office in 1841. Eight members of the Supreme Court were chosen by these two presidents, five by Jackson and three by Van Buren. Of Jackson's appointees, John McLean of Ohio served from 1829 to 1861, Henry Baldwin of Pennsylvania from 1830 to 1844, James M. Wayne of Georgia from 1835 to 1867, Roger Brooke Taney of Maryland succeeded John Marshall as chief justice and served from 1836 to 1864, and Philip P. Barbour of Virginia served from 1836 to 1841. Van Buren's selections were John Catron of Tennessee, who served from 1837 to 1865, John McKinley, of Alabama, 1837 to 1852, and Peter V. Daniel of Virginia, 1841 to 1860. Taney, who had served as Jackson's secretary of the treasury, was bitterly opposed by the Whigs and the supporters of the national bank. He was Jackson's closest ally on the Court.

Conversely, although much of the era between Jackson's first election in 1828 and the Civil War was characterized by vigorous two-party competition between Jacksonian Democrats and Whigs (a competition that divided even the South between the two parties), the Whigs never controlled the presidency as long as the Jacksonians. As a result, Whig opportunities to make Supreme Court appointments were limited to two presidential terms and were not handled as advantageously from a partisan standpoint as those of the Jacksonians. Most Jacksonian appointees were Democrats although the first, McLean, soon became a Whig and ultimately a Republican while on the bench, and the third, Wayne, was a Southern Whig. Of the two Whig appointees, Samuel Nelson of New York (1845–1872) was a Democrat and Benjamin R. Curtis of Massachusetts (1851–1857) was a bona fide Whig. The other Jacksonian appointments preceding the Civil War were made by President Polk (Levi Woodbury of New Hampshire, 1845–1851; Robert C. Grier of Pennsylvania, 1846–1870), by President Pierce (John A. Campbell of Alabama, 1853–1861), and by President Buchanan (Nathan Clifford of Maine, 1858–1881). They were all Democrats. The divisions on the Supreme Court were, nevertheless, often more closely decided because of factional conflicts among Democrats and because of the longevity and consistency of those members who adhered to old Federalist (and National Republican or Whig) principles. After Marshall's death, the most consistent of the neo-Federalists was Joseph Story. The closeness of these divisions was most obvious in legal conflicts involving property rights, commerce, and the institution of slavery.

The most important aspect of this era was the transformation of values and issues that confronted justices conditioned to the political and economic issues of the 1820s and '30s with fundamental choices over issues that were not salient when their political generation emerged. The most significant issues involved the scope of the commerce power, the status of corporations, the contract clause, and, above all, slavery.

Because of the political conflict between the Jackson administration and the Second Bank of the United States and its leader, Nicholas Biddle, economic conservatives feared that Jacksonian domination of the Supreme Court after the death of John Marshall would lead to a weakening of property rights or the erosion of the position of private corporations. But the new composition of the Court, now led by Chief Justice Roger Brooke Taney, neither weakened nor eroded either, and over subsequent decades actually maintained or expanded positions previously taken under Marshall. In 1837, in the Charles River Bridge case, an issue arose that posed the fundamental question whether the contract clause would become an inflexible instrument invoked to resist change. The proprietors of the original Charles River Bridge were granted a state charter in 1786 to charge tolls for 40 years, later extended to 70. In 1828 the Massachusetts legislature, under public pressure, chartered a new bridge near the original to ease congestion. This bridge was to be toll-free in six years. The proprietors of the original bridge claimed that this new Warren Bridge was an unconstitutionl impairment of the obligation of a contract. Chief Justice Taney examined this issue very comprehensively.

PROPRIETORS OF
CHARLES RIVER BRIDGE v. PROPRIETORS
OF WARREN BRIDGE
11 Peters 420 (1837)

The questions involved in this case are of the gravest character, and the court have given to them the most anxious and deliberate consideration. The value of the right claimed by the plaintiffs is large in amount; and many persons may no doubt be seriously affected in their pecuniary interests by any decision which the court may pronounce; and the questions which have been raised as to the power of the several States, in relation to the corporations they have charted, are pregnant with important consequences; not only to the individuals who are concerned in the corporate franchises, but to the communities in which they exist. The court are fully sensible that it is their duty, in exercising the high powers conferred on them by the constitution of the United States, to deal with these great and extensive interests with the utmost caution; guarding, as far as they have the power to do so, the rights of property, and at the same time carefully abstaining from any encroachment on the rights reserved to the States. . . .

Borrowing, as we have done, our system of jurisprudence from the English law; and having adopted, in every other case, civil and criminal, its rules for the construction of statutes; is there any thing in our local situation, or in the nature of our political institutions, which should lead us to depart from the principle where corporations are concerned? Are we to apply to acts of incorporation, a rule of construction differing from that of the English law, and, by implication, make the terms of a charter in one of the States, more unfavorable to the public, than upon an act of parliament, framed in the same words, would be sanctioned in an English court? Can any good reasons be assigned for excepting this particular class of cases from the operation of the general principle; and for introducing a new and adverse rule of construction in favor of corporations, while we adopt and adhere to the rules of construction known to the English common law, in every other case, without exception? We think not; and it would present a singular spectacle, if, while the courts in England are restraining, within the strictest limits, the spirit of monopoly, and exclusive privileges in nature of monopolies, and confining corporations to the privileges plainly given to them in their charter; the courts of this country should be found enlarging these privileges by implication; and construing a statute more unfavorably to the public, and to the rights of the community, than would be done in a case in an English court of justice.

But we are not now left to determine, for the first time, the rules by which public grants are to be construed in this country. The subject has already been considered in this court; and the rule of construction, above stated, fully established. In the case of the United States v. Arredondo, 6 Pct. 738, the leading cases upon this subject are collected together by the learned judge who delivered the opinion of the court; and the principle recognized, that in grants by the public, nothing passes by implication. . . .

But the case most analogous to this, and in which the question came more directly before the court, is the case of the Providence Bank v. Billings. . . .

It may, perhaps, be said, that in the case of the Providence Bank, this court was speaking of the taxing power; which is of vital importance to the very existence of every government. But the object and end of all government is to promote the happiness and prosperity of the community by which it is established; and it can never be assumed, that the government intended to diminish its power of accomplishing the end for which it was created. And in a country like ours, free, active, and enterprising, continually advancing in numbers and wealth, new channels of communication are daily found necessary, both for travel and trade; and are essential to the comfort, convenience, and prosperity of the people. A State ought never to be presumed to surrender this power, because, like the taxing power, the whole community have an interest in preserving it undiminished. And when a corporation alleges, that a State has surrendered for seventy years, its power of improvement and public accommodation, in a great and important line of travel, along which a vast number of its citizens must daily pass; the community have a right to insist, in the language of this court above quoted, "that its abandonment ought not to be presumed, in a case, in which the deliberate purpose of the State to abandon it does not appear." The continued existence of a government would be of no great value, if by implications and presumptions, it was disarmed of the powers necessary to accomplish the ends of its creation; and the functions it was designed to perform, transferred to the hands of privileged corporations. The rule of construction announced by the court, was not confined to the taxing power; nor is it so limited in the opinion delivered. On the contrary, it was distinctly placed on the ground that the interests of the community were concerned in preserving, undiminished, the power then in question; and whenever any power of the State is said to be surrendered or diminished, whether it be the taxing power or any other affecting the public interest, the same principle applies, and the rule of construction must be the same. No one will question that the interests of the great body of the people of the State, would, in this instance, be affected by the surrender of this great line of travel to a single corporation, with the right to exact toll, and exclude competition for seventy years. While the rights of private property are sacredly guarded, we must not forget that the community also have rights, and that the happiness and well being of every citizen depends on their faithful preservation.

Adopting the rule of construction above stated as the settled one, we proceed to apply it to the charter of 1785, to the proprietors of the Charles River Bridge. This act of incorporation is in the usual form, and the privileges such as are commonly given to corporations of that kind. It confers on them the ordinary faculties of a corporation, for the purpose of building the bridge; and establishes certain rates of toll, which the company are authorized to take. This is the whole grant. There is no exclusive privilege given to them over the waters

of Charles River, above or below their bridge. No right to erect another bridge themselves, nor to prevent other persons from erecting one. No engagement from the State that another shall not be erected; and no undertaking not to sanction competition, nor to make improvements that may diminish the amount of its income. Upon all these subjects the charter is silent; and nothing is said in it about a line of travel, so much insisted on in the argument, in which they are to have exclusive privileges. No words are used, from which an intention to grant any of these rights can be inferred. If the plaintiff is entitled to them, it must be implied, simply, from the nature of the grant; and cannot be inferred from the words by which the grant is made.

The relative position of the Warren Bridge has already been described. It does not interrupt the passage over the Charles River Bridge, nor make the way to it or from it less convenient. None of the faculties or franchises granted to that corporation have been revoked by the legislature, and its right to take the tolls granted by the charter remains unaltered. In short, all the franchises and rights of property enumerated in the charter, and there mentioned to have been granted to it, remain unimpaired. But its income is destroyed by the Warren Bridge; which, being free, draws off the passengers and property which would have gone over it, and renders their franchise of no value. This is the gist of the complaint. For it is not pretended that the erection of the Warren Bridge would have done them any injury, or in any degree affected their right of property, if it had not diminished the amount of their tolls. In order then to entitle themselves to relief, it is necessary to show that the legislature contracted not to do the act of which they complain, and that they impaired, or, in other words, violated that contract by the erection of the Warren Bridge.

The inquiry then is, Does the charter contain such a contract on the part of the State? Is there any such stipulation to be found in that instrument? It must be admitted on all hands that there is none,—no words that even relate to another bridge, or to the diminution of their tolls, or to the line of travel. If a contract on that subject can be gathered from the charter, it must be by implication, and cannot be found in the words used. Can such an agreement be implied? The rule of construction before stated is an answer to the question. In charters of this description, no rights are taken from the public, or given to the corporation, beyond those which the words of the charter, by their natural and proper construction, purport to convey. There are no words which import such a contract as the plaintiffs in error contend for, and none can be implied; and the same answer must be given to them that was given by this court to the Providence Bank. . . . The whole community are interested in this inquiry, and they have a right to require that the power of promoting their comfort and convenience, and of advancing the public prosperity, by providing safe, convenient, and cheap ways for the transportation of produce and the purposes of travel, shall not be construed to have been surrendered or diminished by the State, unless it shall appear by plain words that it was intended to be done. . . .

Can the legislature be presumed to have taken upon themselves an implied obligation, contrary to its own acts and declarations contained in the same law? It would be difficult to find a case justifying such an implication, even between individuals; still less will it be found where sovereign rights are concerned, and where the interests of a whole community would be deeply affected by such an implication. It would, indeed, be a strong exertion of judicial power, acting upon its own views of what justice required, and the parties ought to have done, to raise, by a sort of judicial coercion, an implied contract, and infer from it the nature of the very instrument in which the legislature appear to have taken pains to use words which disavow and repudiate any intention, on the part of the State, to make such a contract.

Indeed, the practice and usage of almost every State in the Union, old enough to have commenced the work of internal improvements, is opposed to the doctrine contended for on the part of the plaintiffs in error. Turnpike roads have been made in succession on the same line of travel; the later one interfering materially with the profits of the first. These corporations have, in some instances, been utterly ruined by the introduction of newer and better modes of transportation and travelling. In some cases, railroads have rendered the turnpike roads on the same line of travel so entirely useless, that the franchise of the turnpike corporation is not worth preserving. Yet in none of these cases have the corporation supposed that their privileges were invaded, or any contract violated on the part of the State. Amid the multitude of cases which have occurred, and have been daily occurring for the last forty or fifty years, this is the first instance in which such an implied contract has been contended for, and this court called upon to infer it from an ordinary act of incorporation, containing nothing more than the usual stipulations and provisions to be found in every such law. The absence of any such controversy, when there must have been so many occasions to give rise to

it, proves that neither States, nor individuals, nor corporations, ever imagined that such a contract could be implied from such charters. It shows that the men who voted for these laws, never imagined that they were forming such a contract; and if we maintain that they have made it, we must create it by a legal fiction, in opposition to the truth of the fact, and the obvious intention of the party. We cannot deal thus with the rights reserved to the States, and by legal intendments and mere technical reasoning, take away from them any portion of that power over their own internal police and improvement, which is so necessary to their well being and prosperity.

And what would be the fruits of this doctrine of implied contracts on the part of the States, and of property in a line of travel by a corporation, if it should now be sanctioned by this court? To what results would it lead us? If it is to be found in the charter to this bridge, the same process of reasoning must discover it in the various acts which have been passed, within the last forty years, for turnpike companies. And what is to be the extent of the privileges of exclusion on the different sides of the road? The counsel who have so ably argued this case, have not attempted to define it by any certain boundaries. How far must the new improvement be distant from the old one? How near may you approach without invading its rights in the privileged line? If this court should establish the principles now contended for, what is to become of the numerous railroads established on the same line of travel with turnpike companies; and which have rendered the franchises of the turnpike corporations of no value? Let it once be understood that such charters carry with them these implied contracts, and give this unknown and undefined property in a line of travelling, and you will soon find the old turnpike corporations awakening from their sleep, and calling upon this court to put down the improvements which have taken their place. The millions of property which have been invested in railroads and canals, upon lines of travel which had been before occupied by turnpike corporations, will be put in jeopardy. We shall be thrown back to the improvements of the last century, and obliged to stand still, until the claims of the old turnpike corporations shall be satisfied, and they shall consent to permit these States to avail themselves of the lights of modern science, and to partake of the benefit of those improvements which are now adding to the wealth and prosperity, and the convenience and comfort of every other part of the civilized world. Nor is this all. This court will find itself compelled to fix, by some arbitrary rule, the width of this new kind of property in a line of travel; for if such a right of property exists, unless, indeed, we resort to the old feudal grants, and to the exclusive rights of ferries, by prescription, between towns; and are prepared to decide that when a turnpike road from one town to another had been made, no railroad or canal, between these two points, could afterwards be established. This court are not prepared to sanction principles which must lead to such results. . . .

Again in 1837, a significant commerce clause case came before the Supreme Court. A statute of the state of New York had been passed to cope, in part, with the increasing flood of foreign immigrants. (National legislation dealing with this had not yet been adopted.) The state law required ship captains to provide, upon arrival in New York, a detailed account of the background and health of each immigrant on their vessel. This law was challenged as an unconstitutional violation of Congress' exclusive power to regulate foreign commerce. Justice Phillip Pendleton Barbour wrote the majority opinion while Justice Joseph Story dissented and Justice Smith Thompson wrote a concurring opinion.

NEW YORK v. MILN
11 Peters 102 (1837)

It is contended by the counsel for the defendant, that the act in question is a regulation of commerce; that the power to regulate commerce is, by the constitution of the United States, granted to congress; that this power is exclusive, and that consequently the act is a violation of the constitution of the United States.

On the part of the plaintiff it is argued, that an affirmative grant of power previously existing in the States to congress, is not exclusive; except, 1st, where it is so expressly declared in terms, by the clause giving the power; or 2dly, where a similar power is prohibited to the States; or 3dly, where the power in the States would be repugnant to, and incompatible with, a similar power in congress; that this power falls within neither of these predicaments; that it is not, in terms, declared to be exclusive; that it is not prohibited to the States; and that it is not repugnant to, or incompatible with, a similar power in congress; and that having preexisted in the States, they therefore have a concurrent power in relation to the subject; and that the act in question would be valid, even if it were a regulation of commerce, it not contravening any regulation made by congress.

But they deny that it is a regulation of commerce; on the contrary, they assert that it is a mere regulation of internal police, a power over which is not granted to congress; and which therefore, as well as upon the true construction of the constitution, as by force of the tenth amendment to that instrument, is reserved to, and resides in the several States.

We shall not enter into any examination of the question whether the power to regulate commerce, be or be not exclusive of the States, because the opinion which we have formed renders it unnecessary; in other words, we are of opinion that the act is not a regulation of commerce, but of police; and that being thus considered, it was passed in the exercise of a power which rightfully belonged to the States.

That the State of New York possessed power to pass this law before the adoption of the constitution of the United States, might probably be taken as a truism, without the necessity of proof. . . .

If, as we think, it be a regulation, not of commerce, but police, then it is not taken from the States. To decide this, let us examine its purpose, the end to be attained, and the means of its attainment.

It is apparent, from the whole scope of the law, that the object of the legislature was to prevent New York from being burdened by an influx of persons brought thither in ships; either from foreign countries, or from any other of the States; and for that purpose a report was required of the names, places of birth, &c., of all passengers, that the necessary steps might be taken by the city authorities, to prevent them from becoming chargeable as paupers.

Now, we hold that both the end and the means here used, are within the competency of the States, since a portion of their powers were surrendered to the federal government. Let us see what powers are left with the States. The Federalist, in the 45th number, speaking of this subject, says; the powers reserved to the several States will extend to all the objects which, in the ordinary course of affairs, concern the lives, liberties, and properties of the people; and the internal order, improvement, and prosperity of the State.

And this court, in the case of Gibbons v. Ogden, . . .

in speaking of the inspection laws of the States, say; they form a portion of that immense mass of legislation which embraces every thing within the territory of a State, not surrendered to the general government, all which can be most advantageously exercised by the States themselves. Inspection laws, quarantine laws, health laws of every description, as well as laws for regulating the internal commerce of a State, and those which respect turnpike roads, ferries, &c., are component parts of this mass. . . .

If we look at the persons for whose benefit it was passed, they are the people of New York, for whose protection and welfare the legislature of that State are authorized and in duty bound to provide.

If we turn our attention to the purpose to be attained, it is to secure that very protection, and to provide for that very welfare. . . .

The act of 1819 contains regulations obviously designed for the comfort of the passengers themselves; for this purpose, it prohibits the bringing more than a certain number proportioned to the tonnage of the vessel, and prescribes the kind and quality of provisions, or sea stores, and their quantity, in a certain proportion to the number of the passengers.

Another section requires the master to report to the collector a list of all passengers, designating the age, sex, occupation, the country to which they belong, &c.; which list is required to be delivered to the secretary of state, and which he is directed to lay before congress.

The object of this clause, in all probability, was to enable the government of the United States to form an accurate estimate of the increase of population by emigration; but whatsoever may have been its purpose, it is obvious that these laws only affect, through the power over navigation, the passengers whilst on their voyage, and until they shall have landed. After that, and when they have ceased to have any connection with the ship, and when, therefore, they have ceased to be passengers, we are satisfied that acts of congress, applying to them as such, and only professing to legislate in relation to them as such, have then performed their office, and can, with no propriety of language, be said to come into conflict with the law of a State, whose operation is not even on the same subject, because, although the person on whom it operates is the same, yet, having ceased to be a passenger, he no longer stands in the only relation in which the laws of congress either professed or intended to act upon him.

There is, then, no collision between the law in question and the acts of congress just commented on; and, therefore, if the state law were to be considered as partaking of the nature of a commercial regulation, it would stand the test of the most rigid scrutiny, if tried by the standard laid down in the reasoning of the court, quoted from the case of Gibbons v. Ogden.

But we do not place our opinion on this ground. We choose rather to plant ourselves on what we consider impregnable positions. They are these: That a State has the same undeniable and unlimited jurisdiction over all persons and things within its territorial limits, as any foreign nation, where that jurisdiction is not surrendered or restrained by the constitution of the United States. That, by virtue of this, it is not only the right, but the bounden and solemn duty of a State to advance the safety, happiness, and prosperity of its people, and to provide for its general welfare, by any and every act of legislation, which it may deem to be conducive to these ends, where the power over the particular subject, or the manner of its exercise, is not surrendered or restrained, in the manner just stated. That all those powers which relate to merely municipal legislation, or what may, perhaps, more properly be called internal police, are not thus surrendered or restrained; and that, consequently, in relation to these, the authority of a State is complete, unqualified, and exclusive. . . .

Now, in relation to the section in the act immediately before us, that is obviously passed with a view to prevent her citizens from being oppressed by the support of multitudes of poor persons who come from foreign countries without possessing the means of supporting themselves. There can be no mode in which the power to regulate internal police could be more appropriately exercised. New York, from her particular situation, is, perhaps, more than any other city in the Union, exposed to the evil of thousands of foreign emigrants arriving there, and the consequent danger of her citizens being subjected to a heavy charge in the maintenance of those who are poor. It is the duty of the State to protect its citizens from this evil; they have endeavored to do so, by passing, amongst other things, the section of the law in question. We should, upon principle, say that it had a right to do so. . . .

We think it as competent and as necessary for a State to provide precautionary measures against the moral pestilence of paupers, vagabonds, and possibly convicts, as it is to guard against the physical pestilence which may arise from unsound and infectious articles imported, or from a ship, the crew of which may be laboring under an infectious disease. . . .

We are therefore of opinion . . . that so much of the section of the act of the legislature of New York, as applies to the breaches assigned in the declaration, does not assume to regulate commerce between the port of New York and foreign ports, and that so much of said section is constitutional. . . .

Justice Story objected to what he viewed as a serious weakening of federal constitutional authority. His dissent stated, in part:

> . . . The power given to Congress to regulate commerce with foreign nations, and among the states, has been deemed exclusive, from the nature and objects of the power, and the necessary implications growing out of its exercise. Full power to regulate a particular subject implies the whole power, and leaves no residuum; and a grant of the whole to one is incompatible with a grant to another of a part. . . .[97]

The positions taken by Barbour for the majority and by Story in dissent were for a number of decades to represent polar opposites in the ongoing controversy over the scope of the commerce power.

The ability of states to regulate corporations was especially important in the Jacksonian era because such private institutions, foreign or domestic, were virtually unregulated by the national government. In the 1830s, an attempt by the state of Alabama to exclude out-of-state banks (after such banks had gained ownership of all the banks within Alabama) was challenged on contract clause and interstate comity grounds. Chief Justice Taney wrote a majority opinion that sought an accommodating position.

BANK OF AUGUSTA v. EARLE
13 Peters 519 (1839)

It will at once be seen that the questions brought here for decision are of a very grave character, and they have received from the court an attentive examination. A multitude of corporations for various purposes have been chartered by the several States; a large portion of certain branches of business has been transacted by incorporated companies, or through their agency; and contracts to a very great amount have undoubtedly been made by different corporations out of the jurisdiction of the particular State by which they were created. In deciding the case before us, we in effect determine whether these numerous contracts are valid or not. And if, as has been argued at the bar, a corporation, from its nature and character, is incapable of making such contracts, or if they are inconsistent with the rights and sovereignty of the States in which they are made, they cannot be enforced in the courts of justice. . . .

But it has been urged in the argument, that notwithstanding the powers thus conferred by the terms of the charter, a corporation, from the very nature of its being, can have no authority to contract out of the limits of the State; that the laws of a State can have no extra-territorial operation; and that, as a corporation is the mere creature of a law of the State, it can have no existence beyond the limits in which that law operates;

and that it must necessarily be incapable of making a contract in another place.

It is very true that a corporation can have no legal existence out of the boundaries of the sovereignty by which it is created. It exists only in contemplation of law, and by force of the law; and where that law ceases to operate, and is no longer obligatory, the corporation can have no existence. It must dwell in the place of its creation, and cannot migrate to another sovereignty. But although it must live and have its being in that State only, yet it does not by any means follow that its existence there will not be recognized in other places; and its residence in one State creates no insuperable objection to its power of contracting in another. It is indeed a mere artificial being, invisible and intangible; yet it is a person, for certain purposes in contemplation of law, and has been recognized as such by the decisions of this court. It was so held in the case of The United States v. Amedy, and in Beaston v. The Farmer's Bank of Delaware. Now natural persons, through the intervention of agents, are continually making contracts in countries in which they do not reside; and where they are not personally present when the contract is made; and nobody has ever doubted the validity of these agreements. And what greater objection can there be to the capacity of an artificial person, by its agents, to make a contract within the scope of its limited powers, in a sovereignty in which it does not eside; provided such contracts are permitted to be made by them by the laws of the place?

The corporation must no doubt show that the law of its creation gave it authority to make such contracts, through such agents. Yet, as in the case of a natural person, it is not necessary that it should actually exist in the sovereignty in which the contract is made. It is sufficient that its existence as an artificial person, in the State of its creation, is acknowledged and recognized by the law of the nation where the dealing takes place; and that it is permitted by the laws of that place to exercise there the powers with which it is endowed.

Every power, however, of the description of which we are speaking, which a corporation exercises in another State, depends for its validity upon the laws of the sovereignty in which it is exercised; and a corporation can make no valid contract without their sanction, express or implied. . . .

[W]e proceed to inquire whether, by the comity of nations, foreign corporations are permitted to make contracts within their jurisdiction; and we can perceive no sufficient reason for excluding them, when they are not contrary to the known policy of the State, or injurious to its interests. . . .

We think it is well settled, that by the law of comity among nations, a corporation created by one sovereignty is permitted to make contracts in another, and to sue in its courts; and that the same law of comity prevails among the several sovereignties of this Union. The public and well known and long continued usage of trade; the general acquiescence of the States; the particular legislation of some of them, as well as the legislation of congress; all concur in proving the truth of this proposition.

But we have already said that this comity is presumed from the salient acquiescence of the State. Whenever a State sufficiently indicates that contracts which derive their validity from its comity are repugnant to its policy, or are considered as injurious to its interests; the presumption in favor of its adoption can no longer be made. . . .

Chief Justice Taney's reasoning in the Earle case, while couched in diplomatic terms, was largely supportive of the pro-corporation position of Chancellor James Kent. Kent, a New York conservative and a Federalist, had summed up his views on corporate status in an article in one of the early law journals. This opening question had equated corporate expansion with American nationalism.

Can it be possible in this great American Republic, when we are one nation for all national purposes, and one people in commercial pursuits, with the same common interests, sympathies, intercourse, and principles of jurisprudence, and entitled to an equal intercommunity of "privileges and immunities as citizens" throughout the land, that these corporate associations shall not have the liberty to make contracts, and to have free access to the courts of justice in one State as well as another? He then argued that . . . whenever a civil corporation, duly created in one state or country, enters, by its competent agent, into contracts in another, and such contracts are not in violation of its charter, but within its lawful powers, and consistent with dealings of a like nature, held lawful to the citizens of the State in which they take place, and are not forbidden by positive law to be made by corporate persons, the foreign corporation is entitled of right in every case to the protection and assistance of the courts, equally with resident citizens.[98]

The dissenting opinion of Justice John McKinley in *Bank of Augusta* v. *Earle* not only included his constitutional argument about the rights of the states but harbingered modern center-periphery arguments (emphasizing economic dependence for certain regions) as well. It was not just the issue of "foreign" corporations doing business where they preferred regardless of state policy, but the "corporations of the north" exploiting the cotton producing economy of the south. McKinley's dissent was the first of a series of strong critiques of the expansion of corporate power based upon federal judicial fiat.[99] He argued as follows:

. . . The counsel for the banks contended that the power of Congress to regulate commerce among the several States, deprives Alabama of the power to pass any law restraining the sale and purchase of a bill of exchange; and, by consequence, the whole power belongs to Congress. The court, by the opinion of the majority, does not recognize this doctrine, in terms. But if the power which the court exercised is not derived from that provision of the Constitution, in my opinion it does not exist.

If ever Congress shall exercise this power to the broad extent contended for, the power of the States over commerce, and contracts relating to commerce, will be reduced to very narrow limits. The creation of banks, the making and indorsing of bills of exchange and promissory notes, and the damages on bills of exchange, all relate, more or less, to the commerce among the several States. Whether the exercise of these powers amounts to regulating the commerce among the several States, is not a question for my determination on this occasion. The majority of the court have decided that the comity of nations gives validity to these contracts.

And what are the reasons upon which this doctrine is now established? Why, the counsel for the banks say: We are obliged to concede that these banks had no authority to make these contracts in the State of Alabama, in virtue of the laws of the States creating them, or by the laws of Alabama. Therefore, unless this court will extend to them the benefit of the comity of nations, they must lose all the money now in controversy, they will be deprived hereafter of the benefit of a very profitable branch of their business as bankers, and great public inconvenience will result to the commerce of the country. And besides all this, there are many corporations in the north, which were created for the purpose of carrying on various branches of manufactures, and particularly that of cotton. Those engaged in the manufacture of cotton will be unable to send their agents to the south to sell their manufactured articles, and to purchase cotton to carry on their business, and may lose debts already created. This is the whole amount of the argument, upon which the benefit of this doctrine is claimed.

The late 1830s produced judicial decision-making that transformed and enhanced corporate power, opened a long debate on the scope of the commerce power, and tested the scope of judicial power to force executive action. The latter issue was most clearly demonstrated in the case of *Kendall* v. *United States ex. rel. Stokes.* Amos Kendall was postmaster general under President Andrew Jackson. Upon assuming his post, Kendall had discovered evidence of corruption in postal contracts to a private delivery corporation, Stockon and Stokes, which held contracts to carry mail in post coaches in several eastern states. The corporation had important friends and contacts throughout the national government. One, the solicitor of the treasury, ordered Kendall to pay the corporation $40,000 even though Kendall had evidence that the corporation had failed to perform services for this money. After Stockton and Stokes lobbied Congress unsuccessfully, they turned to the circuit court for the District of Columbia. Postmaster General Kendall was summoned to show cause why he should not be compelled to pay the solicitor's award to Stockton and Stokes. The issue went to the Supreme Court after the circuit court decided against Kendall. Kendall challenged the authority of the circuit court to issue a writ of mandamus compelling him to pay. Peters, the court reporter, did not identify the writer of the majority opinion that is reproduced in part below:

AMOS KENDALL v. UNITED STATES
EX. REL. STOKES ET AL.
12 Peters 524 (1839)

In error to the Circuit Court of the United States in the District of Columbia, for the County of Washington. . . .

[Regarding the attempt to invoke the writ of mandamus as a remedy in the Circuit Court for the District of Columbia, the opinion stated that the authority for such a writ was found]. . .under the general delegation of power "to issue all other writs not specially provided for by statute, which may be necessary for the exercise of their respective jurisdictions, and agreeable to the principles and usages of law." And it is under this power that this court issues the writ to the circuit courts to compel them to proceed to a final judgment or decree in a cause, in order that we may exercise the jurisdiction of review given by the law; and the same power is exercised by the circuit courts over the district courts, where a writ of error or appeal lies to the Circuit Court. But this power is not exercised, as in England, by the King's Bench, as having a general supervising power over inferior courts; but only for the purpose of bringing the case to a final judgment or decree, so that it may be reviewed. The mandamus does not direct the inferior court how to proceed, but only that it must proceed, according to its own judgment, to a final determination; otherwise it cannot be reviewed in the Appellate Court. So that it is in a special, modified manner, in which the writ of mandamus is to be used in this court, and in the circuit courts in the States; and does not stand on the same footing, as in this district, under the general adoption of the laws of Maryland, which included the common law, as altered or modified on the 27th of February, 1801.

Thus far the power of the Circuit Court to issue the writ of mandamus has been considered as derived under the first section of the Act of 27th of February, 1801. But the third and fifth sections are to be taken into consideration in deciding this question. The third section, so far as it relates to the present inquiry, declares: "That there shall be a court in this district, which shall be called the Circuit Court of the District of Columbia; and the said court, and the judges thereof, shall have all the powers by law vested in the circuit courts and the judges of the circuit courts of the United States." And the fifth section declares: "That the said court shall have cognizance of all cases in law and equity between parties, both or either of which shall be resident or be found within the district."

And the power in the court below to exercise this jurisdiction, we think, results irresistibly from the third section of the Act of the 27th of February, 1801, which declares that the said court, and the judges thereof, shall have all the powers by law vested in the circuit courts and the judges of the circuit courts of the United States. The question here is, what circuit courts are referred to. By the Act of the 13th of February, 1801, the circuit courts established under the Judiciary Act of 1789 were abolished, and no other circuit courts were in existence except those established by the Act of 13th February, 1801. It was admitted by the Attorney General, on the argument, that if the language of the law had been, all the powers now vested in the circuit courts, etc., reference would have been made to the Act of the 13th February, 1801, and the courts thereby established. We think that would not have varied the constitution of the act. The reference is to the powers by law vested in the circuit courts. The question necessarily arises, what law? The question admits of no other answer than that it must be some existing law, by which powers are vested, and not a law which had been repealed. And there is no other law in force, vesting powers in circuit courts, except the law of the 13th of February, 1801. And the repeal of this law, fifteen months afterwards, and after the court in this district had been organized and gone into operation, under the Act of 27th of February, 1801, could not, in any manner, affect that law, any further than was provided by the repealing act. To what law was the Circuit Court of this district to look for the powers vested in the circuit courts of the United States, by which the court was to be governed, during the time the Act of the 13th of February was in force? Certainly to none other than that act. And whether the time was longer or shorter before that law was repealed, could make no difference.

It was not an uncommon course of legislation in the States at an early day to adopt, by reference, British statutes; and this has been the course of legislation by Congress in many instances where State practice and State process has been adopted. And such adoption has always been considered as referring to the law existing at the time of adoption; and no subsequent legislation has ever been supposed to affect it. And such must necessarily be the effect and operation of such adoption. No other rule would furnish any certainty as to what was the law, and would be adopting prospectively, all changes that might be made in the law. And this has been the light in which this court has viewed such legislation. . . .

The judgment of the court below is accordingly affirmed with costs, and the cause remanded for further proceedings.

The seriousness of the federal circuit court's challenge to federal executive authority was underscored in the dissents. One of these, by Justice Catron, treated this interesting question: How could a federal court issue a writ of mandamus after the definitive holding in *Marbury* v. *Madison* that Congress' grant of such authority was unconstitutional? Justice Catron's dissent and the court reporter's head note are reproduced below:[100]

[At the January Term of the Supreme Court, in 1838, the following dissenting opinion was delivered by Mr. Justice Catron, in the case of Amos Kendall, Postmaster-General v. The United States, on the relation of William B. Stokes and others. The case is reported in 12 Peters's Reports, 527. This opinion was not received from the clerk of the Supreme Court, with the opinions delivered at the January Term, 1838; it was received by the reporter from Mr. Justice Catron, on the 6th of March, 1839. It is inserted in the present volume with the consent of Mr. Justice Catron; and the reporter avails himself of this occasion to record his regret that it had not its place in the twelfth volume of the reports.]

Justice Catron, dissenting:

In this proceeding of the United States against the Postmaster-General, at the relation of Stockton, Stokes, & Company, I had intended not to intimate that I differed in any respect from the majority, having an aversion to dissenting opinions, save on constitutional questions. But my two brethren, with whom I agree, having determined to do so, it follows I must express a concurrence with the one side or the other.

On the merits, I think the Senate of the United States and the Solicitor of the Treasury construed the special act of Congress correctly, and that the solicitor's award is a final adjudication, and conclusive of the rights of the relators.

But the question whether the Circuit Court of this district had power to compel the Postmaster-General, by mandamus, to enter a credit for the amount awarded, lies at the foundation of our institutions; a question more grave or important rarely arises.

Coercion by the writ of mandamus of the officers and agents of a government, is one of the highest exertions of sovereignty known to the British constitution and common law; it is truly declared to be one of the flowers of the King's Bench (3 Black. Com. 110, note), and in England, can only be enforced by that court, where the King formerly sat in person, and is now deemed to be potentially present.

It is his command, in his own name, directed to a court, person, or corporation, to do a particular thing therein specified, which appertained to their office or duty, as a means of compelling its performance. 3 Black. Com. ch. 7. The proceeding there, as here, is in the name of the government, and not that of the relators; it stands on the foot of contempt, and is intended to reform official delinquency.

By the act of independence, this prerogative and portion of sovereignty, unimpaired, devolved on the different States of this Union; and by the Constitution of the United States, such portion of it as was necessary to coerce the courts, officers, and agents, of the general government, was withdrawn from the States and conferred on the federal sovereignty. Here the power lay dormant until Congress shall act. On the Legislature was imposed the duty to give it effect; it was wide as the land, and extended to every portion of it; and by the Judiciary Act of 1789 (sec. 13), Congress attempted to invest the Supreme Court of the United States with the power to issue writs of mandamus to persons holding office under the authority of the United States. But the Constitution having restricted this court to the exercise of certain original powers, and this not being amongst them, it was holden, in Marbury v. Madison. 1 Cranch, so much of the act was void. The decision was made in 1803; up to that time Congress and the country did not question that a law existed proper and necessary to give effect to the prerogative through the instrumentality of this court, and that it was properly vested in the highest tribunal in the land, exercising a jurisdiction coextensive with our whole territory. So the matter stood when the Act of the 27th February, 1801, was passed, organizing the Circuit Court for the District of Columbia. And the question is, did Congress, by implication, confer or intend to confer this high prerogative, within the ten miles square, on the Circuit Court? That concurrent power with the Supreme Court was intended to be given, it is difficult to believe. . . .

That the power can only be maintained to exist by implication, and not by express enactment, is admitted on all hands. It never was attempted to be conferred in express terms save on the Supreme Court; and is the construction that invokes it for the Circuit Court of this District a strained one? The tenth section of the repealed Act of the 13th of February, 1801, declares "that the circuit courts then established shall have, and are hereby invested with all the powers heretofore granted by law to the Circuit Courts of the United States, unless otherwise provided by this act."

There is no repealing clause to the act. The section quoted refers directly to the fourteenth section of the Act of 1789, for the powers common to all the circuit courts of the Union. They have stood unaltered, and been recognized, with slight exceptions, as the sole powers by which the jurisdiction of the circuit courts has been enforced, from the year 1789 to this time.

It is insisted, however, that the jurisdiction conferred on the Circuit Court by the 11th section of the repealed Act of the 13th of February, 1801, is much broader than that given to them by the eleventh section of the Act of 1789; that the Act of 1801 covers the whole ground of the Constitution. This is certainly true, but the fifth section of the Act of the 27th of February, 1801, declaring what matters shall be cognizable in the Circuit Court for the District of Columbia, confers jurisdiction quite as comprehensive. Its cognizance, or jurisdiction "to hold plea," extends to all cases in law and equity, provided the defendant be found in the district. Thus, as the eleventh sections of the Act of 1789, and the 13th of February, 1801, each have reference to the exercise of jurisdiction in suits or actions between litigant parties, or over matters in some form brought before the court to try and ascertain a contested right, it would be a most unnatural construction to hold; as I think that the phrase, "cognizance of all cases in law and equity," authorized the court to assume the high power of coercing by mandamus one of the secretaries or the Postmaster-General, to the performance of some specific public duty, in case of an ascertained right, by force of the strong arm of sovereign power, because he was a public officer, and who was not a suitor in court, or party to a case in law or equity. . . .

Another consideration prominently presents itself. Congress has jurisdiction, exclusive of the several States, over this district of ten miles square; and so Congress has exclusive jurisdiction over the territories of the United States; and upon the courts of these, as upon the courts of this district, the jurisdiction and powers of the State courts, of which the territories were formerly a part, have been conferred; and, in addition thereto, the territorial courts have been invested with the jurisdiction and powers of the circuit courts of the United States. There are two territories, the courts of which are now exercising such general jurisdiction and powers—Florida and Wisconsin. These courts, having coextensive powers with that of the District of Columbia, it follows if the sovereign prerogative to exert the writ of mandamus to coerce executive officers of the United States pertains to the one court it must to the others; and that congress has, by implication, intrusted to the courts of the two territories named, as well as to the court of this district, powers that have been unquestionably withholden from the federal circuit courts of the twenty-six States. To say Congress never so intended, and if the power exists it was conferred by an oversight in the Legislature, is perhaps asserting what few would be found to deny. The truth (there can be little room for doubt) is, that Congress has been unwilling to expose the action of the government in the administration of its vast and complicated affairs, and its officers, who have charge of their management, to the danger and indignity of being coerced and controlled at the ill-defined discretion of the inferior courts by the writ of mandamus; and that after the decision of Marbury v. Madison in 1803, holding that the Supreme Court had not the power thus to coerce an officer of the United States, it has been permitted to lie dormant, awaiting the action of the Legislature. The supposition is rendered highly probable, when we consider the delicacy its exercise would necessarily involve, and the difficulty of vesting so high and exensive a power in the inferior courts, and especially in those of this district, in a modified and safe form.

Such being my own opinion, I think the order awarding the mandamus against the Postmaster-General should be reversed, for want of jurisdiction in the court below to issue the writ.

The application of the doctrine that a writ of mandamus may issue from a federal court to a cabinet officer of the president of the United States originated with the chief judge of the Circuit Court of the District of Columbia, William Cranch. His career began with a minor patronage job bestowed by an old friend of his family from Massachusetts, John Adams, second president of the United States. When Adams was defeated in 1800, he had picked Cranch as a judge of the newly created Circuit Court for the District of Columbia, where he served initially with James Marshall and the first chief judge of the circuit court, William Kilty. Adams' choice for chief judge, Thomas Johnson, had declined the appointment. Consequently, the incoming president, Thomas Jefferson, chose a distinguished Maryland jurist, William Kilty, who served for six years. When Kilty resigned to become chancellor of the state of Maryland, President Jefferson promoted Cranch to chief judge of the circuit, a lapse of partisan commitment which was, inadvertently to ensure Cranch's conservative, Federalist influence for more than a half a century on the only remaining circuit court with separate judges. From 1801 to 1807, Cranch served as assistant circuit judge. From 1807 to 1856 Cranch was chief judge, influencing the D.C. circuit for an astonishing 55 years. For several years early in his circuit court career, Cranch also served as Supreme Court reporter.[101]

As a result of the Kendall decision, executive power was viewed as severely limited and judicial authority enhanced by invocation of the doctrine that the writ of mandamus may be imposed on a high federal executive despite the decision in *Marbury* v. *Madison.* Justice Catron, in dissent, noted the irony of the latter. President Martin Van Buren, in his annual message of December 3, 1838, severely criticized the decision, pointing out that it had the effect of accepting the issuance of a writ of mandamus in only one circuit jurisdiction while denying it in all others. He suggested that "Congress alone can provide a remedy." In the following year, Congress did so, by enacting a law expressly forbidding the issuance of the writ of mandamus by the courts of the District of Columbia.[102]

The Kendall case is generally treated only as an action involving a special (and subsequently short-lived) judicial restriction on executive authority. There is, however, another important dimension to the Kendall controversy. The Kendall decision never dealt with the issue of corruption accurately raised by the postmaster general. Thus, the case illustrated the growing capacity of private corporations to defy public governmental efforts at curbing unconscionable profiteering or, as in the case of Stockton and Stokes, outright corruption. As commercial and business enterprises multiplied and corporations developed and expanded their activities, the characteristics of the legal profession began to change. More lawyers chose to forego politics and enter corporation law. The prototype of the modern corporate law firm was Cravath, originated in 1819. Later in the 19th century, this firm began the practice of selecting the best law graduates of elite Ivy League law schools and utilizing them in an intensely competitive and rigorous manner until a small proportion of them were chosen as law firm partners.[103]

The transformation in the relative positions of public governments (federal, state, or local) and private "governments"[104] (such as multinational corporations, banking and railroad institutions, and corporate firms) from the early 19th century to the last two decades of the 20th century is tremendous, but the changes were often limited albeit cumulative. The major and most consistent contributor to this development was the Supreme Court of the United States. Basic changes in the status of corporations were crucial elements in this transformation. Two decisions of the Supreme Court in the early 1840s contributed a great deal to this shift.

Swift v. *Tyson,*[105] decided in 1842, extended federal judicial power considerably by adopting the principles of a "general commercial law." Despite the fact that some years earlier the Court had abandoned any claims for a federal common law jurisdiction, the Tyson doctrine, in effect, established such a jurisdiction in cases involving common commercial law that came to federal courts under diversity of citizenship. Thereafter, federal judges were no longer required to apply the common commercial law interpretations of state judges. Instead, they provided their own interpretations in accordance with "general commercial law." In the context of the generally strong anticorporation doctrinal tendencies of several state judiciaries, *Swift* v. *Tyson* afforded private corporations a friendly sanctuary in which doctrines of national commercial law were developed and subsequently expanded. The scope of this expansion of federal juicial power was controlled, of course, by the accessibility of the federal courts to corporations via diversity of citizenship jurisdiction. The Supreme Court obligingly assured corporations a privileged status within two years of the Tyson decision. The occasion was the important case of *Louisville, Cincinnati, and Charleston Railroad Company* v. *Letson*.

The question whether a corporation could bring cases to federal courts under the diversity of citizenship jurisdiction of Article III of the Constitution was initially raised early in the 19th Century. In *Bank of the United States* v. *Deveaux*,[106] the Court provided a very qualified affirmative response. Chief Justice Marshall had held that a corporation "is certainly not a citizen; and, consequently, cannot sue or be sued in the courts of the United States unless the rights of the members, in this respect, can be exercised in their corporate name."[107] This doctrine did not always prevent corporate access to the federal courts but rendered it difficult under a number of circumstances. Jurisdiction was limited to those suits in which all the individual corporate litigants were citizens of a state different from the state of any one of the opposing litigants.

In the Letson case this doctrine was challenged by attorneys for the defendant. Chief Justice Taney was absent. The Supreme Court's opinion was delivered by Associate Justice Wayne of Georgia. He first rejected arguments based upon the Eleventh Amendment. He then dealt with the major argument raised on the basis of the Deveaux doctrine and subsequently abandoned the earlier precedent.

LOUISVILLE, CINCINNATI, AND CHARLESTON RAILROAD COMPANY v. LETSON
2 Howard 497 (1844)

A suit then brought by a citizen of one state against a corporation by its corporate name in the state of its locality, by which it was created and where its business is done by any of the corporators who are chosen to manage its affairs, is a suit, so far as jurisdiction is concerned, between citizens of the state where the suit is brought and a citizen of another state. The corporators as individuals are not defendants in the suit, but they are parties having an interest in the result, and some of them being citizens of the state where the suit is brought, jurisdiction attaches over the corporation,—nor can we see how it can be defeated by some of the members, who cannot be sued, residing in a different state. It may be said that the suit

is against the corporation, and that nothing must be looked at but the legal entity, and then that we cannot view the members except as an artificial aggregate. This is so, in respect to the subject-matter of the suit and the judgment which may be rendered; but if it be right to look to the members to ascertain whether there be jurisdiction or not, the want of appropriate citizenship in some of them to sustain jurisdiction, cannot take it away, when there are other members who are citizens, with the necessary residence to maintain it.

But we are now met and told that the cases of Strawbridge and Curtis, and that of The Bank of the United States and Deveaux, hold a different doctrine.

We do not deny that the language of those decisions do not justify in some degree the inferences which have been made from them, or that the effect of them has been to limit the jurisdiction of the circuit courts in practice to the cases contended for by the counsel for the plaintiff in error. The practice has been, since those cases were decided, that if there be two or more plaintiffs and two or more joint defendants, each of the plaintiffs must be capable of suing each of the defendants in the courts of the United States in order to support the jurisdiction, and in cases of corporation to limit jurisdiction to cases in which all the corporators were citizens of the State in which the suit is brought. The case of Strawbridge and Curtis was decided without argument. That of the Bank and Deveaux, after argument of great ability. But never since that case has the question been presented to this court, with the really distinguished ability of the arguments of the counsel in this, in no way surpassed by those in the former. And now we are called upon in the most imposing way to give our best judgments to the subject, yielding to decided cases every thing that can be claimed for them on the score of authority, except the surrender of conscience.

After mature deliberation, we feel free to say, that the cases of Strawbridge and Curtis, and that of the Bank and Deveaux, were carried too far, and that consequences and inferences have been argumentatively drawn from the reasoning employed in the latter which ought not to be followed. . . . A corporation, created by a State, to perform its functions under the authority of that State, and only suable there, though it may have members out of the State, seems to us to be a person, though an artificial one, inhabiting and belonging to that State, and therefore entitled, for the purpose of suing and being sued, to be deemed a citizen of that State. We remark, too, that the cases of Strawbridge and Curtis, and the Bank and Deveaux, have never been satisfactory to the bar, and that they were not, especially the last, entirely satisfactory to the court that made them. They have been followed always most reluctantly and with dissatisfaction. By no one was the correctness of them more questioned than by the late chief justice who gave them. It is within the knowledge of several of us, that he repeatedly expressed regret that those decisions had been made, adding, whenever the subject was mentioned, that if the point of jurisdiction was an original one, the conclusion would be different. We think we may safely assert, that a majority of the members of this court have at all times partaken of the same regret, and that, whenever a case has occurred on the circuit, involving the application of the case of the Bank and Deveaux, it was yielded to, because the decision had been made, and not because it was thought to be right. We have already said that the case of The Bank of Vicksburgh and Slocomb, 14 Pet. 60, was most reluctantly given, upon mere authority. We are now called upon, upon the authority of those cases alone, to go further in this case than has yet been done. It has led to a review of the principles of all the cases. We cannot follow further, and upon our maturest deliberation we do not think that the cases relied upon for a doctrine contrary to that which this court will here announce, are sustained by a sound and comprehensive course of professional reasoning. Fortunately, a departure from them involves no change in a rule of property. Our conclusion, too, if it shall not have universal acquiescence, will be admitted by all to be coincident with the policy of the constitution and the condition of our country. It is coincident also with the recent legislation of congress, as that is shown by the act of the 28th of February, 1839, in amendment of the acts respecting the judicial system of the United States. We do not hesitate to say, that it was passed exclusively with an intent to rid the courts of the decision in the case of Strawbridge and Curtis. . . .

The judgment of the circuit court below is affirmed.

The Supreme Court report carried no indication of dissent to this far-reaching doctrinal change, but a decade later, Justice Grier, in writing the majority opinion in *Marshall* v. *Baltimore and Ohio Railroad Company*,[108] acknowledged inferentially that there was disagreement with the Letson doctrine but argued for adherence to precedent and stability as follows:

The published report of that case (whatever the fact may have been) exhibits no dissent to the opinion of the Court by any member of it. It has, for the space of ten years, been received by the bar as a final settlement of the questions which have so frequently arisen under this clause of the Constitution; and the practice and forms of pleading in the courts of the United States have been conformed to it. Confiding in its stability, numerous controversies involving property and interests to a large amount have been heard and decided by the Circuit Courts, and by this Court; and many are still pending here where the jurisdiction has been assumed on the faith of the sufficiency of such an averment. If we should now declare these judgments to have been entered without jurisdiction of authority, we should inflict a great and irreparable evil on the community. There are no cases, where an adherence to the maxim of *"stare decisis"* is so absolutely necessary to the peace of society, as those which affect retroactively the jurisdiction of courts. For this reason alone, even if the Court were now of opinion that the principles affirmed in the case just mentioned, and that of *The Bank v. Deveaux*, were not founded on right reason, we should not be justified in overruling them. The practice founded on these decisions, to say the least, injures or wrongs no man; while their reversal could not fail to work wrong and injury to many.[109]

In actuality, the Letson doctrine evoked a series of strong dissents, especially from Justices Peter V. Daniel and Archibald Campbell. Daniel had attacked the doctrinal foundation of the decision, arguing that the majority in Letson

> . . . have not only contravened all the known definitions and adjudications with respect to the nature of corporations, but they have repudiated the doctrines of the civilians as to what is imported by the term *subject* or *citizen*, and repealed, at the same time, that restriction in the Constitution which limited the jurisdiction of the courts of the United States to controversies between "citizens of different states." They have asserted that, "a corporation created by, and transacting business in a State, is to be deemed an inhabitant of the State, capable of being treated as a citizen, for all the purposes of suing and being sued, and that an averment of the facts of its creation, and the place of transacting its business, is sufficient to give the circuit courts jurisdiction."[110]

However, the most concentrated attacks on the Letson doctrine were made by Justice John Archibald Campbell. In dissent in *Marshall v. Baltimore and Ohio Railroad Company*, Campbell argued that

> A corporation is not a citizen. It may be an artificial person, a moral person, a juridical person, a legal entity, a faculty, an intangible, invisible being; but Chief Justice Marshall employed no metaphysical refinements, nor subtlety, nor sophism, but spoke the common sense, "the universal understanding," as he calls it, of the people when he declared the unanimous judgment of this court, "that it certainly is not a citizen." Nor were corporations within the contemplation of the framers of the Constitution when they delegated a jurisdiction over controversies between the citizens of different States.[111]

Campbell also argued that the ultimate political effect of the doctrine would be serious for state autonomy. An advocate of the Calhounian political philosophy, Campbell argued that the doctrine, by enhancing the position of corporations, also strengthened the position of the northern commercial and manufacturing states of the Union. In the same dissent in the Marshall case, Campbell argued that

> . . . It may be safely assumed that no offering could be made to the wealthy, powerful, and ambitious corporations of the populous and commercial States of the Union so valuable, and none which would so serve to enlarge the influence of those States, as the adoption, to its full import, of the conclusion, "that to all intents and purposes, for the objects of their incorporation, these artificial persons are capable of being treated as a citizen as much as a natural person."

The Supreme Court of Kentucky says, truly, "the apparent reciprocity of the power would prove to be a delusion. The competition for extraterritorial advantages would but aggrandize the stronger to the disparagement of the weaker States. Resistance and retaliation would lead to conflict and confusion, and the weaker states must either submit to have their policy controlled, their business monopolized, their domestic institutions reduced to insignificance, or the peace and harmony of the States broken up and destroyed." To this consummation this judgment of the Court is deemed to be a progress.[112]

The tendency to equate a number of issues to the weakening or strengthening of the slave states was not only true of status of corporation issues, but became important in commerce clause cases as well. Advocacy of doctrines providing for expansion of congressional authority in interstate or foreign commerce and for exclusive congressional authority in such commerce was considered by Southern leaders as prima facie evidence of anti–Southern tendencies. In the *Passenger Cases*, the Court attempted to resolve the question whether the states of New York and Massachusetts could levy head taxes on passengers to their seaports. Counsel for the states argued that the taxes were not attempts at interfering with commerce or immigration, but simply devices to defray the costs of caring for foreign paupers. The justices divided on the question of the scope of congressional authority over interstate and foreign commerce. The opinions of Justice McLean and Chief Justice Taney are provided below.

THE PASSENGER CASES
7 Howard 283 (1849)

Justice McLean:

I will consider the case under two general heads:—

1. Is the power of congress to regulate commerce an exclusive power?

2. Is the statute of New York a regulation of commerce? . . .

A concurrent power in the States to regulate commerce is an anomaly not found in the constitution. If such power exists, it may be exercised independently of the federal authority.

It does not follow, as is often said, with little accuracy, that, when a state law shall conflict with an act of congress, the former must yield. On the contrary, except in certain cases named in the federal constitution, this is never correct when the act of the State is strictly within its powers. . . .

A concurrent power excludes the idea of a dependent power. The general government and a State exercise concurrent powers in taxing the people of the State. The objects of taxation may be the same, but the motives and policy of the tax are different, and the powers are distinct and independent. A concurrent

power in two distinct sovereignties, to regulate the same thing, is as inconsistent in principle as it is impracticable in action. It involves a moral and physical impossibility. A joint action is not supposed, and two independent wills cannot do the same thing. The action of one, unless there be an arrangement, must necessarily precede the action of the other; and that which is first, being competent, must establish the rule. If the powers be equal, as must be the case, both being sovereign, one may undo what the other does, and this must be the result of their action.

But the argument is, that a State, acting in a subordinate capacity, wholly inconsistent with its sovereignty, may regulate foreign commerce until congress shall act on the same subject, and that the State must then yield to the paramount authority. A jealousy of the federal powers has often been expressed, and an apprehension entertained that they would impair the sovereignty of the States. But this argument degrades the States by making their legislation, to the extent stated, subject to the will of congress. State powers do not rest upon this basis. Congress can in no respect restrict or enlarge state powers, though they may adopt a state law. State powers are, at all times and under all circumstances, exercised independently of the general government, and are never declared void or inoperative except when they transcend state jurisdiction. And, on the same principle, the federal authority is void when exercised beyond its constitutional limits. . . .

It has been well remarked that the regulation of commerce consists as much in negative as in positive action. There is not a federal power which has been exerted in all its diversified means of operation. And yet it may have been exercised by congress, influenced by a judicious policy and the instruction of the people. Is a commercial regulation open to state action because the federal power has not been exhausted? No ingenuity can provide for every contingency; and if it could, it might not be wise to do so. Shall free goods be taxed by a State because congress have not taxed them? Or shall a State increase the duty, on the ground that it is too low? Shall passengers, admitted by act of congress without a tax, be taxed by a State? The supposition of such a power in a State is utterly inconsistent with a commercial power, either paramount or exclusive, in congress.

That it is inconsistent with the exclusive power will be admitted; but the exercise of a subordinate commercial power by a State is contended for. When this power is exercised, how can it be known that the identical thing has not been duly considered by congress? And how can congress, by any legislation, prevent this interference? A practical enforcement of this system, if system it may be called, would overthrow the federal commercial power. . . .

I come now to inquire, under the second general proposition, Is the statute of New York a regulation of foreign commerce? . . .

Commerce is defined to be "an exchange of commodities." But this definition does not convey the full meaning of the term. It includes "navigation and intercourse." That the transportation of passengers is a part of commerce, is not now an open question. . . .

Except to guard its citizens against diseases and paupers, the municipal power of a State cannot prohibit the introduction of foreigners brought to this country under the authority of congress. . . .

The police power of the State cannot draw within its jurisdiction objects which lie beyond it. It meets the commercial power of the Union in dealing with subjects under the protection of that power, yet it can only be exerted under peculiar emergencies, and to a limited extent. In guarding the safety, the health, and morals of its citizens, a State is restricted to appropriate and constitutional means. If extraordinary expense be incurred, an equitable claim to an indemnity can give no power to a State to tax objects not subject to its jurisdiction. . . .

A tax or duty upon tonnage, merchandise, or passengers is a regulation of commerce, and cannot be laid by a State, except under the sanction of congress and for the purposes specified in the constitution. On the subject of foreign commerce, including the transportation of passengers, congress have adopted such regulations as they deemed proper, taking into view our relations with other countries. And this covers the whole ground. The act of New York which imposes a tax on passengers of a ship from a foreign port, in the manner provided, is a regulation of foreign commerce, which is exclusively vested in congress; and the act is, therefore, void. . . .

Chief Justice Taney dissented:

[T]he first inquiry is, whether, under the constitution of the United States, the federal government has the power to compel the several States to receive, and suffer to remain in association with its citizens, every person or class of persons whom it may be the policy or pleasure of the United States to admit. In my judgment, this question lies at the foundation of the controversy in this case. I do not mean to say that the general government have, by treaty or act of congress, required the State of Massachusetts to permit the aliens in question to land. I think there is no treaty or act of congress which can justly be so construed. But it is not necessary to examine that question until we have first inquired whether congress can lawfully exercise such a power, and whether the States are bound to submit to it. For if the people of the several States of this Union reserved to themselves the power of expelling from their borders any person, or class of persons, whom it might deem dangerous to its peace, or likely to produce a physical or moral evil among its citizens, then any treaty or law of congress invading this right, and authorizing the introduction of any person or description of persons against the consent of the State, would be an usurpation of power which this court could neither recognize nor enforce. . . .

[I]t is equally clear, that, if it may remove from among its citizens any person or description of persons whom it regards as injurious to their welfare, it follows that it may meet them at the threshold and prevent them from entering. . . .

Neither can this be a concurrent power, and whether it belongs to the general or to the state government, the sovereignty which possesses the right must in its exercise be altogether independent of the other. If the United States have the power, then any legislation by the State in conflict with a treaty or act of congress would be void. And if the States possess it, then any act on the subject by the general government, in conflict with the state law, would also be void, and this court bound to disregard it. It must be paramount and absolute in the sovereignty which possesses it. A concurrent and equal power in the United States and the States, as to who should and who should not be permitted to reside in a State, would be a direct conflict of powers repugnant to each other, continually thwarting and defeating its exercise by either, and could result in nothing but disorder and confusion.

Again: if the State has the right to exclude from its borders any person or persons whom it may regard as dangerous to the safety of its citizens, it must necessarily have the right to decide when and towards whom this power is to be exercised. It is in its nature a discretionary power, to be exercised according to the judgment of the party which possesses it. And it must, therefore, rest with the State to determine whether any particular class or description of persons are likely to produce discontents or insurrection in its territory, or to taint the morals of its citizens, or to bring among them contagious diseases, or the evils and burdens of a numerous pauper population. For if the general government can in any respect, or by any form of legislation, control or restrain a State in the exercise of this power, or decide whether it has been exercised with proper discretion, and towards proper persons, and on proper occasions, then the real and substantial power would be in congress, and not in the States. In the cases decided in this court, and herein before referred to, the power of determining who is or who is not dangerous to the interests and well-being of the people of the State has been uniformly admitted to reside in the State. . . .

Undoubtedly, vessels engaged in the transportation of passengers from foreign countries, may be regulated by congress, and are a part of the commerce of the country. Congress may prescribe how the vessel shall be manned, and navigated, and equipped, and how many passengers she may bring, and what provision shall be made for them, and what tonnage she shall pay. But the law of Massachusetts now in question does not in any respect attempt to regulate this trade, or impose burdens upon it. I do not speak of the duty enjoined upon the pilot, because that provision is not now before us, although I see no objection to it. But this law imposes no tonnage duty on the ship, or any tax upon the captain or passengers for entering its waters. It merely refuses permission to the passengers to land until the security demanded by the State for the protection of its own people from the evils of pauperism has been given. If, however, the treaty or act of congress above referred to had attempted to compel the State to receive them without any security, the question would not be on any conflicting regulations of commerce, but upon one far more important to the States, that is, the power of deciding who should or should not be permitted to reside among its citizens. Upon that subject I have already stated my opinion. I cannot believe that it was ever intended to vest in congress, by the general words in relation to the regulation of commerce, this overwhelming power over the States. For if the treaty stipulation before referred to, can receive the construction given to it in the argument, and has that commanding power claimed for it over the States, then the emancipated slaves of the West Indies have at this hour the absolute right to reside, hire houses, and traffic and trade throughout the southern States, in spite of any state law to the contrary; inevitably producing the most serious discontent, and ultimately leading to the most painful consequences. . . .

I may, therefore, safely assume, that, according to the true construction of the constitution, the power granted to congress to regulate commerce, did not in any degree abridge the power of taxation in the States; and that they would at this day have the right to tax the merchandise brought into their ports and harbors by the authority and under the regulations of congress, had they not been expressly prohibited. . . .

The Court held the state statutes unconstitutional in a 5 to 4 decision, but divided so deeply on the issue of the exclusiveness of Congress' commerce power that the court reporter could not identify a single court opinion. Justice McLean asserted that the doctrine of the exclusiveness of federal commerce authority. Justices Wayne, Catron, McKinley, and Grier supported McLean's conclusion that the acts were unconstitutional, but did not commit themselves on the exclusiveness doctrine. Chief Justice Taney and Justices Nelson, Woodbury, and Daniel dissented, emphasizing state authority. McLean's and Taney's opinions represented the polar extremes. Justice Levi Woodbury's opinion incorporated the innovative doctrine of "selective exclusiveness" adopted by a majority of the Court in 1851. Woodbury died before that decision was rendered, and the doctrine he developed was identified with his successor, Justice Benjamin R. Curtis.

The 1851 case, *Cooley* v. *Board of Wardens of the Port of Philadelphia,* involved the validity of a regulation of the qualifications of Philadelphia harbor pilots alleged to be in conflict with Congressional commerce authority. The central issue was whether the states could regulate interstate or foreign commerce under any circumstances. The key portions of Justice Curtis' treatment of this issue are reproduced below.

COOLEY v. BOARD OF WARDENS OF THE PORT OF PHILADELPHIA
12 Howard 299 (1851)

That the power to regulate commerce includes the regulation of navigation, we consider settled. And when we look to the nature of the service performed by pilots, to the relations which that service and its compensations bear to navigation between the several States, and between the ports of the United States and foreign countries, we are brought to the conclusion, that the regulation of the qualifications of pilots, of the modes and times of offering and rendering their services, of the responsibilities which shall rest upon them, of the powers they shall possess, of the compensation they may demand, and of the penalties by which their rights and duties may be enforced, do constitute regulations of navigation, and consequently of commerce, within the just meaning of this clause of the constitution.

The power to regulate navigation is the power to prescribe rules in conformity with which navigation must be carried on. It extends to the persons who conduct it, as well as to the instruments used. Accordingly, the first Congress assembled under the Constitution passed laws, requiring the masters of ships and vessels of the United States to be citizens of the United States, and established many rules for the government and regulation of officers and seamen. These have been from time to time added to and changed, and we are not aware that their validity has been questioned.

Now, a pilot, so far as respects the navigation of the vessel in that part of the voyage which is his pilotage ground, is the temporary master charged with the safety of the vessel and cargo, and of the lives of those on board, and intrusted with the command of the crew. He is not only one of the persons engaged in navigation, but he occupies a most important and responsible place among those thus engaged. And if Congress has power to regulate the seamen who assist the pilot in the management of the vessel, a power never denied, we can perceive no valid reason why the pilot should be beyond the reach of the same power. It is true that, according to the usages of modern commerce on the ocean, the pilot is on board only during a part of the voyage between ports of different states, or between ports of the United States and foreign countries; but if he is on board for such a purpose and during so much of the voyage as to be engaged in navigation, the power to regulate navigation extends to him while thus engaged, as clearly as it would if he were to remain on board throughout the whole passage, from port to port. For it is a power which extends to every part of the voyage, and may regulate those who conduct or assist in conducting navigation in one part of a voyage as much as in another part, or during the whole voyage.

Nor should it be lost sight of, that this subject of the regulation of pilots and pilotage has an intimate connection with, and an important relation to, the general subject of commerce with foreign nations and among the several States, over which it was one main object of the Constitution to create a national control. . . .

. . . And a majority of the court are of opinion that a regulation of pilots is a regulation of commerce, within the grant to congress of the commercial power, contained in the third clause of the eighth section of the first article of the Constitution.

It becomes necessary, therefore, to consider whether this law of Pennsylvania, being a regulation of commerce, is valid.

The Act of Congress of the 7th of August, 1789, sec. 4, is as follows:

"That all pilots in the bays, inlets, rivers, harbors, and ports of the United States shall continue to be regulated in conformity with the existing laws of the States, respectively, wherein such pilots may be, or with such laws as the States may respectively hereafter enact for the purpose, until further legislative provision shall be made by Congress." . . .

. . . We are brought directly and unavoidably to the consideration of the question, whether the grant of the commercial power to Congress, did per se deprive the States of all power to regulate pilots. This question has never been decided by this court, nor, in our judgment, has any case depending upon all the considerations which must govern this one, come before this court. The grant of commercial power to Congress does not contain any terms which exclude the States from exercising an authority over its subject matter. If they are excluded it must be because the nature of the power, thus granted to Congress, requires that a similar authority should not exist in the States. If it were conceded on the one side that the nature of this power, like that to legislate for the District of Columbia, is absolutely and totally repugnant to the existence of similar power in the States, probably no one would deny that the grant of the power to Congress, as effectually and perfectly excludes the States from all future legislation on the subject, as if express words had been used to exclude them. And on the other hand, if it were admitted that the existence of this power in Congress, like the power of taxation, is compatible with the existence of a similar power in the States, then it would be in conformity with the contemporary exposition of the Constitution (Federalist, No. 32), and with the judicial construction given from time to time by this court, after the most deliberate consideration, to hold that the mere grant of such a power to Congress, did not imply a prohibition on the States to exercise the same power; that it is not the mere existence of such a power, but its exercise by Congress, which may be incompatible with the exercise of the same power by the States, and that the States may legislate in the absence of congressional regulations. . . .

The diversities of opinion, therefore, which have existed on this subject, have arisen from the different views taken of the nature of this power. But when the nature of a power like this is spoken of, when it is said that the nature of the power requires that it should be exercised exclusively by Congress, it must be intended to refer to the subjects of that power, and to say they are of such a nature as to require exclusive legislation by Congress. Now, the power to regulate commerce, embraces a vast field, containing not only many, but exceedingly various subjects, quite unlike in their nature; some imperatively demanding a single uniform rule, operating equally on the commerce of the United States in every port; and some, like the subject now in question, as imperatively demanding that diversity, which alone can meet the local necessities of navigation.

Either absolutely to affirm, or deny, that the nature of this power requires exclusive legislation by Congress, is to lose sight of the nature of the subjects of this power, and to assert concerning all of them, what is really applicable but to a part. Whatever subjects of this power are in their nature national, or admit only of one uniform system, or plan of regulation, may justly be said to be of such a nature as to require exclusive legislation by Congress. That this cannot be affirmed of laws for the regulation of pilots and pilotage is plain. The Act of 1789 contains a clear and authoritative declaration by the first Congress, that the nature of this subject is such, that until Congress should find it necessary to exert its power, it should be left to the legislation of the States; that it is local and not national; that it is likely to be the best provided for, not by one system, or plan of regulations, but by as many as the legislative discretion of the several States should deem applicable to the local peculiarities of the ports within their limits. . . .

It is the opinion of a majority of the court that the mere grant to Congress of the power to regulate commerce, did not deprive the States of power to regulate pilots, and that although Congress has legislated on this subject, its legislation manifests an intention, with a single exception, not to regulate this subject, but to leave its regulation to the several States. To these precise questions, which are all we are called on to decide, this opinion must be understood to be confined. It does not extend to the question what other subjects, under the commercial power, are within the exclusive control of Congress, or may be regulated by the States in the absence of all congressional legislation; nor to the general question how far any regulation of a subject by Congress may be deemed to operate as an exclusion of all legislation by the States upon the same subject. We decide the precise questions before us, upon what we deem sound principles, applicable to this particular subject in the state in which the legislation of Congress has left it. We go no farther. . . .

Justice McLean, with Justice Wayne concurring, rendered a dissenting opinion.
Justice Daniel rendered an opinion which differed in reasoning but concurred in the judgment of the Court.

The Taney Court and Jacksonian political principles

The Jacksonian political movement ushered in an era of increased public participation in the electoral process and was generally viewed as putting an end to gentry class political domination. But the machinery of participation and the nature of representation was largely in the control of individual states. Some of these were far less responsive to Jacksonian democratization than others. For example, Rhode Island continued to restrict suffrage by means of property qualifications for voting after many other states had abandoned such restrictions. By 1841, a movement led by Thomas A. Dorr had swept the state. Mass meetings were held and a plan for popular choice of delegates to a state constitutional convention was adopted. It did not conform to the old, existing state constitution. The new constitution was adopted by a majority of voters and Dorr set about installing the new government. The old regime declared martial law, called out the state militia, and asked President Tyler to send federal troops to crush the rebellion. Tyler complied and "Dorr's Rebellion" collapsed. Dorr himself was arrested, tried for treason, sentenced to life imprisonment, and subsequently pardoned. He had attempted to bring the issue to the Supreme Court by means of a writ of habeas corpus, but failed. A civil issue between Luther and Borden did, however, bring the matter before the Court in 1849.

LUTHER v. BORDEN
7 Howard 1 (1849)

Chief Justice Taney
delivered the opinion of the Court:

This case has arisen out of the unfortunate political differences which agitated the people of Rhode Island in 1841 and 1842.

It is an action of trespass brought by Martin Luther, the plaintiff in error, against Luther M. Borden and others, the defendants, in the Circuit Court of the United States for the District of Rhode Island, for breaking and entering the plaintiff's house. The defendants justify upon the ground that large numbers of men were assembled in different parts of the State for the purpose of overthrowing the government by military force, and were actually levying war upon the State; that, in order to defend itself from this insurrection, the State was declared by competent authority to be under martial law; that the plaintiff was engaged in the insurrection; and that the defendants, being in the military service of the State, by command of their superior officer, broke and entered the house and searched the rooms for the plaintiff, who was supposed to be there concealed, in order to arrest him, doing as little damage as possible. The plaintiff replied, that the trespass was committed by the defendants of their own proper wrong, and without any such cause; and upon the issue joined on this replication, the parties proceeded to trial. . . .

The existence and authority of the government under which the defendants acted was called in question; and the plaintiff insists, that, before the acts complained of were committed, that government had been displaced and annulled by the people of Rhode Island, and that the plaintiff was engaged in supporting the lawful authority of the State, and the defendants themselves were in arms against it.

This is a new question in this court, and certainly a very grave one; and at the time when the trespass is alleged to have been committed it had produced a general and painful excitement in the State, and threatened to end in bloodshed and civil war.

The evidence shows that the defendants, in breaking into the plaintiff's house and endeavouring to arrest him, as stated in the pleadings, acted under the authority of the government which was established in Rhode Island at the time of the Declaration of Independence, and which is usually called the charter government. For when the separation from England took place, Rhode Island did not, like the other States, adopt a new constitution, but continued the form of government established by the charter of Charles the Second in 1663; making only such alterations, by acts of the legislature, as were necessary to adapt it to their condition and rights as an independent State.

In this form of government no mode of proceeding was pointed out by which amendments might be made. It authorized the legislature to prescribe the qualification of voters, and in the exercise of this power the right of suffrage was confined to freeholders, until the adoption of the constitution of 1843. . . .

The Circuit Court rejected this evidence, and instructed the jury that the charter government and laws under which the defendants acted were, at the time the trespass is alleged to have been committed, in full force and effect as the form of government and paramount law of the State, and constituted a justification of the acts of the defendants as set forth in their pleas.

It is this opinion of the Circuit Court that we are now called upon to review. It is set forth more at large in the exception, but is in substance as above stated; and the question presented is certainly a very serious one. For, if this court is authorized to enter upon this inquiry as proposed by the plaintiff, and it should be decided that the charter government had no legal existence during the period of time above mentioned,—if it had been annulled by the adoption of the opposing government,—then the laws passed by its legislature during that time were nullities; its taxes wrongfully collected; its salaries and compensation to its officers illegally paid; its public accounts improperly settled; and the judgments and sentences of its courts in civil and criminal cases null and void, and the officers who carried their decisions into operation answerable as trespassers, if not in some cases as criminals.

When the decision of this court might lead to such results, it becomes its duty to examine very carefully its own powers before it undertakes to exercise jurisdiction.

Certainly, the question which the plaintiff proposed to raise by the testimony he offered has not heretofore been recognized as a judicial one in any of the State courts. . . .

Moreover, the Constitution of the United States, as far as it has provided for an emergency of this kind, and authorized the general government to interfere in the domestic concerns of a State, has treated the subject as political in its nature, and placed the power in the hands of that department.

The fourth section of the fourth article of the Constitution of the United States provides that the United States shall guarantee to every state in the Union a republican form of government, and shall protect each of them against invasion; and on the application of the legislature or of the executive (when the legislature cannot be convened) against domestic violence.

Under this article of the Constitution it rests with Congress to decide what government is the established one in a state. For as the United States guarantee to each state a republican government, Congress must necessarily decide what government is established in the state before it can determine whether it is republican or not. And when the Senators and Representatives of a state are admitted into the councils of the Union, the authority of the government under which they are appointed, as well as its republican character, is recognized by the proper constitutional authority. And its decision is binding on every other department of the government, and could not be questioned in a judicial tribunal. It is true that the contest in this case did not last long enough to bring the matter to this issue; and as no Senators or Representatives were elected under the authority of the government of which Mr. Dorr was the head, Congress was not called upon to decide the controversy. Yet the right to decide is placed there, and not in the courts.

So, too, as relates to the clause in the above-mentioned article of the Constitution, providing for cases of domestic violence. It rested with Congress, too, to determine upon the means proper to be adopted to fulfill this guarantee. They might, if they had deemed it most advisable to do so, have placed it in the power of a court to decide when the contingency had happened which required the federal government to interfere. But Congress thought otherwise, and no doubt wisely; and by the act of February 28, 1795, provided that, "in case of any insurrection in any state against the government thereof, it shall be lawful for the President of the United States, on application of the legislature of such state or of the executive (when the legislature cannot be convened) to call forth such number of militia of any other state or states, as may be applied for, as he may judge sufficient to suppress such insurrection."

By this act, the power of deciding whether the exigency had arisen upon which the government of the United States is bound to interfere, is given to the President. He is to act upon the application of the legislature or of the executive, and consequently he must determine what body of men constitute the legislature, and who is the governor, before he can act. The fact that both parties claim the right to the government cannot alter the case, for both cannot be entitled to it. If there is an armed conflict, like the one of which we are speaking, it is a case of domestic violence, and one of the parties must be in insurrection against the lawful government. And the President must, of necessity, decide which is the government, and which party is unlawfully arrayed against it, before he can perform the duty imposed upon him by the act of Congress.

After the President has acted and called out the militia, is a circuit court of the United States authorized to inquire whether his decision was right? Could the court, while the parties were actually contending in arms for the possession of the government, call witnesses before it and inquire which party represented a majority of the people? If it could, then it would become the duty of the court (provided it came to the conclusion that the President had decided incorrectly) to discharge those who were arrested or detained by the troops in the service of the United States or the government which the President was endeavoring to maintain. If the judicial power extends so far, the guarantee contained in the Constitution of the United States is a guarantee of anarchy, and not of order. Yet if this right does not reside in the courts when the conflict is raging, if the judicial power is, at that time, bound to follow the decision of the political, it must be equally bound when the contest is over. It cannot, when peace is restored, punish as offenses and crimes the acts which it before recognized, and was bound to recognize, as lawful.

It is true that in this case the militia were not called out by the President. But upon the application of the governor under the charter government, the President recognized him as the executive power of the state, and took measures to call out the militia to support his authority, if it should be found necessary for the general government to interfere; and it is admitted in the argument that it was the knowledge of this decision that put an end to the armed opposition to the charter government, and prevented any further efforts to establish by force the proposed constitution. The interference of the President, therefore, by announcing his determination, was as effectual as if the militia had been assembled under his orders, and it should be equally authoritative. For certainly no court of the United States, with a knowledge of this decision, would have been justified in recognizing the opposing party as the lawful government, or in treating as wrongdoers or insurgents the officers of the government which the President had recognized, and was prepared to support by an armed force. In the case of foreign nations, the government acknowledged by the President is always recognized in the courts of justice. And this principle has been applied by the act of Congress to the sovereign states of the Union.

It is said that this power in the President is dangerous to liberty, and may be abused. All power may be abused if placed in unworthy hands. But it would be difficult, we think, to point out any other hands in which this power would be more safe, and at the same time equally effectual. When citizens of the same state are in arms against each other, and the constituted authorities unable to execute the laws, the interposition of the United States must be prompt, or it is of little value. The ordinary course of proceedings in courts of justice would be utterly unfit for the crisis. And the elevated office of the President, chosen as he is by the people of the United States, and the high responsibility he could not fail to feel when acting in a case of so much moment, appear to furnish as strong safeguards against a wilful abuse of power as human prudence and foresight could well provide. At all events, it is conferred upon him by the Constitution and laws of the United States, and must, therefore, be respected and enforced in its judicial tribunals. . . . Undoubtedly, if the President, in exercising this power, shall fall into error, or invade the rights of the people of the state, it would be in the power of Congress to apply the proper remedy. But the courts must administer the law as they find it. . . .

Much of the argument on the part of the plaintiff turned upon political rights and political questions, upon which the court has been urged to express an opinion. We decline doing so. The high power has been conferred on this court of passing judgment upon the acts of the state sovereignties, and of the legislative and executive branches of the federal government, and of determining whether they are beyond the limits of power marked out for them respectively by the Constitution of the United States. This tribunal, therefore, should be the last to overstep the boundaries which limit its own jurisdiction. And while it should always be ready to meet any question confided to it by the Constitution, it is equally its duty not to pass beyond its appropriate sphere of action, and to take care not to involve itself in discussions which properly belong to other forums. No one, we believe, has ever doubted the proposition, that, according to the institutions of this country, the sovereignty in every state resides in the people of the state, and that they may alter and change their form of government at their own pleasure. But whether they have changed it or not by abolishing an old government, and establishing a new one in its place, is a question to be settled by the political power. And when that power has decided, the courts are bound to take notice of its decision, and to follow it.

The judgment of the Circuit Court must therefore be affirmed.

The irreconcilable issue: Slavery

Slavery was the issue that tore at the vitals of the nation. The intensity of the conflict increased until by the 1850s, it dominated virtually every forum. But even in the 1830s and 1840s it was important. One significant case was that of a slave ship, the *Amistad*. Technically the issue involved the interpretation of a treaty between Spain and the United States and the application of international law. But the circumstances surrounding the case and the wide newspaper coverage of it made the case much more important. For some years before the Supreme Court's decision in 1841, the House of Representatives had attempted to curtail debate and discussion of various aspects of slavery. After the wide public attention focused on the judicial resolution of the *Amistad* case, it was virtually impossible to limit such discussion.

The case involved the question of whether under the treaty and international law, the government of the United States was obliged to return to alleged Spanish owners a shipload of Africans who had been seized by slave traders in Sierra Leone to be sold in Havana, Cuba, a Spanish colony. En route to Havana, the Africans killed the captain and most of the crew of the slave vessel and ordered the remaining crew members to steer the vessel back to Africa or to a free port. The Spaniards sailed the *Amistad* toward the United States. It was seized by an American naval vessel, the *Washington,* which, in turn, claimed the vessel and its contents as salvage in a federal district court. The Spanish government claimed the vessel and its contents under a treaty and international law, but the district judge granted salvage to the American vessel for virtually everything except the Africans. These he ordered delivered to the president of the United States for transport back to Africa. The attorney general appealed first to a federal circuit court and failing there, ultimately to the Supreme Court of the United States. Because some of President Martin Van Buren's cabinet officers were slave holders, the issues in the case were closely related to contemporary political controversies over slavery.

Former President John Quincy Adams, then a member of the House of Representatives, was persuaded to serve as one of two counsels for the Africans. Adams and Roger Baldwin presented eight days of oral argument. The Court did not, in that era, impose the strict time limitations on oral argument nor did it insist upon limiting such arguments to issues specifically before the Court unlike modern practice. Adams consequently used the occasion to make a wide-ranging attack on slavery in general and its American manifestations in particular. The Court held, in the *United States* v. *The Amistad,*[113] that the Africans had been kidnapped and were being transported to Cuba in violation of Spanish laws and treaties and the laws of the United States. (Both nations had abolished the slave trade.) Justice Joseph Story, writing for the Court, held that the Africans were entitled to their freedom under American domestic and international law and ordered them freed from the custody of the Court. Stories about the odyssey of the Africans were widespread in the newspapers. Antislavery organizations first unsuccessfully asked President Van Buren to provide a government ship to take the Africans home. These organizations then raised sufficient money through donations to pay for their passage to Sierra Leone and the passages of five missionaries who accompanied them.[114]

The *Amistad* decision stimulated a great deal of interest in slavery questions. The following year, another decision seriously divided the Court and provided an opportunity for antislavery justices to force Southern members of Congress to seek federal enforcement of the Fugitive Slave Act.

PRIGG v. PENNSYLVANIA
16 Peters 539 (1842)

Justice Story delivered the majority opinion:

There are two clauses in the constitution upon the subject of fugitives, which stand in juxtaposition with each other, and have been thought mutually to illustrate each other. They are both contained in the 2d section of the 4th article, and are in the following words:

> A person charged in any State with treason, felony, or other crime, who shall flee from justice, and be found in another State, shall, on demand of the executive authority of the State from which he fled, be delivered up, to be removed to the State having jurisdiction of the crime.

> No person held to service or labor in one State under the laws thereof, escaping into another, shall in consequence of any law or regulation therein, be discharged from such service or labor; but shall be delivered up, on claim of the party to whom such service or labor may be due.

The last clause is that, the true interpretation whereof is directly in judgment before us. Historically, it is well known that the object of this clause was to secure to the citizens of the slaveholding States the complete right and title of ownership in their slaves, as property, in very State in the Union into which they might escape from the State where they were held in servitude. The full recognition of this right and title was indispensable to the security of this species of property in all the slaveholding States; and, indeed, was so vital to the preservation of their domestic interests and institutions, that it cannot be doubted that it constituted a fundamental article, without the adoption of which the Union could not have been formed. . . .

[U]nder and in virtue of the constitution, the owner of a slave is clothed with entire authority, in every State in the Union, to seize and recapture his slave, whenever he can do it without any breach of the peace or any illegal violence. In this sense, and to this extent this clause of the constitution may properly be said to execute itself, and to require no aid from legislation, State or national. . . .

If, indeed, the constitution guarantees the right, and if it requires the delivery upon the claim of the owner, (as cannot well be doubted,) the natural inference certainly is, that the national government is clothed with the appropriate authority and functions to enforce it. The fundamental principle, applicable to all cases of this sort, would seem to be, that where the end is required, the means are given; and where the duty is enjoined, the ability to perform it is contemplated to exist on the part of the functionaries to whom it is intrusted. The clause is found in the national constitution, and not in that of any State. It does not point out any state functionaries, or any state action to carry its provisions into effect. The States cannot, therefore, be compelled to enforce them; and it might well be deemed an unconstitutional exercise of the power of interpretation, to insist that the States are bound to provide means to carry into effect the duties of the national government, nowhere delegated or intrusted to them by the constitution. On the contrary, the natural, if not the necessary conclusion is, that the national government, in the absence of all positive provisions to the contrary, is bound, through its own proper departments, legislative, judicial, or executive, as the case may require, to carry into effect all the rights and duties imposed upon it by the constitution. . . .

The remaining question is, whether the power of legislation upon this subject is exclusive in the national government, or concurrent in the States, until it is exercised by congress. In our opinion it is exclusive; and we shall now proceed briefly to state our reasons for that opinion. The doctrine stated by this court, in Sturges *v.* Crowninshield contains the true, although not the sole rule or consideration, which is applicable to this particular subject. "Wherever," said Mr. Chief Justice Marshall, in delivering the opinion of the court, "the terms in which a power is granted to congress, or the nature of the power, require that it should be exercised exclusively by congress, the subject is as completely taken from the state legislatures as if they had been forbidden to act." The nature of the power, and the true objects to be attained by it, are then as important to be weighed, in considering the question of its exclusiveness, as the words in which it is granted.

In the first place, it is material to state, (what has been already incidentally hinted at,) that the right to seize and retake fugitive slaves, and the duty to deliver them up, in whatever State of the Union they may be found, and of course the corresponding power in congress to use the appropriate means to enforce the right and duty, derive their whole validity and obligation exclusively from the constitution of the United States, are are there for the first time, recognized and established in that peculiar character. Before the adoption of the constitution, no State had any power whatsoever over the subject, except within its own territorial limits, and could not bind the sovereignty or the legislation of other States. Whenever the right was acknowledged or the duty enforced in any State, it was a matter of comity and favor, and not as a matter of strict moral, political, or international obligation or duty. . . .

In the next place, the nature of the provision and the objects to be attained by it, require that it should be controlled by one and the same will, and act uniformly by the same system of regulations throughout the Union. If, then, the States have a right, in the absence of legislation by congress, to act upon the subject, each State is at liberty to prescribe just such regulations as suit its own policy, local convenience, and local feelings. The legislation of one State may not only be different from, but utterly repugnant to and incompatible with that of another. The time, and mode, and limitation of the remedy, the proofs of the title, and all other incidents applicable thereto, may be prescribed in one State, which are rejected or disclaimed in another. One State may require the owner to sue in one mode, another in a different mode. One State may make a statute of limitations as to the remedy, in its own tribunals, short and summary; another may prolong the period, and yet restrict the proofs. Nay, some States may utterly refuse to act upon the subject at all; and others may refuse to open its courts to any remedies *in rem*, because they would interfere with their own domestic policy, institutions, or habits. The right, therefore, would never, in a practical sense, be the same in all the States. It would have no unity of purpose, or uniformity of operation. The duty might be enforced in some States; retarded or limited in others; and denied, as compulsory in many, if not in all. Consequences like these must have been foreseen as very likely to occur in the nonslaveholding States, where legislation, if not silent on the subject, and purely voluntary, could scarcely be presumed to be favorable to the exercise of the rights of the owner. . . .

To guard, however, against any possible misconstruction of our views, it is proper to state, that we are by no means to be understood in any manner whatsoever to doubt or to interfere with the police power belonging to the States, in virtue of their general sovereignty. That police power extends over all subjects within the territorial limits of the States, and has never been conceded to the United States. It is wholly distin-

guishable from the right and duty secured by the provision now under consideration, which is exclusively derived from and secured by the constitution of the United States, and owes its whole efficacy thereto. We entertain no doubt whatsoever, that the States, in virtue of their general police power, possess full jurisdiction to arrest and restrain runaway slaves, and remove them from their borders, and otherwise to secure themselves against their depredations and evil example, as they certainly may do in cases of idlers, vagabonds, and paupers. The rights of the owners of fugitive slaves are in no just sense interefered with, or regulated by such a course; and in many cases, the operations of this police power, although designed generally for other purposes, for the protection, safety, and peace of the State, may essentially promote and aid the interests of the owners. But such regulations can never be permitted to interfere with or to obstruct the just rights of the owner to reclaim his slave, derived from the constitution of the United States, or with the remedies prescribed by congress to aid and enforce the same. . . .

Chief Justice Taney dissented:

I concur in the opinion pronounced by the court, that the law of Pennsylvania, under which the plaintiff in error was indicted, is unconstitutional and void; and that the judgment against him must be reversed. But as the questions before us arise upon the construction of the constitution of the United States, and as I do not assent to all the principles contained in the opinion just delivered, it is proper to state the points on which I differ. . . .

The opinion of the court maintains that the power over this subject is so exclusively vested in congress, that no State, since the adoption of the constitution, can pass any law in relation to it. In other words, according to the opinion just delivered, the state authorities are prohibited from interfering for the purpose of protecting the right of the master, and aiding him in the recovery of his property. I think the States are not prohibited; and that, on the contrary, it is enjoined upon them, as a duty, to protect and support the owner when he is endeavoring to obtain possession of his property found within their respective territories.

The language used in the constitution does not, in my judgment, justify the construction given to it by the court. It contains no words prohibiting the several states from passing laws to enforce this right. They are in express terms forbidden to make any regulation that shall impair it. But there the prohibition stops.

And according to the settled rules of construction for all written instruments, the prohibition being confined to laws injurious to the right, the power to pass laws to support and enforce it, is necessarily implied. And the words of the article which direct that the fugitive "shall be delivered up," seem evidently designed to impose it as a duty upon the people of the several States to pass laws to carry into execution, in good faith, the compact into which they thus solemnly entered with each other. The constitution of the United States, and every article and clause in it, is a part of the law of every State in the Union; and is the paramount law. The right of the master, therefore, to seize his fugitive slave, is the law of each State; and no State has the power to abrogate or alter it. And why may not a State protect a right of property, acknowledged by its own paramount law? Besides, the laws of the different States, in all other cases, constantly protect the citizens of other States in their rights of property, when it is found within their respective territories; and no one doubts their power to do so. And in the absence of any express prohibition, I perceive no reason for establishing, by implication, a different rule in this instance; where, by the national compact, this right of property is recognized as an existing right in every State of the Union. . . .

I dissent therefore, upon these grounds, from that part of the opinion of the court which denies the obligation and the right of the state authorities to protect the master, when he is endeavoring to seize a fugitive from his service, in pursuance of the right given to him by the constitution of the United States; provided the state law is not in conflict with the remedy provided by congress.

After the *Amistad* decision and *Prigg* v. *Pennsylvania*, the controversy over slavery dominated politics in America. The 1850s were the setting for the next great transformation in American political alignments and the Supreme Court became more heavily involved in the controversy.

Conclusion

The Jacksonian Democratic justices selected between 1829 and 1860 emerged as very important politically, both in the initial assertion of doctrines modifying traditional Federalist principles and in the later development of doctrines rationalizing slavery. The continuation of such doctrinal tendencies in the face of electoral repudiation in the presidential election of 1860 could have precipitated a serious constitutional crisis. But in contrast to the persistent nature of Federalist–Whig doctrinal influence and judicial longevity, the Jacksonian influence was not destined to endure as a majority position for many years after the last Jacksonian Democratic president left office in early 1861. These personnel developments are summarized in Table 5-1.

The change to the Jacksonian era in 1828 had occurred with no serious involvement for the Supreme Court, but a number of salient issues combining constitutional principles and partisan divisions fully engaged the Court in the political disputes of the 1860s. Of all these, slavery was destined to be the most serious. Before 1828, the Supreme Court had not rendered any decisions which contributed directly to the second critical election, a situation in marked contrast to the judicial role prior to the first critical election of 1800.

But within a few years, as President Jackson consolidated his position, the Federalist and neo-Federalist majority was markedly out of step with Jacksonian principles. When Jackson achieved a majority on the Court, his party had already become embroiled in a number of confrontations with the ideological successors to the Federalists (and to a degree, the National Republicans), the Whigs. The issues generally involved economic matters, especially the second Bank of the

**TABLE 5-1 Judicial political generations and critical elections:
The persistence of Jacksonian Democratic influence, 1829–1881***

Appointing president and party	Chief Justice	Justices chosen in the Jacksonian Democratic era, 1829 through 1860								
		Critical election of 1828: Jacksonian Democrats take control of Congress and the presidency								
Andrew Jackson Jacksonian Democrat 1829–1837	J. Marshall 1801–1835 R. Taney 1836–1864	Vacant; H. Baldwin 1830–1844, nominal Jacksonian Democrat	P. Barbour 1836–1841	J. Story 1811–1845, nominal Republican, doctrinal neo-Federalist,	S. Thompson 1823–1843	J. Wayne 1835–1867, nominal Jacksonian	J. McLean 1829–1861, Whig-Republican (Lincoln)	*Court increased to 9 by act of Congress of March 3, 1837*		
Martin Van Buren Jacksonian Democrat 1837–1841			P. Daniel 1841–1860	became Whig		Democrat, doctrinal Whig		J. Catron 1837–1865	J. McKinley 1837–1852	
William Henry Harrison Whig 1841										
John Tyler Whig-Jeffersonian Republican 1841–1845		Vacant			Vacant S. Nelson 1845–1872					
James K. Polk Jacksonian Democrat 1845–1849		R. Grier 1846–1870		L. Woodbury 1845–1851						
Zachary Taylor Whig 1849–1850										
Millard Fillmore Whig 1850–1853				B. Curtis 1851–1857 Whig						
Franklin Pierce Jacksonian 1853–1857									J. Campbell 1853–1861	
James Buchanan Jacksonian Democrat 1857–1861				N. Clifford 1858–1881						

*Jacksonian Democrats are in italics.

TABLE 5-1 Judicial political generations and critical elections: The persistence of Jacksonian Democratic influence, 1829–1881* (continued)

Appointing president and party	Chief Justice	Justices chosen in the Jacksonian Democratic era, 1829 through 1860						
Critical election of 1860: Republicans take control of Congress and the presidency while, in 1861, the Southern Confederacy secedes								
Abraham Lincoln Republican 1861–1865	S. Chase 1864–1873		Vacant; S. Miller 1862–1890			N. Swayne 1862–1881	D. Davis 1862–1877	*Court increased to 10 by act of Congress;* S. Field 1863–1877
Andrew Johnson Union Democrat 1865–1869						*Court reduced to 7 by act of July 23, 1866*		
Ulysses S. Grant Republican 1869–1877	M. Waite 1874–1888	W. Strong 1870–1880			W. Hunt 1872–1882	*Court increased to 9 by act of Congress April 10, 1869;* J. Bradley 1870–1892		
Rutherford B. Hayes Republican 1877–1881		W. Woods 1880–1887					J. Harlan 1877–1911	
James A. Garfield Republican 1881						S. Matthews 1881–1889		
Chester A. Arthur Republican 1881–1885			H. Gray 1881–1902	S. Blatchford 1882–1893				

*Jacksonian Democrats are in italics.

United States and the status of corporations. Because President Jackson's judicial nominees were, after his earlier appointees, trusted Jacksonian Democratic partisans, judicial appointments became major political battles as well. President Jackson's initial choices were made for reasons often unrelated to his ideological goals. But when he solidified his political control nationally, his Court selections did reflect his ideological preferences. Ironically, the Jacksonian era proved to be one in which the economic battles of Jacksonian Democrats and Whigs soon became overshadowed by the bitter controversy over slavery. While Jacksonian and Whig justices still divided on the Court most bitterly over the economic differences that were salient when their own political generations had achieved prominence in the late 1820s and 1830s, these political and judicial generations were rendered less relevant as slavery became the most divisive of the new issues.

REFERENCES

1. Robert V. Remini, "The Election of 1828," in *The Coming to Power*, ed. Arthur M. Schlesinger, Fred Israel (New York: Chelsea House, 1971), pp. 67–90.
2. In March 1823, Justice Livingston died. President Monroe chose his secretary of war, Smith Thompson, as Livingston's successor.
3. As quoted by George W. Wickersham, "Federal Control of Interstate Commerce," *Harvard Law Review* 23 (February 1910): 243.
4. The privilege was granted to John Fitch in 1787 and then to Livingston and Fulton in 1798; Beveridge, op. cit., p. 399.
5. Warren reported sixteen cases in state courts involving the monopoly; *History*, vol. 1, p. 599, note 1.
6. 9 Wheaton 738 (1824).
7. Ernest L. Bogart, "Taxation of the Second Bank of the United States by Ohio," *The American Historical Review* 18 (January 1912): 313–314.
8. As quoted in Bogart, op. cit., p. 315.
9. *House Journal*, as quoted by Bogart, ibid., p. 324; Historian Bogart denied the assertions of McMaster and Schouler that the Ohio legislation was prompted by the McCulloch decision.
10. Daniel H. Chamberlain, "Osborn v. The Bank of the United States," *Harvard Law Review* 1 (December 1887): 224.
11. Bogart, op. cit., pp. 329–330.
12. Marshall himself did not adhere to this doctrine; see *Governor of Georgia v. Madrazo*, 1 Peters 110 (1828); it was abandoned completely in *Pennover v. McConnaughy*, 140 U.S. 1 (1940); Willoughby, *Constitutional Law*, III, op. cit., p. 1399.
13. Bogart, op. cit., p. 331; Bogart felt that the people of Ohio had not been converted to strict constructionism, even though they resorted to such arguments in the Osborn controversy.
14. Warren, *History*, vol 1, pp. 628–629.
15. 9 Wheaton 904 (1824).
16. *Martin v. Hunter's Lessee* and *Cohens v. Virginia*.
17. *Gelston v. Hoyt*, *Sturgis v. Crowninshield*, and *Gibbons v. Ogden*.
18. *McMillan v. McNeill*.
19. *McCulloch v. Maryland*.
20. *Dartmouth College v. Woodward*.
21. *Farmer's and Mechanic's Bank v. Smith*.
22. *Wayman v. Southard*, *Bank of United States v. Halstead*, *Bank of United States v. January*, and *Greene v. Biddle*.
23. *Society for the Propagation of the Gospel v. New Haven*.
24. *Osborn v. The Bank of the United States*.
25. *Bank of the United States v. Planter's Bank of Georgia*; in addition, South Carolina opposed an important federal circuit court decision, *Elkinson v. Delisseline*.
26. Warren, *History*, vol. 1, pp. 667–669.
27. Haines, *The Role of the Supreme Court in American Government and Politics*, op. cit., pp. 511–512.
28. Carson, *History of the Supreme Court*, op. cit., p. 274.
29. 12 Wheaton 19 (1827).
30. Johnson, *Readings in American Constitutional History, 1776–1876*, op. cit., pp. 261–268.
31. Article I, section 8, clauses 15 and 16 respectively.
32. 12 Wheaton 28 (1827).
33. Ibid.
34. Ibid., p. 29.
35. 12 Wheaton 213 (1827).
36. *Gozler v. Georgetown*, 6 Wheaton 593 (1821).

37. *Mason* v. *Haile*, 12 Wheaton 370 (1827); *Satterlee* v. *Matthewson*, 2 Peters 380 (1829); *Jackson* v. *Lamphire*, 3 Peters 280 (1830); *Providence Bank* v. *Billings*, 4 Peters 514 (1830); *Hawkins* v. *Barney's Lessee*, 5 Peters 457 (1831); *Lessee of Livingston* v. *Moore*, 7 Peters 469 (1833); *Watson* v. *Mercer*, 8 Peters 88 (1834); *Mumma* v. *Potomac Co.*, 8 Peters 281 (1834); and *Beers* v. *Haughton*, 9 Peters 329 (1835); cited in Wright, *Contract Clause*, op. cit., pp. 52–53.

38. Warren, *History*, vol. 1, p. 692; actually Marshall did not state a doctrine of congressional exclusiveness in either the Sturgis or Saunders opinions.

39. 12 Wheaton 340 (1827).

40. Ibid., p. 346.

41. 9 Cranch 43 (1815).

42. 2 Peters 627 (1829).

43. For a complete discussion of the role of natural law in constitutional interpretation, see Benjamin F. Wright, Jr., *American Interpretations of Natural Law* (Cambridge: Harvard University Press, 1931), pp. 280–306.

44. 12 Wheaton 419 (1827).

45. Article I, Section 10.

46. Article I, Section 8.

47. 12 Wheaton 439 (1827).

48. Ibid., p. 442.

49. Ibid., p. 443.

50. Ibid., pp. 447–448; the congressional act was that of March 1799, which laid down duties on the importation of certain foreign commodities.

51. 1 Peters 511 (1828).

52. Ibid., pp. 542–543.

53. Remini, op. cit., p. 498.

54. Stanwood, op. cit., pp. 100–101.

55. Carl Brent Swisher, *Roger B. Taney* (New York: Macmillan, 1935), p. 132.

56. Swisher, op. cit., pp. 580–583.

57. 2 Peters 245 (1829).

58. 2 Peters 380 (1829).

59. 2 Peters 627 (1829); Haines, op. cit., pp. 580–583.

60. Felix Frankfurter, *The Commerce Clause Under Marshall, Taney and Waite* (Chapel Hill: University of North Carolina Press, 1937), p. 29.

61. 2 Peters 449 (1829).

62. 2 Peters 449–450 (1829).

63. 2 Peters 465 (1828).

64. Ibid., pp. 467–469.

65. Hockett, *The Constitutional History of the United States*, II, op. cit., pp. 29–35.

66. Richard Cralle (ed.), "Discourse on the Constitution and Government of the United States," *The Works of John C. Calhoun* 1 (Columbia: General Assembly of South Carolina, 1851), p. 338.

67. The more controversial opinions were given widespread newspaper coverage.

68. Hockett, op. cit., p. 52.

69. 4 Peters 410 (1830); before the 1830 term, Justice Bushrod Washington died. Pennsylvania Judge Gibson, whose dissent in *Eakin* v. *Raub* remains the classic criticism of judicial review, was thought to be Jackson's choice as Washington's successor. To the relief of most nationalists, however, Jackson nominated Henry Baldwin of Pennsylvania; Warren, *History*, vol. 1, pp. 711–712.

70. 4 Peters 437.

71. As quoted in Haines, op. cit., p. 594.

72. Haines, ibid., p. 595.

73. Warren, *History*, vol. 1, p. 769.

74. Ulrich B. Phillips, "Georgia and State Rights," *Annual Report of the American History Association*, vol. 2 (1901), pp. 46–51.

75. Ibid.

76. Ibid., pp. 52–65; McLaughlin, *A Constitutional History of the United States* (New York: D. Appleton-Century Company, 1935), pp. 426–427.

77. As quoted by Phillips, ibid., p. 64.

78. Ibid., p. 69.
79. According to a census taken by the Nation in 1825, the Cherokees east of the Mississippi included 13,563 tribesmen, 147 white men, 73 white women married to Cherokees, and 1,277 Negro slaves; Phillips, ibid., p. 71.
80. In January 1832, Justice Story wrote, "At Philadelphia, I was introduced to two of the Chiefs of the Cherokee Nation so sadly dealt with by the state of Georgia. They are both educated men, and conversed with singular force and propriety of language upon their own case, the law of which they perfectly understood and reasoned upon." Warren, *History*, vol. 1, p. 750, note 1.
81. Phillips, op. cit., p. 75.
82. Beveridge, op. cit., vol. 4, p. 543.
83. 5 Peters 2 (1831); in the same term the Court also exercised its power as final arbiter in a case involving two states. *New Jersey* v. *New York* was the first case involving a boundary dispute between two states. Marshall not only asserted the Supreme Court's right to take original jurisdiction in the case, but also held that should a defendant state fail to appear after due service of process, the complaining state could proceed *ex parte* to a final judgment; 5 Peters 284 (1831); *see also* William C. Coleman, "The State as Defendant," *Harvard Law Review* 31 (December 1917): 220–221.
84. Phillips, op. cit., pp. 78–80.
85. 6 Peters 515 (1832).
86. Ibid., pp. 561–563.
87. Phillips, op. cit., pp. 82–85.
88. Ibid.; Haines, op. cit., p. 603; Beveridge, op. cit., vol. 4.
89. Warren, *History*, vol. 1, pp. 757–766.
90. Ibid., p. 779, note 1.
91. The missionaries had shown a conciliating attitude and had, by January 1833, abandoned attempts to further prosecute their case before the Supreme Court; Phillips, op. cit., p. 83.
92. Bitter opposition to his conservative views arise in *Charles River Bridge* v. *Warren*, *Briscoe* v. *The Bank of Kentucky*, and *New York* v. *Miln*. These cases were destined to be decided by a Court hostile to Marshall's views on the issues, although they were considered by the Court in both the 1834 and 1835 terms; Warren, *History*, vol. 1, pp. 789–790.
93. Haines, op. cit., vol. 1, pp. 628–629.
94. Cralle, op. cit., 1, p. 328.
95. Haines, *The Role of the Supreme Court in American Government and Politics: 1789–1835*, p. 82.
96. John Quincy Adams, *Parties in the United States* (New York: Greenberg, 1941), p. 121.
97. Ibid., p. 161.
98. T. K. Ramsay and L. S. Morin, eds. *Law Reporter* 1 (July 1838): 62.
99. 13 Peters 519, 597–606.
100. 13 Peters 607 (1839).
101. John R. Schmidhauser, *Judges and Justices: The Federal Appellate Judiciary* (Boston: Little, Brown and Company, 1979), pp. 48–49, 138.
102. Haines, op. cit., vol. 2, pp. 292–305.
103. Otto E. Koegel, *Walter S. Carter, Collector of Young Masters or the Progenitor of Many Law Firms* (New York: Round Table Press, 1953); Robert T. Swaine, *The Cravath Firm and its Predecessors, 1819–1964*, 3 vols. (New York: Ad Press, 1964); and Erwin O. Smigel, *The Wall Street Lawyer: Professional Organization Man?* (New York: The Free Press, 1964).
104. *See, for example,* Corinne Lathrop Gilb, *Hidden Hierarchies* (New York: Harper and Row, 1966), pp. 112–156.
105. *Swift* v. *Tyson*, 16 Peters 1 (1842).
106. 5 Cranch 57 (1809).
107. 5 Cranch 86 (1809).
108. 16 Howard 314 (1853).
109. Ibid., pp. 325–326.
110. Dissent in *Rundle* v. *Delaware and Raritan Canal Company*, 14 Howard 80, 100–101 (1852).
111. 16 Howard 314, 351 (1853).
112. Ibid., p. 353.
113. 15 Peters 518 (1841).
114. Haines, op. cit., vol. 2, pp. 98–110.

CHAPTER

6

Slavery, the Court, and
the Emergence of the Republican Party

The Critical Election of 1860

Just as the events of the election of 1824 had set the stage for the critical election of 1828, so did the circumstances influencing the elections of 1852 and especially 1856 set the conditions for the massive political transformation brought about in 1860. The Jacksonian Democratic party was torn asunder by the controversies engendered by the slavery issue and especially the unraveling of the compromise of 1850, passage of the Kansas-Nebraska Act, and the controversies over the Fugitive Slave Act. After its defeat in 1860, the Democratic Party would not capture the presidency until the era of Grover Cleveland. Its long time rival of the 1830s, '40s, and early '50s, the Whig Party, was not only torn asunder, it disappeared as a party.[1]

The era immediately before the critical election of 1828 did not involve Supreme Court decision making that directly contradicted the policy positions of the emerging Jacksonian Democratic victors. But the interaction of the Supreme Court with the political forces that merged to become the victorious Republican Party in the critical election of 1860 was provocative and controversial. Judicial resolution of issues arising out of slavery in the 1840s and '50s generally involved doctrinal positions in opposition to the stands espoused by the newly emerging political coalition that captured control of the executive and legislative branches of government in 1860. A majority of Jacksonian Democratic justices were committed to maintaining the claimed constitutional guarantee to slave owners to maintain their property rights in slaves. Conversely, the national political tides outside of the South were gradually turning away from the values and policy positions of the political generation from which most of the Jacksonian Democratic justices were chosen.

The Court maintains slavery

The Civil War and the issues that brought in its outbreak and its painful duration provided an extremely revealing test of the extent to which the background and career-ladder attributes of justices may be related to their individual decision-making behavior. Justices often served for many years after the most significant events of the era in which their own political generation governed and determined the outcome of political, social, and economic controversies. In Table 6-1, the justices who made decisions involving slavery, the commerce clause, and the status of corporations between 1837 and 1860 are classified by political party and regional background. These doctrinal areas are identified by most historians as fundamental to the discussions between North and South prior to the Civil War. Fifty-two decisions involving these issues were analyzed and the positions of the justices categorized on a pro-Northern–pro-Southern continuum. The divisions are summarized in Table 6-2, where it is apparent that political party and region contributed to a degree of polarization. But the justices tended to be divided more seriously over issues that were salient in the era when they were appointed rather than in the period when regional divisions were dominating congressional debate. Thus, the Court divided more deeply over economic matters that reflected older Jacksonian values than over Northern-Southern issues.[2]

Despite a relatively balanced *overall* record of the Taney Court in dealing with the issues relevent to the sectional crisis of 1837–1860, its position in the Dred Scott decision was a disaster in the estimation of the public. Ironically, the Court had been encouraged by some political leaders to settle definitively in this case an issue that Congress had not been able to resolve satisfactorily. The case involved the status of Dred Scott, a slave owned by one John Sanford in Missouri, a slave state, who claimed freedom on the ground that he had been taken for several years to Rock Island, Illinois, a free state, and to Wisconsin while it was free

TABLE 6-1 **Participating justices classified by party and by regional background**

Name	Years served	Section	Party
Joseph Story	1811–1845	North (Mass.)	Whig
Smith Thompson	1823–1843	North (N.Y.)	Democrat
John McLean	1829–1861	North (Ohio)	Whig
Henry Baldwin	1830–1844	North (Pa.)	Democrat
James M. Wayne	1835–1867	South (Ga.)	Whig
Roger B. Taney	1836–1864	South (Md.)	Democrat
Philip P. Barbour	1836–1841	South (Va.)	Democrat
John Catron	1837–1865	South (Tenn.)	Democrat
John McKinley	1837–1852	South (Ala.)	Democrat
Peter V. Daniel	1841–1860	South (Va.)	Democrat
Samuel Nelson	1845–1872	North (N.Y.)	Democrat
Levi Woodbury	1845–1851	North (N.H.)	Democrat
Robert C. Grier	1846–1870	North (Pa.)	Democrat
Benjamin R. Curtis	1851–1857	North (Mass.)	Whig
John A. Campbell	1853–1861	South (Ala.)	Democrat
Nathan Clifford	1858–1881	North (Maine)	Democrat

TABLE 6-2 **The relationship of scale score to regional and party background**

Category	Scale score	Name	Judicial experience	Section and party
Strong Pro-Northern	29	Story	0	Northern
Score	28	McLean	JE	Whigs
Moderate Pro-Northern	22	Curtis	0	Northern Whig
Score	22	Baldwin	0	Northern Democrat
	20	Wayne	JE	Southern Whig
Neutral Score	16	McKinley	0	Southern Democrat
	14	Woodbury	JE	Northern Democrat
	14	Clifford	0	Northern Democrat
	14	Taney	0	Southern Democrat
Moderate Pro-Southern	12	Grier	JE	Northern
Score	10	Nelson	JE	Democrats
	10	Thompson	JE	
Strong Pro-Southern	4	Catron	JE	Southern
Score	1	Campbell	0	Democrats
	0	Daniel	0	
	0	Barbour	JE	

territory. In considering this issue, the Supreme Court decided to determine the constitutionality of the Missouri Compromise and the status of blacks, issues crucial to the interests of pro- and antislavery advocates. The Court could have avoided these issues but was too divided to accept a limited jurisdictional ruling. The result was not only a bitterly divided Court, but a more deeply divided nation. Each justice wrote a separate opinion. Justices Curtis and McLean dissented. Portions of each of the major arguments are included below.

DRED SCOTT v. SANFORD
19 Howard 393 (1857)

Chief Justice Taney delivered the opinion of the Court:

The question is simply this: Can a negro, whose ancestors were imported into this country, and sold as slaves, become a member of the political community formed and brought into existence by the constitution of the United States, and as such become entitled to all the rights, and privileges, and immunities, guaranteed by that instrument to the citizen? One of which rights is the privilege of suing in a court of the United States in the cases specified in the constitution.

It will be observed, that the plea applies to that class of persons only whose ancestors were negroes of the African race, and imported into this country, and sold and held as slaves. The only matter in issue before the court, therefore, is, whether the descendants of such slaves, when they shall be emancipated, or who are

born of parents who had become free before their birth, are citizens of a State, in the sense in which the word citizen is used in the constitution of the United States. And this being the only matter in dispute on the pleadings, the court must be understood as speaking in this opinion of that class only, that is, of those persons who are the descendants of Africans who were imported into this country; and sold as slaves. . . .

The words "people of the United States" and "citizens" are synonymous terms, and mean the same thing. They both describe the political body who, according to our republican institutions, form the sovereignty, and who hold the power and conduct the government through their representatives. They are what we familiarly call the "sovereign people," and every citizen is one of this people, and a constituent member of this sovereignty. The question before us is, whether the class of persons described in the plea in abatement compose a portion of this people, and are constituent members of this sovereignty? We think they are not, and that they are not included, and were not intended to be included, under the word "citizens" in the constitution, and can therefore claim none of the rights and privileges which that instrument provides for and secures to citizens of the United States. On the contrary, they were at that time considered as a subordinate and inferior class of beings, who had been subjugated by the dominant race, and, whether emancipated or not, yet remained subject to their authority, and had no rights or privileges but such as those who held the power and the government might choose to grant them.

It is not the province of the court to decide upon the justice or injustice, the policy or impolicy, of these laws. The decision of that question belonged to the political or law-making power; to those who formed the sovereignty and framed the constitution. The duty of the court is, to interpret the instrument they have framed, with the best lights we can obtain on the subject, and to administer it as we find it, according to its true intent and meaning when it was adopted.

In discussing this question, we must not confound the rights of citizenship which a State may confer within its own limits, and the rights of citizenship as a member of the Union. It does not by any means follow, because he has all the rights and privileges of a citizen of a State, that he must be a citizen of the United States. He may have all of the rights and privileges of the citizen of a state, and yet not be entitled to the rights and privileges of a citizen in any other State. For, previous to the adoption of the constitution of the United States, every State had the undoubted right to confer on whomsoever it pleased the character of citizen, and to endow him with all its rights. But this character of course was confined to the boundaries of the State, and gave him no rights or privileges in other States beyond those secured to him by the laws of nations and the comity of States. Nor have the several States surrendered the power of conferring these rights and privileges by adopting the constitution of the United States. . . .

It is very clear, therefore, that no State can, by any act or law of its own, passed since the adoption of the constitution, introduce a new member into the political community created by the constitution of the United States. It cannot make him a member of this community by making him a member of its own. And for the same reason it cannot introduce any person, or description of persons, who were not intended to be embraced in this new political family, which the constitution brought into existence, but were intended to be excluded from it.

The question then arises, whether the provisions of the constitution, in relation to the personal rights and privileges to which the citizen of a State should be entitled, embraced the negro African race, at that time in this country, or who might afterwards be imported, who had then or should afterwards be made free in any State; and to put it in the power of a single State to make him a citizen of the United States, and endow him with the full rights of citizenship in every other State without their consent? Does the constitution of the United States act upon him whenever he shall be made free under the laws of a State, and raised there to the rank of a citizen, and immediately clothe him with all the privileges of a citizen in every other State, and in its own courts?

The court think the affirmative of these propositions cannot be maintained. And if it cannot, the plaintiff in error could not be a citizen of the State of Missouri, within the meaning of the constitution of the United States, and, consequently, was not entitled to sue in its courts.

It is true, every person, and every class and description of persons, who were at the time of the adoption of the constitution recognized as citizens in the several States, became also citizens of this new political body; but none other; it was formed by them, and for them and their posterity, but for no one else. And the personal rights and privileges guaranteed to citizens of this new sovereignty were intended to embrace those only who were then members of the several State communities, or who should afterwards by birthright or otherwise become members, according to the provisions of the constitution and the principles on which it was founded. It was the union of those who were at that time members of distinct and separate political communities into one political family, whose power, for certain specified purposes, was to extend over the whole territory of the United States. And it gave to each citizen rights and privileges outside of his State which he did not before possess, and placed him in every other State upon a perfect equality with its own citizens as to rights of person and rights of property; it made him a citizen of the United States. . . .

In the opinion of the court, the legislation and histories of the times, and the language used in the declaration of independence, show, that neither the class of persons who had been imported as slaves, nor their descendants, whether they had become free or not, were then acknowledged as a part of the people, nor intended to be included in the general words used in that memorable instrument. . . .

They had for more than a century before been

regarded as beings of an inferior order, and altogether unfit to associate with the white race, either in social or political relations; and so far inferior, that they had no rights which the white man was bound to respect; and that the negro might justly and lawfully be reduced to slavery for his benefit. . . .

The legislation of the different colonies furnishes positive and indisputable proof of this fact. . . .

The language of the declaration of independence is equally conclusive. . . .

But it is too clear for dispute, that the enslaved African race were not intended to be included, and formed no part of the people who framed and adopted this declaration; for if the language, as understood in that day, would embrace them, the conduct of the distinguished men who framed the declaration of independence would have been utterly and flagrantly inconsistent with the principles they asserted; and instead of the sympathy of mankind, to which they so confidently appealed, they would have deserved and received universal rebuke and reprobation. . . .

This state of public opinion had undergone no change when the constitution was adopted, as is equally evident from its provisions and language. . . .

But there are two clauses in the constitution which point directly and specifically to the negro race as a separate class of persons, and show clearly that they were not regarded as a portion of the people or citizens of the government then formed.

One of these clauses reserves to each of the thirteen States the right to import slaves until the year 1808, if it thinks proper. . . . And by the other provision the States pledge themselves to each other to maintain the right of property of the master, by delivering up to him any slave who may have escaped from his service, and be found within their respective territories. . . .

The only two provisions which point to them and include them, treat them as property, and make it the duty of the government to protect it; no other power, in relation to this race, is to be found in the constitution; and as it is a government of special, delegated, powers, no authority beyond these two provisions can be constitutionally exercised. The government of the United States had no right to interfere for any other purpose but that of protecting the rights of the owner, leaving it altogether with the several States to deal with this race, whether emancipated or not, as each State may think justice, humanity, and the interests and safety of society, require. The States evidently intended to reserve this power exclusively to themselves. . . .

[U]pon a full and careful consideration of the subject,

the court is of opinion, that, upon the facts stated . . . , Dred Scott was not a citizen of Missouri within the meaning of the constitution of the United States, and not entitled as such to sue in its courts; and, consequently, that the circuit court had no jurisdiction of the case, and that the judgment on the plea in abatement is erroneous. . . .

We proceed . . . to inquire whether the facts relied on by the plaintiff entitled him to his freedom. . . .

The act of Congress, upon which the plaintiff relies, declares that slavery and involuntary servitude, except as a punishment for crime, shall be forever prohibited in all that part of the territory ceded by France, under the name of Louisiana, which lies north of thirty-six degrees thirty minutes north latitude and not included within the limits of Missouri. And the difficulty which meets us at the threshold of this part of the inquiry is whether Congress was authorized to pass this law under any of the powers granted to it by the Constitution; for, if the authority is not given by that instrument, it is the duty of this Court to declare it void and inoperative and incapable of conferring freedom upon anyone who is held as a slave under the laws of any one of the states.

The counsel for the plaintiff has laid much stress upon that article in the Constitution which confers on Congress the power "to dispose of and make all needful rules and regulations respecting the territory or other property belonging to the United States"; but, in the judgment of the Court, that provision has no bearing on the present controversy, and the power there given, whatever it may be, is confined, and was intended to be confined, to the territory which at that time belonged to, or was claimed by, the United States and was within their boundaries as settled by the treaty with Great Britain and can have no influence upon a territory afterward acquired from a foreign government. It was a special provision for a known and particular territory, and to meet a present emergency, and nothing more. . . .

We do not mean, however, to question the power of Congress in this respect. The power to expand the territory of the United States by the admission of new states is plainly given; and in the construction of this power by all the departments of the government, it has been held to authorize the acquisition of territory, not fit for admission at the time, but to be admitted as soon as its population and situation would entitle it to admission. It is acquired to become a state and not to be held as a colony and governed by Congress with absolute authority; and, as the propriety of admitting a new state is committed to the sound discretion of

Congress, the power to acquire territory for that purpose, to be held by the United States until it is in a suitable condition to become a state upon an equal footing with the other states, must rest upon the same discretion. It is a question for the political department of the government, and not the judicial; and whatever the political department of the government shall recognize as within the limits of the United States, the judicial department is also bound to recognize, and to administer in it the laws of the United States, so far as they apply, and to maintain in the territory the authority and rights of the government, and also the personal rights and rights of property of individual citizens, as secured by the Constitution. All we mean to say on this point is that, as there is no express regulation in the Constitution defining the power which the general government may exercise over the person or property of a citizen in a territory thus acquired, the Court must necessarily look to the provisions and principles of the Constitution, and its distribution of powers, for the rules and principles by which its decision must be governed.

Taking this rule to guide us, it may be safely assumed that citizens of the United States who migrate to a territory belonging to the people of the United States cannot be ruled as mere colonists, dependent upon the will of the general government, and to be governed by any laws it may think proper to impose. The principle upon which our governments rest, and upon which alone they continue to exist, is the union of states, sovereign and independent within their own limits in their internal and domestic concerns, and bound together as one people by a general government, possessing certain enumerated and restricted powers, delegated to it by the people of the several states, and exercising supreme authority within the scope of the powers granted to it, throughout the dominion of the United States. A power, therefore, in the general government to obtain and hold colonies and dependent territories, over which they might legislate without restriction, would be inconsistent with its own existence in its present form. Whatever it acquires, it acquires for the benefit of the people of the several states who created it. It is their trustee acting for them and charged with the duty of promoting the interests of the whole people of the Union in the exercise of the powers specifically granted. . . .

But the power of Congress over the person or property of a citizen can never be a mere discretionary power under our Constitution and form of government. The powers of the government and the rights and privileges of the citizen are regulated and plainly

defined by the Constitution itself. And, when the territory becomes a part of the United States, the federal government enters into possession in the character impressed upon it by those who created it. It enters upon it with its powers over the citizen strictly defined and limited by the Constitution, from which it derives its own existence, and by virtue of which alone it continues to exist and act as a government and sovereignty. It has no power of any kind beyond it; and it cannot, when it enters a territory of the United States, put off its character and assume discretionary or despotic powers which the Constitution has denied to it. It cannot create for itsef a new character separated from the citizens of the United States and the duties it owes them under the provisions of the Constitution. The territory, being a part of the United States, the government and the citizen both enter it under the authority of the Constitution, with their respective rights defined and marked out; and the federal government can exercise no power over his person or property, beyond what that instrument confers, nor lawfully deny any right which it has reserved. . . .

These powers, and others, in relation to rights of person, which it is not necessary here to enumerate, are, in express and positive terms, denied to the general government; and the rights of private property have been guarded with equal care. Thus the rights of property are united with the rights of person and placed on the same ground by the Fifth Amendment to the Constitution, which provides that no person shall be deprived of life, liberty, and property without due process of law. And an act of Congress which deprives a citizen of the United States of his liberty or property, without due process of law, merely because he came himself or brought his property into a particular territory of the United States, and who had committed no offense against the laws, could hardly be dignified with the name of due process of law. . . .

The powers over person and property of which we speak are not only not granted to Congress but are in express terms denied, and they are forbidden to exercise them. And this prohibition is not confined to the states, but the words are general and extend to the whole territory over which the Constitution gives it power to legislate, including those portions of it remaining under territorial government as well as that covered by states. . . .

It seems, however, to be supposed that there is a difference between property in a slave and other property and that different rules may be applied to it in expounding the Constitution of the United States. And the laws and usages of nations, and the writings of eminent jurists upon the relation of master and slave and their mutual rights and duties, and the powers which governments may exercise over it, have been dwelt upon in the argument.

But, in considering the question before us, it must be borne in mind that there is no law of nations standing between the people of the United States and their government and interfering with their relation to each other. The powers of the government and the rights of the citizen under it are positive and practical regulations plainly written down. The people of the United States have delegated to it certain enumerated powers and forbidden it to exercise others. It has no power over the person or property of a citizen but what the citizens of the United States have granted. And no laws or usages of other nations, or reasoning of statesmen or jurists upon the relations of master and slave, can enlarge the powers of the government or take from the citizens the rights they have reserved. And if the Constitution recognizes the right of property of the master in a slave, and makes no distinction between that description of property and other property owned by a citizen, no tribunal, acting under the authority of the United States, whether it be legislative, executive, or judicial, has a right to draw such a distinction or deny to it the benefit of the provisions and guaranties which have been provided for the protection of private property against the encroachments of the government.

Now, as we have already said in an earlier part of this opinion, upon a different point, the right of property in a slave is distinctly and expressly affirmed in the Constitution. The right to traffic in it, like an ordinary article of merchandise and property, was guaranteed to the citizens of the United States, in every state that might desire it, for twenty years. And the government in express terms is pledged to protect it in all future time if the slave escapes from his owner. That is done in plain words—too plain to be misunderstood. And no word can be found in the Constitution which gives Congress a greater power over slave property or which entitles property of that kind to less protection than property of any other description. The only power conferred is the power coupled with the duty of guarding and protecting the owner in his rights.

Upon these considerations it is the opinion of the Court that the act of Congress which prohibited a citizen from holding and owning property of this kind in the territory of the United States north of the line therein mentioned is not warranted by the Constitution and is therefore void; and that neither Dred Scott himself, nor any of his family, were made free by being carried into this territory; even if they had been carried there by the owner with the intention of becoming a permanent resident. . . .

Portions of the dissenting opinion of Justice McLean:

But it is said, if the court, on looking at the record, shall clearly perceive that the circuit court had no jurisdiction, it is a ground for the dismissal of the case. This may be characterized as rather a sharp practice, and one which seldom, if ever, occurs. . . . No such case, it is believed, can be cited. But if this rule of practice is to be applied in this case, and the plaintiff in error is required to answer and maintain as well the points ruled in his favor, as to show the error of those ruled against him, he has more than an ordinary duty to perform. Under such circumstances, the want of jurisdiction in the circuit court must be so clear as not to admit of doubt. Now, the plea which raises the question of jurisdiction, in my judgment, is radically defective. The gravamen of the plea is this: "That the plaintiff is a negro of African descent, his ancestors being of pure African blood, and were brought into this country, and sold as negro slaves."

There is no averment in this plea which shows or conduces to show an inability in the plaintiff to sue in the circuit court. It does not allege that the plaintiff had his domicil in any other State, nor that he is not a free man in Missouri. He is averred to have had a negro ancestry, but this does not show that he is not a citizen of Missouri, within the meaning of the act of congress authorizing him to sue in the circuit court. It has never been held necessary, to constitute a citizen within the act, that he should have the qualifications of an elector. Females and minors may sue in the federal courts, and so may any individual who has a permanent domicil in the State under whose laws his rights are protected, and to which he owes allegiance. . . .

Portions of the dissenting opinion
of Justice Curtis, on citizenship:

First. That the constitution itself has described what native-born persons shall or shall not be citizens of the United States; or,

Second. That it has empowered congress to do so; or,

Third. That all free persons, born within the several States, are citizens of the United States; or,

Fourth. That it is left to each State to determine what free persons, born within its limits, shall be citizens of such State, and *thereby* be citizens of the United States. . . .

*The opinion of Justice Curtis
on the Missouri Compromise:*

First. That the free native-born citizens of each State are citizens of the United States.

Second. That as free colored persons born within some of the States are citizens of those States, such persons are also citizens of the United States.

Third. That every such citizen, residing in any State, has the right to sue and is liable to be sued in the federal courts, as a citizen of that State in which he resides.

Fourth. That as the plea to the jurisdiction in this case shows no facts, except that the plaintiff was of African descent, and his ancestors were sold as slaves, and as these facts are not inconsistent with his citizenship of the United States, and his residence in the State of Missouri, the plea to the jurisdiction was bad, and the judgment of the circuit court overruling it was correct. . . .

*Justice Curtis' opinion
on Dred Scott's removal to a free state:*

First. The rules of international law respecting the emancipation of slaves, by the rightful operation of the laws of another State or country upon the *status* of the slave, while resident in such foreign State or country, are part of the common law of Missouri, and have not been abrogated by any statute law of that State.

Second. The laws of the United States, constitutionally enacted, which operated directly on and changed the *status* of a slave coming into the territory of Wisconsin with his master, who went thither to reside for an indefinite length of time, in the performance of his duties as an officer of the United States, had a rightful operation on the *status* of the slave, and it is in conformity with the rules of international law that this change of *status* should be recognized everywhere.

Third. The laws of the United States, in operation in the territory of Wisconsin at the time of the plaintiff's residence there, did act directly on the *status* of the plaintiff, and change his *status* to that of a free man.

Fourth. The plaintiff and his wife were capable of contracting, and, with the consent of Dr. Emerson, did contract a marriage in that territory, valid under its laws; and the validity of this marriage cannot be questioned in Missouri, save by showing that it was in fraud of the laws of that State, or of some right derived from them; which cannot be shown in this case, because the master consented to it.

Fifth. That the consent of the master that his slave, residing in a country which does not tolerate slavery, may enter into a lawful contract of marriage, attended with the civil rights and duties which belong to that condition, is an effectual act of emancipation. And the law does not enable Dr. Emerson, or any one claiming under him, to assert a title to the married persons as slaves, and thus destroy the obligation of the contract of marriage, and bastardize their issue, and reduce them to slavery.

Curtis subsequently resigned from the Supreme Court in large part because of his lack of confidence in most of his fellow justices and in part for personal reasons, citing inadequate compensation. His brother later wrote that Justice Curtis "no longer felt that confidence in the Supreme Court which was essential to his useful co-operation with its members."[3]

The Dred Scott decision became one of the salient political issues of the critical election of 1860 and was invoked by both Stephen Douglas and Abraham Lincoln in their famous debates. Lincoln's frequent reference to "Stephen, James, and Roger" linked Douglas with President James Buchanan and Chief Justice Roger Brooke Taney as alleged contrivers of the decision. Actually, Taney did not consult with either, but Associate Justices Catron and Grier had given Buchanan advance knowledge of the decision.

The bitterness engendered by the slavery controversy and federal enforcement of the Fugitive Slave Act led to the last significant decision involving the issue before the Civil War, the case of *Ableman v. Booth.* Sherman Booth, editor of an abolitionist newspaper in Milwaukee, Wisconsin, was convicted in federal district court of assisting in the escape of a fugitive slave in violation of the Fugitive Slave Act of 1850 (whose passage was rendered necessary by the Court's decision in

Prigg v. *Pennsylvania* in 1842). Held in a local jail, Booth successfully got a writ of habeas corpus from a Wisconsin judge who held the relevant federal statutes unconstitutional. The state judge's ruling was upheld by the Supreme Court of Wisconsin. The latter court defiantly obstructed federal judicial process by refusing to honor a writ of error sent it by the Supreme Court of the United States. The attorney general of the United States had to present a copy of the Wisconsin Supreme Court action to the Supreme Court of the United States so that action in the case would proceed. Chief Justice Taney wrote the Court's opinion:

ABLEMAN v. BOOTH
21 Howard 506 (1859)

If the judicial power exercised in this instance has been reserved to the States, no offence against the laws of the United States can be punished by their own courts, without the permission and according to the judgment of the courts of the State in which the party happens to be imprisoned; for, if the Supreme Court of Wisconsin possessed the power it has exercised in relation to offences against the act of Congress in question, it necessarily follows that they must have the same judicial authority in relation to any other law of the United States; and, consequently, their supervising and controlling power would embrace the whole criminal code of the United States, and extend to offences against our revenue laws, or any other law intended to guard the different departments of the General Government from fraud or violence. And it would embrace all crimes, from the highest to the lowest; including felonies, which are punished with death, as well as misdemeanors, which are punished by imprisonment. And, moreover, if the power is possessed by the Supreme Court of the State of Wisconsin, it must belong equally to every other State in the Union, when the prisoner is within its territorial limits; and it is very certain that the State courts would not always agree in opinion; and it would often happen, that an act which was admitted to be an offence, and justly punished, in one State, would be regarded as innocent, and indeed as praiseworthy, in another.

It would seem to be hardly necessary to do more than state the result to which these decisions of the State courts must inevitably lead. It is, of itself, a sufficient and conclusive answer; for no one will suppose that a Government which has now lasted nearly seventy years, enforcing its laws by its own tribunals, and preserving the union of the States, could have lasted a single year, or fulfilled the high trusts committed to it, if offences against its laws could not have been punished without the consent of the State in which the culprit was found.

The judges of the Supreme Court of Wisconsin do not distinctly state from what source they suppose they have derived this judicial power. There can be no such thing as judicial authority, unless it is conferred by a Government or sovereignty; and if the judges and courts of Wisconsin possess the jurisdiction they claim, they must derive it either from the United States or the State. It certainly has not been conferred on them by the United States; and it is equally clear it was not in the power of the State to confer it, even if it had attempted to do so; for no State can authorize one of its judges or courts to exercise judicial power, by *habeas corpus* or otherwise, within the jursidiction of another and independent Government. And although the State of Wisconsin is sovereign within its territorial limits to a certain extent, yet that sovereignty is limited and restricted by the Constitution of the United States. And the powers of the General Government, and of the State, although both exist and are exercised within the same territorial limits, are yet separate and distinct sovereignties, acting separately and independently of each other, within their respective spheres. And the sphere of action appropriated to the United States is as far beyond the reach of the judicial process issued by a State judge or a State court, as if the line of division was traced by landmarks and monuments visible to the eye. And the State of Wisconsin had no more power to authorize these proceedings of its judges and courts, than it would have had if the prisoner had been confined in Michigan, or in any other State of the Union, for an offence against the laws of the State in which he was imprisoned. . . .

But, as we have already said, questions of this kind must always depend upon the Constitution and laws of the United States, and not of a State. The Constitution was not formed merely to guard the State against danger from foreign nations, but mainly to secure union and harmony at home; for if this object could be attained, there would be but little danger from abroad; and to accomplish this purpose, it was felt by the statesmen who framed the Constitution, and by the people who adopted it, that it was necessary that many

of the rights of sovereignty which the States then possessed should be ceded to the General Government;
and that, in the sphere of action assigned to it, it should
be supreme, and strong enough to execute its own
laws by its own tribunals, without interruption from a
State or from State authorities. And it was evident
that anything short of this would be inadequate to the
main objects for which the Government was established; and that local interests, local passions or prejudices, incited and fostered by individuals for sinister
purposes, would lead to acts of aggression and injustice
by one State upon the rights of another, which would
ultimately terminate in violence and force, unless there
was a common arbiter between them, armed with
power enough to protect and guard the rights of all, by
appropriate laws, to be carried into execution peacefully by its judicial tribunals. . . .

But the supremacy thus conferred on this Government could not peacefully be maintained, unless it
was clothed with judicial power, equally paramount in
authority to carry it into execution; for if left to the
courts of justice of the several States, conflicting decisions would unavoidably take place, and the local tribunals could hardly be expected to be always free from
the local influences of which we have spoken. And the
Constitution and laws and treaties of the United
States, and the powers granted to the Federal Government, would soon receive different interpretations in
different States, and the Government of the United
States would soon become one thing in one State and
another thing in another. It was essential, therefore,
to its very existence as a Government, that it should
have the power of establishing courts of justice, altogether independent of State power, to carry into effect
its own laws; and that a tribunal should be established
in which all cases which might arise under the Constitution and laws and treaties of the United States,
whether in a State court or a court of the United
States, should be finally and conclusively decided.
Without such a tribunal, it is obvious that there would
be no uniformity of judicial decision; and that the
supremacy, (which is but another name for independence,) so carefully provided in the clause of the Con-

stitution above referred to, could not possibly be maintained peacefully, unless it was associated with this
paramount judicial authority. . . .

This judicial power was justly regarded as indispensable, not merely to maintain the supremacy of the laws
of the United States, but also to guard the States from
any encroachment upon their reserved rights by the
General Government. And as the Constitution is the
fundamental and supreme law, if it appears that an act
of Congress is not pursuant to and within the limits of
the power assigned to the Federal Government, it is
the duty of the courts of the United States to declare it
unconstitutional and void. The grant of judicial power
is not confined to the administration of laws passed in
pursuance to the provisions of the Constitution, nor
confined to the interpretation of such laws; but, by the
very terms of the grant, the Constitution is under
their view when any act of Congress is brought before
them, and it is their duty to declare the law void, and
refuse to execute it, if it is not pursuant to the legislative powers conferred upon Congress. And as the final
appellate power in all such questions is given to this
court, controversies as to the respective powers of the
United States and the States, instead of being determined by military and physical force, are heard, investigated, and finally settled, with the calmness and deliberation of judicial inquiry. And no one can fail to see,
that if such an arbiter had not been provided, in our
complicated system of government, internal tranquility
could not have been preserved; and if such controversies were left to arbitrament of physical force, our
Government, State and National, would soon cease to
be Governments of laws, and revolutions by force of
arms would take the place of courts of justice and judicial decisions. . . .

But although we think it unnecessary to discuss
these questions, yet, as they have been decided by the
State court, and are before us on the record, and we
are not willing to be misunderstood, it is proper to say
that, in the judgment of this court, the act of Congress
commonly called the fugitive slave law is, in all of its
provisions, fully authorized by the Constitution of the
United States. . . .

Using language similar to that of the Virginia and Kentucky Resolutions of
1798–1799, the Wisconsin legislature resolved that the states could interpose to
prevent enforcement of federal laws deemed unconstitutional. On the eve of Lincoln's election, the Southern states defended constitutional orthodoxy while Wisconsin asserted states' rights, a situation soon to be dramatically reversed.[4]

The credit for averting sectional division in 1850 was associated with the temporarily successful compromises fashioned by Congress, notably the California,
New Mexico, and Utah Acts of September 9, 1850, the Fugitive Slave Act of

September 18, 1850, and the act abolishing the slave trade in the District of Columbia of September 20, 1850. Historians Kelly and Harbison have concluded that after the compromises of 1850, "the day of Congress as the arbiter of constitutional questions was in fact drawing to a close," while the role of the Supreme Court was becoming more influential.[5] But the very factors that had seemingly enhanced the role of the Court in attempting to settle the slavery issue contributed to its severe institutional decline.

From the perspective of the Supreme Court's institutional role in relation to the executive and legislative branches of the federal government, the period 1789 through the eve of the Civil War was most remarkable for *what it did not do* in the assertion of the most significant of the powers it had at its command—the power of judicial review. To be sure, the Court had defined the nature of the power of judicial review in 1803 in *Marbury* v. *Madison*. But there was not another assertion of that power until 1857 in *Dred Scott* v. *Sanford*. The first assertion had rankled Jeffersonian Republicans but was not viewed as a serious threat to the ascendance of that newly emergent political party. After all, the same Federalist Court had, in the same term and in an extremely cryptic opinion, upheld the Jeffersonian abolition of the circuit courts created by the Federalist Judiciary Act of 1801. But the second assertion of judicial review did not occur for more than a half a century. This time the Taney Court, dominated by Southern-leaning Jacksonian Democrats, put the Court in direct contradiction to the major policy position of the newly emergent Republican Party.

The majority's position in holding the Missouri Compromise statute unconstitutional prohibited the Congress from excluding the institution of slavery from federal territories. That position was not only a total victory for Southern advocates of slavery, it placed the new Republican Party in an untenable position constitutionally. In their original national convention in Philadelphia in 1856, the Republicans had adopted as their major plank the position that slavery was illegal in any federal territory because it denied persons of their liberty without due process of the law. Taney had, in effect, turned this argument on its head by ruling that the due process clause of the Fifth Amendment protected the vested property right of slave owners in all of the territories of the United States, an early assertion of substantive due process.

In the presidential campaign of 1860, the Republican Party responded by attacking the Court on a number of points including its doctrinal positions and its members. Many Republican candidates treated the Court's position (and especially Chief Justice Taney's) on slavery in the territories as *obiter dicta*, that is, as statements made in the opinion that are not pertinent or necessary to the decision. They pointedly argued that the *Dred Scott* decision could be reversed by the Court in the future, and they indicated that the election of the Republican presidential candidate, Abraham Lincoln, and Republican majorities in the House and Senate would make fulfillment of this goal possible. The Jacksonian Democratic majority was attacked as being composed of Southerners or "Northern men with Southern principles." In short, the *Dred Scott* decision precipitated a direct and apparently irreconcilable conflict between the old political generation comprising the Court's majority in 1860 and the new leadership comprising the Republican Party in the same year.

Civil war and saving the Union

After the Republicans won, the South rebelled and seceded from the Union. President Buchanan was incapable of meeting the crisis. After Lincoln assumed the presidency, he responded strongly to the South Carolinian attack on Fort Sumter. Lincoln led the Union in direct military response to Sumter and to disunion.

Republican feelings against the old Court majority were strong, and it is conceivable that a court-packing plan might have succeeded if President Lincoln had not had a number of vacancies to fill in his first term. Taney was still viewed (correctly) as a Southern sympathizer. Campbell first sought to help negotiate a settlement with the South to forestall war, and then resigned to join the Confederacy. Most remaining carry-over members of the Supreme Court were still viewed as "Northern men with Southern principles," a description that had been applied to them frequently during the 1860 presidential campaign. Justice McLean had become a Republican. He was 75 years of age in 1860 having served on the Court 31 years. Wayne, 70 years of age, was a 25-year Court veteran and although a Southern Whig, he was a Unionist. Taney, 83, had served 24 years. Catron, 74, had served 23 years. Daniel, 76, had served 19 years; Nelson, 68, 15 years; and Grier, 65, 14 years. Pierce's and Buchanan's appointees, Campbell and Clifford, were age 49, 7 years, and age 52, 2 years, respectively. In 1861, Republican Senator Hale of New Hampshire introduced a resolution recommending "the abolition of the present Supreme Court . . . and establishing, instead thereof, another Supreme Court . . . which, in the opinion of Congress, will meet the requirements of the Constitution."[6] This resolution was not adopted. As a matter of fact, in 1861, President Lincoln had the opportunity to fill three vacancies created by Campbell's resignation and the deaths of Justices McLean (in 1861) and Peter V. Daniel (in 1860). In 1862 Lincoln appointed three strong Republicans to replace them: Noah H. Swayne of Ohio, Samuel Freeman Miller of Iowa, and David Davis of Illinois. In 1863 an additional seat on the Court was created and Stephen J. Field, a Union Democrat from California, was appointed to it.

While the Supreme Court was not subjected to a major attempt at abolition, the single separate circuit court, that of the District of Columbia, was abolished in the Civil War years. The three circuit judges were considered Southern sympathizers and placed under house arrest in a Washington, D.C. hotel. Congress abolished the D.C. circuit court on March 3, 1863, and in the same statute created a new court with precisely the same powers and jurisdiction (which subsequently was reorganized within the federal court of appeals system). President Lincoln and the Republican Senate selected an entirely new complement of judges to man the new court.[7]

The decade of the 1860s confronted the Supreme Court with a novel array of issues related to the previously untested powers of the chief executive to exercise power in a period of civil war. The first major case involved the authority of the president to order a blockade of Southern ports by proclamation. He issued one such proclamation a week after fighting began and gained Congressional approval several months after its issuance. The 37th Congress, which acted upon this as well as other executive actions and proposals, was attended by approximately two-thirds of its House members and only 44 Senators. The remainder had joined the Confederacy. In order to thwart threatened foreign intervention (particularly by Great Britain), the Lincoln administration technically insisted that the Civil War was an insurrection, not a war or a rebellion, thus denying that the Confederate States of America existed. *The Prize Cases* concerned the question, can the legal right to capture ships as prizes exist without a formal state of war? Justice Grier, who delivered the Court's opinion, was the only pre–Civil War Democrat on the Court who did not dissent.

THE PRIZE CASES
2 Black 635 (1863)

Justice Grier delivered the opinion of the court:

Had the President a right to institute a blockade of ports in possession of persons in armed rebellion against the government, on the principles of international law, as known and acknowledged among civilized States? . . .

Neutrals have a right to challenge the existence of a blockade *de facto,* and also the authority of the party exercising the right to institute it. They have a right to enter the ports of a friendly nation for the purposes of trade and commerce, but are bound to recognize the rights of a belligerent engaged in actual war, to use this mode of coercion, for the purpose of subduing the enemy.

That a blockade *de facto* actually existed, and was formally declared and notified by the President on the 27th and 30th of April, 1861, is an admitted fact in these cases.

That the President, as the Executive Chief of the Government and Commander-in-Chief of the Army and Navy, was the proper person to make such notification, has not been, and cannot be disputed.

The right of prize and capture has its origin in the "*jus belli,*" and is governed and adjudged under the laws of nations. To legitimate the capture of a neutral vessel or property on the high seas, a war must exist *de facto,* and the neutral must have a knowledge or notice of the intention of one of the parties belligerent to use this mode of coercion against a port, city or territory, in possession of the other.

Let us inquire whether, at the time this blockade was instituted, a state of war existed which would justify a resort to these means of subduing the hostile force.

War has been well defined to be, "That state in which a nation prosecutes its right by force."

The parties belligerent in a public war are independent nations. But it is not necessary, to constitute war, that both parties should be acknowledged as independent nations or sovereign States. A war may exist where one of the belligerents claims sovereign rights as against the other.

Insurrection against a government may or may not culminate in an organized rebellion, but a civil war always begins by insurrection against the lawful authority of the government. A civil war is never solemnly declared; it becomes such by its accidents—the number, power, and organization of the persons who originate and carry it on. When the party in rebellion occupy and hold in a hostile manner a certain portion of territory; have declared their independence; have cast off their allegiance; have organized armies; have commenced hostilities against their former Sovereign, the world acknowledges them as belligerents, and the contest a war. They claim to be in arms to establish their liberty and independence, in order to become a sovereign State, while the sovereign party treats them as insurgents and rebels who owe allegiance, and who should be punished with death for their treason. . . .

As a civil war is never publicly proclaimed, *eo nomine* against insurgents, its actual existence is a fact in our domestic history which the court is bound to notice and to know. . . .

By the Constitution, Congress alone has the power to declare a national or foreign war. It cannot declare war against a State or any number of States, by virtue of any clause in the Constitution. The Constitution confers on the President the whole executive power. He is bound to take care that the laws be faithfully executed. He is Commander-in-Chief of the Army and Navy of the United States, and of the militia of the several States when called into the actual service of the United States. He has no power to initiate or declare a war either against a foreign nation or a domestic State. But by the Acts of Congress . . . he is authorized to call out the militia and use the military and naval forces of the United States in case of invasion by foreign nations, and to suppress insurrection against the government of a State or of the United States.

If a war be made by invasion of a foreign nation, the President is not only authorized but bound to resist force, by force. He does not initate the war, but is bound to accept the challenge without waiting for any special legislative authority. And whether the hostile party be a foreign invader, or States organized in rebellion, it is none the less a war, although the declaration of it be *"unilateral."* . . .

This greatest of civil wars was not gradually developed by popular commotion, tumultuous assemblies, or local unorganized insurrections. However long may have been its previous conception, it nevertheless sprung forth suddenly from the parent brain, a Minerva in the full panoply of war. The President was bound to meet it in the shape it presented itself, without waiting for Congress to baptize it with a name; and no name given to it by him or them could change the fact.

It is not the less a civil war, with belligerent parties in hostile array, because it may be called an "insurrection" by one side, and the insurgents be considered as rebels or traitors. It is not necessary that the independence of the revolted province or State be acknowledged in order to constitute it a party belligerent in a war according to the law of nations. Foreign nations acknowledge it as war by a declaration of neutrality. The condition of neutrality cannot exist unless there be two belligerent parties. . . .

Whether the President in fulfilling his duties, as Commander-in-Chief, in suppressing an insurrection, has met with such armed hostile resistance, and a civil war of such alarming proportions as will compel him to accord to them the character of belligerents, is a question to be decided by him, and this court must be governed by the decisions and acts of the Political Department of the government to which this power was intrusted. "He must determine what degree of force the crisis demands." The proclamation of blockade is, itself, official and conclusive evidence to the court that a state of war existed which demanded and authorized a recourse to such a measure, under the circumstances peculiar to the case. . . .

If it were necessary to the technical existence of a war, that it should have a legislative sanction, we find it in almost every Act passed at the extraordinary session of the Legislature of 1861, which was wholly employed in enacting laws to enable the government to prosecute the war with vigor and efficiency. And finally, in 1861, we find Congress *"ex majore cautela"* and in anticipation of such astute objections, passing an Act "approving, legalizing and making valid all the acts, proclamations, and orders of the President, &c., as if they had been *issued and done under the previous express authority* and direction of the Congress of the United States." . . .

On this first question, therefore, we are of the opinion that the President had a right, *jure belli*, to institute a blockade of ports in possession of the States in rebellion which neutrals are bound to regard. . . .

The other early confrontation between the judiciary and the president concerned the presidential suspension of the writ of habeas corpus. Lincoln had acted after pro-Southern riots in Baltimore, Maryland, had threatened communications and Union troop movement between the North and Washington, D. C. In his suspension of the writ he authorized the Union general commanding the zone including Baltimore to determine who should be detained. John Merryman was an outspoken advocate of secession and leader of a secessionist military company in Baltimore. The commanding general, Cadwalader, had Merryman arrested at his home and detained in Fort McHenry. Merryman was permitted to secure legal counsel and the latter petitioned Chief Justice Taney for a writ of habeas corpus. Taney issued a writ ordering the general to produce Merryman in the federal circuit court in Baltimore. The general sent a military aide who read a statement. Taney cited the general for contempt of court and sent a U. S. marshal to Fort McHenry, where he was denied admission to the fort. Because the marshal could not raise a posse and storm the fort, Taney relieved him of further responsibility. He then wrote an analysis and sent it to President Lincoln. The analysis emphasized that the writ could be suspended only by an act of Congress. Taney urged Lincoln to fulfill his constitutional obligation. Lincoln sent this analysis to Attorney General Bates for his opinion. Bates ruled that the president did have authority to suspend the writ and authorize military arrests as part of this "duty" to suppress rebellion. Lincoln interpreted congressional silence as agreement. Taney was, in effect, ignored. As a result of the Merryman issue and the outcome of the *Prize Cases*, the Supreme Court made no further attempts to impede or obstruct actions of the Lincoln administration.[8]

No major issue of this kind was decided by the Supreme Court for the duration of the Civil War, but shortly thereafter it decided *Ex Parte Milligan*. Milligan was arrested by order of the commanding general of the military district of Indiana, tried in October 1864 by a military tribunal, convicted of a variety of treasonable activities, and sentenced to hang. Two weeks after he assumed office following the assassination of President Lincoln, President Andrew Johnson approved the sentence. On May 10, 1865, Milligan sought a writ of habeas corpus from a federal circuit court in order to challenge the validity of the proceedings under which he was convicted and sentenced. Consequently, the authority of the president to suspend the writ and to replace civilian courts with military tribunals was challenged directly before the Supreme Court. The majority opinion was written by one of President Lincoln's appointees and close associates, Justice David Davis of Illinois.

EX PARTE MILLIGAN
4 Wallace 2 (1866)

Justice Davis delivered the opinion of the Court:

. . . The importance of the main question presented by this record cannot be overstated; for it involves the very framework of the government and the fundamental principles of American liberty. . . .

The controlling question in the case is this: Upon the facts stated in Milligan's petition, and the exhibits filed, had the military commission mentioned in it jurisdiction, legally, to try and sentence him? Milligan, not a resident of one of the rebellious States, or a prisoner of war, but a citizen of Indiana for twenty years past, and never in the military or naval service, is, while at his home, arrested by the military power of the United States, imprisoned, and, on certain criminal charges preferred against him, tried, convicted, and sentenced to be hanged by a military commission, organized under the direction of the military commander of the military district of Indiana. Had this tribunal the legal power and authority to try and punish this man? . . .

Have any of the rights guaranteed by the Constitution been violated in the case of Milligan? and if so, what are they?

Every trial involves the exercise of judicial power; and from what source did the military commission that tried him derive their authority? Certainly no part of the judicial power of the country was conferred on them; because the Constitution expressly vests it "in one Supreme Court and such inferior courts as the

Congress may from time to time ordain and establish," and it is not pretended that the commission was a court ordained and established by Congress. They cannot justify on the mandate of the President, because he is controlled by law, and has his appropriate sphere of duty, which is to execute, not to make, the laws; and there is "no unwritten criminal code to which resort can be had as a source of jurisdiction."

But it is said that the jurisdiction is complete under the "law and usages of war."

It can serve no useful purpose to inquire what those laws and usages are, whence they originated, where found, and on whom they operate; they can never be applied to citizens in States which have upheld the authority of the government, and where the courts are open and their process unobstructed. This court has judicial knowledge that in Indiana the Federal authority was always unopposed, and its courts always open to hear criminal accusations and redress grievances; and no usage of war could sanction a military trial there for any offense whatever of a citizen in civil life, in nowise connected with the military service. Congress could grant no such power; and to the honor of our national legislature be it said, it has never been provoked by the state of the country even to attempt its exercise. One of the plainest constitutional provisions was, therefore, infringed when Milligan was tried by a court not ordained and established by Congress, and not composed of judges appointed during good behavior.

Why was he not delivered to the Circuit Court of Indiana to be proceeded against according to law? No reason of necessity could be urged against it; because

Congress had declared penalties against the offenses charged, provided for their punishment, and directed that court to hear and determine them. And soon after this military tribunal was ended, the circuit court met, peacefully transacted its business, and adjourned. It needed no bayonets to protect it, and required no military aid to execute its judgments. It was held in a State, eminently distinguished for patriotism, by judges commissioned during the rebellion who were provided with juries, upright, intelligent, and selected by a marshal appointed by the President. The government had no right to conclude that Milligan, if guilty, would not receive in that court merited punishment; for its records disclose that it was constantly engaged in the trial of similar offenses, and was never interrupted in its administration of criminal justice. If it was dangerous, in the distracted condition of affairs, to leave Milligan unrestrained of his liberty, because he "conspired against the government, afforded aid and comfort to rebels, and incited the people to insurrection," the law said, arrest him, confine him closely, render him powerless to do further mischief; and then present his case to the grand jury of the district, with proofs of his guilt, and, if indicted, try him according to the course of the common law. If this had been done, the Constitution would have been vindicated, the law of 1863 enforced, and the securities for personal liberty preserved and defended.

Another guarantee of freedom was broken when Milligan was denied a trial by jury. The great minds of the country have differed on the correct interpretation to be given to the various provisions of the federal Constitution; and judicial decision has been often invoked to settle their true meaning; but until recently no one ever doubted that the right of trial by jury was fortified in the organic law against the power of attack. It is now assailed; but if ideas can be expressed in words, and language has any meaning, this right—one of the most valuable in a free country—is preserved to every one accused of crime who is not attached to the army, or navy, or militia in actual service. The Sixth Amendment affirms that "in all criminal prosecutions the accused shall enjoy the right to a speedy and public trial by an impartial jury,"—language broad enough to embrace all persons and cases; but the Fifth, recognizing the necessity of an indictment, or presentment, before any one can be held to answer for high crimes, "excepts cases arising in the land or naval forces" or in the militia, "when in actual service, in time of war or public danger"; and the framers of the Constitution, doubtless, meant to limit the right of trial by jury, in the Sixth Amendment, to those persons who were subject to indictment or presentment in the Fifth.

It is claimed that martial law covers with its broad mantle the proceedings of this military commission. The proposition is this: that in a time of war the commander of an armed force (if, in his opinion, the exigencies of the country demand it, and of which he is to judge) has the power, within the lines of his military district, to suspend all civil rights and their remedies, and subject citizens as well as soldiers to the rule of his will; and in the exercise of his lawful authority cannot be restrained, except by his superior officer or the President of the United States.

If this position is sound to the extent claimed, then when war exists, foreign or domestic, and the country is subdivided into military departments for mere convenience, the commander of one of them can, if he chooses, within his limits, on the plea of necessity, with the approval of the Executive, substitute military force for, and to the exclusion of, the laws, and punish all persons, as he thinks right and proper, without fixed or certain rules.

The statement of this proposition shows its importance; for, if true, republican government is a failure, and there is an end of liberty regulated by law. Martial law, established on such a basis, destroys every guarantee of the Constitution, and effectually renders the "military independent of, and superior to, the civil power,"—the attempt to do which by the King of Great Britain was deemed by our fathers such an offense, that they assigned it to the world as one of the causes which impelled them to declare their independence. Civil liberty and this kind of martial law cannot endure together; the antagonism is irreconcilable; and, in the conflict, one or the other must perish.

This nation, as experience has proved, cannot always remain at peace, and has no right to expect that it will always have wise and humane rulers, sincerely attached to the principles of the Constitution. Wicked men, ambitious of power, with hatred of liberty and contempt of law, may fill the place once occupied by Washington and Lincoln; and if this right is conceded, and the calamities of war again befall us, the dangers to human liberty are frightful to contemplate. If our fathers had failed to provide for just such a contingency, they would have been false to the trust reposed in them. They knew—the history of the world told them—the nation they were founding, be its existence short or long, would be involved in war; how often or how long continued, human foresight could not tell; and that unlimited power, wherever lodged at such a time, was especially hazardous to freemen. For this, and other equally weighty reasons, they secured the inheritance they had fought to maintain, by incorporating in a written Constitution the safeguards which time had proved were essential to its preservation. Not one of these safeguards can the President, or Congress, or the judiciary disturb, except the one concerning the writ of habeas corpus.

It is essential to the safety of every government that, in a great crisis like the one we have just passed through, there should be a power somewhere of suspending the writ of habeas corpus. In every war, there are men of previously good character, wicked enough to counsel their fellow-citizens to resist the measures deemed necessary by a good government to sustain its just authority and overthrow its enemies; and their influence may lead to dangerous combinations. In the emergency of the times, an immediate public investigation according to law may not be possible; and yet the peril to the country may be too imminent to suffer such persons to go at large. Unquestionably, there is then an exigency which demands that the government, if it should see fit, in the exercise of a proper discretion, to make arrests, should not be required to produce the persons arrested in answer to a writ of habeas corpus. The Constitution goes no further. It does not say after a writ of habeas corpus is denied a citizen, that he shall be tried otherwise than by the course of the common law; if it had intended this result, it was easy by the use of direct words to have accomplished it. The illustrious men who framed that instrument were guarding the foundations of civil liberty against the abuses of unlimited power; they were full of wisdom, and the lessons of history informed them that a trial by an established court, assisted by an impartial jury, was the only sure way of protecting the citizen against oppression and wrong. Knowing this, they limited the suspension to one great right, and left the rest to remain forever inviolable. But, it is insisted that the safety of the country in time of war demands that this broad claim for martial law shall be sustained. If this were true, it could be well said that a country, preserved at the sacrifice of all the cardinal principles of liberty, is not worth the cost of preservation. Happily, it is not so.

It will be borne in mind that this is not a question of the power to proclaim martial law, when war exists in a community and the courts and civil authorities are overthrown. Nor is it a question what rule a military commander, at the head of his army, can impose on States in rebellion to cripple their resources and quell the insurrection. The jurisdiction claimed is much more extensive. The necessities of the service, during the late Rebellion, required that the loyal States should be placed within the limits of certain military districts and commanders appointed in them; and, it is urged, that this, in a military sense, constituted them the theatre of military operations; and, as in this case, Indiana had been and was again threatened with invasion by the enemy, the occasion was furnished to establish martial law. The conclusion does not follow from the premises. If armies were collected in Indiana, they were to be employed in another locality, where the laws were obstructed and the national authority disputed. On her soil there was no hostile foot; if once invaded, that invasion was at an end, and with it all pretext for martial law. Martial law cannot arise from a threatened invasion. The necessity must be actual and present; the invasion real, such as effectually closes the courts and deposes the civil administration.

It is difficult to see how the safety of the country required martial law in Indiana. If any of her citizens were plotting treason, the power of arrest could secure them, until the government was prepared for their trial, when the courts were open and ready to try them. It was as easy to protect witnesses before a civil as a military tribunal; and as there could be no wish to convict, except on sufficient legal evidence, surely an ordained and established court was better able to judge of this than a military tribunal composed of gentlemen not trained to the profession of the law.

It follows, from what has been said on this subject, that there are occasions when martial rule can be properly applied. If, in foreign invasion or civil war, the courts are actually closed, and it is impossible to administer criminal justice according to law, then, on the theatre of active military operations, where war really prevails, there is a necessity to furnish a substitute for the civil authority, thus overthrown, to preserve the safety of the army and society; and as no power is left but the military, it is allowed to govern by martial rule until the laws can have their free course. As necessity creates the rule, so it limits its duration; for, if this government is continued after the courts are reinstated, it is a gross usurpation of power. Martial rule can never exist where the courts are open, and in the proper and unobstructed exercise of their jurisdiction. It is also confined to the locality of actual war. Because, during the late Rebellion it could have been enforced in Virginia, where the national authority was overturned and the courts driven out, it does not follow that it should obtain in Indiana, where that authority was never disputed, and justice was always administered. And so in the case of a foreign invasion, martial rule may become a necessity in one State, when, in another, it would be "mere lawless violence." . . .

The two remaining questions in this case must be answered in the affirmative. The suspension of the privilege of the writ of habeas corpus does not suspend the writ itself. The writ issues as a matter of course;

and on the return made to it the court decides whether the party applying is denied the right of proceeding any further with it.

If the military trial of Milligan was contrary to law, then he was entitled, on the facts stated in his petition, to be discharged from custody by the terms of the Act of Congress of March 3, 1863. The provisions of this law having been considered in a previous part of this opinion, we will not restate the views there presented. Milligan avers he was a citizen of Indiana, not in the military or naval service, and was detained in close confinement, by order of the President, from the 5th day of October, 1864, until the 2d day of January, 1865, when the circuit court for the district of Indiana, with a grand jury, convened in session at Indianapolis; and afterwards, on the 27th day of the same month, adjourned without finding an indictment or present-ment against him. If these averments were true (and their truth is conceded for the purposes of this case), the court was required to liberate him on taking certain oaths prescribed by the law, and entering into recog-nizance for his good behavior.

But it is insisted that Milligan was a prisoner of war, and, therefore, excluded from the privileges of the statute. It is not easy to see how he can be treated as a prisoner of war, when he lived in Indiana for the past twenty years, was arrested there, and had not been, during the late troubles, a resident of any States in rebellion. If in Indiana he conspired with bad men to assist the enemy, he is punishable for it in the courts of Indiana; but, when tried for the offense, he cannot plead the rights of war; for he was not engaged in legal acts of hostility against the government, and only such persons, when captured, are prisoners of war. If he cannot enjoy the immunities attaching to the character of a prisoner of war, how can he be subject to their pains and penalties? . . .

Chief Justice Chase, for himself and Justice Wayne, Justice Swayne, and Justice Miller, delivered an opinion in which he differed from the Court in several important points, but concurred in the judgment in the case:

Four members of the Court, concurring with their brethren in the order heretofore made in this cause,

but unable to concur in some important particulars with the opinion which has just been read, think it their duty to make a separate statement of their views of the whole case.

We do not doubt that the Circuit Court for the District of Indiana had jurisdiction of the petition of Milligan for the writ of habeas corpus. . . .

But the opinion which has just been read goes further and, as we understand it, asserts not only that the military commission held in Indiana was not autho-rized by Congress but that it was not in the power of Congress to authorize it; from which it may be thought to follow that Congress has no power to indemnify the officers who composed the commission against liability in civil courts for acting as members of it.

We cannot agree to this. . . .

Congress has the power not only to raise and sup-port and govern armies but to declare war. It has, therefore, the power to provide by law for carrying on war. This power necessarily extends to all legislation essential to the prosecution of war with vigor and suc-cess, except such as interferes with the command of the forces and the conduct of campaigns. That power and duty belong to the President as commander-in-chief. Both these powers are derived from the Consti-tution, but neither is defined by that instrument. Their extent must be determined by their nature and by the principles of our institutions. . . .

We cannot doubt that, in such a time of public danger, Congress had power, under the Constitution, to provide for the organization of a military commis-sion and for trial by that commission of persons en-gaged in this conspiracy. The fact that the federal courts were open was regarded by Congress as a suffi-cient reason for not exercising the power; but that fact could not deprive Congress of the right to exer-cise it. Those courts might be open and undisturbed in the execution of their functions, and yet wholly in-competent to avert threatened danger, or to punish, with adequate promptitude and certainty, the guilty conspirators. . . .

We have confined ourselves to the question of power. It was for Congress to determine the question of expediency. . . .

Radical Republicans and Reconstruction

The Radical Republicans in control of Congress were determined to impose severe restrictions on the individuals who had engaged in rebellion and upon the states that had comprised the Confederacy. President Lincoln had desired a more concil-iatory policy as did his successor, Andrew Johnson. Military occupation of the

South, reconstruction of Southern politics and society, and the imposition of test oaths were among the most important of the immediate post–Civil War enactments of the Radical Republican Congress. President Andrew Johnson's attempts at opposing those policies led to a narrowly defeated attempt at his impeachment conviction and removal. Southern leaders generally found that the Supreme Court appeared to offer the only means of thwarting the will of the Radical Republican Congress. In *Cummings* v. *Missouri* the constitutional validity of the test oath was considered.

CUMMINGS v. MISSOURI
4 Wallace 277 (1867)

Associate Justice Stephen J. Field delivered the majority opinion:

This case came before us on a writ of error to the Supreme Court of Missouri, and involves a consideration of the test oath imposed by the constitution of that State. The plaintiff in error is a priest of the Roman Catholic Church, and was indicted and convicted in one of the circuit courts of the State of the crime of teaching and preaching as a priest and minister of that religious denomination without having first taken the oath, and was sentenced to pay a fine of five hundred dollars, and to be committed to jail until the same was paid. On appeal to the Supreme Court of the State, the judgment was affirmed. . . .

The oath thus required is, for its severity, without any precedent that we can discover. In the first place, it is retrospective; it embraces all the past from this day; and, if taken years hence, it will also cover all the intervening period. In its retrospective feature we believe it is peculiar to this country. In England and France there have been test oaths, but they were always limited to an affirmation of present belief, or present disposition towards the government, and were never exacted with reference to particular instances of past misconduct. In the second place, the oath is directed not merely against overt and visible acts of hostility to the government, but is intended to reach words, desires, and sympathies, also. And, in the third place, it allows no distinction between acts springing from malignant enmity and acts which may have been prompted by charity, or affection, or relationship. If one has ever expressed sympathy with any who were drawn into the Rebellion, even if the recipients of that sympathy were connected by the closest ties of blood, he is as unable to subscribe to the oath as the most active and the most cruel of the rebels, and is equally debarred from the offices of honor or trust, and the positions and employments specified.

But, as it was observed by the learned counsel who appeared on behalf of the State of Missouri, this court cannot decide the case upon the justice or hardship of these provisions. Its duty is to determine whether they are in conflict with the Constitution of the United States. On behalf of Missouri, it is urged that they only prescribe a qualification for holding certain offices, and practising certain callings, and that it is therefore within the power of the State to adopt them. On the other hand, it is contended that they are in conflict with that clause of the Constitution which forbids any State to pass a bill of attainder or an *ex post facto* law. . . .

Qualifications relate to the fitness or capacity of the party for a particular pursuit or profession. . . . It is evident from the nature of the pursuits and professions of the parties, placed under disabilities by the constitution of Missouri, that many of the acts, from the taint of which they must purge themselves, have no possible relation to their fitness for those pursuits and professions. There can be no connection between the fact that Mr. Cummings entered or left the State of Missouri to avoid enrolment or draft in the military service of the United States and his fitness to teach the doctrines or administer the sacraments of his church; nor can a fact of this kind or the expression of words of sympathy with some of the persons drawn into the Rebellion constitute any evidence of the unfitness of the attorney or counsellor to practice his profession, or of the professor to teach the ordinary branches of education, or of the want of business knowledge or business capacity in the manager of a corporation, or in any director or trustee. It is manifest upon the simple statement of many of the acts and of the professions and pursuits, that there is no such relation between them as to render a denial of the commission of the acts at all appropriate as a condition of allowing the exercise of the professions and pursuits. The oath could not, therefore, have been required as a means of ascertaining whether parties were qualified or not for their respective callings or the trusts with which they were charged. It was required in order to reach the person, not the calling. It was exacted, not from any notion that the several acts designated indicated unfitness for the callings, but because it was thought that the several acts deserved punishment, and that for many of them there was no way to inflict punishment except by depriving the parties, who had committed them, of some of the rights and privileges of the citizen.

The disabilities created by the constitution of Missouri must be regarded as penalties—they constitute punishment. . . .

The theory upon which our political institutions rest is, that all men have certain inalienable rights—that among these are life, liberty, and the pursuit of happiness; and that in the pursuit of happiness all avocations, all honors, all positions, are alike open to every one, and that in the protection of these rights all are equal before the law. Any deprivation or suspension of any of these rights for past conduct is punishment, and can be in no otherwise defined. . . .

" 'No State shall pass any bill of attainder, *ex post facto* law, or law impairing the obligation of contracts.' "

A bill of attainder is a legislative act which inflicts punishment without a judicial trial.

If the punishment be less than death, the act is termed a bill of pains and penalties. Within the meaning of the Constitution, bills of attainder include bills of pains and penalties. In these cases the legislative body, in addition to its legitimate functions, exercises the powers and office of judge; it assumes, in the language of the text-books, judicial magistracy; it pronounces upon the guilt of the party, without any of the forms or safeguards of trial; it determines the sufficiency of the proofs produced, whether conformable to the rules of evidence or otherwise; and it fixes the degree of punishment in accordance with its own notions of the enormity of the offence. . . .

If the clauses of the second article of the constitution of Missouri, to which we have referred, had in terms declared that Mr. Cummings was guilty, or should be held guilty, of having been in armed hostility to the United States, or of having entered that State to avoid being enrolled or drafted into the military service of the United States, and, therefore, should be deprived of the right to preach as a priest of the Catholic Church, or to teach in any institution of learning, there could be no question that the clauses would constitute a bill of attainder within the meaning of the Federal Constitution. If these clauses, instead of mentioning his name, had declared that all priests and clergymen within the State of Missouri were guilty of these acts, or should be held guilty of them, and hence be subjected to the like deprivation, the clauses would be equally open to objection. And, further, if these clauses

had declared that all such priests and clergymen should be so held guilty, and be thus deprived, provided they did not, by a day designated, do certain specified acts, they would be no less within the inhibition of the Federal Constitution.

In all these cases there would be the legislative enactment creating the deprivation without any of the ordinary forms and guards provided for the security of the citizen in the administration of justice by the established tribunals.

The results which would follow from clauses of the character mentioned do follow from the clauses actually adopted. The difference between the last case supposed and the case actually presented is one of form only, and not of substance. The existing clauses presume the guilt of the priests and clergymen, and adjudge the deprivation of their right to preach or teach unless the presumption be first removed by their expurgatory oath—in other words, they assume the guilt and adjudge the punishment conditionally. The clauses supposed differ only in that they declare the guilt instead of assuming it. . . .

By an *ex post facto* law is meant one which imposes a punishment for an act which was not punishable at the time it was committed; or imposes additional punishment to that then prescribed; or changes the rules of evidence by which less or different testimony is sufficient to convict than was then required. . . .

The clauses in the Missouri constitution, which are the subject of consideration, do not, in terms, define any crimes, or declare that any punishment shall be inflicted, but they produce the same result upon the parties, against whom they are directed, as though the crimes were defined and the punishment was declared. They assume that there are persons in Missouri who are guilty of some of the acts designated. They would have no meaning in the constitution were not such the fact. They are aimed at past acts, and not future acts. They were intended especially to operate upon parties who, in some form or manner, by action or words, directly or indirectly, had aided or countenanced the Rebellion, or sympathized with parties engaged in the Rebellion, or had endeavored to escape the proper responsibilities and duties of a citizen in time of war; and they were intended to operate by depriving such persons of the right to hold certain offices and trusts, and to pursue their ordinary and regular avocations. This deprivation is punishment; nor is it any less so because a way is opened for escape from it by the expurgatory oath. The framers of the constitution of Missouri knew at the time that whole classes of individuals would be unable to take the oath prescribed. To them there is no escape provided; to them the deprivation was intended to be, and is, absolute and perpetual. To make the enjoyment of a right dependent upon an impossible condition is equivalent to an absolute denial of the right under any condition, and such denial, enforced for a past act, is nothing less than punishment imposed for that act. It is a misapplication of terms to call it anything else. . . .

The judgment of the Supreme Court of Missouri

must be reversed, and the cause remanded, with directions to enter a judgment reversing the judgment of the Circuit Court, and directing that court to discharge the defendant from imprisonment, and suffer him to depart without delay.

The Chief Justice,
and Justices Swayne, Davis, and Miller dissented.

One of the most direct assaults on the Reconstruction Acts was an attempt by the state of Mississippi to enjoin President Andrew Johnson and the commander of the Military District of Mississippi and Arkansas from executing or carrying out any of the statutes.

MISSISSIPPI v. JOHNSON
4 Wallace 475 (1867)

Chief Justice Chase delivered the opinion of the Court:

A motion was made, some days since, in behalf of the State of Mississippi, for leave to file a bill in the name of the State, praying this court perpetually to enjoin and restrain Andrew Johnson, President of the United States, and E. O. C. Ord, general commanding in the District of Mississippi and Arkansas, from executing, or in any manner carrying out, certain acts of Congress therein named.

The acts referred to are those of March 2d and March 23d, 1867, commonly known as the Reconstruction Acts.

The Attorney-General objected to the leave asked for, upon the ground that no bill which makes a President a defendant, and seeks an injunction against him to restrain the performance of his duties as President, should be allowed to be filed in this court.

This point has been fully argued, and we will now dispose of it.

We shall limit our inquiry to the question presented by the objection, without expressing any opinion on the broader issues discussed in argument, whether, in any case, the President of the United States may be required, by the process of this court, to perform a purely ministerial act under a positive law, or may be held amenable, in any case, otherwise than by impeachment for crime.

The single point which requires consideration is this: Can the President be restrained by injunction from carrying into effect an act of Congress alleged to be unconstitutional?

It is assumed by the counsel for the State of Mis-

sissippi, that the President, in the execution of the Reconstruction Acts, is required to perform a mere ministerial duty. In this assumption there is, we think, a confounding of the terms ministerial and executive, which are by no means equivalent in import.

A ministerial duty, the performance of which may, in proper cases, be required of the head of a department, by judicial process, is one in respect to which nothing is left to discretion. It is a simple, definite duty, arising under conditions admitted or proved to exist, and imposed by law.

The case of *Marbury* v. *Madison, Secretary of State,* furnishes an illustration. A citizen had been nominated, confirmed, and appointed a justice of the peace for the District of Columbia, and his commission had been made out, signed, and sealed. Nothing remained to be done except delivery, and the duty of delivery was imposed by law on the Secretary of State. It was held that the performance of this duty might be enforced by *mandamus* issuing from a court having jurisdiction. . . .

Very different is the duty of the President in the exercise of the power to see that the laws are faithfully executed, and among these laws the acts named in the bill. By the first of these acts he is required to assign generals to command in the several military districts, and to detail sufficient military force to enable such officers to discharge their duties under the law. By the supplementary act, other duties are imposed on the several commanding generals, and these duties must necessarily be performed under the supervision of the President as commander-in-chief. The duty thus imposed on the President is in no just sense ministerial. It is purely executive and political.

An attempt on the part of the judicial department of the government to enforce the performance of such duties by the President might be justly characterized, in the language of Chief Justice Marshall, as "an absurd and excessive extravagance." . . .

It was admitted in the argument that the application now made to us is without a precedent; and this is of much weight against it. . . .

The fact that no such application was ever before made in any case indicates the general judgment of the profession that no such application should be entertained.

It will hardly be contended that Congress can interpose, in any case, to restrain the enactment of an unconstitutional law; and yet how can the right to judicial interposition to prevent such an enactment, when the purpose is evident and the execution of that purpose certain, be distinguished, in principle, from the right to such interposition against the execution of such a law by the President?

The Congress is the legislative department of the government; the President is the executive department. Neither can be restrained in its action by the judicial department; though the acts of both, when performed, are, in proper cases, subject to its cognizance.

The impropriety of such interference will be clearly seen upon consideration of its possible consequences.

Suppose the bill filed and the injunction prayed for allowed. If the President refuse obedience, it is needless to observe that the court is without power to enforce its process. If, on the other hand, the President complies with the order of the court and refuses to execute the acts of Congress, is it not clear that a collision may occur between the executive and legislative departments of the government? May not the House of Representatives impeach the President for such refusal? And in that case could this court interfere, in behalf of the President, thus endangered by compliance with its mandate, and restrain by injunction the Senate of the United States from sitting as a court of impeachment? Would the strange spectacle be offered to the public world of an attempt by this court to arrest proceedings in that court?

These questions answer themselves.

It is true that a State may file an original bill in this court. And it may be true, in some cases, that such a bill may be filed against the United States. But we are fully satisfied that this court has no jurisdiction of a bill to enjoin the President in the performance of his official duties; and that no such bill ought to be received by us.

It has been suggested that the bill contains a prayer that, if the relief sought cannot be had against Andrew Johnson, as President, it may be granted against Andrew Johnson as a citizen of Tennessee. But it is plain that relief as against the execution of an act of Congress by Andrew Johnson, is relief against its execution by the President. A bill praying an injunction against the execution of an act of Congress by the incumbent of the presidential office cannot be received, whether it describes him as President or as a citizen of a State. . . .

A southern newspaper editor, McCardle, sought an ingenious mode of forcing a test of the Reconstruction Acts by invoking a federal statute originally passed to protect blacks and federal officers in the South. This was an action for direct appeal to the Supreme Court of the denial of his petition for a writ of habeas corpus by a federal circuit court. McCardle had sought the writ after he was tried and convicted of sedition by a federal military court. The Court took jurisdiction, whereupon the Radical Republican Congress repealed the statute that provided the basis for that jurisdiction. President Andrew Johnson vetoed this repealer but it was passed over his veto. The Court delayed its decision until the following term and was bitterly criticized by Justices Grier and Field for cowardice. In 1869 the Court acted.

EX PARTE McCARDLE
7 Wallace 506 (1869)

Chief Justice Chase delivered the opinion of the Court:

. . . The first question necessarily is that of jurisdiction; for, if the Act of March 1868, takes away the jurisdiction defined by the Act of February, 1867, it is useless, if not improper, to enter into any discussion of other questions.

It is quite true, as was argued by the counsel for the petitioner, that the appellate jurisdiction of this court is not derived from Acts of Congress. It is, strictly speaking, conferred by the Constitution. But it is conferred "with such exceptions and under such regulations as Congress shall make."

It is unnecessary to consider whether, if Congress had made no exceptions and no regulations, this court might not have exercised general appellate jurisdiction under rules prescribed by itself. From among the earliest Acts of the first Congress, at its first session, was the Act of September 24th, 1789, to establish the judicial courts of the United States. That Act provided for the organization of this court, and prescribed regulations for the exercise of its jurisdiction.

The source of that jurisdiction, and the limitations of it by the Constitution and by statute, have been on several occasions subjects of consideration here. In the case of Durousseau v. United States [1810]; Wiscart v. Dauchy [1796], particularly, the whole matter was carefully examined, and the court held, that while "the appellate powers of this court are not given by the Judicial Act, but are given by the Constitution"; they are, nevertheless, "limited and regulated by that Act, and by such other acts as have been passed on the subject." The court said, further, that the Judicial Act was an exercise of the power given by the Constitution to Congress "of making exceptions to the appellate jurisdiction of the Supreme Court."

"They have described affirmatively," said the court, "its jurisdiction, and this affirmative description has been understood to imply a negation of the exercise of such appellate power as is not comprehended with it."

The principle that the affirmation of appellate jurisdiction implies the negation of all such jurisdiction not affirmed having been thus established, it was an almost necessary consequence that Acts of Congress, providing for the exercise of jurisdiction, should come to be spoken of as Acts granting jurisdiction, and not as Acts making exceptions to the constitutional grant of it.

The exception to appellate jurisdiction in the case before us, however, is not an inference from the affirmation of other appellate jurisdiction. It is made in terms. The provision of the Act of 1867, affirming the appellate jurisdiction of this court in cases of habeas corpus, is expressly repealed. It is hardly possible to imagine a plainer instance of positive exception.

We are not at liberty to inquire into the motives of the Legislature. We can only examine into its power under the Constitution; and the power to make exceptions to the appellate jurisdiction of this court is given by express words.

What, then, is the effect of the repealing Act upon the case before us? We cannot doubt as to this. Without jurisdiction the court cannot proceed at all in any cause. Jurisdiction is power to declare the law, and when it ceases to exist, the only function remaining to the court is that of announcing the fact and dismissing the cause. And this is not less clear upon authority than upon principle.

Several cases were cited by the counsel for the petitioner in support of the position that jurisdiction of this case is not affected by the repealing Act. But none of them, in our judgment, afford any support to it. . . .

On the other hand, the general rule, supported by the best elementary writers . . . is, that "when an Act of the Legislature is repealed, it must be considered, except as to transactions past and closed, as if it never existed." And the effect of repealing Acts upon suits under Acts repealed, has been determined by the adjudications of this court. The subject was fully considered in Norris v. Crocker [1852], and more recently in Insurance Company v. Ritchie [1867]. In both of these cases it was held that no judgment could be rendered in a suit after the repeal of the Act under which it was brought and prosecuted.

It is quite clear, therefore, that this court cannot proceed to pronounce judgment in this case, for it has no longer jurisdiction of the appeal; and judicial duty is not less fitly performed by declining ungranted jurisdiction than in exercising firmly that which the Constitution and the laws confer.

Counsel seem to have supposed, if effect be given to the repealing Act in question, that the whole appellate power of the court, in cases of habeas corpus, is denied. But this is in error. The Act of 1868 does not except from that jurisdiction any cases but appeals from circuit courts under the Act of 1867. It does not affect the jurisdiction which was previously exercised. . . .

The appeal of the petitioner in this case must be dismissed for want of jurisdiction.

The Radical Republican Congress had wanted to treat the states comprising the Confederacy as "conquered provinces," but President Lincoln and many others preferred to be more conciliatory and to restore status as states when possible. The Supreme Court dealt with this issue in *Texas* v. *White*. The post–Civil War government of Texas sought to recover pre–Civil War United States bonds that had been sold by the Confederate government of Texas during the war. The most important issue was whether a state could unilaterally secede from the Union.

TEXAS v. WHITE
7 Wallace 700 (1869)

Chief Justice Chase delivered the opinion of the Court:

The first inquiries to which our attention was directed by counsel, arose upon the allegations . . . that the State, having severed her relations with a majority of the States of the Union, and having by her ordinance of secession attempted to throw off her allegiance to the Constitution and government of the United States, has so far changed her status as to be disabled from prosecuting suits in the National courts. . . .

If, therefore, it is true that the State of Texas was not at the time of filing this bill, or is not now, one of the United States, we have no jurisdiction of this suit, and it is our duty to dismiss it. . . .

In the Constitution the term state most frequently expresses the combined idea just noticed, of people, territory, and government. A state, in the ordinary sense of the Constitution, is a political community of free citizens, occupying a territory of defined boundaries, and organized under a government sanctioned and limited by a written constitution, and established by the consent of the governed. It is the union of such states, under a common constitution, which forms the distinct and greater political unit, which that Constitution designates as the United States, and makes of the people and states which compose it one people and one country. . . .

The Republic of Texas was admitted into the Union, as a State, on the 27th of December, 1845. By this act the new State, and the people of the new State, were invested with all the rights, and became subject to all the responsibilities and duties of the original States under the Constitution.

From the date of admission, until 1861, the State was represented in the Congress of the United States by her senators and representatives, and her relations as a member of the Union remained unimpaired. In that year, acting upon the theory that the rights of a State under the Constitution might be renounced, and her obligations thrown off at pleasure, Texas undertook to sever the bond thus formed, and to break up her constitutional relations with the United States. . . .

The position thus assumed could only be maintained by arms, and Texas accordingly took part, with the other Confederate States, in the war of the rebellion, which these events made inevitable. During the whole of that war there was no governor, or judge, or any other State officer in Texas, who recognized the Na-

tional authority. Nor was any officer of the United States permitted to exercise any authority whatever under the National government within the limits of the State, except under the immediate protection of the National military forces.

Did Texas, in consequence of these acts, cease to be a State? Or, if not, did the State cease to be a member of the Union?

It is needless to discuss, at length, the question whether the right of a State to withdraw from the Union for any cause, regarded by herself as sufficient, is consistent with the Constitution of the United States.

The Union of the States never was a purely artificial and arbitrary relation. It began among the Colonies, and grew out of common origin, mutual sympathies, kindred principles, similar interests, and geographical relations. It was confirmed and strengthened by the necessities of war, and received definite form, and character, and sanction from the Articles of Confederation. By these the Union was solemnly declared to "be perpetual." And when these Articles were found to be inadequate to the exigencies of the country, the Constitution was ordained "to form a more perfect Union." It is difficult to convey the idea of indissoluble unity more clearly than by these words. What can be indissoluble if a perpetual Union, made more perfect, is not?

But the perpetuity and indissolubility of the Union, by no means implies the loss of distinct and individual existence, or of the right of self-government by the States. Under the Articles of Confederation each State retained its sovereignty, freedom, and independence, and every power, jurisdiction, and right not expressly delegated to the United States. Under the Constitution, though the powers of the States were much restricted, still, all powers not delegated to the United States, nor prohibited to the States, are reserved to the States respectively, or to the people. And we have already had occasion to remark at this term, that "the people of each State compose a State, having its own government, and endowed with all the functions essential to separate and independent existence," and that "without the States in union, there could be no such political body as the United States." Not only, therefore, can there be no loss of separate and independent autonomy to the States, through their union under the Constitution, but it may be not unreasonably said that the preservation of the States, and the maintenance of their governments, are as much within the design and care of the Constitution as the preservation of the

Union and the maintenance of the National government. The Constitution, in all its provisions, looks to an indestructible Union, composed of indestructible States.

When, therefore, Texas became one of the United States, she entered into an indissoluble relation. All the obligations of perpetual union, and all the guaranties of republican government in the Union, attached at once to the State. The act which consummated her admission into the Union was something more than a compact; it was the incorporation of a new member into the political body. And it was final. The union between Texas and the other States was as complete, as perpetual, and as indissoluble as the union between the original States. There was no place for reconsideration, or revocation, except through revolution, or through consent of the States.

Considered therefore as transactions under the Constitution, the ordinance of secession, adopted by the convention and ratified by a majority of the citizens of Texas, and all the acts of her legislature intended to give effect to that ordinance, were absolutely null. They were utterly without operation in law. The obligations of the State, as a member of the Union, and of every citizen of the State, as a citizen of the United States, remained perfect and unimpaired. It certainly follows that the State did not cease to be a State, nor her citizens to be citizens of the Union. If this were otherwise, the State must have become foreign, and her citizens foreigners. The war must have ceased to be a war for the suppression of rebellion, and must have become a war for conquest and subjugation.

Our conclusion therefore is, that Texas continued to be a State, and a State of the Union, notwithstanding the transactions to which we have referred. And this conclusion, in our judgment, is not in conflict with any act or declaration of any department of the National government, but entirely in accordance with the whole series of such acts and declarations since the first outbreak of the rebellion.

But in order to the exercise, by a State, of the right to sue in this court, there needs to be a State government, competent to represent the State in its relations with the National government, so far at least as the institution and prosecution of a suit is concerned.

And it is by no means a logical conclusion, from the premises which we have endeavored to establish, that the governmental relations of Texas to the Union remained unaltered. . . . No one has been bold enough to contend that, while Texas was controlled by a government hostile to the United States, and in affiliation with a hostile confederation, waging war upon the United States, senators chosen by her legislature, or representatives elected by her citizens, were entitled to seats in Congress; or that any suit, instituted in her name, could be entertained in this court. All admit that, during this condition of civil war, the rights of the State as a member, and of her people as citizens of the Union, were suspended. The government and the citizens of the State, refusing to recognize their constitutional obligations, assumed the character of enemies, and incurred the consequences of rebellion. . . .

When the war closed there was no government in the State except that which had been organized for the purpose of waging war against the United States. That government immediately disappeared. . . .

There being then no government in Texas in constitutional relations with the Union, it became the duty of the United States to provide for the restoration of such a government. . . .

It is not important to review, at length, the measures which have been taken, under this power, by the executive and legislative departments of the National government. It is proper, however, to observe that almost immediately after the cessation of organized hostilities, and while the war yet smouldered in Texas, the President of the United States issued his proclamation appointing a provisional governor for the State, and providing for the assembling of a convention, with a view to the reestablishment of a republican government, under an amended constitution, and to the restoration of the State to her proper constitutional relations. A convention was accordingly assembled, the constitution amended, elections held, and a State government, acknowledging its obligations to the Union, established.

Whether the action then taken was, in all respects, warranted by the Constitution, it is not now necessary to determine. The power exercised by the President was supposed, doubtless, to be derived from his constitutional functions, as commander-in-chief; and, so long as the war continued, it cannot be denied that he might institute temporary government within insurgent districts, occupied by the National forces, or take measures, in any State, for the restoration of State government faithful to the Union, employing, however, in such efforts, only such means and agents as were authorized by constitutional laws.

But, the power to carry into effect the clause of guaranty is primarily a legislative power, and resides in Congress. . . .

Nothing in the case before us requires the court to pronounce judgment upon the constitutionality of any particular provision of [the Reconstruction] acts. . . .

Another extremely important issue of the Civil War era related to economic stability and the nature of the currency. Lincoln had chosen Salmon Portland Chase as chief justice in part because as secretary of the treasury, Chase had developed and defended the wartime legal tender system. In *Hepburn v. Griswold*, Chief Justice Chase dealt with the currency issue as a member of the Court. Concurrently, President U. S. Grant chose two new justices whose views differed with Chase's on legal tender. A year later in the joint cases of *Knox v. Lee* and *Parker v. Davis*, commonly referred to as the *Legal Tender Cases*, the Court reversed the Hepburn decision, an action that did not enhance the Court's already shaky public and professional reputation.

HEPBURN v. GRISWOLD
8 Wallace 603 (1870)

Chief Justice Chase delivered the opinion of the Court:

The case before us is one of private right. The plaintiff in the court below sought to recover of the defendants a certain sum expressed on the face of a promissory note. The defendants insisted on the right, under the act of February 25th, 1862, to acquit themselves of their obligation by tendering in payment a sum nominally equal in United States notes. But the note had been executed before the passage of the act, and the plaintiff insisted on his right under the Constitution to be paid the amount due in gold and silver. And it has not been, and cannot be, denied that the plaintiff was entitled to judgment according to his claim, unless bound by a constitutional law to accept the notes as coin.

Thus two questions were directly presented: Were the defendants relieved by the act from the obligation assumed in the contract? Could the plaintiff be compelled, by a judgment of the court, to receive in payment a currency of different nature and value from that which was in the contemplation of the parties when the contract was made?

The Court of Appeals resolved both questions in the negative, and the defendants, in the original suit, seek the reversal of that judgment by writ of error.

It becomes our duty, therefore, to detemine whether the act of February 25th, 1862, so far as it makes United States notes a legal tender in payment of debts contracted prior to its passage, is constitutional and valid or otherwise. . . .

It is not necessary . . . in order to prove the existence of a particular authority to show a particular and express grant. The design of the Constitution was to establish a government competent to the direction and administration of the affairs of a great nation, and, at the same time, to mark, by sufficiently definite lines, the sphere of its operations. To this end it was needful only to make express grants of general powers, coupled with a further grant of such incidental and auxiliary powers as might be required for the exercise of the powers expressly granted. These powers are necessarily extensive. It has been found, indeed, in the practical administration of the government, that a very large part, if not the largest part, of its functions have been performed in the exercise of powers thus implied.

But the extension of power by implication was regarded with some apprehension by the wise men who framed, and by the intelligent citizens who adopted, the Constitution. This apprehension is manifest in the terms by which the grant of incidental and auxiliary powers is made. All powers of this nature are included under the description of "power to make all laws necessary and proper for carrying into execution the powers expressly granted to Congress or vested by the Constitution in the government or in any of its departments or officers." . . .

It has not been maintained in argument, nor, indeed, would any one, however slightly conversant with constitutional law, think of maintaining that there is in the Constitution any express grant of legislative power to make any description of credit currency a legal tender in payment of debts.

We must inquire then whether this can be done in the exercise of an implied power.

The rule for determining whether a legislative enactment can be supported as an exercise of an implied power was stated by Chief Justice Marshall, speaking for the whole court, in the case of *McCullough v. The State of Maryland;* and the statement then made has ever since been accepted as a correct exposition of the Constitution. His words were these: "Let the end be legitimate, let it be within the scope of the Constitution, and all means which are appropriate, which are plainly adapted to that end, which are not prohibited, but consistent with the letter and spirit of the Constitution, are constitutional." And in another part of the same opinion the practical application of this rule was thus illustrated: "Should Congress, in the execution of its powers, adopt measures which are prohibited by the Constitution, or should Congress, under the pretext of executing its powers, pass laws for the accomplishment of objects not intrusted to the government, it would be the painful duty of this tribunal, should a case requiring such a decision come before it, to say that such an act was not the law of the land. But where the law is not prohibited, and is really calculated to effect any of the objects intrusted to the government, to undertake here to inquire into the degree of its necessity would be to pass the line which circumscribes the judicial department, and tread on legislative ground."

It must be taken then as finally settled, so far as judicial decisions can settle anything, that the words "all laws necessary and proper for carrying into execution" powers expressly granted or vested, have, in the Constitution, a sense equivalent to that of the words, laws, not absolutely necessary indeed, but appropriate, plainly adapted to constitutional and legitimate ends; laws not prohibited, but consistent with the letter and spirit of the Constitution; laws really calculated to effect objects intrusted to the government.

The question before us, then, resolves itself into this: "Is the clause which makes United States notes a legal tender for debts contracted prior to its enactment, a law of the description stated in the rule?"

It is not doubted that the power to establish a standard of value by which all other values may be measured, or, in other words, to determine what shall be lawful money and a legal tender, is in its nature, and of necessity, a governmental power. It is in all countries exercised by the government. In the United States, so far as it relates to the precious metals, it is vested in Congress by the grant of the power to coin money. But can a power to impart these qualities to notes, or promises to pay money, when offered in discharge of pre-existing debts, be derived from the coinage power, or from any other power expressly given? . . .

[I]t has been maintained in argument that the power to make United States notes a legal tender in payment of all debts is a means appropriate and plainly adapted to the execution of the power to carry on war, of the power to regulate commerce, and of the power to borrow money. If it is, and is not prohibited, nor inconsistent with the letter or spirit of the Constitution, then the act which makes them such legal tender must be held to be constitutional. . . .

It is difficult to say to what express power the authority to make notes a legal tender in payment of pre-existing debts may not be upheld as incidental,

upon the principles of this argument. Is there any power which does not involve the use of money? . . .

We are unable to persuade ourselves that an expedient of this sort is an appropriate and plainly adapted means for the execution of the power to declare and carry on war. If it adds nothing to the utility of the notes, it cannot be upheld as a means to the end in furtherance of which the notes are issued. Nor can it, in our judgment, be upheld as such, if, while facilitating in some degree the circulation of the notes, it debases and injures the currency in its proper use to a much greater degree. And these considerations seem to us equally applicable to the powers to regulate commerce and to borrow money. Both powers necessarily involve the use of money by the people and by the government, but neither, as we think, carries with it as an appropriate and plainly adapted means to its exercise, the power of making circulating notes a legal tender in payment of pre-existing debts.

But there is another view, which seems to us decisive, to whatever express power the supposed implied power in question may be referred. In the rule stated by Chief Justice Marshall, the words appropriate, plainly adapted, really calculated, are qualified by the limitation that the means must be not prohibited, but consistent with the letter and spirit of the Constitution. Nothing so prohibited or inconsistent can be regarded as appropriate, or plainly adapted, or really calculated means to any end.

Let us inquire, then, first, whether making bills of credit a legal tender, to the extent indicated, is consistent with the spirit of the Constitution.

Among the great cardinal principles of that instrument, no one is more conspicuous or more venerable than the establishment of justice. And what was intended by the establishment of justice in the minds of the people who ordained it is, happily, not a matter of disputation. It is not left to inference or conjecture, especially in its relations to contracts. . . .

The . . . principle found . . . expression in that most valuable provision of the Constitution of the United States, ever recognized as an efficient safeguard against injustice, that "no State shall pass any law impairing the obligation of contracts."

It is true that this prohibition is not applied in terms to the government of the United States. Congress has express power to enact bankrupt laws, and we do not say that a law made in the execution of any other express power, which, incidentally, only impairs the obligation of a contract, can be held to be unconstitutional for that reason.

But we think it is clear that those who framed and those who adopted the Constitution, intended that the spirit of this prohibition should pervade the entire body of legislation and that the justice which the Constitution was ordained to establish was not thought by them to be compatible with legislation of an opposite tendency. In other words, we cannot doubt that a law not made in pursuance of an express power, which necessarily and in its direct operation impairs the obligation of contracts, is inconsistent with the spirit of the Constitution.

Another provision, found in the fifth amendment, must be considered in this connection. We refer to that which ordains that private property shall not be taken for public use without compensation. This provision is kindred in spirit to that which forbids legislation impairing the obligation of contracts; but, unlike that, it is addressed directly and solely to the National government. It does not, in terms, prohibit legislation which appropriates the private property of one class of citizens to the use of another class; but if such property cannot be taken for the benefit of all, without compensation, it is difficult to understand how it can be so taken for the benefit of a part without violating the spirit of the prohibition.

But there is another provision in the same amendment, which, in our judgment, cannot have its full and intended effect unless construed as a direct prohibition of the legislation which we have been considering. It is that which declares that "no person shall be deprived of life, liberty, or property, without due process of law."

It is not doubted that all the provisions of this amendment operate directly in limitation and restraint of the legislative powers conferred by the Constitution. The only question is, whether an act which compels all those who hold contracts for the payment of gold and silver money to accept in payment a currency of inferior value deprives such persons of property without due process of law.

It is quite clear, that whatever may be the operation of such an act, due process of law makes no part of it. Does it deprive any person of property? A very large proportion of the property of civilized men exists in the form of contracts. These contracts almost invariably stipulate for the payment of money. And we have already seen that contracts in the United States, prior to the act under consideration, for the payment of money, were contracts to pay the sums specified in gold and silver coin. And it is beyond doubt that the holders of these contracts were and are as fully entitled to the protection of this constitutional provision as the holders of any other description of property. . . .

We are obliged to conclude that an act making mere promises to pay dollars a legal tender in payment of debts previously contracted, is not a means appropriate, plainly adapted, really calculated to carry into effect any express power vested in Congress; that such an act is inconsistent with the spirit of the Constitution; and that it is prohibited by the Constitution. . . .

The reversal came the next year, in 1871, when President Grant appointed Justices William Strong and Joseph Bradley. This situation is often cited as one of the most direct and most successful efforts of a president to choose Court appointees whose ideology and policy positions conformed to his own, thus causing an abrupt change in judicial policy.

THE LEGAL TENDER CASES
12 Wallace 457 (1871)

Justice Strong delivered the opinion of the Court:

Are the acts of Congress, known as the legal tender acts, constitutional when applied to contracts made before their passage; and, secondly, are they valid as applicable to debts contracted since their enactment? These questions have been elaborately argued, and they have received from the court that consideration which their great importance demands. It would be difficult to overestimate the consequences which must follow our decision. They will affect the entire business

of the country, and take hold of the possible continued existence of the government. If it be held by this court that Congress has no constitutional power, under any circumstances, or in any emergency, to make treasury notes a legal tender for the payment of all debts (a power confessedly possessed by every independent sovereignty other than the United States), the government is without those means of self-preservation which, all must admit, may, in certain contingencies, become indispensable, even if they were not when the acts of Congress now called in question were enacted. It is also clear that if we hold the acts invalid as applicable to debts incurred, or transactions which have taken place since their enactment, our decision must cause, throughout the country, great business derangement, widespread distress, and the rankest injustice. . . . And there is no well-founded distinction to be made between the constitutional validity of an act of Congress declaring treasury notes a legal tender for the payment of debts contracted after its passage and that of an act making them a legal tender for the discharge of all debts, as well as those incurred before as those made after its enactment. There may be a difference in the effects produced by the acts, and in the hardship of their operation, but in both cases the fundamental question, that which tests the validity of the legislation, is, can Congress constitutionally give to treasury notes the character and qualities of money? Can such notes be constituted a legitimate circulating medium, having a defined legal value? If they can, then such notes must be available to fulfil all contracts (not expressly excepted) solvable in money, without reference to the time when the contracts were made. . . .

The consequences of which we have spoken, serious as they are, must be accepted, if there is a clear incompatibility between the Constitution and the legal tender acts. But we are unwilling to precipitate them upon the country unless such an incompatibility plainly appears. A decent respect for a co-ordinate branch of the government demands that the judiciary should presume, until the contrary is clearly shown, that there has been no transgression of power by Congress—all the members of which act under the obligation of an oath of fidelity to the Constitution. . . .

Nor can it be questioned that, when investigating the nature and extent of the powers conferred by the Constitution upon Congress, it is indispensable to keep in view the objects for which those powers were granted. This is a universal rule of construction applied alike to statutes, wills, contracts, and constitutions. If the general purpose of the instrument is ascertained, the language of its provisions must be construed with reference to that purpose and so as to subserve it. . . . [T]he powers conferred upon Congress must be regarded as related to each other, and all means for a common end. Each is but part of a system, a constituent of one whole. No single power is the ultimate end for which the Constitution was adopted. It may, in a very proper sense, be treated as a means for the accomplishment of a subordinate object, but that object is itself a means designed for an ulterior purpose. Thus the power to levy and collect taxes, to coin money and regulate its value, to raise and support armies, or to provide for and maintain a navy, are instruments for the paramount object, which was to establish a government, sovereign within its sphere, with capability of self-preservation, thereby forming a union more perfect than that which existed under the old Confederacy.

The same may be asserted also of all the non-enumerated powers included in the authority expressly given "to make all laws which shall be necessary and proper for carrying into execution the specified powers vested in Congress, and all other powers vested by the Constitution in the government of the United States, or in any department or officer thereof." . . .

And here it is to be observed it is not indispensable to the existence of any power claimed for the Federal government that it can be found specified in the words of the Constitution, or clearly and directly traceable to some one of the specified powers. Its existence may be deduced fairly from more than one of the substantive powers expressly defined, or from them all combined. It is allowable to group together any number of them and infer from them all that the power claimed has been conferred. . . .

And it is of importance to observe that Congress has often exercised, without question, powers that are not expressly given nor ancillary to any single enumerated power. Powers thus exercised are what are called by Judge Story in his Commentaries on the Constitution, resulting powers, arising from the aggregate powers of the government. He instances the right to sue and make contracts. Many others might be given. The oath required by law from officers of the government is one. So is building a capitol or a presidential mansion, and so also is the penal code. . . .

Indeed the whole history of the government and of congressional legislation has exhibited the use of a very wide discretion, even in times of peace and in the absence of any trying emergency, in the selection of the necessary and proper means to carry into effect the great objects for which the government was framed, and this discretion has generally been unquestioned, or, if questioned, sanctioned by this court. This is true not only when an attempt has been made to execute a single power specifically given, but equally true when the means adopted have been appropriate to the execution, not of a single authority, but of all the powers created by the Constitution. . . .

We do not propose to dilate at length upon the circumstances in which the country was placed, when Congress attempted to make treasury notes a legal tender. They are of too recent occurrence to justify enlarged description. Suffice it to say that a civil war was then raging which seriously threatened the overthrow of the government and the destruction of the Constitution itself. It demanded the equipment and support of large armies and navies, and the employment of money to an extent beyond the capacity of all ordinary sources of supply. . . .

It was at such a time and in such circumstances that Congress was called upon to devise means for maintaining the army and navy, for securing the large supplies of money needed, and, indeed, for the preservation of the government created by the Constitution. It was at such a time and in such an emergency that the legal tender acts were passed. Now, if it were certain that nothing else would have supplied the absolute necessities of the treasury, that nothing else would have enabled the government to maintain its armies and navies, that nothing else would have saved the government and the Constitution from destruction, while the legal tender acts would, could any one be bold enough to assert that Congress transgressed its powers? . . .

Concluding, then, that the provision which made treasury notes a legal tender for the payment of all debts other than those expressly excepted, was not an inappropriate means for carrying into execution the legitimate powers of the government, we proceed to inquire whether it was forbidden by the letter or spirit of the Constitution. It is not claimed that any express prohibition exists, but it is insisted that the spirit of the Constitution was violated by the enactment. Here those who assert the unconstitutionality of the acts mainly rest their argument. . . . To assert . . . that the clause enabling Congress to coin money and regulate its value tacitly implies a denial of all other power over the currency of the nation, is an attempt to introduce a new rule of construction against the solemn decisions of this court. So far from its containing a lurking prohibition, many have thought it was intended to confer upon Congress that general power over the currency

which has always been an acknowledged attribute of sovereignty in every other civilized nation than our own, especially when considered in connection with the other clause which denies to the States the power to coin money, emit bills of credit, or make anything but gold and silver coin a tender in payment of debts. . . .

We come next to the argument much used, and, indeed, the main reliance of those who assert the unconstitutionality of the legal tender acts. It is that they are prohibited by the spirit of the Constitution because they indirectly impair the obligation of contracts. . . .

That discovery calls for a new reading of the Constitution.

If . . . the legal tender acts were justly chargeable with impairing contract obligations, they would not, for that reason, be forbidden, unless a different rule is to be applied to them from that which has hitherto prevailed in the construction of other powers granted by the fundamental law. But . . . the objection misapprehends the nature and extent of the contract obligation spoken of in the Constitution. As in a state of civil society property of a citizen or subject is ownership, subject to the lawful demands of the sovereign, so contracts must be understood as made in reference to the possible exercise of the rightful authority of the government, and no obligation of a contract can extend to the defeat of legitimate government authority. . . .

We are not aware of anything else which has been advanced in support of the proposition that the legal tender acts were forbidden by either the letter or the spirit of the Constitution. If, therefore, they were, what we have endeavored to show, appropriate means for legitimate ends, they were not transgressive of the authority vested in Congress. . . .

The judicial controversies of the 1860s and early 1870s were largely concerned with issues arising out of the rebellion and immediate post-war reconstruction. A possible serious crisis between a predominantly Democratic Supreme Court and the first Republican president and Congress did not occur in large part for gerontological as well as political reasons. President Abraham Lincoln had a rather distinctive opportunity to control the Court by constitutionally legitimate means. Most presidents who have successfully led their political parties to electoral victory have not had the opportunity to extend their electoral success to control of the judicial branch. Lincoln was only the third president to appoint a Supreme Court majority. Previously only George Washington and Andrew Jackson had achieved a Court majority. As noted above, Lincoln chose Justices Swayne, Miller, and Davis in 1862, Justice Field in 1863 (as the result of the short-term creation of a tenth seat), and Chief Justice Salmon P. Chase in 1864 after the death of Taney. After Justice Catron's death in 1865, the size of the Court reverted to nine members.

The post–Civil War amendments

One of the most significant results of the Union victory in the Civil War was the adoption of three key constitutional amendments designed to eliminate slavery and its related manifestations from the American constitutional system. The first of these, the Thirteenth Amendment, was ratified and officially proclaimed on December 18, 1865. It prohibited slavery and involuntary servitude except for punishment for crime within the United States or any area subject to its jurisdiction, and granted Congress authority to enforce the prohibition. The Fourteenth Amendment, in effect, repudiated Taney's Dred Scott decision by providing that *all* persons born or naturalized in the United States and subject to its jurisdiction were citizens of the United States and of the state in which they resided. The new amendment also prohibited a state from abridging the privileges and immunities of United States citizens, from depriving any person of life, liberty, or property without due process of law, and from denying any person within its jurisdiction the equal protection of the laws. This amendment was ratified and proclaimed on July 28, 1868. The Fifteenth Amendment, ratified and proclaimed on March 30, 1870, prohibited federal or state denial or abridgement of the right of male citizens to vote because of race, color, or previous condition of servitude. Both the Fourteenth and Fifteenth Amendments provided for congressional power to enforce their sections. Supreme Court interpretations of these amendments not only tested the Court's reactions to the Radical Republican congressional positions but had significant implications for the emergent role of private corporations in constitutional interpretations.

The Republican-dominated Supreme Court under Chief Justice Chase had scrupulously avoided head-on clashes with the Radical Republican Congress over reconstruction, but did not hesitate to assert its independence when long-range issues involved the post–Civil War constitutional amendments. The *Slaughterhouse Cases* provided the first judicial interpretation of the privileges and immunities clause of the Fourteenth Amendment. The case arose when the constitutionality of a slaughterhouse monopoly statute enacted by the reconstructed Louisiana legislature was challenged by a group of independent butchers in the city of New Orleans. The challenge was actually based on the Thirteenth Amendment, and the due process and equal protection clauses as well as the privileges and immunities clause of the Fourteenth Amendment. Counsel for the butchers was former Supreme Court Justice John Archibald Campbell, who had joined the Confederacy after the outbreak of the Civil War. Because his argument represented a complete reversal of his pre-war positions on federal-state relations and, especially, because his oral argument sought to establish new bases for the independence of private business from governmental control, some portions of Campbell's oral argument before the Court are reproduced below. Similarly, significant portions of the dissents of Justices Field and Bradley are included as well as the majority opinion

of Justice Miller. Field's and Bradley's views, like some of Campbell's, were har-
bingers of the future positions of the Supreme Court. In many respects, the
controversies discussed in the Slaughterhouse Cases represented the issues of a
new, emergent economic and social era in the United States.

THE SLAUGHTERHOUSE CASES
16 Wallace 36 (1873)

ERROR to the Supreme Court of Louisiana.

The three cases—the parties to which as plaintiffs
and defendants in error, are given specifically as a sub-
title, at the head of this report, but which are reported
together also under the general name which, in common parlance, they had acquired—grew out of an act
of the legislature of the State of Louisiana, entitled:
*"An act to protect the health of the City of New Orleans, to locate
the stock landings and slaughterhouses, and to incorporate 'The
Crescent City Live-Stock Landing and Slaughter-House Company,'"* which was approved on the 8th of March, 1869,
and went into operation on the 1st of June following;
and the three cases were argued together. . . .

*Mr. John A. Campbell argued the case
in behalf of the plaintiffs in error:*

II. *But if this monopoly were not thus void at common law, it
would be so under both the thirteenth and fourteenth amendments.*

The thirteenth amendment prohibits "slavery and
involuntary *servitude*." The expressions are ancient
ones, and were familiar even before the time when
they appeared in the great Ordinance of 1787, for the
government of our vast Northwestern Territory; a
territory from which great States were to arise. In that
ordinance they are associated with enactments affording comprehensive protection for life, liberty, and
property; for the spread of religion, morality, and
knowledge; for maintaining the inviolability of contracts, the freedom of navigation upon the public rivers, and the unrestrained conveyance of property by
contract and devise, and for equality of children in the
inheritance of patrimonial estates. The ordinance became a law after Great Britain, in form the most popular government in Europe, had been expelled from that
territory because of "injuries and usurpations having
in direct object the establishment of an absolute tyranny over the States." Feudalism at that time prevailed
in nearly all the kingdoms of Europe, and serfdom and
servitude and feudal service depressed their people to
the level of slaves. The prohibition of "slavery and
involuntary servitude" in every form and degree,
except as a sentence upon a conviction for crime, comprises much more than the abolition or prohibition of

African slavery. Slavery in the annals of the world had
been the ultimate solution of controversies between
the creditor and debtor; the conqueror and his captive;
the father and his child; the state and an offender
against its laws. The laws might enslave a man to the
soil. The whole of Europe in 1787 was crowded with
persons who were held as vassals to their landlord, and
serfs on his dominions. The American constitution for
that great territory was framed to abolish slavery and
involuntary servitude in all forms, and in all degrees in
which they have existed among men, except as a punishment for crime duly proved and adjudged.

Now, the act of which we complain has made of
three parishes of Louisiana "enthralled ground." "The
seventeen" have *astricted* not only the inhabitants of
those parishes, but of all other portions of the earth
who may have cattle or animals for sale or for food, to
land them at the wharves of that company (if brought
to that territory), to keep them in their pens, yards,
or stables, and to prepare them for market in their
abattoir or slaughter-house. Lest some competitor may
present more tempting or convenient arrangements,
the act directs that all of these shall be closed on a
particular day, and prohibits any one from having,
keeping, or establishing any other; and a peremptory
command is given that all animals shall be sheltered,
preserved, and protected by this corporation, and by
none other, under heavy penalties.

Is not this "a servitude?" Might it not be so considered in a strict sense? . . .

III. *The act is even more plainly in the face of the fourteenth
amendment.* That amendment was a development of the
thirteenth, and is a more comprehensive exposition
of the principles which lie at the foundation of the
thirteenth.

Slavery had been abolished as the issue of the civil
war. More than three millions of a population lately
servile, were liberated without preparation for any
political or civil duty. . . . [Now] the fourteenth amendment does define citizenship and the relations of citizens to the State and Federal government. It ordains
that "all persons born or naturalized in the United
States and subject to the jurisdiction thereof are citizens of the United States and of the State where they
reside." Citizenship in a State is made by residence and
without reference to the consent of the State. Yet, by
the same amendment, when it exists, no State can

abridge its privileges or immunities. The doctrine of the "States-Rights party," led in modern times by Mr. Calhoun, was, that there was no citizenship in the whole United States, except *sub modo* and by the permission of the States. According to their theory the United States had no integral existence except as an incomplete combination among several integers. The fourteenth amendment struck at, and forever destroyed, all such doctrines. . . . By it the national principle has received an indefinite enlargement. The tie between the United States and every citizen in every part of its own jurisdiction has been made intimate and familiar. To the same extent the confederate features of the government have been obliterated. The States in their closest connection with the members of the State, have been placed under the oversight and restraining and enforcing hand of Congress. The purpose is manifest, to establish through the whole jurisdiction of the United States ONE PEOPLE, and that every member of the empire shall understand and appreciate the fact that his privileges and immunities cannot be abridged by State authority; that State laws must be so framed as to secure life, liberty, property from arbitrary violation and secure protection of law to all.

From whatever cause originating, or with whatever special and present or pressing purpose passed, the fourteenth amendment is not confined to the population that had been servile, or to that which had any of the disabilities or disqualifications arising from race or from contract. The vast number of laborers in mines, manufactories, commerce, as well as the laborers on the plantations, are defended against the unequal legislation of the States. Nor is the amendment confined in its application to laboring men. The mandate is universal in its application to persons of every class and every condition. . . .

Campbell not only provided what many Radical Republicans perceived as an ingenious and dangerous set of doctrines to employ their own amendments to defeat the legislation of a Radical Republican-dominated Louisiana state legislature, but he also opened up the long-range prospects for corporate invocation of the amendments for their own economic purposes. Justice Miller's majority opinion rejected Campbell's arguments, but Justices Field and Bradley (the former supported by Chief Justice Chase and Justices Swayne and Bradley) wrote strong dissents embodying many of Campbell's arguments. Most of the majority opinion and portions of each dissent are reproduced below.

Justice Miller delivered the opinion of the court:

The records show that the plaintiffs in error relied upon, and asserted throughout the entire course of the litigation in the State courts, that the grant of privileges in the charter of defendant, which they were contesting, was a violation of the most important provisions of the thirteenth and fourteenth articles of amendment of the Constitution of the United States. The jurisdiction and the duty of this court to review the judgment of the State court on those questions is clear and is imperative.

The statute thus assailed as unconstitutional was passed March 8th, 1869, and is entitled "An act to protect the health of the city of New Orleans, to locate the stock-landings and slaughter-houses, and to incorporate the Crescent City Live-Stock Landing and Slaughter-House Company." . . .

The plaintiffs in error . . . allege that the statute is a violation of the Constitution of the United States in these several particulars:

That it creates an involuntary servitude forbidden by the thirteenth article of amendment;

That it abridges the privileges and immunities of citizens of the United States;

That it denies to the plaintiffs the equal protection of the laws; and,

That it deprives them of their property without due process of law; contrary to the provisions of the first section of the fourteenth article of amendment.

This court is thus called upon for the first time to give construction to these articles.

We do not conceal from ourselves the great responsibility which this duty devolves upon us. No questions so far-reaching and pervading in their consequences, so profoundly interesting to the people of this country, and so important in their bearing upon the relations of the United States, and of the several States to each other and to the citizens of the States and of the United States, have been before this court during the official life of any of its present members. We have given every opportunity for a full hearing at the bar;

we have discussed it freely and compared views among ourselves; we have taken ample time for careful deliberation, and we now propose to announce the judgments which we have formed in the construction of those articles, so far as we have found them necessary to the decision of the cases before us, and beyond that we have neither the inclination nor the right to go.

Twelve articles of amendment were added to the Federal Constitution soon after the original organization of the government under it in 1789. Of these all but the last were adopted so soon afterwards as to justify the statement that they were practically contemporaneous with the adoption of the original; and the twelfth, adopted in eighteen hundred and three, was so nearly so as to have become, like all the others, historical and of another age. But within the last eight years three other articles of amendment of vast importance have been added by the voice of the people to that now venerable instrument.

The most cursory glance at these articles discloses a unity of purpose, when taken in connection with the history of the times, which cannot fail to have an important bearing on any question of doubt concerning their true meaning. Nor can such doubts, when any reasonably exist, be safely and rationally solved without a reference to that history; for in it is found the occasion and the necessity for recurring again to the great source of power in this country, the people of the States, for additional guarantees of human rights; additional powers to the Federal government; additional restraints upon those of the States. Fortunately, that history is fresh within the memory of us all, and its leading features, as they bear upon the matter before us, free from doubt.

The institution of African slavery, as it existed in about half the States of the Union, and the contests pervading the public mind for many years, between those who desired its curtailment and ultimate extinction and those who desired additional safeguards for its security and perpetuation, culminated in the effort, on the part of most of the States in which slavery existed, to separate from the Federal government, and to resist its authority. This constituted the war of the rebellion, and whatever auxiliary causes may have contributed to bring about this war, undoubtedly the overshadowing and efficient cause was African slavery.

In that struggle slavery, as a legalized social relation, perished.

We repeat, then, in the light of this recapitulation of events, almost too recent to be called history, but which are familiar to us all; and on the most casual examination of the language of these amendments, no one can fail to be impressed with the one pervading purpose found in them all, lying at the foundation of each, and without which none of them would have been even suggested; we mean the freedom of the slave race, the security and firm establishment of that freedom, and the protection of the newly-made freeman and citizen from the oppressions of those who had formerly exercised unlimited dominion over him. It is true that only the fifteenth amendment, in terms, mentions the negro by speaking of his color and his slavery. But it is just as true that each of the other articles was addressed to the grievances of that race, and designed to remedy them as the fifteenth.

We do not say that no one else but the negro can share in this protection. Both the language and spirit of these articles are to have their fair and just weight in any question of construction. Undoubtedly while negro slavery alone was in the mind of the Congress which proposed the thirteenth article, it forbids any other kind of slavery, now or hereafter. If Mexican peonage or the Chinese coolie labor system shall develop slavery of the Mexican or Chinese race within our territory, this amendment may safely be trusted to make it void. And so if other rights are assailed by the States which properly and necessarily fall within the protection of these articles, that protection will apply, though the party interested may not be of African descent. But what we do say, and what we wish to be understood is, that in any fair and just construction of any section or phrase of these amendments, it is necessary to look to the purpose which we have said was the pervading spirit of them all, the evil which they were designed to remedy, and the process of continued addition to the Constitution, until that purpose was supposed to be accomplished, as far as constitutional law can accomplish it.

The first section of the fourteenth article, to which our attention is more specially invited, opens with a definition of citizenship—not only citizenship of the United States, but citizenship of the States. No such definition was previously found in the Constitution, nor had any attempt been made to define it by act of Congress. It had been the occasion of much discussion in the courts, by the executive departments, and in the public journals. It had been said by eminent judges that no man was a citizen of the United States, except as he was a citizen of one of the States composing the Union. Those, therefore, who had been born and resided always in the District of Columbia or in the Territories, though within the United States, were not citizens. Whether this proposition was sound or not had never been judicially decided. But it had been held by this court, in the celebrated Dred Scott case, only a few years before the outbreak of the civil war, that a man of African descent, whether a slave or not, was not and could not be a citizen of a State or of the United States. This decision, while it met the condemnation of some of the ablest statesmen and constitutional lawyers of the country, had never been overruled; and if it was to be accepted as a constitutional limitation of the right of citizenship, then all the negro race who had recently been made freemen, were still, not only not citizens, but were incapable of becoming so by anything short of an amendment to the Constitution.

To remove this difficulty primarily, and to establish a clear and comprehensive definition of citizenship which should declare what should constitute citizenship of the United States, and also citizenship of a State, the first clause of the first section was framed.

"All persons born or naturalized in the United States, and subject to the jurisdiction thereof, are citizens of the United States and of the State wherein they reside."

The first observation we have to make on this clause is, that it puts at rest both the questions which we stated to have been the subject of differences of opinion. It declares that persons may be citizens of the United States without regard to their citizenship of a particular State, and it overturns the Dred Scott decision by making *all persons* born within the United States and subject to its jurisdiction citizens of the United States. That its main purpose was to establish the citizenship of the negro can admit of no doubt. The phrase, "subject to its jurisdiction" was intended to exclude from its operation children of ministers, consuls, and citizens or subjects of foreign States born within the United States.

The next observation is more important in view of the arguments of counsel in the present case. It is, that the distinction between citizenship of the United States and citizenship of a State is clearly recognized and established. Not only may a man be a citizen of the United States without being a citizen of a State, but an important element is necessary to convert the former into the latter. He must reside within the State to make him a citizen of it, but it is only necessary that he should be born or naturalized in the United States to be a citizen of the Union.

It is quite clear, then, that there is a citizenship of the United States, and a citizenship of a State, which are distinct from each other, and which depend upon different characteristics or circumstances in the individual.

We think this distinction and its explicit recognition in this amendment of great weight in this argument, because the next paragraph of this same section, which is the one mainly relied on by the plaintiffs in error, speaks only of privileges and immunities of citizens of the United States, and does not speak of those of citizens of the several States. The argument, however, in favor of the plaintiffs rests wholly on the assumption that the citizenship is the same, and the privileges and immunities guaranteed by the clause are the same.

The language is, "No State shall make or enforce any law which shall abridge the privileges or immunities of citizens of *the United States*." It is a little remarkable, if this clause was intended as a protection to the citizen of a State against the legislative power of his own State, that the word citizen of the State should be left out when it is so carefully used, and used in contradistinction to citizens of the United States, in the very sentence which precedes it. It is too clear for argument that the change in phraseology was adopted understandingly and with a purpose.

Of the privileges and immunities of the citizen of the United States, and of the privileges and immunities of the citizen of the State, and what they respectively are, we will presently consider; but we wish to state here that it is only the former which are placed by this clause under the protection of the Federal Constitution, and that the latter, whatever they may be, are not intended to have any additional protection by this paragraph of the amendment.

If, then, there is a difference between the privileges and immunities belonging to a citizen of the United States as such, and those belonging to the citizen of the State as such, the latter must rest for their security and protection where they have heretofore rested; for they are not embraced by this paragraph of the amendment.

The first occurrence of the words "privileges and immunities" in our constitutional history, is to be found in the fourth of the articles of the old Confederation.

It declares "that the better to secure and perpetuate mutual friendship and intercourse among the people of the different States in this Union, the free inhabitants of each of these States, paupers, vagabonds, and fugitives from justice excepted, shall be entitled to all the privileges and immunities of free citizens in the several States; and the people of each State shall have free ingress and regress to and from any other State, and shall enjoy therein all the privileges of trade and commerce, subject to the same duties, impositions, and restrictions as the inhabitants thereof respectively."

In the Constitution of the United States, which superseded the Articles of Confederation, the corresponding provision is found in section two of the fourth article, in the following words: "The citizens of each State shall be entitled to all the privileges and immunities of citizens of the several States."

There can be but little question that the purpose of both these provisions is the same, and that the privileges and immunities intended are the same in each. In the article of the Confederation we have some of these specifically mentioned, and enough perhaps to give some general idea of the class of civil rights meant by the phrase.

Fortunately we are not without judicial construction of this clause of the Constitution. The first and the leading case on the subject is that of *Corfield* v. *Coryell*, decided by Mr. Justice Washington in the Circuit Court for the District of Pennsylvania in 1823.

"The inquiry," he says, "is, what are the privileges and immunities of citizens of the several States? We feel no hesitation in confining these expressions to those privileges and immunities which are *fundamental*; which belong of right to the citizens of all free governments, and which have at all times been enjoyed by citizens of the several States which compose this Union, from the time of their becoming free, independent, and sovereign. What these fundamental principles are, it would be more tedious than difficult to enumerate. They may all, however, be comprehended under the following general heads: protection by the government, with the right to acquire and possess property of every kind, and to pursue and obtain happiness and safety, subject, nevertheless, to such restraints as the government may prescribe for the general good of the whole."

This definition of the privileges and immunities of citizens of the States is adopted in the main by this court in the recent case of *Ward* v. *The State of Maryland*, while it declines to undertake an authoritative definition beyond what was necessary to that decision. The description, when taken to include others not named, but which are of the same general character, embraces nearly every civil right for the establishment and protection of which organized government is instituted. They are, in the language of Judge Washington, those rights which are fundamental. Throughout his opinion, they are spoken of as rights belonging to the individual as a citizen of a State. They are so spoken of in the constitutional provision which he was construing. And they have always been held to be the class of rights which the State governments were created to establish and secure.

In the case of *Paul* v. *Virginia*, the court, in expounding this clause of the Constitution, says that "the privileges and immunities secured to citizens of each State in the several States, by the provision in question, are those privileges and immunities which are common to the citizens in the latter States under their constitution and laws by virtue of their being citizens."

The constitutional provision there alluded to did not create those rights, which it called privileges and immunities of citizens of the States. It threw around them in that clause no security for the citizen of the State in which they were claimed or exercised. Nor did it profess to control the power of the State governments over the rights of its own citizens.

Its sole purpose was to declare to the several States, that whatever those rights, as you grant or establish them to your own citizens, or as you limit or qualify, or impose restrictions on their exercise, the same, neither more nor less, shall be the measure of the rights of citizens of other States within your jurisdiction.

It would be the vainest show of learning to attempt to prove by citations of authority, that up to the adoption of the recent amendments, no claim or pretence was set up that those rights depended on the Federal government for their existence or protection, beyond the very few express limitations which the Federal Constitution imposed upon the States—such, for instance, as the prohibition against ex post facto laws, bills of attainder, and laws impairing the obligation of contracts. But with the exception of these and a few other restrictions, the entire domain of the privileges and immunities of citizens of the States, as above defined, lay within the constitutional and legislative power of the States, and without that of the Federal government. Was it the purpose of the fourteenth amendment, by the simple declaration that no State should make or enforce any law which shall abridge the privileges and immunities of *citizens of the United States*, to transfer the security and protection of all the civil rights which we have mentioned, from the States to the Federal government? And where it is declared that Congress shall have the power to enforce that article, was it intended to bring within the power of Congress the entire domain of civil rights heretofore belonging exclusively to the States?

All this and more must follow, if the proposition of the plaintiffs in error be sound. For not only are these rights subject to the control of Congress whenever in its discretion any of them are supposed to be abridged by State legislation, but that body may also pass laws in advance, limiting and restricting the exercise of legislative power by the States, in their most ordinary and usual functions, as in its judgment it may think proper on all such subjects. And still further, such a construction followed by the reversal of the judgments of the Supreme Court of Louisiana in these cases, would constitute this court a perpetual censor upon all legislation of the States, on the civil rights of their own citizens, with authority to nullify such as it did not approve as consistent with those rights, as they existed at the time of the adoption of this amendment. The argument we admit is not always the most conclusive which is drawn from the consequences urged against the adoption of a particular construction of an instrument. But when, as in the case before us, these consequences are so serious, so far-reaching and pervading, so great a departure from the structure and spirit of our institutions; when the effect is to fetter and degrade the State governments by subjecting them to the control of Congress, in the exercise of powers heretofore universally conceded to them of the most ordinary and fundamental character; when in fact it radically changes the whole theory of the relations of the State and Federal governments to each other and of both these governments to the people; the argument has a force that is irresistible, in the absence of language which expresses such a purpose too clearly to admit of doubt.

We are convinced that no such results were intended by the Congress which proposed these amendments, nor by the legislatures of the States which ratified them.

Having shown that the privileges and immunities relied on in the argument are those which belong to citizens of the States as such, and that they are left to the State governments for security and protection, and not by this article placed under the special care of the Federal government, we may hold ourselves excused from defining the privileges and immunities of citizens of the United States which no State can abridge, until some case involving those privileges may make it necessary to do so.

But lest it should be said that no such privileges and immunities are to be found if those we have been considering are excluded, we venture to suggest some which owe their existence to the Federal government, its National character, its Constitution, or its laws.

One of these is well described in the case of *Crandall v. Nevada*. It is said to be the right of the citizen of this great country, protected by implied guarantees of its Constitution, "to come to the seat of government to assert any claim he may have upon that government, to transact any business he may have with it, to seek its protection, to share its offices, to engage in administering its functions. He has the right of free access to its seaports, through which all operations of foreign commerce are conducted, to the subtreasuries, land

offices, and courts of justice in the several States." And quoting from the language of Chief Justice Taney in another case, it is said "that *for all the great purposes for which the Federal government* was established, we are one people, with one common country, *we are all citizens of the United States;*" and it is, as such citizens, that their rights are supported in this court in *Crandall v. Nevada*.

Another privilege of a citizen of the United States is to demand the care and protection of the Federal government over his life, liberty, and property when on the high seas or within the jurisdiction of a foreign government. Of this there can be no doubt, nor that the right depends upon his character as a citizen of the United States. The right to peaceably assemble and petition for redress of grievances, the privilege of the writ of *habeas corpus*, are rights of the citizen guaranteed by the Federal Constitution. The right to use the navigable waters of the United States, however they may penetrate the territory of the several States, all rights secured to our citizens by treaties with foreign nations, are dependent upon citizenship of the United States, and not citizenship of a State. One of these privileges is conferred by the very article under consideration. It is that a citizen of the United States can, of his own volition, become a citizen of any State of the Union by a *bona fide* residence therein, with the same rights as other citizens of that State. To these may be added the rights secured by the thirteenth and fifteenth articles of amendment, and by the other clause of the fourteenth, next to be considered.

But it is useless to pursue this branch of the inquiry, since we are of opinion that the rights claimed by these plaintiffs in error, if they have any existence, are not privileges and immunities of citizens of the United States within the meaning of the clause of the fourteenth amendment under consideration.

"All persons born or naturalized in the United States, and subject to the jurisdiction thereof, are citizens of the United States and of the State wherein they reside. No State shall make or enforce any law which shall abridge the privileges or immunities of citizens of the United States; nor shall any State deprive any person of life, liberty, or property without due process of law, nor deny to any person within its jurisdiction the equal protection of its laws."

The argument has not been much pressed in these cases that the defendant's charter deprives the plaintiffs of their property without due process of law, or that it denies to them the equal protection of the law. The first of these paragraphs has been in the Constitution since the adoption of the fifth amendment, as a restraint upon the Federal power. It is also to be found in some form of expression in the constitutions of nearly all the States, as a restraint upon the power of the States. This law then, has practically been the same as it now is during the existence of the government, except so far as the present amendment may place the restraining power over the States in this matter in the hands of the Federal government.

We are not without judicial interpretation, therefore, both State and National, of the meaning of this clause. And it is sufficient to say that under no construction of that provision that we have ever seen, or any that we deem admissible, can the restraint imposed by the State of Louisiana upon the exercise of their trade by the butchers of New Orleans be held to be a deprivation of property within the meaning of that provision.

"Nor shall any State deny to any person within its jurisdiction the equal protection of the laws."

In the light of the history of these amendments, and the pervading purpose of them, which we have already discussed, it is not difficult to give a meaning to this clause. The existence of laws in the States where the newly emancipated negroes resided, which discriminated with gross injustice and hardship against them as a class, was the evil to be remedied by this clause, and by it such laws are forbidden.

If, however, the States did not conform their laws to its requirements, then by the fifth section of the article of amendment Congress was authorized to enforce it by suitable legislation. We doubt very much whether any action of a State not directed by way of discrimination against the negroes as a class, or on account of their race, will ever be held to come within the purview of this provision. It is so clearly a provision for that race and that emergency, that a strong case would be necessary for its application to any other. But as it is a State that is to be dealt with, and not alone the validity of its laws, we may safely leave that matter until Congress shall have exercised its power, or some case of State oppression, by denial of equal justice in its courts, shall have claimed a decision at our hands. We find no such case in the one before us, and do not deem it necessary to go over the argument again, as it may have relation to this particular clause of the amendment.

In the early history of the organization of the government, its statesmen seem to have divided on the line which should separate the powers of the National government from those of the State governments, and though this line has never been very well defined in public opinion, such a division has continued from that day to this.

The adoption of the first eleven amendments to the Constitution so soon after the original instrument was accepted, shows a prevailing sense of danger at that time from the Federal power. And it cannot be denied that such a jealousy continued to exist with many patriotic men until the breaking out of the late civil war. It was then discovered that the true danger to the perpetuity of the Union was in the capacity of the State organizations to combine and concentrate all the powers of the State, and of contiguous States, for a determined resistance to the General Government.

Unquestionably this has given great force to the argument, and added largely to the number of those who believe in the necessity of a strong National government.

But, however pervading this sentiment, and however it may have contributed to the adoption of the amendments we have been considering, we do not see in those amendments any purpose to destroy the main features of the general system. Under the pressure of all the excited feeling growing out of the war, our statesmen have still believed that the existence of the States with powers for domestic and local government, including the regulation of civil rights—the rights of person and of property—was essential to the perfect working of our complex form of government, though they have thought proper to impose additional limitations on the States, and to confer additional power on that of the Nation.

But whatever fluctuations may be seen in the history of public opinion on this subject during the period of our national existence, we think it will be found that this court, so far as its functions required, has always held with a steady and an even hand the balance between State and Federal power, and we trust that such may continue to be the history of its relation to that subject so long as it shall have duties to perform which demand of it a construction of the Constitution, or of any of its parts.

The judgments of the Supreme Court of Louisiana in these cases are affirmed.

Justice Field dissented:

I am unable to agree with the majority of the court in these cases, and will proceed to state the reasons of my dissent from their judgment. . . .

No one will deny the abstract justice which lies in the position of the plaintiffs in error; and I shall endeavor to show that the position has some support in the fundamental law of the country.

It is contended in justification for the act in question

that it was adopted in the interest of the city, to promote its cleanliness and protect its health, and was the legitimate exercise of what is termed the police power of the State. That power undoubtedly extends to all regulations affecting the health, good order, morals, peace, and safety of society, and is exercised on a great variety of subjects, and in almost numberless ways. All sorts of restrictions and burdens are imposed under it, and when these are not in conflict with any constitutional prohibitions, or fundamental principles, they cannot be successfully assailed in a judicial tribunal. With this power of the State and its legitimate exercise I shall not differ from the majority of the court. But under the pretence of prescribing a police regulation the State cannot be permitted to encroach upon any of the just rights of the citizen, which the Constitution intended to secure against abridgment.

In the law in question there are only two provisions which can properly be called police regulations—the one which requires the landing and slaughtering of animals below the city of New Orleans, and the other which requires the inspection of the animals before they are slaughtered. When these requirements are complied with, the sanitary purposes of the act are accomplished. In all other particulars the act is a mere grant to a corporation created by it of special and exclusive privileges by which the health of the city is in no way promoted. . . .

The act of Louisiana presents the naked case, unaccompanied by any public considerations, where a right to pursue a lawful and necessary calling, previously enjoyed by every citizen, and in connection with which a thousand persons were daily employed, is taken away and vested exclusively for twenty-five years, for an extensive district and a large population, in a single corporation, or its exercise is for that period restricted to the establishments of the corporation, and there allowed only upon onerous conditions.

If exclusive privileges of this character can be granted to a corporation of seventeen persons, they may, in the discretion of the legislature, be equally granted to a single individual. If they may be granted for twenty-five years they may be equally granted for a century, and in perpetuity. If they may be granted for the landing and keeping of animals intended for sale or slaughter they may be equally granted for the landing and storing of grain and other products of the earth, or for any article of commerce. If they may be granted for structures in which animal food is prepared for market they may be equally granted for structures in which farinaceous or vegetable food is prepared. They may be granted for any of the pursuits of human industry, even in its most simple and common forms. Indeed, upon the theory on which the exclusive privileges granted by the act in question are sustained, there is no monopoly, in the most odious form, which may not be upheld.

The question presented is, therefore, one of the gravest importance, not merely to the parties here, but to the whole country. It is nothing less than the question whether the recent amendments to the Federal Constitution protect the citizens of the United States against the deprivation of their common rights by State legislation. In my judgment the fourteenth amendment does afford such protection, and was so intended by the Congress which framed and the States which adopted it. . . .

The amendment does not attempt to confer any new privileges or immunities upon citizens, or to enumerate or define those already existing. It assumes that there are such privileges and immunities which belong of right to citizens as such, and ordains that they shall not be abridged by State legislation. If this inhibition has no reference to privileges and immunities of this character, but only refers, as held by the majority of the court in their opinion, to such privileges and immunities as were before its adoption specially designated in the Constitution or necessarily implied as belonging to citizens of the United States, it was a vain and idle enactment, which accomplished nothing, and most unnecessarily excited Congress and the people on its passage. With privileges and immunities thus designated or implied no State could ever have interfered by its laws, and no new constitutional provision was required to inhibit such interference. The supremacy of the Constitution and the laws of the United States always controlled any State legislation of that character. But if the amendment refers to the natural and inalienable rights which belong to all citizens, the inhibition has a profound significance and consequence.

What, then, are the privileges and immunities which are secured against abridgment by State legislation?

In the first section of the Civil Rights Act Congress has given its interpretation to these terms, or at least has stated some of the rights which, in its judgment, these terms include; it has there declared that they include the right "to make and enforce contracts, to sue, be parties and give evidence, to inherit, purchase, lease, sell, hold, and convey real and personal property, and to full and equal benefit of all laws and proceedings for the security of person and property." That act, it is true, was passed before the fourteenth amendment, but the amendment was adopted, as I have already said, to obviate objections to the act, or, speaking more accurately, I should say, to obviate objections to legislation of a similar character, extending the protection of the National government over the common rights of all citizens of the United States. Accordingly, after its ratification, Congress re-enacted the act under the belief that whatever doubts may have previously existed of its validity, they were removed by the amendment.

The terms, privileges and immunities, are not new in the amendment; they were in the Constitution before the amendment was adopted. They are found in the second section of the fourth article, which declares that "the citizens of each State shall be entitled to all privileges and immunities of citizens in the several States," and they have been the subject of frequent consideration in judicial decisions. In *Corfield* v. *Coryell,* Mr. Justice Washington said he had "no hesitation in confining these expressions to those privileges and immunities which were, in their nature, fundamental; which belong of right to citizens of all free governments, and which have at all times been enjoyed by the citizens of the several States which compose the Union, from the time of their becoming free, independent, and sovereign;" and, in considering what those fundamental privileges were, he said that perhaps it would be more tedious than difficult to enumerate them, but that they might be "all comprehended under the following general heads: protection by the government; the enjoyment of life and liberty, with the right to acquire and possess property of every kind, and to pursue and obtain happiness and safety, subject, nevertheless, to such restraints as the government may justly prescribe for the general good of the whole." This appears to me to be a sound construction of the clause in question. The privileges and immunities designated are those *which of right belong to the citizens of all free governments.* Clearly among these must be placed the right to pursue a lawful employment in a lawful manner, without other restraint than such as equally affects all persons. In the discussions in Congress upon the passage of the Civil Rights Act repeated reference was made to this language of Mr. Justice Washington. It was cited by Senator Trumbull with the observation that it enumerated the very rights belonging to a citizen of the United States set forth in the first section of the act, and with the statement that all persons born in the United States, being declared by the act citizens of the United States, would thenceforth be entitled to the rights of citizens, and that these were the great fundamental rights set forth in the act; and that they were set forth "as appertaining to every freeman."

The privileges and immunities designated in the second section of the fourth article of the Constitution are, then, according to the decision cited, those which of right belong to the citizens of all free governments, and they can be enjoyed under that clause by the citizens of each State in the several States upon the same terms and conditions as they are enjoyed by the citizens of the latter States. No discrimination can be made by one State against the citizens of other States in their enjoyment, nor can any greater imposition be levied than such as is laid upon its own citizens.

I am authorized by the Chief Justice,
Justice Swayne, and Justice Bradley, to state that
they concur with me in this dissenting opinion.

The narrow interpretation of the privileges and immunities clause of the Fourteenth Amendment was applied later in the 1870s to deny women the right to practice law and to vote. In *Bradwell* v. *Illinois,* even the dissenters in the Slaughterhouse Case supported the result that upheld a state prohibition against the practice of law by women. Justice Bradley's concurring opinion, supported by Field and Swayne, stated that "the natural and proper timidity and delicacy which belongs to the female sex evidently unfits it for many of the occupations of the civil life. . . . [The] paramount destiny and mission of women are to fulfill the noble and benign offices of wife and mother. This is the law of the Creator."[9] In *Minor* v. *Happersett,* the Court rejected an argument that the right to vote was a privilege of national citizenship, which was violated by a state constitutional provision limiting the right to males.[10]

The dissenters in the Slaughterhouse Cases had argued that the constitutional safeguards of the Fourteenth Amendment should extend not only to the former slaves whose newly achieved freedom might be put in jeopardy, but to all others whose occupational or property rights may be denied or infringed by state governmental actions. Issues involving the privileges and rights of the freed slaves continued to be raised, but there was an increasing emphasis upon property and business-related controversies as significant advances in manufacturing, agricultural production, and transportation were made in the post–Civil War years. Railroad corporations had emerged as virtually dominant economic institutions, especially in those sectors of the economy, such as agriculture, that were largely dependent upon modernized modes of transportation and storage for the distribution and profitable sale of seasonal commodities. The excessive manipulation of railroad rates and of the costs of grain elevator storage by corporations controlling the flow of agricultural products to markets in the 1860s and 1870s created an explosive political situation. Western farmers organized the Grange movement, which successfully gained adoption of state laws regulating the charges and services of railroads, grain elevators, and warehouses. After a successful beginning in Illinois in 1871, the movement extended to Minnesota, Iowa, and Wisconsin. In *Munn* v. *Illinois* the constitutionality of an Illinois statute regulating the rates of grain elevators was tested under the due process clause of the Fourteenth Amendment and the commerce clause.

Historically, due process within the context of the original Fifth Amendment and the new Fourteenth Amendment was interpreted as a procedural safeguard. Indeed, before the Civil War, the Dred Scott decision, in part, was the only exception on the federal level, and the New York courts the major exception on the state level. After the Civil War, the Supreme Court under Chief Justice Waite, who succeeded Chase in 1874, began to indicate that the substance of state legislative enactment could and, on occasion, should be limited. A shift from judicial examination of the question of proper or fair procedure to the broader question whether the substantive content of legislation was constitutionally appropriate embodied a quiet but very substantial expansion of federal judicial authority. After the Fourteenth Amendment was ratified, the Court held in *Loan Association* v. *Topeka* that taxes can be levied only for public purposes. The new due process clause was not invoked. Instead, natural law conceptions were applied as follows:

> There are limitations on such power which grow out of the essential nature of all free governments; implied reservations of individual rights, without which the social compact could not exist. . . .[11]

In *Munn* v. *Illinois*, however, the issue of doctrinal use of the due process clause of the Fourteenth Amendment as a substantive limitation on state legislation was squarely confronted. Although the state was sustained, the decision clearly indicated that there were substantive limits to state legislative enactments. Chief Justice Waite wrote the majority opinion sustaining the Illinois statute and Justice Field dissented.

MUNN v. ILLINOIS
94 U. S. 113 (1877)

*Chief Justice Waite delivered the opinion
of the Court, saying in part:*

Every statute is presumed to be constitutional. The courts ought not to declare one to be unconstitutional, unless it is clearly so. If there is doubt, the expressed will of the Legislature should be sustained.

The Constitution contains no definition of the word "deprive," as used in the 14th Amendment. To determine its signification, therefore, it is necessary to ascertain the effect which usage has given it, when employed in the same or a like connection.

While this provision of the Amendment is new in the Constitution of the United States, it is old as a principle of civilized government. It is found in Magna Charta, and, in substance if not in form, in nearly or quite all the constitutions that have been from time to time adopted by the several States of the Union. By the 5th Amendment, it was introduced into the Constitution of the United States as a limitation upon the powers of the National Government, and by the 14th, as a guaranty against any encroachment upon an acknowledged right of citizenship by the Legislatures of the States. . . .

When one becomes a member of society, he necessarily parts with some rights or privileges which, as an individual not affected by his relations to others, he might retain. "A body politic," as aptly defined in the preamble of the Constitution of Massachusetts, "is a social compact by which the whole people covenants with each citizen, and each citizen with the whole people, that all shall be governed by certain laws for the common good." This does not confer power upon the whole people to control rights which are purely and exclusively private . . . , but it does authorize the establishment of laws requiring each citizen to so conduct himself, and so use his own property as not unnecessarily to injure another. This is the very essence of government, and has found expression in the maxim, Sic utere tuo ut alienum non laedas. From this source come the police powers, which . . . "[a]re nothing more or less than the powers of government inherent in every sovereignty, . . . that is to say, . . . the power to govern men and things." Under these powers the government regulates the conduct of its citizens one towards another, and the manner in which each shall use his own property, when such regulation becomes necessary for the public good. In their exercise it has been customary in England from time immemorial, and in this country from its first colonization, to regulate ferries, common carriers, hackmen, bakers, millers, wharfingers, innkeepers, etc., and in so doing to fix a maximum of charge to be made for services rendered, accommodations furnished, and articles sold. To this day, statutes are to be found in many of the states upon some or all these subjects; and we think it has never yet been successfully contended that such legislation came within any of the constitutional prohibitions against interference with private property. . . .

From this it is apparent that, down to the time of the adoption of the 14th Amendment, it was not supposed that statutes regulating the use, or even the price of the use, of private property necessarily deprived an owner of his property without due process of law. Under some circumstances they may, but not under all. The Amendment does not change the law in this particular; it simply prevents the states from doing that which will operate as such a deprivation.

This brings us to inquire as to the principles upon which this power of regulation rests, in order that we may determine what is within and what without its operative effect. Looking, then, to the common law, from whence came the right which the Constitution protects, we find that when private property is "affected with a public interest, it ceases to be juris privati only." This was said by Lord Chief Justice Hale more than two hundred years ago. . . . Property does become clothed with a public interest when used in a manner to make it of public consequence, and affect the community at large. When, therefore, one devotes his property to a use in which the public has an interest, he, in effect, grants to the public an interest in that use, and must submit to be controlled by the public for the common good, to the extent of the interest he has thus created. He may withdraw his grant by discontinuing the use; but, so long as he maintains the use, he must submit to the control. . . .

And the same has been held as to warehouses and warehousemen. . . .

From the same source comes the power to regulate the charges of common carriers, which was done in England as long ago as the third year of the reign of William and Mary, and continued until within a comparatively recent period. . . .

Common carriers exercise a sort of public office, and have duties to perform in which the public is interested. . . .

Their business is, therefore, "affected with a public interest," within the meaning of the doctrine which Lord Hale has so forcibly stated.

But we need not go further. Enough has already been said to show that, when private property is devoted to a public use, it is subject to public regulation. It remains only to ascertain whether the warehouses of these plaintiffs in error, and the business which is carried on there, come within the operation of this principle.

For this purpose we accept as true the statements of fact contained in the elaborate brief of one of the counsel of the plaintiffs in error. From these it appears that ". . . The quantity (of grain) received in Chicago has made it the greatest grain market in the world. This business has created a demand for means by which the immense quantity of grain can be handled or stored, and these have been found in grain warehouses. . . . In this way the largest traffic between the citizens of the country lying on the Atlantic coast north of Washington is in grain which passes through the elevators of Chicago. In this way the trade in grain is carried on by the inhabitants of seven or eight of the great States of the West with four or five of the States lying on the seashore, and forms the largest part of interstate commerce in these States. The grain warehouses or elevators in Chicago are immense structures, holding from 300,000 to 1,000,000 bushels at one time, according to size. . . . It has been found impossible to preserve each owner's grain separate, and this has given rise to a system of inspection and grading, by which the grain of different owners is mixed and receipts issued for the number of bushels which are negotiable, and redeemable in like kind, upon demand. This mode of conducting the business was inaugurated more than twenty years ago, and has grown to immense proportions. The railways have found it impracticable to own such elevators, and public policy forbids the transaction of such business by the carrier; the ownership has, therefore, been by private individuals, who have embarked their capital and devoted their industry to such business as a private pursuit."

In this connection it must also be borne in mind that, although in 1874 there were in Chicago fourteen warehouses adapted to this particular business, and owned by about thirty persons, nine business firms controlled them, and that the prices charged and received for storage were such "as have been from year to year agreed upon and established by the different elevators or warehouses in the city of Chicago, and which rates have been annually published in one or more newspapers printed in said city, in the month of January in each year, as the established rates for the year then next ensuing such publication." Thus it is apparent that all the elevating facilities through which these vast productions "of seven or eight great States of the West" must pass on the way "to four or five of the States on the seashore" may be a "virtual" monopoly.

Under such circumstances it is difficult to see why, if the common carrier, or the miller, or the ferryman, or the innkeeper, or the wharfinger, or the baker, or the cartman, or the hackney-coachman, pursues a public employment and exercises "a sort of public office," these plaintiffs in error do not. They stand, to use again the language of their counsel, in the very "gateway of commerce," and take toll from all who pass. Their business most certainly "tends to a common charge, and is become a thing of public interest and use." . . . Certainly, if any business can be clothed "with a public interest, and cease to be juris privati only," this has been. It may not be made so by the operation of the Constitution of Illinois or this statute, but it is by the facts.

We also are not permitted to overlook the fact that, for some reason, the people of Illinois, when they revised their Constitution in 1870, saw fit to make it the duty of the general assembly to pass laws "for the protection of producers, shippers and receivers of grain and produce," art. XIII., sec. 7; and by sec. 5 of the same article, to require all railroad companies receiving and transporting grain in bulk or otherwise to deliver the same at any elevator to which it might be consigned, that could be reached by any track that was or could be used by such company, and that all railroad companies should permit connections to be made with their tracks, so that any public warehouse, etc., might be reached by the cars on their railroads. This indicates very clearly that during the twenty years in which this peculiar business had been assuming its present "immense proportions," something had occurred which led the whole body of the people to suppose that remedies such as are usually employed to prevent abuses by virtual monopolies might not be inappropriate here. For our purposes we must assume that, if a state of facts could exist that would justify such legislation, it actually did exist when the statute now under consideration was passed. For us the question is one of power, not of expediency. If no state of circumstances could exist to justify such a statute, then we declare this one void, because in excess of the legislative power of the State. But if it could, we must presume it did. Of the propriety of legislative interference within the scope of legislative power, the Legislature is the exclusive judge.

Neither is it a matter of any moment that no precedent can be found for a statute precisely like this. It is conceded that the business is one of recent origin, that its growth has been rapid, and that it is already of great importance. And it must also be conceded that it is a business in which the whole public has a direct and positive interest. It presents, therefore, a case for the application of a long known and well established principle in social science, and this statute simply extends the law so as to meet this new development of commercial progress. There is no attempt to compel these owners to grant the public an interest in their property, but to declare their obligations, if they use it in this particular manner.

It matters not in this case that these plaintiffs in error had built their warehouses and established their business before the regulations complained of were adopted. What they did was, from the beginning, subject to the power of the body politic to require them to conform to such regulations as might be established by the proper authorities for the common good. They entered upon their business and provided themselves with the means to carry it on subject to this condition. If they did not wish to submit themselves to such interference, they should not have clothed the public with an interest in their concerns. . . .

It is insisted, however, that the owner of property is entitled to a reasonable compensation for its use, even though it be clothed with a public interest, and that what is reasonable is a judicial and not a legislative question.

As has already been shown, the practice has been otherwise. In countries where the common law prevails, it has been customary from time immemorial for the Legislature to declare what shall be a reasonable compensation under such circumstances, or, perhaps more properly speaking, to fix a maximum beyond which any charge made would be unreasonable. Undoubtedly, in mere private contracts, relating to matters in which the public has no interest, what is reasonable must be ascertained judicially. But this is because the Legislature has no control over such a contract. So, too, in matters which do affect the public interest, and as to which legislative control may be exercised, if there are no statutory regulations upon the subject, the courts must determine what is reasonable. The controlling fact is the power to regulate at all. If that exists, the right to establish the maximum of charge, as one of the means of regulation, is implied. In fact, the common law rule, which requires the charge to be reasonable, is itself a regulation as to price. Without it the owner could make his rates at will, and compel the public to yield to his terms, or forego the use.

But a mere common law regulation of trade or business may be changed by statute. A person has no property, no vested interest, in any rule of the common law. That is only one of the forms of municipal law, and is no more sacred than any other. Rights of property which have been created by the common law cannot be taken away without due process; but the law itself, as a rule of conduct, may be changed at the will, or even at the whim, of the Legislature, unless prevented by constitutional limitations. Indeed, the great office of statutes is to remedy defects in the common law as they are developed, and to adapt it to the changes of time and circumstances. To limit the rate of charge for services rendered in a public employment, or for the use of property in which the public has an interest, is only changing a regulation which existed before. It establishes no new principle in the law, but only gives a new effect to an old one.

We know that this is a power which may be abused; but that is no argument against its existence. For protection against abuses by Legislatures the people must resort to the polls, not to the courts. . . .

We conclude, therefore, that the statute in question is not repugnant to the Constitution of the United States, and that there is no error in the judgment. . . . Judgment affirmed.

Justice Field, with Justice Strong concurring,
dissented, saying in part:

I am compelled to dissent from the decision of the court in this case, and from the reasons upon which that decision is founded. The principle upon which the opinion of the majority proceeds is, in my judgment, subversive of the rights of private property, heretofore believed to be protected by constitutional guaranties against legislative interference, and is in conflict with the authorities cited in its support. . . .

The declaration of the Constitution of 1870, that private buildings used for private purposes shall be deemed public institutions, does not make them so. The receipt and storage of grain in a building erected by private means for that purpose does not constitute the building a public warehouse. There is no magic in the language, though used by a constitutional convention, which can change a private business into a public one, or alter the character of the building in which the business is transacted.

. . . One might as well attempt to change the nature of colors, by giving them a new designation.

If this be sound law, if there be no protection, either in the principles upon which our republican government is founded, or in the prohibitions of the Constitution against such invasion of private rights, all property and all business in the State are held at the mercy of a majority of its Legislature. The public has no greater interest in the use of buildings for the storage of grain than it has in the use of buildings for the residences of families, nor, indeed, anything like so great an interest; and, according to the doctrine announced, the Legislature may fix the rent of all tenements used for residences, without reference to the cost of their erection. If the owner does not like the rates prescribed, he may cease renting his houses. . . .

By the term "liberty," as used in the provision, something more is meant than mere freedom from physical restraint or the bounds of a prison. It means freedom to go where one may choose, and to act in such manner, not inconsistent with the equal rights of others, as his judgment may dictate for the promotion of his happiness; that is, to pursue such callings and avocations as may be most suitable to develop his capacities, and give to them their highest enjoyment.

The same liberal construction which is required for the protection of life and liberty, in all particulars in which life and liberty are of any value, should be applied to the protection of private property. If the Legislature of a State, under pretense of providing for the public good, or for any other reason, can determine, against the consent of the owner, the use to which private property shall be devoted, or the prices which the owner shall receive for its uses, it can

deprive him of the property as completely as by a special Act for its confiscation or destruction. . . .

There is nothing in the character of the business of the defendants as warehousemen which called for the interference complained of in this case. Their buildings are not nuisances; their occupation of receiving and storing grain infringes upon no rights of others, disturbs no neighborhood, infects not the air, and in no respect prevents others from using and enjoying their property as to them may seem best. The legislation in question is nothing less than a bold assertion of absolute power by the State to control, at its discretion, the property and business of the citizen, and fix the compensation he shall receive. The will of the Legislature is made the condition upon which the owner shall receive the fruits of his property and the just reward of his labor, industry and enterprise. "That government," says Story, "can scarcely be deemed to be free where the rights of property are left solely dependent upon the will of a legislative body without any restraint. The fundamental maxims of a free government seem to require that the rights of personal liberty and private property should be held sacred." Wilkinson v. Leland [1829]. The decision of the court in this case gives unrestrained license to legislative will.

Nearly a decade later the Waite Court again sustained a state statute but employed language that clearly accepted the concept of substantive due process. *Mugler* v. *Kansas* sustained a Kansas statute forbidding the manufacture and sale of intoxicating liquor as a valid exercise of the state police power. The court stated that

> If . . . a statute purposing to have been enacted to protect the public health, the public morals or the public safety, has no real or substantial relation to these subjects, or is a palpable invasion of rights secured by the fundamental law, it is the duty of the courts to so adjudge and thereby give effect to the constitution.[12]

The acceptance of this doctrine came in the decades immediately following the Civil War when interest in extending or protecting the rights of the former slaves began to decline in the North, and concomitantly interest in enhancing property rights and the role of corporations had begun to increase. In terms of the latter, *Santa Clara County* v. *Southern Pacific Railroad Company* established the doctrine that a corporation is a "person" within the meaning of the Fourteenth Amendment.[13] Thus, the status of corporations was enhanced in an era when the status of freed men, for whom the amendments were passed, was being undermined.

The significant trends described in this chapter quite correctly place emphasis upon the interplay of industrialization, corporate power and influence, waning black judicial protection, and growing judicial authority upon Supreme Court doctrinal development. The tone and temper of the latter part of the 19th century was, of course, much more diverse and occasionally unpredictable. The frontiers were closing, but were not shut tight by any means. The unpredictability and occasional violence of that disappearing frontier perspective in American life touched the Supreme Court directly in *In Re Neagle*, decided in 1889. Its importance, however, is not in its exciting circumstances, but in the rather broad grounds for presidential authority to "take care that the laws be faithfully executed" adopted by Justice Miller.

Justice Field, in his capacity as circuit court judge, had presided over the federal circuit court in California in a land title case ultimately decided against the wife of Terry, a former Chief Justice of the Supreme Court of California. Mrs. Terry had bitterly accused Justice Field of selling justice. She and her husband had engaged in a violent struggle with the U.S. Marshal on duty in circuit court and were subsequently held in contempt of court and sentenced to six months imprisonment. When released they publicly threatened to kill Justice Field if he ever set foot in California again. Members of the Supreme Court were then required by law to serve in their assigned circuit court for set terms annually. Consequently, Field was required to return annually to preside over the circuit court in California. The attorney general of the United States, acting under the authority of the United States, had a U.S. Marshal assigned to protect Justice Field's life. While traveling in California in connection with his circuit court responsibilities, Field was attacked by Terry in a railroad restaurant. A deputy U.S. Marshal, Neagle, shot Terry and killed him as Terry was about to draw a knife on the justice. Neagle was arrested by local police and charged with murder. He secured his release on the basis of a writ of habeas corpus issued by the federal court of appeal. The constitutional challenge was brought on the ground that he had not acted under the authority of a specific federal statute.

IN RE NEAGLE
135 U.S. 1 (1889)

Justice Miller delivered the opinion of the Court:

. . . Without a more minute discussion of this testimony, it produces upon us the conviction of a settled purpose on the part of Terry and his wife, amounting to a conspiracy, to murder Justice Field. And we are quite sure that if Neagle had been merely a brother or a friend of Judge Field, traveling with him, and aware of all the previous relations of Terry to the judge,—as he was,—of his bitter animosity, his declared purpose to have revenge even to the point of killing him, he would have been justified in what he did in defense of Mr. Justice Field's life, and possibly of his own.

But such a justification would be a proper subject for consideration on a trial of the case for murder in

the courts of the State of California, and there exists no authority in the courts of the United States to discharge the prisoner while held in custody by the State authorities for this offense, unless there be found in aid of the defense of the prisoner some element of power and authority asserted under the government of the United States.

This element is said to be found in the facts that Mr. Justice Field, when attacked, was in the immediate discharge of his duty as judge of the Circuit Courts of the United States within California; that the assault upon him grew out of the animosity of Terry and wife, arising out of the previous discharge of his duty as Circuit Justice in the case for which they were committed for contempt of court; and that the deputy marshal of the United States, who killed Terry in defense of Field's life, was charged with a duty under the law of the United States to protect Field from the violence which

Terry was inflicting, and which was intended to lead to Field's death.

To the inquiry whether this proposition is sustained by law and the facts which we have recited, we now address ourselves. . . .

We have no doubt that Mr. Justice Field when attacked by Terry was engaged in the discharge of his duties as Circuit Justice of the Ninth Circuit, and was entitled to all the protection under those circumstances which the law could give him.

It is urged, however, that there exists no statute authorizing any such protection as that which Neagle was instructed to give Judge Field in the present case, and indeed no protection whatever against a vindictive or malicious assault growing out of the faithful discharge of his official duties; and that the language of section 753 of the Revised Statutes, that the party seeking the benefit of the writ of habeas corpus must in this connection show that he is "in custody for an act done or omitted in pursuance of a law of the United States," makes it necessary that upon this occasion it should be shown that the act for which Neagle is imprisoned was done by virtue of an Act of Congress. It is not supposed that any special Act of Congress exists which authorizes the marshals or deputy marshals of the United States in express terms to accompany the judges of the Supreme Court through their circuits, and act as a body-guard to them, to defend them against malicious assaults against their persons. But we are of opinion that this view of the statute is an unwarranted restriction of the meaning of a law designed to extend in a liberal manner the benefit of the writ of habeas corpus to persons imprisoned for the performance of their duty. And we are satisfied that if it was the duty of Neagle, under the circumstances, a duty which could only arise under the laws of the United States, to defend Mr. Justice Field from a murderous attack upon him, he brings himself within the meaning of the section we have recited. This view of the subject is confirmed by the alternative provision, that he must be in custody "for an act done or omitted in pursuance of a law of the United States or of an order, process, or decree of a court or judge thereof, or is in custody in violation of the Constitution or of a law or treaty of the United States."

In the view we take of the Constitution of the United States, any obligation fairly and properly inferable from that instrument, or any duty of the marshal to be derived from the general scope of his duties under the laws of the United States, is "a law" within the meaning of this phrase. It would be a great reproach to the system of government of the United

States, declared to be within its sphere sovereign and supreme, if there is to be found within the domain of its powers no means of protecting the judges, in the conscientious and faithful discharge of their duties, from the malice and hatred of those upon whom their judgments may operate unfavorably. . . .

Where, then, are we to look for the protection which we have shown Judge Field was entitled to when engaged in the discharge of his official duties? Not to the courts of the United States; because, as has been more than once said in this court, in the division of the powers of government between the three great departments, executive, legislative and judicial, the judicial is the weakest for the purposes of self-protection and for the enforcement of the powers which it exercises. The ministerial officers through whom its commands must be executed are marshals of the United States, and belong emphatically to the executive department of the government. They are appointed by the President, with the advice and consent of the Senate. They are removable from office at his pleasure. They are subjected by Act of Congress to the supervision and control of the Department of Justice, in the hands of one of the cabinet officers of the President, and their compensation is provided by Acts of Congress. The same may be said of the district attorneys of the United States, who prosecute and defend the claims of the government in the courts.

The legislative branch of the government can only protect the judicial officers by the enactment of laws for that purpose, and the argument we are now combating assumes that no such law has been passed by Congress.

If we turn to the Executive Department of the government, we find a very different condition of affairs. The Constitution, section 3, Article II, declares that the President "shall take care that the laws be faithfully executed," and he is provided with the means of fulfilling this obligation by his authority to commission all the officers of the United States, and, by and with the advice and consent of the Senate, to appoint the most important of them and to fill vacancies. He is declared to be commander-in-chief of the army and navy of the United States. The duties which are thus imposed upon him he is further enabled to perform by the recognition in the Constitution, and the creation by Acts of Congress, of executive departments, which have varied in number from four or five to seven or eight, the heads of which are familiarly called cabinet ministers. These aid him in the performance of the great duties of his office, and represent him in a thousand acts to which it can hardly be supposed his personal attention is called, and thus he is enabled to fulfill the duty of his great department, expressed in the phrase that "he shall take care that the laws be faithfully executed."

Is this duty limited to the enforcement of Acts of Congress or of treaties of the United States according to their express terms, or does it include the rights, duties and obligations growing out of the Constitution itself, our international relations, and all the protection implied by the nature of the government under the Constitution? . . .

We cannot doubt the power of the President to take measures for the protection of a judge of one of the courts of the United States, who, while in the discharge of the duties of his office, is threatened with a personal attack which may probably result in his death, and we think it clear that where this protection is to be afforded through the civil power, the Department of Justice is the proper one to set in motion the necessary means of protection. The correspondence already recited in this opinion between the marshal of the Northern District of California, and the Attorney-General, and the district attorney of the United States for that district, although prescribing no very specific mode of affording this protection by the Attorney-General, is sufficient, we think, to warrant the marshal in taking the steps which he did take, in making the provisions which he did make, for the protection and defense of Mr. Justice Field.

But there is positive law investing the marshals and their deputies with powers which not only justify what Marshal Neagle did in this matter, but which imposed it upon him as a duty. In chapter fourteen of the Revised Statutes of the United States, which is devoted to the appointment and duties of the district attorneys, marshals and clerks of the courts of the United States, section 788 declares:

"The marshals and their deputies shall have, in each State, the same powers, in executing the laws of the United States, as the sheriffs and their deputies in such State may have, by law, in executing the laws thereof."

If, therefore, a sheriff of the State of California was authorized to do in regard to the laws of California what Neagle did, that is, if he was authorized to keep the peace, to protect a judge from assault and murder, then Neagle was authorized to do the same thing in reference to the laws of the United States. . . .

That there is a peace of the United States; that a man assaulting a judge of the United States while in the discharge of his duties violates that peace; that in such case the marshal of the United States stands in the same relation to the peace of the United States which the sheriff of the county does to the peace of the State of California; are questions too clear to need argument to prove them. That it would be the duty of a sheriff, if one had been present at this assault by Terry upon Judge Field, to prevent this breach of the peace, to prevent this assault, to prevent the murder which was contemplated by it, cannot be doubted. And if, in performing this duty, it became necessary for the protection of Judge Field, or of himself, to kill Terry, in a case where, like this, it was evidently a question of the choice of who should be killed, the assailant and violator of the law and disturber of the peace, or the unoffending man who was in his power, there can be no question of the authority of the sheriff to have killed Terry. So the marshal of the United States, charged with the duty of protecting and guarding the judge of the United States court against this special assault upon his person and his life, being present at the critical moment, when prompt action was necessary, found it to be his duty, a duty which he had no liberty to refuse to perform, to take the steps which resulted in Terry's death. This duty was imposed on him by the section of the Revised Statutes which we have recited, in connection with the powers conferred by the State of California upon its peace officers, which become, by this statute, in proper cases, transferred as duties to the marshals of the United States. . . .

The result at which we have arrived upon this examination is, that in the protection of the person and the life of Mr. Justice Field while in the discharge of his official duties, Neagle was authorized to resist the attack of Terry upon him; that Neagle was correct in the belief that without prompt action on his part the assault of Terry upon the judge would have ended in the death of the latter; that such being his well-founded belief, he was justified in taking the life of Terry, as the only means of preventing the death of the man who was intended to be his victim; that in taking the life of Terry, under the circumstances, he was acting under the authority of the law of the United States, and was justified in so doing; and that he is not liable to answer in the courts of California on account of his part in that transaction.

We therefore affirm the judgment of the Circuit Court authorizing his discharge from the custody of the sheriff of San Joaquin County.

*Justice Lamar delivered a
dissenting opinion in which
Chief Justice Fuller concurred.*

The expansion of corporate rights
and the narrowing of noneconomic human rights

While the outcome in *In Re Neagle* assured executive authority to protect the judiciary, the long-range trends related to the weakening of black constitutional protections became more apparent. Most important, the scope of the post-Civil War amendments was narrowed considerably in this era when applied to blacks. *United States* v. *Reese* limited the coverage of the Fifteenth Amendment and the *Civil Rights Cases* curtailed the impact of the Fourteenth.

Voting rights for blacks had been considered essential to reconstruction and federal legislation designed to prevent interference with black use of the right was enacted for that purpose. The Enforcement Act of 1870 was challenged by two Kentucky election inspectors who had been indicted under its authority for refusing to take and count the ballot of a black citizen.

UNITED STATES v. REESE
92 U. S. A. 214 (1876)

Chief Justice Waite delivered the opinion of the Court:

Rights and immunities created by or dependent upon the Constitution of the United States can be protected by Congress. The form and the manner of the protection may be such as Congress, in the legitimate exercise of its legislative discretion, shall provide. These may be varied to meet the necessities of the particular right to be protected.

The Fifteenth Amendment does not confer the right of suffrage upon anyone. It prevents the States, or the United States, however, from giving preference, in this, particular, to one citizen of the United States from voting as it was on account of age, property, or education. Now it is not. If citizens of one race having certain qualifications are permitted by law to vote, those of another having the same qualifications must be. Previous to this amendment, there was no constitutional guarantee against this discrimination: now there is. It follows that the amendment has invested the citizens of the United States with a new constitutional right which is within the protecting power of Congress. The right is exemption from discrimination in the exercise of the elective franchise on account of race, color, or previous condition of servitude. This, under the express provisions of the second section of the amendment, Congress may enforce by "appropriate legislation."

This leads us to inquire whether the act now under consideration is "appropriate legislation" for that purpose. . . .

The statute contemplates a most important change

in the election laws. Previous to its adoption, the States, as a general rule, regulated in their own way all the details of all elections. They prescribed the qualifications of voters, and the manner in which those offering to vote at an election should make known their qualifications to the officers in charge. This act interferes with this practice, and prescribes rules not provided by the laws of the States. It substitutes, under certain circumstances, performance wrongfully prevented for performance itself. If the elector makes and presents his affidavit in the form and to the effect prescribed, the inspectors are to treat this as the equivalent of the specified requirement of the State law. This is a radical change in the practice, and the statute which creates it should be explicit in its terms. Nothing should be left to construction, if it can be avoided. The law ought not to be in such a condition that the elector may act upon one idea of its meaning, and the inspector upon another. . . .

If the legislature undertakes to define by statute a new offence, and provide for its punishment, it should express its will in language that need not deceive the common mind. Every man should be able to know with certainty when he is committing a crime.

But . . . we find . . . no words of limitation, or reference even, that can be construed as manifesting any intention to confine its provisions to the terms of the Fifteenth Amendment. That section has for its object the punishment of all persons, who, by force, bribery, &c., hinder, delay, &c., any person from qualifying or voting. In view of all these facts, we feel compelled to say, that, in our opinion, the language of the third and fourth sections does not confine their operation to unlawful discriminations on account of race, &c. If Congress had the power to provide generally for the punishment of those who unlawfully interfere to prevent the exercise of the elective franchise without regard to such discrimination, the language of these sections would be broad enough for that purpose.

It remains now to consider whether a statute, so general as this in its provisions, can be made available for the punishment of those who may be guilty of unlawful discrimination against citizens of the United States, while exercising the elective franchise, on account of their race, &c.

There is no attempt in the sections now under consideration to provide specifically for such an offence. If the case is provided for at all, it is because it comes under the general prohibition against any wrongful act or unlawful obstruction in this particular. . . .

It would certainly be dangerous if the legislature could set a net large enough to catch all possible offenders, and leave it to the courts to step inside

and say who could be rightfully detained, and who should be set at large. This would, to some extent, substitute the judicial for the legislative department of the government. The courts enforce the legislative will when ascertained, if within the constitutional grant of power. Within its legitimate sphere, Congress is supreme, and beyond the control of the courts; but if it steps outside of its constitutional limitations, and attempts that which is beyond its reach, the courts are authorized to, and when called upon in due course of legal proceedings must, annul its encroachments upon the reserved power of the States and the people. . . .

To limit this statute in the manner now asked for would be to make a new law, not to enforce an old one. This is no part of our duty.

We must, therefore, decide that Congress has not as yet provided by "appropriate legislation" for the punishment of the offence charged in the indictment. . . .

In *Strauder* v. *West Virginia*, portions of the broadly based and very diverse Civil Rights Act were actually upheld. That decision held that a state statute that denied all black citizens the right to serve as jurors because of race violated the equal protection clause of the Fourteenth Amendment.[14] But a few years later, other portions of the Civil Rights Act were held invalid.

This broadly based statute attempted to accomplish three broad purposes. First, state officials were made subject to penalties if they denied blacks rights guaranteed by the Thirteenth and Fourteenth Amendments. Second, the act penalized private individuals if they attempted denials under these amendments. And third, the act spelled out in detail the rights protected by the amendments. In the *Civil Rights Cases*, the majority's narrow constructionist interpretation was presented by Justice Bradley. Justice John Marshall Harlan wrote a moving and ultimately prophetic dissenting opinion.

THE CIVIL RIGHTS CASES
109 U. S. 3 (1883)

Justice Bradley delivered the opinion of the court:

It is obvious that the primary and important question in all the cases is the constitutionality of the law: for if the law is unconstitutional none of the prosecutions can stand.

The sections of the law referred to provide as follows:

"SEC. 1. That all persons within the jurisdiction of the United States shall be entitled to the full and equal enjoyment of the accommodations, advantages, facilities, and privileges of inns, public conveyances on land or water, theatres, and other places of public amusement; subject only to the conditions and limitations

established by law, and applicable alike to citizens of every race and color, regardless of any previous condition of servitude.

"SEC. 2. That any person who shall violate the foregoing section by denying to any citizen, except for reasons by law applicable to citizens of every race and color, and regardless of any previous condition of servitude, the full enjoyment of any of the accommodations, advantages, facilities, or privileges in said section enumerated, or by aiding or inciting such denial, shall for every such offence forfeit and pay the sum of five hundred dollars to the person aggrieved thereby, to be recovered in an action of debt, with full costs; and shall also, for every such offence, be deemed guilty of a misdemeanor, and, upon conviction thereof, shall be fined not less than five hundred nor more than one thousand dollars, or shall be imprisoned not less than thirty days nor more than one year: *Provided,* That all persons may elect to sue for the penalty aforesaid, or to proceed under their rights at common law and by State statutes; and having so elected to proceed in the one mode or the other, their right to proceed in the other jurisdiction shall be barred. But this provision shall not apply to criminal proceedings, either under this act or the criminal law of any State: *And provided further,* That a judgment for the penalty in favor of the party aggrieved, or a judgment upon an indictment, shall be a bar to either prosecution respectively."

Are these sections constitutional? The first section, which is the principal one, cannot be fairly understood without attending to the last clause, which qualifies the preceding part.

The essence of the law is, not to declare broadly that all persons shall be entitled to the full and equal enjoyment of the accommodations, advantages, facilities, and privileges of inns, public conveyances, and theatres; but that such enjoyment shall not be subject to any conditions applicable only to citizens of a particular race or color, or who had been in a previous condition of servitude. In other words, it is the purpose of the law to declare that, in the enjoyment of the accommodations and privileges of inns, public conveyances, theatres, and other places of amusement, colored citizens, whether formerly slaves or not, and citizens of other races, shall have the same accommodations and privileges in all inns, public conveyances, and places of amusement as are enjoyed by white citizens; and *vice versa.* The second section makes it a penal offence in any person to deny to any citizen of any race or color, regardless of previous servitude, any of the accommodations or privileges mentioned in the first section.

Has Congress constitutional power to make such a law? Of course, no one will contend that the power to pass it was contained in the Constitution before the adoption of the last three amendments. The power is sought, first, in the Fourteenth Amendment, and the views and arguments of distinguished Senators, advanced whilst the law was under consideration, claiming authority to pass it by virtue of that amendment, are the principal arguments adduced in favor of the power. We have carefully considered those arguments, as was due to the eminent ability of those who put them forward, and have felt, in all its force, the weight of authority which always invests a law that Congress deems itself competent to pass. But the responsibility of an independent judgment is now thrown upon this court; and we are bound to exercise it according to the best lights we have.

The first section of the Fourteenth Amendment (which is the one relied on), after declaring who shall be citizens of the United States, and of the several States, is prohibitory in its character, and prohibitory upon the States. It declares that:

"No State shall make or enforce any law which shall abridge the privileges or immunities of citizens of the United States; nor shall any State deprive any person of life, liberty, or property without due process of law; nor deny to any person within its jurisdiction the equal protection of the laws."

It is State action of a particular character that is prohibited. Individual invasion of individual rights is not the subject-matter of the amendment. It has a deeper and broader scope. It nullifies and makes void all State legislation, and State action of every kind, which impairs the privileges and immunities of citizens of the United States, or which injures them in life, liberty or property without due process of law, or which denies to any of them the equal protection of the laws. It not only does this, but, in order that the national will, thus declared, may not be a mere *brutum fulmen,* the last section of the amendment invests Congress with power to enforce it by appropriate legislation. To enforce what? To enforce the prohibition. To adopt appropriate legislation for correcting the effects of such prohibited State laws and State acts, and thus to render them effectually null, void, and innocuous. This is the legislative power conferred upon Congress, and this is the whole of it. It does not invest Congress with power to legislate upon subjects which are within the domain of State legislation; but to provide modes of relief against State legislation, or State action, of the kind referred to. It does not authorize Congress to create a code of municipal law for the regulation of private rights; but to provide modes of redress against the operation of State laws, and the action of State officers executive or judicial, when these are subversive of the fundamental rights specified in the amendment. Positive rights and privileges are undoubtedly secured by the Fourteenth Amendment; but they are secured by way of prohibition against State laws and State proceedings affecting those rights and privileges, and by power given to Congress to legislate for the purpose of carrying such prohibition into effect: and such legislation must necessarily be predicated upon such supposed State laws or State proceedings, and be directed to the correction of their operation and effect . . . until some State law has been passed, or some State action through its officers or agents has been taken, adverse to the rights of citizens sought to be protected by the Fourteenth Amendment, no legislation of the United States under said amendment, nor any proceeding under such legislation, can be called into activity; for the prohibitions of the amendment are against State laws and acts done under State authority. Of course, legislation may, and should be, provided in advance to meet the exigency when it arises; but it should be adapted to the mischief and wrong which the amendment was intended to provide against; and that is, State laws, or State action of some kind, adverse to the rights of the citizen secured by the amendment. Such legislation cannot properly cover the whole domain of rights appertaining to life, liberty and property, defining them and providing for their vindication. That would be to establish a code of municipal law regulative of all private rights between man and man in society. It would be to make Congress take the place of the State legislatures and to supersede them. It is absurd to affirm that, because the rights of life, liberty and property (which include all civil rights that men have), are by the amendment sought to be protected against invasion on the part of the State without due process of law. Congress may therefore provide due process of law for their vindication in every case; and that, because the denial by a State to any persons, of the equal protection of the laws, is prohibited by the amendment, therefore Congress may establish laws for their equal protection. In line, the legislation which Congress is authorized to adopt in this behalf is not general legislation upon the rights of the citizen, but corrective legislation, that is, such as may be necessary and proper for counteracting such laws as the States may adopt or enforce, and which, by the amendment, they are prohibited from making or enforcing, or such acts and proceedings as the States may commit or take, and which, by the amendment, they are prohibited from committing or taking. It is not necessary for us to state, if we could, what legislation would be proper for Congress to adopt. It is sufficient for us to examine whether the law in question is of that character.

An inspection of the law shows that it makes no reference whatever to any supposed or apprehended violation of the Fourteenth Amendment on the part of the States. It is not predicated on any such view. It proceeds *ex directo* to declare that certain acts committed by individuals shall be deemed offences, and shall be prosecuted and punished by proceedings in the courts of the United States. It does not profess to be corrective of any constitutional wrong committed by the States; it does not make its operation to depend upon any such wrong committed. It applies equally to cases arising in States which have the justest laws respecting the personal rights of citizens, and whose authorities are ever ready to enforce such laws, as to those which arise in States that may have violated the prohibition of the amendment. In other words, it steps

into the domain of local jurisprudence, and lays down rules for the conduct of individuals in society towards each other, and imposes sanctions for the enforcement of those rules, without referring in any manner to any supposed action of the State or its authorities.

If this legislation is appropriate for enforcing the prohibitions of the amendment, it is difficult to see where it is to stop. Why may not Congress with equal show of authority enact a code of laws for the enforcement and vindication of all rights of life, liberty, and property? If it is supposable that the States may deprive persons of life, liberty, and property without due process of law (and the amendment itself does suppose this), why should not Congress proceed at once to prescribe equal privileges in inns, public conveyances, and theatres? The truth is, that the implication of a power to legislate in this manner is based upon the assumption that if the States are forbidden to legislate or act in a particular way on a particular subject, and power is conferred upon Congress to enforce the prohibition, this gives Congress power to legislate generally upon that subject and not merely power to provide modes of redress against such State legislation or action. The assumption is certainly unsound. It is repugnant to the Tenth Amendment of the Constitution, which declares that powers not delegated to the United States by the Constitution, nor prohibited by it to the States, are reserved to the States respectively or to the people.

We have not overlooked the fact that the fourth section of the act now under consideration has been held by this court to be constitutional. That section declares "that no citizen, possessing all other qualifications which are or may be prescribed by law, shall be disqualified for service as grand or petit juror in any court of the United States, or of any State, on account of race, color, or previous condition of servitude; and any officer or other person charged with any duty in the selection or summoning of jurors who shall exclude or fail to summon any citizen for the cause aforesaid, shall, on conviction thereof, be deemed guilty of a misdemeanor, and be fined not more than five thousand dollars." . . .

In this connection it is proper to state that civil rights, such as are guaranteed by the Constitution against State aggression, cannot be impaired by the wrongful acts of individuals, unsupported by State authority in the shape of laws, customs, or judicial or executive proceedings. The wrongful act of an individual, unsupported by any such authority, is simply a private wrong, or a crime of that individual; an invasion of the rights of the injured party, it is true, whether they affect his person, his property, or his reputation; but if not sanctioned in some way by the State, or not done under State authority, his rights remain in full force, and may presumably be vindicated by resort to the laws of the State for redress. An individual cannot deprive a man of his right to vote, to hold property, to buy and sell, to sue in the courts, or to be a witness or a juror; he may, by force or fraud, interfere with the enjoyment of the right in a particular case; he may commit an assault against the person, or commit murder, or use ruffian violence at the polls, or slander the good name of a fellow citizen; but, unless protected in these wrongful acts by some shield of State law or State authority, he cannot destroy or injure the right; he will only render himself amenable to satisfaction or punishment; and amenable therefore to the laws of the State where the wrongful acts are committed. Hence, in all those cases where the Constitution seeks to protect the rights of citizens against discriminative and unjust laws of the State by prohibiting such laws, it is not individual offences, but abrogation and denial of rights, which it denounces, and for which it clothes the Congress with power to provide a remedy. This abrogation and denial of rights, for which the States alone were or could be responsible, was the great seminal and fundamental wrong which was intended to be remedied. And the remedy to be provided must necessarily be predicated upon that wrong. It must assume that in the cases provided for, the evil or wrong actually committed rests upon some State law or State authority for its excuse and perpetuation.

Of course, these remarks do not apply to those cases in which Congress is clothed with direct and plenary powers of legislation over the whole subject, accompanied with an express or implied denial of such power to the States, as in the regulation of commerce with foreign nations, among the several States, and with the Indian tribes, the coining of money, the establishment of post offices and post roads, the declaring of war, etc. In these cases Congress has power to pass laws for regulating the subjects specified in every detail, and the conduct and transactions of individuals in respect thereof. But where a subject is not submitted to the general legislative power of Congress, but is only submitted thereto for the purpose of rendering effective some prohibition against particular State legislation or State action in reference to that subject, the power given is limited by its object, and any legislation by Congress in the matter must necessarily be corrective in its character, adapted to counteract and redress the operation of such prohibited State laws or proceedings of State officers.

If the principles of interpretation which we have laid down are correct, as we deem them to be . . . it is clear that the law in question cannot be sustained by any grant of legislative power made to Congress by the Fourteenth Amendment. That amendment prohibits the States from denying to any person the equal protection of the laws, and declares that Congress shall have power to enforce by appropriate legislation, the provisions of the amendment. The law in question, without any reference to adverse State legislation on the subject, declares that all persons shall be entitled to equal accommodations and privileges of inns, public conveyances, and places of public amusement, and imposes a penalty upon any individual who shall deny to any citizen such equal accommodations and privileges. This is not corrective legislation; it is primary and direct; it takes immediate and absolute possession of the subject of the right of admission to inns, public conveyances, and places of amusement. It supersedes and displaces State legislation on the same subject, or only allows it permissive force. It ignores such legislation, and assumes that the matter is one that belongs to the domain of national regulation. Whether it would not have been a more effective protection of the rights of citizens to have clothed Congress with plenary power over the whole subject, is not now the question. What we have to decide is, whether such plenary power has been conferred upon Congress by the Fourteenth Amendment; and, in our judgment, it has not . . . But the power of Congress to adopt direct and primary, as distinguished from corrective legislation, on the subject in hand, is sought, in the second place, from the Thirteenth Amendment, which abolishes slavery. This amendment declares "that neither slavery, nor involuntary servitude, except as a punishment for crime, whereof the party shall have been duly convicted, shall exist within the United States, or any place subject to their jurisdiction;" and it gives Congress power to enforce the amendment by appropriate legislation. . . .

The only question under the present head, therefore, is, whether the refusal to any persons of the accommodations of an inn, or a public conveyance, or a place of public amusement, by an individual, and without any sanction or support from any State law or regulation, does inflict upon such persons any manner of servitude, or form of slavery, as those terms are understood in this country? Many wrongs may be obnoxious to the prohibitions of the Fourteenth Amendment which are not, in any just sense, incidents or elements of slavery. Such, for example, would be the taking of private property without due process of law; or allowing persons who have committed certain crimes (horse stealing, for example) to be seized and hung by the *posse comitatus* without regular trial; or denying to any person, or class of persons, the right to pursue any peaceful avocations allowed to others. What is called class legislation would belong to this category, and would be obnoxious to the prohibitions of the Fourteenth Amendment, but would not necessarily be so to the Thirteenth, when not involving the idea of any subjection of one man to another. The Thirteenth Amendment has respect, not to distinctions of race, or class, or color, but to slavery. The Fourteenth Amendment extends its protection to races and classes, and prohibits any State legislation which has the effect of denying to any race or class, or to any individual, the equal protection of the laws.

Now, conceding, for the sake of the argument, that the admission to an inn, a public conveyance, or a place of public amusement, on equal terms with all other citizens, is the right of every man and all classes of men, is it any more than one of those rights which the states by the Fourteenth Amendment are forbidden to deny to any person? And is the Constitution violated until the denial of the right has some State sanction or authority? Can the act of a mere individual, the owner of the inn, the public conveyance or place of amusement, refusing the accommodation, be justly regarded as imposing any badge of slavery or servitude upon the applicant, or only as inflicting an ordinary civil injury, properly cognizable by the laws of the State, and presumably subject to redress by those laws until the contrary appears?

After giving to these questions all the consideration which their importance demands, we are forced to the conclusion that such an act of refusal has nothing to do with slavery or involuntary servitude, and that if it is violative of any right of the party, his redress is to be sought under the laws of the States; or if those laws are adverse to his rights and do not protect him, his remedy will be found in the corrective legislation which Congress has adopted, or may adopt, for counteracting the effect of State laws, or State action, prohibited by the Fourteenth Amendment. It would be running the slavery argument into the ground to make it apply to every act of discrimination which a person may see fit to make as to the guests he will entertain, or as to the people he will take into his coach or cab or car, or admit to his concert or theatre, or deal with in other matters of intercourse or business. Innkeepers and public carriers, by the laws of all the States, so far as we are aware, are bound, to the extent of their facilities, to furnish proper accommodations to all unobjectionable persons who in good faith apply for them. If the laws themselves make any unjust discrimination, amenable to the prohibitions of the Four-teenth Amendment, Congress has full power to afford a remedy under that amendment and in accordance with it.

When a man has emerged from slavery, and by the aid of beneficent legislation has shaken off the inseparable concomitants of that state, there must be some stage in the progress of his elevation when he takes the rank of a mere citizen, and ceases to be the special favorite of the laws, and when his rights as a citizen, or a man, are to be protected in the ordinary modes by which other men's rights are protected. There were thousands of free colored people in this country before the abolition of slavery, enjoying all the essential rights of life, liberty and property the same as white citizens; yet no one, at that time, thought that it was any invasion of his personal status as a freeman because he was not admitted to all the privileges enjoyed by white citizens, or because he was subjected to discriminations in the enjoyment of accommodations in inns, public conveyances and places of amusement. Mere discriminations on account of race or color were not regarded as badges of slavery. If, since that time, the enjoyment of equal rights in all these respects has become established by constitutional enactment, it is not by force of the Thirteenth Amendment (which merely abolishes slavery), but by force of the Thirteenth and Fifteenth Amendments.

On the whole we are of opinion, that no countenance of authority for the passage of the law in question can be found in either the Thirteenth or Fourteenth Amendment of the Constitution; and no other ground of authority for its passage being suggested, it must necessarily be declared void, at least so far as its operation in the several States is concerned. . . .

Justice Harlan dissented:

The opinion in these cases proceeds, it seems to me, upon grounds entirely too narrow and artificial. I cannot resist the conclusion that the substance and spirit of the recent amendments of the Constitution have been sacrificed by a subtle and ingenious verbal criticism. . . .

The court adjudges, I think erroneously, that Congress is without power, under either the Thirteenth or Fourteenth Amendment, to establish such regulations, and that the first and second sections of the statute are, in all their parts, unconstitutional and void. . . .

That there are burdens and disabilities which constitute badges of slavery and servitude, and that the power to enforce by appropriate legislation the Thirteenth Amendment may be exerted by legislation of a direct and primary character, for the eradication, not simply of the institution, but of its badges and incidents, are propositions which ought to be deemed indisputable. They lie at the foundation of the Civil Rights Act of 1866. Whether that act was authorized by the Thirteenth Amendment alone, without the support which it subsequently received from the Fourteenth Amendment, after the adoption of which it was re-enacted with some additions, my brethren do not consider it necessary to inquire. But I submit, with all respect to them, that its constitutionality is conclusively shown by their opinion. They admit, as I have said, that the Thirteenth Amendment established freedom; that there are burdens and disabilities, the necessary incidents of slavery, which constitute its substance and visible form; that Congress, by the act of 1866, passed in view of the Thirteenth Amendment, before the Fourteenth was adopted, undertook to remove certain burdens and disabilities, the necessary incidents of slavery, and to secure to all citizens of every race and color, and without regard to previous servitude, those fundamental rights which are the essence of civil freedom, namely, the same right to make and enforce contracts, to sue, be parties, give evidence, and to inherit, purchase, lease, sell, and convey property as is enjoyed by white citizens; that under the Thirteenth Amendment, Congress has to do with slavery and its incidents; and that legislation, so far as necessary or proper to eradicate all forms and incidents of slavery and involuntary servitude, may be direct and primary, operating upon the acts of individuals, whether sanctioned by State legislation or not. These propositions being conceded, it is impossible, as it seems to me, to question the constitutional validity of the Civil Rights Act of 1866. . . .

I am of the opinion that such discrimination practised by corporations and individuals in the exercise of their public or quasi-public functions is a badge of servitude the imposition of which Congress may prevent under its power, by appropriate legislation, to enforce the Thirteenth Amendment; and, consequently, without reference to its enlarged power under the Fourteenth Amendment, the act of March 1, 1875, is not, in my judgment, repugnant to the Constitution.

It remains now to consider these cases with reference to the power Congress has possessed since the adoption of the Fourteenth Amendment. Much that has been said as to the power of Congress under the Thirteenth Amendment is applicable to this branch of the discussion, and will not be repeated.

Before the adoption of the recent amendments, it had become, as we have seen, the established doctrine of this court that negroes, whose ancestors had been imported and sold as slaves, could not become citizens of a State, or even of the United States, with the rights and privileges guaranteed to citizens by the national Constitution; further, that one might have all the rights and privileges of a citizen of a State without being a citizen in the sense in which that word was used in the national Constitution, and without being entitled to the privileges and immunities of citizens of the several States. Still, further, between the adoption of the Thirteenth Amendment and the proposal by Congress of the Fourteenth Amendment, on June 16, 1866, the statute books of several of the States, as we have seen, had become loaded down with enactments which, under the guise of Apprentice, Vagrant, and Contract regulations. . . .

It is said that any interpretation of the Fourteenth Amendment different from that adopted by the majority of the court, would imply that Congress had authority to enact a municipal code for all the States, covering every matter affecting the life, liberty, and property of the citizens of the several States. Not so. Prior to the adoption of that amendment the constitutions of the several States, without perhaps an exception, secured all *persons* against deprivation of life, liberty, or property, otherwise than by due process of law, and, in some form, recognized the right of all *persons* to the equal protection of the laws. Those rights, therefore, existed before that amendment was proposed or adopted, and were not created by it. If, by reason of that fact, it be assumed that protection in these rights of persons still rests primarily with the States, and that Congress may not interfere except to enforce, by means of corrective legislation, the prohibitions upon State laws or State proceedings inconsistent with those rights, it does not at all follow, that privileges which have been *granted by the nation*, may not be protected by primary legislation upon the part of Congress. The personal rights and immunities recognized in the prohibitive clauses of the amendment were, prior to its adoption, under the protection, primarily, of the States, while rights, created by or derived from the United States, have always been, and, in the nature of things, should always be, primarily, under the protection of the general government. Exemption from race discrimination in respect of the civil rights which are fundamental in *citizenship* in a republican government, is, as we have seen, a new right, created by the nation, with express power in Congress, by legislation, to enforce the constitutional provision from which it is derived. If, in some sense, such race discrimination is, within the letter of the last clause of the first section, a denial of that equal protection of the laws which is secured against State denial to all persons, whether citizens or not, it cannot be possible that a mere prohibition upon such State denial, or a prohibition upon State laws abridging the privileges and immunities of citizens of the United States, takes from the nation the power which it has uniformly exercised of protecting, by direct primary legislation, those privileges and immunities which existed under the Constitution before the adoption of the Fourteenth Amendment, or have been created by that amendment in behalf of those thereby made *citizens* of their respective States.

This construction does not in any degree intrench upon the just rights of the States in the control of their domestic affairs. It simply recognizes the enlarged powers conferred by the recent amendments upon the general government. In the view which I take of those amendments, the States possess the same authority which they have always had to define and regulate the civil rights which their own people, in virtue of State citizenship, may enjoy within their respective limits; except that its exercise is now subject to the expressly granted power of Congress, by legislation, to enforce the provisions of such amendments— a power which necessarily carries with it authority, by national legislation, to protect and secure the privileges and immunities which are created by or are derived from those amendments. That exemption of citizens from discrimination based on race or color, in respect of civil rights, is one of those privileges or immunities, can no longer be deemed an open question in this court. . . .

What I affirm is that no State, nor the officers of any State, nor any corporation or individual wielding power under State authority for the public benefit or the public convenience, can, consistently either with the freedom established by the fundamental law, or with that equality of civil rights which now belongs to every citizen, discriminate against freemen or citizens, in those rights, because of their race, or because they once labored under the disabilities of slavery imposed upon them as a race. The rights which Congress, by the act of 1875, endeavored to secure and protect are legal, not social rights. The right, for instance, of a colored citizen to use the accommodations of a public highway, upon the same terms as are permitted to white citizens, is no more a social right than his right, under the law, to use the public streets of a city or a town, or a turnpike road, or a public market, or a post office, or his right to sit in a public building with others, of whatever race, for the purpose of hearing the political questions of the day discussed. Scarcely a day passes without our seeing in this court-room citizens of the white and black races sitting side by side, watching over the progress of our business. It would never occur to any one that the presence of a colored citizen in a court-house, or court-room, was an invasion of the social rights of white persons who may frequent such places. And yet, such a suggestion would be quite as sound in law—I say it with all respect—as is the suggestion that the claim of a colored citizen to use, upon the same terms as is permitted to white citizens, the accommodations of public highways, or public inns, or places of public amusement, established under the license of the law, is an invasion of the social rights of the white race. . . .

My brethren say, that when a man has emerged from slavery, and by the aid of beneficent legislation has shaken off the inseparable concomitants of that state, there must be some stage in the process of his elevation when he takes the rank of a mere citizen, and ceases to be the special favorite of the laws, and when his rights as a citizen, or a man, are to be protected in the ordinary modes by which other men's rights are protected. It is, I submit, scarcely just to say that the colored race has been the special favorite of the laws. The statute of 1875, now adjudged to be unconstitutional, is for the benefit of citizens of every race and color. What the nation, through Congress, has sought to accomplish in reference to that race, is—what had already been done in every State of the Union for the white race—to secure and protect rights belonging to them as freemen and citizens; nothing more. It was not deemed enough "to help the feeble up, but to support him after." The one underlying purpose of congressional legislation has been to enable the black race to take the rank of mere citizens. The difficulty has been to compel a recognition of the legal right of the black race to take the rank of citizens, and to secure the enjoyment of privileges belonging, under the law, to them as a component part of the people for whose welfare and happiness government is ordained. At every step, in this direction, the nation has been confronted with class tyranny, which a contemporary English historian says is, of all tyrannies, the most intolerable, "for it is ubiquitous in its operation, and weighs, perhaps, most heavily on those whose obscurity or distance would withdraw them from the notice of a single despot." Today, it is the colored race which is denied, by corporations and individuals wielding public authority, rights fundamental in their freedom and citizenship. At some future time, it may be that some other race will fall under the ban of race discrimination. If the constitutional amendments be enforced, according to the intent with which, as I conceive, they were adopted, there cannot be, in this republic, any class of human beings in practical subjection to another class, with power in the latter to dole out to the former just such privileges as they may choose to grant. The supreme law of the land has decreed that no authority shall be exercised in this country upon the basis of discrimination, in respect of civil rights, against free-men and citizens because of their race, color, or pre-vious condition of servitude. To that decree—for the due enforcement of which, by appropriate legislation, Congress has been invested with express power—

every one must bow, whatever may have been, or whatever now are, his individual views as to the wis-dom or policy, either of the recent changes in the fun-damental law, or of the legislation which has been enacted to give them effect.

For the reasons stated I feel constrained to withhold my assent to the opinion of the court.

The gradual change in judicial emphasis from the rights of the freed men to property and corporate expansion actually paralleled a striking political shift, which was completed in the aftermath of the presidential election of 1876. The contested election of that year was settled by the compromise of 1877 in which federal troops were withdrawn from the South, federal support for a southern transcontinental railroad, the Texas Pacific route, was assured, and, in return, several cabinet posts were assured to ex–Confederates and to railroad-oriented political leaders, and a group of ex–Confederate congressmen were to support Republican James Garfield for speaker of the House of Representatives despite a Democratic victory in House elections in 1876. Rutherford Hayes kept the presi-dency in Republican hands, however, and the Republican Party turned away from the cause of the freed slaves and became more deeply committed to the growth and expansion of corporate power and influence.[15] The judicial appointments of Republican presidents reflected this significant shift rather clearly, and the subse-quent doctrinal developments on the Supreme Court ultimately brought about a major redistribution of power and wealth in the nation. The narrow construction provided in the Civil Rights decision was by no means the only example of the judicial dimension of this basic political change. Even before that decision, the Court's handling of race related issues in *Hall* v. *De Cuir* and *Virginia* v. *Rives* indi-cated a shift. The Hall case concerned the validity of a Louisiana reconstruction legislative act banning racial discrimination on any form of transportation.

HALL v. DE CUIR
95 U. S. 498 (1878)

Chief Justice Waite delivered the opinion of the Court:

For the purposes of this case, we must treat the act of Louisiana of Feb. 23, 1869, as requiring those engaged in inter-state commerce to give all persons travelling in that State, upon the public conveyances employed in such business, equal rights and privileges in all parts of the conveyance, without distinction or discrimination on account of race or color. Such was the construction given to that act in the courts below, and it is conclu-sive upon us as the construction of a State law by the State courts. It is with this provision of the statute alone that we have to deal. We have nothing whatever to do with it as a regulation of internal commerce, or as affecting any thing else than commerce among the States.

There can be no doubt but that exclusive power has been conferred upon Congress in respect to the regu-lation of commerce among the several States. The dif-ficulty has never been as to the existence of this power, but as to what is to be deemed an encroach-ment upon it; for, as has been often said, "legislation may in a great variety of ways affect commerce and persons engaged in it without constituting a regula-tion of it within the meaning of the Constitution." . . . By such statutes the States regulate, as a matter of domestic concern, the instruments of commerce situ-ated wholly within their own jurisdictions, and over which they have exclusive governmental control, ex-cept when employed in foreign or inter-state com-merce. As they can only be used in the State, their regulation for all purposes may properly be assumed by the State, until Congress acts in reference to their foreign or inter-state relations. When Congress does act, the State laws are superseded only to the extent that they affect commerce outside the State as it comes within the State. It has also been held that health and inspection laws may be passed by the States. . . . The line which separates the powers of the States from this exclusive power of Congress is not always distinctly marked, and oftentimes it is not easy to determine on which side a particular case belongs. Judges not unfrequently differ in their reasons for a decision in which they concur. Under such circumstances it would be a useless task to undertake to fix an arbitrary rule by which the line must in all cases be located. It is far better to leave a matter of such delicacy to be settled in each case upon a view of the particular rights involved.

But we think it may safely be said that State legislation which seeks to impose a direct burden upon interstate commerce, or to interfere directly with its freedom, does encroach upon the exclusive power of Congress. The statute now under consideration, in our opinion, occupies that position. It does not act upon the business through the local instruments to be employed after coming within the State, but directly upon the business as it comes into the State from without or goes out from within. While it purports only to control the carrier when engaged within the State, it must necessarily influence his conduct to some extent in the management of his business throughout his entire voyage. His disposition of passengers taken up and put down within the State, or taken up within to be carried without, cannot but affect in a greater or less degree those taken up without and brought within, and sometimes those taken up and put down without. A passenger in the cabin set apart for the use of whites without the State must, when the boat comes within, share the accommodations of that cabin with such colored persons as may come on board afterwards, if the law is enforced.

It was to meet just such a case that the commercial clause in the Constitution was adopted. The river Mississippi passes through or along the borders of ten different States, and its tributaries reach many more. The commerce upon these waters is immense, and its regulation clearly a matter of national concern. If each State was at liberty to regulate the conduct of carriers while within its jurisdiction, the confusion likely to follow could not but be productive of great inconvenience and unnecessary hardship. Each State could provide for its own passengers and regulate the transportation of its own freight, regardless of the interests of others. Nay more, it could prescribe rules by which the carrier must be governed within the

State in respect to passengers and property brought from without. On one side of the river or its tributaries he might be required to observe one set of rules, and on the other another. Commerce cannot flourish in the midst of such embarrassments. No carrier of passengers can conduct his business with satisfaction to himself, or comfort to those employing him, if on one side of a State line his passengers, both white and colored, must be permitted to occupy the same cabin, and on the other be kept separate. Uniformity in the regulations by which he is to be governed from one end to the other of his route is a necessity in his business, and to secure it Congress, which is untrammelled by State lines, has been invested with the exclusive legislative power of determining what such regulations shall be. If this statute can be enforced against those engaged in inter-state commerce, it may be as well against those engaged in foreign, and the master of a ship clearing from New Orleans for Liverpool, having passengers on board, would be compelled to carry all, white and colored, in the same cabin during his passage down the river, or be subject to an action for damages, "exemplary as well as actual," by any one who felt himself aggrieved because he had been excluded on account of his color.

This power of regulation may be exercised without legislation as well as with it. By refraining from action, Congress, in effect, adopts as its own regulations those which the common law or the civil law, where that prevails, has provided for the government of such business, and those which the States, in the regulation of their domestic concerns, have established affecting commerce, but not regulating it within the meaning of the Constitution. In fact, congressional legislation is only necessary to cure defects in existing laws, as they are discovered, and to adapt such laws to new developments of trade. As was said by Mr. Justice Field, speaking for the court in *Welton* v. *The State of Missouri*, 91 U. S. 282, "inaction [by Congress] . . . is equivalent to a declaration that interstate commerce shall remain free and untrammelled." Applying that principle to the circumstances of this case, congressional inaction left [the boatowner] . . . at liberty to adopt such reasonable rules and regulations for the disposition of passengers upon his boat, while pursuing her voyage within Louisiana or without, as seemed to him most for the interest of all concerned. The statute under which this suit is brought, as construed by the State court, seeks to take away from him that power so long as he is within Louisiana; and while recognizing to the fullest extent the principle which sustains a statute, unless its unconstitutionality is clearly established, we think this statute, to the extent that it requires those engaged in the transportation of passengers among the States to carry colored passengers in Louisiana in the same cabin with whites, is unconstitutional and void. If the public good requires such legislation, it must come from Congress and not from the States. . . .

In the Rives case, systematic exclusion of blacks from juries by custom rather than statute was considered. The Court obviously was not eager to examine the realities.

VIRGINIA v. RIVES
100 U. S. 313 (1880)

Justice Strong delivered the opinion of the Court:

Section 641 of the Revised Statutes provides for a removal "when any civil suit or prosecution is commenced in any State court, for any cause whatsoever, against any person who is denied or cannot enforce in the judicial tribunals of the State, or in the part of the State where such suit or prosecution is pending, any right secured to him by any law providing for the equal civil rights of citizens of the United States," &c. It declares that such a case may be removed before trial or final hearing. . . .

It rests upon the Fourteenth Amendment of the Constitution and the legislation to enforce its provisions. That amendment declares that no State shall make or enforce any law which shall abridge the privileges or immunities of citizens of the United States, nor shall any State deprive any person of life, liberty, or property, without due process of law, nor deny to any person within its jurisdiction the equal protection of the laws. It was in pursuance of these constitutional provisions that the civil rights statutes were enacted. . . .

The provisions of the Fourteenth Amendment of the Constitution we have quoted all have reference to State action exclusively, and not to any action of private individuals. It is the State which is prohibited from denying to any person within its jurisdiction the equal protection of the laws, and consequently the statutes partially enumerating what civil rights colored men shall enjoy equally with white persons, founded as they are upon the amendment, are intended for protection against State infringement of those rights. Sect. 641 was also intended for their protection against State action, and against that alone. . . .

The statute authorizes a removal of the case only before trial, not after a trial has commenced. It does not, therefore, embrace many cases in which a colored man's right may be denied. It does not embrace a case in which a right may be denied by judicial action during the trial, or by discrimination against him in the sentence, or in the mode of executing the sentence. But the violation of the constitutional provisions, when made by the judicial tribunals of a State, may be, and generally will be, after the trial has commenced. It is then, during or after the trial, that denials of a defendant's right by judicial tribunals occur. Not often until then. Nor can the defendant know until then that the equal protection of the laws will not be extended to him. Certainly until then he cannot affirm that it is denied, or that he cannot enforce it, in the judicial tribunals.

It is obvious, therefore, that to such a case—that is, a judicial infraction of the constitutional inhibitions, after trial or final hearing has commenced—sect. 641 has no applicability. It was not intended to reach such cases. It left them to the revisory power of the higher courts of the State, and ultimately to review of this court. We do not say that Congress could not have authorized the removal of such a case into the Federal courts at any stage of its proceeding, whenever a ruling should be made in it denying the equal protection of the laws to the defendant. Upon that subject it is unnecessary to affirm any thing. It is sufficient to say now that sect. 641 does not.

It is evident, therefore, that the denial or inability to enforce in the judicial tribunals of a State, rights secured to a defendant by any law providing for the equal civil rights of all persons citizens of the United States, of which sect. 641 speaks, is primarily, if not exclusively, a denial of such rights, or an inability to enforce them, resulting from the Constitution or laws of the State, rather than a denial first made manifest at the trial of the case. In other words, the statute has reference to a legislative denial or an inability resulting from it. Many such cases of denial might have been excluded by law from any jury summoned to try persons of their race, or the law might have denied to them the testimony of colored men in their favor, or process for summoning witnesses. Numerous other illustrations might be given. In all such cases a defendant can affirm, on oath, before trial, that he is denied the equal protection of the laws or equality of civil rights. But in the absence of constitutional or legislative impediments he cannot swear before his case comes to trial that his enjoyment of all his civil rights is denied to him. When he has only an apprehension that such rights will be withheld from him when his case shall come to trial, he cannot affirm that they are actually denied, or that he cannot enforce them. Yet such an affirmation is essential to his right to remove his case. By the express requirement of the statute his petition must set forth the facts upon which he bases his claim to have his case removed, and not merely his belief that he cannot enforce his rights at a subsequent stage of the proceedings. The statute was not, therefore, intended as a corrective of errors or wrongs committed by judicial tribunals in the administration of the law at the trial.

The petition of the two colored men for the removal of their case into the Federal court does not appear to have made any case for removal, if we are correct in our reading of the act of Congress. It did not assert, nor is it claimed now, that the Constitution or laws of Virginia denied to them any civil right, or stood in the way of their enforcing the equal protection of the laws. The law made no discrimination against them because of their color, nor any discrimination at all. The complaint is that there were no colored men in the jury that indicted them, nor in the petit jury summoned to try them. The petition expressly admitted that by the laws of the State all male citizens twenty-one years of age and not over sixty, who are entitled to vote and hold office under the Constitution and laws thereof, are made liable to serve as jurors. And it affirms (what is undoubtedly true) that this law allows the right, as well as requires the duty, of the race to which the petitioners belong to serve as jurors. It does not exclude colored citizens.

Now, conceding as we do, and as we endeavored to maintain in the case of *Strauder* v. *West Virginia,* that discrimination by law against the colored race, because of their color, in the selection of jurors, is a denial of the equal protection of the laws to a negro when he is put upon trial for an alleged criminal offence against a State, the laws of Virginia make no such discrimination. . . . If, as in this case, the subordinate officer whose duty it is to select jurors fails to discharge that duty in the true spirit of the law; if he

excludes all colored men solely because they are colored; or if the sheriff to whom a *venire* is given, composed of both white and colored citizens, neglects to summon the colored jurors only because they are colored; or if a clerk whose duty it is to take the twelve names from the box rejects all the colored jurors for the same reason,—it can with no propriety be said the defendant's right is denied by the State and cannot be enforced in the judicial tribunals. . . . We cannot think such cases are within the provisions of section 641. . . .

The assertions in the petition for removal, that the grand jury by which the petitioners were indicted, as well as the jury summoned to try them, were composed wholly of the white race, and that their race had never been allowed to serve as jurors in the county of Patrick in any case in which a colored man was interested, fall short of showing that any civil right was denied, or that there had been any discrimination against the defendants because of their color or race. The facts may have been as stated, and yet the jury which indicted them, and the panel summoned to try them, may have been impartially selected.

Nor did the refusal of the court and of the counsel for the prosecution allow a modification of the *venire,* by which one-third of the jury, or a portion of it, should be composed of persons of the petitioners' own race, amount to any denial of a right secured to them by any law providing for the equal civil rights of citizens of the United States. The privilege for which they moved, and which they also asked from the prosecution, was not a right given or secured to them, or to any person, by the law of the State, or by any act of Congress, or by the Fourteenth Amendment of the Constitution. It *is* a right to which every colored man is entitled, that, in the selection of jurors to pass upon his life, liberty, or property, there shall be no exclusion of his race, and no discrimination against them because of their color. But this is a different thing from the right which it is asserted was denied to the petitioners by the State Court, viz. a right to have the jury composed in part of colored men. A mixed jury in a particular case is not essential to the equal protection of the laws, and the right to it is not given by any law of Virginia, or by any Federal statute. It is not, therefore, guaranteed by the Fourteenth Amendment, or within the purview of sect. 641.

It follows that the petition for a removal stated no facts that brought the case within the provisions of this section, and, consequently, no jurisdiction of the case was acquired by the Circuit Court of the United States. . . .

Not all the decisions illustrating the absence of great judicial concern for noneconomic human rights involved blacks. But all exemplified a judicial unwillingness to construe the post–Civil War amendments broadly where human noneconomic rights were concerned. Thus, in the Hurtado decision, the Supreme Court ruled decisively that noneconomic portions of the Bill of Rights could not be invoked against the states through application of the due process clause of the Fourteenth Amendment. Technically, *Hurtado* v. *California* involved the fundamental question whether an individual convicted of murder and sentenced to be hanged was denied due process because these results were reached by indictment by information by a prosecuting attorney instead of by a grand jury.

HURTADO v. CALIFORNIA
110 U. S. 516 (1884)

Justice Matthews delivered the opinion of the Court:

. . . The proposition of law we are asked to affirm is, that an indictment or presentment by a grand jury, as known to the common law of England, is essential to that "due process of law," when applied to prosecutions for felonies, which is secured and guaranteed by this provision of the Constitution of the United States, and which accordingly it is forbidden to the States respectively to dispense with in the administration of criminal law.

. . . It is maintained on behalf of the plaintiff in error that the phrase "due process of law" is equivalent to "law of the land," as found in the [thirty-]ninth chapter of Magna Charta; that, by immemorial usage, it has acquired a fixed, definite and technical meaning; that it refers to and includes, not only the general principles of public liberty and private right, which lie at the foundation of all free government, but the very institutions which, venerable by time and custom, have been tried by experience and found fit and necessary for the preservation of those principles, and which, having been the birthright and inheritance of every English subject, crossed the Atlantic with the colonists and were transplanted and established in the fundamental laws of the State; that, having been originally introduced into the Constitution of the United States as a limitation upon the powers of the government, brought into being by that instrument, it has now been added as an additional security to the individual against oppression by the States themselves; that one of these institutions is that of the grand jury, an indictment or presentment by which against the accused in cases of alleged felonies is an essential part of due process of law, in order that he may not be

harassed or destroyed by prosecutions founded only upon private malice or popular fury. . . .

It is urged upon us, however, in argument, that the claim made in behalf of the plaintiff in error is supported by the decision of this court in Murray's Lessee v. Hoboken Land & Improvement Company [1856]. There, Mr. Justice Curtis delivering the opinion of the court, after showing that due process of law must mean something more than the actual existing law of the land, for otherwise it would be no restraint upon legislative power, proceeds as follows: "To what principle, then, are we to resort to ascertain whether this process, enacted by Congress, is due process? To this the answer must be twofold. We must examine the Constitution itself to see whether this process be in conflict with any of its provisions. If not found to be so, we must look to those settled usages and modes of proceeding existing in the common and statute law of England before the emigration of our ancestors, and which are shown not to have been unsuited to their civil and political condition by having been acted on by them after the settlement of this country."

This, it is argued, furnishes an indispensable test of what constitutes "due process of law"; that any proceeding otherwise authorized by law, which is not thus sanctioned by usage, or which supersedes and displaces one that is, cannot be regarded as due process of law.

But this inference is unwarranted. The real syllabus of the passage quoted is, that a process of law, which is not otherwise forbidden, must be taken to be due process of law, if it can show the sanction of settled usage both in England and in this country; but it by no means follows, that nothing else can be due process of law. The point in the case cited arose in reference to a summary proceeding, questioned on that account, as not due process of law. The answer was: however exceptional it may be, as tested by definitions and principles of ordinary procedure, nevertheless, this, in substance, has been immemorially the actual law of the land, and, therefore, is due process of law. But to hold that such a characteristic is essential to due process of law, would be to deny every quality of the law but its age, and to render it incapable of progress or improvement. It would be to stamp upon our jurisprudence the unchangeableness attributed to the laws of the Medes and Persians.

This would be all the more singular and surprising, in this quick and active age, when we consider that, owing to the progressive development of legal ideas and institutions in England, the words of Magna Charta stood for very different things at the time of the separation of the American Colonies from what they represented originally. . . .

The Constitution of the United States was ordained, it is true, by descendants of Englishmen, who inherited the traditions of English law and history; but it was made for an undefined and expanding future, and for a people gathered and to be gathered from many Nations and of many tongues. And while we take just pride in the principles and institutions of the common law, we are not to forget that in lands where other systems of jurisprudence prevail, the ideas and processes of civil justice are also not unknown. Due process of law, in spite of the absolutism of continental governments, is not alien to that Code which survived the Roman Empire as the foundation of modern civilization in Europe, and which has given us that fundamental maxim of distributive justice, *suum cuique tribuere.* There is nothing in Magna Charta, rightly construed as a broad charter of public right and law, which ought to exclude the best ideas of all systems and of every age; and as it was the characteristic principle of the common law to draw its inspiration from every fountain of justice, we are not to assume that the sources of its supply have been exhausted. On the contrary, we should expect that the new and various experiences of our own situation and system will mold and shape it into new and not less useful forms. . . .

The concessions of Magna Charta were wrung from the King as guaranties against the oppressions and usurpations of his prerogative. It did not enter into the minds of the barons to provide security against their own body or in favor of the Commons by limiting the power of Parliament; so that bills of attainder, *ex post facto* laws, laws declaring forfeitures of estates, and other arbitrary acts of legislation which occur so frequently in English history, were never regarded as inconsistent with the law of the land; for notwithstanding what was attributed to Lord Coke in *Bonham's Case,* 8 Rep. 115, 118 *a,* the omnipotence of Parliament over the common law was absolute, even against common right and reason. The actual and practical security for English liberty against legislative tyranny was the power of a free public opinion represented by the Commons.

In this country written constitutions were deemed essential to protect the rights and liberties of the people against the encroachments of power delegated to their governments, and the provisions of Magna Charta were incorporated into Bills of Rights. They were limitations upon all the powers of government, legislative as well as executive and judicial.

It necessarily happened, therefore, that as these broad and general maxims of liberty and justice held in our system a different place and performed a different function from their position and office in English constitutional history and law, they would receive and justify a corresponding and more comprehensive interpretation. Applied in England only as guards against executive usurpation and tyranny, here they have become bulwarks also against arbitrary legislation; but, in that application, as it would be incongruous to measure and restrict them by the ancient customary English law, they must be held to guarantee not particular forms of procedure, but the very substance of individual rights to life, liberty, and property. . . .

We are to construe this phrase in the Fourteenth Amendment by the *usus loquendi* of the Constitution itself. The same words are contained in the Fifth Amendment. That article makes specific and express provision for perpetuating the institution of the grand jury, so far as relates to prosecutions for the more aggravated crimes under the laws of the United States. It declares that:

No person shall be held to answer for a capital or otherwise infamous crime, unless on a presentment or indictment of a grand jury, except in cases arising in the land or naval forces, or in the militia when in actual service in time of war or public danger; nor shall any person be subject for the same offence to be twice put in jeopardy of life or limb; nor shall he be compelled in any criminal case to be witness against himself. [It then immediately adds]: Nor be deprived of life, liberty, or property, without due process of law.

According to a recognized canon of interpretation, especially applicable to formal and solemn instruments of constitutional law, we are forbidden to assume, without clear reason to the contrary, that any part of this most important amendment is superfluous. The natural and obvious inference is, that in the sense of the Constitution, "due process of law" was not meant or intended to include, *ex vi termini*, the institution and procedure of a grand jury in any case. The conclusion is equally irresistible, that when the same phrase was employed in the Fourteenth Amendment to restrain the action of the States, it was used in the same sense and with no greater extent; and that if in the adoption of that amendment it had been part of its purpose to perpetuate the institution of the grand jury in all the States, it would have embodied, as did the Fifth Amendment, express declarations to that effect. . . .

But it is not to be supposed that these legislative powers are absolute and despotic, and that the amendment prescribing due process of law is too vague and indefinite to operate as a practical restraint. It is not every act, legislative in form, that is law. Law is something more than mere will exerted as an act of power. It must be not a special rule for a particular person or a particular case, but in the language of Mr. Webster, in his familiar definition, "the general law, a law which hears before it condemns, which proceeds upon inquiry, and renders judgment only after trial," so "that every citizen shall hold his life, liberty, property and immunities under the protection of the general rules which govern society," and thus excluding, as not due process of law, acts of attainder, bills of pains and penalties, acts of confiscation, acts reversing judgments, and acts directly transferring one man's estate to another, legislative judgments and decrees, and other similar special, partial and arbitrary exertions of power under the forms of legislation. Arbitrary power, enforcing its edicts to the injury of the persons and property of its subjects, is not law, whether manifested as the decree of a personal monarch or of an impersonal multitude. And the limitations imposed by our constitutional law upon the action of the governments, both State and national, are essential to the preservation of public and private rights, notwithstanding the representative character of our political institutions. The enforcement of these limitations by judicial process is the device of self-governing communities to protect the rights of individuals and minorities, as well against the power of numbers, as against the violence of public agents transcending the limits of

lawful authority, even when acting in the name and wielding the force of the government. . . .

It follows that any legal proceeding enforced by public authority, whether sanctioned by age and custom, or newly devised in the discretion of the legislative power, in furtherance of the general public good, which regards and preserves these principles of liberty and justice, must be held to be due process of law. . . .

Tried by these principles, we are unable to say that the substitution for a presentment or indictment by a grand jury of the proceeding by information, after examination and commitment by a magistrate, certifying to the probable guilt of the defendant, with the right on his part to the aid of counsel, and to the cross-examination of the witnesses produced for the prosecution, is not due process of law. It is, as we have seen, an ancient proceeding at common law, which might include every case of an offense of less grade than a felony, except misprision of treason; and in every circumstance of its administration, as authorized by the Statute of California, it carefully considers and guards the substantial interest of the prisoner. It is merely a preliminary proceeding, and can result in no final judgment, except as the consequence of a regular judicial trial, conducted precisely as in cases of indictments. . . .

For these reasons, finding no error therein, the judgment of the Supreme Court of California is affirmed.

Justice Harlan, dissented, saying in part:

. . . I cannot agree that the State may, consistently with due process of law, require a person to answer for a capital offense, except upon the presentment or indictment of a grand jury. . . .

. . . To what principles are we to resort to ascertain whether this process . . . is due process? To this the answer must be twofold. We must examine the Constitution itself to see whether this process be in conflict with any of its provisions. If not found to be so, we must look *"to those settled usages and modes of proceeding existing in the common and statute law of England before the emigration of our ancestors, and which are shown not to have been unsuited to their civil and political condition by having been acted on by them after the settlement of this country."* . . .

Yick Wo v. Hopkins provided a direct test of the scope of the equal protection of the laws clause of the Fourteenth Amendment. In terms of the decision-making tendencies of the era, however, the decision exhibited an unusual emphasis upon the rights of an uninfluential minority.

YICK WO v. HOPKINS
118 U. S. 356 (1886)

Justice Matthews delivered the opinion of the court:

In the case of the petitioner, brought here by writ of error to the Supreme Court of California, our jurisdiction is limited to the question whether the plaintiff in error has been denied a right in violation of the Constitution, laws, or treaties of the United States.

The ordinance drawn in question in the present case does not prescribe a rule and conditions, for the regulation of the use of property for laundry purposes, to which all similarly situated may conform. It allows without restriction the use for such purposes of buildings of brick or stone; but, as to wooden buildings, constituting nearly all those in previous use, it divides the owners or occupiers into two classes, not having respect to their personal character and qualifications for the business, nor the situation and nature and adaptation of the buildings themselves, but merely by an arbitrary line, on one side of which are those who are permitted to pursue their industry by the mere will and consent of the supervisors, and on the other those from whom that consent is withheld, at their mere will and pleasure. And both classes are alike only in this: that they are tenants at will, under the supervisors, of their means of living. The ordinance, therefore, also differs from the not unusual case, where discretion is lodged by law in public officers or bodies to grant or withhold licenses to keep taverns, or places for the sale of spirituous liquors, and the like, when one of the conditions is that the applicant shall be a fit person for the exercise of the privilege, because in such cases the fact of fitness is submitted to the judgment of the officer, and calls for the exercise of a discretion of a judicial nature.

The rights of the petitioners, as affected by the proceedings of which they complain, are not less because they are aliens and subjects of the Emperor of China. By the third article of the Treaty between this government and that of China, concluded November 17, 1880, 22 Stat. at L. 827, it is stipulated: "If Chinese laborers, or Chinese of any other class, now either permanently or temporarily residing in the territory of the United States, meet with ill treatment at the hands of any other persons, the Government of the United States will exert all its powers to devise measures for their protection, and to secure to them the same rights, privileges, immunities and exemptions as may be enjoyed by the citizens or subjects of the most favored nation, and to which they are entitled by treaty."

The Fourteenth Amendment to the Constitution is not confined to the protection of citizens. It says: "Nor shall any State deprive any person of life, liberty, or property without due process of law; nor deny to any person within its jurisdiction the equal protection of the laws." These provisions are universal in their application, to all persons within the territorial jurisdiction, without regard to any differences of race, of color, or of nationality; and the equal protection of the laws is a pledge of the protection of equal laws. It is accordingly enacted by section 1977 of the Revised Statutes, that "All persons within the jurisdiction of the United States shall have the same right in every State and Territory to make and enforce contracts, to sue, be parties, give evidence, and to the full and equal benefit of all laws and proceedings for the security of persons and property as is enjoyed by white citizens, and shall be subject to like punishments, pains, penalties, taxes, licenses and exactions of every kind, and to no other." The questions we have to consider and decide in these cases, therefore, are to be treated as involving the rights of every citizen of the United States equally with those of the strangers and aliens who now invoke the jurisdiction of the court. . . . In the present cases, we are not obliged to reason from the probable to the actual and pass upon the validity of the ordinances complained of, as tried merely by the opportunities which their terms afford, of unequal and unjust discrimination in their administration. For the cases present the ordinances in actual operation, and the facts shown establish an administration directed so exclusively against a particular class of persons as to warrant and require the conclusion that whatever may have been the intent of the ordinances as adopted, they are applied by the public authorities charged with their administration, and thus representing the State itself, with a mind so unequal and oppressive as to amount to a practical denial by the State of that equal protection of the laws which is secured to the petitioners, as to all other persons, by the broad and benign provisions of the Fourteenth Amendment to the Constitution of the United States. Though the law itself be fair on its face and impartial in appearance, yet, if it is applied and administered by public authority with an evil eye and an unequal hand, so as practically to make unjust and illegal discriminations between persons in similar circumstances, material to their rights, the denial of equal justice is still within the prohibition of the Constitution. . . .

The present cases, as shown by the facts disclosed in the record, are within this class. It appears that both petitioners have complied with every requisite, deemed by the law or by the public officers charged with its administration necessary for the protection of neighboring property from fire, or as a precaution against injury to the public health. No reason whatever, except the will of the supervisors, is assigned why they should not be permitted to carry on, in the accustomed manner their harmless and useful occupation, on which they depend for a livelihood. And while this consent of the supervisors is withheld from them and from two hundred others who have also petitioned, all of whom happened to be Chinese subjects, eighty others, not Chinese subjects, are permitted to carry on the same business under similar conditions. The fact of this discrimination is admitted. No reason for it is shown, and the conclusion cannot be resisted, that no reason for it exists except hostility to the race and nationality to which the petitioners belong, and which in the eye of the law is not justified. The discrimination is therefore illegal, and the public administration which enforces it is a denial of the equal protection of the laws and a violation of the Fourteenth Amendment of the Constitution. The imprisonment of the petitioners is therefore illegal, and they must be discharged.

To this end, the judgment of the Supreme Court of California in the case of Yick Wo, and that of the Circuit Court of the United States for the District of California in the case of Wo Lee, are severally reversed, and the cases remanded, each to the proper court, with directions to discharge the petitioners from custody and imprisonment.

As the post–Civil War era evolved, the positions taken by the Supreme Court occasionally demonstrated a curious ambivalence regarding federal-state relations. In *Collector* v. *Day*, a doctrine of intergovernmental tax immunity was adopted over the strong dissent of Justice Bradley.

COLLECTOR v. DAY
11 Wallace 113 (1870)

Justice Nelson delivered the opinion of the court:

This is a writ of error to the circuit court of the United States for the district of Massachusetts.

Day, the plaintiff in the court below and defendant in error, brought a suit against Buffington, collector of the internal revenue, to recover back $61.51 and interest, assessed upon his salary in the years 1866 and 1867, as judge of the court of probate and insolvency for the county of Barnstable, state of Massachusetts, paid under protest. The salary is fixed by law, and payable out of the treasury of the state. The case was submitted to the court below on an agreed statement of facts, and upon which judgment was rendered for the plaintiff. It is now here for re-examination. It presents the question, whether or not it is competent for Congress, under the Constitution of the United States, to impose a tax upon the salary of a judicial officer of a state.

In the case of *Dobbins* v. *Erie Co.* 16 Pet. 135, it was decided that it was not competent for the legislature of a state to levy a tax upon the salary or emoluments of an officer of the United States. The decision was placed mainly upon the ground that the officer was a means or instrumentality employed for carrying into effect some of the legitimate powers of the government, which could not be interfered with by taxation or otherwise by the states, and that the salary or compensation for the service of the officer was inseparably connected with the office; that if the officer, as such, was exempt, the salary assigned for his support or maintenance while holding the office, was also, for like reasons, equally exempt.

The cases of *McCulloch* v. *Md.* 4 Wheat. 316, and *Weston* v. *Charleston*, 2 Pet. 449, were referred to as settling the principle that governed the case, namely: "that the state governments cannot lay a tax upon the constitutional means employed by the government of the Union to execute its constitutional powers." The soundness of this principle is happily illustrated by the Chief Justice in *McCulloch* v. *Md.* "If the states," he observes, "may tax one instrument employed by the government in the execution of its powers, they may tax any and every other instrument. They may tax the mail; they may tax the mint; they may tax patent rights; they may tax judicial process; they may tax all the means employed by the government to an excess which would defeat all the ends of the government." "This," he observes, "was not intended by the American people. They did not design to make their government dependent on the states." Again, p. 427,

"That the power of taxing it (the bank) by the states may be exercised so far as to destroy it, is too obvious to be denied." And, in *Weston* v. *Charleston*, he observes: "If the right to impose the tax exists, it is a right which, in its nature, acknowledges no limits. It may be carried to any extent within the jurisdiction of the state or corporation which imposes it which the will of each state and corporation may presribe."

It is conceded in the case of *McCulloch* v. *Md.* that the power of taxation by the states was not abridged by the grant of a similar power to the government of the Union; that it was retained by the states, and that the power is to be concurrently exercised by the two governments; and also that there is no express constitutional prohibition upon the states against taxing the means or instrumentalities of the general government. But, it was held, and we agree properly held, to be prohibited by necessary implication; otherwise, the states might impose taxation to an extent that would impair, if not wholly defeat, the operations of the Federal authorities when acting in their appropriate sphere.

These views, we think, abundantly establish the soundness of the decision of the case of *Dobbins* v. *Erie Co. supra,* which determined that the states were prohibited, upon a proper construction of the Constitution, from taxing the salary or emoluments of an officer of the government of the United States. And we shall now proceed to show that, upon the same construction of that instrument, and for like reasons, that government is prohibited from taxing the salary of the judicial officer of a state.

It is a familiar rule of construction of the Constitution of the Union, that the sovereign powers vested in the state governments by their respective constitutions, remained unaltered and unimpaired except so far as they were granted to the government of the United States. That the intention of the framers of the Constitution in this respect might not be misunderstood this rule of interpretation is expressly declared in the 10th article of the Amendments, namely: "The powers not delegated to the United States are reserved to the states respectively, or to the people." The government of the United States, therefore, can claim no powers which are not granted to it by the Constitution, and the powers actually granted must be such as are expressly given, or given by necessary implication.

The general government, and the states, although both exist within the same territorial limits, are separable and distinct sovereignties, acting separately and independently of each other, within their respective spheres. The former, in its appropriate sphere, is supreme; but the states within the limits of their powers

not granted; or, in the language of the 10th Amendment, "reserved," are as independent of the general government as that government within its sphere is independent of the states. The relations existing between the two governments are well stated by the present Chief Justice in the case of *Lane Co.* v. *Oregon*, 7 Wall. 76, 19 L. ed. 104. "Both the states and the United States," he observed, "existed before the Constitution. The people, through that instrument, established a more perfect union, by substituting a national government, acting with ample powers directly upon the citizens, instead of the confederate government, which acted with powers, greatly restricted, only upon the states. But, in many of the articles of the Constitution, the necessary existence of the states, and within their proper spheres, the independent authority of the states are distinctly recognized. To them nearly the whole charge of interior regulation is committed or left; to them, and to the people, all powers, not expressly delegated to the national government, are reserved." Upon looking into the Constitution it will be found that but a few of the articles in that instrument could be carried into practical effect without the existence of the states.

Two of the great departments of the government, the executive and legislative, depend upon the exercise of the powers, or upon the people of the states. The Constitution guarantees to the states a republican form of government, and protects each against invasion or domestic violence. Such being the separate and independent condition of the states in our complex system, as recognized by the Constitution, and the existence of which is so indispensable, that, without them, the general government itself would disappear from the family of nations, it would seem to follow, as a reasonable, if not a necessary consequence, that the means and instrumentalities employed for carrying on the operations of their governments for preserving their existence, and fulfilling the high and responsible duties assigned to them in the Constitution, should be left free and unimpaired; should not be liable to be crippled, much less defeated by the taxing power of another government, which power acknowledges no limits but the will of the legislative body imposing the tax. And, more especially, those means and instrumentalities which are the creation of their sovereign and reserved rights, one of which is the establishment of the judicial department, and the appointment of officers to administer their laws. Without this power, and the exercise of it, we risk nothing in saying that no one of the states, under the form of government guaranteed by the Constitution could long preserve its existence. A despotic government might. We have said that one of the reserved powers was that to establish a judicial department, it would have been more accurate, and in accordance with the existing state of things at the time, to have said the power to maintain a judicial department. All of the thirteen states were in the possession of this power, and had exercised it at the adoption of the Constitution; and it is not pretended that any grant of it to the general government is found in that instrument. It is, therefore, one of the sovereign powers vested in the states by their constitutions which remained unaltered and unimpaired, and in respect to which the state is as independent of the general government as that government is independent of the states.

The supremacy of the general government, therefore, so much relied on in the argument of the counsel for the plaintiff in error, in respect to the question before us, cannot be maintained. The two governments are upon an equality, and the question is whether the power "to lay and collect taxes" enables the general government to tax the salary of a judicial officer of the state, which officer is a means or instrumentality employed to carry into execution one of its most important functions, the administration of the laws, and which concerns the exercise of a right reserved to the states.

We do not say the mere circumstance of the establishment of the judicial department, and the appointment of officers to administer the laws, being among the reserved powers of the state, disables the general government from levying the tax, as that depends upon the express power "to lay and collect taxes," but it shows that it is an original inherent power never parted with, and in respect to which the supremacy of that government does not exist, and is of no importance in determining the question; and further, that being an original and reserved power, and the judicial officers appointed under it being a means or instrumentality employed to carry it into effect, the right and necessity of its unimpaired exercise, and the exemption of the officer from taxation by the general government, stand upon as solid a ground and are maintained by principles and reasons as cogent as those which led to the exemption of the Federal officer in *Dobbins* v. *Erie Co. supra*, from taxation by the state; for, in this respect, that is, in respect to the reserved powers, the state is as sovereign and independent as the general government. And if the means and instrumentalities employed by that government to carry into operation the powers granted to it are necessarily, and, for the sake of self-preservation, exempt from taxation by the states, why are not those of the states depending upon their reserved powers, for like reasons, equally exempt from Federal taxation? Their unimpaired existence in the one case is as essential as in the other. It is admitted that there is no express provision in the Constitution that prohibits the general government from taxing the means and instrumentalities of the states, nor is there any prohibiting the states from taxing the means and instrumentalities of that government. In both cases the exemption rests upon necessary implication, and is upheld by the great law of self-preservation; as any government, whose means employed in conducting its operations, if subject to the control of another and distinct government, can exist only at the mercy of that government. Of what avail are these means if another power may tax them at discretion?

But we are referred to *The Veazie Bk.* v. *Fenno,* 8 Wall. 533, 91 L. ed. 482, in support of this power of taxation. That case furnishes a strong illustration of the position taken by the Chief Justice in *McCulloch* v. *Md. supra,* namely, "that the power to tax involves the power to destroy."

The power involved was one which had been exercised by the states since the foundation of the government and had been, after the lapse of three quarters of a century, annihilated from excessive taxation by the general government, just as the judicial office in the present case might be, if subject, at all, to taxation by that government. But notwithstanding the sanction of this taxation by a majority of the court, it is conceded, in the opinion, that "the reserved rights of the states, such as the right to pass laws; to give effect to laws through executive action; to administer justice through the courts, and to employ all necessary agencies for legitimate purposes of state government, are not proper subjects of the taxing power of Congress." This concession covers the case before us, and adds the authority of this court in support of the doctrine which we have endeavored to maintain.

The judgment of the court below is affirmed.

Justice Bradley dissented:

I dissent from the opinion of the court in this case, because it seems to me that the general government has the same power of taxing the income of officers of the state governments as it has of taxing that of its own officers. It is the common government of all alike; and every citizen is presumed to trust his own government in the matter of taxation. No man ceases to be a citizen of the United States by being an officer under the state government. I cannot accede to the doctrine that the general government is to be regarded as in any sense foreign or antagonistic to the state governments, their officers, or people; nor can I agree that a presumption can be admitted that the general government will act in a manner hostile to the existence or functions of the state governments, which are constituent parts of the system or body politic forming the basis on which the general government is founded. The taxation by the state governments of the instruments employed by the general government in the exercise of its powers is a very different thing. Such taxation involves an interference with the powers of a government in which other states and their citizens are equally interested with the state which imposes the taxation. In my judgment, the limitation of the power of taxation in the general government, which the present decision establishes, will be found very difficult to control. Where are we to stop in enumerating the functions of the state governments which will be interfered with by Federal taxation? If a state incorporates a railroad to carry out its purposes of internal improvement, or a bank to aid its financial arrangements, reserving, perhaps, a percentage on the stock or profits, for the supply of its own treasury, will the bonds or stock of such an institution be free from Federal taxation? How can we now tell what the effect of this decision will be? I cannot but regard it as founded on a fallacy, and that it will lead to mischievous consequences. I am as much opposed as anyone can be to any interference by the general government with the just powers of the state governments. But no concession of any of the just powers of the general government can easily be recalled. I, therefore, consider it my duty to at least record my dissent when such concession appears to be made. An extended discussion of the subject would answer no useful purpose.

The post–Civil War era had changed in its political and social emphases as dramatized by the electoral Compromise of 1877. The shift to corporate influence and private corporate freedom from governmental control was underscored in the Wabash case and in *Kilbourn* v. *Thompson*.

The Wabash decision represented a dramatic landmark in the Supreme Court's long and often unpredictable development of the law of the commerce clause. It definitely enhanced federal authority. The key question was the constitutionality of an Illinois statute regulating the rates of interstate railroad carriers. The Illinois state legislature was attempting to end what was widely acknowledged as ruinous rate discrimination practiced by profit-conscious railroad corporations. The Supreme Court acknowleged the "obvious injustice" of the rate discriminations, but struck down the Illinois law on the basis of the doctrine that even where Congress has not acted, whenever the subject to be regulated required "general and national" supervision, the states cannot constitutionally regulate. The decision contributed to growing national sentiment that the Court allowed national corporations to operate relatively free from either national or state supervision. The decision is credited with contributing to subsequent congressional adoption of the Interstate Commerce Act in 1887. But the Interstate Commerce Commission created under the act proved relatively ineffective for a number of years.

WABASH, ST. LOUIS, AND PACIFIC RAILWAY COMPANY v. ILLINOIS
118 U. S. 557 (1886)

Justice Miller delivered the opinion of the Court:

The question of the right of the State to regulate the rate of fares and tolls on railroads, and how far that right was affected by the commerce clause of the Constitution of the United States, was presented to the court in [the Granger] cases. And it must be admitted that, in a general way, the court treated the cases then before it as belonging to that class of regulations of commerce which, like pilotage, bridging navigable rivers, and many others, could be acted upon by the States in the absence of any legislation by Congress on the same subject.

By the slightest attention to the matter it will be readily seen that the circumstances under which a bridge may be authorized across a navigable stream within the limits of a State, for the use of a public highway, and the local rules which shall govern the conduct of the pilot of each of the varying harbors of the coasts of the United States, depend upon principles far more limited in their application and importance than those which should regulate the transportation of persons and property across the half or the whole of the continent, over the territories of half a dozen States, through which they are carried without change of car or breaking bulk. . . .

[T]he great question to be decided, and which was decided, and which was argued in all those cases, was the right of the State within which a railroad company did business to regulate or limit the amount of any of these traffic charges.

The importance of that question overshadowed all others; and the case of *Munn* v. *Illinois* was selected by the court as the most appropriate one in which to give its opinion on that subject, because that case presented the question of a private citizen, or unincorporated partnership, engaged in the warehousing business in Chicago, free from any claim of right or contract under an act of incorporation of any State whatever, and free from the question of continuous transportation through several States. And in that case the court was presented with the question, which it decided, whether any one engaged in a public business, in which all the public had a right to require his service, could be regulated by acts of the legislature in the exercise of this public function and public duty, so far as to limit the amount of charges that should be made for such services.

The railroad companies set up another defence, apart from denying the general right of the legislature to regulate transportation charges, namely, that in their charters from the States they each had a contract, express or implied, that they might regulate and establish their own fares and rates of transportation. These two questions were of primary importance; and though it is true that, as incidental or auxiliary to these, the question of the exclusive right of Congress to make such regulations of charges as any legislative power had the right to make, to the exclusion of the States, was presented, it received but little attention at the hands of the court, and was passed over with the remarks in the opinions of the court which have been cited. . . .

It cannot be too strongly insisted upon that the right of continuous transportation from one end of the country to the other is essential in modern times to that freedom of commerce from the restraints which the State might choose to impose upon it, that the commerce clause was intended to secure. This clause, giving to Congress the power to regulate commerce among the States and with foreign nations, as this court has said before, was among the most important of the subjects which prompted the formation of the Constitution. . . . And it would be a very feeble and almost useless provision, but poorly adapted to secure the entire freedom of commerce among the States which was deemed essential to a more perfect union by the framers of the Constitution, if, at every stage of the transportation of goods and chattels through the country, the State within whose limits a part of this transportation must be done could impose regulations concerning the price, compensation, or taxation, or any other restrictive regulation interfering with and seriously embarrassing this commerce.

The argument on this subject can never be better stated than it is by Chief Justice Marshall in *Gibbons* v. *Ogden*. . . . He there demonstrates that commerce among the States, like commerce with foreign nations, is necessarily a commerce which crosses State lines, and extends into the States, and the power of Congress to regulate it exists wherever that commerce is found. Speaking of navigation as an element of commerce, which it is, only, as a means of transportation, now largely superseded by railroads, he says: "The power of Congress, then, comprehends navigation within the limits of every State in the Union, so far as that navigation may be, in any manner, connected with 'commerce with foreign nations, or among the several States, or with the Indian tribes.' It may, of consequence, pass the jurisdictional line of New York and act upon the very waters [the Hudson River] to which the prohibition now under consideration applies. . . ." So the same power may pass the line of the State of Illinois and act upon its restriction upon the right of transportation extending over several States, including that one. . . .

We must, therefore, hold that it is not, and never has been, the deliberate opinion of a majority of this court that a statute of a State which attempts to regulate the fares and charges by railroad companies within its limits, for a transportation which constitutes a part of commerce among the States, is a valid law.

Let us see precisely what is the degree of interference with transportation of property or persons from one State to another which this statute proposes. A citizen of New York has goods which he desires to have transported by the railroad companies from that city to the interior of the State of Illinois. A continuous line of rail over which a car loaded with these goods can be carried, and is carried habitually, connects the place of shipment with the place of delivery. He undertakes to make a contract with a person engaged in the carrying business at the end of this route from whence the goods are to start, and he is told by the carrier,

"I am free to make a fair and reasonable contract for this carriage to the line of the State of Illinois, but when the car which carries these goods is to cross the line of that State, pursuing at the same time this continuous tract, I am met by a law of Illinois which forbids me to make a free contract concerning this transportation within that State, and subjects me to certain rules by which I am to be governed as to the charges which the same railroad company in Illinois may make, or has made, with reference to other persons and other places of delivery."

So that while that carrier might be willing to carry these goods from the city of New York to the city of Peoria at the rate of fifteen cents per hundred pounds, he is not permitted to do so because the Illinois railroad company has already charged at the rate of twenty-five cents per hundred pounds for carriage to Gilman, in Illinois, which is eighty-six miles shorter than the distance to Peoria.

So, also, in the present case, the owner of corn, the principal product of the country, desiring to transport it from Peoria, in Illinois, to New York, finds a railroad company willing to do this at the rate of fifteen cents per hundred pounds for a car-load, but is compelled to pay at the rate of twenty-five cents per hundred pounds, because the railroad company has received from a person residing at Gilman twenty-five cents per hundred pounds for the transportation of a car-load of the same class of freight over the same line of road from Gilman to New York. This is the result of the statute of Illinois, in its endeavor to prevent unjust discrimination, as construed by the Supreme Court of that State. The effect of it is, that whatever may be the rate of transportation per mile charged by the railroad company from Gilman to Sheldon, a distance

of twenty-three miles, in which the loading and the unloading of the freight is the largest expense incurred by the railroad company, the same rate per mile must be charged from Peoria to the city of New York.

The obvious injustice of such a rule as this, which railroad companies are by heavy penalties compelled to conform to, in regard to commerce among the States, when applied to transportation which includes Illinois in a long line of carriage through several States, shows the value of the constitutional provision which confides the power of regulating interstate commerce to the Congress of the United States, whose enlarged view of the interests of all the States, and of the railroads concerned, better fits it to establish just and equitable rules.

Of the justice or propriety of the principle which lies at the foundation of the Illinois statute it is not the province of this court to speak. . . . But when it is attempted to apply to transportation through an entire series of States a principle of this kind, and each one of the States shall attempt to establish its own rates of transportation, its own methods to prevent discrimination in rates, or to permit it, the deleterious influence upon the freedom of commerce among the States and upon the transit of goods through those States cannot be overestimated. That this species of regulations is one which must be, if established at all, of a general and national character, and cannot be safely and wisely remitted to local rules and local regulations, we think is clear from what has already been said. And if it be a regulation of commerce, as we think we have demonstrated it is, and as the Illinois court concedes it to be, it must be of that national character, and the regulation can only appropriately exist by general rules and principles, which demand that it should be done by Congress of the United States under the commerce clause of the Constitution. . . .

Another manifestation of relatively uncontrolled corporate excesses in this era was in fund manipulations by banks. The Jay Cooke banking corporation was a depository of federal funds. It failed in 1876 and a House committee investigated the relationship of Cooke and his firm with a "real estate pool" managed by one Kilbourn. When asked to be a witness before the committee about the pool and documents related to it, Kilbourn refused to reply or provide the requested materials. The House of Representatives had him jailed in a District of Columbia jail for 45 days for contempt. Kilbourn challenged the authority of the House, claiming false imprisonment. Justice Miller, for the Court, had Kilbourn released on the ground that the legislature had exercised judicial powers. He wrote that

. . . [The Constitution vests no judicial power] in the Congress or either branch of it, save in the cases specifically enumerated. . . . If the [Committee's investigation] was judicial in its character, if it related to a matter wherein relief or redress could be had only by a judicial proceeding, [it is clear] that the power attempted to be exercised was one confided by the Constitution to the judicial and not to the legislative department of the government. . . .

In all the argument of the case no suggestion has been made of what [Congress] could have done in the way of remedying the wrong or securing the creditors of Jay Cooke & Co., or even the United States. Was it to be simply a fruitless investigation into the personal affairs of individuals? If so, the House of Representatives had no power or authority in the matter more than any other equal number of gentlemen interested for the government of their country. By 'fruitless' we mean that it could result in no valid legislation on the subject to which the inquiry referred.

What was this committee charged to do? To inquire into the nature and history of the real-estate pool. How indefinite! What was the real-estate pool? Is it charged with any crime of offence? If so, the courts alone can punish the members of it. Is it charged with a fraud against the government? Here, again, [only the courts] can afford a remedy. . . . what authority has the House to enter upon this investigation into the private affairs of individuals who hold no office under the government?[16]

Conclusion

By the end of the 1880s the great transformation symbolized by the Compromise of 1877 had become more pronounced. Black rights were afforded less protection. By virtue of Wabash, corporations were able to operate relatively free from either state or federal control. And the elements in the American political system that were increasingly critical of the imbalances developing in the economic, social, and political sectors of the nation began to coalesce. After two decades of post–Civil War defeats, the Democratic Party had emerged as capable of mounting successful presidential campaigns.

Significant changes had taken place in the composition of the Supreme Court since Abraham Lincoln's appointment of a new majority with the selections of Swayne, Davis, Miller, Field, and Chase. President Andrew Johnson made no appointments. During his two terms, President Ulysses S. Grant made four selections to the Supreme Court: Chief Justice Morrison R. Waite (1874), Associate Justice Ward Hunt (1872), Associate Justice William Strong (1870), and Associate Justice Joseph P. Bradley (1870). President Hayes chose Associate Justices John Marshall Harlan (1877) and William Burnham Woods (1880). The brief Presidency of James Garfield produced the appointment of Stanley Matthews (1881). Garfield's successor, Chester Arthur, chose Horace Gray (1881) and Samuel Blatchford (1882). All were chosen by Republican presidents, but with the exception of Harlan, the appointees after Lincoln were ideologically closer to the pro-corporation positions of Stephen J. Field than to the more critical positions of Samuel Freeman Miller.

In his private correspondence to Ballinger, his son-in-law, Miller confidentially described the internal conditions on the Supreme Court in the years leading to the fourth significant political transformation in the United States after the American Revolution, the critical election of 1896. More than 20 years before this election, Justice Miller wrote:

It is vain to contend with judges who have been at the bar the advocates for forty
years of railroad companies, and all the forms of associated capital, when they are
called upon to decide cases where such interests are in contest. All their training, all
their feelings are from the start in favor of those who need no such influence.[17]

The era accentuated by the Compromise of 1877 has been characterized as
one of "capitalist ambition, industrial might, and sectional rigidity." Sidney I.
Pomerantz suggested that

> the outcome of the War and the promise of the Reconstruction forged a new nation-
> alism, with party and section vying for favor at the seat of government and in the
> councils of northern business interests committed to sound money, protective tariffs,
> state and federal subsidies, especially for internal improvements, and all this, para-
> doxically, in a *laissez-faire* political and economic environment.[18]

The Supreme Court's decisions contributed a great deal to the creation of that
paradox. In 1896, as in 1860, the decision-making tendencies of the Supreme
Court became salient in the realignment of political parties, platforms, and, ultimately, sectional behavior.

But the pattern for the selection of economic conservatives—primarily Republican, but occasionally Democratic as in the Presidency of Grover Cleveland—was
established firmly during the terms of President Ulysses S. Grant. Although
seriously challenged on public policy and ethical grounds in the critical election
of 1896, that election did not introduce such Republican doctrinal conservatism
to the Supreme Court but reinstated and reinforced it. The enduring nature of
such conservatism is summarized in Table 6-3, in which Republican conservative
appointees are italicized and Democratic conservative appointees are underlined.
Such conservative influence encompasses the many decades between 1869 and
1937, when a New Deal Democratic majority controlled the court.

REFERENCES

1. Roy F. Nichols and Philip S. Klein, "The Election of 1856" and Elting Morrison, "The
   Election of 1860," in *The Coming to Power*, ed. Arthur M. Schlesinger, Fred Israel (New York:
   Chelsea House, 1971), pp. 91–117 and 118–142, respectively.
2. This discussion and Tables 1 and 2 are adapted from John R. Schmidhauser, "Judicial
   Behavior and the Sectional Crisis of 1837–1860," *Journal of Politics*, 23 (1961): 616–638.
3. 2 Haines and Sherwood, op. cit., pp. 423–430, note 93.
4. John R. Schmidhauser, *The Supreme Court as Final Arbiter in Federal State Relations*, 1789–1957
   (Chapel Hill: University of North Carolina Press, 1958), pp. 51–52.
5. Alfred H. Kelly and Winfred A. Harbison, *The American Constitution*, 5th ed. (New York:
   W. W. Norton and Co., 1976), pp. 350–353.
6. *Congressional Globe*, 37th Congress, 2nd session (December 9, 1861), p. 26.
7. Schmidhauser, *Judges and Justices*, op. cit., p. 46.
8. Charles Grove Haines and Foster Sherwood, *The Role of the Supreme Court in American Government and Politics, 1835–1864* (Berkeley, Los Angeles: University of California Press, 1957),
   pp. 454–481.
9. 16 Wallace 130 (1872).
10. 21 Wallace 162 (1874).
11. 20 Wallace 655 (1874).
12. 123 U. S. 623 (1887).

13. 118 U. S. 394 (1886).
14. 100 U. S. 303 (1879).
15. Sidney I. Pomerantz, "The Election of 1876" in Schlesinger and Israel, (eds.) *The Coming to Power*, op. cit., pp. 168–224; this political transformation bears a remarkable resemblance to the fate of the predecessor of post–Civil War Reconstruction—the Port Royal experiment conducted on the sea islands off Charleston, South Carolina; see Willie Lee Rose, *Rehearsal for Reconstruction: the Port Royal Experiment* (New York: Vintage Books, 1967).
16. *Kilbourn v. Thompson*, 103 U. S. 168 (1881).
17. Cited in Charles Fairman, *Mr. Justice Miller and the Supreme Court* (Cambridge: Harvard University Press, 1939), p. 374.
18. Sidney I. Pomerantz, "The Election of 1876," op. cit., pp. 222–223.

TABLE 6–3 Judicial political generations and critical elections: The persistence of Conservative Republican influence, 1869–1937*

Appointing president and party	Chief Justice	Justices chosen in the era of economic conservatism							
Ulysses S. Grant Republican 1869–1877	M. Waite 1874–1888	*W. Strong* 1870–1880			*W. Hunt* 1872–1882			S. Field 1863–1897, economic conservative appointed by Lincoln	*Court incr. to 9 by act of April 10, 1869* *J. Bradley* 1870–1892
Rutherford B. Hayes Republican 1877–1881		*W. Woods* 1880–1887					J. Harlan 1877–1911, not economic conservative		
James A. Garfield Republican 1881					*S. Matthews* 1881–1889				
Chester A. Arthur Republican 1881–1885				*H. Gray* 1881–1902	*S. Blatchford* 1882–1893				
Grover Cleveland Democrat 1885–1889	M. Fuller 1888–1910	L. Lamar 1888–1893							
Benjamin Harrison Republican 1889–1893		H. Jackson 1893–1895	*H. Brown* 1890–1906			*D. Brewer* 1889–1910			*G. Shiras* 1892–1903
Grover Cleveland Democrat 1893–1897		R. Peckham 1895–1909			E. White 1894–1910 To. C. J.				

*Conservative Republicans are in italics, Conservative Democrats are underlined.

**TABLE 6-3 Judicial political generations and critical elections:
The persistence of Conservative Republican influence, 1869–1937* (continued)**

Appointing president and party	Chief Justice	Justices chosen in the era of economic conservatism							
notes									

Appointing president and party	Chief Justice								
Critical election of 1896: Republicans reassert control over Congress and the presidency									
William McKinley Republican 1897–1901								*J. McKenna 1898–1925*	
Theodore Roosevelt Republican 1901–1909			W. Moody 1906–1910	O. Holmes 1902–1932					*W. Day 1903–1922*
William H. Taft Republican 1909–1913	<u>E. White 1910–1921</u>	<u>H. Lurton 1910–1916</u>	<u>J. Lamar 1910–1916</u>		*W. Devanter 1910–1937*	C. Hughes 1910–1916	*M. Pitney 1912–1922*		
Woodrow Wilson Democrat 1913–1921		<u>J. McReynolds 1914–1941</u>	L. Brandeis 1916–1939			J. Clarke 1906–1922			
Warren G. Harding Republican 1921–1923	*W. Taft 1921–1930*					*G. Sutherland 1922–1938*		*E. Sanford 1923–1930*	*P. Butler 1922–1939*
Calvin Coolidge Republican 1923–1929								H. Stone 1925–1941 (to C.J.)	
Herbert Hoover Republican 1929–1933	*C. Hughes 1930–1941*			B. Cardozo 1932–1938			*W. Roberts 1930–1945*		
Critical election of 1932: Democrats take control of Congress and the presidency									
Franklin D. Roosevelt Democrat 1933–1945	H. Stone 1941–1946	J. Byrnes 1941–1942 W. Rutledge 1943–1949	W. Douglas 1939–1975	F. Frankfurter 1939–1962	H. Black 1937–1971	S. Reed 1938–1957		R. Jackson 1941–1954	F. Murphy 1940–1949

*Conservative Republicans are in italics, Conservative Democrats are underlined.

CHAPTER

7

The Supreme Court and the
Critical Election of 1896

The Triumph of Conservative Principles and
the Decline of Public Participation and Confidence

The era of Republican political dominance ushered in by the critical election of 1860 and accentuated by the Civil War appeared to be coming to an end by the mid–1870s, when the Democrats registered substantial gains in Congress and narrowly missed capturing the presidency. Grover Cleveland's two non-consecutive presidential elections in 1884 and 1892 represented the only Democratic presidential victories since the Civil War. But Cleveland was, in many respects, as conservative as many Republican leaders in this era, and the Democratic justices he appointed were ideologically similar to the appointees chosen by the Republican presidents of the period. Consequently, the growing economic conservatism of the Supreme Court was not interrupted, but accentuated by Cleveland's selections.

By the late 1880s and early 1890s, a largely unheralded but major transformation had taken place on the Supreme Court. Although considerable political attention had been focused upon the replacement of elderly Jacksonian Democrats after their deaths or resignations, the most significant change that took place was the selection of political conservatives with corporate law firm backgrounds. Most of the old Jacksonians had left the Court by the early 1860s—Daniel in 1860, McLean in 1861, Campbell in 1861, Taney in 1864, Catron in 1865, and Wayne in 1867. Grier left in 1870 and Nelson in 1872. Clifford, Buchanan's appointee, survived until 1881. But some of Lincoln's Republican appointees also had left the Court before the 1880s—Chase in 1873 and Davis in 1877. The generation of conservatives committed to keeping a constitutional balance between state and federal governmental authority—Nathan Clifford, David Davis, Ward Hunt, Samuel F. Miller, William Strong, Noah H. Swayne, and Morrison R. Waite—all left the Court between 1877 and 1890.[1] Their Republican and Democratic successors generally were less interested in protecting black minority rights, and more interested in protecting private corporations from *either* state or federal authority. John Marshall Harlan, a Hayes appointee, was the major exception. But Republicans Horace Gray and Samuel Blatchford (both appointed by Arthur in 1882), Democrats Melville W. Fuller, Lucius Q. C. Lamar, Edward D. White, and Rufus W. Peckham (appointed by Cleveland in 1888, 1888, 1894, and 1895, respectively), and Republicans David J. Brewer and Henry B. Brown (appointed by Harrison in 1889 and 1890) fitted this description quite accurately. If Republican and Democratic Court appointees shared common ideological assumptions, why would the doctrinal positions of the Supreme Court figure prominently in the third critical election—that of 1896? Primarily because control of the Democratic nominating convention was wrested from the conservative Democrats (aligned with Cleveland's approach) by the Populist-oriented wing of the party led by William Jennings Bryan. When the Democratic convention was over, the conservative Supreme Court had become a central issue in the 1896 election.

The conflict involved a number of complex issues. Declining agricultural prices, ruinous railroad rates, and the acute economic distress of small and medium-sized communities directly affected by instability in agricultural areas created recurring crises in the last three decades of the 19th century. Although financial institutions and railroad corporations frequently contributed to these problems by speculative ventures and discriminatory price fixing, such institutions and corporations generally were successful in invoking the contract clause in municipal bond default issues, and in devising arguments that permitted them to evade public control and regulation. Conditions of laboring people in a rapidly industrialized society also stimulated discontent, which was accentuated by Court decisions that were virtually all antilabor.

Alan Westin provided a dramatic account of the Supreme Court's influence and the sharp reaction to it in the critical election of 1896. His description detailed the climactic economic struggles over railroad rates, agricultural economic instability, the emergent role of organized labor, and financial policy, which became more intense by the mid-1890s. His analysis of the Democratic national convention of 1896 underscored the fact that the conservative doctrines of the Supreme Court became a major campaign issue.[2] When William Jennings Bryan captured the nomination, the convention adopted most elements of the Populist Party's anti–Court position. Mark Hanna, Republican party leader, seized the opportunity to seek conservative Democratic defectors who recoiled from attacking the Court. But labor and many farmers were influenced by the anti–Court platform of the Bryan Democrats. Several Court decisions—notably the Minnesota Rate Case, *U. S.* v. *E. C. Knight,* called the Sugar Trust Case, *In Re Debs, Pollak* v. *Farmer's Loan and Trust Company,* and *Plessy* v. *Ferguson*—illustrate the conservative doctrinal positions that provoked direct attacks on the Court by Bryan Democrats and Populists.

The Minnesota Rate Case, decided in 1890, virtually overruled *Munn* v. *Illinois* and substituted the Supreme Court's standards for those of the Minnesota legislature in a public policy arena bristling with political and economic controversy.

The decision was perceived by the Court's proregulatory opponents as providing railroad corporations with a virtual guarantee of immunity from state regulation. Most important, the Court asserted its own primacy in this policy arena, thus further weakening state legislative authority.

CHICAGO, MILWAUKEE, AND ST. PAUL RAILWAY COMPANY v. MINNESOTA
134 U. S. 418 (1890)

Justice Blatchford delivered the opinion of the Court:

The construction put upon the statute by the Supreme Court of Minnesota must be accepted by this court, for the purpose of the present case, as conclusive and not to be reëxamined here as to its propriety or accuracy. The Supreme Court authoritatively declares that it is the expressed intention of the legislature of Minnesota, by the statute, that the rates recommended and published by the commission, if it proceeds in the manner pointed out by the act, are not simply advisory, nor merely *prima facie* equal and reasonable, but final and conclusive as to what are equal and reasonable charges; that the law neither contemplates nor allows any issue to be made or inquiry to be had as to their equality or reasonableness in fact; that, under the statute, the rates published by the commission are the only ones that are lawful, and therefore, in contemplation of law the only ones that are equal and reasonable; and that, in a proceeding for a mandamus under the statute, there is no fact to traverse except the violation of law in not complying with the recommendations of the commission. In other words, although the railroad company is forbidden to establish rates that are not equal and reasonable, there is no power in the courts to stay the hands of the commission, if it chooses to establish rates that are unequal and unreasonable.

This being the construction of the statute by which we are bound in considering the present case, we are of opinion that, so construed, it conflicts with the Constitution of the United States in the particulars complained of by the railroad company. It deprives the company of its right to a judicial investigation, by due process of law, under the forms and with the machinery provided by the wisdom of successive ages for the investigation judicially of the truth of a matter in controversy, and substitutes therefore, as an absolute finality, the action of a railroad commission which, in view of the powers conceded to it by the state court, cannot be regarded as clothed with judicial functions or possessing the machinery of a court of justice. . . .

By the second section of the statute in question, it is provided that all charges made by a common carrier for the transportation of passengers or property shall be equal and reasonable. Under this provision, the carrier has a right to make equal and reasonable charges for such transportation. In the present case, the return alleged that the rate of charge fixed by the commission was not equal or reasonable, and the Supreme Court held that the statute deprived the company of the right to show that judicially. The question of the reasonableness of a rate of charge for transportation by a railroad company, involving as it does the element of reasonableness both as regards the company and as regards the public, is eminently a question for judicial investigation, requiring due process of law for its determination. If the company is deprived of the power of charging reasonable rates for the use of its property, and such deprivation takes place in the absence of an investigation by judicial machinery, it is deprived of the lawful use of its property, and thus, in substance and effect, of the property itself, without due process of law and in violation of the Constitution of the United States; and in so far as it is thus deprived, while other persons are permitted to receive reasonable profits upon their invested capital, the company is deprived of the equal protection of the laws. . . .

Justice Bradley, with whom concurred Justice Gray and Justice Lamar, dissented:

I cannot agree to the decision of the court in this case. It practically overrules *Munn v. Illinois*, and the several railroad cases that were decided at the same time. The governing principle of those cases was that the regulation and settlement of the fares of railroads and other public accommodations is a legislative prerogative and not a judicial one. This is a principle which I regard as of great importance. . . .

It is always a delicate thing for the courts to make an issue with the legislative department of the government, and they should never do so if it is possible to avoid it. By the decision now made we declare, in effect, that the judiciary, and not the legislature, is the final arbiter in the regulation of fares and freights of railroads and the charges of other public accommodations. It is an assumption of authority on the part of the judiciary which . . . it has no right to make. . . .

Whatever tribunal has jurisdiction, its decisions are final and conclusive unless an appeal is given therefrom. The important question always is, what is the lawful tribunal for the particular case? In my judgement, in the present case, the proper tribunal was the legislature, or the board of commissioners which it created for the purpose. . . .

The triumph of conservatism in race, taxation, and labor issues

The year 1895 represented a climax of major conservative decision making. The scope and objectives of antitrust legislation were central to conservative judicial policymaking. The Sherman Antitrust Act had been passed in 1890 during Benjamin Harrison's second term, but President Harrison, Attorney General William H. H. Miller, and Solicitor General William Howard Taft were not very enthusiastic about enforcing the act. The strong public and congressional responses to corporate abuse of economic power were summed up earlier by President Grover Cleveland in his annual message of December 3, 1888:

> As we view the achievements of aggregated capital we discover the existence of trusts, combinations, and monopolies, while the citizen is struggling far in the rear or is trampled to death beneath an iron heel. Corporations which should be the carefully restrained creatures of the law and the servants of the people, are fast becoming the people's masters. [Their arrogance] appears in the sordid disregard of all but personal interests, in the refusal to abate for the benefit of others one iota of selfish advantage, and in combinations to perpetuate such advantages through efforts to control legislation and improperly influence the suffrages of the people.[3]

Although Grover Cleveland had strongly criticized trusts and monopolies, he selected as his attorney general Richard Olney, a lawyer who had served as counsel for the whiskey interests in the so-called Whiskey Trust Case that ended when the indictment was held "insufficient." Shortly after taking office, Olney indicated to Secretary of the Treasury John G. Carlisle that a group of Boston bankers and merchants were willing to support repeal of the Antitrust Act with money and work. Olney requested a list of Senators "who might be persuaded to see the thing in the right light."[4] As attorney general, Olney did not begin any antitrust action, but chose a pending case involving the sugar trust to test the act's validity. Federal attorneys were later criticized for a weak presentation of the case against the trust, especially concerning the relationship of local refining and interstate commerce. Olney indicated he was pleased at the outcome! In 1895, President Cleveland replaced him with a more vigorous antitrust lawyer, Judson Harmon. Nevertheless, under Presidents Harrison, Cleveland, and McKinley the Sherman Antitrust Act was not invoked very effectively against corporations.

The E. C. Knight case emasculated the Sherman Antitrust Act by defining production so narrowly as to leave it outside the scope of the act. The Sherman Antitrust Act in simple and direct terms had declared that "every contract, combination in the form of trust or otherwise, or conspiracy, in restraint of trade or commerce among the several states, or with foreign nations, is hereby declared illegal." By the Court's new narrow definition, the American Sugar Refining Company, which had gained control of 94 percent of all sugar refining inside the nation, did not fall within the scope of the act.

UNITED STATES v. E. C. KNIGHT COMPANY
156 U. S. 1 (1895)

Chief Justice Fuller delivered the opinion of the court:

. . . The fundamental question is, whether conceding that the existence of a monopoly in manufacture is established by the evidence, that monopoly can be directly suppressed under the act of congress in the mode attempted by this bill.

It cannot be denied that the power of a State to protect the lives, health, and property of its citizens, and to preserve good order and the public morals, "the power to govern men and things within the limits of its dominion," is a power originally and always belonging to the States, not surrendered by them to the general government, nor directly restrained by the Constitution of the United States, and essentially exclusive. The relief of the citizens of each State from the burden of monopoly and the evils resulting from the restraint of trade among such citizens was left with the States to deal with, and this court has recognized their possession of that power even to the extent of holding that an employment or business carried on by private individuals, when it becomes a matter of such public interest and importance as to create a common charge or burden upon the citizen; in other words, when it becomes a practical monopoly, to which the citizen is compelled to resort and by means of which a tribute can be exacted from the community, is subject to regulation by state legislative power. On the other hand, the power of Congress to regulate commerce among the several States is also exclusive. The Constitution does not provide that interstate commerce shall be free, but, by the grant of this exclusive power to regulate it, it was left free except as Congress might impose restraints. Therefore it has been determined that the failure of Congress to exercise this exclusive power in any case is an expression of its will that the subject shall be free from restrictions or impositions upon it by the several States, and if a law passed by a State in the exercise of its acknowledged powers comes into conflict with that will, the Congress and the State cannot occupy the position of equal opposing sovereignties, because the Constitution declares its supremacy and that of the laws passed in pursuance thereof; and that which is not supreme must yield to that which is supreme. "Commerce, undoubtedly, is traffic," said Chief Justice Marshall, "but it is something more; it is intercourse. It describes the commercial intercourse between nations and parts of nations in all its branches, and is regulated by prescribing rules for carrying on that intercourse." That which belongs to commerce is within the jurisdiction of the police power of the State. . . .

The argument is that the power to control the manufacture of refined sugar is a monopoly over a necessary of life, to the enjoyment of which by a large part of the population of the United States interstate commerce is indispensable, and that, therefore, the general government in the exercise of the power to regulate commerce may repress such monopoly directly and set aside the instruments which have created it. But this argument cannot be confined to necessaries of life merely, and must include all articles of general consumption. Doubtless the power to control the manufacture of a given thing involves in a certain sense the control of its disposition, but this is a secondary and not the primary sense; and although the exercise of that power may result in bringing the operation of commerce into play, it does not control it, and affects it only incidentally and indirectly. Commerce succeeds to manufacture, and is not a part of it. The power to regulate commerce is the power to prescribe the rule by which commerce shall be governed, and is a power independent of the power to suppress monopoly. But it may operate in repression of monopoly whenever that comes within the rules by which commerce is governed or whenever the transaction is itself a monopoly of commerce.

It is vital that the independence of the commercial power and of the police power, and the delimitation between them, however sometimes perplexing, should always be recognized and observed, for while the one furnishes the strongest bond of union, the other is essential to the preservation of the autonomy of the States as required by our dual form of government; and acknowledged evils, however grave and urgent they may appear to be, had better be borne, than the risk be run, in the effort to suppress them, of more serious consequences by resort to expedients of even doubtful constitutionality. . . .

It will be perceived how far reaching the proposition is that the power of dealing with a monopoly directly may be exercised by the general government whenever interstate or international commerce may be ultimately affected. The regulation of commerce applies to the subjects of commerce and not to matters of internal police. Contracts to buy, sell, or exchange goods to be transported among the several states, the transportation and its instrumentalities, and articles bought, sold, or exchanged for the purpose of such transit among the states, or put in the way of transit, may be regulated, but this is because they form part of interstate trade or commerce. The fact that an article is manufactured for export to another state does not of itself make it an article of interstate commerce, and the intent of the manufacture does not determine the time when the article or product passes from the control of the state and belongs to commerce. . . .

Contracts, combinations, or conspiracies to control domestic enterprise in manufacture, agriculture, mining, production in all its forms, or to raise or lower prices or wages, might unquestionably tend to restrain external as well as domestic trade, but the restraint would be an indirect result, however inevitable and whatever its extent, and such result would not necessarily determine the object of the contract, combination, or conspiracy.

Again, all the authorities agree that in order to vitiate a contract or combination it is not essential that its result should be a complete monopoly; it is sufficient if it really tends to that end and to deprive the public of the advantages which flow from free competition. Slight reflection will show that if the national power extends to all contracts and combinations in manufacture, agriculture, mining, and other productive industries, whose ultimate result may affect external commerce, comparatively little of business operations and affairs would be left for state control.

It was in the light of well-settled principles that the act of July 2, 1890, was framed. Congress did not attempt thereby to assert the power to deal with monopoly directly as such; or to limit and restrict the rights of corporations created by the States or the citizens of the States in the acquisition, control, or disposition of property; or to regulate or prescribe the price or prices at which such property or the products thereof should be sold; or to make criminal the acts of persons in the acquisition and control of property which the States of their residence or creation sanctioned or permitted. Aside from the provisions applicable where Congress might exercise municipal power, what the law struck at was combinations, contracts, and conspiracies to monopolize trade and commerce among the several States or with foreign nations; but the contracts and acts of the defendants related exclusively to the acquisition of the Philadelphia refineries and the business of sugar refining in Pennsylvania, and bore no direct relation to commerce between the States or with foreign nations. . . . There was nothing in the proofs to indicate any intention to put a restraint upon trade or commerce, and the fact, as we have seen, that trade or commerce might be indirectly affected was not enough to entitle complainants to a decree. . . .

Justice Harlan dissented:

. . . While the opinion of the court in this case does not declare the Act of 1890 to be unconstitutional, it defeats the main object for which it was passed. For, it is, in effect, held that the statute would be unconstitutional if interpreted as embracing such unlawful restraints upon the purchasing of goods in one state to be carried to another state as necessarily arise from the *existence* of combinations formed for the purpose and with the effect, not only monopolizing the ownership of all such goods in every part of the country, but of controlling the prices for them in all the states. This view of the scope of the Act leaves the public, so far as national power is concerned, entirely at the mercy of combinations which arbitrarily control the prices of articles purchased to be transported from one state to another state. I cannot assent to that view. In my judgment, the general government is not placed by the Constitution in such a condition of helplessness that it must fold its arms and remain inactive while capital combines, under the name of a corporation, to destroy competition, not in one state only, but throughout the entire country, in the buying and selling of articles— especially the necessaries of life—that go into commerce among the states. The doctrine of the autonomy of the states cannot properly be invoked to justify a denial of power in the national government to meet such an emergency, involving as it does that freedom of commercial intercourse among the states which the Constitution sought to attain.

It is said that there are no proofs in the record which indicate an intention upon the part of the American Sugar Refining Company and its associates to put a restraint upon trade or commerce. Was it necessary that formal proof be made that the persons engaged in this combination admitted, in words, that they intended to restrain trade or commerce? Did any one expect to find in the written agreements which resulted in the formation of this combination a distinct expression of a purpose to restrain interstate trade or commerce? Men who form and control these combinations are too cautious and wary to make such admissions orally or in writing. Why, it is conceded that the object of this combination was to obtain control of the business of making and selling refined sugar throughout the entire country. Those interested in its operations will be satisfied with nothing less than to have the whole population of America pay tribute to them.

That object is disclosed upon the very face of the transactions described in the bill. And it is proved—indeed, is conceded—that the object has been accomplished to the extent that the American Sugar Refining Company now controls ninety-eight per cent of all the sugar refining business in the country, and therefore controls the price of that article everywhere. Now, the mere existence of a combination having such an object and possessing such extraordinary power is itself, under settled principles of law—there being no adjudged case to the contrary in this country—a direct restraint of trade in the article for the control of the sales of which in this country that combination was organized. And that restraint is felt in all the states, for the reason, known to all, that the article in question goes, was intended to go, and must always go, into commerce among the several states, and into the homes of people in every condition of life.

A decree recognizing the freedom of commercial intercourse as embracing the right to buy goods to be transported from one state to another, without buyers being burdened by unlawful restraints imposed by combinations of corporations or individuals, so far from disturbing or endangering, would tend to preserve the autonomy of the states, and protect the people of all the states against dangers so portentous as to excite apprehension for the safety of our liberties. If this be not a sound interpretation of the Constitution, it is easy to perceive that interstate traffic, so far as it involves the price to be paid for articles necessary to the comfort and well being of the people in all the states, may pass under the absolute control of overshadowing combinations having financial resources without limit and an audacity in the accomplishment of their objects that recognizes none of the restraints of moral obligations controlling the action of individuals; combinations governed entirely by the law of greed and selfishness—so powerful that no single state is able to overthrow them and give the required protection to the whole country, and so all-pervading that they threaten the integrity of our institutions.

We have before us the case of a combination which absolutely controls, or may, at its discretion, control the price of all refined sugar in this country. Suppose another combination, organized for private gain and to control prices, should obtain possession of all the large flour mills in the United States; another, of all the grain elevators; another, of all the oil territory; another, of all the salt producing regions; another, of all the cotton mills; and another, of all the great establishments for slaughtering animals, and the preparation of meats. What power is competent to protect the

people of the United States against such dangers except a national power—one that is capable of exerting its sovereign authority throughout every part of the territory and over all the people of the nation?

To the general government has been committed the control of commercial intercourse among the states, to the end that it may be free at all times from any restraints except such as Congress may impose or permit for the benefit of the whole country. The common government of all the people is the only one that can adequately deal with a matter which directly and injuriously affects the entire commerce of the country, which concerns equally all the people of the Union, and which, it must be confessed, cannot be adequately controlled by any one state. Its authority should not be so weakened by construction that it cannot reach and eradicate evils that, beyond all question, tend to defeat an object which that government is entitled, by the Constitution, to accomplish. "Powerful and ingenious minds," this court has said, "taking, as postulates, that the powers expressly granted to the government of the Union, are to be contracted by construction into the narrowest possible compass, and that the original powers of the states are retained if any possible construction will retain them, may, by a course of well digested, but refined and metaphysical reasoning, founded on these premises, explain away the Constitution of our country, and leave it, a magnificent structure, indeed, to look at, but totally unfit for use. They may so entangle and perplex the understanding as to obscure principles which were before thought quite plain, and induce doubts where, if the mind were to pursue its own course, none would be perceived." . . .

While a decree annulling the contracts under which the combination in question was formed, may not, in view of the facts disclosed, be effectual to accomplish the object of the Act of 1890, I perceive no difficulty in the way of the court passing a decree declaring that that combination imposes an unlawful restraint upon trade and commerce among the states, and perpetually enjoining it from further prosecuting any business pursuant to the unlawful agreements under which it was formed or by which it was created. Such a decree would be within the scope of the bill, and is appropriate to the end which Congress intended to accomplish, namely, to protect the freedom of commercial intercourse among the states against combinations and conspiracies which impose unlawful restraints upon such intercourse.

For the reasons stated I dissent from the opinion and judgment of the court.

While attempts to invoke the Sherman Act against business corporations were singularly unsuccessful, the legislation was utilized tellingly against organized labor. A federal district judge granted an injunction against a union upon the request of President Harrison's attorney general. In *United States* v. *Workingman's Amalgamated Council*, the judge made the following statutory interpretation:

> I think the congressional debates show that the statute had its origin in the evils of massed capital; but, when Congress came to formulating the prohibition which is the yardstick for measuring one complaintant's right to the injunction, it expressed it in these words: "Every contract or combination in the form of trust, or otherwise in restraint of trade or commerce among the several states or with foreign nations, is hereby declared to be illegal." The subject had so broadened in the minds of the legislators that the source of the evil was not regarded as material, and the evil in its entirety dealt with. They made the interdiction include combinations of labor. . . .[5]

During the bitterly fought Pullman strike, Attorney General Olney was reluctant to invoke the Sherman Act against railroad corporations charged with deliberately refraining from rail operations to provoke federal strike-breaking intervention. A Chicago circuit court handed down a broad injunction against the strikers based in part on the Sherman Act. Ultimately, the Supreme Court's validation of this injunction in *In Re Debs* was based on broader grounds. There is ample evidence, however, that in the first decade of the Antitrust Act's application, it did not become the basis for effective injunctive action against the evils for which it was enacted—corporate trusts and monopolies. Instead, the injunction— a court order directing an individual, group, or organization to do or stop doing something—became a favorite weapon invoked by corporations against labor unions for several decades and was invoked more recently in the 1982 Iowa Beef Corporation strike in Dakota City, Nebraska. *In Re Debs* was viewed in the 1890s as a stunning judicial setback to organized labor.

IN RE DEBS
158 U. S. 564 (1895)

Justice Brewer delivered the opinion of the Court:

Congress has exercised the power granted in respect to interstate commerce in a variety of legislative acts. . . .

Under the power vested in Congress to establish post offices and post roads, Congress has, by a mass of legislation, established the great post office system of the country, with all its detail of organization, its machinery for the transaction of business, defining what shall be carried and what not, and the prices of carriage, and also prescribing penalties for all offences against it.

Obviously these powers given to the national government over interstate commerce and in respect to the transportation of the mails were not dormant and unused. Congress had taken hold of these two matters, and by various and specific acts had assumed and exercised the powers given to it, and was in the full discharge of its duty to regulate interstate commerce and carry the mails. The validity of such exercise and the exclusiveness of its control had been again and again presented to this court for consideration. It is curious to note the fact that in a large proportion of the cases in respect to interstate commerce brought to this court the question presented was of the validity of state legislation in its bearings upon interstate commerce, and the uniform course of decision has been to declare that it is not within the competency of a State to legislate in such a manner as to obstruct interstate commerce. If a State with its recognized powers of sovereignty is impotent to obstruct interstate commerce, can it be that any mere voluntary association of individuals within the limits of that State has a power which the State itself does not possess?

As, under the Constitution, power over interstate commerce and the transportation of the mails is vested in the national government, and Congress by virtue of such grant has assumed actual and direct control, it follows that the national government may prevent any unlawful and forcible interference therewith. But how shall this be accomplished? Doubtless, it is within the competency of Congress to prescribe by legislation that any interference with these matters shall be offences against the United States, and prosecuted and punished by indictment in the proper courts. But is that the only remedy? Have the vast interests of the nation in interstate commerce, and in the transportation of the mails, no other protection than lies in the possible punishment of those who interfere with it? To ask the question is to answer it. . . .

The entire strength of the nation may be used to enforce in any part of the land the full and free exercise of all national powers and the security of all rights entrusted by the Constitution to its care. The strong arm of the national government may be put forth to brush away all obstructions to the freedom of interstate commerce on the transportation of the mails. If the emergency arises, the army of the nation and all its militia are at the service of the Nation to compel obedience to its laws.

But passing to the second question, is there no other alternative than the use of force on the part of the executive authorities whenever obstructions arise to the freedom of interstate commerce or the transportation of the mails? Is the army the only instrument by which rights of the public can be enforced and the peace of the nation preserved? Grant that any public nuisance may be forcibly abated either at the instance of the authorities, or by any individual suffering private damage therefrom, the existence of this right of forcible abatement is not inconsistent with nor does it destroy the right of appeal in an orderly way to the courts for a judicial determination, and an exercise of their powers by writ of injunction and otherwise to accomplish the same result. . . .

Neither can it be doubted that the government has such an interest in the subject-matter as enables it to appear as party plaintiff in this suit. It is said that equity only interferes for the protection of property, and that the government has no property interest. A sufficient reply is that the United States have a property in the mails, the protection of which was one of the purposes of this bill. . . .

We do not care to place our decision upon this ground alone. Every government, entrusted, by the very terms of its being, with powers and duties to be exercised and discharged for the general welfare, has a right to apply to its own courts for any proper assistance in the exercise of the one and the discharge of the other, and it is no sufficient answer to its appeal to one of those courts that it has no pecuniary interest in the matter. The obligations which it is under to promote the interest of all, and to prevent the wrongdoing of one resulting in injury to the general welfare, is often of itself sufficient to give it a standing in court. This proposition in some of its relations has heretofore received the sanction of this court. . . .

Again, it is objected that it is outside of the jurisdiction of a court of equity to enjoin the commission of crimes. This, as a general proposition, is unquestioned. A chancellor has no criminal jurisdiction. Something more than the threatened commission of an offense against the laws of the land is necessary to call into exercise the injunctive powers of the court. There must be some interferences, actual or threatened, with property or rights of a pecuniary nature, but when such interferences appear the jurisdiction of a court of equity arises, and is not destroyed by the fact that they are accompanied by or are themselves violations of the criminal law. . . .

Further, it is said by counsel in their brief:

"No case can be cited where such a bill in behalf of the sovereign has been entertained against riot and mob violence, though occurring on the highway. It is not such fitful and temporary obstruction that constitutes a nuisance. The strong hand of executive power is required to deal with such lawless demonstrations.

"The courts should stand aloof from them and not invade executive prerogative, nor even at the behest or request of the executive travel out of the beaten path of well-settled judicial authority. A mob cannot be suppressed by injunction; nor can its leaders be tried, convicted, and sentenced in equity.

"It is too great a strain upon the judicial branch of the government to impose this essentially executive and military power upon courts of chancery."

We do not perceive that this argument questions the jurisdiction of the court, but only the expediency of the action of the government in applying for its process. . . . But does not counsel's argument imply too much? Is it to be assumed that these defendants were conducting a rebellion or inaugurating a revolution, and that they and their associates were thus placing themselves beyond the reach of the civil process of the courts? . . .

We enter into no examination of the [Sherman] act . . . upon which the Circuit Court relied mainly to sustain its jurisdiction. It must not be understood from this that we dissent from the conclusions of that court in reference to the scope of the act, but simply that we prefer to rest our judgment on the broader ground which has been discussed in this opinion, believing it of importance that the principles underlying it should be fully stated and affirmed. . . .

When Congress adopted a federal income tax statute in 1894, the law was immediately challenged in a test case. A stockholder sued a corporation to prevent payment of the tax on the ground that it was a direct tax, which must be apportioned among the states by population. A Civil War federal income tax had been upheld against a similar challenge in *Springer* v. *the United States*.[6] But in *Pollack* v. *Farmers' Loan and Trust Company*, the majority reversed that position and rendered the highly controversial decision that led to adoption of the income tax amendment (the 16th) in 1913.

The legislative history of the income tax was one of bitter antagonism. Opponents predicted that the Supreme Court would hold the measure unconstitutional, and proponents retorted that if long-standing precedents (those established in the Hylton and Springer cases) were overturned, it would be evidence that the power of corporate wealth extended beyond the Congress to the Supreme Court.[7] Shortly after the income tax statute went into effect on January 1, 1895, a number of corporate attorneys arranged several suits to test the constitutionality of the act before the collection of the tax took place. They persuaded a stockholder to bring suit against a corporation to prohibit a breach of trust by alleged illegal payment of the income tax by the treasurer of the corporation. A formidable group of leading corporate lawyers rushed the test case to the Supreme Court, where it was argued in March 1895 and decided in the same year. Chief Justice Fuller wrote the majority opinion, striking down the statute. Major portions of his opinion and parts of the dissents of Justices Harlan and White are included below.

POLLACK v. FARMER'S LOAN AND TRUST COMPANY
158 U. S. 601 (1895)

Chief Justice Fuller delivered the opinion of the Court:

The Constitution divided Federal taxation into two great classes, the class of direct taxes, and the class of duties, imports, and excises; and prescribed two rules which qualified the grant of power as to each class.

The power to lay direct taxes apportioned among the several States in proportion to their representation in the popular branch of Congress, a representation based on population as ascertained by the census, was plenary and absolute, but to lay direct taxes without apportionment was forbidden. The power to lay duties, imposts, and excises was subject to the qualification that the imposition must be uniform throughout the United States.

Our previous decision was confined to the consideration of the validity of the tax on the income from real estate, and on the income from municipal bonds. The question thus limited was whether such taxation was direct or not, in the meaning of the Constitution; and

the court went no farther, as to the tax on the income from real estate, than to hold that it fell within the same class as the source whence the income was derived, that is, that a tax upon the realty and a tax upon the receipts therefrom were alike direct; while as to the income from municipal bonds, that could not be taxed because of want of power to tax the source, and no reference was made to the nature of the tax as being direct or indirect.

We are now permitted to broaden the field of inquiry, and to determine to which of the two great classes a tax upon a person's entire income, whether derived from rents, or products, or otherwise, or real estate, or from bonds, stocks, or other forms of personal property, belongs; and we are unable to conclude that the enforced subtraction from the yield of all the owner's real or personal property, in the manner prescribed, is so different from a tax upon the property itself, that it is not a direct, but an indirect tax, in the meaning of the Constitution. . . .

The Constitution prohibits any direct tax, unless in proportion to numbers as ascertained by the census; . . . is it not an evasion of that prohibition to hold that a general unapportioned tax, imposed upon all property owners as a body for or in respect of their property, is not direct, in the meaning of the Constitution, because confined to the income therefrom?

Whatever the speculative views of political economists or revenue reformers may be, can it be properly held that the Constitution, taken in its plain and obvious sense, and with due regard to the circumstances attending the formation of the government, authorizes a general unapportioned tax on the products of the farm and the rents of real estate, although imposed merely because of ownership and with no possible means of escape from payment, as belonging to a totally different class from that which includes the property from whence the income proceeds?

There can be but one answer, unless the constitutional restriction is to be treated as utterly illusory and futile, and the object of its framers defeated. We find it impossible to hold that a fundamental requisition, deemed so important as to be enforced by two provisions, one affirmative and one negative, can be refined away by forced distinctions between that which gives value to property, and the property itself.

Nor can we perceive any ground why the same reasoning does not apply to capital in personalty held for the purpose of income or ordinarily yielding income, and to the income therefrom. All the real estate of the country, and all its invested personal property, are open to the direct operation of the taxing power if an apportionment be made according to the Constitution. The Constitution does not say that no direct tax shall be laid by apportionment on any other property than land; on the contrary, it forbids all unapportioned direct taxes; and we know of no warrant for excepting personal property from the exercise of the power, or any reason why an apportioned direct tax cannot be laid and assessed, as Mr. Gallatin said in his report when Secretary of the Treasury in 1812, "upon the same objects of taxation on which the direct taxes levied under the authority of the State are laid and assessed."

Personal property of some kind is of general distribution; and so are incomes, though the taxable range thereof might be narrowed through large exemptions. . . .

We have unanimously held in this case that, so far as this law operates on the receipts from municipal bonds, it cannot be sustained, because it is a tax on the power of the States, and on their instrumentalities to borrow money, and consequently repugnant to the Constitution. But if, as contended, the interest when received has become merely money in the recipient's pocket, and taxable as such without reference to the source from which it came, the question is immaterial whether it could have been originally taxed at all or not. This was admitted by the Attorney General with characteristic candor; and it follows that, if the revenue derived from municipal bonds cannot be taxed because the source cannot be, the same rule applies to revenue from any other source not subject to the tax; and the lack of power to levy any but an apportioned tax on real and personal property equally exists as to the revenue therefrom.

Admitting that this act taxes the income of property irrespective of its source, still we cannot doubt that such a tax is necessarily a direct tax in the meaning of the Constitution. . . .

Being direct, and therefore to be laid by apportionment, is there any real difficulty in doing so? Cannot Congress, if the necessity exist of raising thirty, forty, or any other number of million dollars for the support of the government, in addition to the revenue from duties, imposts, and excises, apportion the quota of each State upon the basis of the census, and thus advise it of the payment which must be made, and proceed to assess that amount on all the real and personal property and the income of all persons in the State, and collect the same if the State does not in the meantime assume and pay its quota and collect the amount according to its own system and in its own way? Cannot Congress do this, as respects either or all these subjects of taxation, and deal with each in such manner as might be deemed expedient . . . ? Inconveniences might possibly attend the levy of an income tax, notwithstanding the listing of receipts, when adjusted, furnishes its own valuation; but that it is apportionable is hardly denied, although it is asserted that it would operate so unequally as to be undesirable. . . .

We are not here concerned with the question whether an income tax be or be not desirable, nor whether such a tax would enable the government to diminish taxes on consumption and duties on imports, and to enter upon what may be believed to be a reform of its fiscal and commercial system. Questions of that character belong to the controversies of political parties, and cannot be settled by judicial decision. In these cases our province is to determine whether this income tax on the revenue from property does or does not belong to the class of direct taxes. If it does, it is, being unapportioned, in violation of the Constitution, and we must so declare.

Differences have often occurred in this court— differences exist now—but there has never been a time in its history when there has been a difference of opinion as to its duty to announce its deliberate conclusions unaffected by considerations not pertaining to the case in hand. . . .

Our conclusions may, therefore, be summed up as follows:

First. We adhere to the opinion already announced, that, taxes on real estate being indisputably direct taxes, taxes on the rents or income of real estate are equally direct taxes.

Second. We are of opinion that taxes on personal property, or on the income of personal property, are likewise direct taxes.

Third. The tax imposed by sections twenty-seven to thirty-seven, inclusive, of the act of 1894, so far as it falls on the income of real estate and of personal property, being a direct tax within the meaning of the Constitution, and, therefore, unconstitutional and void because not apportioned according to representation, all those sections, constituting one entire scheme of taxation, are necessarily invalid. . . .

Here I close my opinion. I could not say less in view of questions of such gravity that go down to the very foundation of the government. If the provisions of the Constitution can be set aside by an Act of Congress, where is the course of usurpation to end? The present assault upon capital is but the beginning. It will be but the stepping-stone to others, larger and more sweeping, till our political contests will become a war of the poor against the rich; a war constantly growing in intensity and bitterness. "If the court sanctions the power of discriminating taxation, and nullifies the uniformity mandate of the Constitution," as said by one who has been all his life a student of our institutions, "it will mark the hour when the sure decadence of our present government will commence." If the purely arbitrary limitation of $4000 in the present law can be sustained, none having less than that amount of income being assessed or taxed for the support of the government, the limitation of future Congresses may be fixed at a much larger sum, at five or ten or twenty thousand dollars, parties possessing an income of that amount alone being bound to bear the burdens of government; or the limitation may be designated at such an amount as a board of "walking delegates" may deem necessary. There is no safety in allowing the limitation to be adjusted except in strict compliance with the mandates of the Constitution which requires its taxation, if imposed by direct taxes, to be apportioned among the states according to their representation, and if imposed by indirect taxes, to be uniform in operation and, so far as practicable, in proportion to their property, equal upon all citizens. Unless the rule of the Constitution governs, a majority may fix the limitation at such rate as will not include any of their own number.

I am of opinion that the whole law of 1894 should be declared void and without any binding force . . .

Justice White dissented:

. . . My strong convictions forbid that I take part in a conclusion which seems to me so full of peril to the country. I am unwilling to do so, without reference to the question of what my personal opinion upon the subject might be if the question were a new one, and was thus unaffected by the action of the framers, the history of the government, and the long line of decisions by this court. The wisdom of our forefathers in adopting a written Constitution has often been impeached upon the theory that the interpretation of a written instrument did not afford as complete protection to liberty as would be enjoyed under a Constitution made up of the traditions of a free people. Writing, it has been said, does not insure greater stability than tradition does, while it destroys flexibility. The answer has always been that by the foresight of the fathers the construction of our written Constitution was ultimately confided to this body, which, from the nature of its judicial structure, could always be relied upon to act with perfect freedom from the influence of faction and to preserve the benefits of consistent interpretation. The fundamental conception of a judicial body is that of one hedged about by precedents which are binding on the court without regard to the personality of its members. Break down this belief in judicial continuity, and let it be felt that on great constitutional questions this court is to depart from the settled conclusions of its predecessors, and to determine them all according to the mere opinion of those who temporarily fill its bench, and our Constitution will, in my judgment, be bereft of value and become a most dangerous instrument to the rights and liberties of the people. . . .

Justice Harlan also dissented:

In my judgment—to say nothing of the disregard of the former adjudications of this court, and of the settled practice of the government—this decision may well excite the gravest apprehensions. It strikes at the very foundations of national authority, in that it denies to the general government a power which is, or may become, vital to the very existence and preservation of the Union in a national emergency, such as that of war with a great commercial nation, during which the collection of all duties upon imports will cease or be materially diminished. It tends to reëstablish that condition of helplessness in which Congress found itself during the period of the Articles of Confederation, when it was without authority by laws operating directly upon individuals, to lay and collect, through its own agents, taxes sufficient to pay the debts and defray the expenses of government, but was dependent, in all such matters, upon the good will of the States, and their promptness in meeting requisitions made upon them by Congress.

Why do I say that the decision just rendered impairs or menaces the national authority? The reason is so apparent that it need only be stated. In its practical operation this decision withdraws from national taxation not only all incomes derived from real estate, but tangible personal property, "*invested* personal property, bonds, stocks, investments of all kinds," and the income that may be derived from such property. This results from the fact that by the decision of the court, all such personal property and all incomes from real estate and personal property, are placed beyond national taxation otherwise than by *apportionment* among the States *on the basis* simply *of population.* No such apportionment can possibly be made without doing gross injustice to the many for the benefit of the favored few in particular States. . . .

I cannot assent to an interpretation of the Constitution that impairs and cripples the just powers of the National Government in the essential matter of taxation, and at the same time discriminates against the greater part of the people of our country.

The practical effect of the decision to-day is to give to certain kinds of property a position of favoritism and advantage inconsistent with the fundamental principles of our social organization, and to invest them with power and influence that may be perilous to that portion of the American people upon whom rests the larger part of the burdens of the government, and who ought not to be subjected to the dominion of aggregated wealth any more than the property of the country should be at the mercy of the lawless.

The exhortative language employed by Chief Justice Fuller and by Justices White and Harlan in the Pollack decision denote the mounting tensions in this divisive era. One of the most deep-seated issues, race relations, was not yet a major political issue. Although some Republican politicians invoked the Civil War and the treatment afforded blacks by Southern Democrats, after the Hayes-Tilden controversy was resolved in Hayes' favor, most national Republican leaders accepted the reestablishment of white political and social domination in the South. Southern efforts to establish caste-like distinctions short of slavery were not a major issue between Bryan and McKinley. Thus, when the Supreme Court decided that a Louisiana statute providing for "separate but equal" seating on railway cars was constitutional, the question did not play a significant role in the critical election of 1896. Ironically, Justice Brown, a Northern Republican from Michigan, wrote the majority opinion in the case involving the issue, while Justice John Marshall Harlan, a former Kentucky slaveholder and Democrat turned Republican, dissented strongly. Major portions of the majority and dissenting opinions are reproduced below:

PLESSY v. FERGUSON
163 U. S. 537 (1896)

Justice Brown delivered the opinion of the court:

This case turns upon the constitutionality of an act of the General Assembly of the State of Louisiana, passed in 1890, providing for separate railway carriages for the white and colored races. . . .

The information filed in the criminal District Court charged in substance that Plessy, being a passenger between two stations within the State of Louisiana, was assigned by officers of the company to the coach used for the race to which he belonged, but he insisted upon going into a coach used by the race to which he did not belong. Neither in the information nor plea was his particular race or color averred.

The petition for the writ of prohibition averred that petitioner was seven eighths Caucasian and one eighth African blood; that the mixture of colored blood was not discernible in him, and that he was entitled to every right, privilege and immunity secured to citizens of the United States of the white race; and that, upon such theory, he took possession of a vacant seat in a coach where passengers of the white race were accommodated, and was ordered by the conductor to vacate said coach and take a seat in another assigned to persons of the colored race, and having refused to comply with such demand he was forcibly ejected with the aid of a police officer, and imprisoned in the parish jail to answer a charge of having violated the above act.

The constitutionality of this act is attacked upon the ground that it conflicts both with the Thirteenth Amendment of the Constitution, abolishing slavery, and the Fourteenth Amendment, which prohibits certain restrictive legislation on the part of the States.

1. That it does not conflict with the Thirteenth Amendment, which abolished slavery and involuntary servitude, except as a punishment for crime, is too clear for argument. Slavery implies involuntary servitude— a state of bondage; the ownership of mankind as a chattel, or at least the control of the labor and services of one man for the benefit of another, and the absence of a legal right to the disposal of his own person, property and services. This amendment was said in the *Slaughter-house cases* . . . to have been intended primarily to abolish slavery, as it had been previously known in this country, and that it equally forbade Mexican peonage or the Chinese coolie trade, when they amounted to slavery or involuntary servitude, and that the use of the word "servitude" was intended to prohibit the use of all forms of involuntary slavery, of whatever class or name. It was intimated, however, in that case that this amendment was regarded by the statesmen of that day as insufficient to protect the colored race from certain laws which had been enacted in the Southern States, imposing upon the colored race onerous disabilities and burdens, and curtailing their rights in the pursuit of life, liberty and property to such an extent that their freedom was of little value; and that the Fourteenth Amendment was devised to meet this exigency.

So, too, in the *Civil Rights cases*, . . . it was said that the act of a mere individual, the owner of an inn, a public conveyance or place of amusement, refusing accommodations to colored people, cannot be justly regarded as imposing any badge of slavery or servitude upon the applicant, but only as involving an ordinary civil injury, properly cognizable by the laws of the State, and presumably subject to redress by those laws until the contrary appears. "It would be running the slavery argument into the ground," said Mr. Justice Bradley, "to make it apply to every act of discrimination which a person may see fit to make as to the

guests he will entertain, or as to the people he will take into his coach or cab or car, or admit to his concert or theatre, or deal with in other matters of intercourse or business."

A statute which implies merely a legal distinction between the white and colored races—a distinction which is founded in the color of the two races, and which must always exist so long as white men are distinguished from the other race by color—has no tendency to destroy the legal equality of the two races, or reestablish a state of involuntary servitude. Indeed, we do not understand that the Thirteenth Amendment is strenuously relied upon by the plaintiff in error in this connection.

2. By the Fourteenth Amendment, all persons born or naturalized in the United States, and subject to the jurisdiction thereof, are made citizens of the United States and of the State wherein they reside; and the States are forbidden from making or enforcing any law which shall abridge the privileges or immunities of citizens of the United States, or shall deprive any person of life, liberty or property without due process of law, or deny to any person within their jurisdiction the equal protection of the laws.

The proper construction of this amendment was first called to the attention of this court in the *Slaughterhouse cases*, . . . which involved, however, not a question of race, but one of exclusive privileges. The case did not call for any expression of opinion as to the exact rights it was intended to secure to the colored race, but it was said generally that its main purpose was to establish the citizenship of the negro; to give definitions of citizenship of the United States and of the States, and to protect from the hostile legislation of the States the privileges and immunities of citizens of the United States, as distinguished from those of citizens of the States.

The object of the amendment was undoubtedly to enforce the absolute equality of the two races before the law, but in the nature of things it could not have been intended to abolish distinctions based upon color, or to enforce social, as distinguished from political equality, or a commingling of the two races upon terms unsatisfactory to either. Laws permitting, and even requiring, their separation in places where they are liable to be brought into contact do not necessarily imply the inferiority of either race to the other, and have been generally, if not universally, recognized as within the competency of the state legislatures in the exercise of their police power. The most common instance of this is connected with the establishment of separate schools for white and colored children, which has been held to be a valid exercise of the legislative power even by courts of States where the political rights of the colored race have been longest and most earnestly enforced.

One of the earliest of these cases is that of *Roberts* v. *City of Boston,* . . . in which the Supreme Judicial Court of Massachusetts held that the general school committee of Boston had power to make provision for the instruction of colored children in separate schools established exclusively for them, and to prohibit their attendance upon the other schools. "The great principle," said Chief Justice Shaw, p. 206, "advanced by the learned and eloquent advocate for the plaintiff," (Mr. Charles Sumner,) "is, that by the constitution and laws of Massachusetts, all persons without distinction of age or sex, birth or color, origin or condition, are equal before the law. . . . But, when this great principle comes to be applied to the actual and various conditions of persons in society, it will not warrant the assertion, that men and women are legally clothed with the same civil and political powers, and that children and adults are legally to have the same functions and be subject to the same treatment; but only that the rights of all, as they are settled and regulated by law, are equally entitled to the paternal consideration and protection of the law for their maintenance and security." It was held that the powers of the committee extended to the establishment of separate schools for children of different ages, sexes and colors, and that they might also establish special schools for poor and neglected children, who have become too old to attend the primary school, and yet have not acquired the rudiments of learning, to enable them to enter the ordinary schools. Similar laws have been enacted by Congress under its general power of legislation over the District of Columbia, . . . as well as by the legislatures of many of the States, and have been generally, if not uniformly, sustained by the courts. . . .

So far, then, as a conflict with the Fourteenth Amendment is concerned, the case reduces itself to the question whether the statute of Louisiana is a reasonable regulation, and with respect to this there must necessarily be a large discretion on the part of the legislature. In determining the question of reasonableness it is at liberty to act with reference to the established usages, customs and traditions of the people, and with a view to the promotion of their comfort, and the preservation of the public peace and good order. Gauged by this standard, we cannot say that a law which authorizes or even requires the separation of the two races in public conveyances is unreasonable, or more obnoxious to the Fourteenth Amendment than the acts of Congress requiring separate schools for colored children in the District of Columbia, the constitutionality of which does not seem to have been questioned, or the corresponding acts of state legislatures.

We consider the underlying fallacy of the plaintiff's argument to consist in the assumption that the enforced separation of the two races stamps the colored race with a badge of inferiority. If this be so, it is not by reason of anything found in the act, but solely because the colored race chooses to put that construction upon it. The argument necessarily assumes that if, as has been more than once the case, and is not unlikely to be so again, the colored race should become the dominant power in the state legislature, and should enact a law in precisely similar terms, it would thereby relegate the white race to an inferior position. We imagine that the white race, at least, would not acquiesce in this assumption. The argument also assumes that social prejudices may be overcome by legislation, and that equal rights cannot be secured to the negro except by an enforced commingling of the two races. We cannot accept this proposition. If the two races are to meet upon terms of social equality, it must be the result of natural affinities, a mutual appreciation of each other's merits and a voluntary consent of individuals. . . . Legislation is powerless to eradicate racial instincts or to abolish distinctions based upon physical differences, and the attempt to do so can only result in accentuating the difficulties of the present situation. If the civil and political rights of both races be equal one cannot be inferior to the other civilly or politically. If one race be inferior to the other socially, the Constitution of the United States cannot put them upon the same plane.

It is true that the question of the proportion of colored blood necessary to constitute a colored person, as distinguished from a white person, is one upon which there is a difference of opinion in the different States, some holding that any visible admixture of black blood stamps the person as belonging to the colored race, . . . others that it depends upon the preponderance of blood, and still others that the predominance of white blood must only be in the proportion of three fourths. . . . But these are questions to be determined under the laws of each State and are not properly put in issue in this case. Under the allegations of his petition it may undoubtedly become a question of importance whether, under the laws of Louisiana, the petitioner belongs to the white or colored race.

The judgment of the court below is, therefore, Affirmed.

Justice Harlan dissented:

. . . It was said in argument that the statute of Louisiana does not discriminate against either race, but prescribes a rule applicable alike to white and colored citizens. But this argument does not meet the difficulty. Every one knows that the statute in question had its origin in the purpose, not so much to exclude white persons from railroad cars occupied by blacks, as to exclude colored people from coaches occupied by or assigned to white persons. Railroad corporations of Louisiana did not make discrimination among whites in the matter of accommodation for travellers. The thing to accomplish was, under the guise of giving equal accommodation for whites and blacks, to compel the latter to keep to themselves while travelling in railroad passenger coaches. No one would be so wanting in candor as to assert the contrary. The fundamental objection, therefore, to the statute is that it interferes with the personal freedom of citizens. "Personal liberty," it has been well said, "consists in the power of locomotion, of changing situation, or removing one's person to whatsoever places one's own inclination may direct, without imprisonment or restraint, unless by due course of law." . . .

If a white man and a black man choose to occupy the same public conveyance on a public highway, it is their right to do so, and no government, proceeding alone on grounds of race, can prevent it without infringing the personal liberty of each.

The white race deems itself to be the dominant race in this country. And so it is, in prestige, in achievements, in education, in wealth and in power. So, I doubt not, it will continue to be for all time, if it remains true to its great heritage and holds fast to the principles of constitutional liberty. But in view of the Constitution, in the eye of the law, there is in this country no superior, dominant, ruling class of citizens. There is no caste here. Our Constitution is color-blind, and neither knows nor tolerates classes among citizens. In respect of civil rights, all citizens are equal before the law. The humblest is the peer of the most powerful. The law regards man as man, and takes no account of his surroundings or of his color when his civil rights as guaranteed by the supreme law of the land are involved. It is, therefore, to be regretted that this high tribunal, the final expositor of the fundamental law of the land, has reached the conclusion that it is competent for a State to regulate the enjoyment by citizens of their civil rights solely upon the basis of race.

In my opinion, the judgment this day rendered will, in time, prove to be quite as pernicious as the decision made by this tribunal in the *Dred Scott case*. It was adjudged in that case that the descendants of Africans who were imported into this country and sold as slaves were not included nor intended to be included under the word "citizens" in the Constitution, and could not claim any of the rights and privileges which that instrument provided for and secured to citizens of the United States; that at the time of the adoption of the Constitution they were "considered as a subordinate and inferior class of beings, who had been subjugated by the dominant race, and, whether emancipated or not, yet remained subject to their authority, and had no rights or privileges but such as those who held the power and the government might choose to grant them." . . . The recent amendments of the Constitution, it was supposed, had eradicated these principles from our institutions. But it seems that we have yet, in some of the States, a dominant race—a superior class of citizens, which assumes to regulate the enjoyment of civil rights, common to all citizens, upon the basis of race. The present decision, it may well be apprehended, will not only stimulate aggressions, more or less brutal and irritating, upon the admitted rights of colored citizens, but will encourage the belief that it is possible, by means of state enactments, to defeat the beneficent purposes which the people of the United States had in view when they adopted the recent amendments of the Constitution, by one of which the blacks of this country were made citizens of the United States and of the States in which they respectively reside, and whose privileges and immunities, as citizens, the States are forbidden to abridge. Sixty millions of whites are in no danger from the presence here of eight millions of blacks. The destinies of the two races, in this country, are indissolubly linked together, and the interests of both require that the common government of all shall not permit the seeds of race hate to be planted under the sanction of law. What can more certainly arouse race hate, what more certainly create and perpetuate a feeling of distrust between these races, than state enactments, which, in fact, proceed on the ground that colored citizens are so inferior and degraded that they cannot be allowed to sit in public coaches occupied by white citizens? That, as all will admit, is the real meaning of such legislation as was enacted in Louisiana.

The sure guarantee of the peace and security of each race is the clear, distinct, unconditional recognition by our governments, National and State, of every right that inheres in civil freedom, and of the equality before the law of all citizens of the United States without regard to race. State enactments, regulating the enjoyment of civil rights, upon the basis of race, and cunningly devised to defeat legitimate results of the war, under the pretence of recognizing equality of rights, can have no other result than to render permanent peace impossible, and to keep alive a conflict of races, the continuance of which must do harm to all concerned. This question is not met by the suggestion that social equality cannot exist between the white and black races in this country. That argument, if it can be properly regarded as one, is scarcely worthy of consideration; for social equality no more exists between two races when travelling in a passenger coach or a public highway than when members of the same races sit by each other in a street car or in the jury box, or stand or sit with each other in a political assembly, or when they use in common the streets of a city or town, or when they are in the same room for the purpose of having their names placed on the registry of voters, or when they approach the ballot-box in order to exercise the high privilege of voting.

There is a race so different from our own that we do not permit those belonging to it to become citizens of the United States. Persons belonging to it are, with few exceptions, absolutely excluded from our country. I allude to the Chinese race. But by the statute in question, a Chinaman can ride in the same passenger coach with white citizens of the United States, while citizens of the black race in Louisiana, many of whom, perhaps, risked their lives for the preservation of the Union, who are entitled, by law, to participate in the political control of the State and nation, who are not excluded, by law or by reason of their race, from public stations of any kind, and who have all the legal rights that belong to white citizens, are yet declared to be criminals, liable to imprisonment, if they ride in a public coach occupied by citizens of the white race. It is scarcely just to say that a colored citizen should not object to occupying a public coach assigned to his own race. He does not object, nor, perhaps, would he object to separate coaches for his race, if his rights under the law were recognized. But he objects, and ought never to cease objecting to the proposition, that citizens of the white and black races can be adjudged criminals because they sit, or claim the right to sit, in the same public coach on a public highway.

The arbitrary separation of citizens, on the basis of race, while they are on a public highway, is a badge of servitude wholly inconsistent with the civil freedom and the equality before the law established by the Constitution. It cannot be justified upon any legal grounds.

If evils will result from the commingling of the two races upon public highways established for the benefit of all, they will be infinitely less than those that will surely come from state legislation regulating the en-joyment of civil rights upon the basis of race. We boast of the freedom enjoyed by our people above all other peoples. But it is difficult to reconcile that boast with a state of the law which, practically, puts the brand of servitude and degradation upon a large class of our fellow-citizens, our equals before the law. The thin disguise of "equal" accommodations for passengers in railroad coaches will not mislead any one, nor atone for the wrong this day done.

The result of the whole matter is, that while this court has frequently adjudged, and at the present term has recognized the doctrine, that a State cannot, consistently with the Constitution of the United States, prevent white and black citizens, having the required qualifications for jury service, from sitting in the same jury box, it is now solemnly held that a State may prohibit white and black citizens from sitting in the same passenger coach on a public highway, or may require that they be separated by a "partition," when in the same passenger coach. May it not now be reasonably expected that astute men of the dominant race, who affect to be disturbed at the possibility that the integrity of the white race may be corrupted, or that its supremacy will be imperilled, by contact on public highways with black people, will endeavor to procure statutes requiring white and black jurors to be separated in the jury box by a "partition," and that, upon retiring from the court room to consult as to their verdict, such partition, if it be a moveable one, shall be taken to their consultation room, and set up in such way as to prevent black jurors from coming too close to their brother jurors of the white race. If the "partition" used in the court room happens to be stationary, provision could be made for screens with openings through which jurors of the two races could confer as to their verdict without coming into personal contact with each other. I cannot see but that, according to the principles this day announced, such state legislation, although conceived in hostility to, and enacted for the purpose of humiliating citizens of the United States of a particular race, would be held to be consistent with the Constitution.

I do not deem it necessary to review the decisions of state courts to which reference was made in argument. Some, and the most important, of them are wholly inapplicable, because rendered prior to the adoption of the last amendments of the Constitution, when colored people had very few rights which the dominant race felt obliged to respect. Others were made at a time when public opinion, in many localities, was dominated by the institution of slavery; when it would not have been safe to do justice to the black man; and when, so far as the rights of blacks were concerned, race prejudice was, practically, the supreme law of the land. Those decisions cannot be guides in the era introduced by the recent amendments of the supreme law, which established universal civil freedom, gave citizenship to all born or naturalized in the United States and residing here, obliterated the race line from our systems of governments, National and State, and placed our free institutions upon the broad and sure foundation of the equality of all men before the law.

I am of opinion that the statute of Louisiana is inconsistent with the personal liberty of citizens, white and black, in that State, and hostile to both the spirit and letter of the Constitution of the United States. If laws of like character should be enacted in the several States of the Union, the effect would be in the highest degree mischievous. Slavery, as an institution tolerated by law would, it is true, have disappeared from our country, but there would remain a power in the States, by sinister legislation, to interfere with the full enjoyment of the blessings of freedom; to regulate civil rights, common to all citizens, upon the basis of race; and to place in a condition of legal inferiority a large body of American citizens, now constituting a part of the political commuity called the People of the United States, for whom, and by whom through representatives, our government is administered. Such a system is inconsistent with the guarantee given by the Constitution to each State of a republican form of government, and may be stricken down by Congressional action, or by the courts in the discharge of their solemn duty to maintain the supreme law of the land, anything in the constitution or laws of any State to the contrary notwithstanding.

For the reasons stated, I am constrained to withhold my assent from the opinion and judgment of the majority.

Justice Brewer did not hear the argument or participate in the decision of this case.

In 1896, William Jennings Bryan and the Democratic Party were decisively defeated. But the racially regressive, antiregulatory, and antilabor decisions of the Court continued to engender strong opposition.

In retrospect, the Supreme Court of the United States was a center of controversy in two of the three previous critical elections, those of 1800 and 1860 (but not 1828). In those two critical elections, controversial positions associated with the Supreme Court—such as Federalist Alien and Sedition Act enforcement and the development of a federal common law jurisdiction before 1800, and the Dred Scott decision before 1860—were convincingly repudiated at the polls. But after 1896, the opponents of the Court were thoroughly defeated and a resurgent conservative Republican Party was destined for several more years of control. Criticism of the Court did not end, however, and in the 1890s and first decades of the 20th century, the impact of the Court's conservative doctrines stimulated thoughtful reappraisal of the role of the Supreme Court not only among the antagonistic Populists and the more temperate Progressives, but also by students of American institutions who basically supported judicial review. Perhaps the most perceptive of the latter was James Bradley Thayer, whose 1901 views on judicial review strongly influenced some modern jurists. The following excerpt is taken from *For Judicial Self-Restraint as a Function of Democratic Trust in the People.*

When one reflects upon the multitude, variety, and complexity of the questions relating to the regulation of interstate commerce, upon the portentous and ever increasing flood of litigation to which the Fourteenth Amendment has given rise; upon the new problems in business, government, and police which have come in with steam and electricity, and their ten thousand applications; upon the growth of corporations of wealth, the changes of opinion on social questions, such as the relation of capital and labor, and upon the recent expansions of our control over great and distant islands,—we seem to be living in a different world from Marshall's.

Under these new circumstances, what is happening in the region of constitutional law? Very serious things, indeed.

The people of the states, when making new constitutions, have long been adding more and more prohibitions and restraints upon their legislatures. The courts, meantime, in many places, enter into the harvest thus provided for them with a light heart, and too promptly and easily proceed to this distrust, and more and more readily incline to justify it, and to shed the consideration of constitutional restraints,— certainly as concerning the exact extent of these restrictions,—turning that subject over to the courts; and, what is worse, they insensibly fall into a habit of assuming that whatever they can constitutionally do they may do,—as if honor and fair dealing and common honesty were not relevant to their inquiries.

The people, all this while, become careless as to whom they send to the legislature; too often they cheerfully vote for men whom they would not trust with an important private affair, and when these unfit persons are found to pass foolish and bad laws, and the courts step in and disregard them, the people are glad that these few wiser gentlemen on the bench are so ready to protect them against their more immediate representatives.

From these causes there has developed a vast and growing increase of judicial interference with legislation. This is a very different state of things from what our fathers contemplated, a century and more ago, in framing the new system. Seldom, indeed, as they imagined, under our system, would this great, novel, tremendous power of the courts be exerted,—would this sacred ark of the covenant be taken from within the veil. Marshall himself expressed truly one aspect of the matter, when he said in one of the later years of his life: "No questions can be brought before a judicial tribunal of greater delicacy than those which involve the constitutionality of legislative acts. If they become indispensably necessary to the case, the court must meet and decide them; but if the case may be determined on other grounds, a just respect for the legislature requires that the obligation of its laws should not be unneccessarily and wantonly assailed." And again, a little earlier than this, he laid down the one true rule of duty for the courts. When he went to Philadelphia at the end of September, in 1831, on that painful errand of which I have spoken, in answering a cordial tribute from the bar of that city he remarked that if he might be permitted to claim for himself and his associates any part of the kind things they had said, it would be this, that they had "never sought to enlarge the judicial power beyond its proper bounds, nor feared to carry it to the fullest extent that duty required."

That is the safe twofold rule; nor is the first part of it any whit less important than the second; nay, more; to-day it is the part which most requires to be emphasized. For just here comes in a consideration of very great weight. Great and, indeed, inestimable as are the advantages in a popular government of this conservative influence,—the power of the judiciary to disregard unconstitutional legislation,—it should be remembered that the exercise of it, even when unavoidable, is always attended with a serious evil, namely, that the correction of legislative mistakes comes from the outside, and the people thus lose the political experience, and the moral education and stimulus that come from fighting the question out in the ordinary way, and correcting their own errors. . . .[8]

James Bradley Thayer

A formidable array of Supreme Court decisions substantiated Thayer's carefully reasoned judgment. Some contributed to the crisis that led to the political confrontation in 1896, while others continued to create the generally accurate impression that the Court in this era invariably supported the rich and the powerful, especially when those attributes were organized in the "artificial" person of a corporation. Supreme Court failure to find grounds to protect the public interest in railroad rate cases was one continuing area of criticism. Interestingly enough, several Justices chosen early in the 20th century were strong proponents of judicial respect for the experimental role of legislatures. The most notable of these were Justices Oliver Wendell Holmes and Louis D. Brandeis. In the 1890s, however, the strong tendency for judicial intervention, often for conservative public policy considerations, continued unabated.

The expansion of judicial authority

The critical election of 1896 put the Supreme Court in political consistency with the conservative political leaders who were swept into executive and legislative offices in that year along with President William McKinley. Thus, it is not surprising that the Court continued its conservative doctrinal approach after 1896. The remaining years of the 1890s were notable for further expansion of judicial power in railroad rate cases and a major judicial definition of citizenship. The first of these was *Interstate Commerce Commission* v. *Cincinnati, New Orleans, and Texas Pacific Railway Company*, a case in which the Court interpreted the commission's authority very narrowly. Justice Brewer's majority opinion follows:

INTERSTATE COMMERCE COMMISSION v. CINCINNATI, NEW ORLEANS, AND TEXAS PACIFIC RAILWAY COMPANY
167 U. S. 479 (1897)

Justice Brewer delivered the opinion of the Court:

Before the passage of the [Interstate Commerce] act it was generally believed that there were great abuses in railroad management and railroad transportation, and the grave question which Congress had to consider was how those abuses should be corrected and what control should be taken of the business of such corporations. The present inquiry is limited to the question as to what it determined should be done with reference to the matter of rates. There were three obvious and dissimilar courses open for consideration. Congress might itself prescribe the rates; or it might commit to some subordinate tribunal this duty; or it might leave with the companies the right to fix rates, subject to regulations and restrictions, as well as to that rule which is as old as the existence of common carriers, to wit, that rates must be reasonable. There is nothing in the act fixing rates. Congress did not attempt to exercise that power, and if we examine the legislative and public history of the day it is apparent that there was no serious thought of doing so.

The question debated is whether it vested in the commission the power and the duty to fix rates; and the fact that this is a debatable question, and has been most strenuously and earnestly debated, is very persuasive that it did not. The grant of such a power is never to be implied. The power itself is so vast and comprehensive, so largely affecting the rights of carrier and shipper, as well as indirectly all commercial transactions, the language by which the power is given had been so often used and was so familiar to the legislative mind and is capable of such definite and exact statement, that no just rule of construction would tolerate a grant of such power by mere implication. . . .

It is one thing to inquire whether the rates which have been charged and collected are reasonable—that is a judicial act; but an entirely different thing to prescribe rates which shall be charged in the future—that is a legislative act. . . .

It will be perceived that in this case the Interstate Commerce Commission assumed the right to prescribe rates which should control in the future, and their application to the court was for a mandamus to compel the companies to comply with their decision; that is, to abide by their legislative determination as to the maximum rates to be observed in the future. Now, nowhere in the interstate commerce act do we find words similar to those in the statutes referred to, giving to the commission power to "increase or reduce any of the rates"; "to establish rates of charges"; "to make and fix reasonable and just rates of freight and passenger tariffs"; "to make a schedule of reasonable maximum rates of charges"; "to fix tables of maximum charges"; to compel the carrier "to adopt such rate, charge or classification as said commissioners shall declare to be equitable and reasonable." The power, therefore, is not expressly given. . . . Congress did not intend to give to the commission the power to prescribe any tariff and determine what for the future should be reasonable and just rates. The power given is the power to execute and enforce, not to legislate. The power given is partly judicial, partly executive and administrative, but not legislative. . . .

We have, therefore, these considerations presented: First. The power to prescribe a tariff of rates for carriage by a common carrier is a legislative and not an administrative or judicial function, and, having respect to the large amount of property invested in railroads, the various companies engaged therein, the thousands of miles of road, and the millions of tons of freight carried, the varying and diverse conditions attaching to such carriage, is a power of supreme delicacy and importance. Second. That Congress has transferred such a power to any administrative body is not to be presumed or implied from any doubtful and uncertain language. The words and phrases efficacious to make such a delegation of power are well understood and have been frequently used, and if Congress had intended to grant such a power to the Interstate Commerce Commission it cannot be doubted that it would have used language open to no misconstruction, but clear and direct. Third. Incorporating into a statute the common law obligation resting upon the carrier to make all its charges reasonable and just, and directing the commission to execute and enforce the provisions of the act, does not by implication carry to the commissioner or invest it with the power to exercise the legislative function of prescribing rates which shall control in the future. Fourth. Beyond the inference which irresistibly follows from the omission to grant in express terms to the commission this power of fixing rates, is the clear language of section 6, recognizing the right of the carrier to establish rates, to increase or reduce them, and prescribing the conditions upon which such increase or reduction may be made, and requiring, as the only conditions of its action, first, publication, and, second, the filing of the tariff with the commission. The grant to the commission of the power to prescribe the form of the schedules, and to direct the place and manner of publication of joint rates, thus specifying the scope and limit of its functions in this respect, strengthens the conclusion that the power to prescribe rates or fix any tariff for the future is not among the powers granted to the commission.

The considerations convince us that under the interstate commerce act the commission has no power to prescribe the tariff of rates which shall control in the future, and, therefore, cannot invoke a judgement in mandamus from the courts to enforce any such tariff by it prescribed. . . .

By denying the ICC the power to set rates, the Court seriously curtailed federal authority. One year later, the Supreme Court virtually replaced state commissions as rate-makers, thus substantially increasing judicial authority, by insisting that the courts would determine the "reasonableness" of railroad rates set by these state commissions. *Smythe* v. *Ames* embodied this far-reaching doctrine. In striking down a Nebraska law setting intrastate freight rates, the Court barred state rate-making action. The Ames decision's emphasis upon substantive due process reached its broadest scope in this era.

SMYTHE v. AMES
169 U. S. 466 (1898)

Justice Harlan delivered the opinion of the Court:

We are now to inquire whether the Nebraska statute is repugnant to the Constitution of the United States.

By the Fourteenth Amendment it is provided that no State shall deprive any person of property without due process of law, nor deny to any person within its jurisdiction the equal protection of the laws. That corporations are persons within the meaning of this Amendment is now settled. . . . What amounts to deprivation of property without due process of law or what is a denial of the equal protection of the laws is often difficult to determine, especially where the question relates to the property of a *quasi* public corporation and the extent to which it may be subjected to public control. But this court, speaking by Chief Justice Waite, has said that, while a State has power to fix the charges by railroad companies for the transportation of persons and property within its own jurisdiction, unless restrained by valid contract, or unless what is done amounts to a regulation of foreign or interstate commerce, such power is not without limit; and that, "under pretence of regulating fares and freights, the State cannot require a railroad corporation to carry persons or property without reward, neither can it do that which in law amounts to the taking of private property for public use without just compensation, or without due process of law." . . .

These principles must be regarded as settled:

1. A railroad corporation is a person within the meaning of the Fourteenth Amendment declaring that no State shall deprive any person of property without due process of law, nor deny to any person within its jurisdiction the equal protection of the laws.

2. A state enactment, or regulations made under the authority of a state enactment, establishing rates for the transportation of persons or property by railroad that will not admit of the carrier earning such compensation as under all the circumstances is just to it and to the public, would deprive such carrier of its property without due process of law and deny to it the equal protection of the laws, and would therefore be repugnant to the Fourteenth Amendment of the Constitution of the United States.

3. While rates for the transportation of persons and property within the limits of a State are primarily for its determination, the question whether they are so unreasonably low as to deprive the carrier of its property without such compensation as the Constitution secures, and therefore without due process of law, cannot be so conclusively determined by the legislature of the State or by regulations adopted under its authority, that the matter may not become the subject of judicial inquiry.

The cases before us directly present the important question last stated. . . .

What are the considerations to which weight must be given when we seek to ascertain the compensation that a railroad company is entitled to receive, and a prohibition upon the receiving of which may be fairly deemed a deprivation by legislative decree of property without due process of law? Undoubtedly that question could be more easily determined by a commission composed of persons whose special skill, observation and experience qualifies them to so handle great problems of transportation as to do justice both to the public and to those whose money has been used to

construct and maintain highways for the convenience and benefit of the people. But despite the difficulties that confessedly attend the proper solution of such questions, the court cannot shrink from the duty to determine whether it be true, as alleged, that the Nebraska statute invades or destroys rights secured by the supreme law of the land. . . .

[T]he plaintiffs contended that a railroad company is entitled to exact such charges for transportation as will enable it, at all times, not only to pay operating expenses, but also to meet the interest regularly accruing upon all its outstanding obligations, and justify a dividend upon all its stock; and that to prohibit it from maintaining rates or charges for transportation adequate to *all* those ends will deprive it of its property without due process of law, and deny to it the equal protection of the laws. This contention was the subject of elaborate discussion; and, as it bears upon each case in its important aspects, it should not be passed without examination.

In our opinion, the broad proposition advanced by counsel involves some misconception of the relations between the public and a railroad corporation. It is unsound in that it practically excludes from consideration the fair value of the property used, omits altogether any consideration of the right of the public to be exempt from unreasonable exactions, and makes the interests of the corporation maintaining a public highway the sole test in determining whether the rates established by or for it are such as may be rightfully prescribed as between it and the public. . . .

What was said in *Covington & Lexington Turnpike Road Co. v. Sandford*, . . . is pertinent to the question under consideration. It was there observed: "It cannot be said that a corporation is entitled, as of right, and without reference to the interests of the public, to realize a given per cent upon its capital stock. When the question arises whether the legislature has exceeded its constitutional power in prescribing rates to be charged by a corporation controlling a public highway, stockholders are not the only persons whose rights or interests are to be considered. The rights of the public are not to be ignored. It is alleged here that the rates prescribed are unreasonable and unjust to the company and its stockholders. But that involves an inquiry as to what is reasonable and just for the public. . . . The public cannot properly be subjected to unreasonable rates in order simply that stockholders may earn dividends. The legislature has the authority, in every case, where its power has not been restrained by contract, to proceed upon the ground that the public may not rightfully be required to submit to unreasonable exactions for the use of a public highway established and maintained under legislative authority. If a corporation can not maintain such a highway and earn dividends for stockholders, it is a misfortune for it and them which the Constitution does not require to be remedied by imposing unjust burdens upon the public." . . .

We hold . . . that the basis of all calculations as to the reasonableness of rates to be charged by a corporation maintaining a highway under legislative sanction must be the fair value of the property being used by it for the convenience of the public. And in order to ascertain that value, the original cost of construction, the amount expended in permanent improvements, the amount and market value of its bonds and stock, the present as compared with the original cost of construction, the probable earning capacity of the property under particular rates prescribed by statute, and the sum required to meet operating expenses, are all matters for consideration, and are to be given such weight as may be just and right in each case. We did not say that there may not be other matters to be regarded in estimating the value of the property. What the company is entitled to ask is a fair return upon the value of that which it employs for the public convenience. On the other hand, what the public is entitled to demand is that no more be exacted from it for the use of a public highway than the services rendered by it are reasonably worth. . . .

As the century closed, the Supreme Court confronted in the case of *United States v. Wong Kim Ark* the question whether the child born to Chinese nationals in the United States was a citizen of the United States under the provisions of the first clause of the Fourteenth Amendment. In those states in which large numbers of Chinese laborers had been brought to work on railroads, there was bitter political and social conflict over their presence. The contrast between Justice Gray's majority opinion and Fuller's and Harlan's dissent reflected these public policy differences.

UNITED STATES v. WONG KIM ARK
169 U.S. 649 (1898)

Justice Gray delivered the opinion of the court:

The facts of this case, as agreed by the parties, are as follows: Wong Kim Ark was born in 1873 in the city of San Francisco, in the State of California and United States of America, and was and is a laborer. His father and mother were persons of Chinese descent, and subjects of the Emperor of China; they were at the time of his birth domiciled residents of the United States, having previously established and still enjoying a permanent domicil and residence therein at San Francisco; they continued to reside and remain in the United States until 1890, when they departed for China; and during all the time of their residence in the United States they were engaged in business, and were never employed in any diplomatic or official capacity under the Emperor of China. Wong Kim Ark, ever since his birth, has had but one residence, to wit, in California, within the United States, and has there resided, claiming to be a citizen of the United States, and has never lost or changed that residence, or gained or acquired another residence; and neither he, nor his parents acting for him, ever renounced his allegiance to the United States, or did or committed any act or thing to exclude him therefrom. In 1890 (when he must have been about seventeen years of age) he departed for China on a temporary visit and with the intention of returning to the United States, and did return thereto by sea in the same year, and was permitted by the collector of customs to enter the United States, upon the sole ground that he was a native-born citizen of the United States. After such return, he remained in the United States, claiming to be a citizen thereof, until 1894, when he (being about twenty-one years of age, but whether a little above or a little under that age does not appear) again departed for China on a temporary visit and with the intention of returning to the United States; and he did return thereto by sea in August, 1895, and applied to the collector of customs for permission to land; and was denied such permission, upon the sole ground that he was not a citizen of the United States.

It is conceded that, if he is a citizen of the United States, the acts of Congress, known as the Chinese Exclusion Acts, prohibiting persons of the Chinese race, and especially Chinese laborers, from coming into the United States, do not and cannot apply to him.

The question presented by the record is whether a child born in the United States, of parents of Chinese descent, who, at the time of his birth, are subjects of the Emperor of China, but have a permanent domicil and residence in the United States, and are there carrying on business, and are not employed in any diplomatic or official capacity under the Emperor of China, becomes at the time of his birth a citizen of the United States, by virtue of the first clause of the Fourteenth Amendment of the Constitution, "All persons born or naturalized in the United States, and subject to the jurisdiction thereof, are citizens of the United States and of the State wherein they reside."

The Fourteenth Amendment of the Constitution, in the declaration that "all persons born or naturalized in the United States, and subject to the jurisdiction thereof, are citizens of the United States and of the State wherein they reside," contemplates two sources of citizenship, and two only: birth and naturalization. Citizenship by naturalization can only be acquired by naturalization under the authority and in the forms of law. But citizenship by birth is established by the mere fact of birth under the circumstances defined in the Constitution. Every person born in the United States, and subject to the jurisdiction thereof, becomes at once a citizen of the United States, and needs no naturalization. A person born out of the jurisdiction of the United States can only become a citizen by being naturalized, either by treaty, as in the case of the annexation of foreign territory; or by authority of Congress, exercised either by declaring certain classes of persons to be citizens, as in the enactments conferring citizenship upon foreign-born children of citizens, or by enabling foreigners individually to become citizens by proceedings in the judicial tribunals, as in the ordinary provisions of the naturalization acts.

The power of naturalization, vested in Congress by the Constitution, is a power to confer citizenship, not a power to take it away. "A naturalized citizen," said Chief Justice Marshall, "becomes a member of the society, possessing all the rights of a native citizen, and standing, in the view of the Constitution, on the footing of a native. The Constitution does not authorize Congress to enlarge or abridge those rights. The simple power of the National Legislature is to prescribe a uniform rule of naturalization, and the exercise of this power exhausts it, so far as respects the individual. The Constitution then takes him up, and, among other rights, extends to him the capacity of suing in the courts of the United States, precisely under the same circumstances under which a native might sue." *Osborn v. United States Bank*, 9 Wheat. 738, 827. Congress having no power to abridge the rights conferred by the Constitution upon those who have become naturalized citizens by virtue of acts of Congress, *a fortiori* no act or omission of Congress, as to providing for the naturalization of parents or children of a particular race, can affect citizenship acquired as a birthright, by virtue of the Constitution itself, without any aid of legislation. The Fourteenth Amendment, while it leaves the power, where it was before, in Congress, to regulate naturalization, has conferred no authority upon Congress to restrict the effect of birth, declared by the Constitution to constitute a sufficient and complete right to citizenship.

No one doubts that the Amendment, as soon as it was promulgated, applied to persons of African descent born in the United States, wherever the birthplace of their parents might have been; and yet, for two years afterwards, there was no statute authorizing persons of that race to be naturalized. If the omission or the refusal of Congress to permit certain classes of persons to be made citizens by naturalization could be allowed the effect of correspondingly restricting the classes of persons who should become citizens by birth, it would be in the power of Congress, at any time, by striking negroes out of the naturalization laws, and limiting those laws, as they were formerly limited, to white persons only, to defeat the main purpose of the Constitutional Amendment.

The fact, therefore, that acts of Congress or treaties have not permitted Chinese persons born out of this country to become citizens by naturalization, cannot exclude Chinese persons born in this country from the operation of the broad and clear words of the Constitution, "All persons born in the United States, and subject to the jurisdiction thereof, are citizens of the United States."

VII. Upon the facts agreed in this case, the American citizenship which Wong Kim Ark acquired by birth within the United States has not been lost or taken away by anything happening since his birth. No doubt he might himself, after coming of age, renounce this citizenship, and become a citizen of the country of his parents, or of any other country; for by our law, as solemnly declared by Congress, "the right of expatriation is a natural and inherent right of all people," and "any declaration, instruction, opinion, order or direction of any officer of the United States, which denies, restricts, impairs or questions the right of expatriation, is declared inconsistent with the fundamental principles of the Republic." . . .

Whether any act of himself, or of his parents, during his minority, could have the same effect, is at least doubtful. But it would be out of place to pursue that inquiry; inasmuch as it is expressly agreed that his residence has always been in the United States, and not elsewhere; that each of his temporary visits to China, the one for some months when he was about seventeen years old, and the other for something like a year about the time of his coming of age, was made with the intention of returning, and was followed by his actual return, to the United States; and "that said Wong Kim Ark has not, either by himself or his parents acting for him, ever renounced his allegiance to the United States, and that he has never done or committed any act or thing to exclude him therefrom."

The evident intention, and the necessary effect, of the submission of this case to the decision of the court upon the facts agreed by the parties, were to present for determination the single question, stated at the beginning of this opinion, namely, whether a child born in the United States, of parents of Chinese descent, who, at the time of his birth, are subjects of the Emperor of China, but have a permanent domicil and residence in the United States, and are there carrying on business, and are not employed in any diplomatic or official capacity under the Emperor of China, becomes at the time of his birth a citizen of the United States. For the reasons above stated, this court is of opinion that the question must be answered in the affirmative. Order affirmed.

Chief Justice Fuller dissented,
with the concurrence of Justice Harlan:

I cannot concur in the opinion and judgment of the court in this case.

The proposition is that a child born in this country of parents who were not citizens of the United States, and under the laws of their own country and of the United States could not become such—as was the fact from the beginning of the Government in respect of the class of aliens to which the parents in this instance belonged—is, from the moment of his birth a citizen of the United States, by virtue of the first clause of the Fourteenth Amendment, any act of Congress to the contrary notwithstanding. . . .

In *Fong Yue Ting* v. *United States*, . . . it was said in respect of the treaty of 1868: "After some years' experience under that treaty, the Government of the United States was brought to the opinion that the presence within our territory of large numbers of Chinese laborers, of a distinct race and religion, remaining strangers in the land, residing apart by themselves, tenaciously adhering to the customs and usages of their own country, unfamiliar with our institutions, and apparently incapable of assimilating with our people, might endanger good order, and be injurious to the public interests; and therefore requested and obtained from China a modification of the treaty."

It is not to be admitted that the children of persons so situated become citizens by the accident of birth. On the contrary, I am of opinion that the President and Senate by treaty, and the Congress by naturalization, have the power, notwithstanding the Fourteenth Amendment, to prescribe that all persons of a particular race, or their children, cannot become citizens, and that it results that the consent to allow such persons to come into and reside within our geographical limits does not carry with it the imposition of citizenship upon children born to them while in this country under such consent, in spite of treaty and statute.

In other words, the Fourteenth Amendment does not exclude from citizenship by birth children born in the United States of parents permanently located therein, and who might themselves become citizens; nor, on the other hand, does it arbitrarily make citizens of children born in the United States of parents who, according to the will of their native government and of this Government, are and must remain aliens.

Tested by this rule, Wong Kim Ark never became and is not a citizen of the United States, and the order of the District Court should be reversed.

I am authorized to say that Justice Harlan
concurs in this dissent. Justice McKenna, not having
been a member of the court when this case was argued,
took no part in the decision.

The raising of Progressive hopes

The election of William McKinley in 1896 brought a four-year term of high tariff, sound money, Republican economic orthodoxy, and the heady adventure in imperialism in which the United States acquired several Caribbean and Asiatic possessions at the end of the Spanish-American War. Although McKinley did not respond positively to the domestic reactions against his conservative policies, he won reelection handily in 1900. Many critics of Republican economic orthodoxy were critics of the conservative doctrines of the Supreme Court as well. Republican ascendancy did not end when McKinley was assassinated in 1901, but his successor, Theodore Roosevelt, was responsive in a number of respects to the Progressive movement.

The conservatism of the Supreme Court of the 1890s had helped considerably to stimulate Progressivism, a movement that made inroads in Congress and was espoused by President Theodore Roosevelt and, later, President Woodrow Wilson. Several decisions handed down early in the 20th century raised hopes that the Court would develop broader constructionist doctrines under the commerce clause and the taxing power. In *Champion* v. *Ames*, the Court upheld congressional authority to prohibit the transportation of lottery tickets across state lines. A portion of Justice Harlan's majority opinion is provided below.

CHAMPION v. AMES
188 U. S. 321 (1903)

Justice Harlan delivered the opinion of the Court:

It was said in argument that lottery tickets are not of any real or substantial value in themselves, and therefore are not subjects of commerce. If that were conceded to be the only legal test as to what are to be deemed subjects of the commerce that may be regulated by Congress, we cannot accept as accurate the broad statement that such tickets are of no value. Upon their face they showed that the lottery company offered a large capital prize, to be paid to the holder of the ticket winning the prize at the drawing advertised to be held at Asuncion, Paraguay. Money was placed on deposit in different banks in the United States to be applied by the agents representing the lottery company to the prompt payment of prizes. These tickets were the subject of traffic; they could have been sold; and the holder was assured that the company would pay to him the amount of the prize drawn. . . . In short, a lottery ticket is a subject of traffic, and is so designated in the act of 1895. . . .

We are of opinion that lottery tickets are subjects of traffic and therefore are subjects of commerce, and the regulation of the carriage of such tickets from State to State, at least by independent carriers, is a regulation of commerce among the several States.

But it is said that the statute in question does not regulate the carrying of lottery tickets from State to State, but by punishing those who cause them to be so carried Congress in effect prohibits such carrying; that in respect of the carrying from one State to another of articles or things that are, in fact, or according to usage in business, the subjects of commerce, the authority given Congress was not to *prohibit*, but only to *regulate*.

This view was earnestly pressed at the bar by learned counsel and must be examined. . . .

We have said that the carrying from State to State of lottery tickets constitutes interstate commerce, and that the regulation of such commerce is within the power of Congress under the Constitution. Are we prepared to say that a provision which is, in effect, a *prohibition* of the carriage of such articles from State to State is not a fit or appropriate mode for the *regulation* of that particular kind of commerce? If lottery traffic, *carried on through interstate commerce*, is a matter of which Congress may take cognizance and over which its power may be exerted, can it be possible that it must tolerate the traffic, and simply regulate the manner in which it may be carried on? Or may not Congress, for the protection of the people of all the States, and under the power to regulate interstate commerce, devise such means, within the scope of the Constitution, and not prohibited by it, as will drive that traffic out of commerce among the States?

In determining whether regulation may not under some circumstances properly take the form or have the effect of prohibition, the nature of the interstate traffic which it was sought by the act of May 2, 1895, to suppress cannot be overlooked. . . . In other cases we have adjudged that authority given by legislative enactment to carry on a lottery, although based upon a consideration in money, was not protected by the contract clause of the Constitution; this, for the reason that no State may bargain away its power to protect the public morals, nor excuse it failure to perform a public duty by saying that it had agreed, by legislative enactment, not to do so. . . .

If a State, when considering legislation for the suppression of lotteries within its own limits, may properly take into view the evils that inhere in the raising of money, in that mode, why may not Congress, invested with the power to regulate commerce among the several States, provide that such commerce shall not be polluted by the carrying of lottery tickets from one State to another? . . .

It is said, however, that if, in order to suppress lotteries carried on through interstate commerce, Congress may exclude lottery tickets from such commerce, that principle leads necessarily to the conclusion that Congress may arbitrarily exclude from commerce among the States any article, commodity or thing, of whatever kind or nature, or however useful or valuable, which it may choose, no matter with what motive, to declare shall not be carried from one State to another. It will be time enough to consider the constitutionality of such legislation when we must do so. The present case does not require the court to declare the full extent of the power that Congress may exercise in the regulation of commerce among the States. We may, however, repeat, in this connection, what the court has heretofore said, that the power of Congress to regulate commerce among the States, although plenary, cannot be deemed arbitrary, since it is subject to such limitations or restrictions as are prescribed by the Constitution. This power, therefore, may not be exercised so as to infringe rights secured or protected by that instrument. It would not be difficult to imagine legislation that would be justly liable to such an objection as that stated, and be hostile to the objects for the accomplishment of which Congress was invested with the general power to regulate commerce among the several States. But, as often said, the possible abuse of a power is not an argument against its existence. There is probably no governmental power that may

not be exerted to the injury of the public. If what is done by Congress is manifestly in excess of the powers granted to it, then upon the courts will rest the duty of adjudging that its action is neither legal nor binding upon the people. But if what Congress does is within the limits of its power, and is simply unwise or injurious, the remedy is that suggested by Chief Justice Marshall in *Gibbons* v. *Ogden*, when he said: "The wisdom and the discretion of Congress, their identity with the people, and the influence which their constituents possess at elections are, in this, as in many other instances, as that, for example, of declaring war, the sole restraints on which they have relied, to secure them from its abuse. They are the restraints on which the people must often rely solely, in all representative governments."

The whole subject is too important, and the questions suggested by its consideration are too difficult of solution, to justify any attempt to lay down a rule for determining in advance the validity of every statute, that may be enacted under the commerce clause. We decide nothing more in the present case than that lottery tickets are subjects of traffic among those who choose to sell or buy them; . . . [and] that under its power to regulate commerce among the several States Congress . . . may prohibit the carriage of such tickets from State to State; and that legislation to that end, and of that character, is not inconsistent with any limitation or restriction imposed upon the exercise of the powers granted to Congress. . . .

Chief Justice Fuller dissented with the concurrence of Justices Brewer, Shiras, and Peckham.

Such decisions were viewed by some Progressives as precedents for the use of federal commerce power and taxing power to fulfill objectives previously handled under state police authority. Another example of a broad constructionist approach occurred in 1904. In this instance, Congressional tax power was upheld in *McCray* v. *United States* in a 1902 statute that taxed oleomargarine colored to look like butter (but did not tax oleo that was not colored). The dairy lobby was a major factor in imposing the tax. A portion of Justice White's majority opinion is included.

McCRAY v. UNITED STATES
195 U. S. 27 (1904)

Justice White delivered the opinion of the Court:

The summary which follows embodies the propositions contained in the assignments of error, and the substance of the elaborate argument by which those

assignments are deemed to be sustained. Not denying the general power of Congress to impose excise taxes, and conceding that the acts in question, on their face, purport to levy taxes of that character, the propositions are these:

(a) That the power of internal taxation which the Constitution confers on Congress is given to that body for the purpose of raising revenue, and that the

tax on artificially colored oleomargarine is void becaus
it is of such an onerous character as to make it manifest that the purpose of Congress in levying it was not
to raise revenue but to suppress the manufacture of
the taxed article.

(b) The power to regulate the manufacture and sale
of oleomargarine being solely reserved to the several
States, it follows that the acts in question, enacted by
Congress for the purpose of suppressing the manufacture and sale of oleomargarine, when artificially colored, are void, because usurping the reserved power of
the States, and therefore exerting an authority not
delegated to Congress by the Constitution.

(c) Whilst it is true—so the argument proceeds—
that Congress in exerting the taxing power conferred
upon it may use all means appropriate to the exercise
of such power, a tax which is fixed at such a high rate
as to suppress the production of the article taxed, is
not a legitimate means to the lawful end, and is therefore beyond the scope of the taxing power. . . .

To avoid confusion and repetition we shall consider
these distinct contentions separately, and we hence
come, first, to ascertain how far, if at all, the motives
or purposes of Congress are open to judicial inquiry in
considering the power of that body to enact the laws in
question. Having determined the question of our right
to consider motive or purpose we shall then approach
the propositions relied on by the light of the correct
rule on the subject of purpose or motive.

Whilst, as a result of our written constitution, it is
axiomatic that the judicial department of the government is charged with the solemn duty of enforcing
the Constitution, and therefore in cases properly presented, of determining whether a given manifestation
of authority has exceeded the power conferred by
that instrument, no instance is afforded from the
foundation of the government where an act, which
was within a power conferred, was declared to be
repugnant to the Constitution, because it appeared
to the judicial mind that the particular exertion of
constitutional power was either unwise or unjust. To
announce such a principle would amount to declaring
that in our constitutional system the judiciary was not
only charged with the duty of upholding the Constitution but also with the responsibility of correcting
every possible abuse arising from the exercise by the
other departments of their conceded authority. So
to hold would be to overthrow the entire distinction between the legislative, judicial and executive
departments of the government, upon which our
system is founded, and would be a mere act of judicial
usurpation. . . .

It is, of course, true, as suggested, that if there be no
authority in the judiciary to restrain a lawful exercise
of power by another department of the government,
where a wrong motive or purpose has impelled to the
exertion of the power, that abuses of a power conferred may be temporarily effectual. The remedy for
this, however, lies, not in the abuse by the judicial
authority of its functions, but in the people, upon
whom, after all, under our institutions, reliance must
be placed for the correction of abuses committed in the
exercise of a lawful power. . . .

It being thus demonstrated that the motive or purpose of Congress in adopting the acts in question may
not be inquired into, we are brought to consider the
contentions relied upon to show that the acts assailed
were beyond the power of Congress, putting entirely
out of view all considerations based upon purpose or
motive.

1. Undoubtedly, in determining whether a particular act is within a granted power, its scope and effect
are to be considered. Applying this rule to the acts
assailed, it is self-evident that on their face they levy
an excise tax. That being their necessary scope and
operation, it follows that the acts are within the grant
of power. The argument to the contrary rests on the
proposition that, although the tax be within the power,
as enforcing it will destroy or restrict the manufacture
of artificially colored oleomargarine, therefore the
power to levy the tax did not obtain. This, however,
is but to say that the question of power depends,
not upon the authority conferred by the Constitution,
but upon what may be the consequence arising from
the exercise of the lawful authority.

Since, as pointed out in all the decisions referred to,
the taxing power conferred by the Constitution knows
no limits except those expressly stated in that instrument, it must follow, if a tax be within the lawful
power, the exertion of that power may not be judicially restrained because of the results to arise from its
exercise. The proposition now relied upon was urged
in *Knowlton* v. *Moore,* . . . and was overruled. . . .

2. The proposition that where a tax is imposed
which is within the grant of powers, and which does
not conflict with any express constitutional limitation,
the courts may hold the tax to be void because it is
deemed that the tax is too high, is absolutely disposed
of by the opinions in the cases hitherto cited, and
which expressly hold, to repeat again the language of
one of the cases, . . . that "The judicial department
cannot prescribe to the legislative department limitations upon the exercise of its acknowledged powers.
The power to tax may be exercised oppressively upon

persons; but the responsibility of the legislature is not to the courts, but to the people by whom its members are elected." . . .

3. Whilst undoubtedly both the Fifth and Tenth Amendments qualify, in so far as they are applicable, all the provisions of the Constitution, nothing in those amendments operates to take away the grant of power to tax conferred by the Constitution upon Congress. The contention on this subject rests upon the theory that the purpose and motive of Congress in exercising its undoubted powers may be inquired into by the courts, and the proposition is therefore disposed of by what has been said on that subject.

The right of Congress to tax within its delegated power being unrestrained, except as limited by the Constitution, it was within the authority conferred on Congress to select the objects upon which an excise should be laid. It therefore follows that, in exerting its power, no want of due process of law could possibly result, because that body chose to impose an excise on artificially colored oleomargarine and not upon natural butter artificially colored. The judicial power may not usurp the functions of the legislative in order to control that branch of the government in the performance of its lawful duties. This was aptly pointed out in the extract heretofore made from the opinion in *Treat* v. *White* . . .

But it is urged that artificially colored oleomargarine and artificially colored natural butter are in substance and in effect one and the same thing, and from this it is deduced that to lay an excise tax only on oleomargarine artificially colored and not on butter so colored is violative of the due process clause of the Fifth Amendment, because, as there is no possible distinction between the two, the act of Congress was a mere arbitrary imposition of an excise on the one article and not on the other, although essentially of the same class. Conceding merely for the sake of argument that the due process clause of the Fifth Amendment, would avoid an exertion of the taxing power which, without any basis for classification, arbitrarily taxed one article and excluded an article of the same class, such concession would be wholly inapposite to the case in hand. The distinction between natural butter artificially colored, and oleomargarine artificially colored so as to cause it to look like butter, has been pointed out in previous adjudications of this court. . . . Indeed, in the cases referred to the distinction between the two products was held to be so marked, and the aptitude of oleomargarine when artificially colored, to deceive the public into believing it to be butter, was decided to be so great that it was held no violation of the due process

clause of the Fourteenth Amendment was occasioned by state legislation absolutely forbidding the manufacture, within the State, of oleomargarine artificially colored. As it has been thus decided that the distinction between the two products is so great as to justify the absolute prohibition of the manufacture of oleomargarine artificially colored, there is no foundation for the proposition that the difference between the two was not sufficient, under the extremest view, to justify a classification, distinguishing between them.

4. Lastly we come to consider the argument that, even though as a general rule a tax of the nature of the one in question would be within the power of Congress, in this case the tax should be held not to be within such power, because of its effect. This is based on the contention that, as the tax is so large as to destroy the business of manufacturing oleomargarine artificially colored, to look like butter, it thus deprives the manufacturers of that article of their freedom to engage in a lawful pursuit, and hence, irrespective of the distribution of powers made by the Constitution, the taxing laws are void, because they violate those fundamental rights which it is the duty of every free government to safeguard, and which, therefore, should be held to be embraced by implied though none the less potential guaranties, or in any event to be within the protection of the due process clause of the Fifth Amendment.

Let us concede, for the sake of argument only, the premise of fact upon which the proposition is based. Moreover, concede for the sake of argument only, that even although a particular exertion of power by Congress was not restrained by any express limitation of the Constitution, if by the perverted exercise of such power so great an abuse was manifested as to destroy fundamental rights which no free government could consistently violate, that it would be the duty of the judiciary to hold such acts to be void upon the assumption that the Constitution by necessary implication forbade them.

Such concession, however, is not controlling in this case. This follows when the nature of oleomargarine, artificially colored to look like butter, is recalled. As we have said, it has been conclusively settled by this court that the tendency of that article to deceive the public into buying it for butter is such that the States may, in the exertion of their police powers, without violating the due process clause of the Fourteenth Amendment, absolutely prohibit the manufacture of the article. It hence results, that even although it be true that the effect of the tax in question is to repress the manufacture of artificially colored oleomargarine, it cannot be said that such repression destroys rights which no free government could destroy, and, therefore, no ground exists to sustain the proposition that the judiciary may invoke an implied prohibition, upon the theory that to do so is essential to save such rights from destruction. And the same considerations dispose of the contention based upon the due process clause of the Fifth Amendment. That provision, as we have previously said, does not withdraw or expressly limit the grant of power to tax conferred upon Congress by the Constitution. From this it follows, as we have also previously declared, that the judiciary is without authority to void an act of Congress exerting the taxing power, even in a case where to the judicial mind it seems that Congress had in putting such power in motion abused its lawful authority by levying a tax which was unwise or oppressive, or the result of the enforcement of which might be to indirectly affect subjects not within the powers delegated to Congress.

Let us concede that if a case was presented where the abuse of the taxing power was so extreme as to be beyond the principles which we have previously stated, and where it was plain to the judicial mind that the power had been called into play not for revenue but solely for the purpose of destroying rights which could not be rightfully destroyed consistently with the principles of freedom and justice upon which the Constitution rests, that it would be the duty of the courts to say that such an arbitrary act was not merely an abuse of a delegated power, but was the exercise of an authority not conferred. This concession, however, like the one previously made, must be without influence upon the decision of this cause for the reasons previously stated; that is, that the manufacture of artificially colored oleomargarine may be prohibited by a free government without a violation of fundamental rights. . . .

Chief Justice,
Justice Brown and Justice Peckham dissent.

In *Northern Securities Company v. United States,* the Court narrowly upheld a Justice Department action under the Sherman Antitrust Act against a Morgan-Harriman railroad combine. But the narrowness of the division and the inability of Progressives to anticipate consistent antitrust support from justices chosen because of their purported adherence to antitrust principles served as indicators of the uncertainty of Progressive judicial influence. Progressive hopes had been buoyed by President Theodore Roosevelt's judicial selections of Oliver Wendell Holmes, Jr., in 1902, William Rufus Day in 1903, and William Henry Moody in 1906. The decisions of Holmes, as chief justice of the Supreme Judicial Court of Massachusetts, had indicated more understanding of the position of labor than was demonstrated by most appellate judges in that era. These decisions drew strong criticism from corporations, but Theodore Roosevelt was impressed by that record. He wrote to Senator Henry Cabot Lodge that

> The ablest lawyers and greatest judges were men whose past has naturally brought them into close relationship with the wealthiest and most powerful clients, and I am glad when I can find a judge who has been able to preserve his aloofness of mind so as to keep his broad humanity of feeling and his sympathy for the class from which he has not drawn his clients. I think it eminently desirable that our Supreme Court should show in unmistakable fashion their entire sympathy with all proper effort to secure the most favorable possible consideration for the men who most need that consideration.[9]

Two years later, President Roosevelt was bitterly disappointed when Holmes dissented in the Northern Securities case. The majority opinion by Justice John Marshall Harlan is reproduced in part below:

NORTHERN SECURITIES COMPANY v. UNITED STATES
193 U. S. 197 (1904)

This suit was brought by the United States against the Northern Securities Company, a corporation of New Jersey. . . .

Its general object was to enforce, as against the defendants, the provisions of the statute of July 2, 1890, commonly known as the Anti-Trust Act, and entitled, "An act to protect trade and commerce against unlawful restraints and monopolies." . . .

The Government charges that if the combination was held not to be in violation of the act of Congress then all efforts of the National Government to preserve to the people the benefits of free competition among carriers engaged in interstate commerce will be wholly unavailing and all transcontinental lines, indeed the entire railway systems of the country, may be absorbed, merged and consolidated, thus placing the public at the absolute mercy of the holding corporation. . . .

In our judgment, the evidence fully sustains the material allegations of the bill, and shows a violation of the act of Congress, in so far as it declares illegal every combination or conspiracy in restraint of commerce among the several States and with foreign nations, and forbids attempts to monopolize such commerce or any part of it. . . .

Is the act to be construed as forbidding every combination or conspiracy in restraint of trade or commerce among the States or with foreign nations? Or, does it embrace only such restraints as are unreasonable in their nature? Is the motive with which a forbidden combination or conspiracy was formed at all material when it appears that the necessary tendency of the particular combination or conspiracy in question is to restrict or suppress free competition between competing railroads engaged in commerce among the States? Does the act of Congress prescribe, as a *rule* for *interstate* or *international* commerce, that the operation of the natural laws of competition between those engaged in *such* commerce shall not be restricted or interfered with by any contract, combination or conspiracy? . . .

We will not encumber this opinion by extended extracts from the former opinions of this court. It is sufficient to say that from the decisions . . . certain propositions are plainly deducible and embrace the present case. Those propositions are:

That although the act of Congress known as the Anti-Trust Act has no reference to the mere manufac-ture or production of articles or commodities within the limits of the several States, it does embrace and declare to be illegal every contract, combination or conspiracy, in whatever form, of whatever nature, and whoever may be parties to it, which directly or necessarily operates *in restraint* of trade or commerce *among the several States or with foreign nations;*

That the act is not limited to restraints of interstate and international trade or commerce that are unreasonable in their nature, but embraces *all* direct *restraints* imposed by any combination, conspiracy or monopoly upon such trade or commerce;

That railroad carriers engaged in interstate or international trade or commerce are embraced by the act;

That combinations even among *private* manufacturers or dealers whereby *interstate or international commerce* is restrained are equally embraced by the act;

That Congress has the power to establish *rules* by which *interstate and international* commerce shall be governed, and, by the Anti-Trust Act, has prescribed the rule of free competition among those engaged in such commerce;

That *every* combination or conspiracy which would extinguish competition between otherwise competing railroads engaged in *interstate trade or commerce,* and which would *in that way* restrain *such* trade or commerce, is made illegal by the act;

That the natural effect of competition is to increase commerce, and an agreement whose direct effect is to prevent this play of competition restrains instead of promotes trade and commerce;

That to vitiate a combination, such as the act of Congress condemns, it need not be shown that the combination, in fact, results or will result in a total suppression of trade or in a complete monopoly, but it is only essential to show that by its necessary operation it tends to restrain interstate or international trade or commerce or tends to create a monopoly in such trade or commerce and to deprive the public of the advantages that flow from free competition;

That the constitutional guarantee of liberty of contract does not prevent Congress from prescribing the rule of free competition for those engaged in *interstate and international* commerce; and

That under its power to regulate commerce among the several States and with foreign nations, Congress had authority to enact the statute in question. . . .

The means employed in respect of the combinations forbidden by the Anti-Trust Act, and which Congress deemed germane to the end to be accomplished, was to prescribe as *a rule* for *interstate and international* commerce (not for domestic commerce), that it should not be vexed by combinations, conspiracies or monopolies which restrain commerce by destroying or restricting competition. We say that Congress has prescribed such a rule, because in all the prior cases in this court the Anti-Trust Act has been construed as forbidding any combination which by its necessary operation destroys or restricts free competition among those engaged in interstate commerce; in other words, that to destroy or restrict free competition in interstate commerce was to restrain such commerce. Now, can this court say that such a rule is prohibited by the Constitution or is not one that Congress could appropriately prescribe when exerting its power under the commerce clause of the Constitution? Whether the free operation of the normal laws of competition is a wise and wholesome rule for trade and commerce is an economic question which this court need not consider or determine. Undoubtedly, there are those who think that the general business interests and prosperity of the country will be best promoted if the rule of competition is not applied. But there are others who believe that such a rule is more necessary in these days of enormous wealth than it ever was in any former period of our history. Be all this as it may, Congress has, in effect, recognized the rule of free competition by declaring illegal every combination or conspiracy in restraint of interstate and international commerce.

We cannot agree that Congress may strike down combinations among manufacturers and dealers in iron pipe, tiles, grates and mantels that restrain commerce among the States in such articles, but may not strike down combinations among stockholders of competing railroad carriers, which restrain commerce as involved in the transportation of passengers and property among the several States. If private parties may not, by combination among themselves, restrain interstate and international commerce in violation of an act of Congress, much less can such restraint be tolerated when imposed or attempted to be imposed upon commerce as carried on over public highways. Indeed, if the contentions of the defendants are sound why may not *all* the railway companies in the United States, that are engaged, under state charters, in interstate and international commerce, enter into a combination such as the one here in question, and by the device of a holding corporation obtain the absolute control throughout the entire country of rates for passengers and freight, beyond the power of Congress to protect the public against their exactions? The argument in behalf of the defendants necessarily leads to such results, and places Congress, although invested by the people of the United States with full authority to regu-

late interstate and international commerce, in a condition of utter helplessness, so far as the protection of the public against such combinations is concerned. . . .

Many suggestions were made in argument based upon the thought that the Anti-Trust Act would in the end prove to be mischievous in its consequences. Disaster to business and wide-spread financial ruin, it has been intimated, will follow the execution of its provisions. Such predictions were made in all the cases heretofore arising under that act. But they have not been verified. It is the history of monopolies in this country and in England that predictions of ruin are habitually made by them when it is attempted, by legislation, to restrain their operations and to protect the public against their exactions. In this, as in former cases, they seek shelter behind the reserved rights of the States and even behind the constitutional guarantee of liberty of contract. But this court has heretofore adjudged that the act of Congress did not touch the rights of the States, and that liberty of contract did not involve a right to deprive the public of the advantages of free competition in trade and commerce. Liberty of contract does not imply liberty in a corporation or individuals to defy the national will, when legally expressed. Nor does the enforcement of a legal enactment of Congress infringe, in any proper sense, the general inherent right of every one to acquire and hold property. That right, like all other rights, must be exercised in subordination to the law. . . .

It was said in argument that the circumstances under which the Northern Securities Company obtained the stock of the constituent companies imported simply an investment in the stock of other corporations, a purchase of that stock; which investment or purchase, it is contended, was not forbidden by the charter of the company and could not be made illegal by any act of Congress. This view is wholly fallacious, and does not comport with the actual transaction. There was no actual investment, in any substantial sense, by the Northern Securities Company in the stock of the two constituent companies. If it was, in form, such a transaction, it was not, in fact, one of that kind. However that company may have acquired for itself any stock in the Great Northern and Northern Pacific Railway companies, no matter how it obtained the means to do so, all the stock it held or acquired in the constituent companies was acquired and held to be used in suppressing competition between those companies. It came into existence only for that purpose. . . .

Guided by these long-established rules of construction, it is manifest that if the Anti-Trust Act is held not to embrace a case such as is now before us, the plain intention of the legislative branch of the Government will be defeated. If Congress has not, by the words used in the act, described this and like cases, it would, we apprehend, be impossible to find words that would describe them. . . .

Although Theodore Roosevelt was reported to be irked by Holmes' dissent to the point of suggesting that the justice would no longer be welcome at the White House,[10] Holmes and several justices chosen in the Progressive era did frequently contribute doctrinal innovations or support to regulatory statutes. Justice Holmes made such a contribution in a meat-packing corporation conspiracy case. In this instance in 1905, the Supreme Court distinguished a conspiracy by meat packers from the E. C. Knight precedent, thus substantially increasing the scope of congressional regulatory authority under the commerce clause. The Swift case was perceived as a significant regulatory victory. Major portions of Justice Holmes' majority opinion are provided:

SWIFT AND COMPANY v. UNITED STATES
196 U. S. 375 (1905)

The scheme as a whole seems to us to be within reach of the law. The constituent elements, as we have stated them, are enough to give to the scheme a body and, for all that we can say, to accomplish it. Moreover, whatever we may think of them separately when we take them up as distinct charges, they are alleged sufficiently as elements of the scheme. It is suggested that the several acts charged are lawful and that intent can make no difference. But they are bound together as the parts of a single plan. The plan may make the parts unlawful. . . . The statute gives this proceeding against combinations in restraint of commerce among the States and against attempts to monopolize the same. Intent is almost essential to such a combination and is essential to such an attempt. Where acts are not sufficient in themselves to produce a result which the law seeks to prevent—for instance, the monopoly—but require further acts in addition to the mere forces of nature to bring that result to pass, an intent to bring it to pass is necessary in order to produce a dangerous probability that it will happen. . . . But when that intent and the consequent dangerous probability exist, this statute, like many others and like the common law in some cases, directs itself against that dangerous probability as well as against the completed result. . . .

One further observation should be made. Although the combination alleged embraces restraint and monopoly of trade within a single State, its effect upon commerce among the States is not accidental, secondary, remote or merely probable. On the allegations of the bill the latter commerce no less, perhaps even more, than commerce within a single State is an object of attack. . . . Moreover, it is a direct object, it is that for the sake of which the several specific acts and courses of conduct are done and adopted. Therefore the case is not like *United States v. E. C. Knight Co.*, where the subject matter of the combination was manufacture and the direct object monopoly of manufacture within a State. However likely monopoly of commerce among the States in the article manufactured was to follow from the agreement it was not a necessary consequence nor a primary end. Here the subject matter is sales and the very point of the combination is to restrain and monopolize commerce among the States in respect of such sales. The two cases are near to each other, as sooner or later always must happen where lines are to be drawn, but the line between them is distinct. . . .

[W]e are of opinion that the carrying out of the scheme alleged, by the means set forth, properly may be enjoined, and that the bill cannot be dismissed. . . .

It is said that this charge is too vague and that it does not set forth a case of commerce among the States. Taking up the latter objection first, commerce among the States is not a technical legal conception, but a practical one, drawn from the course of business. When cattle are sent for sale from a place in one State, with the expectation that they will end their transit, after purchase, in another, and when in effect they do so, with only the interruption necessary to find a purchaser at the stockyard, and when this is a typical, constantly recurring course, the current thus existing is a current of commerce among the States, and the purchase of the cattle is a part and incident of such commerce. . . . Commerce among the States is not a technical legal conception, but a practical one, drawn from the course of business. . . .

Hostility toward labor: Adair, Lawlor, and Lochner

The broad constructionist approach taken in the Swift case was abandoned in the decisions involving state or federal legislative efforts to better the working or bargaining conditions of organized labor. The Adair, Lawlor, and Lochner decisions all illustrated the deep conservatism and latent hostility to labor of a majority of the Court. *Adair* v. *the United States* involved the validity of the Erdman Act of 1898, which prohibited "yellow dog" contracts in which railroad corporations required employees to sign an agreement not to belong to or join a union as a condition of employment. The employee in the case was discharged because he was a member of the Order of Locomotive Firemen. Portions of Justice Harlan's opinion striking down the Erdman Act are provided below:

ADAIR v. UNITED STATES
208 U. S. 161 (1908)

May Congress make it a criminal offense against the United States—as by the tenth section of the act of 1898 it does—for an agent or officer of an interstate carrier, having full authority in the premises from the carrier, to discharge an employé from service simply because of his membership in a labor organization?

This question is admittedly one of importance, and has been examined with care and deliberation. And the court has reached a conclusion which, in its judgment, is consistent with both the words and spirit of the Constitution and is sustained as well by sound reason.

The first inquiry is whether the part of the tenth section of the act of 1898 upon which the first count of the indictment was based is repugnant to the Fifth Amendment of the Constitution declaring that no person shall be deprived of liberty or property without due process of law. In our opinion that section, in the particular mentioned, is an invasion of the personal liberty, as well as of the right of property, guaranteed by that Amendment. Such liberty and right embraces the right to make contracts for the purchase of the labor of others and equally the right to make contracts for the sale of one's own labor; each right, however, being subject to the fundamental condition that no contract, whatever its subject matter, can be sustained which the law, upon reasonable grounds, forbids as inconsistent with the public interests or as hurtful to the public order or as detrimental to the common good. . . .

In *Lochner* v. *New York* . . . the court said: "The general right to make a contract in relation to his business is part of the liberty of the individual protected by the Fourteenth Amendment of the Federal Constitution." . . .

While, as already suggested, the rights of liberty and property guaranteed by the Constitution against deprivation without due process of law, are subject to such reasonable restraints as the common good or the general welfare may require, it is not within the functions of government—at least in the absence of contract between the parties—to compel any person in the course of his business and against his will to accept or retain the personal services of another, or to compel any person, against his will, to perform personal services for another. The right of a person to sell his labor upon such terms as he deems proper is, in its essence, the same as the right of the purchaser of labor to prescribe the conditions upon which he will accept such labor from the person offering to sell it. So the right of the employé to quit the service of the employer, for whatever reason, is the same as the right of the employer, for whatever reason, to dispense with the services of such employé. It was the legal right of the defendant Adair—however unwise such a course might have been—to discharge Coppage because of his being a member of a labor organization, as it was the legal right of Coppage, if he saw fit to do so—however unwise such a course on his part might have been—to quit the service in which he was engaged, because the defendant employed some persons who were not members of a labor organization. In all such particulars the employer and the employé have equality of right, and any legislation that disturbs that equality is an arbitrary interference with the liberty of contract which no government can legally justify in a free land. . . .

But it is suggested that the authority to make it a crime for an agent or officer of an interstate carrier, having authority in the premises from his principal, to discharge an employé from service to such carrier, simply because of his membership in a labor organization, can be referred to the power of Congress to regulate interstate commerce, without regard to any question of personal liberty or right of property arising under the Fifth Amendment. This suggestion can have no bearing in the present discussion unless the statute, in the particular just stated, is within the meaning of the Constitution a regulation of commerce among the States. If it be not, then clearly the Government cannot invoke the commerce clause of the Constitution as sustaining the indictment against Adair.

Let us inquire what is commerce, the power to regulate which is given to Congress?

This question has been frequently propounded in this court, and the answer has been—and no more specific answer could well have been given—that commerce among the several States comprehends traffic, intercourse, trade, navigation, communication, the transit of persons and the transmission of messages by telegraph—indeed, every species of commercial intercourse among the several States, but not to that commerce "completely internal, which is carried on between man and man, in a State, or between different parts of the same State, and which does not extend to or affect other States." . . . Manifestly, any rule prescribed for the conduct of interstate commerce, in order to be within the competency of Congress under its power to regulate commerce among the States, must have some real or substantial relation to or connection with the commerce regulated. But what possible legal or logical connection is there between an employé's membership in a labor organization and the carrying on of interstate commerce? Such relation to a labor organization cannot have, *in itself* and in the eye

of the law, any bearing upon the commerce with which the employé is connected by his labor and services. Labor associations, we assume, are organized for the general purpose of improving or bettering the conditions and conserving the interests of its members as wage-earners—an object entirely legitimate and to be commended rather than condemned. But surely those associations as labor organizations have nothing to do with interstate commerce as such. One who engages in the service of an interstate carrier will, it must be assumed, faithfully perform his duty, whether he be a member or not a member of a labor organization. His fitness for the position in which he labors and his diligence in the discharge of his duties cannot in law or sound reason depend in any degree upon his being or not being a member of a labor organization. It cannot be assumed that his fitness is assured, or his diligence increased, by such membership, or that he is less fit or less diligent because of his not being a member of such an organization. It is the employé as a man and not as a member of a labor organization who labors in the service of an interstate carrier. . . .

It results, on the whole case, that the provision of the statute under which the defendant was convicted must be held to be repugnant to the Fifth Amendment and as not embraced by nor within the power of Congress to regulate interstate commerce, but under the guise of regulating interstate commerce and as applied to this case it arbitrarily sanctions an illegal invasion of the personal liberty as well as the right of property of the defendant Adair. . . .

Organized labor hopes were further dashed in the same year by the Danbury Hatter's case (*Loewe* v. *Lawlor*), which reasserted a broader Congressional authority by extending the scope of the Antitrust Act to labor unions. Chief Justice Fuller's majority opinion is reproduced below:

LOEWE v. LAWLOR
208 U. S. 274 (1908)

In our opinion, the combination described in the declaration is a combination "in restraint of trade or commerce among the several States," in the sense in which those words are used in the act, and the action can be maintained accordingly.

And that conclusion rests on many judgments of this court, to the effect that the act prohibits any combination whatever to secure action which essentially obstructs the free flow of commerce between the States, or restricts, in that regard, the liberty of a trader to engage in business.

The combination charged falls within the class of restraints of trade aimed at compelling third parties and strangers involuntarily not to engage in the course of trade except on conditions that the combination imposes; and there is no doubt that (to quote from the well-known work of Chief Justice Erle on Trade Unions) "at common law every person has individually, and the public also has collectively, a right to require that the course of trade should be kept free from unreasonable obstruction." But the objection here is to the jurisdiction, because, even conceding that the declaration states a case good at common law, it is contended that it does not state one within the statute. Thus, it is said, that the restraint alleged would operate to entirely destroy plaintiffs' business and thereby include intrastate trade as well; that physical obstruction is not alleged as contemplated; and that defendants are not themselves engaged in interstate trade.

We think none of these objections are tenable, and that they are disposed of by previous decisions of this court.

United States v. *Trans-Missouri Freight Association,* . . . *United States* v. *Joint Traffic Association,* . . . and *Northern Securities Company* v. *United States,* . . . hold in effect that the Anti-Trust law has a broader application than the prohibition of restraints of trade unlawful at common law. . . .

We do not pause to comment on cases such as *United States* v. *Knight,* . . . in which the undisputed facts showed that the purpose of the agreement was not to obstruct or restrain interstate commerce. The object and intention of the combination determined its legality. . . .

The averments here are that there was an existing interstate traffic between plaintiffs and citizens of other States, and that for the direct purpose of destroying such interstate traffic defendants combined not merely to prevent plaintiffs from manufacturing articles then and there intended for transportation beyond the State, but also to prevent the vendees from reselling the hats which they had imported from Connecticut, or from further negotiating with plaintiffs for the purchase and intertransportation of such hats from Connecticut to the various places of destination. So that, although some of the means whereby the interstate traffic was to be destroyed were acts within a State, and some of them were in themselves as a part of their obvious purpose and effect beyond the scope of Federal authority, still, as we have seen, the acts must be considered as a whole, and the plan is open to condemnation, notwithstanding a negligible amount of intrastate business might be affected in carrying it out. If the purposes of the combination were, as alleged, to prevent any interstate transportation at all, the fact that the means operated at one end before physical transportation commenced and at the other end after the physical transportation ended was immaterial.

Nor can the act in question be held inapplicable because defendants were not themselves engaged in interstate commerce. The act made no distinction between classes. It provided that "every" contract, combination or conspiracy in restraint of trade was illegal. The records of Congress show that several efforts were made to exempt, by legislation, organizations of farmers and laborers from the operation of the act and

that all these efforts failed, so that the act remained as we have it before us. . . .

The subject had so broadened in the minds of the legislators that the source of the evil was not regarded as material, and the evil in its entirety is dealt with. They made the interdiction include combinations of labor, as well as of capital; in fact, all combinations in restraint of commerce, without reference to the character of the persons who entered into them. It is true this statute has not been much expounded by judges, but, as it seems to me, its meaning, as far as relates to the sort of combinations to which it is to apply, is manifest, and that it includes combinations which are composed of laborers acting in the interest of laborers. . . .

At the risk of tediousness, we repeat that the complaint averred that plaintiffs were manufacturers of hats in Danbury, Connecticut, having a factory there, and were then and there engaged in an interstate trade in some twenty States other than the State of Connecticut; that they were practically dependent upon such interstate trade to consume the product of their factory, only a small percentage of their entire output being consumed in the State of Connecticut; that at the time the alleged combination was formed they were in the process of manufacturing a large number of hats for the purpose of fulfilling engagements then actually made with consignees and wholesale dealers in States other than Connecticut, and that if prevented from carrying on the work of manufacturing these hats they would be unable to complete their engagements.

That defendants were members of a vast combination called The United Hatters of North America, comprising about 9,000 members and including a large number of subordinate unions, and that they were combined with some 1,400,000 others into another association known as The American Federation of Labor, of which they were members, whose members resided in all the places in the several States where the wholesale dealers in hats and their customers resided and did business; that defendants were "engaged in a combined scheme and effort to force all manufacturers of fur hats in the United States, including the plaintiffs, against their will and their previous policy of carrying on their business, to organize their workmen in the departments of making and finishing, in each of their factories, into an organization, to be part and parcel of the said combination known as The United Hatters of North America, or as the defendants and their confederates term it, to unionize their shops, with the intent thereby to control the employment of labor in and the operation of said factories, and to subject the same to the direction and control of persons other than the owners of the same, in a manner extremely onerous and distasteful to such owners and to carry out such scheme, effort and purpose, by restraining and destroying the interstate trade and commerce of such manufacturers, by means of intimidation of and threats made to such manufacturers and their customers in the several States, of boycotting them, their product and their customers, using therefor all the powerful means at their command, as aforesaid, until such time as, from the damage and loss of business resulting therefrom, the said manufacturers should yield to the said demand to unionize their factories." . . .

[T]he defendants proceeded to carry out their combination to restrain and destroy interstate trade and commerce between plaintiffs and their customers in other States by employing the identical means contrived for that purpose; and that by reason of those acts plaintiffs were damaged in their business and property in some $80,000.

Although the Supreme Court occasionally appeared to be indecisive in its applications of doctrinal restraints on state and national regulation of business and labor during the first two decades of the 20th century, the main thrust of its decisions remained probusiness, antilabor, and antiregulatory. One of the most important manifestations of its underlying antilabor tendency was the 1905 decision in *Lochner* v. *New York*. The case involved a New York statute that, in order to protect the health of bakers, limited work in bakeries to 10 hours a day and 60 hours a week. The rigid conservatism of the Court's majority is summed up in Justice Peckham's majority opinion. Portions of Justice Harlan's and Holmes' separate dissents are also reproduced.

LOCHNER v. NEW YORK
198 U. S. 45 (1905)

Justice Peckham delivered the opinion of the Court:

The statute necessarily interferes with the right of contract between the employer and employés, concerning the number of hours in which the latter may labor in the bakery of the employer. The general right to make a contract in relation to his business is part of the liberty of the individual protected by the Fourteenth Amendment of the Federal Constitution. *Allgeyer* v. *Louisiana.* . . . Under that provision no State can deprive any person of life, liberty or property without due process of law. The right to purchase or to sell labor is part of the liberty protected by this amendment, unless there are circumstances which exclude the right. There are, however, certain powers, existing in the sovereignty of each State in the Union, somewhat vaguely termed police powers, the exact description and limitation of which have not been attempted by the courts. Those powers, broadly stated and without, at present, any attempt at a more specific limitation, relate to the safety, health, morals and general welfare of the public. Both property and liberty are held on such reasonable conditions as may be imposed by the governing power of the State in the exercise of those powers, and with such conditions the Fourteenth Amendment was not designed to interfere. . . .

The State, therefore, has power to prevent the individual from making certain kinds of contracts, and in regard to them the Federal Constitution offers no protection. If the contract be one which the State, in the legitimate exercise of its police power, has the right to prohibit, it is not prevented from prohibiting it by the Fourteenth Amendment. Contracts in violation of a statute, either of the Federal or state government, or a contract to let one's property for immoral purposes, or to do any other unlawful act, could obtain no protection from the Federal Constitution, as coming under the liberty of person or free contract. Therefore, when the State, by its legislature, in the assumed exercise of its police powers, has passed an act which seriously limits the right to labor or the right of contract in regard to their means of livelihood between persons who are *sui juris* (both the employer and employé), it becomes of great importance to determine which shall prevail—the right of the individual to labor for such time as he may choose, or the right of the State to prevent the individual from laboring or from entering into any contract to labor, beyond a certain time prescribed by the State.

This court has recognized the existence and upheld

the exercise of the police powers of the States in many cases which might fairly be considered as border ones, and it has, in the course of its determination of questions regarding the asserted invalidity of such statutes, on the ground of their violation of the rights secured by the Federal Constitution, been guided by rules of a very liberal nature, the application of which has resulted, in numerous instances, in upholding the validity of state statutes thus assailed. . . .

It must, of course, be conceded that there is a limit to the valid exercise of the police power by the State. There is no dispute concerning this general proposition. . . . In every case that comes before this court, therefore, where legislation of this character is concerned and where the protection of the Federal Constitution is sought, the question necessarily arises: Is this a fair, reasonable and appropriate exercise of the police power of the State, or is it an unreasonable, unnecessary and arbitrary interference with the right of the individual to his personal liberty or to enter into those contracts in relation to labor which may seem to him appropriate or necessary for the support of himself and his family? Of course the liberty of contract relating to labor includes both parties to it. The one has as much right to purchase as the other to sell labor.

This is not a question of substituting the judgment of the court for that of the legislature. If the act be within the power of the State it is valid, although the judgment of the court might be totally opposed to the enactment of such a law. But the question would still remain: Is it within the police power of the State? and that question must be answered by the court.

The question whether this act is valid as a labor law, pure and simple, may be dismissed in a few words. There is no reasonable ground for interfering with the liberty of person or the right of free contract, by determining the hours of labor, in the occupation of a baker. There is no contention that bakers as a class are not equal in intelligence and capacity to men in other trades or manual occupations, or that they are not able to assert their rights and care for themselves without the protecting art of the State, interfering with their independence of judgment and of action. They are in no sense wards of the State. . . . The law must be upheld, if at all, as a law pertaining to the health of the individual engaged in the occupation of a baker. It does not affect any other portion of the public than those who are engaged in that occupation. Clean and wholesome bread does not depend upon whether the baker works but ten hours per day or only sixty hours a week. The limitation of the hours of labor does not come within the police power on that ground.

It is a question of which of two powers or rights shall prevail—the power of the State to legislate or the right of the individual to liberty of person and freedom of contract. . . .

We think the limit of the police power has been reached and passed in this case. There is, in our judgment, no reasonable foundation for holding this to be necessary or appropriate as a health law to safeguard the public health or the health of the individuals who are following the trade of a baker. If this statute be valid, and if, therefore, a proper case is made out in which to deny the right of an individual, *sui juris*, as employer or employé, to make contracts for the labor of the latter under the protection of the provisions of the Federal Constitution, there would seem to be no length to which legislation of this nature might not go. . . .

We think that there can be no fair doubt that the trade of a baker, in and of itself, is not an unhealthy one to that degree which would authorize the legislature to interfere with the right to labor, and with the right of free contract on the part of the individual, either as employer or employé. In looking through statistics regarding all trades and occupations, it may be true that the trade of a baker does not appear to be as healthy as some other trades, and is also vastly more healthy than still others. To the common understanding the trade of a baker has never been regarded as an unhealthy one. Very likely physicians would not recommend the exercise of that or of any other trade as a remedy for ill health. Some occupations are more healthy than others, but we think there are none which might not come under the power of the legislature to supervise and control the hours of working therein, if the mere fact that the occupation is not absolutely and perfectly healthy is to confer that right upon the legislative department of the Government. It might be safely affirmed that almost all occupations more or less affect the health. . . . But are we all, on that account, at the mercy of legislative majorities? . . .

Statutes of the nature of that under review, limiting the hours in which grown and intelligent men may labor to earn their living, are mere meddlesome interferences with the rights of the individual, and they are not saved from condemnation by the claim that they are passed in the exercise of the police power and upon the subject of the health of the individual whose rights are interfered with, unless there be some fair ground, reasonable in and of itself, to say that there is material danger to the public health or to the health of the employés, if the hours of labor are not curtailed. If this be not clearly the case the individuals, whose rights are thus made the subject of legislative interference, are under the protection of the Federal Constitution regarding their liberty of contract as well as of person; and the legislature of the State has no power to limit their right as proposed in this statute. . . .

It was further urged on the argument that restricting the hours of labor in the case of bakers was valid because it tended to cleanliness on the part of the workers, as a man was more apt to be cleanly when not overworked, and if cleanly then his "output" was also more likely to be so. . . . In our judgment it is not possible in fact to discover the connection between the number of hours a baker may work in the bakery and the healthful quality of the bread made by the workman. The connection, if any exists, is too shadowy and thin to build any argument for the interference of the legislature. If the man works ten hours a day it is all right, but if ten and a half or eleven his health is in danger and his bread may be unhealthful, and, therefore, he shall not be permitted to do it. This, we think, is unreasonable and entirely arbitrary. . . .

It is manifest to us that the limitation of the hours of labor as provided for in this section of the statute under which the indictment was found, and the plaintiff in error convicted, has no such direct relation to and no such substantial effect upon the health of the employé, as to justify us in regarding the section as really a health law. It seems to us that the real object and purpose were simply to regulate the hours of labor between the master and his employés (all being men, *sui juris*), in a private business, not dangerous in any degree to morals or in any real and substantial degree, to the health of the employés. Under such circumstances the freedom of master and employé to contract with each other in relation to their employment, and in defining the same, cannot be prohibited or interfered with, without violating the Federal Constitution. . . .

Justice Harlan dissented, with Justice White and Justice Day concurring:

While this court has not attempted to mark the precise boundaries of what is called the police power of the State, the existence of the power has been uniformly recognized, both by the Federal and state courts.

All the cases agree that this power exter.ds at least to the protection of the lives, the health and the safety of the public against the injurious exercise by any citizen of his own rights. . . .

It is plain that this statute was enacted in order to protect the physical well-being of those who work in bakery and confectionery establishments. It may be that the statute had its origin, in part, in the belief that employers and employés in such establishments were not upon an equal footing, and that the necessities of the latter often compelled them to submit to such exactions as unduly taxed their strength. Be this as it may, the statute must be taken as expressing the belief of the people of New York that, as a general rule, and in the case of the average man, labor in excess of sixty hours during a week in such establishments may endanger the health of those who thus labor. Whether or not this be wise legislation it is not the province of the court to inquire. Under our systems of government the courts are not concerned with the wisdom or policy of legislation. So that in determining the question of power to interfere with liberty of contract, the court may inquire whether the means devised by the State are germane to an end which may be lawfully accomplished and have a real or substantial relation to the protection of health, as involved in the daily work of the persons, male and female, engaged in bakery and confectionery establishments. . . . I submit that this court will transcend its foundations if it assumes to annul the statute of New York. It must be remembered that this statute does not apply to all kinds of business. It applies only to work in bakery and confectionery establishments, in which, as all know, the air constantly breathed by workmen is not as pure and healthful as that to be found in some other establishments or out of doors.

Professor Hirt in his treatise on the "Diseases of the Workers" has said:

"The labor of the bakers is among the hardest and most laborious imaginable, because it has to be performed under conditions injurious to the health of those engaged in it. It is hard, very hard work, not only because it requires a great deal of physical exertion in an overheated workshop and during unreasonably long hours, but more so because of the erratic demands of the public, compelling the baker to perform the greater part of his work at night, thus depriving him of an opportunity to enjoy the necessary rest and sleep, a fact which is highly injurious to his health."

Another writer says:

"The constant inhaling of flour dust causes inflammation of the lungs and of the bronchial tubes. The eyes also suffer through this dust, which is responsible for the many cases of running eyes among the bakers. The long hours of toil to which all bakers are subjected produce rheumatism, cramps and swollen legs. . . ."

In the Eighteenth Annual Report by the New York Bureau of Statistics of Labor it is stated that among the occupations involving exposure to conditions that interfere with nutrition is that of a baker. . . .

There are many reasons of a weighty, substantial character, based upon the experience of mankind, in support of the theory that, all things considered, more than ten hours' steady work each day, from week to week, in a bakery or confectionery establishment, may endanger the health, and shorten the lives of the workmen, thereby diminishing their physical and mental capacity to serve the State, and to provide for those dependent upon them.

If such reasons exist that ought to be the end of this case, for the State is not amenable to the judiciary, in respect of its legislative enactments, unless such enactments are plainly, palpably, beyond all question, inconsistent with the Constitution of the United States. We are not to presume that the State of New York has acted in bad faith. Nor can we assume that its legislature acted without due deliberation, or that it did not determine this question upon the fullest attainable information, and for the common good. We cannot say that the State has acted without reason nor ought we to proceed upon the theory that its action is a mere sham. Our duty, I submit, is to sustain the statute as not being in conflict with the Federal Constitution, for the reason—and such is an all-sufficient reason—it is not shown to be plainly and palpably inconsistent with that instrument. Let the State alone in the management of its purely domestic affairs, so long as it does not appear beyond all question that it has violated the Federal Constitution. This view necessarily results from the principle that the health and safety of the people of a State are primarily for the State to guard and protect.

I take leave to say that the New York statute, in the particulars here involved, cannot be held to be in conflict with the Fourteenth Amendment, without enlarging the scope of the Amendment far beyond its original purpose and without bringing under the supervision of this court matters which have been supposed to belong exclusively to the legislative departments of the several States when exerting their conceded power to guard the health and safety of their citizens by such regulations as they in their wisdom deem best. . . . A decision that the New York statute is void under the Fourteenth Amendment will, in my opinion, involve consequences of a far-reaching and mischievous character; for such a decision would seriously cripple the inherent power of the States to care for the lives, health and well-being of their citizens. . . .

Justice Holmes wrote a separate dissent:

I regret sincerely that I am unable to agree with the judgment in this case, and I think it my duty to express my dissent.

This case is decided upon an economic theory which a large part of the country does not entertain. If it were a question whether I agreed with that theory, I should desire to study it further and long before making up my mind. But I do not conceive that to be my duty, because I strongly believe that my agreement or disagreement has nothing to do with the right of a majority to embody their opinions in law. It is settled by various decisions of this court that state constitutions and state laws may regulate life in many ways which we as legislators might think as injudicious, or if you like as tyrannical, as this, and which equally with this, interfere with the liberty to contract. Sunday laws and usury laws are ancient examples. A more modern one is the prohibition of lotteries. The liberty of the citizen to do as he likes so long as he does not interfere with the liberty of others to do the same, which has been a shibboleth for some well-known writers, is interfered with by school laws, by the Postoffice, by every state or municipal institution which takes his money for purposes thought desirable, whether he likes it or not. The 14th Amendment does not enact Mr. Herbert Spencer's Social Statics. The other day we sustained the Massachusetts vaccination law. . . . United States and state statutes and decisions cutting down the liberty to contract by way of combination are familiar to this court. . . .

. . . Two years ago we upheld the prohibition of sales of stocks on margins, or for future delivery, in the Constitution of California. . . . The decision sustaining an eight-hour law for miners is still recent. . . . Some of these laws embody convictions or prejudices which judges are likely to share. Some may not. But a Constitution is not intended to embody a particular economic theory, whether of paternalism and the organic relation of the citizen to the state or of laissez faire. It is made for people of fundamentally differing views, and the accident of our finding certain opinions natural and familiar, or novel, and even shocking, ought not to conclude our judgment upon the question whether statutes embodying them conflict with the Constitution of the United States.

General propositions do not decide concrete cases. The decision will depend on a judgment or intuition more subtle than any articulate major premise. But I think that the proposition just stated, if it is accepted, will carry us far toward the end. Every opinion tends to become a law. I think that the word "liberty," in the 14th Amendment, is perverted when it is held to prevent the natural outcome of a dominant opinion, unless it can be said that a rational and fair man necessarily would admit that the statute proposed would infringe fundamental principles as they have been understood by the traditions of our people and our law. It does not need research to show that no such sweeping condemnation can be passed upon the statute before us. A reasonable man might think it a proper measure on the score of health. Men whom I certainly could not pronounce unreasonable would uphold it as a first instalment of a general regulation of the hours of work. Whether in the latter aspect it would be open to the charge of inequality I think it unnecessary to discuss.

The Progressive forces that sought to achieve social change by improving working conditions though state or federal legislation were aided by a remarkably able attorney, Louis D. Brandeis, who developed the important concept of the factual brief, a legal brief employing factual economic, health, and social evidence. As counsel for the state of Oregon he and his supporters in the Consumer League amassed a compelling array of social, economic, and physiological information in a brief prepared to defend the validity of an Oregon statute limiting the work day for women to ten hours. In *Muller* v. *Oregon* this approach succeeded, despite the generally prevailing conservatism of the Court's majority.

MULLER v. OREGON
208 U. S. 412 (1908)

Justice Brewer delivered the opinion of the Court:

The single question is the constitutionality of the statute under which the defendant was convicted so far as it affects the work of a female in a laundry. . . .

We held in *Lochner* v. *New York* . . . that a law providing that no laborer shall be required or permitted to work in a bakery not more than sixty hours in a week or ten hours in a day was not as to men a legitimate exercise of the police power of the State, but an unreasonable, unnecessary and arbitrary interference with the right and liberty of the individual to contract in relation to his labor, and as such was in conflict with, and void under, the Federal Constitution. That decision is invoked by plaintiff in error as decisive of the question before us. But this assumes that the difference between the sexes does not justify a different rule respecting a restriction of the hours of labor.

In patent cases counsel are apt to open the argument with a discussion of the state of the art. It may not be amiss, in the present case, before examining the constitutional question, to notice the course of legislation as well as expressions of opinion from other than judicial sources. In the brief filed by Mr. Louis D. Brandeis, for the defendant in error, is a very copious collection of all these matters. . . .

The legislation and opinions referred to . . . may not be, technically speaking, authorities, and in them is little or no discussion of the constitutional question presented to us for determination, yet they are signifi-cant of a widespread belief that woman's physical structure, and the functions she performs in consequence thereof, justify special legislation restricting or qualifying the conditions under which she should be permitted to toil. Constitutional questions, it is true, are not settled by even a consensus of present public opinion, for it is the peculiar value of a written constitution that it places in unchanging form limitations upon legislative action, and thus gives a permanence and stability to popular government which otherwise would be lacking. At the same time, when a question of fact is debated and debatable, and the extent to which a special constitutional limitation goes is affected by the truth in respect to that fact, a widespread and long continued belief concerning it is worthy of consideration. We take judicial cognizance of all matters of general knowledge.

It is undoubtedly true, as more than once declared by this court, that the general right to contract in relation to one's business is part of the liberty of the individual, protected by the Fourteenth Amendment to the Federal Constitution; yet it is equally well settled that this liberty is not absolute and extending to all contracts, and that a State may, without conflicting with the provisions of the Fourteenth Amendment, restrict in many respects the individual's power of contract. . . .

That woman's physical structure and the performance of maternal functions place her at a disadvantage in the struggle for subsistence is obvious. This is especially true when the burdens of motherhood are upon her. Even when they are not, by abundant testimony of the medical fraternity continuance for a long time on her feet at work, repeating this from day to day, tends to injurious effects upon the body, and as healthy mothers are essential to vigorous offspring, the physical well-being of woman becomes an object of public interest and care in order to preserve the strength and vigor of the race.

Still again, history discloses the fact that woman has always been dependent upon man. . . . The two sexes differ in structure of body, in the functions to be performed by each, in the amount of physical strength, in the capacity for long-continued labor, particularly when done standing, the influence of vig-orous health upon the future well-being of the race, the self-reliance which enables one to assert full rights, and in the capacity to maintain the struggle for subsistence. This difference justifies a difference in legislation and upholds that which is designed to compensate for some of the burdens which rest upon her. . . .

For these reasons, and without questioning in any respect the decision in *Lochner* v. *New York*, we are of the opinion that it cannot be adjudged that the act in question is in conflict with the Federal Constitution, so far as it respects the work of a female in a laundry. . . .

A few years later, Progressives received more encouragement because of the successful defense of another Oregon law providing regulation of the working hours of men as well as women and wage regulations for time and one half for overtime. A factual brief again was important to the outcome, but the optimism of Progressives was destined to be short-lived. Justice McKenna's majority opin-ion in *Bunting* v. *Oregon* is reproduced in part:

BUNTING v. OREGON
243 U. S. 426 (1917)

The consonance of the Oregon law with the Four-teenth Amendment is the question in the case, and this depends upon whether it is a proper exercise of the police power of the State, as the Supreme Court of the State decided that it is.

That the police power extends to health regulations is not denied, but it is denied that the law has such purpose or justification. It is contended that it is a wage law, not a health regulation, and takes the prop-erty of plaintiff in error without due process. The con-tention presents two questions: (1) Is the law a wage law, or an hours of service law? And (2) if the latter, has it equality of operation?

Section 1 of the law expresses the policy that im-pelled its enactment to be the interest of the State in the physical well-being of its citizens and that it is injurious to their health for them to work "in any mill, factory or manufacturing establishment" more than ten hours in any one day; and § 2, as we have seen, forbids their employment in those places for a longer time. If, therefore, we take the law at its word there can be no doubt of its purpose, and the Supreme Court of the State has added the confirmation of its decision, by declaring that "the aim of the statute is to fix the maximum hours of service in certain industries. The act makes no attempt to fix the standard of wages. No maximum or minimum wage is named. That is left wholly to the contracting parties." . . .

First, as to plaintiff in error's attack upon the law. He says: "The law is not a ten-hour law; it is a thirteen-hour law designed solely for the purpose of compelling the employer of labor in mills, factories and manufacturing establishments to pay more for labor than the actual market value thereof." And fur-ther: "It is a ten-hour law for the purpose of taking the employer's property from him and giving it to the employé; it is a thirteen-hour law for the purpose of protecting the health of the employé." To this plaintiff in error adds that he was convicted, not for working an employee during a busy season for more than ten hours, but for not paying him more than the market value of his services. . . .

There is a certain verbal plausibility in the conten-tion that it was intended to permit 13 hours' work if there be 15½ hours' pay, but the plausibility disap-pears upon reflection. The provision for overtime is permissive, in the same sense that any penalty may be said to be permissive. Its purpose is to deter by its burden and its adequacy for this was a matter of legis-lative judgment under the particular circumstances. It may not achieve its end, but its insufficiency can-not change its character from penalty to permission. Besides, it is to be borne in mind that the legislature was dealing with a matter in which many elements were to be considered. It might not have been possible, it might not have been wise, to make a rigid pro-hibition. We can easily realize that the legislature deemed it sufficient for its policy to give to the law an adaptation to occasions different from special cases of emergency for which it provided, occasions not of such imperative necessity, and yet which should have some accommodation—abuses prevented by the requirement of higher wages. Or even a broader contention might be made that the legislature considered it a proper policy to meet the conditions long existent by a tentative restraint of conduct rather than by an absolute restraint, and achieve its purpose through the interest of those affected rather than by the positive fiat of the law.

We cannot know all of the conditions that impelled the law or its particular form. The Supreme Court, nearer to them, describes the law as follows: "It is clear that the intent of the law is to make 10 hours a regular day's labor in the occupations to which reference is made. Apparently the provisions for permitting labor for the overtime on express conditions were made in order to facilitate the enforcement of the law, and in the nature of a mild penalty for employing one not more than three hours overtime. It might be regarded as more difficult to detect violations of the law by an employment for a shorter time than for a longer time. This penalty also goes to the employee in case the employer avails himself of the overtime clause."

But we need not cast about for reasons for the legislative judgment. We are not required to be sure of the precise reasons for its exercise or be convinced of the wisdom of its exercise. . . . It is enough for our decision if the legislation under review was passed in the exercise of an admitted power of government; and that it is not as complete as it might be, not as rigid in its prohibitions as it might be, gives perhaps evasion too much play, is lighter in its penalties than it might be, is no impeachment of its legality. This may be a blemish, giving opportunity for criticism and difference in characterization, but the constitutional validity of legislation cannot be determined by the degree of exactness of its provisions or remedies. New policies are usually tentative in their beginnings, advance in firmness as they advance in acceptance. They do not at a particular moment of time spring full-perfect in extent or means from the legislative brain. Time may be necessary to fashion them to precedent customs and conditions and as they justify themselves or otherwise they pass from militancy to triumph or from question to repeal.

But passing general considerations and coming back to our immediate concern, which is the validity of the particular exertion of power in the Oregon law, our judgment of it is that it does not transcend constitutional limits. . . .

Federalism, inherent powers, and state equality

Some modern scholars compare 20th century decision making unfavorably with the magisterial style and the clear sense of nationalistic purpose characteristic of the decisions of Chief Justice John Marshall. Differences in style were indeed marked, although they did not account for all variations in decision making. But the 20th century jurist was not confronted with the clear-cut choices in federal-state relations or separation of powers that confronted the young Court in the early 1800s. In comparison to the delineation given by Marshall in *McCulloch* v. *Maryland*, most issues of federalism in the 20th century were considerably less clear-cut and less dramatic. *South Carolina* v. *United States* is illustrative. Justice Brewer's majority opinion addressed itself as much to Brewer's fear of Socialism as it did to the issue of federalism.

SOUTH CAROLINA v. UNITED STATES
199 U. S. 437 (1905)

The important question in this case is whether persons who are selling liquor are relieved from liability for the internal revenue tax by the fact that they have no interest in the profits of the business, and are simply the agents of a state which, in the exercise of its sovereign power, has taken charge of the business of selling intoxicating liquors. . . .

The right of South Carolina to control the sale of liquor by the dispensary system has been sustained. . . . The profits from the business in the year 1901, as appears from the findings of fact, were over half a million of dollars. Mingling the thought of profit with the necessity of regulation may induce the state to take possession, in like manner, of tobacco, oleomargarine, and all other objects of internal revenue tax. If one state finds it thus profitable, other states may follow, and the whole body of internal revenue tax be thus stricken down.

More than this. There is a large and growing movement in the country in favor of the acquisition and management by the public of what are termed "public utilities," including not merely therein the supply of gas and water, but also the entire railroad system. Would the state, by taking into possession these public utilities, lose its republican form of government?

We may go even a step further. There are some insisting that the state shall become the owner of all property and the manager of all business. Of course, this is an extreme view, but its advocates are earnestly contending that thereby the best interests of all citizens will be subserved. If this change should be made in any state, how much would that state contribute to the revenue of the nation? If this extreme action is not to be counted among the probabilities, consider the result of one much less so. Suppose a state assumes, under its police power, the control of all those matters subject to the internal revenue tax, and also engages in the business of importing all foreign goods. The same argument which would exempt the sale by a state of liquor, tobacco, etc., from a license tax, would exempt the importation of merchandise by a state from import duty. While the state might not prohibit importations, as it can the sale of liquor, by private individuals, yet, paying no import duty, it could undersell all individuals, and so monopolize the importation and sale of foreign goods.

Obviously, if the power of the state is carried to the extent suggested, and with it is relief from all Federal taxation, the national government would be largely crippled in its revenues. Indeed, if all the states should concur in exercising their powers to the full extent, it would be almost impossible for the nation to collect any revenues. In other words, in this indirect way it would be within the competency of the states to practically destroy the efficiency of the national government. . . .

There is something of a conflict between the full power of the nation in respect to taxation and the exemption of the state from Federal taxation in respect to its property and a discharge of all its functions. Where and how shall the line between them be drawn? We have seen that the full power of collecting license taxes is in terms granted to the national government, with only the limitations of uniformity and the public benefit. The exemption of the state's property and its functions from Federal taxation is implied from the dual character of our Federal system and the necessity of preserving the state in all its efficiency. In order to determine to what extent that implication will go we must turn to the condition of things at the time the Constitution was framed. What, in the light of that condition, did the framers of the convention intend should be exempt? Certain is it that modern notions as to the extent to which the functions of a state may be carried had then no hold. . . .

Looking, therefore, at the Constitution in the light of the conditions surrounding [it] at the time of its adoption, it is obvious that the framers, in granting full power over license taxes to the national government, meant that that power should be complete, and never thought that the states, by extending their functions, could practically destroy it. . . .

It is also worthy of remark that the cases in which the invalidity of a Federal tax has been affirmed were those in which the tax was attempted to be levied upon property belonging to the state, or one of its municipalities, or was a charge upon the means and instrumentalities employed by the state, in the discharge of its ordinary functions as a government. . . .

These decisions, while not controlling the question before us, indicate that the thought has been that the exemption of state agencies and instrumentalities from national taxation is limited to those which are of a strictly governmental character, and does not extend to those which are used by the state in the carrying on of an ordinary private business. . . .

For these reasons we think that the license taxes charged by the Federal government upon persons selling liquor are not invalidated by the fact that they are the agents of the state, which has itself engaged in that business.

The judgment of the Court of Claims is affirmed.

Justice White, with whom Justice Peckham and Justice McKenna concurred, wrote a dissenting opinion.

Early 20th century treatment of the issues of federalism embraced far more than the early limitations of the doctrine of intergovernmental tax immunity developed in *South Carolina* v. *the United States*. *Kansas* v. *Colorado* provided a rather interesting situation in which the Supreme Court found itself responding to a political crisis largely of its own making. After the Wabash decision and others inhibited its ability to regulate, for example, the Interstate Commerce Commission, in its 1897 Annual Report, stated candidly that

> . . . But by virtue of judicial decision, it [the Commission] has ceased to be a body for the regulation of interstate carriers. It is proper that the Congress should understand this. The people should no longer look to this Commission for a protection which it is powerless to extend.[11]

A few years later, President Theodore Roosevelt drew upon a doctrine originally discussed by one of the founding fathers who became a member of the Supreme Court—James Wilson—that the national government possesses inherent power to deal with any major problem even though the authority to act is not specified in the Constitution. Roosevelt charged that the Supreme Court had created a "twilight zone" in federal-state relations in which predatory economic interests could operate without either federal or state control. In a speech dedicating the state capitol building in Harrisburg, Pennsylvania, President Roosevelt argued that

> . . . Certain judicial decisions have done just what Wilson feared; they have, as a matter of fact, left vacancies, left blanks between the limits of actual national jurisdiction over the control of the great business corporations. . . . Actual experience has shown that the states are wholly powerless to deal with this subject; and any action or decision that deprives the nation of the power to deal with it, simply results in leaving the corporations absolutely free to work without any effective supervision whatever; and such a course is fraught with untold danger to the future of our whole system of government and indeed, to our whole civilization.[12]

In *Kansas* v. *Colorado*, the doctrine was introduced by Attorney General Charles V. Bonaparte intervening on behalf of the Roosevelt administration. The Court unequivocally rejected the doctrine. Justice Brewer's opinion follows (with his extensive discussion of reclamation policy omitted).

KANSAS v. COLORADO
206 U. S. 46 (1907)

. . . Counsel for the government relies upon "the doctrine of sovereign and inherent power," adding, "I am aware that in advancing this doctrine I seem to challenge great decisions of the court, and I speak with deference." His argument runs substantially along this line: All legislative power must be vested in either the state or the national government; no legislative powers belong to a state government other than those which affect solely the internal affairs of that state; consequently all powers which are national in their scope must be found vested in the Congress of the United States. But the proposition that there are legislative powers affecting the nation as a whole which belong to, although not expressed in, the grants of powers, is in direct conflict with the doctrine that this is a government of enumerated powers. That this is such a government clearly appears from the Constitution, independently of the Amendments, for otherwise there would be an instrument granting certain specified things made operative to grant other and distinct things. This natural construction of the original body of the Constitution is made absolutely certain by the 10th Amendment. This Amendment, which was seemingly adopted with prescience of just such contention as the present, disclosed the widespread fear that the national government might, under the pressure of a supposed general welfare, attempt to exercise powers which had not been granted. With equal determination the framers intended that no such assumption should ever find jurisdiction in the organic act, and that if, in the future, further powers seemed necessary, they should be granted by the people in the manner they had provided for amending that act. It reads: "The powers not delegated to the United States by the Constitution, nor prohibited by it to the states, are reserved to the states respectively, or to the people." The argument of counsel ignores the principal factor in this article, to wit, "the people." Its principal purpose was not the distribution of power between the United States and the states, but a reservation to the people of all powers not granted. The preamble of the Constitution declares who framed it,—"We, the people of the United States," not the people of one state, but the people of all the states; and article 10 reserves to the people of all the states the powers not delegated to the United States. The powers affecting the internal affairs of the states not granted to the United States by the Constitution, nor prohibited by it to the states,

are reserved to the states respectively, and all powers of a national character which are not delegated to the national government by the Constitution are reserved to the people of the United States. The people who adopted the Constitution knew that in the nature of things they could not foresee all the questions which might arise in the future, all the circumstances which might call for the exercise of further national powers than those granted to the United States, and, after making provision for an amendment to the Constitution by which any needed additional powers would be granted, they reserved to themselves all powers not so delegated. This article 10 is not to be shorn of its meaning by any narrow or technical construction, but is to be considered fairly and liberally so as to give effect to its scope and meaning. . . .

In 1910 the territory of Arizona was initially denied admission as a state. President Taft had vetoed the Congressional enabling act because he was strongly opposed to a single provision of the proposed state constitution, the section for recall of judges. Arizona was then admitted to statehood after removing the objectionable section, but immediately restored it after achieving statehood. This rapid turnabout was not challenged, but a year later, Oklahoma's postadmission turnabout on the location of its new state capital and the abandonment of a public expenditure restriction was challenged before the Supreme Court in *Coyle* v. *Smith*.

COYLE v. SMITH
221 U. S. 559 (1911)

Justice Lurton delivered the opinion of the Court:

. . . The only question for review by us is whether the provision of the enabling act was a valid limitation upon the power of the State after its admission, which overrides any subsequent state legislation repugnant thereto.

The power to locate its own seat of government, and to determine when and how it shall be changed from one place to another, and to appropriate its own public funds for that purpose, are essentially and peculiarly state powers. That one of the original thirteen States could now be shorn of such powers by an act of Congress would not be for a moment entertained. The question, then, comes to this: Can a State be placed upon a plane of inequality with its sister States in the Union if the Congress chooses to impose conditions which so operate, at the time of its admission? The argument is, that while Congress may not deprive a State of any power which it possesses, it may, as a

condition to the admission of a new State, constitutionally restrict its authority, to the extent, at least, of suspending its powers for a definite time in respect to the location of its seat of government. This contention is predicated upon the constitutional power of admitting new States to this Union, and the constitutional duty of guaranteeing to "every State in this Union a republican form of government." The position of counsel for the appellants is substantially this: That the power of Congress to admit new States, and to determine whether or not its fundamental law is republican in form, are political powers, and as such, uncontrollable by the courts. That Congress may, in the exercise of such power, impose terms and conditions upon the admission of the proposed new State, which, if accepted, will be obligatory, although they operate to deprive the State of powers which it would otherwise possess, and, therefore, not admitted upon "an equal footing with the original States."

The power of Congress in respect to the admission of new States is found in the 3rd section of the 4th article of the Constitution. That provision is that, "new states may be admitted by the Congress into this Union." The only expressed restriction upon this power is that no new State shall be formed within the jurisdiction of any other State, nor by the junction of two or more States, or parts of States, without the consent of such States, as well as of the Congress.

But what is this power? It is not to admit political organizations which are less or greater, or different in dignity or power, from those political entities which constitute the Union. It is, as strongly put by counsel, a "power to admit States."

The definition of "a state" is found in the powers possessed by the original states which adopted the Constitution,—a definition emphasized by the term employed in all subsequent acts of Congress admitting new States into the Union. The first two States admitted into the Union were the States of Vermont and Kentucky, one as of March 4, 1791, and the other as of June 1, 1792. No terms or conditions were exacted from either. Each act declares that the State is admitted "as a new and *entire member* of the United States of America." . . . Emphatic and significant as is the phrase admitted as "an entire member," even stronger was the declaration upon the admission in 1796 of Tennessee as the third new State, it being declared to be "one of the United States of America," "on an equal footing with the original States in all respects whatsoever,"—phraseology which has ever since been substantially followed in admission acts, concluding with the Oklahoma act, which declares that Oklahoma shall be admitted "on an equal footing with the original states."

The power is to admit "new States into *this* Union."

"This Union" was and is a union of States, equal in power, dignity, and authority, each competent to exert that residuum of sovereignty not delegated to the United States by the Constitution itself. To maintain otherwise would be to say that the Union, through the power of Congress to admit new States, might come to be a union of States unequal in power, as including States whose powers were restricted only by the Constitution, with others whose powers had been further restricted by an act of Congress accepted as a condition of admission. Thus it would result, first, that the powers of Congress would not be defined by the Constitution alone, but in respect to new States, enlarged or restricted by the conditions imposed upon new States by its own legislation admitting them into the Union; and, second, that such new States might not exercise all of the powers which had not been delegated by the Constitution, but only such as had not been further bargained away as conditions of admission.

The argument that Congress derives from the duty of "guaranteeing to each State in this Union a republican form of government," power to impose restrictions upon a new State which deprive it of equality with other members of the Union, has no merit. It may imply the duty of such new State to provide itself with such state government, and impose upon Congress the duty of seeing that such form is not changed to one anti-republican, . . . but it obviously does not confer power to admit a new State which shall be any less a State than those which compose the Union.

We come now to the question as to whether there is anything in the decisions of this court which sanctions the claim that Congress may, by the imposition of conditions in an enabling act, deprive a new State of any of those attributes essential to its equality in dignity and power with other States. In considering the decisions of this court bearing upon the question, we must distinguish, first, between provisions which are fulfilled by the admission of the State; second, between compacts or affirmative legislation intended to operate in futuro, which are within the scope of the conceded powers of Congress over the subject; and third, compacts or affirmative legislation which operates to restrict the powers of such new States in respect of matters which would otherwise be exclusively within the sphere of state power.

As to requirements in such enabling acts as relate only to the contents of the constitution for the proposed new State, little needs to be said. The constitutional provision concerning the admission of new States is not a mandate, but a power to be exercised with discretion. From this alone it would follow that Congress may require, under penalty of denying admission, that the organic laws of a new State at the time of admission shall be such as to meet its approval. A constitution thus supervised by Congress, would, after all, be a constitution of a State, and as such subject to alteration and amendment by the State after admission. Its force would be that of a state constitution, and not that of an act of Congress. . . .

So far as this court has found occasion to advert to the effect of enabling acts as affirmative legislation affecting the power of new states after admission, there is to be found no sanction for the contention that any state may be deprived of any of the power constitutionally possessed by other states, as states, by reason of the terms in which the acts admitting them to the Union have been framed. . . . [Here follows discussion of a case involving the construction of the act under which Alabama was admitted to the Union.]

The plain deduction from this case is that when a new state is admitted into the Union, it is so admitted with all of the powers of sovereignty and jurisdiction which pertain to the original states, and that such powers may not be constitutionally diminished, impaired, or shorn away by any conditions, compacts, or stipulations embraced in the act under which the new state came into the union, which would not be valid and effectual if the subject of congressional legislation after admission. . . .

It may well happen that Congress should embrace in an enactment introducing a new state into the union legislation intended as a regulation of commerce among the states, or with Indian tribes situated within the limits of such new state, or regulations touching the sole care and disposition of the public lands or reservations therein which might be upheld as legislation within the sphere of the plain power of Congress. But in every such case such legislation would derive its force not from any agreement or compact with the proposed new state, nor by reason of its acceptance of such enactment as a term of admission, but solely because the power of Congress extended to the subject, and therefore would not operate to restrict the state's legislative power in respect of any matter which was not plainly within the regulative power of Congress. . . .

No such question is presented here. The legislation in the Oklahoma enabling act relating to the location of the capital of the state, if construed as forbidding a removal by the state after its admission as a state, is referable to no power granted to Congress over the subject, and if it is to uphold at all, it must be implied from the power to admit new states. If power to impose such a restriction upon the general and undelegated power of a state be conceded as implied from the power to admit a new state, where is the line to be drawn against restrictions imposed upon new states? . . .

. . . If anything was needed to complete the argument against the assertion that Oklahoma has not been admitted to the Union upon an equality of power, dignity, and sovereignty with Massachusetts or Virginia, it is afforded by the express provision of the act of admission, by which it is declared that when the people of the proposed new state have complied with the terms of the act, that it shall be the duty of the President to issue his proclamation, and that "thereupon the proposed state of Oklahoma shall be deemed admitted by Congress into the Union under and by virtue of this act, *on an equal footing with the original states.*" The proclamation has been issued and the Senators and Representatives from the state admitted to their seats in the Congress.

Has Oklahoma been admitted upon an equal footing with the original states? If she has, she, by virtue of her jurisdictional sovereignty as such a state, may determine for her own people the proper location of the local seat of government. She is not equal in power to them if she cannot. . . .

To this we may add that the constitutional equality of the states is essential to the harmonious operation of the scheme upon which the Republic was organized. When that equality disappears we may remain a free people, but the Union will not be the Union of the Constitution.

Judgment affirmed.

Justice McKenna and Justice Holmes dissent.

In terms of the major, enduring political issue that divided Progressives and conservatives in both political parties in the early 20th century—whether government, state or federal, could effectively regulate large corporations in the public interest—the Supreme Court usually opted for corporate freedom from control. Thus, in the controversial Standard Oil Case, the Court introduced another doctrine, the "rule of reason," reiterating its earlier preoccupation with judicial supervision of Congressional regulation of business under the revised Sherman Antitrust Act. Portions of Chief Justice White's majority opinion are reproduced below.

STANDARD OIL COMPANY OF NEW JERSEY v. UNITED STATES
221 U. S. 1 (1911)

Chief Justice White delivered the opinion of the Court:

First. *The text of the [Sherman Anti-Trust] act and its meaning.*

We quote the text of the first and second sections of the act, as follows:

"SECTION 1. Every contract, combination in the form of trust or otherwise, or conspiracy, in restraint of trade or commerce, among the several States, or with foreign nations, is hereby declared to be illegal. Every person who shall make any such contract, or engage in any such combination or conspiracy, shall be deemed guilty of a misdemeanor, and, on conviction thereof, shall be punished by fine not exceeding five thousand dollars, or by imprisonment not exceeding one year, or by both said punishments, in the discretion of the court.

"SEC. 2. Every person who shall monopolize, or attempt to monopolize, or combine or conspire with any other person or persons, to monopolize any part of the trade or commerce among the several States, or with foreign nations, shall be deemed guilty of a misdemeanor, and, on conviction thereof, shall be punished by fine not exceeding five thousand dollars, or by imprisonment not exceeding one year, or by both said punishments, in the discretion of the court."

The [legislative] debates show that doubt as to whether there was a common law of the United States which governed the subject in the absence of legislation was among the influences leading to the passage of the act. They conclusively show, however, that the main cause which led to the legislation was the thought that it was required by the economic condition of the times, that is, the vast accumulation of wealth in the hands of corporations and individuals, the enormous development of corporate organization, the facility for combination which such organizations afforded, the fact that the facility was being used, and that combinations known as trusts were being multiplied, and the widespread impression that their power had been and would be exerted to oppress individuals and injure the public generally. Although debates may not be used as a means for interpreting a statute . . . that rule in the nature of things is not violated by resorting to debates as a means of ascertaining the environment at the time of the enactment of a particular law, that is, the history of the period when it was adopted.

There can be no doubt that the sole subject with which the first section deals is restraint of trade as therein contemplated, and that the attempt to monopolize and monopolization is the subject with which the second section is concerned. It is certain that those terms, at least in their rudimentary meaning, took their origin in the common law, and were also familiar in the law of this country prior to and at the time of the adoption of the act in question. . . .

Without going into detail and but very briefly surveying the whole field, it may be with accuracy said that the dread of enhancement of prices and of other wrongs which it was thought would flow from the undue limitation on competitive conditions caused by contracts or other acts of individuals or corporations, led, as a matter of public policy, to the prohibition or treating as illegal all contracts or acts which were unreasonably restrictive of competitive conditions, either from the nature or character of the contract or act or where the surrounding circumstances were such as to justify the conclusion that they had not been entered into or performed with the legitimate purpose of reasonably forwarding personal interest and developing trade, but on the contrary were of such a character as to give rise to the inference or presumption that they had been entered into or done with the intent to do wrong to the general public and to limit the right of individuals, thus restraining the free flow of commerce and tending to bring about the evils such as enhancement of prices, which were considered to be against public policy. It is equally true to say that the survey of the legislation in this country on this subject from the beginning will show, depending as it did upon the economic conceptions which obtained at the time when the legislation was adopted or judicial decision was rendered, that contracts or acts were at one time deemed to be of such a character as to justify the inference of wrongful intent which were at another period thought not to be of that character. . . .

In view of the common law and the law in this country as to restraint of trade, which we have reviewed, and the illuminating effect which that history must have under the rule to which we have referred, we think it results:

a. That the context manifests that the statute was drawn in the light of the existing practical conception of the law of restraint of trade, because it groups as within that class, not only contracts which were in restraint of trade in the subjective sense, but all contracts or acts which theoretically were attempts to monopolize, yet which in practice had come to be considered as in restraint of trade in a broad sense.

b. That in view of the many new forms of contracts and combinations which were being evolved from existing economic conditions, it was deemed essential by an all-embracing enumeration to make sure that no form of contract or combination by which an undue restraint of interstate or foreign commerce was brought about could save such restraint from condemnation. The statute under this view evidenced the intent not to restrain the right to make and enforce contracts, whether resulting from combination or otherwise, which did not unduly restrain interstate or foreign commerce, but to protect that commerce from being restrained by methods, whether old or new, which would constitute an interference that is an undue restraint.

c. And as the contracts or acts embraced in the provision were not expressly defined, since the enumeration addressed itself simply to classes of acts, those classes being broad enough to embrace every conceivable contract or combination which could be made concerning trade or commerce or the subjects of such commerce, and thus caused any act done by any of the enumerated methods anywhere in the whole field of human activity to be illegal if in restraint of trade, it inevitably follows that the provision necessarily called for the exercise of judgment which required that some standard should be resorted to for the purpose of determining whether the prohibitions contained in the statute had or had not in any given case been violated. Thus not specifying but indubitably contemplating and requiring a standard, it follows that it was intended that the standard of reason which had been applied at the common law and in this country in dealing with subjects of the character embraced by the statute, was intended to be the measure used for the purpose of determining whether in a given case a particular act had or had not brought about the wrong against which the statute provided. . . .

Undoubtedly, the words "to monopolize" and "monopolize" as used in the section reach every act bringing about the prohibited results. The ambiguity, if any, is involved in determining what is intended by monopolize. But this ambiguity is readily dispelled in the light of the previous history of the law of restraint of trade to which we have referred and the indication which it gives of the practical evolution by which monopoly and the acts which produce the same result as monopoly, that is, an undue restraint of the course of trade, all came to be spoken of as, and to be indeed synonymous with, restraint of trade. In other words, having by the first section forbidden all means of monopolizing trade, that is, unduly restraining it by means of every contract, combination, etc., the second section seeks, if possible, to make the prohibitions of the act all the more complete and perfect by embracing all attempts to reach the end prohibited by the first section, that is, restraints of trade, by any attempt to monopolize, or monopolization thereof, even although the acts by which such results are attempted to be brought about or are brought about be not embraced within the general enumeration of the first section. And, of course, when the second section is thus harmonized with and made as it was intended to be the complement of the first, it becomes obvious that the criteria to be resorted to in any given case for the purpose of ascertaining whether violations of the section have been committed, is the rule of reason guided by the established law and by the plain duty to enforce the prohibitions of the act and thus the public policy which its restrictions were obviously enacted to subserve. . . .

Justice Harlan concurred in part, and dissented in part:

All who recall the condition of the country in 1890 will remember that there was everywhere, among the people generally, a deep feeling of unrest. The Nation had been rid of human slavery—fortunately, as all now feel—but the conviction was universal that the country was in real danger from another kind of slavery sought to be fastened on the American people, namely, the slavery that would result from aggregations of capital in the hands of a few individuals and corporations. . . .

On reading the opinion just delivered, the first inquiry will be, that as the court is unanimous in holding that the particular things done by the Standard Oil Company and its subsidiary companies, in this case, were illegal under the Anti-trust Act, whether those things were in reasonable or unreasonable restraints of interstate commerce, why was it necessary to make an elaborate argument, as is done in the opinion, to show that according to the "rule of reason" the act as passed by Congress should be interpreted as if it contained the word "unreasonable" or the word "undue"? The only answer which, in frankness, can be given to this question is, that the court intends to decide that its deliberate judgment, fifteen years ago, to the effect that the act permitted no restraint whatever of interstate commerce, whether reasonable or unreasonable, was not in accordance with the "rule of reason." In effect the court says, that it will now, for the first time, bring the discussion under the "light of reason" and apply the "rule of reason" to the questions to be decided. I have the authority of this court for saying that such a course of proceeding on its part would be "judicial legislation." . . .

The disposition of the case under consideration, according to the views of the defendants, will, it is claimed, quiet and give rest to "the business of the country." On the contrary, I have a strong conviction that it will throw the business of the country into confusion and invite widely-extended and harassing litigation, the injurious effects of which will be felt for many years to come. When Congress prohibited *every* contract, combination or monopoly, in restraint of commerce, it prescribed a simple, definite rule that all could understand, and which could be easily applied by everyone wishing to obey the law, and not to conduct their business in violation of law. But now, it is to be feared, we are to have, in cases without number, the constantly recurring inquiry—difficult to solve by proof—whether the particular contract, combination, or trust involved in each case is or is not an "unreasonable" or "undue" restraint of trade. Congress, in effect, said that there should be *no* restraint of trade, *in any form,* and this court solemnly adjudged many years ago that Congress meant what it thus said in clear and explicit words, and that it *could not* add to the words of the act. . . .

The Shreveport Rate Case was one of an occasional, but by no means consistent, broadening of the scope of congressional commerce power. The circumstances of the case, fully described in then Associate Justice Charles Evans Hughes' decision, indicated a determination not to permit interference with interstate commerce under the guise of purely intrastate regulation. But, like the Standard Oil Company decision, the Court's decision upheld a major corporation's contentions and rates.

The case provided an interesting example of successful corporate resistance to regulatory authority, while the scope of the commerce power was upheld. Charles Evans Hughes, serving as an associate justice (before his try for the presidency in 1916), wrote the majority opinion:

THE SHREVEPORT RATE CASE: HOUSTON, EAST AND WEST TEXAS RAILWAY COMPANY v. UNITED STATES 234 U. S. 342 (1914)

These suits were brought in the commerce court by the Houston, East & West Texas Railway Company and the Houston & Shreveport Railroad Company, and by the Texas & Pacific Railway Company, respectively, to set aside an order of the Interstate Commerce Commission, dated March 11, 1912, upon the ground that it exceeded the Commission's authority. . . .

The order of the Interstate Commerce Commission was made in a proceeding initiated in March, 1911, by the Railroad Commission of Louisiana. The complaint was that the appellants, and other interstate carriers, maintained unreasonable rates from Shreveport, Louisiana, to various points in Texas, and further, that these carriers, in the adjustment of rates over their respective lines, unjustly discriminated in favor of traffic within the state of Texas, and against similar traffic between Louisiana and Texas. The carriers filed answers; numerous pleas of intervention by shippers and commercial bodies were allowed; testimony was taken and arguments were heard.

The gravamen of the complaint, said the Interstate Commerce Commission, was that the carriers made rates out of Dallas and other Texas points into eastern Texas which were much lower than those which they extended into Texas from Shreveport. The situation may be briefly described: Shreveport, Louisiana, is about 40 miles from Houston, Texas, on the line of the Houston, East & West Texas and Houston & Shreveport Companies (which are affiliated in interest); it is 189 miles from Dallas, Texas, on the line of the Texas & Pacific. Shreveport competes with both cities for the trade of the intervening territory. The rates on these lines from Dallas and Houston, respectively, eastward to intermediate points in Texas, were much less, according to distance, than from Shreveport westward to the same points. It is undisputed that the difference was substantial, and injuriously affected the commerce of Shreveport. It appeared, for example, that a rate of 60 cents carried first-class traffic a distance of 160 miles to the eastward from Dallas, while the same rate would carry the same class of traffic only 55 miles into Texas from Shreveport. . . . The rate on wagons from Dallas to Marshall, Texas, 147.7 miles, was 36.8 cents, and from Shreveport to Marshall, 42 miles, 56 cents. . . . These instances of differences in rates are merely illustrative; they serve to indicate the character of the rate adjustment.

. . . The Interstate Commerce Commission . . . found that the carriers maintained "higher rates from Shreveport to points in Texas" than were in force "from cities in Texas to such points under substantially similar conditions and circumstances," and that thereby "an unlawful and undue preference and advantage" was given to the Texas cities, and a "discrimination" that was "undue and unlawful" was effected against Shreveport. In order to correct this discrimination, the carriers were directed to desist from charging higher rates for the transportation of any commodity from Shreveport to Dallas and Houston, respectively, and intermediate points, than were contemporaneously charged for the carriage of such commodity from Dallas and Houston toward Shreveport for equal distances, as the Commission found that relation of rates to be reasonable. . . .

. . . There are, it appears, commodity rates fixed by the Railroad Commission of Texas for intrastate hauls, which are substantially less than the class, or standard, rates prescribed by that Commission; and thus the commodity rates charged by the carriers from Dallas and Houston eastward to Texas points are less than the rates which they demand for the transportation of the same articles for like distances from Shreveport into Texas. The present controversy relates to these commodity rates.

The point of the objection to the order is that, as the discrimination found by the Commission to be unjust arises out of the relation of intrastate rates, maintained under state authority, to interstate rates that have been upheld as reasonable, its correction was beyond the Commission's power. Manifestly the order might be complied with, and the discrimination avoided, either by reducing the interstate rate from Shreveport to the level of the competing intrastate rates, or by raising these intrastate rates to the level of the interstate rates, or by such reduction in the one case and increase in the other as would result in equality. But it is urged that, so far as the interstate rates were sustained by the Commission as reasonable, the Commission was without authority to compel their reduction in order to equalize them with the lower intrastate rates. The holding of the commerce court was that the order relieved the appellants from further obligation to observe the intrastate rates, and that they were at liberty to comply with the Commission's requirements by increasing these rates sufficiently to remove the forbidden discrimination. The invalidity of the order in this aspect is challenged upon two grounds:

(1) That Congress is impotent to control the intrastate charges of an interstate carrier even to the extent necessary to prevent injurious discrimination against interstate traffic; and

(2) That, if it be assumed that Congress has this power, still it has not been exercised, and hence the action of the Commission exceeded the limits of the authority which has been conferred upon it.

First. It is necessary to repeat what has frequently been said by this court with respect to the complete and paramount character of the power confided to Congress to regulate commerce among the several states. It is of the essence of this power that, where it exists, it dominates. Interstate trade was not left

to be destroyed or impeded by the rivalries of local government. The purpose was to make impossible the recurrence of the evils which had overwhelmed the Confederation, and to provide the necessary basis of national unity by insuring "uniformity of regulation against conflicting and discriminating state legislation." By virtue of the comprehensive terms of the grant, the authority of Congress is at all times adequate to meet the varying exigencies that arise, and to protect the national interest by securing the freedom of interstate commercial intercourse from local control. . . .

Congress is empowered to regulate,—that is, to provide the law for the government of interstate commerce; to enact "all appropriate legislation" for its "protection and advancement" . . .; to adopt measures "to promote its growth and insure its safety." Its authority, extending to these interstate carriers as instruments of interstate commerce, necessarily embraces the right to control their operations in all matters having such a close and substantial relation to interstate traffic that the control is essential or appropriate to the security of that traffic, to the efficiency of the interstate service, and to the maintenance of conditions under which interstate commerce may be conducted upon fair terms and without molestation or hindrance. As it is competent for Congress to legislate to these ends, unquestionably it may seek their attainment by requiring that the agencies of interstate commerce shall not be used in such manner as to cripple, retard, or destroy it. The fact that carriers are instruments of intrastate commerce, as well as of interstate commerce, does not derogate from the complete and paramount authority of Congress over the latter, or preclude the Federal power from being exerted to prevent the intrastate operations of such carriers from being made a means of injury to that which has been confided to Federal care. Wherever the interstate and intrastate transactions of carriers are so related that the government of the one involves the control of the other, it is Congress, and not the state, that is entitled to prescribe the final and dominant rule, for otherwise Congress would be denied the exercise of its constitutional authority, and the state, and not the nation, would be supreme within the national field. . . .

. . . This is not to say that Congress possesses the authority to regulate the internal commerce of a state, as such, but that it does possess the power to foster and protect interstate commerce, and to take all measures necessary or appropriate to that end, although intrastate transactions of interstate carriers may thereby be controlled.

This principle is applicable here. We find no reason

to doubt that Congress is entitled to keep the highways of interstate communication open to interstate traffic upon fair and equal terms. That an unjust discrimination in the rates of a common carrier, by which one person or locality is unduly favored as against another under substantially similar conditions of traffic, constitutes an evil, is undeniable; and where this evil consists in the action of an interstate carrier in unreasonably discriminating against interstate traffic over its line, the authority of Congress to prevent it is equally clear. It is immaterial, so far as the protecting power of Congress is concerned, that the discrimination arises from intrastate rates as compared with interstate rates. The use of the instrument of interstate commerce in a discriminatory manner so as to inflict injury upon that commerce, or some part thereof, furnishes abundant ground for Federal intervention. Nor can the attempted exercise of state authority alter the matter, where Congress has acted, for a state

may not authorize the carrier to do that which Congress is entitled to forbid and has forbidden. . . .

In conclusion: Reading the order in the light of the report of the Commission, it does not appear that the Commission attempted to require the carriers to reduce their interstate rates out of Shreveport below what was found to be a reasonable charge for that service. So far as these interstate rates conformed to what was found to be reasonable by the Commission, the carriers are entitled to maintain them, and they are free to comply with the order by so adjusting the other rates, to which the order relates, as to remove the forbidden discrimination. But this result they are required to accomplish.

The decree of the Commerce Court is affirmed in each case.

Affirmed.

Justice Lurton and Justice Pitney dissent.

A judicial face of stone against child labor laws

Since the turn of the century, both presidents and Congress have occasionally reacted strongly to the conservatism of the Supreme Court and the inferior federal judiciary. President Theodore Roosevelt had made a pointed reference to this problem in his annual message of 1907. In 1910 Congress adopted a statute designed to limit "government by injunction" by prohibiting an injunction against a state officer on the basis of the unconstitutionality of a state statute unless a hearing was held before a three-judge court including a justice or circuit court judge.[13] In addition, Congress had proposed that corporations be stripped of their status as citizens within the diversity of citizenship jurisdiction of the federal judiciary. This proposal aroused considerable discussion in the 1890s, but all legislative efforts failed.[14] Such presidential and congressional efforts had little long-range influence on the ideological conservatism of the Supreme Court. In fact, during the second decade of the 20th century the Court struck down a very significant statute that prohibited the transportation in interstate commerce of any product resulting from child labor or from an establishment using such labor. The statute was the Keating-Owen Act of 1916.

Many members of Congress had been encouraged by *Champion* v. *Ames* or the McCray decision to believe that Congressional commerce or taxing power could be expanded as a kind of federal "police power." Such police power could be employed to protect the health, safety, and general welfare more effectively than the states traditionally exercised such power (when it was exercised at all). The Progressive era had brought a significant number of congressional enactments that were accepted as exercises of federal police power under the commerce clause. These included farmer and consumer protection legislation such as the Animal Contagion Disease and Quarantine Acts in 1903 and 1905, Plant Quarantine Acts in 1905, 1912, 1915, and 1917, the Meat Inspection Act of 1907, the

Apple Grading Act and the Adulterated-Seed Act of 1912, and the Warehouse Act and the Grain Standards Act of 1916.

Others in the federal police power category were the Metals Hallmark Acts of 1905 and 1906, the Narcotics Acts of 1909 and 1914, the White Slave Traffic Act of 1910, the Insecticide Act of 1910, and the Serums and Toxins Act of 1913.[15] The response of the Supreme Court to the Child Labor Act of 1916 was, therefore, a shock and surprise.

HAMMER v. DAGENHART
247 U. S. 251 (1918)

Justice Day delivered the opinion of the Court:

The attack upon the act rests upon three propositions: First. It is not a regulation of interstate and foreign commerce. Second. It contravenes the 10th Amendment to the Constitution. Third. It conflicts with the 5th Amendment to the Constitution.

The controlling question for decision is: Is it within the authority of Congress in regulating commerce among the states to prohibit the transportation in interstate commerce of manufactured goods, the product of a factory in which, within thirty days prior to their removal therefrom, children under the age of fourteen have been employed or permitted to work, or children between the ages of fourteen and sixteen years have been employed or permitted to work more than eight hours in any day, or more than six days in any week, or ofter the hour of 7 o'clock p.m. or before the hour of 6 o'clock a.m.?

The power essential to the passage of this act, the government contends, is found in the commerce clause of the Constitution which authorizes Congress to regulate commerce with foreign nations and among the states.

In Gibbons v. Ogden [1824], Chief Justice Marshall, speaking for this court, and defining the extent and nature of the commerce power, said: "It is the power to regulate,—that is, to prescribe the rule by which commerce is to be governed." In other words, the power is one to control the means by which commerce is carried on, which is directly the contrary of the assumed right to forbid commerce from moving and thus destroy it as to particular commodities. But it is insisted that adjudged cases in this court establish the doctrine that the power to regulate given to Congress incidently includes the authority to prohibit the movement of ordinary commodities, and therefore the subject is not open for discussion. The cases demonstrate the contrary. They rest upon the character of the particular subjects dealt with and the fact that the

scope of governmental authority, state or national, possessed over them, is such that the authority to prohibit is, as to them, but the exertion of the power to regulate. [The Court then discusses the several cases mentioned in the note introducing this case.] . . .

In each of these instances the use of interstate transportation was necessary to the accomplishment of harmful results. In other words, although the power over interstate transportation was to regulate, that could only be accomplished by prohibiting the use of the facilities of interstate commerce to effect the evil intended.

This element is wanting in the present case. The thing intended to be accomplished by this statute is the denial of the facilities of interstate commerce to those manufacturers in the states who employ children within the prohibited ages. The act in its effect does not regulate transportation among the states, but aims to standardize the ages at which children may be employed in mining and manufacturing within states. The goods shipped are of themselves harmless. The act permits them to be freely shipped after thirty days from the time of their removal from the factory. When offered for shipment, and before transportation begins, the labor of their production is over, and the mere fact that they were intended for interstate commerce transportation does not make their production subject to Federal control under the commerce power.

Commerce "consists of intercourse and traffic . . . and includes the transportation of persons and property, as well as the purchase, sale and exchange of commodities." The making of goods and the mining of coal are not commerce, nor does the fact that these things are to be afterwards shipped, or used in interstate commerce, make their production a part thereof. . . .

Over interstate transportation, or its incidents, the regulatory power of Congress is ample, but the production of articles intended for interstate commerce is a matter of local regulation. "When the commerce begins is determined not by the character of the commodity, nor by the intention of the owner to transfer it to another state for sale, nor by his preparation of it for transportation, but by its actual delivery to a common carrier for transportation, or the actual commencement of its transfer to another state." . . . This principle has been recognized often in this court. . . . If it were otherwise, all manufacture intended for interstate shipment would be brought under federal control to the practical exclusion of the authority of the states,—a result certainly not contemplated by the framers of the Constitution when they vested in Congress the authority to regulate commerce among the states. . . .

It is further contended that the authority of Congress may be exerted to control interstate commerce in the shipment of child-made goods because of the effect of the circulation of such goods in other states where the evil of this class of labor has been recognized by local legislation, and the right to thus employ child labor has been more rigorously restrained than in the state of production. In other words, that the unfair competition thus engendered may be controlled by closing the channels of interstate commerce to manufacturers in those states where the local laws do not meet what Congress deems to be the more just standard of other states.

There is no power vested in Congress to require the states to exercise their police power so as to prevent possible unfair competition. Many causes may cooperate to give one state, by reason of local laws or conditions, an economic advantage over others. The commerce clause was not intended to give to Congress a general authority to equalize such conditions. In some of the states laws have been passed fixing minimum wages for women, in others the local law regulates the hours of labor of women in various employments. Business done in such states may be at an economic disadvantage when compared with states which have no such regulation; surely, this fact does not give Congress the power to deny transportation in interstate commerce to those who carry on business where the hours of labor and the rate of compensation for women have not been fixed by a standard in use in other states and approved by Congress.

The grant of power to Congress over the subject of interstate commerce was to enable it to regulate such commerce, and not to give it authority to control the states in their exercise of the police power over local trade and manufacture.

The grant of authority over a purely Federal matter was not intended to destroy the local power always existing and carefully reserved to the states in the 10th Amendment of the Constitution.

Police regulations relating to the internal trade and affairs of the states have been uniformly recognized as within such control. "This," said this court in United States v. Dewitt [1870], "has been so frequently declared by this court, results so obviously from the terms of the Constitution, and has been so fully explained and supported on former occasions, that we think it unnecessary to enter again upon the discussion." . . .

That there should be limitations upon the right to employ children in mines and factories in the interest of their own and the public welfare, all will admit. That such employment is generally deemed to require regulation is shown by the fact that the brief of counsel states that every state in the Union has a law upon the subject, limiting the right to thus employ children. In North Carolina, the state wherein is located the factory in which the employment was had in the present case, no child under twelve years of age is permitted to work.

It may be desirable that such laws be uniform, but our Federal government is one of enumerated powers. . . .

In interpreting the Constitution it must never be forgotten that the nation is made up of states, to which are intrusted the powers of local government. And to them and to the people the powers not expressly delegated to the national government are reserved. . . . The power of the states to regulate their purely internal affairs by such laws as seem wise to the local authority is inherent, and has never been surrendered to the general government. . . . To sustain this statute would not be, in our judgment, a recognition of the lawful exertion of congressional authority over interstate commerce, but would sanction an invasion by the federal power of the control of a matter purely local in its character, and over which no authority has been delegated to Congress in conferring the power to regulate commerce among the states.

We have neither authority nor disposition to question the motives of Congress in enacting this legislation. The purposes intended must be attained consistently with constitutional limitations, and not by an invasion of the powers of the states. This court has no more important function than that which devolves upon it the obligation to preserve inviolate the constitutional limitations upon the exercise of authority, federal and state, to the end that each may continue to discharge, harmoniously with the other, the duties intrusted to it by the Constitution.

In our view the necessary effect of this act is, by means of a prohibition against the movement in interstate commerce of ordinary commercial commodities, to regulate the hours of labor of children in factories and mines within the states, a purely state authority. Thus the act in a twofold sense is repugnant to the Constitution. It not only transcends the authority delegated to Congress over commerce, but also exerts a power as to a purely local matter to which the Federal authority does not extend. The far-reaching result of upholding the act cannot be more plainly indicated than by pointing out that if Congress can thus regulate matters intrusted to local authority by prohibition of the movement of commodities in interstate commerce, all freedom of commerce will be at an end, and the power of the states over local matters may be eliminated, and thus our system of government be practically destroyed.

For these reasons we hold that this law exceeds the constitutional authority of Congress. It follows that the decree of the District Court must be affirmed.

Justice Holmes dissented:

The single question in this case is whether Congress has power to prohibit the shipment in interstate or foreign commerce of any product of cotton mill [etc.]. . . . The objection urged against the power is that the states have exclusive control over their methods of production and that Congress cannot meddle with them, and taking the proposition in the sense of direct intermeddling I agree to it and suppose that no one denies it. But if an act is within the powers specifically conferred upon Congress, it seems to me that it is not made any less constitutional because of the indirect effects that it may have, however obvious it may be that it will have those effects; and that we are not at liberty upon such grounds to hold it void.

The first step in my argument is to make plain what no one is likely to dispute,—that the statute in question is within the power expressly given to Congress if considered only as to its immediate effects, and that if invalid it is so only upon some collateral ground. The statute confines itself to prohibiting the carriage of certain goods in interstate or foreign commerce. Congress is given power to regulate such commerce in unqualified terms. It would not be argued to-day that the power to regulate does not include the power to prohibit. Regulation means the prohibition of something, and when interstate commerce is the matter to be regulated I cannot doubt that the regulations may prohibit any part of such commerce that Congress sees fit to forbid. At all events it is established by the Lottery Case and others that have followed it that a law is not beyond the regulative power of Congress merely because it prohibits certain transportation out

and out. Champion v. Ames. . . . So I repeat that this statute in its immediate operation is clearly within the Congress's constitutional power.

The question, then, is narrowed to whether the exercise of its otherwise constitutional power by Congress can be pronounced unconstitutional because of its possible reaction upon the conduct of the states in a matter upon which I have admitted that they are free from direct control. I should have thought that that matter had been disposed of so fully as to leave no room for doubt. I should have thought that the most conspicuous decisions of this court had made it clear that the power to regulate commerce and other constitutional powers could not be cut down or qualified by the fact that it might interfere with carrying out of the domestic policy of any state.

The manufacture of oleomargarine is as much a matter of state regulation as the manufacture of cotton cloth. Congress levied a tax upon the compound when colored so as to resemble butter that was so great as obviously to prohibit the manufacture and sale. In a very elaborate discussion the present Chief Justice excluded any inquiry into the purpose of an act which, apart from that purpose, was within the power of Congress. McCray v. United States. . . . Fifty years ago a tax on state banks, the obvious purpose and actual effect of which was to drive them, or at least their circulation, out of existence, was sustained, although the result was one that Congress had no constitutional power to require. The court made short work of the argument as to the purpose of the act. "The judicial cannot prescribe to the legislative departments of the government limitations upon the exercise of its acknowledged powers. . . ."

And to come to cases upon interstate commerce, notwithstanding United States v. E. C. Knight Co. . ., the Sherman Act has been made an instrument for the breaking up of combinations in restraint of trade and monopolies, using the power to regulate commerce as a foothold, but not proceeding because the commerce was the end actually in mind. The objection that the control of the states over production was interfered with was urged again and again, but always in vain. . . .

The Pure Food and Drug Act was sustained in Hipolite Egg Co. v. United States. . ., with the intimation that "no trade can be carried on between the states to which it [the power of Congress to regulate commerce] does not extend," applies not merely to articles that the changing opinions of the time condemn as intrinsically harmful, but to others innocent in themselves, simply on the ground that the order for them was induced by a preliminary fraud. . . . It does not matter whether the supposed evil precedes or follows the transportation. It is enough that, in the opinion of Congress, the transportation encourages the evil. . . .

The notion that prohibition is any less prohibition when applied to things now thought evil I do not understand. But if there is any matter upon which civilized countries have agreed,—far more unanimously than they have with regard to intoxicants and some other matters over which this country is now emotionally aroused,—it is the evil of premature and excessive child labor. I should have thought that if we were to introduce our own moral conceptions where, in my opinion, they do not belong, this was pre-eminently a case for upholding the exercise of all its powers by the United States.

But I had thought that the propriety of the exercise of a power admitted to exist in some cases was for the consideration of Congress alone, and that this court always had disavowed the right to intrude its judgment upon questions of policy or morals. It is not for this court to pronounce when prohibition is necessary to regulation if it ever may be necessary,—to say that it is permissible as against strong drink, but not as against the product of ruined lives.

The act does not meddle with anything belonging to the states. They may regulate their internal affairs and their domestic commerce as they like. But when they seek to send their products across the state line they are no longer within their rights. If there were no Constitution and no Congress their power to cross the line would depend upon their neighbors. Under the Constitution such commerce belongs not to the states, but to Congress to regulate. It may carry out its views of public policy whatever indirect effect they may have upon the activities of the states. Instead of being encountered by a prohibitive tariff at her boundaries, the state encounters the public policy of the United States which it is for Congress to express. The public policy of the United States is shaped with a view to the benefit of the nation as a whole. If, as has been the case within the memory of men still living, a state should take a different view of the propriety of sustaining a lottery from that which generally prevails, I cannot believe that the fact would require a different decision from that reached in Champion v. Ames. Yet in that case it would be said with quite as much force as in this that Congress was attempting to intermeddle with the state's domestic affairs. The national welfare as understood by Congress may require a different attitude within its sphere from that of some self-seeking state. It seems to me entirely constitutional for Congress to enforce its understanding by all the means at its command.

Justice McKenna, Justice Brandeis, and Justice Clarke concur in this opinion.

The use of the taxing power for regulatory purposes had been upheld in a number of instances and was sustained again after *Hammer* v. *Dagenhart*. In 1919 the Court, by a five to four margin, upheld the Harrison Narcotic Drug Act of 1914. The act taxed the transfer of opium and coca leaves or their derivatives nominally in order to prohibit the sale of drugs by persons other than physicians or pharmacists. All persons dealing in drugs were required to pay a one dollar a year tax but also to comply with a detailed record-keeping program administered by the Bureau of Internal Revenue. Severe penalties for noncompliance were included in the nominal tax statute.

UNITED STATES v. DOREMUS
249 U. S. 86 (1919)

Justice Day delivered the opinion of the Court:

The only limitation upon the power of Congress to levy excise taxes of the character now under consideration is geographical uniformity throughout the United States. This court has often declared it cannot add others. Subject to such limitation Congress may select the subjects of taxation, and may exercise the power conferred at its discretion. . . . Of course, Congress may not, in the exercise of Federal power, exert authority wholly reserved to the states. Many decisions of this court have so declared. And from an early day the court has held that the fact that other motives may impel the exercise of Federal taxing power does not authorize the courts to inquire into that subject. If the legislation enacted has some reasonable relation to the exercise of the taxing authority conferred by the

Constitution, it cannot be invalidated because of the supposed motives which induced it. Veazie Bank v. Fenno [1869], in which case this court sustained a tax on a state bank issue of circulating notes. McCray v. United States [1904], where the power was thoroughly considered, and an act levying a special tax upon oleomargarine artificially colored was sustained. . . .

Nor is it sufficient to invalidate the taxing authority given to the Congress by the Constitution that the same business may be regulated by the police power of the state. License Tax Cases [1867].

The act may not be declared unconstitutional because its effect may be to accomplish another purpose as well as the raising of revenue. If the legislation is within the taxing authority of Congress—that is sufficient to sustain it. In re Kollock [1897].

The legislation under consideration was before us in a case concerning § 8 of the act, and in the course of the decision we said: "It may be assumed that the statute has a moral end as well as revenue in view, but we are of opinion that the district court, in treating those ends as to be reached only through a revenue measure and within the limits of a revenue measure, was right." . . . Considering the full power of Congress over excise taxation the decisive question here is: Have the provisions in question any relation to the raising of revenue? That Congress might levy an excise tax upon such dealers and others who are named in § 1 of the act cannot be successfully disputed. The provisions of § 2 to which we have referred, aim to confine sales to registered dealers and to those dispensing the drugs as physicians, and to those who come to dealers with legitimate prescriptions of physicians. Congress, with full power over the subject, short of arbitrary and unreasonable action, which is not to be assumed, inserted these provisions in an act specifically providing for the raising of revenue. Considered of themselves, we think they tend to keep the

traffic aboveboard and subject to inspection by those authorized to collect the revenue. They tend to diminish the opportunity of unauthorized persons to obtain the drugs and sell them clandestinely without paying the tax imposed by the Federal law. This case well illustrates the possibility which may have induced Congress to insert the provisions limiting sales to registered dealers, and requiring patients to obtain these drugs as a medicine from physicians or upon regular prescriptions. Ameris, being, as the indictment charges, an addict, may not have used this great number of doses for himself. He might sell some to others without paying the tax; at least, Congress may have deemed it wise to prevent such possible dealings because of their effect upon the collection of the revenue.

We cannot agree with the contention that the provisions of § 2, controlling the disposition of these drugs in the ways described, can have nothing to do with facilitating the collection of the revenue, as we should be obliged to do if we were to declare this act beyond the power of Congress, acting under its constitutional authority, to impose excise taxes. It follows that the judgment of the District Court must be reversed.

Reversed.

Chief Justice White dissented:

Chief Justice White dissents because he is of opinion that the court below correctly held the act of Congress, in so far as it embraced the matters complained of, to be beyond the constitutional power of Congress to enact because to such extent the statute was a mere attempt by Congress to exert a power not delegated; that is, the reserved police power of the states.

*Justice McKenna, Justice Van Devanter,
and Justice McReynolds concur in this dissent.*

Progressive forces in Congress were angered but undaunted by the Dagenhart decision. Under Title 12 of the Revenue Act of February 24, 1919, Congress levied a tax of 10 percent on the annual net profits of persons or corporations who knowingly employed child labor for any portion of a year. Like the tax on oleomargarine colored to look like butter, the child labor tax was designed to change social policy rather than raise revenue. But in contrast to the McCray decision upholding the oleomargarine act and the recent Doremus decision, the Court struck down the Child Labor Tax Act as decisively as the Child Labor Act based on the commerce power. The *Bailey* decision was written by Chief Justice William Howard Taft.

BAILEY v. DREXEL FURNITURE COMPANY
259 U. S. 20 (1922)

The law is attacked on the ground that it is a regulation of the employment of child labor in the states,—an exclusively state function under the Federal Constitution and within the reservations of the 10th Amendment. It is defended on the ground that it is a mere excise tax, levied by the Congress of the United States under its broad power of taxation conferred by § 8, article I, of the Federal Constitution. We must construe the law and interpret the intent and meaning of Congress from the language of the act. The words are to be given their ordinary meaning unless the context shows that they are differently used. Does this law impose a tax with only that incidental restraint and regulation which a tax must inevitably involve? Or does it regulate by the use of a so-called tax as a penalty? If a tax, it is clearly an excise. If it were an excise on a commodity or other thing of value we might not be permitted, under previous decisions of this court, to infer solely from its heavy burden, that the act intends a prohibition instead of a tax. But this act is more. It provides a heavy exaction for a departure from a detailed and specified course of conduct in business. That course of business is that employers shall employ in mines and quarries, children of an age greater than sixteen years; in mills and factories, children of an age greater than fourteen years; and shall prevent children of less than sixteen years in mills and factories from working more than eight hours a day or six days in the week. If an employer departs from this prescribed course of business, he is to pay to the government one tenth of his entire net income in the business for a full year. The amount is not to be proportioned in any degree to the extent or frequency of the departures, but is to be paid by the employer in full measure whether he employs five hundred children for a year, or employs only one for a day. Moreover, if he does not know the child is within the named age limit, he is not to pay; that is to say, it is only where he knowingly departs from the prescribed course that payment is to be exacted. Scienters are associated with penalties, not with taxes. The employer's factory is to be subject to inspection at any time not only by the taxing officers of the Treasury, the Department normally charged with the collection of taxes, but also by the Secretary of Labor and his subordinates, whose normal function is the advancement and protection of the welfare of the workers. In the light of these features of the act, a court must be blind not to see that the so-called tax is imposed to stop the employment of children within the age limits prescribed. Its prohibitory and regulatory effect and purpose are palpable. All others can see and understand this. How can we properly shut our minds to it?

It is the high duty and function of this court in cases regularly brought to its bar to decline to recognize or enforce seeming laws of Congress, dealing with subjects not intrusted to Congress, but left or committed by the supreme law of the land to the control of the states. We cannot avoid the duty even though it require us to refuse to give effect to legislation designed to promote the highest good. The good sought in unconstitutional legislation is an insidious feature because it leads citizens and legislators of good purpose to promote it without thought of the serious breach it will make in the ark of our covenant, or the harm which will come from breaking down recognized standards. In the maintenance of self-government, on the one hand, and the national power, on the other, our country has been able to endure and prosper for near a century and a half.

Out of proper respect for the acts of a co-ordinate branch of the government, this Court has gone far to sustain taxing acts as such, even though there has been ground for suspecting, from the weight of the tax, it was intended to destroy its subject. But in the act before us, the presumption of validity cannot prevail, because the proof of the contrary is found on the very face of its provisions. Grant the validity of this law, and all that Congress would need to do hereafter, in seeking to take over to its control any one of the great number of subjects of public interest, jurisdiction of which the states have never parted with, and which are reserved to them by the 10th Amendment, would be to enact a detailed measure of complete regulation of the subject and enforce it by a so-called tax upon departures from it. To give such magic to the word "tax" would be to break down all constitutional limitation of the powers of Congress and completely wipe out the sovereignty of the states.

The difference between a tax and a penalty is sometimes difficult to define, and yet the consequences of the distinction in the required method of their collection often are important. Where the sovereign enacting the law has power to impose both tax and penalty, the difference between revenue production and mere regulation may be immaterial; but not so when one sovereign can impose a tax only, and the power of regulation rests in another. Taxes are occasionally imposed in the discretion of the legislature on proper subjects with the primary motive of obtaining revenue from them, and with the incidental motive of discouraging them by making their continuance onerous. They do not lose their character as taxes because of the incidental motive. But there comes a time in the extension of the penalizing features of the so-called tax when it loses its character as such and becomes a mere penalty, with the characteristics of regulation and punishment. Such is the case in the law before us. Although Congress does not invalidate the contract of employment, or expressly declare that the employment within the mentioned ages is illegal, it does exhibit its intent practically to achieve the latter result by adopting the criteria of wrongdoing, and imposing its principal consequence on those who transgress its standard.

The case before us cannot be distinguished from that of Hammer v. Dagenhart. . . .

In the case at the bar, Congress, in the name of a tax which, on the face of the act, is a penalty, seeks to do the same thing, and the effort must be equally futile.

The analogy of the Dagenhart case is clear. The congressional power over interstate commerce is, within its proper scope, just as complete and unlimited as the congressional power to tax; and the legislative motive in its exercises is just as free from judicial suspicion and inquiry. Yet when Congress threatened to stop interstate commerce in ordinary and necessary commodities, unobjectionable as subjects of transportation, and to deny the same to the people of a state, in order to coerce them into compliance with Congress's regulation of state concerns, the court said this was not in fact regulation of interstate commerce, but rather that of state concerns, and was invalid. So here the so-called tax is a penalty to coerce people of a state to act as Congress wishes them to act in respect of a matter completely the business of the state government under the Federal Constitution. This case requires, as did the Dagenhart case, the application of the principle announced by Chief Justice Marshall in M'Culloch v. Maryland. . . , in a much-quoted passage:

"Should Congress, in the execution of its powers, adopt measures which are prohibited by the Constitution, or should Congress, under the pretext of executing its powers, pass laws for the accomplishment of objects not intrusted to the government, it would become the painful duty of this tribunal, should a case requiring such a decision come before it, to say that such an act was not the law of the land." . . .

For the reasons given, we must hold the Child Labor Tax Law invalid, and the judgment of the District Court is affirmed.

Justice Clarke dissented.

The *Dagenhart* and *Bailey* decisions underscored the basic paradox Congress and the state legislatures confronted when both were thwarted by national judicial decisions limiting federal action under commerce or taxation authority and by the harsh realities of corporate competition for special economic privileges among the states. This judicially enforced free competition among the states discouraged social experimentation by state legislatures who feared that competing states, offering cheap labor incentives by permitting child labor, would gain economic advantage through the migration of industries or the sale of products at lower prices. In 1924 the Congress passed a Child Labor Amendment to the Constitution but it was not ratified for the same economic competitive reasons that thwarted state social experimentation. By 1930, only five states had ratified the amendment. It was not until New Deal justices brought about a transformation in doctrinal values that child labor legislation was sanctioned by the Supreme Court.[16]

Determining the scope of intergovernmental tax immunity and presidential power

Although the Supreme Court had utilized the Tenth Amendment as a restriction on federal police power control of child labor in *Dagenhart* and *Bailey*, it further narrowed but did not abandon the doctrine of intergovernmental tax immunity in

Metcalf and Eddy v. *Mitchell.* Justice Harlan Fiske Stone wrote the Court's opinion, in which the facts of the case are fully explained.

METCALF AND EDDY v. MITCHELL
269 U. S. 514 (1926)

Metcalf & Eddy, the plaintiffs below, were consulting engineers who, either individually or as copartners, were professionally employed to advise states or subdivisions of states with reference to proposed water supply and sewage disposal systems. During 1917 the fees received by them for these services were paid over to the firm and became a part of its gross income. Upon this portion of their net income they paid, under protest, the tax assessed on the net income of copartnerships under the War Revenue Act of 1917. They then brought suit in the United States district court of Massachusetts to recover the tax paid on the items in question, on the ground that they were expressly exempted from the tax by the act itself, and on the further ground that Congress had no power under the Constitution to tax the income in question. . . .

All of the items of income were received by the taxpayers as compensation for their services as consulting engineers under contracts with states or municipalities, or water or sewage districts created by state statute. In each case the service was rendered in connection with a particular project for water supply or sewage disposal, and the compensation was paid in some instances on an annual basis, in others on a monthly or daily basis, and in still others on the basis of a gross sum for the whole service.

The War Revenue Act provided for the assessment of a tax on net income, but § 201 (a) contains a provision for exemption from the tax as follows:

"This title shall apply to all trades or businesses of whatever description, whether continuously carried on or not, except—

"(a) In the case of officers and employees under the United States, or any state, territory, or the District of Columbia, or any local subdivision thereof, the compensation or fees received by them as such officers or employees." . . .

We think it clear that neither of the plaintiffs in error occupied any official position in any of the undertakings to which their writ of error . . . relates. They took no oath of office; they were free to accept any other concurrent employment; none of their engagements was for work of a permanent or continuous character; some were of brief duration and some from year to year, others for the duration of the particular work undertaken. Their duties were prescribed by

their contracts and it does not appear to what extent, if at all, they were defined or prescribed by statute. We therefore conclude that plaintiffs in error have failed to sustain the burden cast upon them of establishing that they were officers of a state or a subdivision of a state within the exception of § 201 (a). . . .

Nor do ⸴he facts stated in the bill of exception establish that the plaintiffs were "employees" within the meaning of the statute. So far as appears, they were in the position of independent contractors. The record does not reveal to what extent, if at all, their services were subject to the direction or control of the public boards or officers engaging them. In each instance the performance of their contract involved the use of judgment and discretion on their part and they were required to use their best professional skill to bring about the desired result. This permitted to them liberty of action which excludes the idea [of] that control or right of control by the employer . . . and differentiates the employee or servant from the independent contractor. . . .

We pass to the more difficult question whether Congress had the constitutional power to impose the tax in question, and this must be answered by ascertaining whether its effect is such as to bring it within the purview of those decisions holding that the very nature of our constitutional system of dual sovereign governments is such as impliedly to prohibit the Federal government from taxing the instrumentalities of a state government, and in a similar manner to limit the power of the states to tax the instrumentalities of the Federal government. . . .

Just what instrumentalities of either a state or the Federal government are exempt from taxation by the other cannot be stated in terms of universal application. But this court has repeatedly held that those agencies through which either government immediately and directly exercises its sovereign powers are immune from the taxing power of the other. Thus, the employment of officers who are agents to administer its laws . . . are all so intimately connected with the necessary functions of government, as to fall within the established exemption; and when the instrumentality is of that character, the immunity extends not only to the instrumentality itself but to income derived from it . . . and forbids an occupation tax imposed on its use. . . .

When, however, the question is approached from the other end of the scale, it is apparent that not every person who uses his property or derives a profit, in his dealings with the government, may clothe himself with immunity from taxation on the theory that either he or his property is an instrumentality of government within the meaning of the rule. . . .

As cases arise lying between the two extremes, it becomes necessary to draw the line which separates those activities having some relation to government, which are nevertheless subject to taxation, from those which are immune. Experience has shown that there is no formula by which that line may be plotted with precision in advance. But recourse may be had to the reason upon which the rule rests, and which must be the guiding principle to control its operation. Its origin was due to the essential requirement of our constitutional system that the Federal government must exercise its authority within the territorial limits of the states; and it rests on the conviction that each government, in order that it may administer its affairs within its own sphere, must be left free from undue interference by the other. . . .

In a broad sense, the taxing power of either government, even when exercised in a manner admittedly necessary and proper, unavoidably has some effect upon the other. The burden of Federal taxation necessarily sets an economic limit to the practical operation of the taxing power of the states, and vice versa. Taxation by either state or the Federal government affects in some measure the cost of operation of the other.

But neither government may destroy the other nor curtail in any substantial manner the exercise of its powers. Hence, the limitation upon the taxing power of each, so far as it affects the other, must receive a practical construction which permits both to function with the minimum of interference each with the other; and that limitation cannot be so varied or extended as seriously to impair either the taxing power of the government imposing the tax . . . or the appropriate exercise of the functions of the government affected by it. . . .

While it is evident that in one aspect the extent of the exemption must finally depend upon the effect of the tax upon the functions of the government alleged to be affected by it, still the nature of the governmental agencies or the mode of their constitution may not be disregarded in passing on the question of tax exemption; for it is obvious that an agency may be of such a character or so intimately connected with the exercise of a power or the performance of a duty by the one government, that any taxation of it by the other would be such a direct interference with the functions of government itself as to be plainly beyond the taxing power.

It is on this principle that, as we have seen, any taxation by one government of the salary of an officer of the other, or the public securities of the other, or an agency created and controlled by the other, exclusively to enable it to perform a governmental function . . . is prohibited. But here the tax is imposed on the income of one who is neither an officer nor an employee of government and whose only relation to it is that of contract, under which there is an obligation to furnish service; for practical purposes not unlike a contract to sell and deliver a commodity. The tax is imposed without discrimination upon income whether derived from services rendered to the state or services rendered to private individuals. In such a situation it cannot be said that the tax is imposed upon an agency of government in any technical sense, and the tax itself cannot be deemed to be an interference with government, or an impairment of the efficiency of its agencies in any substantial way. . . .

As was said by this court in Baltimore Shipbuilding Co. v. Baltimore [1904] (in holding that a state might tax the interest of a corporation in a dry dock which the United States had the right to use under a contract entered into with the corporation):

"It seems to us extravagant to say that an independent private corporation for gain created by a state is exempt from state taxation either in its corporate person or its property because it is employed by the United States, even if the work for which it is employed is important and takes much of its time."

And as was said in Fidelity & Deposit Co. v. Pennsylvania [1916], in holding valid a state tax on premiums collected by bonding insurance companies on surety bonds required of United States officials:

"But mere contracts between private corporations and the United States do not necessarily render the former essentially government agencies and confer freedom from state control."

Despite the uses of the Tenth Amendment to forestall federal limitation of child labor, the Supreme Court did uphold congressional authority to regulate the killing of migratory birds provided by federal statute in 1918. Interestingly enough, an earlier statute, passed in 1913 had been declared unconstitutional in two federal district court decisions, *United States* v. *Shauver* (1914) and *United States* v.

McCullach (1915). The new statute was passed in accordance with a treaty with Great Britain (regarding Canada) adopted in 1916. The treaty relationship proved crucial, as the following opinion by Justice Oliver Wendell Holmes indicated.

MISSOURI v. HOLLAND
252 U. S. 416 (1920)

Justice Holmes delivered the opinion of the Court:

. . . As we have said, the question raised is the general one whether the treaty and statute are void as an interference with the rights reserved to the states.

To answer this question it is not enough to refer to the 10th Amendment, reserving the powers not delegated to the United States, because by article 2, § 2, the power to make treaties is delegated expressly, and by article 6, treaties made under the authority of the United States, along with the Constitution and laws of the United States, made in pursuance thereof, are declared the supreme law of the land. If the treaty is valid, there can be no dispute about the validity of the statute under article 1, § 8, as a necessary and proper means to execute the powers of the government. The language of the Constitution as to the supremacy of treaties being general, the question before us is narrowed to an inquiry into the ground upon which the present supposed exception is placed.

It is said that a treaty cannot be valid if it infringes the Constitution; that there are limits, therefore, to the treaty-making power; and that one such limit is that what an act of Congress could not do unaided, in derogation of the powers reserved to the states, a treaty cannot do. An earlier act of Congress that attempted by itself, and not in pursuance of a treaty, to regulate the killing of migratory birds within the states, had been held bad in the district court. United States v. Shauver [1914]; United States v. McCullach [1915]. Those decisions were supported by arguments that migratory birds were owned by the states in their sovereign capacity, for the benefit of their people, and that under cases like Geer v. Connecticut [1896], this control was one that Congress had no power to displace. The same argument is supposed to apply now with equal force.

Whether the two cases cited were decided rightly or not, they cannot be accepted as a test of the treaty power. Acts of Congress are the supreme law of the land only when made in pursuance of the constitution, while treaties are declared to be so when made under the authority of the United States. It is open to question whether the authority of the United States means more than the formal acts prescribed to make the con-

vention. We do not mean to imply that there are no qualifications to the treaty-making power; but they must be ascertained in a different way. It is obvious that there may be matters of the sharpest exigency for the national well-being that an act of Congress could not deal with, but that a treaty followed by such an act could, and it is not lightly to be assumed that, in matters requiring national action, "a power which must belong to and somewhere reside in every civilized government" is not to be found. . . . We are not yet discussing the particular case before us, but only are considering the validity of the test proposed. With regard to that, we may add that when we are dealing with words that also are a constituent act, like the Constitution of the United States, we must realize that they have called into life a being the development of which could not have been foreseen completely by the most gifted of its begetters. It was enough for them to realize or to hope that they had created an organism; it has taken a century and has cost their successors much sweat and blood to prove that they created a nation. The case before us must be considered in the light of our whole experience, and not merely in that of what was said a hundred years ago. The treaty in question does not contravene any prohibitory words to be found in the Constitution. The only question is whether it is forbidden by some invisible radiation from the general terms of the 10th Amendment. We must consider what this country has become in deciding what that amendment has reserved.

The state, as we have intimated, founds its claim of exclusive authority upon an assertion of title to migratory birds,—an assertion that is embodied in statute. No doubt it is true that, as between a state and its inhabitants, the state may regulate the killing and sale of such birds, but it does not follow that its authority is exclusive of paramount powers. To put the claim of the state upon title is to lean upon a slender reed. Wild birds are not in the possession of anyone; and possession is the beginning of ownership. The whole foundation of the state's rights is the presence within their jurisdiction of birds that yesterday had not arrived, tomorrow may be in another state, and in a week a thousand miles away. If we are to be accurate, we cannot put the case of the state upon higher ground than that the treaty deals with creatures that for the moment are within the state borders, that it must be carried out by officers of the United States within the same territory, and that, but for the treaty, the state would be free to regulate this subject itself.

As most of the laws of the United States are carried out within the states, and as many of them deal with matters which, in the silence of such laws, the state might regulate, such general grounds are not enough to support Missouri's claim. Valid treaties, of course, "are as binding within the territorial limits of the states as they are effective throughout the dominion of the United States." . . . No doubt the great body of private relations usually falls within the control of the state, but a treaty may override its power. . . .

Here a national interest of very nearly the first magnitude is involved. It can be protected only by national action in concert with that of another power. The subject-matter is only transitorily within the state, and has no permanent habitat therein. But for the treaty and the statute, there soon might be no birds for any powers to deal with. We see nothing in the Constitution that compels the government to sit by while a food supply is cut off and the protectors of our forests and our crops are destroyed. It is not sufficient to rely upon the states. The reliance is vain, and were it otherwise, the question is whether the United States is forbidden to act. We are of opinion that the treaty and statute must be upheld. . . .

Decree affirmed.

Justice Van Devanter and Justice Pitney dissent.

A major case decided by the Supreme Court in the 1920s resulted from President Wilson's removal of the postmaster of Portland, Oregon, a political appointee, from his post before his four-year term was completed. This issue, decided in *Myers v. the United States,* was a major test of the presidential removal power. Although the decision was handed down in 1926, the statutory basis for the constitutional challenge to President Wilson's authority was a reconstruction-era act of 1876 that sought to limit presidential power by making removal of first, second, and third class postmasters subject to the consent of the Senate. The Court handled the question several years after Wilson had left office. Chief Justice William Howard Taft, a former president, supported a broad interpretation of executive power that not only provided grounds for invalidating the statute, but also suggested that presidents could remove quasi-judicial officials. Major portions of Chief Justice Taft's majority opinion and Justice Holmes' dissent are reproduced below.

MYERS v. UNITED STATES
272 U. S. 52 (1926)

Chief Justice Taft delivered the opinion of the Court:

[After a detailed review of three quarters of a century of practice and experience, the chief justice summed up the power of the president as follows:]

Made responsible under the Constitution for the effective enforcement of the law, the President needs as an indispensable aid to meet it the disciplinary influence upon those who act under him of a reserve power of removal. . . .

In all such cases, the discretion to be exercised is that of the President in determining the national public interest and in directing the action to be taken by his executive subordinates to protect it. In this field his cabinet officers must do his will. He must place in each member of his official family, and his chief executive subordinates, implicit faith. The moment that he loses confidence in the intelligence, ability, judgment or loyalty of any one of them, he must have the power to remove him without delay. To require him to file charges and submit them to the consideration of the Senate might make impossible that unity and coordination in executive administration essential to effective action.

The duties of the heads of departments and bureaus in which the discretion of the President is exercised and which we have described, are the most important in the whole field of executive action of the government. There is nothing in the Constitution which permits a distinction between the removal of the head of the department or a bureau, when he discharges a political duty of the President or exercises his discretion, and the removal of executive officers engaged in the discharge of their other normal duties. The imperative reasons requiring an unrestricted power to remove the most important of his subordinates in their most important duties must, therefore, control the interpretation of the Constitution as to all appointed by him.

But this is not to say that there are not strong reasons why the President should have a like power to remove his appointees charged with other duties than those above described. The ordinary duties of officers prescribed by statute come under the general administrative control of the President by virtue of the general grant to him of the executive power, and he may properly supervise and guide their construction of the statutes under which they act in order to secure that unitary and uniform execution of the laws which article 2 of the Constitution evidently contemplated in vesting general executive power in the President alone. Laws are often passed with specific provisions for the adoption of regulations by a department or bureau head to make the law workable and effective. The ability and judgment manifested by the official thus empowered, as well as his energy and stimulation of his subordinates, are subjects which the President must consider and supervise in his administrative control. Finding such officers to be negligent and inefficient, the President should have the power to remove them. Of course there may be duties so peculiarly and specifically committed to the discretion of a particular officer as to raise a question whether the President may overrule or revise the officer's interpretation of his statutory duty in a particular instance. Then there may be duties of a quasi-judicial character imposed on executive officers and members of executive tribunals whose decisions after hearing affect interests of individuals, the discharge of which the President can not in a particular case properly influence or control. But even in such a case he may consider the decision after its rendition as a reason for removing the officer, on the ground that the discretion regularly entrusted to that officer by statute has not been on the whole intelligently or wisely exercised. Otherwise he does not discharge his own constitutional duty of seeing that the laws be faithfully executed. . .

. . . It is further pressed on us that, even though the legislative decision of 1789 included inferior officers, yet under the legislative power given Congress with respect to such officers, it might directly legislate as to the method of their removal without changing their method of appointment by the President with the consent of the Senate. We do not think the language of the Constitution justifies such a contention. . . .

The power to remove inferior executive officers, like that to remove superior executive officers, is an incident of the power to appoint them, and is in its nature an executive power. The authority of Congress given by the excepting clause to vest the appointment of such inferior officers in the heads of departments carries with it authority incidentally to invest the heads of departments with power to remove. It has been the practice of Congress to do so and this court has recognized that power. The court also has recognized in the Perkins case that Congress, in committing the appointment of such inferior officers to the heads of departments, may prescribe incidental regulations controlling and restricting the latter in the exercise of the power of removal. But the court never has held, nor reasonably could hold, although it is argued to the contrary on behalf of the appellant, that the excepting clause enables Congress to draw to itself, or to either branch of it, the power to remove or the right to participate in the exercise of that power. To do this would be to go beyond the words and implications of that clause and to infringe the constitutional principle of the separation of governmental powers. . . .

Summing up, then, the facts as to acquiescence by all branches of the Government in the legislative decision of 1789, as to executive officers, whether superior or inferior, we find that from 1789 until 1863, a period of seventy-four years, there was no act of Congress, no executive act, and no decision of this court at variance with the declaration of the First Congress, but there was, as we have seen, clear, affirmative recognition of it by each branch of the Government. . . .

We come now to a period in the history of the Government when both houses of Congress attempted to reverse this constitutional construction and to subject the power of removing executive officers appointed by the President and confirmed by the Senate to the control of the Senate—indeed, finally, to the assumed power in Congress to place the removal of such officers anywhere in the Government.

This reversal grew out of the serious political difference between the two houses of Congress and President Johnson. There was a two-thirds majority of the Republican party in control of each house of Congress, which resented what it feared would be Mr. Johnson's obstructive course in the enforcement of the reconstruction measures, in respect of the States whose people had lately been at war against the National Government. This led the two houses to enact legislation to curtail the then acknowledged powers of the President. . . .

But the chief legislation in support of the reconstruction policy of Congress was the Tenure of Office Act, of March 2, 1867, providing that all officers appointed by and with the consent of the Senate should hold their offices until their successors should have in like manner been appointed and qualified, and that certain heads of departments, including the Secretary of War, should hold their offices during the term of the President by whom appointed and one month thereafter subject to removal by consent of the Senate. The Tenure of Office Act was vetoed, but it was passed over the veto. The House of Representatives preferred articles of impeachment against President Johnson for refusal to comply with, and for conspiracy to defeat, the legislation above referred to, but he was acquitted for lack of a two-thirds vote for conviction in the Senate. . . .

. . . The feeling growing out of the controversy with President Johnson retained the act on the statute book until 1887, when it was repealed. During this interval, on June 8, 1872, Congress passed an act reorganizing and consolidating the Post Office Department, and provided that the Postmaster General and his three assistants should be appointed by the President by and with the advice and consent of the Senate and might be removed in the same manner. In 1876 the act here under discussion was passed, making the consent of the Senate necessary both to the appointment and removal of first, second and third class postmasters.

An argument ab inconvenienti has been made against our conclusion in favor of the executive power of removal by the President, without the consent of the Senate—that it will open the door to a reintroduction of the spoils system. The evil of the spoils system aimed at in the civil service law and its amendments is in respect of inferior offices. It has never been attempted to extend that law beyond them. Indeed, Congress forbids its extension to appointments confirmed by the Senate, except with the consent of the Senate. . . . It may still be enlarged by further legislation. The independent power of removal by the President alone, under present conditions, works no practical interference with the merit system. Political appointments of inferior officers are still maintained in one important class, that of the first, second and third class postmasters, collectors of internal revenue, marshals, collectors of customs and other officers of that kind, distributed through the country. They are appointed by the President with the consent of the Senate. It is the intervention of the Senate in their appointments, and not in their removal, which prevents their classification into the merit system. If such appointments were vested in the heads of departments to which they belong, they could be entirely removed from politics, and that is what a number of Presidents have recommended. . . . The extension of the merit system rests with Congress. . . .

. . . Without animadverting on the character of the measures taken, we are certainly justified in saying that they should not be given the weight affecting proper constitutional construction to be accorded to that reached by the First Congress of the United States during a political calm and acquiesced in by the whole Government for three-quarters of a century, especially when the new construction contended for has never been acquiesced in by either the executive or the judicial departments. While this court has studiously avoided deciding the issue until it was presented in such a way that it could not be avoided, in the references it has made to the history of the question, and in the presumptions it has indulged in favor of a statutory construction not inconsistent with the legislative decision of 1789, it has indicated a trend of view that we should not and can not ignore. When, on the merits, we find our conclusion strongly favoring the view which prevailed in the First Congress, we have no hesitation in holding that conclusion to be correct; and it therefore follows that the Tenure of Office Act of 1867, in so far as it attempted to prevent the President from removing executive officers who had been appointed by him by and with the advice and consent of the Senate, was invalid, and that subsequent legislation of the same effect was equally so.

For the reasons given, we must therefore hold that the provision of the law of 1876, by which the unrestricted power of removal of first class postmasters is denied to the President, is in violation of the Constitution, and invalid. This leads to an affirmance of the judgment of the Court of Claims. . . .

Judgment affirmed.

Justice Holmes dissented, saying in part:

The arguments drawn from the executive power of the President and from his duty to appoint officers of the United States (when Congress does not vest the appointment elsewhere), to take care that the laws be faithfully executed, and to commission all officers of the United States, seem to me spider's webs inadequate to control the dominant facts.

We have to deal with an office that owes its existence to Congress and that Congress may abolish tomorrow. Its duration and the pay attached to it while it lasts depend on Congress alone. Congress alone confers on the President the power to appoint to it and at any time may transfer the power to other hands. With such power over its own creation, I have no more trouble in believing that Congress has power to prescribe a term of life for it free from any interference than I have in accepting the undoubted power of

Congress to decree its end. I have equally little trouble in accepting its power to prolong the tenure of an incumbent until Congress or the Senate shall have assented to his removal. The duty of the President to see that the laws be executed is a duty that does not go beyond the laws or require him to achieve more than Congress sees fit to leave within his power.

*In a separate dissenting opinion,
Justice McReynolds said in part:*

. . . The long struggle for civil service reform and the legislation designed to insure some security of official tenure ought not to be forgotten. Again and again Congress has enacted statutes prescribing restrictions on removals and by approving them many Presidents have affirmed its power therein. . . .

Nothing short of language clear beyond serious disputation should be held to clothe the President with authority wholly beyond congressional control arbitrarily to dismiss every officer whom he appoints except a few judges. There are no such words in the Constitution, and the asserted inference conflicts with the heretofore accepted theory that this government is one of carefully enumerated power under an intelligible charter. . . .

If the phrase "executive power" infolds the one now claimed, many others heretofore totally unsuspected may lie there awaiting future supposed necessity; and no human intelligence can define the field of the President's permissible activities. "A masked battery of constructive powers would complete the destruction of liberty." . . .

Corruption and the scope of legislative investigative power

The scandals of the Harding era provided the setting for a major constitutional test of congressional investigative authority. For several decades such legislative authority had been restricted by the decision handed down in the 19th century in *Kilbourn* v. *Thompson*. The complex circumstances brought about by widespread political corruption provided the basis for a new judicial approach. The so-called Ohio gang associated with President Warren G. Harding had been accused, often by opposition Progressive or Democratic senators, of appointment scandals, bribery, and misuse of federal funds. In early 1924, the Senate established an investigating committee to inquire about the ties of the "Ohio gang" with Attorney General Harry M. Daugherty and the failure of the Justice Department to enforce the criminal statutes of the United States in relation to the "gang." Although Attorney General Daugherty thereafter resigned under fire, the Senate committee had traced some of the corrupt activity to a small-town bank in Ohio managed by Mally S. Daugherty, the attorney general's brother. Subsequently Mally failed to appear, as requested by the committee, as a witness in the investigation of Justice Department failures to investigate and prosecute scandals in naval oil leases, the Veterans Bureau, and enforce the antitrust acts. The Senate had to order the sergeant-at-arms to arrest him and bring him to the Senate to testify. McGrain, a deputy sergeant-at-arms, arrested Mally in Ohio. Mally asked for a writ of habeas corpus and a federal district court had him released. The issue was then taken to the Supreme Court, where Justice Van Devanter wrote the majority opinion.

McGRAIN v. DAUGHERTY
273 U. S. 135 (1927)

This is an appeal from the final order in a proceeding in habeas corpus discharging a recusant witness held in custody under process of attachment issued from the United States Senate in the course of an investigation which it was making of the administration of the Department of Justice. . . .

The first of the principal questions—the one which the witness particularly presses on our attention—is, as before shown, whether the Senate—or the House of Representatives, both being on the same plane in this regard—has power, through its own process, to compel a private individual to appear before it or one of its committees and give testimony needed to enable it efficiently to exercise a legislative function belonging to it under the Constitution.

The Constitution provides for a Congress consisting of a Senate and House of Representatives and invests it with "all legislative powers" granted to the United States, and with power "to make all laws which shall be necessary and proper" for carrying into execution these powers and "all other powers" vested by the Constitution in the United States or in any department or officer thereof. Article I, sections 1, 8. . . . But there is no provision expressly investing either house with power to make investigations and exact testimony to the end that it may exercise its legislative function advisedly and effectively. So the question arises whether this power is so far incidental to the legislative function as to be implied.

In actual legislative practice power to secure needed information by such means has long been treated as an attribute of the power to legislate. It was so regarded in the British Parliament and in the colonial legislatures before the American Revolution; and a like view has prevailed and been carried into effect in both houses of Congress and in most of the state legislatures.

This power was both asserted and exerted by the House of Representatives in 1792, when it appointed a select committee to inquire into the St. Clair expedition and authorized the committee to send for necessary persons, papers and records. Mr. Madison, who had taken an important part in framing the Constitution only five years before, and four of his associates in that work, were members of the House of Representatives at the time, and all voted for the inquiry. . . . Other exertions of the power by the House of Representatives, as also by the Senate, are shown in the citations already made. Among those by the Senate, the inquiry ordered in 1859 respecting the raid by John Brown and his adherents on the armory and arsenal of the United States at Harper's Ferry is of special significance. The resolution directing the inquiry authorized the committee to send for persons and papers, to inquire into the facts pertaining to the raid and the means by which it was organized and supported, and to report what legislation, if any, was necessary to preserve the peace of the country and protect the public property. The resolution was briefly discussed and adopted without opposition. . . . Later on the committee reported that Thaddeus Hyatt, although sub-poenaed to appear as a witness, had refused to do so, whereupon the Senate ordered that he be attached and brought before it to answer for his refusal. When he was brought in he answered by challenging the power of the Senate to direct the inquiry and exact testimony to aid it in exercising its legislative function. The question of power thus presented was thoroughly discussed by several senators—Mr. Sumner of Massachusetts taking the lead in denying the power, and Mr. Fessenden of Maine in supporting it. Sectional and party lines were put aside and the question was debated and determined with special regard to principle and precedent. The vote was taken on a resolution pronouncing the witness's answer insufficient and directing that he be committed until he should signify that he was ready and willing to testify. The resolution was adopted—forty-four senators voting for it and ten against. . . .

The deliberate solution of the question on that occasion has been accepted and followed on other occasions by both houses of Congress, and never has been rejected or questioned by either.

The state courts quite generally have held that the power to legislate carries with it by necessary implication ample authority to obtain information needed in the rightful exercise of that power, and to employ compulsory process for the purpose. . . .

We have referred to the practice of the two houses of Congress; and we now shall notice some significant congressional enactments. . . .

[The Court here reviews the congressional statutes leading up to the passage of the Compulsory Testimony Act of 1857.]

. . . They show very plainly that Congress intended thereby (a) to recognize the power of either house to institute inquiries and exact evidence touching subjects within its jurisdiction and on which it was disposed to act; (b) to recognize that such inquiries may be conducted through committees; (c) to subject defaulting and contumacious witnesses to indictment and punishment in the courts, and thereby to enable either house to exert the power of inquiry "more effectually"; and (d) to open the way for obtaining evidence in such an inquiry, which otherwise could not be obtained, by exempting witnesses required to give evidence therein from criminal and penal prosecutions in respect of matters disclosed by their evidence.

Four decisions of this court are cited and more or less relied on, and we now turn to them.

The first decision was in Anderson v. Dunn [1821]. The question there was whether, under the Constitution, the House of Representatives has power to attach and punish a person other than a member for contempt of its authority—in fact, an attempt to bribe one of its members. The court regarded the power as essential to the effective exertion of other powers expressly granted, and therefore as implied. . . .

The next decision was in Kilbourn v. Thompson [1881]. The question there was whether the House of Representatives had exceeded its power in directing one of its committees to make a particular investigation. The decision was that it had. The principles announced and applied in the case are—that neither house of Congress possesses a "general power of making inquiry into the private affairs of the citizen"; that the power actually possessed is limited to inquiries relating to matters of which the particular house "has jurisdiction," and in respect of which it rightfully may take other actions; that if the inquiry relates to "a matter wherein relief or redress could be had only by a judicial proceeding" it is not within the range of this power, but must be left to the courts, conformably to the constitutional separation of governmental powers; and that for the purpose of determining the essential character of the inquiry recourse may be had to the resolution or order under which it is made. The court examined the resolution which was the basis of the particular inquiry, and ascertained therefrom that the inquiry related to a private real-estate pool or partnership in the District of Columbia. Jay Cook & Company had had an interest in the pool, but had become bankrupt, and their estate was in course of administration in a federal bankruptcy court in Pennsylvania. The United States was one of their creditors. The trustee in the bankruptcy proceeding had effected a settlement of the bankrupts' interest in the pool, and of course his action was subject to examination and approval or disapproval by the bankruptcy court. Some of the creditors, including the United States, were dissatisfied with the settlement. In these circumstances, disclosed in the preamble, the resolution directed the committee "to inquire into the matter and history of said real-estate pool and the character of said settlement, with the amount of property involved in which Jay Cook & Company were interested, and the amount paid or to be paid in said settlement, with power to send for persons and papers and report to the House." The court pointed out that the resolution contained no suggestion of contemplated legislation; that the matter was one in respect to which no valid legislation could be had; that the bankrupts' estate and the trustee's settlement were still pending in the bankruptcy court; and that the United States and other creditors were free to press their claims in that proceeding. And

on these grounds the court held that in undertaking the investigation "the House of Representatives not only exceeded the limit of its own authority, but assumed power which could only be properly exercised by another branch of the government, because it was in its nature clearly judicial." . . .

[The Court also reviewed In re Chapman . . . and Marshall v. Gordon. . . , involving the power to compel testimony and punish for contempt.]

While these cases are not decisive of the question we are considering, they definitely settle two propositions which we recognize as entirely sound and having a bearing on its solution: One, that the two houses of Congress, in their separate relations, possess not only such powers as are expressly granted to them by the Constitution, but such auxiliary powers as are necessary and appropriate to make the express powers effective; and, the other, that neither house is invested with "general" power to inquire into private affairs and compel disclosures, but only with such limited power of inquiry as is shown to exist when the rule of constitutional interpretation just stated is rightly applied. . . .

With this review of the legislative practice, congressional enactments and court decisions, we proceed to a statement of our conclusions on the question.

We are of opinion that the power of inquiry—with process to enforce it—is an essential and appropriate auxiliary to the legislative function. It was so regarded and employed in American legislatures before the constitution was framed and ratified. Both houses of Congress took this view of it early in their history— the House of Representatives with the approving votes of Mr. Madison and other members whose service in the convention which framed the Constitution gives special significance to their action—and both houses have employed the power accordingly up to the present time. The acts of 1798 and 1857, judged by their comprehensive terms, were intended to recognize the existence of this power in both houses and to enable them to employ it "more effectually" then before. So, when their practice in the matter is appraised according to the circumstances in which it was begun and to those in which it has been continued, it falls nothing short of a practical construction, long continued, of the constitutional provisions respecting their powers, and therefore should be taken as fixing the meaning of those provisions, if otherwise doubtful.

We are further of opinion that the provisions are not of doubtful meaning, but, as was held by this court in the cases we have reviewed, are intended to be effectively exercised, and therefore to carry with them such auxiliary powers as are necessary and appropriate to that end. While the power to exact information in aid of the legislative function was not involved in those cases, the rule of interpretation applied there is applicable here. A legislative body cannot legislate wisely or effectively in the absence of information respecting the conditions which the legislation is intended to affect or change; and where the legislative body does not itself possess the requisite information—which not infrequently is true—recourse must be had to others who do possess it. Experience has taught that mere requests for such information often are unavailing, and also that information which is volunteered is not always accurate or complete; so some means of compulsion are essential to obtain what is needed. . . .

The contention is earnestly made on behalf of the witness that this power of inquiry, if sustained, may be abusively and oppressively exerted. If this be so, it affords no ground for denying the power. . . . And it is a necessary deduction from the decisions in Kilbourn v. Thompson and Re Chapman that a witness rightfully may refuse to answer where the bounds of the power are exceeded or the questions are not pertinent to the matter under inquiry.

We come now to the question whether it sufficiently appears that the purpose for which the witness's testimony was sought was to obtain information in aid of the legislative function. The court below answered the question in the negative, and put its decision largely on this ground, as is shown by the following excerpts from its opinion:

"It will be noted that in the second resolution the Senate has expressly avowed that the investigation is in aid of other action than legislation. Its purpose is to 'obtain information necessary as a basis for such legislative and other action as the Senate may deem necessary and proper.' This indicates that the Senate is contemplating the taking of action other than legislative, as the outcome of the investigation, at least the possibility of so doing. The extreme personal cast of the original resolutions; the spirit of hostility towards the then Attorney General which they breathe; that it was not avowed that legislative action was had in view until after the action of the Senate had been challenged; and that the avowal then was coupled with an avowal that other action was had in view—are calculated to create the impression that the idea of legislative action being in contemplation was an afterthought. . . .

"That the Senate has in contemplation the possibility of taking action other than legislation as an outcome of the investigation, as thus expressly avowed,

would seem of itself to invalidate the entire proceeding. But, whether so or not, the Senate's action is invalid and absolutely void, in that, in ordering and conducting the investigation, it is exercising the judicial function, and power to exercise that function, in such a case as we have here, has not been conferred upon it expressly or by fair implication. What it is proposing to do is to determine the guilt of the Attorney General of the shortcomings and wrongdoings set forth in the resolutions. It is 'to hear, adjudge, and condemn.' In so doing it is exercising the judicial function. . . .

"What the Senate is engaged in doing is not investigating the Attorney General's office; it is investigating the former Attorney General. What it has done is to put him on trial before it. In so doing it is exercising the judicial function. This it has no power to do."

We are of opinion that the court's ruling on this question was wrong, and that it sufficiently appears, when the proceedings are rightly interpreted, that the object of the investigation and of the effort to secure the witness's testimony was to obtain information for legislative purposes.

It is quite true that the resolution directing the investigation does not in terms avow that it is intended to be in aid of legislation; but it does show that the subject to be investigated was the administration of the Department of Justice—whether its functions were being properly discharged or were being neglected or misdirected, and particularly whether the Attorney General and his assistants were performing or neglecting their duties in respect of the institution and prosecution of proceedings to punish crimes and enforce appropriate remedies against the wrongdoers—specific instances of alleged neglect being recited. Plainly the subject was one on which legislation could be had and would be materially aided by the information which the investigation was calculated to elicit. This becomes manifest when it is reflected that the functions of the Department of Justice, the powers and duties of the Attorney General and the duties of his assistants, are all subject to regulation by congressional legislation, and that the department is maintained and its activities are carried on under such appropriations as in the judgment of Congress are needed from year to year.

The only legitimate object the Senate could have in ordering the investigation was to aid it in legislating; and we think the subject-matter was such that the presumption should be indulged that this was the real object. An express avowal of the object would have been better; but in view of the particular subject-matter was not indispensable. . . .

We conclude that the investigation was ordered

for a legitimate object; that the witness wrongfully refused to appear and testify before the committee and was lawfully attached; that the Senate is entitled to have him give testimony pertinent to the inquiry, either at its bar or before the committee; and that the

district court erred in discharging him from custody under the attachment. . . .

Final order reversed.

Justice Stone did not participate in the case.

War, patriotism, and a new approach: Clear and present danger

The thrust of Progessive domestic legislative efforts was not only blunted by the conservative doctrines of the Supreme Court, but ultimately was overshadowed by the channeling of national efforts into the first World War. Concomitantly, law development and political interest turned dramatically toward concepts of patriotism, the obligation for military service, and for the first time in many decades, the Bill of Rights. Congressional enactment of the Espionage Act of 1917 and a major amendment to it, generally referred to as the Sedition Act of 1918, brought about postal censorship of treasonable and seditious materials. Later the states enacted measures that duplicated the federal legislation but occasionally went considerably farther by prohibiting criminal anarchy and criminal syndicalism as well. This legislation stimulated constitutional challenges long after World War I had ended.

Interestingly enough, the first major war-related constitutional issue involved the validity of the Selective Draft Act of 1917. Although the United States had been involved in several major conflicts since 1789, the constitutionality of military conscription had never been tested. Chief Justice White wrote the majority opinion in the *Selective Draft Law Cases* in 1918. One indication of the intense emotions of that era occurred during oral argument before the Supreme Court. When an attorney opposed conscription on the grounds that the statute required individuals to take part in a war that had not received public approval, Chief Justice White retorted that

I don't think your statement has anything to do with legal arguments and should not have been said in this Court. It is a very unpatriotic statement to make. . . .[17]

SELECTIVE DRAFT LAW CASES
245 U. S. 366 (1918)

Chief Justice White delivered the opinion of the Court:

The possession of authority to enact the statute must be found in the clauses of the Constitution giving Congress power "to declare war; . . . to raise and support armies, but no appropriation of money to that use shall be for a longer term than two years; . . . to make rules for the government and regulation of the land and naval forces." Article I, § 8. And of course the powers conferred by these provisions like all other powers given carry with them as provided by the Constitution the authority "to make all laws which shall be

necessary and proper for carrying into execution the foregoing powers." Article I, § 8.

As the mind cannot conceive an army without the men to compose it, on the face of the Constitution the objection that it does not give power to provide for such men would seem to be too frivolous for further notice. It is said, however, that since under the Constitution as originally framed state citizenship was primary and United States citizenship but derivative and dependent thereon, therefore the power conferred upon Congress to raise armies was only coterminous with United States citizenship and could not be exerted so as to cause that citizenship to lose its dependent character and dominate state citizenship. But the proposition simply denies to Congress the power to raise armies which the Constitution gives. That power by the very terms of the Constitution, being delegated, is supreme. Article VI. In truth the contention simply assails the wisdom of the framers of the Constitution in conferring authority on Congress and in not retaining it as it was under the Confederation in the several States. Further it is said, the right to provide is not denied by calling for volunteer enlistments, but it does not and cannot include the power to exact enforced military duty by the citizen. This however but challenges the existence of all power, for a governmental power which has no sanction to it and which therefore can only be exercised provided the citizen consents to its exertion is in no substantial sense a power. It is argued, however, that although this is abstractly true, it is not concretely so because as compelled military service is repugnant to a free government and in conflict with all the great guarantees of the Constitution as to individual liberty, it must be assumed that the authority to raise armies was intended to be limited to the right to call an army into existence counting alone upon the willingness of the citizen to do his duty in time of public need, that is, in time of war. But the premise of this proposition is so devoid of foundation that it leaves not even a shadow of ground upon which to base the conclusion. Let us see if this is not at once demonstrable. It may not be doubted that the very conception of a just government and its duty to the citizen includes the reciprocal obligation of the citizen to render military service in case of need and the right to compel it. Vattel, Law of Nations, Book III, c. 1 & 2. To do more than state the proposition is absolutely unnecessary in view of the practical illustration afforded by the almost universal legislation to that effect now in force. . . .

In the Colonies before the separation from England there cannot be the slightest doubt that the right to enforce military service was unquestioned and that practical effect was given to the power in many cases. Indeed the brief of the Government contains a list of Colonial acts manifesting the power and its enforcement in more than two hundred cases. And this exact situation existed also after the separation. Under the Articles of Confederation it is true Congress had no such power, as its authority was absolutely limited to making calls upon the States for the military forces needed to create and maintain the army, each State

being bound for its quota as called. But it is indisputable that the States in response to the calls made upon them met the situation when they deemed it necessary by directing enforced military service on the part of the citizens. In fact the duty of the citizen to render military service and the power to compel him against his consent to do so was expressly sanctioned by the constitutions of at least nine of the States. . . . While it is true that the States were sometimes slow in exerting the power in order to fill their quotas—that fact serves to demonstrate instead a challenge to the existence of the authority. A default in exercising a duty may not be resorted to as a reason for denying its existence.

When the Constitution came to be formed it may not be disputed that one of the recognized necessities for its adoption was the want of power in Congress to raise an army and the dependence upon the States for their quotas. In supplying the power it was manifestly intended to give it all and leave none to the States, since besides the delegation to Congress of authority to raise armies the Constitution prohibited the States, without the consent of Congress, from keeping troops in time of peace or engaging in war. . . .

Thus sanctioned as is the act before us by the text of the Constitution, and by its significance as read in the light of the fundamental principles with which the subject is concerned, by the power recognized and carried into effect in many civilized countries, by the authority and practice of the colonies before the Revolution, of the States under the Confederation and of the Government since the formation of the Constitution, the want of merit in the contentions that the act in the particulars which we have been previously called upon to consider was beyond the constitutional power of Congress, is manifest. . . .

Finally, as we are unable to conceive upon what theory the exaction by government from the citizen of the performance of his supreme and noble duty of contributing to the defense of the rights and honor of the nation, as the result of a war declared by the great representative body of the people, can be said to be the imposition of involuntary servitude in violation of the prohibitions of the Thirteenth Amendment, we are constrained to the conclusion that the contention to that effect is refuted by its mere statement.

Affirmed.

The strong feelings unleashed by World War I had a direct impact upon a wide range of civil liberties. Congress passed a wide-ranging Espionage Act, which, among other things, provided penalties for (1) the making or dissemination of false reports in aid of the enemy, (2) the encouragement of disobedience in the armed forces, and (3) the willful obstruction of military recruitment. Additional acts or amendments, such as the Trading with the Enemy Act of 1917, and the Sedition Act of 1918, were added later. Sweeping investigations such as those by the American Protective League sometimes resulted in illegal detention or unreasonable searches and seizures, many of which were not challenged in the courts.

Some proposals for harsh legislation were defeated through the opposition of civil liberties organizations or by the determined opposition of President Wilson. For example, Assistant Attorney General Charles Warren drafted and sent to Congress, without the authorization of the Department of Justice, a bill that designated the entire United States as "part of the zone of operations conducted by the enemy." Thus, any person deemed a spy would be subject to military rather than civilian courts and subject to the death penalty or other severe punishment designated by the military tribunal. President Woodrow Wilson's critical letter to a key senator helped defeat the bill. Wilson indicated that he was

> . . . wholly and unalterably opposed to such legislation. . . . I think it is not only unconstitutional, but that in character it would put us upon the level of the very people we are fighting and affecting to despise. It would be altogether inconsistent with the spirit and the practice of America, and in view of the recent legislation, the espionage bill, the sabotage bill, and the woman spy bill, I think it is unnecessary and uncalled for. . . .[18]

The Supreme Court considered a number of important cases involving war-time civil liberties issues. Since the Court had not directly addressed itself to many of these issues, its responses initiated a whole new area of judicial policymaking. A case involving alleged conspiracy to violate the Espionage Act reached the Court in 1919 and was decided in that year. The act was challenged on the ground that it violated First Amendment freedoms. In the majority opinion in *Schenck* v. *The United States*, Oliver Wendell Holmes enunciated the "clear and present danger" doctrine, which provided the first truly significant criterion for determining the special circumstances under which First Amendment freedoms may be limited. Justice Holmes' rationale for *not* applying these standards to strike down the Espionage Act of 1917, that "the character of every act depends upon the circumstances in which it is done," was later adapted to a number of circumstances in which the justice himself was more inclined to protect the freedom rather than restrict free speech. Holmes' doctrinal innovation was incisive, but subject to the peculiarities of other justices who were occasionally inclined to manipulate the seemingly "clear" doctrine. The lines were drawn between justices fearful that the clear and present danger doctrine would dangerously weaken current standards for limiting basic freedoms such as speech, and a small number who emerged as careful protagonists of the basic freedoms. In the political context in which it arose, during World War I and early 1920s when the emphasis was on "Americanism," the Court needed to distinguish circumstances under which First Amendment freedoms might be limited, to examine the 20th century meaning of those freedoms, and to assert, in the face of transient pressures to the contrary, the rationale for preserving these basic freedoms.

The clear and present danger doctrine appears in the following opinion by Justice Holmes:

SCHENCK v. THE UNITED STATES
249 U. S. 47 (1919)

This is an indictment in three counts. The first charges a conspiracy to violate the Espionage Act of June 15, 1917, . . . by causing and attempting to cause insubordination, &c., in the military and naval forces of the United States, and to obstruct the recruiting and enlistment service of the United States, when the United States was at war with the German Empire, to-wit, that the defendants wilfully conspired to have printed and circulated to men who had been called and accepted for military service under the Act of May 18, 1917, a document set forth and alleged to be calculated to cause such insubordination and obstruction. The count alleges overt acts in pursuance of the conspiracy, ending in the distribution of the document set forth. The second count alleges a conspiracy to commit an offence against the United States, to-wit, to use the mails for the transmission of matter declared to be non-mailable by Title XII, § 2 of the Act of June 15, 1917, to-wit, the above mentioned document, with an averment of the same overt acts. The third count charges an unlawful use of the mails for the transmission of the same matter and otherwise as above. The defendants were found guilty on all the counts. They set up the First Amendment to the Constitution forbidding Congress to make any law abridging the freedom of speech, or of the press, and bringing the case here on that ground have argued some other points also of which we must dispose.

It is argued that the evidence, if admissible, was not sufficient to prove that the defendant Schenck was concerned in sending the documents. According to the testimony Schenck said he was general secretary of the Socialist party and had charge of the Socialist headquarters from which the documents were sent. He identified a book found there as the minutes of the Executive Committee of the party. The book showed a resolution of August 13, 1917, that 15,000 leaflets should be printed on the other side of one of them in use, to be mailed to men who had passed exemption boards, and for distribution. Schenck personally attended to the printing. On August 20 the general secretary's report said "Obtained new leaflets from printer and started work addressing envelopes" &c.; and there was a resolve that Comrade Schenck be allowed $125 for sending leaflets through the mail. He said that he had about fifteen or sixteen thousand printed. There were files of the circular in question in the inner office which he said were printed on the other side of the one sided circular and were there for

distribution. Other copies were proved to have been sent through the mails to drafted men. Without going into confirmatory details that were proved, no reasonable man could doubt that the defendant Schenck was largely instrumental in sending the circulars about. As to the defendant Baer there was evidence that she was a member of the Executive Board and that the minutes of its transactions were hers. The argument as to the sufficiency of the evidence that the defendants conspired to send the documents only impairs the seriousness of the real defence. . . .

The document in question upon its first printed side recited the first section of the Thirteenth Amendment, said that the idea embodied in it was violated by the Conscription Act and that a conscript is little better than a convict. In impassioned language it intimated that conscription was despotism in its worst form and a monstrous wrong against humanity in the interest of Wall Street's chosen few. It said "Do not submit to intimidation," but in form at least confined itself to peaceful measures such as a petition for the repeal of the act. The other and later printed side of the sheet was headed "Assert Your Rights." It stated reasons for alleging that any one violated the Constitution when he refused to recognize "your right to assert your opposition to the draft," and went on "If you do not assert and support your rights, you are helping to deny or disparage rights which it is the solemn duty of all citizens and residents of the United States to retain." It described the arguments on the other side as coming from cunning politicians and a mercenary capitalist press, and even silent consent to the conscription law as helping to support an infamous conspiracy. It denied the power to send our citizens away to foreign shores to shoot up the people of other lands, and added that words could not express the condemnation such cold-blooded ruthlessness deserves, &c., &c., winding up "You must do your share to maintain, support and uphold the rights of the people of this country." Of course the document would not have been sent unless it had been intended to have some effect, and we do not see what effect it could be expected to have upon persons subject to the draft except to influence them to obstruct the carrying of it out. The defendants do not deny that the jury might find against them on this point.

But it is said, suppose that that was the tendency of this circular, it is protected by the 1st Amendment to the Constitution. Two of the strongest expressions are said to be quoted respectively from well-known public men. It well may be that the prohibition of laws abridging the freedom of speech is not confined to previous restraints, although to prevent them may have been the main purpose, as intimated in Patterson v. Colorado [1907]. We admit that in many places and in ordinary times the defendants, in saying all that was said in the circular, would have been within their constitutional rights. But the character of every act depends upon the circumstances in which it is done. The most stringent protection of free speech would not protect a man in falsely shouting fire in a theatre, and causing a panic. It does not even protect a man from an injunction against uttering words that may have all the effect of force . . .

The question in every case is whether the words used are used in such circumstances and are of such a nature as to create a clear and present danger that they will bring about the substantive evils that Congress has a right to prevent. It is a question of proximity and degree. When a nation is at war many things that might be said in time of peace are such a hindrance to its effort that their utterance will not be endured so long as men fight, and that no court could regard them as protected by any constitutional right. It seems to be admitted that if an actual obstruction of the recruiting service were proved, liability for words that produced that effect might be enforced. The statute of 1917, in § 4, punishes conspiracies to obstruct as well as actual obstruction. If the act (speaking, or circulating a paper), its tendency and the intent with which it is done, are the same, we perceive no ground for saying that success alone warrants making the act a crime. . . .

Judgments affirmed.

Many state legislatures sought to duplicate or complement congressional actions in this field. State actions to punish and prevent criminal syndicalism, for example, spread from coast to coast. The first major test of such state laws involved a criminal anarchy statute of New York adopted in 1902, but similar in certain respects to the syndicalism statutes adopted during World War I. In *Gitlow* v. *New York*, Justice Sanford wrote the majority opinion and Justices Holmes and Brandeis dissented. Holmes' dissent invoked the standards enunciated in Schenck, but succeeded in gaining only Brandeis' support.

The most significant development in the First Amendment case law of the 20th century was the virtually off-hand acceptance by both majority and minority justices of the heretofore unprecedented doctrine that the First Amendment's freedom of speech and press are protected against state action by the Fourteenth Amendment's due process clause. This doctrinal incorporation of portions of the Bill of Rights as applicable against state actions was a direct repudiation of the position taken by the Court nearly a century earlier in *Barron* v. *Baltimore*. Although the justices in both *Schenck* and *Gitlow* did not discuss very fully the grounds for this fundamental shift, the applicability of some portions of the Bill of Rights against state action is, indeed, the most significant judicial act toward the nationalization of the Bill of Rights. The development of doctrinal grounds for asserting, expanding, and upholding these fundamental freedoms came initially from the dissents of Holmes, Brandeis, and, later, Stone.

GITLOW v. NEW YORK
268 U. S. 652 (1925)

Justice Sanford delivered the opinion of the Court:

Benjamin Gitlow was indicted in the supreme court of New York, with three others, for the statutory crime of criminal anarchy. . . .

The contention here is that the statute, by its terms and as applied in this case, is repugnant to the due process clause of the 14th Amendment. Its material provisions are:

"§ 160. Criminal anarchy defined.—Criminal anarchy is the doctrine that organized government should be overthrown by force or violence, or by assassination of the executive head or of any of the executive officials of government, or by any unlawful means. The advocacy of such doctrine either by word of mouth or writing is a felony.

"§ 161. Advocacy of criminal anarchy.—Any person who:

"1. By word of mouth or writing advocates, advises or teaches the duty, necessity or propriety of overthrowing or overturning organized government by force or violence, or by assassination of the executive head or of any of the executive officials of government, or by any unlawful means; or

"2. Prints, publishes, edits, issues or knowingly circulates, sells, distributes or publicly displays any book, paper, document, or written or printed matter in any form, containing or advocating, advising or teaching the doctrine that organized government should be overthrown by force, violence or any unlawful means, . . .

"Is guilty of a felony and punishable" by imprisonment or fine, or both.

The indictment was in two counts. The first charged that the defendants had advocated, advised, and taught the duty, necessity, and propriety of overthrowing and overturning organized government by force, violence, and unlawful means, by certain writings therin set forth, entitled, "The Left Wing Manifesto"; the second, that he had printed, published, and knowingly circulated and distributed a certain paper called "The Revolutionary Age," containing the writings set forth in the first count, advocating, advising, and teaching the doctrine that organized government should be overthrown by force, violence, and unlawful means.

. . . It was admitted that the defendant signed a card subscribing to the Manifesto and Program of the Left Wing, which all applicants were required to sign before being admitted to membership; that he went to different parts of the state to speak to branches of the Socialist party about the principles of the Left Wing, and advocated their adoption; and that he was responsible [as business manager] for the Manifesto as it appeared, that "he knew of the publication, in a general way, and he knew of its publication afterwards, and is responsible for its circulation."

There was no evidence of any effect resulting from the publication and circulation of the Manifesto.

No witnesses were offered in behalf of the defendant.

Extracts from the Manifesto are set forth in the margin. Coupled with a review of the rise of Socialism, it condemned the dominant "moderate Socialism" for its recognition of the necessity of the democratic parliamentary state; repudiated its policy of introducing Socialism by legislative measures; and advocated, in plain and unequivocal language, the necessity of accomplishing the "Communist Revolution" by a militant and "revolutionary Socialism," based on "the class struggle" and mobilizing the "power of the proletariat in action," through mass industrial revolts developing into mass political strikes and "revolutionary mass action" for the purpose of conquering and destroying the parliamentary state and establishing in its place, through a "revolutionary dictatorship of the proletariat," the system of Communist Socialism. The then recent strikes in Seattle and Winnipeg were cited as instances of a development already verging on revolutionary action and suggestive of proletarian dictatorship, in which the strike workers were "trying to usurp the functions of municipal government"; and Revolutionary Socialism, it was urged, must use these mass industrial revolts to broaden the strike, make it general and militant, and develop it into mass political strikes and revolutionary mass action for the annihilation of the parliamentary state.

. . . The sole contention here is, essentially, that, as there was no evidence of any concrete result flowing from the publication of the Manifesto, or of circumstances showing the likelihood of such result, the statute as construed and applied by the trial court penalizes the mere utterance, as such, of "doctrine" having no quality of incitement, without regard either to the circumstances of its utterance or to the likelihood of unlawful sequences; and that, as the exercise of the right of free expression with relation to government is only punishable "in circumstances involving likelihood of substantive evil," the statute contravenes the due process clause of the Forteenth Amendment. The argument in support of this contention rests primarily upon the following propositions: 1st, that the "liberty" protected by the 14th Amendment includes the liberty of speech and of the press; and 2d, that while liberty of expression "is not absolute," it may be restrained "only in circumstances where its exercise bears a causal relation with some substantive evil, consummated, attempted, or likely"; and as the statute "takes no account of circumstances," it unduly restrains this liberty, and is therefore unconstitutional.

The precise question presented, and the only question which we can consider under this writ of error, then, is whether the statute, as construed and applied in this case by the state courts, deprived the defendant of his liberty of expression, in violation of the due process clause of the 14th Amendment.

The statute does not penalize the utterance or publication of abstract "doctrine" or academic discussion having no quality of incitement to any concrete action. It is not aimed against mere historical or philosophical essays. It does not restrain the advocacy of changes in the form of government by constitutional and lawful means. What it prohibits is language advocating, advising, or teaching the overthrow of organized government by unlawful means. These words imply urging to action. Advocacy is defined in the Century Dictionary as: "1. The act of pleading for, supporting, or recommending; active espousal." It is not the abstract "doctrine" of overthrowing organized government by unlawful means which is denounced by the statute, but the advocacy of action for the accomplishment of that purpose. . . .

The Manifesto, plainly, is neither the statement of abstract doctrine nor, as suggested by counsel, mere prediction that industrial disturbances and revolutionary mass strikes will result spontaneously in an inevitable process of evolution in the economic system. It advocates and urges in fervent language mass action which shall progressively foment industrial disturbances, and through political mass strikes and revolutionary mass action, overthrow and destroy organized parliamentary government. It concludes with a call to action in these words: "The proletariat revolution and the Communist reconstruction of society—*the struggle for these*—is now indispensable. . . . The Communist International calls the proletariat of the world to the final struggle!" This is not the expression of philosophical abstraction, the mere prediction of future events: it is the language of direct incitement.

The means advocated for bringing about the destruction of organized parliamentary government, namely, mass industrial revolts usurping the functions of municipal government, political mass strikes directed against the parliamentary state, and revolutionary mass action for its final destruction, necessarily imply the use of force and violence, and in their essential nature are inherently unlawful in a constitutional government of law and order. That the jury were warranted in finding that the Manifesto advocated not merely the abstract doctrine of overwhelming organized government by force, violence, and unlawful means, but action to that end, is clear.

For present purposes we may and do assume that freedom of speech and of the press—which are protected by the 1st Amendment from abridgment by Congress—are among the fundamental personal rights and "liberties" protected by the due process clause of the 14th Amendment from impairment by the states. . . .

It is a fundamental principle, long established, that

freedom of speech and of the press which is secured by the Constitution does not confer an absolute right to speak or publish, without responsibility, whatever one may choose, or an unrestricted and unbridled license that gives immunity for every possible use of language, and prevents the punishment of those who abuse this freedom.

. . . Reasonably limited, it was said by Story in the passage cited, this freedom is an inestimable privilege in a free government; without such limitation, it might become the scourge of the Republic.

That a state, in the exercise of its police power, may punish those who abuse this freedom by utterances inimical to the public welfare, tending to corrupt public morals, incite to crime, or disturb the public peace, is not open to question. . . . Thus it was held by this court in the Fox Case . . . that a state may punish publications advocating and encouraging a breach of its criminal laws; and, in the Gilbert Case that a state may punish utterances teaching or advocating that its citizens should not assist the United States in prosecuting or carrying on war with its public enemies.

And, for yet more imperative reasons, a state may punish utterances endangering the foundations of organized government and threatening its overthrow by unlawful means. These imperil its own existence as a constitutional state. Freedom of speech and press, said Story (supra), does not protect disturbances of the public peace or the attempt to subvert the government. It does not protect publications or teachings which tend to subvert or imperil the government, or to impede or hinder it in the performance of its governmental duties. . . . It does not protect publications prompting the overthrow of government by force; the punishment of those who publish articles which tend to destroy organized society being essential to the security of freedom and the stability of the state. . . . And a state may penalize utterances which openly advocate the overthrow of the representative and constitutional form of government of the United States and the several states, by violence or other unlawful means. . . . In short, this freedom does not deprive a state of the primary and essential right of self-preservation, which, so long as human governments endure, they cannot be denied. . . . .

By enacting the present statute the state has determined, through its legislative body, that utterances advocating the overthrow of organized government by force, violence, and unlawful means, are so inimical to the general welfare, and involve such danger of substantive evil, that they may be penalized in the exercise of its police power. That determination must be given great weight. Every presumption is to be indulged in favor of the validity of the statute. . . . That utterances inciting to the overthrow of organized government by unlawful means present a sufficient danger of substantive evil to bring their punishment within the range of legislative discretion is clear. Such utterances, by their very nature, involve danger to the public peace and to the security of the state. They threaten breaches of the peace and ultimate revolution. And the immediate danger is none the less real and substantial because the effect of a given utterance cannot be accurately foreseen. The state cannot reasonably be required to measure the danger from every such utterance in the nice balance of a jeweler's scale. A single revolutionary spark may kindle a fire that, smoldering for a time, may burst into a sweeping and destructive conflagration. It cannot be said that the state is acting arbitrarily or unreasonably when, in the exercise of its judgment as to the measures necessary to protect the public peace and safety, it seeks to extinguish the spark without waiting until it has enkindled the flame or blazed into the conflagration. It cannot reasonably be required to defer the adopting of measures for its own peace and safety until the revolutionary utterances lead to actual disturbances of the public peace or imminent and immediate danger of its own destruction; but it may, in the exercise of its judgment, suppress the threatened danger in its incipiency. . . .

We cannot hold that the present statute is an arbitrary or unreasonable exercise of the police power of the state, unwarrantably infringing the freedom of speech or press; and we must and do sustain its constitutionality.

This being so it may be applied to every utterance—not too trivial to be beneath the notice of the law—which is of such a character and used with such intent and purpose as to bring it within the prohibition of the statute. . . . In other words, when the legislative body has determined generally, in the constitutional exercise of its discretion, that utterances of a certain kind involve such danger of substantive evil that they may be punished, the question whether any specific utterance coming within the prohibited class is likely, in and of itself, to bring about the substantive evil, is not open to consideration. It is sufficient that the statute itself be constitutional, and that the use of the language comes within its prohibition.

It is clear that the question in such cases is entirely different from that involved in those cases where the statute merely prohibits certain acts involving the danger of substantive evil, without any reference to language itself, and it is sought to apply its provisions to language used by the defendant for the purpose of bringing about prohibited results. There, if it be contended that the statute cannot be applied to the language used by the defendant because of its protection by the freedom of speech or press, it must necessarily be found, as an original question, without any previous determination by the legislative body, whether the specific language used involved such likelihood of bringing about the substantive evil as to deprive it of the constitutional protection. In such cases it has been held that the general provisions of the statute may be constitutionally applied to the specific utterance of the defendant if its natural tendency and probable effect were to bring about the substantive evil which the legislative body might prevent. Schenck v. United States [1919]; Debs v. United States [1919]. And the general statement in the Schenck Case that the "question in every case is whether the words are used in such circumstances and are of such a nature as to create a clear and present danger that they will bring about the substantive evils,"—upon which great reliance is placed in the defendant's argument,—was manifestly intended, as shown by the context, to apply only in cases of this class, and has no application to those like the present, where the legislative body itself has previously determined the danger of substantive evil arising from utterances of a specified character. . . .

And finding, for the reasons stated, that the statute is not in itself unconstitutional, and that it has not been applied in the present case in derogation of any constitutional right, the judgment of the Court of Appeals is affirmed.

Justice Holmes dissented:

Justice Brandeis and I are of the opinion that this judgment should be reversed. The general principle of free speech, it seems to me, must be taken to be included in the 14th Amendment, in view of the scope that has been given to the word "liberty" as there used, although perhaps it may be accepted with a somewhat larger latitude of interpretation than is allowed to Congress by the sweeping language that governs, or ought to govern, the laws of the United States. If I am right, then I think that the criterion sanctioned by the full court in Schenck v. United States, applies: "The question in every case is whether the words used are used in such circumstances and are of such a nature as to create a clear and present danger that they will bring about the substantive evils that [the state] has a right to prevent." It is true that in my opinion this criterion was departed from in Abrams v. United States . . . but the convictions that I expressed in that case are too deep for it to be possible for me as yet to believe that it and Schaefer v. United States . . . have settled the law. If what I think the correct test is applied, it is manifest that there was no present danger of an attempt to overthrow the government by force on the part of the admittedly small minority who shared the defendant's views. It is said that this Manifesto was more than a theory, that it was an incitement. Every idea is an incitement. It offers itself for belief, and, if believed, it is acted on unless some other belief outweighs it, or some failure of energy stifles the movement at its birth. The only difference between the expression of an opinion and an incitement in the narrower sense is the speaker's enthusiasm for the result. Eloquence may set fire to reason. But whatever may be thought of the redundant discourse before us, it had no chance of starting a present conflagration. If, in the long run, the beliefs expressed in proletarian dictatorship are destined to be accepted by the dominant forces of the community, the only meaning of free speech is that they should be given their chance and have their way.

If the publication of this document had been laid as an attempt to induce an uprising against government at once, and not at some indefinite time in the future, it would have presented a different question. The object would have been one with which the law might deal, subject to the doubt whether there was any danger that the publication could produce any result; or, in other words, whether it was not futile and too remote from possible consequences. But the indictment alleges the publication and nothing more.

Although the majority had rejected Gitlow's contentions, it is significant that they did accept the principle "that freedom of speech and of the press—which are protected by the First Amendment from abridgment by Congress—are among the fundamental personal rights and 'liberties' protected by the due process clause of the Fourteenth Amendment from impairment by the states." This doctrine ushered in an entirely novel approach to these issues and greatly increased the supervisory role of the Supreme Court over the states.

These decisions and others involving freedom of the press and the right to counsel were products of a Supreme Court still dominated by economic conservatives before the advent of the so-called New Deal Court. The principle of the incorporation of First Amendment freedoms as rights and liberties protected against state action by the due process clause of the Fourteenth Amendment was applied in *Near* v. *Minnesota*. The process of incorporation had been very gradual and not very clear. The statement of the principle in the Gitlow case did not make clear whether the incorporation was accepted in an unusual set of circumstances, or was intended to push positively for an enduring enunciation of the doctrine. In Near the majority quietly dropped the qualifier "for present purposes" that had left matters uncertain in Gitlow.

Chief Justice Hughes wrote the majority opinion in Near while Justice Pierce Butler, a Minnesotan, dissented strongly, supported by Justices Van Devanter, McReynolds, and Sutherland. The rejection of prior restraint, a doctrine central to Blackstone, the influential British law analyst, was adopted as a major doctrinal consideration in freedom of the press cases. Crucial to acceptance of the doctrine in the Near case was recognition that the practical effect of previous restraint of publications was often effective censorship. The facts of the case are summarized and discussed fully in the decision.

NEAR v. MINNESOTA
283 U. S. 697 (1931)

Chief Justice Hughes delivered the opinion of the Court:

Chapter 285 of the Session Laws of Minnesota for the year 1925 provides for the abatement, as a public nuisance, of a "malicious, scandalous and defamatory newspaper, magazine or other periodical." Section one of the Act is as follows:

"Section 1. Any person who, as an individual, or as a member or employee of a firm, or association or organization, or as an officer, director, member or employee of a corporation, shall be engaged in the business of regularly or customarily producing, publishing or circulating, having in possession, selling or giving away.

(a) an obscene, lewd and lascivious newspaper, magazine, or other periodical, or

(b) a malicious, scandalous and defamatory newspaper, magazine or other periodical, is guilty of a nuisance, and all persons guilty of such nuisance may be enjoined, as hereinafter provided.

"Participation in such business shall constitute a commission of such nuisance and render the participant liable and subject to the proceedings, orders and judgments provided for in this Act. Ownership, in whole or in part, directly or indirectly, of any such periodical, or of any stock or interest in any corporation or organization which owns the same in whole or in part, or which publishes the same, shall constitute such participation. . . ."

Section two provides that whenever any such nuisance is committed or exists, the County Attorney of any county where any such periodical is published or circulated, or, in case of his failure or refusal to proceed upon written request in good faith of a reputable citizen, the Attorney General, or upon like failure or refusal of the latter, any citizen of the county, may maintain an action in the district court of the county in the name of the State to enjoin perpetually the persons committing or maintaining any such nuisance from further committing or maintaining it. Upon such evidence as the court shall deem sufficient, a temporary injunction may be granted. The defendants have the right to plead by demurrer or answer, and the plaintiff may demur or reply as in other cases.

The action, by section three, is to be "governed by the practice and procedure applicable to civil actions for injunctions," and after trial the court may enter judgment permanently enjoining the defendants found

guilty of violating the Act from continuing the violation and, "in and by such judgment, such nuisance may be wholly abated." The court is empowered, as in other cases of contempt, to punish disobedience to a temporary or permanent injunction by fine of not more than $1,000 or by imprisonment in the county jail for not more than twelve months.

Under this statute, clause (b), the County Attorney of Hennepin County brought this action to enjoin the publication of what was described as a "malicious, scandalous and defamatory newspaper, magazine and periodical," known as "The Saturday Press," published by the defendants in the city of Minneapolis. . . .

Without attempting to summarize the contents of the voluminous exhibits attached to the complaint, we deem it sufficient to say that the articles charged in substance that a Jewish gangster was in control of gambling, bootlegging and racketeering in Minneapolis, and that law enforcing officers and agencies were not energetically performing their duties. Most of the charges were directed against the Chief of Police; he was charged with gross neglect of duty, illicit relations with gangsters, and with participation in graft. The County Attorney was charged with knowing the existing conditions and with failure to take adequate measures to remedy them. The Mayor was accused of inefficiency and dereliction. One member of the grand jury was stated to be in sympathy with the gangsters. A special grand jury and a special prosecutor were demanded to deal with the situation in general, and, in particular, to investigate an attempt to assassinate one Guilford, one of the original defendants, who, it appears from the articles, was shot by gangsters after the first issue of the periodical had been published. There is no question but that the articles made serious accusations against the public officers named and others in connection with the prevalence of crimes and the failure to expose and punish them. . . .

[The trial court issued an injunction, which was affirmed by the State Supreme Court.]

From the judgment as thus affirmed, the defendant Near appeals to this Court.

This statute, for the suppression as a public nuisance of a newspaper or periodical, is unusual, if not unique, and raises questions of grave importance transcending the local interest involved in the particular action. It is no longer open to doubt that the liberty of the press, and of speech, is within the liberty safeguarded by the due process clause of the Fourteenth Amendment from invasion by state action. . . . In maintaining this guaranty, the authority of the State to enact laws to promote the health, safety, morals and general welfare of its people is necessarily admitted. The limits of this sovereign power must always be determined with appropriate regard to the particular subject of its exercise. . . . Liberty of speech, and of the press, is also not an absolute right, and the State may punish its abuse. . . . Liberty, in each of its phases, has its history and connotation and, in the present instance, the inquiry is as to the historic conception of the liberty of the press and whether the statute under review violates the essential attributes of that liberty. . . .

With respect to these contentions it is enough to say that in passing upon constitutional questions the Court has regard to substance and not to mere matters of form, and that, in accordance with familiar principles, the statute must be tested by its operation and effect. . . . That operation and effect we think is clearly shown by the record in this case. We are not concerned with mere errors of the trial court, if there be such, in going beyond the direction of the statute as construed by the Supreme Court of the State. It is thus important to note precisely the purpose and effect of the statute as the state court has construed it.

First. The statute is not aimed at the redress of individual or private wrongs. Remedies for libel remain available and unaffected. The statute, said the state court, "is not directed at threatened libel but at an existing business which, generally speaking, involves more than libel." It is aimed at the distribution of scandalous matter as "detrimental to public morals and to the general welfare," tending "to disturb the peace of the community" and "to provoke assaults and the commission of crime." In order to obtain an injunction to suppress the future publication of the newspaper or periodical, it is not necessary to prove the falsity of the charges that have been made in the publication condemned. In the present action there was no allegation that the matter published was not true. It is alleged, and the statute requires the allegation, that the publication was "malicious." But, as in prosecutions for libel, there is no requirement of proof by the State of malice in fact as distinguished from malice inferred from the mere publication of the defamatory matter. The judgment in this case proceeded upon the mere proof of publication. The statute permits the defense, not of the truth alone, but only that the truth was published with good motives and for justifiable ends. It is apparent that under the statute the publication is to be regarded as defamatory if it injures reputation, and that it is scandalous if it circulates charges of reprehensible conduct, whether criminal or otherwise, and

the publication is thus deemed to invite public reprobation and to constitute a public scandal. The court sharply defined the purpose of the statute, bringing out the precise point, in these words: "There is no constitutional right to publish a fact merely because it is true. It is a matter of common knowledge that prosecutions under the criminal libel statutes do not result in efficient repression or suppression of the evils of scandal. Men who are the victims of such assaults seldom resort to the courts. This is especially true if their sins are exposed and the only question relates to whether it was done with good motives and for justifiable ends. This law is not for the protection of the person attacked nor to punish the wrongdoer. It is for the protection of the public welfare."

Second. The statute is directed not simply at the circulation of scandalous and defamatory statements with regard to private citizens, but at the continued publication by newspapers and periodicals of charges against public officers of corruption, malfeasance in office, or serious neglect of duty. Such charges by their very nature create a public scandal. They are scandalous and defamatory within the meaning of the statute, which has its normal operation in relation to publications dealing prominently and chiefly with the alleged derelictions of public officers.

Third. The object of the statute is not punishment, in the ordinary sense, but suppression of the offending newspaper or periodical. The reason for the enactment, as the state court has said, is that prosecutions to enforce penal statutes for libel do not result in "efficient repression or suppression of the evils of scandal." Describing the business of publication as a public nuisance, does not obscure the substance of the proceeding which the statute authorizes. It is the continued publication of scandalous and defamatory matter that constitutes the business and the declared nuisance. In the case of public officers, it is the reiteration of charges of official misconduct, and the fact that the newspaper or periodical is principally devoted to that purpose, that exposes it to suppression. In the present instance, the proof was that nine editions of the newspaper or periodical in question were published on successive dates, and that they were chiefly devoted to charges against public officers and in relation to the prevalence and protection of crime. In such a case, these officers are not left to their ordinary remedy in a suit for libel, or the authorities to a prosecution for criminal libel. Under this statute, a publisher of a newspaper or periodical, undertaking to conduct a campaign to expose and to censure official derelictions, and devoting his publication principally to that purpose, must face not simply the possibility of a verdict against him in a suit or prosecution for libel, but a determination that his newspaper or periodical is a public nuisance to be abated, and that this abatement and suppression will follow unless he is prepared with legal evidence to prove the truth of the charges and also to satisfy the court that, in addition to being true, the matter was published with good motives and for justifiable ends.

This suppression is accomplished by enjoining publication and that restraint is the object and effect of the statute.

Fourth. The statute not only operates to suppress the offending newspaper or periodical but to put the publisher under an effective censorship. When a newspaper or periodical is found to be "malicious, scandalous and defamatory," and is suppressed as such, resumption of publication is punishable as a contempt of court by fine or imprisonment. Thus, where a newspaper or periodical has been suppressed because of the circulation of charges against public officers of official misconduct, it would seem to be clear that the renewal of the publication of such charges would constitute a contempt and that the judgment would lay a permanent restraint upon the publisher, to escape which he must satisfy the court as to the character of a new publication. Whether he would be permitted again to publish matter deemed to be derogatory to the same or other public officers would depend upon the court's ruling. In the present instance the judgment restrained the defendants from "publishing, circulating, having in their possession, selling or giving away any publication whatsoever which is a malicious, scandalous or defamatory newspaper, as defined by law." The law gives no definition except that covered by the words "scandalous and defamatory," and publications charging official misconduct are of that class. While the court, answering the objection that the judgment was too broad, saw no reason for construing it as restraining the defendants "from operating a newspaper in harmony with the public welfare to which all must yield," and said that the defendants had not indicated "any desire to conduct their business in the usual and legitimate manner," the manifest inference is that, at least with respect to a new publication directed against official misconduct, the defendant would be held, under penalty of punishment for contempt as provided in the statute, to a manner of publication which the court considered to be "usual and legitimate" and consistent with the public welfare.

If we cut through mere details of procedure, the operation and effect of the statute in substance is that public authorities may bring the owner or publisher of a newspaper or periodical before a judge upon a charge of conducting a business of publishing scandalous and defamatory matter—in particular that the matter consists of charges against public officers of official dereliction—and unless the owner or publisher is able and disposed to bring competent evidence to satisfy the judge that the charges are true and are published with good motives and for justifiable ends, his newspaper or periodical is suppressed and further publication is made punishable as a contempt. This is of the essence of censorship.

The question is whether a statute authorizing such proceedings in restraint of publication is consistent with the conception of the liberty of the press as historically conceived and guaranteed. In determining the extent of the constitutional protection, it has been generally, if not universally, considered that it is the chief purpose of the guaranty to prevent previous restraints upon publication. The struggle in England, directed against the legislative power of the licenser, resulted in renunciation of the censorship of the press. The liberty deemed to be established was thus described by Blackstone: "The liberty of the press is indeed essential to the nature of a free state; but this consists in laying no *previous* restraints upon publications, and not in freedom from censure for criminal matter when published. Every freeman has an undoubted right to lay what sentiments he pleases before the public; to forbid this, is to destroy the freedom of the press; but if he publishes what is improper, mischievous or illegal, he must take the consequence of his own temerity." . . .

The criticism upon Blackstone's statement has not been because immunity from previous restraint upon publication has not been regarded as deserving of special emphasis, but chiefly because that immunity cannot be deemed to exhaust the conception of the liberty guaranteed by state and federal constitutions. The point of criticism has been "that the mere exemption from previous restraints cannot be all that is secured by the constitutional provisions"; and that "the liberty of the press might be rendered a mockery and a delusion, and the phrase itself a byword, if, while every man was at liberty to publish what he pleased, the public authorities might nevertheless punish him for harmless publications." . . . But it is recognized that punishment for the abuse of the liberty accorded to the press is essential to the protection of the public, and that the common law rules that subject the libeler to responsibility for the public offense, as well as for the private injury, are not abolished by the protection extended in our constitutions. . . . In the present case, we have no occasion to inquire as to the permissible scope of subsequent punishment. For whatever wrong the appellant has committed or may commit, by his publications, the State appropriately affords both public and private redress by its libel laws. As has been noted, the statute in question does not deal with punishments; it provides for no punishment, except in case of contempt for violation of the court's order, but for suppression and injunction, that is, for restraint upon publication.

The objection has also been made that the principle as to immunity from previous restraint is stated too broadly, if every such restraint is deemed to be prohibited. That is undoubtedly true; the protection even as to previous restraint is not absolutely unlimited. But the limitation has been recognized only in exceptional cases: "When a nation is at war many things that might be said in time of peace are such a hindrance to its effort that their utterance will not be endured so long as men fight and that no Court could regard them as protected by any constitutional right." *Schenck* v. *United States* [1919]. . . . No one would question but that a government might prevent actual obstruction to its recruiting service or the publication of the sailing dates of transports or the number and location of troops. On similar grounds, the primary requirements of decency may be enforced against obscene publications. The security of the community life may be protected against incitements to acts of violence and the overthrow by force of orderly government. The constitutional guaranty of free speech does not "protect a man from an injunction against uttering words that may have all the effect of force." . . .

The exceptional nature of its limitations places in a strong light the general conception that liberty of the press, historically considered and taken up by the Federal Constitution, has meant, principally although not exclusively, immunity from previous restraints or censorship. The conception of the liberty of the press in this country had broadened with the exigencies of the colonial period and with the efforts to secure freedom from oppressive administration. That liberty was especially cherished for the immunity it afforded from previous restraint of the publication of censure of public officers and charges of official misconduct. . . .

The importance of this immunity has not lessened. While reckless assaults upon public men, and efforts to bring obloquy upon those who are endeavoring faithfully to discharge official duties, exert a baleful influence and deserve the severest condemnation in public opinion, it cannot be said that this abuse is greater, and

it is believed to be less, than that which characterized the period in which our institutions took shape. Meanwhile, the administration of government has become more complex, the opportunities for malfeasance and corruption have multiplied, crime has grown to most serious proportions, and the danger of its protection by unfaithful officials and of the impairment of the fundamental security of life and property by criminal alliances and official neglect, emphasizes the primary need of a vigilant and courageous press, especially in great cities. The fact that the liberty of the press may be abused by miscreant purveyors of scandal does not make any the less necessary the immunity of the press from previous restraint in dealing with official misconduct. Subsequent punishment for such abuses as may exist is the appropriate remedy, consistent with constitutional privilege. . . .

The statute in question cannot be justified by reason of the fact that the publisher is permitted to show, before injunction issues, that the matter published is true and is published with good motives and for justifiable ends. If such a statute, authorizing suppression and injunction on such a basis, is constitutionally valid, it would be equally permissible for the legislature to provide that at any time the publisher of any newspaper could be brought before a court, or even an administrative officer (as the constitutional protection may not be regarded as resting on mere procedural details) and required to produce proof of the truth of his publication, or of what he intended to publish, and of his motives, or stand enjoined. If this can be done, the legislature may provide machinery for determining in the complete exercise of its discretion what are justifiable ends and restrain publication accordingly. And it would be but a step to a complete system of censorship. The recognition of authority to impose previous restraint upon publication in order to protect the community against the circulation of charges of misconduct, and especially of official misconduct, necessarily would carry with it the admission of the authority of the censor against which the constitutional barrier was erected. The preliminary freedom, by virtue of the very reason for its existence, does not depend, as this Court has said, on proof of truth. . . .

Equally unavailing is the insistence that the statute is designed to prevent the circulation of scandal which tends to disturb the public peace and to provoke assaults and the commission of crime. Charges of reprehensible conduct, and in particular of official malfeasance, unquestionably create a public scandal, but the theory of the constitutional guaranty is that even a more serious public evil would be caused by authority to prevent publication. . . . There is nothing new in the fact that charges of reprehensible conduct may create resentment and the disposition to resort to violent means of redress, but this well-understood tendency did not alter the determination to protect the press against censorship and restraint upon publication. . . . The danger of violent reactions becomes greater with effective organization of defiant groups resenting exposure, and if this consideration warranted legislative interference with the initial freedom of publication, the constitutional protection would be reduced to a mere form of words.

For these reasons we hold the statute, so far as it authorized the proceedings in this action under clause (b) of section one, to be an infringement of the liberty of the press guaranteed by the Fourteenth Amendment. We should add that this decision rests upon the operation and effect of the statute, without regard to the question of the truth of the charges contained in the particular periodical. The fact that the public officers named in this case, and those associated with the charges of official dereliction, may be deemed to be impeccable, cannot affect the conclusion that the statute imposes an unconstitutional restraint upon publication.

Judgment reversed.

Justice Butler dissented:

. . . The Minnesota statute does not operate as a *previous* restraint on publication within the proper meaning of that phrase. It does not authorize administrative control in advance such as was formerly exercised by the licensers and censors but prescribes a remedy to be enforced by a suit in equity. In this case there was previous publication made in the course of the business of regularly producing malicious, scandalous and defamatory periodicals. The business and publications unquestionably constitute an abuse of the right of free press. The statute denounces the things done as a nuisance on the ground, as stated by the state supreme court, that they threaten morals, peace and good order. There is no question of the power of the State to denounce such transgressions. The restraint authorized is only in respect of continuing to do what has been duly adjudged to constitute a nuisance. . . .

It is well known, as found by the state supreme court, that existing libel laws are inadequate effectively to suppress evils resulting from the kind of business and publications that are shown in this case. The doctrine that measures such as the one before us are invalid because they operate as previous restraints to infringe freedom of press exposes the peace and good order of every community and the business and private affairs of every individual to the constant and protracted false and malicious assaults of any insolvent publisher who may have purpose and sufficient capacity to contrive and put into effect a scheme or program for oppression, blackmail or extortion.

The judgment should be affirmed.

Justice Van Devanter, Justice McReynolds, and Justice Sutherland concur in this opinion.

Right to counsel and the Powell case

The fundamental problem that members of an unpopular, and often unprotected, minority under certain circumstances would be denied fair treatment in some local or state criminal justice systems had troubled the Supreme Court of the United States in the 19th as well as 20th century. But the Court's responses were not always consistent. By the early 1930s, the Court began to lay down more comprehensive guidelines. One such approach, in *Powell* v. *Alabama*, concerned important right to counsel issues arising out of the action of an Alabama court that sentenced several illiterate young black men to death for the alleged rape of two white women while all were riding in a railroad flatcar. The trial within the Alabama judicial system had attracted nationwide attention, combining the elements of racial bias in Alabama justice with a significant issue involving the right to counsel. Justice Sutherland wrote a strong majority opinion.

POWELL v. ALABAMA
287 U. S. 45 (1932)

The petitioners, hereinafter referred to as defendants, are negroes charged with the crime of rape, committed upon the persons of two white girls. The crime is said to have been committed on March 25, 1931. The indictment was returned in a state court of first instance on March 31, and the record recites that on the same day the defendants were arraigned and entered pleas of not guilty. There is a further recital to the effect that upon the arraignment they were represented by counsel. But no counsel had been employed, and aside from a statement made by the trial judge several days later during a colloquy immediately preceding the trial, the record does not disclose when, or under what circumstances, an appointment of counsel was made, or who was appointed. During the colloquy referred to, the trial judge, in response to a question, said that he had appointed all the members of the bar for the purpose of arraigning the defendants and then of course anticipated that the members of the bar would continue to help the defendants if no counsel appeared. Upon the argument here both sides accepted that as a correct statement of the facts concerning the matter.

There was a severance upon the request of the state, and the defendants were tried in three separate groups, as indicated above. As each of the three cases was called for trial, each defendant was arraigned, and, having the indictment read to him, entered a plea of not guilty. Whether the original arraignment and pleas were regarded as ineffective is not shown. Each of the three trials was completed within a single day. Under the Alabama statute the punishment for rape is to be fixed by the jury, and in its discretion may be from ten years imprisonment to death. The juries found defendants guilty and imposed the death penalty upon all. The trial court overruled motions for new trials and sentenced the defendants in accordance with the verdicts. The judgments were affirmed by the state supreme court. Chief Justice Anderson thought the defendants had not been accorded a fair trial and strongly dissented. . . .

In this Court the judgments are assailed upon the grounds that the defendants, and each of them, were denied due process of law and the equal protection of the laws, in contravention of the Fourteenth Amendment, specifically as follows: (1) they were not given a fair, impartial and deliberate trial; (2) they were denied the right of counsel, with the accustomed incidents of consultation and opportunity of preparation for trial; and (3) they were tried before juries from which qualified members of their own race were systematically excluded. These questions were properly raised and saved in the courts below.

The only one of the assignments which we shall consider is the second, in respect of the denial of counsel; and it becomes unnecessary to discuss the facts of the case or the circumstances surrounding the prosecution except in so far as they reflect light upon that question.

The record shows that on the day when the offense is said to have been committed, these defendants, together with a number of other negroes, were upon a freight train on its way through Alabama. On the same train were seven white boys and the two white girls. A fight took place between the negroes and the white boys, in the course of which the white boys, with the exception of one named Gilley, were thrown off the train. A message was sent ahead, reporting the fight and asking that every negro be gotten off the train. The participants in the fight, and the two girls, were in an open gondola car. The two girls testified that each of them was assaulted by six different negroes in turn, and they identified the seven defendants as having been among the number. None of the white boys was called to testify, with the exception of Gilley, who was called in rebuttal.

Before the train reached Scottsboro, Alabama, a sheriff's posse seized the defendants and two other negroes. Both girls and the negroes then were taken to Scottsboro, the county seat. Word of their coming and of the alleged assault had preceded them, and they were met at Scottsboro by a large crowd. It does not sufficiently appear that the defendants were seriously threatened with, or that they were actually in danger of, mob violence; but it does appear that the attitude of the community was one of great hostility. The sheriff thought it necessary to call for the militia to assist in safeguarding the prisoners. Chief Justice Anderson pointed out in his opinion that every step taken from the arrest and arraignment to the sentence was accompanied by the military. Soldiers took the defendants to Gadsden for safekeeping, brought them back to Scottsboro for arraignment, returned them to Gadsden for safekeeping while awaiting trial, escorted them to Scottsboro for trial a few days later, and guarded the court house and grounds at every stage of the proceedings. It is perfectly apparent that the proceedings, from beginning to end, took place in an atmosphere of tense, hostile and excited public sentiment.

During the entire time, the defendants were closely confined or were under military guard. The record does not disclose their ages, except that one of them was nineteen; but the record clearly indicates that most, if not all, of them were youthful, and they are constantly referred to as "the boys." They were ignorant and illiterate. All of them were residents of other states, where alone members of their families or friends resided.

However guilty defendants, upon due inquiry, might prove to have been, they were, until convicted, presumed to be innocent. It was the duty of the court having their cases in charge to see that they were denied no necessary incident of a fair trial. With any error of the state court involving alleged contravention of the state statutes or constitution we, of course, have nothing to do. The sole inquiry which we are permitted to make is whether the federal Constitution was contravened . . .; and as to that, we confine ourselves, as already suggested, to the inquiry whether the defendants were in substance denied the right of counsel, and if so, whether such denial infringes the due process clause of the Fourteenth Amendment.

First. The record shows that immediately upon the return of the indictment defendants were arraigned and pleaded not guilty. Apparently they were not asked whether they had, or were able to employ, counsel, or wished to have counsel appointed; or whether they had friends or relatives who might assist in that regard if communicated with. That it would not have been an idle ceremony to have given the defendants reasonable opportunity to communicate with their families and endeavor to obtain counsel is demonstrated by the fact that, very soon after conviction, able counsel appeared in their behalf. This was pointed out by Chief Justice Anderson in the course of his dissenting opinion. "They were nonresidents," he said, "and had little time or opportunity to get in touch with their families and friends who were scattered throughout two other states, and time has demonstrated that they could or would have been represented by able counsel had a better opportunity been given by a reasonable delay in the trial of the cases, judging from the number and activity of counsel that appeared immediately or shortly after their conviction." . . .

It is hardly necessary to say that, the right to counsel being conceded, a defendant should be afforded a fair opportunity to secure counsel of his own choice. Not only was that not done here, but such designation of counsel as was attempted was either so indefinite or so close upon the trial as to amount to a denial of effective and substantial aid in that regard. This will be amply demonstrated by a brief review of the record.

April 6, six days after indictment, the trials began. When the first case was called, the court inquired whether the parties were ready for trial. The state's attorney replied that he was ready to proceed. No one answered for the defendants or appeared to represent or defend them. Mr. Roddy, a Tennessee lawyer not a member of the local bar, addressed the court, saying that he had not been employed, but that people who were interested had spoken to him about the case. He was asked by the court whether he intended to appear for the defendants, and answered that he would like to appear along with counsel that the court might appoint. The record then proceeds:

"The Court: If you appear for these defendants, then I will not appoint counsel; if local counsel are willing to appear and assist you under the circumstances all right, but I will not appoint them.

"Mr. Roddy: Your Honor has appointed counsel, is that correct?

"The Court: I appointed all the members of the bar for the purpose of arraigning the defendants and then of course I anticipated them to continue to help them if no counsel appears.

"Mr. Moody: I am willing to go ahead and help Mr. Roddy in anything I can do about it, under the circumstances.

"The Court: All right, all the lawyers that will; of course I would not require a lawyer to appear if—

"Mr. Moody: I am willing to do that for him as a member of the bar; I will go ahead and help do anything I can do.

"The Court: All right."

And in this casual fashion the matter of counsel in a capital case was disposed of.

It thus will be seen that until the very morning of the trial no lawyer had been named or definitely designated to represent the defendants. Prior to that time, the trial judge had "appointed all the members of the bar" for the limited "purpose of arraigning the defendants." Whether they would represent the defendants thereafter if no counsel appeared in their behalf, was a matter of speculation only, or, as the judge indicated, of mere anticipation on the part of the court. Such a designation, even if made for all purposes, would, in our opinion, have fallen far short of meeting, in any proper sense, a requirement for the appointment of counsel. How many lawyers were members of the bar does not appear; but, in the very nature of things, whether many or few, they would not, thus collectively named, have been given that clear appreciation of responsibility or impressed with that individual sense of duty which should and naturally would accompany the appointment of a selected member of the bar, specifically named and assigned. . . .

. . . In any event, the circumstance lends emphasis to the conclusion that during perhaps the most critical period of the proceedings against these defendants, that is to say, from the time of their arraignment until the beginning of their trial, when consultation, thoroughgoing investigation and preparation were vitally important, the defendants did not have the aid of counsel in any real sense, although they were as much entitled to such aid during that period as at the trial itself. . . .

In the light of the facts outlined in the forepart of this opinion—the ignorance and illiteracy of the defendants, their youth, the circumstances of public hostility, the imprisonment and the close surveillance of the defendants by the military forces, the fact that their friends and families were all in other states and communication with them necessarily difficult, and above all that they stood in deadly peril of their lives—we think the failure of the trial court to give them reasonable time and opportunity to secure counsel was a clear denial of due process.

But passing that, and assuming their inability, even if opportunity had been given, to employ counsel, as the trial court evidently did assume, we are of opinion that, under the circumstances just stated, the necessity of counsel was so vital and imperative that the failure of the trial court to make an effective appointment of counsel was likewise a denial of due process within the meaning of the Fourteenth Amendment. Whether this would be so in other criminal prosecutions, or under other circumstances, we need not determine. All that it is necessary now to decide, as we do decide, is that in

a capital case, where the defendant is unable to employ counsel, and is incapable adequately of making his own defense because of ignorance, feeble mindedness, illiteracy, or the like, it is the duty of the court, whether requested or not, to assign counsel for him as a necessary requisite of due process of law; and that duty is not discharged by an assignment at such a time or under such circumstances as to preclude the giving of effective aid in the preparation and trial of the case. To hold otherwise would be to ignore the fundamental postulate, already adverted to, "that there are certain immutable principles of justice which inhere in the very idea of free government which no member of the Union may disregard." . . . In a case such as this, whatever may be the rule in other cases, the right to have counsel appointed, when necessary, is a logical corollary from the constitutional right to be heard by counsel. . . .

The United States by statute and every state in the Union by express provision of law, or by the determination of its courts, make it the duty of the trial judge, where the accused is unable to employ counsel, to appoint counsel for him. In most states the rule applies broadly to all criminal prosecutions, in others it is limited to the more serious crimes, and in a very limited number, to capital cases. A rule adopted with such unanimous accord reflects, if it does not establish, the inherent right to have counsel appointed, at least in cases like the present, and lends convincing support to the conclusion we have reached as to the fundamental nature of that right.

The judgments must be reversed and the causes remanded for further proceedings not inconsistent with this opinion.

Judgments reversed.

Justice Butler wrote a dissenting opinion in which Justice McReynolds concurred.

The Powell decision not only broke new ground doctrinally, it asserted a procedural safeguard for young men who ordinarily would have been dealt with summarily and unequally by the usual standards of regional justice. For its time, the Powell decision thus broke new ground symbolically as well.

Economic conservatism remains the hallmark

The contributions to civil liberties and rights of the conservative-dominated Supreme Court in the last two decades before the critical election of 1932 were significant enough to set the pattern for subsequent development. But the main thrust of the era following the conservative Republican victory in the critical election of 1896 was the protection of corporate business from state or federal regulation and from the claims of organized labor. Doctrines that weakened the position of labor were the hallmark of the Court as the long period begun in 1896 was coming to an end. Three decisions handed down in the early 1920s exemplified these tendencies—*Truax* v. *Corrigan*, *Adkin's* v. *Children's Hospital*, and *Wolff Packing Company* v. *Court of Industrial Relations*. The first of these decisions, *Truax* v. *Corrigan*, struck down an Arizona statute that authorized secondary boycotts on the ground that it deprived business owners of their property without due process under the Fourteenth Amendment. Chief Justice Taft wrote the majority opinion while Holmes dissented.

TRUAX v. CORRIGAN
257 U. S. 312 (1921)

Chief Justice Taft delivered the opinion of the Court:

Plaintiffs' business is a property right . . . and free access for employees, owner and customers to his place of business is incident to such right. Intentional injury caused to either right or both by a conspiracy is a tort. Concert of action is a conspiracy if its object is unlawful or if the means used are unlawful. . . . Intention to inflict the loss and the actual loss caused are clear. The real question here is, were the means used illegal? The . . . recital of what the defendants did, can leave no doubt of that. The libelous attacks upon the plaintiffs, their business, their employees, and their customers, and the abusive epithets applied to them were palpable wrongs. They were uttered in aid of the plan to induce plaintiffs' customers and would-be customers to refrain from patronizing the plaintiffs. The patrolling of defendants immediately in front of the restaurant on the main street and within five feet of plaintiffs' premises continuously during business hours, with the banners announcing plaintiffs' unfairness; the attendance by the picketers at the entrance to the restaurant and their insistent and loud appeals all day long, the constant circulation by them of the libels and epithets applied to employees, plaintiffs and customers, and the threats of injurious consequences to future customers, all linked together in a campaign, were an unlawful annoyance and a hurtful nuisance in respect of the free access to the plaintiffs' place of business. It was not lawful persuasion or inducing. It was not a mere appeal to the sympathetic aid of would-be customers by a simple statement of the fact of the strike and a request to withhold patronage. It was compelling every customer or would-be customer to run the gauntlet of most uncomfortable publicity, aggressive and annoying importunity, libelous attacks and fear of injurious consequences, ille-

gally inflicted, to his reputation and standing in the community. No wonder that a business of $50,000 was reduced to only one-fourth of its former extent. Violence could not have been more effective. It was moral coercion by illegal annoyance and obstruction and it thus was plainly a conspiracy. . . .

A law which operates to make lawful such a wrong as is described in plaintiffs' complaint deprives the owner of the business and the premises of his property without due process, and can not be held valid under the Fourteenth Amendment. . . .

It is to be observed that this is not the mere case of a peaceful secondary boycott as to the illegality of which courts have differed and States have adopted different statutory provisions. A secondary boycott of this kind is where many combine to injure one in his business by coercing third persons against their will to cease patronizing him by threats of similar injury. In such a case the many have a legal right to withdraw their trade from the one, they have the legal right to withdraw their trade from third persons, and they have the right to advise third persons of their intention to do so when each act is considered singly. The question in such cases is whether the moral coercion exercised over a stranger to the original controversy by steps in themselves legal becomes a legal wrong. But here the illegality of the means used is without doubt and fundamental. The means used are the libelous and abusive attacks on the plaintiffs' reputation, like attacks on their employees and customers, threats of such attacks on would-be customers, picketing and patrolling of the entrance to their place of business, and the consequent obstruction of free access thereto—all with the purpose of depriving the plaintiffs of their business. To give operation to a statute whereby serious losses inflicted by such unlawful means are in effect made remediless, is, we think, to disregard fundamental rights of liberty and property and to deprive the person suffering the loss of due process of law. . . .

This brings us to consider the effect in this case of

that provision of the Fourteenth Amendment which forbids any State to deny to any person the equal protection of the laws. The clause is associated in the Amendment with the due process clause and it is customary to consider them together. It may be that they overlap, that a violation of one may involve at times the violation of the other, but the spheres of the protection they offer are not coterminous. The due process clause, brought down from Magna Carta, was found in the early state constitutions, and later in the Fifth Amendment to the Federal Constitution as a limitation upon the executive, legislative and judicial powers of the Federal Government, while the equality clause does not appear in the Fifth Amendment and so does not apply to congressional legislation. The due process clause requires that every man shall have the protection of his day in court, and the benefit of the general law, a law which hears before it condemns, which proceeds not arbitrarily or capriciously but upon inquiry, and renders judgment only after trial, so that every citizen shall hold his life, liberty, property and immunities under the protection of the general rules which govern society. . . .

It, of course, tends to secure equality of law in the sense that it makes a required minimum of protection for every one's right of life, liberty and property, which the Congress or the legislature may not withhold. Our whole system of law is predicated on the general, fundamental principle of equality of application of the law. "All men are equal before the law," "This is a government of laws and not of men," "No man is above the law," are all maxims showing the spirit in which legislatures, executives and courts are expected to make, execute and apply laws. But the framers and adopters of this Amendment were not content to depend on a mere minimum secured by the due process clause, or upon the spirit of equality which might not be insisted on by local public opinion. They therefore embodied that spirit in a specific guaranty.

The guaranty was aimed at undue favor and individual or class privilege, on the one hand, and at hostile discrimination or the oppression of inequality, on the other. It sought an equality of treatment of all persons, even though all enjoyed the protection of due process. . . . Thus the guaranty was intended to secure equality of protection not only for all but against all similarly situated. Indeed, protection is not protection unless it does so. Immunity granted to a class, however limited, having the effect to deprive another class, however limited, of a personal or property right, is just as clearly a denial of equal protection of the laws to the latter class as if the immunity were in favor of, or the deprivation of right permitted worked against, a larger class. . . .

With these views of the meaning of the equality clause, it does not seem possible to escape the conclusion that by the clauses of Paragraph 1464 of the Revised Statutes of Arizona, here relied on by the defendants, as construed by its Supreme Court, the plaintiffs have been deprived of the equal protection of the law. . . .

Justice Holmes dissented
and was joined by Justices Brandeis and Clarke.

The strongest and most discouraging setback for organized labor and Progressive leaders was the rather unexpected reassertion of the Lochner doctrine to strike down a congressional minimum wage law for women in the District of Columbia. Justice Sutherland's majority opinion in *Adkins* v. *Children's Hospital* provoked strong dissents from Justice Holmes and from Chief Justice Taft. The latter, especially, invoked the Mueller doctrine in his criticism of the majority.

ADKINS v. CHILDREN'S HOSPITAL
261 U. S. 525 (1923)

Justice Sutherland delivered the opinion of the Court:

The statute now under consideration is attacked upon the ground that it authorizes an unconstitutional interference with the freedom of contract included within the guaranties of the due process clause of the Fifth Amendment. That the right to contract about one's affairs is a part of the liberty of the individual protected by this clause, is settled by the decisions of this Court and is no longer open to question. . . .

Within this liberty are contracts of employment of labor. In making such contracts, generally speaking, the parties have an equal right to obtain from each other the best terms they can as the result of private bargaining. . . .

There is, of course, no such thing as absolute freedom of contract. It is subject to a great variety of restraints. But freedom of contract is, nevertheless, the general rule and restraint the exception; and the exercise of legislative authority to abridge it can be justified only by the existence of exceptional circumstances. Whether these circumstances exist in the present case constitutes the question to be answered. It will be helpful to this end to review some of the decisions where the interference has been upheld and consider the grounds upon which they rest.

(1) *Those dealing with statutes fixing rates and charges to be exacted by businesses impressed with a public interest.* There are many cases, but it is sufficient to cite *Munn* v. *Illinois*, . . . The power here rests upon the ground that where property is devoted to a public use the owner thereby, in effect, grants to the public an interest in the use which may be controlled by the public for the common good to the extent of the interest thus created. It is upon this theory that these statutes have been upheld and, it may be noted in passing, so upheld even in respect of their incidental and injurious or destructive effect upon preëxisting contracts. . . . In the case at bar the statute does not depend upon the existence of a public interest in any business to be affected, and this class of cases may be laid aside as inapplicable.

(2) *Statutes relating to contracts for the performance of public work. Atkin* v. *Kansas*, . . . *Heim* v. *McCall*, . . . *Ellis* v. *United States*, . . . These cases sustain such statutes as depending, not upon the right to condition private contracts, but upon the right of the government to prescribe the conditions upon which it will permit work of a public character to be done for it, or, in the case of a State, for its municipalities. We may, therefore, in like manner, dismiss these decisions from consideration as inapplicable.

(3) *Statutes prescribing the character, methods and time for payment of wages.* Under this head may be included *McLean* v. *Arkansas*, . . . sustaining a state statute requiring coal to be measured for payment of miners' wages before screening; *Knoxville Iron Co.* v. *Harbison*, . . . sustaining a Tennessee statute requiring the redemption in cash of store orders issued in payment of wages; *Erie R. R. Co.* v. *Williams*, . . . upholding a statute regulating the time within which wages shall be paid to employees in certain specified industries; and other cases sustaining statutes of like import and effect. In none of the statutes thus sustained, was the liberty of employer or employee to fix the amount of wages the one was willing to pay and the other willing to receive interfered with. Their tendency and purpose was to prevent unfair and perhaps fraudulent methods in the payment of wages and in no sense can they be said to be, or to furnish a precedent for, wage-fixing statutes.

(4) *Statutes fixing hours of labor.* It is upon this class that the greatest emphasis is laid in argument and therefore, and because such cases approach most nearly the line of principle applicable to the statute here involved, we shall consider them more at length. In some instances the statute limited the hours of labor for men in certain occupations and in others it was confined in its application to women. No statute has thus far been brought to the attention of this Court which by its terms, applied to all occupations. In *Holden* v. *Hardy*, 169 U. S. 366, the Court considered an act of the Utah legislature, restricting the hours of labor in mines and smelters. This statute was sustained as a legitimate exercise of the police power, on the ground that the legislature had determined that these particular employments, when too long pursued, were injurious to the health of the employees, and that, as there were reasonable grounds for supporting this determination on the part of the legislature, its decision in that respect was beyond the reviewing power of the federal courts.

That this constituted the basis of the decision is emphasized by the subsequent decision in *Lochner* v. *New York*, 198 U. S. 45, reviewing a state statute which restricted the employment of all persons in bakeries to ten hours in any one day. The Court referred to *Holden* v. *Hardy*, *supra*, and, declaring it to be inapplicable, held the statute unconstitutional as an unreasonable, unnecessary and arbitrary interference with the liberty of contract and therefore void under the Constitution. . . .

Subsequent cases in this Court have been distinguished from that decision [*Lochner*], but the principles therein stated have never been disapproved. . . .

The essential characteristics of the statute now under consideration, which differentiate it from the laws fixing hours of labor, will be made to appear as we proceed. It is sufficient now to point out that the latter as well as the statutes mentioned under paragraph (3), deal with incidents of the employment having no necessary effect upon the heart of the contract, that is, the amount of wages to be paid and received. A law forbidding work to continue beyond a given number of hours leaves the parties free to contract about wages and thereby equalize whatever additional burdens may be imposed upon the employer as a result of the restrictions as to hours, by an adjustment in respect of the amount of wages. Enough has been said to show that the authority to fix hours of labor cannot be exercised except in respect of those occupations where work of long continued duration is detrimental to health. This Court has been careful in every case where the question has been raised, to place its decision upon this limited authority of the legislature to regulate hours of labor and to disclaim any purpose to uphold the legislation as fixing wages, thus recognizing an essential difference between the two. It seems plain that these decisions afford no real support for any form of law establishing minimum wages.

If now, in the light furnished by the foregoing exceptions to the general rule forbidding legislative interference with freedom of contract, we examine and analyze the statute in question, we shall see that it differs from them in every material respect. It is not a law dealing with any business charged with a public interest or with public work, or to meet and tide over a temporary emergency. It has nothing to do with the character, methods or periods of wage payments. It does not prescribe hours of labor or conditions under which labor is to be done. It is not for the protection of persons under legal disability or for the prevention of fraud. It is simply and exclusively a price-fixing law, confined to adult women (for we are not now considering the provisions relating to minors), who are legally as capable of contracting for themselves as men. It forbids two parties having lawful capacity—under penalties as to the employer—to freely contract with one another in respect of the price for which one shall render service to the other in a purely private employment where both are willing, perhaps anxious, to agree, even though the consequence may be to oblige one to surrender a desirable engagement and the other to dispense with the services of a desirable employee. The price fixed by the board need have no relation to the capacity or earning power of the employee, the number of hours which may happen to constitute the day's work, the character of the place where the work is to be done, or the circumstances or surroundings of the employment; and, while it has no other basis to support its validity than the assumed necessities of the employee, it takes no account of any independent resources she may have. It is based wholly on the opinions of the members of the board and their advisers—perhaps an average of their opinions, if they do not precisely agree—as to what will be necessary to provide a living for a woman, keep her in health and preserve her morals. It applies to any and every occupation in the District, without regard to its nature or the character of the work. . . .

The feature of this statute which, perhaps more than any other, puts upon it the stamp of invalidity is that it exacts from the employer an arbitrary payment for a purpose and upon a basis having no causal connection with his business, or the contract or the work the employee engages to do. The declared basis, as already pointed out, is not the value of the service rendered, but the extraneous circumstance that the employee needs to get a prescribed sum of money to insure her subsistence, health and morals. The ethical right of every worker, man or woman, to a living wage may be conceded. One of the declared and important purposes of trade organizations is to secure it. And with that principle and with every legitimate effort to realize it in fact, no one can quarrel; but the fallacy of the proposed method of attaining it is that it assumes that every employer is bound at all events to furnish it. The moral requirement implicit in every contract of employment, viz., that the amount to be paid and the service to be rendered shall bear to each other some relation of just equivalence, is completely ignored. The necessities of the employee are alone considered and these arise outside of the employment, and the same when there is no employment, and as great in one occupation as in another. Certainly the employer by paying a fair equivalent for the service rendered, though not sufficient to support the employee, has neither caused nor contributed to her poverty. On the contrary, to the extent of what he pays he has relieved it. In principle, there can be no difference between the case of selling labor and the case of selling goods. If one goes to the butcher, the baker or grocer to buy food, he is morally entitled to obtain the worth of his money but he is not entitled to more. If what he gets is worth what he pays he is not justified in demanding more simply because he needs more; and the shopkeeper, having dealt fairly and honestly in that transaction, is not concerned in any peculiar sense with the question of his customer's necessities. Should a statute undertake to vest in a commission power to determine the quantity of food necessary for individual support and require the shopkeeper, if he sell to the individual at all, to furnish that quantity at not more than a fixed maximum, it would undoubtedly fall before the constitutional test. The fallacy of any argument in support of the validity of such a statute would be quickly exposed. The argument in support of that now being considered is equally fallacious, though the weakness of it may not be so plain. A statute requiring an employer to pay in money, to pay at prescribed and regular intervals, to pay the value of the services rendered, even to pay with fair relation to the extent of the benefit obtained from the service, would be understandable. But a statute which prescribes payment without regard to any of these things and solely with relation to circumstances apart from the contract of employment, the business affected by it and the work done under it, is so clearly the product of a naked, arbitrary exercise of power that it cannot be allowed to stand under the Constitution of the United States.

We are asked, upon the one hand, to consider the fact that several States have adopted similar statutes, and we are invited, upon the other hand, to give weight to the fact that three times as many States, presumably as well informed and as anxious to promote the health and morals of their people, have refrained from enacting such legislation. We have also been furnished with a large number of printed opinions approving the policy of the minimum wage, and our own reading has disclosed a large number to the contrary. These are all proper enough for the consideration of the lawmaking bodies, since their tendency is to establish the desirability or undesirability of the legislation; but they reflect no legitimate light upon the question of its validity, and that is what we are called upon to decide. The elucidation of that question cannot be aided by counting heads.

It is said that great benefits have resulted from the operation of such statutes, not alone in the District of Columbia but in the several States, where they have been in force. A mass of reports, opinions of special observers and students of the subject, and the like, has been brought before us in support of this statement, all of which we have found interesting but only mildly persuasive. That the earnings of women now are greater than they were formerly and that conditions affecting women have become better in other respects may be conceded, but convincing indications of the logical relation of these desirable changes to the law in question are significantly lacking. They may be, and quite probably are, due to other causes. We cannot close our eyes to the notorious fact that earnings everywhere in all occupations have greatly increased—not alone in States where the minimum wage law obtains but in the country generally—quite as much or more among men as among women and in occupations outside the reach of the law as in those governed by it. No real test of the economic value of the law can be had during periods of maximum employment, when general causes keep wages up to or above the minimum; that will come in periods of depression and struggle for employment when the efficient will be employed at the minimum rate while the less capable may not be employed at all.

Finally, it may be said that if, in the interest of the public welfare, the police power may be invoked to justify the fixing of a minimum wage, it may, when the public welfare is thought to require it, be invoked to justify a maximum wage. The power to fix high wages connotes, by like course of reasoning, the power to fix low wages. If, in the face of the guaranties of the Fifth Amendment, this form of legislation shall be legally justified, the field for the operation of the police power will have been widened to a great and dangerous degree. If, for example, in the opinion of future lawmakers, wages in the building trades shall become so high as to preclude people of ordinary means from building and owning homes, an authority which sustains the minimum wage will be invoked to support a maximum wage for building laborers and artisans, and the same argument which has been here urged to strip the employer of his constitutional liberty of contract in one direction will be utilized to strip the employee of his constitutional liberty of contract in the opposite direction. A wrong decision does not end with itself: it is a precedent, and, with the swing of sentiment, its bad influence may run from one extremity of the arc to the other.

It has been said that legislation of the kind now under review is required in the interest of social justice, for whose ends freedom of contract may lawfully be subjected to restraint. The liberty of the individual to do as he pleases, even in innocent matters, is not absolute. It must frequently yield to the common good, and the line beyond which the power of interference may not be pressed is neither definite nor unalterable but may be made to move, within limits not well defined, with changing need and circumstance. Any attempt to fix a rigid boundary would be unwise as well as futile. But, nevertheless, there are limits to the power, and when these have been passed, it becomes the plain duty of the courts in the proper exercise of their authority to so declare. To sustain the individual freedom of action contemplated by the Constitution, is not to strike down the common good but to exalt it; for surely the good of society as a whole cannot be better served than by the preservation against arbitrary restraint of the liberties of its constituent members. . . .

Justice Holmes dissented:

. . . I confess that I do not understand the principle on which the power to fix a minimum for the wages of women can be denied by those who admit the power to fix a maximum for their hours of work. [The] bargain is equally affected whichever half you regulate. [It] will need more than the 19th Amendment to convince me that there are no differences between men and women, or that legislation cannot take those differences into account. . . .

Chief Justice Taft, dissenting:

I regret much to differ from the Court in these cases.

The boundary of the police power beyond which its exercise becomes an invasion of the guaranty of liberty under the Fifth and Fourteenth Amendments to the Constitution is not easy to mark. Our Court has been laboriously engaged in pricking out a line in successive cases. We must be careful, it seems to me, to follow that line as well as we can and not to depart from it by suggesting a distinction that is formal rather than real.

Legislatures in limiting freedom of contract between employee and employer by a minimum wage proceed on the assumption that employees, in the class receiving least pay, are not upon a full level of equality of choice with their employer and in their necessitous circumstances are prone to accept pretty much anything that is offered. They are peculiarly subject to the overreaching of the harsh and greedy employer. The evils of the sweating system and of the long hours and low wages which are characteristic of it are well known. Now, I agree that it is a disputable question in the field of political economy how far a statutory requirement of maximum hours or minimum wages may be a useful remedy for these evils, and whether it may not make the case of the oppressed employee worse than it was before. But it is not the function of this Court to hold congressional acts invalid simply because they are passed to carry out economic views which the Court believes to be unwise or unsound.

Legislatures which adopt a requirement of maximum hours or minimum wages may be presumed to believe that when sweating employers are prevented from paying unduly low wages by positive law they will continue their business, abating that part of their profits, which were wrung from the necessities of their employees, and will concede the better terms required by the law; and that while in individual cases hardship may result, the restriction will enure to the benefit of the general class of employees in whose interest the law is passed and so to that of the community at large.

The right of the legislature under the Fifth and Fourteenth Amendments to limit the hours of employment on the score of the health of the employee, it seems to me, has been firmly established. As to that, one would think, the line had been pricked out so that it has become a well formulated rule. In *Holden* v. *Hardy* . . . it was applied to miners and rested on the unfavorable environment of employment in mining and smelting. In *Lochner* v. *New York* . . . it was held that restricting those employed in bakeries to ten hours a day was an arbitrary and invalid interference with the liberty of contract secured by the Fourteenth Amendment. Then followed a number of cases beginning with *Muller* v. *Oregon* . . . sustaining the validity of a limit on maximum hours of labor for women . . . , and following these cases came *Bunting* v. *Oregon* . . . In that case, this Court sustained a law limiting the hours of labor of any person, whether man or woman, working in any mill, factory or manufacturing establishment to ten hours a day with a proviso as to further hours to which I shall hereafter advert. The law covered the whole field of industrial employment and certainly covered the case of persons employed in bakeries. Yet the opinion in the *Bunting Case* does not mention the *Lochner Case*. No one can suggest any constitutional distinction between employment in a bakery and one in any other kind of a manufacturing establishment which should make a limit of hours in the one invalid, and the same limit in the other permissible. It is impossible for me to reconcile the *Bunting Case* and the *Lochner Case* and I have always supposed that the *Lochner Case* was thus overruled *sub silentio*. Yet the opinion of the Court herein in support of its conclusion quotes from the opinion in the *Lochner Case* as one which has been sometimes distinguished but never overruled. Certainly there was no attempt to distinguish it in the *Bunting Case*.

However, the opinion herein does not overrule the *Bunting Case* in express terms, and therefore I assume that the conclusion in this case rests on the distinction between a minimum of wages and a maximum of hours in the limiting of liberty to contract. I regret to be at variance with the Court as to the substance of this distinction. In absolute freedom of contract the one term is as important as the other, for both enter equally into the consideration given and received, a restriction as to one is not any greater in essence than the other, and is of the same kind. One is the multiplier and the other the multiplicand.

If it be said that long hours of labor have a more direct effect upon the health of the employee than the low wage, there is very respectable authority from close observers, disclosed in the record and in the literature on the subject quoted at length in the briefs, that they are equally harmful in this regard. Congress took this view and we can not say it was not warranted in so doing.

With deference to the very able opinion of the Court and my brethren who concur in it, it appears to me to exaggerate the importance of the wage term of the contract of employment as more inviolate than its other terms. Its conclusion seems influenced by the fear that the concession of the power to impose a minimum wage must carry with it a concession of the power to fix a maximum wage. This, I submit, is a *non sequitur*. A line of distinction like the one under discussion in this case is, as the opinion elsewhere admits, a matter of degree and practical experience and not of pure logic. Certainly the wide difference between prescribing a minimum wage and a maximum wage could as a matter of degree and experience be easily affirmed. . . .

Without, however, expressing an opinion that a minimum wage limitation can be enacted for adult men, it is enough to say that the case before us involves only the application of the minimum wage to women. If I am right in thinking that the legislature can find as much support in experience for the view that a sweating wage has as great and as direct a tendency to bring about an injury to the health and morals of workers, as for the view that long hours injure their health, then I respectfully submit that *Muller* v. *Oregon,* 208 U. S. 412, controls this case. The law which was there sustained forbade the employment of any female in any mechanical establishment or factory or laundry for more than ten hours. This covered a pretty wide field in women's work and it would not seem that any sound distinction between that case and this can be built up on the fact that the law before us applies to all occupations of women with power in the board to make certain exceptions. Mr. Justice Brewer, who spoke for the Court in *Muller* v. *Oregon,* based its conclusion on the natural limit to women's physical strength and the likelihood that long hours would therefore injure her health, and we have had since a series of cases which may be said to have established a rule of decision. . . .

I am not sure from a reading of the opinion whether the Court thinks the authority of *Muller* v. *Oregon* is shaken by the adoption of the Nineteenth Amendment. The Nineteenth Amendment did not change the physical strength or limitations of women upon which the decision in *Muller* v. *Oregon* rests. The Amendment did give women political power and makes more certain that legislative provisions for their protection will be in accord with their interests as they see them. But I don't think we are warranted in varying constitutional construction based on physical differences between men and women, because of the Amendment. . . .

The third of these era-ending decisions underscored "freedom of contract" as a dominant judicial doctrine. On this basis, a Kansas law providing for compulsory arbitration in certain labor-management disputes was held invalid in *Wolff Packing Company* v. *Kansas Court of Industrial Relations.* Chief Justice Taft had unanimous support for his opinion:

WOLFF PACKING COMPANY v. COURT OF INDUSTRIAL RELATIONS
262 U. S. 522 (1923)

The necessary postulate of the Industrial Court Act is that the State, representing the people, is so much interested in their peace, health and comfort that it may compel those engaged in the manufacture of food, and clothing, and the production of fuel, whether owners or workers, to continue in their business and employment on terms fixed by an agency of the State if they can not agree. Under the construction adopted by the State Supreme Court the act gives the Industrial Court authority to permit the owner or employer to go out of the business, if he shows that he can only continue on the terms fixed at such heavy loss that collapse will follow; but this privilege under the circumstances is generally illusory. . . . A laborer dissatisfied with his wages is permitted to quit, but he may not agree with his fellows to quit or combine with others to induce them to quit.

These qualifications do not change the essence of the act. It curtails the right of the employer on the one hand, and of the employee on the other, to contract about his affairs. This is part of the liberty of the individual protected by the guaranty of the due process clause of the Fourteenth Amendment. . . . While there is no such thing as absolute freedom of contract and it is subject to a variety of restraints, they must not be arbitrary or unreasonable. Freedom is the general rule, and restraint the exception. The legislative authority to abridge can be justified only by exceptional circumstances. . . .

It is argued for the State that such exceptional circumstances exist in the present case and that the act is neither arbitrary nor unreasonable. Counsel maintain:

First. The act declares that the preparation of human food is affected by a public interest and the power of the legislature so to declare and then to regulate the business is established in *Munn* v. *Illinois*. . . .

Second. The power to regulate a business affected with a public interest extends to fixing wages and terms of employment to secure continuity of operation. . . .

Businesses said to be clothed with a public interest justifying some public regulation may be divided into three classes:

(1) Those which are carried on under the authority of a public grant of privileges which either expressly or impliedly imposes the affirmative duty of rendering a public service demanded by any member of the public. Such are the railroads, other common carriers and public utilities.

(2) Certain occupations, regarded as exceptional, the public interest attaching to which, recognized from earliest times, has survived the period of arbitrary laws by Parliament or Colonial legislatures for regulating all trades and callings. Such are those of the keepers of inns, cabs and grist mills. . . .

(3) Businesses which though not public at their inception may be fairly said to have risen to be such and have become subject in consequence to some government regulation. They have come to hold such a peculiar relation to the public that this is superimposed upon them. In the language of the cases, the owner by devoting his business to the public use, in effect grants the public an interest in that use and subjects himself to public regulation to the extent of that interest although the property continues to belong to its private owner and to be entitled to protection accordingly. *Munn* v. *Illinois*. . . .

It is manifest from an examination of the cases cited under the third head that the mere declaration by a legislature that a business is affected with a public interest is not conclusive of the question whether its attempted regulation on that ground is justified. The circumstances of its alleged change from the status of a private business and its freedom from regulation into one in which the public have come to have an interest are always a subject of judicial inquiry. . . .

It has never been supposed, since the adoption of the Constitution, that the business of the butcher, or the baker, the tailor, the wood chopper, the mining operator or the miner was clothed with such a public interest that the price of his product or his wages could be fixed by State regulation. It is true that in the days of the early common law an omnipotent Parliament did regulate prices and wages as it chose, and occasionally a colonial legislature sought to exercise the same power; but nowadays one does not devote one's property or business to the public use or clothe it with a public interest merely because one makes commodities for, and sells to, the public in the common callings of which those above mentioned are instances. . . .

It is very difficult under the cases to lay down a working rule by which readily to determine when a business has become "clothed with a public interest." All business is subject to some kinds of public regulation; but when the public becomes so peculiarly dependent upon a particular business that one engaging therein subjects himself to a more intimate public regulation is only to be determined by the process of exclusion and inclusion and to gradual establishment of a line of distinction. . . .

To say that a business is clothed with a public interest, is not to determine what regulation may be permissible in view of the private rights of the owner. The extent to which an inn or a cab system may be regulated may differ widely from that allowable as to a railroad or other common carrier. It is not a matter of legislative discretion solely. It depends on the nature of the business, on the feature which touches the public, and on the abuses reasonably to be feared. To say that a business is clothed with a public interest is not to import that the public may take over its entire management and run it at the expense of the owner. (The extent to which regulation may reasonably go varies with different kinds of business.) The regulation of rates to avoid monopoly is one thing. The regulation of wages is another. A business may be of such character that only the first is permissible, while another may involve such a possible danger of monopoly on the one hand, and such disaster from stoppage on the other, that both come within the public concern and power of regulation. . . .

Conclusion

Despite the persistence of conservative judicial ideology on the Supreme Court, the long period from the reinstatement of conservative Republican electoral ascendancy in the critical election of 1896 to the emergence of the New Deal in the critical election of 1932 was an era of significant doctrinal innovation. The acceptance of the concept of the factual brief (commonly referred to as the Brandeis brief after its orginator) in cases like Muller and Bunting proved to be temporary with the resurgence of stronger conservative influence after President Harding's electoral victory in 1920. The hardening of conservative resolve and the addition of more conservatives contributed to the rejection of a factual approach in favor of a restatement of older judicial ideological principles in the Atkins decision. But the Brandeis innovation was destined to have great influence in subsequent judicial development despite the setback of the 1920s.

The most important innovation of the era was the incorporation of several fundamental freedoms protected against national governmental action by provisions of the Bill of Rights into the definition of the due process clause of the Fourteenth Amendment, thus affording identical protection against state action. Whether this extension was truly an innovation or merely an expansion of the principle to human noneconomic rights may be open to some question. The bitter dissent of Justice John Marshall Harlan in the Chicago, Burlington, and Quincy Railroad Rate case recognized the extension of Bill of Rights provision for just compensation to due process protection against state action but deplored the fact that the principle was denied in human nonproperty situations. He then concluded that "it would seem that the protection of private property is of more consequence than the life and liberty of the citizen."[19] In many respects and despite many promising progressive beginnings, Harlan's comment captured the main thrust of this long judicial era.

Throughout the decades between 1896 and 1932, judicial selection was virtually a monopoly of conservatives, generally of Republican political persuasion, except for some of the appointees of Theodore Roosevelt and Woodrow Wilson. One of Roosevelt's appointees, Oliver Wendell Holmes, Jr., played a tremendously influential role during his long career on the Supreme Court. Roosevelt's other appointees were less significant and had briefer careers. Wilson appointed three justices, of whom one, James Clark McReynolds, proved to be as rock-ribbed a conservative as the subsequent appointees of Harding. His second appointee, Louis D. Brandeis, was, like Roosevelt's choice of Holmes, an outstanding one. The nomination of Brandeis had itself sparked an intense and bitter campaign by corporate leaders, conservative politicians, and conservative leaders of the American Bar Association to defeat him in the Senate. Wilson ultimately prevailed and secured Brandeis' nomination. After Charles Evans Hughes resigned to accept the Republican presidential nomination to run against President Wilson, Wilson selected a Progressive Democratic leader from Ohio, John H. Clarke, to replace Hughes.

The major impact of Holmes, Brandeis, and to a lesser extent, Clarke, was in their eloquent and carefully reasoned dissenting opinions. In the first three decades of the 20th century these dissents laid the intellectual groundwork for greater state and federal participation in the economy. Benjamin N. Cardozo, a Hoover appointee, also supported and contributed to the doctrinal approaches of Holmes and Brandeis. Cardozo was an outstanding jurist from the New York Court of Appeals. Hoover's nominations elicited a great deal of attention. Chief Justice William Howard Taft was succeeded by Chief Justice Charles Evans Hughes during the Hoover administration only after some Progressive Senate attacks on Hughes' corporate background. In addition to Cardozo, Hoover appointed

Owen J. Roberts, another corporate law firm attorney. Hoover's choice of Circuit Judge John J. Parker was the first nomination defeated in the Senate in the 20th century. Parker's defeat was attributed to a procivil rights and prolabor coalition, which cited racist remarks made by Parker as a gubernatorial candidate in North Carolina and his alleged antilabor bias in circuit court decision making. Most of Hoover's Supreme Court nominations were subjected to sharp Progressive scrutiny as the decades of conservative domination were closing.

The long era that had begun with the critical election of 1896 finally came to an end in the early 1930s. When Herbert Hoover was defeated by Franklin Delano Roosevelt in 1932, the overwhelmingly conservative, largely Republican federal judiciary was ideologically opposed to federal governmental intervention in the deeply depressed economy. Ironically, the Supreme Court and inferior federal courts were *not* significant issues in the election campaign of 1932—in sharp contrast to the situation in the last critical election, that of 1896.

REFERENCES

1. Kelly and Harbison, op. cit., p. 484.
2. Alan Westin, "The Supreme Court, The Populist Movement, and the Campaign of 1896," *Journal of Politics* 15 (February 1953): 30–41.
3. Grover Cleveland, *Messages and Papers of the Presidents*, vol. 11 (Washington, D. C.: Government Printing Office, 1935), pp. 5359–5360.
4. Carl Brent Swisher, *American Constitutional Development*, 2nd ed., (Westport, Conn.: Greenwood Press, 1978), p. 428.
5. *United States v. Workingman's Amalgamated Council*, 54 Fed. 994, 996 (1893).
6. 102 U. S. 586 (1881).
7. *Congressional Record* 26, Senate, 1st session (1894); see especially the arguments of Senator William V. Allen of Nebraska, p. 6707. For a thorough analysis, see George Tunell, "The Legislative History of the Second Income Tax Law," *Journal of Political Economy* 3 (June 1895), pp. 311–337.
8. James Bradley Thayer, *John Marshall* (Boston: Houghton, Mifflin, 1901), pp. 102–104.
9. Letter of Theodore Roosevelt to Henry Cabot Lodge, July 10, 1902, in *Selections from Correspondence of Theodore Roosevelt and Henry Cabot Lodge* (Boston: George Putnam's Sons, 1925) p. 517.
10. Swisher, *American Constitutional Development*, p. 519.
11. Cited in Carl McFarland, *Judicial Control of the Federal Trade Commission and the Interstate Commerce Commission* (Cambridge: Harvard University Press, 1933), p. 110.
12. Cited in Westel W. Willoughby, *I Constitutional Law*, op. cit., p. 31.
13. Charles Warren, *The Supreme Court in United States History*, vol. 3, (Boston: Little, Brown, 1923), p. 439.
14. Ibid, p. 427.
15. Ibid, pp. 458–459.
16. Kelly and Harbison, op. cit., pp. 671–672; see especially Stephen B. Wood, *Constitutional Politics in the Progressive Era: Child Labor and the Law* (Chicago: University of Chicago Press, 1968).
17. *New York Times*, December 14, 1917, quoted in Swisher, *American Constitutional Development*, op. cit., p. 602.
18. *New York Times*, April 28, 1918, quoted in Swisher, *American Constitutional Development*, op. cit., p. 618.
19. *Chicago, Burlington, and Quincy Railroad Company v. Chicago*, 16 U. S. 226 (1897) in his dissent in *Maxwell v. Dow* 176 U. S. 581, 614 (1900). For an excellent discussion of this and of the entire incorporation process, see Richard C. Cortner, *The Supreme Court and the Second Bill of Rights: The Fourteenth Amendment and the Nationalization of Civil Liberties* (Madison: University of Wisconsin Press, 1981), p. 36.

8

The New Deal and the
Supreme Court Crisis: Its Dimensions
and Its Aftermath

In his 1932 campaign for the Presidency, Franklin D. Roosevelt exploited President Hoover's weaknesses successfully without provoking an open conflict with the federal judiciary. Roosevelt's program was cautious. Near the end of the campaign, however, Roosevelt made a speech that included a passing reference to Republican control of the three branches of government—Presidency, Congress, and Court—while characterizing Republican leadership as consisting of "Destruction, Delay, Deceit, and Despair." President Hoover immediately tried to inject the Supreme Court as a campaign issue, arguing that

> . . . Aside from the fact that the charge that the Supreme Court has been controlled by any political party is an atrocious one, there is a deeper implication in that statement. Does it disclose the Democratic candidate's conception of the functions of the Supreme Court? Does it expect the Supreme Court to be subservient to him and his party? . . .[1]

Roosevelt was persuaded by his advisors not to rebut Hoover's charges and went on to a landslide victory, capturing 42 states and 472 electoral votes to Hoover's 6 states and 59 electoral votes. Of popular votes, Roosevelt gained 22.8 million (57.4 percent) to Hoover's 15.7 million (39.7 percent) with minor party candidates gaining 1.2 million (2.9 percent).[2] There was a fundamental electoral realignment to Democratic control.

Confronted by a continually deteriorating economy, the newly elected president immediately launched a wide series of relief measures to stabilize the weakening economic community and stimulate recovery. In March, 1933, shortly after taking office, Roosevelt called Congress into special session. In the first hundred days, federal banking, currency, and deposit insurance legislation, an agricultural reform act, a light wine and beer bill, an abandonment of the gold standard act, public works and civilian conservation corps measures, a securities regulation measure, a Tennessee Valley Authority measure, and a mortgage foreclosure bill were introduced. New Deal officials were apprehensive about the reactions of the conservative Supreme Court. At the outset of Roosevelt's first term, the Court included four strong conservatives, Justices McReynolds, Van Devanter, Butler, and Sutherland. Chief Justice Hughes and Justice Roberts were less rigid, but often voted with the conservatives. Justices Brandeis, Stone and Cardozo were thus the only members generally supportive of governmental intervention in the economy.

The Court enters like a lamb, but soon roars like a lion

Interestingly enough, the Supreme Court did not immediately assert its constitutional and public policy opposition to governmental intervention in the early days of the New Deal. In the beginning of President Roosevelt's first term, for example, the Supreme Court handed down a couple of decisions that appeared to respond to the extreme distress of the serious economic depression. Partly in response to persuasive dissenting criticisms first by Holmes and then by Brandeis and Stone, but primarily because of the impact of the depression, the Court completely discarded the doctrine that price controls must be justified constitutionally because the businesses so controlled are "affected with a public interest" in the traditional sense. This action was taken in 1934 in *Nebbia* v. *New York*.

NEBBIA v. NEW YORK
291 U. S. 502 (1934)

Justice Roberts delivered the opinion of the Court:

The Legislature of New York established a Milk Control Board with power, among other things, to "fix minimum and maximum . . . retail prices to be charged by . . . stores to consumers for consumption off the premises where sold." The Board fixed nine cents as the price to be charged by a store for a quart of milk. Nebbia, the proprietor of a grocery store in Rochester, sold two quarts and a five cent loaf of bread for eighteen cents; and was convicted for violating the Board's order. At his trial he asserted the statute and order contravened the equal protection clause and the due process clause. . . .

The question for decision is whether the Federal Constitution prohibits a state from so fixing the selling price of milk. We first inquire as to the occasion for the legislation and its history.

During 1932 the prices received by farmers for milk were much below the cost of production. The decline in prices during 1931 and 1932 was much greater than that of prices generally. The situation of the families of dairy producers had become desperate and called for

state aid similar to that afforded the unemployed, if conditions should not improve.

On March 10, 1932, the senate and assembly resolved "That a joint legislative committee is hereby created . . . to investigate the causes of the decline of the price of milk to producers and the resultant effect of the low prices upon the dairy industry. . . ."

In part those conclusions [of the committee] are:

Milk is an essential item of diet. It cannot long be stored. It is an excellent medium for growth of bacteria. These facts necessitate safeguards in its production and handling for human consumption which greatly increase the cost of the business. Failure of producers to receive a reasonable return for their labor and investment over an extended period threatens a relaxation of vigilance against contamination.

The production and distribution of milk is a paramount industry of the state, and largely affects the health and prosperity of its people. Dairying yields fully one-half of the total income from all farm products. Dairy farm investment amounts to approximately $1,000,000,000. Curtailment or destriction of the dairy industry would cause a serious economic loss to the people of the state.

In addition to the general price decline, other causes for the low price of milk include a periodic increase in the number of cows and in milk production, the prevalence of unfair and destructive trade practices in the distribution of milk, leading to a demoralization of prices in the metropolitan area and other markets, and the failure of transportation and distribution charges to be reduced in proportion to the reduction in retail prices for milk and cream.

The fluid milk industry is affected by factors of instability peculiar to itself which call for special methods of control. . . . [The Court here analyzes these factors in detail.]

The legislature adopted chapter 158 [creating a Milk Control Board with power to fix prices] as a method of correcting the evils, which the report of the committee showed could not be expected to right themselves through the ordinary play of the forces of supply and demand, owing to the peculiar and uncontrollable factors affecting the industry. . . .

First. The appellant urges that the order of the Milk Control Board denies him the equal protection of the laws. It is shown that the order requires him, if he purchases his supply from a dealer, to pay eight cents per quart and five cents per pint, and to resell at not less than nine and six, whereas the same dealer may buy his supply from a farmer at lower prices and deliver milk to consumers at ten cents the quart and six cents the pint. We think the contention that the discrimination deprives the appellant of equal protection is not well founded. For aught that appears, the appellant purchased his supply of milk from a farmer as do distributors, or could have procured it from a farmer if he so desired. There is therefore no showing that the order placed him at a disadvantage, or in fact affected him adversely, and this alone is fatal to the claim of denial of equal protection. But if it were shown that the appellant is compelled to buy from a distributor, the difference in the retail price he is required to charge his customers from that prescribed for sales by distributors is not on its face arbitrary or unreasonable, for there are obvious distinctions between the two sorts of merchants which may well justify a difference of treatment, if the legislature possesses the power to control the prices to be charged for fluid milk. . . .

Second. The more serious question is whether in the light of the conditions disclosed. . . . [the price-regulation] denied the appellant the due process secured to him by the Fourteenth amendment. . . .

Under our form of government the use of property and the making of contracts are normally matters of private and not of public concern. The general rule is that both shall be free of governmental interference. But neither property rights nor contract rights are absolute; for government cannot exist if the citizen may at will use his property to the detriment of his fellows, or exercise his freedom of contract to work them harm. Equally fundamental with the private right is that of the public to regulate it in the common interest. . . .

The milk industry in New York has been the subject of long-standing and drastic regulation in the public interest. The legislative investigation of 1932 was persuasive of the fact that for this and other reasons unrestricted competition aggravated existing evils and the normal law of supply and demand was insufficient to correct maladjustments detrimental to the community. The inquiry disclosed destructive and demoralizing competitive conditions and unfair trade practices which resulted in retail price cutting and reduced the income of the farmer below the cost of production. We do not understand the appellant to deny that in these circumstances the legislature might reasonably consider further regulation and control desirable for protection of the industry and the consuming public. That body believed conditions could be improved by preventing destructive price-cutting by stores which, due to the flood of surplus milk, were able to buy at much lower prices than the larger distributors and to sell without incurring the delivery costs of the latter. In the order of which complaint is made the Milk Control Board fixed a price of ten cents per quart for sales by a distributor to a consumer, and nine cents by a store to a consumer, thus recognizing the lower costs of the store, and endeavoring to establish a differential which would be just to both. In the light of the facts the order appears not to be unreasonable or arbitrary, or without relation to the purpose to prevent ruthless competition from destroying the wholesale price structure on which the farmer depends for his livelihood, and the community for an assured supply of milk.

But we are told that because the law essays to control prices it denies due process. Notwithstanding the admitted power to correct existing economic ills by appropriate regulation of business, even though an indirect result may be a restriction of the freedom of contract or a modification of charges for services or the price of commodities, the appellant urges that direct fixation of prices is a type of regulation absolutely forbidden. His position is that the Fourteenth Amendment requires us to hold the challenged statute void for this reason alone. The argument runs that the public control of rates or prices is per se unreasonable and unconstitutional, save as applied to businesses affected with a public interest; that a business so affected is one in which property is devoted to an enterprise of a sort which the public itself might appropriately undertake, or one whose owner relies on a public grant or franchise for the right to conduct the business, or in which he is bound to serve all who apply; in short, such as is commonly called a public utility; or a business in its nature a monopoly. The milk industry, it is said, possesses none of these characteristics, and, therefore, not being affected with a public interest, its charges may not be controlled by the state. Upon the soundness of this contention the appellant's case against the statute depends.

We may as well say at once that the dairy industry is not, in the accepted sense of the phrase, a public utility. We think the appellant is also right in asserting that there is in this case no suggestion of any monopoly or monopolistic practice. It goes without saying that those engaged in the business are in no way dependent upon public grants or franchises for the privilege of conducting their activities. But if, as must be conceded, the industry is subject to regulation in the public interest, what constitutional principle bars the state from correcting existing maladjustments by legislation touching prices? We think there is no such principle. The due process clause makes no mention of sales or of prices any more than it speaks of business or contracts or buildings or other incidents of property. The thought seems nevertheless to have persisted that there is something peculiarly sacrosanct about the price one may charge for what he makes or sells, and that, however able to regulate other elements of manufacture or trade, with incidental effect upon price, the state is incapable of directly controlling the price itself. This view was negatived many years ago. . . .

It is clear that there is no closed class or category of businesses affected with a public interest, and the function of courts in the application of the Fifth and Fourteenth Amendments is to determine in each case whether circumstances vindicate the challenged regulation as a reasonable exertion of governmental authority or condemn it as arbitrary or discriminatory. . . . The phrase "affected with a public interest" can, in the nature of things, mean no more than that an industry, for adequate reason, is subject to control for the public good. In several of the decisions of this court wherein the expressions "affected with a public interest," and "clothed with a public use," have been brought forward as the criteria of the validity of price control, it has been admitted that they are not susceptible of definition and form an unsatisfactory test of the constitutionality of legislation directed at business practices or prices. These decisions must rest, finally, upon the basis that the requirements of due

process were not met because the laws were found arbitrary in their operation and effect. But there can be no doubt that upon proper occasion and by appropriate measures the state may regulate a business in any of its aspects, including the prices to be charged for the products or commodities it sells.

So far as the requirement of due process is concerned, and in the absence of other constitutional restriction, a state is free to adopt whatever economic policy may reasonably be deemed to promote public welfare, and to enforce that policy by legislation adapted to its purpose. The courts are without authority either to declare such policy, or, when it is declared by the legislature, to override it. . . .

. . . The constitution does not secure to any one liberty to conduct his business in such fashion as to inflict injury upon the public at large, or upon any substantial group of the people. Price control, like any other form of regulation, is unconstitutional only if arbitrary, discriminatory, or demonstrably irrelevant to the policy the legislature is free to adopt, and hence an unnecessary and unwarranted interference with individual liberty.

Tested by these considerations we find no basis in the due process clause of the Fourteenth Amendment for condemning the provisions of the Agriculture and Markets Law here drawn into question.

The judgment is affirmed.

Justice McReynolds dissented in an opinion concurred in by Justices Van Devanter, Sutherland, and Butler:

Regulation to prevent recognized evils in business has long been upheld as permissible legislative action. But fixation of the price at which "A," engaged in an ordinary business, may sell, in order to enable "B," a producer, to improve his condition, has not been regarded as within legislative power. This is not regulation, but management, control, dictation—it amounts to the deprivation of the fundamental right which one has to conduct his own affairs honestly and along customary lines. . . .

The statement by the court below that—"Doubtless the statute before us would be condemned by an earlier generation as a temerarious interference with the rights of property and contract . . .; with the natural law of supply and demand," is obviously correct. But another, that "statutes . . . aiming to stimulate the production of a vital food product by fixing living standards of prices for the producer, are to be interpreted with that degree of liberality which is essential to the attainment of the end in view," conflicts with views of constitutional rights accepted since the beginning. An end although apparently desirable cannot justify inhibited means. Moreover the challenged act was not designed to stimulate production—there was too much milk for the demand and no prospect of less for several years; also "standards of prices" at which the producer might sell were not prescribed. The Legislature cannot lawfully destroy guaranteed rights of one man with the prime purpose of enriching another, even if for the moment, this may seem advantageous to the public. And the adoption of any "concept of jurisprudence" which permits facile disregard of the Constitution as long interpreted and respected will inevitably lead to its destruction. Then, all rights will be subject to the caprice of the hour; government by stable laws will pass.

The language utilized by the majority did not suggest that the Court was ready to support any sort of government intervention uncritically. The impact of the deep economic depression and judicial recognition of careful state legislative fact-finding were important elements in the successful defense of the state statute.

Similarly, a Minnesota Mortgage Moratorium statute was upheld even though the delay in fulfillment of legal obligations would undoubtedly have been held in violation of the contract clause under ordinary economic circumstances. Indeed, it resembled the "stay" laws that had stimulated the movement toward adoption of the contract clause in 1787. *Home Building and Loan Association* v. *Blaisdell*, like the Nebbia decision, was decided narrowly by a majority of five to four. Justice Sutherland wrote a sharp dissent. But again in 1934, the success of the narrow majority in Blaisdell led to early hope that the growing array of New Deal measures would pass constitutional muster. The background of the litigation and the deep significance of the economic depression were discussed fully in the majority opinion of Chief Justice Hughes:

HOME BUILDING AND LOAN ASSOCIATION v. BLAISDELL
290 U. S. 398 (1934)

Appellant contests the validity of Chapter 339 of the Laws of Minnesota of 1933, p. 514, approved April 18, 1933, called the Minnesota Mortgage Moratorium Law, as being repugnant to the contract clause . . . and the due process and equal protection clauses of the Fourteenth Amendment, of the Federal Constitution. The statute was sustained by the Supreme Court of Minnesota . . . and the case comes here on appeal.

The Act provides that, during the emergency declared to exist, relief may be had through authorized judicial proceedings with respect to foreclosures of mortgages, and execution sales, of real estate; that sales may be postponed and periods of redemption may be extended. The Act does not apply to mortgages subsequently made nor to those made previously which shall be extended for a period ending more than a year after the passage of the Act (Part One, § 8). . . . The Act is to remain in effect "only during the continuance of the emergency and in no event beyond May 1, 1935." . . .

In determining whether the provision for this temporary and conditional relief exceeds the power of the State by reason of the clause in the Federal Constitution prohibiting impairment of the obligations of contracts, we must consider the relation of emergency to constitutional power, the historical setting of the contract clause, the development of the jurisprudence of this Court in the construction of that clause, and the principles of construction which we may consider to be established.

Emergency does not create power. Emergency does not increase granted power or remove or diminish the restrictions imposed upon power granted or reserved. The Constitution was adopted in a period of grave emergency. Its grants of power to the Federal Government and its limitations of the power of the States were determined in the light of emergency and they are not altered by emergency. What power was thus granted and what limitations were thus imposed are questions which have always been, and always will be, the subject of close examination under our constitutional system.

While emergency does not create power, emergency may furnish the occasion for the exercise of power. . . . The constitutional question presented in the light of an emergency is whether the power possessed embraces the particular exercise of it in response to particular conditions. . . . When the provisions of the Constitution, in grant or restriction, are specific, so particularized as not to admit of construction, no question is presented. . . . But where constitutional grants and limitations of power are set forth in general clauses, which afford a broad outline, the process of construction is essential to fill in the details. That is true of the contract clause. . . .

But full recognition of the occasion and general purpose of the clause does not suffice to fix its precise scope. Nor does an examination of the details of prior legislation in the States yield criteria which can be considered controlling. To ascertain the scope of the constitutional prohibition we examine the course of judicial decisions in its application. These put it beyond question that the prohibition is not an absolute one and is not to be read with literal exactness like a mathematical formula. . . .

Not only is the constitutional provision qualified by the measure of control which the State retains over remedial processes, but the State also continues to possess authority to safeguard the vital interests of its people. It does not matter that legislation appropriate to that end "has the result of modifying or abrogating contracts already in effect." . . . Not only are existing laws read into contracts in order to fix obligations as between the parties, but the reservation of essential attributes of sovereign power is also read into contracts as a postulate of the legal order. The policy of protecting contracts against impairment presupposes the maintenance of a government by virtue of which contractual relations are worth while,—a government which retains adequate authority to secure the peace and good order of society. This principle of harmonizing the constitutional prohibition with the necessary residuum of state power has had progressive recognition in the decisions of this Court. . . .

Undoubtedly, whatever is reserved of state power must be consistent with the fair intent of the constitutional limitation of that power. The reserved power cannot be construed so as to destroy the limitation, nor is the limitation to be construed to destroy the reserved power in its essential aspects. They must be construed in harmony with each other. This principle precludes a construction which would permit the State to adopt as its policy the repudiation of debts or the destruction of contracts or the denial of means to enforce them. But it does not follow that conditions may not arise in which a temporary restraint of enforcement may be consistent with the spirit and purpose of the constitutional provision and thus be found to be within the range of the reserved power of the State to protect the vital interests of the community.

It cannot be maintained that the constitutional prohibition should be so construed as to prevent limited and temporary interpositions with respect to the enforcement of contracts if made necessary by a great public calamity such as fire, flood, or earthquake. . . . The reservation of state power appropriate to such extraordinary conditions may be deemed to be as much a part of all contracts, as is the reservation of state power to protect the public interest in the other situations to which we have referred. And if state power exists to give temporary relief from the enforcement of contracts in the presence of disasters due to physical causes such as fire, flood or earthquake, that power cannot be said to be non-existent when the urgent public need demanding such relief is produced by other and economic causes. . . .

It is manifest from this review . . . that there has been a growing appreciation of public needs and of the necessity of finding ground for a rational compromise between individual rights and public welfare. The settlement and consequent contraction of the public domain, the pressure of a constantly increasing density of population, the interrelation of the activities of our people and the complexity of our economic interests, have inevitably led to an increased use of the organization of society in order to protect the very bases of individual opportunity. Where, in earlier days, it was thought that only the concerns or of individuals or of classes were involved and that those of the State itself were touched only remotely, it has later been found that the fundamental interests of the state are directly affected; and that the question is no longer merely that of one party to a contract as against another, but of the use of reasonable means to safeguard the economic structure upon which the good of all depends.

It is no answer to say that this public need was not apprehended a century ago, or to insist that what the provision of the Constitution meant to the vision of that day it must mean to the vision of our time. If by the statement that what the Constitution meant at the time of its adoption it means to-day, it is intended to say that the great clauses of the Constitution must be confined to the interpretation which the framers, with the conditions and outlook of their time, would have placed upon them, the statement carries its own refutation. It was to guard against such a narrow conception that Chief Justice Marshall uttered the memorable warning—"We must never forget that it is *a constitution* we are expounding" . . . —"a constitution intended to endure for ages to come, and consequently, to be adapted to the various *crises* of human affairs." . . .

Nor is it helpful to attempt to draw a fine distinction between the intended meaning of the words of the Constitution and their intended application. When we consider the contract clause and the decisions which have expounded it in harmony with the essential reserved power of the States to protect the security of their peoples, we find no warrant for the conclusion that the clause has been warped by these decisions from its proper significance or that the founders of our Government would have interpreted the clause differently had they had occasion to assume that responsibility in the conditions of the later day. The vast body of law which has been developed was unknown to the fathers, but it is believed to have preserved the essential content and the spirit of the Constitution. With a growing recognition of public needs and the relation of individual right to public security, the court has sought to prevent the perversion of the clause through its use as an instrument to throttle the capacity of the States to protect their fundamental interests. This development is a growth from the seeds which the fathers planted. . . . The principle of this development is, as we have seen, that the reservation of the reasonable exercise of the protective power of the State is read into all contracts. . . .

Applying the criteria established by our decisions we conclude:

1. An emergency existed in Minnesota which furnished a proper occasion for the exercise of the reserved power of the State to protect the vital interests of the community. . . .

2. The legislation was addressed to a legitimate end, that is, the legislation was not for the mere advantage of particular individuals but for the protection of a basic interest of society.

3. In view of the nature of the contracts in question—mortgages of unquestionable validity—the relief afforded and justified by the emergency, in order not to contravene the constitutional provision, could only be of a character appropriate to that emergency and could be granted only upon reasonable conditions. . . .

We are of the opinion that the Minnesota statute as here applied does not violate the contract clause of the Federal Constitution. Whether the legislation is wise or unwise as a matter of policy is a question with which we are not concerned. . . .

The judicial ordeal of the New Deal

However great the optimism the Nebbia and Blaisdell decisions generated among supporters of the New Deal, the legislation upheld in each decision was state, not federal, and the margin of success for each statute was the narrowest possible, five to four. As in the early years of Jefferson's first presidential term, the composition of the Supreme Court had not changed to coincide with the fundamental shift in political power and ideological perspective brought about by the critical election of 1932. The fundamental conservatism of the Court was still its most consistent characteristic. Four members of the Supreme Court were doggedly opposed to any modifications of constitutional interpretation to accommodate the great problems of the depression—Justices Pierce Butler, James McReynolds, George Sutherland, and Willis Van Devanter. Chief Justice Charles Evans Hughes and Justices Louis D. Brandeis, Benjamin N. Cardozo, Owen J. Roberts, and Harlan Fiske Stone were receptive to depression-related needs in Nebbia and Blaisdell. These early decisions were constitutional tests of state statutes. The New Deal legislation was not challenged before 1935. But after the tests began, eight major statutes out of ten tested before the Supreme Court were struck down in the brief span of 16 months. In addition, the president suffered a serious setback in relation to his exercise of the removal power, a decision that prevented his replacement of regulators who did not share his more aggressive approach.

The first major action by the Court was the decision in January 1935 declaring the "hot oil" provisions of the National Industrial Recovery Act invalid as a delegation of legislative authority to the president. In *Panama Refining Company* v. *Ryan*,[3] in response to critical questions raised by Justice Brandeis, government counsel conceded that the executive orders under which petroleum industry officials had been penalized had not been promulgated. The admission not only made the negative Court decision a foregone conclusion, but also led immediately to the establishment of an orderly and predictable mode for promulgation of all executive orders—by publication in the newly created *Federal Register*.[4]

Although there were serious procedural difficulties in the administration of the program to take the nation off the gold standard, the Roosevelt administration won an important victory in the *Gold Clause Cases*[5] in which congressional authority to eliminate the "payment in gold" provision of public and private contracts was sustained. While these decisions were pending, several key members of the Roosevelt administration discussed the possibility of enlarging the Supreme Court in the event the conservative Court held the Gold Clause Act unconstitutional. According to Harold Ickes, Attorney General Homer Cummings, among others, was deeply concerned that an adverse decision would trigger a massive economic disaster within the framework of an already severely depressed economy.[6] The Court did not strike down the Gold Clause Act, but neither did the Roosevelt administration's victory harbinger an era of good executive-judicial relations.

In May of 1935, the most serious early confrontations between the New Deal and the Court took place in three decisions that struck down New Deal statutes. In *Railroad Retirement Board* v. *Alton RailRoad Company*,[7] the Court, by a five to four decision, held the Railroad Retirement Pension Act an unconstitutional violation of the due process clause of the Fifth Amendment. Later in May, the Court invalidated the Frazier-Lemke Mortgage Act as a violation of the Fifth Amendment in *Louisville Bank* v. *Radford*.[8] But the most dramatic decision was the invalidation of the National Industrial Recovery Act (NIRA) in *Schechter Poultry Corporation* v. *The United States*, the so-called Sick Chicken Case. The unanimous opinion was written by Chief Justice Hughes.

SCHECHTER POULTRY CORPORATION v. UNITED STATES
295 U. S. 495 (1935)

Petitioners . . . were convicted in the District Court of the United States for the Eastern District of New York on eighteen counts of an indictment charging violations of what is known as the "Live Poultry Code," and on an additional count for conspiracy to commit such violations. . . .

New York City is the largest live-poultry market in the United States. Ninety-six per cent of the live poultry there marketed comes from other States. Three-fourths of this amount arrives by rail and is consigned to commission men or receivers. . . . The commission men transact by far the greater part of the business on a commission basis. . . . They sell to slaughterhouse operators who are also called market-men.

The defendants are slaughterhouse operators of the latter class. . . . Defendants ordinarily purchase their live poultry from commission men at the West Washington Market in New York City or at the railroad terminals serving the city, but occasionally they purchase from commission men in Philadelphia. They buy the poultry for slaughter and resale. After the poultry is trucked to their slaughterhouse markets in Brooklyn, it is there sold, usually within twenty-four hours, to retail poultry dealers and butchers who sell directly to consumers. The poultry purchased from defendants is immediately slaughtered, prior to delivery, by shochtim in defendant's employ. Defendants do not sell poultry in interstate commerce.

The "Live Poultry Code" was promulgated under § 3 of the National Industrial Recovery Act. That section . . . authorizes the President to approve "codes of fair competition." . . . The "Live Poultry Code" was approved by the President on April 13, 1934. . . .

. . . The Code is established as "a code for fair competition for the live poultry industry of the metropolitan area in and about the City of New York." . . .

The Code fixes the number of hours for workdays. It provides that no employee, with certain exceptions, shall be permitted to work in excess of forty (40) hours in any one week, and that no employee save as stated, "shall be paid in any pay period less than at the rate of fifty (50) cents per hour." The article containing "general labor provisions" prohibits the employment of any person under sixteen years of age, and declares that employees shall have the right of "collective bargaining" and freedom of choice with respect to labor organizations, in terms of § 7 a of the Act. The minimum number of employees who shall be employed by slaughterhouse operators is fixed, the numbers being graduated according to the average volume of weekly sales. . . .

The seventh article, containing "trade practice provisions," prohibits various practices which are said to constitute "unfair methods of competition." . . .

The President approved the Code by an executive order. . . .

Of the eighteen counts of the indictment upon which the defendants were convicted, aside from the count for conspiracy, two counts charged violation of the minimum wage and maximum hour provisions of the Code, and ten counts were for violation of the requirement (found in the "trade practice provisions") of "straight killing." This requirement was really one of "straight" selling. The term "straight killing" was defined in the Code as "the practice of requiring persons purchasing poultry for resale to accept the run of any half coop, coop, or coops, as purchased by slaughterhouse operators, except for culls." The charges in the ten counts, respectively, were that the defendants in selling to retail dealers and butchers had permitted "selections of individual chickens taken from particular coops and half coops."

Of the other six counts, one charged the sale to a butcher of an unfit chicken; two counts charged the making of sales without having the poultry inspected or approved in accordance with regulations or ordinances of the City of New York; two counts charged the making of false reports or the failure to make reports relating to the range of daily prices and volume of sales for certain periods; and the remaining count was for sales to slaughterers or dealers who were without licenses required by the ordinances and regulations of the City of New York. . . .

Second. The question of the delegation of legislative power. . . . The Constitution provides that "all legislative powers herein granted shall be vested in a Congress of the United States, which shall consist of a Senate and House of Representatives." Art. 1, § I. And the Congress is authorized "to make all laws which

shall be necessary and proper for carrying into execution" its general power. Art. 1, § 8, par. 18. The Congress is not permitted to abdicate or to transfer to others the essential legislative functions with which it is thus vested. We have repeatedly recognized the necessity of adapting legislation to complex conditions involving a host of details with which the national Legislature cannot deal directly. We pointed out in the Panama Company case that the Constitution has never been regarded as denying to Congress the necessary resources of flexibility and practicality, which will enable it to perform its function in laying down policies and establishing standards, while leaving to selected instrumentalities the making of subordinate rules within prescribed limits and the determination of facts to which the policy as declared by the Legislature is to apply. But we said that the constant recognition of the necessity and validity of such provisions, and the wide range of administrative authority which has been developed by means of them, cannot by allowed to obscure the limitations of the authority to delegate, if our constitutional system is to be maintained.

Accordingly we look to the statute to see whether Congress has overstepped these limitations,—whether Congress in authorizing "codes of fair competition" has itself established the standards of legal obligation, thus performing its essential legislative function, or, by the failure to enact such standards, has attempted to transfer that function to others. . . .

What is meant by "fair competition" as the term is used in the Act? Does it refer to a category established in the law, and is the authority to make codes limited accordingly? Or is it used as a convenient designation for whatever set of laws the formulators of a code for a particular trade or industry may propose and the President may approve (subject to certain restrictions), or the President may himself prescribe, as being wise and beneficent provisions for the government of the trade or industry in order to accomplish the broad purposes of rehabilitation, correction and expansion which are stated in the first section of Title I?

The Act does not define "fair competition." "Unfair competition" as known to common law is a limited concept, primarily, and strictly, it relates to the palming off of one's goods as those of a rival trader. . . . In recent years its scope has been extended. It has been held to apply to misappropriation as well as misrepresentation, to the selling of another's goods as one's own—to misappropriation of what equitably belongs to a competitor. . . . Unfairness in competition has been predicated of acts which lie outside the ordinary course of business and are tainted by fraud, or coercion, or conduct otherwise prohibited by law. But it is evident that in its widest range "unfair competition," as it has been understood in the law, does not reach the objectives of the codes which are authorized by the National Industrial Recovery Act. The codes may, indeed, cover conduct which existing law condemns, but they are not limited to conduct of that sort. The Government does not contend that the Act contemplates such a limitation. It would be opposed both to the declared purposes of the Act and to its administrative construction. . . . [Here follows an analysis of the term "unfair methods of competition" used in the Federal Trade Commission Act as construed by judicial decisions.]

. . . We cannot regard the "fair competition" of the codes as antithetical to the "unfair methods of competition" of the Federal Trade Commission Act. The "fair competition" of the codes has a much broader range and a new significance. . . .

For a statement of the authorized objectives and content of the "codes of fair competition" we are referred repeatedly to the "Declaration of Policy" in § 1 of Title I of the Recovery Act. Thus the approval of a code by the President is conditioned on his finding that it "will tend to effectuate the policy of this title." § 3 (a). The President is authorized to impose such conditions "for the protection of consumers, competitors, employees and others, and in furtherance of the public interest, and may provide such exceptions to and exemptions from the provisions of such code as the President in his discretion deems necessary to effectuate the policy herein declared." The "policy herein declared" is manifestly that set forth in § 1. That declaration embraces a broad range of objectives. Among them we find the elimination of "unfair competitive practices." But even if this clause were taken to relate to practices which fall under the ban of existing law, either common law or statute, it is still only one of the authorized aims described in § 1. It is there declared to be "the policy of Congress"—"to remove obstructions to the free flow of interstate and foreign commerce which tend to diminish the amount thereof; and to provide for the general welfare by promoting the organization of industry for the purpose of cooperative action among trade groups, to induce and maintain united action of labor and management under adequate governmental sanctions and supervision, to eliminate unfair competitive practices, to promote the fullest possible utilization of the present productive capacity of industries, to avoid undue restriction of production

(except as may be temporarily required), to increase the consumption of industrial and agricultural products by increasing purchasing power, to reduce and relieve unemployment, to improve standards of labor, and otherwise to rehabilitate industry and to conserve natural resources."

Under § 3, whatever "may tend to effectuate" these general purposes may be included in the "codes of fair competition." We think the conclusion is inescapable that the authority sought to be conferred by § 3 was not merely to deal with "unfair competitive practices" which offend against existing law, and could be the subject of judicial condemnation without further legislation, or to create administrative machinery for the application of established principles of law to particular instances of violation. Rather, the purpose is clearly disclosed to authorize new and controlling prohibitions through codes of laws which would embrace what the formulators would propose, and what the President would approve, or prescribe, as wise and beneficent measures for the government of trades and industries in order to bring about their rehabilitation, correction and development, according to the general declaration of policy in § 1. . . .

The government urges that the code will "consist of rules of competition deemed fair for each industry by representative members of that industry, by the persons most vitally concerned and most familiar with its problems." Instances are cited in which Congress has availed itself of such assistance: as e.g., in the exercise of its authority over the public domain, with respect to the recognition of local customs or rules of miners as to mining claims or in matters of a more or less technical nature, as in designating the standard height of drawbars. But would it be seriously contended that Congress could delegate its legislative authority to trade or industrial associations or groups so as to empower them to enact the laws they deem to be wise and beneficent for the rehabilitation and expansion of their trade or industries? Could trade or industrial associations or groups be constituted legislative bodies for that purpose because such associations or groups are familiar with the problems of their enterprises? And, could an effort of that sort be made valid by such a preface of generalities as to permissible aims as we find in § 1 of Title I? The answer is obvious. Such a delegation of legislative power is unknown to our law and is utterly inconsistent with the constitutional prerogatives and duties of Congress.

The question, then, turns upon the authority which § 3 of the Recovery Act vests in the President to approve or prescribe. If the codes have standing as penal statutes, this must be due to the effect of the executive action. But Congress cannot delegate legislative power to the President to exercise an unfettered discretion to make whatever laws he thinks may be needed or advisable for the rehabilitation and expansion of trade or industry. . . .

Accordingly we turn to the Recovery Act to ascertain what limits have been set to the exercise of the President's discretion. *First*, the President, as a condition of approval, is required to find that the trade or industrial associations or groups which propose a code "impose no inequitable restrictions on admission to membership" and are "truly representative." That condition, however, relates only to the status of the initiators of the new laws and not to the permissible scope of such laws. *Second*, the President is required to find that the code is not "designed to promote monopolies or to eliminate or oppress small enterprises and will not operate to discriminate against them." And to this is added a proviso that the code "shall not permit monopolies or monopolistic practices." But these restrictions leave virtually untouched the field of policy envisaged by § 1, and in that wide field of legislative possibilities the proponents of a code, refraining from monopolistic designs, may roam at will and the President may approve or disapprove their proposals as he may see fit. . . .

To summarize and conclude upon this point: § 3 of the Recovery Act is without precedent. It supplies no standards for any trade, industry or activity. It does not undertake to prescribe rules of conduct to be applied to particular states of fact determined by appropriate administrative procedure. Instead of prescribing rules of conduct, it authorizes the making of codes to prescribe them. For that legislative undertaking, § 3 sets up no standards, aside from the statement of the general aims of rehabilitation, correction and expansion described in § 1. In view of the scope of that broad declaration, and of the nature of the few restrictions that are imposed, the discretion of the President in approving or prescribing codes, and thus enacting laws for the government of trade and industry throughout the country, is virtually unfettered. We think that the code-making authority thus conferred is an unconstitutional delegation of legislative power. . . .

Third. The question of the application of the provisions of the Live Poultry Code to intrastate transactions. Although the validity of the codes (apart from the question of delegation) rests upon the commerce clause of the Constitution, § 3 (a) is not in terms limited to interstate and foreign commerce. From the generality of terms, and from the argument of the Government at the bar it would appear that § 3 (a) was designed to authorize codes without that limitation. But under § 3 (f) penalties are confined to violations of a code provision "in any transaction in or affecting interstate or foreign commerce." This aspect of the case presents the question whether the particular provisions of the Live Poultry Code, which the defendants were convicted for violating and for having conspired to violate, were within the regulating power of Congress.

These provisions relate to the hours and wages of those employed by defendants in their slaughterhouses in Brooklyn and to the sales there made to retail dealers and butchers.

(1) Were these transactions "*in*" interstate commerce? Much is made of the fact that almost all the poultry coming to New York is sent there from other States. But the code provisions, as here applied, do not concern the transportation of the poultry from other States to New York, or the transactions of the commission men or others to whom it is consigned, or the sales made by such consignees to defendants. When defendants had made their purchases, whether at the West Washington Market in New York City or at the railroad terminals serving the city, or elsewhere, the poultry was trucked to their slaughterhouses in Brooklyn for local disposition. The interstate transactions in relation to that poultry then ended. Defendants held the poultry at their slaughterhouse markets for slaughter and local sale to retail dealers and butchers, who in turn sold directly to consumers. Neither the slaughtering nor the sales by defendants were transactions in interstate commerce. . . .

The undisputed facts thus afford no warrant for the argument that the poultry handled by defendants at their slaughterhouse markets was in a "*current*" or "*flow*" of interstate commerce and was thus subject to congressional regulation. The mere fact that there may be a constant flow of commodities into a State does not mean that the flow continues after the property has arrived and has become commingled with the mass of property within the State and is there held solely for local disposition and use. So far as the poultry herein questioned is concerned, the flow in interstate commerce has ceased. The poultry had come to a permanent rest within the State. It was not held, used or sold by defendants in relation to any further transactions in interstate commerce and was not destined for transportation to other states. Hence, decisions which deal with a stream of interstate commerce—and with the regulations of transactions involved in that practical continuity of movement, are not applicable here. . . .

(2) Did the defendants' transactions directly "affect" interstate commerce so as to be subject to Federal regulation? The power of Congress extends not only to the regulation of transactions which are part of interstate commerce, but to the protection of that commerce from injury. It matters not that the injury may be due to the conduct of those engaged in intrastate operations. Thus, Congress may protect the safety of those employed in interstate transportation "no matter what may be the source of the dangers which threaten it." . . . , We said in Second Employers' Liability Cases that it is the "effect upon interstate commerce," not "the source of the injury," which is "the criterion of congressional power." We have held that, in dealing with common carriers engaged in both interstate and intrastate commerce, the dominant authority of Congress necessarily embraces the right to control their intrastate operations in all matters having such a close and substantial relation to interstate traffic that the control is essential or appropriate to secure the freedom of that traffic from interference or unjust discrimination and to promote the efficiency of the interstate service. The Shreveport Case . . . and combinations and conspiracies to restrain interstate commerce, or to monopolize any part of it, are none the less within the reach of the Anti-Trust Act, because the conspirators seek to attain their end by means of intrastate activities. . . .

. . . This is not a prosecution for a conspiracy to restrain or monopolize interstate commerce in violation of the Anti-Trust Act. Defendants have been convicted, not upon direct charges of injury to interstate commerce or of interference with persons engaged in that commerce, but of violations of certain provisions of the Live Poultry Code and of conspiracy to commit these violations. Interstate commerce is brought in only upon the charge that violations of these provisions—as to hours and wages of employes and local sales—"*affected*" interstate commerce.

In determining how far the Federal Government may go in controlling intrastate transactions upon the ground that they "affect" interstate commerce, there is a necessary and well-established distinction between direct and indirect effects. The precise line can be drawn only as individual cases arise, but the distinction is clear in principle. Direct effects are illustrated by the railroad cases we have cited, as, e.g., the effect of failure to use prescribed safety appliances on railroads which are the highways of both interstate and intra-

state commerce, injury to an employe engaged in interstate transportation by the negligence of an employe engaged in an intrastate movement, the fixing of rates for intrastate transportation which unjustly discriminate against interstate commerce. But where the effect of intrastate transactions upon interstate commerce is merely indirect, such transactions remain within the domain of state power. If the commerce clause were construed to reach all enterprises and transactions which could be said to have an indirect effect upon interstate commerce, the Federal authority would embrace practically all the activities of the people and the authority of the State over its domestic concerns would exist only by sufferance of the Federal Government. Indeed, on such a theory, even the development of the State's commercial facilities would be subject to Federal control. . . .

The question of chief importance relates to the provisions of the Code as to the hours and wages of those employed in defendants' slaughterhouse markets. It is plain that these requirements are imposed in order to govern the details of defendants' management of their local business. The persons employed in slaughtering and selling in local trade are not employed in interstate commerce. Their hours and wages have no direct relation to interstate commerce. The question of how many hours these employes should work and what they should be paid differs in no essential respect from similar questions in other local businesses which handle commodities brought into a State and there dealt in as a part of its internal commerce. This appears from an examination of the considerations urged by the Government with respect to conditions in the poultry trade. Thus, the Government argues that hours and wages affect prices; that slaughterhouse men sell at a small margin above operating costs; that labor represents 50 to 60 per cent of these costs; that a slaughterhouse operator paying lower wages or reducing his cost by exacting long hours of work translates his saving into lower prices; that this results in demands for a cheaper grade of goods, and that the cutting of prices brings about a demoralization of the price structure. Similar conditions may be adduced in relation to other businesses. The argument of the Government proves too much. If the Federal Government may determine the wages and hours of employes in the internal commerce of a State, because of their relation to cost and prices and their indirect effect upon interstate commerce, it would seem that a similar control might be exerted over other elements of cost, also affecting prices, such as the number of employes, rents, advertising, methods of doing business, etc. All the processes of production and distribution that enter into cost could likewise be controlled. If the cost of doing an intrastate business is in itself the permitted object of Federal control, the extent of the regulation of cost would be a question of discretion and not of power.

The Government also makes the point that efforts to enact State legislation establishing high labor standards have been impeded by the belief that unless similar action is taken generally, commerce will be diverted from the States adopting such standards, and that this fear of diversion has led to demands for Federal legislation on the subject of wages and hours. The apparent implication is that the Federal authority under the commerce clause should be deemed to extend to the establishment of rules to govern wages and hours in intrastate trade and industry generally throughout the country, thus overriding the authority of the States to deal with domestic problems arising from labor conditions in their internal commerce.

It is not the province of the Court to consider the economic advantages or disadvantages of such a centralized system. It is sufficient to say that the Federal Constitution does not provide for it. Our growth and development have called for wide use of the commerce power of the Federal Government in its control over the expanded activities of interstate commerce and in protecting that commerce from burdens, interferences and conspiracies to restrain and monopolize it. But the authority of the Federal Government may not be pushed to such an extreme as to destroy the distinction, which the commerce clause itself establishes, between commerce "among the several States" and the internal concerns of a State. The same answer must be made to the contention that is based upon the serious economic situation which led to the passage of the Recovery Act—the fall in prices, the decline in wages and employment, and the curtailment of the market for commodities. Stress is laid upon the great importance of maintaining wage distributions which would provide the necessary stimulus in starting "the cumulative forces making for expanding commercial activity." Without in any way disparaging this motive, it is enough to say that the recuperative efforts of the Federal Government must be made in a manner consistent with the authority granted by the Constitution.

We are of the opinion that the attempt through the provisions of the Code to fix the hours and wages of employes of defendants in their intrastate business was not a valid exercise of Federal power.

On both the grounds we have discussed, the attempted delegation of legislative power and the attempted regulation of intrastate transactions which affect interstate commerce only indirectly, we hold the code provisions here in question to be invalid and that the judgment of conviction must be reversed.

[Justice Cardozo concurred.]

Because of the poor manner in which the legislation was drafted and the broad and sweeping nature of the legislation, the attorneys for the New Deal had not persuaded a single member on the Court in Schechter, not even those members who had frequently supported government intervention in the past. This first major setback for the New Deal was soon followed by a second defeat that was viewed by some as a retreat from the Myers decision. The question whether the Humphrey decision actually was a retreat from the broad grant of presidential removal authority handed down in the Myers decision turned on whether some of Chief Justice Taft's remarks were an essential part of his decision; most scholars agree that these remarks were simply additional commentary.

Humphrey's Executor (Rathbun) v. *The United States* was a stunning judicial limitation on President Roosevelt's power to remove carry-over officials of regulatory agencies. Humphrey, a Hoover appointee to the Federal Trade Commission, died before the legal action was completed, and consequently, Rathbun, his executor, was technically the plaintiff in the final court action.

In the context of the New Deal efforts to stimulate economic recovery and create greater confidence in prospects for the future, the timing of the Schechter and Humphrey decisions was particularly discouraging. Both decisions were handed down in a single day (as was a third decision rendering a farm bankruptcy law void).[9] The facts leading to the constitutional confrontation were presented in Justice Sutherland's majority opinion:

HUMPHREY'S EXECUTOR (RATHBUN)
v. UNITED STATES
295 U. S. 602 (1935)

Plaintiff brought suit in the Court of Claims against the United States to recover a sum of money alleged to be due the deceased for salary as a federal trade commissioner from October 8, 1933, when the President undertook to remove him from office, to the time of his death on February 14, 1934. The court below has certified to this court two questions . . . in respect of the power of the President to make the removal. The material facts which give rise to the question are as follows:

William E. Humphrey, the decedent, on December 10, 1931, was nominated by President Hoover to succeed himself as a member of the Federal Trade Commission and was confirmed by the United States Senate. He was duly commissioned for a term of seven years expiring September 25, 1938; and, after taking the required oath of office, entered upon his duties. On July 25, 1933, President Roosevelt addressed a letter to the commissioner asking for his resignation, on the ground "that the aims and purposes of the Administration with respect to the work of the commission can be carried out most effectively with personnel of my own selection," but disclaiming any reflection upon the commissioner personally or upon his services. The commissioner replied, asking time to consult his friends. After some further correspondence upon the subject, the President, on August 31, 1933, wrote the commissioner expressing the hope that the resignation would be forthcoming and saying:

"You will, I know, realize that I do not feel that your mind and my mind go along together on either the policies or the administering of the Federal Trade Commission, and, frankly, I think it is best for the people of this country that I should have a full confidence."

The commissioner declined to resign, and on October, 7, 1933, the President wrote him:

"Effective as of this date, you are hereby removed from the office of Commissioner of the Federal Trade Commission."

Humphrey never acquiesced in this action, but continued thereafter to insist that he was still a member of the commission, entitled to perform its duties and receive the compensation provided by law at the rate of $10,000 per annum. Upon these and other facts set forth in the certificate which we deem it unnecessary to recite, the following questions are certified:

"1. Do the provisions of § 1 of the Federal Trade Commission Act, stating that 'any commissioner may be removed by the President for inefficiency, neglect of duty or malfeasance in office,' restrict or limit the power of the President to remove a commissioner except upon one or more of the causes named?

"If the foregoing question is answered in the affirmative, then—

"2. If the power of the President to remove a commissioner is restricted or limited as shown by the foregoing interrogatory and the answer made thereto, is such a restriction or limitation valid under the Constitution of the United States?"

The Federal Trade Commission Act . . . creates a commission of five members to be appointed by the President by and with the advice and consent of the Senate, and § 1 provides:

"Not more than three of the commissioners shall be members of the same political party. The first commissioners appointed shall continue in office for terms of three, four, five, six and seven years, respectively, from the date of the taking effect of this act, the term of each to be designated by the President, but their successors shall be appointed for terms of seven years, except that any person chosen to fill a vacancy shall be appointed only for the unexpired term of the commissioner whom he shall succeed. The commission shall choose a chairman from its own membership. No commissioner shall engage in any other business, vocation, or employment. Any commissioner may be removed by the President for inefficiency, neglect of duty, or malfeasance in office."

Section 5 of the act in part provides:

"Unfair methods of competition in commerce are hereby declared unlawful.

"The commission is hereby empowered and directed to prevent persons, partnerships or corporations, except banks and common carriers subject to the acts to regulate commerce, from using unfair methods of competition in commerce."

In exercising this power the commission must issue a complaint stating its charges and giving notice of hearing upon a day to be fixed. A person, partnership or corporation proceeded against is given the right to appear at the time and place fixed and show cause why an order to cease and desist should not be issued. There is provision for intervention by others interested. If the commission finds the method of competition is one prohibited by the act it is directed to make a report in writing stating its findings as to the facts, and to issue and cause to be served a cease and desist order. If the order is disobeyed the commission may apply to the appropriate circuit court of appeals for its enforcement. This party subject to the order may seek and obtain a review in the circuit court of appeals in a manner provided by the act.

Section 6, among other things, gives the commission wide powers of investigation in respect of certain corporations subject to the act, and in respect of other matters, upon which it must report to Congress with recommendations. Many such investigations have been made, and some have served as the basis of congressional legislation.

Section 7 provides:

"That in any suit in equity brought by or under the direction of the Attorney General, as provided in the antitrust acts, the court may, upon the conclusion of the testimony therein if it shall be then of opinion that the complainant is entitled to relief, refer said suit to the commission, as a master in chancery, to ascertain and report an appropriate form of decree therein. The commission shall proceed upon such notice to the parties and under such rules of procedure as the court may prescribe and upon the coming in of such report such exceptions may be filed and such proceedings had in relation thereto as upon the report of a master in other equity causes, but the court may adopt or reject such report, in whole or in part, and enter such decree as the nature of the case may in its judgment require."

First. The question to be considered is whether, by the provisions of § 1 of the Federal Trade Commission Act already quoted, the President's power is limited to removal for the specific causes enumerated therein. . . .

. . . The statute fixes a term of office in accordance with many precedents. The first commissioners appointed are to continue in office for terms of three, four, five, six and seven years, respectively; and their successors are to be appointed for terms of seven years—any commissioner being subject to removal by the President for inefficiency, neglect of duty or malfeasance in office. The words of the act are definite and unambiguous.

The government says the phrase "continue in office" is of no legal significance, and moreover, applies only to the first commissioners. We think it has significance. It may be that, literally, its application is restricted as suggested; but it, nevertheless, lends support to a view contrary to that of the government as to the meaning of the entire requirement in respect of tenure; for it is not easy to suppose that Congress intended to secure the first commissioners against removal except for the causes specified and deny like security to their successors. Putting this phrase aside, however, the fixing of a definite term subject to removal for cause, unless there be some countervailing provision or cir-

cumstance indicating the contrary, which here we are unable to find, is enough to establish the legislative intent that the term is not to be curtailed in the absence of such cause. But if the intention of Congress that no removal should be made during the specified term except for one or more of the enumerated causes were not clear upon the face of the statute, as we think it is, it would be made clear by a consideration of the character of the commission and the legislative history which accompanied and preceded the passage of the act.

The commission is to be nonpartisan; and it must, from the very nature of its duties, act with entire impartiality. It is charged with the enforcement of no policy except the policy of the law. Its duties are neither political nor executive, but predominantly quasi-judicial and quasi-legislative. Like the Interstate Commerce Commission, its members are called upon to exercise the trained judgment of a body of experts "appointed by law and informed by experience." . . .

The legislative reports in both houses of Congress clearly reflect the view that a fixed term was necessary to the effective and fair administration of the law. . . .

The debates in both houses demonstrate that the prevailing view was that the commission was not to be "subject to anybody in the government but . . . only to the people of the United States," free from "political domination or control," or the "probability or possibility of such a thing"; to be "separate and apart from any existing department of the government—not subject to the orders of the President." . . .

Thus, the language of the act, the legislative reports and the general purposes of the legislation as reflected by the debates, all combine to demonstrate the Congressional intent to create a body of experts who shall gain experience by length of service—a body which shall be independent of Executive authority, *except in its selection*, and free to exercise its judgment without the leave or hindrance of any other official or any department of the government. To the accomplishment of these purposes it is clear that Congress was of opinion that length and certainty of tenure would vitally contribute. And to hold that, nevertheless, the members of the commission continue in office at the mere will of the President, might be to thwart, in large measure, the very ends which Congress sought to realize by definitely fixing the term of office.

We conclude that the intent of the act is to limit the executive power of removal to the causes enumerated, the existence of none of which is claimed here; and we pass to the second question.

Second. To support its contention that the removal

provision of § 1, as we have just construed it, is an unconstitutional interference with the executive power of the President, the government's chief reliance is Myers v. United States. . . . Nevertheless, the narrow point actually decided was only that the President had power to remove a postmaster of the first class, without the advice and consent of the Senate, as required by the act of Congress. In the course of the opinion of the court, expressions occur which tend to sustain the government's contention, but these are beyond the point involved, and therefore, do not come within the rule of stare decisis. In so far as they are out of harmony with the views here set forth, these expressions are disapproved. . . .

The office of a postmaster is so essentially unlike the office now involved that the decision in the Myers case cannot be accepted as controlling our decision here. A postmaster is an executive officer restricted to the performance of executive functions. He is charged with no duty at all related to either the legislative or judicial power. The actual decision in the Myers case finds support in the theory that such an officer is merely one of the units in the executive department and, hence, inherently subject to the exclusive and illimitable power of removal by the Chief Executive, whose subordinate and aid he is. Putting aside *dicta*, which may be followed if sufficiently persuasive but which are not controlling, the necessary reach of the decision goes far enough to include all purely executive officers. It goes no farther;—much less does it include an officer who occupies no place in the executive department and who exercises no part of the executive power vested by the Constitution in the President.

The Federal Trade Commission is an administrative body created by Congress to carry into effect legislative policies embodied in the statute in accordance with the legislative standard therein prescribed, and to perform other specified duties as a legislative or as a judicial aid. Such a body cannot in any proper sense be characterized as an arm or an eye of the executive. Its duties are performed without executive leave and, in the contemplation of the statute, must be free from executive control. In administering the provisions of the statute in respect of "unfair methods of competition"—that is to say in filling in and administering the details embodied by the general standard— the commission acts in part quasi-legislatively and in part quasi-judicially. In making investigations and reports thereon for the information of Congress under § 6, in aid of the legislative power it acts as a legislative agency. Under § 7, which authorizes the commission to act as a master in chancery under rules prescribed

by the court, it acts as an agency of the judiciary. To the extent that it exercises any executive function—as distinguished from executive power in the constitutional sense—it does so in the discharge and effectuation of its quasi-legislative or quasi-judicial powers, or as an agency of the legislative or judicial departments of the government.

If Congress is without authority to prescribe causes for removal of members of the Trade Commission and limit executive power of removal accordingly, that power at once becomes practically all inclusive in respect of civil officers, with the exception of the judiciary provided for by the Constitution. The Solicitor General, at the bar, apparently recognizing this to be true, with commendable candor agreed that his view in respect of the removability of members of the Federal Trade Commission necessitated a like view in respect of the Interstate Commerce Commission and the Court of Claims. We are thus confronted with the serious question whether not only the members of these quasi-legislative and quasi-judicial bodies, but the judges of the legislative Court of Claims, exercising judicial power . . . continue in office only at the pleasure of the President.

We think it plain under the Constitution that illimitable power of removal is not possessed by the President in respect of officers of the character of those just named. The authority of Congress, in creating quasi-legislative or quasi-judicial agencies, to require them to act in discharge of their duties independently of executive control, cannot well be doubted and that authority includes, as an appropriate incident, power to fix the period during which they shall continue, and to forbid their removal except for cause in the meantime. For it is quite evident that one who holds his office only during the pleasure of another cannot be depended upon to maintain an attitude of independence against the latter's will.

The fundamental necessity of maintaining each of the three general departments of government entirely free from the control or coercive influence, direct or indirect, of either of the others, has often been stressed and is hardly open to serious question. So much is implied in the very fact of the separation of the powers of these departments by the Constitution, and in the rule which recognizes their essential co-equality. The sound application of a principle that makes one master in his own house precludes him from imposing his control in the house of another who is master there. . . .

The power of removal here claimed for the President falls within this principle, since its coercive influence threatens the independence of a commission, which is not only wholly disconnected from the executive department, but which, as already fully appears, was created by Congress as a means of carrying into operation legislative and judicial powers, and as an agency of the legislative and judicial departments.

In the light of the question now under consideration, we have reexamined the precedents referred to in the Myers case, and find nothing in them to justify a conclusion contrary to that which we have reached. . . .

The result of what we now have said is this: Whether the power of the President to remove an officer shall prevail over the authority of Congress to condition the power by fixing a definite term and precluding a removal except for cause will depend upon the character of the office. The Myers decision, affirming the power of the President alone to make the removal is confined to purely executive officers.

And as to officers of the kind here under consideration, we hold that no removal can be made during the prescribed term for which the officer is appointed, except for one or more of the causes named in the applicable statute.

To the extent that, between the decision in the Myers case, which sustains the unrestrictable power of the President to remove purely executive officers, and our present decision that such power does not extend to an office such as that here involved there shall remain a field of doubt, we leave such cases as may fall within it for future consideration and determination as they arise.

In accordance with the foregoing the questions submitted are answered.

Question No. 1, Yes.

Question No. 2, Yes.

The Court's actions in 1936 were initially as negative as the major anti–New Deal decisions of 1935. The negative impact of conservative Supreme Court action eliminated the chief legislative effort of the Congress to alleviate the severe effects of the depression in the agricultural sector of the economy. Congressional and executive leaders had felt that legislation based upon the taxing power would fare better than the use of the commerce power. But in *United States* v. *Butler*, the Court, in an opinion by Justice Roberts, invoked the Child Labor Tax opinion to strike down the Agricultural Adjustment Act of 1935, one of the most successful of the early New Deal efforts to reinvigorate the depressed economy. Robert Jackson, in his *Struggle for Judicial Supremacy*, cited significant economic gains as a result of the Agricultural Adjustment Act.[10] The conservative majority again was not influenced by such considerations. Justice Stone's dissent, supported by Cardozo and Brandeis, strongly criticized the majority's position on grounds that ultimately provided the basis for broad constructionist approval of similar legislative efforts.

UNITED STATES v. BUTLER
297 U. S. 1 (1936)

Justice Roberts delivered the opinion of the Court:

It is inaccurate and misleading to speak of the exaction from processors prescribed by the challenged act as a tax, or to say that as a tax it is subject to no infirmity. A tax, in the general understanding of the term, and as used in the Constitution, signifies an exaction for the support of the Government. The word has never been thought to connote the expropriation of money from one group for the benefit of another. We may concede that the latter sort of imposition is constitutional when imposed to effectuate regulation of a matter in which both groups are interested and in respect of which there is a power of legislative regulation. But manifestly no justification for it can be found unless as an integral part of such regulation. The exaction cannot be wrested out of its setting, denominated an excise for raising revenue and legalized by ignoring its purpose as a mere instrumentality for bringing about a desired end. To do this would be to shut our eyes to what all others than we can see and understand. . . .

We conclude that the act is one regulating agricultural production; that the tax is a mere incident of such regulation and that the respondents have standing to challenge the legality of the exaction. . . .

Second. The Government asserts that even if the respondents may question the propriety of the appropriation embodied in the statute their attack must fail because Article I, § 8 of the Constitution authorizes the contemplated expenditure of the funds raised by the tax. This contention presents the great and the controlling question in the case. We approach its decision with a sense of our grave responsibility to render judgment in accordance with the principles established for the governance of all three branches of the Government.

There should be no misunderstanding as to the function of this court in such a case. It is sometimes said that the court assumes a power to overrule or control the action of the people's representatives. This is a misconception. The Constitution is the supreme law of the land ordained and established by the people. All legislation must conform to the principles it lays down. When an act of Congress is appropriately challenged in the courts as not conforming to the constitutional mandate the judicial branch of the Government has only one duty,—to lay the article of the Constitution which is invoked beside the statute which is challenged and to decide whether the latter squares with the former. All the court does, or can do, is to announce its considered judgment upon the question. The only power it has, if such it may be called, is the power of judgment. This court neither approves nor condemns any legislative policy. Its delicate and difficult office is to ascertain and declare whether the legislation is in accordance with, or in contravention of, the provisions of the Constitution; and, having done that, its duty ends.

The question is not what power the federal Government ought to have but what powers in fact have been given by the people. It hardly seems necessary to reiterate that ours is a dual form of government; that in every state there are two governments,—the state and the United States. Each State has all governmental powers save such as the people, by their Constitution, have conferred upon the United States, denied to the States, or reserved to themselves. The federal union is a government of delegated powers. It has only such as are expressly conferred upon it and such as are reasonably to be implied from those granted. In this respect we differ radically from nations where all legislative power, without restriction or limitation, is vested in a parliament or other legislative body subject to no restrictions except the discretion of its members.

Article I, § 8, of the Constitution vests sundry powers in the Congress. But two of its clauses have any bearing upon the validity of the statute under review.

The third clause endows the Congress with power "to regulate Commerce . . . among the several States." Despite a reference in its first section to a burden upon, and an obstruction of the normal currents of commerce, the act under review does not purport to regulate transactions in interstate or foreign commerce. Its stated purpose is the control of agricultural production, a purely local activity, in an effort to raise the prices paid the farmer. Indeed, the Government does not attempt to uphold the validity of the act on the basis of the commerce clause, which, for the purpose of the present case, may be put aside as irrelevant.

The clause thought to authorize the legislation,— the first,—confers upon the Congress power "to lay and collect Taxes, Duties, Imposts and Excises, to pay the Debts and provide for the common Defence and general Welfare of the United States. . . ." It is not contended that this provision grants power to regulate agricultural production upon the theory that such legislation would promote the general welfare. The Government concedes that the phrase "to provide for the general welfare" qualifies the power "to lay and collect taxes." The view that the clause grants power to provide for the general welfare, independently of the taxing power, has never been authoritatively accepted. Mr. Justice Story points out that if it were adopted "it is obvious that under color of the generality of the words, to 'provide for the common defence and general welfare,' the government of the United States is, in reality, a government of general and unlimited powers, notwithstanding the subsequent enumeration of specific powers." The true construction undoubtedly is that the only thing granted is the power to tax for the purpose of providing funds for payment of the nation's debts and making provision for the general welfare.

Nevertheless the Government asserts that warrant is found in this clause for the adoption of the Agricultural Adjustment Act. The argument is that Congress may appropriate and authorize the spending of moneys for the "general welfare"; that the phrase should be liberally construed to cover anything conducive to national welfare; that decision as to what will promote such welfare rests with Congress alone, and the courts may not review its determination; and finally that the appropriation under attack was in fact for the general welfare of the United States.

The Congress is expressly empowered to lay taxes to provide for the general welfare. Funds in the Treasury as a result of taxation may be expended only through appropriation (Art. I, § 9, cl. 7.) They can never accomplish the objects for which they were collected unless the power to appropriate is as broad as the power to tax. The necessary implication from the terms of the grant is that the public funds may be appropriated "to provide for the general welfare of the United States." These words cannot be meaningless, else they would not have been used. The conclusion must be that they were intended to limit and define the granted power to raise and to expend money. How shall they be construed to effectuate the intent of the instrument?

Since the foundation of the nation sharp differences of opinion have persisted as to the true interpretation of the phrase. Madison asserted it amounted to no more than a reference to the other powers enumerated in the subsequent clauses of the same section; that, as the United States is a government of limited and enumerated powers, the grant of power to tax and spend for the general national welfare must be confined to the enumerated legislative fields committed to the Congress. In this view the phrase is mere tautology, for taxation and appropriation are or may be necessary incidents of the exercise of any of the enumerated legislative powers. Hamilton, on the other hand, maintained the clause confers a power separate and distinct from those later enumerated, is not restricted in meaning by the grant of them, and Congress consequently has a substantive power to tax and to appropriate, limited only by the requirement that it shall be exercised to provide for the general welfare of the United States. Each contention has had the support of those whose views are entitled to weight. This court has noticed the question, but has never found it necessary to decide which is the true construction. Mr. Justice Story, in his Commentaries, espouses the Hamiltonian position. We shall not review the writings of public men and commentators or discuss the legislative practice. Study of all these leads us to conclude that the reading advocated by Mr. Justice Story is the correct one. While, therefore, the power to tax is not unlimited, its confines are set in the clause which confers it, and not in those of § 8 which bestow and define the legislative powers of the Congress. It results that the power of Congress to authorize expenditure of public moneys for public purposes is not limited by the direct grants of legislative power found in the Constitution. . . .

We are not now required to ascertain the scope of the phrase "general welfare of the United States" or to determine whether an appropriation in aid of agriculture falls within it. Wholly apart from that question, another principle embedded in our constitution prohibits the enforcement of the Agricultural Adjustment Act. The act invades the reserved rights of the

states. It is a statutory plan to regulate and control agricultural production, a matter beyond the powers delegated to the federal government. The tax, the appropriation of the funds raised, and the direction of their disbursement, are but parts of the plan. They are but means to an unconstitutional end.

From the accepted doctrine that the United States is a government of delegated powers, it follows that those not expressly granted, or reasonably to be implied from such as are conferred, are reserved to the states or to the people. To forestall any suggestion to the contrary, the Tenth Amendment was adopted. The same proposition, otherwise stated, is that powers not granted are prohibited. None to regulate agricultural production is given, and therefore legislation by Congress for that purpose is forbidden.

It is an established principle that the attainment of a prohibited end may not be accomplished under the pretext of the exertion of powers which are granted. "Should Congress, in the execution of its powers, adopt measures which are prohibited by the constitution; or should Congress, under the pretext of executing its powers, pass laws for the accomplishment of objects not intrusted to the government; it would become the painful duty of this tribunal, should a case requiring such a decision come before it, to say that such an act was not the law of the land. . . ."

"Congress cannot, under the pretext of executing delegated power, pass laws for the accomplishment of objects not intrusted to the federal Government. And we accept as established doctrine that any provision of an act of Congress ostensibly enacted under power granted by the Constitution, not naturally and reasonably adapted to the effective exercise of such power but solely to the achievement of something plainly within power reserved to the States, is invalid and cannot be enforced. . . ."

These principles are as applicable to the power to lay taxes as to any other federal power. Said the court, in *M'Culloch* v. *Maryland*:

"Let the end be legitimate, let it be within the scope of the constitution, and all means which are appropriate, which are plainly adapted to that end, which are not prohibited, but consist with the letter and spirit of the constitution, are constitutional."

The power of taxation, which is expressly granted, may, of course, be adopted as a means to carry into operation another power also expressly granted. But resort to the taxing power to effectuate an end which is not legitimate, not within the scope of the Constitution, is obviously inadmissible. . . .

Third. If the taxing power may not be used as the instrument to enforce a regulation of matters of state concern with respect to which the Congress has no authority to interfere, may it, as in the present case, be employed to raise the money necessary to purchase a compliance which the Congress is powerless to command? The Government asserts that whatever might be said against the validity of the plan, if compulsory, it is constitutionally sound because the end is accomplished by voluntary cooperation. There are two sufficient answers to the contention. The regulation is not in fact voluntary. The farmer, of course, may refuse to comply, but the price of such refusal is the loss of benefits. The amount offered is intended to be sufficient to exert pressure on him to agree to the proposed regulation. *The power to confer or withhold unlimited benefits is the power to coerce or destroy.* If the cotton grower elects not to accept the benefits, he will receive less for his crops; those who receive payments will be able to undersell him. The result may well be financial ruin. The coercive purpose and intent of the state is not obscured by the fact that it has not been perfectly successful. It is pointed out that, because there still remained a minority whom the rental and benefit payments were insufficient to induce to surrender their independence of action, the Congress has gone further and, in the Bankhead Cotton Act, used the taxing power in a more directly minatory fashion to compel submission. This progression only serves more fully to expose the coercive purpose of the so-called tax imposed by the present act. It is clear that the Department of Agriculture has properly described the plan as one to keep a non-cooperating minority in line. This is coercion by economic pressure. The asserted power of choice is illusory. . . .

But if the plan were one for purely voluntary cooperation it would stand no better so far as federal power is concerned. At best it is a scheme for purchasing with federal funds submission to federal regulation of a subject reserved to the states.

It is said that Congress has the undoubted right to appropriate money to executive officers for expenditure under contracts between the government and individuals; that much of the total expenditures is so made. But appropriations and expenditures under contracts for proper governmental purposes cannot justify contracts which are not within federal power. And contracts for the reduction of acreage and the control of production are outside the range of that power. An appropriation to be expended by the United States under contracts calling for a violation of a state law clearly would offend the Constitution. Is a statute less objectionable which authorizes expenditure of federal moneys to induce action in a field in which the United States has no power to intermeddle? The Congress cannot invade state jurisdiction to compel individual action; no more can it purchase such action.

We are referred to numerous types of federal appropriation which have been made in the past, and it is asserted no question has been raised as to their validity. We need not stop to examine or consider them. As was said in *Massachusetts* v. *Mellon* [1923]:

"As an examination of the acts of Congress will disclose, a large number of statutes appropriating or involving the expenditure of moneys for nonfederal purposes have been enacted and carried into effect."

As the opinion points out, such expenditures have not been challenged because no remedy was open for testing their constitutionality in the courts.

We are not here concerned with a conditional appropriation of money, nor with a provision that if certain conditions are not complied with the appropriation shall no longer be available. By the Agricultural Adjustment Act the amount of the tax is appropriated to be expended only in payment under contracts whereby the parties bind themselves to regulation by the federal government. There is an obvious difference between a statute stating the conditions upon which moneys shall be expended and one effective only upon assumption of a contractual obligation to submit to a regulation which otherwise could not be enforced. Many examples pointing the distinction might be cited. We are referred to appropriations in aid of education, and it is said that no one has doubted the power of Congress to stipulate the sort of education for which money shall be expended. But an appropriation to an educational institution which by its terms is to become available only if the beneficiary enters into a contract to teach doctrines subversive of the Constitution is clearly bad. An affirmance of the authority of Congress so to condition the expenditure of an appropriation would tend to nullify all constitutional limitations upon legislative power. . . .

Congress has no power to enforce its commands on the farmer to the ends sought by the Agricultural Adjustment Act. It must follow that it may not indirectly accomplish those ends by taxing and spending to purchase compliance. The Constitution and the entire plan of our government negative any such use of the power to tax and to spend as the act undertakes to authorize. It does not help to declare that local conditions throughout the nation have created a situation of national concern; for this is but to say that whenever there is a widespread similarity of local conditions, Congress may ignore constitutional limitations upon its own powers and usurp those reserved to the states. If, in lieu of compulsory regulation of subjects within the states' reserved jurisdiction, which is prohibited, the Congress could invoke the taxing and spending power as a means to accomplish the same end, clause 1 of § 8 of Article I would become the instrument for total subversion of the governmental powers reserved to the individual states.

If the act before us is a proper exercise of the federal taxing power, evidently the regulation of all industry throughout the United States may be accomplished by similar exercises of the same power. It would be possible to exact money from one branch of an industry and pay it to another branch in every field of activity which lies within the province of the states. The mere threat of such a procedure might well induce the surrender of rights and the compliance with federal regulation as the price of continuance in business. . . .

Until recently no suggestion of the existence of any such power in the Federal Government has been advanced. The expressions of the framers of the Constitution, the decisions of this court interpreting that instrument, and the writings of great commentators will be searched in vain for any suggestion that there exists in the clause under discussion or elsewhere in the Constitution, the authority whereby every provision and every fair implication from that instrument may be subverted, the independence of the individual states obliterated, and the United States converted into a central government exercising uncontrolled police power in every state of the Union, superseding all local control or regulation of the affairs or concerns of the states. . . .

Justice Stone dissented:

I think the judgment should be reversed.

The present stress of widely held and strongly expressed differences of opinion of the wisdom of the Agricultural Adjustment Act makes it important, in the interest of clear thinking and sound result, to emphasize at the outset certain propositions which should have controlling influence in determining the validity of the Act. They are:

1. The power of courts to declare a statute unconstitutional is subject to two guiding principles of decision which ought never to be absent from judicial consciousness. One is that courts are concerned only with the power to enact statutes, not with their wisdom. The other is that while unconstitutional exercise of power by the executive and legislative branches of the government is subject to judicial restraint, the only check upon our own exercise of power is our own sense of self-restraint. For the removal of unwise laws from the statute books appeal lies not to the courts but to the ballot and to the processes of democratic government.

2. The constitutional power of Congress to levy an excise tax upon the processing of agricultural products is not questioned. The present levy is held invalid, not for any want of power in Congress to lay such a tax to defray public expenditures, including those for the general welfare, but because the use to which its proceeds are put is disapproved.

3. As the present depressed state of agriculture is nation wide in its extent and effects, there is no basis for saying that the expenditure of public money in aid of farmers is not within the specifically granted power of Congress to levy taxes to "provide for the . . . general welfare." The opinion of the Court does not declare otherwise. . . .

Of the assertion that the payments to farmers are coercive, it is enough to say that no such contention is pressed by the taxpayer, and no such consequences were to be anticipated or appear to have resulted from the administration of the Act. The suggestion of coercion finds no support in the record or in any data showing the actual operation of the Act. Threat of loss, not hope of gain, is the essence of economic coercion. . . .

It is upon the contention that state power is infringed by purchased regulation of agricultural production that chief reliance is placed. It is insisted that, while the Constitution gives to Congress, in specific and unambiguous terms, the power to tax and spend, the power is subject to limitations which do not find their origin in any express provision of the Constitution and to which other expressly delegated powers are not subject. . . .

. . . The power of Congress to spend is inseparable from persuasion to action over which Congress [has authority] . . . That the governmental power of the purse is a great one is not now for the first time announced. . . . The suggestion that it must now be curtailed by judicial fiat because it may be abused by unwise use hardly rises to the dignity of argument. So may judicial power be abused. . . .

A tortured construction of the Constitution is not to be justified by recourse to extreme examples of reckless congressional spending which might occur if courts could not prevent—expenditures which, even if they could be thought to effect any national purpose, would be possible only by action of a legislature lost to all sense of public responsibility. Such suppositions are addressed to the mind accustomed to believe that it is the business of courts to sit in judgment on the wisdom of legislative action. Courts are not the only agency of government that must be assumed to have capacity to govern. Congress and the courts both unhappily may falter or be mistaken in the performance of their constitutional duty. But interpretation of our great charter of government which proceeds on any assumption that the responsibility for the preservation of our institutions is the exclusive concern of any one of the three branches of government, or that it alone can save them from destruction is far more likely, in the long run, "to obliterate the constituent members" of "an indestructible union of indestructible states" than the frank recognition that language, even of a constitution, may mean what it says: that the power to tax and spend includes the power to relieve a nationwide economic maladjustment by conditional gifts of money.

The New Deal plan for the sale of surplus power generated at Wilson Dam by the newly created Tennessee Valley Authority was upheld on national defense and traditional river navigation grounds in February 1936.[11] But by May another major New Deal program embodied in the Bituminous Coal Act of 1935 (Guffey Act) was struck down in *Carter* v. *Carter Coal Company.* Justice Sutherland delivered the majority opinion, supported by Justices Pierce Butler, James Clark McReynolds, Willis Van Devanter, and Owen Roberts. Chief Justice Hughes wrote a separate concurring opinion. Justice Benjamin Cardozo wrote a strong dissent, supported by Justices Holmes and Stone. The majority opinion contained an extremely narrow interpretation of the commerce clause.

CARTER v. CARTER COAL COMPANY
298 U. S. 238 (1936)

Justice Sutherland delivered the opinion of the Court:

The purposes of the "Bituminous Coal Conservation Act of 1935," involved in these suits, as declared by the title, are to stabilize the bituminous coal-mining industry and promote its interstate commerce; to provide for a drawback under certain conditions; to declare the production, distribution, and use of such coal to be affected with a national public interest; to conserve the national resources of such coal; to provide for the general welfare, and for other purposes. . . . The constitutional validity of the act is challenged in each of the suits. . . .

It is very clear that the "excise tax" is not imposed for revenue but exacted as a penalty to compel compliance with the regulatory provisions of the act. The whole purpose of the exaction is to coerce what is called an agreement—which, of course, it is not, for it lacks the essential element of consent. One who does a thing in order to avoid a monetary penalty does not agree; he yields to compulsion precisely the same as though he did so to avoid a term in jail.

The exaction here is a penalty and not a tax within the test laid down by the court in numerous cases. . . .

Certain recitals contained in the act plainly suggest that its makers were of opinion that its constitutionality could be sustained under some general federal power, thought to exist, apart from the specific grants of the Constitution. . . .

The ruling and firmly established principle is that the powers which the general government may exercise are only those specifically enumerated in the Constitution, and such implied powers as are necessary and proper to carry into effect the enumerated powers. Whether the end sought to be attained by an act of Congress is legitimate is wholly a matter of constitutional power and not at all of legislative discretion. Legislative congressional discretion begins with the choice of means and ends with the adoption of methods and details to carry the delegated powers into effect. The distinction between these two things—power and discretion—is not only very plain but very important. For while the powers are rigidly limited to the enumerations of the Constitution, the means which may be employed to carry the powers into effect are not restricted, save that they must be appropriate, plainly adapted to the end, and not prohibited by, but consistent with, the letter and spirit of the Constitution. . . . Thus, it may be said that to a constitutional end many ways are open; but to an end not within the terms of the Constitution, all ways are closed.

The proposition, often advanced and as often discredited, that the power of the federal government inherently extends to purposes affecting the nation as a whole with which the states severally cannot deal or cannot adequately deal, and the related notion that Congress, entirely apart from those powers delegated by the Constitution, may enact laws to promote the general welfare, have never been accepted but always definitely rejected by this court. . . .

Since the validity of the act depends upon whether it is a regulation of interstate commerce, the nature and extent of the power conferred upon Congress by the commerce clause becomes the determinative question in this branch of the case. . . .

We have seen that the word "commerce" is the equivalent of the phrase "intercourse for the purposes of trade." Plainly, the incidents leading up to and culminating in the mining of coal do not constitute such intercourse. The employment of men, the fixing of their wages, hours of labor and working conditions, the bargaining in respect of these things—whether carried on separately or collectively—each and all constitute intercourse for the purposes of production, not of trade. The latter is a thing apart from the relation of employer and employee, which in all producing occupations is purely local in character. Extraction of coal from the mine is the aim and the completed result of local activities. Commerce in the coal mined is not brought into being by force of these activities, but by negotiations, agreements, and circumstances entirely apart from production. Mining brings the subject matter of commerce into existence. Commerce disposes of it.

A consideration of the foregoing, and of many cases which might be added to those already cited, renders inescapable the conclusion that the effect of the labor provisions of the act, including those in respect of minimum wages, wage agreements, collective bargaining, and the Labor Board and its powers, primarily falls upon production and not upon commerce; and confirms the further resulting conclusion that production is a purely local activity. It follows that none of these essential antecedents of production constitutes a transaction in or forms any part of interstate commerce. . . . Everything which moves in interstate commerce has had a local origin. Without local production somewhere, interstate commerce, as now carried on, would practically disappear. Nevertheless, the local character of mining, of manufacturing and of crop growing is a fact, and remains a fact, whatever may be done with the products.

The government's contentions in defense of the labor provisions are really disposed of adversely by our decision in the *Schechter* case. . . . The only perceptible difference between that case and this is that in the *Schechter* case the federal power was asserted with respect to commodities which had come to rest after their interstate transportation; while here, the case deals with commodities at rest before interstate commerce has begun. That difference is without significance. The federal regulatory power ceases when interstate commercial intercourse ends; and, correlatively, the power does not attach until interstate commercial intercourse begins. There is no basis in law or reason for applying different rules to the two situations. No such distinction can be found in anything said in the *Schechter* case. On the contrary, the situations were recognized as akin. In the opinion, . . . after calling attention to the fact that if the commerce clause could be construed to reach transactions having an indirect effect upon interstate commerce the federal authority would embrace practically all the activities of the people, and the authority of the state over its domestic concerns would exist only by sufferance of the federal government, we said: "Indeed, on such a theory, even the development of the State's commercial facilities would be subject to federal control." And again, after pointing out that hours and wages have no direct relation to interstate commerce and that if the federal government had power to determine the wages and hours of employees in the internal commerce of a state because of their relation to cost and prices and their indirect effect upon interstate commerce, we said . . . : "All the processes of production and distribution that enter into cost could likewise be controlled. If the cost of doing an intrastate business is in itself the permitted object of federal control, the extent of the regulation of cost would be a question of discretion and not of power." A reading of the entire opinion makes clear, what we now declare, that the want of power on the part of the federal government is the same whether the wages, hours of service, and working conditions, and the bargaining about them, are related to production before interstate commerce has begun, or to sale and distribution after it has ended. . . .

Finally, we are brought to the price-fixing provisions of the code. The necessity of considering the question of their constitutionality will depend upon whether they are separable from the labor provisions so that they can stand independently. Section 15 of the act provides:

"If any provision of this Act, or the application thereof to any person or circumstances, is held invalid, the remainder of the Act and the application of such provisions to other persons or circumstances shall not be affected thereby." . . .

[T]he primary contemplation of the act is stabilization of the industry through the regulation of labor *and* the regulation of prices; for, since both were adopted, we must conclude that both were thought essential. The regulations of labor on the one hand and prices on the other furnish mutual aid and support; and their associated force—not one or the other but both combined—was deemed by Congress to be necessary to achieve the end sought. The statutory mandate for a code upheld by two legs at once suggests the improbability that Congress would have assented to a code supported by only one.

This seems plain enough; for Congress must have been conscious of the fact that elimination of the labor provisions from the act would seriously impair, if not destroy, the force and usefulness of the price provisions. The interdependence of wages and prices is manifest. Approximately two-thirds of the cost of producing a ton of coal is represented by wages. Fair

prices necessarily depend upon the cost of production; and since wages constitute so large a proportion of the cost, prices cannot be fixed with any proper relation to cost without taking into consideration this major element. If one of them becomes uncertain, uncertainty with respect to the other necessarily ensues. . . .

The conclusion is unavoidable that the price-fixing provisions of the code are so related to and dependent upon the labor provisions as conditions, considerations or compensations, as to make it clearly probable that the latter being held bad, the former would not have been passed. The fall of the latter, therefore, carries down with it the former. . . .

The devastating legal setbacks dealt the New Deal by the conservatives on the Supreme Court had been anticipated in part by several equally conservative federal district judges. Even before the NIRA had been struck down by the highest tribunal, federal district judges had issued numerous restraining orders curtailing governmental action under New Deal legislation. Several judges openly invoked their personal conservative political philosophy when issuing such orders. Thus, prior to the Schechter case, Merrill E. Otis, judge in the Western District of Missouri, stated flatly that the scope of the commerce clause did not permit congressional prohibition of "the movement in commerce of harmless things because forsooth, they are manufactured by child labor or by vegetarians, or by teetotalers." Charles I. Dawson, judge of the Western District of Kentucky, asserted that "the scheme of regulation of the strictly local affairs of the citizens of the country attempted to be set up and enforced under the Recovery Act (NIRA) has no place in our system of government."[12]

The prospects of widespread delay and interference with New Deal economic legislation by antagonistic federal district judges selected by conservative Presidents Harding, Coolidge, and Hoover was noted early by New Deal supporters in Congress. Senator Hugo L. Black of Alabama, for example, introduced a bill requiring direct appeals to the Supreme Court whenever a federal district court held an act of Congress unconstitutional. The Supreme Court was required to hear the case within ten days and prepare an opinion within a defined time span. Black thus sought to curtail lengthy dilatory actions. Chief Justice Hughes and Justices Brandeis and Van Devanter later appeared before a Senate Judiciary subcommittee to oppose the bill on the grounds that it would interfere with the work of the Supreme Court.[13] The bill was not acted upon, but other modifications of federal district court procedure, where constitutional questions were involved, were made subsequently.

President Roosevelt's initial reactions to the negative series of Supreme Court actions on New Deal legislation were critical of the Court but basically cautious. After the Schechter decision, he referred to the narrow interpretation of the commerce clause as one that would return the nation to "the horse-and-buggy age." The phrase appeared in many headlines, but Roosevelt was more directly

concerned about the basic issue of federalism: whether or not the national government could cope with national problems. Within the Roosevelt administration,
discussion of what to do about the Supreme Court was guarded. After all, the
three adverse decisions handed down on "Black Monday," May 27, 1935, were all
unanimous. Later, when the Court was narrowly divided, often striking down
legislation by a margin of one vote, more internal commentary took place. But
Roosevelt himself was patient and careful. He was well aware of the potential
dangers of adverse public reaction, as suggested in an early Gallup Poll. He had
observed the conflicts between Theodore Roosevelt's Progressives and the William
Howard Taft conservatives over recall of judges and judicial decisions in the early
years of his political career. Also he clearly did not want to endanger prospects for
continued Democratic control of both houses of Congress in the pending 1936
election. Nevertheless, the president was deeply interested in finding constitutionally acceptable and politically feasible means of persuading the Court to accept
the New Deal.[14]

The main thrust of the conservative Supreme Court's anti–New Deal decision
making had been to defeat efforts that would expand federal authority. But in
June of 1936 in *Morehead* v. *New York ex rel Tipaldo*, it reimposed strong limits on
state authority as well. By a five to four margin the Court struck down a state
minimum wage law for women as a violation of liberty of contract "protected by
the due process clause." Roosevelt spoke out, even though he had earlier remained
silent to avoid jeopardizing his legislative majority in the pending election:

> . . . It seems to be fairly clear, as a result of this decision and former decisions . . .
> that the 'no-man's-land' where no government—State or Federal—can function is
> being more clearly defined. . . .[15]

It has been often argued that the conservatives on the Court during the first
four years of the Roosevelt presidency were true products of the historical era in
which they had entered political life. Franklin D. Roosevelt was a product of virtually the same political generation, but he had drawn considerably different conclusions from the main developments of that era. Leuchtenburg indicated that
"Franklin Roosevelt began his political career at the time that his distant cousin,
Theodore, was assaulting the sanctity of the courts. . . ."[16] Franklin's response to
Tipaldo was virtually a restatement of Theodore Roosevelt's earlier contention
that the Supreme Court, through conservative decision making, had sought to
create a twilight zone in which corporations could exploit people and resources
free of federal and state authority.

Roosevelt resumed and maintained a discreet public silence on the problems
with the Court until after the election of 1936. Re-elected by a landslide and
maintaining a strong majority in the House and Senate, President Roosevelt
emerged from the election in a strong position. Shortly before he left for a South
American trip in November, he asked Attorney General Homer Cummings to
prepare a plan for dealing with the conservative Court. Cummings had a long
memorandum prepared in the Justice Department, but it was inconclusive. Cummings also discussed specific approaches with Professor Edward D. Corwin of

Princeton University. Corwin emphasized, among other things, a retirement proposal. The publication of Drew Pearson and Robert S. Allen's *The Nine Old Men*, a widely read journalistic critique of the Court, added interest to the retirement idea. Attorney General Cummings was still unsure of the precise form by which the principle could be applied. Cummings then discovered, in his own manuscript co-authored with Carl McFarland, *Federal Justice*, a recommendation that appeared to provide the desired solution. Ironically, it was a recommendation originally made by James C. McReynolds when he served as attorney general under President Woodrow Wilson in 1913. In his report for the fiscal year ending June 30, 1913, McReynolds urged that

> . . . Judges of the United States Courts, at the age of 70, after having served 10 years, may retire upon full pay. In the past, many judges have availed themselves of this privilege. Some, however, have remained upon the bench long beyond the time that they are able to adequately discharge their duties, and in consequence the administration of justice has suffered.
>
> . . . I suggest an act providing that when any judge of a Federal court below the Supreme Court fails to avail himself of the privilege of retiring now granted by law, that the President be required, with the advice and consent of the Senate, to appoint another judge, who would preside over the affairs of the court and have precedence over the older one. This will insure at all times the presence of a judge sufficiently active to discharge promptly and adequately the duties of the court. . . .[17]

Cummings concluded that the principle should be applied to Supreme Court members. By applying the age of 70 as the retirement age, President Roosevelt would be able to name six additional Court members, insuring a working majority in the event that the elderly conservatives decided to remain on the Court, as they were expected to do. By the end of 1936, the stage was set for a direct political and constitutional confrontation between the president and the Supreme Court. An important decision was made regarding strategy: The Court would not be attacked directly because of the conservatism of a majority of its current members. Instead, the advanced age, incapacity, and inefficiency of both the justices and the lower court judges of the federal judicial system were made the ostensible targets.[18] In February 1937, the proposal was unveiled in the form of a bill, and a tremendous battle for Congressional votes and public support began.

The conflict with the Court was intense. The judicial dismantling of New Deal legislation had been viewed as devastating by the architects of these programs. But the Court had, interestingly enough, reserved its negative responses entirely for the domestic efforts of the New Deal.

The Court and foreign affairs

While dismantling major portions of the New Deal domestic program, the Court strongly supported executive power in foreign affairs. In *United States* v. *Curtiss-Wright Export Corporation*, Congress and the president supported a concept of peacekeeping that has been virtually abandoned since World War II. In the postwar era, it is generally assumed that peace is somehow maintained by supplying sufficient arms and sophisticated weapons to potential adversaries to deter aggression. Such arms sales are authorized by the government. In the early 1930s, it was assumed that the best way to deter conflict was to prohibit the sale of arms and new equipment in order to render conflict difficult and generally unlikely. In 1934, in accordance with that assumption, Congress authorized the President to impose an embargo on arms sales and shipments to countries at war in the Chaco (between Paraguay and Bolivia) if he found facts to indicate that this embargo "may contribute in the reestablishment of peace between these countries." Violation of such an embargo was made a crime. The Curtiss-Wright Export Company committed such a violation. Justice Sutherland wrote for a seven-man majority. Justice McReynolds dissented and Justice Stone abstained.

UNITED STATES v. CURTISS-WRIGHT EXPORT CORPORATION
299 U. S. 304 (1936)

Justice Sutherland delivered the opinion of the Court:

On January 27, 1936, an indictment was returned in the court below, the first count of which charges that appellees, beginning with the 29th day of May, 1934, conspired to sell in the United States certain arms of war, namely, fifteen machine guns, to Bolivia, a country then engaged in armed conflict in the Chaco, in violation of the Joint Resolution of Congress approved May 28, 1934, and the provisions of a proclamation issued on the same day by the President of the United States pursuant to authority conferred by § 1 of the resolution. In pursuance of the conspiracy, the commission of certain overt acts was alleged, details of which need not be stated. The Joint Resolution follows:

"Resolved by the Senate and House of Representatives of the United States of America in Congress assembled, That if the President finds that the prohibition of the sale of arms and munitions of war in the United States to those countries now engaged in armed conflict in the Chaco may contribute to the reestablishment of peace between those countries, and if after consultation with the governments of other American Republics and with their cooperation, as well as that of such other governments as he may deem necessary, he makes proclamation to that effect, it shall be unlawful to sell, except under such limitations and exceptions as the President prescribes, any arms or munitions of war in any place in the United States to the countries now engaged in that armed conflict, or to any person, company, or association acting in the interest of either country, until otherwise ordered by the President or by Congress.

"Sec. 2. Whoever sells any arms or munitions of war in violation of section 1 shall, on conviction, be punished by a fine not exceeding $10,000 or by imprisonment not exceeding two years, or both." . . .

Appellees severally demurred to the first count of the indictment on the grounds that (1) it did not charge facts sufficient to show the commission by appellees of any offense against any law of the United States;

. . . The points urged in support of the demurrers were, first, that the joint resolution effects an invalid delegation of legislative power to the Executive; second, that the joint resolution never became effective because of the failure of the President to find essential jurisdictional facts; . . .

The court below sustained the demurrers upon the first point, but overruled them on the second and third points. . . . The government appealed to this court under the provisions of the Criminal Appeals Act of March 2, 1907. . . . That act authorizes the United States to appeal from a district court direct to this court in criminal cases where, among other things, the decision sustaining a demurrer to the indictment or any count thereof is based upon the invalidity or construction of the statute upon which the indictment is founded.

First. It is contended that by the Joint Resolution the going into effect and continued operation of the resolution was conditioned (a) upon the President's judgment as to its beneficial effect upon the reestablishment of peace between the countries engaged in armed conflict in the Chaco; (b) upon the making of a proclamation, which was left to his unfettered discretion, thus constituting an attempted substitution of the President's will for that of Congress; (c) upon the making of a proclamation putting an end to the operation of the resolution, which again was left to the President's unfettered discretion; and (d) further, that the extent of its operation in particular cases was subject to limitation and exception by the President, controlled by no standard. In each of these particulars, appellees urge that Congress abdicated its essential functions and delegated them to the Executive.

Whether, if the Joint Resolution had related solely to internal affairs, it would be open to the challenge that it constituted an unlawful delegation of legislative power to the Executive, we find it unnecessary to determine. The whole aim of the resolution is to affect a situation entirely external to the United States, and falling within the category of foreign affairs. The determination which we are called to make, therefore, is whether the Joint Resolution, as applied to that situation, is vulnerable to attack under the rule that forbids a delegation of the lawmaking power. In other words, assuming (but not deciding) that the challenged delegation, if it were confined to internal affairs, would be invalid, may it nevertheless be sustained on the ground that its exclusive aim is to afford a remedy for a hurtful condition within foreign territory?

It will contribute to the elucidation of the question if we first consider the differences between the powers of the Federal government in respect of foreign or external affairs and those in respect of domestic or internal affairs. That there are differences between them, and that these differences are fundamental, may not be doubted.

The two classes of powers are different, both in respect of their origin and their nature. The broad statement that the Federal government can exercise no powers except those specifically enumerated in the Constitution, and such implied powers as are necessary and proper to carry into effect the enumerated powers, is categorically true only in respect of our internal affairs. In that field, the primary purpose of the Constitution was to carve from the general mass of legislative powers *then possessed by the states* such portions as it was thought desirable to vest in the Federal government, leaving those not included in the enumeration still in the states. Carter v. Carter Coal Co. [1936]. That this doctrine applies only to powers which the states had is self-evident. And since the states severally never possessed international powers, such powers could not have been carved from the mass of state powers but obviously were transmitted to the United States from some other source. During the colonial period, those powers were possessed exclusively by and were entirely under the control of the Crown. By the Declaration of Independence, "the Representatives of the United States of America" declared the United [not the several] Colonies to be free and independent states, and as such to have "full Power to levy War, conclude Peace, contract Alliances, establish Commerce and to do all other Acts and Things which Independent States may of right do."

As a result of the separation from Great Britain by the colonies, acting as a unit, the powers of external sovereignty passed from the Crown not to the colonies severally, but to the colonies in their collective and corporate capacity as the United States of America. Even before the Declaration, the colonies were a unit in foreign affairs, acting through a common agency— namely, the Continental Congress, composed of delegates from the thirteen colonies. That agency exercised the powers of war and peace, raised an army, created a navy, and finally adopted the Declaration of Independence. Rulers come and go; governments end and forms of government change; but sovereignty survives. A political society cannot endure without a supreme will somewhere. Sovereignty is never held in suspense. When, therefore, the external sovereignty of Great Britain in respect of the colonies ceased, it immediately passed to the Union. . . . That fact was given practical application almost at once. The treaty of peace, made on September 3, 1783, was concluded between his Britannic Majesty and the "United States of America." . . .

The Union existed before the Constitution, which was ordained and established among other things to form "a more perfect Union." Prior to that event, it is clear that the Union, declared by the Articles of Confederation to be "perpetual," was the sole possessor of external sovereignty and in the Union it remained without change save in so far as the Constitution in express terms qualified its exercise. . . .

It results that the investment of the Federal government with the powers of external sovereignty did not depend upon the affirmative grants of the Constitution. The powers to declare and wage war, to conclude peace, to make treaties, to maintain diplomatic relations with other sovereignties, if they had never been mentioned in the Constitution, would have vested in the Federal government as necessary concomitants of nationality. Neither the Constitution nor the laws passed in pursuance of it have any force in foreign territory unless in respect of our own citizens . . . ; and operations of the nation in such territory must be governed by treaties, international understandings and compacts, and the principles of international law. As a member of the family of nations, the right and power of the United States in that field are equal to the right and power of the other members of the international family. Otherwise, the United States is not completely sovereign. The power to acquire territory by discovery and occupation (Jones v. United States [1890]), the power to expel undesirable aliens (Fong Yue Ting v. United States [1893]), the power to make such international agreements as do not constitute treaties in the constitutional sense (Altman & Co. v. United States [1912] . . .), none of which is expressly affirmed by the Constitution, nevertheless exist as inherently inseparable from the conception of nationality. This the court recognized, and in each of the cases cited found the warrant for its conclusions not in the provisions of the Constitution, but in the law of nations. . . .

Not only, as we have shown, is the Federal power over external affairs in origin and essential character different from that over internal affairs, but participation in the exercise of the power is significantly limited. In this vast external realm, with its important, complicated, delicate and manifold problems, the President alone has the power to speak or listen as a representative of the nation. He *makes* treaties with the advice and consent of the Senate; but he alone negotiates. Into the field of negotiation the Senate cannot intrude; and Congress itself is powerless to invade it. . . .

It is important to bear in mind that we are here dealing not alone with an authority vested in the President by an exertion of legislative power, but with such an authority plus the very delicate, plenary and exclusive power of the President as the sole organ of the Federal government in the field of international relations—a power which does not require as a basis for its exercise an act of Congress, but which, of course, like every other governmental power, must be exercised in subordination to the applicable provisions of the Constitution. It is quite apparent that if, in the maintenance of our international relations, embarrassment—perhaps serious embarrassment—is to be avoided and success for our aims achieved, congressional legislation which is to be made effective through negotiation and inquiry within the international field must often accord to the President a degree of discretion and freedom from statutory restriction which would not be admissible were domestic affairs alone involved. Moreover, he, not Congress, has the better opportunity of knowing the conditions which prevail in foreign countries, and especially is this true in time of war. He has his confidential sources of information. He has his agents in the form of diplomatic, consular and other officials. Secrecy in respect of information gathered by them may be highly necessary, and the premature disclosure of it productive of harmful results. . . .

In the light of the foregoing observations, it is evident that this court should not be in haste to apply a general rule which will have the effect of condemning legislation like that under review as constituting an unlawful delegation of legislative power. The principles which justify such legislation find overwhelming support in the unbroken legislative practice which has prevailed almost from the inception of the national government to the present day. . . .

Practically every volume of the United States Statutes contains one or more acts or joint resolutions of Congress authorizing action by the President in respect of subjects affecting foreign relations, which either leave the exercise of the power to his unrestricted judgment, or provide a standard far more general than that which has always been considered requisite with regard to domestic affairs. . . .

. . . A legislative practice such as we have here, evidenced not by only occasional instances, but marked by the movement of a steady stream for a century and a half of time, goes a long way in the direction of proving the presence of unassailable ground for the constitutionality of the practice, to be found in the origin and history of the power involved, or in its nature, or in both combined. . . .

We deem it unnecessary to consider, seriatim, the several clauses which are said to evidence the unconstitutionality of the Joint Resolution as involving an unlawful delegation of legislative power. It is enough to summarize by saying that, both upon principle and in accordance with precedent, we conclude there is sufficient warrant for the broad discretion vested in the President to determine whether the enforcement of the statute will have a beneficial effect upon the reestablishment of peace in the affected countries; whether he shall make proclamation to bring the resolution into operation; whether and when the resolution shall cease to operate and to make proclamation accordingly; and to prescribe limitations and exceptions to which the enforcement of the resolution shall be subject.

Second. The second point raised by the demurrer was that the Joint Resolution never became effective because the President failed to find essential jurisdictional facts. . . .

1. The Executive proclamation recites, "I have found that the prohibition of the sale of arms and munitions of war in the United States to those countries now engaged in armed conflict in the Chaco may contribute to the reestablishment of peace between those countries, and that I have consulted with the governments

of other American Republics and have been assured of the cooperation of such governments as I have deemed necessary as contemplated by the said joint resolution." This finding satisfies every requirement of the Joint Resolution. There is no suggestion that the resolution is fatally uncertain or indefinite; and a finding which follows its language, as this finding does, cannot well be challenged as insufficient. . . .

The judgment of the court below must be reversed and the cause remanded for further proceedings in accordance with the foregoing opinion.

Reversed.

The Court's decision in *United States* v. *Belmont* reestablished the principle that a presidential executive agreement has the same status as a treaty. President Roosevelt recognized the government of the Soviet Union in 1933, received the Soviet ambassador and, in turn, sent an American ambassador to Russia. Following this act of recognition, claims and counterclaims between the nations dating from the October Revolution of 1918 were negotiated by international compact called the *Litvinov assignments*. The president's executive agreement to such compact was not subject to Senate approval as required for a treaty. Money and property held in Belmont's Bank in New York City had been part of the assets of the Petrograd Metal Works when the company was confiscated by the Soviet government when it nationalized such companies in 1918. The Litvinov assignments required that Soviet assets be assigned to the government of the United States. Belmont brought action successfully in a federal district court on the ground that the act of nationalization was merely confiscation and took property in violation of New York State and federal policy. Justice Sutherland, who was in the forefront of opponents to President Roosevelt's domestic program, wrote the majority opinion, in which Justices Stone, Brandeis, and Cardozo concurred. Sutherland reversed the district court decision.

UNITED STATES v. BELMONT
301 U. S. 324 (1937)

Justice Sutherland delivered the opinion of the Court:

. . . *First.* We do not pause to inquire whether in fact there was any policy of the State of New York to be infringed, since we are of opinion that no state policy can prevail against the international compact here involved.

This court has held . . . that every sovereign state must recognize the independence of every other sovereign state: and that the courts of one will not sit in judgment upon the acts of the government of another, done within its own territory.

. . . This court held that the conduct of foreign relations was committed by the Constitution to the political departments of the government, and the propriety of what may be done in the exercise of this political power was not subject to judicial inquiry or decision; that who is the sovereign of a territory is not a judicial question, but one the determination of which by the political departments conclusively binds the courts; and that recognition by these departments is retroactive and validates all actions and conduct of the government so recognized from the commencement of its existence. . . .

We take judicial notice of the fact that coincident with the assignment set forth in the complaint, the President recognized the Soviet government, and normal diplomatic relations were established between that government and the government of the United States, followed by an exchange of ambassadors. The effect of this was to validate, so far as this country is concerned, all acts of the Soviet government here involved from the commencement of its existence. The recognition, establishment of diplomatic relations, the assignment, and agreements with respect thereto, were all parts of one transaction, resulting in an international compact between the two governments. That the negotiations, acceptance of the assignment and agreements and understandings in respect thereof were within the competence of the President may not be doubted. Governmental power over internal affairs is distributed between the national government and the several states. Governmental power over external affairs is not distributed, but is vested exclusively in the national government. And in respect of what was done here, the Executive had authority to speak as the sole organ of that government. The assignment and the agreements in connection therewith did not, as in the case of treaties, as that term is used in the treaty making clause of the constitution (Article II, § 2), require the advice and consent of the Senate.

A treaty signifies "a compact made between two or more independent nations, with a view to the public welfare." . . . But an international compact, as this was, is not always a treaty which requires the participation of the Senate. There are many such compacts, of which a protocol, a modus vivendi, a postal convention, and agreements like that now under consideration are illustrations. . . . The distinction was pointed out by this court in the Altman case which arose under § 3 of the Tariff Act of 1897, authorizing the President to conclude commercial agreements with foreign countries in certain specified matters. We held that although this might not be a treaty requiring ratification by the Senate, it was a compact negotiated and proclaimed under the authority of the President, and as such was a "treaty" within the meaning of the Circuit Court of Appeals Act, the construction of which might be reviewed upon direct appeal to this court.

Plainly, the external powers of the United States are to be exercised without regard to state laws or policies. The supremacy of a treaty in this respect has been recognized from the beginning. Mr. Madison, in the Virginia Convention, said that if a treaty does not supersede existing state laws, as far as they contravene its operation, the treaty would be ineffective. "To counteract it by the supremacy of the state laws, would bring on the Union the just charge of national perfidy, and involve us in war." . . . And while this rule in respect of treaties is established by the express language of clause 2, Art. VI, of the Constitution, the

same rule would result in the case of all international compacts and agreements from the very fact that complete power over international affairs is in the national government and is not and cannot be subject to any curtailment or interference on the part of the several states. . . . In respect of all international negotiations and compacts, and in respect of our foreign relations generally, state lines disappear. As to such purposes the state of New York does not exist. Within the field of its powers, whatever the United States rightfully undertakes, it necessarily has warrant to consummate. And when judicial authority is invoked in aid of such consummation, state constitutions, state laws, and state policies are irrelevant to the inquiry and decision. It is inconceivable that any of them can be interposed as an obstacle to the effective operation of a federal constitutional power. . . .

Second. The public policy of the United States relied upon as a bar to the action is that declared by the Constitution, namely, that private property shall not be taken without just compensation. But the answer is that our Constitution, laws, and policies have no extraterritorial operation, unless in respect of our own citizens. . . . What another country has done in the way of taking over property of its nationals, and especially of its corporations, is not a matter for judicial consideration here. Such nationals must look to their own government for any redress to which they may be entitled. So far as the record shows, only the rights of the Russian corporation have been affected by what has been done; and it will be time enough to consider the rights of our nationals when, if ever, by proper judicial proceeding, it shall be made to appear that they are so affected as to entitle them to judicial relief. The substantive right to the moneys, as now disclosed, became vested in the Soviet Government as the successor to the corporation; and this right that government has passed to the United States. It does not appear that respondents have any interest in the matter beyond that of a custodian. Thus far no question under the Fifth Amendment is involved. . . .

"The switch in time that saved nine"

On the domestic front, many observers felt that the moment the president openly mounted his drive for congressional approval of his court-packing plan, he committed a series of serious political blunders that doomed any chance of its acceptance. His plan was designed to obtain a majority committed to the New Deal programs by increasing the size of the Supreme Court, ostensibly in order to permit appointment of an additional justice where a sitting justice had failed to retire either after ten years service or after attainment of 70.5 years of age.

Opposition to this plan was virtually inevitable because of the constitutional commitment to tenure on good behavior. Justices and judges chosen by presidents attuned to the principles of an earlier political generation often find it difficult to adjust to or understand the novel experiences of newer political generations. Ultimately, despite wide public support for his program and his leadership, Roosevelt was forced to withdraw the plan. But the basic reason for its development, the intransigence of a majority of the justices, also disappeared, coincidentally, after the New Deal landslide of 1936. Irreverently called "the switch in time that saved nine," a couple of Supreme Court members, Justice Roberts and Chief Justice Hughes, modified their opposition to New Deal legislation. Constitutional historians Kelley and Harbison described the turnabout by the court as "the most abrupt change of face in its entire history, (accepting) all the major constitutional postulates underlying the New Deal."[19] Roosevelt's court-packing plan failed, but the ideological battle was won in the Court.

Among the highlights of this change was *West Coast Hotel Company* v. *Parrish* in which the Court upheld a Washington minimum wage law similar to those it previously had held invalid. Chief Justice Hughes and Justice Roberts joined the earlier dissenters. Hughes wrote the majority opinion and Justice Sutherland wrote a bitter dissent, criticizing the idea that "the meaning of the Constitution changes with the ebb and flow of economic events."

WEST COAST HOTEL COMPANY v. PARRISH
300 U. S. 379 (1937)

*Chief Justice Hughes
delivered the opinion of the court:*

This case presents the question of the constitutional validity of the minimum wage law of the State of Washington.

The Act, entitled "Minimum Wages for Women," authorizes the fixing of minimum wages for women and minors. . . . It provides:

"SECTION 1. The welfare of the State of Washington demands that women and minors be protected from conditions of labor which have a pernicious effect on their health and morals. The State of Washington, therefore, exercising herein its police and sovereign power declares that inadequate wages and unsanitary conditions of labor exert such pernicious effect.

"SEC. 2. It shall be unlawful to employ women or minors in any industry or occupation within the State of Washington under conditions of labor detrimental to their health or morals; and it shall be unlawful to employ women workers in any industry within the State of Washington at wages which are not adequate for their maintenance.

"SEC. 3. There is hereby created a commission to be known as the 'Industrial Welfare Commission' for the State of Washington, to establish such standards of wages and conditions of labor for women and minors employed within the State of Washington, as shall be held hereunder to be reasonable and not detrimental to health and morals, and which shall be sufficient for the decent maintenance of women."

Further provisions required the Commission to ascertain the wages and conditions of labor of women and minors within the State. . . .

The appellant conducts a hotel. The appellee Elsie Parrish was employed as a chambermaid and (with her husband) brought this suit to recover the difference between the wages paid her and the minimum wage fixed pursuant to the state law. The minimum wage was $14.50 per week of 48 hours. The appellant challenged the act as repugnant to the due process clause of the Fourteenth Amendment of the Constitution of the United States. The Supreme Court of the State, reversing the trial court, sustained the statute and directed judgment for the plaintiffs. . . .

The appellant relies upon the decision of this Court in *Adkins v. Children's Hospital,* . . . which held invalid the District of Columbia Minimum Wage Act, which was attacked under the due process clause of the Fifth Amendment. . . .

The principle which must control our decision is not in doubt. The constitutional provision invoked is the due process clause of the Fourteenth Amendment governing the States, as the due process clause invoked in the *Adkins* case governed Congress. In each case the violation alleged by those attacking minimum wage regulation for women is deprivation of freedom of contract. What is this freedom? The Constitution does not speak of freedom of contract. It speaks of liberty and prohibits the deprivation of liberty without due process of law. In prohibiting that deprivation the Constitution does not recognize an absolute and uncontrollable liberty. Liberty in each of its phases has its history and connotation. But the liberty safeguarded is liberty in a social organization which requires the protection of law against the evils which menace the health, safety, morals and welfare of the people. Liberty under the Constitution is thus necessarily subject to the restraints of due process, and regulation which is reasonable in relation to its subject and is adopted in the interests of the community is due process.

This essential limitation of liberty in general governs freedom of contract in particular. More than twenty-five years ago we set forth the applicable principle in these words, after referring to the cases where the liberty guaranteed by the Fourteenth Amendment had been broadly described:

"But it was recognized in the cases cited, as in many others, that freedom of contract is a qualified and not an absolute right. There is no absolute freedom to do as one wills or to contract as one chooses. The guaranty of liberty does not withdraw from legislative supervision that wide department of activity which consists of the making of contracts, or deny to government the power to provide restrictive safeguards. Liberty implies the absence of arbitrary restraint, not immunity from reasonable regulations and prohibitions imposed in the interests of the community." . . .

This power under the constitution to restrict freedom of contract has had many illustrations. That it may be exercised in the public interest with respect to contracts between employer and employee is undeniable. . . .

The point that has been strongly stressed that adult employees should be deemed competent to make their own contracts was decisively met nearly forty years ago in *Holden* v. *Hardy*, . . . where we pointed out the inequality in the footing of the parties. We said . . . :

"The legislature has also recognized the fact, which the experience of legislators in many States has corroborated, that the proprietors of these establishments and their operatives do not stand upon an equality, and that their interests are, to a certain extent, conflicting. The former naturally desire to obtain as much labor as possible from their employes, while the latter are often induced by the fear of discharge to conform to regulations which their judgment, fairly exercised, would pronounce to be detrimental to their health or strength. In other words, the proprietors lay down the rules and the laborers are practically constrained to obey them. In such cases self-interest is often an unsafe guide, and the legislature may properly interpose its authority."

And we added that the fact "that both parties are of full age and competent to contract does not necessarily deprive the State of the power to interfere where the parties do not stand upon an equality, or where the public health demands that one party to the contract shall be protected against himself." . . .

It is manifest that this established principle is peculiarly applicable in relation to the employment of women in whose protection the State has a special interest. That phase of the subject received elaborate consideration in *Muller* v. *Oregon*, . . . where the constitutional authority of the State to limit the working hours of women was sustained. We emphasized the consideration that "women's physical structure and the performance of maternal functions place her at a disadvantage in the struggle for subsistence" and that her physical well being "becomes an object of public interest and care in order to preserve the strength and vigor of the race." We emphasized the need of protecting women against oppression despite her possession of contractual rights. We said that

"though limitations upon personal and contractual rights may be removed by legislation, there is that in her disposition and habits of life which will operate against a full assertion of those rights. She will still be where some legislation to protect her seems necessary to secure a real equality of right."

Hence she was "properly placed in a class by herself, and legislation designed for her protection may be sustained even when like legislation is not necessary for men and could not be sustained." We concluded that the limitations which the statute there in question "placed upon her contractual powers, upon her right to agree with her employer as to the time she shall labor" were "not imposed solely for her benefit, but also largely for the benefit of all." . . .

This array of precedents and the principles they applied were thought by the dissenting Justices in the *Adkins* case to demand that the minimum wage statute be sustained. The validity of the distinction made by the Court between a minimum wage and a maximum of hours in limiting liberty of contract was especially challenged. . . . That challenge persists and is without any satisfactory answer. As Chief Justice Taft observed: "In absolute freedom of contract the one term is as important as the other, for both enter equally into the consideration given and received, a restriction as to the one is not greater in essence than the other and is of the same kind. One is the multiplier and the other the multiplicand." And Mr. Justice Holmes, while recognizing that "the distinctions of the law are distinctions of degree," could "perceive no difference in the kind or degree of interference with liberty, the only matter with which we have any concern, between the one case and the other. The bargain is equally affected whichever half you regulate." . . .

The minimum wage to be paid under the Washington statute is fixed after full consideration by representatives of employers, employees and the public. It may be assumed that the minimum wage is fixed in consideration of the services that are performed in the particular occupations under normal conditions. Provision is made for special licenses at less wages in the case of women who are incapable of full service. The statement of Mr. Justice Holmes in the *Adkins* case is pertinent: "This statute does not compel anybody to pay anything. It simply forbids employment at rates below those fixed as the minimum requirement of health and right living. It is safe to assume that women will not be employed at even the lowest wages allowed unless they earn them, or unless the employer's business can sustain the burden. In short the law in its character and operation is like hundreds of so-called police laws that have been upheld." . . . And Chief Justice Taft forcibly pointed out the consideration which is basic in a statute of this character: "Legislatures which adopt a requirement of maximum hours or minimum wages may be presumed to believe that when sweating employers are prevented from paying unduly low wages by positive law they will continue their business, abating that part of their profits, which were wrung from the necessities of their employees, and will concede the better terms required by the law; and that while in individual cases hardship may result, the restriction will enure to the benefit of the general class of employees in whose interest the law is passed and so to that of the community at large." . . .

We think that the views thus expressed are sound and that the decision in the *Adkins* case was a departure from the true application of the principles governing the regulation by the State of the relation of employer and employed. . . .

With full recognition of the earnestness and vigor which characterize the prevailing opinion in the *Adkins* case, we find it impossible to reconcile that ruling with these well considered declarations. What can be closer to the public interest than the health of women and their protection from unscrupulous and overreaching employers? And if the protection of women is a legitimate end of the exercise of state power, how can it be said that the requirement of the payment of a minimum wage fairly fixed in order to meet the very necessities of existence is not an admissible means to that end? The legislature of the State was clearly entitled to consider the situation of women in employment, the fact that they are in the class receiving the least pay, that their bargaining power is relatively weak, and that they are the ready victims of those who would take advantage of their necessitous circumstances. The legislature was entitled to adopt measures to reduce the evils of the "sweating system," the exploiting of workers at wages so low as to be insufficient to meet the bare cost of living, thus making their very helplessness the occasion of a most injurious competition. The legislature had the right to consider that its minimum wage requirements would be an important aid in carrying out its policy of protection. The adoption of similar requirements by many States evidences a deepseated conviction both as to the presence of the evil and as to the means adapted to check it. Legislative response to that conviction cannot be regarded as arbitrary or capricious, and that is all we have to decide. Even if the wisdom of the policy be regarded as debatable and its effects uncertain, still the legislature is entitled to its judgment.

There is an additional and compelling consideration which recent economic experience has brought into a strong light. The exploitation of a class of workers who are in an unequal position with respect to bargaining power and are thus relatively defenceless against the denial of a living wage is not only detrimental to their health and well being but casts a direct burden for their support upon the community. What these workers lose in wages the taxpayers are called upon to pay. The bare cost of living must be met. We may take judicial notice of the unparalleled demands for relief which arose during the recent period of depression and still continue to an alarming extent despite the degree of economic recovery which has been achieved. It is unnecessary to cite official statistics to establish what is of common knowledge through the length and breadth of the land. While in the instant case no factual brief has been presented, there is no reason to doubt that the State of Washington has encountered the same social problem that is present elsewhere. The community is not bound to provide what is in effect a subsidy for unconscionable employers. The community may direct its law-making power to correct the abuse which springs from their selfish disregard of the public interest. The argument that the legislation in question constitutes an arbitrary discrimination, because it does not extend to men, is unavailing. This Court has frequently held that the legislative authority, acting within its proper field, is not bound to extend its regulation to all cases which it might possibly reach. The legislature "is free to recognize degrees of harm and it may confine its restrictions to those classes of cases where the need is deemed to be clearest." If "the law presumably hits the evil where it is most felt, it is not to be overthrown because there are other instances to which it might have been applied." There is no "doctrinaire requirement" that the legislation should be couched in all embracing terms. . . .

Our conclusion is that the case of *Adkins* v. *Children's Hospital* . . . should be, and it is, overruled. . . .

Justice Sutherland dissented:

Mr. Justice Van Devanter, Mr. Justice McReynolds, Mr. Justice Butler and I think the judgment of the court below should be reversed. . . .

The suggestion that the only check upon the exercise of the judicial power, when properly invoked, to declare a constitutional right superior to an unconstitutional statute is the judge's own faculty of self-restraint, is both ill considered and mischievous. Self-restraint belongs in the domain of will and not of judgment. The check upon the judge is that imposed by his oath of office, by the Constitution and by his own conscientious and informed convictions; and since he has the duty to make up his own mind and adjudge accordingly, it is hard to see how there could be any other restraint. This court acts as a unit. It cannot act in any other way; and the majority (whether a bare majority or a majority of all but one of its members), therefore, establishes the controlling rule as the decision of the court, binding, so long as it remains unchanged, equally upon those who disagree and upon those who subscribe to it. Otherwise, orderly administration of justice would cease. But it is the right of those in the minority to disagree, and sometimes, in matters of grave importance, their imperative duty to voice their disagreement at such length as the occasion demands—always, of course, in terms which, however forceful, do not offend the proprieties or impugn the good faith of those who think otherwise.

It is urged that the question involved should now receive fresh consideration, among other reasons, because of "the economic conditions which have supervened"; but the meaning of the Constitution does not change with the ebb and flow of economic events. We frequently are told in more general words that the Constitution must be construed in the light of the present. If by that it is meant that the Constitution is made up of living words that apply to every new condition which they include, the statement is quite true. But to say, if that be intended, that the words of the Constitution mean today what they did not mean when written—that is, that they do not apply to a situation now to which they would have applied then—is to rob that instrument of the essential element which continues it in force as the people have made it until they, and not their official agents, have made it otherwise. . . .

The judicial function is that of interpretation; it does not include the power of amendment under the guise of interpretation. To miss the point of difference between the two is to miss all that the phrase "supreme law of the land" stands for and to convert what was intended as inescapable and enduring mandates into mere moral reflections.

If the Constitution, intelligently and reasonably construed in the light of these principles, stands in the way of desirable legislation, the blame must rest upon that instrument, and not upon the court for enforcing it according to its terms. The remedy in that situation—and the only true remedy—is to amend the Constitution. . . .

This decision was one of four handed down on March 29, 1937, that reversed previous conservative positions concerning state or federal authority. In addition to the Parrish decision, the court narrowly upheld the revised Frazier-Lemke farm bankruptcy act in *Wright* v. *Vinton Branch*[20] and an amended railroad labor act in *Virginia Railroad Company* v. *System Federation.*[21] But the most important decision was *National Labor Relations Board* v. *Jones and Laughlin Steel Corporation.* In this instance, the use of the commerce power as a positive source of Congressional regulatory authority in labor-management relations was upheld. Politically, the success of the National Labor Relations Act brought long-term Democratic electoral advantages. But the immediate impact of these four decisions was to undercut, rather effectively, the already faltering effort of the Roosevelt administration to secure passage of its court-packing bill. To be sure, President Roosevelt's uncharacteristically poor political strategy compounded the difficulty. The indirectness of his statement of purpose, his failure to lay groundwork adequately among both congressional leaders and liberal allies all contributed to his defeat. Conversely,

Roosevelt's legislative opponents, the Republicans and conservative Southern Democrats, rejuvenated the conservative coalition ostensibly to save the Court but ultimately to contain or defeat New Deal legislative efforts.[22] The most effective strategist opposing court-packing may well have been the chief justice himself. Charles Evans Hughes not only employed excellent timing in the announcement of the four decisions, but he prepared a crucial letter that was read to the Senate Judiciary Committee on March 22, 1937 (one week before the four modifying decisions were handed down). The letter rebutted point by point the key assumptions of the court-packing bill, concluding that an enlargement in the size of the Supreme Court would decrease rather than increase efficiency.[23] The testimony of Hughes and Brandeis regarding the manageability of the case load also was important.

In the most important of the four decisions handed down on March 29, Chief Justice Hughes wrote the majority opinion. Justice McReynolds wrote a strong dissent supported by Justices Van Devanter, Sutherland, and Butler.

NATIONAL LABOR RELATIONS BOARD v. JONES & LAUGHLIN STEEL CORPORATION
301 U. S. 1 (1937)

Chief Justice Hughes delivered the opinion of the Court:

First. The scope of the Act.—The Act is challenged in its entirety as an attempt to regulate all industry, thus invading the reserved powers of the States over their local concerns. It is asserted that the references in the Act to interstate and foreign commerce are colorable at best; that the Act is not a true regulation of such commerce or of matters which directly affect it but on the contrary has the fundamental object of placing under the compulsory supervision of the federal government all industrial labor relations within the nation. The argument seeks support in the broad words of the preamble . . . and in the sweep of the provisions of the Act, and it is further insisted that its legislative history shows an essential universal purpose in the light of which its scope cannot be limited by either construction or by the application of the separability clause.

If this conception of terms, intent and consequent inseparability were sound, the Act would necessarily fall by reason of the limitation upon the federal power which inheres in the constitutional grant, as well as because of the explicit reservation of the Tenth Amendment. *Schechter Corp. v. United States,* . . . The authority of the federal government may not be pushed to such an extreme as to destroy the distinction, which the commerce clause itself establishes, between commerce "among the several States" and the internal concerns of a State. That distinction between what is national and what is local in the activities of commerce is vital to the maintenance of our federal system. . . .

We think it clear that the National Labor Relations Act may be construed so as to operate within the sphere of constitutional authority. The jurisdiction conferred upon the Board, and invoked in this instance, is found in § 10 (a), which provides:

"SEC. 10 (a). The Board is empowered, as hereinafter provided, to prevent any person from engaging in any unfair labor practice (listed in section 8) affecting commerce."

The critical words of this provision, prescribing the limits of the Board's authority in dealing with the labor practices, are "affecting commerce." The Act specifically defines the "commerce" to which it refers (§ 2 (6)):

"The term 'commerce' means trade, traffic, commerce, transportation, or communication among the several States, or between the District of Columbia or any Territory of the United States and any State or other Territory, or between any foreign country and any State, Territory, or the District of Columbia, or within the District of Columbia or any Territory, or between points in the same State but through any other State or any Territory or the District of Columbia or any foreign country."

There can be no question that the commerce thus contemplated by the Act (aside from that within a Territory or the District of Columbia) is interstate and foreign commerce in the constitutional sense. The Act also defines the term "affecting commerce" (§ 2 (7)):

"The term 'affecting commerce' means in commerce, or burdening or obstructing commerce or the free flow of commerce, or having led or tending to lead to a labor dispute burdening or obstructing commerce or the free flow of commerce."

This definition is one of exclusion as well as inclusion. The grant of authority to the Board does not purport to extend to the relationship between all industrial employees and employers. Its terms do not impose collective bargaining upon all industry regardless of effects upon interstate or foreign commerce. It purports to reach only what may be deemed to burden or obstruct that commerce and, thus qualified, it must be construed as contemplating the exercise of control within constitutional bounds. It is a familiar principle that acts which directly burden or obstruct interstate or foreign commerce, or its free flow, are within the reach of the congressional power. Acts having that effect are not rendered immune because they grow out of labor disputes. . . . It is the effect upon commerce, not the source of the injury, which is the criterion. . . . Whether or not particular action does affect commerce in such a close and intimate fashion as to be subject to federal control, and hence to lie within the authority conferred upon the Board, is left by the statute to be determined as individual cases arise. We are thus to inquire whether in the instant case the constitutional boundary has been passed.

Second. The unfair labor practices in question—The unfair labor practices found by the Board are those defined in § 8, subdivisions (1) and (3). These provide:

Sec. 8. It shall be an unfair labor practice for an employer—

"(1) To interfere with, restrain, or coerce employees in the exercise of the rights guaranteed in section 7."

"(3) By discrimination in regard to hire or tenure of employment or any term or condition of employment to encourage or discourage membership in any labor organization: . . ."

Section 8, subdivision (1), refers to § 7, which is as follows:

"SEC. 7. Employees shall have the right to self-organization, to form, join, or assist labor organizations, to bargain collectively through representatives of their own choosing, and to engage in concerted activities, for the purpose of collective bargaining or other mutual aid or protection."

Thus, in its present application, the statute goes no further than to safeguard the right of employees to self-organization and to select representatives of their own choosing for collective bargaining or other mutual protection without restraint or coercion by their employer.

That is a fundamental right. Employees have as clear a right to organize and select their representatives for lawful purposes as the respondent has to organize its business and select its own officers and agents. Discrimination and coercion to prevent the free exercise of the right of employees to self-organization and representation is a proper subject for condemnation by

competent legislative authority. Long ago we stated the reason for labor organizations. We said that they were organized out of the necessities of the situation; that a single employee was helpless in dealing with an employer; that he was dependent ordinarily on his daily wage for the maintenance of himself and family; that if the employer refused to pay him the wages that he thought fair, he was nevertheless unable to leave the employ and resist arbitrary and unfair treatment; that union was essential to give laborers opportunity to deal on an equality with their employer. . . . Fully recognizing the legality of collective action on the part of employees in order to safeguard their proper interests, we [have] said that Congress was not required to ignore this right but could safeguard it. Congress could seek to make appropriate collective action of employees an instrument of peace rather than of strife. We said that such collective action would be a mockery if representation were made futile by interference with freedom of choice. Hence the prohibition by Congress of interference with the selection of representatives for the purpose of negotiation and conference between employees and employees, "instead of being an invasion of the constitutional right of either, was based on the recognition of the rights of both." . . .

Third. The application of the Act to employees engaged in production.—The principle involved—Respondent says that whatever may be said of employees engaged in interstate commerce, the industrial relations and activities in the manufacturing department of respondent's enterprise are not subject to federal regulation. The argument rests upon the proposition that manufacturing in itself is not commerce. . . .

The Government distinguishes these cases. The various parts of respondent's enterprise are described as interdependent and as thus involving

"a great movement of iron ore, coal and limestone along well-defined paths to the steel mills, thence through them, and thence in the form of steel products into the consuming centers of the country—a definite and well-understood course of business."

It is urged that these activities constitute a "stream" or "flow" of commerce, of which the Aliquippa manufacturing plant is the focal point, and that industrial strife at that point would cripple the entire movement. Reference is made to our decision sustaining the Packers and Stockyards Act. *Stafford* v. *Wallace*, . . . The Court found that the stockyards were but a "throat" through which the current of commerce flowed and the transactions which there occurred could not be separated from that movement. Hence the sales at the stock-yards were not regarded as merely local transactions, for while they created "a local change of title" they did not "stop the flow," but merely changed the private interests in the subject of the current. Distinguishing the cases which upheld the power of the State to impose a non discriminatory tax upon property which the owner intended to transport to another State, but which was not in actual transit and was held within the State subject to the disposition of the owner, the Court remarked:

"The question, it should be observed, is not with respect to the extent of the power of Congress to regulate interstate commerce, but whether a particular exercise of state power in view of its nature and operation must be deemed to be in conflict with this paramount authority." . . .

Respondent contends that the instant case presents material distinctions. Respondent says that the Aliquippa plant is extensive in size and represents a large investment in buildings, machinery and equipment. The raw materials which are brought to the plant are delayed for long periods and, after being subjected to manufacturing processes, "are changed substantially as to character, utility and value." The finished products which emerge "are to a large extent manufactured without reference to preexisting orders and contracts and are entirely different from the raw materials which enter at the other end." Hence respondent argues that "If importation and exportation in interstate commerce do not singly transfer purely local activities into the field of congressional regulation, it should follow that their combination would not alter the local situation." . . .

We do not find it necessary to determine whether these features of defendant's business dispose of the asserted analogy to the "stream of commerce" cases. The instances in which that metaphor has been used are but particular, and not exclusive, illustrations of the protective power which the Government invokes in support of the present Act. The congressional authority to protect interstate commerce from burdens and obstructions is not limited to transactions which can be deemed to be an essential part of a "flow" of interstate or foreign commerce. Burdens and obstructions may be due to injurious action springing from other sources. The fundamental principle is that the power to regulate commerce is the power to enact "all appropriate legislation" for "its protection and advancement" . . .; to adopt measures "to promote its growth and insure its safety" . . .; "to foster, protect, control and restrain." That power is plenary and may be exerted to protect interstate commerce "no matter what the source of the dangers which threaten it."

Although activities may be intrastate in character when separately considered, if they have such a close and substantial relation to interstate commerce that their control is essential or appropriate to protect that commerce from burdens and obstructions, Congress cannot be denied the power to exercise that control. . . . Undoubtedly the scope of this power must be considered in the light of our dual system of government and may not be extended so as to embrace effects upon interstate commerce so indirect and remote that to embrace them, in view of our complex society, would effectually obliterate the distinction between what is national and what is local and create a completely centralized government. . . . The question is necessarily one of degree. . . .

That intrastate activities, by reason of close and intimate relation to interstate commerce, may fall within federal control is demonstrated in the case of carriers who are engaged in both interstate and intrastate transportation. There federal control has been found essential to secure the freedom of interstate traffic from interference or unjust discrimination and to promote the efficiency of the interstate service. . . .

. . . It is manifest that intrastate rates deal *primarily* with a local activity. But in rate-making they bear such a close relation to interstate rates that effective control of the one must embrace some control over the other. . . . Under the Transportation Act, 1920, Congress went so far as to authorize the Interstate Commerce Commission to establish a state-wide level of intrastate rates in order to prevent an unjust discrimination against interstate commerce. . . .

The close and intimate effect which brings the subject within the reach of federal power may be due to activities in relation to productive industry although the industry when separately viewed is local. This has been abundantly illustrated in the application of the federal Anti-Trust Act. In the *Standard Oil* and *American Tobacco* cases, . . . that statute was applied to combinations of employers engaged in productive industry. . . .

Upon the same principle, the Anti-Trust Act has been applied to the conduct of employees engaged in production. . . .

It is thus apparent that the fact that the employees here concerned were engaged in production is not determinative. The question remains as to the effect upon interstate commerce of the labor practice involved. In the *Schechter* case, *supra*, we found that the effect there was so remote as to be beyond the federal power. To find "immediacy or directness" there was to find it "almost everywhere," a result inconsistent with the maintenance of our federal system. . . .

Fourth. Effects of the unfair labor practice in respondent's enterprise.—Giving full weight to respondent's contention with respect to a break in the complete continuity of the "stream of commerce" by reason of respondent's manufacturing operations, the fact remains that the stoppage of those operations by industrial strife would have a most serious effect upon interstate commerce. In view of respondent's far-flung activities, it is idle to say that the effect would be indirect or remote. It is obvious that it would be immediate and might be catastrophic. We are asked to shut our eyes to the plainest facts of our national life and to deal with the question of direct and indirect effects in an intellectual vacuum. Because there may be but indirect and remote effects upon interstate commerce in connection with a host of local enterprises throughout the country, it does not follow that other industrial activities do not have such a close and intimate relation to interstate commerce as to make the presence of industrial strife a matter of the most urgent national concern. When industries organize themselves on a national scale, making their relation to interstate commerce the dominant factor in their activities, how can it be maintained that their industrial labor relations constitute a forbidden field into which Congress may not enter when it is necessary to protect interstate commerce from the paralyzing consequences of industrial war? We have often said that interstate commerce itself is a practical conception. It is equally true that interferences with that commerce must be appraised by a judgment that does not ignore actual experience.

Experience has abundantly demonstrated that the recognition of the right of employees to self-organization and to have representatives of their own choosing for the purpose of collective bargaining is often an essential condition of industrial peace. Refusal to confer and negotiate has been one of the most prolific causes of strife. . . .

These questions have frequently engaged the attention of Congress and have been the subject of many inquiries. The steel industry is one of the great basic industries of the United States, with ramifying activities affecting interstate commerce at every point. The Government aptly refers to the steel strike of 1919–1920 with its far-reaching consequences. The fact that there appears to have been no major disturbance in that industry in the more recent period did not dispose of the possibilities of future and like dangers to interstate commerce which Congress was entitled to foresee and to exercise its protective power to forestall. It is not necessary again to detail the facts as to respondent's enterprise. Instead of being beyond the pale, we think that it presents in a most striking way the close and intimate relation which a manufacturing industry may have to interstate commerce and we have no doubt that Congress had constitutional authority to safeguard the right of respondent's employees to self-organization and freedom in the choice of representatives for collective bargaining.

Fifth. The means which the Act employs.—Questions under the due process clause and other constitutional restrictions.— Respondent asserts its right to conduct its business in an orderly manner without being subjected to arbitrary restraints. What we have said points to the fallacy in the argument. Employees have their correlative right to organize for the purpose of securing the redress of grievances and to promote agreements with employers relating to rates of pay and conditions of work. . . . Restraint for the purpose of preventing an unjust interference with that right cannot be considered arbitrary or capricious. . . .

The Act does not compel agreements between employers and employees. It does not compel any agreement whatever. It does not prevent the employer "from refusing to make a collective contract and hiring individuals on whatever terms" the employer "may by unilateral action determine." The Act expressly provides in § 9 (a) that any individual employee or group of employees shall have the right at any time to present grievances to their employer. The theory of the Act is that free opportunity for negotiation with accredited representatives of employees is likely to promote industrial peace and may bring about the adjustments and agreements which the Act in itself does not attempt to compel. . . . The Act does not interfere with the normal exercise of the right of the employer to select its employees or to discharge them. The employer may not, under cover of that right, intimidate or coerce its employees with respect to their self-organization and representation, and, on the other hand, the Board is not entitled to make its authority a pretext for interference with the right of discharge when that right is exercised for other reasons than such intimidation and coercion. The true purpose is the subject of investigation with full opportunity to show the facts. It would seem that when employers freely recognize the right of their employees to their own organizations and their unrestricted right of representation there will be much less occasion for controversy in respect to the free and appropriate exercise of the right of selection and discharge.

The Act has been criticised as one-sided in its application; that it subjects the employer to supervision and restraint and leaves untouched the abuses for which employees may be responsible; that it fails to provide a more comprehensive plan,—with better assurances of fairness to both sides and with increased chances of success in bringing about, if not compelling, equitable solutions of industrial disputes affecting interstate commerce. But we are dealing with the power of Congress, not with a particular policy or with the extent to which policy should go. We have frequently said that the legislative authority, exerted within its proper field, need not embrace all the evils within its reach. The Constitution does not forbid "cautious advance, step by step," in dealing with the evils which are exhibited in activities within the range of legislative power. . . . The question in such cases is whether the legislature, in what it does prescribe, has gone beyond constitutional limits.

The procedural provisions of the Act are assailed. But these provisions, as we construe them, do not offend against the constitutional requirements governing the creation and action of administrative bodies. . . .

Our conclusion is that the order of the Board was within its competency and that the Act is valid as here applied. The judgment of the Circuit Court of Appeals is reversed and the cause is remanded for further proceedings in conformity with this opinion.

Reversed.

Another major victory for the New Deal came with the five to four decision in *Steward Machine Company* v. *Davis*. This decision upheld the taxation portions of the Social Security Act passed in 1935. Because this act was one of the cornerstones of the New Deal program, its defeat would have been extremely serious. In a companion case, *Helvering* v. *Davis*, the social security tax to provide old age benefits was upheld.[24] These decisions again enhanced the New Deal program, but in the context of the court-packing controversy made victory even more remote. Just prior to these decisions, Justice Van Devanter resigned, again making the proposal less needed. And most important, the Senate Judiciary Committee issued a strong rejection of Roosevelt's proposal, stating that the bill was "a needless, futile, and utterly dangerous abandonment of constitutional principle."[25] Roosevelt doggedly attempted to keep the fight going. In this setting, the Steward Machine Company decision was handed down by Justice Cardozo:

STEWARD MACHINE COMPANY v. DAVIS
301 U. S. 548 (1937)

. . . The assault on the statute proceeds on an extended front. Its assailants take the ground that the tax is not an excise; that it is not uniform throughout the United States as excises are required to be; that its exceptions are so many and arbitrary as to violate the Fifth Amendment; that its purpose was not revenue, but an unlawful invasion of the reserved powers of the states; and that the states in submitting to it have yielded to coercion and have abandoned governmental functions which they are not permitted to surrender.

The objections will be considered seriatim with such further explanation as may be necessary to make their meaning clear.

First. The tax, which is described in the statute as an excise, is laid with uniformity throughout the United States as a duty, an impost or an excise upon the relation of employment.

1. We are told that the relation of employment is one so essential to the pursuit of happiness that it may not be burdened with a tax. Appeal is made to history. From the precedents of colonial days we are supplied with illustrations of excises common in the colonies. They are said to have been bound up with the enjoyment of particular commodities. Appeal is also made to principle or the analysis of concepts. An excise, we are told, imports a tax upon a privilege; employment, it is said, is a right, not a privilege, from which it follows that employment is not subject to an excise. Neither the one appeal nor the other leads to the desired goal.

As to the argument from history: Doubtless there were many excises in colonial days and later that were associated, more or less intimately, with the enjoyment or the use of property. This would not prove, even if no others were then known, that the forms then accepted were not subject to enlargement. . . .

But in truth other excises *were* known, and known since early times. . . .

The historical prop failing, the prop or fancied prop of principle remains. We learn that employment for lawful gain is a "natural" or "inherent" or "inalienable" right, and not a "privilege" at all. But natural rights, so called, are as much subject to taxation as rights of less importance. An excise is not limited to vocations or activities that may be prohibited altogether. It is not limited to those that are the outcome of a franchise. It extends to vocations or activities pursued as of common right. What the individual does in the operation of a business is amenable to taxation just as much as what he owns, at all events if the classification is not tyrannical or arbitrary. "Business is as legitimate an object of the taxing powers as property." . . .

The statute books of the states are strewn with illustrations of taxes laid on occupations pursued of common right. We find no basis for a holding that the power in that regard which belongs by accepted practice to the legislatures of the states, has been denied by the Constitution to the Congress of the nation.

2. The tax being an excise, its imposition must conform to the canon of uniformity. There has been no departure from this requirement. According to the settled doctrine the uniformity exacted is geographical, not intrinsic. . . .

Second. The excise is not invalid under the provisions of the Fifth Amendment by force of its exemptions.

The statute does not apply, as we have seen, to employers of less than eight. It does not apply to agricultural labor, or domestic service in a private home or to some other classes of less importance. Petitioner contends that the effect of these restrictions is an arbitrary discrimination vitiating the tax.

The Fifth Amendment unlike the Fourteenth has no equal protection clause. . . . But even the states, though subject to such a clause, are not confined to a formula of rigid uniformity in framing measures of taxation. . . . They may tax some kinds of property at one rate, and others at another, and exempt others altogether. . . . They may lay an excise on the operations of a particular kind of business, and exempt some other kind of business closely akin thereto. . . . If this latitude of judgment is lawful for the states, it is lawful, *a fortiori,* in legislation by the Congress, which is subject to restraints less narrow and confining. . . .

The classifications and exemptions directed by the statute now in controversy have support in considerations of policy and practical convenience that cannot be condemned as arbitrary. The classifications and exemptions would therefore be upheld if they had been adopted by a state and the provisions of the Fourteenth Amendment were invoked to annul them. . . . The act of Congress is therefore valid, so far at least as its system of exemptions is concerned, and this though we must assume that discrimination, if gross enough, is equivalent to confiscation and subject under the Fifth Amendment to challenge and annulment.

Third. The excise is not void as involving the coercion of the States in contravention of the Tenth Amendment or of restrictions implicit in our federal form of government.

The proceeds of the excise when collected are paid into the Treasury at Washington, and thereafter are subject to appropriation like public moneys generally. . . . No presumption can be indulged that they will be misapplied or wasted. Even if they were collected in the hope or expectation that some other collateral good would be furthered as an incident, that without more would not make the act invalid. . . . This indeed is hardly questioned. The case for the petitioner is built on the contention that here an ulterior aim is wrought into the very structure of the act, and what is even more important that the aim is not only ulterior, but essentially unlawful. In particular, the 90 per cent credit is relied upon as supporting that conclusion. But before the statute succumbs to an assault upon these lines, two propositions must be made out by the assailant. . . . There must be a showing in the first place that separated from the credit the revenue provisions are incapable of standing by themselves. There must be a showing in the second place that the tax and the credit in combination are weapons of coercion, destroying or impairing the autonomy of the states. The truth of each proposition being essential to the success of the assault, we pass for convenience to a consideration of the second, without pausing to inquire whether there has been a demonstration of the first.

To draw the line intelligently between duress and inducement there is need to remind ourselves of facts as to the problem of unemployment that are now matters of common knowledge. . . .

The relevant statistics are gathered in the brief of counsel for the Government. Of the many available figures a few only will be mentioned. During the years 1929 to 1936, when the country was passing through a cyclical depression, the number of the unemployed mounted to unprecedented heights. Often the average was more than 10 million; at times a peak was attained of 16 million or more. Disaster to the breadwinner meant disaster to dependents. Accordingly the roll of the unemployed, itself formidable enough, was only a partial roll of the destitute or needy. The fact developed quickly that the states were unable to give the requisite relief. The problem had become national in area and dimensions. There was need of help from the nation if the people were not to starve. It is too late today for the argument to be heard with tolerance that in a crisis so extreme the use of the moneys of the nation to relieve the unemployed and their dependents is a use for any purpose narrower than the promotion of the general welfare. . . .

In the presence of this urgent need for some remedial expedient, the question is to be answered whether the expedient adopted has overlept the bounds of power. The assailants of the statute say that its dominant end and aim is to drive the state legislatures under the whip of economic pressure into the enactment of unemployment compensation laws at the bidding of the central government. Supporters of the statute say that its operation is not constraint, but the creation of a larger freedom, the states and the nation joining in a coöperative endeavor to avert a common evil. . . .

The Social Security Act is an attempt to find a method by which all these public agencies may work together to a common end. Every dollar of the new taxes will continue in all likelihood to be used and needed by the nation as long as states are unwilling, whether through timidity or for other motives, to do what can be done at home. At least the inference is permissible that Congress so believed, though retaining undiminished freedom to spend the money as it pleased. On the other hand fulfilment of the home duty will be lightened and encouraged by crediting the taxpayer upon his account with the Treasury of the nation to the extent that his contributions under the laws of the locality have simplified or diminished the problem of relief and the probable demand upon the resources of the fisc. Duplicated taxes, or burdens that approach them, are recognized hardships that government, state or national, may properly avoid. . . . If Congress believed that the general welfare would better be promoted by relief through local units than by the system then in vogue, the coöperating localities ought not in all fairness to pay a second time.

Who then is coerced through the operation of this statute? Not the taxpayer. He pays in fulfilment of the mandate of the local legislature. Not the state. Even now she does not offer a suggestion that in passing the unemployment law she was affected by duress. . . . For all that appears she is satisfied with her choice, and would be sorely disappointed if it were now to be annulled. The difficulty with the petitioner's contention is that it confuses motive with coercion. "Every tax is in some measure regulatory. To some extent it interposes an economic impediment to the activity taxed as compared with others not taxed." . . . In like manner every rebate from a tax when conditioned upon conduct is in some measure a temptation. But to hold that motive or temptation is equivalent to coercion is to plunge the law in endless difficulties. The outcome of such a doctrine is the acceptance of a philosophical determinism by which choice becomes impossible. Till now the law has been guided by a robust common sense which assumes the freedom of the will as a working hypothesis in the solution of its problems. The wisdom of the hypothesis has illustration in this case. Nothing in the case suggests the exertion of a power akin to undue influence, if we assume that such a concept can ever be applied with fitness to the relations between state and nation. Even on that assumption the location of the point at which pressure turns into compulsion, and ceases to be inducement, would be a question of degree,—at times, perhaps, of fact. The point had not been reached when Alabama made her choice. We cannot say that she was acting, not of her unfettered will, but under the strain of a persuasion equivalent to undue influence, when she chose to have relief administered under laws of her own making, by agents of her own selection, instead of under federal laws, administered by federal officers, with all the ensuing evils, at least to many minds, of federal patronage and power. There would be a strange irony, indeed, if her choice were now to be annulled on the basis of an assumed duress in the enactment of a statute which her courts have accepted as a true expression of her will. . . . We think the choice must stand.

In ruling as we do, we leave many questions open. We do not say that a tax is valid, when imposed by act of Congress, if it is laid upon the condition that a state may escape its operation through the adoption of a statute unrelated in subject matter to activities fairly within the scope of national policy and power. No such question is before us. In the tender of this credit Congress does not intrude upon fields foreign to its function. The purpose of its intervention, as we have shown, is to safeguard its own treasury and as an incident to that protection to place the states upon a footing of equal opportunity. Drains upon its own resources are to be checked; obstructions to the freedom of the state are to be leveled. It is one thing to impose a tax dependent upon the conduct of the taxpayers, or of the state in which they live, where the conduct to be stimulated or discouraged is unrelated to the fiscal need subserved by the tax in its normal operation, or to any other end legitimately national. . . . It is quite another thing to say that a tax will be abated upon the doing of an act that will satisfy the fiscal need, the tax and the alternative being approximate equivalents. In such circumstances, if in no others, inducement or persuasion does not go beyond the bounds of power. We do not fix the outermost line. Enough for present purposes that wherever the line may be, this statute is within it. Definition more precise must abide the wisdom of the future. . . .

A new generation of New Deal justices

It was clear by May of 1937 that Roosevelt's court-packing bill had no chance of passage. President Roosevelt insisted upon keeping up the fight until after the unexpected death of the bill's Senate leader, Senator Joe Robinson of Arkansas, an ideological opponent of the bill who had worked for its passage in the hopes of receiving an appointment to the Supreme Court. By the end of the summer, the bill was withdrawn. But the bitterness and political controversy over the proposal did not end with the demise of the bill. One aspect of the continued controversy concerned the nomination of Senator Hugo Lafayette Black of Alabama to replace Justice Willis Van Devanter. Black's opponents argued that his selection represented solely a reward for his strong legislative support of the New Deal in general and the court-packing plan in particular. Black's membership in the Ku Klux Klan and his vote for a bill increasing the retirement pay of Supreme Court justices also became issues. Nevertheless, Black was confirmed on August 17, 1937 by a vote of 63 to 16. Another major attack on Black occurred after he was confirmed. When he returned from a European vacation, he made a national radio address in which he indicated that he had joined the Klan early in his political career, then had resigned and never rejoined.[26] Black did not resign from the Court but went on to compile an outstanding civil liberties record.

In January 1938 Justice George Sutherland resigned. President Roosevelt immediately nominated his solicitor general, Stanley A. Reed, to fill the vacancy. Reed received senatorial approval rapidly and without dissent. Within six months, Justice Cardozo had died, and on January 5, 1939, Felix Frankfurter was nominated. Although subjected to some unfriendly questions, Frankfurter was confirmed without an opposition vote on January 17. Within two weeks of Frankfurter's swearing in, Justice Louis D. Brandeis resigned. William O. Douglas, law school professor and member of the Securities and Exchange Commission, was chosen as his successor.[27] Justice Pierce Butler died in November of 1939 and was succeeded in February of 1940 by the new attorney general, Frank Murphy.

Thus, in the four years between the devastating rejections of New Deal statutes in 1936 and Murphy's selection in 1940, two major judicial transformations had occurred. Justice Roberts and Chief Justice Hughes had initially modified their doctrinal positions, thus switching the majority from the conservatives. But the deaths and resignations of Sutherland, Cardozo, Brandeis, and Butler, and Van Devanter's retirement provided President Roosevelt five key judicial appointments, three of which replaced conservatives. During this four-year period, however, Roosevelt had not ended all political combat regarding the Court. In several Democratic primary elections in 1938, the President campaigned against Democratic opponents of his court-packing bill. In most instances, such as his effort against Senator Guy Gillette of Iowa, he failed. Thus, the Court controversy continued to affect the balance of power within the Democratic legislative majority.

In the early 1940s, President Roosevelt was able to expand these fundmental personnel changes. In 1941 two additional vacancies occurred with the resignations of James C. McReynolds in February and of Charles Evans Hughes in June. McReynolds was replaced by Senator James Byrnes of South Carolina. After the promotion of Harlan Fiske Stone to the chief justiceship, Roosevelt's attorney general, Robert H. Jackson, filled his vacancy in the ranks of associate justices. Byrnes resigned in October 1942 and was replaced by Circuit Judge and former Iowa Law School Dean Wiley Rutledge. Well before all of these personnel changes were completed, however, the changes in the positions of Hughes and Roberts and the initial substantial increase in liberal justices brought about a fundmental shift in doctrinal emphasis. One important example was in the Darby case. This case involved the Fair Labor Standards Act of 1938, which extended and expanded federal regulation of labor-management relations. It prohibited the shipment in interstate commerce of goods produced by child labor, established a national minimum wage schedule, and regulated overtime. This act was challenged in *United States* v. *Darby Lumber Company. Hammer* v. *Dagenhart* was decisively overruled and a broad constructionist interpretation of the scope of congressional commerce power was reinstated. Justice Harlan Fiske Stone wrote the majority opinion:

UNITED STATES v. DARBY LUMBER COMPANY
312 U. S. 100 (1941)

The two principal questions raised by the record in this case are, *first*, whether Congress has constitutional power to prohibit the shipment in interstate commerce of lumber manufactured by employees whose wages are less than a prescribed minimum or whose weekly hours of labor at that wage are greater than a prescribed maximum, and, *second*, whether it has power to prohibit the employment of workmen in the production of goods "for interstate commerce" at other than prescribed wages and hours. A subsidiary question is whether in connection with such prohibitions Congress can require the employer subject to them to keep records showing the hours worked each day and week by each of his employees including those engaged "in the production and manufacture of goods to-wit, lumber, for 'interstate commerce.'" . . .

The prohibition of shipment of the prescribed goods in interstate commerce. . . .

While manufacture is not of itself interstate commerce, the shipment of manufactured goods interstate is such commerce and the prohibition of such shipment by Congress is indubitably a regulation of the commerce. The power to regulate commerce is the power "to prescribe the rule by which commerce is governed." *Gibbons* v. *Ogden*, 9 Wheat. 1, 196. It extends not only to those regulations which aid, foster and protect the commerce, but embraces those which prohibit it. . . . It is conceded that the power of Congress to prohibit transportation in interstate commerce includes noxious articles, . . . stolen articles, . . . kidnapped persons, . . . and articles such as intoxicating liquor or convict-made goods, traffic in which is forbidden or restricted by the laws of the state of destination. . . .

But it is said that the present prohibition falls within the scope of none of these categories; that while the prohibition is nominally a regulation of the commerce its motive or purpose is regulation of wages and hours of persons engaged in manufacture, the control of which has been reserved to the states and upon which Georgia and some of the states of destination have placed no restriction; that the effect of the present statute is, . . . under the guise of a regulation of interstate commerce, . . . to regulate wages and hours within the state contrary to the policy of the state which has elected to leave them unregulated.

The power of Congress over interstate commerce "is complete in itself, may be exercised to its utmost extent, and acknowledges no limitations other than are prescribed in the Constitution." *Gibbons* v. *Ogden*. That power can neither be enlarged nor diminished by the exercise or non-exercise of state power. . . . Congress, following its own conception of public policy concerning the restrictions which may appropriately be imposed on interstate commerce, is free to exclude from the commerce articles whose use in the states for which they are destined it may conceive to be injurious to the public health, morals or welfare, even though the state has not sought to regulate their use. . . .

Such regulation is not a forbidden invasion of state power merely because either its motive or its consequence is to restrict the use of articles of commerce within the states of destination; and is not prohibited unless by other Constitutional provisions. It is no objection to the assertion of the power to regulate interstate commerce that its exercise is attended by the same incidents which attend the exercise of the police power of the states. . . .

The motive and purpose of the present regulation are plainly to make effective the Congressional conception of public policy that interstate commerce should not be made the instrument of competition in the distribution of goods produced under substandard labor conditions, which competition is injurious to the commerce and to the states from and to which the commerce flows. The motive and purpose of a regulation of interstate commerce are matters for the legislative judgment upon the exercise of which the Constitution places no restriction and over which the courts are given no control. . . . Whatever their motive and purpose, regulations of commerce which do not infringe some constitutional prohibition are within the plenary power conferred on Congress by the Commerce Clause. Subject only to that limitation, presently to be considered, we conclude that the prohibition of the shipment interstate of goods produced under the forbidden substandard labor conditions is within the constitutional authority of Congress.

In the more than a century which has elapsed since the decision of *Gibbons* v. *Ogden,* these principles of constitutional interpretation have been so long and repeatedly recognized by this Court as applicable to the Commerce Clause, that there would be little occasion for repeating them now were it not for the decision of this Court twenty-two years ago in *Hammer* v. *Dagenhart.* . . . In that case it was held by a bare majority of the Court over the powerful and now classic dissent of Mr. Justice Holmes setting forth the fundamental issues involved, that Congress was without power to exclude the products of child labor from interstate commerce. The reasoning and conclusion of the Court's opinion there cannot be reconciled with the conclusion which we have reached, that the power of Congress under the Commerce Clause is plenary to exclude any article from interstate commerce subject only to the specific prohibitions of the Constitution.

Hammer v. *Dagenhart* has not been followed. The distinction on which the decision was rested that Congressional power to prohibit interstate commerce is limited to articles which in themselves have some harmful or deleterious property—a distinction which was novel when made and unsupported by any provision of the Constitution—has long since been abandoned. . . . The thesis of the opinion that the motive of the prohibition or its effect to control in some measure the use or production within the states of the article thus excluded from the commerce can operate to deprive the regulation of its constitutional authority has long since ceased to have force. . . . And finally we have declared "The authority of the federal government over interstate commerce does not differ in

extent or character from that retained by the states over intrastate commerce." . . .

The conclusion is inescapable that *Hammer* v. *Dagenhart* was a departure from the principles which have prevailed in the interpretation of the Commerce Clause both before and since the decision and that such vitality, as a precedent, as it then had has long since been exhausted. It should be and now is overruled.

Validity of the wage and hour requirements. Section 15 (a) (2) and §§ 6 and 7 require employers to conform to the wage and hour provisions with respect to all employees engaged in the production of goods for interstate commerce. . . .

There remains the question whether such restriction on the production of goods for commerce is a permissible exercise of the commerce power. The power of Congress over interstate commerce is not confined to the regulation of commerce among the states. It extends to those activities intrastate which so affect interstate commerce or the exercise of the power of Congress over it as to make regulation of them appropriate means to the attainment of a legitimate end, the exercise of the granted power of Congress to regulate interstate commerce. . . .

Congress, having by the present Act adopted the policy of excluding from interstate commerce all goods produced for the commerce which do not conform to the specified labor standards, it may choose the means reasonably adapted to the attainment of the permitted end, even though they involved control of intrastate activities. . . .

The Sherman Act and the National Labor Relations Act are familiar examples of the exertion of the commerce power to prohibit or control activities wholly intrastate because of their effect on interstate commerce. . . .

The means adopted for the protection of interstate commerce by the suppression of the production of the condemned goods for interstate commerce is so related to the commerce and so affects it as to be within the reach of the commerce power. . . . Congress, to attain its objective in the suppression of nationwide competition in interstate commerce by goods produced under substandard labor conditions, has made no distinction as to the volume or amount of shipments in the commerce or of production for commerce by any particular shipper or producer. It recognized that in present day industry, competition by a small part may affect the whole and that the total effect of the competition of many small producers may be great. . . .

So far as *Carter* v. *Carter Coal Co.* . . . is inconsistent with this conclusion, its doctrine is limited in principle by the decisions under the Sherman Act and the National Labor Relations Act, which we have cited and which we follow. . . .

Our conclusion is unaffected by the Tenth Amendment. . . . The amendment states but a truism that all is retained which has not been surrendered. There is nothing in the history of its adoption to suggest that it was more than declaratory of the relationship between the national and state governments as it had been established by the Constitution before the amendment or that its purpose was other than to allay fears that the new national government might seek to exercise powers not granted, and that the states might not be able to exercise fully their reserved powers. . . .

From the beginning and for many years the amendment has been construed as not depriving the national government of authority to resort to all means for the exercise of a granted power which are appropriate and plainly adapted to the permitted end. . . .

Validity of the wage and hour provisions under the Fifth Amendment. Both provisions are minimum wage requirements compelling the payment of a minimum standard wage with a prescribed increased wage for overtime of "not less than one and one-half times the regular rate" at which the worker is employed. Since our decision in *West Coast Hotel Co.* v. *Parrish,* . . . it is no longer open to question that the fixing of a minimum wage is within the legislative power and that the bare fact of its exercise is not a denial of due process under the Fifth more than under the Fourteenth Amendment. Nor is it any longer open to question that it is within the legislative power to fix maximum hours. . . .

The Act is sufficiently definite to meet constitutional demands. One who employs persons, without conforming to the prescribed wage and hour conditions, to work on goods which he ships or expects to ship across state lines, is warned that he may be subject to the criminal penalties of the Act. No more is required. . . .

Yet another example of the significance of New Deal doctrinal change was *Wickard* v. *Filburn*, which sustained the Agricultural Adjustment Act of 1938. The Filburn case demonstrated the extent to which the broad construction of the commerce clause could be carried, and above all, it underscored the turnabout in personnel and doctrine. The decision became a cause celebre for conservative farm groups. The Court's opinion was prepared by Justice Jackson, one of the new majority of Roosevelt appointees.

WICKARD v. FILBURN
317 U. S. 111 (1942)

It is urged that under the Commerce Clause of the Constitution, Article I, clause 3, Congress does not possess the power it has in this instance sought to exercise. The question would merit little consideration since our decision in *United States* v. *Darby* . . . sustaining the federal power to regulate production of goods for commerce, except for the fact that this Act extends federal regulation to production not intended in any part for commerce but wholly for consumption on the farm. The Act includes a definition of "market" and its derivatives, so that as related to wheat, in addition to its conventional meaning, it also means to dispose of "by feeding (in any form) to poultry or livestock which, or the products of which, are sold, bartered, or exchanged, or to be so disposed of." Hence, marketing quotas not only embrace all that may be sold without penalty but also what may be consumed on the premises. Wheat produced on excess acreage is designated as "available for marketing" as so defined, and the penalty is imposed thereon. Penalties do not depend upon whether any part of the wheat, either within or without the quota, is sold or intended to be sold. The sum of this is that the Federal Government fixes a quota including all that the farmer may harvest for sale or for his own farm needs, and declares that wheat produced on excess acreage may neither be disposed of nor used except upon payment of the penalty, or except it is stored as required by the Act or delivered to the Secretary of Agriculture.

Appellee says that this is a regulation of production and consumption of wheat. Such activities are, he urges, beyond the reach of Congressional power under the Commerce Clause, since they are local in character, and their effects upon interstate commerce are at most "indirect." In answer the Government argues that the statute regulates neither production nor consumption, but only marketing; and, in the alternative, that if the act does go beyond the regulation of marketing it is sustainable as a "necessary and proper" implementation of the power of Congress over interstate commerce.

The Government's concern lest the Act be held to be a regulation of production or consumption, rather than of marketing, is attributable to a few dicta and decisions of this Court which might be understood to lay it down that activities such as "production," "manufacturing," and "mining" are strictly "local" and, except in special circumstances which are not present here, cannot be regulated under the commerce power because their effects upon interstate commerce are, as matter of law, only "indirect." Even today, when this power has been held to have great latitude, there is no decision of this Court that such activities may be regulated where no part of the product is intended for interstate commerce or intermingled with the subjects thereof. We believe that a review of the course of decision under the Commerce Clause will make plain, however, that questions of the power of Congress are not to be decided by reference to any formula which would give controlling force to nomenclature such as "production" and "indirect" and foreclose consideration of the actual effects of the activity in question upon interstate commerce. . . .

. . . For nearly a century, however, decisions of this Court under the Commerce Clause dealt rarely with questions of what Congress might do in the exercise of its granted power under the Clause, and almost entirely with the permissibility of state activity which it was claimed discriminated against or burdened interstate commerce. During this period there was perhaps little occasion for the affirmative exercise of the commerce power, and the influence of the Clause on American life and law was a negative one, resulting almost wholly from its operation as a restraint upon the powers of the states. In discussion and decision the point of reference, instead of being what was "necessary and proper" to the exercise by Congress of its granted power, was often some concept of sovereignty thought to be implicit in the status of statehood. Certain activities such as "production," "manufacturing," and "mining" were occasionally said to be within the province of state governments and beyond the power of Congress under the Commerce Clause.

It was not until 1887, with the enactment of the Interstate Commerce Act, that the interstate commerce power began to exert positive influence in American law and life. This first important federal resort to the commerce power was followed in 1890 by the Sherman Anti-Trust Act and, thereafter, mainly after 1903, by many others. These statutes ushered in new phases of adjudication, which required the Court to approach the interpretation of the Commerce Clause in the light of an actual exercise by Congress of its power thereunder.

When it first dealt with this new legislation, the Court adhered to its earlier pronouncements, and allowed but little scope to the power of Congress. *United States* v. *Knight Co.* . . . . These earlier pronouncements also played an important part in several of the five cases in which this Court later held that Acts of Congress under the Commerce Clause were in excess of its power.

Even while important opinions in this line of restrictive authority were being written, however, other cases called forth broader interpretations of the Commerce Clause destined to supersede the earlier ones, and to bring about a return to the principles first enunciated by Chief Justice Marshall. . . .

Not long after the decision of *United States* v. *Knight Co.*, . . . Mr. Justice Holmes, in sustaining the exercise of national power over intrastate activity, stated for the Court that "commerce among the States is not a technical legal conception, but a practical one, drawn from the course of business." *Swift & Co.* v. *United States* . . . It was soon demonstrated that the effects of many kinds of intrastate activity upon interstate commerce were such as to make them a proper subject of federal regulation. In some cases sustaining the exercise of federal power over intrastate matters the term "direct" was used for the purpose of stating, rather than of reaching, a result; in others it was treated as synonymous with "substantial" or "material"; and in others it was not used at all. Of late its use has been abandoned in cases dealing with questions of federal power under the Commerce Clause.

In the *Shreveport Rate Cases*. . . . the Court held that railroad rates of an admittedly intrastate character and fixed by authority of the state might, nevertheless, be revised by the Federal Government because of the economic effects which they had upon interstate commerce. The opinion of Mr. Justice Hughes found federal intervention constitutionally authorized because of "matters having such a close and substantial relation to interstate traffic that the control is essential or appropriate to the security of that traffic, to the efficiency of the interstate service, and to the maintenance of conditions under which interstate commerce may be conducted upon fair terms and without molestation or hindrance." . . .

The Court's recognition of the relevance of the economic effects in the application of the commerce clause, exemplified by this statement, made the mechanical application of legal formulas no longer feasible. Once an economic measure of the reach of the power granted to Congress in the Commerce Clause is accepted, questions of federal power cannot be decided simply by finding the activity in question to be "production," nor can consideration of its economic effects be foreclosed by calling them "indirect." The present Chief Justice [Stone] has said in summary of the present state of the law:

"The commerce power is not confined in its exercise to the regulation of commerce among the states. It extends to those activities intrastate which so affect interstate commerce, or the exertion of the power of Congress over it, as to make regulation of them appropriate means to the attainment of a legitimate end, the effective execution of the granted power to regulate interstate commerce. . . . The power of Congress over interstate commerce is plenary and complete in itself, may be exercised to its utmost extent, and acknowledges no limitations other than are prescribed in the Constitution. . . . It follows that no form of state activity can constitutionally thwart the regulatory power granted by the commerce clause to Congress. Hence the reach of that power extends to those intrastate activities which in a substantial way interfere with or obstruct the exercise of the granted power." . . .

Whether the subject of the regulation in question was "production," "consumption," or "marketing" is, therefore, not material for purposes of deciding the question of federal power before us. That an activity is of local character may help in a doubtful case to determine whether Congress intended to reach it. The same consideration might help in determining whether in the absence of Congressional action it would be permissible for the state to exert its power on the subject matter, even though in so doing it to some degree affected interstate commerce. But even if appellee's activity be local and though it may not be regarded as commerce, it may still, whatever its nature, be reached by Congress if it exerts a substantial economic effect on interstate commerce, and this irrespective of whether such effect is what might at some earlier time have been defined as "direct" or "indirect."

The parties have stipulated a summary of the economics of the wheat industry. Commerce among the states in wheat is large and important. Although wheat is raised in every state but one, production in most states is not equal to consumption. Sixteen states on average have had a surplus of wheat above their own requirements for feed, seed, and food. Thirty-two states and the District of Columbia, where production has been below consumption, have looked to those surplus-producing states for their supply as well as for wheat for export and carry-over.

The wheat industry has been a problem industry for some years. Largely as a result of increased foreign production and import restrictions, annual exports of wheat and flour from the United States during the ten-year period ending in 1940 averaged less than 10 per cent. The decline in the export trade has left a large surplus in production which, in connection with an abnormally large supply of wheat and other grains in recent years, caused congestion in a number of markets; tied up railroad cars; and caused elevators in some instances to turn away grains, and railroads to institute embargoes to prevent further congestion.

Many countries, both importing and exporting, have sought to modify the impact of the world market conditions on their own economy. Importing countries have taken measures to stimulate production and self-sufficiency. The four large exporting countries of Argentina, Australia, Canada, and the United States have all undertaken various programs for the relief of growers. Such measures have been designed, in part at least, to protect the domestic price received by producers. Such plans have generally evolved towards control by the central government.

In the absence of regulation, the price of wheat in the United States would be much affected by world conditions. During 1941, producers who coöperated with the Agricultural Adjustment program received an average price on the farm of about $1.16 a bushel, as compared with the world market price of 40 cents a bushel.

Differences in farming conditions, however, make these benefits mean different things to different wheat growers. There are several large areas of specialization in wheat, and the concentration on this crop reaches 27 per cent of the crop land, and the average harvest runs as high as 155 acres. Except for some use of wheat as stock feed and for seed, the practice is to sell the crop for cash. Wheat from such areas constitutes the bulk of the interstate commerce therein.

On the other hand, in some New England states less than one per cent of the crop land is devoted to wheat, and the average harvest is less than five acres per farm. In 1940 the average percentage of the total wheat production that was sold in each state, as measured by value, ranged from 29 per cent thereof in Wisconsin to 90 per cent in Washington. Except in regions of large scale production, wheat is usually grown in rotation with other crops; for a nurse crop for grass seeding; and as a cover crop to prevent soil erosion and leaching. Some is sold, some kept for seed, and a percentage of the total production much larger than in areas of specialization is consumed on the farm and grown for such purpose. Such farmers, while growing some wheat, may even find the balance of their interest on the consumer's side.

The effect of consumption of home-grown wheat on interstate commerce is due to the fact that it constitutes the most variable factor in the disappearance of the wheat crop. Consumption on the farm where grown appears to vary in an amount greater than 20 per cent of average production. The total amount of wheat consumed as food varies but relatively little, and use as seed is relatively constant.

The maintenance by government regulation of a price for wheat undoubtedly can be accomplished as effectively by sustaining or increasing the demand as by limiting the supply. The effect of the statute before us is to restrict the amount which may be produced for market and the extent as well to which one may forestall resort to the market by producing to meet his own needs. That appellee's own contribution to the demand for wheat may be trivial by itself is not enough to remove him from the scope of federal regulation where, as here, his contribution, taken together with that of many others similarly situated, is far from trivial. . . .

It is well established by decisions of this Court that the power to regulate commerce includes the power to regulate the prices at which commodities in that commerce are dealt in and practices affecting such prices. One of the primary purposes of the Act in question was to increase the market price of wheat, and to that end to limit the volume thereof that could affect the market. It can hardly be denied that a factor of such volume and variability as home-consumed wheat would have a substantial influence on price and market conditions. This may arise because being in marketable condition such wheat overhangs the market and, if induced by rising prices, tends to flow into the market and check price increases. But if we assume that it is never marketed, it supplies a need of the man who grew it which would otherwise be reflected by purchases in the open market. Home-grown wheat in this sense competes with wheat in commerce. The stimulation of commerce is a use of the regulatory function quite as definitely as prohibitions or restrictions thereon. This record leaves us in no doubt that Congress may properly have considered that wheat consumed on the farm where grown, if wholly outside the scheme of regulation, would have a substantial effect in defeating and obstructing its purpose to stimulate trade therein at increased prices.

It is said, however, that this Act, forcing some farmers into the market to buy what they could provide for themselves, is an unfair promotion of the markets and prices of specializing wheat growers. It is of the essence of regulation that it lays a restraining hand on the self-interest of the regulated and that advantages from the regulation commonly fall to others. The conflicts of economic interest between the regulated and those who advantage by it are wisely left under our system to resolution by the Congress under its more flexible and responsible legislative process. Such conflicts rarely lend themselves to judicial determination. And with the wisdom, workability, or fairness, of the plan of regulation we have nothing to do. . . .

In retrospect, it is ironic that the major 20th century political confrontation between an economically conservative Supreme Court and a progressive and often liberal presidency and Congress was resolved before major changes in the membership of this Court had occurred. Periodic replacement of justices based upon normal turnover (deaths, retirements, and occasional resignations) was identified by Robert Dahl as the chief means for avoiding major conflicts. But key modifications of anti–New Deal positions by a majority of the conservative Court came in 1937, well before such "normal" turnover took place.

During the political and ideological battles surrounding Franklin Roosevelt's selections to the Supreme Court, great significance and attention was focused on the fact that not a single corporation lawyer was appointed. This represented a very significant departure from the pattern of several previous decades. (Wilson's two progressive appointees, Clarke and Brandeis, were, in fact, corporation lawyers, albeit unusual ones.) But if the shift in appointment patterns was viewed (as it was by many uneasy conservatives) as beginning a doctrinal shift toward undoing the truly fundamental institutional and doctrinal advantages achieved by corporations since the chief justiceships of Marshall and Taney, the reality was far less dramatic. To be sure, the Court assumed a stronger regulatory stance and an initial prolabor stance in civil liberties cases (which it soon modified). But the significant advantages that were unique only to corporations, such as their status as a person under the Fourteenth Amendment, were not even seriously threatened. Justice Black's dissent in *Connecticut General Life Insurance Company* v. *Johnson* (1938) is illustrative.

CONNECTICUT GENERAL LIFE INSURANCE COMPANY v. JOHNSON
303 U. S. 77 (1938)

. . . This Court has also frequently sustained the right of a state to impose conditions on foreign corporations in order to favor its own corporations. If a state did not have this privilege it could not protect the domestic business of its own corporations from undesirable competition by foreign corporations. The state of California has the constitutional right to limit the privileges of its own corporations and to reserve the right to control their privileges and to define and limit their activities. If California has the lawful constitutional right (as this Court has many times said it has) to impose conditions upon foreign corporations so as to protect domestic corporations, its own elected legislative representatives should be the judges of what is reasonable and proper in a democracy. . . .

. . . But it is contended that the due process clause of the Fourteenth Amendment prohibits California from determining what terms and conditions should be imposed upon this Connecticut corporation to promote the welfare of the people of California. . . .

I do not believe the word "person" in the Fourteenth Amendment includes corporations. "The doctrine of stare decisis, however appropriate and even necessary at times, has only a limited application in the field of constitutional law." This Court has many times changed its interpretations of the Constitution when the conclusion was reached that an improper construction had been adopted. . . .

Neither the history nor the language of the Fourteenth Amendment justifies the belief that corporations are included within its protection. . . .

In 1949 Justice William O. Douglas dissented in *Wheeling Steel Corporation* v. *Glander* in order to indicate his agreement with Justice Black's 1938 argument. Only Black supported Douglas' dissent in Glander.[28]

The Connecticut Insurance decision is perhaps more important for what it rejected in Justice Black's dissent than for its majority holding. To be sure, the new justices were strong in their support of New Deal principles and generally were positively disposed to uphold regulation of business. But like the New Deal program itself, the new Court majority was not seriously inclined to attack the more fundamental special privileges that American corporations had gained and expanded since early in the 19th century.

The growing significance of civil rights and liberties tempered by war

In the midst of the political controversies surrounding the changes in judicial attitudes and voting behavior, a significant civil liberties issue concerning freedom of speech arose in the late 1930s in the case of *De Jonge* v. *Oregon*. The essential facts leading to the constitutional test of an Oregon criminal syndicalism statute are contained in Chief Justice Hughes' majority opinion.

De JONGE v. OREGON
299 U. S. 353 (1937)

It thus appears that, while defendant was a member of the Communist Party, he was not indicted for participating in its organization, or for joining it, or for soliciting members or for distributing its literature. He was not charged with teaching or advocating criminal syndicalism or sabotage or any unlawful acts, either at the meeting or elsewhere. He was accordingly deprived of the benefit of evidence as to the orderly and lawful conduct of the meeting and that it was not called or used for the advocacy of criminal syndicalism or sabotage or any unlawful action. His sole offense as charged, and for which he was convicted and sentenced to imprisonment for seven years, was that he had assisted in the conduct of a public meeting, albeit otherwise lawful, which was held under the auspices of the Communist Party.

The broad reach of the statute as thus applied is plain. While defendant was a member of the Communist Party, the membership was not necessary to conviction on such a charge. A like fate might have attended any speaker, although not a member, who "assisted in the conduct" of the meeting. However innocuous the object of the meeting, however lawful the subjects and tenor of the addresses, however reasonable and timely the discussion, all those assisting in the conduct of the meeting would be subject to imprisonment as felons if the meeting were held by the Communist Party. This manifest result was brought out sharply at this bar by the concessions which the Attorney General made, and could not avoid, in the light of the decision of the state court. Thus if the Communist Party had called a public meeting in Portland to discuss the tariff, or the foreign policy of the Government, or taxation, or relief, or candidacies for the offices of President, members of Congress, Governor, or state legislators, every speaker who assisted in the conduct of the meeting would be equally guilty with the defendant in this case, upon the charge as here defined and sustained. The list of illustrations might be indefinitely extended to every variety of meetings under the auspices of the Communist Party although held for the discussion of political issues or to adopt protests and pass resolutions of an entirely innocent and proper character.

While the States are entitled to protect themselves from the abuse of the privileges of our institutions through an attempted substitution of force and violence in the place of peaceful political action in order to effect revolutionary changes in government, none of our decisions go to the length of sustaining such a curtailment of the right of free speech and assembly as the Oregon statute demands in its present application. . . .

Freedom of speech and of the press are fundamental rights which are safeguarded by the due process clause of the Fourteenth Amendment of the Federal Constitution. . . . The right of peaceable assembly is a right cognate to those of free speech and free press and is equally fundamental. As this Court said in *United States* v. *Cruikshank*, . . . "The very idea of a government, republican in form, implies a right on the part of its citizens to meet peaceably for consultation in respect to public affairs and to petition for a redress

of grievances." The First Amendment of the Federal Constitution expressly guarantees that right against abridgment by Congress. But explicit mention there does not argue exclusion elsewhere. For the right is one that cannot be denied without violating those fundamental principles of liberty and justice which lie at the base of all civil and political institutions,—principles which the Fourteenth Amendment embodies in the general terms of its due process clause. . . .

These rights may be abused by using speech or press or assembly in order to incite to violence and crime. The people through their legislatures may protect themselves against that abuse. But the legislative intervention can find constitutional justification only by dealing with the abuse. The rights themselves must not be curtailed. The greater the importance of safeguarding the community from incitements to the overthrow of our institutions by force and violence, the more imperative is the need to preserve inviolate the constitutional rights of free speech, free press and free assembly in order to maintain the opportunity for free political discussion, to the end that government may be responsive to the will of the people and that changes, if desired, may be obtained by peaceful means. Therein lies the security of the Republic, the very foundation of constitutional government.

It follows from these considerations that, consistently with the Federal Constitution peaceable assembly for lawful discussion cannot be made a crime. The holding of meetings for peaceable political action cannot be proscribed. Those who assist in the conduct of such meetings cannot be branded as criminals on that score. The question, if the rights of free speech and peaceable assembly are to be preserved, is not as to the auspices under which the meeting is held but as to its purpose; not as to the relations of the speakers, but whether their utterances transcend the bounds of the freedom of speech which the Constitution protects. If the persons assembling have committed crimes elsewhere, if they have formed or are engaged in a conspiracy against the public peace and order, they may be prosecuted for their conspiracy or other violation of valid laws. But it is a different matter when the State, instead of prosecuting them for such offenses, seizes upon mere participation in a peaceable assembly and a lawful public discussion as the basis for a criminal charge.

We are not called upon to review the findings of the state court as to the objectives of the Communist Party. Notwithstanding those objectives, the defendant still enjoyed his personal right of free speech and to take part in a peaceable assembly having a lawful purpose, although called by that Party. The defendant was none the less entitled to discuss the public issues of the day and thus in a lawful manner, without incitement to violence or crime, to seek redress of alleged grievances. That was of the essence of his guaranteed personal liberty.

We hold that the Oregon statute as applied to the particular charge as defined by the state court is repugnant to the due process clause of the Fourteenth Amendment. . . .

In the midst of the rapid and surprising transformation of judicial values in 1937, Justice Cardozo contributed an opinion that provided the basis for an entirely different sort of change unrelated to the bitter controversies surrounding the New Deal legislation. Drawing upon the earlier doctrinal suggestions of Justice Moody, Cardozo established a broad and compelling basis for further incorporation of some fundamental freedoms protected against federal action by the Bill of Rights within the meaning of "liberty" in the due process clause of the Fourteenth Amendment. As in the World War I era, such incorporation therefore limited state action. Cardozo's doctrine paved the way for a significant expansion of such incorporation, and thus provided the basis for subsequent federal supervision of the state judicial systems. This development aroused significant political controversy in the 1940s, 1950s, and 1960s and led to a major confrontation in the 1970s. The occasion for Cardozo's doctrinal innovation was his majority opinion in *Palko* v. *Connecticut*. The facts of the case are included in Justice Cardozo's introduction.

PALKO v. CONNECTICUT
302 U. S. 319 (1937)

Justice Cardozo delivered the opinion of the Court:

. . . Appellant was indicted . . . for the crime of murder in the first degree. A jury found him guilty of murder in the second degree, and he was sentenced to confinement in the state prison for life. Thereafter the State of Connecticut, with the permission of the judge presiding at the trial, gave notice of appeal to the Supreme Court of Errors. This it did pursuant to an act adopted in 1886. . . . Upon such appeal, the Supreme Court of Errors reversed the judgment and ordered a new trial. . . . It found that there had been error of law to the prejudice of the state. . . .

. . . [The] defendant was brought to trial again. Before a jury was impaneled and also at later stages of the case he made the objection that the effect of the new trial was to place him twice in jeopardy for the same offense, and in so doing to violate the Fourteenth Amendment of the Constitution of the United States. Upon the overruling of the objection the trial proceeded. The jury returned a verdict of murder in the first degree, and the court sentenced the defendant to the punishment of death. . . . The case is here upon appeal. . . .

1. The execution of the sentence will not deprive

appellant of his life without the process of law assured to him by the Fourteenth Amendment of the Federal Constitution.

The argument for appellant is that whatever is forbidden by the Fifth Amendment is forbidden by the Fourteenth also. The Fifth Amendment, which is not directed to the states, but solely to the federal government, creates immunity from double jeopardy. No person shall be "subject for the same offense to be twice put in jeopardy of life or limb." The Fourteenth Amendment ordains, "nor shall any State deprive any person of life, liberty, or property, without due process of law." To retry a defendant, though under one indictment and only one, subjects him, it is said, to double jeopardy in violation of the Fifth Amendment, if the prosecution is one on behalf of the United States. From this the consequence is said to follow that there is a denial of life or liberty without due process of law, if the prosecution is one on behalf of the People of a State. . . .

We have said that in appellant's view the Fourteenth Amendment is to be taken as embodying the prohibitions of the Fifth. His thesis is even broader. Whatever would be a violation of the original Bill of Rights (Amendments I to VIII) if done by the federal government is now equally unlawful by force of the Fourteenth Amendment if done by a state. There is no such general rule.

The Fifth Amendment provides, among other things, that no person shall be held to answer for a capital or otherwise infamous crime unless on presentment or indictment of a grand jury. This Court has held that, in prosecutions by a state, presentment or indictment by a grand jury may give way to informations at the instance of a public officer. *Hurtado v. California* [1884]. . . . The Fifth Amendment provides also that no person shall be compelled in any criminal case to be a witness against himself. This Court has said that, in prosecution by a state, the exemption will fail if the state elects to end it. *Twining v. New Jersey* [1908]. . . . The Sixth Amendment calls for a jury trial in criminal cases and the Seventh for a jury trial in civil cases at common law where the value in controversy shall exceed twenty dollars. This Court has ruled that consistently with those amendments trial by jury may be modified by a state or abolished altogether. *Walker v. Sauvinet* [1876] . . . *Maxwell v. Dow* [1900]. . . .

On the other hand, the due process clause of the Fourteenth Amendment may make it unlawful for a state to abridge by its statutes the freedom of speech which the First Amendment safeguards against encroachment by the Congress, *De Jonge v. Oregon* [1937] . . .; or the like freedom of the press, *Grosjean v. American Press Co.* [1936] . . .; or the free exercise of religion, *Hamilton v. Regents* [1934] . . .; or the right of peaceable assembly, without which speech would be unduly trammeled, *De Jonge v. Oregon* . . .; or the right of one accused of crime to the benefit of counsel, *Powell v. Alabama* [1932]. . . . In these and other situations immunities that are valid as against the federal government by force of the specific pledges of particular amendments have been found to be implicit in the concept of ordered liberty, and thus, through the Fourteenth Amendment, become valid as against the states.

The line of division may seem to be wavering and broken if there is a hasty catalogue of the cases on the one side and the other. Reflection and analysis will induce a different view. There emerges the perception of a rationalizing principle which gives to discrete instances a proper order and coherence. The right to trial by jury and the immunity from prosecution except as the result of an indictment may have value and importance. Even so, they are not of the very essence of a scheme of ordered liberty. To abolish them is not to violate a "principle of justice so rooted in the traditions and conscience of our people as to be ranked as fundamental." . . . Few would be so narrow or provincial as to maintain that a fair and enlightened system of justice would be impossible without them. What is

true of jury trials and indictments is true also, as the cases show, of the immunity from compulsory self-incrimination. *Twining v. New Jersey*. This too might be lost, and justice still be done. Indeed, today as in the past there are students of our penal system who look upon the immunity as a mischief rather than a benefit, and who would limit its scope, or destroy it altogether. . . . The exclusion of these immunities and privileges from the privileges and immunities protected against the action of the states has not been arbitrary or casual. It has been dictated by a study and appreciation of the meaning, the essential implications, of liberty itself.

We reach a different plane of social and moral values when we pass to the privileges and immunities that have been taken over from the earlier articles of the federal bill of rights and brought within the Fourteenth Amendment by a process of absorption. These in their origin were effective against the federal government alone. If the Fourteenth Amendment has absorbed them, the process of absorption has had its source in the belief that neither liberty nor justice would exist if they were sacrificed. *Twining v. New Jersey*. This is true, for illustration, of freedom of thought, and speech. Of that freedom one may say that it is the matrix, the indispensable condition, of nearly every other form of freedom. With rare aberrations a pervasive recognition of that truth can be traced in our history, political and legal. So it has come about that the domain of liberty, withdrawn by the Fourteenth Amendment from encroachment by the states, has been enlarged by latter-day judgments to include liberty of the mind as well as liberty of action. . . . Fundamental too in the concept of due process, and so in that of liberty, is the thought that condemnation shall be rendered only after trial. . . . The hearing, moreover, must be a real one, not a sham or a pretense. *Moore v. Dempsey* [1923]. . . . For that reason, ignorant defendants in a capital case were held to have been condemned unlawfully when in truth, though not in form, they were refused the aid of counsel. *Powell v. Alabama* [1932]. . . . The decision did not turn upon the fact that the benefit of counsel would have been guaranteed to the defendants by the provisions of the Sixth Amendment if they had been prosecuted in a federal court. The decision turned upon the fact that in the particular situation laid before us in the evidence the benefit of counsel was essential to the substance of a hearing.

Our survey of the cases serves, we think, to justify the statement that the dividing line between them, if not unfaltering throughout its course, has been true for the most part to a unifying principle. On which side of the line the case made out by the appellant has appropriate location must be the next inquiry and the final one. Is that kind of double jeopardy to which the statute has subjected him a hardship so acute and shocking that our polity will not endure it? Does it violate those "fundamental principles of liberty and justice which lie at the base of all our civil and political institutions"? . . . The answer surely must be "no." What the answer would have to be if the state were permitted after a trial free from error to try the accused over again or to bring another case against him, we have no occasion to consider. We deal with the statute before us and no other. The state is not attempting to wear the accused out by a multitude of cases with accumulated trials. It asks no more than this, that the case against him shall go on until there shall be a trial free from the corrosion of substantial legal error. . . . This is not cruelty at all, nor even vexation in any immoderate degree. If the trial had been infected with error adverse to the accused, there might have been review at his instance, and as often as necessary to purge the vicious taint. A reciprocal privilege, subject at all times to the discretion of the presiding judge . . . has now been granted to the state. There is here no seismic innovation. The edifice of justice stands, its symmetry, to many, greater than before.

2. The conviction of appellant is not in derogation of any privileges or immunities that belong to him as a citizen of the United States. . . .

The judgment is affirmed.

Justice Butler dissented.

From Justice Cardozo's significant analysis of the special characteristics of freedom of thought and speech as the "matrix, the indispensable condition, of nearly every other form of freedom," the conception of a category of preferred freedoms began to emerge. In *United States* v. *Carolene Products Company*,[29] Justice Harlan Fiske Stone made the concept more explicit in a now famous footnote. He called for a "narrower scope of operations" for the ordinary presumption of constitutionality in situations that were "within a specific prohibition of the Constitution, such as those of the first ten amendments, which are deemed equally specific when held to be embraced within the Fourteenth." In short, constitutional provisions, particularly those in the First Amendment, should be treated as "preferred freedoms." Cardozo's and Stone's contributions were landmarks in the significant shift by a majority of the New Deal Court from emphasis upon economic issues to those of human rights and civil liberties.

Within a short time after the New Deal appointments of the late 1930s or early 1940s, the depression was overshadowed by World War II. The judicial values that emerged with its advent, in some instances, had little to do with the New Deal. Especially in wartime, issues related to loyalty and patriotism tended to overshadow domestic economic issues. The exception was the broad area involving wartime emergency powers over the domestic economy. One major example was the broad constitutional challenge brought against the Emergency Price Control Act of 1942. A section of the statute that authorized the price administrator to promulgate price-fixing regulations that "in his judgment will be generally fair and equitable and will effectuate the purposes" of the act was attacked as an improper delegation of legislative authority to the executive branch. In *Yakus* v. *The United States*,[30] the New Deal majority upheld the act, noting that the principle of separation of powers did not impose a straitjacket on Congress and suggesting that the delegation doctrine could no longer be invoked to bar expansion of federal police power. Justice Roberts dissented with the observation that the majority's decision meant that the function of legislation may be surrendered to an autocrat whose "judgment" will constitute the law.

The tensions of war often bear heavily on minorities who by religious, ideological, or ethical conviction object to the majority's commitment to combat or to the symbols of national authority. In 1940, in *Minersville School District* v. *Gobitis*,[31] a majority of eight justices upheld a school board rule requiring all children attending public schools in the school district to give the salute to the flag of the United States at the opening of each school day regardless of their religious convictions. Some of the children were Jehovah's Witnesses, and their religion prohibited such salutes. Justice Frankfurter wrote the majority opinion and Justice Stone wrote a vigorous dissent stating that "by this law the state seeks to coerce these children to express a sentiment, which as they interpret it, they do not entertain, and which violates their deepest religious convictions." Three years later, the Court provided a remarkable reversal of its position in *West Virginia State Board of Education* v. *Barnette*. Justice Jackson wrote the majority opinion. Justices Black and Douglas concurred in a separate opinion. Justice Murphy also concurred in a separate opinion. Justices Roberts and Reed and Frankfurter dissented.

WEST VIRGINIA STATE BOARD OF EDUCATION v. BARNETTE
319 U. S. 624 (1943)

Justice Jackson delivered the opinion of the Court:

Following the decision by this Court on June 3, 1940, in *Minersville School District* v. *Gobitis* . . . the West Virginia legislature amended its statutes to require all schools therein to conduct courses of instruction in history, civics, and in the Constitutions of the United States and of the State "for the purpose of teaching, fostering and perpetuating the ideals, principles and spirit of Americanism, and increasing the knowledge of the organization and machinery of the government." . . .

The Board of Education on January 9, 1942, adopted a resolution containing recitals taken largely from the Court's *Gobitis* opinion and ordering that the salute to the flag become "a regular part of the program of activities in the public schools," that all teachers and pupils "shall be required to participate in the salute honoring the Nation represented by the Flag; provided, however, that refusal to salute the Flag be regarded as an act of insubordination, and shall be dealt with accordingly."

The resolution originally required the "commonly accepted salute to the Flag" which it defined. Objections to the salute as "being too much like Hitler's" were raised by the Parent and Teachers Association, the Boy and Girl Scouts, the Red Cross, and the Federation of Women's Clubs. Some modification appears to have been made in deference to these objections, but no concession was made to Jehovah's Witnesses. What is now required is the "stiff-arm" salute, the saluter to keep the right hand raised with palm turned up while the following is repeated: "I pledge allegiance to the Flag of the United States of America and to the Republic for which it stands; one Nation, indivisible, with liberty and justice for all."

Failure to conform is "insubordination" dealt with by expulsion. Readmission is denied by statute until compliance. Meanwhile the expelled child is "unlawfully absent" and may be proceeded against as a delinquent. His parents or guardians are liable to prosecution, and if convicted are subject to fine not exceeding $50 and jail term not exceeding thirty days.

Appellees, citizens of the United States and of West Virginia, brought suit in the United States District Court for themselves and others similarly situated asking its injunction to restrain enforcement of these laws and regulations against Jehovah's Witnesses. The Witnesses are an unincorporated body teaching that the obligation imposed by law of God is superior to that of laws enacted by temporal government. Their religious beliefs include a literal version of Exodus, Chapter 20, verses 4 and 5, which says: "Thou shalt not make unto thee any graven image, or any likeness of anything that is in heaven above, or that is in the earth beneath, or that is in the water under the earth; thou shalt not bow down thyself to them nor serve them." They consider that the flag is an "image" within this command. For this reason they refuse to salute it.

Children of this faith have been expelled from school and are threatened with exclusion for no other cause. Officials threaten to send them to reformatories maintained for criminally inclined juveniles. Parents of such children have been prosecuted and are threatened with prosecutions for causing delinquency. . . .

This case calls upon us to reconsider a precedent decision, as the Court throughout its history often has been required to do. Before turning to the *Gobitis* case, however, it is desirable to notice certain characteristics by which this controversy is distinguished.

The freedom asserted by these appellees does not bring them into collision with rights asserted by any other individual. It is such conflicts which most frequently require intervention of the State to determine where the rights of one end and those of another begin. But the refusal of these persons to participate in the ceremony does not interfere with or deny rights of others to do so. Nor is there any question in this case that their behavior is peaceable and orderly. The sole conflict is between authority and rights of the individual. The State asserts power to condition access to public education on making a prescribed sign and profession and at the same time to coerce attendance by punishing both parent and child. The latter stand on a right of self-determination in matters that touch individual opinion and personal attitude.

As the present Chief Justice [Stone] said in dissent in the *Gobitis* case, the State may "require teaching by instruction and study of all in our history and in the structure and organization of our government, including the guaranties of civil liberty, which tend to inspire patriotism and love of country." . . . Here, however, we are dealing with a compulsion of students to declare a belief. They are not merely made acquainted with the flag salute so that they may be informed as to what it is or even what it means. The issue here is whether this slow and easily neglected route to aroused loyalties constitutionally may be short-cut by substituting a compulsory salute and slogan. . . .

There is no doubt that, in connection with the pledges, the flag salute is a form of utterance. Symbolism is a primitive but effective way of communicating ideas. The use of an emblem or flag to symbolize some system, idea, institution, or personality, is a short cut from mind to mind. Causes and nations, political parties, lodges and ecclesiastical groups seek to knit the loyalty of their followings to a flag or banner, a color or design. The State announces rank, function, and authority through crowns and maces, uniforms and black robes; the church speaks through the Cross, the Crucifix, the altar and shrine, and clerical raiment. Symbols of State often convey political ideas just as religious symbols come to convey theological ones. Associated with many of these symbols are appropriate gestures of acceptance or respect: a salute, a bowed or bared head, a bended knee. A person gets from a symbol the meaning he puts into it, and what is one man's comfort and inspiration is another's jest and scorn.

Over a decade ago Chief Justice Hughes led this Court in holding that the display of a red flag as a symbol of opposition by peaceful and legal means to organized government was protected by the free speech guaranties of the Constitution. *Stromberg* v. *California* [1931]. . . . Here it is the State that employs a flag as a symbol of adherence to government as presently organized. It requires the individual to communicate by word and sign his acceptance of the political ideas it thus bespeaks. Objection to this form of communication when coerced is an old one, well known to the framers of the Bill of Rights.

It is also to be noted that the compulsory flag salute and pledge requires affirmation of a belief and an attitude of mind. It is not clear whether the regulation contemplates that pupils forego any contrary convictions of their own and become unwilling converts to the prescribed ceremony or whether it will be acceptable if they simulate assent by words without belief and by gesture barren of meaning. It is now a commonplace that censorship or suppression of expression of opinion is tolerated by our Constitution only when the expression presents a clear and present danger of action of a kind the State is empowered to prevent and punish. It would seem that involuntary affirmation could be commanded only on even more immediate and urgent grounds than silence. But here the power of compulsion is invoked without any allegation that remaining passive during a flag salute ritual creates a clear and present danger that would justify an effort even to muffle expression. . . .

1. It was said that the flag-salute controversy confronted the Court with "the problem which Lincoln cast in memorable dilemma: 'Must a government of necessity be too *strong* for the liberties of its people, or too *weak* to maintain its own existence?'" and that the answer must be in favor of strength. . . .

We think these issues may be examined free of pressure or restraint growing out of such considerations.

It may be doubted whether Mr. Lincoln would have thought that the strength of government to maintain itself would be impressively vindicated by our confirming power of the State to expel a handful of children from school. Such oversimplification, so handy in political debate, often lacks the precision necessary to postulates of judicial reasoning. If validly applied to this problem, the utterance cited would resolve every issue of power in favor of those in authority and would require us to override every liberty thought to weaken or delay execution of their policies.

Government of limited power need not be anemic government. Assurance that rights are secure tends to diminish fear and jealousy of strong government, and by making us feel safe to live under it makes for its better support. Without promise of a limiting Bill of Rights it is doubtful if our Constitution could have mustered enough strength to enable its ratification. To enforce those rights today is not to choose weak government over strong government. It is only to adhere as a means of strength to individual freedom of mind in preference to officially disciplined uniformity for which history indicates a disappointing and disastrous end.

The subject now before us exemplifies this principle. Free public education, if faithful to the ideal of secular instruction and political neutrality, will not be partisan or enemy of any class, creed, party, or faction. If it is to impose any ideological discipline, however, each party or denomination must seek to control, or failing that, to weaken the influence of the education system. Observance of the limitations of the Constitution will not weaken government in the field appropriate for its exercise.

2. It was also considered in the *Gobitis* case that functions of educational officers in States, counties and school districts were such that to interfere with their authority "would in effect make us the school board for the country."

The Fourteenth Amendment, as now applied to the States, protects the citizen against the State itself and all of its creatures—Boards of Education not excepted. These have, of course, important, delicate, and highly discretionary functions, but none that they may not perform within the limits of the Bill of Rights. That they are educating the young for citizenship is reason for scrupulous protection of Constitutional freedoms of the individual, if we are not to strangle the free mind at its source and teach youth to discount important principles of our government as mere platitudes.

Such Boards are numerous and their territorial jurisdiction often small. But small and local authority may feel less sense of responsibility to the Constitution, and agencies of publicity may be less vigilant in calling it to account. The action of Congress in making flag observance voluntary and respecting the conscience of the objector in a matter so vital as raising the Army contrasts sharply with these local regulations in matters relatively trivial to the welfare of the nation. There are village tyrants as well as village Hampdens, but none who acts under color of law is beyond reach of the Constitution.

3. The *Gobitis* opinion reasoned that this is a field "where courts possess no marked and certainly no controlling competence," that it is committed to the legislatures as well as the courts to guard cherished liberties and that it is constitutionally appropriate to "fight out the wise use of legislative authority in the forum of public opinion and before legislative assemblies rather than to transfer such a contest to the judicial arena," since all the "effective means of inducing political changes are left free."

The very purpose of a Bill of Rights was to withdraw certain subjects from the vicissitudes of political controversy, to place them beyond the reach of majorities and officials and to establish them as legal principles to be applied by the courts. One's right to life, liberty, and property, to free speech, a free press, freedom of worship and assembly, and other fundamental rights may not be submitted to vote; they depend on the outcome of no elections.

In weighing arguments of the parties it is important to distinguish between the due process clause of the Fourteenth Amendment as an instrument for transmitting the principles of the First Amendment and those cases in which it is applied for its own sake. The test of legislation which collides with the Fourteenth Amendment, because it also collides with the principles of the First, is much more definite than the test when only the Fourteenth is involved. Much of the vagueness of the due process clause disappears when the specific prohibitions of the First become standard. The right of a State to regulate, for example, a public utility may well include, so far as the due process test is concerned, power to impose all of the restrictions which a legislature may have a "rational basis" for adopting. But freedoms of speech and of press, of assembly, and of worship may not be infringed on such slender grounds. They are susceptible of restriction only to prevent grave and immediate danger to interests which the State may lawfully protect. It is important to note that while it is the Fourteenth Amendment which bears directly upon the State it is the more specific limiting principles of the First Amendment that finally govern this case.

Nor does our duty to apply the Bill of Rights to assertions of official authority depend upon our possession of marked competence in the field where the invasion of rights occurs. True, the task of translating the majestic generalities of the Bill of Rights, conceived as part of the pattern of liberal government in the eighteenth century, into concrete restraints on officials dealing with the problems of the twentieth century, is one to disturb self-confidence. These principles grew in soil which also produced a philosophy that the individual was the center of society, that his liberty was attainable through mere absence of governmental restraints, and that government should be entrusted with few controls and only the mildest supervision over men's affairs. We must transplant these rights to a soil in which the *laissez-faire* concept or principle of non-interference has withered at least as to economic affairs, and social advancements are increasingly sought through closer integration of society and through expanded and strengthened governmental controls. These changed conditions often deprive precedents of reliability and cast us more than we would choose upon our own judgment. But we act in these matters not by authority of our competence but by force of our commissions. We cannot, because of modest estimates of our competence in such specialties as public education, withhold the judgment that history authenticates as the function of this Court when liberty is infringed.

4. Lastly, and this is the very heart of the *Gobitis* opinion, it reasons that "National unity is the basis of national security," that the authorities have, "the right to select appropriate means for its attainment," and hence reaches the conclusion that such compulsory measures toward "national unity" are constitutional. Upon the verity of this assumption depends our answer in this case.

National unity as an end which officials may foster by persuasion and example is not in question. The problem is whether under our Constitution compulsion as here employed is a permissible means for its achievement.

Struggles to coerce uniformity of sentiment in support of some end thought essential to their time and country have been waged by many good as well as by evil men. Nationalism is a relatively recent phenomenon but at other times and places the ends have been racial or territorial security, support of a dynasty or regime, and particular plans for saving souls. As first and moderate methods to attain unity have failed, those bent on its accomplishment must resort to an ever-increasing severity. As governmental pressure toward unity becomes greater, so strife becomes more bitter as to whose unity it shall be. Probably no deeper division of our people could proceed from any provocation than from finding it necessary to choose what doctrine and whose program public educational officials shall compel youth to unite in embracing. Ultimate futility of such effort from the Roman drive to stamp out Christianity as a disturber of its pagan unity, the Inquisition as a means to religious and dynastic unity, the Siberian exiles as a means to Russian unity, down to the fast failing efforts of our present totalitarian enemies. Those who begin coercive elimination of dissent soon find themselves exterminating dissenters. Compulsory unification of opinion achieves only the unanimity of the graveyard.

It seems trite but necessary to say that the First Amendment to our Constitution was designed to avoid these ends by avoiding these beginnings. There is no mysticism in the American concept of the State or of the nature or origin of its authority. We set up government by consent of the governed, and the Bill of Rights denies those in power any legal opportunity to coerce that consent. Authority here is to be controlled by public opinion, not public opinion by authority.

The case is made difficult not because the principles of its decision are obscure but because the flag involved is our own. Nevertheless, we apply the limitations of the Constitution with no fear that freedom to be intellectually and spiritually diverse or even contrary will disintegrate the social organization. To believe that patriotism will not flourish if patriotic ceremonies are voluntary and spontaneous instead of a compulsory routine is to make an unflattering estimate of the appeal of our institutions to free minds. We can have intellectual individualism and the rich, cultural diversities that we owe to exceptional minds only at the price of occasional eccentricity and abnormal attitudes. When they are so harmless to others or to the State as those we deal with here, the price is not too great. But freedom to differ is not limited to things that do not matter much. That would be a mere shadow of freedom. The test of its substance is the right to differ as to things that touch the heart of the existing order.

If there is any fixed star in our constitutional constellation, it is that no official, high or petty, can prescribe what shall be orthodox in politics, nationalism, religion, or other matters of opinion or force citizens to confess by word or act their faith therein. If there are any circumstances which permit an exception, they do not now occur to us.

We think the action of the local authorities in compelling the flag salute and pledge transcends constitutional limitations on their power and invades the sphere of intellect and spirit which it is the purpose of the First Amendment to our Constitution to reserve from all official control.

The decision of this Court in *Minersville School District v. Gobitis* . . . [is] overruled, and the judgment enjoining enforcement of the West Virginia Regulation is affirmed.

Justice Frankfurter dissented:

One who belongs to the most vilified and persecuted minority in history is not likely to be insensible to the freedoms guaranteed by our Constitution. Were my purely personal attitude relevant I should wholeheartedly associate myself with the general libertarian views in the Court's opinion, representing as they do the thought and action of a lifetime. But as judges we are neither Jew nor Gentile, neither Catholic or agnostic. We owe equal attachment to the Constitution and are equally bound by our judicial obligations whether we derive our citizenship from the earliest or the latest immigrants to these shores. . . . As a member of this Court I am not justified in writing my private notions of policy into the Constitution, no matter how deeply I may cherish them or how mischievous I may deem their disregard. The duty of a judge who must decide which of two claims before the Court shall prevail, that of a State to enact and enforce laws within its general competence or that of an individual to refuse obedience because of the demands of his conscience, is not that of the ordinary person. It can never be emphasized too much that one's own opinion about the wisdom or evil of a law should be excluded altogether when one is doing one's duty on the bench. The only opinion of our own even looking in that direction that is material is our opinion whether legislators could in reason have enacted such a law. In the light of all the circumstances, including the history of this question in this Court, it would require more daring than I possess to deny that reasonable legislators could have taken the action which is before us for review. Most unwillingly, therefore, I must differ from my brethren with regard to legislation like this. I cannot bring my mind to believe that the "liberty" secured by the Due Process Clause gives this Court authority to deny to the State of West Virginia the attainment of that which we all recognize as a legitimate legislative end, namely, the promotion of good citizenship, by employment of the means here chosen. . . .

Justice Jackson's opinion contained a moving analysis of the relationship between freedom of conscience and the compelling necessity for national unity in time of war. But the sentiments expressed by the majority in *Barnette* were not applied in a war-related decision involving the evacuation and detention of Japanese nationals living on the West Coast and persons of Japanese ancestry who were American citizens. Justice Black wrote the majority opinion in *Korematsu* v. *The United States* and Justice Murphy wrote a courageous and powerful dissenting opinion.

KOREMATSU v. UNITED STATES
323 U. S. 214 (1944)

Justice Black delivered the opinion of the Court:

In the light of the principles we announced in the *Hirabayashi* case, we are unable to conclude that it was beyond the war power of Congress and the Executive to exclude those of Japanese ancestry from the West Coast war area at the time they did. True, exclusion from the area in which one's home is located is a far greater deprivation than constant confinement to the home from 8 P.M. to 6 A.M. Nothing short of apprehension by the proper military authorities of the gravest imminent danger to the public safety can constitutionally justify either. But exclusion from a threatened area, no less than curfew, has a definite and close relationship to the prevention of espionage and sabotage. The military authorities, charged with the primary responsibility of defending our shores, concluded that curfew provided inadequate protection and ordered exclusion. They did so, as pointed out in our *Hirabayashi* opinion, in accordance with Congressional authority to the military to say who should, and who should not, remain in the threatened areas.

In this case the petitioner challenges the assumptions upon which we rested our conclusions in the *Hirabayashi* case. He also urges that by May 1942, when Order No. 34 was promulgated, all danger of Japanese invasion of the West Coast had disappeared. After careful consideration of these contentions we are compelled to reject them.

Here, as in the *Hirabayashi* case, . . . ". . . we cannot reject as unfounded the judgment of the military authorities and of Congress that there were disloyal members of that population, whose number and strength could not be precisely and quickly ascertained. We cannot say that the war-making branches of the Government did not have ground for believing that in a critical hour such persons could not readily be isolated and separately dealt with, and constituted a menace to the national defense and safety, which demanded that prompt and adequate measures be taken to guard against it."

Like curfew, exclusion of those of Japanese origin was deemed necessary because of the presence of an unascertained number of disloyal members of the group, most of whom we have no doubt were loyal to this country. It was because we could not reject the finding of the military authorities that it was impossible to bring about an immediate segregation of the disloyal from the loyal that we sustained the validity of the curfew order as applying to the whole group. In the instant case, temporary exclusion of the entire group was rested by the military on the same ground. The judgment that exclusion of the whole group was for the same reason a military imperative answers the contention that the exclusion was in the nature of group punishment based on antagonism to those of Japanese origin. That there were members of the group who retained loyalties to Japan has been confirmed by investigations made subsequent to the exclusion. Approximately five thousand American citizens of Japanese ancestry refused to swear unqualified allegiance to the United States and to renounce allegiance to the Japanese Emperor, and several thousand evacuees requested repatriation to Japan.

We uphold the exclusion order as of the time it was made and when the petitioner violated it. . . . In doing so, we are not unmindful of the hardships imposed by it upon a large group of American citizens. . . . But hardships are part of war, and war is an aggregation of hardships. All citizens alike, both in and out of uniform, feel the impact of war in greater or lesser measure. Citizenship has its responsibilities as well as its privileges, and in time of war the burden is always heavier. Compulsory exclusion of large groups of citizens from their homes, except under circumstances of direst emergency and peril, is inconsistent with our basic governmental institutions. But when under conditions of modern warfare our shores are threatened by hostile forces, the power to protect must be commensurate with the threatened danger. . . .

We are . . . being asked to pass at this time upon the whole subsequent detention program in both assembly and relocation centers, although the only issues framed at the trial related to petitioner's remaining in the prohibited area in violation of the exclusion order. Had petitioner here left the prohibited area and gone to an assembly center we cannot say either as a matter of fact or law that his presence in that center would have resulted in his detention in a relocation center. Some who did report to the assembly center were not sent to relocation centers, but were released upon condition that they remain outside the prohibited zone until the military orders were modified or lifted. This illustrates that they pose different problems and may be governed by different principles. The lawfulness of one does not necessarily determine the lawfulness of the others. This is made clear when we analyze the requirements of the separate provisions of the separate orders. These separate requirements were that those of Japanese ancestry (1) depart from the area; (2) report to and temporarily remain in an assembly center; (3) go under military control to a relocation center there to remain for an indeterminate period until released conditionally or unconditionally by the military authorities. Each of these requirements, it will be noted, imposed distinct duties in connection with the separate steps in a complete evacuation program. Had Congress directly incorporated into one Act the language of these separate orders, and provided sanctions for their violations, disobedience of any one would have constituted a separate offense. There is no reason why violations of these orders, insofar as they were promulgated pursuant to Congressional enactment, should not be treated as separate offenses. . . .

It is said that we are dealing here with the case of imprisonment of a citizen in a concentration camp solely because of his ancestry, without evidence or inquiry concerning his loyalty and good disposition towards the United States. Our task would be simple, our duty clear, were this a case involving the imprisonment of a loyal citizen in a concentration camp because of racial prejudice. Regardless of the true nature of the assembly and relocation centers—and we deem it unjustifiable to call them concentration camps with all the ugly connotations that term implies—we are dealing specifically with nothing but an exclusion order. To cast this case into outlines of racial prejudice, without reference to the real military dangers which were presented, merely confuses the issue. Korematsu was not excluded from the Military Area because of hostility to him or his race. He *was* excluded because we are at war with the Japanese Empire, because the properly constituted military authorities feared an invasion of our West Coast and felt constrained to take proper security measures, because they decided that the military urgency of the situation demanded that all citizens of Japanese ancestry be segregated from the West Coast temporarily, and finally, because Congress, reposing its confidence in this time of war in our military leaders—as inevitably it must—determined that they should have the power to do just this. . . . We cannot—by availing ourselves of the calm perspective of hindsight—now say that at that time these actions were unjustified.

Justice Frankfurther concurred,
Justice Roberts dissented:

I dissent, because I think the indisputable facts exhibit a clear violation of constitutional rights.

This is not a case of keeping people off the streets at night as was *Hirabayashi* v. *United States,* . . . nor a case of temporary exclusion of a citizen from an area for his own safety or that of the community, nor a case of offering him an opportunity to go temporarily out of an area where his presence might cause danger to himself or to his fellows. On the contrary, it is the case of convicting a citizen as a punishment for not submitting to imprisonment in a concentration camp, based on his ancestry, and solely because of his ancestry, without evidence or inquiry concerning his loyalty and good disposition towards the United States. If this be a correct statement of the facts disclosed by this record, and facts of which we take judicial notice, I need hardly labor the conclusion that Constitutional rights have been violated. . . .

Justice Murphy dissented:

This exclusion of "all persons of Japanese ancestry, both alien and non-alien," from the Pacific Coast area on a plea of military necessity in the absence of martial law ought not to be approved. Such exclusion goes over "the very brink of constitutional power" and falls into the ugly abyss of racism.

In dealing with matters relating to the prosecution and progress of a war, we must accord great respect and consideration to the judgments of the military authorities who are on the scene and who have full knowledge of the military facts. The scope of their discretion must, as a matter of necessity and common sense, be wide. And their judgments ought not to be overruled lightly by those whose training and duties ill-equip them to deal intelligently with matters so vital to the physical security of the nation.

At the same time, however, it is essential that there be definite limits to military discretion, especially where martial law has not been declared. Individuals must not be left impoverished of their constitutional rights on a plea of military necessity that has neither substance nor support. Thus, like other claims conflicting with the asserted constitutional rights of the individual, the military claim must subject itself to the judicial process of having its reasonableness determined and its conflicts with other interests reconciled.

. . . Being an obvious racial discrimination, the order deprives all those within its scope of the equal protection of the laws as guaranteed by the Fifth Amendment. It further deprives these individuals of their constitutional rights to live and work where they will, to establish a home where they choose and to move about freely. In excommunicating them without benefit of hearings, this order also deprives them of all their constitutional rights to procedural due process. Yet no reasonable relation to an "immediate, imminent, and impending" public danger is evident to support this racial restriction which is one of the most sweeping and complete deprivations of constitutional

rights in the history of this nation in the absence of martial law.

It must be conceded that the military and naval situation in the spring of 1942 was such as to generate a very real fear of invasion of the Pacific Coast, accompanied by fears of sabotage and espionage in that area. The military command was therefore justified in adopting all reasonable means necessary to combat these dangers. In adjudging the military action taken in light of the then apparent dangers, we must not erect too high or too meticulous standards; it is necessary only that the action have some reasonable relation to the removal of the dangers of invasion, sabotage and espionage. But the exclusion, either temporarily or permanently, of all persons with Japanese blood in their veins has no such reasonable relation. And that relation is lacking because the exclusion order necessarily must rely for its reasonableness upon the assumption that *all* persons of Japanese ancestry may have a dangerous tendency to commit sabotage and espionage and to aid our Japanese enemy in other ways. It is difficult to believe that reason, logic or experience could be marshalled in support of such an assumption.

That this forced exclusion was the result in good measure of this erroneous assumption of racial guilt rather than bona fide military necessity is evidenced by the Commanding General's Final Report on the evacuation from the Pacific Coast area. In it he refers to all individuals of Japanese descent as "subversive," as belonging to "an enemy race" whose "racial strains are undiluted," and as constituting "over 112,000 potential enemies . . . at large today" along the Pacific Coast. In support of this blanket condemnation of all persons of Japanese descent, however, no reliable evidence is cited to show that such individuals were generally disloyal, or had generally so conducted themselves in this area as to constitute a special menace to defense installations or war industries, or had otherwise by their behavior furnished reasonable ground for their exclusion as a group.

Justification for the exclusion is sought, instead, mainly upon questionable racial and sociological grounds not ordinarily within the realm of expert military judgment. . . .

The main reasons relied upon by those responsible for the forced evacuation, therefore, do not prove a reasonable relation between the group characteristics of Japanese Americans and the dangers of invasion, sabotage and espionage. The reasons appear, instead, to be largely an accumulation of much of the misinformation, half-truths and insinuations that for years have been directed against Japanese Americans by people with racial and economic prejudices—the same people who have been among the foremost advocates of the evacuation. A military judgment based upon such racial and sociological considerations is not entitled to the great weight ordinarily given the judgments based upon strictly military considerations. Especially is this so when every charge relative to race, religion, culture, geographical location, and legal and economic status has been substantially discredited by independent studies made by experts in these matters.

The military necessity which is essential to the validity of the evacuation order thus resolves itself into a few intimations that certain individuals actively aided the enemy, from which it is inferred that the entire group of Japanese Americans could not be trusted to be or remain loyal to the United States. No one denies, of course, that there were some disloyal persons of Japanese descent on the Pacific Coast who did all in their power to aid their ancestral land. Similar disloyal activities have been engaged in by many persons of German, Italian and even more pioneer stock in our country. But to infer that examples of individual disloyalty prove group disloyalty and justify discriminatory action against the entire group is to deny that under our system of law individual guilt is the sole basis for deprivation of rights. Moreover, this inference, which is at the very heart of the evacuation orders, has been used in support of the abhorrent and despicable treatment of minority groups by the dictatorial tyrannies which this nation is now pledged to destroy. To give constitutional sanction to that inference in this case, however well-intentioned may have been the military command on the Pacific Coast, is to adopt one of the cruelest of the rationales used by our enemies to destroy the dignity of the individual and to encourage and open the door to discriminatory actions against other minority groups in the passions of tomorrow.

No adequate reason is given for the failure to treat these Japanese Americans on an individual basis by holding investigations and hearings to separate the loyal from the disloyal, as was done in the case of persons of German and Italian ancestry. . . . It is asserted merely that the loyalties of this group "were unknown and time was of the essence." Yet nearly four months elapsed after Pearl Harbor before the first exclusion order was issued: nearly eight months went by until the last order was issued; and the last of these "subversive" persons was not actually removed until almost eleven months had elapsed. Leisure and deliberation seem to have been more of the essence than speed. And the fact that conditions were not such as to warrant a declaration of martial law adds strength to the belief that the factors of time and military necessity were not as urgent as they have been represented to be. . . .

The limitations under which courts always will labor in examining the necessity for a military order are illustrated by this case. How does the Court know that these orders have a reasonable basis in necessity? No evidence whatever on that subject has been taken by this or any other court. There is sharp controversy as to the credibility of the DeWitt report. So the Court, having no real evidence before it, has no choice but to accept General DeWitt's own unsworn, self-serving statement, untested by any cross-examination, that what he did was reasonable. And thus it will always be when courts try to look into the reasonableness of a military order.

In the very nature of things, military decisions are not susceptible of intelligent judicial appraisal. They do not pretend to rest on evidence, but are made on information that often would not be admissible and on assumptions that could not be proved. Information in support of an order could not be disclosed to courts without danger that it would reach the enemy. Neither can courts act on communications made in confidence. Hence courts can never have any real alternative to accepting the mere declaration of the authority that issued the order that it was reasonably necessary from a military viewpoint.

Much is said of the danger to liberty from the Army program for deporting and detaining these citizens of Japanese extraction. But a judicial construction of the due process clause that will sustain this order is a far more subtle blow to liberty than the promulgation of the order itself. A military order, however unconstitutional, is not apt to last longer than the military emergency. Even during that period a succeeding commander may revoke it all. But once a judicial opinion rationalizes such an order to show that it conforms to the Constitution, or rather rationalizes the Constitution to show that the Constitution sanctions such an order, the Court for all time has validated the principle of racial discrimination in criminal procedure and of transplanting American citizens. The principle then lies about like a loaded weapon ready for the hand of any authority that can bring forward a plausible claim of an urgent need. Every repetition imbeds that principle more deeply in our law and thinking and expands it to new purposes. All who observe the work of courts are familiar with what Judge Cardozo described as "the tendency of a principle to expand itself to the limit of its logic." A military commander may overstep the bounds of constitutionality, and it is an incident. But if we review and approve, that passing incident becomes the doctrine of the Constitution. There it has a generative power of its own, and all that it creates will be in its own image. Nothing better illustrates this danger than does the Court's opinion in this case.

It argues that we are bound to uphold the conviction of Korematsu because we upheld one in *Hirabayashi* v. *United States,* . . . when we sustained these orders in so far as they applied a curfew requirement to a citizen of Japanese ancestry. I think we should learn something from that experience.

In that case we were urged to consider only the curfew feature, that being all that technically was involved, because it was the only count necessary to sustain Hirabayashi's conviction and sentence. We yielded, and the Chief Justice guarded the opinion as carefully as language will do. He said: "Our investigation here does not go beyond the inquiry whether, in the light of all the relevant circumstances preceding and attending their promulgation, the challenged orders and statute *afforded a reasonable basis for the action taken in imposing the curfew.*" . . . "We decide only the issue as we have defined it—we decide only that the *curfew order* as applied, and at the time it was applied, was within the boundaries of the war power." . . . And again: "It is unnecessary to consider whether or to what extent *such findings would support orders differing from the curfew order.*" . . . (Italics supplied.) However, in spite of our limiting words we did validate a discrimination on the basis of ancestry for mild and temporary deprivation of liberty. Now the principle of racial discrimination is pushed from support of mild measures to very harsh ones, and from temporary deprivations to indeterminate ones. And the precedent which it is said requires us to do so is *Hirabayashi.* The Court is now saying that in *Hirabayashi* we did decide the very things we there said we were not deciding. Because we said that these citizens could be made to stay in their homes during the hours of dark, it is said we must require them to leave home entirely; and if that, we are told they may also be taken into custody for deportation; and if that, it is argued they may also be held for some undetermined time in detention camps. How far the principle of this case would be extended before plausible reasons would play out, I do not know.

I should hold that a civil court cannot be made to enforce an order which violates constitutional limitations even if it is a reasonable exercise of military authority. The courts can exercise only the judicial power, can apply only law, and must abide by the Constitution, or they cease to be civil courts and become instruments of military policy.

Of course the existence of a military power resting on force, so vagrant, so centralized, so necessarily heedless of the individual, is an inherent threat to liberty. But I would not lead people to rely on this Court for a review that seems to be wholly delusive. The military reasonableness of these orders can only be determined by military superiors. If the people ever let command of the war power fall into irresponsible and unscrupulous hands, the courts wield no power equal to its restraint. The chief restraint upon those who command the physical forces of the country, in the future as in the past, must be their responsibility to the political judgments of their contemporaries and to the moral judgments of history.

My duties as a justice as I see them do not require me to make a military judgment as to whether General DeWitt's evacuation and detention program was a reasonable military necessity. I do not suggest that the courts should have attempted to interfere with the Army in carrying out its task. But I do not think they may be asked to execute a military expedient that has no place in law under the Constitution. I would reverse the judgment and discharge the prisoner.

Although war-related issues and New Deal economics were the primary concerns of the Court in the 1940s, the problem of racism also continued to trouble the nation and the Court. The relationship of racism to political participation in the South had been handled indecisively in 1935 when, in *Grovey* v. *Townsend,*[32] the Texas Democratic Party's restrictions on membership (whites only) was challenged under the equal protection of the laws clause, and the Court decided that such action by a political party did not constitute the state action necessary to invoke the Fourteenth Amendment. In *Smith* v. *Allwright,* decided in 1944, however, the New Deal Court examined the realities of Texas statutory provisions for party primaries. Its findings provided a basis for striking down the discriminatory actions, recognizing that the political parties were, in practice, agencies of the state, and consequently, their discriminatory actions constituted state action in violation of the equal protection clause of the Fourteenth Amendment. Justice Reed's majority opinion was thus a significant step toward the significant civil rights revolution supported by the Court in the 1950s.

SMITH v. ALLWRIGHT
321 U. S. 649 (1944)

Justice Reed delivered the opinion of the Court:

This writ of certiorari brings here for review a claim for damages in the sum of $5,000 on the part of the petitioner, a Negro citizen of the 48th precinct of Harris County, Texas, for the refusal of respondents, election and associate election judges respectively of that precinct, to give petitioner a ballot or to permit him to cast a ballot in the primary election of July 27, 1940, for the nomination of Democratic candidates for the United States Senate and House of Representatives, and Governor and other state officers. The refusal is alleged to have been solely because of the race and color of the proposed voter. . . .

Texas is free to conduct her elections and limit her electorate as she may deem wise, save only as her action may be affected by the prohibitions of the United States Constitution or in conflict with powers delegated to and exercised by the National Government. The Fourteenth Amendment forbids a state from making or enforcing any law which abridges the privileges or immunities of citizens of the United States and the Fifteenth Amendment specifically interdicts any denial or abridgement by a state of the right of citizens to vote on account of color. Respondents appeared in the District Court and the Circuit Court of Appeals and defended on the ground that the Democratic party of Texas is a voluntary organization with members banded together for the purpose of selecting individuals of the group representing the common political beliefs as candidates in the general election. As such a voluntary organization, it was claimed, the Democratic party is free to select its own membership and limit to whites participation in the party primary. Such action, the answer asserted, does not violate the Fourteenth, Fifteenth or Seventeenth Amendment as officers of government cannot be chosen at primaries and the Amendments are applicable only to general elections where governmental officers are actually elected. Primaries, it is said, are political party affairs, handled by party, not governmental, officers. No appearance for respondents is made in this Court. Arguments presented here by the Attorney General of Texas and the Chairman of the State Democratic Executive Committee of Texas, as amici curiae, urged substantially the same grounds as those advanced by the respondents. . . .

In *Grovey* v. *Townsend* [1935] . . . this Court had before it another suit for damages for the refusal in a primary of a county clerk, a Texas officer with only public functions to perform, to furnish petitioner, a Negro, an absentee ballot. The refusal was solely on the ground of race. . . . This Court went on to announce that to deny a vote in a primary was a mere refusal of party membership with which "the state need have no concern," . . . while for a state to deny a vote in a general election on the ground of race or color violated the Constitution. Consequently, there was found no ground for holding that the county clerk's refusal of a ballot because of racial ineligibility for party membership denied the petitioner any right under the Fourteenth or Fifteenth Amendments.

Since *Grovey* v. *Townsend* and prior to the present suit, no case from Texas involving primary elections has been before this Court. We did decide, however, *United States* v. *Classic* [1941]. . . . We there held that § 4 of Article I of the Constitution authorized Congress to regulate primary as well as general elections, . . . "where the primary is by law made an integral part of the election machinery." . . . The fusing by the *Classic* case of the primary and general elections into a single instrumentality for choice of officers has a definite bearing on the permissibility under the Constitution of excluding Negroes from primaries. This is not to say that the *Classic* case cuts directly into the rationale of *Grovey* v. *Townsend*. This latter case was not mentioned in the opinion. *Classic* bears upon *Grovey* v. *Townsend* not because exclusion of Negroes from primaries is any more or less state action by reason of the unitary character of the electoral process but because the recognition of the place of the primary in the electoral scheme makes clear that state delegation to a party of the power to fix the qualifications of primary elections is delegation of a state function that may make the party's action the action of the state. When *Grovey* v. *Townsend* was written, the Court looked upon the denial of a vote in a primary as a mere refusal by a party of party membership. . . . As the Louisiana statutes for holding primaries are similar to those of Texas, our ruling in *Classic* as to the unitary character of the electoral process calls for a re-examination as to whether or not the exclusion of Negroes from a Texas party primary was state action. . . .

It may now be taken as a postulate that the right to vote in such a primary for the nomination of candidates without discrimination by the State, like the right to vote in a general election, is a right secured by the Constitution. . . . By the terms of the Fifteenth Amendment that right may not be abridged by any state on account of race. Under our Constitution the great privilege of the ballot may not be denied a man by the State because of his color. . . .

Primary elections are conducted by the party under state statutory authority. The county executive committee selects precinct election officials and the county, district or state executive committees, respectively, canvass the returns. These party committees or the state convention certify the party's candidates to the appropriate officers for inclusion on the official ballot for the general election. No name which has not been so certified may appear upon the ballot for the general election as a candidate of a political party. No other name may be printed on the ballot which has not been placed in nomination by qualified voters who must take oath that they did not participate in a primary for the selection of a candidate for the office for which the nomination is made.

The state courts are given exclusive original jurisdiction of contested elections and of mandamus proceedings to compel party officers to perform their statutory duties. . . .

The United States is a constitutional democracy. Its organic law grants to all citizens a right to participate in the choice of elected officials without restriction by any state because of race. This grant to the people of the opportunity for choice is not to be nullified by a state through casting its electoral process in a form which permits a private organization to practice racial discrimination in the election. Constitutional rights would be of little value if they could be thus indirectly denied. . . .

The privilege of membership in a party may be, as this Court said in *Grovey* v. *Townsend*, . . . no concern of a state. But when, as here, that privilege is also the essential qualification for voting in a primary to select nominees for a general election, the state makes the action of the party the action of the state. In reaching this conclusion we are not unmindful of the desirability of continuity of decision in constitutional questions. However, when convinced of former error, this Court has never felt constrained to follow precedent. In constitutional questions, where correction depends upon amendment and not upon legislative action, this Court throughout its history has freely exercised its power to re-examine the basis of its constitutional decisions. This has long been accepted practice, and this practice has continued to this day. This is particularly true when the decision believed erroneous is the application of a constitutional principle rather than an interpretation of the Constitution to extract the principle itself. Here we are applying, contrary to the recent decision in *Grovey* v. *Townsend*, the well established principle of the Fifteenth Amendment, forbidding the abridgement by a state of a citizen's right to vote. *Grovey* v. *Townsend* is overruled. . . .

The Fair Deal, the president's authority, and the Cold War

The resurgence of Republican congressional strength in 1946 coincided with a significant change in the leadership of the Supreme Court. Soon after he succeeded President Roosevelt, President Harry S. Truman had the opportunity to make an appointment because Justice Roberts resigned. Truman chose a moderate Republican, Harold Burton of Ohio. Burton's appointment, made in 1945, was obviously an attempt at bipartisanship. But Republican midterm congressional victories ended the brief honeymoon in 1946. In August of that year, Chief Justice Harlan Fiske Stone died. In the same year, President Harry Truman chose Fred Vinson of Kentucky as the new Chief Justice.

Vinson had begun his career as a prosecuting attorney in Kentucky, served two terms in Congress and six years as a judge of the federal Circuit Court of Appeals for the District of Columbia. He then held a number of increasingly important administrative posts under Presidents Roosevelt and Truman. The former appointed Vinson Director of Economic Stabilization in 1943. Later Vinson headed the Reconstruction Finance Corporation, then directed War Mobilization and Reconversion, and finally joined President Truman's cabinet as secretary of the treasury.

Vinson confronted a difficult internal situation on the Court. Especially after the last of the conservatives had left the court, the members of the highest tribunal, totally manned by appointees of Roosevelt, divided, often seriously, over a variety of doctrinal approaches. When New Deal justices had generally united against the once dominant conservatives, they were effective. But when this unity was no longer necessary, they disagreed among themselves over substantive issues and especially over the extent to which the Court should actively develop social policy through doctrinal change. Justices Black and Douglas frequently led the activist wing and Justice Frankfurter often spoke for judicial restraint. In this setting two activist members of the New Deal Court died suddenly, both in their midfifties, and both in the same year, 1949. Frank Murphy and Wiley B. Rutledge were replaced by Attorney General Tom Clark of Texas and Sherman Minton of Indiana, a New Deal senator, White House administrative assistant, and Circuit Court of Appeals judge. After 1937, all of the Roosevelt and Truman appointees were strong supporters of federal and state intervention in economics, business, and labor relations. But they differed considerably over many issues that became salient after the Court's opposition to the New Deal ceased. The Truman (Fair Deal) appointees generally opposed many of the manifestations of judicial activism demonstrated by Justices Black and Douglas.

By the late 1940s, the Republican party had experienced a dramatic resurgence, making great gains in congressional seats in 1946 and anticipating a decisive presidential victory in 1948. Thomas E. Dewey waged an initially strong campaign against President Truman's Fair Deal, but relaxed near the end of the campaign while Truman, despite seemingly insurmountable odds, continued his vigorous and effective "whistle-stop" campaign. But after Truman's surprise victory in 1948, his administration came under increasing attack. It was blamed for the fall of mainland China to the Communist Revolution under Mao, for internal security problems, and after the initial unity of the Korean conflict, for mishandling the Korean War.

The war precipitated a major constitutional confrontation. The Supreme Court confronted a major issue involving presidential authority when President Truman seized many of the nation's steel mills to prevent a work stoppage in steel production, which could have interfered with the conduct of the Korean War.

In *Youngstown Sheet and Tube Company* v. *Sawyer*, the Court, composed of an overwhelming New Deal/Fair Deal majority, struck down the presidential order. Justice Black wrote the majority opinion supported by separate concurring opinions by Justices Frankfurter, Douglas, Jackson, Burton and Clark. Chief Justice Vinson, joined by Justices Reed and Minton, dissented. Portions of Justice Black's majority opinion and Chief Justice Vinson's dissenting opinion are reproduced below:

YOUNGSTOWN SHEET AND TUBE COMPANY v. SAWYER
343 U. S. 579 (1952)

Justice Black delivered the opinion of the Court:

We are asked to decide whether the President was acting within his constitutional power when he issued an order directing the Secretary of Commerce to take possession of and operate most of the Nation's steel mills. The mill owners argue that the President's order amounts to lawmaking, a legislative function which the Constitution has expressly confided to the Congress and not to the President. The Government's position is that the order was made on findings of the President that his action was necessary to avert a national catastrophe which would inevitably result from a stoppage of steel production, and that in meeting this grave emergency the President was acting within the aggregate of his constitutional powers as the Nation's Chief Executive and the Commander in Chief of the Armed Forces of the United States. . . .

II

The President's power, if any, to issue the order must stem either from an act of Congress or from the Constitution itself. There is no statute that expressly authorizes the President to take possession of property as he did here. Nor is there any act of Congress to which our attention has been directed from which such a power can fairly be implied. Indeed, we do not understand the Government to rely on statutory authorization for this seizure. There are two statutes which do authorize the President to take both personal and real property under certain conditions. However, the Government admits that these conditions were not met and that the President's order was not rooted in either of the statutes. The Government refers to the seizure provisions of one of these statutes (§ 201 (b) of the Defense Production Act) as "much too cumbersome, involved, and time-consuming for the crisis which was at hand."

Moreover, the use of the seizure technique to solve labor disputes in order to prevent work stoppages was not only unauthorized by any congressional enactment; prior to this controversy, Congress had refused to adopt that method of settling labor disputes. When the Taft-Hartley Act was under consideration in 1947, Congress rejected an amendment which would have authorized such governmental seizures in cases of emergency. Apparently it was thought that the technique of seizure, like that of compulsory arbitration, would interfere with the process of collective bargaining. Consequently, the plan Congress adopted in that Act did not provide for seizure under any circumstances. Instead, the plan sought to bring about settlements by use of the customary devices of mediation, conciliation, investigation by boards of inquiry, and public reports. In some instances temporary injunctions were authorized to provide cooling-off periods. All this failing, unions were left free to strike after a secret vote by employees as to whether they wished to accept their employers' final settlement offer.

It is clear that if the President had authority to issue the order he did, it must be found in some provision of the Constitution. And it is not claimed that express constitutional language grants this power to the President. The contention is that presidential power should be implied from the aggregate of his powers under the Constitution. Particular reliance is placed on provisions in Article II which say that "The executive Power shall be vested in a President . . ."; that "he shall take Care that the Laws be faithfully executed"; and that he "shall be Commander in Chief of the Army and Navy of the United States."

The order cannot properly be sustained as an exercise of the President's military power as Commander in Chief of the Armed Forces. The Government attempts to do so by citing a number of cases upholding broad powers in military commanders engaged in day-to-day fighting in a theater of war. Such cases need not concern us here. Even though "theater of war" be an expanding concept, we cannot with faithfulness to our constitutional system hold that the Commander in Chief of the Armed Forces has the ultimate power as such to take possession of private property in order to keep labor disputes from stopping production. This is a job for the Nation's lawmakers, not for its military authorities.

Nor can the seizure order be sustained because of the several constitutional provisions that grant executive power to the President. In the framework of our Constitution, the President's power to see that the laws are faithfully executed refutes the idea that he is to be a lawmaker. The Constitution limits his functions in the lawmaking process to the recommending of laws he thinks wise and the vetoing of laws he thinks bad. And the Constitution is neither silent nor equivocal about who shall make laws which the President is to execute. The first section of the first article says that "All legislative Powers herein granted shall be vested in a Congress of the United States. . . ."

The President's order does not direct that a congressional policy be executed in a manner prescribed by Congress—it directs that a presidential policy be executed in a manner prescribed by the President. The preamble of the order itself, like that of many statutes, sets out reasons why the President believes certain policies should be adopted, proclaims these policies as rules of conduct to be followed, and again, like a statute, authorizes a government official to promulgate additional rules and regulations consistent with the policy proclaimed and needed to carry that policy into execution. The power of Congress to adopt such public policies as those proclaimed by the order is beyond question. It can authorize the taking of private property for public use. It can make laws regulating the relationships between employers and employees, prescribing rules designed to settle labor disputes, and fixing wages and working conditions in certain fields of our economy. The Constitution does not subject this lawmaking power of Congress to presidential or military supervision or control.

It is said that other Presidents without congressional authority have taken possession of private business enterprises in order to settle labor disputes. But even if this be true, Congress has not thereby lost its exclusive constitutional authority to make laws necessary and proper to carry out the powers vested by the Constitution "in the Government of the United States, or any Department or Officer thereof."

The Founders of this Nation entrusted the lawmaking power to the Congress alone in both good and bad times. It would do no good to recall the historical events, the fears of power and the hopes for freedom that lay behind their choice. Such a review would but confirm our holding that this seizure order cannot stand.

The judgment of the District Court is affirmed.

Chief Justice Vinson dissented:

. . . One is not here called upon even to consider the possibility of executive seizure of a farm, a corner grocery store or even a single industrial plant. Such considerations arise only when one ignores the central fact of this case—that the Nation's entire basic steel production would have shut down completely if there had been no Government seizure. . . .

Accordingly, if the President has any power under the Constitution to meet a critical situation in the absence of express statutory authorization, there is no basis whatever for criticizing the exercise of such power in this case. . . .

. . . We are not called upon today to expand the Constitution to meet a new situation. For, in this case, we need only look to history and time-honored princi-

ples of constitutional law—principles that have been applied consistently by all branches of the Government throughout our history. It is those who assert the invalidity of the Executive Order who seek to amend the Constitution in this case.

III

A review of executive action demonstrates that our Presidents have on many occasions exhibited the leadership contemplated by the Framers when they made the President Commander in Chief, and imposed upon him the trust to "take Care that the Laws be faithfully executed." With or without explicit statutory authorization, Presidents have at such times dealt with national emergencies by acting promptly and resolutely to enforce legislative programs, at least to save those programs until Congress could act. Congress and the courts have responded to such executive initiative with consistent approval.

Our first President displayed at once the leadership contemplated by the Framers. When the national revenue laws were openly flouted in some sections of Pennsylvania, President Washington, without waiting for a call from the state government, summoned the militia and took decisive steps to secure the faithful execution of the laws. When international disputes engendered by the French revolution threatened to involve this country in war, and while congressional policy remained uncertain, Washington issued his Proclamation of Neutrality. . . .

Jefferson's initiative in the Louisiana Purchase, the Monroe Doctrine, and Jackson's removal of Government deposits from the Bank of the United States further serve to demonstrate by deed what the Framers described by word when they vested the whole of the executive power in the President.

Without declaration of war, President Lincoln took energetic action with the outbreak of the War Between the States. He summoned troops and paid them out of the Treasury without appropriation therefore. He proclaimed a naval blockade of the Confederacy and seized ships violating that blockade. Congress, far from denying the validity of these acts, gave them express approval. The most striking action of President Lincoln was the Emancipation Proclamation, issued in aid of the successful prosecution of the War Between the States, but wholly without statutory authority.

In an action furnishing a most apt precedent for this case, President Lincoln without statutory authority directed the seizure of rail and telegraph lines leading to Washington. Many months later, Congress recognized and confirmed the power of the President to seize railroads and telegraph lines and provided criminal penalties for interference with Government operation. . . .

In *In Re Neagle* [1890] this Court held that a federal officer had acted in line of duty when he was guarding a Justice of this Court riding circuit. It was conceded that there was no specific statute authorizing the President to assign such a guard. In holding that such a statute was not necessary, the Court broadly stated the question as follows:

[The President] is enabled to fulfil the duty of his great department, expressed in the phrase that "he shall take care that the laws be faithfully executed."

Is this duty limited to the enforcement of acts of Congress or of treaties of the United States according to their *express terms*, or does it include the rights, duties and obligations growing out of the Constitution itself, our international relations, and all the protection implied by the nature of the government under the Constitution?

The latter approach was emphatically adopted by the Court.

President Hayes authorized the widespread use of federal troops during the Railroad Strike of 1877. President Cleveland also used the troops in the Pullman Strike of 1895 and his action is of special significance. No statute authorized this action. No call for help had issued from the Governor of Illinois; indeed Governor Altgeld disclaimed the need for supplemental forces. But the President's concern was that federal laws relating to the free flow of interstate commerce and the mails be continuously and faithfully executed without interruption. To further this aim his agents sought and obtained the injunction upheld by this Court in *In Re Debs* [1895].

During World War I, President Wilson established a War Labor Board without awaiting specific direction by Congress. With William Howard Taft and Frank P. Walsh as co-chairmen, the Board had as its purpose the prevention of strikes and lockouts interfering with the production of goods needed to meet the emergency. Effectiveness of War Labor Board decision was accomplished by Presidential action, including seizure of industrial plants. Seizure of the Nation's railroads was also ordered by President Wilson.

Beginning with the Bank Holiday Proclamation and continuing through World War II, executive leadership and initiative were characteristic of President Franklin D. Roosevelt's administration. . . .

Some six months before Pearl Harbor, a dispute at a single aviation plant at Inglewood, California, interrupted a segment of the production of military aircraft. . . . President Roosevelt ordered the seizure of the plant "pursuant to the powers vested in [him] by the Constitution and laws of the United States, as

President of the United States of America and Commander in Chief of the Army and Navy of the United States." The Attorney General (Jackson) vigorously proclaimed that the President had the moral duty to keep this Nation's defense effort a "going concern." His ringing moral justification was coupled with a legal justification equally well stated:

The Presidential proclamation rests upon the aggregate of the Presidential powers derived from the Constitution itself and from statutes enacted by the Congress. . . .

[Before and after Pearl Harbor] . . . industrial concerns were seized to avert interruption of needed production. During the same period, the President directed seizure of the Nation's coal mines to remove an obstruction to the effective prosecution of the war. . . .

At the time of the seizure of the coal mines . . . [a] bill to provide a statutory basis for seizures . . . [was] before Congress. As stated by its sponsor, the purpose of the bill was not to augment Presidential power, but to "let the country know that the Congress is squarely behind the President." . . .

This is but a cursory summary of executive leadership. But it amply demonstrates that Presidents have taken prompt action to enforce the laws and protect the country whether or not Congress happened to provide in advance for the particular method of execution. . . . The fact that Congress and the courts have consistently recognized and given their support to such executive action indicates that such a power of seizure has been accepted throughout our history. . . .

Much of the argument in this case has been directed at straw men. We do not now have before us the case of a President acting solely on the basis of his own notions of the public welfare. Nor is there any question of unlimited executive power in this case. The President himself closed the door to any such claim when he sent his Message to Congress stating his purpose to abide by any action of Congress, whether approving or disapproving his seizure action. Here, the President immediately made sure that Congress was fully informed of the temporary action he had taken only to preserve the legislative programs from destruction until Congress could act.

The absence of a specific statute authorizing seizure of the steel mills as a mode of executing the laws—both the military procurement program and the anti-inflation program—has not until today been thought to prevent the President from executing the laws. Unlike an administrative commission confined to the enforcement of the statute under which it was created, or the head of a department when administering a particular statute, the President is a constitutional officer charged with taking care that a "mass of legislation" be executed. Flexibility as to mode of execution to meet critical situations is a matter of practical necessity. . . .

. . . In this case, there is no statute prohibiting the action taken by the President in a matter not merely important but threatening the very safety of the Nation. Executive inaction in such a situation, courting national disaster, is foreign to the concept of energy and initiative in the Executive as created by the Founding Fathers. . . .

The broad executive power granted by Article II to an officer on duty 365 days a year cannot, it is said, be invoked to avert disaster. Instead, the President must confine himself to sending a message to Congress recommending action. Under this messenger-boy concept of the office, the President cannot even act to preserve legislative programs from destruction so that Congress will have something left to act upon. . . .

Along with its many changes in constitutional doctrine and political ideology, the Court had adopted a new mode of decision making. Decision making by means of a single majority opinion, a mode established by Chief Justice John Marshall in 1800, was not totally abandoned, but it was considerably modified by the widespread use of separate opinions. The New Deal and Fair Deal justices were subjected to criticism on both professional and partisan grounds because of the multiplicity of separate concurring and dissenting opinions. Justice William O. Douglas and several other members of the Court wrote strong and spirited defenses of the new practice, often arguing that the dissenting opinion was an important safeguard of democracy.[33] The dissents by Justices Black and Douglas in *Dennis* v. *The United States* are illustrative.

During the later 1940s and early '50s, Congress and the press carried on intense political controversy over internal security. Heightened concern about these issues was demonstrated by highly controversial investigations by the House Un-American Activities Committee and the Senate Internal Security Committee and, especially, by passage of the Smith Act of 1940, which provided that it is unlawful for any individual

(1) To knowingly or willfully advocate, abet, advise, or to teach the duty, necessity, desirability, or propriety of overthrowing or destroying any government in the United States by force or violence . . . ; (2) With intent to cause the overthrow or destruction of any government in the United States, to print, publish, edit, issue, circulate, sell, distribute, or publicly display any written or printed matter advocating, advising, or teaching the duty, necessity, desirability, or propriety of overthrowing or destroying any government in the United States by force or violence; (3) To organize or help to organize any society, group, or assembly of persons who teach, advocate, or encourage the overthrow or destruction of any government in the United States by force or violence; or to be or become a member of, or affiliate with, any such society . . . knowing the purposes thereof.

In a narrowly decided case, Chief Justice Vinson wrote the majority opinion in a major test of the constitutionality of this act, *Dennis* v. *The United States*, and was supported by separate concurring opinions by Justices Frankfurter and Jackson. Justice Clark did not participate. Justices Black and Douglas wrote separate dissenting opinions. Chief Justice Vinson's majority opinion was endorsed by Justices Reed, Burton, and Minton.

DENNIS v. UNITED STATES
341 U. S. 494 (1951)

Chief Justice Vinson delivered the opinion of the Court:

Petitioners were indicted in July, 1948, for violation of the conspiracy provisions of the Smith Act . . . during the period of April 1945, to July, 1948. . . . A verdict of guilty as to all the petitioners was returned by the jury on October 14, 1949. The Court of Appeals affirmed. . . . We granted certiorari, . . . limited to the following two questions: (1) Whether either § 2 or § 3 of the Smith Act, inherently or as construed and applied in the instant case, violates the First Amendment and other provisions of the Bill of Rights; (2) whether either § 2 or § 3 of the act, inherently or as construed and applied in the instant case, violates the First and Fifth Amendments because of indefiniteness.

I

It will be helpful in clarifying the issues to treat next the contention that the trial judge improperly interpreted the statute by charging that the statute required an unlawful intent before the jury could convict. . . .

The structure and purpose of the statute demand the inclusion of intent as an element of the crime. Congress was concerned with those who advocate and organize for the overthrow of the Government. Certainly those who recruit and combine for the purpose of advocating overthrow intend to bring about that overthrow. We hold that the statute requires as an essential element of the crime proof of the intent of those who are charged with its violation to overthrow the Government by force and violence. . . .

II

The obvious purpose of the statute is to protect existing Government, not from change by peaceable, lawful and constitutional means, but from change by violence, revolution and terrorism. That it is within the *power* of Congress to protect the Government of the United States from armed rebellion is a proposition which requires little discussion. Whatever theoretical merit there may be to the argument that there is a "right" to rebellion against dictatorial governments is without force where the existing structure of the government provides for peaceful and orderly change. We reject any principle of governmental helplessness in the face of preparation for revolution, which principle, carried to its logical conclusion, must lead to anarchy.

No one could conceive that it is not within the power of Congress to prohibit acts intended to overthrow the Government by force and violence. The question with which we are concerned here is not whether Congress has such *power*, but whether the *means* which it has employed conflict with the First and Fifth Amendments to the Constitution.

One of the bases for the contention that the means which Congress has employed are invalid takes the form of an attack on the face of the statute on the grounds that by its terms it prohibits academic discussion of the merits of Marxism-Leninism, that it stifles ideas and is contrary to all concepts of a free speech and a free press. Although we do not agree that the language itself has that significance, we must bear in mind that it is the duty of the federal courts to interpret federal legislation in a manner not inconsistent with the demands of the Constitution. . . . This is a federal statute which we must interpret as well as judge.

The very language of the Smith Act negates the interpretation which petitioners would have us impose on that Act. It is directed at advocacy, not discussion. Thus, the trial judge properly charged the jury that they could not convict if they found that petitioners did "no more than pursue peaceful studies and discussions or teaching and advocacy in the realm of ideas." He further charged that it was not unlawful "to conduct in an American college or university a course explaining the philosophical theories set forth in the books which have been placed in evidence." Such a charge is in strict accord with the statutory language, and illustrates the meaning to be placed on those words. Congress did not intend to eradicate the free discussion of political theories, to destroy the traditional rights of Americans to discuss and evaluate ideas without fear of governmental sanction. Rather Congress was concerned with the very kind of activity in which the evidence showed these petitioners engaged.

III

But although the statute is not directed at the hypothetical cases which petitioners have conjured, its application in this case has resulted in convictions for the teaching and advocacy of the overthrow of the Government by force and violence, which, even though coupled with the intent to accomplish that overthrow, contains an element of speech. For this reason, we must pay special heed to the demands of the First Amendment marking out the boundaries of speech.

We pointed out in *Douds* . . . that the basis of the First Amendment is the hypothesis that speech can rebut speech, propaganda will answer propaganda, free debate of ideas will result in the wisest governmental policies. It is for this reason that this Court has recognized the inherent value of free discourse. An analysis of the leading cases in this Court which have involved direct limitations on speech, however, will demonstrate that both the majority of the Court and the dissenters in particular cases have recognized that this is not an unlimited, unqualified right, but that the societal value of speech must, on occasion, be subordinated to other values and considerations. . . .

. . . Although no case subsequent to *Whitney* and *Gitlow* has expressly overruled the majority opinions in those cases, there is little doubt that subsequent opinions have inclined toward the Holmes-Brandeis rationale. And in *American Communications Assn.* v. *Douds,* [1950] . . . [w]e pointed out that Congress did not intend to punish belief, but rather intended to regulate the conduct of union affairs. We therefore held that any indirect sanction on speech which might arise from the oath requirement did not present a proper case for the "clear and present danger" test, for the regulation was aimed at conduct rather than speech. In discussing the proper measure of evaluation of this kind of legislation, we suggest that the Holmes-Brandeis philosophy insisted that where there was a direct restriction upon speech, a "clear and present danger" that the substantive evil would be caused was necessary before the statute in question could be constitutionally applied. And, we stated, "[The First] Amendment requires that one is permitted to believe what he will. It requires that one be permitted to advocate what he will unless there is a clear and present danger that a substantial public evil will result therefrom." But we further suggested that neither Justice Holmes nor Justice Brandeis ever envisioned that a shorthand phrase should be crystallized into a rigid rule to be applied inflexibly without regard to the circumstances of each case. Speech is not an absolute, above and beyond control by the legislature when its judgment, subject to review here, is that certain kinds of speech are so undesirable as to warrant criminal sanction. Nothing is more certain in modern society than the principle that there are no absolutes, that a name, a phrase, a standard has meaning only when associated with the considerations which gave birth to the nomenclature. . . . To those who would paralyze our government in the face of impending threat by encasing it in a semantic strait jacket we must reply that all concepts are relative.

In this case we are squarely presented with the application of the "clear and present danger" test, and must decide what the phrase imports. We first note that many of the cases in which this Court has reversed convictions by use of this or similar tests have been based on the fact that the interest which the State was attempting to protect was itself too insubstantial to warrant restriction of speech. . . . Overthrow of the Government by force and violence is certainly a substantial enough interest for the Government to limit speech. Indeed, this is the ultimate value of any society, for if a society cannot protect its very structure from armed internal attack, it must follow that no subordinate value can be protected. If, then, this interest may be protected, the literal problem which is presented is what has been meant by the use of the phrase "clear and present danger" of the utterances bringing about the evil within the power of Congress to punish.

Obviously, the words cannot mean that before the Government may act, it must wait until the *putsch* is about to be executed, the plans have been laid and the signal is awaited. If Government is aware that a group aiming at its overthrow is attempting to indoctrinate its members and to commit them to a course whereby they will strike when the leaders feel the circumstances permit, action by the Government is required. The argument that there is no need for Government to concern itself, for Government is strong, it possesses ample powers to put down a rebellion, it may defeat the revolution with ease needs no answer. For that is not the question. Certainly an attempt to overthrow the Government by force, even though doomed from the outset because of inadequate numbers or powers of revolutionists, is a sufficient evil for Congress to prevent. The damage which such attempts create both physically and politically to a nation makes it impossible to measure the validity in terms of the probability of success, or the immediacy of a successful attempt. In the instant case the trial judge charged the jury that they could not convict unless they found that petitioners intended to overthrow the Government "as speedily as circumstances would permit." This does not mean, and could not properly mean, that they would not strike until there was certainty of success. What was meant was that the revolutionists would strike when they thought the time was ripe. We must therefore reject the contention that success or probability of success is the criterion.

The situation with which Justices Holmes and Brandeis were concerned in *Gitlow* was a comparatively isolated event, bearing little relation in their minds to any substantial threat to the safety of the community. . . . They were not confronted with any situation comparable to the instant one—the development of an apparatus designed and dedicated to the overthrow of the Government, in the context of world crisis after crisis.

Chief Judge Learned Hand, writing for the majority

below, interpreted the phrase as follows: "In each case [courts] must ask whether the gravity of the 'evil,' discounted by its improbability, justifies such invasion of free speech as is necessary to avoid the danger." 183 F. 2d at 212. We adopt this statement of the rule. As articulated by Chief Judge Hand, it is as succinct and inclusive as any other we might devise at this time. It takes into consideration those factors which we deem relevant, and relates their significances. More we cannot expect from words.

Likewise, we are in accord with the court below, which affirmed the trial court's finding that the requisite danger existed. The mere fact that from the period 1945 to 1948 petitioners' activities did not result in an attempt to overthrow the Government by force and violence is of course no answer to the fact that there was a group that was ready to make the attempt. The formation by petitioners of such a highly organized conspiracy, with rigidly disciplined members subject to call when the leaders, these petitioners, felt that the time had come for action, coupled with the inflammable nature of world conditions, similar uprisings in other countries, and the touch-and-go nature of our relations with countries with whom petitioners were in the very least ideologically attuned, convince us that their convictions were justified on this score. And this analysis disposes of the contention that a conspiracy to advocate, as distinguished from the advocacy itself, cannot be constitutionally restrained, because it comprises only the preparation. It is the existence of the conspiracy which creates the danger. . . . If the ingredients of the reaction are present, we cannot bind the Government to wait until the catalyst is added.

IV

. . . The argument that the action of the trial court is erroneous, in declaring as a matter of law that such violation shows sufficient danger to justify the punishment despite the First Amendment, rests on the theory that a jury must decide a question of the application of the First Amendment. We do not agree.

When facts are found that establish the violation of a statute, the protection against conviction afforded by the First Amendment is a matter of law. The doctrine that there must be a clear and present danger of substantive evil that Congress has a right to prevent is a judicial rule to be applied as a matter of law by the courts. The guilt is established by proof of facts. Whether the First Amendment protects the activity which constitutes the violation of the statute must depend upon a judicial determination of the scope of the First Amendment applied to the circumstances of the case.

We hold that the statute may be applied where there is a "clear and present danger" of the substantive evil which the legislature had the right to prevent. Bearing, as it does, the marks of a "question of law," the issue is properly one for the judge to decide.

V

There remains to be discussed the question of vagueness—whether the statute as we have interpreted it is too vague, not sufficiently advising those who would speak of the limitations upon their activity. . . .

We hold that § § 2 (a)(1), 2 (a)(3) and 3 of the Smith Act do not inherently, or as construed or applied in the instant case, violate the First Amendment and other provisions of the Bill of Rights, or the First and Fifth Amendments because of indefiniteness. Petitioners intended to overthrow the Government of the United States as speedily as the circumstances would permit. Their conspiracy to organize the Communist Party and to teach and advocate the overthrow of the Government of the United States by force and violence created a "clear and present danger" of an attempt to overthrow the Government by force and violence. They were properly and constitutionally convicted for violation of the Smith Act. The judgments of conviction are affirmed.

Justice Douglas dissented:

If this were a case where those who claimed protection under the First Amendment were teaching the techniques of sabotage, the assassination of the President, the filching of documents from public files, the planting of bombs, the art of street warfare, and the like, I would have no doubts. The freedom to speak is not absolute; the teaching of methods of terror and other seditious conduct should be beyond the pale along with obscenity and immorality. This case was argued as if those were the facts. The argument imported much seditious conduct into the record. That is easy and it has popular appeal, for the activities of Communists in plotting and scheming against the free world are common knowledge. But the fact is that no such evidence was introduced at the trial. There is a statute which makes a seditious conspiracy unlawful. Petitioners, however, were not charged with a "conspiracy to overthrow" the Government. They were charged with a conspiracy to form a party and groups and assemblies of people who teach and advocate the overthrow of our Government by force or violence and with a conspiracy to advocate and teach its overthrow by force and violence. It may well be that indoctrination in the techniques of terror to destroy the Government would be indictable under either statute. But the teaching which is condemned here is of a different character. . . .

The vice of treating speech as the equivalent of overt acts of a treasonable or seditious character is emphasized by a concurring opinion, which by invoking the law of conspiracy makes speech do service for deeds which are dangerous to society. The doctrine of conspiracy has served divers and oppressive purposes and in its broad reach can be made to do great evil. But never until today has anyone seriously thought that the ancient law of conspiracy could constitutionally be used to turn speech into seditious conduct. Yet that is precisely what is suggested. I repeat that we deal here with speech alone, not with speech *plus* acts of sabotage or unlawful conduct. Not a single seditious act is charged in the indictment. To make a lawful speech unlawful because two men conceive it is to raise the law of conspiracy to appalling proportions. That course is to make a radical break with the past and to violate one of the cardinal principles of our constitutional scheme. . . .

There comes a time when even speech loses its constitutional immunity. Speech innocuous one year may at another time fan such destructive flames that it must be halted in the interests of the safety of the Republic. That is the meaning of the clear and present danger test. When conditions are so critical that there will be no time to avoid the evil that the speech threatens, it is time to call a halt. Otherwise, free speech which is the strength of the Nation will be the cause of its destruction.

Yet free speech is the rule, not the exception. The restraint to be constitutional must be based on more than fear, on more than passionate opposition against the speech, on more than a revolted dislike for its contents. There must be some immediate injury to society that is likely if speech is allowed. . . .

The First Amendment provides that "Congress shall make no law . . . abridging the freedom of speech." The Constitution provides no exception. This does not mean, however, that the Nation need hold its hand until it is in such weakened condition that there is no time to protect itself from incitement to revolution. Seditious conduct can always be punished. But the command of the First Amendment is so clear that we should not allow Congress to call a halt to free speech except in the extreme case of peril from the speech itself. The First Amendment makes confidence in the common sense of our people and in their maturity of judgment the great postulate of our democracy. Its philosophy is that violence is rarely, if ever, stopped by denying civil liberties to those advocating resort to force. The First Amendment reflects the philosophy of Jefferson "that it is time enough for the rightful purposes of civil government, for its officers to interfere when principles break out into overt acts against peace and good order." The political censor has no place in our public debates. Unless and until extreme and necessitous circumstances are shown, our aim should be to keep speech unfettered and to allow the processes of law to be invoked only when the provocateurs among us move from speech to action.

Vishinsky wrote in 1938 in The Law of the Soviet State, "In our state, naturally, there is and can be no place for freedom of speech, press, and so on for the foes of socialism."

Our concern should be that we accept no such standard for the United States. Our faith should be that our people will never give support to these advocates of revolution, so long as we remain loyal to the purposes for which our Nation was founded.

Conclusion

The election of 1932 was a critical election in terms of the size of the mandate accorded Franklin D. Roosevelt, the accompanying Democratic victories in the House and in the Senate, and most important, the fundamental shift in voter preference that occurred in that election and kept the Democratic party in power through several others. The conservative Supreme Court that Roosevelt inherited from three Republican predecessors was not a meaningful issue in the 1932 election, but a combination of crucial factors led to a devastating series of judicial setbacks for the Roosevelt administration: the intransigence of the four most conservative members, the initial tendency of more flexible conservatives to strike down New Deal legislation, and the slipshod legislative draftsmanship of the New Deal architects.

Because of the longevity of the conservatives and their desire to remain on the Court, Roosevelt had no vacancies to fill until October 1937. Between 1937 and

1940, only four vacancies represented potential changes in ideology and voting behavior; Roosevelt replaced Van Devanter in October 1937, Sutherland in January 1938, Butler in February 1940, and McReynolds in October 1941. Thus, the "normal turnover" discussed by Robert Dahl did not occur immediately during the postelection period when relations between the President and the Court were strained to the breaking point. A graceful but abrupt doctrinal transition by Justices Hughes and Roberts helped to turn the tide in favor of the New Deal. The Court's doctrinal direction was accurately described by Justice William O. Douglas in his comment about the late Senator Joseph Robinson:

> . . . In terms of the constitutionality of economic and social legislation, Joe Robinson might have passed muster, and it was by that standard that FDR was making his selections. Yet the standard was irrelevant to the demands of the coming years. Substantive due process was on the decline and the emerging problems dealt with civil rights. On these issues Robinson would have been on a par with any of the old wheel horses of the South. . . .[34]

By 1941 the change in personnel, doctrinal values, and judicial voting behavior was complete. Table 8–1 summarizes the enduring influence of the New Deal, Fair Deal, and subsequent liberal Court appointees, including some highly influential liberal Republicans.

On the eve of the 1952 presidential election, the controversies of the 1930s appeared to be resolved. The New Deal/Fair Deal Court was committed to permitting legislative intervention in the economy, to unrestrained diversity in judicial decision making, and to the broader assertion of judicial protection of civil rights and liberties. Would the Court become a major issue in the coming presidential election? And if Eisenhower won the election, how would a change in partisan control of the White House affect the selection of judges?

REFERENCES

1. Frank Freidel, "The Election of 1932," in Schlesinger and Israel, op. cit., pp. 352–353.
2. Freidel, op. cit., pp. 322–354.
3. 293 U.S. 388 (1935).
4. William F. Swindler, *Court and Constitution in the Twentieth Century: The New Legality, 1932–1968* (Indianapolis: Bobbs-Merrill, 1970), p. 33.
5. *Norman* v. *Baltimore and Ohio Railroad Company*, 294 U.S. 240 (1935); *United States* v. *Bankers Trust Company*, 294 U.S. 240 (1935); *Perry* v. *United States*, 294 U.S. 330 (1935); and *Nortz* v. *United States*, 294 U.S. 317 (1935).
6. Harold Ickes, *Secret Diary*, vol. 1 (New York: 1954), pp. 273–274.
7. 295 U.S. 330 (1935).
8. 295 U.S. 555 (1935).
9. *Louisville Bank* v. *Radford*, 295 U.S. 555 (1935).
10. *The Struggle for Judicial Supremacy*, op. cit., pp. 157–164.
11. 297 U.S. 288 (1936).
12. Cited in Swindler, op. cit., pp. 46–47; from *Hart Coal Company* v. *Sparks*, 7 F.S. 16, 28 (1934) and *Penn* v. *Glenn*, 10 F.S. 483, 487 (1935).
13. See *Congressional Record* 69: 9524, and Swindler, op. cit., pp. 38–39.
14. Swindler, op. cit., p. 45, and especially, William E. Leuchtenberg, "The Origins of Franklin D. Roosevelt's 'Court-Packing' Plan," *The Supreme Court Review* (Chicago: University of Chicago Press, 1966), pp. 347–375.

**TABLE 8-1 Judicial political generations and critical elections:
The persistence of Liberal Democratic influence, 1937–1983***

Appointing president and party	Chief Justice	Justices chosen in the post-1932 Democratic era, 1932–1968							
Critical election of 1932: Democrats take control of Congress and the presidency									
Franklin D. Roosevelt Democrat 1933–1945	H. Stone 1941–1946	*J. Byrnes* 1941–1942 *W. Rutledge* 1943–1949	*W. Douglas* 1939–1975	*F. Frankfurter* 1939–1962	*H. Black* 1937–1971	*S. Reed* 1938–1957		*R. Jackson* 1941–1954	*F. Murphy* 1940–1949
Harry S. Truman Democrat 1945–1953	*F. Vinson* 1946–1953	*S. Minton* 1949–1950					H. Burton 1945–1958		*T. Clark* 1949–1967
Dwight D. Eisenhower Republican 1953–1961	E. Warren 1953–1969	*W. Brennan* 1956–present				*C. Whittaker* 1957–1962	*P. Stewart* 1959–1981	*J. Harlan* 1955–1971	
John F. Kennedy Democrat 1961–1963				*A. Goldberg* 1962–1965		*B. White* 1962–present			
Lyndon B. Johnson Democrat 1963–1969				*A. Fortas* 1965–1969					*T. Marshall* 1967–present
Richard M. Nixon Republican 1969–1974	W. Burger 1969–present				H. Blackmun 1970–present	L. Powell 1972–present		W. Rehnquist 1972–present	
Gerald R. Ford Republican 1974–1977			J. Stevens 1975–present						
Jimmy Carter Democrat 1977–1981									
Ronald Reagan Republican 1981–present							S. O'Connor 1981–present		

*New Deal, Fair Deal, and Liberal Democratic Justices are in italics, Liberal Republicans are underlined.

15. Cited in Leuchtenberg, op. cit., p. 378.
16. Ibid., p. 348.
17. Cited in Leuchtenberg, op. cit., p. 391.
18. Ibid., pp. 393–396.
19. Kelley and Harbison, op. cit., p. 718; for a full discussion of the crisis see William E. Leuchtenberg, "Franklin D. Roosevelt's Supreme 'Court-Packing' Plan" in *Essays on the New Deal,* ed. Harold M. Hollingsworth and William F. Holmes (Austin: University of Texas Press, 1969).
20. 300 U. S. 440 (1937).
21. 300 U. S. 515 (1937).
22. Leuchtenberg, *Essays,* op. cit.; and Swindler op. cit., pp. 62–76.
23. For the full text of the chief justice's letter see U. S. Senate Judiciary Committee, *Hearings on the Reorganization of the Federal Courts, S. 1392* (March 10–16, 1937).
24. 301 U. S. 619 (1937).
25. U. S. Senate Judiciary Committee, *Adverse Report on S. 1392* (Washington: U. S. Government Printing Office, 1937).
26. Leuchtenberg, *Essays,* op. cit.; and Swindler, op. cit., pp. 81–87.
27. Swindler, op. cit., pp. 81–97.
28. William O. Douglas, *The Court Years, 1939–1975: The Autobiography of William O. Douglas* (New York: Random House, 1980), p. 155; see *Wheeling Steel Corporation* v. *Glander,* 337 U. S. 562 (1949).
29. 304 U. S. 144 (1938).
30. 321 U. S. 414 (1944), see also *Bowles* v. *Willingham,* 321 U. S. 503 (1944).
31. 310 U. S. 586 (1940).
32. 295 U. S. 45 (1935).
33. William O. Douglas, "The Dissent: A Safeguard of Democracy," *Journal of the American Judicature Society* 32 (December 1948); for a detailed discussion of the politics of the Court's internal procedures see, Schmidhauser, *Judges and Justices,* op. cit., pp. 105–200.
34. Douglas, *The Court Years,* op. cit., p. 18.

CHAPTER
9

The Transformation of Judicial Values in the 1950s and 1960s

A Judicial Revolution without a Critical Election

Dwight David Eisenhower's victory in the presidential campaign of 1952 was a decisive ending of the Fair Deal, a conclusion underscored by the size of the popular vote margin—Eisenhower's 33.9 million to Adlai Stevenson's 27.3 million. Although the Supreme Court had been subjected to rather serious congressional attack throughout Harry Truman's second term, the Court itself did not figure prominently in the presidential contest. Since General Eisenhower was not identified with any political position during the long years of his military career, it was not clear how he would deal with the Supreme Court. Initially, after his election, all of the justices were New Deal/Fair Deal appointees: Chief Justice Fred Vinson, Felix Frankfurter, Hugo L. Black, Sherman Minton, William O. Douglas, Stanley Reed, Tom Clark, Harold Burton, and Robert Jackson. The prospects for immediate change did not appear to be great. But unlike Franklin Roosevelt, Eisenhower had a major opportunity before the end of his first year in office.

In September 1953 Chief Justice Vinson died suddenly. Within the Eisenhower Administration, Attorney General Herbert Brownell, Jr., was given chief responsibility for compiling a list of potential nominees. Earl Warren's administrative ability and his standing as a notable western Republican were important considerations in his selection. After serving as chief justice on the basis of an interim appointment, on March 1, 1954 Earl Warren was confirmed by the Senate unanimously. The selection was momentous because Warren proved to be a liberal and an activist.

Less than a year later, Justice Robert Jackson died suddenly. President Eisenhower had established close ties with the American Bar Association. Brownell developed a list of candidates approved by a committee of the ABA, and Presidential Assistant Sherman Adams cleared potential nominees with the Republican

National Committee. The successor to Jackson was John Marshall Harlan, grandson of the justice who had dissented in *Plessy* v. *Ferguson* and the Income Tax Case. Although identified, as was Warren, with the moderate Thomas Dewey wing of the Republican party, Harlan was a corporate law firm member who served as a circuit judge. His confirmation was delayed by conservative Southern Democrats and Northern Republicans who were critical of his purported liberal views. Harlan was confirmed on March 28, 1955 and proved to be a moderate conservative. Justice Sherman Minton retired in the fall of 1956. William J. Brennan, a Roman Catholic Democrat and a distinguished member of the Supreme Court of New Jersey, was chosen as his successor on October 16, 1956. Because of McCarthyist attacks, his confirmation was held up until March 19, 1957. Brennan, like Warren, was a liberal and an activist. President Eisenhower's fourth nominee, midwestern corporate lawyer Charles E. Whittaker, who succeeded the resigning Stanley Reed in March of 1957, had no serious opposition from Senate conservatives. He was a conservative who labored at his opinions. The president had yet another appointment to make when Justice Burton resigned in 1958. An Ohio Republican and former State Supreme Court member, Potter Stewart, was chosen in October of 1958 but gained Senate confirmation only by a vote of 70 to 17.[1] Stewart was a moderate conservative. Thus, within six years Eisenhower was able to reshape the Court.

Internal security and the Eisenhower era

The significance of these new appointments soon became apparent. The Dennis decision's application of the clear and present danger doctrine had aroused concerns about future Smith Act indictments. Later in the 1950s, after most of the Eisenhower appointments, that application was carefully reappraised in the context of a different set of circumstances in *Yates* v. *The United States*. The majority opinion established a distinction between Dennis and the facts in the Yates case. Justices Black and Douglas concurred and dissented in part. Justice Burton concurred, and Justice Clark dissented without an opinion. Justices Brennan and Whittaker did not take part in the case.

YATES v. UNITED STATES
354 U. S. 298 (1957)

Justice Harlan delivered the opinion of the Court:

We brought these cases here to consider certain questions arising under the Smith Act which have not heretofore been passed upon by this Court, and otherwise to review the convictions of these petitioners for conspiracy to violate that Act. Among other things, the convictions are claimed to rest upon an application of the Smith Act which is hostile to the principles upon which its constitutionality was upheld in *Dennis* v. *United States*. . . .

. . . The conspiracy is alleged to have originated in 1940 and continued down to the date of the in-

dictment in 1951. The indictment charged that in carrying out the conspiracy the defendants and their co-conspirators would (a) become members and officers of the Communist Party, with knowledge of its unlawful purposes, and assume leadership in carrying out its policies and activities; (b) cause to be organized units of the Party in California and elsewhere; (c) write and publish, in the "Daily Worker" and other Party organs, articles on the proscribed advocacy and teaching; (d) conduct schools for the indoctrination of Party members in such advocacy and teaching, and (e) recruit new Party members, particularly from among persons employed in the key industries of the nation. Twenty-three overt acts in furtherance of the conspiracy were alleged. . . .

We conclude . . . that since the Communist Party came into being in 1945, and the indictment was not returned until 1951, the three-year statute of limitations had run on the "organizing" charge, and required the withdrawal of that part of the indictment from the jury's consideration. . . .

Petitioners contend that the instructions to the jury were fatally defective in that the trial court refused to charge that, in order to convict, the jury must find that the advocacy which the defendants conspired to promote was of a kind calculated to "incite" persons to action for the forcible overthrow of the Government. It is argued that advocacy of forcible overthrow as mere *abstract doctrine* is within the free speech protection of the First Amendment; that the Smith Act, consistently with that constitutional provision, must be taken as proscribing only the sort of advocacy which incites to illegal *action*; and that the trial court's charge, by permitting conviction for mere advocacy, unrelated to its tendency to produce forcible action, resulted in an unconstitutional application of the Smith Act. The Government, which at the trial also requested the court to charge in terms of "incitement," now takes the position, however, that the true constitutional dividing line is not between inciting and abstract advocacy of forcible overthrow, but rather between advocacy as such, irrespective of its inciting qualities, and the mere discussion or exposition of violent overthrow as an abstract theory. . . .

We are . . . faced with the question whether the Smith Act prohibits advocacy and teaching of forcible overthrow as an abstract principle, divorced from any effort to instigate action to that end, so long as such advocacy or teaching is engaged in with evil intent. We hold that it does not.

The distinction between advocacy of abstract doctrine and advocacy directed at promoting unlawful action is one that has been consistently recognized in the opinions of this Court. . . . This distinction was heavily underscored in *Gitlow* v. *New York* [1925] . . . in which the statute involved was nearly identical with the one now before us. . . .

. . . The legislative history of the Smith Act and related bills shows beyond all question that Congress was aware of the distinction between the advocacy or teaching of abstract doctrine and the advocacy or teaching of action, and that it did not intend to disregard it. The statute was aimed at the advocacy and teaching of concrete action for the forcible overthrow of the Government, and not of principles divorced from action. . . .

In failing to distinguish between advocacy of forcible overthrow as an abstract doctrine and advocacy of action to that end, the District Court appears to have been led astray by the holding in *Dennis* that advocacy of violent action to be taken at some future time was enough. It seems to have considered that, since "inciting" speech is usually thought of as something calculated to induce immediate action, and since *Dennis* held advocacy of action for future overthrow sufficient, this meant that advocacy, irrespective of its tendency to generate action, is punishable, provided only that it is uttered with a specific intent to accomplish overthrow. In other words, the District Court apparently thought that *Dennis* obliterated the traditional dividing line between advocacy of abstract doctrine and advocacy of action. . . .

. . . As one of the concurring opinions in *Dennis* put it: "Throughout our decisions there has recurred a distinction between the statement of an idea which may prompt its hearers to take unlawful action, and advocacy that such action be taken." . . . There is nothing in *Dennis* which makes that historic distinction obsolete. . . .

On this basis we have concluded that the evidence against [five of the] petitioners . . . is so clearly insufficient that their acquittal should be ordered. . . .

. . . [W]e find no adequate evidence in the record which would permit a jury to find that they were members of such a conspiracy. For all purposes relevant here, the sole evidence as to them was that they had long been members, officers or functionaries of the Communist Party of California. . . . So far as this record shows, none of them has engaged in or been associated with any but what appear to have been wholly lawful activities or has ever made a single remark or been present when someone else made a remark, which would tend to prove the charges against them. . . .

Moreover, apart from the inadequacy of the evidence to show, at best, more than the abstract advocacy and teaching of forcible overthrow by the Party, it is difficult to perceive how the requisite specific intent to accomplish such overthrow could be deemed proved by a showing of mere membership or the holding of office in the Communist Party. We therefore think that as to these petitioners the evidence was entirely too meagre to justify putting them to a new trial, and that their acquittal should be ordered. . . .

For the foregoing reasons we think that the way must be left open for a new trial to the extent indicated. . . . It is so ordered.

Members of Congress generally voting with the conservative coalition were incensed at the modification of the Dennis decision. They had been outraged at what they described as a blatant Supreme Court invasion of states' rights in *Nelson v. Pennsylvania*. This case involved a Pennsylvania sedition act that had provided the basis for the indictment and conviction of Steve Nelson, a member of the Communist party. The Supreme Court of Pennsylvania had reversed Nelson's conviction on the ground that the federal Smith Act preempted state legislation prohibiting sedition against the United States. There was no evidence that Nelson had conspired against the state of Pennsylvania. Although it was the state Supreme Court that had applied this federal preemption doctrine, (and the U.S. Supreme Court had upheld this position in the decision reproduced below), congressional conservatives' anger and attempts at legislative retaliation were directed against the federal Supreme Court.

PENNSYLVANIA v. NELSON
350 U.S. 497 (1956)

*Chief Justice Warren
delivered the opinion of the Court:*

The respondent Steve Nelson, an acknowledged member of the Communist Party, was convicted . . . of a violation of the Pennsylvania Sedition Act and sentenced to imprisonment for twenty years and to a fine of $10,000. . . . The Superior Court affirmed the conviction. . . . The Supreme Court of Pennsylvania, recognizing but not reaching many alleged serious trial errors and conduct of the trial court infringing upon the respondent's right to due process of law, decided the case on the narrow issue of supersession of the state law by the Federal Smith Act. In its opinion, the court stated:

And, while the Pennsylvania statute proscribes sedition against either the Government of the United States or the Government of Pennsylvania, it is only alleged sedition against the United States with which the instant case is concerned. Out of all the voluminous testimony, we have not found, nor has anyone pointed to, a single word indicating a seditious act or even utterance directed against the Government of Pennsylvania.

The precise holding of the court, and all that is before us for review, is that the Smith Act of 1940, as amended in 1948, which prohibits the knowing advocacy of the overthrow of the Government of the United States by force and violence, supersedes the enforceability of the Pennsylvania Sedition Act which proscribes the same conduct. . . .

It should be said at the outset that the decision in this case does not affect the right of States to enforce their sedition laws at times when the Federal Government has not occupied the field and is not protecting the entire country from seditious conduct. The distinction between the two situations was clearly recognized by the court below. Nor does it limit the jurisdiction of the States where the Constitution and Congress have specifically given them concurrent jurisdiction, as was done under the Eighteenth Amendment and the Volstead Act. . . . Neither does it limit the right of the State to protect itself at any time against sabotage or attempted violence of all kinds. Nor does it prevent the State from prosecuting where the same act constitutes both a federal offense and a state offense under the police power. . . .

Where, as in the instant case, Congress has not stated specifically whether a federal statute has occupied a field in which the States are otherwise free to legislate, different criteria have furnished touchstones for decision. Thus,

[T]his Court, in considering the validity of state laws in the light of . . . federal laws touching the same subject, has made use of the following expressions: conflicting; contrary to; occupying the field; repugnance; difference; irreconcilability; inconsistency; violation; curtailment; and interference. But none of these expressions provides an infallible constitutional test or an exclusive constitutional yardstick. In the final analysis, there can be no one crystal clear distinctly marked formula.

. . . In this case, we think that each of several tests of supersession is met.

First, "[t]he scheme of federal regulation [is] so pervasive as to make reasonable the inference that Congress left no room for the States to supplement it." . . . The Congress determined in 1940 that it was necessary for it to re-enter the field of antisubversive legislation, which had been abandoned by it in 1921. In that year, it enacted the Smith Act which proscribes advocacy of the overthrow of any government—federal, state or local—by force and violence and organization of and knowing membership in a group which so advocates. Conspiracy to commit any of these acts is punishable under the general criminal conspiracy provisions in 18 U. S. C. § 371. . . .

We examine these Acts only to determine the congressional plan. Looking to all of them in the aggregate, the conclusion is inescapable that Congress has intended to occupy the field of sedition. Taken as a whole, they evince a congressional plan which makes it reasonable to determine that no room has been left for the States to supplement it. Therefore, a state sedition statute is superseded regardless of whether it purports to supplement the federal law. . . .

Second, the federal statutes "touch a field in which the federal interest is so dominant that the federal system [must] be assumed to preclude enforcement of state laws on the same subject." . . . Congress has devised an all-embracing program for resistance to the various forms of totalitarian aggression. Our external defenses have been strengthened, and a plan to protect against internal subversion has been made by it. It has appropriated vast sums, not only for our own protection, but also to strengthen freedom throughout the world. It has charged the Federal Bureau of Investigation and the Central Intelligence Agency with responsibility for intelligence concerning Communist seditious activities against our Government, and has denominated such activities as part of a world conspiracy. It accordingly proscribed sedition against all government in the nation—national, state and local. Congress declared that these steps were taken "to provide for the common defense, to preserve the sovereignty of the United States as an independent nation, and to guarantee to each State a republican form of government. . . ." Congress having thus treated seditious conduct as a matter of vital national concern, it is in no sense a local enforcement problem. . . .

Third, enforcement of state sedition acts presents a serious danger of conflict with the administration of the federal program. Since 1939, in order to avoid a hampering of uniform enforcement of its program by sporadic local prosecutions, the Federal Government has urged local authorities not to intervene in such matters, but to turn over to the federal authorities immediately and unevaluated all information concerning subversive activities. The President made such a request on September 6, 1939, when he placed the Federal Bureau of Investigation in charge of investigation in this field. . . . Should the States be permitted to exercise a concurrent jurisdiction in this area, federal enforcement would encounter not only the difficulties mentioned by Mr. Justice Jackson, but the added conflict engendered by different criteria of substantive offenses.

Since we find that Congress has occupied the field to the exclusion of parallel state legislation, that the dominant interest of the Federal Government precludes state intervention, and that administration of state Acts would conflict with the operation of the federal plan, we are convinced that the decision of the Supreme Court of Pennsylvania is unassailable.

We are not unmindful of the risk of compounding punishments which would be created by finding concurrent state power. In our view of the case, we do not reach the question whether double or multiple punishment for the same overt acts directed against the United States has constitutional sanction. Without compelling indication to the contrary, we will not assume that Congress intended to permit the possibility of double punishment. . . .

The judgment of the Supreme Court of Pennsylvania is affirmed.

Justice Reed, joined by
Justices Burton and Minton, dissented:

. . . Congress has not, in any of its statutes relating to sedition, specifically barred the exercise of state power to punish the same Acts under state law. And, we read the majority opinion to assume for this case that, absent federal legislation, there is no constitutional bar to punishment of sedition against the United States by both a State and the Nation. The majority limits to the federal courts the power to try charges of sedition against the Federal Government. . . .

[I]t is quite apparent that since 1940 Congress has been keenly aware of the magnitude of existing state legislation proscribing sedition. It may be validly assumed that in these circumstances this Court should not void state legislation without a clear mandate from Congress.

We cannot agree that the federal criminal sanctions against sedition directed at the United States are of such a pervasive character as to indicate an intention to void state action.

Secondly, the Court states that the federal sedition statutes touch a field "in which the federal interest is so dominant" they must preclude state laws on the same subject. This concept is suggested in a comment on *Hines* v. *Davidowitz.* . . . The Court in *Davidowitz* ruled that federal statutes compelling alien registration preclude enforcement of state statutes requiring alien registration. We read *Davidowitz* to teach nothing more than that, when the Congress provided a single nation-wide integrated system of regulation so complete as that for aliens' registration (with fingerprinting, a scheduling of activities, and continuous information as to their residence), the Act bore so directly on our foreign relations as to make it evident that Congress intended only one uniform national alien registration system. . . .

Thirdly, the Court finds ground for abrogating Pennsylvania's antisedition statute because, in the Court's view, the State's administration of the Act may hamper the enforcement of the federal law. Quotations are inserted from statements of President Roosevelt and Mr. Hoover, the Director of the Federal Bureau of Investigation, to support the Court's position. But a reading of the quotations leads us to conclude that their purpose was to gain prompt knowledge of evidence of subversive activities so that the federal agency could be fully advised. We find no suggestion from any official source that state officials should be less alert to ferret out or punish subversion. The Court's attitude as to interference seems to us quite contrary to that of the Legislative and Executive Departments. Congress was advised of the existing state

sedition legislation when the Smith Act was enacted and has been kept current with its spread. No declaration of exclusiveness followed. . . .

Finally, and this one point seems in and of itself decisive, there is an independent reason for reversing the Pennsylvania Supreme Court. The Smith Act appears in Title 18 of the United States Code, which Title codifies the federal criminal laws. Section 3231 of that Title provides:

Nothing in this title shall be held to take away or impair the jurisdiction of the courts of the several States under the laws thereof.

That declaration springs from the federal character of our Nation. It recognizes the fact that maintenance of order and fairness rests primarily with the States. The section was first enacted in 1825 and has appeared successively in the federal criminal laws since that time. This Court has interpreted the section to mean that States may provide concurrent legislation in the absence of explicit congressional intent to the contrary. . . . The majority's position in this case cannot be reconciled with that clear authorization of Congress. . . .

The Court's decision in the Nelson case stimulated, additionally, strong negative reactions among conservative Congressmen (many of whom had already opposed the desegregation decision of *Brown* v. *Board of Education*). Congressman Howard Smith of Virginia, chairman of the House Rules Committee, introduced a strong anti–Court bill in 1957. This bill provided that

No act of Congress shall be construed as indicating an intent on the part of Congress to occupy the field in which such act operates, to the exclusion of any state laws on the same subject matter, unless such act contains an express provision to the effect or unless there is a direct and positive conflict between such act and the state law, so that the two cannot be reconciled or consistently stand together.

The House passed this bill in 1958 and in 1959 but it was opposed by the Eisenhower administration and ultimately failed in the Senate.

Another important issue concerned Congressional authority to investigate internal security problems. In *Watkins* v. *The United States*, the Supreme Court considered an appeal from a labor union official's contempt conviction based upon his failure to testify on certain matters before the House Un-American Activities Committee. The majority opinion reversed the conviction. Justice Frankfurter wrote a separate concurring opinion; Justices Burton and Whittaker took no part in the case, and Justice Clark wrote a sharp dissent.

WATKINS v. UNITED STATES
354 U. S. 178 (1957)

Chief Justice Warren
delivered the opinion of the Court:

. . . We start with several basic premises on which there is general agreement. The power of the Congress to conduct investigations is inherent in the legislative process. That power is broad. It encompasses inquiries concerning the administration of existing laws as well as proposed or possibly needed statutes. It includes surveys of defects in our social, economic or political system for the purpose of enabling the Congress to remedy them. It comprehends probes into departments of the Federal Government to expose corruption, inefficiency or waste. But broad as is this power of inquiry, it is not unlimited. There is no general authority to expose the private affairs of individuals without justification in terms of the functions of the Congress. This was freely conceded by the Solicitor General in his argument of this case. Nor is the Congress a law enforcement or trial agency. These are functions of the executive and judicial departments of government. No inquiry is an end in itself; it must be related to and in furtherance of a legitimate task of the Congress. Investigations conducted solely for the personal aggrandizement of the investigators or to "punish" those investigated are indefensible.

It is unquestionably the duty of all citizens to cooperate with the Congress in its efforts to obtain the facts needed for intelligent legislative action. It is their unremitting obligation to respond to subpoenas, to respect the dignity of the Congress and its committees and to testify fully with respect to matters within the province of proper investigation. This, of course, assumes that the constitutional rights of witnesses will be respected by the Congress as they are in a court of justice.

The Bill of Rights is applicable to investigations as to all forms of governmental action. Witnesses cannot be compelled to give evidence against themselves. They cannot be subjected to unreasonable search and seizure. Nor can the First Amendment freedoms of speech, press, religion, or political belief and association be abridged. . . .

In the decade following World War II, there appeared a new kind of congressional inquiry unknown in prior periods of American history. Principally this was the result of the various investigations into the threat of subversion of the United States Government, but other subjects of congressional interest also contributed to the changed scene. This new phase of legislative inquiry involved a broad-scale intrusion into the lives and affairs of private citizens. It brought before the courts novel questions of the appropriate limits of congressional inquiry. . . . In the more recent cases, the emphasis shifted to problems of accommodating the interest of the Government with the rights and privileges of individuals. The central theme was the application of the Bill of Rights as a restraint upon the assertion of governmental power in this form.

It was during this period that the Fifth Amendment privilege against self-incrimination was frequently invoked and recognized as a legal limit upon the authority of a committee to require that a witness answer its questions. Some early doubts as to the applicability of that privilege before a legislative committee never matured. When the matter reached this Court, the Government did not challenge in any way that the Fifth Amendment protection was available to the witness, and such a challenge could not have prevailed. It confined its argument to the character of the answers sought and to the adequacy of the claim of privilege. . . .

A far more difficult task evolved from the claim by witnesses that the committees' interrogations were infringements upon the freedoms of the First Amendment. Clearly, an investigation is subject to the command that the Congress shall make no law abridging freedom of speech or press or assembly. While it is true that there is no statute to be reviewed, and that an investigation is not a law, nevertheless an investigation is part of lawmaking. It is justified solely as an adjunct to the legislative process. The First Amendment may be invoked against infringement of the protected freedoms by law or by law-making.

Abuses of the investigative process may imperceptibly lead to abridgment of protected freedoms. The mere summoning of a witness and compelling him to testify, against his will, about his beliefs, expressions or associations is a measure of governmental interference. And when those forced revelations concern matters that are unorthodox, unpopular, or even hateful to the general public, the reaction in the life of the witness may be disastrous. This effect is even more harsh when it is past beliefs, expressions or associations that are disclosed and judged by current standards rather than those contemporary with the matters exposed. Nor does the witness alone suffer the consequences. Those who are identified by witnesses and thereby placed in the same glare of publicity are equally subject to public stigma, scorn and obloquy. Beyond that, there is the more subtle and immeasurable effect upon those who tend to adhere to the most orthodox and uncontroversial views and associations in order to avoid a similar fate at some future time. That this impact is partly the result of non-governmental activity by private persons cannot relieve the investigators of their responsibility for initiating the reaction. . . .

Accommodation of the congressional need for particular information with the individual and personal interest in privacy is an arduous and delicate task for any court. We do not underestimate the difficulties that would attend such an undertaking. It is manifest, that despite the adverse effects which follow upon compelled disclosure of private matters, not all such inquiries are barred. . . . The critical element is the existence of, and the weight to be ascribed to, the interest of the Congress in demanding disclosures from an unwilling witness. We cannot simply assume, however, that every congressional investigation is justified by a public need that overbalances any private rights affected. To do so would be to abdicate the responsibility placed by the Constitution upon the judiciary to insure that the Congress does not unjustifiably encroach upon an individual's right to privacy nor abridge his liberty of speech, press, religion or assembly.

Petitioner has earnestly suggested that the difficult questions of protecting these rights from infringement by legislative inquiries can be surmounted in this case because there was no public purpose served in his interrogation. His conclusion is based upon the thesis that the Subcommittee was engaged in a program of exposure for the sake of exposure. . . .

We have no doubt that there is no congressional power to expose for the sake of exposure. The public is, of course, entitled to be informed concerning the workings of its government. That cannot be inflated into a general power to expose where the predominant result can only be an invasion of the private rights of individuals. But a solution to our problem is not to be found in testing the motives of committee members for this purpose. Such is not our function. Their motives alone would not vitiate an investigation which had been instituted by a House of Congress if that assembly's legislative purpose is being served.

. . . The theory of a committee inquiry is that the committee members are serving as the representatives of the parent assembly in collecting information for a

legislative purpose. Their function is to act as the eyes and ears of the Congress in obtaining facts upon which the full legislature can act. . . .

An essential premise in this situation is that the House or Senate shall have instructed the committee members on what they are to do with the power delegated to them. It is the responsibility of the Congress, in the first instance, to insure that compulsory process is used only in furtherance of a legislative purpose. That requires that the instructions to an investigating committee spell out that group's jurisdiction and purpose with sufficient particularity. Those instructions are embodied in the authorizing resolution. That document is the committee's charter. Broadly drafted and loosely worded, however, such resolutions can leave tremendous latitude to the discretion of the investigators. The more vague the committee's charter is, the greater becomes the possibility that the committee's specific actions are not in conformity with the will of the parent House of Congress.

The authorizing resolution of the Un-American Activities Committee was adopted in 1938 when a select committee, under the chairmanship of Representative Dies, was created. Several years later, the Committee was made a standing organ of the House with the same mandate. It defines the Committee's authority as follows:

"The Committee on Un-American Activities, as a whole or by subcommittee, is authorized to make from time to time investigations of (i) the extent, character, and objects of un-American propaganda activities in the United States, (ii) the diffusion within the United States of subversive and un-American propaganda that is instigated from foreign countries or of a domestic origin and attacks the principle of the form of government as guaranteed by our Constitution, and (iii) all other questions in relation thereto that would aid Congress in any necessary remedial legislation."

It would be difficult to imagine a less explicit authorizing resolution. Who can define the meaning of "un-American"? What is that single, solitary "principle of the form of government as guaranteed by our Constitution"? There is no need to dwell upon the language, however. At one time, perhaps, the resolution might have been read narrowly to confine the Committee to the subject of propaganda. The events that have transpired in the fifteen years before the interrogation of petitioner make such a construction impossible at this date.

The members of the Committee have clearly demonstrated that they did not feel themselves restricted in any way to propaganda in the narrow sense of the word. Unquestionably the Committee conceived of its task in the grand view of its name. Un-American activities were its target, no matter how or where manifested. Notwithstanding the broad purview of the Committee's experience, the House of Representatives repeatedly approved its continuation. . . .

Combining the language of the resolution with the construction it has been given, it is evident that the preliminary control of the Committee exercised by the House of Representatives is slight or non-existent. No one could reasonably deduce from the charter the kind of investigation that the Committee was directed to make. As a result, we are asked to engage in a process of retroactive rationalization. Looking backward from the events that transpired, we are asked to uphold the Committee's actions unless it appears that they were clearly not authorized by the charter. As a corollary to this inverse approach, the Government urges that we must view the matter hospitably to the power of the Congress—that if there is any legislative purpose which might have been furthered by the kind of disclosure sought, the witness must be punished for withholding it. No doubt every reasonable indulgence of legality must be accorded to the actions of a coordinate branch of our Government. But such deference cannot yield to an unnecessary and unreasonable dissipation of precious constitutional freedoms.

The Government contends that the public interest at the core of the investigations of the Un-American Activities Committee is the need by the Congress to be informed of efforts to overthrow the Government by force and violence so that adequate legislative safeguards can be erected. From this core, however, the Committee can radiate outward infinitely to any topic thought to be related in some way to armed insurrection. The outer reaches of this domain are known only by the content of "un-American activities." . . .

The consequences that flow from this situation are manifold. In the first place, a reviewing court is unable to make the kind of judgment made by the Court in *United States* v. *Rumely* [1953]. . . . The Committee is allowed, in essence, to define its own authority, to choose the direction and focus of its activities. In deciding what to do with the power that has been conferred upon them, members of the Committee may act pursuant to motives that seem to them to be the highest. Their decisions, nevertheless, can lead to ruthless exposure of private lives in order to gather data that is neither desired by the Congress nor useful to it. Yet it is impossible in this circumstance, with constitutional freedoms in jeopardy, to declare that the Committee has ranged beyond the area committed to it by its parent assembly because the boundaries are so nebulous.

More important and more fundamental than that, however, it insulates the House that has authorized the investigation from the witnesses who are subjected to the sanctions of compulsory process. There is a wide gulf between the responsibility for the use of investigative power and the actual exercise of that power. This is an especially vital consideration in assuring respect for constitutional liberties. Protected freedoms should not be placed in danger in the absence of a clear determination by the House or the Senate that a particular inquiry is justified by a specific legislated need.

. . . An excessively broad charter, like that of the House Un-American Activities Committee, places the courts in an untenable position if they are to strike a balance between the public need for a particular interrogation and the right of citizens to carry on their affairs free from unnecessary governmental interference. It is impossible in such a situation to ascertain whether any legislative purpose justifies the disclosures sought and, if so, the importance of that information to the Congress in furtherance of its legislative function. The reason no court can make this critical judgment is that the House of Representatives itself has never made it. Only the legislative assembly initiating an investigation can assay the relative necessity of specific disclosures.

Absence of the qualitative consideration of petitioner's questioning by the House of Representatives aggravates a serious problem, revealed in this case, in the relationship of congressional investigating committees and the witnesses who appear before them. Plainly these committees are restricted to the missions delegated to them, i.e., to acquire certain data to be used by the House or the Senate in coping with a problem that falls within its legislative sphere. No witness can be compelled to make disclosures on matters outside that area. This is a jurisdiction concept of pertinency drawn from the nature of a congressional committee's source of authority. It is not wholly different from nor unrelated to the element of pertinency embodied in the criminal statute under which petitioner was prosecuted. When the definition of jurisdiction pertinency is as uncertain and wavering as in the case of the Un-American Activities Committee, it becomes extremely difficult for the Committee to limit its inquiries to statutory pertinency.

Since World War II, the Congress has practically abandoned its original practice of utilizing the coercive sanction of contempt proceedings at the bar of the House. The sanction there imposed is imprisonment by the House until the recalcitrant witness agrees to testify or disclose the matters sought, provided that the incarceration does not extend beyond adjournment. The Congress has instead invoked the aid of the federal judicial system in protecting itself against contumacious conduct. It has become customary to refer these matters to the United States Attorneys for prosecution under criminal law. . . .

In fulfillment of their obligation under this statute, the courts must accord to the defendants every right which is guaranteed to defendants in all other criminal cases. Among these is the right to have available, through a sufficiently precise statute, information revealing the standard of criminality before the commission of the alleged offense. Applied to persons prosecuted under § 192, this raises a special problem in that the statute defines the crime as refusal to answer "any question pertinent to the question under inquiry." Part of the standard of criminality, therefore, is the pertinency of the questions propounded to the witness.

The problem attains proportion when viewed from the standpoint of the witness who appears before a congressional committee. He must decide at the time the questions are propounded whether or not to answer. As the Court said in *Sinclair v. United States* [1929] . . . the witness acts at his peril. He is ". . . bound rightly to construe the statute." . . . An erroneous determination on his part, even if made in the utmost good faith, does not exculpate him if the court should later rule that the questions were pertinent to the question under inquiry.

It is obvious that a person compelled to make this choice is entitled to have knowledge of the subject to which the interrogation is deemed pertinent. That knowledge must be available with the same degree of explicitness and clarity that the Due Process Clause requires in the expression of any element of a criminal offense. The "vice of vagueness" must be avoided here as in all other crimes. There are several sources that can outline the "question under inquiry" in such a way that the rules against vagueness are satisfied. The authorizing resolution, the remarks of the chairman or members of the committee, or even the nature of the proceedings themselves might sometimes make the topic clear. This case demonstrates, however, that these sources often leave the matter in grave doubt.

The first possibility is that the authorizing resolution itself will so clearly declare the "question under inquiry" that a witness can understand the pertinency of questions asked him. The Government does not contend that the authorizing resolution of the Un-American Activities Committee could serve such a purpose. Its confusing breadth is amply illustrated by the innumerable and diverse questions into which the Committee has inquired under this charter since 1938. If the "question under inquiry" were stated with such

sweeping and uncertain scope, we doubt that it would withstand an attack on the ground of vagueness. . . .

No aid is given as to the "question under inquiry" in the action of the full Committee that authorized the creation of the Subcommittee before which petitioner appeared. The Committee adopted a formal resolution giving the Chairman the power to appoint subcommittees ". . . for the purpose of performing any and all acts which the Committee as a whole is authorized to do." In effect, this was a device to enable the investigations to proceed with a quorum of one or two members and sheds no light on the relevancy of the questions asked of petitioner.

The Government believes that the topic of inquiry before the Subcommittee concerned Communist infiltration in labor. In his introductory remarks, the Chairman made reference to a bill, then pending before the Committee, which would have penalized labor unions controlled or dominated by persons who were, or had been, members of a "Communist-action" organization, as defined in the Internal Security Act of 1950. The Subcommittee, it is contended, might have been endeavoring to determine the extent of such a problem. . . .

Having exhausted the several possible indicia of the "question under inquiry," we remain unenlightened as to the subject to which the questions asked petitioner were pertinent. Certainly, if the point is that obscure after trial and appeal, it was not adequately revealed to petitioner when he had to decide at his peril whether or not to answer. Fundamental fairness demands that no witness be compelled to make such a determination with so little guidance. Unless the subject matter has been made to appear with undisputable clarity, it is the duty of the investigative body, upon objection of the witness on grounds of pertinency, to state for the record the subject under inquiry at that time and the manner in which the propounded questions are pertinent thereto. To be meaningful, the explanation must describe what the topic under inquiry is and the connective reasoning whereby the precise questions asked relate to it. . . .

The statement of the Committee Chairman in this case, in response to petitioner's protest, was woefully inadequate to convey sufficient information as to the pertinency of the questions to the subject under inquiry. Petitioner was thus not accorded a fair opportunity to determine whether he was within his rights in refusing to answer, and his conviction is necessarily invalid under the Due Process Clause of the Fifth Amendment.

The judgment of the Court of Appeals is reversed, and the case is remanded to the District Court with instructions to dismiss the indictment. It is so ordered.

The thrust of the Supreme Court's internal security decisions appeared to be far too permissive to its severe congressional critics. Yet within the Court, dialogue continued between the advocates of judicial activism and judicial restraint. Thus, while the Watkins decision extended limits on congressional investigative authority, *Barenblatt v. The United States* upheld such congressional authority over the sharp dissents of Justices Black and Douglas. Justice Harlan's majority opinion upheld congressional authority and narrowly construed the scope of the Watkins ruling.

BARENBLATT v. UNITED STATES
360 U. S. 109 (1959)

Justice Harlan delivered the opinion of the Court:

Once more the Court is required to resolve the conflicting constitutional claims of congressional power and of an individual's right to resist its exercise. The congressional power in question concerns the internal process of Congress in moving within its legislative domain; it involves the utilization of its committees to secure "testimony needed to enable it efficiently to exercise a legislative function belonging to it under the Constitution." . . . The power of inquiry has been employed by Congress throughout our history, over the whole range of the national interests concerning which Congress might legislate or decide upon due investigation not to legislate; it has similarly been utilized in determining what to appropriate from the national purse, or whether to appropriate. The scope of the power of inquiry, in short, is as penetrating and far-reaching as the potential power to enact and appropriate under the Constitution.

Broad as it is, the power is not, however, without limitations. Since Congress may only investigate into those areas in which it may potentially legislate or appropriate, it cannot inquire into matters which are within the exclusive province of one of the other branches of the Government. Lacking the judicial power given to the Judiciary, it cannot inquire into matters that are exclusively the concern of the Judiciary. Neither can it supplant the Executive in what exclusively belongs to the Executive. And the Congress, in common with all branches of the Government, must exercise its powers subject to the limitations placed by the Constitution on governmental action, more particularly in the context of this case the relevant limitations of the Bill of Rights.

The congressional power of inquiry, its range and scope, and an individual's duty in relation to it, must be viewed in proper perspective. . . . The power and the right of resistance to it are to be judged in the concrete, not on the basis of abstractions. In the present

case congressional efforts to learn the extent of a nationwide, indeed world wide, problem have brought one of its investigating committees into the field of education. Of course, broadly viewed, inquiries cannot be made into the teaching that is pursued in any of our educational institutions. When academic teaching-freedom and its corollary learning-freedom, so essential to the well-being of the Nation, are claimed, this Court will always be on the alert against intrusion by Congress into this constitutionally protected domain. But this does not mean that the Congress is precluded from interrogating a witness merely because he is a teacher. An educational institution is not a constitutional sanctuary from inquiry into matters that may otherwise be within the constitutional legislative domain merely for the reason that inquiry is made of someone within its walls.

In the setting of this framework of constitutional history, practice and legal precedents, we turn to the particularities of this case.

We here review petitioner's conviction under 2 U. S. C. § 192 for contempt of Congress, arising from his refusal to answer certain questions put to him by a Subcommittee of the House Committee on Un-American Activities during the course of an inquiry concerning alleged Communist infiltration into the field of education. . . .

Petitioner's various contentions resolve themselves into three propositions: First, the compelling of testimony by the Subcommittee was neither legislatively authorized nor constitutionally permissible because of the vagueness of Rule XI of the House of Representatives, Eighty-third Congress, the charter of authority of the parent Committtee. Second, petitioner was not adequately apprised of the pertinency of the Subcommittee's questions to the subject matter of the inquiry. Third, the questions petitioner refused to answer infringed rights protected by the First Amendment. . . .

At the outset it should be noted that Rule XI authorized this Subcommittee to compel testimony within the framework of the investigative authority conferred on the Un-American Activities Committee. Petitioner contends that *Watkins* v. *United States* nevertheless held the grant of this power in all circumstances ineffective because of the vagueness of Rule XI in delineating the Committee jurisdiction to which its exercise was to be appurtenant. This view of *Watkins* was accepted by two of the dissenting judges below.

The *Watkins* case cannot properly be read as standing for such a proposition. A principal contention in *Watkins* was that the refusals to answer were justified because the requirement of 2 U.S.C. § 192 that the questions asked be "pertinent to the question under inquiry" had not been satisfied. . . . This Court reversed the conviction soley on that ground, holding that Watkins had not been adequately apprised of the subject matter of the Subcommittee's investigation on the pertinency thereto of the questions he refused to answer. . . . In so deciding the Court drew upon Rule XI only as one of the facets in the total mise en scéne in its search for the "question under inquiry" in that particular investigation. . . . The Court, in other words, was not dealing with Rule XI at large, and indeed in effect stated that no such issue was before it. . . . That the vagueness of Rule XI was not alone determinative is also shown by the Court's further statement that aside from the Rule "the remarks of the chairman or members of the committee, or even the nature of the proceedings themselves, might sometimes make the topic [under inquiry] clear." In short, while *Watkins* was critical of Rule XI, it did not involve the broad and inflexible holding petitioner now attributes to it.

Petitioner also contends, independently of *Watkins,* that the vagueness of Rule XI deprived the Subcommittee of the right to compel testimony in this investigation into Communist activity. We cannot agree with this contention, which in its furthest reach would mean that the House Un-American Activities Committee under its existing authority has no right to compel testimony in any circumstances. Granting the vagueness of the Rule, we may not read it in isolation from its long history in the House of Representatives. Just as legislation is often given meaning by the gloss of legislative reports, administrative interpretation, and long usage, so the proper meaning of an authorization to a congressional committee is not to be derived alone from its abstract terms unrelated to the definite content furnished them by the course of congressional actions. The Rule comes to us with a "persuasive gloss of legislative history," . . . which shows beyond doubt that in pursuance of its legislative concerns in the domain of "national security" the House has clothed the Un-American Activities Committee with pervasive authority to investigate Communist activities in this country. . . .

In the context of these unremitting pursuits, the House has steadily continued the life of the Committee at the commencement of each new Congress; it has never narrowed the powers of the Committee, whose authority has remained throughout identical with that contained in Rule XI; and it has continuingly supported the Committee's activities with substantial appropriations. Beyond this, the Committee was raised to the level of a standing committee of the House in 1945, it having been but a special committee prior to that time.

In light of this long and illuminating history it can hardly be seriously argued that the investigation of Communist activities generally, and the attendant use of compulsory process, was beyond the purview of the Committee's intended authority under Rule XI.

We are urged, however, to construe Rule XI so as at least to exclude the field of education from the Committee's compulsory authority. . . .

In this framework of the Committee's history we must conclude that its legislative authority to conduct the inquiry presently under consideration is unassailable, and that independently of whatever bearing the broad scope of Rule XI may have on the issue of "pertinency" in a given investigation into Communist activities, as in *Watkins,* the Rule cannot be said to be constitutionally infirm on the score of vagueness. The constitutional permissibility of that authority otherwise is a matter to be discussed later. . . . Undeniably a conviction for contempt under 2 U.S.C. § 192 cannot stand unless the questions asked are pertinent to the subject matter of the investigation. . . . But the factors which led us to rest decision on this ground in *Watkins* were very different from those involved here.

In *Watkins* the petitioner had made specific objection to the Subcommittee's questions on the ground of pertinency; the question under inquiry had not been disclosed in any illuminating manner; and the questions asked the petitioner were not only amorphous on their face, but in some instances clearly foreign to the alleged subject matter of the investigation— "Communism in labor." . . .

In contrast, petitioner in the case before us raised no objections on the ground of pertinency at the time any of the questions were put to him. . . .

We need not, however, rest decision on petitioner's failure to object on this score, for here "pertinency" was made to appear "with undisputable clarity." . . .

First of all, it goes without saying that the scope of the Committee's authority was for the House, not a witness, to determine, subject to the ultimate reviewing responsibility of this Court. What we deal with here is whether petitioner was sufficiently apprised of "the topic under inquiry" thus authorized "and the connective reasoning whereby the precise questions asked relate[d] to it." . . .

In light of his prepared memorandum of constitutional objections there can be no doubt that this petitioner was well aware of the Subcommittee's authority and purpose to question him as it did. . . . In addition the other sources of this information which we recognized in *Watkins* . . . leave no room for a "pertinency" objection on this record. The subject matter of the inquiry had been identified at the commencement of the investigation as Communist infiltration into the field of education. Just prior to petitioner's appearance before the Subcommittee, the scope of the day's hearings had been announced as "in the main Communism in education and the experiences and background in the party by Francis X. T. Crowley. It will deal with activities in Michigan, Boston, and in some small degree, New York." Petitioner had heard the Subcommittee interrogate the witness Crowley along the same lines as he, petitioner, was evidently to be questioned, and had listened to Crowley's testimony identifying him as a former member of an alleged Communist student organization at the University of Michigan while they both were in attendance there. Further, petitioner had stood mute in the face of the Chairman's statement as to why he had been called as a witness by the Subcommittee. And, lastly, unlike *Watkins*, . . . petitioner refused to answer questions as to his own Communist Party affiliations, whose pertinency of course was clear beyond doubt.

Petitioner's contentions on this aspect of the case cannot be sustained. . . . Our function, at this point, is purely one of constitutional adjudication in the particular case and upon the particular record before us, not to pass judgment upon the general wisdom of efficacy of the activities of this Committee in a vexing and complicated field.

The precise constitutional issue confronting us is whether the Subcommittee's inquiry into petitioner's past or present membership in the Communist Party transgressed the provisions of the First Amendment, which of course reach and limit congressional investigations. . . . The Court's past cases establish sure guides to decision. Undeniably, the First Amendment in some circumstances protects an individual from being compelled to disclose his associational relationships. However, the protections of the First Amendment, unlike a proper claim of the privilege against self-incrimination under the Fifth Amendment, do not afford a witness the right to resist inquiry in all

circumstances. Where First Amendment rights are asserted to bar governmental interrogation resolution of the issue always involves a balancing by the courts of the competing private and public interests at stake in the particular circumstances shown. These principles were recognized in the *Watkins Case*. . . .

The first question is whether this investigation was related to a valid legislative purpose, for Congress may not constitutionally require an individual to disclose his political relationships or other private affairs except in relation to such a purpose. . . .

That Congress has wide power to legislate in the field of Communist activity in this Country, and to conduct appropriate investigations in aid thereof, is hardly debatable. The existence of such power has never been questioned by this Court, and it is sufficient to say, without particularization, that Congress has enacted or considered in this field a wide range of legislative measures, not a few of which have stemmed from recommendations of the very Committee whose actions have been drawn in question here. In the last analysis this power rests on the right of self-preservation, "the ultimate value of any society," . . . Justification for its exercise in turn rests on the long and widely accepted view that the tenets of the Communist Party include the ultimate overthrow of the Government of the United States by force and violence, a view which has been given formal expression by the Congress. . . .

. . . To suggest that because the Communist Party may also sponsor peaceable political reforms the constitutional issues before us should now be judged as if that Party were just an ordinary political party from the standpoint of national security, is to ask this Court to blind itself to world affairs which have determined the whole course of our national policy since the close of World War II, . . . and to the vast burdens which these conditions have entailed for the entire Nation.

We think that investigatory power in this domain is not to be denied Congress solely because the field of education is involved. Nothing in the prevailing opinions in *Sweezy* v. *New Hampshire* . . . stands for a contrary view. The vice existing there was that the questioning of Sweezy, who had not been shown ever to have been connected with the Communist Party, as to the contents of a lecture he had given at the University of New Hampshire, and as to his connections with the Progressive Party, then on the ballot as a normal political party in some 26 States, was too far removed from the premises on which the constitutionality of the State's investigation had to depend to withstand attack under the Fourteenth Amendment. . . . This is a very different thing from inquiring into the extent to which the Communist Party has succeeded in infiltrating into our universities, or elsewhere, persons and groups committed to furthering the objective of overthrow. Indeed we do not understand petitioner here to suggest that Congress in no circumstances may inquire into Communist activity in the field of education.

Rather, his position is in effect that this particular investigation was aimed not at the revolutionary aspects but at the theoretical classroom discussion of communism.

In our opinion this position rests on a too constricted view of the nature of the investigatory process, and is not supported by a fair assessment of the record before us. An investigation of advocacy of or preparation for overthrow certainly embraces the right to identify a witness as a member of the Communist Party . . . and to inquire into the various manifestations of the Party's tenets. The strict requirements of a prosecution under the Smith Act, . . . are not the measure of the permissible scope of a congressional investigation into "overthrow," for of necessity the investigatory process must proceed step by step. Nor can it fairly be concluded that this investigation was directed at controlling what is being taught at our universities rather than at overthrow. The statement of the Subcommittee Chairman at the opening of the investigation evinces no such intention, and so far as this record reveals nothing thereafter transpired which would justify our holding that the thrust of the investigation later changed. The record discloses considerable testimony concerning the foreign domination and revolutionary purposes and efforts of the Communist Party . . . and to inquire into the various manifestations of the Party's tenets. The strict requirements of a prosecution under the Smith Act, . . . are not the measure of the permissible scope of a congressional investigation into "overthrow," for of necessity the that the questioning of petitioner would have exceeded permissible bounds had he not shut off the Subcommittee at the threshold.

Nor can we accept the further contention that this investigation should not be deemed to have been in furtherance of a legislative purpose because the true objective of the Committee and of the Congress was purely "exposure." So long as Congress acts in pursuance of its constitutional power, the Judiciary lacks authority to intervene on the basis of the motives which spurred the exercise of that power. . . . "It is, of course, true," as was said in *McCray* v. *United States* . . . "that if there be no authority in the judiciary to restrain a lawful exercise of power by another

department of the government, where a wrong motive or purpose has impelled to the exertion of the power, that abuses of a power conferred may be temporarily effectual. The remedy for this, however, lies, not in the abuse by the judicial authority of its functions, but in the people, upon whom, after all, under our institutions, reliance must be placed for the correction of abuses committed in the exercise of a lawful power." These principles of course apply as well to committee investigations into the need for legislation as to the enactments which such investigations may produce. . . . Thus, in stating in the *Watkins* case that "there is no congressional power to expose for the sake of exposure," we at the same time declined to inquire into the "motives of committee members," and recognized that their "motives alone would not vitiate an investigation which had been instituted by a House of Congress if that assembly's legislative purpose is being served." Having scrutinized this record we cannot say that the unanimous panel of the Court of Appeals which first considered this case was wrong in concluding that "the primary purposes of the inquiry were in aid of legislative process," 240 F2d, at 881. Certainly this is not a case like *Kilbourn* v. *Thompson* . . . where "the House of Representatives not only exceeded the limit of its own authority, but assumed a power which could only be properly exercised by another branch of the government, because it was in its nature clearly judicial." . . . The constitutional legislative power of Congress in this instance is beyond question.

Finally, the record is barren of the factors which in themselves might sometimes lead to the conclusion that the individual interests at stake were not subordinate to those of the state. There is no indication in this record that the Subcommittee was attempting to pillory witnesses. Nor did petitioner's appearance as a witness follow from indiscriminate dragnet procedures, lacking in probable cause for belief that he possessed information which might be helpful to the Subcommittee. And the relevancy of the questions put to him by the Subcommittee is not open to doubt.

We conclude that the balance between the individual and the governmental interests here at stake must be struck in favor of the latter, and that therefore the provisions of the First Amendment have not been offended.

We hold that petitioner's conviction for contempt of Congress discloses no infirmity, and that the judgment of the Court of Appeals must be affirmed.

Chief Justice Warren and Justice Douglas concurred with Justice Black, who dissented:

. . . The Court today affirms, and thereby sanctions the use of the contempt power to enforce questioning by congressional committees in the realm of speech and association. I cannot agree with this disposition of the case for I believe that the resolution establishing the House Un-American Activities Committee and the questions that Committee asked Barenblatt violate the Constitution in several respects. (1) Rule XI creating the Committee authorizes such a sweeping, unlimited, all-inclusive and undiscriminating compulsory examination of witnesses in the field of speech, press, petition and assembly that it violates the procedural requirements of the Due Process Clause of the Fifth Amendment. (2) Compelling an answer to the questions asked Barenblatt abridges freedom of speech and association in contravention of the First Amendment. (3) The Committee proceedings were part of a legislative program to stigmatize and punish by public identification and exposure all witnesses considered by the Committee to be guilty of Communist affiliations, as well as all witnesses who refused to answer Committee questions on constitutional grounds; the Committee was thus improperly seeking to try, convict, and punish suspects, a task which the Constitution expressly denies to Congress and grants exclusively to the courts, to be exercised by them only after indictment and in full compliance with all safeguards provided by the Bill of Rights. . . .

The First Amendment says in no equivocal language that Congress shall pass no law abridging freedom of speech, press, assembly or petition. The activities of this Committee, authorized by Congress, do precisely that, through exposure, obloquy and public scorn. . . .

To apply the Court's balancing test under such circumstances is to read the First Amendment to say "Congress shall pass no law abridging freedom of speech, press, assembly and petition, unless Congress and the Supreme Court reach the joint conclusion that on balance the interest of the Government in stifling these freedoms is greater than the interest of the people in having them exercised." This is closely akin to the notion that neither the First Amendment nor any other provision of the Bill of Rights should be enforced unless the Court believes it is *reasonable* to do so. Not only does this violate the genius of our *written* Constitution, but it runs expressly counter to the injunction to Court and Congress made by Madison when he introduced the Bill of Rights. "If they [the first ten amendments] are incorporated into the Constitution, independent tribunals of justice will consider themselves in a peculiar manner the guardians of those rights; they will be an impenetrable bulwark against *every* assumption of power in the Legislative or Executive; they will be naturally led to resist *every* encroachment upon rights expressly stipulated for in the Constitution by the declaration of rights." Unless we return to this view of our judicial function, unless we once again accept the notion that the Bill of Rights means what it says and that this Court must enforce that meaning, I am of the opinion that our great charter of liberty will be more honored in the breach than in the observance. . . .

Justice Brennan dissented in a separate opinion:

I would reverse this conviction. It is sufficient that I state my complete agreement with my Brother Black that no purpose for the investigation of Barenblatt is revealed by the record except exposure purely for the sake of exposure. This is not a purpose to which Barenblatt's rights under the First Amendment can validly be subordinated. An investigation in which the process of law-making and law-evaluating are submerged entirely in exposure of individual behavior—in adjudication, of a sort, through the exposure process—is outside the constitutional pale of congressional inquiry. . . .

Although internal security issues aroused serious conservative criticism of the Supreme Court in Congress, such opposition was restrained compared to regional reaction to the Court's major civil rights decision.

Civil rights become paramount

The keystone of these civil rights decisions was *Brown* v. *Board of Education of Topeka,* which overturned the separate but equal doctrine established in *Plessy* v. *Ferguson* in 1896. But, in retrospect, a long line of decisions led to the repudiation of "separate but equal." The road to such repudiation was not direct and, indeed, included several setbacks. Even as late as the 1930s, the victories for equal and fair treatments of blacks appeared to be particularistic, limited to specific situations, with outcomes unlikely to change fundamentally the overall status of black people in American society. Among the victories were *Aldridge* v. *United States*[2] in which a black defendant charged with murder of a white was sustained in his effort to examine prospective jurors for racial prejudice. A year later, in 1932, the Fourteenth Amendment was successfully invoked to strike down a Texas statute that permitted political parties to determine the qualifications of primary election voters, thus creating white primaries. The action by the parties was ruled state action within the scope of the amendment.[3] In the same year, *Powell* v. *Alabama* underscored the right to counsel principle in the controversial Scottsboro trial.[4] Three years later the Fourteenth Amendment was again invoked successfully in *Norris* v. *Alabama*. A black defendant's conviction was struck down because blacks had been excluded from the local grand and trial juries.[5] In the same year, however, the trend toward black equality in voting rights was temporarily stopped in *Grovey* v. *Townsend*, in which denial of a black voter of the right to vote in a primary election was upheld as private rather than state action.[6]

The first major break in the relatively solid judicial acceptance of racial segregation in public education came in 1938 in *Missouri ex rel Gaines* v. *Canada*. Missouri was compelled to provide substantially similar higher education to black residents of the state if it provided such opportunities in white segregated public universities or colleges.[7] In 1941 a crucial decision relating to the meaning of state action was handed down in *United States* v. *Classic*,[8] a case that did not involve race. The Court adopted the doctrine that the activities within a dominant political party organization that controlled the primary election (which in a one-party state was tantamount to selection in the general election) was state action. Thus, the Court had opened the way for elimination of racial discrimination in primary elections. State officials illegally tampering with ballot boxes were subject to federal control. In *Smith* v. *Allwright*, *Grovey* v. *Townsend* was reversed and Texas Democratic party rules barring blacks were held to be unconstitutional state action prohibited by the Fifteenth Amendment.[9]

In 1948 state court enforcement of racially restrictive residential covenants was held state action in violation of the Fourteenth Amendment in *Shelley* v. *Kraemer*.[10] In 1950 two significant decisions involving segregation in higher education were handed down. In *Sweatt* v. *Painter*, the Court held that a white state-supported university must admit black students when the separate black university was unequal in facilities.[11] In the same year, the case of *McLaurin* v. *Oklahoma Regents* virtually assured a direct test of the old "separate but equal" doctrine because it struck down in-school segregation as well.[12] The *Brown* v. *Board of Education of Topeka* and its companion cases originating in Delaware, the District of Columbia, South Carolina, and Virginia emerged at a time in modern history when positive doctrinal change at last seemed possible. The Brown case was argued first before Fred Vinson and later, after his death, before the new chief justice, Earl Warren. The basic questions were framed by the Vinson Court in preparation for the cases.[13] Consequently, it was not until 1954 that segregation in secondary public schools was directly challenged before the Supreme Court. When the Court finally acted, it did unanimously. When Chief Justice Warren wrote the Court's opinion, he included the background of the combined cases.

BROWN v. BOARD
OF EDUCATION OF TOPEKA
347 U. S. 483 (1954)

These cases come to us from the States of Kansas, South Carolina, Virginia, and Delaware. They are premised on different facts and different local conditions, but a common legal question justifies their consideration together in this consolidated opinion.

In each of the cases, minors of the Negro race, through their legal representatives, seek the aid of the courts in obtaining admission to the public schools of their community on a nonsegregated basis. In each instance, they had been denied admission to schools attended by white children under laws requiring or permitting segregation according to race. This segregation was alleged to deprive the plaintiffs of the equal protection of the laws under the Fourteenth Amendment. In each of the cases other than the Delaware case, a three-judge federal district court denied relief to the plaintiffs on the so-called "separate but equal" doctrine announced by this Court in *Plessy* v. *Ferguson*. . . . Under that doctrine, equality of treatment is accorded when the races are provided substantially equal facilities, even though these facilities be separate. In the Delaware case, the Supreme Court of Delaware adhered to that doctrine, but ordered that the plaintiffs be admitted to the white schools because of their superiority to the Negro school.

The plaintiffs contend that segregated public schools are not "equal" and cannot be made "equal," and that hence they are deprived of the equal protection of the laws. Because of the obvious importance of the question present, the Court took jurisdiction. Argument was heard in the 1952 Term, and reargument was heard this Term on certain questions propounded by the Court.

Reargument was largely devoted to the circumstances surrounding the adoption of the Fourteenth Amendment in 1868. It covered exhaustively consideration of the Amendment in Congress, ratification by the states, then existing practices in racial segregation, and the views of proponents and opponents of the Amendment. This discussion and our own investigation convince us that, although these sources cast some light, it is not enough to resolve that problem with which we are faced. At best, they are inconclusive. The most avid proponents of the post-War Amendments undoubtedly intended them to remove all legal distinctions among "all persons born or naturalized in the United States." Their opponents, just as certainly, were antagonistic to both the letter and the spirit of the Amendments and wished them to have the most limited effect. What others in Congress and the State legislatures had in mind cannot be determined with any degree of certainty.

An additional reason for the inconclusive nature of the Amendment's history, with respect to segregated schools, is the status of public education at that time. In the South, the movement toward free common schools, supported by general taxation, had not yet taken hold. Education of white children was largely in the hands of private groups. Education of Negroes was almost nonexistent, and practically all of the race were illiterate. In fact, any education of Negroes was forbidden by law in some states. Today, in contrast, many Negroes have achieved outstanding success in the arts and sciences as well as in the business and professional world. It is true that public school education at the time of the Amendment had advanced further in the North, but the effect of the Amendment on Northern States was generally ignored in the congressional debates. Even in the North, the conditions of public education did not approximate those existing today. The curriculum was usually rudimentary; ungraded schools were common in rural areas; the school term was but three months a year in many states; and compulsory school attendance was virtually unknown. As a consequence, it is not surprising that there should be so little in the history of the Fourteenth Amendment relating to its intended effect on public education.

In the first cases in this Court construing the Fourteenth Amendment, decided shortly after its adoption, the Court interpreted it as proscribing all state-imposed discriminations against the Negro race. The doctrine of "separate but equal" did not make its appearance in this Court until 1896 in the case of *Plessy* v. *Ferguson* involving not education but transportation. American courts have since labored with the doctrine for over half a century. In this Court, there have been six cases involving the "separate but equal" doctrine in the field of public education. In *Cumming* v. *County Board of Education* . . . and *Gong Lum* v. *Rice* . . . the validity of the doctrine itself was not challenged. In more recent cases, all on the graduate school level, inequality was found in that specific benefits enjoyed by white students were denied to Negro students of the same educational qualifications. . . .

. . . In none of these cases was it necessary to re-examine the doctrine to grant relief to the Negro plaintiff. And in *Sweatt* v. *Painter* the Court expressly reserved decision on the question whether *Plessy* v. *Ferguson* should be held inapplicable to public education.

In the instant cases, that question is directely presented. Here, unlike *Sweatt* v. *Painter*, there are findings below that the Negro and white schools involved have been equalized, or are being equalized, with respect to buildings, curricula, qualifications and salaries of teachers, and other "tangible" factors. Our decision, therefore, cannot turn on merely a comparison of these tangible factors in the Negro and white schools involved in each of the cases. We must look instead to the effect of segregation itself on public education.

In approaching this problem, we cannot turn the clock back to 1868 when the Amendment was adopted, or even to 1896 when *Plessy* v. *Ferguson* was written. We must consider public education in the light of its full development and its present place in American life throughout the Nation. Only in this way can it be determined if segregation in public schools deprives these plaintiffs of the equal protection of the laws.

Today, education is perhaps the most important function of state and local governments. Compulsory school attendance laws and the great expenditures for education both demonstrate our recognition of the importance of education to our democratic society. It is required in the performance of our most basic public responsibilities, even service in the armed forces. It is the very foundation of good citizenship. Today it is a principal instrument in awakening the child to cultural values, in preparing him for later professional training, and in helping him to adjust normally to his environment. In these days, it is doubtful that any child may reasonably be expected to succeed in life if he is denied the opportunity of an education. Such an opportunity, where the state has undertaken to provide it, is a right which must be made available to all on equal terms.

We come then to the question presented: Does segregation of children in public schools solely on the basis of race, even though the physical facilities and other "tangible" factors may be equal, deprive the children of the minority group of equal educational opportunities? We believe that it does.

In *Sweatt* v. *Painter*, in finding that a segregated law school for Negroes could not provide them equal educational opportunities, this Court relied in large part on "those qualities which are incapable of objective measurement but which make for greatness in a law school." In *McLaurin* v. *Oklahoma State Regents*, the Court, in requiring that a Negro admitted to a white graduate school be treated like all other students, again resorted to intangible considerations: ". . . his ability to study, to engage in discussions and exchange views with other students, and, in general, to learn his profession." Such considerations apply with added force to children in grade and high schools. To separate them from others of similar age and qualifications solely because of their race generates a feeling of inferiority as to their status in the community that may affect their hearts and minds in a way unlikely ever to be undone. The effect of this separation on their educational opportunities was well stated by a finding in the Kansas case by a court which nevertheless felt compelled to rule against the Negro plaintiffs:

Segregation of white and colored children in public schools has a detrimental effect upon the colored children. The impact is greater when it has the sanction of the law; for the policy of separating the races is usually interpreted as denoting the inferiority of the negro group. A sense of inferiority affects the motivation of a child to learn. Segregation with the sanction of law, therefore, has a tendency to [retard] the educational and mental development of negro children and to deprive them of some of the benefits they would receive in a racial[ly] integrated school system.

Whatever may have been the extent of psychological knowledge at the time of *Plessy* v. *Ferguson*, this finding is amply supported by modern authority. Any language in *Plessy* v. *Ferguson* contrary to this finding is rejected.

We conclude that in the field of public education the doctrine of "separate but equal" has no place. Separate educational facilities are inherently unequal. Therefore, we hold that the plaintiffs and others similarly situated for whom the actions have been brought are, by reason of the segregation complained of, deprived of the equal protection of the laws guaranteed by the Fourteenth Amendment. This disposition makes unnecessary any discussion whether such segregation also violates the Due Process Clause of the Fourteenth Amendment.

Because these are class actions, because of the wide applicability of this decision, and because of the great variety of local conditions, the formulation of decrees in these cases presents problems of considerable complexity. On reargument, the consideration of appropriate relief was necessarily subordinated to the primary question—the constitutionality of segregation in public education. We have now announced that such segregation is a denial of the equal protection of the laws. In order that we may have the full assistance of the parties in formulating decrees, the cases will be restored to the docket, and the parties are requested to present further argument on Questions 4 and 5 [concerning the process of implementation] previously propounded by the Court for the reargument this Term. The Attorney General of the United States is again invited to participate. The Attorneys General of the states requiring or permitting segregation in public education will also be permitted to appear as *amici curiae* upon request to do so by September 15, 1954, and submission of briefs by October 1, 1954. It is so ordered.

The most immediate formal reaction to the Brown decision was the organization of oral arguments and briefs by the counsel for several states for the second
Brown v. *Board of Education*. Although a great deal of attention was focused upon the
doctrinal basis of the first Brown decision, once the separate but equal doctrine
had been rejected, the next significant question was how the Court should implement its doctrinal position. At the conclusion of the first Brown decision, the
Court had set the stage for the second set of arguments. William Swindler accurately noted that the dramatic elements in the oral arguments for the first *Brown*
v. *Board of Education* vividly illustrated the personal characteristics of two opposing
counsel. Eighty-year-old John W. Davis, special counsel for South Carolina and
Virginia, was a corporation lawyer who had served as Woodrow Wilson's solicitor
general and as a conservative Democratic presidential nominee in 1924. Davis
symbolized and represented the past when he argued that it was beyond the
scope of federal judicial authority to alter a system that had "stood legally for
three quarters of a century." In contrast, 45-year-old Thurgood Marshall, chief
counsel for the National Association for the Advancement of Colored People and
grandson of a slave, argued that the post–Civil War amendments forced resolution of the question "whether the [segregationist] mores of South Carolina and
Virginia, or the provisions of the Constitution, shall prevail."

When the Court considered implementation a year later, the truly daring and
innovative arguments were made by counsel for a labor organization rather than
for the NAACP. The two major positions were for (1) gradualism, or (2) all
deliberate speed. But Arthur Goldberg, Thomas E. Harris, and David E. Feller of
the Congress for Industrial Organizations presented a third position in an *amicus
curiae* brief—desegregation forthwith. The CIO *amicus curiae* brief, which is ex-
cerpted below, is a remarkable example of interest-group policy innovation.

INTEREST GROUPS AND POLICY INNOVATION:
THE CIO AND DESEGREGATION

This Brief *amicus curiae* is submitted by the Congress of Industrial Organizations
with the consent of the parties.

The CIO is dedicated to the protection of our democratic system of government,
and, hence of the civil rights of all Americans. Therefore, it supports the elimination
of racial segregation and discrimination from every phase of American life.

The CIO's interest in the specific issues before the Court in this case is two-fold.

First, racial segregation in the public schools directly affects the millions of CIO
members whose children attend these schools. The CIO is convinced that school
segregation is harmful to the Negro children who are thus treated as inferior, to the
white children in whom attitudes of racial hostility and discrimination are thus
engendered and encouraged at an early age, and to the community as a whole.
School segregation is a weakening and divisive force in American life. At the CIO's
International Convention in November of this year, the delegates unanimously declared their opposition to school segregation, and their support for the position taken
by the plaintiffs in these cases.

Secondly, the outcome of these cases will have indirect effects of great importance to the CIO. The CIO is endeavoring to practice non-segregation and non-
discrimination in the everyday conduct of its union business. This effort has repeatedly been obstructed by statutes, ordinances and regulations which require

segregation in public meeting halls, public dining places, toilet facilities, etc. These laws seek to require CIO unions to maintain "equal but separate" facilities even in their own buildings, despite our membership's repudiation of segregation in any form. Since the constitutionality of these laws rests on basically the same line of reasoning which is put forward to justify school segregation, the decision of this Court in these school cases will, in all probability, have far-reaching implications as to the validity of these other segregation laws.

More broadly, school segregation, and the general pattern of government enforced segregation of which it is a part, fosters an atmosphere of inter-racial hostility which makes it more difficult for the CIO to carry out its own non-segregation policy. Further, this atmosphere of inter-racial hostility is used by anti-labor employers in opposing CIO organizing drives: invariably these employers stress the CIO's opposition to segregation and discrimination.

THE QUESTION DISCUSSED

In prior briefs *amicus curiae*, last year in *Brown* v. *Board of Education of Topeka*, and earlier in other school segregation cases, the CIO argued that segregation in public schools on the basis of race violates the Fourteenth Amendment *per se*. That is still our view, and we wholeheartedly subscribe to the arguments in support of it advanced by counsel for the appellants in Nos. 1, 2, and 4, and for the respondents in No. 10. Instead of repeating those arguments, however, we have concluded that it would be most helpful to the Court for us to confine our discussion to one particular issue on which the CIO has a certain amount of special experience and expert knowledge.

That issue, set out in paragraph 4 of the Court's Order of June 8, 1953, is what the Court should do if it concludes that segregation in the public schools violates the Fourteenth Amendment, i.e., whether the Court should order segregation terminated "forthwith" or permit "gradual adjustment."

This issue is very similar to the problem which the CIO and its affiliated unions have repeatedly faced as to how best to put into effect the non-segregation and non-discrimination policies of the national organizations in localities where segregation and discrimination have theretofore prevailed. It is our experience in the handling of this problem that we wish to lay before the Court.

ARGUMENT

Non-Segregation Could Be Effectuated with Less Disturbance
by a "Forthwith" Decree Than by "Gradual Adjustment"

This memorandum seeks to summarize for the Court the experience and conclusions of unions and employers as to the best way to effectuate non-discrimination or non-segregation policies, and specifically as to how "forthwith" enforcement compares with "gradual adjustment." The bulk of this experience, both union and employer, relates to the institution or enforcement of a policy of non-discrimination and non-segregation in employment. The unions have, however, also had some experience with respect to desegregation in other fields, such as use of meeting halls and other union facilities.

As will be seen, all of this experience, union and employer, reinforces this central point: if a union or an employer wants to put into effect a policy of non-discrimination or non-segregation, it should do it "forthwith," firmly and decisively, and should avoid "gradual adjustment" or any other formula of indefinite postponement. If the policy of non-discrimination or non-segregation is put into effect concurrently with its announcement, and if it is enforced with firmness and decisiveness, there is every likelihood that the policy will be generally accepted and that any substantial degree of inter-racial friction will be avoided. The bulk of the people in any community or plant or office are influenced in their attitudes on racial discrimination by the current practice in the community or plant or office. If the practice is changed, and if the change be made unequivocally, they accept the new practice and their attitudes come to reflect it. Thus traditional Southern attitudes on racial segregation largely mirror, according to our experience, simply the prevailing practices, rather than deeply or strongly held individual convictions. Once the practice is changed, beliefs as to what the practice should be will change too.

Conversely, "gradual adjustment" to a new policy of non-segregation or non-discrimination is apt to work less well. Long drawn out discussion of a contemplated ultimate end of segregation or discrimination may serve only to exacerbate racial tensions. Division along racial lines may harden and people may be led to take more extreme and adamant stands than they would have if the issue had been disposed of promptly, once and for all. For example, in a plant where Negro workers have customarily been excluded from certain types of jobs it may prove extremely difficult to persuade the white workers, through a program of education and discussion, that the time has come to end this discrimination. Such a program may serve only to accentuate inter-racial tension by keeping the issue alive and in suspension. On the other hand, if the union and employer firmly announce that henceforth there will be no job discrimination, the new policy will, in our experience, be accepted by the workers with little friction, and the issue will be disposed of once and for all.

We do not mean that education and discussion do not serve a purpose in this field; they do. But they should accompany the effective implementation of a policy of non-discrimination and non-segregation. Absent such effective implementation, endless discussion and the indefinite postponements of "gradual adjustment" may serve only to freeze or accentuate attitudes. If no fixed terminal date for segregation is set, its proponents will regard the issue as really still open, and the controversy is likely only to become more intense with the passage of time.

Our experience suggests, we think, one further point: The CIO and its unions have put non-segregation and non-discrimination policies into effect in all parts of the country. No major strife has resulted within these organizations—and they are voluntary organizations, whose officers are elected by the membership and whose very existence depends upon the continued good will of the membership. If the non-segregation policies of these voluntary organizations, when promptly and firmly implemented, can win such acceptance, then, *a fortiori*, a definitive decree of the highest Court of the land will receive general acceptance. . . .

CONCLUSION

For the reasons stated, we respectfully suggest to the Court, that if it concludes, as we think it should, that segregation in public schools violates the Fourteenth Amendment, it would be preferable for it to implement this conclusion by directing the cessation of segregation "forthwith" rather than by "gradual adjustment."[14]

In the second *Brown* v. *Board of Education of Topeka,* the Supreme Court retained the unanimity it had achieved in the first Brown decision but, in another opinion by Chief Justice Warren, chose all deliberate speed as its mode of implementation.

(SECOND) BROWN v. BOARD OF
EDUCATION OF TOPEKA
349 U. S. 294 (1955)

Chief Justice Warren
delivered the opinion of the Court:

These cases were decided on May 17, 1954. The opinions of that date, declaring the fundamental principle that racial discrimination in public education is unconstitutional, are incorporated herein by reference. All provisions of federal, state, or local law requiring or permitting such discrimination must yield to this principle. There remains for consideration the manner in which relief is to be accorded.

Because these cases arose under different local conditions and their disposition will involve a variety of local problems, we requested further argument on the question of relief. In view of the nationwide importance of the decision, we invited the Attorney General of the United States and the Attorneys General of all states requiring or permitting racial discrimination in public education to present their views on that question. The parties, the United States, and the States of Florida, North Carolina, Arkansas, Oklahoma, Maryland, and Texas filed briefs and participated in the oral argument.

These presentations were informative and helpful to the court in its consideration of the complexities arising from the transition to a system of public education freed of racial discrimination. The presentations also demonstrated that substantial steps to eliminate racial discrimination in public schools have already been taken, not only in some of the communities in which these cases arose, but in some of the states appearing as *amici curiae*, and in other states as well. Substantial progress has been made in the District of Columbia and in the communities in Kansas and Delaware involved in this litigation. The defendants in the cases coming to us from South Carolina and Virginia are awaiting the decision of this Court concerning relief.

Full implementation of these constitutional principles may require solution of varied local school problems. School authorities have the primary responsibility for elucidating, assessing, and solving these problems; courts will have to consider whether the action of school authorities constitutes good faith implementation of the governing constitutional principles. Because of their proximity to local conditions and the possible need for further hearings, the courts

which originally heard these cases can best perform this judicial appraisal. Accordingly, we believe it appropriate to remand the cases to those courts.

In fashioning and effectuating the decrees, the courts will be guided by equitable principles. Traditionally, equity has been characterized by a practical flexibility in shaping its remedies and by a facility for adjusting and reconciling public and private needs. These cases call for the exercise of these traditional attributes of equity power. At stake is the personal interest of the plaintiffs in admission to public schools as soon as practicable on a nondiscriminatory basis. To effectuate this interest may call for elimination of a variety of obstacles in making the transition to school systems operated in accordance with the constitutional principles set forth in our May 17, 1954, decision. Courts of equity may properly take into account the public interest in the elimination of such obstacles in a systematic and effective manner. But it should go without saying that the vitality of these constitutional principles cannot be allowed to yield simply because of disagreement with them.

While giving weight to these public and private considerations, the courts will require that the defendants make a prompt and reasonable start toward full compliance with our May 17, 1954, ruling. Once such a start has been made, the courts may find that additional time is necessary to carry out the ruling in an effective manner. The burden rests upon the defendants to establish that such time is necessary in the public interest and is consistent with good faith compliance at the earliest practicable date. To that end, the courts may consider problems related to administration, arising from the physical condition of the school plant, the school transportation system, personnel, revision of school districts and attendance areas into compact units to achieve a system of determining admission to the public schools on a nonracial basis, and revision of local laws and regulations which may be necessary in solving the foregoing problems. They will also consider the adequacy of any plans the defendants may propose to meet these problems and to effectuate a transition to a racially nondiscriminatory school system. During this period of transition, the courts will retain jurisdiction of these cases.

The judgments below, except that in the Delaware case, are accordingly reversed and the cases are remanded to the District Courts to take such proceedings and enter such orders and decrees consistent with this opinion as are necessary and proper to admit to public schools on a racially nondiscriminatory basis with all deliberate speed the parties to these cases. The judgment in the Delaware case—ordering the immediate admission of the plaintiffs to schools previously attended only by white children—is affirmed on the basis of the principles stated in our May 17, 1954, opinion, but the case is remanded to the Supreme Court of Delaware for such further proceedings as that Court may deem necessary in light of this opinion. It is so ordered.

Despite the Court's selection of the middle ground alternative, all deliberate speed, in contrast to the extremes, gradualism or implementation forthwith, the doctrinal basis of the first Brown decision was subjected to a storm of criticism, especially from Southern congressional leaders. A number of plans were devised to resist implementation, not the least of which was the Virginia plan of massive resistance, which was based upon a neo–Calhounian doctrine of state interposition. More drastic attempts were made to continue segregation by force. Arkansas called out the National Guard to keep Central High School of Little Rock "off limits" to black students, who had been granted access by a federal district court order. In *Cooper* v. *Aaron*, the Supreme Court upheld the federal district court and asserted once again the doctrine of federal supremacy. Chief Justice Warren wrote the opinion of the unanimous Court.

COOPER v. AARON
358 U. S. 1 (1958)

. . . As this case reaches us it raises questions of the highest importance to the maintenance of our federal system of government. It necessarily involves a claim by the Governor and Legislature of a State that there is no duty on state officials to obey federal court orders resting on this Court's considered interpretation of the United States Constitution. . . . We are urged to uphold a suspension of the Little Rock School Board's plan to do away with segregated public school in Little Rock until state laws and efforts to upset and nullify our holding in *Brown* v. *Board of Education* have been further challenged and tested in the courts. We reject these contentions. . . .

In affirming the judgment of the Court of Appeals which reversed the District Court we have accepted without reservation the position of the School Board, the Superintendent of Schools, and their counsel that they displayed entire good faith in the conduct of these proceedings and in dealing with the unfortunate and distressing sequence of events which has been outlined. We likewise have accepted the findings of the District Court as to the conditions at Central High School during the 1957—1958 school year, and also the findings that the educational progress of all the students, white and colored, of that school has suffered and will continue to suffer if the conditions which prevailed last year are permitted to continue.

The significance of these findings, however, is to be considered in light of the fact, indisputably revealed by the record before us, that the conditions they depict are directly traceable to the actions of legislators and executive officials of the State of Arkansas, taken in their official capacities, which reflect their own determination to resist this Court's decision in the *Brown* case and which have brought about violent resistance to that decision in Arkansas. In its petition for certiorari filed in this Court, the School Board itself describes the situation in this language: "The legislative, executive, and judicial departments of the state government opposed the desegregation of Little Rock schools by enacting laws, calling out troops, making statements villifying federal law and federal courts, and failing to utilize state law enforcement agencies and judicial processes to maintain public peace."

One may well sympathize with the position of the Board in the face of the frustrating conditions which have confronted it, but, regardless of the Board's good faith, the actions of the other state agencies responsible for those conditions compel us to reject the Board's legal position. Had Central High School been under the direct management of the State itself, it could hardly be suggested that those immediately in charge of the school should be heard to assert their own good faith as a legal excuse for delay in implementing the constitutional rights of these respondents, when vindication of those rights was rendered difficult or impossible by the actions of other state officials.

The situation here is in no different posture because the members of the School Board and the Superintendent of Schools are local officials; from the point of view of the Fourteenth Amendment, they stand in this litigation as the agents of the State.

The constitutional rights of respondents are not to be sacrificed or yielded to the violence and disorder which have followed upon the actions of the Governor and Legislature. . . .

The controlling legal principles are plain. The command of the Fourteenth Amendment is that no "State" shall deny to any person within its jurisdiction the equal protection of the laws. "A State acts by its legislative, its executive, or its judicial authorities. It can act in no other way. The constitutional provision, therefore, must mean that no agency of the State, or of the officers or agents by whom its powers are exerted, shall deny to any person within its jurisdiction the equal protection of the laws. Whoever, by virtue of public position under a State government . . . denies or takes away the equal protection of the laws, violates the constitutional inhibition; and as he acts in the name and for the State, and is clothed with the State's power, his act is that of the State. This must be so, or the constitutional prohibition has no meaning." . . . Thus the prohibitions of the Fourteenth Amendment extend to all action of the State denying equal protection of the laws; whatever the agency of the State taking the action. . . . In short, the constitutional rights of children not to be discriminated against in school admission on grounds of race or color declared by this Court in the *Brown* case can neither be nullified openly and directly by state legislators or state executive or judicial officers, nor nullified indirectly by them through evasive schemes for segregation whether attempted "ingeniously or ingenuously." . . .

What has been said, in the light of the facts developed, is enough to dispose of the case. However, we should answer the premise of the actions of the Governor and Legislature that they are not bound by our holding in the *Brown* case. It is necessary only to recall some basic constitutional propositions which are settled doctrine.

Article VI of the Constitution makes the Constitution the "supreme Law of the Land." In 1803, Chief Justice Marshall, speaking for a unanimous Court, referring to the Constitution as "the fundamental and paramount law of the nation," declared in the notable case of *Marbury* v. *Madison* . . . that "It is emphatically the province and duty of the judicial department to say what the law is." This decision declared the basic principle that the federal judiciary is supreme in the exposition of the law of the Constitution, and that principle has ever since been respected by this Court and the Country as a permanent and indispensable feature of our constitutional system. It follows that the interpretation of the Fourteenth Amendment enunciated by this Court in the *Brown* case is the supreme law of the land, and Art. VI of the Constitution makes it of binding effect on the States "any Thing in the Constitution or Laws of any State to the Contrary notwithstanding." Every state legislator and executive and judicial officer is solemnly committed by oath taken pursuant to Art. VI, § 3 "to support this Constitution." . . .

No state legislator or executive or judicial officer can war against the Constitution without violating his undertaking to support it. Chief Justice Marshall spoke for a unanimous Court in saying that: "If the legislatures of the several states may, at will, annul the judgments of the court of the United States, and destroy the rights acquired under those judgments, the constitution itself becomes a solemn mockery. . . ." A Governor who asserts a power to nullify a federal court order is similarly restrained. . . .

The strong reaction of Southern conservatives to the thrust of Supreme Court actions in the 1950s extended into the 1960s but some changes in the composition of the House and Senate and John F. Kennedy's narrow electoral victory for the presidency in 1960 created a new climate in Congress and new expectations for the Supreme Court itself. During Kennedy's brief and ultimately tragic experience in the presidency, he was afforded two opportunities to fill vacancies. Following the resignation of Justice Whittaker in April 1962, President Kennedy nominated Assistant Attorney General Byron White. In August of 1962, an ailing Justice Frankfurter resigned; he was succeeded in early October by Secretary of Labor Arthur Goldberg. In each instance, an advocate of doctrinal restraint was replaced by a more liberal justice.

Reapportionment and congressional criticism

The storm of opposition to desegregation also took the form of a "Southern Manifesto" in Congress. But race was not the only issue that stimulated anti-Court opposition in the national legislature. The legislative reapportionment issue and its judicial resolution, for example, pitted a majority of the Supreme Court against the entrenched forces that dominated malapportioned state legislatures and the interest groups that benefited from such domination. Critics viewed *Baker v. Carr* as an inappropriate intrusion into matters best left to the political branches, while its supporters saw it as a courageous breakthrough for fair representation. Justice Brennan wrote the majority opinion concurred in separately by Justices Douglas, Clark, and Stewart. Justice Whittaker did not participate in the case. Justice Frankfurter dissented in an opinion joined by Justice Harlan. Frankfurter's invocation of the doctrine of political questions in *Colegrove* v. *Green*[15] was overturned, and his admonition to the Court to stay out of the "political thicket" of legislative reapportionment was rejected in *Baker* v. *Carr*. The background of the issues in *Baker* is summarized in the opinion of Justice Brennan.

BAKER v. CARR
369 U. S. 186 (1962)

Justice Brennan delivered the opinion of the Court:

This civil action was brought . . . to redress the alleged deprivation of federal constitutional rights. The complaint, alleging that by means of a 1901 statute of Tennessee apportioning the members of the General Assembly among the State's 95 counties, "these plaintiffs and others similarly situated, are denied the equal protection of the laws accorded them by the Fourteenth Amendment to the Constitution of the United States by virtue of the debasement of their votes," was dismissed by a three-judge court. . . . We hold that the dismissal was error, and remand the cause to the District Court for trial and further proceedings consistent with this opinion.

The General Assembly of Tennessee consists of the Senate with 33 members and the House of Representatives with 99 members. . . .

. . . Tennessee's standard for allocating legislative representation among her counties is the total number of qualified voters resident in the respective counties, subject only to minor qualifications. . . . In 1901 the General Assembly abandoned separate enumeration in favor of reliance upon the Federal Census and passed the Apportionment Act here in controversy. In the more than 60 years since that action, all proposals in both Houses of the General Assembly for reapportionment have failed to pass.

Between 1901 and 1961, Tennessee has experienced substantial growth and redistribution of her population. In 1901 the population was 2,020,616, of whom 487,380 were eligible to vote. The 1960 Federal Census reports the State's population at 3,567,089, of whom 2,092,891 are eligible to vote. The relative standings of the counties in terms of qualified voters have changed significantly. It is primarily the continued application of the 1901 Apportionment Act to this shifted and enlarged voting population which gives rise to the present controversy.

Indeed, the complaint alleges that the 1901 statute, even as of the time of its passage, "made no apportionment of Representatives and Senators in accordance with the constitutional formula . . . , but instead arbitrarily and capriciously apportioned representatives in the Senate and House without reference . . . to any logical or reasonable formula whatever." It is further alleged that "because of the population changes since 1900, and the failure of the Legislature to reapportion itself since 1901," the 1901 statute became "unconstitutional and obsolete." Appellants also argue that, because of the composition of the legislature effected by the 1901 Apportionment Act, redress in the form of a state constitutional amendment to change the entire mechanism for reapportioning, or any other change short of that, is difficult or impossible. The complaint concludes that "these plaintiffs and others similarly situated, are denied the equal protection of the laws accorded them by the Fourteenth Amendment to the Constitution of the United States by virtue of the debasement of their votes." They seek a declaration that the 1901 statute is unconstitutional and an injunction restraining the appellees from acting to conduct any further elections under it. They also pray that unless and until the General Assembly enacts a valid reapportionment, the District Court should either decree a reapportionment by mathematical application of the Tennessee constitutional formulae to the most recent Federal Census figures, or direct the appellees to conduct legislative elections, primary and general, at large. They also pray for such other and further relief as may be appropriate.

I

THE DISTRICT COURT'S OPINION AND ORDER OF DISMISSAL

In light of the District Court's treatment of the case, we hold today only (a) that the court possessed jurisdiction of the subject matter; (b) that a justiciable cause of action is stated upon which appellants would be entitled to appropriate relief; and (c) because appellees raise the issue before this Court, that the appellants have standing to challenge the Tennessee apportionment statutes. Beyond noting that we have no cause at this stage to doubt the District Court will be able to fashion relief if violations of constitutional rights are found, it is improper now to consider what remedy would be most appropriate if appellants prevail at the trial.

II

JURISDICTION OF THE SUBJECT MATTER

The District Court was uncertain whether our cases withholding federal judicial relief rested upon a lack of federal jurisdiction or upon the inappropriateness of the subject matter for judicial consideration—what we have designated "nonjusticiability." The distinction between the two grounds is significant. In the instance of nonjusticiability, consideration of the cause is not wholly and immediately foreclosed; rather, the Court's inquiry necessarily proceeds to the point of deciding whether the duty asserted can be judicially identified and its breach judicially determined, and whether protection for the right asserted can be judicially molded. In the instance of lack of jurisdiction the cause either does not "arise under" the Federal Constitution, laws or treaties (or fall within one of the other enumerated categories of Art. III, § 2), or is not a "case or controversy" within the meaning of that section; or the cause is not one described by any jurisdictional statute. Our conclusion, *infra*, that this cause presents no nonjusticiable "political question" settles the only possible doubt that it is a case or controversy. Under the present heading of "Jurisdiction of the Subject Matter" we

hold only that the matter set forth in the complaint does arise under the Constitution. . . .

Article III, § 2, of the Federal Constitution provides that "The judicial Power shall extend to all Cases, in Law and Equity, arising under this Constitution, the laws of the United States, and treaties made, or which shall be made, under their Authority. . . ." It is clear that the cause of action is one which "arises under" the Federal Constitution. The complaint alleges that the 1901 statute effects an apportionment that deprives the appellants of the equal protection of the laws in violation of the Fourteenth Amendment. Dismissal of the complaint upon the ground of lack of jurisdiction of the subject matter would, therefore, be justified only if that claim were "so attenuated and unsubstantial as to be absolutely devoid of merit." . . . Since the District Court obviously and correctly did not deem the asserted federal constitutional claim unsubstantial and frivolous, it should not have dismissed the complaint for want of jurisdiction of the subject matter. And of course no further consideration of the merits of the claim is relevant to a determination of the court's jurisdiction of the subject matter. . . .

An unbroken line of our precedents sustains the federal courts' jurisdiction of the subject matter of federal constitutional claims of this nature. The first cases involved the redistricting of States for the purpose of electing Representatives to the Federal Congress. When the Ohio Supreme Court sustained Ohio legislation against an attack for repugnancy to Art. I, § 4, of the Federal Constitution, we affirmed on the merits and expressly refused to dismiss for want of jurisdiction "In view . . . of the subject-matter of the controversy and the Federal characteristics which inhere in it. . . ." When the Minnesota Supreme Court affirmed the dismissal of a suit to enjoin the Secretary of State of Minnesota from acting under Minnesota redistricting legislation, we reviewed the constitutional merits of the legislation and reversed the State Supreme Court. . . .

The appellees refer to *Colegrove* v. *Green* as authority that the District Court lacked jurisdiction of the subject matter. Appellees misconceive the holding of that case. The holding was precisely contrary to their reading of it. Seven members of the Court participated in the decision. Unlike many other cases in this field which have assumed without discussion that there was jurisdiction, all three opinions filed in *Colegrove* discussed the question. Two of the opinions expressing the views of four of the Justices, a majority, flatly held that there was jurisdiction of the subject matter. Mr. Justice Black joined by Mr. Justice Douglas and Mr. Justice Murphy stated: "It is my judgment that the

District Court had jurisdiction. . . ." Mr. Justice Rutledge, writing separately, expressed agreement with this conclusion. . . .

We hold that the District Court has jurisdiction of the subject matter of the federal constitutional claim asserted in the complaint.

III
STANDING

A federal court cannot "pronounce any statute, either of a State or of the United States, void, because irreconcilable with the Constitution, except as it is called upon to adjudge the legal rights of litigants in actual controversies." . . . Have the appellants alleged such a personal stake in the outcome of the controversy as to assure that concrete adverseness which sharpens the presentation of issues upon which the court so largely depends for illumination of difficult constitutional questions? This is the gist of the question of standing. It is, of course, a question of federal law. . . .

We hold that the appellants do have standing to maintain this suit. Our decisions plainly support this conclusion. Many of the cases have assumed rather than articulated the premise in deciding the merits of similar claims. And Colegrove v. Green squarely held that voters who allege facts showing disadvantage to themselves as individuals have standing to sue. . . .

These appellants seek relief in order to protect or vindicate an interest of their own, and of those similarly situated. Their constitutional claim is, in substance, that the 1901 statute constitutes arbitrary and capricious state action, offensive to the Fourteenth Amendment in its irrational disregard of the standard of apportionment prescribed by the State's Constitution or of any standard, effecting a gross disproportion of representation of voting population. The injury which appellants assert is that this classification disfavors the voters in the counties in which they reside, placing them in a position of constitutionally unjustifiable inequality vis-a-vis voters in irrationally favored counties. A citizen's right to a vote free of arbitrary impairment by state action has been judicially recognized as a right secured by the Constitution, when such impairment resulted from dilution by a false tally, . . . or by a refusal to count votes from arbitrarily selected precincts . . . or by a stuffing of the ballot box. . . .

It would not be necessary to decide whether appellants' allegations of impairment of their votes by the 1901 apportionment will, ultimately, entitle them to any relief, in order to hold that they have standing to seek it. If such impairment does produce a legally cognizable injury, they are among those who have sustained it. They are asserting "a plain, direct and adequate interest in maintaining the effectiveness of their votes," . . . not merely a claim of "the right, possessed by every citizen, to require that the Government be administered according to law. . . ." . . . They are entitled to a hearing and to the District Court's decision on their claims. "The very essence of civil liberty certainly consists in the right of every individual to claim the protection of the laws, whenever he receives an injury." . . .

IV
JUSTICIABILITY

In holding that the subject matter of this suit was not justiciable, the District Court relied on Colegrove v. Green and subsequent per curiam cases. The court stated: "From a review of these decisions there can be no doubt that the federal rule . . . is that the federal courts . . . will not intervene in cases of this type to compel legislative reapportionment." We understand the District Court to have read the cited cases as compelling the conclusion that since the appellants sought to have a legislative apportionment held unconstitutional, their suit presented a "political question" and was therefore nonjusticiable. We hold that this challenge to an apportionment presents no nonjusticiable "political question." The cited cases do not hold the contrary.

Of course the mere fact that the suit seeks protection of a political right does not mean it presents a political question. Such an objection "is little more than a play upon words." . . . Rather, it is argued that apportionment cases, whatever the actual wording of the complaint, can involve no federal constitutional right except one resting on the guaranty of a republican form of government, and that complaints based on that clause have been held to present political questions which are nonjusticiable.

We hold that the claim pleaded here neither rests upon nor implicates the Guaranty Clause and that its justiciability is therefore not foreclosed by our decisions of cases involving that clause. The District Court misinterpreted Colegrove v. Green and other decisions of this Court on which it relied. Appellants' claim that they are being denied equal protection is justiciable, and if "discrimination is sufficiently shown, the right to relief under the equal protection clause is not diminished by the fact that the discrimination relates to political rights." . . . To show why we reject the argument based on the Guaranty Clause, we must examine the authorities under it. But because there appears to be some uncertainty as to why those cases did present political questions, and specifically as to whether this apportionment case is like those cases, we deem it necessary first to consider the contours of the "political question" doctrine.

Our discussion, even at the price of extending this opinion, requires review of a number of political question cases, in order to expose the attributes of the doctrine—attributes which, in various settings, diverge, combine, appear, and disappear in seeming disorderliness. Since that review is undertaken solely to demonstrate that neither singly nor collectively do these cases support a conclusion that this apportionment case is nonjusticiable, we of course do not explore their implications in other contexts. That review reveals that in the Guaranty Clause cases and in the other "political question" cases, it is the relationship between the judiciary and the coordinate branches of the Federal Government, and not the federal judiciary's relationship to the States, which gives rise to the "political question."

We have said that "In determining whether a question falls within [the political question] category, the appropriateness under our system of government of attributing finality to the action of the political departments, and also the lack of satisfactory criteria for a judicial determination are dominant considerations." . . . The nonjusticiability of a political question is primarily a function of the separation of powers. Much confusion results from the capacity of the "political question" label to obscure the need for case-by-case inquiry. Deciding whether a matter has in any measure been committed by the Constitution to another branch of government, or whether the action of that branch exceeds whatever authority has been committed, is itself a delicate exercise in constitutional interpretation, and is a responsibility of this Court as ultimate interpreter of the Constitution. To demonstrate this requires no less than to analyze representative cases and to infer from them the analytical threads that make up the political question doctrine. We shall then show that none of those threads catches this case. . . .

We come, finally, to the ultimate inquiry whether our precedents as to what constitutes a nonjusticiable "political question" brings the case before us under the umbrella of that doctrine. A natural beginning is to note whether any of the common characteristics which we have been able to identify and label descriptively are present. We find none: The question here is the consistency of state action with the Federal Constitution. We have no question decided, or to be decided, by a political branch of government coequal with this

Court. Nor do we risk embarrassment of our government abroad, or grave disturbance at home if we take issue with Tennessee as to the constitutionality of her action here challenged. Nor need the appellants, in order to succeed in this action, ask the Court to enter upon policy determinations for which judicially manageable standards are lacking. Judicial standards under the Equal Protection Clause are well developed and familiar, and it has been open to courts since the enactment of the Fourteenth Amendment to determine, if on the particular facts they must, that a discrimination reflects *no* policy, but simply arbitrary and capricious action. . . .

We conclude that the complaint's allegations of a denial of equal protection present a justiciable constitutional cause of action upon which appellants are entitled to a trial and a decision. The right asserted is within the reach of judicial protection under the Fourteenth Amendment.

The judgment of the District Court is reversed and the cause is remanded for further proceedings consistent with this opinion.

Reversed and remanded.

Justice Frankfurter, joined by
Justice Harlan, dissented as follows:

The Court today reverses a uniform course of decision established by a dozen cases, including one by which the very claim now sustained was unanimously rejected only five years ago. The impressive body of rulings thus cast aside reflected the equally uniform course of our political history regarding the relationship between population and legislative representation —a wholly different matter from denial of the franchise to individuals because of race, color, religion or sex. Such a massive repudiation of the experience of our whole past in asserting destructively novel judicial power demands a detailed analysis of the role of this Court in our constitutional scheme. Disregard of inherent limits in the effective exercise of the Court's "judicial Power" not only presages the futility of judicial intervention in the essentially political conflict of forces by which the relation between population and representation has time out of mind been and now is determined. It may well impair the Court's position as the ultimate organ of "the supreme Law of the Land" in that vast range of legal problems, often strongly entangled in popular feeling, on which this Court must pronounce. The Court's authority—possessed of neither the purse nor the sword—ultimately rests on sustained public confidence in its moral sanction. Such feeling must be nourished by the Court's complete detachment, in fact and in appearance, from political entanglements and by abstention from injecting itself into the clash of political forces in political settlements. . . .

The Framers carefully and with deliberate forethought refused so to enthrone the judiciary. In this situation, as in others of like nature, appeal for relief does not belong here. Appeal must be to an informed, civically militant electorate. In a democratic society like ours, relief must come through an aroused popular conscience that sears the conscience of the people's representatives. In any event there is nothing judicially more unseemly nor more self-defeating than for this Court to make *in terrorem* pronouncements, to indulge in merely empty rhetoric, sounding a word of promise to the ear, sure to be disappointing to the hope. . . .

Standards of fair representation were not determined in *Baker* v. *Carr.* Criteria for congressional districts were established in *Wesberry* v. *Sanders,* and for state legislative districts in *Reynolds* v. *Sims.* The criteria in Wesberry aroused bitter criticism from several established members of Congress whose safe House seats were threatened as a result of the new, fairer standards. Justice Black wrote the majority opinion in Wesberry with Justice Clark concurring in part and dissenting in part. Justice Harlan dissented.

WESBERRY v. SANDERS
376 U. S. 1 (1964)

Justice Black delivered the opinion of the Court:

Appellants are citizens and qualified voters of Fulton County, Georgia, and as such are entitled to vote in Congressional elections in Georgia's Fifth Congressional District. That district, one of ten created by a 1931 Georgia statute, includes Fulton, DeKalb, and Rockdale Counties and has a population according to the 1960 census of 823,680. The average population of the ten districts is 394,312, less than half that of the Fifth. One district, the Ninth, has only 272,154 people, less than one-third as many as the Fifth. Since there is only one Congressman for each district, this inequality of population means that the Fifth District's Congressman has to represent from two to three times as many people as do Congressmen from some of the other Georgia districts.

Claiming that these population disparities deprive them and voters similarly situated of the right under the federal Constitution to have their votes for Congressmen given the same weight as the votes of other Georgians, the appellants brought this action . . . asking that the Georgia statute be declared invalid and that the appellees, the Governor and Secretary of the state of Georgia, be enjoined from conducting elections under it. The complaint alleged that appellants were deprived of the full benefit of their right to vote, in violation of (1) Art. I, §2 of the Constitution of the United States, which provides that "The House of Representatives shall be composed of members chosen every second year by the People of the several States . . ."; (2) the Due Process, Equal Protection, and Privileges and Immunities Clauses of the Fourteenth Amendment; and (3) that part of Section 2 of the Fourteenth Amendment which provides that "Representatives shall be apportioned among the several States according to their respective numbers. . . ."

The case was heard by a three-judge District Court, which found unanimously, from facts not disputed, that:

It is clear by any standard . . . that the population of the Fifth District is grossly out of balance with that of the other nine congressional districts of Georgia and in fact, so much so that the removal of DeKalb and Rockdale Counties from the District, leaving only Fulton with a population of 556,326, would leave it exceeding the average by slightly more than forty per cent.

Notwithstanding these findings, a majority of the court dismissed the complaint, citing as their guide Mr. Justice Frankfurter's minority opinion in *Colegrove* v. *Green,* an opinion stating that challenges to apportionment of congressional districts raised only "political" questions, which were not justiciable. Although the majority below said that the dismissal here was based on "want of equity" and not on justiciability, they relied on no circumstances which were peculiar to the present case; instead, they adopted the language and reasoning of Mr. Justice Frankfurter's *Colegrove* opinion in concluding that the appellants had presented a wholly "political" question. Judge Tuttle, disagreeing with the court's reliance on that opinion, dissented from the dismissal, though he would have denied an injunction at that time in order to give the Georgia Legislature ample opportunity to correct the "abuses" in the apportionment. He relied on *Baker* v. *Carr*, which, after full discussion of Colegrove and all the opinions in it, held that allegations of disparities of population in state legislative districts raise justiciable claims on which courts may grant relief. We noted probable jurisdiction. . . . We agree with Judge Tuttle that in debasing the weight of appellants' votes the state had abridged the right to vote for members of Congress guaranteed them by the United States Constitution, that the District Court should have entered a declaratory judgment to that effect, and that it was therefore error to dismiss this suit. The question of what relief should be given we leave for further consideration and decision by the District Court in light of existing circumstances. . . .

This statement in *Baker*, which referred to our past decisions holding Congressional apportionment cases to be justiciable, we believe was wholly correct and we adhere to it. Mr. Justice Frankfurter's *Colegrove* opinion contended that Art. I, §4, of the Constitution had given Congress "exclusive authority" to protect the right of citizens to vote for Congressmen, but we made it clear in *Baker* that nothing in the language of that article gives support to a construction that would immunize state Congressional apportionment laws which debase a citizen's right to vote from the power of courts to protect the constitutional rights of individuals from legislative destruction. . . . The right to vote is too important in our free society to be stripped of judicial protection by such an interpretation of Article I. This dismissal can no more be justified on the ground of "want of equity" than on the ground of "nonjusticiability." We therefore hold that the District Court erred in dismissing the complaint.

This brings us to the merits. We agree with the District Court that the 1931 Georgia apportionment grossly discriminates against voters in the Fifth Congressional District. A single Congressman represents from two to three times as many Fifth District voters as are represented by each of the Congressmen from the other Georgia Congressional districts. The apportionment statute thus contracts the value of some votes and expands that of others. If the federal Constitution intends that when qualified voters elect members of Congress each vote be given as much weight as any other vote, then this statute cannot stand.

We hold that, construed in its historical context, the command of Art. I, §2, that Representatives be chosen "by the People of the several States" means that as nearly as is practicable one man's vote in a congressional election is to be worth as much as another's. This rule is followed automatically, of course, when Representatives are chosen as a group on a statewide basis, as was a widespread practice in the first fifty years of our nation's history. It would be extraordinary to suggest that in such statewide elections the votes of inhabitants of some parts of a state, for example, Georgia's thinly populated Ninth District, could be weighed at two or three times the value of the votes of people living in more populous parts of the state, for example, the Fifth District around Atlanta. We do not believe that the framers of the Constitution intended to permit the same vote-diluting discrimination to be accomplished through the device of districts containing widely varied numbers of inhabitants. To say that a vote is worth more in one district than in another would not only run counter to our fundamental ideas of democratic government, it would cast aside the principle of the House of Representatives elected "by the People," a principle tenaciously fought over and established at the Constitutional Convention. The history of the Constitution, particularly that part of it relating to the adoption of Art. I, §2, reveals that those who framed the Constitution meant that, no matter what the mechanics of an election, whether statewide or by districts, it was population which was to be the basis of the House of Representatives. . . .

The debates at the Convention make at least one fact abundantly clear: that when the delegates agreed that the House should represent "people" they intended that in allocating Congressmen the number assigned to each state should be determined solely by the number of the state's inhabitants. The Constitution embodied Edmund Randolph's proposal for a periodic census to ensure "fair representation of the people," an idea endorsed by Mason as assuring that "numbers of inhabitants" should always be the measure of representation in the House of Representatives. The Convention also overwhelmingly agreed to a resolution offered by Randolph to base future apportionment squarely on numbers and to delete any reference to wealth. And the delegates defeated a motion made by Elbridge Gerry to limit the number of Representatives from newer Western states so that it would never exceed the number from the original states.

It would defeat the principle solemnly embodied in the Great Compromise—equal representation in the House of equal numbers of people—for us to hold that, within the states, legislatures may draw the lines of Congressional districts in such a way as to give some voters a greater voice in choosing a Congressman than others. The House of Representatives, the Convention agreed, was to represent the people as individuals, and on a basis of complete equality for each voter. The delegates were quite aware of what Madison called the "vicious representation" in Great Britain whereby "rotten boroughs" with few inhabitants were represented in Parliament on or almost on a par with cities of greater population. Wilson urged that people must be represented as individuals, so that America would escape the evils of the English system under which one man could send two members to Parliament to represent the borough of Old Sarum while London's million people sent but four. The delegates referred to rotten borough apportionments in some of the state legislatures as the kind of objectionable governmental action that the Constitution should not tolerate in the election of congressional representatives. . . .

It is in the light of such history that we must construe Art. I, §2, of the Constitution, which, carrying out the ideas of Madison and those of like views, provides that Representatives shall be chosen "by the People of the several States" and shall be "apportioned among the several States . . . according to their respective numbers." It is not surprising that our Court has held that this Article gives persons qualified to vote a constitutional right to vote and to have their votes counted. *United States* v. *Mosley* [1915] . . . *Ex parte Yarbrough* [1884] . . . Not only can this right to vote not be denied outright, it cannot, consistently with Article I, be destroyed by alteration of ballots, see *United States* v. *Classic* [1941] . . . or diluted by stuffing of the ballot box. . . . No right is more precious in a free country than that of having a voice in the election of those who make the laws under which, as good citizens, we must live. Other rights, even the most basic, are illusory if the right to vote is undermined. Our Constitution leaves no room for classification of people in a way that unnecessarily abridges this right. In urging the people to adopt the Constitution, Madison said in No. 57 of *The Federalist*:

Who are to be the electors of the Federal Representatives? Not the rich more than the poor; not the learned more than the ignorant; not the haughty heirs of distinguished names, more than the humble sons of obscure and unpropitious fortune. The electors are to be the great body of the people of the United States.

Readers surely could have fairly taken this to mean, "one person, one vote."

While it may not be possible to draw Congressional districts with mathematical precision, that is no excuse for ignoring our Constitution's plain objective of making equal representation for equal numbers of people the fundamental goal for the House of Representatives. That is the high standard of justice and common sense which the founders set for us.

Reversed and remanded.

Justice Harlan dissented:

I had not expected to witness the day when the Supreme Court of the United States would render a decision which cast grave doubt on the constitutionality of the composition of the House of Representatives. It is not an exaggeration to say that such is the effect of today's decision. The Court's holding that the Constitution requires states to select Representatives either by elections at large or by elections in districts composed "as nearly as is practicable" of equal population places in jeopardy the seats of almost all the members of the present House of Representatives. . . . Only a demonstration which could not be avoided would justify this Court in rendering a decision the effect of which, inescapably as I see it, is to declare constitutionally defective the very composition of a coordinate branch of the federal government. The Court's opinion not only fails to make such a demonstration. It is unsound logically on its face and demonstrably unsound historically. . . .

. . . [T]he language of Art. I, §§2 and 4, the surrounding text, and the relevant history are all in strong and consistent direct contradiction of the Court's holding. The constitutional scheme vests in the states plenary power to regulate the conduct of elections for Representatives, and, in order to protect the federal government, provides for Congressional supervision of the states' exercise of their power. Within this scheme, the appellants do not have the right which they assert, in the absence of provision for equal districts by the Georgia Legislature or the Congress. The constitutional right which the Court creates is manufactured out of whole cloth.

The unstated premise of the Court's conclusion quite obviously is that the Congress has not dealt, and the Court believes it will not deal, with the problem of Congressional apportionment in accordance with what the Court believes to be sound political principles. Laying aside for the moment the validity of such a consideration as a factor in constitutional interpretation, it becomes relevant to examine the history of Congressional action under Art. I, § 4. This history reveals that the Court is not simply undertaking to exercise a power which the Constitution reserves to the Congress; it is also overruling Congressional judgment. . . .

Today's decision has portents for our society and the Court itself which should be recognized. This is not a case in which the Court vindicates the kind of individual rights that are assured by the Due Process Clause of the Fourteenth Amendment, whose "vague contours," . . . of course leave much room for constitutional developments necessitated by changing conditions in a dynamic society. Nor is this a case in which an emergent set of facts requires the Court to frame new principles to protect recognized constitutional rights. The claim for judicial relief in this case strikes at one of the fundamental doctrines of our system of government, the separation of powers. In upholding the claim, the Court attempts to effect reforms in a field which the Constitution, as plainly as can be, has committed exclusively to the political process.

This Court, no less than all other branches of the government, is bound by the Constitution. The Constitution does not confer on the Court blanket authority to step into every situation where the political branch may be thought to have fallen short. The stability of this institution ultimately depends not only upon its being alert to keep the other branches of government within constitutional bounds but equally upon recognition of the limitations on the Court's own functions in the Constitutional system.

What is done today saps the political process. The promise of judicial intervention in matters of this sort cannot but encourage popular inertia in efforts for political reform through the political process, with the inevitable result that the process is itself weakened. By yielding to the demand for a judicial remedy in this instance, the Court in my view does a disservice both to itself and to the broader values of our system of government.

Believing that the complaint fails to disclose a constitutional claim, I would affirm the judgment below dismissing the complaint.

Justice Stewart dissented also:

I think it is established that "this Court has power to afford relief in a case of this type as against the objection that the issues are not justiciable," and I cannot subscribe to any possible implication to the contrary which may lurk in Mr. Justice Harlan's dissenting opinion. With this single qualification I join the dissent because I think Mr. Justice Harlan has unanswerably demonstrated that Art. I, § 2, of the Constitution gives no mandate to this Court or to any court to ordain that Congressional districts within each state must be equal in population.

The Reynolds case, which set criteria for state legislative districts, aroused even more political opposition than Wesberry because it threatened long-established rural political machines largely dominated by the Farm Bureau Federation. Farm Bureau lobbyists and their congressional allies, such as then Representative Robert Dole, sought to gain approval for a constitutional amendment to overturn Reynolds and establish "one house on population and one house on area," the so-called federal analogy.

REYNOLDS v. SIMS
377 U. S. 533 (1964)

*Chief Justice Warren
delivered the opinion of the Court:*

II

. . . Undeniably the Constitution of the United States protects the right of all qualified citizens to vote, in state as well as in federal elections. A consistent line of decisions by this Court in cases involving attempts to deny or restrict the right of suffrage has made this indelibly clear. . . . The right to vote freely for the candidate of one's choice is of the essence of a demo-cratic society, and any restrictions on that right strike at the heart of representative government. And the right of suffrage can be denied by a debasement or dilution of the weight of a citizen's vote just as effectively as by wholly prohibiting the free exercise of the franchise. . . .

Gray and *Wesberry* are of course not dispositive of or directly controlling on our decision in these cases involving state legislative apportionment controversies. Admittedly, those decisions, in which we held that, in statewide and in congressional elections, one person's vote must be counted equally with those of all other voters in a State, were based on different constitutional considerations and were addressed to rather distinct problems. But neither are they wholly inapposite. *Gray*, though not determinative here since involving the weighting of votes in statewide elections, established the basic principle of equality among voters within a State, and held that voters cannot be classified, constitutionally, on the basis of where they live, at least with respect to voting in statewide elections. And our decision in *Wesberry* was of course grounded on that language of the Constitution which prescribes that members of the Federal House of Representatives are to be chosen "by the People," while attacks on state legislative apportionment schemes, such as that involved in the instant cases, are principally based on the Equal Protection Clause of the Fourteenth Amendment. Nevertheless, *Wesberry* clearly established that the fundamental principle of representative government in this country is one of equal representation for equal numbers of people, without regard to race, sex, economic status, or place of residence within a state. Our problem, then, is to ascertain, in the instant cases, whether there are any constitutionally cognizable principles which would justify departures from the basic standard of equality among voters in the apportionment of seats in state legislatures.

III

A predominant consideration in determining whether a State's legislative apportionment scheme constitutes an invidious discrimination violative of rights asserted under the Equal Protection Clause is that the rights allegedly impaired are individual and personal in nature. . . .[T]he judicial focus must be concentrated upon ascertaining whether there has been any discrimination against certain of the State's citizens which constitutes an impermissible impairment of their constitutionally protected right to vote. Like *Skinner* v. *Oklahoma* [1942] . . . such a case "touches a sensitive and important area of human rights," and "involves one of the basic civil rights of man," presenting questions of alleged "invidious discriminations . . . against groups or types of individuals in violation of the constitutional guaranty of just and equal laws." . . . Undoubtedly, the right of suffrage is a fundamental matter in a free and democratic society. Especially since the right to exercise the franchise in a free and unimpaired manner is preservative of other basic civil and political rights, any alleged infringement of the right of citizens to vote must be carefully and meticulously scrutinized. . . .

Legislators represent people, not trees or acres. Legislators are elected by voters, not farms or cities or economic interests. As long as ours is a representative form of government, and our legislatures are those instruments of government elected directly by and directly representative of the people, the right to elect legislators in a free and unimpaired fashion is a bedrock of our political system. It could hardly be gainsaid that a constitutional claim had been asserted by an allegation that certain otherwise qualified voters had been entirely prohibited from voting for members of their state legislature. And, if a State should provide that the votes of citizens in one part of the State should be given two times, or five times, or 10 times the weight of votes of citizens in another part of the State, it could hardly be contended that the right to vote of those residing in the disfavored area had not been effectively diluted. It would appear extraordinary to suggest that a State could be constitutionally permitted to enact a law providing that certain of the State's voters could vote two, five, or 10 times for their legislative representatives, while voters living elsewhere could vote only once. And it is inconceivable that a state law to the effect that, in counting votes for legislators, the votes of citizens in one part of the State would be multiplied by two, five, or 10, while the votes of persons in another area would be counted only at face value, could be constitutionally sustainable. Of course, the effect of state legislative districting schemes which give the same number of representatives to unequal numbers of constituents is identical. Overweighting and overvaluation of the votes of those living here has the certain effect of dilution and undervaluation of the votes of those living there. The resulting discrimination against those individual voters living in disfavored areas is easily demonstrable mathematically. Their right to vote is simply not the same right to vote as that of those living in a favored part of the State. Two, five, or 10 of them must vote before the effect of their voting is equivalent to that of their favored neighbor. Weighting the votes of citizens differently, by any method or means, merely because of where they happen to reside, hardly seems justifiable. . . .

State legislatures are, historically, the fountainhead of representative government in this country. . . . Most citizens can achieve [full and effective] participation only as qualified voters through the election of legislators to represent them. Full and effective participation by all citizens in state government requires, therefore, that each citizen have an equally effective voice in the election of members of his state legislature. Modern and viable state government needs, and the Constitution demands, no less.

Logically, in a society ostensibly grounded on representative government, it would seem reasonable that a majority of the people of a State could elect a majority of that State's legislators. To conclude differently, and to sanction minority control of state legislative bodies, would appear to deny majority rights in a way that far surpasses any possible denial of minority rights that might otherwise be thought to result. Since legislatures are responsible for enacting laws by which all citizens are to be governed, they should be bodies which are collectively responsive to the popular will. And the concept of equal protection has been traditionally viewed as requiring the uniform treatment of persons standing in the same relation to the governmental action questioned or challenged. With respect to the allocation of legislative representation, all voters, as citizens of a state, stand in the same relation regardless of where they live. Any suggested criteria for the differentiation of citizens are insufficient to justify any discrimination, as to the weight of their votes, unless relevant to the permissible purposes of legislative apportionment. Since the achieving of fair and effective representation for all citizens is concededly the basic aim of legislative apportionment, we conclude that the Equal Protection Clause guarantees the opportunity for equal participation by all voters in the election of state legislators. Diluting the weight of votes because of place of residence impairs basic constitutional rights under the Fourteenth Amendment just as much as invidious discriminations based upon factors such as race, . . . or economic status. . . . Our constitutional system amply provides for the protection of minorities by means other than giving them majority control of state legislatures. And the democratic ideals of equality and majority rule, which have served this nation so well in the past, are hardly of any less significance for the present and the future.

We are told that the matter of apportioning representation in a state legislature is a complex and many-faceted one. We are advised that States can rationally consider factors other than population in apportioning legislative representation. We are admonished not to restrict the power of the States to impose differing views as to political philosophy on their citizens. We are cautioned about the dangers of entering into political thickets and mathematical quagmires. Our answer is this: a denial of constitutionally protected rights demands judicial protection; our oath and our office require no less of us. . . . To the extent that a citizen's right to vote is debased, he is that much less a citizen. The fact that an individual lives here or there is not a legitimate reason for overweighting or diluting the efficacy of his vote. The complexions of societies and civilizations change, often with amazing rapidity. A nation once primarily rural in character becomes predominantly urban. Representation schemes once fair

and equitable become archaic and outdated. But the basic principle of representative government remains, and must remain, unchanged—the weight of a citizen's vote cannot be made to depend on where he lives. Population is, of necessity, the starting point for consideration and the controlling criterion for judgment in legislative apportionment controversies. A citizen, a qualified voter, is no more nor no less so because he lives in the city or on the farm. This is the clear and strong command of our Constitution's Equal Protection Clause. This is an essential part of the concept of a government of laws and not men. This is at the heart of Lincoln's vision of "government of the people, by the people, [and] for the people." The Equal Protection Clause demands no less than substantially equal state legislative representation for all citizens, of all places as well as of all races.

IV

We hold that, as a basic constitutional standard, the Equal Protection Clause requires that the seats in both houses of a bicameral state legislature must be apportioned on a population basis. Simply stated, an individual's right to vote for state legislators is unconstitutionally impaired when its weight is in a substantial fashion diluted when compared with votes of citizens living in other parts of the State. . . .

Much has been written since our decision in *Baker v. Carr* about the applicability of the so-called federal analogy to state legislative apportionment arrangements. After considering the matter, the court below concluded that no conceivable analogy could be drawn between the federal scheme and the apportionment of seats in the Alabama Legislature under the proposed constitutional amendment. We agree with the District Court, and find the federal analogy inapposite and irrelevant to state legislative districting schemes. Attempted reliance on the federal analogy appears often to be little more than an after-the-fact rationalization offered in defense of maladjusted state apportionment arrangements. . . .

The system of representation in the two Houses of the Federal Congress is one ingrained in our Constitution, as part of the law of the land. It is one conceived out of compromise and concession indispensable to the establishment of our federal republic. Arising from unique historical circumstances, it is based on the consideration that in establishing our type of federalism a group of formerly independent states bound themselves together under one national government. . . .

Political subdivisions of States—counties, cities, or whatever—never were and never have been considered as sovereign entities. Rather, they have been traditionally regarded as subordinate governmental instrumentalities created by the State to assist in the carrying out of state governmental functions. . . .

Since we find the so-called federal analogy inapposite to a consideration of the institutional validity of state legislative apportionment schemes, we necessarily hold that the Equal Protection Clause requires both houses of a state legislature to be apportioned on a population basis. The right of a citizen to equal representation and to have his vote weighted equally with those of all other citizens in the election of members of one house of a bicameral state legislature would amount to little if States could effectively submerge the equal-population principle in the apportionment of seats in the other house. If such a scheme were permissible, an individual citizen's ability to exercise an effective voice in the only instrument of state government directly representative of the people might be almost as effectively thwarted as if neither house were apportioned on a population basis. . . .

We do not believe that the concept of bicameralism is rendered anachronistic and meaningless when the predominant basis of representation in the two state legislative bodies is required to be the same—population. A prime reason for bicameralism, modernly considered, is to insure mature and deliberate consideration of, and to prevent precipitate action on, proposed legislative measures. Simply because the controlling criterion for apportioning representation is required to be the same in both houses does not mean that there will be no differences in the composition and complexion of the two bodies. . . .

VI

By holding that as a federal constitutional requisite both houses of a state legislature must be apportioned on a population basis, we mean that the Equal Protection Clause requires that a State make an honest and good faith effort to construct districts, in both houses of its legislature, as nearly of equal population as is practicable. We realize that it is a practical impossibility to arrange legislative districts so that each one has an identical number of residents, or citizens, or voters. Mathematical exactness or precision is hardly a workable constitutional requirement. . . .

. . . So long as the divergences from a strict population standard are based on legitimate considerations incident to the effectuation of a rational state policy, some deviations from the equal-population principle are constitutionally permissible with respect to the apportionment of seats in either or both of the two houses of a bicameral state legislature. But neither history alone, nor economic or other sorts of group interests, are permissible factors in attempting to justify disparities from population-based representation. Citizens, not history or economic interests, cast votes. Considerations of area alone provide an insufficient justification for deviations from the equal-population principle. Again, people, not land or trees or pastures, vote. Modern developments and improvements in transportation and communications make rather hollow, in the mid-1960's, most claims that deviations from population-based representation can validly be based solely on geographical considerations. Arguments for allowing such deviations in order to insure effective representation for sparsely settled areas and to prevent legislative districts from becoming so large that the availability of access of citizens to their representatives is impaired are today, for the most part, unconvincing.

A consideration that appears to be of more substance in justifying some deviations from population-based representation in state legislatures is that of insuring some voice to political subdivisions, as political subdivisions. . . . In many States much of the legislature's activity involves the enactment of so-called local legislation, directed only to the concerns of particular political subdivisions. And a State may legitimately desire to construct districts along political subdivision lines to deter the possibilities of gerrymandering. But if, even as a result of a clearly rational state policy of according some legislative representation to political subdivisions, population is submerged as the controlling consideration in the apportionment of seats in the particular legislative body, then the right of all of the State's citizens to cast an effective and adequately weighted vote would be unconstitutionally impaired. . . .

We find, therefore, that the action taken by the District Court in this case, in ordering into effect a reapportionment of both houses of the Alabama Legislature for purposes of the 1962 primary and general elections, by using the best parts of the two proposed plans which it had found, as a whole, to be invalid, was an appropriate and well-considered exercise of judicial power. [W]e affirm the judgment below and remand the cases for further proceedings consistent with the views stated in this opinion.

It is so ordered.

Justices Clark and Stewart concurred in separate opinions, while Justice Harlan dissented:

The Court's constitutional discussion, . . . is remarkable . . . for its failure to address itself at all to the Fourteenth Amendment as a whole or to the legislative history of the Amendment pertinent to the matter at hand. Stripped of aphorisms, the Court's argument boils down to the assertion that appellees' right to vote has been invidiously "debased" or "diluted" by systems of apportionment which entitle them to vote for fewer legislators than other voters, an assertion which is tied to the Equal Protection Clause only by the constitutionally frail tautology that "equal" means "equal."

Had the Court paused to probe more deeply into the matter, it would have found that the Equal Protection Clause was never intended to inhibit the States in choosing any democratic method they pleased for the apportionment of their legislatures. . . .

The history of the adoption of the Fourteenth Amendment provides conclusive evidence that neither those who proposed nor those who ratified the Amendment believed that the Equal Protection Clause limited the power of the States to apportion their legislatures as they saw fit. Moreover, the history demonstrates that the intention to leave this power undisturbed was deliberate and was widely believed to be essential to the adoption of the Amendment. [An extensive review of the history follows.]

Although the Court—necessarily, as I believe—provides only generalities in elaboration of its main thesis, its opinion nevertheless fully demonstrates how far removed these problems are from fields of judicial competence. Recognizing that "indiscriminate districting" is an invitation to "partisan gerrymandering," . . . the Court nevertheless excludes virtually every basis for the formation of electoral districts other than "indiscriminate districting." In one or another of today's opinions, the Court declares it unconstitutional for a State to give effective consideration to any of the following in establishing legislative districts:

1. history;
2. "economic or other sorts of group interests";
3. area;
4. geographical considerations;
5. a desire "to insure effective representation for sparsely settled areas";
6. "availability of access of citizens to their representatives";
7. theories of bicameralism (except those approved by the Court);
8. occupation;
9. "an attempt to balance urban and rural power";
10. the preference of a majority of voters in the State.

So far as presently appears, the *only* factor which a state may consider, apart from numbers, is political subdivisions. But even "a clearly rational state policy" recognizing this factor is unconstitutional if "population is submerged as the controlling consideration. . . ."

I know of no principle of logic or practical or theoretical politics, still less any constitutional principle, which establishes all or any of these exclusions. Certain it is that the Court's opinion does not establish them. So far as the Court says anything at all on this score, it says only the "legislators represent people, not trees or acres," . . . that "citizens, not history or economic interests, cast votes." . . . that "people, not land or trees or pastures, vote." . . . All this may be conceded. But it is surely equally obvious, and, in the context of elections, more meaningful to note that people are not ciphers and that legislators can represent their electors only by speaking for their interests—economic, social, political—many of which do reflect the place where the electors live. The Court does not establish, or indeed even attempt to make a case for the proposition that conflicting interests within a state can only be adjusted by disregarding them when voters are grouped for purposes of representation. . . .

The political consequences of the reapportionment cases were far reaching. Concerted attempts were made to secure congressional approval of legislation that would defeat or delay implementation of key legislative reapportionment decisions. Some, like the Tuck bill, passed the House by a large margin but failed to gain Senate approval. Senator Everett Dirksen of Illinois led the most determined of these efforts, but despite his employment of complicated parliamentary maneuvers and the services of the public relations firm of Whittaker and Baxter, he too failed.[16]

The expansion of congressional civil rights authority

The intensity of conservative congressional opposition to the Supreme Court was increased as the Court carried its expansion of equal protection and commerce power decisions to their fullest scope in order to limit racial discrimination. Conversely, Congress itself, despite fierce conservative reaction, began to pass civil rights legislation. Thus, the expansion of the concept of equal protection as a prohibition against racial segregation in public education was the result, not only of judicial decisions, but of belated but significant congressional actions. *Heart of Atlanta Motel, Inc.* v. *The United States* and *Katzenbach* v. *McClung* were tests of the scope of Congress' commerce power as a basis for legislative prohibitions on racial segregation in privately owned businesses that provide public accommodations such as lodging or food. Justice Clark wrote the majority opinion in *Heart of Atlanta Motel*.

HEART OF ATLANTA MOTEL, INC. v. UNITED STATES
379 U. S. 241 (1964)

This is a declaratory judgment action . . . attacking the constitutionality of Title II of the Civil Rights Act of 1964. . . . Appellees counterclaimed for enforcement under § 206 (a) of the Act and asked for a three-judge district court under § 206 (b). A three-judge court, . . . sustained the validity of the Act and issued a permanent injunction on appellees' counter-claim restraining appellant from continuing to violate the Act. . . . We affirm the judgment.

1. THE FACTUAL BACKGROUND AND CONTENTIONS OF THE PARTIES

The case comes here on admissions and stipulated facts. Appellant owns and operates the Heart of Atlanta Motel which has 216 rooms available to transient guests. The motel is located on Courtland Street, two blocks from downtown Peachtree Street. It is readily accessible to interstate highways 75 and 85 and state highways 23 and 41. Appellant solicits patronage from outside the State of Georgia through various national advertising media, including magazines of national circulation; it maintains over 50 billboards and highway signs within the State, soliciting patronage for the motel; it accepts convention trade from outside Georgia and approximately 75% of its registered guests are from out of State. Prior to passage of the Act the motel had followed a practice of refusing to rent rooms to Negroes, and it alleged that it intended to continue to do so. In an effort to perpetuate that policy this suit was filed.

The appellant contends that Congress in passing this Act exceeded its power to regulate commerce under Art. I, § 8, cl. 3, of the Constitution of the United States; that the Act violates the Fifth Amendment because appellant is deprived of the right to choose its customers and operate its business as it

wishes, resulting in a taking of its liberty and property without due process of law and taking of its property without just compensation; and, finally, that by requiring appellant to rent available rooms to Negroes against its will, Congress is subjecting it to involuntary servitude in contravention of the Thirteenth Amendment. . . .

2. THE HISTORY OF THE ACT

. . . The Act as finally adopted was most comprehensive, undertaking to prevent through peaceful and voluntary settlement discrimination in voting, as well as in places of accommodation and public facilities, federally secured programs and in employment. Since Title II is the only portion under attack here, we confine our consideration to those public accommodation provisions.

3. TITLE II OF THE ACT

This Title is divided into seven sections beginning with § 201 (a) which provides that:

All persons shall be entitled to the full and equal enjoyment of the goods, services, facilities, privileges, advantages, and accommodations of any place of public accommodation, as defined in this section, without discrimination or segregation on the ground of race, color, religion, or national origin.

There are listed in § 201 (b) four classes of business establishments, each of which "serves the public" and "is a place of public accommodation" within the meaning of § 201 (a) "if its operations affect commerce, or if discrimination or segregation by it is supported by State action." The covered establishments are:

(1) any inn, hotel, motel, or other establishment which provides lodging to transient guests, other than an establishment located within a building which contains not more than five rooms for rent or hire and which is actually occupied by the proprietor of such establishment as his residence;
(2) any restaurant, cafeteria . . . [not here involved];

(3) any motion picture house . . . [not here involved];

(4) any establishment . . . which is physically located within the premises of any establishment otherwise covered by this subsection, or . . . within the premises of which is physically located any such covered establishment . . . [not here involved].

Section 201 (c) defines the phrase "affect commerce" as applied to the above establishment. It first declares that "any inn, hotel, motel, or other establishment which provides lodging to transient guests" affects commerce *per se*. . . .

Finally, § 203 prohibits the withholding or denial, etc., of any right or privilege secured by § 201 . . . or the intimidation, threatening or coercion of any person with the purpose of interfering with any such right or the punishing, etc., of any person for exercising or attempting to exercise any such right.

The remaining sections of the Title are remedial ones for violations of any of the previous sections. Remedies are limited to civil actions for preventive relief. The Attorney General may bring suit where he has "reasonable cause to believe that any person or group of persons is engaged in a pattern or practice of resistance to the full enjoyment of any of the rights secured by this title, and that the pattern or practice is of such a nature and is intended to deny the full exercise of the rights herein described. . . ."

4. APPLICATION OF TITLE II TO HEART OF ATLANTA MOTEL

It is admitted that the operation of the motel brings it within the provisions of § 201 (a) of the Act and that appellant refused to provide lodging for transient Negroes because of their race or color and that it intends to continue that policy unless restrained.

The sole question posed is, therefore, the constitutionality of the Civil Rights Act of 1964 as applied to these facts. The legislative history of the Act indicates that Congress based the Act on § 5 and the Equal Protection Clause of the Fourteenth Amendment as well as its power to regulate interstate commerce under Art. I, § 8, cl. 3, of the Constitution.

The Senate Commerce Committee made it quite clear that the fundamental object of Title II was to vindicate "the deprivation of personal dignity that surely accompanies denials of equal access to public establishments." At the same time, however, it noted that such an objective has been and could be readily achieved "by congressional action based on the commerce power of the Constitution." . . . Our study of the legislative record, made in the light of prior cases,

has brought us to the conclusion that Congress possessed ample power in this regard, and we have therefore not considered the other grounds relied upon. This is not to say that the remaining authority upon which it acted was not adequate, a question upon which we do not pass, but merely that since the commerce power is sufficient for our decision here we have considered it alone. . . .

5. THE CIVIL RIGHTS CASES, 109 U. S. 3 (1883), AND THEIR APPLICATION

In light of our ground for decision, it might be well at the outset to discuss the *Civil Rights Cases*, . . . which declared provisions of the Civil Rights Act of 1875 unconstitutional. . . . We think that decision inapposite, and without precedential value in determining the constitutionality of the present Act. Unlike Title II of the present legislation, the 1875 Act broadly proscribed discrimination in "inns, public conveyances on land or water, theaters, and other places of public amusement," without limiting the categories of affected businesses to those impinging upon interstate commerce. In contrast, the applicability of Title II is carefully limited to enterprises having a direct and substantial relation to the interstate flow of goods and people, except where state action is involved. Further, the fact that certain kinds of businesses may not in 1875 have been sufficiently involved in interstate commerce to warrant bringing them within the ambit of the commerce power is not necessarily dispositive of the same question today. Our populace had not reached its present mobility, nor were facilities, goods and services circulating as readily in interstate commerce as they are today. Although the principles which we apply today are those first formulated by Chief Justice Marshall in *Gibbons* v. *Ogden* . . . , the conditions of transportation and commerce have changed dramatically, and we must apply those principles to the present state of commerce. The sheer increase in volume of interstate traffic alone would give discriminatory practices which inhibit travel a far larger impact upon the Nation's commerce than such practices had on the economy of another day. . . .

6. THE BASIS OF CONGRESSIONAL ACTION

While the Act as adopted carried no congressional findings the record of its passage through each house is replete with evidence of the burdens that discrimination by race or color places upon interstate commerce. . . . This testimony included the fact that our people have become increasingly mobile with millions of people of all races traveling from State to State; that

Negroes in particular have been the subject of discrimination in transient accommodations, having to travel great distances to secure the same; that often they have been unable to obtain accommodations and have had to call upon friends to put them up overnight, . . . and that these conditions had become so acute as to require the listing of available lodging for Negroes in a special guidebook which was itself "dramatic testimony to the difficulties" Negroes encounter in travel. . . . These exclusionary practices were found to be nationwide, the Under Secretary of Commerce testifying that there is "no question that the discrimination in the North still exists to a large degree" and in the West and Midwest as well. . . . This testimony indicated a qualitative as well as quantitative effect on interstate travel by Negroes. The former was the obvious impairment of the Negro traveler's pleasure and convenience that resulted when he continually was uncertain of finding lodging. As for the latter, there was evidence that this uncertainty stemming from racial discrimination had the effect of discouraging travel on the part of a substantial portion of the Negro community. . . . This was the conclusion not only of the Under Secretary of Commerce but also of the Administrator of the Federal Aviation Agency who wrote the Chairman of the Senate Commerce Committee that it was his "belief that air commerce is adversely affected by the denial to a substantial segment of the traveling public of adequate and desegregated public accommodations." . . . We shall not burden this opinion with further details since the voluminous testimony presents overwhelming evidence that discrimination by hotels and motels impedes interstate travel.

7. THE POWER OF CONGRESS OVER INTERSTATE TRAVEL

The power of Congress to deal with these obstructions depends on the meaning of the Commerce Clause. Its meaning was first enunciated 140 years ago by the great Chief Justice John Marshall in *Gibbons* v. *Ogden*. . . .

. . . In short, the determinative test of the exercise of power by Congress under the Commerce Clause is simply whether the activity sought to be regulated is "commerce which concerns more States than one" and has a real and substantial relation to the national interest. Let us now turn to this facet of the problem.

That the "intercourse" of which the Chief Justice spoke included the movement of persons through more States than one was settled as early as 1849, in the *Passenger Cases* [1849] . . . where Mr. Justice McLean stated: "That the transportation of passengers is a part of commerce is not now an open question." Again in

1913 Mr. Justice McKenna, speaking for the Court, said: "Commerce among the States, we have said, consists of intercourse and traffic between their citizens, and includes the transportation of persons and property." *Hoke* v. *United States.* . . . And only four years later in 1917 in *Caminetti* v. *United States* . . . Mr. Justice Day held for the Court:

The transportation of passengers in interstate commerce, it has long been settled, is within the regulatory power of Congress, under the commerce clause of the Constitution, and the authority of Congress to keep the channels of interstate commerce free from immoral and injurious uses has been frequently sustained, and is no longer open to question.

Nor does it make any difference whether the transportation is commercial in character. In *Morgan* v. *Virginia* [1946] . . . Mr. Justice Reed observed as to the modern movement of persons among the States:

The recent changes in transportation brought about by the coming of automobiles [do] not seem of great significance in the problem. People of all races travel today more extensively than in 1878 when this Court first passed upon state regulation of racial segregation in commerce. [It but] emphasizes the soundness of this Court's early conclusion in *Hall* v. *DeCuir* [1878] . . .

The same interest in protecting interstate commerce which led Congress to deal with segregation in interstate carriers and the white-slave traffic has prompted it to extend the exercise of its power to gambling . . .; to criminal enterprises . . .; to deceptive practices in the sale of products . . .; to fraudulent security transactions . . .; to misbranding of drugs . . .; to wages and hours . . .; to members of labor unions . . .; to crop control . . .; to discrimination against shippers . . .; to the protection of small business from injurious price cutting . . .; to resale price maintenance . . .; to professional football . . .; and to racial discrimination by owners and managers of terminal restaurants. . . .

That Congress was legislating against moral wrongs in many of these areas rendered its enactments no less valid. In framing Title II of this Act Congress was also dealing with what it considered a moral problem. But that fact does not detract from the overwhelming evidence of the disruptive effect that racial discrimination has had on commercial intercourse. It was this burden which empowered Congress to enact appropriate legislation, and, given this basis for the exercise of its power, Congress was not restricted by the fact that the particular obstruction to interstate commerce with which it was dealing was also deemed a moral and social wrong.

It is said that the operation of the motel here is of a purely local character. But, assuming this to be true, "[i]f it is interstate commerce that feels the pinch, it does not matter how local the operation which applies the squeeze." . . . As Chief Justice Stone put it in *United States* v. *Darby:*

The power of Congress over interstate commerce is not confined to the regulation of commerce among the states. It extends to those activities intrastate which so affect interstate commerce or the exercise of the power of Congress over it as to make regulation of them appropriate means to the attainment of a legitimate end, the exercise of the granted power of Congress to regulate interstate commerce. . . .

Thus the power of Congress to promote interstate commerce also includes the power to regulate the local incidents thereof, including local activities in both the States of origin and destination, which might have a substantial and harmful effect upon that commerce. One need only examine the evidence which we have discussed above to see that Congress may—as it has—prohibit racial discrimination by motels serving travelers, however "local" their operations may appear.

Nor does the Act deprive appellant of liberty or property under the Fifth Amendment. The commerce power invoked here by the Congress is a specific and plenary one authorized by the Constitution itself. The only questions are: (1) whether Congress had a rational basis for finding that racial discrimination by motels affected commerce, and (2) if it had such a basis, whether the means it selected to eliminate that evil are reasonable and appropriate. If they are, appellant has no "right" to select its guests as it sees fit, free from governmental regulation.

There is nothing novel about such legislation. Thirty-two States now have it on their books either by statute or executive order and many cities provide such regulation. Some of these Acts go back fourscore years. It has been repeatedly held by this Court that such laws do not violate the Due Process Clause of the Fourteenth Amendment. . . .

. . . As a result the constitutionality of such state statutes stands unquestioned. "The authority of the Federal Government over interstate commerce does not differ . . . in extent or character from that retained by the states over intrastate commerce." . . .

It is doubtful if in the long run appellant will suffer economic loss as a result of the Act. Experience is to the contrary where discrimination is completely obliterated as to all public accommodations. But whether this be true or not is of no consequence since this Court has specifically held that the fact that a "member of the class which is regulated may suffer economic losses not shared by others . . . has never been a barrier" to such legislation. . . . Likewise in a long line of cases this Court has rejected the claim that the prohibition of racial discrimination in public accommodations interferes with personal liberty. . . .

We find no merit in the remainder of appellant's contentions, including that of "involuntary servitude." . . .

We, therefore, conclude that the action of the Congress in the adoption of the Act as applied here to a motel which concededly serves interstate travelers is within the power granted it by the Commerce Clause of the Constitution, as interpreted by this Court for 140 years. It may be argued that Congress would have pursued other methods to eliminate the obstructions it found in interstate commerce caused by racial discrimination. But this is a matter of policy that rests entirely with the Congress not with the courts. How obstructions in commerce may be removed—what means are to be employed—is within the sound and exclusive discretion of the Congress. It is subject only to one caveat—that the means chosen by it must be reasonably adapted to the end permitted by the Constitution. We cannot say that its choice here was not so adapted. The Constitution requires no more.

[The separate concurring opinions of Justice Black, Douglas, and Goldberg emphasized the constitutional authority of Congress to accomplish the goals of the Act of 1964 under the Fourteenth Amendment.]

Justice Clark also wrote the companion decision in *Katzenbach* v. *McClung*. Justices Black, Goldberg, and Douglas wrote separate concurring opinions.

KATZENBACH v. McCLUNG
379 U. S. 294 (1964)

Justice Clark delivered the opinion of the Court:

This case was argued with *Heart of Atlanta Motel* v. *United States* . . . in which we upheld the constitutional validity of Title II of the Civil Rights Act of 1964 against an attack by hotels, motels, and like establishments. This complaint for injunctive relief against appellants attacks the constitutionality of the Act as applied to a restaurant. . . .

2. THE FACTS

Ollie's Barbecue is a family-owned restaurant in Birmingham, Alabama, specializing in barbecued meats and homemade pies, with a seating capacity of 220 customers. It is located on a state highway 11 blocks from an interstate one and a somewhat greater distance from railroad and bus stations. The restaurant caters to a family and white-collar trade with a takeout service for Negroes. It employs 36 persons, two thirds of whom are Negroes.

In the 12 months preceding the passage of the Act, the restaurant purchased locally approximately $150,000 worth of food, $69,683 or 46% of which was meat that it bought from a local supplier who had procured it from outside the State. The District Court expressly found that a substantial portion of the food served in the restaurant had moved in interstate commerce. The restaurant has refused to serve Negroes in its dining accommodation since its original opening in 1927, and since July 2, 1964, it has been operating in violation of the Act. The court below concluded that if it were required to serve Negroes it would lose a substantial amount of business.

On the merits, the District Court held that the Act could not be applied under the Fourteenth Amendment because it was conceded that the State of Alabama was not involved in the refusal of the restaurant to serve Negroes. . . . As to the Commerce Clause, the court found . . . that the clause was also a grant of power "to regulate intrastate activities, but only to the extent that action on its part is necessary or appropriate to the effective execution of its expressly granted power to regulate interstate commerce." There must be, it said, close and substantial relation between local activities and interstate commerce which requires control of the former in the protection of the latter. The court concluded, however, that the Congress, rather than finding facts sufficient to meet this rule, had legislated a conclusive presumption that a restaurant affects interstate commerce if it serves or offers to serve interstate travelers or if a substantial portion of the food which it serves has moved in commerce. This, the court held, it could not do because there was no demonstrable connection between food purchased in interstate commerce and sold in a restaurant and the conclusion of Congress that discrimination in the restaurant would affect that commerce. . . .

3. THE ACT AS APPLIED

Section 201 (a) of Title II commands that all persons shall be entitled to the full and equal enjoyment of the goods and services of any place of public accommodation without discrimination or segregation on the ground of race, color, religion or national origin; and § 201 (b) defines establishments as places of public accommodation if their operations affect commerce or segregation by them is supported by state action. Sections 201 (b) (2) and (c) place any "restaurant . . .

principally engaged in selling food for consumption on the premises" under the Act "if . . . it serves or offers to serve interstate travelers or a substantial portion of the food which it serves . . . has moved in commerce."

Ollie's Barbecue admits that it is covered by these provisions of the Act. The Government makes no contention that the discrimination at the restaurant was supported by the State of Alabama. There is no claim that interstate travelers frequented the restaurant. The sole question, therefore, narrows down to whether Title II, as applied to a restaurant annually receiving about $70,000 worth of food which has moved in commerce, is a valid exercise of the power of Congress. The Government has contended that Congress had ample basis upon which to find that racial discrimination at restaurants which receive from out of state a substantial portion of the food served does, in fact, impose commercial burdens of national magnitude upon interstate commerce. The appellees' major argument is directed to this premise. They urge that no such basis existed. It is to that question that we now turn.

4. THE CONGRESSIONAL HEARINGS

As we noted in *Heart of Atlanta Motel* both Houses of Congress conducted prolonged hearings on the Act. And, as we said there, while no formal findings were made, which of course are not necessary, it is well that we make mention of the testimony at these hearings the better to understand the problem before Congress and determine whether the Act is a reasonable and appropriate means toward its solution. The record is replete with testimony of the burdens placed on interstate commerce by racial discrimination in restaurants. A comparison of per capita spending by Negroes in restaurants, theaters, and like establishments indicated less spending, after discounting income differences, in areas where discrimination is widely practiced. This condition, which was especially aggravated in the South, was attributed in the testimony of the Under Secretary of Commerce to racial segregation. . . . This diminutive spending springing from a refusal to serve Negroes and their total loss as customers has, regardless of the absence of direct evidence, a close connection to interstate commerce. The fewer customers a restaurant enjoys the less food it sells and consequently the less it buys. . . . In addition, the Attorney General testified that this type of discrimination imposed "an artificial restriction on the market" and interfered . . . with the flow of merchandise. . . . In addition, there were many references to discriminatory situations causing wide unrest and having a depressant effect on general business conditions in the respective communities. . . .

Moreover there was an impressive array of testimony that discrimination in restaurants had a direct and highly restrictive effect upon interstate travel by Negroes. This resulted, it was said, because discriminatory practices prevent Negroes from buying prepared food served on the premises while on a trip, except in isolated and unkempt restaurants and under most unsatisfactory and often unpleasant conditions. This obviously discourages travel and obstructs interstate commerce for one can hardly travel without eating. Likewise, it was said, that discrimination deterred professional, as well as skilled, people from moving into areas where such practices occurred and thereby caused industry to be reluctant to establish there. . . .

We believe that this testimony afforded ample basis for the conclusion that established restaurants in such areas sold less interstate goods because of the discrimination, that interstate travel was obstructed directly by it, that business in general suffered and that many new businesses refrained from establishing there as a result of it. Hence the District Court was in error in concluding that there was no connection between discrimination and the movement of interstate commerce. The court's conclusion that such a connection is outside "common experience" flies in the face of stubborn fact.

It goes without saying that, viewed in isolation, the volume of food purchased by Ollie's Barbecue from sources supplied from out of state was insignificant when compared with the total foodstuffs moving in commerce. But, as our late Brother Jackson said for the Court in *Wickard* v. *Filburn* [1942] . . .

That appellee's own contribution to the demand for wheat may be trivial by itself is not enough to remove him from the scope of federal regulation where, as here, his contribution, taken together with that of many others similarly situated, is far from trivial.

We noted in *Heart of Atlanta Motel* that a number of witnesses attested to the fact that racial discrimination was not merely a state or regional problem but was one of nationwide scope. Against this background, we must conclude that while the focus of the legislation was on the individual restaurant's relation to interstate commerce, Congress appropriately considered the importance of that connection with the knowledge that the discrimination was but "representative of many others throughout the country, the total incidence of which if left unchecked may well become far-reaching in its harm to commerce." . . .

With this situation spreading as the record shows, Congress was not required to await the total dislocation of commerce. . . .

5. THE POWER OF CONGRESS
TO REGULATE LOCAL ACTIVITIES

Article I, § 8, cl. 3, confers upon Congress the power "[t]o regulate Commerce . . . among the several States" and Clause 18 of the same Article grants it the power "[t]o make all Laws which shall be necessary and proper for carrying into Execution the foregoing Powers. . . ." This grant, as we have pointed out in *Heart of Atlanta Motel* "extends to those activities intrastate which so affect interstate commerce, or the exertion of the power of Congress over it, as to make regulation of them appropriate means to the attainment of a legitimate end, the effective execution of the granted power to regulate interstate commerce." . . . Much is said about a restaurant business being local but "even if appellee's activity be local and though it may not be regarded as commerce, it may still, whatever its nature, be reached by Congress if it exerts a substantial economic effect on interstate commerce. . . ." *Wickard* v. *Filburn* . . . The activities that are beyond the reach of Congress are "those which are completely within a particular State, which do not affect other States, and with which it is not necessary to interfere, for the purpose of executing some of the general powers of the government." . . . This rule is as good today as it was when Chief Justice Marshall laid it down almost a century and a half ago. . . .

Nor are the cases holding that interstate commerce ends when goods come to rest in the State of destination apposite here. That line of cases has been applied with reference to state taxation or regulation but not in the field of federal regulation.

The appellees contend that Congress has arbitrarily created a conclusive presumption that all restaurants meeting the criteria set out in the Act "affect commerce." Stated another way, they object to the omission of a provision for a case-by-case determination—judicial or administrative—that racial discrimination in a particular restaurant affects commerce.

But Congress' action in framing this Act was not unprecedented. In *United States* v. *Darby,* [1941] . . . this Court held constitutional the Fair Labor Standards Act of 1938. There Congress determined that the payment of substandard wages to employees engaged in the production of goods for commerce, while not itself commerce, so inhibited it as to be subject to federal regulation. The appellees in that case argued, as do the appellees here, that the Act was invalid because it included no provision for an independent inquiry regarding the effect on commerce of substandard wages in a particular business. . . . But the Court rejected the argument, observing that:

[S]ometimes Congress itself has said that a particular activity affects the commerce, as it did in the present Act, the Safety Appliance Act and the Railway Labor Act. In passing on the validity of legislation of the class last mentioned the only function of courts is to determine whether the particular activity regulated or prohibited is within the reach of the federal power.

Here, as there, Congress has determined for itself that refusals of service to Negroes have imposed burdens both upon the interstate flow of food and upon the movement of products generally. Of course, the mere fact that Congress has said when particular activity shall be deemed to affect commerce does not preclude further examination by this Court. But where we find that the legislators, in light of the facts and testimony before them, have a rational basis for finding a chosen regulatory scheme necessary to the protection of commerce, our investigation is at an end. The only remaining question—one answered in the affirmative by the court below—is whether the particular restaurant either serves or offers to serve interstate travelers or serves food a substantial portion of which has moved in interstate commerce. . . .

Confronted as we are with the facts laid before Congress, we must conclude that it has a rational basis for finding that racial discrimination in restaurants had a direct and adverse effect on the free flow of interstate commerce. Insofar as the sections of the Act here relevant are concerned, §§ 201 (b) (2) and (c), Congress prohibited discrimination only in those establishments having a close tie to interstate commerce, i.e., those, like the McClungs', serving food that has come from out of the State. We think in so doing that Congress acted well within its power to protect and foster commerce in extending the coverage of Title II only to those restaurants offering to serve interstate travelers or serving food, a substantial portion of which has moved in interstate commerce.

The absence of direct evidence connecting discriminatory restaurant service with the flow of interstate food, a factor on which the appellees place much reliance, is not, given the evidence as to the effect of such practices on other aspects of commerce, a crucial matter.

The power of Congress in this field is broad and sweeping; where it keeps within its sphere and violates no express constitutional limitation it has been the rule of this Court, going back almost to the founding days of the Republic, not to interfere. The Civil Rights Act of 1964, as here applied, we find to be plainly appropriate in the resolution of what the Congress found to be a national commercial problem of the first magnitude. We find it in no violation of any express limitations of the Constitution and we therefore declare it valid.

The judgment is therefore reversed.

After years of piecemeal Congressional action to remove restrictions to voting rights based upon racial discrimination (such as the statutes of 1957, 1960, and 1964), in 1965 the 89th Congress decided to enact a comprehensive voting rights act that would eliminate literacy tests, poll taxes, and other ingenious devices designed to restrict suffrage racially. The attorney general was given considerable discretion to deal with voting discrimination including power to send federal examiners to any county in which 50 percent or more of the voting age population was not registered. The state of South Carolina brought an action charging that some portions of the act were unconstitutional and seeking an injunction against enforcement of certain provisions by the attorney general of the United States. Chief Justice Earl Warren wrote the majority opinion in *South Carolina* v. *Katzenbach, Attorney General*, the facts of which are summarized in the opinion.

SOUTH CAROLINA v. KATZENBACH, ATTORNEY GENERAL
383 U. S. 301 (1966)

By leave of the Court, . . . South Carolina has filed a bill of complaint, seeking a declaration that selected provisions of the Voting Rights Act of 1965 violate the Federal Constitution, and asking for an injunction against enforcement of these provisions by the Attorney General. . . .

The Voting Rights Act was designed by Congress to banish the blight of racial discrimination in voting, which has infected the electoral process in parts of our country for nearly a century. The Act creates stringent new remedies for voting discrimination where it persists on a pervasive scale, and in addition the statute strengthens existing remedies for pockets of voting discrimination elsewhere in the country. Congress assumed the power to prescribe these remedies from § 2 of the Fifteenth Amendment, which authorizes the National Legislature to effectuate by "appropriate" measures the constitutional prohibition against racial discrimination in voting. We hold that the sections of the Act which are properly before us are an appropriate means for carrying out Congress' constitutional responsibilities and are consonant with all other provisions of the Constitution. We therefore deny South Carolina's request that enforcement of these sections of the Act be enjoined.

The constitutional propriety of the Voting Rights Act of 1965 must be judged with reference to the historical experience which it reflects. . . .

Two points emerge vividly from the voluminous legislative history of the Act contained in the committee hearings and floor debates. First: Congress felt itself confronted by an insidious and pervasive evil which had been perpetuated in certain parts of our country through unremitting and ingenious defiance of the Constitution. Second: Congress concluded that the unsuccessful remedies which it had prescribed in the past would have to be replaced by sterner and more elaborate measures in order to satisfy the clear commands of the Fifteenth Amendment. . . .

The Voting Rights Act of 1965 reflects Congress' firm intention to rid the country of racial discrimination in voting. The heart of the Act is a complex scheme of stringent remedies aimed at areas where voting discrimination has been most flagrant. Section 4 (a)—(d) lays down a formula defining the States and political subdivisions to which these new remedies apply. The first of the remedies, contained in § 4 (a), is the suspension of literacy tests and similar voting qualifications for a period of five years from the last occurrence of substantial voting discrimination. Section 5 prescribes a second remedy, the suspension of all new voting regulations pending review by federal authorities to determine whether their use would perpetuate voting discrimination. The third remedy, covered in §§ 6 (b), 7, 9, and 13 (a), is the assignment of federal examiners on certification by the Attorney General to list qualified applicants who are thereafter entitled to vote in all elections.

Other provisions of the Act prescribe subsidiary cures for persistent voting discrimination. Section 8 authorizes the appointment of federal poll-watchers in places to which federal examiners have already been assigned. Section 10 (d) excuses those made eligible to vote in sections of the country covered by § 4 (b) of the Act from paying accumulated past poll taxes for state and local elections. Section 12 (e) provides for balloting by persons denied access to the polls in areas where federal examiners have been appointed.

The remaining remedial portions of the Act are aimed at voting discrimination in any area of the country where it may occur. Section 2 broadly prohibits the use of voting rules to abridge exercise of the franchise on racial grounds. Sections 3, 6 (a), and 13 (b) strengthen existing procedures for attacking voting discrimination by means of litigation. Section 4 (e) excuses citizens educated in American schools conducted in a foreign language from passing English-language literacy tests. Section 10 (a)—(c) facilitates constitutional litigation challenging the imposition of all poll taxes for state and local elections. Sections 11 and 12 (a)—(d) authorize civil and criminal sanctions against interference with the exercise of rights guaranteed by the Act. . . .

These provisions of the Voting Rights Act of 1965 are challenged on the fundamental grounds that they exceed the powers of Congress and encroach on an area reserved to the States by the Constitution. . . . Has Congress exercised its power under the Fifteenth Amendment in an appropriate manner with relation to the States?

The ground rules for resolving this question are clear. The language and purpose of the Fifteenth Amendment, the prior decisions construing its several provisions, and the general doctrine of constitutional interpretation, all point to one fundamental principle. As against the reserved powers of the States, Congress may use any rational means to effectuate the constitutional prohibition of racial discrimination in voting. . . .

Section 1 of the Fifteenth Amendment declares that "[t]he right of citizens of the United States to vote shall not be denied or abridged by the United States or by any state on account of race, color, or previous condition of servitude." This declaration has always been treated as self-executing and has repeatedly been construed, without further legislative specification, to invalidate state voting qualifications or procedures which are discriminatory on their face or in practice. . . .

§ 2 of the Fifteenth Amendment expressly declares that "Congress shall have power to enforce this article by appropriate legislation." By adding this authorization, the Framers indicated that Congress was to be chiefly responsible for implementing the rights created in § 1. . . .

Congress has repeatedly exercised these powers in

the past, and its enactments have repeatedly been upheld. For recent examples, see the Civil Rights Act of 1957, which was sustained in *United States* v. *Raines*. . . .

Congress exercised its authority under the Fifteenth Amendment in an inventive manner when it enacted the Voting Rights Act of 1965. First: The measure prescribes remedies for voting discrimination which go into effect without any need for prior adjudication. This was clearly a legitimate response to the problem, for which there is ample precedent under other constitutional provisions. . . . Congress had found that case-by-case litigation was inadequate to combat widespread and persistent discrimination in voting, because of the inordinate amount of time and energy required to overcome the obstructionist tactics invariably encountered in these lawsuits. After enduring nearly a century of systematic resistance to the Fifteenth Amendment, Congress might well decide to shift the advantage of time and inertia from the perpetrators of the evil to its victims. The question remains, of course, whether the specific remedies prescribed in the Act were an appropriate means of combatting the evil, and to this question we shall presently address ourselves.

Second: The Act intentionally confines these remedies to a small number of States and political subdivisions which in most instances were familiar to Congress by name. This, too, was a permissible method of dealing with the problem. Congress had learned that substantial voting discrimination presently occurs in certain sections of the country, and it knew no way of accurately forecasting whether the evil might spread elsewhere in the future. In acceptable legislative fashion, Congress chose to limit its attention to the geographic areas where immediate action seemed necessary. . . . The doctrine of the equality of States, invoked by South Carolina, does not bar this approach, for that doctrine applies only to the terms upon which States are admitted to the Union, and not to the remedies for local evils which have subsequently appeared. . . .

COVERAGE FORMULA

We now consider the related question of whether the specific States and political subdivisions within § 4 (b) of the Act were an appropriate target for the new remedies. South Carolina contends that the coverage formula is awkwardly designed in a number of respects and that it disregards various local conditions which have nothing to do with racial discrimination. . . .

The areas, . . . for which there was evidence of actual voting discrimination, share two characteristics incorporated by Congress into the coverage formula:

the use of tests and devices for voter registration, and a voting rate in the 1964 presidential election at least 12 points below the national average. Tests and devices are relevant to voting discrimination because of their long history as a tool for perpetrating the evil; a low voting rate is pertinent for the obvious reason that widespread disenfranchisement must inevitably affect the number of actual voters. Accordingly, the coverage formula is rational in both practice and theory. . . .

SUSPENSION OF TESTS

We now arrive at consideration of the specific remedies prescribed by the Act for areas included within the coverage formula. . . . The record shows that in most of the States covered by the Act, including South Carolina, various tests and devices have been instituted with the purpose of disenfranchising Negroes, have been framed in such a way as to facilitate this aim, and have been administered in a discriminatory fashion for many years. Under these circumstances, the Fifteenth Amendment has clearly been violated. . . .

The Act suspends literacy tests and similar devices for a period of five years from the last occurrence of substantial voting discrimination. This was a legitimate response to the problem, for which there is ample precedent in Fifteenth Amendment cases. . . . Underlying the response was the feeling that States and political subdivisions which had been allowing white illiterates to vote for years could not sincerely complain about "dilution" of their electorates through the registration of Negro illiterates. Congress knew that continuance of the tests and devices in use at the present time, no matter how fairly administered in the future, would freeze the effect of past discrimination in favor of unqualified white registrants. Congress permissibly rejected the alternative of requiring a complete re-registration of all voters, believing that this would be too harsh on many whites who had enjoyed the franchise for their entire adult lives.

REVIEW OF NEW RULES

The Act suspends new voting regulations pending scrutiny by federal authorities to determine whether their use would violate the Fifteenth Amendment. This may have been an uncommon exercise of congressional power, as South Carolina contends, but the Court has recognized that exceptional conditions can justify legislative measures not otherwise appropriate. . . . Congress knew that some of the States covered by § 4 (b) of the Act had resorted to the extraordinary stratagem of contriving new rules of various kinds for the sole purpose of perpetuating voting discrimination in the face of adverse federal court decrees. Congress had reason to suppose that these States might try similar maneuvers in the future in order to evade the remedies for voting discrimination contained in the Act itself. Under the compulsion of these unique circumstances, Congress responded in a permissibly decisive manner. . . .

FEDERAL EXAMINERS

The Act authorizes the appointment of federal examiners to list qualified applicants who are thereafter entitled to vote, subject to an expeditious challenge procedure. This was clearly an appropriate response to the problem, closely related to remedies authorized in prior cases. . . . In many of the political subdivisions covered by § 4 (b) of the Act, voting officials have persistently employed a variety of procedural tactics to deny Negroes the franchise, often in direct defiance or evasion of federal court decress. Congress realizes that merely to suspend voting rules which have been misused or are subject to misuse might leave this localized evil undisturbed. As for the briskness of the challenge procedure, Congress knew that in some of the areas affected, challenges had been persistently employed to harass registered Negroes. It chose to forestall this abuse, at the same time providing alternative ways for removing persons listed through error or fraud. In addition to the judicial challenge procedure, § 7 (d) allows for the removal of names by the examiner himself, and § 11 (c) makes it a crime to obtain a listing through fraud. . . .

After enduring nearly a century of widespread resistance to the Fifteenth Amendment, Congress has marshalled an array of potent weapons against the evil, with authority in the Attorney General to employ them effectively. Many of the areas directly affected by this development have indicated their willingness to abide by any restraints legitimately imposed upon them. We here hold that the portions of the Voting Rights Act properly before us are a valid means for carrying out the commands of the Fifteenth Amendment. Hopefully, millions of non-white Americans will now be able to participate for the first time on an equal basis in the government under which they live. We may finally look forward to the day when truly "[t]he right of citizens of the United States to vote shall not be denied or abridged by the United States or by any State on account of race, color, or previous condition of servitude."

The bill of complaint is dismissed.

Freedom of the press was placed under considerable pressure during the 1960s, especially because of issues that arose out of the major public policy controversies of the decade—the civil rights movement and the Vietnam conflict. *New York Times Company v. Sullivan* involved the question whether a partially erroneous *New York Times* advertisement very critical of Montgomery, Alabama, municipal officials and police provided grounds for libel against four of the black signers of the ad and the New York Times Company. Key portions of Justice Brennan's majority opinion are reproduced below:

NEW YORK TIMES COMPANY v. SULLIVAN
376 U. S. 254 (1964)

Under Alabama law as applied in this case, a publication is "libelous per se" if the words "tend to injure a person . . . in his reputation" or to "bring [him] into public contempt"; the trial court stated that the standard was met if the words were such as to "injure him in his public office, or impute misconduct to him in his office, or want of official integrity, or want of fidelity to a public trust. . . ." The jury must find that the words were published "of and concerning" the plaintiff, but where the plaintiff is a public official his place in the governmental hierarchy is sufficient evidence to support a finding that his reputation has been affected by statements that reflect upon the agency of which he is in charge. Once "libel per se" has been established, the defendant has no defense as to stated facts unless he can persuade the jury that they were true in all their particulars. . . . His privilege of "fair comment" for expressions of opinion depends on the truth of the facts upon which the comment is based. . . . Unless he can discharge the burden of proving truth, general damages are presumed, and may be awarded without proof of pecuniary injury. A showing of actual malice is apparently a prerequisite to recovery of punitive damages, and the defendant may in any event forestall a punitive award by a retraction meeting the statutory requirements. Good motives and belief in truth do not negate an inference of malice, but are relevant only in mitigation of punitive damages if the jury chooses to accord them weight. . . .

The question before us is whether this rule of liability, as applied to an action brought by a public official against critics of his official conduct, abridges the freedom of speech and of the press that is guaranteed by the First and Fourteenth Amendments.

Respondent relies heavily, as did the Alabama courts, on statements of this Court to the effect that the Constitution does not protect libelous publications. Those statements do not foreclose our inquiry here. None of the cases sustained the use of libel laws to impose sanctions upon expression critical of the official conduct of public officials. . . .

[W]e consider this case against the background of a profound national commitment to the principle that debate on public issues should be uninhibited, robust, and wide-open, and that it may well include vehement, caustic, and sometimes unpleasantly sharp attacks on government and public officials. . . . The present advertisement, as an expression of grievance and protest on one of the major public issues of our time, would seem clearly to qualify for the constitutional protection. The question is whether it forfeits that protection by the falsity of some of its factual statements and by its alleged defamation of respondent.

Authoritative interpretations of the First Amendment guarantees have consistently refused to recognize an exception for any test of truth—whether administered by judges, juries, or administrative officials—and especially one that puts the burden of proving truth on the speaker. . . . The constitutional protection does not turn upon "the truth, popularity, or social utility of the ideas and beliefs which are offered." . . . As Madison said, "Some degree of abuse is inseparable from the proper use of every thing; and in no instance is this more true than in that of the press." . . . That erroneous statement is inevitable in free debate, and that it must be protected if the freedoms of expression are to have the "breathing space" that they "need . . . to survive." . . .

Injury to official reputation affords no more warrant for repressing speech that would otherwise be free than does factual error. Where judicial officers are involved, this Court has held that concern for the dignity and reputation of the courts does not justify the punishment as criminal contempt of criticism of the judge or his decision. . . . This is true even though the utterance contains "half-truths" and "misinformation." . . . Such repression can be justified, if at all, only by a clear and present danger of the obstruction of justice. . . . If judges are to be treated as "men of fortitude, able to thrive in a hardy climate," . . . surely the same must be true of other government officials, such as elected city commissioners. Criticism of their official conduct does not lose its constitutional protection merely because it is effective criticism and hence diminishes their official reputations.

If neither factual error nor defamatory content suffices to remove the constitutional shield from criticism of official conduct, the combination of the two elements is no less inadequate. This is the lesson to be drawn from the great controversy over the Sedition Act of 1798, . . . which first crystallized a national awareness of the central meaning of the First Amendment. . . .

A rule compelling the critic of official conduct to guarantee the truth of all his factual assertions—and to do so on pain of libel judgments virtually unlimited in amount—leads to a comparable "self-censorship." Allowance of the defense of truth, with the burden of proving it on the defendant, does not mean that only false speech will be deterred. Even courts accepting this defense as an adequate safeguard have recognized the difficulties of adducing legal proofs that the alleged libel was true in all its factual particulars. . . . Under such a rule, would-be critics of official conduct may be deterred from voicing their criticism, even though it is believed to be true and even though it is in fact true, because of doubt whether it can be proved in court or fear of the expense of having to do so. They tend to make only statements which "steer far wider of the unlawful zone." . . . The rule thus dampens the vigor and limits the variety of public debate. It is inconsistent with the First and Fourteenth Amendments.

The constitutional guarantees require, we think, a federal rule that prohibits a public official from recovering damages for a defamatory falsehood relating to his official conduct unless he proves that the statement was made with "actual malice"—that is, with knowledge that it was false or with reckless disregard of whether it was false or not. . . .

The procedural rights revolution

Legislative reapportionment and civil rights were by no means the only decision-making arenas that engendered determined conservative congressional attacks. Indeed, of all the issues that aroused political reactions against the Supreme

Court in the 1950s, 1960s, and 1970s, the decisions that extended Bill of Rights protection to criminal defendants were perhaps the most significant. *Mapp* v. *Ohio* is a landmark decision in such extension. Justice Clark's majority opinion evoked sharp dissent from Justice Harlan. The facts of the case are included in the opinion.

MAPP v. OHIO
367 U. S. 643 (1961)

Justice Clark delivered the opinion of the Court:

Appellant stands convicted of knowingly having had in her possession and under her control certain lewd and lascivious books, pictures, and photographs in violation of § 2905.34 of Ohio's Revised Code. . . . [T]he Supreme Court of Ohio found that her conviction was valid though "based primarily upon the introduction in evidence of lewd and lascivious books and pictures unlawfully seized during an unlawful search of defendant's home. . . ." . . .

On May 23, 1957, three Cleveland police officers arrived at appellant's residence in that city pursuant to information that "a person [was] hiding out in the home, who was wanted for questioning in connection with a recent bombing, and that there was a large amount of policy paraphernalia being hidden in the home." . . . Upon their arrival at that house, the officers knocked on the door and demanded entrance but appellant, after telephoning her attorney, refused to admit them without a search warrant. They advised their headquarters of the situation and undertook a surveillance of the house.

The officers again sought entrance some three hours later when four or more additional officers arrived on the scene. When Miss Mapp did not come to the door immediately, at least one of the several doors to the house was forcibly opened and the policemen gained admittance. Meanwhile Miss Mapp's attorney arrived, but the officers, having secured their own entry, and continuing in their defiance of the law, would permit him neither to see Miss Mapp nor to enter the house. It appears that Miss Mapp was halfway down the stairs from the upper floor to the front door when the officers, in this highhanded manner, broke into the hall. She demanded to see the search warrant. A paper, claimed to be a warrant, was held up by one of the officers. She grabbed the "warrant" and placed it in her bosom. A struggle ensued in which the officers recovered the piece of paper and as a result of which they handcuffed appellant because she had been "belligerent" in resisting their official rescue of the

"warrant" from her person. Running roughshod over appellant, a policeman "grabbed" her, "twisted [her] hand," and she "yelled [and] pleaded with him" because "it was hurting." Appellant, in handcuffs, was then forcibly taken upstairs to her bedroom where the officers searched a dresser, a chest of drawers, a closet and some suitcases. They also looked into a photo album and through personal papers belonging to the appellant. The search spread to the rest of the second floor including . . . the living room, the kitchen and a dinette. The basement of the building and a trunk found therein were also searched. The obscene materials for possession of which she was ultimately convicted were discovered in the course of that widespread search.

At the trial no search warrant was produced by the prosecution, nor was the failure to produce one explained or accounted for. At best, "There is, in the record, considerable doubt as to whether there ever was any warrant for the search of defendant's home." . . .

The State says that even if the search were made without authority, or otherwise unreasonably, it is not prevented from using the unconstitutionally seized evidence at trial, citing *Wolf* v. *Colorado* . . . , in which this Court did indeed hold "that in a prosecution in a State court for a State crime the Fourteenth Amendment does not forbid the admission of evidence obtained by an unreasonable search and seizure." . . . On this appeal, . . . it is urged once again that we review that holding. . . .

There are in the cases of this Court some passing references to the *Weeks* v. *United States* . . . rule as being one of evidence. But the plain and unequivocal language of *Weeks*—and its later paraphrase in *Wolf*—to the effect that the *Weeks* rule is of constitutional origin, remains entirely undisturbed. . . . The Court, in *Olmstead* v. *United States*, . . . in unmistakable language restated the *Weeks* rule:

The striking outcome of the *Weeks* case and those which followed it was the sweeping declaration that the Fourth Amendment, although not referring to or limiting the use of evidence in courts, really forbade its introduction if obtained by government officers through a violation of the Amendment.

II

In 1949, 35 years after *Weeks* was announced, this Court, in *Wolf* v. *Colorado* again for the first time, discussed the effect of the Fourth Amendment upon the States through the operation of the Due Process Clause of the Fourteenth Amendment. It said:

[W]e have no hesitation in saying that were a State affirmatively to sanction such police incursion into privacy it would run counter to the guaranty of the Fourteenth Amendment.

Nevertheless, after declaring that the "security of one's privacy against arbitrary intrusion by the police" is "implicit in the concept of ordered liberty and as such enforceable against the States through the Due Process Clause" . . ., the Court decided that the *Weeks* exclusionary rule would not then be imposed upon the States as "an essential ingredient of the right." . . . The Court's reasons for not considering essential to the right to privacy, as a curb imposed upon the States by the Due Process Clause, that which decades before had been posited as part and parcel of the Fourth Amendment's limitation upon federal encroachment of individual privacy, were bottomed on factual considerations.

While they are not basically relevant to a decision that the exclusionary rule is an essential ingredient of the Fourth Amendment as the right it embodies is vouch-safed against the States by the Due Process Clause, we will consider the current validity of the factual grounds upon which *Wolf* was based.

The Court in *Wolf* first stated that "[t]he contrariety of views of the States" on the adoption of the exclusionary rule of *Weeks* was "particularly impressive" and, in this connection, that it could not "brush aside the experience of States which deem the incidence of such conduct by the police too slight to call for a deterrent remedy . . . by overriding the [States'] relevant rules of evidence." . . . While in 1949, prior to the *Wolf* case, almost two-thirds of the States were opposed to the use of the exclusionary rule, now, despite the *Wolf* case, more than half of those since passing upon it, by their own legislative or judicial decision, have wholly or partly adopted or adhered to the *Weeks* rule. . . . Significantly, among those now following the rule is California, which, according to its highest court, was "compelled to reach that conclusion because other remedies have completely failed to secure compliance with the constitutional provisions. . . ." . . . In connection with this California case, we note that the second basis elaborated in *Wolf* in support of its failure to enforce this exclusionary doctrine against the States was that "other means of protection" have been afforded "the right to privacy." . . . The experience

of California that such other remedies have been worthless and futile is buttressed by the experience of other States. The obvious futility of relegating the Fourth Amendment to the protection of other remedies has, moreover, been recognized by this Court since *Wolf*. . . .

Likewise, time has set its face against what *Wolf* called the "weighty testimony" of *People* v. *Defore*, . . . There Justice (then Judge) Cardozo, rejecting adoption of the *Weeks* exclusionary rule in New York, had said that "[t]he Federal rule as it stands is either too strict or too lax." . . . However, the force of that reasoning has been largely vitiated by later decisions of this Court. . . .

It, therefore, plainly appears that the factual considerations supporting the failure of the *Wolf* Court to include the *Weeks* exclusionary rule when it recognized the enforceability of the right to privacy against the States in 1949, while not basically relevant to the constitutional consideration, could not, in any analysis, now be deemed controlling. . . .

III

. . . Today we once again examine *Wolf's* constitutional documentation of the right to privacy free from unreasonable state intrusion, and, after its dozen years on our books, are led by it to close the only courtroom door remaining open to evidence secured by official lawlessness in flagrant abuse of that basic right, reserved to all persons as a specific guarantee against that very same unlawful conduct. We hold that all evidence obtained by searches and seizures in violation of the Constitution is, by that same authority, inadmissible in a state court.

IV

Since the Fourth Amendment's right of privacy has been declared enforceable against the States through the Due Process Clause of the Fourteenth, it is enforceable against them by the same sanction of exclusion as is used against the Federal Government. Were it otherwise, then just as without the *Weeks* rule the assurance against unreasonable federal searches and seizures would be "a form of words," valueless and undeserving of mention in a perpetual charter of inestimable human liberties, so too, without that rule the freedom from state invasions of privacy would be so ephemeral and so neatly severed from its conceptual nexus with the freedom from all brutish means of coercing evidence as not to merit this Court's high regard as a freedom "implicit in the concept of ordered liberty." At the time that the Court held in *Wolf* that the Amendment was applicable to the States through the Due Process Clause, the cases of this Court, as we have seen, had steadfastly held that as to federal officers the Fourth Amendment included the exclusion of the evidence seized in violation of its provisions. Even *Wolf* "stoutly adhered" to that proposition. The right to privacy, when conceded operatively enforceable against the States, was not susceptible of destruction by avulsion of the sanction upon which its protection and enjoyment had always been deemed dependent. . . . Therefore, in extending the substantive protections of due process to all constitutionally unreasonable searches—state or federal—it was logically and constitutionally necessary that the exclusion doctrine—an essential part of the right to privacy—be also insisted upon as an essential ingredient of the right newly recognized by the *Wolf* case. In short, the admission of the new constitutional right by *Wolf* could not consistently tolerate denial of its most important constitutional privilege, namely, the exclusion of the evidence which an accused had been forced to give by reason of the unlawful seizure. To hold otherwise is to grant the right but in reality to withhold its privilege and enjoyment. Only last year the Court itself recognized that the purpose of the exclusionary rule "is to deter—to compel respect for the constitutional guaranty in the only effectively available way—by removing the incentive to disregard it." . . .

Indeed, we are aware of no restraint, similar to that rejected today, conditioning the enforcement of any other basic constitutional right. The right to privacy, no less important than any other right carefully and particularly reserved to the people, would stand in marked contrast to all other rights declared as "basic to a free society." . . . This Court has not hesitated to enforce as strictly against the States as it does against the Federal Government the rights of free speech and of a free press, the rights to notice and to a fair, public trial, including, as it does, the right not to be convicted by use of a coerced confession, however logically relevant it be, and without regard to its reliability. . . . And nothing could be more certain than that when a coerced confession is involved, "the relevant rules of evidence" are overridden without regard to "the incidence of such conduct by the police," slight or frequent. Why should not the same rule apply to what is tantamount to coerced testimony by way of unconstitutional seizure of goods, papers, effects, documents, etc.? We find that, as to the Federal Government, the Fourth and Fifth Amendments and, as to the States, the freedom from unconscionable invasions of privacy and the freedom from convictions based upon coerced confessions do enjoy an "intimate relation" in their perpetuation of "principles of humanity and civil liberty [secured] . . . only after years of struggle," . . . .

V

Moreover, our holding that the exclusionary rule is an essential part of both the Fourth and Fourteenth Amendments is not only the logical dictate of prior cases, but it also makes very good sense. There is no war between the Constitution and common sense. Presently, a federal prosecutor may make no use of evidence illegally seized, but a State's attorney across the street may, although he supposedly is operating under the enforceable prohibitions of the same Amendment. Thus the State, by admitting evidence unlawfully seized, serves to encourage disobedience to the Federal Constitution which it is bound to uphold. Moreover, as was said in *Elkins*, "[t]he very essence of a healthy federalism depends upon the avoidance of needless conflict between state and federal courts." . . . Yet the double standard recognized until today hardly put such a thesis into practice. In nonexclusionary States, federal officers, being human, were by it invited to and did, as our cases indicate, step across the street to the State's attorney with their unconstitutionally seized evidence. Prosecution on the basis of that evidence was then had in a state court in utter disregard of the enforceable Fourth Amendment. If the fruits of an unconstitutional search had been inadmissible in both state and federal courts, this inducement to evasion would have been sooner eliminated. . . .

Federal-state cooperation in the solution of crime under constitutional standards will be promoted, if only by recognition of their now mutual obligation to respect the same fundamental criteria in their approaches. "However much in a particular case insistence upon such rules may appear as a technicality that inures to the benefit of a guilty person, the history of the criminal law proves that tolerance of shortcut methods in law enforcement impairs its enduring effectiveness." . . . Denying shortcuts to only one of two cooperating law enforcement agencies tends naturally to breed legitimate suspicion of "working arrangements" whose results are equally tainted. . . .

There are those who say, as did Justice (then Judge) Cardozo, that under our constitutional exclusionary doctrine "[t]he criminal is to go free because the constable has blundered." . . . In some cases this will undoubtedly be the result. But, as was said in *Elkins*, "there is another consideration—the imperative of judicial integrity." . . . The criminal goes free, if he must, but it is the law that sets him free. Nothing can destroy a government more quickly than its failure to observe its own laws, or worse, its disregard of the charter of its own existence. . . .

The ignoble shortcut to conviction left open to the State tends to destroy the entire system of constitutional restraints on which the liberties of the people rest. Having once recognized that the right to privacy embodied in the Fourth Amendment is enforceable against the States, and that the right to be secure against rude invasions of privacy by state officers is, therefore, constitutional in origin, we can no longer permit that right to remain an empty promise. Because it is enforceable in the same manner and to like effect as other basic rights secured by the Due Process Clause, we can no longer permit it to be revocable at the whim of any police officer who, in the name of law enforcement itself, chooses to suspend its enjoyment. Our decision, founded on reason and truth, gives to the individual no more than that which the Constitution guarantees him, to the police officer no less than that to which honest law enforcement is entitled, and to the courts, that judicial integrity so necessary in the true administration of justice.

The judgment of the Supreme Court of Ohio is reversed and the cause remanded for further proceedings not inconsistent with this opinion.

Reversed and remanded.

[The separate concurring opinions of Justices Black and Douglas and the memorandum of Justice Stewart partly dissenting and partly concurring were omitted.]

Justice Harlan, whom Justices
Frankfurter and Whittaker joined, dissented:

In overruling the *Wolf* case the Court, in my opinion, has forgotten the sense of judicial restraint which, with due regard for the *stare decisis*, is one element that should enter into deciding whether a past decision of this Court should be overruled. Apart from that I also believe that the *Wolf* rule represents sounder Constitutional doctrine than the new rule which now replaces it.

I

From the Court's statement of the case one would gather that the central, if not controlling, issue on this appeal is whether illegally state-seized evidence is Constitutionally admissible in a state prosecution, an issue which would of course face us with the need for re-examining *Wolf*. However, such is not the situation. For, although that question was indeed raised here and below among appellant's subordinate points, the new and pivotal issue brought to the Court by this appeal is whether § 2905.34 of the Ohio Revised Code making criminal the *mere* knowing possession or control of obscene material, and under which appellant has been convicted, is consistent with the rights of free thought and expression assured against state action by the Fourteenth Amendment. That was the principal issue

which was decided by the Ohio Supreme Court and which was briefed and argued in this Court.

In this posture of things, I think it fair to say that five members of this Court have simply "reached out" to overrule *Wolf*. With all respect for the views of the majority, and recognizing that *stare decisis* carries different weight in Constitutional adjudication than it does in nonconstitutional decision, I can perceive no justification for regarding this case as an appropriate occasion for re-examining *Wolf*. . . .

II

Essential to the majority's argument against *Wolf* is the proposition that the rule of *Weeks v. United States* . . . excluding in federal criminal trials the use of evidence obtained in violation of the Fourth Amendment, derives not from the "supervisory power" of this Court over the federal judicial system, but from Constitutional requirement. This is so because no one, I suppose, would suggest that this Court possesses any general supervisory power over the state courts. Although I entertain considerable doubt as to the soundness of this foundational proposition of the majority . . . , I shall assume, for present purposes, that the *Weeks* rule "is of constitutional origin."

At the heart of the majority's opinion in this case is the following syllogism: (1) the rule excluding in federal criminal trials evidence which is the product of an illegal search and seizure is "part and parcel" of the Fourth Amendment; (2) *Wolf* held that the "privacy" assured against federal action by the Fourth Amendment is also protected against state action by the Fourteenth Amendment; and (3) it is therefore "logically and constitutionally necessary" that the *Weeks* exclusionary rule should be enforced against the States.

This reasoning ultimately rests on the unsound premise that because *Wolf* carried into the States, as part of "the concept of ordered liberty" embodied in the Fourteenth Amendment, the principle of "privacy" underlying the Fourth Amendment . . . , it must follow that whatever configurations of the Fourth Amendment have been developed in the particularizing federal precedents are likewise to be deemed a part of "ordered liberty," and as such are enforceable against the States. For me, this does not follow at all.

It cannot be too much emphasized that what was recognized in *Wolf* was not that the Fourth Amendment as *such* is enforceable against the States as a facet of due process, a view of the Fourteenth Amendment which, as *Wolf* itself pointed out . . . , has long since been discredited, but the principle of privacy "which is at the core of the Fourth Amendment." . . . It would not be proper to expect or impose any precise equivalence, either as regards the scope of the right or the means of its implementation, between the requirements of the Fourth and Fourteenth Amendments. For the Fourth, unlike what was said in *Wolf* of the Fourteenth, does not state a general principle only; it is a particular command, having its setting in a pre-existing legal context on which both interpreting decisions and enabling statutes must at least build. . . .

. . . [H]ere we are reviewing not a determination that what the state police did was Constitutionally permissible (since the state court quite evidently assumed that it was not), but a determination that appellant was properly found guilty of conduct which, for present purposes, it is to be assumed the State could Constitutionally punish. Since there is not the slightest suggestion that Ohio's policy is "affirmatively to sanction . . . police incursion into privacy" . . . what the Court is now doing is to impose upon the States not only federal substantive standards of "search and seizure " but also the basic federal remedy for violation of those standards. For I think it entirely clear that the *Weeks* exclusionary rule is but a remedy which, by penalizing past official misconduct, is aimed at deterring such conduct in the future.

I would not impose upon the States this federal exclusionary remedy. The reasons given by the majority for now suddenly turning its back on *Wolf* seem to me notably unconvincing.

First, it is said that "the factual grounds upon which *Wolf* was based" have since changed, in that more States now follow the *Weeks* exclusionary rule than was so at the time *Wolf* was decided. While that is true, a recent survey indicates that at present one-half of the States still adhere to the common-law non-exclusionary rule, and one, Maryland, retains the rule as to felonies. . . . But in any case, surely all this is beside the point, as the majority itself indeed seems to recognize. . . .

The preservation of a proper balance between state and federal responsibility in the administration of criminal justice demands patience on the part of those who might like to see things move faster among the States in this respect. Problems of criminal law enforcement vary widely from State to State. One State, in considering the totality of its legal picture, may conclude that the need for embracing the *Weeks* rule is pressing because other remedies are unavailable or inadequate to secure compliance with the substantive constitutional principle involved. Another, though equally solicitous of Constitutional rights, may choose to pursue one purpose at a time, allowing all evidence relevant to guilt to be brought into a criminal trial, and dealing with Constitutional infractions by other means. Still another may consider the exclusionary rule too rough-and-ready a remedy, in that it reaches only unconstitutional intrusions which eventuate in criminal prosecution of the victims. Further, a State after experimenting with the *Weeks* rule for a time may, because of unsatisfactory experience with it, decide to revert to a non-exclusionary rule. And so on. From the standpoint of Constitutional permissibility in pointing a State in one direction or another, I do not see at all why "time has set its face against" the considerations which led Mr. Justice Cardozo, then chief judge of the New York Court of Appeals, to reject for New York in *People* v. *Defore* . . . the *Weeks* exclusionary rule. For us the question remains, as it has always been, one of state power, not one of passing judgment on the wisdom of one state course or another. In my view the Court should continue to forbear from fettering the States with an adamant rule which may embarrass them in coping with their own peculiar problems in criminal law enforcement.

Further, we are told that imposition of the *Weeks* rule on the States makes "very good sense," in that it will promote recognition by state and federal officials of their "mutual obligation to respect the same fundamental criteria" in their approach to law enforcement, and will avoid "'needless conflict between state and federal courts.'" . . .

An approach which regards the issue as one of achieving procedural symmetry or of serving administrative convenience surely disfigures the boundaries of this Court's functions in relation to the state and federal courts. . . . I do not believe that the Fourteenth Amendment empowers this Court to mould state remedies effectuating the right to freedom from "arbitrary intrusion by the police" to suit its own notions of how things should be done. . . .

. . . I do not see how it can be said that a trial becomes unfair simply because a State determines that evidence may be considered by the trier of fact, regardless of how it was obtained, if it is relevant to the one issue with which the trial is concerned, the guilt or innocence of the accused. Of course, a court may use its procedures as an incidental means of pursuing other ends than the correct resolution of the controversies before it. Such indeed is the *Weeks* rule, but if a State does not choose to use its courts in this way, I do not believe that this Court is empowered to impose this much-debated procedure on local courts, however efficacious we may consider the *Weeks* rule to be as a means of securing Constitutional rights.

Finally, it is said that the overruling of *Wolf* is supported by the established doctrine that the admission in evidence of an involuntary confession renders a state conviction Constitutionally invalid. Since such a confession may often be entirely reliable, and therefore of the greatest relevance to the issue of the trial, the argument continues, this doctrine is ample warrant in precedent that the way evidence was obtained, and not just its relevance, is Constitutionally significant to the fairness of a trial. I believe this analogy is not a true one. The "coerced confession" rule is certainly not a rule that any illegally obtained statements may not be used in evidence. . . .

The point, then, must be that in requiring exclusion of an involuntary statement of an accused, we are concerned not with an appropriate remedy for what the police have done, but with something which is regarded as going to the heart of our concepts of fairness in judicial procedure. . . . The pressures brought to bear against an accused leading to a confession, unlike an unconstitutional violation of privacy, do not, apart from the use of the confession at trial, necessarily involve independent Constitutional violations. What is crucial is that the trial defense to which an accused is

entitled should not be rendered an empty formality by reason of statements wrung from him, for then "a prisoner . . . [has been] made the deluded instrument of his own conviction." . . . That this is a *procedural right*, and that its violation occurs at the time his improperly obtained statement is admitted at trial, is manifest. For without this right all the careful safeguards erected around the giving of testimony, whether by an accused or any other witness, would become empty formalities in a procedure where the most compelling possible evidence of guilt, a confession, would have already been obtained at the unsupervised pleasure of the police.

This, and not the disciplining of the police, as with illegally seized evidence, is surely the true basis for excluding a statement of the accused which was unconstitutionally obtained. In sum, I think the coerced confession analogy works strongly *against* what the Court does today. . . .

The process of determining the scope of federal judicial supervision of state criminal justice systems continued with significant expansion of federal restrictions on the states. *Gideon* v. *Wainwright* was an important expansion of the right to counsel concept. In terms of doctrinal evolution, the significant brief by Abe Fortas was yet another landmark in a doctrinal odyssey that included *Powell* v. *Alabama* and *Betts* v. *Brady*. The relevant facts in the case are summarized in the opinion.

GIDEON v. WAINWRIGHT
372 U. S. 335 (1963)

Justice Black delivered the opinion of the Court:

Petitioner was charged in a Florida state Court with having broken and entered a poolroom with intent to commit a misdemeanor. This offense is a felony under Florida law. Appearing in court without funds and without a lawyer, petitioner asked the court to appoint counsel for him, whereupon the following colloquy took place:

The COURT: Mr. Gideon, I am sorry, but I cannot appoint Counsel to represent you in this case. Under the laws of the State of Florida the only time the Court can appoint Counsel to represent a Defendant is when that person is charged with a capital offense. I am sorry, but I will have to deny your request to appoint Counsel to defend you in this case.

The DEFENDANT: The United States Supreme Court says I am entitled to be represented by Counsel.

Put to trial before a jury, Gideon conducted his defense about as well as could be expected from a lay-

man. He made an opening statement to the jury, cross-examined the State's witnesses, presented witnesses in his own defense, declined to testify himself, and made a short argument "emphasizing his innocence to the charge contained in the Information filed in this case." The jury returned a verdict of guilty, and petitioner was sentenced to serve five years in the state prison. . . . Since 1942, when *Betts* v. *Brady* . . . was decided by a divided Court, the problem of a defendant's federal constitutional right to counsel in a state court has been a continuing source of controversy and litigation in both state and federal courts. To give this problem another review here, we granted certiorari. . . . Since Gideon was proceeding *in forma pauperis*, we appointed counsel to represent him and requested both sides to discuss in their briefs and oral arguments the following: "Should this Court's holding in *Betts* v. *Brady* . . . be reconsidered?"

I

The facts upon which Betts claimed that he had been unconstitutionally denied the right to have counsel appointed to assist him are strikingly like the facts upon which Gideon here bases his federal constitutional claim. Betts was indicted for robbery in a Maryland state court. On arraignment, he told the trial judge of his lack of funds to hire a lawyer and asked the court to appoint one for him. Betts was advised that it was not the practice in the county to appoint counsel for indigent defendants except in murder and rape cases. He then pleaded not guilty, had witnesses summoned, cross-examined the State's witnesses, examined his own, and chose not to testify himself. He was found guilty by the judge, sitting without a jury, and sentenced to eight years in prison. Like Gideon, Betts sought release by habeas corpus, alleging that he had been denied the right to assistance of counsel in violation of the Fourteenth Amendment. Betts was denied any relief, and on review this Court affirmed. It was held that a refusal to appoint counsel for an indigent defendant charged with a felony did not necessarily violate the Due Process Clause of the Fourteenth Amendment, which for reasons given the Court deemed to be the only applicable federal constitutional provision. The Court said:

Asserted denial [of due process] is to be tested by an appraisal of the totality of facts in a given case. That which may, in one setting, constitute a denial of fundamental fairness, shocking to the universal sense of justice, may in other circumstances, and in the light of other considerations, fall short of such denial. . . .

Treating due process as "a concept less rigid and more fluid than those envisaged in other specific and particular provisions of the Bill of Rights," the Court held that refusal to appoint counsel under the particular facts and circumstances in the *Betts* case was not so "offensive to the common and fundamental ideas of fairness" as to amount to a denial of due process. Since the facts and circumstances of the two cases are so nearly indistinguishable, we think the *Betts* v. *Brady* holding if left standing would require us to reject Gideon's claim that the Constitution guarantees him the assistance of counsel. Upon full reconsideration we conclude that *Betts* v. *Brady* should be overruled.

II

The Sixth Amendment provides, "In all criminal prosecutions, the accused shall enjoy the right . . . to have the Assistance of Counsel for his defence." We have construed this to mean that in federal courts counsel must be provided for defendants unable to employ counsel unless the right is competently and intelligently waived. Betts argued that this right is extended to indigent defendants in state courts by the Fourteenth Amendment. In response the Court stated that,

while the Sixth Amendment laid down "no rule for the conduct of the States, the question recurs whether the constraint laid by the Amendment upon the national courts expresses a rule so fundamental and essential in a fair trial, and so, to due process of law, that it is made obligatory upon the States by the Fourteenth Amendment." . . . In order to decide whether the Sixth Amendment's guarantee of counsel is of this fundamental nature, the Court in *Betts* set out and considered "[r]elevant data on the subject . . . afforded by constitutional and statutory provisions subsisting in the colonies and the States prior to the inclusion of the Bill of Rights in the national Constitution, and in the constitutional, legislative, and judicial history of the States to the present date." . . . On the basis of this historical data the Court concluded that "appointment of counsel is not a fundamental right, essential to a fair trial." . . . It was for this reason the *Betts* Court refused to accept the contention that the Sixth Amendment's guarantee of counsel for indigent federal defendants was extended to or, in the words of that Court, "made obligatory upon the States by the Fourteenth Amendment." Plainly, had the Court concluded that appointment of counsel for an indigent criminal defendant was "a fundamental right, essential to a fair trial," it would have held that the Fourteenth Amendment requires appointment of counsel in a state court, just as the Sixth Amendment requires in a federal court.

We think the Court in *Betts* had ample precedent for acknowledging that those guarantees of the Bill of Rights which are fundamental safeguards of liberty immune from federal abridgment are equally protected against state invasion by the Due Process Clause of the Fourteenth Amendment. This same principle was recognized, explained, and applied in *Powell* v. *Alabama*, . . . a case upholding the right of counsel, where the Court held that despite sweeping language to the contrary in *Hurtado* v. *California* . . . the Fourteenth Amendment "embraced" those "'Fundamental principles of liberty and justice which lie at the base of all our civil and political institutions,'" even though they had been "specifically dealt with in another part of the federal Constitution." . . . In many cases other than *Powell* and *Betts*, this Court has looked to the fundamental nature of original Bill of Rights guarantees to decide whether the Fourteenth Amendment makes them obligatory on the States. Explicitly recognized to be of this "fundamental nature" and therefore made immune from state invasion by the Fourteenth, or some part of it, are the First Amendment's freedoms of speech, press, religion, assembly, association, and petition for redress of grievances. For the same reason, though not always in precisely the same terminology, the Court has made obligatory on the States the Fifth Amendment's command that private property shall not be taken for public use without just compensation, the Fourth Amendment's prohibition of unreasonable searches and seizures, and the Eighth's ban on cruel and unusual punishment. On the other hand, this Court in *Palko* v. *Connecticut* . . . refused to hold that the Fourteenth Amendment made the double jeopardy provision of the Fifth Amendment obligatory on the States. In so refusing, however, the Court, speaking through Mr. Justice Cardozo, was careful to emphasize that "immunities that are valid as against the federal government by force of the specific pledges of particular amendments have been found to be implicit in the concept of ordered liberty, and thus, through the Fourteenth Amendment, become valid as against the states" and that guarantees "in their origin . . . effective against the federal government alone" had by prior cases "been taken over from the earlier articles of the federal bill of rights and brought within the Fourteenth Amendment by a process of absorption." . . .

We accept *Betts* v. *Brady's* assumption, based as it was on our prior cases, that a provision of the Bill of Rights which is "fundamental and essential to a fair trial" is made obligatory upon the States by the Fourteenth Amendment. We think the Court in *Betts* was wrong, however, in concluding that the Sixth Amendment's guarantee of counsel is not one of these fundamental rights. Ten years before *Betts* v. *Brady*, this Court, after full consideration of all the historical data examined in *Betts*, had unequivocally declared that "the right to the aid of counsel is of this fundamental character." . . . While the Court at the close of its *Powell* opinion did by its language, as this Court frequently does, limit its holding to the particular facts and circumstances of that case, its conclusions about the fundamental nature of the right to counsel are unmistakable. Several years later, in 1936, the Court re-emphasized what it had said about the fundamental nature of the right to counsel in this language:

We concluded that certain fundamental rights, safeguarded by the first eight amendments against federal action, were also safeguarded against state action by the due process of law clause of the Fourteenth Amendment, and among them the fundamental right of the accused to the aid of counsel in a criminal prosecution. *Grosjean* v. *American Press Co.* . . .

And again in 1938 this Court said:

[The assistance of counsel] is one of the safeguards of the Sixth Amendment deemed necessary to insure fundamental human rights of life and liberty. . . . The Sixth Amendment stands as a constant admonition that if the constitutional safeguards it provides be lost, justice will not still be done. . . .

In light of these and many other prior decisions of this Court, it is not surprising that the *Betts* Court, when faced with the contention that "one charged with crime, who is unable to obtain counsel, must be furnished counsel by the State," conceded that "[e]xpressions in the opinions of this court lend color to the argument. . . ."

The fact is that in deciding as it did—that "appointment of counsel is not a fundamental right, essential to a fair trial"—the Court in *Betts* v. *Brady* made an abrupt break with its own well-considered precedents. In returning to these old precedents, sounder we believe than the new, we but restore constitutional principles established to achieve a fair system of justice. Not only these precedents but also reason and reflection require us to recognize that in our adversary system of criminal justice, any person haled into court, who is too poor to hire a lawyer, cannot be assured a fair trial unless counsel is provided for him. This seems to us to be an obvious truth. Governments, both state and federal, quite properly spend vast sums of money to establish machinery to try defendants accused of crime. Lawyers to prosecute are everywhere deemed essential to protect the public's interest in an orderly society. Similarly, there are few defendants charged with crime, few indeed, who fail to hire the best lawyers they can get to prepare and present their defenses. That government hires lawyers to prosecute and defendants who have the money hire lawyers to defend are the strongest indications of the widespread belief that lawyers in criminal courts are necessities, not luxuries. The right of one charged with crime to counsel may not be deemed fundamental and essential to fair trials in some countries, but it is in ours. From the very beginning, our state and national constitutions and laws have laid great emphasis on procedural and substantive safeguards designed to assure fair trials before impartial tribunals in which every defendant stands equal before the law. This noble ideal cannot be realized if the poor man charged with crime has to face his accusers without a lawyer to assist him. A defendant's need for a lawyer is nowhere better stated than in the moving words of Mr. Justice Sutherland in *Powell* v. *Alabama*:

The right to be heard would be, in many cases, of little avail if it did not comprehend the right to be heard by counsel. Even the intelligent and educated layman has small and sometimes no skill in the science of law. If charged with crime, he is incapable, generally, of determining for himself whether the indictment is good or bad. He is unfamiliar with the rules of evidence. Left without the aid of counsel he may be put on trial without a proper charge, and convicted upon incompetent evidence, or evidence irrelevant to the issue or otherwise inadmissible. He lacks both the skill and knowledge adequately to prepare his defense, even though he have a perfect one. He requires the guiding hand of counsel at every step in the proceedings against him. Without it, though he be not guilty, he faces the danger of conviction because he does not know how to establish his innocence. . . .

The Court in *Betts* v. *Brady* departed from the sound wisdom upon which the Court's holding in *Powell* v. *Alabama* rested. Florida, supported by two other States, has asked that *Betts* v. *Brady* be left intact. Twenty-two States, as friends of the Court, argue that *Betts* was "an anachronism when handed down" and that it should now be overruled. We agree.

The judgment is reversed and the cause is remanded to the Supreme Court of Florida for further action not inconsistent with this opinion. Reversed.
[Separate concurring opinions by Justices Douglas and Clark are omitted.]

Justice Harlan concurred:

I agree that *Betts* v. *Brady* should be overruled, but consider it entitled to a more respectful burial than has been accorded, at least on the part of those of us who were not on the Court when that case was decided.

I cannot subscribe to the view that *Betts* v. *Brady* represented "an abrupt break with its own well-considered precedents." . . . In 1932, in *Powell* v. *Alabama* . . . a capital case, this Court declared that under the particular facts there presented—"the ignorance and illiteracy of the defendants, their youth, the circumstances of public hostility . . . and above all that they stood in deadly peril of their lives" . . .—the state court had a duty to assign counsel for the trial as a necessary requisite of due process of law. It is evident that these limiting facts were not added to the opinion as an afterthought; they were repeatedly emphasized . . . and were clearly regarded as important to the result.

Thus when this Court, a decade later, decided *Betts* v. *Brady*, it did no more than to admit to the possible existence of special circumstances in noncapital as well as capital trials, while at the same time insisting that such circumstances be shown in order to

establish a denial of due process. The right to appointed counsel had been recognized as being considerably broader in federal prosecutions, . . . but to have imposed these requirements on the States would indeed have been "an abrupt break" with the almost immediate past. The declaration that the right to appointed counsel in state prosecutions, as established in *Powell* v. *Alabama*, was not limited to capital cases was in truth not a departure from, but an extension of, existing precedent. . . .

. . . The Court has come to recognize, in other words, that the mere existence of a serious criminal charge constituted in itself special circumstances requiring the services of counsel at trial. In truth the *Betts* v. *Brady* rule is no longer a reality.

This evolution, however, appears not to have been fully recognized by many state courts, in this instance charged with the front-line responsibility for the enforcement of constitutional rights. To continue a rule which is honored by this Court only with lip service is not a healthy thing and in the long run will do disservice to the federal system. . . .

In agreeing with the Court that the right to counsel in a case such as this should now be expressly recognized as a fundamental right embraced in the Fourteenth Amendment, I wish to make a further observation. When we hold a right or immunity, valid against the Federal Government, to be "implicit in the concept of ordered liberty" and thus valid against the States, I do not read our past decisions to suggest that by so holding, we automatically carry over an entire body of federal law and apply it in full sweep to the States. Any such concept would disregard the frequently wide disparity between the legitimate interests of the States and of the Federal Government, the divergent problems that they face, and the significantly different consequences of their actions. . . . In what is done today I do not understand the Court to depart from the principles laid down in *Palko* v. *Connecticut*, . . . or to embrace the concept that the Fourteenth Amendment "incorporates" the Sixth Amendment as such.

On these premises I join in the judgment of the Court.

Conflict over greater federal Supreme Court supervision of the state criminal justice systems aroused both strong support and strong opposition from the 1950s and thereafter. Advocates argued that conditions in the states warranted this supervision. Detractors deplored the consequences in terms of costs as well as loss of state autonomy. The charge that "law and order" was weakened became the basis for a political movement to eliminate "softness on crime" by judges. The advocacy of Professor Francis Allen and the politically significant rebuttal of a large majority of the state chief justices are important illustrations from the late 1950s. The Conference of State Chief Justices voted 36 to 8 (with 6 abstentions) for the critical report of 1958. Like other advocates of state reform of criminal justice systems and supporters of Supreme Court intervention such as the Griffin decision, Allen said empirical evidence established that "it can fairly be said that the Court has been one of the most important factors in recent efforts at reform of various aspects of American criminal-law administration." In contrast, a majority of the state chief justices argued that "the practical problems which flow from the decision in *Griffin* v. *Illinois* are, however, almost unlimited and are now only in course of development and possible solution." Both are cited below:

FOR INTERVENTION BY THE SUPREME COURT[17]

No precise measure of the impact of the Court's decisions on local law-enforcement practices is available. Obviously, the lines of communication between the courts and the police are dangerously imperfect. There are no data upon which to base an estimate of the Court's influence, if any, on general public attitudes toward the issues litigated in the state criminal cases or in the development of what appears to be a quickening public interest in the administration of criminal justice. Nevertheless, the Court's influence on state criminal justice has been substantial. This influence has not been of equal significance in all states or with reference to all issues. But it can fairly be said that the Court has been one of the most important factors in recent efforts at reform of various aspects of American criminal-law administration. It is important to note how this influence has operated. By identifying and dramatizing aspects of the criminal process in a particular state, the Court has often succeeded in opening the way for local legislative action. This is no mere conjecture. The experience in Illinois provides a concrete example. In the course of a decade and a half, these changes, among others, have been produced: Practices relating to the appointment of counsel have been liberalized. Time for filing of exceptions in the review process has been extended by rule of the Illinois supreme court. A new statute to meet a critical problem of post-conviction remedies was enacted by the legislature. A rule of the Illinois prison system that barred state prisoners from direct access to the courts was withdrawn. The state supreme court eliminated barriers that blocked impoverished defendants from appellate review of their convictions. It is perfectly clear that all these measures were the direct or indirect product of judicial supervision of Illinois criminal procedures by the United States Supreme Court. It may also be asserted that these alterations in the existing law were necessary and desirable.

THE STATE CHIEF JUSTICES IN REBUTTAL[18]

. . . We shall not comment in this report upon the broad sweep which the Supreme Court now gives to habeas corpus proceedings. . . .

We cannot, however, completely avoid any reference at all to habeas corpus matters because what is probably the most far reaching decision of recent years on state criminal procedure which has been rendered by the Supreme Court is itself very close to a habeas corpus case. That is the case of *Griffin* v. *Illinois*, . . . which arose under the Illinois Post Conviction Procedure Act. The substance of the holding in that case may perhaps be briefly and accurately stated in this way: If a transcript of the record, or its equivalent, is essential to an effective appeal, and if a state permits an appeal by those able to pay for the cost of the record or its equivalent, then the state must furnish without expense to an indigent defendant either a transcript of the record at his trial, or an equivalent thereof, in order that the indigent defendant may have an equally effective right of appeal. Otherwise, the inference seems clear, the indigent defendant must be released upon habeas corpus or similar proceedings. Probably no one would dispute the proposition that the poor man should not be deprived of the opportunity for a meritorious appeal simply because of his poverty. The practical problems which flow from the decision in *Griffin* v. *Illinois* are, however, almost unlimited and are now only in course of development and possible solution. This was extensively discussed at the 1957 meeting of this conference of Chief Justices in New York.

We may say at this point that in order to give full effect to the doctrine of *Griffin* v. *Illinois*, we see no basis for distinction between the cost of the record and other expenses to which the defendant will necessarily be put in the prosecution of an appeal. These include filing fees, the cost of printing the brief and of such part of the record as may be necessary, and counsel fees. . . .

As the Court asserted and expanded what its literate critics called its policymaking role, new issues arising out of fundamental changes in lifestyles or in public attitudes demanded judicial resolution.

The new social issues

During the 1960s, a period of social change, controversies arose over changing lifestyles. Contraception was an issue that stimulated an innovative doctrinal approach. Private behavior probably had never coincided with political and legal requirements, but by the 1960s Americans had begun to challenge social legislation instead of accepting it meekly. The differences among the justices over the meaning of "right to privacy" in the Connecticut contraception case—*Griswold* v. *Connecticut*—reflected the divisions in society over this issue. The doctrine enunciated by Justice Douglas once again aroused criticism from conservatives in Congress. The facts of *Griswold* are included in the majority opinion.

GRISWOLD v. CONNECTICUT
381 U. S. 479 (1965)

Justice Douglas delivered the opinion of the Court:

Appellant Griswold is Executive Director of the Planned Parenthood League of Connecticut. Appellant Buxton is a licensed physician and a professor at the Yale Medical School who served as Medical Director for the League at its Center in New Haven—a center open and operating from November 1 to November 10, 1961, when appellants were arrested.

They gave information, instruction, and medical advice to *married persons* as to the means of preventing conception. They examined the wife and prescribed the best contraceptive device or material for her use. Fees were usually charged, although some couples were serviced free.

The statutes whose constitutionality is involved in this appeal are §§ 53–32 and 54–196 of the General Statutes of Connecticut (1958 rev). The former provides:

Any person who uses any drug, medicinal article or instrument for the purpose of preventing conception shall be fined not less than fifty dollars or imprisoned not less than sixty days nor more than one year or be both fined and imprisoned.

Section 54–196 provides:

Any person who assists, abets, counsels, causes, hires or commands another to commit any offense may be prosecuted and punished as if he were the principal offender.

The appellants were found guilty as accessories and fined $100 each, against the claim that the accessory statute as so applied violated the Fourteenth Amendment. . . .

We think that appellants have standing to raise the constitutional rights of the married people with whom they had a professional relationship. *Tileston* v. *Ullman* [1943] . . . is different, for there the plaintiff seeking to represent others asked for a declaratory judgment. In that situation we thought that the requirements of standing should be strict, lest the standards of "case or controversy" in Article III of the Constitution become blurred. Here those doubts are removed by reason of a criminal conviction for serving married couples in violation of an aiding-and-abetting statute. Certainly the accessory should have standing to assert that the offense which he is charged with assisting is not, or cannot constitutionally be, a crime. . . .

Coming to the merits, we are met with a wide range of questions that implicate the Due Process Clause of the Fourteenth Amendment. Overtones of some arguments suggest that *Lochner* v. *New York* [1905] . . . should be our guide. But we decline that invitation as we did in *West Coast Hotel Co.* v. *Parrish* [1937]. . . . We do not sit as a super-legislature to determine the wisdom, need, and propriety of laws that touch economic problems, business affairs, or social conditions. This law, however, operates directly on an intimate relation of husband and wife and their physician's role in one aspect of that relation.

The association of people is not mentioned in the Constitution nor in the Bill of Rights. The right to educate a child in a school of the parents' choice— whether public or private or parochial—is also not mentioned. Nor is the right to study any particular subject or any foreign language. Yet the First Amendment has been construed to include certain of those rights.

By *Pierce* v. *Society of Sisters* [1925] . . . the right to educate one's children as one chooses is made applicable to the States by the force of the First and Fourteenth Amendments. By *Meyer* v. *Nebraska* [1923] . . . the same dignity is given the right to study the German language in a private school. In other words, the State may not, consistently with the spirit of the First Amendment, contract the spectrum of available knowledge. The right of freedom of speech and press includes not only the right to utter or to print, but the right to distribute, the right to receive, the right to read . . . and freedom of inquiry, freedom of thought, and freedom to teach . . .—indeed the freedom of the entire university community. . . .

Without those peripheral rights the specific rights would be less secure. And so we reaffirm the principle of the *Pierce* and the *Meyer* cases.

In *NAACP* v. *Alabama* [1958] we protected the "freedom to associate and privacy in one's associations," noting that freedom of association was a peripheral First Amendment right. Disclosure of membership lists of a constitutionally valid association, we held, was invalid "as entailing the likelihood of a substantial restraint upon the exercise by petitioner's members of their right to freedom of association." . . . In other words, the First Amendment has a penumbra where privacy is protected from governmental intrusion. In like context, we have protected forms of "association" that are not political in the customary sense but pertain to the social, legal, and economic benefit of the members. *NAACP* v. *Button* [1963]. . . . In *Schware* v. *Board of Bar Examiners* [1957] . . . we held it not permissible to bar a lawyer from practice, because he had once been a member of the Communist Party. The main "association with that Party" was not shown to be "anything more than a political faith in a political party" . . . and was not action of a kind proving bad moral character. . . .

Those cases involved more than the "right of assembly"—a right that extends to all irrespective of their race or ideology. . . . The right of "association," like the right of belief, . . . is more than the right to attend a meeting; it includes the right to express one's attitudes or philosophies by membership in a group or by affiliation with it or by other lawful means. Association in that context is a form of expression of opinion; and while it is not expressly included in the First Amendment its existence is necessary in making the express guarantees fully meaningful.

The foregoing cases suggest that specific guarantees in the Bill of Rights have penumbras, formed by emanations from those guarantees that help give them life and substance. . . . Various guarantees create zones of privacy. The right of association contained in the penumbra of the First Amendment is one, as we have seen. The Third Amendment in its prohibition against the quartering of soldiers "in any house" in time of peace without the consent of the owner is another facet of that privacy. The Fourth Amendment explicitly affirms the "right of the people to be secure in their persons, houses, papers, and effects, against unreasonable searches and seizures." The Fifth Amendment in its Self-Incrimination Clause enables the citizen to create a zone of privacy which government may not force him to surrender to his detriment. The Ninth Amendment provides: "The enumeration in the Constitution, of certain rights, shall not be construed to deny or disparage others retained by the people." . . .

The present case, then, concerns a relationship lying within the zone of privacy created by several fundamental constitutional guarantees. And it concerns a law which, in forbidding the *use* of contraceptives rather than regulating their manufacture or sale, seeks to achieve its goals by means having a maximum destructive impact upon that relationship. Such a law cannot stand in light of the familiar principle, so often applied by this Court, that a "governmental purpose to control or prevent activities constitutionally subject to state regulation may not be achieved by means which sweep unnecessarily broadly and thereby invade the area of protected freedoms." *NAACP* v. *Alabama* [1964]. . . . Would we allow the police to search the sacred precincts of marital bedrooms for telltale signs of the use of contraceptives? The very idea is repulsive to the notions of privacy surrounding the marriage relationship.

We deal with a right of privacy older than the Bill of Rights—older than our political parties, older than our school system. Marriage is a coming together for better or for worse, hopefully enduring, and intimate to the degree of being sacred. It is an association that promotes a way of life, not causes; a harmony in living, not political faiths; a bilateral loyalty, not commercial or social projects. Yet it is an association for as noble a purpose as any involved in our prior decisions. Reversed.

Chief Justice Warren and Justice Brennan concurred in an opinion written by Justice Goldberg:

While this Court has had little occasion to interpret the Ninth Amendment, "[i]t cannot be presumed that any clause in the Constitution is intended to be without effect." *Marbury* v. *Madison.* . . . To hold that a right so basic and fundamental and so deep-rooted in our society as the right of privacy in marriage may be infringed because that right is not guaranteed in so many words by the first eight amendments to the Constitution is to ignore the Ninth Amendment and to give it no effect whatsoever. Moreover, a judicial construction that this fundamental right is not protected by the Constitution because it is not mentioned in explicit terms by one of the first eight amendments or elsewhere in the Constitution would violate the Ninth Amendment, which specifically states that "[t]he enumeration in the Constitution, of certain rights, shall not be *construed* to deny or disparage others retained by the people." (Emphasis added.)

. . . I do not take the position of my Brother Black . . . that the entire Bill of Rights is incorporated in the Fourteenth Amendment, and I do not mean to imply that the Ninth Amendment is applied against the States by the Fourteenth. Nor do I mean to state that the Ninth Amendment constitutes an independent source of rights protected from infringement by either the States or the Federal Government. Rather, the Ninth Amendment shows a belief of the Constitution's authors that fundamental rights exist that are not expressly enumerated in the first eight amendments and an intent that the list of rights included there not be deemed exhaustive. . . .

. . . In sum, the Ninth Amendment simply lends strong support to the view that the "liberty" protected by the Fifth and Fourteenth Amendments from infringement by the Federal Government or the States is not restricted to rights specifically mentioned in the first eight amendments. . . .

Justice Harlan also concurred:

I fully agree with the judgment of reversal, but find myself unable to join the Court's opinion. The reason is that it seems to me to evince an approach to this case very much like that taken by my Brothers Black and Stewart in dissent, namely: the Due Process Clause of the Fourteenth Amendment does not touch this Connecticut statute unless the enactment is found to violate some right assured by the letter or penumbra of the Bill of Rights.

In other words, what I find implicit in the Court's opinion is that the "incorporation" doctrine may be used to *restrict* the reach of Fourteenth Amendment Due Process. For me this is just as unacceptable constitutional doctrine as is the use of the "incorporation" approach to *impose* upon the States all the requirements of the Bill of Rights as found in the provisions of the first eight amendments and in the decisions of this Court interpreting them. . . .

In my view, the proper constitutional inquiry in this case is whether this Connecticut statute infringes the Due Process Clause of the Fourteenth Amendment because the enactment violates basic values "implicit in the concept of ordered liberty." . . .

*Justice Black, with whom
Justice Stewart joined, dissented:*

The Court talks about a constitutional "right of privacy" as though there is some constitutional provision or provisions forbidding any law ever to be passed which might abridge the "privacy" of individuals. But there is not. There are, of course, guarantees in certain specific constitutional provisions which are designed in part to protect privacy at certain times and places with respect to certain activities. Such, for example, is the Fourth Amendment's guarantee against "unreasonable searches and seizures." But I think it belittles that

Amendment to talk about it as though it protects nothing but "privacy." To treat it that way is to give it a niggardly interpretation, not the kind of liberal reading I think any Bill of Rights provision should be given. The average man would very likely not have his feelings soothed any more by having his property seized openly than by having it seized privately and by stealth. He simply wants his property left alone. And a person can be just as much, if not more, irritated, annoyed and injured by an unceremonious public arrest by a policeman as he is by a seizure in the privacy of his office or home.

One of the most effective ways of diluting or expanding a constitutionally guaranteed right is to substitute for the crucial word or words of a constitutional guarantee another word or words more or less flexible and more or less restricted in meaning. This fact is well illustrated by the use of the term "right of privacy" as a comprehensive substitute for the Fourth Amendment's guarantee against "unreasonable searches and seizures." "Privacy" is a broad, abstract and ambiguous concept which can easily be shrunken in meaning but which can also, on the other hand, easily be interpreted as a constitutional ban against many things other than searches and seizures. I have expressed the view many times that First Amendment freedoms, for example, have suffered from a failure of the courts to stick to the simple language of the First Amendment in construing it, instead of invoking multitudes of words substituted for those the Framers used. . . .

I realize that many good and able men have eloquently spoken and written, sometimes in rhapsodical strains, about the duty of this Court to keep the Constitution in tune with the times. The idea is that the Constitution must be changed from time to time and that this Court is charged with a duty to make those changes. For myself, I must with all deference reject that philosophy. The Constitution makers knew the need for change and provided for it. Amendments suggested by the people's elected representatives can be submitted to the people or their selected agents for ratification. That method of change was good for our Fathers, and being somewhat old-fashioned I must add it is good enough for me. And so, I cannot rely on the Due Process Clause or the Ninth Amendment or any mysterious and uncertain natural law concept as a reason for striking down this state law. The Due Process Clause with an "arbitrary and capricious" or "shocking to the conscience" formula was liberally used by this Court to strike down economic legislation in the early decades of this century, threatening, many people thought, the tranquility and stability of the Nation. See, e.g., *Lochner v. New York* [1905]. . . . That formula, based on subjective considerations of "natural justice," is no less dangerous when used to enforce this Court's views about personal rights than those about economic rights. I had thought that we had laid that formula, as a means for striking down state legislation, to rest once and for all in cases like *West Coast Hotel Co. v. Parrish* [1937]. . . .

[Justice Stewart's dissent is omitted.]

The Court, the Congress, and Adam Clayton Powell

Perhaps the most significant aspect of Supreme Court decision making after it began to reflect the doctrinal tendencies of President Richard Nixon's appointees was manifested in cases directly involving political activity and the behavior of elected officials. But before Nixon's election, during Lyndon B. Johnson's presidency, the issue arose in *Powell v. McCormack*. On March 1, 1967, the House of Representatives refused to seat Adam Clayton Powell, Jr., a black congressman who had represented Harlem for many years. In 1969, the Supreme Court, in an unprecedented action, took jurisdiction in what had generally been assumed a controversy solely under the authority of the House of Representatives itself. The Court overturned a federal Court of Appeals ruling handed down by Judge Warren Burger, subsequently chosen by President Nixon to become Earl Warren's successor. As Judge of the Court of Appeals for the District of Columbia, Burger had held that Adam Clayton Powell had no standing to appeal to the court because the action of the House of Representatives in excluding Powell involved a "political question." It was also argued that Supreme Court intervention would precipitate a major confrontation between Congress and the Court.[19]

POWELL v. McCORMACK
395 U. S. 486 (1969)

Chief Justice Warren
delivered the opinion of the Court:

In November 1966, petitioner Adam Clayton Powell, Jr., was duly elected from the 18th Congressional District of New York to serve in the United States House of Representatives for the 90th Congress. However, pursuant to a House resolution, he was not permitted to take his seat. Powell (and some of the voters of his district) then filed suit in Federal District Court, claiming that the House could exclude him only if it found he failed to meet the standing requirements of age, citizenship, and residence contained in Art. I, § 2, of the Constitution—requirements the House specifically found Powell met—and thus had excluded him unconstitutionally. The District Court dismissed petitioners' complaint "for want of jurisdiction of the subject matter." A panel of the Court of Appeals affirmed the dismissal, although on somewhat different grounds, each judge filing a separate opinion. We have determined that it was [in] error to dismiss the complaint, and that petitioner Powell is entitled to a declaratory judgment that he was unlawfully excluded from the 90th Congress. . . .

Having concluded that the Court of Appeals correctly ruled that the District Court had jurisdiction over the subject matter, we turn to the question whether the case is justiciable. Two determinations must be made in this regard. First, we must decide whether the claim presented and the relief sought are of the type which admit of judicial resolution. Second, we must determine whether the structure of the Federal Government renders the issue presented a "political question"—that is, a question which is not justiciable in federal court because of the separation of powers provided by the Constitution.

GENERAL CONSIDERATIONS

In deciding generally whether a claim is justiciable, a court must determine whether "the duty asserted can be judicially identified and its breach judicially determined, and whether protection for the right asserted can be judicially molded." . . . Respondents do not seriously contend that the duty asserted and its alleged breach cannot be judicially determined. If petitioners are correct, the House had a duty to seat Powell once it determined he met the standing requirements set forth in the Constitution. It is undisputed that he met those requirements and that he was nevertheless excluded.

Respondents do maintain, however, that this case is not justiciable because, they assert, it is impossible for a federal court to "mold effective relief for resolving this case." Respondents emphasize that petitioners asked for coercive relief against the officers of the House, and, they contend, federal courts cannot issue mandamus or injunctions compelling officers or employees of the House to perform specific official acts. Respondents rely primarily on the Speech or Debate Clause to support this contention.

We need express no opinion about the appropriateness of coercive relief in this case, for petitioners sought a declaratory judgment, a form of relief the District Court could have issued. The Declaratory Judgment Act, 28 USC § 2201, provides that a district court may "declare the rights . . . of any interested party . . . whether or not further relief is or could be sought." The availability of declaratory relief depends on whether there is a live dispute between the parties . . . and a request for declaratory relief may be considered independently of whether other forms of relief are appropriate. . . . We thus conclude that in terms of the general criteria of justiciability, this case is justiciable. . . .

. . . We have concluded that Art. I, § 5, is at most a "textually demonstrable commitment" to Congress to judge only the qualifications expressly set forth in the Constitution. Therefore, the "textual commitment" formulation of the political question doctrine does not bar federal courts from adjudicating petitioners' claims.

OTHER CONSIDERATIONS

Respondents' alternate contention is that the case presents a political question because judicial resolution of petitioners' claim would produce a "potentially embarrassing confrontation between coordinate branches" of the Federal Government. But, as our interpretation of Art. I, § 5, discloses, a determination of petitioner Powell's right to sit would require no more than an interpretation of the Constitution. Such a determination falls within the traditional role accorded courts to interpret the law, and does not involve a "lack of the respect due [a] coordinate [branch] of government," nor does it involve an "initial policy determination of a kind clearly for nonjudicial discretion." *Baker* v. *Carr* . . . Our system of government requires that federal courts on occasion interpret the Constitution in a manner at variance with the construction given the document by another branch. The alleged conflict that such an adjudication may cause cannot justify the courts' avoiding their constitutional responsibility. . . .

Nor are any of the other formulations of a political question "inextricable from the case at bar." . . . Petitioners seek a determination that the House was without power to exclude Powell from the 90th Congress, which, we have seen, requires an interpretation of the Constitution—a determination for which clearly there are "judicially . . . manageable standards." Finally, a judicial resolution of petitioners' claim will not result in "multifarious pronouncements by various departments on one question." For, as we noted in *Baker* v. *Carr* . . . it is the responsibility of this Court to act as the ultimate interpreter of the Constitution. *Marbury* v. *Madison* [1803]. Thus, we conclude that petitioners' claim is not barred by the political question doctrine, and, having determined that the claim is otherwise generally justiciable, we hold that the case is justiciable. . . . To summarize, we have determined the following: (1) This case has not been mooted by Powell's seating in the 91st Congress. (2) Although this action should be dismissed against respondent Congressmen, it may be sustained against their agents. (3) The 90th Congress' denial of membership to Powell cannot be treated as an expulsion. (4) We have jurisdiction over the subject matter of this controversy. (5) The case is justiciable.

Further, analysis of the "textual commitment" under Art. I, § 5 has demonstrated that in judging the qualifications of its members Congress is limited to the

standing qualifications prescribed in the Constitution. Respondents concede that Powell met these. Thus, there is no need to remand this case to determine whether he was entitled to be seated in the 90th Congress. Therefore, we hold that, since Adam Clayton Powell, Jr., was duly elected by the voters of the 18th Congressional District of New York and was not ineligible to serve under any provision of the Constitution, the House was without power to exclude him from its membership.

Petitioners seek additional forms of equitable relief, including mandamus for the release of petitioner Powell's back pay. The propriety of such remedies, however, is more appropriately considered in the first instance by the courts below. Therefore, as to respondents McCormack, Albert, Ford, Celler, and Moore, the judgment of the Court of Appeals for the District of Columbia Circuit is affirmed. As to respondents Jennings, Johnson, and Miller, the judgment of the Court of Appeals for the District of Columbia Circuit is reversed and the case is remanded to the United States District Court for the District of Columbia with instructions to enter a declaratory judgment and for further proceedings consistent with this opinion. It is so ordered.

The emergence of "law and order" issues

As the 1960s came to a close, the criminal justice system became a significant issue not only in the politics of congressional-Court relations but in the electoral politics of the 1968 presidential campaign. "Crime in the streets" became a center of controversy with Richard M. Nixon, Republican candidate, attacking the alleged permissiveness of the Supreme Court. Candidate Nixon picked up many themes emphasized by leading congressional critics such as Senator Strom Thurmond of South Carolina. During the 1960s several major decisions protecting the procedural rights of criminal defendants provided targets for attacks on the Court. One of the most important of these cases was *Miranda* v. *Arizona*. In this case the Supreme Court imposed specific procedural safeguards during police interrogations. The case involved a 23-year-old indigent who confessed to a kidnapping and forcible rape during interrogation by Phoenix, Arizona, police after the victim had identified him in a police line-up. Four members, Clark, Harlan, Stewart, and White, dissented. Chief Justice Warren wrote the majority opinion. In Miranda and companion cases, admissibility of evidence obtained in police interrogation was challenged under the Fifth, Sixth, and Fourteenth Amendments.

MIRANDA v. ARIZONA
377 U. S. 201 (1966)

The cases before us raise questions which go to the roots of our concepts of American criminal jurisprudence: the restraints society must observe consistent

with the Federal Constitution in prosecuting individuals for crime. More specifically, we deal with the admissibility of statements obtained from an individual who is subjected to custodial police interrogation and the necessity for procedures which assure that the individual is accorded his privilege under the Fifth

Amendment to the Constitution not to be compelled to incriminate himself. . . .

The constitutional issue we decide in each of these cases is the admissibility of statements obtained from a defendant questioned while in custody or otherwise deprived of his freedom of action in any significant way. In each, the defendant was questioned by police officers, detectives, or a prosecuting attorney in a room in which he was cut off from the outside world. In none of these cases was the defendant given a full and effective warning of his rights at the outset of the interrogation process. In all the cases, the questioning elicited oral admissions, and in three of them, signed statements as well which were admitted at their trials. They all thus share salient features—incommunicado interrogation of individuals in a police-dominated atmosphere, resulting in self-incriminating statements without full warnings of constitutional rights.

An understanding of the nature and setting of this in-custody interrogation is essential to our decisions today. The difficulty in depicting what transpires at such interrogations stems from the fact that in this country they have largely taken place incommunicado. From extensive factual studies undertaken in the early 1930's, including the famous Wickersham Report to Congress by a Presidential Commission, it is clear that police violence and the "third degree" flourished at that time. In a series of cases decided by this Court long after these studies, the police resorted to physical brutality—beatings, hanging, whipping—and to sustained and protracted questioning incommunicado in order to extort confessions. The Commission on Civil Rights in 1961 found much evidence to indicate that "some policemen still resort to physical force to obtain confessions. . . ."

The examples given above are undoubtedly the exception now, but they are sufficiently widespread to be the object of concern. Unless a proper limitation upon custodial interrogation is achieved—such as these decisions will advance—there can be no assurance that practices of this nature will be eradicated in the forseeable future. . . .

. . . [W]e stress that the modern practice of in-custody interrogation is psychologically rather than physically oriented. As we have stated before, "Since Chambers v. State of Florida, . . . this Court has recognized that coercion can be mental as well as physical, and that the blood of the accused is not the only hallmark of an unconstitutional inquisition." . . . Interrogation still takes place in privacy. Privacy results in secrecy and this in turn results in a gap in our knowledge as to what in fact goes on in the interrogation

rooms. A valuable source of information about present police practices, however, may be found in various police manuals and texts which document procedures employed with success in the past, and which recommend various other effective tactics. These texts are used by law enforcement agencies themselves as guides. It should be noted that these texts professedly present the most enlightened and effective means presently used to obtain statements through custodial interrogation. By considering these texts and other data, it is possible to describe procedures observed and noted around the country. . . .

From . . . representative samples of interrogation techniques, the setting prescribed by the manuals and observed in practice becomes clear. In essence, it is this: To be alone with the subject is essential to prevent distraction and to deprive him of any outside support. The aura of confidence in his guilt undermines his will to resist. He merely confirms the preconceived story the police seek to have him describe. Patience and persistence, at times relentless questioning, are employed. To obtain a confession, the interrogator must "patiently maneuver himself or his quarry into a position from which the desired objective may be attained." When normal procedures fail to produce the needed result, the police may resort to deceptive stratagems such as giving false legal advice. It is important to keep the subject off balance, for example, by trading on his insecurity about himself or his surroundings. The police then persuade, trick, or cajole him out of exercising his constitutional rights. . . .

Even without employing brutality, the "third degree" or the specific stratagems described above, the very fact of custodial interrogation exacts a heavy toll on individual liberty and trades on the weakness of individuals. . . .

. . . [T]he constitutional foundation underlying the privilege [against self-incrimination] is the respect a government—state or federal—must accord to the dignity and integrity of its citizens. To maintain a "fair state-individual balance," to require the government "to shoulder the entire load," . . . to respect the inviolability of the human personality, our accusatory system of criminal justice demands that the government seeking to punish an individual produce the evidence against him by its own independent labors, rather than by the cruel, simple expedient of compelling it from his own mouth. . . . In sum, the privilege is fulfilled only when the person is guaranteed the right "to remain silent unless he chooses to speak in the unfettered exercise of his own will." . . .

. . . The question in these cases is whether the privilege is fully applicable during a period of custodial interrogation. In this Court, the privilege has consistently been accorded a liberal construction. . . . We are satisfied that all the principles embodied in the privilege apply to informal compulsion exerted by law-enforcement officers during in-custody questioning. An individual swept from familiar surroundings into police custody, surrounded by antagonistic forces, and subjected to the techniques of persuasion described above cannot be otherwise than under compulsion to speak. As a practical matter, the compulsion to speak in the isolated setting of the police station may well be greater than in courts or other official investigations, where there are often impartial observers to guard against intimidation or trickery. . . .

. . . Today, then, there can be no doubt that the Fifth Amendment privilege is available outside of criminal court proceedings and serves to protect persons in all settings in which their freedom of action is curtailed in any significant way from being compelled to incriminate themselves. We have concluded that without proper safeguards the in-custody interrogation of persons suspected or accused of crime contains inherently compelling pressures which work to undermine the individual's will to resist and to compel him to speak where he would not otherwise do so freely. In order to combat these pressures and to permit a full opportunity to exercise the privilege against self-incrimination, the accused must be adequately and effectively apprised of his rights and the exercise of those rights must be fully honored.

It is impossible for us to foresee the potential alternatives for protecting the privilege which might be devised by Congress or the States in the exercise of their creative rule-making capacities. Therefore we cannot say that the Constitution necessarily requires adherence to any particular solution for the inherent compulsions of the interrogation process as it is presently conducted. Our decision in no way creates a constitutional straitjacket which will handicap sound efforts at reform, nor is it intended to have this effect. We encourage Congress and the States to continue their laudable search for increasingly effective ways of protecting the rights of the individual while promoting efficient enforcement of our criminal laws. However, unless we are shown other procedures at least as effective in apprising accused persons of their right of silence and in assuring a continuous opportunity to exercise it, the following safeguards must be observed. . . .

At the outset, if a person in custody is to be subjected to interrogation, he must first be informed in clear and unequivocal terms that he has the right to remain silent. For those unaware of the privilege, the warning is needed simply to make them aware of it—the threshold requirement for an intelligent decision as to its exercise. More important, such a warning is an absolute prerequisite in overcoming the inherent pressures of the interrogation atmosphere. . . .

. . . To summarize, we hold that when an individual is taken into custody or otherwise deprived of his freedom by the authorities in any significant way and is subjected to questioning, the privilege against self-incrimination is jeopardized. Procedural safeguards must be employed to protect the privilege and unless other fully effective means are adopted to notify the person of his right of silence and to assure that the exercise of the right will be scrupulously honored, the following measures are required. He must be warned prior to any questioning that he has the right to remain silent, that anything he says can be used against him in a court of law, that he has the right to the presence of an attorney, and that if he cannot afford an attorney one will be appointed for him prior to any questioning if he so desires. Opportunity to exercise these rights must be afforded to him throughout the interrogation. After such warnings have been given, and such opportunity afforded him, the individual may knowingly and intelligently waive these rights and agree to answer questions or make a statement. But unless and until such warnings and waiver are demonstrated by the prosecution at trial, no evidence obtained as a result of interrogation can be used against him. . . .

. . . In announcing these principles, we are not unmindful of the burdens which law enforcement officials must bear, often under trying circumstances. We also fully recognize the obligation of all citizens to aid in enforcing the criminal laws. This Court, while protecting individual rights, has always given ample latitude to law enforcement agencies in the legitimate exercise of their duties. The limits we have placed on the interrogation process should not constitute an undue interference with a proper system of law enforcement. As we have noted, our decision does not in any way preclude police from carrying out their traditional investigatory functions. Although confessions may play an important role in some convictions, the cases before us present graphic examples of the overstatement of the "need" for confessions. In each case authorities conducted interrogations ranging up to five days in duration despite the presence, through standard investigating practices, of considerable evidence against each defendant. . . .

Reversed.

Justice Harlan, joined by
Justice Stewart and Justice White, dissented:

I believe the decision of the Court represents poor constitutional law and entails harmful consequences for the country at large. How serious these consequences may prove to be only time can tell. But the basic flaws in the Court's justification seem to me readily apparent now once all sides of the problem are considered.

While the fine points of this scheme are far less clear than the Court admits, the tenor is quite apparent. The new rules are not designed to guard against police brutality or other unmistakably banned forms of coercion. Those who use third-degree tactics and deny them in court are equally able and destined to lie as skillfully about warnings and waivers. Rather, the thrust of the new rules is to negate all pressures, to reinforce the nervous or ignorant suspect, and ultimately to discourage any confession at all. The aim in short is toward "voluntariness" in a utopian sense, or to view it from a different angle, voluntariness with a vengeance. . . .

Viewed as a choice based on pure policy, these new rules prove to be a highly debatable, if not one-sided, appraisal of the competing interests, imposed over widespread objection, at the very time when judicial restraint is most called for by the circumstances.

Without at all subscribing to the generally black picture of police conduct painted by the Court, I think it must be frankly recognized at the outset that police questioning allowable under due process precedents may inherently entail some pressure on the suspect and may seek advantage in his ignorance or weaknesses. The atmosphere and questioning techniques, proper and fair though they be, can in themselves exert a tug on the suspect to confess, and in this light "[t]o speak of any confessions of crime made after arrest as being 'voluntary' or 'uncoerced' is somewhat inaccurate, although traditional. A confession is wholly and incontestably voluntary only if a guilty person gives himself up to the law and becomes his own accuser." . . .

. . . Until today, the role of the Constitution has been only to sift out *undue* pressure, not to assure spontaneous confessions. . . .

. . . What the Court largely ignores is that its rules impair, if they will not eventually serve wholly to frustrate, an instrument of law enforcement that has long and quite reasonably been thought worth the price paid for it. There can be little doubt that the Court's new code would markedly decrease the number of confessions. To warn the suspect that he may remain silent and remind him that his confession may be used in court are minor obstructions. To require also an express waiver by the suspect and an end to questioning whenever he demurs must heavily handicap questioning. And to suggest or provide counsel for the suspect simply invites the end of the interrogation. . . .

How much harm this decision will inflict on law enforcement cannot fairly be predicted with accuracy. Evidence on the role of confessions is notoriously incomplete. . . . We do know that some crimes cannot be solved without confessions, that ample expert testimony attests to their importance in crime control, and that the Court is taking a real risk with society's welfare in imposing its new regime on the country. The social costs of crime are too great to call the new rules anything but a hazardous experimentation.

While passing over the costs and risks of its experiment, the Court portrays the evils of normal police questioning in terms which I think are exaggerated. Albeit stringently confined by the due process standards interrogation is no doubt often inconvenient and unpleasant for the suspect. However, it is no less so for a man to be arrested and jailed, to have his house searched, or to stand trial in court, yet all this may properly happen to the most innocent given probable cause, a warrant, or an indictment. Society has always paid a stiff price for law and order, and peaceful interrogation is not one of the dark moments of the law.

This brief statement of the competing considerations seems to me ample proof that the Court's preference is highly debatable at best and therefore not to be read into the Constitution. . . .

. . . Nothing in the letter or the spirit of the Constitution or in the precedents squares with the heavy-handed and one-sided action that is so precipitously taken by the Court in the name of fulfilling its constitutional responsibilities. . . .

Conclusion

Decisions like Miranda not only divided the Court deeply, but divided the country and provided fuel for bitter political debate on the issue whether the courts, state as well as federal, had become, in the parlance of the more direct political attackers, "soft on crime." The election of 1968 brought such attacks to the level of presidential campaigning. Several aspects of Supreme Court decision making became issues in the campaign.

The era of liberal experimentation in constitutional law had, of course, produced determined opponents. It is fashionable and, indeed, convenient to identify the end of Earl Warren's chief justiceship as the dramatic high point of that opposition. To be sure, Warren's replacement by Chief Justice Warren E. Burger marked the beginning of a new era, but the strength, tenacity, and occasional bitterness of conservative opposition to progressive or liberal change in the Supreme Court's doctrinal interpretations marked the entire period from the late 1930s to the late 1960s. The big difference was that after the 1968 election, the Court had a determined critic in the White House.

It is clear that there can be a judicial doctrinal revolution without the intervention of a critical election. In the long periods between some of the critical elections of the past, judicial doctrinal changes of great social, economic, and political significance have occurred. Some, like the disastrous slavery doctrines, helped stimulate the next critical election. The doctrinal cross currents of the 1950s and 1960s clearly contributed to the political realignment, short of a critical change, that occurred near the end of the 1960s. The pent-up conservative coalition resentment of decisions rendered by the Supreme Court under Vinson and especially under Warren included adverse reaction to the determination of many internal security cases as well as decisions about regulation of private corporations. But such adverse political reaction was restrained compared to the bitter attacks upon the Warren decisions that were made as a result of civil rights, legislative reapportionment, and rights of criminal defendants issues. Between 1950 and 1968, such attacks were generally not limited to one political party and because, as noted above, such criticism was not espoused by an occupant of the White House, the Supreme Court seemed to be immune from serious political injury.

Chapter 10 examines the nature of the Supreme Court's presidential opposition and the judicial response to it, the major doctrinal transformations of the 1970s and 1980s, and a projection of the future of the Court and its political and doctrinal relations with Congress and the president.

REFERENCES

1. William F. Swindler, *Court and Constitution in the Twentieth Century* (Indianapolis: Bobbs-Merrill, 1970), pp. 215–227; and J. W. Anderson, *Eisenhower, Brownell, and the Congress* (University Station: University of Alabama Press, 1964).
2. 283 U. S. 308 (1931).
3. *Nixon* v. *Condon*, 286 U. S. 73 (1932).
4. 287 U. S. 45 (1932).
5. 294 U. S. 587 (1935).
6. 295 U. S. 45 (1935).
7. 305 U. S. 337 (1938).
8. 313 U. S. 299 (1941).
9. 321 U. S. 649 (1944).
10. 334 U. S. 1 (1948).
11. 339 U. S. 629 (1950).

12. 339 U. S. 637 (1950).
13. Swindler, op. cit., pp. 264–267.
14. Arthur J. Goldberg, Thomas E. Harris, and David E. Feller, Brief for the Congress of Industrial Organizations as Amicus Curiae in *Gebhart* v. *Belton,* submitted to the Supreme Court of the United States, October Term, 1953.
15. 328 U. S. 549 (1946).
16. Swindler, op. cit., pp. 325–328.
17. Francis A. Allen, "The Supreme Court, Federalism, and State Systems of Criminal Justice," *University of Chicago Law School Record,* vol. 8 (Autumn 1958), p. 18.
18. Report by the 1958 Conference of State Chief Justices. See *Harvard Law Record,* special ed., October 23, 1958.
19. *Powell* v. *McCormack,* 395 F. 2nd. 577 (1968); for a thorough discussion of the background and significance of the Powell case, see P. Allen Dionisopoulos, *Rebellion, Racism, and Representation: The Adam Clayton Powell Case and Its Antecedents* (Dekalb, Ill.: University of Northern Illinois Press, 1970).

10

The Nixon, Carter, and Reagan Presidencies

The Return of Conservative Tendencies

After the switch in doctrinal positions during the court-packing crisis of 1937, the Supreme Court was free of presidential attack for many years but frequently under attack from Congress. Although most of the attacks were turned back, the persistence of the opposition and the weakening of congressional defenders suggested that the advent of a bona fide Court critic in the White House would be a serious development. In the presidential election of 1968, the electorate chose a president who was an open and severe critic of the Supreme Court and its positions—Richard Milhous Nixon. Although Nixon's margin of victory was small, he claimed a public mandate on issues related to "crime in the streets" because the third candidate for the presidency, George C. Wallace of Alabama, had taken an even more extreme position on crime. Nixon had, indeed, defeated his Democratic opponent narrowly in popular votes by 31.7 million (43.42 percent) to 31.2 million (42.72 percent), but Wallace had gained 9.9 million (13.53 percent), capturing 46 electoral votes from Alabama, Arkansas, Georgia, Louisiana, and Mississippi (plus a single vote from North Carolina). Nixon's electoral vote margin was large: 301 to Humphrey's 191. When the electoral and popular votes of Nixon and Wallace were combined and interpreted (by Nixon and his admirers) as an anticrime mandate, the total looked significant: 347 electoral college votes; 41.6 million popular votes; and 56.85 percent of the total participating in the 1968 presidential balloting.[1] When he assumed office, Nixon treated the result as if it were a critical election, thus assuming that a fundamental realignment had taken place. Because of the weakness of the major parties, the Republicans did not sweep all major elective offices, but Nixon claimed a sweeping mandate.

Opponents of the Supreme Court, whether supporters of Nixon or not, had opened a series of formidable attacks on the Court in the months before the election. The upsurge of such activity was in part the result of President Johnson's surprise announcement that he would not run again, but it predominantly reflected deep antagonism toward the Court itself. The battle to determine the membership of the Court had begun several months before the November election. In June 1968, the 77-year-old chief justice submitted his resignation to President Lyndon Johnson, a resignation contingent upon Senate confirmation of his successor. On June 26, President Johnson nominated Associate Justice Abe Fortas as Warren's successor. He also nominated Court of Appeals Judge Thornberry as Associate Justice to replace Fortas. The Fortas nomination precipitated a firestorm of conservative doctrinal criticism and organized parliamentary maneuvering to defeat the nominee.

During the 1968 campaign, while Richard Nixon aggressively exploited themes of alleged judicial permissiveness and the need for greater emphasis upon the rights of victims, congressional conservatives targeted both Fortas and the civil libertarian doctrines of the Warren Court for direct and bitter attacks. In addition, some claimed that the circumstances of Warren's resignation and President Johnson's subsequent nomination of Fortas were open to serious question because Johnson was a lame-duck president. Vice-president Spiro Agnew not only made the latter argument, he also criticized Warren, a Republican appointee, for lacking a sense of obligation to a possible Republican president succeeding Johnson. Warren might have felt loyal to a Republican candidate other than Nixon, but in realistic political terms, their past political differences on substantive issues presumably precluded such sense of obligation in 1968. Historically, of course, a number of justices had "hung on" or attempted to do so until presidents of their respective parties took office. President James Buchanan's last appointee, Justice Nathan Clifford, stayed on tenaciously and pathetically—as he became senile—after the critical election of 1860, but fell short of Grover Cleveland's election by a few years. But John Danaher, a former Republican Senator, GOP fundraiser, and lobbyist who had received President Eisenhower's first federal appellate nomination (to the U.S. Court of Appeals for the District of Columbia), did return the favor. In December of 1968, Danaher, perhaps as a partisan retort to Warren, announced that although he was eligible to retire, he would do so after January 20, 1969, to enable President-elect Nixon to fill the vacancy. In December 1968, Danaher stated that it was "entirely fitting for me to return the vacancy" to the Republican party.[2]

The major issues in the battle for Justice Fortas' appointment for chief justice of the United States were the substantive positions taken by Fortas and other judicial activists on the Court. Concurrent with congressional attacks on decisions defending the procedural rights of criminal defendants, candidate Nixon kept up a drumroll of criticism, such as his reference to the "barbed wire of legalism erected by the Supreme Court" to thwart law enforcement efforts. But congressional opposition covering a wide range of issues had descended to personal attacks such as Congressman Rarick's reference to Justice Fortas as "Mr. Obscenity."[3] Fortas was criticized for his close ties with President Lyndon Johnson (the "cronyism" charge) and for alleged conflict of interest involving the funding of his American

University lecture fees. But ultimately the most effective weapon of the opposition was the Senate filibuster. After months of extended debate, on October 1, 1968, the Senate defeated a motion to stop debate on the nomination of Abe Fortas as Chief Justice of the United States. The margin was 45–43. Two days later, Senator Mike Mansfield placed in the *Congressional Record* a press statement on Justice Fortas' request to President Johnson that his nomination be withdrawn.

In May 1969, the second Fortas controversy was initiated by a *Life* magazine article indicating that Justice Fortas had accepted a $20,000 gift from financier Louis Wolfson's foundation in January 1966, a few months after being appointed to the Supreme Court. Wolfson was indicted and was subsequently convicted of financial offenses. Although Fortas had returned the money, the circumstances led to numerous calls for his resignation or impeachment. On May 15, 1969, Fortas resigned.

The bitter conflicts of the last half of 1968 and first half of 1969 resulted in a remarkable change in the personnel and doctrinal prospects of the liberal and activist Supreme Court. In January 1968, the Court comprised virtually a solid phalanx of justices committed to state and federal governmental intervention in the economy, judicial supervision of state criminal justice systems, and racial equality. Chief Justice Earl Warren had presided through three presidencies. Justices Black and Douglas, the last of the Roosevelt-era members, were still working productively, while Justices Brennan, Stewart, and Harlan were Eisenhower-era members, the latter two the leading advocates of judicial restraint. They were frequently but not inevitably supported by the last Kennedy-era justice, Byron White. The large activist contingent had been augmented by two Johnson appointees, Abe Fortas and Thurgood Marshall. Yet by mid–1969, Richard Nixon (rather than Hubert Humphrey) had succeeded Lyndon Johnson in the White House, and the tone and temper of the administration of justice had changed dramatically. Attorney General Ramsay Clark was succeeded by John Mitchell. Along with the nomination of Abe Fortas, the concomitant nomination of Texas Circuit Judge Homer Thornberry to succeed Fortas as associate justice was defeated by filibuster in the Senate in October 1968. Chief Justice Earl Warren soon announced, in December of 1968, that he would resign at the end of the current Court term, in June 1969. Thus, to Richard Nixon fell the greatest judicial prize, the chief justiceship. On June 23, 1969, Warren E. Burger became chief justice of the United States.

Burger had served since the Eisenhower administration as a federal Court of Appeals judge for the District of Columbia. During his years on the appeals bench, Burger had been a consistent law-and-order conservative counterpoint to the liberal appeals court majority led by judges such as David Bazelon. Thus, he embodied many of the judicial principles sought by President Nixon. Despite the bitterness engendered among Senate liberals, Burger's nomination encountered little overt opposition. He was confirmed by the overwhelming margin of 74 to 3. But when President Nixon sought to fulfill a widely discussed "Southern strategy," he ran into strong opposition. His first nominee to fill Fortas' vacant associate justiceship was another Court of Appeals judge, Clement Haynsworth of the

Fourth Circuit, a conservative South Carolinian who was defeated, 45 to 55, on judicial ethical grounds. Nixon's second nominee, Harrold Carswell, also a judge of a federal court of appeals, this time in the Fifth Circuit, was defeated 45 to 51, on qualitative grounds as well as on the basis of his previous segregationist positions. Finally, President Nixon, after accusing his Senate opponents of regional bias, nominated Judge Harry A. Blackmun of the federal Court of Appeals for the Eighth Circuit, like Burger a Minnesotan, and indeed, a close friend of the chief justice. His approval did not come until 1970.

Republicans in Congress counterattacked with Republican House Minority Leader Gerald R. Ford initiating impeachment proceedings against Justice William O. Douglas because of his involvement with the Parvin Foundation. This effort failed when the House Judiciary Committee reported that there was no basis for impeachment.[4]

In 1971 President Nixon had two additional opportunities to make Supreme Court appointments. In September of that year Justice Black retired because of failing health. He died eight days later. At the end of the same month Justice John Marshall Harlan also announced his retirement. After several discussions of potential nominees with a judicial screening committee of the American Bar Association, Nixon's initial choices were designated "not qualified." Ultimately, President Nixon nominated Lewis Powell, a Virginia corporate law firm member and former president of the American Bar Association, and William H. Rehnquist, a conservative Arizona lawyer who was serving as assistant attorney general. Both were confirmed in December 1971, Rehnquist by a margin of 68–26.

Law and order and the weakening of procedural rights

The new appointees shared a common determination to toughen judicial doctrines related to crime. They succeeded in a variety of doctrinal settings. But the modification of the Miranda doctrine was a major objective. In *Harris* v. *New York*, the new chief justice wrote a majority opinion significantly weakening Miranda and Justice Brennan wrote a strong dissent.

HARRIS v. NEW YORK
401 U. S. 222 (1971)

Chief Justice Burger delivered the opinion of the Court:

We granted the writ in this case to consider petitioner's claim that a statement made by him to police under circumstances rendering it inadmissible to establish the prosecution's case in chief under *Miranda* v. *Arizona*, . . . may not be used to impeach his credibility.

The State of New York charged petitioner in a two-count indictment with twice selling heroin to an undercover police officer. At a subsequent jury trial the officer was the State's chief witness, and he testified as to details of the two sales. A second officer verified collateral details of the sales, and a third

offered testimony about the chemical analysis of the heroin.

Petitioner took the stand in his own defense. He admitted knowing the undercover police officer but denied a sale on January 4, 1966. He admitted making a sale of contents of a glassine bag to the officer on January 6 but claimed it was baking powder and part of a scheme to defraud the purchaser.

On cross-examination petitioner was asked seriatim whether he had made specified statements to the police immediately following his arrest on Jaunary 7—statements that partially contradicted petitioner's direct testimony at trial. In response to the cross-examination, petitioner testified that he could not remember virtually any of the questions or answers recited by the prosecutor. At the request of petitioner's counsel the written statement from which the prosecutor had read questions and answers in his impeaching process was placed in the record for possible use on appeal; the statement was not shown to the jury.

The trial judge instructed the jury that the statements attributed to petitioner by the prosecution could be considered only in passing on petitioner's credibility and not as evidence of guilt. In closing summations both counsel argued the substance of the impeaching statements. The jury then found petitioner guilty on the second count of the indictment. The New York Court of Appeals affirmed. . . .

At trial the prosecution made no effort in its case in chief to use the statements allegedly made by petitioner, conceding that they were inadmissible under *Miranda* v. *Arizona.* . . . The transcript of the interrogation used in the impeachment, but not given to the jury, shows that no warning of a right to appointed counsel was given before questions were put to petitioner when he was taken into custody. Petitioner makes no claim that the statements made to the police were coerced or involuntary.

Some comments in the *Miranda* opinion can indeed be read as indicating a bar to use of an uncounseled statement for any purpose, but discussion of that issue was not at all necessary to the Court's holding and cannot be regarded as controlling. *Miranda* barred the prosecution from making its case with statements of an accused made while in custody prior to having or effectively waiving counsel. It does not follow from *Miranda* that evidence inadmissible against an accused in the prosecution's case in chief is barred for all purposes, provided of course that the trustworthiness of the evidence satisfies legal standards.

In *Walder* v. *United States,* . . . the Court permitted physical evidence, inadmissible in the case in chief, to be used for impeachment purposes.

"It is one thing to say that the Government cannot make an affirmative use of evidence unlawfully obtained. It is quite another to say that the defendant can turn the illegal method by which evidence in the Government's possession was obtained to his own advantage, and provide himself with a shield against contradiction of his untruths. Such an extension of the *Weeks* doctrine would be a perversion of the Fourth Amendment.

"[T]here is hardly justification for letting the defendant affirmatively resort to perjurious testimony in reliance on the Government's disability to challenge his credibility."

It is true that Walder was impeached as to collateral matters included in his direct examination, whereas petitioner here was impeached as to testimony bearing more directly on the crimes charged. We are not persuaded that there is a difference in principle that warrants a result different from that reached by the Court in *Walder.* Petitioner's testimony in his own behalf concerning the events of January 7 contrasted sharply with what he told the police shortly after his arrest. The impeachment process here undoubtedly provided valuable aid to the jury in assessing petitioner's credibility, and the benefits of this process should not be lost, in our view, because of the speculative possibility that impermissible police conduct will be encouraged thereby. Assuming that the exclusionary rule has a deterrent effect on proscribed police conduct, sufficient deterrence flows when the evidence in question is made unavailable to the prosecution in its case in chief.

Every criminal defendant is privileged to testify in his own defense, or to refuse to do so. But that privilege cannot be construed to include the right to commit perjury. . . . Having voluntarily taken the stand, petitioner was under an obligation to speak truthfully and accurately, and the prosecution here did no more than utilize the traditional truth-testing devices of the adversary process. Had inconsistent statements been made by the accused to some third person, it could hardly be contended that the conflict could not be laid before the jury by way of cross-examination and impeachment.

The shield provided by *Miranda* cannot be perverted into a license to use perjury by way of a defense, free from the risk of confrontation with prior inconsistent utterances. We hold, therefore, that petitioner's credibility was appropriately impeached by use of his earlier conflicting statements.

[Justice Black's dissenting opinion is omitted.]

Justice Brennan, joined by Justices Douglas and Marshall, dissented as follows:

It is conceded that the question-and-answer statement used to impeach petitioner's direct testimony was, under *Miranda* v. *Arizona,* . . . constitutionally inadmissible as part of the State's direct case against petitioner. I think that the Constitution also denied the State the use of the statement on cross-examination to impeach the credibility of petitioner's testimony given in his own defense. . . .

The objective of deterring improper police conduct is only part of the larger objective of safeguarding the integrity of our adversary system. The "essential mainstay" of that system, *Miranda* v. *Arizona,* . . . is the privilege against self-incrimination, which for that reason has occupied a central place in our jurisprudence since before the Nation's birth. Moreover, "we may view the historical development of the privilege as one which groped for the proper scope of governmental power over the citizen. . . . All these policies point to one overrriding thought: the constitutional foundation underlying the privilege is the respect a government . . . must accord to the dignity and integrity of its citizens." *Ibid.* These values are plainly jeopardized if an exception against admission of tainted statements is made for those used for impeachment purposes. Moreover, it is monstrous that courts should aid or abet the law-breaking police officer. It is abiding truth that "[n]othing can destroy a government more quickly than its failure to observe its own laws,

or worse, its disregard of the charter of its own existence." . . .

Thus, even to the extent that *Miranda* was aimed at deterring police practices in disregard of the Constitution, I fear that today's holding will seriously undermine the achievement of that objective. The Court today tells the police that they may freely interrogate an accused incommunicado and without counsel and know that although any statement they obtain in violation of *Miranda* cannot be used on the State's direct case, it may be introduced if the defendant has the temerity to testify in his own defense. This goes far toward undoing much of the progress made in conforming police methods to the Constitution. I dissent.

Vietnam and the Pentagon Papers

The New York Times Company was again in litigation in the early 1970s in the highly significant Pentagon Papers case. The constitutional question arose out of the serialization by the *New York Times* and the *Washington Post* of the hitherto secret documents known as the Pentagon Papers—formally, "History of U.S. Decision-Making Process on Viet-Nam Policy." The federal government sought, by action brought by Attorney General John Mitchell, to enjoin further publication of the series in the *New York Times*. The Supreme Court permitted the injunction to stand a few days while it heard oral arguments and then responded in a *per curiam* opinion. The justices then indicated, in concurring or dissenting opinions, their constitutional views on the issue. The two Nixon appointees (Chief Justice Burger, 1969, and Justice Blackmun, 1970) and Justice Harlan, an Eisenhower appointee (1955), dissented. All the other justices agreed that an injunction against the two newspapers would violate their First Amendment rights.

NEW YORK TIMES COMPANY
v. UNITED STATES
403 U. S. 713 (1971)

PER CURIAM:

We granted certiorari in these cases in which the United States seeks to enjoin *The New York Times* and the *Washington Post* from publishing the contents of a classified study entitled "History of U. S. Decision-Making Process on Vietnam Policy." . . .

"Any system of prior restraints of expression comes to this Court bearing a heavy presumption against its constitutional validity." . . .

The Government "thus carries a heavy burden of showing justification for the imposition of such a restraint." . . .

The District Court for the Southern District of New York in *The New York Times* case and the District Court for the District of Columbia and the Court of

Appeals for the District of Columbia Circuit in the *Washington Post* case held that the Government had not met that burden. We agree.

The judgment of the Court of Appeals for the District of Columbia Circuit is therefore affirmed. The order of the Court of Appeals for the Second Circuit is reversed and the case is remanded with directions to enter a judgment affirming the judgment of the District Court for the Southern District of New York. The stays entered June 25, 1971, by the Court are vacated. The judgments shall issue forthwith. So ordered.

Justice Black, whom Justice Douglas joined, concurred:

I adhere to the view that the Government's case against the *Washington Post* should have been dismissed and that the injunction against the *New York*

Times should have been vacated without oral argument when the cases were first presented to this Court. I believe that every moment's continuance of the injunctions against these newspapers amounts to a flagrant, indefensible, and continuing violation of the First Amendment.

. . . I agree completely that we must affirm the judgment of the Court of Appeals for the District of Columbia Circuit and reverse the judgment of the Court of Appeals for the Second Circuit for the reasons stated by my Brothers Douglas and Brennan. In my view it is unfortunate that some of my Brethren are apparently willing to hold that the publication of news may sometimes be enjoined. Such a holding would make a shambles of the First Amendment. . . .

Now, for the first time in the 182 years since the founding of the Republic, the federal courts are asked to hold that the First Amendment does not mean what it says, but rather means that the Government can halt the publication of current news of vital importance to the people of this country.

In seeking injunctions against these newspapers and in its presentation to the Court, the Executive Branch seems to have forgotten the essential purpose and history of the First Amendment. When the Constitution was adopted, many people strongly opposed it because the document contained no Bill of Rights to safeguard certain basic freedoms. They especially feared that the new powers granted to a central government might be interpreted to permit the government to curtail freedom of religion, press, assembly, and speech. In response to an overwhelming public clamor, James Madison offered a series of amendments to satisfy citizens that these great liberties would remain safe and beyond the power of government to abridge. . . . The amendments were offered to *curtail* and *restrict* the general powers granted to the Executive, Legislative, and Judicial Branches two years before in the original Constitution. The Bill of Rights changed the original Constitution into a new charter under which no branch of government could abridge the people's freedoms of press, speech, religion, and assembly. Yet the Solicitor General argues and some members of the Court appear to agree that the general powers of the Government adopted in the original Constitution should be interpreted to limit and restrict the specific and emphatic guarantees of the Bill of Rights adopted later. I can imagine no greater perversion of history. Madison and the other Framers of the First Amendment, able men that they were, wrote in language they earnestly believed could never be misunderstood: "Congress shall make no law . . . abridging the freedom . . . of the press. . . ." Both the

history and language of the First Amendment support the view that the press must be left free to publish news, whatever the source, without censorship, injunctions, or prior restraints.

In the First Amendment the Founding Fathers gave the free press the protection it must have to fulfill its essential role in our democracy. The press was to serve the governed, not the governors. The Government's power to censor the press was abolished so that the press would remain forever free to censure the Government. The press was protected so that it could bare the secrets of government and inform the people. Only a free and unrestrained press can effectively expose deception in government. And paramount among the responsibilities of a free press is the duty to prevent any part of the government from deceiving the people and sending them off to distant lands to die of foreign fevers and foreign shot and shell. In my view, far from deserving condemnation for their courageous reporting, *The New York Times*, the *Washington Post*, and other newspapers should be commended for serving the purpose that the Founding Fathers saw so clearly. In revealing the workings of government that led to the Vietnam war, the newspapers nobly did precisely that which the Founders hoped and trusted they would do.

The Government's case here is based on premises entirely different from those that guided the Framers of the First Amendment. . . . And the Government argues in its brief that in spite of the First Amendment, "[t]he authority of the Executive Department to protect the nation against publication of information whose disclosure would endanger the national security stems from two interrelated sources: the constitutional power of the President over the conduct of foreign affairs and his authority as Commander-in-Chief." . . .

To find that the President has "inherent power" to halt the publication of news by resort to the courts would wipe out the First Amendment and destroy the fundamental liberty and security of the very people the Government hopes to make "secure." No one can read the history of the adoption of the First Amendment without being convinced beyond any doubt that it was injunctions like those sought here that Madison and his collaborators intended to outlaw in this Nation for all time.

The word "security" is a broad, vague generality whose contours should not be invoked to abrogate the fundamental law embodied in the First Amendment. The guarding of military and diplomatic secrets at the expense of informed representative government provides no real security for our Republic. The Framers of the First Amendment, fully aware of both the need to defend a new nation and the abuses of the English and Colonial governments, sought to give this new society strength and security by providing that freedom of speech, press, religion, and assembly should not be abridged. This thought was eloquently expressed in 1937 by Mr. Chief Justice Hughes—great man and great Chief Justice that he was—when the Court held a man could not be punished for attending a meeting run by Communists.

The greater the importance of safeguarding the community from incitements to the overthrow of our institutions by force and violence, the more imperative is the need to preserve inviolate the constitutional rights of free speech, free press and free assembly in order to maintain the opportunity for free political discussion, to the end that government may be responsive to the will of the people and that changes, if desired, may be obtained by peaceful means. Therein lies the security of the Republic, the very foundation of constitutional government.

Chief Justice Burger dissented:

So clear are the constitutional limitations on prior restraint against expression, that from the time of *Near* v. *Minnesota* . . . until recently . . . we have had little occasion to be concerned with cases involving prior restraints against news reporting on matters of public interest. There is, therefore, little variation among the members of the Court in terms of resistance to prior restraints against publication. Adherence to this basic constitutional principle, however, does not make these cases simple. In these cases, the imperative of a free and unfettered press comes into collision with another imperative, the effective functioning of a complex modern government and specifically the effective exercise of certain constitutional powers of the Executive. Only those who view the First Amendment as an absolute in all circumstances— a view I respect, but reject—can find such cases as these to be simple or easy.

These cases are not simple for another and more immediate reason. We do not know the facts of the cases. No District Judge knew all the facts. No Court of Appeals judge knew all the facts. No member of this Court knows all the facts.

Why are we in this posture, in which only those judges to whom the First Amendment is absolute and permits of no restraint in any circumstances or for any reason, are really in a position to act?

I suggest we are in this posture because these cases have been conducted in unseemly haste. Mr. Justice Harlan covers the chronology of events demonstrating

the hectic pressures under which these cases have been processed and I need not restate them. The prompt setting of these cases reflects our universal abhorrence of prior restraint. But prompt judicial action does not mean unjudicial haste.

Here, moreover, the frenetic haste is due in large part to the manner in which the *Times* proceeded from the date it obtained the purloined documents. It seems reasonably clear now that the haste precluded reasonable and deliberate judicial treatment of these cases and was not warranted. The precipitate action of this Court aborting trials not yet completed is not the kind of judicial conduct that ought to attend the disposition of a great issue.

The newspapers make a derivative claim under the First Amendment; they denominate this right as the public "right to know"; by implication, the *Times* asserts a sole trusteeship of that right by virtue of its journalistic "scoop." The right is asserted as an absolute, as Justice Holmes so long ago pointed out in his aphorism concerning the right to shout "fire" in a crowded theater if there was no fire. There are other exceptions, some of which Chief Justice Hughes mentioned by way of example in *Near* v. *Minnesota*. There are no doubt other exceptions no one has had occasion to describe or discuss. Conceivably such exceptions may be lurking in these cases and would have been flushed had they been properly considered in the trial courts, free from unwarranted deadlines and frenetic pressures. An issue of this importance should be tried and heard in a judicial atmosphere conducive to thoughtful, reflective deliberation, especially when haste, in terms of hours, is unwarranted in light of the long period the *Times*, by its own choice, deferred publication.

It is not disputed that the *Times* has had unauthorized possession of the documents for three to four months, during which it has had its expert analysts studying them, presumably digesting them and preparing the material for publication. During all of this time, the *Times*, presumably in its capacity as trustee of the public's "right to know," has held up publication for purposes it considered proper and thus public knowledge was delayed. No doubt this was for a good reason; the analysis of 7,000 pages of complex material drawn from a vastly greater volume of material would inevitably take time and the writing of good news stories takes time. But why should the United States Government, from whom this information was illegally acquired by someone, along with all the counsel, trial judges, and appellate judges be placed under needless pressure? After these months of deferral, the alleged "right to know" has somehow and suddenly become a right that must be vindicated instanter.

Would it have been unreasonable, since the newspaper could anticipate the Government's objections to release of secret material, to give the Government an opportunity to review the entire collection and determine whether agreement could be reached on publication? Stolen or not, if security was not in fact jeopardized, much of the material could no doubt have been declassified, since it spans a period ending in 1968. With such an approach—one that great newspapers have in the past practiced and stated editorially to be the duty of an honorable press—the newspapers and Government might well have narrowed the area of disagreement as to what was and was not publishable, leaving the remainder to be resolved in orderly litigation, if necessary. To me it is hardly believable that a newspaper long regarded as a great institution in American life would fail to perform one of the basic and simple duties of every citizen with respect to the discovery or possession of stolen property or secret goverment documents. That duty, I had thought—perhaps naively—was to report forthwith, to responsible public officers. This duty rests on taxi drivers, Justices, and The New York Times. The course followed by the Times, whether so calculated or not, removed any possibility of orderly litigation of the issues. If the action of the judges up to now has been correct, that result is sheer happenstance.

Our grant of the writ of certiorari before final judgment in the Times case aborted the trial in the District Court before it had made a complete record pursuant to the mandate of the Court of Appeals for the Second Circuit.

The consequence of all this melancholy series of events is that we literally do not know what we are acting on. As I see it, we have been forced to deal with litigation concerning rights of great magnitude without an adequate record, and surely without time for adequate treatment either in the prior proceedings or in this Court. It is interesting to note that counsel on both sides, in oral argument before this Court, were frequently unable to respond to questions on factual points. Not surprisingly they pointed out that they had been working literally "around the clock" and simply were unable to review the documents that give rise to these cases and were not familiar with them. This Court is in no better posture. I agree generally with Mr. Justice Harlan and Mr. Justice Blackmun but I am not prepared to reach the merits.

I would affirm the Court of Appeals for the Second Circuit and allow the District Court to complete the trial aborted by our grant of certiorari, meanwhile preserving the status quo in the Post case. I would direct that the District Court on remand give priority to the Times case to the exclusion of all other business of that court but I would not set arbitrary deadlines.

I should add that I am in general agreement with much of what Mr. Justice White has expressed with respect to penal sanctions concerning communication or retention of documents or information relating to the national defense.

We all crave speedier judicial processes but when judges are pressured as in these cases the result is a parody of the judicial function.

Narrowing the Commerce Clause

After the New Deal justices had consolidated the doctrinal affirmations that came with the changes of heart of Chief Justice Hughes and Justice Roberts in 1937, it was generally assumed that a broad constructionist interpretation of the scope of congressional commerce power authority was a permanent feature in American constitutional law. But after the Nixon appointees (plus older conservatives) had gained effective control of the Court, this assumption proved premature. Justice Rehnquist's majority opinion in National League of Cities v. Usery indicated the new conservative rationale for limiting congressional authority.

NATIONAL LEAGUE OF CITIES v. USERY
426 U. S. 833 (1976)

Justice Rehnquist delivered the opinion of the Court:

. . . In 1974, Congress again broadened the coverage of the [Fair Labor Standards] Act. . . . The Act . . . imposes upon almost all public employment the min-

imum wage and maximum hour requirements previously restricted to employees engaged in interstate commerce. These requirements are essentially identical to those imposed upon private employers. . . .

. . . [T]he District Court granted appellee Secretary of Labor's motion to dismiss the complaint for failure to state a claim upon which relief might be granted.

The District Court states it was "troubled" by appellants' contentions that the amendments would intrude upon the States' performance of essential governmental functions. The court went on to say that it considered their contentions

substantial and that it may well be that the Supreme Court will feel it appropriate to draw back from the far-reaching implications of [*Maryland* v. *Wirtz*]; but that is a decision that only the Supreme Court can make, and as a Federal district court we feel obliged to apply the *Wirtz* opinion as it stands. . . .

We noted probable jurisdiction in order to consider the important questions recognized by the District Court. . . . We agree with the District Court that the appellants' contentions are substantial. Indeed upon full consideration of the question we have decided that the "far-reaching implications" of *Wirtz* should be overruled, and that the judgment of the District Court must be reversed.

II

It is established beyond peradventure that the Commerce Clause of Art. I of the Constitution is a grant of plenary authority to Congress. That authority is, in the words of Mr. Chief Justice Marshall in *Gibbons* v. *Ogden*, . . . "the power to regulate; that is, to prescribe the rule by which commerce is to be governed." . . .

Congressional power over areas of private endeavor, even when its exercise may pre-empt express state-law determinations contrary to the result which has commended itself to the collective wisdom of Congress, has been held to be limited only by the requirement that "the means chosen by [Congress] must be reasonably adapted to the end permitted by the Constitution." . . .

Appellants in no way challenge these decisions establishing the breadth of authority granted Congress under the commerce power. Their contention, on the contrary, is that when Congress seeks to regulate directly the activities of States as public employers, it transgresses an affirmative limitation on the exercise of its power akin to other commerce power affirmative limitations contained in the Constitution. Congressional enactments which may be fully within the grant of legislative authority contained in the Commerce Clause may nonetheless be invalid because found to offend against the Sixth [and] . . . Fifth Amendment[s] . . . Appellants' essential contention is that the 1974 amendments to the Act, while undoubtedly within the scope of the Commerce Clause, encounter a similar constitutional barrier because they are to be applied directly to the States and subdivisions of States as employers.

This Court has never doubted that there are limits upon the power of Congress to override state sovereignty, even when exercising its otherwise plenary powers to tax or to regulate commerce which are conferred by Art. I of the Constitution. In *Wirtz*, for example, the Court took care to assure the appellants that it had "ample power to prevent . . . 'the utter destruction of the State as a sovereign political entity,'" which they feared. . . . Appellee Secretary in this case, both in his brief and upon oral argument, has agreed that our federal system of government imposes definite limits upon the authority of Congress to regulate the activities of the States as States by means of the commerce power. . . . In *Fry*, the Court recognized that an express declaration of this limitation is found in the Tenth Amendment:

While the Tenth Amendment has been characterized as a 'truism,' stating merely that 'all is retained which has not been surrendered,' *United States* v. *Darby* [1941] . . . , it is not without significance. The Amendment expressly declares the constitutional policy that Congress may not exercise power in a fashion that impairs the States' integrity or their ability to function effectively in a federal system. . . .

In *New York* v. *United States* [1946], Mr. Chief Justice Stone, speaking for four Members of an eight-Member Court in rejecting the proposition that Congress could impose taxes on the States so long as it did so in a nondiscriminatory manner, observed:

A State may, like a private individual, own real property and receive income. But in view of our former decisions we could hardly say that a general non-discriminatory real estate tax (apportioned), or an income tax laid upon citizens and States alike could be constitutionally applied to the State's capitol, its State-house, its public school houses, public parks, or its revenues from taxes or school lands, even though all real property and all income of the citizen is taxed. . . .

The expressions in these more recent cases trace back to earlier decisions of this Court recognizing the essential role of the States in our federal system of government. Mr. Chief Justice Chase, perhaps because of the particular time at which he occupied that office, had occasion more than once to speak for the Court on this point. In *Texas* v. *White*, [1869], he declared that "[t]he Constitution, in all its provisions, looks to an indestructible Union, composed of indestructible States." In *Lane County* v. *Oregon* [1869], his opinion for the Court said: . . .

[I]n many articles of the Constitution the necessary existence of the States, and, within their proper spheres, the independent authority of the States, is distinctly recognized. . . .

In *Metcalf & Eddy* v. *Mitchell* [1926], the Court likewise observed that "neither government may destroy the other nor curtail in any substantial manner the exercise of its powers." . . .

Appellee Secretary argues that the cases in which this Court has upheld sweeping exercises of authority by Congress, even though those exercises pre-empted state regulation of the private sector, have already curtailed the sovereignty of the States quite as much as the 1974 amendments to the Fair Labor Standards Act. We do not agree. It is one thing to recognize the authority of Congress to enact laws regulating individual businesses necessarily subject to the dual sovereignty of the government of the Nation and of the State in which they reside. It is quite another to uphold a similar exercise of congressional authority directed, not to private citizens, but to the States as States. We have repeatedly recognized that there are attributes of sovereignty attaching to every state government which may not be impaired by Congress, not because Congress may lack an affirmative grant of legislative authority to reach the matter, but because the Constitution prohibits it from exercising the authority in that manner. In *Coyle* v. *Oklahoma* [1911], the Court gave this example of such an attribute:

The power to locate its own seat of government and to determine when and how it shall be changed from one place to another, and to appropriate its own public funds for that purpose, are essentially and peculiarly state powers. . . .

One undoubted attribute of state sovereignty is the States' power to determine the wages which shall be paid to those whom they employ in order to carry out their governmental functions, what hours those persons will work, and what compensation will be provided where these employees may be called upon to work overtime. The question we must resolve here, then, is whether these determinations are "'functions essential to separate and independent existence,'" quoting from *Lane County* v. *Oregon* . . . so that Congress may not abrogate the States' otherwise plenary authority to make them.

In their complaint appellants advanced estimates of substantial costs which will be imposed upon them by the 1974 amendments. . . .

Judged solely in terms of increased costs in dollars, these allegations show a significant impact on the functioning of the governmental bodies involved. . . .

Quite apart from the substantial costs imposed upon the States and their political subdivisions, the Act displaces state policies regarding the manner in which they will structure delivery of those governmental services which their citizens require. The Act, speaking directly to the States *qua* States, requires that they shall pay all but an extremely limited minority

of their employees the minimum wage rates currently chosen by Congress. It may well be that as a matter of economic policy it would be desirable that States, just as private employers, comply with these minimum wage requirements. But it cannot be gainsaid that the federal requirement directly supplants the considered policy choices of the States' elected officials and administrators as to how they wish to structure pay scales in state employment. The State might wish to employ persons with little or no training, or those who wish to work on a casual basis, or those who for some other reason do not possess minimum employment requirements, and pay them less than the federally prescribed minimum wage. It may wish to offer part-time or summer employment to teenagers at a figure less than the minimum wage, and if unable to do so may decline to offer such employment at all. But the Act would forbid such choices by the States. The only "discretion" left to them under the Act is either to attempt to increase their revenue to meet the additional financial burden imposed upon them by paying congressionally prescribed wages to their existing complement of employees, or to reduce that complement to a number which can be paid the federal minimum wage without increasing revenue.

This dilemma presented by the minimum wage restrictions may seem not immediately different from that faced by private employers, who have long been covered by the Act and who must find ways to increase their gross income if they are to pay higher wages while maintaining current earnings. The difference, however, is that a State is not merely a factor in the "shifting economic arrangements" of the private sector of the economy . . . but is itself a coordinate element in the system established by the Framers for governing our Federal Union. . . .

Our examination of the effect of the 1974 amendments, as sought to be extended to the States and their political subdivisions, satisfies us that both the minimum wage and the maximum hour provisions will impermissibly interfere with the integral governmental functions of these bodies. . . .

III

One final matter requires our attention. Appellee has vigorously urged that we cannot, consistently with the Court's decisions in *Maryland* v. *Wirtz* . . . , rule against him here. It is important to examine this contention so that it will be clear what we hold today, and what we do not.

With regard to *Fry,* we disagree with appellee. There the Court held that the Economic Stabilization Act of 1970 was constitutional as applied to temporarily freeze the wages of state and local government employees. The Court expressly noted that the degree of intrusion upon the protected area of state sovereignty was in that case even less than that worked by the amendments to the FLSA which were before the Court in *Wirtz.* The Court recognized that the Economic Stabilization Act was "an emergency measure to counter severe inflation that threatened the national economy." . . .

We think our holding today quite consistent with *Fry.* The enactment at issue there was occasioned by an extremely serious problem which endangered the well-being of all the component parts of our federal system and which only collective action by the National Government might forestall. The means selected were carefully drafted so as not to interfere with the States' freedom beyond a very limited, specific period of time. The effect of the across-the-board freeze authorized by that Act, moreover, displaced no state choices as to how governmental operations should be structured, nor did it force the States to remake such choices themselves. Instead, it merely required that the wage scales and employment relationships which the States themselves had chosen be maintained during the period of the emergency. Finally, the Economic Stabilization Act operated to reduce the pressures upon state budgets rather than increase them. These factors distinguish the statute in *Fry* from the provisions at issue here. The limits imposed upon the commerce power when Congress seeks to apply it to the States are not so inflexible as to preclude temporary enactments tailored to combat a national emergency. "[A]lthough an emergency may not call into life a power which has never lived, nevertheless emergency may afford a reason for the exertion of a living power already enjoyed." . . .

With respect to the Court's decision in *Wirtz,* we reach a different conclusion. . . . There are undoubtedly factual distinctions between the two situations, but in view of the conclusions expressed earlier in this opinion we do not believe the reasoning in *Wirtz* may any longer be regarded as authoritative.

Wirtz relied heavily on the Court's decision in *United States* v. *California* [1936]. The opinion quotes the following language from that case:

[We] look to the activities in which the states have traditionally engaged as marking the boundary of the restriction upon the federal taxing power. But there is no such limitation upon the plenary power to regulate commerce. The state can no more deny the power if its exercise has been authorized by Congress than can an individual. . . .

But we have reaffirmed today that the States as States stand on quite different footing from an individual or a corporation when challenging the exercise of Congress' power to regulate commerce. We think the dicta from *United States* v. *California,* simply wrong. Congress may not exercise that power so as to force directly upon the States its choices as to how essential decisions regarding the conduct of integral governmental functions are to be made. We agree that such assertions of power, if unchecked, would indeed, as Mr. Justice Douglas cautioned in his dissent in *Wirtz,* allow "the National Government [to] devour the essentials of state sovereignty," and would therefore transgress the bounds of the authority granted Congress under the Commerce Clause. While there are obvious differences between the schools and hospitals involved in *Wirtz,* and the fire and police departments affected here, each provides an integral portion of those governmental services which the States and their political subdivisions have traditionally afforded their citizens. We are therefore persuaded that *Wirtz* must be overruled.

[Justice Blackmun's concurring opinion is omitted.]

Justice Brennan, with whom Justice White
and Justice Marshall joined, dissented:

The Court concedes, as of course it must, that Congress enacted the 1974 amendments pursuant to its exclusive power under Art. I, § 8, cl. 3, of the Constitution "[t]o regulate Commerce . . . among the several States." It must therefore be surprising that my Brethren should choose this bicentennial year of our independence to repudiate principles governing judicial interpretation of our Constitution settled since the time of Mr. Chief Justice John Marshall, discarding his postulate that the Constitution contemplates that restraints upon exercise by Congress of its plenary commerce power lie in the political process and not in the judicial process. For 152 years ago Mr. Chief Justice Marshall enunciated that principle to which, until today, his successors on this Court have been faithful. . . .

[T]he power over commerce . . . is vested in Congress as absolutely as it would be in a single government, having in its constitution the same restrictions on the exercise of the power as are found in the constitution of the United States. *The wisdom and the discretion of Congress, their identity with the people, and the influence which their constituents possess at elections, are . . . the sole restraints on which they have relied, to secure them from its abuse. They are the restraints on which the people must often rely solely, in all representative governments.* Gibbons v. Odgen . . . [emphasis added].

Only 34 years ago, *Wickard* v. *Filburn* [1942] . . . reaffirmed that "[a]t the beginning Chief Justice Marshall . . . made emphatic the embracing and penetrating nature of [Congress' commerce] power by warning that effective restraints on its exercise must proceed from political rather than from judicial processes."

My Brethren do not successfully obscure today's patent usurpation of the role reserved for the political process by their purported discovery in the Constitution of a restraint derived from sovereignty of the States on Congress' exercise of the commerce power. Mr. Chief Justice Marshall recognized that limitations "prescribed in the Constitution," . . . restrain Congress' exercise of the power. . . . Thus laws within the commerce power may not infringe individual liberties protected by the First Amendment . . . the Fifth Amendment . . . or the Sixth Amendment. . . . But there is no restraint based on state sovereignty requiring or permitting judicial enforcement anywhere expressed in the Constitution; our decisions over the last century and a half have explicitly rejected the existence of any such restraint on the commerce power.

We said in *United States* v. *California* [1936] . . . for example: "The sovereign power of the states is necessarily diminished to the extent of the grants of power to the federal government in the Constitution. . . . [T]he power of the state is subordinate to the constitutional exercise of the granted federal power." This but echoed another principle emphasized by Mr. Chief Justice Marshall:

If any one proposition could command the universal assent of mankind, we might expect it would be this—that the government of the Union, though limited in its powers, is supreme within its sphere of action. . . .

The commerce power "is an affirmative power commensurate with the national needs." . . . "There is no room in our scheme of government for the assertion of state power in hostility to the authorized exercise of Federal power." . . .

My Brethren thus have today manufactured an abstraction without substance, founded neither in the words of the Constitution nor on precedent. An abstraction having such profoundly pernicious consequences is not made less so by characterizing the 1974 amendments as legislation directed against the "States *qua* States." . . . Of course, regulations that this Court can say are not regulations of "commerce" cannot stand, . . . and in this sense "[t]he Court has ample power to prevent . . . 'the utter destruction of the State as a sovereign political entity.'" . . . But my Brethren make no claim that the 1974 amendments are not regulations of "commerce"; rather they overrule *Wirtz* in disagreement with historic principles. . . . Clearly, therefore, my Brethren are also repudiating the long line of our precedents holding that a judicial finding that Congress has not unreasonably regulated

a subject matter of "commerce" brings to an end the judicial role. . . .

The reliance of my Brethren upon the Tenth Amendment as "an express declaration of [a state sovereignty] limitation," . . . not only suggests that they overrule governing decisions of this Court that address this question but must astound scholars of the Constitution. For not only early decisions, *Gibbons* v. *Ogden* . . . *McCulloch* v. *Maryland* . . . and *Martin* v. *Hunter's Lessee* . . . , hold that nothing in the Tenth Amendment constitutes a limitation on congressional exercise of powers delegated by the Constitution to Congress. . . . Rather, as the Tenth Amendment's significance was more recently summarized:

The amendment states but a truism that all is retained which has not been surrendered. . . .

My Brethren purport to find support for their novel state-sovereignty doctrine in the concurring opinion of Mr. Chief Justice Stone in *New York* v. *United States.* . . . That reliance is plainly misplaced. . . . [T]he Chief Justice was addressing not the question of a state-sovereignty restraint upon the exercise of the commerce power, but rather the principle of implied immunity of the States and Federal Government from taxation by the other: "The counterpart of such undue interference has been recognized since Marshall's day as the implied immunity of each of the dual sovereignties of our constitutional system from taxation by the other." . . .

Today's repudiation of this unbroken line of precedents that firmly reject my Brethren's ill-conceived abstraction can only be regarded as a transparent cover for invalidating a congressional judgment with which they disagree. The only analysis even remotely resembling that adopted today is found in a line of opinions dealing with the Commerce Clause and the Tenth Amendment that ultimately provoked a constitutional crisis for the Court in the 1930s. . . . We tend to forget that the Court invalidated legislation during the Great Depression, not solely under the Due Process Clause, but also and primarily under the Commerce Clause and the Tenth Amendment. It may have been the eventual abandonment of that overly restrictive construction of the commerce power that spelled defeat for the Court-packing plan, and preserved the integrity of this institution . . . but my Brethren today are transparently trying to cut back on that recognition of the scope of the commerce power. My Brethren's approach to this case is not far different from the dissenting opinions in the cases that averted the crisis. . . .

That no precedent justifies today's result is particularly clear from the awkward extension of the doctrine of state immunity from federal taxation—an immunity conclusively distinguished by Mr. Justice Stone in *California*, and an immunity that is "narrowly limited" because "the people of all the states have created the national government and are represented in Congress," *Helvering v. Gerhardt* [1938]—to fashion a judicially enforceable restraint on Congress' exercise of the commerce power that the Court has time and again rejected as having no place in our constitutional jurisprudence. . . .

Certainly the paradigm of sovereign action—action *qua* State—is in the enactment and enforcement of state laws. Is it possible that my Brethren are signaling abandonment of the heretofore unchallenged principle that Congress "can, if it chooses, entirely displace the States to the full extent of the far-reaching Commerce Clause"? . . . Indeed, that principle sometimes invalidates state laws regulating subject matter of national importance even when Congress has been silent. . . . In either case the ouster of state laws obviously curtails or prohibits the States' prerogatives to make policy choices respecting subjects clearly of greater significance to the "State *qua* State" than the minimum wage paid to state employees. The Supremacy Clause dictates this result under "the federal system of government embodied in the Constitution." . . .

My Brethren do more than turn aside longstanding constitutional jurisprudence that emphatically rejects today's conclusion. More alarming is the startling restructuring of our federal system, and the role they create therein for the federal judiciary. This Court is simply not at liberty to erect a mirror of its own conception of desirable governmental structure. If the 1974 amendments have any "vice," . . . my Brother Stevens is surely right that it represents "merely . . . a policy issue which has been firmly resolved by the branches of government having power to decide such questions." . . . It bears repeating "that effective restraints on . . . exercise [of the commerce power] must proceed from political rather than from judicial processes." . . .

It is unacceptable that the judicial process should be thought superior to the political process in this area. Under the Constitution the Judiciary has no role to play beyond finding that Congress has not made an unreasonable legislative judgment respecting what is "commerce." My Brother Blackmun suggests that controlling judicial supervision of the relationship between the States and our National Government by use of a balancing approach diminishes the ominous implications of today's decision. Such an approach, however,

is a thinly veiled rationalization for judicial supervision of a policy judgment that our system of government reserves to Congress.

Judicial restraint in this area merely recognizes that the political branches of our Government are structured to protect the interests of the States, as well as the Nation as a whole, and that the States are fully able to protect their own interests in the premises. Congress is constituted of representatives in both the Senate and House *elected from the States*. . . . Decisions upon the extent of federal intervention under the Commerce Clause into the affairs of the States are in that sense decisions of the States themselves. Judicial redistribution of powers granted the National Government by the terms of the Constitution violates the fundamental tenet of our federalism that the extent of federal intervention into the States' affairs in the exercise of delegated powers shall be determined by the States' exercise of political power through their representatives in Congress. . . .

We are left then with a catastrophic judicial body blow at Congress' power under the Commerce Clause. Even if Congress may nevertheless accomplish its objectives—for example, by conditioning grants of federal funds upon compliance with federal minimum wage and overtime standards, cf. *Oklahoma v. CSC* [1947]—there is an ominous portent of disruption of our constitutional structure implicit in today's mischievous decision. I dissent.

Justice Stevens dissented:

The Court holds that the Federal Government may not interfere with a sovereign State's inherent right to pay a substandard wage to the janitor at the state capitol. The principle on which the holding rests is difficult to perceive.

The Federal Government may, I believe, require the State to act impartially when it hires or fires the janitor, to withhold taxes from his paycheck, to observe safety regulations when he is performing his job, to forbid him from burning too much soft coal in the capitol furnace, from dumping untreated refuse in an adjacent waterway, from overloading a state-owned garbage truck, or from driving either the truck or the Governor's limousine over 55 miles an hour. Even though these and many other activities of the capitol janitor are activities of the State *qua* State, I have no doubt that they are subject to federal regulation.

I agree that it is unwise for the Federal Government to exercise its power in the ways described in the

Court's opinion. For the proposition that regulation of the minimum price of a commodity—even labor—will increase the quantity consumed is not one that I can readily understand. That concern, however, applies with even greater force to the private sector of the economy where the exclusion of the marginally employable does the greatest harm and, in all events, merely reflects my views on a policy issue which has been firmly resolved by the branches of government having power to decide such questions. As far as the complexities of adjusting police and fire departments to this sort of federal control are concerned, I presume that appropriate tailor-made regulations would soon solve their most pressing problems. After all, the interests adversely affected by this legislation are not without political power.

My disagreement with the wisdom of this legislation may not, of course, affect my judgment with respect to its validity. On this issue there is no dissent from the proposition that the Federal Government's power over the labor market is adequate to embrace these employees. Since I am unable to identify a limitation on that federal power that would not also invalidate federal regulation of state activities that I consider unquestionably permissible, I am persuaded that this statute is valid. Accordingly, with respect and a great deal of sympathy for the views expressed by the Court, I dissent from its constitutional holding.

Mixed signals on civil rights and equal protection

The impact of President Nixon's appointees on racial desegregation was less consistent than some of the 1968 campaign analysts had predicted. In some areas the Court continued the thrust of the Warren Court years, while in others there were quite important differences with a marked deemphasis upon desegregation. *Swann* v. *Charlotte Mecklenburg Board of Education* involved *de jure* segregation and, among a number of complex issues, the question whether court-ordered busing would be continued. Chief Justice Burger wrote the majority opinion continuing the desegregation program, including busing.

SWANN v. CHARLOTTE-MECKLENBURG BOARD OF EDUCATION
402 U. S. 1 (1971)

We granted certiorari in this case to review important issues as to the duties of school authorities and the scope of powers of federal courts under this Court's mandates to eliminate racially separate public schools established and maintained by state action. . . .

This case and those argued with it arose in States having a long history of maintaining two sets of schools in a single school system deliberately operated to carry out a governmental policy to separate pupils in schools solely on the basis of race. That was what *Brown* v. *Board of Education* was all about. These cases present us with the problem of defining in more precise terms than heretofore the scope of the duty of school authorities and district courts in implementing *Brown I* and the mandate to eliminate dual systems and establish unitary systems at once. Meanwhile district courts and courts of appeals have struggled in hundreds of cases with a multitude and variety of problems under this Court's general directive. Understandably, in an area of evolving remedies, those courts had to improvise and experiment without detailed or specific guidelines. This Court, in *Brown I*, appropriately dealt with the large constitutional principles; other federal courts had to grapple with the flinty, intractable realities of day-to-day implementation of those constitutional commands. Their efforts, of necessity, embraced a process of "trial and error," and our effort to formulate guidelines must take into account their experience.

V

The central issue in this case is that of student assignment, and there are essentially four problem areas:

(1) to what extent racial balance or racial quotas may be used as an implement in a remedial order to correct a previously segregated system;

(2) whether every all-Negro and all-white school must be eliminated as an indispensable part of a remedial process of desegregation;

(3) what the limits are, if any, on the rearrangement of school districts and attendance zones, as a remedial measure; and

(4) what the limits are, if any, on the use of transportation facilities to correct state-enforced racial school segregation.

(1) RACIAL BALANCES OR RACIAL QUOTAS

The constant theme and thrust of every holding from *Brown I* to date is that state-enforced separation of races in public schools is discrimination that violates the Equal Protection Clause. The remedy commanded was to dismantle dual school systems.

We are concerned in these cases with the elimination of the discrimination inherent in the dual school systems, not with myriad factors of human existence which can cause discrimination in a multitude of ways on racial, religious, or ethnic grounds. The target of the cases from *Brown I* to the present was the dual school system. The elimination of racial discrimination in public schools is a large task and one that should not be retarded by efforts to achieve broader purposes lying beyond the jurisdiction of school authorities. One vehicle can carry only a limited amount of baggage. . . .

Our objective in dealing with the issues presented by these cases is to see that school authorities exclude no pupil of a racial minority from any school, directly or indirectly, on account of race; it does not and cannot embrace all the problems of racial prejudice, even when those problems contribute to disproportionate racial concentrations in some schools.

In this case it is urged that the District Court has imposed a racial balance requirement of 71 percent–29 percent on individual schools. . . .

If we were to read the holding of the District Court to require, as a matter of substantive constitutional right, any particular degree of racial balance or mixing, that approach would be disapproved and we would be obliged to reverse. The constitutional command to desegregate schools does not mean that every school in every community must always reflect the racial composition of the school system as a whole. . . .

. . . [T]he use made of mathematical ratios was no more than a starting point in the process of shaping a remedy, rather than an inflexible requirement. From that starting point the District Court proceeded to frame a decree that was within its discretionary powers, as an equitable remedy for the particular circumstances. As we said in *Green*, a school authority's remedial plan or a district court's remedial decree is to be judged by its effectiveness. Awareness of the racial composition of the whole school system is likely to be a useful starting point in shaping a remedy to correct past constitutional violations. In sum, the very limited use made of mathematical ratios was within the equitable remedial discretion of the District Court.

(2) ONE-RACE SCHOOLS

The record in this case reveals the familiar phenomenon that in metropolitan areas minority groups are often found concentrated in one part of the city. In some circumstances certain schools may remain all or largely of one race until new schools can be provided or neighborhood patterns change. Schools all or predominately of one race in a district of mixed population will require close scrutiny to determine that school assignments are not part of state-enforced segregation.

In light of the above, it should be clear that the existence of some small number of one-race, or virtually one-race, schools within a district is not in and of itself the mark of a system that still practices segregation by law. . . . Where the school authority's proposed plan for conversion from a dual to a unitary system contemplates the continued existence of some schools that are all or predominately of one race, they have the burden of showing that such school assignments are genuinely nondiscriminatory. The court should scrutinize such schools, and the burden upon the school authorities will be to satisfy the court that their racial composition is not the result of present or past discriminatory action on their part.

An optional majority-to-minority transfer provision has long been recognized as a useful part of every desegregation plan. Provision for optional transfer to those in the majority racial group of a particular school to other schools where they will be in the minority is an indispensable remedy for those students willing to transfer to other schools in order to lessen the impact on them of the state-imposed stigma of segregation. In order to be effective, such a transfer arrangement must grant the transferring student free transportation and space must be made available in the school to which he desires to move. . . . The court orders in this and the companion *Davis* case now provide such an option.

(3) REMEDIAL ALTERING OF ATTENDANCE ZONES

The maps submitted in these cases graphically demonstrate that one of the principal tools employed by school planners and by courts to break up the dual school system has been a frank—and sometimes drastic—gerrymandering of school districts and attendance zones. An additional step was pairing, "clustering," or "grouping" of schools with attendance assignments made deliberately to accomplish the transfer of Negro students out of formerly segregated Negro schools and transfer of white students to formerly all-Negro schools. More often than not, these zones are neither compact nor contiguous; indeed they may be on opposite ends of the city. As an interim corrective measure, this cannot be said to be beyond the broad remedial powers of a court.

Absent a constitutional violation there would be

no basis for judicially ordering assignment of students on a racial basis. All things being equal, with no history of discrimination, it might well be desirable to assign pupils to schools nearest their homes. But all things are not equal in a system that has been deliberately constructed and maintained to enforce racial segregation. . . .

No fixed or even substantially fixed guidelines can be established as to how far a court can go, but it must be recognized that there are limits. The objective is to dismantle the dual school system. "Racially neutral" assignment plans proposed by school authorities to a district court may be inadequate; such plans may fail to counteract the continuing effects of past school segregation resulting from discriminatory location of school sites or distortion of school size in order to achieve or maintain an artificial racial separation. When school authorities present a district court with a "loaded game board," affirmative action in the form of remedial altering of attendance zones is proper to achieve truly nondiscriminatory assignments. In short, an assignment plan is not acceptable simply because it appears to be neutral. . . .

We hold that the pairing and grouping of noncontiguous school zones is a permissible tool and such action is to be considered in light of the objectives sought. . . .

(4) TRANSPORTATION OF STUDENTS

The scope of permissible transportation of students as an implement of a remedial decree has never been defined by this Court and by the very nature of the problem it cannot be defined with precision. . . .

The importance of bus transportation as a normal and accepted tool of educational policy is readily discernible in this and the companion case. The Charlotte school authorities did not purport to assign students on the basis of geographically drawn zones until 1965 and then they allowed almost unlimited transfer privileges. The District Court's conclusion that assignment of children to the school nearest their home serving their grade would not produce an effective dismantling of the dual system is supported by the record.

Thus the remedial techniques used in the District Court's order were within that court's power to provide equitable relief; implementation of the decree is well within the capacity of the school authority.

The decree provided that the buses used to implement the plan would operate on direct routes. Students would be picked up at schools near their homes and transported to the schools they were to attend. The trips for elementary school pupils average about seven miles and the District Court found that they would take "not over 35 minutes at the most." This system compares favorably with the transportation plan previously operated in Charlotte under which each day 23,600 students on all grade levels were transported an average of 15 miles one way for an average trip requiring over an hour. In these circumstances, we find no basis for holding that the local school authorities may not be required to employ bus transportation as one tool of school desegregation. Desegregation plans cannot be limited to the walk-in school. . . .

At some point, these school authorities and others like them should have achieved full compliance with this Court's decision in *Brown I*. The systems would then be "unitary" in the sense required by our decisions in *Green* and *Alexander* [v. *Holmes County Board of Education* (1968)].

It does not follow that the communities served by such systems will remain demographically stable, for in a growing, mobile society, few will do so. Neither school authorities nor district courts are constitutionally required to make year-by-year adjustments of the racial composition of student bodies once the affirmative duty to desegregate has been accomplished and racial discrimination through official action is eliminated from the system. This does not mean that federal courts are without power to deal with future problems; but in the absence of a showing that either the school authorities or some other agency of the State has deliberately attempted to fix or alter demographic patterns to affect the racial composition of the schools, further intervention by a district court should not be necessary. . . . It is so ordered.

The Court's doctrinal reasoning in *Swann* to uphold busing and other methods of achieving desegregation was not a general rationale for expanding such desegregation plans to areas surrounding inner cities. In *Milliken* v. *Bradley*,[5] the Court, by a five to four margin, struck down a court-ordered busing plan for 53 suburban school districts and the Detroit city schools. Thurgood Marshall's dissent ended in a sober prophecy:

Desegregation is not and was never expected to be an easy task. Racial attitudes engrained in our nation's childhood and adolescence are not quickly thrown aside in its middle years. But just as the inconvenience of some cannot be allowed to stand in the way of rights of others, so public opposition, no matter how strident, cannot be permitted to divert this Court from the enforcement of the constitutional principles at issue in this case. Today's holding, I fear, is more a reflection of a perceived public mood that we have gone far enough in enforcing the constitutional guarantee of equal justice than it is the product of neutral principles of law. In the short run, it may seem to be the easier course to allow our great metropolitan areas to be divided up each into two cities—one white, the other black—but it is a course I predict our people will ultimately regret.[6]

The constitutional question whether racial discrimination practiced in a private club was state action forbidden by the equal protection clause was met in *Moose Lodge No. 107* v. *Irvis*. Justice Rehnquist wrote the majority opinion while Justice Douglas wrote a sharp dissent. A portion of Rehnquist's negative answer to the constitutional question is reproduced below.

MOOSE LODGE NO. 107 v. IRVIS
407 U. S. 162 (1972)

Moose Lodge is a private club in the ordinary meaning of that term. It is a local chapter of a national fraternal organization having well-defined requirements for membership. It conducts all of its activities in a building that is owned by it. It is not publicly funded. Only members and guests are permitted in any lodge of the order; one may become a guest only by invitation of a member or upon invitation of the house committee.

Appellee, while conceding the right of private clubs to choose members upon a discriminatory basis, asserts that the licensing of Moose Lodge to serve liquor by the Pennsylvania Liquor Control Board amounts to such state involvement with the club's activities as to make its discriminatory practices forbidden by the Equal Protection Clause of the Fourteenth Amendment. The relief sought and obtained by appellee in the District Court was an injunction forbidding the licensing by the liquor authority of Moose Lodge until it ceased its discriminatory practices. We conclude that Moose Lodge's refusal to serve food and beverages to a guest by reason of the fact that he was a Negro does not, under the circumstances here presented, violate the Fourteenth Amendment.

In 1883, this Court in *The Civil Rights Cases*, . . . set forth the essential dichotomy between discriminatory action by the State, which is prohibited by the Equal Protection Clause, and private conduct, "however discriminatory or wrongful," against which the clause "erects no shield," *Shelley* v. *Kraemer*, . . . That dichotomy has been subsequently reaffirmed in *Shelley* v. *Kraemer, supra*, and in *Burton* v. *Wilmington Parking Authority*. . . .

While the principle is easily stated, the question of whether particular discriminatory conduct is private, on the one hand, or amounts to "state action," on the other hand, frequently admits of no easy answer. "Only by sifting facts and weighing circumstances can the nonobvious involvement of the State in private conduct be attributed its true significance." . . .

Our cases make clear that the impetus for the forbidden discrimination need not originate with the State if it is state action that enforces privately originated discrimination. *Shelley* v. *Kraemer, supra*. The Court held in *Burton* v. *Wilmington Parking Authority, supra*, that a private restaurant owner who refused service because of a customer's race violated the Fourteenth Amendment, where the restaurant was located in a building owned by a state-created parking authority and leased from the authority. The Court, after a comprehensive review of the relationship between the lessee and the parking authority concluded that the latter had "so far insinuated itself into a position of interdependence with Eagle [the restaurant owner] that it must be recognized as a joint participant in the challenged activity, which, on that account, cannot be considered to have been so 'purely private' as to fall without the scope of the Fourteenth Amendment." . . .

The Court has never held, of course, that discrimination by an otherwise private entity would be violative of the Equal Protection Clause if the private entity receives any sort of benefit or service at all from the State, or if it is subject to state regulation in any degree whatever. Since state-furnished services include such necessities of life as electricity, water, and police and fire protection, such a holding would utterly emasculate the distinction between private as distinguished from state conduct set forth in *The*

Civil Rights Cases, supra, and adhered to in subsequent decisions. Our holdings indicate that where the impetus for the discrimination is private, the State must have "significantly involved itself with invidious discriminations," . . . in order for the discriminatory action to fall within the ambit of the constitutional prohibition.

Our prior decisions dealing with discriminatory refusal of service in public eating places are significantly different factually from the case now before us . . . dealt with the trespass prosecution of persons who "sat in" at a restaurant to protest its refusal of service to Negroes. There the Court held that although the ostensible initiative for the trespass prosecution came from the proprietor, the existence of a local ordinance requiring segregation of races in such places was tantamount to the State having "commanded a particular result," . . . With one exception, which is discussed infra, at 178-179, there is no suggestion in this record

that the Pennsylvania statutes and regulations governing the sale of liquor are intended either overtly or covertly to encourage discrimination. . . .

With the exception hereafter noted, the Pennsylvania Liquor Control Board plays absolutely no part in establishing or enforcing the membership or guest policies of the club that it licenses to serve liquor. There is no suggestion in this record that Pennsylvania law, either as written or as applied, discriminates against minority groups either in their right to apply for club licenses themselves or in their right to purchase and be served liquor in places of public accommodation. The only effect that the state licensing of Moose Lodge to serve liquor can be said to have on the right of any other Pennsylvanian to buy or be served liquor on premises other than those of Moose Lodge is that for some purposes club licenses are counted in the maximum number of licenses that may be issued in a given municipality. . . .

In 1974 the Supreme Court of California in *Serrano* v. *Priest* determined that the property tax basis for financing public school districts was fundamentally discriminatory on the basis of wealth and consequently violated the equal protection clauses of the federal and state constitutions.[7] In *San Antonio School District* v. *Rodriguez*, a majority of the Supreme Court of the United States, in an opinion by Justice Lewis Powell, dealt with a similar issue in a different manner, evoking several strong dissents.

SAN ANTONIO SCHOOL DISTRICT v. RODRIGUEZ
411 U. S. 1 (1973)

Justice Powell delivered the opinion of the Court:

This suit attacking the Texas system of financing public education was initiated by Mexican-American parents whose children attend the elementary and the secondary schools in the Edgewood Independent School District, an urban school district in San Antonio, Texas. They brought a class action on behalf of school children throughout the State who are members of minority groups or who are poor and reside in school districts having a low property tax base. Named as defendants were the State Board of Education, the Commissioner of Education, the State Attorney General, and the Bexar County (San Antonio) Board of Trustees. The complaint was filed in the summer of 1968 and a three-judge court was impaneled in January 1969. In December 1971 the panel rendered its judgment in a per curiam opinion holding the

Texas school finance system unconstitutional under the Equal Protection Clause of the Fourteenth Amendment. The State appealed, and we noted probable jurisdiction to consider the far-reaching constitutional questions presented. For the reasons stated in this opinion we reverse the decision of the District Court.

I

. . . [S]ubstantial interdistrict disparities in school expenditures found by the District Court to prevail in San Antonio and in varying degrees throughout the State still exist. And it was these disparities, largely attributable to differences in the amounts of money collected through local property taxation, that led the District Court to conclude that Texas' dual system of public school financing violated the Equal Protection Clause. The District Court held that the Texas system discriminates on the basis of wealth in the manner in which education is provided for its people. . . . Finding that wealth is a "suspect" classification and that education is a "fundamental" interest, the District Court held that the Texas system could be sustained only if the State could show that it was premised upon some compelling state interest. . . . On this issue the court concluded that "[n]ot only are defendants unable to demonstrate compelling state interests . . . they fail even to establish a reasonable basis for these classifications." . . .

This, then, establishes the framework for our analysis. We must decide, first, whether the Texas system of financing public education operates to the disadvantage of some suspect class or impinges upon a fundamental right explicitly or implicitly protected by the Constitution, thereby requiring state judicial scrutiny. If so, the judgment of the District Court should be affirmed. If not, the Texas scheme must still be examined to determine whether it rationally furthers some legitimate, articulated state purpose and therefore does not constitute an invidious discrimination in violation of the Equal Protection Clause of the Fourteenth Amendment.

II

The wealth discrimination discovered by the District Court in this case, and by several other courts that have recently struck down school-financing laws in other States, is quite unlike any of the forms of wealth discrimination heretofore reviewed by this Court. Rather than focusing on the unique features of the alleged discrimination, the courts in these cases have virtually assumed their findings of a suspect classification through a simplistic process of analysis: since, under the traditional systems of financing public schools, some poorer people receive less expensive educations than other more affluent people, these systems discriminate on the basis of wealth. This approach largely ignores the hard threshold questions, including whether it makes a difference for purposes of consideration under the Constitution that the class of disadvantaged "poor" cannot be identified or defined in customary equal protection terms, and whether the relative—rather than absolute—nature of the asserted deprivation is of significant consequence. Before a State's laws and the justifications for the classifications they create are subjected to strict judicial scrutiny, we think these threshold considerations must be analyzed more closely than they were in the court below.

The case comes to us with no definitive description of the classifying facts or delineation of the disfavored class. Examination of the District Court's opinion and of appellees' complaint, briefs, and contentions at oral argument suggests, however, at least three ways in which the discrimination claimed here might be described. The Texas system of school financing might be regarded as discriminating (1) against "poor" persons whose incomes fall below some identifiable level of poverty or who might be characterized as functionally "indigent," or (2) against those who are relatively poorer than others, or (3) against all those who, irrespective of their personal incomes, happen to reside in relatively poorer school districts. Our task must be to ascertain whether, in fact, the Texas system has been shown to discriminate on any of these possible bases and, if so, whether the resulting classification may be regarded as suspect.

The precedents of this Court provide the proper starting point. The individuals, or groups of individuals, who constituted the class discriminated against in our prior cases shared two distinguishing characteristics: because of their impecunity they were completely unable to pay for some desired benefit, and as a consequence, they sustained an absolute deprivation of a meaningful opportunity to enjoy that benefit. In *Griffin* v. *Illinois* [1956] . . . and its progeny, the Court invalidated state laws that prevented an indigent criminal defendant from acquiring a transcript, or an adequate substitute for a transcript, for use at several stages of the trial and appeal process. The payment requirements in each case were found to occasion *de facto* discrimination against those who, because of their indigency, were totally unable to pay for transcripts. . . .

Likewise, in *Douglas* v. *California* [1963] . . . , a decision establishing an indigent defendant's right to court-appointed counsel on direct appeal, the Court dealt only with defendants who could not pay for counsel from their own resources and who had no other way of gaining representation. . . .

Williams v. *Illinois* [1970] . . . struck down criminal penalties that subjected indigents to incarceration simply because of their inability to pay a fine. Again, the disadvantaged class was composed only of persons who were totally unable to pay the demanded sum. . . .

Finally, in *Bullock* v. *Carter* [1972] . . . the Court invalidated the Texas filing-fee requirement for primary elections. Both of the relevant classifying facts found in the previous cases were present there. The size of the fee, often running into the thousands of dollars and, in at least one case, as high as $8,900, effectively barred all potential candidates who were unable to pay the required fee. As the system provided "no reasonable alternative means of access to the ballot" inability to pay occasioned an absolute denial of a position on the primary ballot.

Only appellees' first possible basis for describing the class disadvantaged by the Texas school-financing system—discrimination against a class of definably "poor" persons—might arguably meet the criteria established in these prior cases. Even a cursory examination, however, demonstrates that neither of the two distinguishing characteristics of wealth classifications can be found here. First, in support of their charge that the system discriminates against the "poor," appellees have made no effort to demonstrate that it operates to the peculiar disadvantage of any class fairly definable as indigent, or as composed of persons whose incomes are beneath any designated poverty level. Indeed, there is reason to believe that the poorest families are not necessarily clustered in the poorest property districts. A recent and exhaustive study of school districts in Connecticut concluded that "[i]t is clearly incorrect . . . to contend that the 'poor' live in 'poor' districts. . . . Thus, the major factual assumption of *Serrano*—that the educational financing system discriminates against the 'poor'—is simply false in Connecticut." Defining "poor" families as those below the Bureau of the Census "poverty level," the Connecticut study found, not surprisingly, that the poor were clustered around commercial and industrial areas—those same areas that provide the most attractive sources of property tax income for school districts. Whether a similar pattern would be discovered in Texas is not known, but there is no basis on the record in this case for assuming that the poorest people—defined by reference to any level of absolute impecunity—are concentrated in the poorest districts.

Second, neither appellees nor the District Court addressed the fact that, unlike each of the foregoing cases, lack of personal resources has not occasioned an absolute deprivation of the desired benefit. The argument here is not that the children in districts having relatively low assessable property values are receiving no public education; rather, it is that they are receiving a poorer quality education than that available to children in districts having more assessable wealth. Apart from the unsettled and disputed question whether the quality of education may be determined by the amount of money expended for it, a sufficient answer to appellees' argument is that, at least where wealth is involved, the Equal Protection Clause does not require absolute equality of precisely equal advantages. . . . The State repeatedly asserted in its briefs in this Court that . . . it now assures "every child in every school district an adequate education." No proof was offered at trial persuasively discrediting or refuting the State's assertion.

For these two reasons—the absence of any evidence that the financing system discriminates against any definable category of "poor" people or that it results in the absolute deprivation of education—the disadvantaged class is not susceptible of identification in traditional terms. . . .

This brings us, then, to the third way in which the classification scheme might be defined—*district* wealth discrimination. Since the only correlation indicated by the evidence is between district property wealth and expenditures, it may be argued that discrimination might be found without regard to the individual income characteristics of district residents. Assuming a perfect correlation between district property wealth and expenditures from top to bottom, the disadvantaged class might be viewed as encompassing every child in every district except the district that has the most assessable wealth and spends the most on education. . . .

However described, it is clear that appellees' suit asks this Court to extend its most exacting scrutiny to review a system that allegedly discriminates against a large, diverse, and amorphous class, unified only by the common factor of residence in districts that happen to have less taxable wealth than other districts. The system of alleged discrimination and the class it defines have none of the traditional indicia of suspectness: the class is not saddled with such disabilities, or subjected to such a history of purposeful unequal treatment, or relegated to such a position of political powerlessness as to command extraordinary protection from the majoritarian political process.

We thus conclude that the Texas system does not operate to the peculiar disadvantage of any suspect class. But in recognition of the fact that this Court has never heretofore held that wealth discrimination alone provides an adequate basis for invoking strict scrutiny, appellees have not relied solely on this contention. They also assert that the State's system impermissibly interferes with the exercise of a "fundamental" right and that accordingly the prior decisions of this Court require the application of the strict standard of judicial review. . . . It is this question—whether education is a fundamental right, in the sense that it is among the rights and liberties protected by the Constitution—which has so consumed the attention of courts and commentators in recent years. . . .

Education, of course, is not among the rights afforded explicit protection under our Federal Constitution. Nor do we find any basis for saying it is implicitly so protected. As we have said, the undisputed importance of education will not alone cause this Court to depart from the usual standard for reviewing a State's social and economic legislation. It is appellees' contention, however, that education is distinguishable from other services and benefits provided by the State because it bears a peculiarly close relationship to other rights and liberties accorded protection under the Constitution. Specifically, they insist that education is itself a fundamental personal right because it is essential to the effective exercise of First Amendment freedoms and to intelligent utilization of the right to vote. . . .

We need not dispute any of these propositions. The Court has long afforded zealous protection against unjustifiable governmental interference with the individual's rights to speak and to vote. Yet we have never presumed to possess either the ability or the authority to guarantee to the citizenry the most *effective* speech or the most *informed* electoral choice. . . .

Even if it were conceded that some identifiable quantum of education is a constitutionally protected prerequisite to the meaningful exercise of either right, we have no indication that the present levels of educational expenditures in Texas provide an education that falls short. . . .

We have carefully considered each of the arguments supportive of the District Court's finding that education is a fundamental right or liberty and have found those arguments unpersuasive. In one further respect we find this a particularly inappropriate case in which to subject state action to strict judicial scrutiny. The present case, in another basic sense, is significantly different from any of the cases in which the Court has applied strict scrutiny to state or federal legislation touching upon constitutionally protected rights. Each of our prior cases involved legislation which "deprived," "infringed," or "interfered" with the free exercise of some such fundamental personal right or liberty. . . . A critical distinction between those cases and the one now before us lies in what Texas is endeavoring to do with respect to education. . . . Every step leading to the establishment of the system Texas utilizes today—including the decisions permitting localities to tax and expend locally, and creating and continuously expanding state aid—was implemented in an effort to *extend* public education and to improve its quality. Of course, every reform that benefits some more than others may be criticized for what it fails to accomplish. But we think it plain that, in substance, the thrust of the Texas system is affirmative and reformatory and, therefore, should be scrutinized under judicial principles sensitive to the nature of the State's efforts and to the rights reserved to the States under the Constitution.

It should be clear, for the reasons stated above and in accord with the prior decisions of this Court, that

this is not a case in which the challenged state action must be subjected to the searching judicial scrutiny reserved for laws that create suspect classifications or impinge upon constitutionally protected rights. . . .

. . . In sum, to the extent that the Texas system of school financing results in unequal expenditures between children who happen to reside in different districts, we cannot say that such disparities are the product of a system that is so irrational as to be invidiously discriminatory. . . .

. . . One also must remember that the system here challenged is not peculiar to Texas or to any other State. In its essential characteristics, the Texas plan for financing public education reflects what many educators for a half century have thought was an enlightened approach to a problem for which there is no perfect solution. We are unwilling to assume for ourselves a level of wisdom superior to that of legislators, scholars, and educational authorities in 50 States, especially where the alternatives proposed are only recently conceived and nowhere yet tested. The constitutional standard under the Equal Protection Clause is whether the challenged state action rationally furthers a legitimate state purpose or interest. . . . We hold that the Texas plan abundantly satisfies this standard. . . .

Reversed.

[Justice Stewart, concurring, and Justice Brennan, dissenting, omitted.]

Justice White, with whom Justice Douglas and Justice Brennan join, dissented:

The Texas public schools are financed through a combination of state funding, local property tax revenue, and some federal funds. Concededly, the system yields wide disparity in per-pupil revenue among the various districts. In a typical year, for example, the Alamo Heights district had total revenues of $594 per pupil, while the Edgewood district had only $356 per pupil. The majority and the State concede, as they must, the existence of major disparities in spendable funds. But the State contends that the disparities do not invidiously discriminate against children and families in districts such as Edgewood, because the Texas scheme is designed "to provide an adequate education for all, with local autonomy to go beyond that as individual school districts desire and are able. . . . It leaves to the people of each district the choice whether to go beyond the minimum and, if so, by how much." The majority advances this rationalization: "While assuring a basic education for every child in the State, it permits and encourages a large measure of participation in and control of each district's schools at the local level."

I cannot disagree with the proposition that local control and local decision making play an important part in our democratic system of government. . . .

The difficulty with the Texas system, however, is that it provides a meaningful option to Alamo Heights and like school districts but almost none to Edgewood and those other districts with a low per-pupil real estate tax base. In these latter districts, no matter how desirous parents are of supporting their schools with greater revenues, it is impossible to do so through the use of the real estate property tax. In these districts, the Texas system utterly fails to extend a realistic choice to parents because the property tax, which is the only revenue-raising mechanism extended to school districts, is practically and legally unavailable. That this is the situation may be readily demonstrated. . . .

In order to equal the highest yield in any other Bexar County district, Alamo Heights would be required to tax at the rate of 68¢ per $100 of assessed valuation. Edgewood would be required to tax at the prohibitive rate of $5.76 per $100. But state law places a $1.50 per $100 ceiling on the maintenance tax rate, a limit that would surely be reached long before Edgewood attained an equal yield. Edgewood is thus precluded in law, as well as in fact, from achieving a yield even close to that of some other districts.

The Equal Protection Clause permits discriminations between classes but requires that the classification bear some rational relationship to a permissible object sought to be attained by the statute. It is not enough that the Texas system before us seeks to achieve the valid, rational purpose of maximizing local initiative; the means chosen by the State must also be rationally related to the end sought to be achieved. . . .

Neither Texas nor the majority heeds this rule. If the State aims at maximizing local initiative and local choice, by permitting school districts to resort to the real property tax if they choose to do so, it utterly fails in achieving its purpose in districts with property tax bases so low that there is little if any opportunity for interested parents, rich or poor, to augment school district revenues. Requiring the State to establish only that unequal treatment is in furtherance of a permissible goal, without also requiring the State to show that the means chosen to effectuate that goal are rationally related to its achievement, makes equal protection analysis no more than an empty gesture. In my view, the parents and children in Edgewood, and in like districts, suffer from an invidious discrimination violative of the Equal Protection Clause. . . .

There is no difficulty in identifying the class that is subject to the alleged discrimination and that is entitled to the benefits of the Equal Protection Clause. I need go no farther than the parents and children in the Edgewood district, who are plaintiffs here and who assert that they are entitled to the same choice as Alamo Heights to augment local expenditures for schools but are denied that choice by state law. This group constitutes a class sufficiently definite to invoke the protection of the Constitution. They are as entitled to the protection of the Equal Protection Clause as were the voters in allegedly underrepresented counties in the reapportionment cases. . . . And in *Bullock* v. *Carter* [1972] . . . where a challenge to the Texas candidate filing fee on equal protection grounds was upheld, we noted that the victims of alleged discrimination wrought by the filing fee "cannot be described by reference to discrete and precisely defined segments of the community as is typical of inequities challenged under the Equal Protection Clause," but concluded that "we would ignore reality were we not to recognize that this system falls with unequal weight on voters, as well as candidates, according to their economic status." Similarly, in the present case we would blink reality to ignore the fact that school districts, and students in the end, are differentially affected by the Texas school-financing scheme with respect to their capability to supplement the Minimum Foundation School Program. At the very least, the law discriminates against those children and their parents who live in districts where the per-pupil tax base is sufficiently low to make impossible the provision of comparable school revenues by resort to the real property tax which is the only device the State extends for this purpose.

[Justice Marshall, with whom Justice Douglas concurred, dissented.]

As racial desegregation was undertaken in the North as well as the South in the decades since *Brown* v. *Board of Education*, rather complex issues involving charges of "reverse discrimination" arose. The *Regents of the University of California* v. *Bakke* involved a major reverse discrimination constitutional issue. The California Supreme Court had held the medical school admissions program at University of California, Davis, in violation of the equal protection of the laws clause of the Fourteenth Amendment. In 1973 the medical school, which began in 1968, had admitted 16 minority students by a special admissions procedure that distinguished minorities from all other students. The 84 regular students admitted had median science grade point averages of 3.51, median quantitative MCAT scores at the 76th percentile, and median science MCAT scores at the 83rd percentile. The minority admittees had median science grade point scores of 2.62, median quantitative MCAT scores at the 24th percentile, and median science MCAT scores at the 35th percentile. Allan Bakke, a white 36-year-old engineer who had scores of 3.44, 94th, and 97th percentiles, respectively, was denied admission both in 1973 and in 1974. He filed suit in the California Superior Court, which rejected his request for an order of admission. He then appealed to the California Supreme Court, which held the admissions program unconstitutional.[8] In *Regents of the University of California* v. *Bakke*, the Supreme Court of the United States upheld the California Supreme Court decision in part and rejected it in part. Justice Powell wrote the majority opinion. Justices Brennan, White, and Marshall concurred in part and dissented in part.

REGENTS OF THE UNIVERSITY OF CALIFORNIA v. BAKKE
438 U. S. 265 (1978)

Justice Powell delivered the opinion of the Court:

For the reasons stated in the following opinion, I believe that so much of the judgment of the California court as holds petitioner's special admissions program unlawful and directs that respondent be admitted to the Medical School must be affirmed. For the reasons expressed in a separate opinion, my Brothers The Chief Justice, Mr. Justice Stewart, Mr. Justice Rehnquist, and Mr. Justice Stevens concur in this judgment.

I also conclude for the reasons stated in the following opinion that the portion of the court's judgment enjoining petitioner from according any consideration to race in its admissions process must be reversed. For reasons expressed in separate opinions, my Brothers Mr. Justice Brennan, Mr. Justice White, Mr. Justice Marshall, and Mr. Justice Blackmun concur in this judgment.

Affirmed in part and reversed in part. . . .

Petitioner does not deny that decisions based on race or ethnic origin by faculties and administrations of state universities are reviewable under the Fourteenth Amendment. . . . For his part, respondent does not argue that all racial or ethnic classifications are *per se* invalid. . . . The parties do disagree as to the level of judicial scrutiny to be applied to the special admissions program. Petitioner argues that the court below erred in applying strict scrutiny, as this inexact term has been applied in our cases. . . .

En route to this crucial battle over the scope of judicial review, the parties fight a sharp preliminary action over the proper characterization of the special admissions program. Petitioner prefers to view it as establishing a "goal" of minority representation in the Medical School. Respondent, echoing the courts below, labels it a racial quota.

This semantic distinction is beside the point: The special admissions program is undeniably a classification based on race and ethnic background. To the extent that there existed a pool of at least minimally qualified minority applicants to fill the 16 special admissions seats, white applicants could compete only for 84 seats in the entering class, rather than the 100 open to minority applicants. Whether this limitation is described as a quota or a goal, it is a line drawn on the basis of race and ethnic status.

The guarantees of the Fourteenth Amendment extend to all persons. Its language is explicit: "No State shall . . . deny to any person within its jurisdiction the equal protection of the laws." It is settled beyond question that the "rights created by the first section of the Fourteenth Amendment are, by its terms, guaranteed to the individual. The rights established are personal rights." . . . The guarantee of equal protection cannot mean one thing when applied to one individual and something else when applied to a person of another color. If both are not accorded the same protection, then it is not equal.

Nevertheless, petitioner argues that the court below erred in applying strict scrutiny to the special admissions program because white males, such as respondent, are not a "discrete and insular minority" requiring extraordinary protection from the majoritarian political process. . . . This rationale, however, has never been invoked in our decisions as a prerequisite to subjecting racial or ethnic distinctions to strict scrutiny. Nor has this Court held that discreteness and insularity constitute necessary preconditions to a holding that a particular classification is invidious. . . . These characteristics may be relevant in deciding whether or not to add new types of classifications to the list of "suspect" categories or whether a particular classification survives close examination. . . . Racial and ethnic classifications, however, are subject to stringent examination without regard to these additional characteristics. We declared as much in the first cases explicitly to recognize racial distinctions as suspect:

Distinctions between citizens solely because of their ancestry are by their very nature odious to a free people whose institutions are founded upon the doctrine of equality. . . .

[A]ll legal restrictions which curtail the civil rights of a single racial group are immediately suspect. That is not to say that all such restrictions are unconstitutional. It is to say that courts must subject them to the most rigid scrutiny. . . .

The Court has never questioned the validity of those pronouncements. Racial and ethnic distinctions of any sort are inherently suspect and thus call for the most exacting judicial examination. . . .

Petitioner urges us to adopt for the first time a more restrictive view of the Equal Protection Clause and hold that discrimination against members of the white "majority" cannot be suspect if its purpose can be characterized as "benign." The clock of our liberties, however, cannot be turned back to 1868. . . . It is far too late to argue that the guarantee of equal protection to *all* persons permits the recognition of special wards entitled to a degree of protection greater than that accorded others. "The Fourteenth Amendment is not directed solely against discrimination due to a 'two-class theory'—that is, based upon differences between 'white' and Negro." . . .

Once the artificial line of a "two-class theory" of the Fourteenth Amendment is put aside, the difficulties entailed in varying the level of judicial review according to a perceived "preferred" status of a particular racial or ethnic minority are intractable. The concepts of "majority" and "minority" necessarily reflect temporary arrangements and political judgments. As observed above, the white "majority" itself is composed of various minority groups, most of which can lay claim to a history of prior discrimination at the hands of the State and private individuals. Not all of these groups can receive preferential treatment and corresponding judicial tolerance of distinctions drawn in terms of race and nationality, for then the only "majority" left would be a new minority of white Anglo-Saxon Protestants. There is no principled basis for deciding which groups would merit "heightened judicial solicitude" and which would not. Courts would be asked to evaluate the extent of the prejudice and consequent harm suffered by various minority groups. Those whose societal injury is thought to exceed some arbitrary level of tolerability then would be entitled to preferential classifications at the expense of individuals belonging to other groups. Those classifications would be free from exacting judicial scrutiny. As these preferences began to have their desired effect, and the consequences of past discrimination were undone, new judicial rankings would be necessary. The kind of variable sociological and political analysis necessary to produce such rankings simply does not lie within the judicial competence—even if they otherwise were politically feasible and socially desirable.

Moreover, there are serious problems of justice connected with the idea of preference itself. First, it may not always be clear that a so-called preference is in fact benign. . . . Second, preferential programs may only reinforce common stereotypes holding that certain groups are unable to achieve success without special protection based on a factor having no relationship to individual worth. . . . Third, there is a measure of inequity in forcing innocent persons in respondent's position to bear the burdens of redressing grievances not of their making.

By hitching the meaning of the Equal Protection Clause to these transitory considerations, we would be holding, as a constitutional principle, that judicial scrutiny of classifications touching on racial and ethnic background may vary with the ebb and flow of political forces. Disparate constitutional tolerance of such classifications well may serve to exacerbate racial and ethnic antagonisms rather than alleviate them. . . . Also, the mutability of a constitutional principle, based upon shifting political and social judgments, undermines the chances for consistent application of the Constitution from one generation to the next, a critical feature of its coherent interpretation. . . .

If it is the individual who is entitled to judicial protection against classifications based upon his racial or ethnic background because such distinctions impinge upon personal rights, rather than the individual only because of his membership in a particular group, then constitutional standards may be applied consistently. Political judgments regarding the necessity for the particular classification may be weighed in the constitutional balance, . . . but the standard of justification will remain constant. This is as it should be, since those political judgments are the product of rough compromise struck by contending groups within the democratic process. When they touch upon an individual's race or ethnic background, he is entitled to a judicial determination that the burden he is asked to bear on that basis is precisely tailored to serve a compelling governmental interest. The Constitution guarantees that right to every person regardless of his background. . . .

Petitioner contends that on several occasions this Court has approved preferential classifications without applying the most exacting scrutiny. Most of the cases upon which petitioner relies are drawn from three areas: school desegregation, employment discrimination, and sex discrimination. Each of the cases cited presented a situation materially different from the facts of this case.

The school desegregation cases are inapposite. Each involved remedies for clearly determined constitutional violations. . . .

If petitioner's purpose is to assure within its student body some specified percentage of a particular group merely because of its race or ethnic origin, such a preferential purpose must be rejected not as insubstantial but as facially invalid. Preferring members of any one group for no reason other than race or ethnic origin is discrimination for its own sake. This the Constitution forbids. . . .

The State certainly has a legitimate and substantial interest in ameliorating, or eliminating where feasible, the disabling effects of identified discrimination. The line of school desegregation cases, commencing with *Brown*, attests to the importance of this state goal and the commitment of the judiciary to affirm all lawful means toward its attainment. In the school cases, the States were required by court order to redress the wrongs worked by specific instances of racial discrimination. That goal was far more focused than the remedying of the effects of "societal discrimination," an amorphous concept of injury that may be ageless in its reach into the past.

We have never approved a classification that aids persons perceived as members of relatively victimized groups at the expense of other innocent individuals in the absence of judicial, legislative, or administrative findings of constitutional or statutory violations. . . . After such findings have been made, the governmental interest in preferring members of the injured groups at the expense of others is substantial, since the legal rights of the victims must be vindicated. In such a case, the extent of the injury and the consequent remedy will have been judicially, legislatively, or administra-

tively defined. Also, the remedial action usually remains subject to continuing oversight to assure that it will work the least harm possible to other innocent persons competing for the benefit. Without such findings of constitutional or statutory violations, it cannot be said that the government has any greater interest in helping one individual than in refraining from harming another. Thus, the government has no compelling justification for inflicting such harm.

Petitioner does not purport to have made, and is in no position to make, such findings. Its broad mission is education, not the formulation of any legislative policy or the adjudication of particular claims of illegality. . .

Hence, the purpose of helping certain groups whom the faculty of the Davis Medical School perceived as victims of "societal discrimination" does not justify a classification that imposes disadvantages upon persons like respondent, who bear no responsibility for whatever harm the beneficiaries of the special admissions program are thought to have suffered. To hold otherwise would be to convert a remedy heretofore reserved for violations of legal rights into a privilege that all institutions throughout the Nation could grant at their pleasure to whatever groups are perceived as victims of societal discrimination. That is a step we have never approved. . . .

Petitioner identifies, as another purpose of its program, improving the delivery of health-care services to communities currently underserved. It may be assumed that in some situations a State's interest in facilitating the health care of its citizens is sufficiently compelling to support the use of a suspect classification. But there is virtually no evidence in the record indicating that petitioner's special admissions program is either needed or geared to promote that goal. The court below addressed this failure of proof:

The University concedes it cannot assure that minority doctors who entered under the program, all of whom expressed an 'interest' in practicing in a disadvantaged community, will actually do so. It may be correct to assume that some of them will carry out this intention, and that it is more likely they will practice in minority communities than the average white doctor. . . . Nevertheless, there are more precise and reliable ways to identify applicants who are genuinely interested in the medical problems of minorities than by race. An applicant of whatever race who has demonstrated his concern for disadvantaged minorities in the past and who declares that practice in such a community is his primary professional goal would be more likely to contribute to alleviation of the medical shortage than one who is chosen entirely on the basis of race and disadvantage. In short, there is no empirical data to demonstrate that any one race is more selflessly socially oriented or by contrast that another is more selfishly acquisitive. . . .

Petitioner simply has not carried its burden of demonstrating that it must prefer members of particular ethnic groups over all other individuals in order to promote better health-care delivery to deprived citizens. Indeed, petitioner has not shown that its preferential classification is likely to have any significant effect on the problem.

The fourth goal asserted by petitioner is the attainment of a diverse student body. This clearly is a constitutionally permissible goal for an institution of higher education. Academic freedom, though not a specifically enumerated constitutional right, long has been viewed as a special concern of the First Amendment. . . . The atmosphere of "speculation, experiment and creation"—so essential to the quality of higher education—is widely believed to be promoted by a diverse student body. As the Court noted in *Keyishian* . . . , it is not too much to say that the "nation's future depends upon leaders trained through wide exposure" to the ideas and mores of students as diverse as this Nation of many peoples.

Thus, in arguing that its universities must be accorded the right to select those students who will contribute the most to the "robust exchange of ideas," petitioner invokes a countervailing constitutional interest, that of the First Amendment. In this light, petitioner must be viewed as seeking to achieve a goal that is of paramount importance in the fulfillment of its mission.

It may be argued that there is greater force to these views at the undergraduate level than in a medical school where the training is centered primarily on professional competency. But even at the graduate level, our tradition and experience lend support to the view that the contribution of diversity is substantial. . . . Physicians serve a heterogeneous population. An otherwise qualified medical student with a particular background—whether it be ethnic, geographic, culturally advantaged or disadvantaged—may bring to a professional school of medicine experiences, outlooks, and ideas that enrich the training of its student body and better equip its graduates to render with understanding their vital service to humanity. . . .

. . . As the interest of diversity is compelling in the context of a university's admissions program, the question remains whether the program's racial classification is necessary to promote this interest. . . .

V

It may be assumed that the reservation of a specified number of seats in each class for individuals from the preferred ethnic groups would contribute to the attainment of considerable ethnic diversity in the student body. But petitioner's argument that this is the only effective means of serving the interest of diversity is seriously flawed. In a most fundamental sense the argument misconceives the nature of the state interest that would justify consideration of race or ethnic background. It is not an interest in simple ethnic diversity, in which a specified percentage of the student body is in effect guaranteed to be members of selected ethnic groups, with the remaining percentage an undifferentiated aggregation of students. The diversity that furthers a compelling state interest encompasses a far broader array of qualifications and characteristics of which racial or ethnic origin is but a single though important element. Petitioner's special admissions program, focused *solely* on ethnic diversity, would hinder rather than further attainment of genuine diversity.

Nor would the state interest in genuine diversity be served by expanding petitioner's two-track system into a multitrack program with a prescribed number of seats set aside for each identifiable category of applicants. Indeed, it is inconceivable that a university would thus pursue the logic of petitioner's two-track program to the illogical end of insulating each category of applicants with certain desired qualifications from competition with all other applicants.

The experience of other university admissions programs, which take race into account in achieving the educational diversity valued by the First Amendment, demonstrates that the assignment of a fixed number of places to a minority group is not a necessary means toward that end. An illuminating example is found in the Harvard College program:

In recent years Harvard College has expanded the concept of diversity to include students from disadvantaged economic, racial and ethnic groups. Harvard College now recruits not only Californians or Louisianans but also blacks and Chicanos and other minority students. . . .

In practice, this new definition of diversity has meant that race has been a factor in some admission decisions. When the Committee on Admissions reviews the large middle group of applicants who are 'admissible' and deemed capable of doing good work in their courses, the race of an applicant may tip the balance in his favor just as geographic origin or a life spent on a farm may tip the balance in other candidates' cases. A farm boy from Idaho can bring something to Harvard College that a Bostonian cannot offer. Similarly, a black student can usually bring something that a white person cannot offer. . . .

In Harvard college admissions the Committee has not set target-quotas for the number of blacks, or of musicians, football players, physicists, or Californians to be admitted in a given year. . . . But that awareness [of the necessity of including more than a token number of black students] does not mean that the Committee sets a minimum number of blacks or of people from west of the Mississippi who are to be admitted. It means only that in choosing among thousands of applicants who are not only 'admissible' academically but have other strong qualities, the Committee, with a number of criteria in mind, pays some attention to distribution among many types and categories of students. . . .

In such an admissions program, race or ethnic background may be deemed a "plus" in a particular applicant's file, yet it does not insulate the individual from comparison with all other candidates for the available seats. The file of a particular black applicant may be examined for his potential contribution to diversity without the factor of race being decisive when compared, for example, with that of an applicant identified as an Italian-American if the latter is thought to exhibit qualities more likely to promote beneficial educational pluralism. Such qualities could include exceptional personal talents, unique work or service experience, leadership potential, maturity, demonstrated compassion, a history of overcoming disadvantage, ability to communicate with the poor, or other qualifications deemed important. In short, an admissions program operated in this way is flexible enough to consider all pertinent elements of diversity in light of the particular qualifications of each applicant, and to place them on the same footing for consideration, although not necessarily according them the same weight. Indeed, the weight attributed to a particular quality may vary from year to year depending upon the "mix" both of the student body and the applicants for the incoming class.

This kind of program treats each applicant as an individual in the admissions process. The applicant who loses out on the last available seat to another candidate receiving a "plus" on the basis of ethnic background will not have been foreclosed from all consideration for that seat simply because he was not the right color or had the wrong surname. It would mean only that his combined qualifications, which may have included similar nonobjective factors, did not outweigh those of the other applicant. His qualifications would have been weighed fairly and competitively, and he would have no basis to complain of unequal treatment under the Fourteenth Amendment.

It has been suggested that an admissions program which considers race only as one factor is simply a subtle and more sophisticated—but no less effective—means of according racial preference than the Davis program. A facial intent to discriminate, however, is evident in petitioner's preference program and not denied in this case. No such facial infirmity exists in an admissions program where race or ethnic background is simply one element—to be weighed fairly against

other elements—in the selection process. "A boundary line," as Mr. Justice Frankfurter remarked in another connection, "is none the worse for being narrow." . . . And a court would not assume that a university, professing to employ a facially nondiscriminatory admissions policy, would operate it as a cover for the functional equivalent of a quota system. In short, good faith would be presumed in the absence of a showing to the contrary in the manner permitted by our cases. . . .

In summary, it is evident that the Davis special admissions program involves the use of an explicit racial classification never before countenanced by this Court. It tells applicants who are not Negro, Asian, or Chicano that they are totally excluded from a specific percentage of the seats in an entering class. No matter how strong their qualifications, quantitative and extracurricular, including their own potential for contribution to educational diversity, they are never afforded the chance to compete with applicants from the preferred groups for the special admissions seats. At the same time, the preferred applicants have the opportunity to compete for every seat in the class.

The fatal flaw in petitioner's preferential program is its disregard of individual rights as guaranteed by the Fourteenth Amendment. . . . Such rights are not absolute. But when a State's distribution of benefits or imposition of burdens hinges on ancestry or the color of a person's skin or ancestry, that individual is entitled to a demonstration that the challenged classification is necessary to promote a substantial state interest. Petitioner has failed to carry this burden. For this reason, that portion of the California court's judgment holding petitioner's special admissions program invalid under the Fourteenth Amendment must be affirmed.

By enjoining petitioner from ever considering the race of any applicant, however, the courts below failed to recognize that the State has a substantial interest that legitimately may be served by a properly devised admissions program involving the competitive consideration of race and ethnic origin. For this reason, so much of the California court's judgment as enjoins petitioner from any consideration of the race of any applicant must be reversed.

Opinion of Justice Brennan, Justice White,
Justice Marshall, and Justice Blackmun, concurring
in the judgment in part and dissenting in part:

Davis' articulated purpose of remedying the effects of past societal discrimination is, under our cases, sufficiently important to justify the use of race-conscious admissions programs where there is a sound basis for concluding that minority underrepresentation is substantial and chronic, and that the handicap of past discrimination is impeding access of minorities to the Medical School. . . .

Finally, Davis' special admissions program cannot be said to violate the Constitution simply because it has set aside a predetermined number of places for qualified minority applicants rather than using minority status as a positive factor to be considered in evaluating the applications of disadvantaged minority applicants. For purposes of constitutional adjudication, there is no difference between the two approaches. In any admissions program which accords special consideration to disadvantaged racial minorities, a determination of the degree of preference to be given is unavoidable, and any given preference that results in the exclusion of a white candidate is no more or less constitutionally acceptable than a program such as that at Davis. . . .

The "Harvard" program, as those employing it readily concede, openly and successfully employs a racial criterion for the purpose of ensuring that some of the scarce places in institutions of higher education are allocated to disadvantaged minority students. That the Harvard approach does not also make public the extent of the preference and the precise workings of the system while the Davis program employs a specific, openly stated number, does not condemn the latter plan for purposes of the Fourteenth Amendment adjudication. It may be that the Harvard plan is more acceptable to the public than is the Davis "quota." If it is, any State, including California, is free to adopt it in preference to a less acceptable alternative, just as it is generally free, as far as the Constitution is concerned, to abjure granting any racial preferences in its admissions program. But there is no basis for preferring a particular preference program simply because in achieving the same goals that the Davis Medical School is pursuing, it proceeds in a manner that is not immediately apparent to the public.

Accordingly, we would reverse the judgment of the Supreme Court of California holding the Medical School's special admissions program unconstitutional and directing respondent's admission, as well as that portion of the judgment enjoining the Medical School from according any consideration to race in the admissions process.

Justice Marshall:

II

The position of the Negro today in America is the tragic but inevitable consequence of centuries of un-

equal treatment. Measured by any bench mark of comfort or achievement, meaningful equality remains a distant dream for the Negro.

A Negro child today has a life expectancy which is shorter by more than five years than that of a white child. The Negro child's mother is over three times more likely to die of complications in childbirth, and the infant mortality rate for Negroes is nearly twice that for whites. The median income of the Negro family is only 60% that of the median of a white family, and the percentage of Negroes who live in families with incomes below the poverty line is nearly four times greater than that of whites.

When the Negro child reaches working age, he finds that America offers him significantly less than it offers his white counterpart. For Negro adults, the unemployment rate is twice that of whites, and the unemployment rate for Negro teenagers is nearly three times that of white teenagers. A Negro male who completes four years of college can expect a median annual income of merely $110 more than a white male who has only a high school diploma. Although Negroes represent 11.5% of the population, they are only 1.2% of the lawyers and judges, 2% of the physicians, 2.3% of the dentists, 1.1% of the engineers and 2.6% of the college and university professors.

The relationship between those figures and the history of unequal treatment afforded to the Negro cannot be denied. At every point from birth to death the impact of the past is reflected in the still disfavored position of the Negro.

In light of the sorry history of discrimination and its devastating impact on the lives of Negroes, bringing the Negro into the mainstream of American life should be a state interest of the highest order. To fail to do so is to ensure that America will forever remain a divided society.

III

I do not believe that the Fourteenth Amendment requires us to accept that fate. Neither its history nor our past cases lend any support to the conclusion that a university may not remedy the cumulative effects of society's discrimination by giving consideration to race in an effort to increase the number and percentage of Negro doctors. . . .

While I applaud the judgment of the Court that a university may consider race in its admissions process, it is more than a little ironic that, after several hundred years of class-based discrimination against Negroes, the Court is unwilling to hold that a class-based remedy for that discrimination is permissible. In declining to so hold, today's judgment ignores the fact that for several hundred years Negroes have been discriminated against, not as individuals, but rather solely because of the color of their skins. It is unnecessary in 20th century America to have individual Negroes demonstrate that they have been victims of racial discrimination; the racism of our society has been so pervasive that none, regardless of wealth or position, has managed to escape its impact. The experience of Negroes in America has been different in kind, not just in degree, from that of other ethnic groups. It is not merely the history of slavery alone but also that a whole people were marked as inferior by the law. And that mark has endured. The dream of America as the great melting pot has not been realized for the Negro; because of his skin color he never even made it into the pot.

These differences in the experience of the Negro make it difficult for me to accept that Negroes cannot be afforded greater protection under the Fourteenth Amendment where it is necessary to remedy the effects of past discrimination. In the *Civil Rights Cases* . . . the Court wrote that the Negro emerging from slavery must cease "to be the special favorite of the laws." . . . We cannot in light of the history of the last century yield to that view. Had the Court in that decision and others been willing to "do for human liberty and the fundamental rights of American citizenship, what it did . . . for the protection of slavery and the rights of the master of fugitive slaves," . . . we would not need now to permit the recognition of any "special wards."

Most importantly, had the Court been willing in 1896, in *Plessy* v. *Ferguson*, to hold that the Equal Protection Clause forbids differences in treatment based on race, we would not be faced with this dilemma in 1978.

We must remember, however, that the principle that the "Constitution is colorblind" appeared only in the opinion of the lone dissenter. . . . The majority of the Court rejected the principle of color blindness, and for the next 60 years, from *Plessy* to *Brown* v. *Board of Education,* ours was a Nation where, *by law,* an individual could be given "special" treatment based on the color of his skin.

It is because of a legacy of unequal treatment that we now must permit the institutions of this society to give consideration to race in making decisions about who will hold the positions of influence, affluence, and prestige in America. For far too long, the doors to those positions have been shut to Negroes. If we are ever to become a fully integrated society, one in which the color of a person's skin will not determine the opportunities available to him or her, we must be willing to take steps to open those doors. I do not believe that anyone can truly look into America's past and still find that a remedy for the effects of that past is impermissible. . . .

I fear that we have come full circle. After the Civil War our Government started several "affirmative action" programs. This Court in the *Civil Rights Cases* and *Plessy* v. *Ferguson* destroyed the movement toward complete equality. For almost a century no action was taken, and this nonaction was with the tacit approval of the courts. Then we had *Brown* v. *Board of Education* and the Civil Rights Acts of Congress, followed by numerous affirmative action programs. *Now,* we have this Court again stepping in, this time to stop affirmative action programs of the type used by the University of California. . . .

The lack of unanimity of the justices, commented upon by Justice Powell in his announcement of the decision, of necessity left the Court with a number of unresolved issues. Sindler summed up the key results as follows: "Bakke won, quotas lost, and affirmative action by universities was upheld."[9] Among the issues left unsettled was the question, how strong a remedy can be applied when racial discrimination in higher education is judicially proven?

Equal protection issues involving women also assumed greater importance during the Chief Justiceship of Warren Burger. The removal of legal impediments to equality in employment for women and the elimination of gender discrimination in other aspects of law brought an increasing number of equal protection of the law challenges before the Supreme Court in the 1970s. *Reed* v. *Reed* involved the question of inequality based on sex in an Idaho state probate proceeding. Chief Justice Burger wrote the majority opinion.

REED v. REED
404 U. S. 71 (1971)

Richard Lynn Reed, a minor, died intestate in Ada County, Idaho, on March 29, 1967. His adoptive parents, who had separated sometime prior to his death, are the parties to this appeal. Approximately seven months after Richard's death, his mother, appellant Sally Reed, filed a petition in the Probate Court of Ada County, seeking appointment as administratrix of her son's estate. Prior to the date set for a hearing on the mother's petition, appellee Cecil Reed, the father of the decedent, filed a competing petition seeking to have himself appointed administrator of the son's estate. The probate court held a joint hearing on the two petitions and thereafter ordered that letters of administration be issued to appellee Cecil Reed upon his taking the oath and filing the bond required by law. The court treated § 15–312 and 15–314 of the Idaho Code as the controlling statutes and read those sections as compelling a preference for Cecil Reed because he was a male.

Section 15–312 designates the persons who are entitled to administer the estate of one who dies intestate. In making these designations, that section lists 11 classes of persons who are so entitled and provides, in substance, that the order in which those classes are listed in the section shall be determinative of the relative rights of competing applicants for letters of administration. One of the 11 classes so enumerated is "[t]he father or mother" of the person dying intestate. Under this section then appellant and appellee, being members of the same entitlement class, would seem to have been equally entitled to administer their son's estate. Section 15–314 provides, however, that

[o]f several persons claiming and equally entitled [under § 15–312] to administer, males must be preferred to females, and relatives of the whole to those of the half blood.

In issuing its order, the probate court implicitly recognized the equality of entitlement of the two applicants under § 15–312 and noted that neither of the applicants was under any legal disability; the court ruled, however, that appellee, being a male, was to be preferred to the female appellant "by reason of Section 15–314 of the Idaho Code." In stating this conclusion, the probate judge gave no indication that he had attempted to determine the relative capabilities of the competing applicants to perform the functions incident to the administration of an estate. It seems clear the probate judge considered himself bound by

statute to give preference to the male candidate over the female, each being otherwise "equally entitled."

Sally Reed appealed from the probate court order, and her appeal was treated by the District Court of the Fourth Judicial District of Idaho as a constitutional attack on § 15–314. In dealing with the attack, that court held that the challenged section violated the Equal Protection Clause of the Fourteenth Amendment and was, therefore, void; the matter was ordered "returned to the Probate Court for its determination of which of the two parties" was better qualified to administer the estate.

This order was never carried out, however, for Cecil Reed took a further appeal to the Idaho Supreme Court, which reversed the District Court and reinstated the original order naming the father administrator of the estate. In reaching this result, the Idaho Supreme Court first dealt with the governing statutory law and held that under § 15–312 "a father and mother are 'equally entitled' to letters of administration," but the preference given to males by § 15–314 is "mandatory" and leaves no room for the exercise of a probate court's discretion in the appointment of administrators. Having thus definitively and authoritatively interpreted the statutory provisions involved, the Idaho Supreme Court then proceeded to examine, and reject, Sally Reed's contention that § 15–314 violates the Equal Protection Clause by giving a mandatory preference to males over females, without regard to their individual qualifications as potential estate administrators. . . .

Sally Reed thereupon appealed for review by this Court . . . and we noted probable jurisdiction. . . . Having examined the record and considered the briefs and oral arguments of the parties, we have concluded that the arbitrary preference established in favor of males by § 15–314 of the Idaho Code cannot stand in the face of the Fourteenth Amendment's command that no State deny the equal protection of the laws to any person within its jurisdiction.

Idaho does not, of course, deny letters of administration to women altogether. Indeed, under § 15–312, a woman whose spouse dies intestate has a preference over a son, father, brother, or any other male relative of the decedent. Moreover, we can judicially notice that in this country, presumably due to the greater longevity of women, a large proportion of estates, both intestate and under wills of decedents, are administered by surviving widows.

Section 15–314 is restricted in its operation to those situations where competing applications for letters of administration have been filed by both male and female members of the same entitlement class established by § 15–312. In such situations, § 15–314 provides that different treatment be accorded to the applicants on the basis of their sex; it thus establishes a classification subject to scrutiny under the Equal Protection Clause.

In applying that clause, this Court has consistently recognized that the Fourteenth Amendment does not deny to States the power to treat different classes of persons in different ways.... The Equal Protection Clause of that amendment does, however, deny to States the power to legislate that different treatment be accorded to persons placed by a statute into different classes on the basis of criteria wholly unrelated to the objective of that statute. A classification "must be reasonable, not arbitrary, and must rest upon some ground of difference having a fair and substantial relation to the object of the legislation, so that all persons similarly circumstanced shall be treated alike." *Royster Guano Co.* v. *Virginia* [1920].... The question presented by this case, then, is whether a difference in the sex of competing applicants for letters of administration bears a rational relationship to a state objective that is sought to be advanced by the operation of §§ 15–312 and 15–314.

In upholding the latter section, the Idaho Supreme Court concluded that its objective was to eliminate one area of controversy when two or more persons, equally entitled under § 15–312, seek letters of administration and thereby present the probate court "with the issue of which one should be named." The court also concluded that where such persons are not of the same sex, the elimination of females from consideration "is neither an illogical nor arbi-

trary method devised by the legislature to resolve an issue that would otherwise require a hearing as to the relative merits . . . of the two or more petitioning relatives. . . ."

Clearly the objective of reducing the workload on probate courts by eliminating one class of contests is not without some legitimacy. The crucial question, however, is whether § 15–314 advances that objective in a manner consistent with the command of the Equal Protection Clause. We hold that it does not. To give a mandatory preference to members of either sex over members of the other, merely to accomplish the elimination of hearings on the merits, is to make the very kind of arbitrary legislative choice forbidden by the Equal Protection Clause of the Fourteenth Amendment....

. . . We note finally that if § 15–314 is viewed merely as a modifying appendage to § 15–312 and as aimed at the same objective, its constitutionality is not thereby saved. The objective of § 15–312 clearly is to establish degrees of entitlement of various classes of persons in accordance with their varying degrees and kinds of relationship to the intestate. Regardless of their sex, persons within any one of the enumerated classes of that section are similarly situated with respect to that objective. By providing dissimilar treatment for men and women who are thus similarly situated, the challenged section violates the Equal Protection Clause....

The judgment of the Idaho Supreme Court is reversed and the case remanded for further proceedings not inconsistent with this opinion. Reversed and remanded.

Reed v. *Reed* dealt with discrimination favoring males. The opposite side of the coin, discrimination favoring females, was the salient issue in *Orr* v. *Orr*. Justice Brennan wrote the majority opinion, which summarizes the facts of the case.

ORR v. ORR
440 U. S. 268 (1979)

The question presented is the constitutionality of Alabama alimony statutes which provide that husbands, but not wives, may be required to pay alimony upon divorce.

On February 26, 1974, a final decree of divorce was entered, dissolving the marriage of William and Lillian Orr. That decree directed appellant, Mr. Orr, to pay appellee, Mrs. Orr, $1,240 per month in alimony. On

July 28, 1976, Mrs. Orr initiated a contempt proceeding in the Circuit Court of Lee County, Ala., alleging that Mr. Orr was in arrears in his alimony payments. On August 19, 1976, at the hearing on Mrs. Orr's petition, Mr. Orr submitted in his defense a motion requesting that Alabama's alimony statutes be declared unconstitutional because they authorize courts to place an obligation of alimony upon husbands but never upon wives. . . . [The Alabama courts sustained the statutes, and the plaintiff appealed to the Supreme Court] We now hold the challenged Alabama statutes unconstitutional and reverse. . . .

II

In authorizing the imposition of alimony obligations on husbands, but not on wives, the Alabama statutory scheme "provides that different treatment be accorded . . . on the basis of . . . sex; it thus establishes a classification subject to scrutiny under the Equal Protection Clause." . . . The fact that the classification expressly discriminates against men rather than women does not protect it from scrutiny. . . . "To withstand scrutiny" under the Equal Protection Clause, "'classifications by gender must serve important governmental objectives and must be substantially related to achievement of those objectives.'" . . . We shall, therefore, examine the three governmental objectives that might arguably be served by Alabama's statutory scheme.

Appellant views the Alabama alimony statutes as effectively announcing the State's preference for an allocation of family responsibilities under which the wife plays a dependent role, and as seeking for their objective the reinforcement of that model among the State's citizens. . . . [But] the "old notion" that "generally it is the man's primary responsibility to provide a home and its essentials," can no longer justify a statute that discriminates on the basis of gender. "No longer is the female destined solely for the home and the rearing of the family, and only the male for the marketplace, and world of ideas,". . . . If the statute is to survive constitutional attack, therefore, it must be validated on some other basis.

The opinion of the Alabama Court of Civil Appeals suggests other purposes that the statute may serve. Its opinion states that the Alabama statutes were "designed" for "the wife of a broken marriage who needs financial assistance. . . ." This may be read as asserting either of two legislative objectives. One is a legislative purpose to provide help for needy spouses, using sex as a proxy for need. The other is a goal of compensating women for past discrimination during marriage, which assertedly has left them unprepared to fend for themselves in the working world following divorce. We concede, of course, that assisting needy spouses is a legitimate and important governmental objective. We have also recognized "[r]eduction of the disparity in economic condition between men and women caused by the long history of discrimination against women . . . as . . . an important governmental objective." . . . It only remains, therefore, to determine whether the classification at issue here is "substantially related to achievement of those objectives."

Ordinarily, we would begin the analysis of the "needy spouse" objective by considering whether sex is a sufficiently "accurate proxy" . . . for dependency to establish that the gender classification rests "'upon some ground of difference having a fair and substantial relation to the object of the legislation,'" *Reed* v. *Reed.* . . . Similarly, we would initially approach the "compensation" rationale by asking whether women had in fact been significantly discriminated against in the sphere to which the statute applied a sex-based classification, leaving the sexes "*not* similarly situated with respect to opportunities" in that sphere. . . .

But in this case, even if sex were a reliable proxy for need, and even if the institution of marriage did discriminate against women, these factors still would "not adequately justify the salient features of" Alabama's statutory scheme. . . . Under the statute, individualized hearings at which the parties' relative financial circumstances are considered *already* occur. . . . There is no reason, therefore, to use sex as a proxy for need. Needy males could be helped along with needy females with little if any additional burden on the State. In such circumstances, not even an administrative convenience rationale exists to justify operating by generalization or proxy. Similarly, since individualized hearings can determine which women were in fact discriminated against vis à vis their husbands, as well as which family units defied the stereotype and left the husband dependent on the wife, Alabama's alleged compensatory purpose may be effectuated without placing burdens solely on husbands. Progress toward fulfilling such a purpose would not be hampered, and it would cost the State nothing more, if it were to treat men and women equally by making alimony burdens independent of sex. "Thus, the gender-based distinction is gratuitous; without it the statutory scheme would only provide benefits to those men who are in fact similarly situated to the women the statute aids," . . . and the effort to help those women would not in any way be compromised.

Moreover, use of a gender classification actually produces perverse results in this case. As compared to a gender-neutral law placing alimony obligations on the spouse able to pay, the present Alabama statutes give an advantage only to the financially secure wife whose husband is in need. Although such a wife might have to pay alimony under a gender-neutral statute, the present statutes exempt her from that obligation. Thus "[t]he [wives] who benefit from the disparate treatment are those who were . . . nondependent on their husbands. . . . ." They are precisely those who are not "needy spouses" and who are "least likely to have been victims of . . . discrimination" by the institution of marriage. A gender-based classification which, as compared to a gender-neutral one, generates additional benefits only for those it has no reason to prefer cannot survive equal protection scrutiny.

Legislative classifications which distribute benefits and burdens on the basis of gender carry the inherent risk of reinforcing stereotypes about the "proper place" of women and their need for special protection. . . . Thus, even statutes purportedly designed to compensate for and ameliorate the effects of past discrimination must be carefully tailored. Where, as here, the State's compensatory and ameliorative purposes are as well served by a gender-neutral classification as one that gender-classifies and therefore carries with it the baggage of sexual stereotypes, the State cannot be permitted to classify on the basis of sex. And this is doubly so where the choice made by the State appears

to redound—if only indirectly—to the benefit of those without need for special solicitude.

III

Having found Alabama's alimony statutes unconstitutional, we reverse the judgment below and remand the cause for futher proceedings not inconsistent with this opinion. . . . [I]t is open to the Alabama courts on remand to consider whether Mr. Orr's stipulated agreement to pay alimony, or other grounds of gender-neutral state law, bind him to continue his alimony payments. Reversed.

[The concurring opinions of Justices Blackmun and Stevens and the dissenting opinions of Justices Powell and Rehnquist (supported by Chief Justice Burger) are omitted.]

The social issues and the radical right

The abortion decision, *Roe* v. *Wade,* became one of the most controversial issues of the 1970s and 80s. Positions on its outcome differentiated President Jimmy Carter and successful presidential challenger, Ronald Reagan, in 1980. The issue came to the Supreme Court as a result of challenges to Texas statutes that, according to their opponents, invaded the right of pregnant women to choose to terminate their pregnancies. Justice Blackmun, former resident counsel to the Mayo Clinic, wrote the majority opinion, which, in effect, invalidated abortion statutes in 46 of the 50 states. Justice Rehnquist dissented. The decision itself is perhaps the most symbolic of the wide variety of Court actions that have transformed and often deeply divided the nation. The social attitudes and behavior of groups holding significantly different moral, political, and practical positions on abortion have had a tremendous impact not only upon law but upon modes of political action itself. The concept of the single-issue Political Action Committee is one of the consequences of the continuing controversy.

ROE v. WADE
410 U. S. 113 (1973)

Justice Blackmun delivered the opinion of the Court:

. . . The principal thrust of appellant's attack on the Texas statutes is that they improperly invade a right, said to be possessed by the pregnant woman, to choose to terminate her pregnancy. Appellant would discover this right in the concept of personal "liberty" embodied in the Fourteenth Amendment's Due Process Clause; or in personal, marital, familial, and sexual privacy said to be protected by the Bill of Rights or its penumbras . . . or among those rights reserved to the people by the Ninth Amendment. . . .

Before addressing this claim, we feel it desirable briefly to survey, in several aspects, the history of

abortion, for such insight as that history may afford us, and then to examine the state purposes and interests behind the criminal abortion laws.

It perhaps is not generally appreciated that the restrictive criminal abortion laws in effect in a majority of States today are of relatively recent vintage. Those laws, generally proscribing abortion or its attempt at any time during pregnancy except when necessary to preserve the pregnant woman's life, are not of ancient or even of common-law origin. Instead, they derive from statutory changes effected, for the most part, in the latter half of the 19th century. . . .

Three reasons have been advanced to explain historically the enactment of criminal abortion laws in the 19th century and to justify their continued existence.

It has been argued occasionally that these laws were the product of a Victorian social concern to discourage illicit sexual conduct. Texas, however, does not advance this justification in the present case, and it appears that no court or commentator has taken the argument seriously. The appellants and amici contend, moreover, that this is not a proper state purpose at all and suggest that, if it were, the Texas statutes are overbroad in protecting it since the law fails to distinguish between married and unwed mothers.

A second reason is concerned with abortion as a medical procedure. When most criminal abortion laws were first enacted, the procedure was a hazardous one for the woman. This was particularly true prior to the development of antisepsis. Antiseptic techniques, of course, were based on discoveries by Lister, Pasteur, and others first announced in 1867, but were not generally accepted and employed until about the turn of the century. Abortion mortality was high. Even after 1900, and perhaps until as late as the development of antibiotics in the 1940's, standard modern techniques such as dilation and curettage were not nearly so safe as they are today. Thus, it has been argued that a State's real concern in enacting a criminal abortion law was to protect the pregnant woman, that is, to restrain her from submitting to a procedure that placed her life in serious jeopardy.

Modern medical techniques have altered this situation. Appellants and various amici refer to medical data indicating that abortion in early pregnancy, this is, prior to the end of the first trimester, although not without its risk, is now relatively safe. Mortality rates for women undergoing early abortions, where the procedure is legal, appear to be as low as or lower than the rates for normal childbirth. Consequently, any interest of the State in protecting the woman from an inherently hazardous procedure, except when it would be equally dangerous for her to forgo it, has largely disappeared. Of course, important state interests in the area of health and medical standards do remain.

The State has a legitimate interest in seeing to it that abortion, like any other medical procedure, is performed under circumstances that insure maximum safety for the patient. This interest obviously extends at least to the performing physician and his staff, to the facilities involved, to the availability of aftercare, and to adequate provision for any complication or emergency that might arise. The prevalence of high mortality rates at illegal "abortion mills" strengthens, rather than weakens, the State's interest in regulating the conditions under which abortions are performed. Moreover, the risk to the woman increases as her pregnancy continues. Thus, the State retains a definite interest in protecting the woman's own health and safety when an abortion is proposed at a late stage of pregnancy.

The third reason is the State's interest—some phrase it in terms of duty—in protecting prenatal life. Some of the argument for this justification rests on the theory that a new human life is present from the moment of conception. The State's interest and general obligation to protect life then extends, it is argued, to prenatal life. Only when the life of the pregnant mother herself is at stake, balanced against the life she carries within her, should the interest of the embryo or fetus not prevail. Logically, of course, a legitimate state interest in this area need not stand or fall on acceptance of the belief that life begins at conception or at some other point prior to live birth. In assessing the State's interest, recognition may be given to the less rigid claim that as long as at least *potential* life is involved, the State may assert interests beyond the protection of the pregnant woman alone.

Parties challenging state abortion laws have sharply disputed in some courts the contention that a purpose of these laws, when enacted, was to protect prenatal life. . . .

It is with these interests, and the weight to be attached to them, that this case is concerned.

The Constitution does not explicitly mention any right of privacy. In a line of decisions, however, going back perhaps as far as *Union Pacific R. Co.* v. *Botsford* [1891] . . . , the Court has recognized that a right of personal privacy, or a guarantee of certain areas of zones of privacy, does exist under the Constitution. In varying contexts, the Court or individual Justices have, indeed, found at least the roots of that right in the First Amendment, *Stanley* v. *Georgia* [1969] . . . ; in the Fourth and Fifth Amendments, *Terry* v. *Ohio* [1968] . . . , *Katz* v. *United States* [1967] . . . ; in the penumbras of the Bill of Rights, *Griswold* v. *Connecticut* [1965] . . . ; in the Ninth Amendment, id., at 486, . . . (Goldberg, J., concurring); or in the concept of liberty guaranteed by the first section of the Fourteenth Amendment, see *Meyer* v. *Nebraska* [1923]. . . . These decisions make it clear that only personal rights that can be deemed "fundamental" or "implicit in the concept of ordered liberty," *Palko* v. *Connecticut* [1937] . . . , are included in this guarantee of personal privacy. They also make it clear that the right has some extension to activities relating to marriage, *Loving* v. *Virginia* [1967] . . . ; procreation, *Skinner* v. *Oklahoma* [1942] . . . ; contraception, *Eisenstadt* v. *Baird* [1972]. . . .

This right of privacy, whether it be founded in the Fourteenth Amendment's concept of personal liberty and restrictions upon state action, as we feel it is, or, as the District Court determined, in the Ninth Amendment's reservation of rights to the people, is broad enough to encompass a woman's decision whether or not to terminate her pregnancy. The detriment that the State would impose upon the pregnant woman by denying this choice altogether is apparent. Specific and direct harm medically diagnosable even in early pregnancy may be involved. Maternity, or additional offspring, may force upon the woman a distressful life and future. Psychological harm may be imminent. Mental and physical health may be taxed by child care. There is also the distress, for all concerned, associated with the unwanted child, and there is the problem of bringing a child into a family already unable, psychologically and otherwise, to care for it. In other cases, as in this one, the additional difficulties and continuing stigma of unwed motherhood may be involved. All these are factors the woman and her responsible physician necessarily will consider in consultation.

On the basis of elements such as these, appellant and some amici argue that the woman's right is absolute and that she is entitled to terminate her pregnancy at whatever time, in whatever way, and for whatever reason she alone chooses. With this we do not agree. Appellant's arguments that Texas either has no valid interest at all in regulating the abortion decision, or no interest strong enough to support any limitation upon the woman's sole determination, is unpersuasive. The Court's decisions recognizing a right of privacy also acknowledge that some state regulation in areas protected by that right is appropriate. As noted above, a State may properly assert important interests in safeguarding health, in maintaining medical standards, and in protecting potential life. At some point in pregnancy, these respective interests become sufficiently compelling to sustain regulation of the factors that govern the abortion decision. The privacy right involved, therefore, cannot be said to be absolute. In fact, it is not clear to us that the claim asserted by some amici that one has an unlimited right to do with one's body as one pleases bears a close relationship to the right of privacy previously articulated in the Court's decisions. The Court has refused to recognize an unlimited right of this kind in the past. *Jacobson* v. *Massachusetts* [1905] . . . (vaccination); *Buck* v. *Bell* [1927] . . . (sterilization).

We, therefore, conclude that the right of personal privacy includes the abortion decision, but that this right is not unqualified and must be considered against important state interests in regulation.

Where certain "fundamental rights" are involved, the Court has held that regulation limiting these

rights may be justified only by a "compelling state interest," . . . and that legislative enactments must be narrowly drawn to express only the legitimate state interests at stake. . . .

The District Court held that the appellee failed to meet his burden of demonstrating that the Texas statute's infringement upon Roe's rights was necessary to support a compelling state interest. . . . Appellee argues that the State's determination to recognize and protect prenatal life from and after conception constitutes a compelling state interest. As noted above, we do not agree fully with either formulation.

A. The appellee and certain amici argue that the fetus is a "person" within the language and meaning of the Fourteenth Amendment. In support of this, they outline at length and in detail the well-known facts of fetal development. If this suggestion of personhood is established, the appellant's case, of course, collapses, for the fetus' right to life is then guaranteed specifically by the Amendment. The appellant conceded as much on reargument. On the other hand, the appellee conceded on reargument that no case could be cited that holds that a fetus is a person within the meaning of the Fourteenth Amendment.

The Constitution does not define "person" in so many words. Section 1 of the Fourteenth Amendment contains three references to "person." The first, in defining "citizens," speaks of "persons born or naturalized in the United States." The word also appears both in the Due Process Clause and in the Equal Protection Clause. "Person" is used in other places in the Constitution. . . . But in nearly all these instances, the use of the word is such that it has application only postnatally. None indicates, with any assurance, that it has any possible prenatal application.

All this, together with our observation, supra, that throughout the major portion of the 19th century prevailing legal abortion practices were far freer than they are today, persuades us that the word "person," as used in the Fourteenth Amendment, does not include the unborn. . . .

B. The pregnant woman cannot be isolated in her privacy. She carries an embryo, and, later, a fetus, if one accepts the medical definitions of the developing young in the human uterus. . . . The situation therefore is inherently different from marital intimacy, or bedroom possession of obscene material, or marriage, or procreation, or education, with which *Eisenstadt*, *Griswold*, *Stanley*, *Loving*, *Skinner*, *Pierce*, and *Meyer* were respectively concerned. As we have intimated above, it is reasonable and appropriate for a State to decide that at some point in time another interest, that of health of the mother or that of potential human life, becomes significantly involved. The woman's privacy is no longer sole and any right of privacy she possesses must be measured accordingly.

Texas urges that, apart from the Fourteenth Amendment, life begins at conception and is present throughout pregnancy, and that, therefore, the State has a compelling interest in protecting that life from and after conception. We need not resolve the difficult question of when life begins. When those trained in the respective disciplines of medicine, philosophy, and theology are unable to arrive at any consensus, the judiciary, at this point in the development of man's knowledge, is not in a position to speculate as to the answer.

It should be sufficient to note briefly the wide divergence of thinking on this most sensitive and difficult question. . . .

In view of all this, we do not agree that, by adopting one theory of life, Texas may override the rights of the pregnant woman that are at stake. We repeat, however, that the State does have an important and legitimate interest in preserving and protecting the health of the pregnant woman, whether she be a resident of the State or a nonresident who seeks medical consultation and treatment there, and that it has still *another* important and legitimate interest in protecting the potentiality of human life. These interests are separate and distinct. Each grows in substantiality as the woman approaches term and, at a point during pregnancy, each becomes "compelling."

With respect to the State's important and legitimate interest in the health of the mother, the "compelling" point, in the light of present medical knowledge, is at approximately the end of the first trimester. This is so because of the now-established medical fact, referred to above . . . that until the end of the first trimester mortality in abortion may be less than mortality in normal childbirth. It follows that, from and after this point, a State may regulate the abortion procedure to the extent that the regulation reasonably relates to the preservation and protection of maternal health. Examples of permissible state regulation in this area are requirements as to the qualifications of the person who is to perform the abortion; as to the licensure of that person; as to the facility in which the procedure is to be performed, that is, whether it must be a hospital or may be a clinic or some other place of less-than-hospital status; as to the licensing of the facility; and the like.

This means, on the other hand, that, for the period of pregnancy prior to this "compelling" point, the attending physician, in consultation with his patient, is free to determine, without regulation by the State, that, in his medical judgment, the patient's pregnancy should be terminated. If that decision is reached, the judgment may be effectuated by an abortion free of interference by the State.

With respect to the State's important and legitimate interest in potential life, the "compelling" point is at viability. This is so because the fetus then presumably has the capability of meaningful life outside the mother's womb. State regulation protective of fetal life after viability thus has both logical and biological justifications. If the State is interested in protecting fetal life after viability, it may go so far as to proscribe abortion during that period, except when it is necessary to preserve the life or health of the mother.

Measured against these standards, Art. 1196 of the Texas Penal Code, in restricting legal abortions to those "procured or attempted by medical advice for the purpose of saving the life of the mother," sweeps too broadly. The statute makes no distinction between abortions performed early in pregnancy and those performed later, and it limits to a single reason, "saving" the mother's life, the legal justification for the procedure. The statute, therefore, cannot survive the constitutional attack made upon it here. . . .

To summarize and repeat:

1. A state criminal abortion statute of the current Texas type, that excepts from criminality only a *lifesaving* procedure on behalf of the mother, without regard to pregnancy stage and without recognition of the other interests involved, is violative of the Due Process Clause of the Fourteenth Amendment.

(a) For the stage prior to approximately the end of the first trimester, the abortion decision and its effectuation must be left to the medical judgment of the pregnant woman's attending physician.

(b) For the stage subsequent to approximately the end of the first trimester, the State, in promoting its interest in the health of the mother, may, if it chooses, regulate the abortion procedure in ways that are reasonably related to maternal health.

(c) For the stage subsequent to viability, the State in promoting its interest in the potentiality of human life may, if it chooses, regulate, and even proscribe, abortion except where it is necessary, in appropriate medical judgment, for the preservation of the life or health of the mother.

2. The State may define the term "physician," as it has been employed in the preceding numbered paragraphs of this Part XI of this opinion, to mean only a physician currently licensed by the State, and may

proscribe any abortion by a person who is not a physician as so defined.

In *Doe* v. *Bolton* [1973] . . . procedural requirements contained in one of the modern abortion statutes are considered. That opinion and this one, of course, are to be read together. . . .

Justice Stewart concurred:

In 1963, this Court, in *Ferguson* v. *Skrupa,* . . . purported to sound the death knell for the doctrine of substantive due process, a doctrine under which many state laws had in the past been held to violate the Fourteenth Amendment. As Mr. Justice Black's opinion for the Court in *Skrupa* put it: "We have returned to the original constitutional proposition that courts do not substitute their social and economic beliefs for the judgment of legislative bodies, who are elected to pass laws." . . .

Barely two years later, in *Griswold* v. *Connecticut,* . . . the Court held a Connecticut birth control law unconstitutional. In view of what had been so recently said in *Skrupa,* the Court's opinion in *Griswold* understandably did its best to avoid reliance on the Due Process Clause of the Fourteenth Amendment as the ground for decision. Yet, the Connecticut law did not violate any provision of the Bill of Rights, nor any other specific provision of the Constitution. So it was clear to me then, and it is equally clear to me now, that the *Griswold* decision can be rationally understood only as a holding that the Connecticut statute substantively invaded the "liberty" that is protected by the Due Process Clause of the Fourteenth Amendment. As so understood, *Griswold* stands as one in a long line of pre-Skrupa cases decided under the doctrine of substantive due process, and I now accept it as such.

"In a Constitution for a free people, there can be no doubt that the meaning of 'liberty' must be broad indeed." . . . The Constitution nowhere mentions a specific right of personal choice in matters of marriage and family life, but the "liberty" protected by the Due Process Clause of the Fourteenth Amendment covers more than those freedoms explicitly named in the Bill of Rights. . . .

Several decisions of this Court make clear that freedom of personal choice in matters of marriage and family life is one of the liberties protected by the Due Process Clause of the Fourteenth Amendment. . . . In *Eisenstadt* v. *Baird,* . . . we recognized "the right of the *individual,* married or single, to be free from unwarranted governmental intrusion into matters so fundamentally affecting a person as the decision whether to bear or beget a child." That right necessarily includes the right of a woman to decide whether or not to terminate her pregnancy. "Certainly the interests of a woman in giving of her physical and emotional self during pregnancy and the interests that will be affected throughout her life by the birth and raising of a child are of a far greater degree of significance and personal intimacy than the right to send a child to private school protected in *Pierce* v. *Society of Sisters* [1925] . . ., or the right to teach a foreign language protected in *Meyer* v. *Nebraska.* . . ."

Justice Rehnquist dissented:

. . . I have difficulty in concluding, as the Court does, that the right of "privacy" is involved in this case. Texas, by the statute here challenged, bars the performance of a medical abortion by a licensed physician on a plaintiff such as Roe. A transaction resulting in an operation such as this is not "private" in the ordinary usage of that word. . . .

If the Court means by the term "privacy" no more than that the claim of a person to be free from unwanted state regulation of consensual transactions may be a form of "liberty" protected by the Fourteenth Amendment, there is no doubt that similar claims have been upheld in our earlier decisions on the basis of that liberty. I agree with the statement of Mr. Justice Stewart in his concurring opinion that the "liberty," against deprivation of which without due process the Fourteenth Amendment protects, embraces more than the rights found in the Bill of Rights. But that liberty is not guaranteed absolutely against deprivation, only against deprivation without due process of law. The test traditionally applied in the area of social and economic legislation is whether or not a law such as that challenged has a rational relation to a valid state objective. . . . But the Court's sweeping invalidation of any restrictions on abortion during the first trimester is impossible to justify under that standard, and the conscious weighing of competing factors that the Court's opinion apparently substitutes for the established test is far more appropriate to a legislative judgment than to a judicial one.

The Court eschews the history of the Fourteenth Amendment in its reliance on the "compelling state interest" test. . . . But the Court adds a new wrinkle to this test by transposing it from the legal considerations associated with the Equal Protection Clause of the Fourteenth Amendment to this case arising under the Due Process Clause of the Fourteenth Amendment. Unless I misapprehend the consequences of this transplanting of the "compelling state interest test," the Court's opinion will accomplish the seemingly impossible feat of leaving this area of the law more confused than it found it.

While the Court's opinion quotes from the dissent of Mr. Justice Holmes in *Lochner* v. *New York,* the result it reaches is more closely attuned to the majority opinion of Mr. Justice Peckham in that case. As in *Lochner* and similar cases applying substantive due process standards to economic and social welfare legislation, the adoption of the compelling state interest standard will inevitably require this Court to examine the legislative policies and pass on the wisdom of these policies in the very process of deciding whether a particular state interest put forward may or may not be "compelling." The decision here to break pregnancy into three distinct terms and to outline the permissible restrictions the State may impose in each one, for example, partakes more of judicial legislation than it does of a determination of the intent of the drafters of the Fourteenth Amendment.

The fact that a majority of the States reflecting, after all the majority sentiment in those States, have had restrictions on abortions for at least a century is a strong indication, it seems to me, that the asserted right to an abortion is not "so rooted in the traditions and conscience of our people as to be ranked as fundamental." . . . Even today, when society's views on abortion are changing, the very existence of the debate is evidence that the "right" to an abortion is not so universally accepted as the appellant would have us believe.

To reach its result, the Court necessarily has had to find within the scope of the Fourteenth Amendment a right that was apparently completely unknown to the drafters of the Amendment. As early as 1821, the first state law dealing directly with abortion was enacted by the Connecticut Legislature. . . . By the time of the adoption of the Fourteenth Amendment in 1868, there were at least 36 laws enacted by state or territorial legislatures limiting abortion. While many States have amended or updated their laws, 21 of the laws on the books in 1868 remain in effect today. . . .

. . . The only conclusion possible from this history is that the drafters did not intend to have the Fourteenth Amendment withdraw from the States the power to legislate with respect to this matter. . . .

In the context of New Right opposition to Supreme Court decisions relating to the changing lifestyles and attitudes of large segments of the American public, the writing of the majority opinion in *Roe* by a Nixon appointee was ironic. If all of President Nixon's appointees had reflected his ideology, they presumably would have joined Rehnquist in his dissent.

Another major area of severe anti–Court criticism, clearly exemplified in the Fortas chief justiceship confirmation fight, involved judicial definitions of obscenity. It is an understatement to say that the Court found it difficult to agree on the criteria for obscenity. The case of *Miller* v. *California* provides an excellent example. Chief Justice Burger wrote the majority opinion and Justices Douglas and Brennan dissented.

MILLER v. CALIFORNIA
413 U. S. 15 (1973)

Chief Justice Burger delivered the opinion of the Court:

This is one of a group of "obscenity-pornography" cases being reviewed by the Court in a re-examination of standards enunciated in earlier cases involving what Mr. Justice Harlan called "the intractable obscenity problem." . . .

Appellant conducted a mass mailing campaign to advertise the sale of illustrated books, euphemistically called "adult" material. After a jury trial, he was convicted of violating California Penal Code § 311.2 (a),

a misdemeanor, by knowingly distributing obscene matter. . . . Appellant's conviction was specifically based on his conduct in causing five unsolicited advertising brochures to be sent through the mail in an envelope addressed to a restaurant in Newport Beach, California. The envelope was opened by the manager of the restaurant and his mother. They had not requested the brochures; they complained to the police.

The brochures advertise four books entitled "Intercourse," "Man-Woman," "Sex Orgies Illustrated," and "An Illustrated History of Pornography," and a film entitled "Marital Intercourse." While the brochures contain some descriptive printed material, primarily they consist of pictures and drawings very explicitly depicting men and women in groups of two or more engaging in a variety of sexual activities, with genitals often prominently displayed.

I

This case involves the application of a State's criminal obscenity statute to a situation in which sexually explicit materials have been thrust by aggressive sales action upon unwilling recipients who had in no way indicated any desire to receive such materials. This Court has recognized that the States have a legitimate interest in prohibiting dissemination or exhibition of obscene material when the mode of dissemination carries with it a significant danger of offending the sensibilities of unwilling recipients or of exposure to juveniles. . . . It is in this context that we are called on to define the standards which must be used to identify obscene material that a State may regulate without infringing on the First Amendment as applicable to the States through the Fourteenth Amendment.

The dissent of Mr. Justice Brennan reviews the background of the obscenity problem, but since the Court now undertakes to formulate standards more concrete than those in the past, it is useful for us to focus on two of the landmark cases in the somewhat tortured history of the Court's obscenity decisions. In *Roth* v. *United States* . . . the Court sustained a conviction under a federal statute punishing the mailing of "obscene, lewd, lascivious or filthy . . ." materials. The key to that holding was the Court's rejection of the claim that obscene materials were protected by the First Amendment. . . .

Nine years later, in *Memoirs* v. *Massachusetts* . . . the Court veered sharply away from the *Roth* concept and, with only three Justices in the plurality opinion, articulated a new test of obscenity. . . .

The sharpness of the break with *Roth* . . . was . . . underscored when the *Memoirs* plurality [stated] . . . "A book cannot be proscribed unless it is found to be *utterly* without redeeming social value." . . .

While *Roth* presumed "obscenity" to be "utterly without redeeming social importance," *Memoirs* required that to prove obscenity it must be affirmatively established that the material is "*utterly* without redeeming social value." Thus, even as they repeated the words of *Roth*, the *Memoirs* plurality produced a drastically altered test that called on the prosecution to prove a negative, *i. e.*, that the material was "*utterly* without redeeming social value"—a burden virtually impossible to discharge under our criminal standards of proof. Such considerations caused Mr. Justice Harlan to wonder if the "*utterly* without redeeming social value" test had any meaning at all. . . .

Apart from the initial formulation in the *Roth* case, no majority of the Court has at any given time been able to agree on a standard to determine what constitutes obscene, pornographic material subject to regulation under the States' police power. . . . We have seen "a variety of views among the members of the Court unmatched in any other course of constitutional adjudication." . . . This is not remarkable, for in the area of freedom of speech and press the courts must always remain sensitive to any infringement on genuinely serious literary, artistic, political, or scientific expression. This is an area in which there are few eternal verities.

The case we now review was tried on the theory that the California Penal Code § 311 approximately incorporates the three-stage *Memoirs* test. . . . But now the *Memoirs* test has been abandoned as unworkable by its author, and no Member of the Court today supports the *Memoirs* formulation.

II

This much has been categorically settled by the Court, that obscene material is unprotected by the First Amendment. . . . We acknowledge, however, the inherent dangers of undertaking to regulate any form of expression. State statutes designed to regulate obscene materials must be carefully limited. . . . As a result, we now confine the permissible scope of such regulations to works which depict or describe sexual conduct. That conduct must be specifically defined by the applicable state law, as written or authoritatively construed. A state offense must also be limited to works which, taken as a whole, appeal to the prurient interest in sex, which portray sexual conduct in a patently offensive way, and which, taken as a whole, do not have serious literary, artistic, political, or scientific value.

The basic guidelines for the trier of fact must be: (a) whether "the average person, applying contemporary community standards" would find that the work taken as a whole, appeals to the prurient interest . . . ; (b) whether the work depicts or describes, in a patently offensive way, sexual conduct specifically defined by the applicable state law; and (c) whether the work, taken as a whole, lacks serious literary, artistic, political, or scientific value. We do not adopt as a constitutional standard the "*utterly* without redeeming social value" test of *Memoirs* v. *Massachusetts* . . . ; that concept has never commanded the adherence of more than three Justices at one time. . . . If a state law that regulates obscene material is thus limited, as written or construed, the First Amendment values applicable to the States through the Fourteenth Amendment are adequately protected by the ultimate power of appellate courts to conduct an independent review of constitutional claims when necessary. . . .

We emphasize that it is not our function to propose regulatory schemes for the States. That must await their concrete legislative efforts. It is possible, however, to give a few plain examples of what a state statute could define for regulation under part (b) of the standard announced in this opinion, *supra:*

(a) Patently offensive representations or descriptions of ultimate sexual acts, normal or perverted, actual or simulated.

(b) Patently offensive representations or descriptions of masturbation, excretory functions, and lewd exhibition of the genitals.

Sex and nudity may not be exploited without limit by films or pictures exhibited or sold in places of public accommodation any more than live sex and nudity can be exhibited or sold without limit in such public places. At a minimum, prurient, patently offensive depiction or description of sexual conduct must have serious literary, artistic, political, or scientific value to merit First Amendment protection. . . . For example, medical books for the education of physicians and related personnel necessarily use graphic illustrations and descriptions of human anatomy. In resolving the inevitably sensitive questions of fact and law, we must continue to rely on the jury system, accompanied by the safeguards that judges, rules of evidence, presumption of innocence, and other protective features provide, as we do with rape, murder, and a host of other offenses against society and its individual members.

Mr. Justice Brennan, author of the opinions of the Court, or the plurality opinions, in *Roth* v. *United States* . . . and *Memoirs* v. *Massachussetts* has abandoned his former position and now maintains that no formulation of this Court, the Congress, or the States can adequately distinguish obscene material unprotected by the First Amendment from protected expression. . . . Paradoxically, Mr. Justice Brennan indicates that suppression of unprotected obscene material is permissible to avoid exposure to unconsenting adults, as in this case, and to juveniles, although he gives no indication of how the division between protected and nonprotected materials may be drawn with greater precision for these purposes than for regulation of commercial exposure to consenting adults only. Nor does he indicate where in the Constitution he finds the authority to distinguish between a willing "adult" one month past the state law age of majority and a willing "juvenile" one month younger.

Under the holdings announced today, no one will be subject to prosecution for the sale or exposure of obscene materials unless these materials depict or describe patently offensive "hard core" sexual conduct specifically defined by the regulating state law, as written or construed. We are satisfied that these specific prerequisites will provide fair notice to a dealer in such materials that his public and commercial activities may bring prosecution. . . . If the inability to define regulated materials with ultimate, god-like precision altogether removes the power of the States or the Congress to regulate, then "hard core" pornography may be exposed without limit to the juvenile, the passerby, and the consenting adult alike, as, indeed, Mr. Justice Douglas contends. . . . In this belief, however, Mr. Justice Douglas now stands alone.

Mr. Justice Brennan also emphasizes "institutional stress" in justification of his change of view. Noting that "[t]he number of obscenity cases on our docket gives ample testimony to the burden that has been placed upon this Court," he quite rightly remarks that the examination of contested materials "is hardly a source of edification to the members of this Court." . . . He also notes, and we agree, that "uncertainty of the standards creates a continuing source of tension between state and federal courts. . . ." "The problem is . . . that one cannot say with certainty that material is obscene until at least five members of this Court, applying inevitably obscure standards, have pronounced it so." . . .

It is certainly true that the absence, since *Roth,* of a single majority view of this Court as to proper standards for testing obscenity has placed a strain on both state and federal courts. But today, for the first time since *Roth* was decided in 1957, a majority of this Court has agreed on concrete guidelines to isolate "hard core" pornography from expression protected by the First Amendment. Now we may . . . attempt to provide positive guidance to federal and state courts alike.

This may not be an easy road, free from difficulty. But no amount of "fatigue" should lead us to adopt a convenient "institutional" rationale—an absolutist, "anything goes" view of the First Amendment —because it will lighten our burdens. "Such an abnegation of judicial supervision in this field would be inconsistent with our duty to uphold the constitutional guarantees." . . . Nor should we remedy "tension between state and federal courts" by arbitrarily depriving the States of a power reserved to them under the Constitution, a power which they have enjoyed and exercised continuously from before the adoption of the First Amendment to this day. . . . "Our duty admits of no 'substitute for facing up to the tough individual problems of constitutional judgment involved in every obscenity case.'" . . .

III

Under a National Constitution, fundamental First Amendment limitations on the powers of the States do not vary from community to community, but this does not mean that there are, or should or can be, fixed, uniform national standards of precisely what appeals to the "prurient interest" or is "patently offensive." These are essentially questions of fact, and our Nation is simply too big and too diverse for this Court to reasonably expect that such standards could be articulated for all 50 States in a single formulation, even assuming the prerequisite consensus exists. When triers of fact are asked to decide whether "the average person, applying contemporary community standards" would consider certain materials "prurient," it would be unrealistic to require that the answer be based on some abstract formulation. The adversary system, with lay jurors as the usual ultimate factfinders in criminal prosecutions, has historically permitted triers of fact to draw on the standards of their community, guided always by limiting instructions on the law. To require a State to structure obscenity proceedings around evidence of a *national* "community standard" would be an exercise in futility. . . .

It is neither realistic nor constitutionally sound to read the First Amendment as requiring that the people of Maine or Mississippi accept public depiction of conduct found tolerable in Las Vegas, or New York City. . . . People in different States vary in their tastes and attitudes, and this diversity is not to be strangled by the absolutism of imposed uniformity. . . . [T]he primary concern with requiring a jury to apply the standard of "the average person, applying contemporary community standards" is to be certain that, so far as material is not aimed at a deviant group, it will be judged by its impact on an average person, rather than a particularly susceptible or sensitive person—or indeed a totally insensitive one. . . . We hold that the requirement that the jury evaluate the materials with reference to "contemporary standards of the State of California" serves this protective purpose and is constitutionally adequate.

IV

The dissenting Justices sound the alarm of repression. But, in our view, to equate the free and robust exchange of ideas and political debate with commercial exploitation of obscene material demeans the grand conception of the First Amendment and its high purposes in the historic struggle for freedom. It is a "mis-

use of the great guarantees of free speech and free press. . . ." . . . The First Amendment protects works which, taken as a whole, have serious literary, artistic, political, or scientific value, regardless of whether the government or a majority of the people approve of the ideas these works represent. "The protection given speech and press was fashioned to assure unfettered interchanges of *ideas* for the bringing about of political and social changes desired by the people." . . . But the public portrayal of hard-core sexual conduct for its own sake, and for the ensuing commercial gain, is a different matter.

There is no evidence, empirical or historical, that the stern 19th century American censorship of public distribution and display of material relating to sex . . . in any way limited or affected expression of serious literary, artistic, political, or scientific ideas. On the contrary, it is beyond any question that the era following Thomas Jefferson to Theodore Roosevelt was an "extraordinarily vigorous period," not just in economics and politics, but in *belles lettres* and in "the outlying fields of social and political philosophies." We do not see the harsh hand of censorship of ideas—good or bad, sound or unsound—and "repression" of political liberty lurking in every state regulation of commercial exploitation of human interest in sex.

Mr. Justice Brennan finds "it is hard to see how state-ordered regimentation of our minds can ever be forestalled." . . . These doleful anticipations assume that the courts cannot distinguish commerce in ideas, protected by the First Amendment, from commercial exploitation of obscene material. Moreover, state regulation of hard-core pornography so as to make it unavailable to nonadults, a regulation which Mr. Justice Brennan finds constitutionally permissible, has all the elements of "censorship" for adults; indeed even more rigid enforcement techniques may be called for with such dichotomy of regulation. . . . One can concede that the "sexual revolution" of recent years may have had useful byproducts in striking layers of prudery from a subject long irrationally kept from needed ventilation. But it does not follow that no regulation of patently offensive "hard core" materials is needed or permissible; civilized people do not allow unregulated access to heroin because it is a derivative of medicinal morphine.

In sum, we (a) reaffirm the *Roth* holding that obscene material is not protected by the First Amendment; (b) hold that such material can be regulated by the States, subject to the specific safeguards enunciated above, without a showing that the material is *"utterly"* without redeeming social value"; and (c) hold that obscenity is to be determined by applying "contemporary community standards" . . . not "national standards." . . .

Vacated and remanded.

Justice Douglas dissented:

I

Today we leave open the way for California to send a man to prison for distributing brochures that advertise books and a movie under freshly written standards defining obscenity which until today's decision were never the part of any law.

The Court has worked hard to define obscenity and concededly has failed. In *Roth* v. *United States* . . . it ruled that "[o]bscene material is material which deals with sex in a manner appealing to prurient interest." . . . Obscenity, it was said, was rejected by the First Amendment because it is "utterly without redeeming social importance." . . . The presence of a "prurient interest" was to be determined by "contemporary community standards." . . . That test, it has been said, could not be determined by one standard here and another standard there. . . .

Today the Court retreats from the earlier formulations of the constitutional test and undertakes to make new definitions. This effort, like the earlier ones, is earnest and well intentioned. The difficulty is that we do not deal with constitutional terms, since "obscenity" is not mentioned in the Constitution or Bill of Rights. And the First Amendment makes no such exception from "the press" which it undertakes to protect nor, as I have said on other occasions, is an exception necessarily implied, for there was no recognized exception to the free press at the time the Bill of Rights was adopted which treated "obscene" publications differently from other types of papers, magazines, and books. So there are no constitutional guidelines for deciding what is and what is not "obscene." The Court is at large because we deal with tastes and standards of literature. What shocks me may be sustenance for my neighbor. What causes one person to boil up in rage over one pamphlet or movie may reflect only his neurosis, not shared by others. We deal here with a regime of censorship which, if adopted, should be done by constitutional amendment after full debate by the people.

Obscenity cases usually generate tremendous emotional outbursts. They have no business being in the courts. If a constitutional amendment authorized censorship, the censor would probably be an administrative agency. Then criminal prosecutions could follow as, if, and when publishers defied the censor and sold their literature. Under that regime a publisher would know when he was on dangerous ground. Under the present regime—whether the old standards or the new ones are used—the criminal law becomes a trap. A brand new test would put a publisher behind bars under a new law improvised by the courts after the publication. . . .

III

While the right to know is the corollary of the right to speak or publish, no one can be forced by government to listen to disclosure that he finds offensive. . . . There is no "captive audience" problem in these obscenity cases. No one is being compelled to look or to listen. Those who enter newsstands or bookstalls may be offended by what they see. But they are not compelled by the State to frequent those places; and it is only state or governmental action against which the First Amendment, applicable to the States by virtue of the Fourteenth, raises a ban.

The idea that the First Amendment permits government to ban publications that are "offensive" to some people puts an ominous gloss on freedom of the press. That test would make it possible to ban any paper or any journal or magazine in some benighted place. The First Amendment was designed "to invite dispute," to induce "a condition of unrest," to "create dissatisfaction with conditions as they are," and even to stir "people to anger." . . . The idea that the First Amendment permits punishment for ideas that are "offensive" to the particular judge or jury sitting in judgment is astounding. No greater leveler of speech or literature has ever been designed. To give the power to the censor, as we do today, is to make a sharp and radical break with the traditions of a free society. The First Amendment was not fashioned as a vehicle for dispensing tranquilizers to the people. Its prime function was to keep debate open to "offensive" as well as to "staid" people. The tendency throughout history has been to subdue the individual and to exalt the power of government. The use of the standard "offensive" gives authority to government that cuts the very vitals out of the First Amendment. As is intimated by the Court's opinion, the materials before us may be garbage. But so is much of what is said in political campaigns, in the daily press, on TV, or over the radio. By reason of the First Amendment—and solely because of it—speakers and publishers have not been threatened or subdued because their thoughts and ideas may be "offensive" to some. . . .

If there are to be restraints on what is obscene, then a constitutional amendment should be the way of achieving the end. There are societies where religion and mathematics are the only free segments. It would be a dark day for America if that were our destiny. But the people can make it such if they choose to write obscenity into the Constitution and define it.

We deal with highly emotional, not rational, questions. To many the Song of Solomon is obscene. I do not think we, the judges, were ever given the constitutional power to make definitions of obscenity. If it is to be defined, let the people debate and decide by a consti-

tutional amendment what they want to ban as obscene and what standards they want the legislatures and the courts to apply. Perhaps the people will decide that the path towards a mature, integrated society requires that all ideas competing for acceptance must have no censor. Perhaps they will decide otherwise. Whatever the choice, the courts will have some guidelines. Now we have none except our own predilections.

[The dissent by Justice Brennan, joined by Justices Stewart and Marshall, is omitted.]

Judicial independence and presidential authority

A serious Fourth Amendment issue arose in the 1970s as a result of a Nixon administration decision to conduct wide electronic surveillance of domestic political activists. The administration acted on the basis of a section of the Omnibus Crime Control and Safe Streets Act of 1968. This activity was challenged in a federal district court when defendants in a case involving the bombing of a CIA office in Ann Arbor, Michigan, asked the Court to compel the federal government to produce any evidence gained by such surveillance. Attorney General John Mitchell indicated that such evidence was gathered but refrained from complying because disclosure "would prejudice the national interest." The District Court rejected his argument, held for disclosure, and ruled that the surveillance violated the Fourth Amendment. The federal government took the issue to the Supreme Court in *United States* v. *District Court for the Eastern District of Michigan*. The government argued that the surveillance was a lawful and constitutional use of presidential power even though it was conducted without prior judicial approval. This argument was refuted in the majority opinion, a forthright rejection of President Nixon's attempt to claim the power to wiretap Americans without judicial supervision if "national security" is allegedly involved. Justice Powell wrote the majority decision soon after Nixon had appointed him to the Supreme Court.

UNITED STATES v. DISTRICT COURT FOR THE EASTERN DISTRICT OF MICHIGAN
407 U. S. 297 (1972)

We think the language of § 2511 (3), as well as the legislative history of the statute, refutes this interpretation. The relevant language is that:

"Nothing contained in this chapter . . . shall limit the constitutional power of the President to take such measures as he deems necessary to protect . . ."

against the dangers specified. At most, this is an implicit recognition that the President does have certain powers in the specified areas. Few would doubt this, as the section refers—among other things—to protection "against actual or potential attack or other hostile acts of a foreign power." But so far as the use of the President's electronic surveillance power is concerned, the language is essentially neutral.

Section 2511 (3) certainly confers no power, as the language is wholly inappropriate for such a purpose. It merely provides that the Act shall not be interpreted to limit or disturb such power as the President may have under the Constitution. In short, Congress simply left presidential powers where it found them. . . .

One could hardly expect a clearer expression of congressional neutrality. The debate above explicitly indicates that nothing in § 2511 (3) was intended to *expand* or to *contract* or to *define* whatever presidential surveillance powers existed in matters affecting the national security. If we could accept the Government's characterization of § 2511 (3) as a congressionally prescribed exception to the general requirement of a warrant, it would be necessary to consider the question of whether the surveillance in this case came within the exception and, if so, whether the statutory exception was itself constitutionally valid. But viewing § 2511 (3) as a congressional disclaimer and expression of neutrality, we hold that the statute is not the measure of the executive authority asserted in this case. Rather, we must look to the constitutional powers of the President. . . .

We begin the inquiry by noting that the President of the United States has the fundamental duty, under Art. II, § 1, of the Constitution, to "preserve, protect and defend the Constitution of the United States." Implicit in that duty is the power to protect our Government against those who would subvert or overthrow it by unlawful means. In the discharge of this duty, the President—through the Attorney General—may find it necessary to employ electronic surveillance to obtain intelligence information on the plans of those who plot unlawful acts against the Government. The use of such surveillance in internal security cases has been sanctioned more or less continuously by various Presidents and Attorneys General since July 1946. . . .

Though the Government and respondents debate their seriousness and magnitude, threats and acts of sabotage against the Government exist in sufficient number to justify investigative powers with respect to them. The covertness and complexity of potential unlawful conduct against the Government and the necessary dependency of many conspirators upon the telephone make electronic surveillance an effective investigatory instrument in certain circumstances. The marked acceleration in technological developments and sophistication in their use have resulted in new techniques for the planning, commission, and concealment of criminal activities. It would be contrary to the public interest for Government to deny to itself the prudent and lawful employment of those very techniques which are employed against the Government and its law-abiding citizens. . . .

But a recognition of these elementary truths does not make the employment by Government of electronic surveillance a welcome development—even when employed with restraint and other judicial supervision. There is, understandably, a deep-seated uneasiness and apprehension that this capability will be used to intrude upon cherished privacy of law-abiding citizens. We look to the Bill of Rights to safeguard this privacy. Though physical entry of the home is the chief evil against which the wording of the Fourth Amendment is directed, its broader spirit now shields private speech from unreasonable surveillance. . . .

National security cases, moreover, often reflect a convergence of First and Fourth Amendment values not present in cases of "ordinary" crime. Though the investigative duty of the executive may be stronger in such cases, so also is there greater jeopardy to constitutionally protected speech. "Historically the struggle for freedom of speech and press in England was bound up with the issue of the scope of the search and seizure power," . . . History abundantly documents the tendency of Government—however benevolent and benign its motives—to view with suspicion those who most fervently dispute its policies. Fourth Amendment protections become the more necessary when the targets of official surveillance may be those suspected of unorthodoxy in their political beliefs. The danger to political dissent is acute where the Government attempts to act under so vague a concept as the power to protect "domestic security." Given the difficulty of defining the domestic security interest, the danger of abuse in acting to protect that interest becomes apparent. . . . The price of lawful public dissent must not be a dread of subjection to an unchecked surveillance power. Nor must the fear of unauthorized official eavesdropping deter vigorous citizen dissent and discussion of Government action in private conversation. For private dissent, no less than open public discourse, is essential to our free society.

As the Fourth Amendment is not absolute in its terms, our task is to examine and balance the basic values at stake in this case: the duty of Government to protect the domestic security, and the potential danger posed by unreasonable surveillance to individual privacy and free expression. If the legitimate need of Government to safeguard domestic security requires the use of electronic surveillance, the question is whether the needs of citizens for privacy and free expression may not be better protected by requiring a warrant before such surveillance is undertaken. We must also ask whether a warrant requirement would unduly frustrate the efforts of Government to protect itself from acts of subversion and overthrow directed against it. . . .

. . . Fourth Amendment freedoms cannot properly be guaranteed if domestic security surveillances may be conducted solely within the discretion of the Executive Branch. The Fourth Amendment does not contemplate the executive officers of Government as neutral and disinterested magistrates. Their duty and responsibility are to enforce the laws, to investigate, and to prosecute. . . . But those charged with this investigative and prosecutorial duty shall not be the sole judges of when to utilize constitutionally sensitive means in pursuing their tasks. The historical judgment, which the Fourth Amendment accepts, is that unreviewed executive discretion may yield too readily to pressures to obtain incriminating evidence and overlook potential invasions of privacy and protected speech.

It may well be that, in the instant case, the Government's surveillance of Plamondon's conversations was a reasonable one which readily would have gained prior judicial approval. But . . . the Fourth Amendment contemplates a prior judicial judgment, not the risk that executive discretion may be reasonably exercised. This judicial role accords with our basic constitutional doctrine that individual freedoms will best be preserved through a separation of powers and division of functions among the different branches and levels of Government. . . . The independent check upon executive discretion is not satisfied, as the Government argues, by "extremely limited" post-surveillance judicial review. Indeed, post-surveillance review would never reach the surveillances which failed to result in prosecutions. Prior review by a neutral and detached magistrate is the time-tested means of effectuating Fourth Amendment rights. . . .

The Government argues that the special circumstances applicable to domestic security surveillances necessitate a further exception to the warrant requirement. It is urged that the requirement of prior judicial review would obstruct the President in the discharge of his constitutional duty to protect domestic security. We are told further that these surveillances are directed primarily to the collecting and maintaining of intelligence with respect to subversive forces, and are not an attempt to gather evidence for specific criminal prosecutions. It is said that this type of surveillance should not be subject to traditional warrant requirements which were established to govern investigation of criminal activity, not ongoing intelligence gathering. . . .

The Government further insists that courts "as a practical matter would have neither the knowledge nor the techniques necessary to determine whether there was probable cause to believe that surveillance was necessary to protect national security." These security problems, the Government contends, involve "a large number of complex and subtle factors" beyond the competence of courts to evaluate. . . .

As a final reason for exemption from a warrant requirement, the Government believes that disclosure to a magistrate of all or even a significant portion of the information involved in domestic security surveillances "would create serious potential dangers to the national security and to the lives of informants and agents. . . . Secrecy is the essential ingredient in intelligence gathering; requiring prior judicial authorization would create a greater 'danger of leaks . . . ,

because in addition to the judge, you have the clerk, the stenographer and some other officer like a law assistant or bailiff who may be apprised of the nature' of the surveillance." . . .

These contentions in behalf of a complete exemption from the warrant requirement, when urged on behalf of the President and the national security in its domestic implications, merit the most careful consideration. We certainly do not reject them lightly, especially at a time of worldwide ferment and when civil disorders in this country are more prevalent than in the less turbulent periods of our history. There is, no doubt, pragmatic force to the Government's position.

But we do not think a case has been made for the requested departure from Fourth Amendment standards. The circumstances described do not justify complete exemption of domestic security surveillance from prior judicial scrutiny. Official surveillance, whether its purpose be criminal investigation or ongoing intelligence gathering, risks infringement of constitutionally protected privacy of speech. Security surveillances are especially sensitive because of the inherent vagueness of the domestic security concept, the necessarily broad and continuing nature of intelligence gathering, and the temptation to utilize such surveillances to oversee political dissent. We recognize, as we have before, the constitutional basis of the President's domestic security role, but we think it must be exercised in a manner compatible with the Fourth Amendment. In this case we hold that this requires an appropriate prior warrant procedure.

We cannot accept the Government's argument that internal security matters are too subtle and complex for judicial evaluation. Courts regularly deal with the most difficult issues of our society. There is no reason to believe that federal judges will be insensitive to or uncomprehending of the issues involved in domestic security cases. Certainly courts can recognize that domestic security surveillance involves different considerations from the surveillance of "ordinary crime." If the threat is too subtle or complex for our senior law enforcement officers to convey its significance to a court, one may question whether there is probable cause for surveillance.

Nor do we believe prior judicial approval will fracture the secrecy essential to official intelligence gathering. The investigation of criminal activity has long involved imparting sensitive information to judicial officers who have respected the confidentialities involved. Judges may be counted upon to be especially conscious of security requirements in national security cases. Title III of the Omnibus Crime Control and Safe

Streets Act already has imposed this responsibility on the judiciary in connection with such crimes as espionage, sabotage, and treason, §§ 2516 (1) (a) and (c), each of which may involve domestic as well as foreign security threats. Moreover, a warrant application involves no public or adversary proceedings: it is an *ex parte* request before a magistrate or judge. Whatever security dangers clerical and secretarial personnel may pose can be minimized by proper administrative measures, possibly to the point of allowing the Government itself to provide the necessary clerical assistance.

Thus, we conclude that the Government's concerns do not justify departure in this case from the customary Fourth Amendment requirement of judicial approval prior to initiation of a search or surveillance. Although some added burden will be imposed upon the Attorney General, this inconvenience is justified in a free society to protect constitutional values. Nor do we think the Government's domestic surveillance powers will be impaired to any significant degree. A prior warrant establishes presumptive validity of the surveillance and will minimize the burden of justification in post-surveillance judicial review. By no means of least importance will be the reassurance of the public generally that indiscriminate wiretapping and bugging of law-abiding citizens cannot occur.

We emphasize, before concluding this opinion, the scope of our decision. As stated at the outset, this case involves only the domestic aspects of national security. We have not addressed, and express no opinion as to, the issues which may be involved with respect to activities of foreign powers or their agents. . . .

The electronic surveillance decision suggested that the Nixon appointees would not support the administration on issues involving blatant invasions of fundamental freedoms and ignoring traditional judicial controls. This proved to be true when the Watergate controversy led to an unprecedented confrontation. The crisis grew out of the capture of seven individuals who had broken into the offices of the Democratic National Committee in the Watergate building in Washington, D. C., on June 17, 1972. When the seven pleaded guilty, federal district judge John Sirica read a letter from one of the defendants, James N. McCord, Jr., implicating others in the conspiracy leading to the break-in. A Senate investigating committee heard not only McCord's testimony but also the dramatic revelations of former White House counsel, John W. Dean, directly involving the White House staff and President Nixon himself in planning or covering up the break-in. Yet another dramatic disclosure came with the revelation that presidential discussions on these and other matters had been recorded for two years on tapes. Judge Sirica ordered that the tapes be turned over to him for *in camera* examination so that unprivileged information could be turned over to a grand jury. President Nixon ordered Special Prosecutor Archibald Cox "not to pursue the matter further." Cox refused and, in yet another dramatic confrontation, was fired by Solicitor General Robert H. Bork—after Attorney General Elliot Richardson resigned and Deputy Attorney General William Ruckelshaus was fired for refusing to fire Cox. These events were described as the "Saturday Night Massacre." After strong negative public reaction, President Nixon finally turned over the tapes (with some omissions and "gaps") and Leon Jaworski became the new special prosecutor with greater independence.

The House Judiciary Committee subsequently subpoenaed 42 additional conversations on tape and Special Prosecutor Jaworski, 64 more. But President Nixon refused to comply and challenged Jaworski's subpoena before the Supreme Court. He claimed authority to determine what evidence he would give or withhold from Jaworski because the latter was allegedly under executive control. More important, he claimed an unprecedentedly large area protected by executive privilege. In

United States v. *Nixon* the Court, in a unanimous opinion written by Chief Justice Burger, rejected this claim.

UNITED STATES v. NIXON
418 U. S. 683 (1974)

IV. THE CLAIM OF PRIVILEGE

A

Having determined that the requirements of Rule 17 (c) were satisfied, we turn to the claim that the subpoena should be quashed because it demands "confidential conversations between a President and his close advisers that it would be inconsistent with the public interest to produce." The first contention is a broad claim that the separation of powers doctrine precludes judicial review of a President's claim of privilege. The second contention is that if he does not prevail on the claim absolute privilege, the court should hold as a matter of constitutional law that the privilege prevails over the subpoena duces tecum.

In the performance of assigned constitutional duties each branch of the Government must initially interpret the Constitution, and the interpretation of its powers by any branch is due great respect from the others. The President's counsel, as we have noted, reads the Constitution as providing an absolute privilege of confidentiality for all Presidential communications. Many decisions of this Court, however, have unequivocally reaffirmed the holding of Marbury v. Madison (1803) that "[i]t is emphatically the province and duty of the judicial department to say what the law is."

No holding of the Court has defined the scope of judicial power specifically relating to the enforcement of a subpoena for confidential Presidential communications for use in a criminal prosecution, but other exercises of power by the Executive Branch and the Legislative Branch have been found invalid as in conflict with the Constitution . . . Youngstown Sheet & Tube. In a series of cases, the Court interpreted the explicit immunity conferred by express provisions of the Constitution on Members of the House and Senate by the Speech or Debate Clause, U. S. Const. Art. I §6. . . . Since this Court has consistently exercised the power to construe and delineate claims arising under express powers, it must follow that the Court has authority to interpret claims with respect to powers alleged to derive from enumerated powers.

Our system of government "requires that federal courts on occasion interpret the Constitution in a manner at variance with the construction given the document by another branch." . . .

And in Baker v. Carr [1962], the Court stated: "Deciding whether a matter has in any measure been committed by the Constitution to another branch of government, or whether the action of that branch exceeds whatever authority has been committed, is itself a delicate exercise in constitutional interpretation, and is a responsibility of this Court as ultimate interpreter of the Constitution." Notwithstanding the deference each branch must accord the others, the "judicial Power of the United States" vested in the federal courts by Art. III, §1, of the Constitution can no more be shared with the Executive Branch than the Chief Executive, for example, can share with the Judiciary the veto power, or the Congress share with the Judiciary the power to override a Presidential veto. Any other conclusion would be contrary to the basic concept of separation of powers and the checks and balances that flow from the scheme of a tripartite government. . . . We therefore reaffirm that it is the province and duty of this Court "to say what the law is" with respect to the claim of privilege presented in this case. Marbury v. Madison.

B

In support of his claim of absolute privilege, the President's counsel urges two grounds, one of which is common to all governments and one of which is peculiar to our system of separation of powers. The first ground is the valid need for protection of communications between high Government officials and those who advise and assist them in the performance of their manifold duties; the importance of this confidentiality is too plain to require further discussion. Human experience teaches that those who expect public dissemination of their remarks may well temper candor with a concern for appearances and for their own interests to the detriment of the decisionmaking process. Whatever the nature of the privilege of confidentiality of Presidential communications in the exercise of Art. II powers, the privilege can be said to derive from the supremacy of each branch within its own assigned area of constitutional duties. Certain powers and privileges flow from the nature of enumerated powers; the protection of the confidentiality of Presidential communications has similar constitutional underpinnings.

The second ground asserted by the President's counsel in support of the claim of absolute privilege rests on the doctrine of separation of powers. Here it is argued that the independence of the Executive Branch within its own sphere, Humphrey's Executor v. United States (1935); Kilbourn v. Thompson (1881), insulates a President from a judicial subpoena in an ongoing criminal prosecution, and thereby protects confidential Presidential communications.

However, neither the doctrine of separation of powers, nor the need for confidentiality of high-level communications, without more, can sustain an absolute, unqualified Presidential privilege of immunity from judicial process under all circumstances. The President's need for complete candor and objectivity from advisers calls for great deference from the courts. However, when the privilege depends solely on the broad, undifferentiated claim of public interest in the confidentiality of such conversations, a confrontation with other values arises. Absent a claim of need to protect military, diplomatic, or sensitive national security secrets, we find it difficult to accept the argument that even the very important interest in confidentiality of Presidential communications is significantly diminished by production of such material for in camera inspection with all the protection that a district court will be obliged to provide.

The impediment that an absolute, unqualified privilege would place in the way of the primary constitutional duty of the Judicial Branch to do justice in criminal prosecutions would plainly conflict with the function of the courts under Art. III. In designing the structure of our Government and dividing and allocating the sovereign power among three co-equal branches, the Framers of the Constitution sought to provide a comprehensive system, but the separate powers were not intended to operate with absolute independence.

While the Constitution diffuses power the better to secure liberty, it also contemplates that practice will integrate the dispersed powers into a workable government. It enjoins upon its branches separateness but interdependence, autonomy but reciprocity. . . .

C

Since we conclude that the legitimate needs of the judicial process may outweigh Presidential privilege, it is necessary to resolve those competing interests in a manner that preserves the essential functions of each branch. The right and indeed the duty to resolve that question does not free the judiciary from according high respect to the representations made on behalf of the President. . . .

The expectation of a President to the confidentiality of his conversations and correspondence, like the claim of confidentiality of jucidial deliberations, for example, has all the values to which we accord deference for the privacy of all citizens and added to those values the necessity for protection of the public interest in candid, objective, and even blunt or harsh opinions in Presidential decision making. . . . These are the considerations justifying a presumptive privilege for Presidential communications. The privilege is fundamental to the operation of government and inextricably rooted in the separation of powers under the Constitution. In Nixon v. Sirica [1973] . . . the Court of Appeals held that such Presidential communications are "presumptively privileged," . . . and this position is accepted by both parties in the present litigation. We agree with Mr. Chief Justice Marshall's observation, therefore, that "[i]n no case of this kind would a court be required to proceed against the President as against an ordinary individual." . . .

But this presumptive privilege must be considered in light of our historic commitment to the rule of law. This is nowhere more profoundly manifest than in our view that "the twofold aim [of criminal justice] is that guilt shall not escape or innocence suffer." . . . We have elected to employ an adversary system of criminal justice in which the parties contest all issues before a court of law. The need to develop all relevant facts in the adversary system is both fundamental and comprehensive. The ends of criminal justice would be defeated if judgments were to be founded on a partial or speculative presentation of the facts. The very integrity of the judicial system and public confidence in the system depend on full disclosure of all the facts, within the framework of the rules of evidence. To ensure that justice is done, it is imperative to the function of courts that compulsory process be available for the production of evidence needed either by the prosecution or by the defense. . . .

. . . In this case the President challenges a subpoena served on him as a third party requiring the production of materials for use in a criminal prosecution; he does so on the claim that he has a privilege against disclosure of confidential communications. He does not place his claim of privilege on the ground they are military or diplomatic secrets. As to these areas of Art. II duties the courts have traditionally shown the utmost deference to Presidential responsibilities. In C. & S. Air Lines v. Waterman Steamship Corp. (1948), dealing with Presidential authority involving foreign policy considerations, the Court said: "The President, both as Commander-in-Chief and as the Nation's organ for foreign affairs, has available intelligence services whose reports are not and ought not to be published to the world. It would be intolerable that courts, without the relevant information, should review and perhaps nullify actions of the Executive taken on information properly held secret." In United States v. Reynolds (1953), dealing with a claimant's demand for evidence in a damage case against the Government the Court said: "It may be possible to satisfy the court, from all the circumstances of the case, that there is a reasonable danger that compulsion of the evidence will expose military matters which, in the interest of national security, should not be divulged. When this is the case, the occasion for the privilege is appropriate, and the court should not jeopardize the security which the privilege is meant to protect by insisting upon an examination of the evidence, even by the judge alone, in chambers." No case of the Court, however, has extended this high degree of deference to a President's generalized interest in confidentiality. Nowhere in the Constitution, as we have noted earlier, is there any explicit reference to a privilege of confidentiality, yet to the extent this interest relates to the effective discharge of a President's powers, it is constitutionally based.

The right to the production of all evidence at a criminal trial similarly has constitutional dimensions. The Sixth Amendment explicitly confers upon every defendant in a criminal trial the right "to be confronted with the witnesses against him" and "to have compulsory process for obtaining witnesses in his favor." Moreover, the Fifth Amendment also guarantees that no person shall be deprived of liberty without due process of law. It is the manifest duty of the courts to vindicate those guarantees, and to accomplish that it is essential that all relevant and admissible evidence be produced.

In this case we must weigh the importance of the general privilege of confidentiality of Presidential communications in performance of his responsibilities against the inroads of such a privilege on the fair administration of criminal justice. The interest in preserving confidentiality is weighty indeed and entitled to great respect. However, we cannot conclude that advisers will be moved to temper the candor of their remarks by the infrequent occasions of disclosure because of the possibility that such conversations will be called for in the context of a criminal prosecution.

On the other hand, the allowance of the privilege to withhold evidence that is demonstrably relevant in a criminal trial would cut deeply into the guarantee of due process of law and gravely impair the basic function of the courts. A President's acknowledged need for confidentiality in the communications of his office is general in nature, whereas the constitutional need for production of relevant evidence in a criminal proceeding is specific and central to the fair adjudication of a particular criminal case in the administration of justice. Without access to specific facts a criminal prosecution may be totally frustrated. The President's broad interest in confidentiality of communications will not be vitiated by disclosure of a limited number of conversations preliminarily shown to have some bearing on the pending criminal cases.

We conclude that when the ground for asserting privilege as to subpoenaed matrials sought for use in a criminal trial is based only on the generalized interest in confidentiality, it cannot prevail over the fundamental demands of due process of law in the fair administration of criminal justice. The generalized assertion of privilege must yield to the demonstrated, specific need for evidence in a pending criminal trial.

D

We have earlier determined that the District Court did not err in authorizing the issuance of the subpoena. If a President concludes that compliance with a subpoena would be injurious to the public interest he may properly, as was done here, invoke a claim of privilege on the return of the subpoena. Upon receiving a claim of privilege from the Chief Executive, it became the further duty of the District Court to treat the subpoenaed material as presumptively privileged and to require the Special Prosecutor to demonstrate that the Presidential material was "essential to the justice of the [pending criminal] case." United States v. Burr. Here the District Court treated the material as presumptively privileged, proceeded to find that the Special Prosecutor has made sufficient showing to rebut the presumption, and ordered an in camera examination of the subpoenaed material. On the basis of our examination of the record we are unable to conclude that the District Court erred in ordering the inspection. Accordingly we affirm the order of the District Court that subpoenaed materials be transmitted to that court. We now turn to the important question of the District Court's responsibilities in conducting the in camera examination of Presidential materials or communications delivered under the compulsion of the subpoena duces tecum.

E

Enforcement of the subpoena duces tecum was stayed pending this Court's resolution of the issues raised by the petitions for certiorari. Those issues now having been disposed of, the matter of implementation will rest with the District Court. "[T]he guard, furnished to [the President] to protect him from being harassed by vexations and unnecessary subpoenas, is to be looked for in the conduct of a [district] court after those subpoenas have issued; not in any circumstances which is to precede their being issued." United States v. Burr. Statements that meet the test of admissibility and relevance must be isolated; all other material must be excised. At this stage the District Court is not limited to representations of the Special Prosecutor as to the evidence sought by the subpoena; the material will be available to the District Court. It is elementary that in camera inspection of evidence is always a procedure calling for scrupulous protection against any release or publication of material not found by the court, at that stage, probably admissible in evidence and relevant to the issues of the trial for which it is sought. That being true of an ordinary situation, it is obvious that the District Court has a very heavy responsibility to see to it that Presidential conversations, which are either not relevant or not admissible, are accorded that high degree of respect due the President of the United States. Mr. Chief Justice Marshall sitting as a trial judge in the Burr case was extraordinarily careful to point out that "[i]n no case of this kind would a court be required to proceed against the president as against an ordinary individual." Marshall's statement cannot be read to mean in any sense that a President is above the law, but relates to the singularly unique role under Art. II of a President's communications and activities, related to the performance of duties under that Article. Moreover, a President's communications and activities encompass a vastly wider range of sensitive material than would be true of any "ordinary individual." It is therefore necessary in the public interest to afford Presidential confidentiality the greatest protection consistent with the fair administration of justice. The need for confidentiality even as to idle conversations with associates in which casual reference might be made concerning political leaders within the country or foreign statesmen is too obvious to call for further treatment. We have no doubt that the District Judge will at all times accord to Presidential records that high degree of deference suggested in United States v. Burr and will discharge his responsibility to see to it that until released to the Special Prosecutor no in camera material is revealed to anyone. This burden applies with even greater force to excised material; once the decision is made to excise, the material is restored to its privileged status and should be returned under seal to its lawful custodian.

Since this matter came before the Court during the pendency of a criminal prosecution, and on representations that time is of the essence, the mandate shall issue forthwith.

Affirmed.

[Justice Rehnquist took no part in the consideration or decision of these cases.]

The Nixon appointees participating in the decision united with the other justices to present a unified rejection of President Nixon's claims. His resignation followed. His pardon by President Gerald Ford brought to a close one of the most serious constitutional crises of modern times. In 1975, after more than a year in the presidency, Ford had an opportunity to fill a Supreme Court vacancy when Justice William O. Douglas retired. On December 1, President Ford nominated moderate conservative Judge John Paul Stevens of the Seventh Circuit Court of Appeals.

The new laissez faire: Money and influence in elections

Congress' authority to control money in elections was the subject of the next major decision in which the Court considered the nature of the political system. In *Buckley* v. *Valeo*, the decision was *per curiam*. The statute creating a federal election commission withstood First Amendment challenges to portions that established monetary limits on campaign contributions of individuals and political committees, public financing of presidential primary and general election campaigns, disclosure of campaign contributions of over $100, and campaign expenditures of more than $10. But the campaign spending limits imposed on individuals and campaign groups, including the personal spending of candidates, was held in violation of First Amendment rights of association and free expression.

BUCKLEY v. VALEO
424 U. S. 1 (1976)

PER CURIAM:

These appeals present constitutional challenges to the key provisions of the Federal Election Campaign Act of 1971, . . . as amended in 1974 . . .

[The provisions include requirements that] individual political contributions are limited to $1,000 to any single candidate per election, with an overall annual limitation of $25,000 by any contributor; independent expenditures by individuals and groups "relative to a clearly identified candidate" are limited to $1,000 a year; campaign spending by candidates for various federal offices and spending for national conventions by political parties are subject to prescribed limits; (b) contributions and expenditures above certain threshold levels must be reported and publicly disclosed; (c) a system for public funding of Presidential campaign activities is established; . . . (d) a Federal Election Commission is established to administer and enforce the Act. . . . [Regarding Contributions and expenditures the majority ruled:]

A. *General Principles.* The Act's contribution and expenditure limitations operate in an area of the most fundamental First Amendment activities. Discussion of public issues and debate on the qualifications of candidates are integral to the operation of the system of government established by our Constitution. . . . upholding the constitutional validity of the Act's contribution and expenditure provisions on the ground that those provisions should be viewed as regulating conduct not speech, the Court of Appeals relied upon United States v. O'Brien (p. 1306 above). [We] cannot share the view that the present Act's contribution and expenditure limitations are comparable to the restrictions on conduct upheld in O'Brien. The expenditure of money simply cannot be equated with such conduct as destruction of a draft card. Some forms of communication made possible by the giving and spending of money involve speech alone, some involve conduct primarily, and some involve a combination of the two. Yet this Court has never suggested that the dependence of a communication on the expenditure of money operates itself to introduce a nonspeech element or to reduce the exacting scrutiny required by the First Amendment. . . .

Even if the categorization of the expenditure of money as conduct were accepted, the limitations challenged here would not meet the O'Brien test because the governmental interests advanced in support of the Act involve "suppressing communication." The interests served by the Act include restricting the voices of people and interest groups who have money to spend and reducing the overall scope of federal election campaigns. Although the Act does not focus on the ideas expressed by persons or groups subjected to its regulations, it is aimed in part at equalizing the relative ability of all voters to affect electoral outcomes by placing a ceiling on expenditures for political expression by citizens and groups. Unlike O'Brien, where the Selective Service System's administrative interest in the preservation of draft cards was wholly unrelated to their use as a means of communication, it is beyond dispute that the interest in regulating the alleged "conduct" of giving or spending money "arises in some measure because the communication allegedly integral to the conduct is itself thought to be harmful."

Nor can the Act's contribution and expenditure limitations be sustained, as some of the parties suggest, by reference to the constitutional principles reflected in such decisions as Cox v. Louisiana II, Adderley v. Florida, and Kovacs v. Cooper. Those cases stand for the proposition that the government may adopt reasonable time, place, and manner regulations, which do not discriminate between speakers or ideas, in order to further an important governmental interest unrelated to the restriction of communication. In contrast to O'Brien, where the method of expression was held to be subject to prohibition, Cox, Adderley, and Kovacs involved place or manner restrictions on legitimate modes of expression—picketing, parading, demonstrating, and using a soundtruck. The critical difference between this case and those time, place and manner cases is that the present Act's contribution and expenditure limitations impose direct quantity restrictions on political communication and association by persons, groups, candidates and political parties in addition to any reasonable time, place, and manner regulations otherwise imposed.

A restriction on the amount of money a person or group can spend on political communication during a campaign necessarily reduces the quantity of expression by restricting the number of issues discussed, the depth of their exploration, and the size of the audience reached. This is because virtually every means of communicating ideas in today's mass society requires the expenditure of money. . . . expenditure limitations contained in the Act represent substantial rather than merely theoretical restraints on the quantity and diversity of political speech. [The] $1,000 ceiling on spending "relative to a clearly identified candidate" would appear to exclude all citizens and groups except candidates, political parties and the institutional press from any significant use of the most effective means of communication. . . .

By contrast with a limitation upon expenditures for political expression, a limitation upon the amount that any one person or group may contribute to a candidate or political committee entails only a marginal restriction upon the contributor's ability to engage in free communication. A contribution serves as a general expression of support for the candidate and his views, but does not communicate the underlying basis for the support. The quantity of communication by the contributor does not increase perceptibly with the size of his contribution, since the expression rests solely on the undifferentiated, symbolic act of contributing. At most, the size of the contribution provides a very rough index of the intensity of the contributor's support for the candidate. A limitation on the amount of money a person may give to a candidate or campaign organization thus involves little direct restraint on his political communication, for it permits the symbolic expression of support evidenced by a contribution but does not in any way infringe the contributor's freedom to discuss candidates and issues. While contributions may result in political expression if spent by a candidate or an association to present views to the voters, the transformation of contributions into political debate involves speech by someone other than the contributor.

Given the important role of contributions in financing political campaigns, contribution restrictions could have a severe impact on political dialogue if the limitations prevented candidates and political committees from amassing the resources necessary for effective advocacy. There is no indication, however, that the contribution limitations imposed by the Act would have any dramatic adverse effect on the funding of campaigns and political associations. The overall effect of the Act's contribution ceilings is merely to require candidates and political committees to raise funds from a greater number of persons and to compel people who would otherwise contribute amounts greater than the statutory limits to expend such funds on direct political expression, rather than to reduce the total amount of money potentially available to promote political expression.

The Act's contribution and expenditure limitations also impinge on protected associational freedoms. Making a contribution, like joining a political party, serves to affiliate a person with a candidate. In addition, it enables like-minded persons to pool their re-

sources in furtherance of common political goals. The Act's contribution ceilings thus limit one important means of associating with a candidate or committee, but leave the contributor free to become a member of any political association and to assist personally in the association's efforts on behalf of candidates. And the Act's contribution limitations permit associations and candidates to aggregate large sums of money to promote effective advocacy. By contrast, the Act's $1,000 limitation on independent expenditures "relative to a clearly identified candidate" precludes most associations from effectively amplifying the voice of their adherents. [In] sum, although the Act's contribution and expenditure limitations both implicate fundamental First Amendment interests, its expenditure ceilings impose significantly more severe restrictions on protected freedoms of political expression and association than do its limitations on financial contributions.

B. *Contribution Limitations.* 1. *The $1,000 Limitation on Contributions by Individuals and Groups to Candidates and Authorized Campaign Committees.* [T]he primary First Amendment problem raised by the Act's contribution limitations is their restriction of one aspect of the contributor's freedom of political association. [G]overnmental "action which may have the effect of curtailing the freedom to associate is subject to the closest scrutiny." NAACP v. Alabama [p. 1455 below]. Yet, [e]ven a "'significant interference' with protected rights of political association" may be sustained if the State demonstrates a sufficiently important interest and employs means closely drawn to avoid unnecessary abridgment of associational freedoms.

It is unnecessary to look beyond the Act's primary purpose—to limit the actuality and appearance of corruption resulting from large individual financial contributions—in order to find a constitutionally sufficient justification for the $1,000 contribution limitation. [To] the extent that large contributions are given to secure political quid pro quos from current and potential officeholders, the integrity of our system of representative democracy is undermined. Although the scope of such pernicious practices can never be reliably ascertained, the deeply disturbing examples surfacing after the 1972 election demonstrate that the problem is not an illusory one. [Of] almost equal concern as the danger of actual quid pro quo arrangements is the impact of the appearance of corruption stemming from public awareness of the opportunities for abuse inherent in a regime of large individual financial contributions. [Appellants] contend that the contribution limitations must be invalidated because bribery laws and narrowly-drawn disclosure requirements constitute a less restrictive means of dealing with "proven and suspected quid pro quo arrangements." But laws making criminal the giving and taking of bribes deal with only the most blatant and specific attempts of those with money to influence governmental action. And [Congress] was surely entitled to conclude that disclosure was only a partial measure, and that contribution ceilings were a necessary legislative concomitant to deal with the reality or appearance of corruption. . . .

The Act's $1,000 contribution limitation focuses precisely on the problem of large campaign contributions—the narrow aspect of political association where the actuality and potential for corruption have been identified—while leaving persons free to engage in independent political expression, to associate actively through volunteering their services, and to assist to a limited but nonetheless substantial extent in supporting candidates and committees with financial resources. Significantly, the Act's contribution limitations in themselves do not undermine to any material degree the potential for robust and effective discussion of candidates and campaign issues by individual citizens, associations, the institutional press, candidates, and political parties. We find that, under the rigorous standard of review established by our prior decisions, the weighty interests served by restricting the size of financial contributions to political candidates are sufficient to justify the limited effect upon First Amendment freedoms caused by the $1,000 contribution ceiling.

Appellants' first overbreadth challenge to the contribution ceiling rests on the proposition that most large contributors do not seek improper influence over a candidate's position or an officeholder's action. Although the truth of that proposition may be assumed, it does not undercut the validity of the $1,000 contribution limitation. Not only is it difficult to isolate suspect contributions but, more importantly, Congress was justified in concluding that the interest in safeguarding against the appearance of impropriety requires that the opportunity for abuse inherent in the process of raising large monetary contributions be eliminated. A second, related overbreadth claim is that the $1,000 restriction is unrealistically low because much more than that amount would still not be enough to enable an unscrupulous contributor to exercise improper influence over a candidate or officeholder, especially in campaigns for statewide or national office. While the contribution limitation provisions might well have been structured to take account

of the graduated expenditure limitations for House, Senate and Presidential campaigns, Congress' failure to engage in such fine tuning does not invalidate the legislation. . . .

Apart from these First Amendment concerns, appellants argue that the contribution limitations work such an invidious discrimination between incumbents and challengers that the statutory provisions must be declared unconstitutional on their face. There is [no] evidence to support the claim that the contribution limitations in themselves discriminate against major-party challengers to incumbents. The charge of discrimination against minor-party and independent candidates is more troubling, but the record provides no basis for concluding that the Act invidiously disadvantages such candidates. [T]he restriction would appear to benefit minor-party and independent candidates relative to their major-party opponents because major-party candidates receive far more money in large contributions. Although there is some force to appellants' response that minor-party candidates are primarily concerned with their ability to amass the resources necessary to reach the electorate rather than with their funding position relative to their major-party opponents, the record is virtually devoid of support for the claim that the $1,000 contribution limitation will have a serious effect on the initiation and scope of minor-party and independent candidacies. . . . [The Court also rejected similar challenges to the $5000 limit on contributions by "political committees," the limits on volunteers' incidental expenses, and the $25,000 limit on total contributions by an individual during a calendar year.]

C. *Expenditure Limitations.* The Act's expenditure ceilings impose direct and substantial restraints on the quantity of political speech. [It] is clear that a primary effect of these expenditure limitations is to restrict the quantity of campaign speech by individuals, groups, and candidates. The restrictions, while neutral as to the ideas expressed, limit political expression "at the core of our electoral process and of First Amendment freedoms."

1. *The $1,000 limitation on expenditures "relative to a clearly identified candidate."* Section 608 (e) (1) provides that "[n]o person may make any expenditure . . . relative to a clearly identified candidate during a calendar year which, when added to all other expenditures made by such person during the year advocating the election or defeat of such candidate, exceeds $1,000." The plain effect of § 608 (e) (1) is to prohibit all individuals, who are neither candidates nor owners of institutional

press facilities, and all groups, except political parties and campaign organizations, from voicing their views "relative to a clearly identified candidate" through means that entail aggregate expenditures of more than $1,000 during a calendar year. The provision, for example, would make it a federal criminal offense for a person or association to place a single one-quarter page advertisement "relative to a clearly identified candidate" in a major metropolitan newspaper. . . .

[Unconstitutional vagueness] can be avoided only by reading § 608 (e) (1) as limited to communications that include explicit words of advocacy of election or defeat of a candidate. [We] turn then to the basic First Amendment question—whether § 608 (e) (1), even as thus narrowly and explicitly construed, impermissibly burdens the constitutional right of free expression. The Court of Appeals summarily held the provision constitutionally valid on the ground that "section 608 (e) is a loophole-closing provision only" that is necessary to prevent circumvention of the contribution limitations. We cannot agree. [T]he constitutionality of § 608 (e) (1) turns on whether the governmental interests advanced in its support satisfy the exacting scrutiny applicable to limitations on core First Amendment rights of political expression.

We find that the governmental interest in preventing corruption and the appearance of corruption is inadequate to justify § 608 (e) (1)'s ceiling on independent expenditures. First, assuming arguendo that large independent expenditures pose the same dangers of actual or apparent quid pro quo arrangements as do large contributions, § 608 (e) (1) does not provide an answer that sufficiently relates to the elimination of those dangers. Unlike the contribution limitations' total ban on the giving of large amounts of money to candidates, § 608 (e) (1) prevents only some large expenditures. So long as persons and groups eschew expenditures that in express terms advocate the election or defeat of a clearly identified candidate, they are free to spend as much as they want to promote the candidate and his views. [It] would naively underestimate the ingenuity and resourcefulness of persons and groups desiring to buy influence to believe that they would have much difficulty devising expenditures that skirted the restriction on express advocacy of election or defeat but nevertheless benefited the candidate's campaign. [Second], the independent advocacy restricted by the provision does not presently appear to pose dangers of real or apparent corruption comparable to those identified with large campaign contributions. The parties defending § 608 (e) (1) contend that it is necessary to prevent would-be contributors from

avoiding the contribution limitations by the simple expedient of paying directly for media advertisements or for other portions of the candidate's campaign activities. [But] controlled or coordinated expenditures are treated as contributions rather than expenditures under the Act [and are restricted by the valid § 608 (b).] By contrast, § 608 (e) (1) limits expenditures for express advocacy of candidates made totally independently of the candidate and his campaign. Unlike contributions, such independent expenditures may well provide little assistance to the candidate's campaign and indeed may prove counterproductive. The absence of prearrangement and coordination of an expenditure with the candidate or his agent not only undermines the value of the expenditure to the candidate, but also alleviates the danger that expenditures will be given as a quid pro quo for improper commitments from the candidate. Rather than preventing circumvention of the contribution limitations, § 608 (e) (1) severely restricts all independent advocacy despite its substantially diminished potential for abuse. While the independent expenditure ceiling thus fails to serve any substantial governmental interest in stemming the reality or appearance of corruption in the electoral process, it heavily burdens core First Amendment expression. [Advocacy] of the election or defeat of candidates for federal office is no less entitled to protection under the First Amendment than the discussion of political policy generally or advocacy of the passage or defeat of legislation.

It is argued, however, that the ancillary governmental interest in equalizing the relative ability of individuals and groups to influence the outcome of elections serves to justify [this limitation]. But the concept that government may restrict the speech of some elements of our society in order to enhance the relative voice of others is wholly foreign to the First Amendment, which was designed "to secure the 'the widest possible dissemination of information from diverse and antagonistic sources,'" and "'to assure unfettered interchange of ideas for the bringing about of political and social changes desired by the people.'" . . . The First Amendment's protection against governmental abridgment of free expression cannot properly be made to depend on a person's financial ability to engage in public discussion.

The Court's decisions in Mills v. Alabama . . . and in Tornillo . . . held that legislative restrictions on advocacy of the election or defeat of political candidates are wholly at odds with the guarantees of the First Amendment. In Mills, the Court addressed the question whether "a State, consistently with the United

States Constitution, can make it a crime for the editor of a daily newspaper to write and publish an editorial *on election day* urging people to vote a certain way on issues submitted to them." We held that "no test of reasonableness could save . . . a state law from invalidation as a violation of the First Amendment." Yet the prohibition on election day editorials invalidated in Mills is clearly a lesser intrusion on constitutional freedom than a $1,000 limitation on the amount of money any person or association can spend *during an entire election year* in advocating the election or defeat of a candidate for public office. [The] legislative restraint [invalidated] in Tornillo pales in comparison to the limitations imposed by § 608 (e) (1). [We] conclude that § 608 (e) (1)'s independent expenditure limitation is unconstitutional under the First Amendment.

2. *Limitation on expenditures by candidates from personal or family resources.* The Act also sets limits on expenditures by a candidate "from his personal funds, or the personal funds of his immediate family, in connection with his campaigns during any calendar year." § 608 (a) (1). These ceilings vary from $50,000 for Presidential or Vice Presidential candidates to $35,000 for Senate candidates, and $25,000 for most candidates for the House of Representatives. [The] candidate, no less than any other person, has a First Amendment right to engage in the discussion of public issues and vigorously and tirelessly to advocate his own election and the election of other candidates. [The] ceiling on personal expenditures by a candidate in furtherance of his own candidacy thus clearly and directly interferes with constitutionally protected freedoms. The primary governmental interest served by the Act—the prevention of actual and apparent corruption of the political process—does not support the limitation on the candidate's expenditure of his own personal funds. [T]he use of personal funds reduces the candidate's dependence on outside contributions and thereby counteracts the coercive pressures and attendant risks of abuse to which the Act's contribution limitations are directed.

The ancillary interest in equalizing the relative financial resources of candidates competing for elective office, therefore, provides the sole relevant rationale for Section 608 (a)'s expenditure ceiling. That interest is clearly not sufficient to justify the provision's infringement of fundamental First Amendment rights. First, the limitation may fail to promote financial equality among candidates. A candidate who spends less of his personal resources on his campaign may nonetheless outspend his rival as a result of more suc-cessful fundraising efforts. Indeed, a candidate's personal wealth may impede his efforts to persuade others that he needs their financial contributions or volunteer efforts to conduct an effective campaign. Second, and more fundamentally, the First Amendment simply cannot tolerate § 608 (a)'s restriction upon the freedom of a candidate to speak without legislative limit on behalf of his own candidacy. . . .

3. *Limitations on campaign expenditures.* Section 608 (c) of the Act places limitations on overall campaign expenditures by candidates seeking nomination for election and election to federal office. Presidential candidates may spend $10,000,000 in seeking nomination for office and an additional $20,000,000 in the general election campaign. [There are also ceilings for campaigns for the House and Senate.] [No] governmental interest that has been suggested is sufficient to justify [these restrictions] on the quantity of political expression. [The] campaign expenditure ceilings appear to be designed primarily to serve the governmental interests in reducing the allegedly skyrocketing costs of political campaigns. [T]he mere growth in the cost of federal election campaigns in and of itself provides no basis for governmental restrictions on the quantity of campaign spending and the resulting limitation on the scope of federal campaigns. The First Amendment denies government the power to determine that spending to promote one's political views is wasteful, excessive, or unwise. In the free society ordained by our Constitution it is not the government but the people—individually as citizens and candidates and collectively as associations and political committees—who must retain control over the quantity and range of debate on public issues in a political campaign. [W]e hold that § 608 (c) is constitutionally invalid.

In sum, the [contribution limits] are constitutionally valid. These limitations along with the disclosure provisions, constitute the Act's primary weapons against the reality or appearance of improper influence stemming from the dependence of candidates on large campaign contributions. The contribution ceilings thus serve the basic governmental interest in safeguarding the integrity of the electoral process without directly impinging upon the rights of individual citizens and candidates to engage in political debate and discussion. By contrast, the First Amendment requires the invalidation of the Act's independent expenditure ceiling, its limitation on a candidate's expenditures from his own personal funds, and its ceilings on overall campaign expenditures. These provisions place substantial and direct restrictions on the ability of candidates, citizens, and associations to engage in protected political expression, restrictions that the First Amendment cannot tolerate. . . .

[Chief Justice Burger's partial concurrence and partial dissent is omitted.]

Justice White concurred in part and dissented in part:

I dissent [from] the Court's view that the expenditure limitations [violate] the First Amendment. Concededly, neither the limitations on contributions nor those on expenditures directly or indirectly purport to control the content of political speech by candidates or by their supporters or detractors. What the Act regulates is giving and spending money, acts that have First Amendment significance not because they are themselves communicative with respect to the qualifications of the candidate, but because money may be used to defray the expenses of speaking or otherwise communicating about the merits or demerits of federal candidates for election. The act of giving money to political candidates, however, may have illegal or other undesirable consequences: it may be used to secure the express or tacit understanding that the giver will enjoy political favor if the candidate is elected. Both Congress and this Court's cases have recognized this as a moral danger against which effective preventive and curative steps must be taken.

Since the contribution and expenditure limitations are neutral as to the content of speech and are not motivated by fear of the consequences of the political speech of particular candidates or of political speech in general, this case depends on whether the nonspeech interests of the Federal Government in regulating the use of money in political campaigns are sufficiently urgent to justify the incidental effects that the limitations visit upon the First Amendment interests of candidates and their supporters. Despite its seeming struggle with the standard by which to judge this case, this is essentially the question the Court asks and answers in the affirmative with respect to the limitations on contributions. [The] Court thus accepts the congressional judgment that the evils of unlimited contributions are sufficiently threatening to warrant restriction regardless of the impact of the limits on the contributor's opportunity for effective speech and in turn on the total volume of the candidate's political communications by reason of his inability to accept large sums from those willing to give.

The congressional judgment, which I would also accept, was that other steps must be taken to counter the corrosive effects of money in federal election campaigns. One of these steps is § 608 (e) [the contribution limits]. Congress was plainly of the view that these expenditures also have corruptive potential; but the Court strikes down the provision, strangely enough claiming more insight as to what may improperly influence candidates than is possessed by the majority of Congress that passed this Bill and the President who signed it. [It] would make little sense to me, and apparently made none to Congress, to limit the amounts an individual may give to a candidate or spend with his approval but fail to limit the amounts that could be spent on his behalf. Yet the Court permits the former while striking down the latter limitation. . . .

Let us suppose that each of two brothers spends one million dollars on TV spot announcements that he has individually prepared and in which he appears, urging the election of the same named candidate in identical words. One brother has sought and obtained the approval of the candidate; the other has not. The former may validly be prosecuted under § 608 (e); under the Court's view, the latter may not, even though the candidate could scarcely help knowing about and appreciating the expensive favor. For constitutional purposes it is difficult to see the difference between the two situations. I would take the word of those who know—that limiting independent expenditures is essential to prevent transparent and widespread evasion of the contribution limits.

In sustaining the contribution limits, the Court recognizes the importance of avoiding public misapprehension about a candidate's reliance on large contributions. It ignores that consideration in invalidating § 608 (e). In like fashion, it says that Congress was entitled to determine that the criminal provisions against bribery and corruption, together with the disclosure provisions, would not in themselves be adequate to combat the evil and that limits on contributions should be provided. Here, the Court rejects the identical kind of judgment made by Congress as to the need for utility of expenditure limits. I would not do so.

The Court also rejects Congress' judgment manifested in § 608 (c) that the federal interest in limiting total campaign expenditures by individual candidates justifies the incidental effect on their opportunity for effective political speech. I disagree both with the Court's assessment of the impact on speech and with its narrow view of the values the limitations will serve. [As] an initial matter, the argument that money is speech and that limiting the flow of money to the speaker violates the First Amendment proves entirely too much. Compulsory bargaining and the right to strike, both provided for or protected by federal law, inevitably have increased the labor costs of those who publish newspapers, which are in turn an important factor in the recent disappearance of many daily papers. . . . But it has not been suggested, nor could it be successfully, that these laws, and many others, are invalid because they siphon off or prevent the accumulation of large sums that would otherwise be available for communicative activities.

In any event, as it should be unnecessary to point out, money is not always equivalent to or used for speech, even in the context of political campaigns. I accept the reality that communicating with potential voters is the heart of an election campaign and that widespread communication has become very expensive. There are, however, many expensive campaign activities that are not themselves communicative or remotely related to speech. Furthermore, campaigns differ among themselves. Some seem to spend much less money than others and yet communicate as much or more than those supported by enormous bureaucracies with unlimited financing. The record before us no more supports the conclusion that the communicative efforts of congressional and Presidential candidates will be crippled by the expenditure limitations than it supports the contrary. The judgment of Congress was that reasonably effective campaigns could be conducted within the limits established by the Act and that the communicative efforts of these campaigns would not seriously suffer. In this posture of the case, there is no sound basis for invalidating the expenditure limitations, so long as the purposes they serve are legitimate and sufficiently substantial, which in my view they are.

In the first place, expenditure ceilings reinforce the contribution limits and help eradicate the hazard of corruption. [It] should be added that many successful candidates would also be saved from large, overhanging campaign debts which must be paid off with money raised while holding public office and at a time when they are already preparing or thinking about the next campaign. The danger to the public interest in such situations is self-evident. Besides backing up the contribution [limits], expenditure limits have their own potential for preventing the corruption of federal elec-

tions themselves. [The] corrupt use of money by candidates is as much to be feared as the corrosive influence of large contributions. [I] have little doubt in addition that limiting the total that can be spent will ease the candidate's understandable obsession with fundraising, and so free him and his staff to communicate in more places and ways unconnected with the fundraising function. [It] is also important to restore and maintain public confidence in federal elections. It is critical to obviate or dispel the impression that federal elections are purely and simply a function of money, that federal offices are bought and sold or that political races are reserved for those who have the facility—and the stomach—for doing whatever it takes to bring together those interests, groups, and individuals that can raise or contribute large fortunes in order to prevail at the polls.

The ceiling on candidate expenditures represents the considered judgment of Congress that elections are to be decided among candidates none of whom has an overpowering advantage by reason of a huge campaign war chest. At least so long as the ceiling placed upon the candidates is not plainly too low, elections are not to turn on the difference in the amounts of money that candidates have to spend. This seems an acceptable purpose and the means chosen a common sense way to achieve it. . . .

I also disagree with the Court's judgment that § 608 (a), which limits the amount of money that a candidate or his family may spend on his campaign, violates the Constitution. Although it is true that this provision does not promote any interest in preventing the corruption of candidates, the provision does, nevertheless, serve salutary purposes related to the integrity of federal campaigns. By limiting the importance of personal wealth, § 608 (a) helps to assure that only individuals with a modicum of support from others will be viable candidates. This in turn would tend to discourage any notion that the outcome of elections is primarily a function of money. Similarly, § 608 (a) tends to equalize access to the political arena, encouraging the less wealthy, unable to bankroll their own campaigns, to run for political office. As with the campaign expenditure limits, Congress was entitled to determine that personal wealth ought to play a less important role in political campaigns than it has in the past. Nothing in the First Amendment stands in the way of that determination. . . .

The majority acknowledged that the Federal Election Campaign Act was "aimed in part at equalizing the relative ability of all voters to affect electoral outcomes by placing a ceiling on expenditures for political expression by citizens and groups."

But despite strong dissents by Justices White and Marshall, key portions of the act were struck down. In 1978, the Supreme Court struck down a Massachusetts statute that had provided strong criminal penalties for business corporations that spent corporate funds "for the purpose of . . . influencing or affecting the vote on any question submitted to the voters, other than one materially affecting any of the property, business, or assets of the corporation." The First National Bank of Boston and other corporations brought suit against the state attorney general arguing that their First Amendment rights were violated. They wished to contribute corporate money to oppose a proposed amendment to the Massachusetts Constitution that authorized a graduated personal income tax, a provision affecting all taxpayers and not related to the contributing corporations. The Supreme Judicial Court of Massachusetts upheld the statute and rejected the principle that a corporation could claim First Amendment rights in a manner similar to natural persons. Justice Lewis Powell dismissed that issue as irrelevant and rephrased the basic constitutional issue in his majority opinion in *First National Bank of Boston* v. *Bellotti*. Justice Rehnquist wrote a strong dissent.

FIRST NATIONAL BANK OF BOSTON v. BELLOTTI
435 U. S. 765 (1978)

Justice Powell delivered the opinion of the Court:

. . . The court below framed the principal question in this case as whether and to what extent corporations have First Amendment rights. We believe that the court posed the wrong question. The Constitution often protects interests broader than those of the party seeking their vindication. The First Amendment, in particular, serves significant societal interests. The proper question therefore is not whether corporations "have" First Amendment rights and, if so, whether they are coextensive with those of natural persons. Instead, the question must be whether § 8 [the statute] abridges expression that the First Amendment was meant to protect. We hold that it does.

The speech proposed by appellants is at the heart of the First Amendment's protection.

We . . . find no support in the First or Fourteenth Amendments, or in the decisions of this Court, for the proposition that speech that otherwise would be within the protection of the First Amendment loses that protection simply because its source is a corporation that cannot prove, to the satisfaction of a court, a material effect on its business or property. The "materially affecting" requirement is not an identification of the boundaries of corporate speech etched by the Constitution itself. Rather, it amounts to an impermissible legislative prohibition of speech based on the identity of the interests that spokesmen may represent in public debate over controversial issues and a requirement that the speaker have a sufficiently great interest in the subject to justify communication.

Section 8 permits a corporation to communicate to the public its views on certain referendum subjects—those materially affecting its business—but not others. It also singles out one kind of ballot question—individual taxation—as a subject about which corporations may never make their ideas public. The legislature has drawn the line between permissible and impermissible speech according to whether there is a sufficent nexus, as defined by the legislature, between the issue presented to the voters and the business interests of the speaker.

In the realm of protected speech, the legislature is constitutionally disqualified from dictating the subjects about which persons may speak and the speakers who may address a public issue. . . . If a legislature may direct business corporations to "stick to business," it also may limit other corporations—religious, charitable, or civic—to their respective "business" when addressing the public. Such power in government to channel the expression of views is unacceptable under the First Amendment. Especially where, as here, the legislature's suppression of speech suggests an attempt to give one side of a debatable public question an advantage in expressing its views to the people, the First Amendment is plainly offended. Yet the State contends that its action is necessitated by governmental interests of the highest order. We next consider these asserted interests.

The constitutionality of § 8's prohibition of the "exposition of ideas" by corporations turns on whether it can survive the exacting scrutiny necessitated by a state-imposed restriction of freedom of speech. Especially where, as here, a prohibition is directed at speech itself, and the speech is intimately related to the process of governing, "the State may prevail only upon showing a subordinating interest which is compelling" . . . "and the burden is on the Government to show the existence of such an interest." . . . Even then, the State must employ means "closely drawn to avoid unnecessary abridgment.". . .

. . . Appellee . . . advances two principal justifications for the prohibition of corporate speech. The first is the State's interest in sustaining the active role of the individual citizen in the electoral process and thereby preventing diminution of the citizen's confidence in government. The second is the interest in protecting the rights of shareholders whose views differ from those expressed by management on behalf of the corporation. However weighty these interests may be in the context of partisan candidate elections, they either are not implicated in this case or are not served at all, or in other than a random manner, by the prohibition in § 8.

Preserving the integrity of the electoral process, preventing corruption, and "sustain[ing] the active, alert responsibility of the individual citizen in a democracy for the wise conduct of government" are interests of the highest importance. . . . Preservation of the individual citizen's confidence in government is equally important. . . .

Appellee advances a number of arguments in support of his view that these interests are endangered by corporate participation in discussion of a referendum issue. They hinge upon the assumption that such participation would exert an undue influence on the outcome of a referendum vote, and—in the end—destroy the confidence of the people in the democratic process and the integrity of government. According to appellee, corporations are wealthy and powerful and their views may drown out other points of view. If appellee's arguments were supported by record or legislative findings that corporate advocacy threatened imminently to undermine democratic processes, thereby denigrating rather than serving First Amendment interests, these arguments would merit our consideration. . . . But there has been no showing that the relative voice of corporations has been overwhelming or even significant in influencing referenda in

Massachusetts, or that there has been any threat to the confidence of the citizenry in government. . . .

Nor are appellee's arguments inherently persuasive or supported by the precedents of this Court. Referenda are held on issues, not candidates for public office. The risk of corruption perceived in cases involving candidate elections . . . simply is not present in a popular vote on a public issue. To be sure, corporate advertising may influence the outcome of the vote; this would be its purpose. But the fact that advocacy may persuade the electorate is hardly a reason to suppress it: The Constitution "protects expression which is eloquent no less than that which is unconvincing." . . . We noted only recently that "the concept that government may restrict the speech of some elements of our society in order to enhance the relative voice of others is wholly foreign to the First Amendment." . . . Moreover, the people in our democracy are entrusted with the responsibility for judging and evaluating the relative merits of conflicting arguments. They may consider, in making their judgment, the source and credibility of the advocate. But if there be any danger that the people cannot evaluate the information and arguments advanced by appellants, it is a danger contemplated by the Framers of the First Amendment . . . In sum, "[a] restriction so destructive of the right of public discussion [as § 8], without greater or more imminent danger to the public interest than existed in this case, is incompatible with the freedoms secured by the First Amendment."

Finally, the State argues that § 8 protects corporate shareholders, an interest that is both legitimate and traditionally within the province of state law. . . . The statute is said to serve this interest by preventing the use of corporate resources in furtherance of views with which some shareholders may disagree. This purpose is belied, however, by the provisions of the statute, which are both under- and over-inclusive.

The under-inclusiveness of the statute is self-evident. Corporate expenditures with respect to a referendum are prohibited, while corporate activity with respect to the passage or defeat of legislation is permitted . . . even though corporations may engage in lobbying more often than they take positions on ballot questions submitted to the voters. Nor does § 8 prohibit a corporation from expressing its views, by the expenditure of corporate funds, on any public issue until it becomes the subject of a referendum, though the displeasure of disapproving shareholders is unlikely to be any less.

The fact that a particular kind of ballot question has been singled out for special treatment undermines the likelihood of a genuine state interest in protecting shareholders. It suggests instead that the legislature may have been concerned with silencing corporations on a particular subject. Indeed, appellee has conceded that "the legislative and judicial history of the statute indicates . . . that the second crime was 'tailor-made' to prohibit corporate campaign contributions to oppose a graduated income tax amendment.". . .

Nor is the fact that § 8 is limited to banks and business corporations without relevance. Excluded from its provisions and criminal sanctions are entities or organized groups in which numbers of persons may hold an interest or membership, and which often have resources comparable to those of large corporations. Minorities in such groups or entities may have interests with respect to institutional speech quite comparable to those of minority shareholders in a corporation. Thus the exclusion of Massachusetts business trusts, real estate investment trusts, labor unions, and other associations undermines the plausibility of the State's purported concern for the persons who happen to be shareholders in the banks and corporations covered by § 8.

The over-inclusiveness of the statute is demonstrated by the fact that § 8 would prohibit a corporation from supporting or opposing a referendum proposal even if its shareholders unanimously authorized the contribution or expenditure. Ultimately shareholders may decide, through the procedures of corporate democracy, whether their corporation should engage in debate on public issues. Acting through their power to elect the board of directors or to insist upon protective provisions in the corporation's charter, shareholders normally are presumed competent to protect their own interests. In addition to intra-corporate remedies, minority shareholders generally have access to the judicial remedy of a derivative suit to challenge corporate disbursements alleged to have been made for improper corporate purposes or merely to further the personal interests of management.

Assuming, *arguendo,* that protection of shareholders is a "compelling" interest under the circumstances of this case, we find "no substantially relevant correlation between the governmental interest asserted and the State's effort" to prohibit appellants from speaking. . . .

Because § 8 prohibits protected speech in a manner

unjustified by a compelling state interest, it must be invalidated. The judgment of the Supreme Judicial Court is Reversed.

[The concurring opinion of Chief Justice Burger . . . is omitted.]

Justices Brennan and Marshall
joined Justice White in his dissent:

There is now little doubt that corporate communications come within the scope of the First Amendment. This, however, is merely the starting point of analysis, because an examination of the First Amendment values corporate expression furthers and the threat to the functioning of a free society it is capable of posing reveals that it is not fungible with communications emanating from individuals and is subject to restrictions which individual expression is not. Indeed, what some have considered to be the principal function of the First Amendment, the use of communication as a means of self-expression, self-realization and self-fulfillment, is not at all furthered by corporate speech. It is clear that the communications of profitmaking corporations are not "an integral part of the development of ideas, of mental exploration and of the affirmation of self." They do not represent a manifestation of individual freedom or choice. Undoubtedly, as this court has recognized . . . there are some corporations formed for the express purpose of advancing certain ideological causes shared by all their members, or, as in the case of the press, of disseminating information and ideas. Under such circumstances, association in a corporate form may be viewed as merely a means of achieving effective self-expression. But this is hardly the case generally with corporations operated for the purpose of making profits. Shareholders in such entities do not share a common set of political or social views, and they certainly have not invested their money for the purpose of advancing political or social causes or in an enterprise engaged in the business of disseminating news and opinion. In fact . . . the government has a strong interest in assuring that investment decisions are not predicated upon agreement or disagreement with the activities of corporations in the political arena.

Of course, it may be assumed that corporate investors are united by a desire to make money, for the value of their investment to increase. Since even communications which have no purpose other than that of enriching the communicator have some First Amendment protection, activities such as advertising and other communications integrally related to the operation of the corporation's business may be viewed as a means of furthering the desires of individual shareholders. This unanimity of purpose breaks down, however, when corporations make expenditures or undertake activities designed to influence the opinion or votes of the general public on political and social issues that have no material connection with or effect upon their business, property, or assets. Although it is arguable that corporations make such expenditures because their managers believe that it is in the corporations' economic interest to do so, there is no basis whatsoever for concluding that these views are expressive of the heterogeneous beliefs of their shareholders whose convictions on many political issues are undoubtedly shaped by considerations other than a desire to endorse any electoral or ideological cause which would tend to increase the value of a particular corporate investment. This is particularly true where, as in this case, whatever the belief of the corporate managers may be, they have not been able to demonstrate that the issue involved has any material connection with the corporate business. Thus when a profitmaking corporation contributes to a political candidate this does not further the self-expression or self-fulfillment of its shareholders in the way that expenditures from them as individuals would.

The self-expression of the communicator is not the only value encompassed by the First Amendment. One of its functions, often referred to as the right to hear or receive information, is to protect the interchange of ideas. Any communication of ideas, and consequently any expenditure of funds which makes the communication of ideas possible, it can be argued, furthers the purposes of the First Amendment. This proposition does not establish, however, that the right of the general public to receive communications financed by means of corporate expenditures is of the same dimension as that to hear other forms of expression. In the first place . . . , corporate expenditures designed to further political causes lack the connection with individual self-expression which is one of the principal justifications for the constitutional protection of speech provided by the First Amendment. Ideas which are not a product of individual choice are entitled to less First Amendment protection. Secondly, the restriction of corporate speech concerned with political matters impinges much less severely upon the availability of ideas to the general public than do restrictions upon individual speech. Even the complete curtailment of corporate communications concerning

political or ideological questions not integral to day-to-day business functions would leave individuals, including corporate shareholders, employees, and customers, free to communicate their thoughts. Moreover, it is unlikely that any significant communication would be lost by such a prohibition. These individuals would remain perfectly free to communicate any ideas which could be conveyed by means of the corporate form. Indeed, such individuals could even form associations for the very purpose of promoting political or ideological causes. . . .

The governmental interest in regulating corporate political communications, especially those relating to electoral matters, also raises considerations which differ significantly from those governing the regulation of individual speech. Corporations are artificial entities created by law for the purpose of furthering certain economic goals. In order to facilitate the achievement of such ends, special rules relating to such matters as limited liability, perpetual life, and the accumulation, distribution, and taxation of assets are normally applied to them. States have provided corporations with such attributes in order to increase their economic viability and thus strengthen the economy generally. It has long been recognized however, that the special status of corporations has placed them in a position to control vast amounts of economic power which may, if not regulated, dominate not only the economy but also the very heart of our democracy, the electoral process. Although Buckley v. Valeo . . . provides support for the position that the desire to equalize the financial resources available to candidates does not justify the limitation upon the expression of support which a restriction upon individual contributions entails, the interest of Massachusetts and the many other States which have restricted corporate political activity is quite different. It is not one of equalizing the resources of opposing candidates or opposing positions but rather of preventing institutions which have been permitted to amass wealth as a result of special advantages extended by the State for certain economic purposes from using that wealth to acquire an unfair advantage in the political process, especially where, as here, the issue involved has no material connection with the business of the corporation. The State need not permit its own creation to consume it. Massachusetts could permissibly conclude that not to impose limits upon the political activities of corporations would have placed it in a position of departing from neutrality and indirectly assisting the propagation of corporate views because of the advantages its laws give to the corporate acquisition of funds to finance such activities. Such expenditures may be viewed as seriously threatening the role of the First Amendment as a guarantor of a free marketplace of ideas. Ordinarily, the expenditure of funds to promote political causes may be assumed to bear some relation to the fervency with which they are held. Corporate political expression, however, is not only divorced from the convictions of individual corporate shareholders, but also, because of the ease with which corporations are permitted to accumulate capital, bears no relation to the conviction with which the ideas expressed are held by the communicator.

The Court's opinion appears to recognize at least the possibility that fear of corporate domination of the electoral process would justify restrictions upon corporate expenditures and contributions in connection with referenda but brushes this interest aside by asserting that "there has been no showing that the relative voice of corporations has been overwhelming or even significant in influencing referenda in Massachusetts," . . . and by suggesting that the statute in issue represents an attempt to give an unfair advantage to those who hold views in opposition to positions which would otherwise be financed by corporations. . . . It fails even to allude to the fact, however, that Massachussetts' most recent experience with unrestrained corporate expenditures in connection with ballot questions establishes precisely the contrary. In 1972, a proposed amendment to the Massachusetts Constitution which would have authorized the imposition of a graduated income tax on both individuals and corporations was put to the voters. The Committee for Jobs and Government Economy, an organized political committee, raised and expended approximately $120,000 to oppose the proposed amendment, the bulk of it raised through large corporate contributions. Three of the present appellant corporations each contributed $3,000 to this committee. In contrast, the Coalition for Tax Reform, Inc., the only political committee organized to support the 1972 amendment, was able to raise and expend only approximately $7,000. . . . Perhaps these figures reflect the Court's view of the appropriate role which corporations should play in the Massachusetts electoral process, but it nowhere explains why it is entitled to substitute its judgment for that of Massachusetts and other States, as well as the United States, which have acted to correct or prevent similar domination of the electoral process by corporate wealth.

This Nation has for many years recognized the need for measures designed to prevent corporate domination of the political process. The Corrupt Practices Act, first enacted in 1907, has consistently barred corporate contributions in connection with federal elections. This Court has repeatedly recognized that one of the principal purposes of this prohibition is "to avoid the deleterious influences on federal elections resulting from the use of money by those who exercise control over large aggregations of capital." . . . Although this Court has never adjudicated the constitutionality of the Act, there is no suggestion in its cases construing it . . . that this purpose is in any sense illegitimate or deserving of other than the utmost respect; indeed, the thrust of its opinions, until today, has been to the contrary. . . .

There is an additional overriding interest related to the prevention of corporate domination which is substantially advanced by Massachusetts' restrictions upon corporate contributions: assuring that shareholders are not compelled to support and financially further beliefs with which they disagree where, as is the case here, the issue involved does not materially affect the business, property, or other affairs of the corporation. The State has not interfered with the prerogatives of corporate management to communicate about matters that have material impact on the business affairs entrusted to them, however much individual stockholders may disagree on economic or ideological grounds. Nor has the State forbidden management from formulating and circulating its views at its own expense or at the expense of others, even where the subject at issue is irrelevant to corporate business affairs. But Massachusetts has chosen to forbid corporate management from spending corporate funds in referenda elections absent some demonstrable effect of the issue on the economic life of the company. In short, corporate management may not use corporate monies to promote what does not further corporate affairs but in the last analysis are the purely personal views of the management, individually or as a group. . . .

I would affirm the judgment of the Supreme Judicial Court for the Commonwealth of Massachusetts.

Justice Rehnquist dissented:

The question presented today, whether business corporations have a constitutionally protected liberty to engage in political activities, has never been squarely addressed by any previous decision of this Court. However, the General Court of the Commonwealth of Massachusetts, the Congress of the United States, and the legislatures of 30 other States of this Republic have considered the matter, and have concluded that restrictions upon the political activity of business corporations are both politically desirable and constitutionally permissible. The judgment of such a broad consensus of governmental bodies expressed over a period of many decades is entitled to considerable deference from this Court. I think it quite probable that their judgment may properly be reconciled with our controlling precedents, but I am certain that under my views of the limited application of the First Amendment to the States, which I share with the two immediately preceding occupants of my seat on the Court, but not with my present colleagues, the judgment of the Supreme Judicial Court of Massachusetts should be affirmed. . . .

. . . A State grants to a business corporation the blessings of potentially perpetual life and limited liability to enhance its efficiency as an economic entity. It might reasonably be concluded that those properties, so beneficial in the economic sphere, pose special dangers in the political sphere: Furthermore, it might be argued that liberties of political expression are not at all necessary to effectuate the purposes for which States permit commercial corporations to exist. So long as the Judicial Branches of the State and Federal Governments remain open to protect the corporation's interest in its property, it has no need, though it may have the desire, to petition the political branches for similar protection. Indeed, the States might reasonably fear that the corporations would use its economic power to obtain further benefits beyond those already bestowed. I would think that any particular form of organization upon which the State confers special privileges or immunities different from those of natural persons would be subject to like regulation, whether the organization is a labor union, a partnership, a trade association, or a corporation.

I can see no basis for concluding that the liberty of a corporation to engage in political activity with regard to matters having no material effect on its business is necessarily incidental to the purposes for which the Commonwealth permitted these corporations to be organized or admitted within its boundaries. Nor can I disagree with the Supreme Judicial Court's factual finding that no such effect has been shown by these appellants. Because the statute as construed provides at least as much protection as the Fourteenth Amendment requires, I believe it is constitutionally valid.

Buckley v. *Valeo* and the Bellotti case underscored an emerging resurgence of neo-conservative doctrinal tendencies. Both decisions resemble *Lochner* v. *New York*. Both, like Lochner, assert, with no empirical basis whatsoever, judicial determination to substitute the predilections of a majority of the Court for the public policy preferences of the national Congress or the state legislature. Both, like Lochner, tilt the scales of justice toward an ever-widening imbalance in favor of corporate power and family wealth. Both, like Lochner, ignore the constitutional issue of the relative status of the powerful and the wealthy, in contrast to the status of the ordinary individual participant in the political process. As a result, the constitutional principle of equality has been virtually eliminated. Justice White touched upon this aspect of the problem in his dissent in Bellotti, but, in fact, the remaining liberals on the Court had conceded the point by accepting the majority position in the *per curiam* decision in *Buckley* v. *Valeo*. Money in elections has indeed become curiously confused with First Amendment freedom. But the thrust of the majority positions compounds that confusion just as it consistently ignores the considerable empirical evidence that judicial enhancement of the influence of individual and corporate wealth in the electoral process undermines the integrity of the entire democratic system.

An important concomitant development is the revival of the contract clause as an instrument for Supreme Court policy, leaving intrusion into "economic and policy matters" largely to the states for the past four decades. In *United States Trust Company* v. *New Jersey*,[10] Justice Harry Blackmun wrote a majority opinion embodying a doctrinal rationale that would have reversed the outcome of the Charles River bridge case of 1837! Holding that a New Jersey statute violated its own state obligation, Blackmun fashioned a judicial oversight formula reminiscent of the conservative doctrines of the 1890s. Whenever a state law violated a state obligation it must be deemed "reasonable and necessary to serve an important purpose" by the Supreme Court in order to pass constitutional muster. The case involved a statutory covenant agreed upon in 1962 by the states of New York and New Jersey to prohibit the Port Authority of New York and New Jersey from subsidizing rail passenger transportation from Port Authority revenues and reserves. The policy consideration of that era included highly optimistic governmental assumptions about the viability and the economic and environmental significance of increased automobile traffic, highly pessimistic assumptions about rail passenger use, and the assumption that bondholders needed assurance that bond revenues would not be used to support unprofitable rail passenger operations.

The repeal of the 1962 covenant in 1974 reflected rather different state legislative assumptions—economic and environmental considerations had made development of rail passenger service an important state policy consideration. These and other factors provided the basis for an outright rejection of the contract clause contentions by the New Jersey courts, which held that the 1974 repeal was "a reasonable exercise [of] state police power." These courts accepted the arguments presented by New Jersey and New York that "mass transportation, energy conservation, and environmental protection" are "goals so important that any harm to bondholders from the repeal of the 1962 covenant is greatly outweighed by the public benefit."

Conversely, Justice Blackmun rejected these considerations completely, and suggested that the state policy objectives could be met by alternative means such as taxes on automobiles and parking, the revenue from which could be used to subsidize mass transit. Prefacing his doctrinal rationale, Blackmun asserted that "whether or not the protection of contract rights comports with current views of wise public policy, the contract clause remains a part of our written Constitution." A key doctrinal argument was Blackmun's assertion that when state impairment of its own obligations occurs, the customary deference accorded to "legislative judgment as to the necessity and reasonableness of a particular measure" [regarding private contracts] is not appropriate. He stated that "as with laws impairing the obligations of private contracts, an impairment [of state obligation] may be constitutional if it is reasonable and necessary to serve an important public purpose. In applying this standard, however, complete deference to a legislative assessment of reasonableness and necessity is not appropriate because the state's self-interest is at stake." Thus, the Blackmun majority not only struck down a state statute by invoking the contract clause for the first time in nearly four decades, but it substantially broadened the conditions that states must meet in order to avoid a decision of unconstitutionality.

Justice Brennan wrote a strongly critical dissent (supported by Justices Marshall and White). He charged that Blackmun's decision

> . . . remolds the Contract Clause into a potent instrument for overseeing important policy determinations of the state legislature. At the same time, by creating a constitutional safe haven for property rights embodied in a contract, the decision substantially distorts modern constitutional jurisprudence governing regulation of

private economic interests. I might understand, though I could not accept, this revival of the Contract Clause were it in accordance with some coherent and constructive view of public policy. But elevation of the Clause to the status of regulator of the municipal bond market at the heavy price of frustration of sound legislative policymaking is as demonstrably unwise as it is unnecessary. . . .

. . . [This decision] regrettably departs from the virtually unbroken line of our cases that remained true to the principle that all private rights of property, even if acquired through contract with the State, are subordinated to reasonable exercises of the States' lawmaking powers in the areas of health, environmental protection, and transportation. . . .

. . . [He also argued that] if today's case signals return to substantive constitutional review of States' policies, and a new resolve to protect property owners whose interest or circumstances may happen to appeal to Members of this Court, then more than the citizens of New Jersey and New York will be the losers. . . .

Brennan concluded with the admonition that

. . . [The] Court should have learned long ago that the Constitution—be it through the Contract or Due Process Clause—can actively intrude into such economic and policy matters only if my Brethren are prepared to bear enormous institutional and social costs. [I] consider the potential dangers of such judicial interference to be intolerable.

The Port Authority issue was decided narrowly by a margin of four to three with Justices Powell and Stewart not taking part. But two years later, these justices joined the supporters of Blackmun's decision to strike down a Minnesota statute that attempted to protect the pension fund rights of discharged workers when their employer terminated the plan or closed its Minnesota facility. Justice Stewart wrote for the five-member majority while Justice Brennan, supported by Justices White and Marshall, dissented. Justice Blackmun did not participate.

Justice Stewart's majority opinion in this case, *Allied Structural Steel Company* v. *Spannaus*,[11] held that the Minnesota law, by retroactively modifying the pension payment obligations of Allied Structural Steel Company, severely impaired its private contract rights and was, therefore, void. Justice Brennan protested that

. . . Today's conversion of the Contract Clause into a limitation on the power of States to enact laws that impose duties additional to obligations assumed under private contracts must inevitably produce results difficult to square with any rational conception of a constitutional order. Under the Court's opinion, any law that may be characterized as "superimposing" new obligations on those provided for by contract is to be regarded as creating "sudden, substantial, and unanticipated burdens" and then to be subjected to the most exacting scrutiny. The validity of such a law will turn upon whether it is temporary (as few will be) or permanent, whether it operates in an area previously subject to regulation, and, finally, whether its duties apply to a broad class of persons. The necessary consequence of the extreme malleability of these rather vague criteria is to vest judges with broad subjective discretion to protect property interests that happen to appeal to them. [There] is nothing sacrosanct about expectations rooted in contract that justify according them a constitutional immunity denied other property rights. . . .

The ebb and flow of presidential and congressional authority: The legislative veto

In the aftermath of Watergate and the Vietnam conflict, it was frequently argued that presidential authority had seriously declined and that, concomitantly, the role of Congress was considerably enhanced. One institutional device, originally developed and utilized in the 1930s, was the legislative veto, the practice of establishing by statute the power of Congress to authorize presidential or administrative actions which could be taken only if a majority of one or both houses of Congress did not vote to stop the action. As the detailed analysis of Justice White (in dissent) indicates below, the legislative veto was utilized with increased intensity as a congressional response to assertions of an imperial presidency. But on June 23, 1983, the Supreme Court, in *Immigration and Naturalization Service* v. *Jagdish Rai Chadha*, handed down a decision holding the legislative veto an unconstitutional violation of separation of powers.[12] The occasion was not a major confrontation between the executive and legislative branches, but a challenge to section 244 (c) (2) of the Immigration and Nationality Act brought by Jagdish Rai Chadha, an alien who had been admitted to the United States in 1966 on a nonimmigrant student visa. His role is described in detail in the introductory portions of Chief Justice Burger's majority opinion. The most complete treatment of the development and uses of the legislative veto is provided in Justice White's dissent. Chief Justice Burger was joined in the majority by Justices Brennan, Marshall, Blackmun, Stevens, and O'Connor. Justice Powell wrote a concurring opinion, while Justices White and Rehnquist wrote dissenting opinions.

IMMIGRATION AND NATURALIZATION SERVICE v. JAGDISH RAI CHADHA
103 Supreme Court Reporter 2764 (1983)

Chief Justice Burger delivered the opinion of the court:

We granted certiorari in Nos. 80-2170 and 80-2171, and postponed consideration of the question of jurisdiction in No. 80-1832. Each presents a challenge to the constitutionality of the provision in § 244 (c) (2) of the Immigration and Nationality Act. . . . authorizing one House of Congress, by resolution, to invalidate the decision of the Executive Branch, pursuant to authority delegated by Congress to the Attorney General of the United States, to allow a particular deportable alien to remain in the United States.

I

Chadha is an East Indian who was born in Kenya and holds a British passport. He was lawfully admitted to the United States in 1966 on a nonimmigrant student visa. His visa expired on June 30, 1972. On October 11, 1973, the District Director of the Immigration and Naturalization Service ordered Chadha to show cause why he should not be deported for having

"remained in the United States for a longer time than permitted." . . . Pursuant to § 242 (b) of the Immigration and Nationality Act . . . a deportation hearing was held before an immigration judge on January 11, 1974. Chadha conceded that he was deportable for overstaying his visa and the hearing was adjourned to enable him to file an application for suspension of deportation under § 244 (a) (1) of the Act. . . . Section 244 (a) (1) provides:

"(a) As hereinafter prescribed in this section, the Attorney General may, in his discretion, suspend deportation and adjust the status to that of an alien lawfully admitted for permanent residence, in the case of an alien who applies to the Attorney General for suspension of deportation and—

(1) is deportable under any law of the United States except the provisions specified in paragraph (2) of this subsection; has been physically present in the United States for a continuous period of not less than seven years immediately preceding the date of such application, and proves that during all of such period he was and is a person of good moral character; and is a person whose deportation would, in the opinion of the Attorney General, result in extreme hardship to the alien or to his spouse, parent, or child, who is a citizen of the United States or an alien lawfully admitted for permanent residence."

After Chadha submitted his application for suspension of deportation, the deportation hearing was resumed on February 7, 1974. On the basis of evidence adduced at the hearing, affidavits submitted with the application, and the results of a character investigation conducted by the INS, the immigration judge, on June 25, 1974, ordered that Chadha's deportation be suspended. The immigration judge found that Chadha met the requirements of § 244 (a) (1): he had resided continuously in the United States for over seven years, was of good moral character, and would suffer "extreme hardship" if deported.

Pursuant to § 244 (c) (1) of the Act . . . the immigration judge suspended Chadha's deportation and a report of the suspension was transmitted to Congress. Section 244 (c) (1) provides:

"Upon application by any alien who is found by the Attorney General to meet the requirements of subsection (a) of this section the Attorney General may in his discretion suspend deportation of such alien. If the deportation of any alien is suspended under the provisions of this subsection, a complete and detailed statement of the facts and pertinent provisions of law in the case shall be reported to the Congress with the reasons for such suspension. Such reports shall be submitted on the first day of each calendar month in which Congress is in session."

Once the Attorney General's recommendation for suspension of Chadha's deportation was conveyed to Congress, Congress had the power under § 244 (c) (2) of the Act . . . to veto the Attorney General's determination that Chadha should not be deported. Section 244 (c) (2) provides:

"(2) In the case of an alien specified in paragraph (1) of subsection (a) of this subsection—if during the session of the Congress at which a case is reported, or prior to the close of the session of the Congress next following the session at which a case is reported, either the Senate or the House of Representatives passes a resolution stating in substance that it does not favor the suspension of such deportation, the Attorney General shall thereupon deport such alien or authorize the alien's voluntary departure at his own expense under the order of deportation in the manner provided by law. If, within the time above specified, neither the Senate nor the House of Representatives shall pass such a resolution, the Attorney General shall cancel deportation proceedings."

The June 25, 1974 order of the immigration judge suspending Chadha's deportation remained outstanding as a valid order for a year and a half. For reasons not disclosed by the record, Congress did not exercise the veto authority reserved to it under § 244 (c) (2) until the first session of the 94th Congress. This was the final session in which Congress, pursuant to

§ 244 (c) (2), could act to veto the Attorney General's determination that Chadha should not be deported. The session ended on December 19, 1975. . . . Absent Congressional action, Chadha's deportation proceedings would have been cancelled after this date and his status adjusted to that of a permanent resident alien. . . .

On December 12, 1975, Representative Eilberg, Chairman of the Judiciary Subcommittee on Immigration, Citizenship, and International Law, introduced a resolution opposing "the granting of permanent residence in the United States to [six] aliens," including Chadha. . . . The resolution was referred to the House Committee on the Judiciary. On December 16, 1975, the resolution was discharged from further consideration by the House Committee on the Judiciary and submitted to the House of Representatives for a vote. . . . The resolution had not been printed and was not made available to other Members of the House prior to or at the time it was voted on. . . . So far as the record before us shows, the House consideration of the resolution was based on Representative Eilberg's statement from the floor that

"[i]t was the feeling of the committee, after reviewing 340 cases, that the aliens contained in the resolution [Chadha and five others] did not meet these statutory requirements, particularly as it relates to hardship; and it is the opinion of the committee that their deportation should not be suspended." . . .

The resolution was passed without debate or recorded vote. Since the House action was pursuant to § 244 (c) (2), the resolution was not treated as an Article I legislative act; it was not submitted to the Senate or presented to the President for his action.

After the House veto of the Attorney General's decision to allow Chadha to remain in the United States, the immigration judge reopened the deportation proceedings to implement the House order deporting Chadha. Chadha moved to terminate the proceedings on the ground that § 244 (c) (2) is unconstitutional. The immigration judge held that he had no authority to rule on the constitutional validity of § 244 (c) (2). On November 8, 1976, Chadha was ordered deported pursuant to the House action.

Chadha appealed the deportation order to the Board of Immigration Appeals again contending that § 244 (c) (2) is unconstitutional. The Board held that it had "no power to declare unconstitutional an act of Congress" and Chadha's appeal was dismissed. . . .

Pursuant to § 106 (a) of the Act . . . Chadha filed a petition for review of the deportation order in the United States Court of Appeals for the Ninth Circuit.

The Immigration and Naturalization Service agreed with Chadha's position before the Court of Appeals and joined him in arguing that § 244 (c) (2) is unconstitutional. In light of the importance of the question, the Court of Appeals invited both the Senate and the House of Representatives to file briefs *amici curiae.*

After full briefing and oral argument, the Court of Appeals held that the House was without constitutional authority to order Chadha's deportation; accordingly it directed the Attorney General "to cease and desist from taking any steps to deport this alien based upon the resolution enacted by the House of Representatives." . . . The essence of its holding was that § 244 (c) (2) violates the constitutional doctrine of separation of powers.

[Portions of the majority opinion dealing with questions of appellate jurisdiction, severability of portions of the challenged act, standing, alternative relief, and whether this was a *bona fide* case or controversy are omitted].

POLITICAL QUESTION

. . . It is also argued that this case presents a nonjusticiable political question because Chadha is merely challenging Congress' authority under the Naturalization Clause, U. S. Const. art. I, § 8, cl. 4, and the Necessary and Proper Clause, U. S. Const. art. I, § 8, cl. 18. It is argued that Congress' Article I power "To establish a uniform Rule of Naturalization," combined with the Necessary and Proper Clause, grants it unreviewable authority over the regulation of aliens. The plenary authority of Congress over aliens under Art. I, § 8, cl. 4 is not open to question, but what is challenged here is whether Congress has chosen a constitutionally permissible means of implementing that power. As we made clear in *Buckley* v. *Valeo,* . . . "Congress has plenary authority in all cases in which it has substantive legislative jurisdiction, *M'Culloch* v. *Maryland,* . . . so long as the exercise of that authority does not offend some other constitutional restriction." . . .

A brief review of those factors which may indicate the presence of a nonjusticiable political question satisfies us that our assertion of jurisdiction over this case does no violence to the political question doctrine. As identified in *Baker* v. *Carr* . . . a political question may arise when any one of the following circumstances is present:

"a textually demonstrable constitutional commitment of the issue to a coordinate political department; or a lack of judicially discoverable and manageable standards for resolving it; or the impossibility of deciding without an initial policy determination of a kind clearly for nonjudicial discretion; or

the impossibility of a court's undertaking independent resolution without expressing lack of the respect due coordinate branches of government; or an unusual need for unquestioning adherence to a political decision already made; or the potentiality of embarrassment from multifarious pronouncements by various departments on one question."

Congress apparently directs its assertion of nonjusticiability to the first of the *Baker* factors by asserting that Chadha's claim is "an assault on the legislative authority to enact Section 244 (c) (2)." Brief for the United States House of Representatives 48. But if this turns the question into a political question virtually every challenge to the constitutionality of a statute would be a political question. Chadha indeed argues that one House of Congress cannot constitutionally veto the Attorney General's decision to allow him to remain in this country. No policy underlying the political question doctrine suggests that Congress or the Executive, or both acting in concert and in compliance with Art. I, can decide the constitutionality of a statute; that is a decision for the courts.

Other *Baker* factors are likewise inapplicable to this case. As we discuss more fully below, Art. I provides the "judicially discoverable and manageable standards" of *Baker* for resolving the question presented by this case. Those standards forestall reliance by this Court on nonjudicial "policy determinations" or any showing of disrespect for a coordinate branch. Similarly, if Chadha's arguments are accepted, § 244 (c) (2) cannot stand, and, since the constitutionality of that statute is for this Court to resolve, there is no possibility of "multifarious pronouncements" on this question.

It is correct that this controversy may, in a sense, be termed "political." But the presence of constitutional issues with significant political overtones does not automatically invoke the political question doctrine. Resolution of litigation challenging the constitutional authority of one of the three branches cannot be evaded by courts because the issues have political implications in the sense urged by Congress. *Marbury* v. *Madison* . . . was also a "political" case, involving as it did claims under a judicial commission alleged to have been duly signed by the President but not delivered. But "courts cannot reject as 'no law suit' a bona fide controversy as to whether some action denominated 'political' exceeds constitutional authority." *Baker* v. *Carr.* . . .

. . . We turn now to the question whether action of one House of Congress under § 244 (c) (2) violates strictures of the Constitution. We begin, of course, with the presumption that the challenged statute is valid. Its wisdom is not the concern of the courts; if a challenged action does not violate the Constitution, it must be sustained:

"Once the meaning of an enactment is discerned and its constitutionality determined, the judicial process comes to an end. We do not sit as a committee of review, nor are we vested with the power of veto." . . .

By the same token, the fact that a given law or procedure is efficient, convenient, and useful in facilitating functions of government, standing alone, will not save it if it is contrary to the Constitution. Convenience and efficiency are not the primary objectives—or the hallmarks—of democratic government and our inquiry is sharpened rather than blunted by the fact that Congressional veto provisions are appearing with increasing frequency in statutes which delegate authority to executive and independent agencies:

"Since 1932, when the first veto provision was enacted into law, 295 congressional veto-type procedures have been inserted in 196 different statutes as follows: from 1932 to 1939, five statutes were affected; from 1940–1949, nineteen statutes; between 1950–1959, thirty-four statutes; and from 1960–1969, forty-nine. From the year 1970 through 1975, at least one hundred sixty-three such provisions were included in eighty-nine laws."

Justice White undertakes to make a case for the proposition that the one-House veto is a useful "political invention" . . . and we need not challenge that assertion. We can even concede this utilitarian argument although the long range political wisdom of this "invention" is arguable. It has been vigorously debated and it is instructive to compare the views of the protagonists. . . . But policy arguments supporting even useful "political inventions" are subject to the demands of the Constitution which defines powers and, with respect to this subject, sets out just how those powers are to be exercised.

Explicit and unambiguous provisions of the Constitution prescribe and define the respective functions of the Congress and of the Executive in the legislative process. Since the precise terms of those familiar provisions are critical to the resolution of this case, we set them out verbatim. Art. I provides:

"All legislative Powers herein granted shall be vested in a Congress of the United States, which shall consist of a Senate *and* a House of Representatives. Art. I, § 1. (Emphasis added).

"Every Bill which shall have passed the House of Representatives *and* the Senate, *shall*, before it becomes a Law, be presented to the President of the United States; . . ." Art. I, § 7, cl. 2. (Emphasis added).

"*Every* Order, Resolution, or Vote to which the Concurrence of the Senate and House of Representatives may be necessary (except on a question of Adjournment) *shall be* presented to the President of the United States; and before the Same shall take Effect, *shall be* approved by him, or being disapproved by him, *shall be* repassed by two thirds of the Senate and House of Representatives, according to the Rules and Limitations prescribed in the Case of a Bill." Art. I, § 7, cl. 3. (Emphasis added).

These provisions of Art. I are integral parts of the constitutional design for the separation of powers. We have recently noted that "[t]he principle of separation of powers was not simply an abstract generalization in the minds of the Framers; it was woven into the documents that they drafted in Philadelphia in the summer of 1787." . . . Just as we relied on the textual provision of Art. II, § 2, cl. 2, to vindicate the principle of separation of powers in *Buckley,* we find that the purposes underlying the Presentment Clauses, Art. I, § 7, cls. 2, 3, and the bicameral requirement of Art. I, § 1 and § 7, cl. 2, guide our resolution of the important question presented in this case. The very structure of the articles delegating and separating powers under Arts. I, II, and III exemplify the concept of separation of powers and we now turn to Art. I.

THE PRESENTMENT CLAUSES

The records of the Constitutional Convention reveal that the requirement that all legislation be presented to the President before becoming law was uniformly accepted by the Framers. Presentment to the President and the Presidential veto were considered so imperative that the draftsmen took special pains to assure that these requirements could not be circumvented. During the final debate on Art. I, § 7, cl. 2, James Madison expressed concern that it might easily be evaded by the simple expedient of calling a proposed law a "resolution" or "vote" rather than a "bill." . . . As a consequence, Art. I, § 7, cl. 3, *ante,* at 25, was added. . . .

The decision to provide the President with a limited and qualified power to nullify proposed legislation by veto was based on the profound conviction of the Framers that the powers conferred on Congress were the Powers to be most carefully circumscribed. It is beyond doubt that lawmaking was a power to be shared by both Houses and the President. In The Federalist No. 73 . . . Hamilton focused on the President's role in making laws:

"If even no propensity had ever discovered itself in the legislative body to invade the rights of the Executive, the rules of just reasoning and theoretic propriety would of themselves teach us that the one ought not to be left to the mercy of the other, but ought to possess a constitutional and effectual power of self-defense." . . .

See also The Federalist No. 51. In his Commentaries on the Constitution, Joseph Story makes the same point. . . .

The President's role in the lawmaking process also reflects the Framers' careful efforts to check whatever propensity a particular Congress might have to enact oppressive, improvident, or ill-considered measures. The President's veto role in the legislative process was described later during public debate on ratification:

"It establishes a salutary check upon the legislative body, calculated to guard the community against the effects of faction, precipitancy, or of any impulse unfriendly to the public good which may happen to influence a majority of that body. . . . The primary inducement to conferring the power in question upon the Executive is to enable him to defend himself; the secondary one is to increase the chances in favor of the community against the passing of bad laws through haste, inadvertence, or design. . . ."

The Court also has observed that the Presentment Clauses serve the important purpose of assuring that a "national" perspective is grafted on the legislative process:

"The President is a representative of the people just as the members of the Senate and of the House are, and it may be, at some times, on some subjects, that the President elected by all the people is rather more representative of them all than are the members of either body of the Legislature whose constituencies are local and not countrywide. . . "

BICAMERALISM

The bicameral requirement of Art. I, §§ 1, 7 was of scarcely less concern to the Framers than was the Presidential veto and indeed the two concepts are interdependent. By providing that no law could take effect without the concurrence of the prescribed majority of the Members of both Houses, the Framers reemphasized their belief, already remarked upon in connection with the Presentment Clauses, that legislation should not be enacted unless it has been carefully and fully considered by the Nation's elected officials. In the Constitutional Convention debates on the need for a bicameral legislature, James Wilson, later to become a Justice of this Court, commented:

"Despotism comes on mankind in different shapes. Sometimes in an Executive, sometimes in a military, one. Is there danger of a Legislative despotism? Theory & practice both proclaim it. If the Legislative authority be not restrained, there can be neither liberty nor stability; and it can only be restrained by dividing it within itself, into distinct and independent branches. In a single house there is no check, but the inadequate one, of the virtue & good sense of those who compose it. . . ."

Hamilton argued that a Congress comprised of a single House was antithetical to the very purposes of the Constitution. Were the Nation to adopt a Constitution providing for only one legislative organ, he warned:

"we shall finally accumulate, in a single body, all the most important prerogatives of sovereignty, and thus entail upon our posterity one of the most execrable forms of government that human infatuation ever contrived. Thus we should create in reality that very tyranny which the adversaries of the new Constitution either are, or affect to be, solicitous to avert. . . ."

This view was rooted in a general skepticism regarding the fallibility of human nature later commented on by Joseph Story:

"Public bodies, like private persons, are occasionally under the dominion of strong passions and excitements; impatient, irritable, and impetuous. . . . If [a legislature] feels no check but its own will, it rarely has the firmness to insist upon holding a question long enough under its own view, to see and mark it in all its bearings and relations to society." 1 J. Story, *supra*, at 383–384.

These observations are consistent with what many of the Framers expressed, none more cogently than Hamilton in pointing up the need to divide and disperse power in order to protect liberty:

"In republican government, the legislative authority necessarily predominates. The remedy for this inconveniency is to divide the legislature into different branches; and to render them, by different modes of election and different principles of action, as little connected with each other as the nature of their common functions and their common dependence on the society will admit. . . ."

However familiar, it is useful to recall that apart from their fear that special interests could be favored at the expense of public needs, the Framers were also concerned, although not of one mind, over the apprehensions of the smaller states. Those states feared a commonality of interest among the larger states would work to their disadvantage; representatives of the larger states, on the other hand, were skeptical of a legislature that could pass laws favoring a minority of the people. . . . It need hardly be repeated here that the Great Compromise, under which one House was viewed as representing the people and the other the states, allayed the fears of both the large and small states.

We see therefore that the Framers were acutely conscious that the bicameral requirement and the Presentment Clauses would serve essential constitutional functions. The President's participation in the legislative process was to protect the Executive Branch from

Congress and to protect the whole people from improvident laws. The division of the Congress into two distinctive bodies assures that the legislative power would be exercised only after opportunity for full study and debate in separate settings. The President's unilateral veto power, in turn, was limited by the power of two thirds of both Houses of Congress to overrule a veto thereby precluding final arbitrary action of one person. . . . It emerges clearly that the prescription for legislative action in Art. I, §§ 1, 7 represents the Framers' decision that the legislative power of the Federal government be exercised in accord with a single, finely wrought and exhaustively considered, procedure.

IV

The Constitution sought to divide the delegated powers of the new federal government into three defined categories, legislative, executive and judicial, to assure, as nearly as possible, that each Branch of government would confine itself to its assigned responsibility. The hydraulic pressure inherent within each of the separate Branches to exceed the outer limits of its power, even to accomplish desirable objectives, must be resisted.

Although not "hermetically" sealed from one another . . . the powers delegated to the three Branches are functionally identifiable. When any Branch acts, it is presumptively exercising the power the Constitution has delegated to it. . . . When the Executive acts, it presumptively acts in an executive or administrative capacity as defined in Art. II. And when, as here, one House of Congress purports to act, it is presumptively acting within its assigned sphere.

Beginning with this presumption, we must nevertheless establish that the challenged action under § 244 (c) (2) is of the kind to which the procedural requirements of Art. I, § 7 apply. Not every action taken by either House is subject to the bicameralism and presentment requirements of Art. I. See *post*, at 35. Whether actions taken by either House are, in law and fact, an exercise of legislative power depends not on their form but upon "whether they contain matter which is properly to be regarded as legislative in its character and effect. . . ."

Examination of the action taken here by one House pursuant to § 244 (c) (2) reveals that it was essentially legislative in purpose and effect. In purporting to exercise power defined in Art. I, § 8, cl. 4 to "establish an uniform Rule of Naturalization," the House took action that had the purpose and effect of altering the legal rights, duties and relations of persons, including the Attorney General, Executive Branch officials and Chadha, all outside the legislative branch. Section 244 (c) (2) purports to authorize one House of Congress to require the Attorney General to deport an individual alien whose deportation otherwise would be cancelled under § 244. The one-House veto operated in this case to overrule the Attorney General and mandate Chadha's deportation; absent the House action, Chadha would remain in the United States. Congress has *acted* and its action has altered Chadha's status.

The legislative character of the one-House veto in this case is confirmed by the character of the Congressional action it supplants. Neither the House of Representatives nor the Senate contends that, absent the veto provision in § 244 (c) (2), either of them, or both of them acting together, could effectively require the Attorney General to deport an alien once the Attorney General, in the exercise of legislatively delegated authority, had determined the alien should remain in the United States. Without the challenged provision in § 244 (c) (2), this could have been achieved, if at all, only by legislation requiring deportation. Similarly, a veto by one House of Congress under § 244 (c) (2) cannot be justified as an attempt at amending the standards set out in § 244 (a) (1), or as a repeal of § 244 as applied to Chadha. Amendment and repeal of statutes, no less than enactment, must conform with Art. I.

The nature of the decision implemented by the one-House veto in this case further manifests its legislative character. After long experience with the clumsy, time consuming private bill procedure, Congress made a deliberate choice to delegate to the Executive Branch, and specifically to the Attorney General, the authority to allow deportable aliens to remain in this country in certain specified circumstances. It is not disputed that this choice to delegate authority is precisely the kind of decision that can be implemented only in accordance with the procedures set out in Art. I. Disagreement with the Attorney General's decision on Chadha's deportation—that is, Congress' decision to deport Chadha—no less than Congress' original choice to delegate to the Attorney General the authority to make that decision, involves determinations of policy that Congress can implement in only one way; bicameral passage followed by presentment to the President. Congress must abide by its delegation of authority until that delegation is legislatively altered or revoked.

Finally, we see that when the Framers intended to authorize either House of Congress to act alone and outside of its prescribed bicameral legislative role, they

THE NIXON, CARTER, AND REAGAN PRESIDENCIES

narrowly and precisely defined the procedure for such action. There are but four provisions in the Constitution, explicit and unambiguous, by which one House may act alone with the unreviewable force of law, not subject to the President's veto:

(a) The House of Representatives alone was given the power to initiate impeachments. Art. I, § 2, cl. 6;

(b) The Senate alone was given the power to conduct trials following impeachment on charges initiated by the House and to convict following trial. Art. I, § 3, cl. 5;

(c) The Senate alone was given final unreviewable power to approve or to disapprove presidential appointments. Art. II, § 2, cl. 2;

(d) The Senate alone was given unreviewable power to ratify treaties negotiated by the President. Art. II, § 2, cl. 2.

Clearly, when the Draftsmen sought to confer special powers on one House, independent of the other House, or of the President, they did so in explicit, unambiguous terms. These carefully defined exceptions from presentment and bicameralism underscore the difference between the legislative functions of Congress and other unilateral but important and binding one-House acts provided for in the Constitution. These exceptions are narrow, explicit, and separately justified; none of them authorize the action challenged here. On the contrary, they provide further support for the conclusion that Congressional authority is not to be implied and for the conclusion that the veto provided for in § 244 (c) (2) is not authorized by the constitutional design of the powers of the Legislative Branch.

Since it is clear that the action by the House under § 244 (c) (2) was not within any of the express constitutional exceptions authorizing one House to act alone, and equally clear that it was an exercise of legislative power, that action was subject to the standards prescribed in Article I. The bicameral requirement, the Presentment Clauses, the President's veto, and Congress' power to override a veto were intended to erect enduring checks on each Branch and to protect the people from the improvident exercise of power by mandating certain prescribed steps. To preserve those checks, and maintain the separation of powers, the carefully defined limits on the power of each Branch must not be eroded. To accomplish what has been attempted by one House of Congress in this case requires action in conformity with the express procedures of the Constitution's prescription for legislative action: passage by a majority of both Houses and presentment to the President.

The veto authorized by § 244 (c) (2) doubtless has been in many respects a convenient shortcut; the "sharing" with the Executive by Congress of its authority over aliens in this manner is, on its face, an appealing compromise. In purely practical terms, it is obviously easier for action to be taken by one House without submission to the President; but it is crystal clear from the records of the Convention, contemporaneous writings and debates, that the Framers ranked other values higher than efficiency. The records of the Convention and debates in the States preceding ratification underscore the common desire to define and limit the exercise of the newly created federal powers affecting the states and the people. There is unmistakable expression of a determination that legislation by the national Congress be a step-by-step, deliberate and deliberative process.

The choices we discern as having been made in the Constitutional Convention impose burdens on governmental processes that often seem clumsy, inefficient, even unworkable, but those hard choices were consciously made by men who had lived under a form of government that permitted arbitrary governmental acts to go unchecked. There is no support in the Constitution or decisions of this Court for the proposition that the cumbersomeness and delays often encountered in complying with explicit Constitutional standards may be avoided, either by the Congress or by the President. . . . With all the obvious flaws of delay, untidiness, and potential for abuse, we have not yet found a better way to preserve freedom than by making the exercise of power subject to the carefully crafted restraints spelled out in the Constitution.

V

We hold that the Congressional veto provision in § 244 (c) (2) is severable from the Act and that it is unconstitutional. Accordingly, the judgment of the Court of Appeals is affirmed.

Justice Powell, concurring
in the judgment, said in part:

The Court's decision, based on the Presentment Clauses, Art. I, § 7, cl. 2 and 3, apparently will invalidate every use of the legislative veto. The breadth of this holding gives one pause. Congress has included the veto in literally hundreds of statutes, dating back to the 1930s. Congress clearly views this procedure as essential to controlling the delegation of power to administrative agencies. One reasonably may disagree with Congress' assessment of the veto's utility, but the respect due its judgment as a coordinate branch of Government cautions that our holding should be no more extensive than necessary to decide this case. In my view, the case may be decided on a narrower ground. When Congress finds that a particular person does not satisfy the statutory criteria for permanent residence in this country it has assumed a judicial function in violation of the principle of separation of powers. Accordingly, I concur in the judgment. . . .

[Chief Justice Burger was joined in the majority by Justices Brennan, Marshall, Blackmun, Stevens, and O'Connor. Justices White and Rehnquist wrote dissenting opinions. The most complete treatment of the development and use of the legislative veto is provided in Justice White's dissent.]

Justice White dissented:

Today the Court not only invalidates § 244 (c) (2) of the Immigration and Nationality Act but also sounds the death knell for nearly 200 other statutory provisions in which Congress has reserved a "legislative veto." For this reason, the Court's decision is of surpassing importance. And it is for this reason that the Court would have been well-advised to decide the case, if possible, on the narrower grounds of separation of powers, leaving for full consideration the constitutionality of other congressional review statutes operating on such varied matters as war powers and agency rulemaking, some of which concern the independent regulatory agencies.

The prominence of the legislative veto mechanism in our contemporary political system and its importance to Congress can hardly be overstated. It has become a central means by which Congress secures the accountability of executive and independent agencies. Without the legislative veto, Congress is faced with a Hobson's choice: either to refrain from delegating the necessary authority, leaving itself with a hopeless task of writing laws with the requisite specificity to cover endless special circumstances across the entire policy landscape, or in the alternative, to abdicate its lawmaking function to the executive branch and independent agencies. To choose the former leaves major national problems unresolved; to opt for the latter risks unaccountable policymaking by those not elected to fill that role. Accordingly, over the past five decades, the legislative veto has been placed in nearly 200 statutes. The device is known in every field of governmental concern: reorganization, budgets, foreign affairs, war powers, and regulation of trade, safety, energy, the environment and the economy.

I

The legislative veto developed initially in response to the problems of reorganizing the sprawling government structure created in response to the Depression. The Reorganization Acts established the chief model for the legislative veto. When President Hoover requested authority to reorganize the government in 1929, he coupled his request that the "Congress be willing to delegate its authority over the problem (subject to defined principles) to the Executive" with a proposal for legislative review. He proposed that the Executive "should act upon approval of a joint committee of Congress or with the reservation of power of revision by Congress within some limited period adequate for its consideration." Pub. Papers 432 (1929). Congress followed President Hoover's suggestion and authorized reorganization subject to legislative review. . . . Although the reorganization authority reenacted in 1933 did not contain a legislative veto provision, the provision returned during the Roosevelt Administration and has since been renewed numerous times. Over the years, the provision was used extensively. Presidents submitted 115 reorganization plans to Congress of which 23 were disapproved by Congress pursuant to legislative veto provisions. . . .

Shortly after adoption of the Reorganization Act of 1939 . . . Congress and the President applied the legislative veto procedure to resolve the delegation problem for national security and foreign affairs. World War II occasioned the need to transfer greater authority to the President in these areas. The legislative veto offered the means by which Congress could confer additional authority while preserving its own constitutional role. During World War II, Congress enacted over thirty statutes conferring powers on the Executive with legislative veto provisions. President Roosevelt accepted the veto as the necessary price for obtaining exceptional authority.

Over the quarter century following World War II, Presidents continued to accept legislative vetoes by one or both Houses as constitutional, while regularly denouncing provisions by which Congressional committees reviewed Executive activity. The legislative veto balanced delegations of statutory authority in new areas of governmental involvement: the space program, international agreements on nuclear energy, tariff arrangements, and adjustment of federal pay rates.

During the 1970's the legislative veto was important in resolving a series of major constitutional disputes between the President and Congress over claims of the President to broad impoundment, war, and national emergency powers. The key provision of the War Powers Resolution . . . authorizes the termination by concurrent resolution of the use of armed forces in hostilities. A similar measure resolved the problem posed by Presidential claims of inherent power to impound appropriations. . . .

In conference, a compromise was achieved under which permanent impoundments, termed "rescissions," would require approval through enactment of legislation. In contrast, temporary impoundments, or "deferrals," would become effective unless disapproved by one House. This compromise provided the President with flexibility, while preserving ultimate Congressional control over the budget. Although the War Powers Resolution was enacted over President Nixon's veto, the Impoundment Control Act was enacted with the President's approval. These statutes were followed by others resolving similar problems: the National Emergencies Act . . . resolving the longstanding problems with unchecked Executive emergency power; the Arms Export Control Act . . . resolving the problem of foreign arms sales; and the Nuclear Non-Proliferation Act of 1978 . . . resolving the problem of exports of nuclear technology.

In the energy field, the legislative veto served to balance broad delegations in legislation emerging from the energy crisis of the 1970's. In the educational field, it was found that fragmented and narrow grant programs "inevitably lead to Executive-Legislative confrontations" because they inaptly limited the Commissioner of Education's authority. . . . The response was to grant the Commissioner of Education rulemaking authority, subject to a legislative veto. In the trade regulation area, the veto preserved Congressional authority over the Federal Trade Commission's broad mandate to make rules to prevent businesses from engaging in "unfair or deceptive acts or practices in commerce."

Even this brief review suffices to demonstrate that the legislative veto is more than "efficient, convenient, and useful." *Ante,* at 23. It is an important if not indispensable political invention that allows the President and Congress to resolve major constitutional and policy differences, assures the accountability of independent regulatory agencies, and preserves Congress' control over lawmaking. Perhaps there are other means of accommodation and accountability, but the increasing reliance of Congress upon the legislative veto suggests that the alternatives to which Congress must now turn are not entirely satisfactory.

The history of the legislative veto also makes clear that it has not been a sword with which Congress has struck out to aggrandize itself at the expense of the other branches—the concerns of Madison and Hamilton. Rather, the veto has been a means of defense, a reservation of ultimate authority necessary if Congress is to fulfill its designated role under Article I as the nation's lawmaker. While the President has often objected to particular legislative vetoes, generally those left in the hands of congressional committees, the Executive has more often agreed to legislative review as the price for a broad delegation of authority. To be sure, the President may have preferred unrestricted power, but that could be precisely why Congress thought it essential to retain a check on the exercise of delegated authority.

II

For all these reasons, the apparent sweep of the Court's decision today is regretable. The Court's Article I analysis appears to invalidate all legislative vetoes irrespective of form or subject. Because the legislative veto is commonly found as a check upon rulemaking by administrative agencies and upon broad-based policy decisions of the Executive Branch, it is particularly unfortunate that the Court reaches its decision in a case involving the exercise of a veto over deportation decisions regarding particular individuals. Courts should always be wary of striking statutes as unconstitutional; to strike an entire class of statutes based on consideration of a somewhat atypical and more-readily indictable exemplar of the class is irresponsible. It was for cases such as this one that Justice Brandeis wrote:

"The Court has frequently called attention to the 'great gravity and delicacy' of its function in passing upon the validity of an act of Congress. . . . The Court will not 'formulate a rule of constitutional law broader than is required by the precise facts to which it is to be applied.'

Unfortunately, today's holding is not so limited."

If the legislative veto were as plainly unconstitutional as the Court strives to suggest, its broad ruling today would be more comprehensible. But, the constitutionality of the legislative veto is anything but clearcut. The issue divides scholars, courts, attorneys general, and the two other branches of the National Government. If the veto devices so flagrantly disregarded the requirements of Article I as the Court today suggests, I find it incomprehensible that Congress, whose members are bound by oath to uphold the Constitution, would have placed these mechanisms in nearly 200 separate laws over a period of 50 years.

The reality of the situation is that the constitutional question posed today is one of immense difficulty over which the executive and legislative branches—as well as scholars and judges—have understandably dis-agreed. That disagreement stems from the silence of the Constitution on the precise question: The Constitution does not directly authorize or prohibit the legislative veto. Thus, our task should be to determine whether the legislative veto is consistent with the purposes of Art. I and the principles of Separation of Powers which are reflected in that Article and throughout the Constitution. We should not find the lack of a specific constitutional authorization for the legislative veto surprising, and I would not infer disapproval of the mechanism from its absence. From the summer of 1787 to the present the government of the United States has become an endeavor far beyond the contemplation of the Framers. Only within the last half century has the complexity and size of the Federal Government's responsibilities grown so greatly that the Congress must rely on the legislative veto as the most effective if not the only means to insure their role as the nation's lawmakers. But the wisdom of the Framers was to anticipate that the nation would grow and new problems of governance would require different solutions. Accordingly, our Federal Government was intentionally chartered with the flexibility to respond to contemporary needs without losing sight of fundamental democratic principles. This was the spirit in which Justice Jackson penned his influential concurrence in the *Steel Seizure Case*:

"The actual art of governing under our Constitution does not and cannot conform to judicial definitions of the power of any of its branches based on isolated clauses or even single Articles torn from context. While the Constitution diffuses power the better to secure liberty, it also contemplates that practice will integrate the dispersed powers into a workable government."

This is the perspective from which we should approach the novel constitutional questions presented by the legislative veto. In my view, neither Article I of the Constitution nor the doctrine of separation of powers is violated by this mechanism by which our elected representatives preserve their voice in the governance of the nation.

III

The Court holds that the disapproval of a suspension of deportation by the resolution of one House of Congress is an exercise of legislative power without compliance with the prerequisites for lawmaking set forth in Art. I of the Constitution. Specifically, the Court maintains that the provisions of § 244 (c) (2) are inconsistent with the requirement of bicameral approval, implicit in Art. I, § 1, and the requirement that all bills and resolutions that require the concurrence of both Houses be presented to the President, Art. I, § 7, cl. 2 and 3.

I do not dispute the Court's truismatic exposition of these clauses. There is no question that a bill does not become a law until it is approved by both the House and the Senate, and presented to the President. Similarly, I would not hesitate to strike an action of Congress in the form of a concurrent resolution which constituted an exercise of original lawmaking authority. I agree with the Court that the President's qualified veto power is a critical element in the distribution of powers under the Constitution, widely endorsed among the Framers, and intended to serve the President as a defense against legislative encroachment and to check the "passing of bad laws through haste, inadvertence, or design. . . ." The records of the Convention reveal that it is the first purpose which figured most prominently but I acknowledge the vitality of the second. . . . I also agree that the bicameral approval required by Art. I, §§ 1, 7 "was of scarcely less concern to the Framers than was the Presidential veto" . . . and that the need to divide and disperse legislative power figures significantly in our scheme of Government. All of this, the Third Part of the Court's opinion, is entirely unexceptionable.

It does not, however, answer the constitutional question before us. The power to exercise a legislative veto is not the power to write new law without bicameral approval or presidential consideration. The veto must be authorized by statute and may only negative what an Executive department or independent agency has proposed. On its face, the legislative veto no more allows one House of Congress to make law than does the presidential veto confer such power upon the President. Accordingly, the Court properly recognizes that it "must establish that the challenged action under § 244 (c) (2) is of the kind to which the procedural requirements of Art. I, § 7 apply" and admits that "not every action taken by either House is subject to the bicameralism and presentation requirements of Art. I. . . .

The terms of the Presentment Clauses suggest only that bills and their equivalent are subject to the requirements of bicameral passage and presentment to the President. Article I, § 7, cl. 2, stipulates only that "Every Bill which shall have passed the House of Representatives and the Senate, shall before it becomes a Law, be presented to the President" for approval or disapproval, his disapproval then subject to being overridden by a two-thirds vote of both houses. Section 7, cl. 3 goes further:

"Every Order, Resolution, or Vote to which the Concurrence of the Senate and House of Representatives may be necessary (except on a question of Adjournment) shall be presented to the President of the United States; and before the same shall take Effect, shall be approved by him, or being disapproved by him, shall be repassed by two-thirds of the Senate and House of Representatives, according to the Rules and Limitations prescribed in the Case of a Bill."

Although the Clause does not specify the actions for which the concurrence of both Houses is "necessary," the proceedings at the Philadelphia Convention suggest its purpose was to prevent Congress from circumventing the presentation requirement in the making of new legislation. James Madison observed that if the President's veto was confined to bills, it could be evaded by calling a proposed law a "resolution" or "vote" rather than a "bill." Accordingly, he proposed that "or resolve" should be added after "bill" in what is now clause 2 of § 7. . . . After a short discussion on the subject, the amendment was rejected. On the following day, however, Randolph renewed the proposal in the substantial form as it now appears, and the motion passed. . . . The chosen language, Madison's comment, and the brevity of the Convention's consideration, all suggest a modest role was intended for the Clause and no broad restraint on Congressional authority was contemplated. . . . This reading is consistent with the historical background of the Presentation Clause itself which reveals only that the Framers were concerned with limiting the methods for enacting new legislation. The Framers were aware of the experience in Pennsylvania where the legislature had evaded the requirements attached to the passing of legislation by the use of "resolves," and the criticisms directed at this practice by the Council of Censors. There is no record that the Convention contemplated, let alone intended, that these Article I requirements would someday be invoked to restrain the scope of Congressional authority pursuant to duly-enacted law.

When the Convention did turn its attention to the scope of Congress' lawmaking power, the Framers were expansive. The Necessary and Proper Clause, Art. I, § 8, cl. 18, vests Congress with the power "to make all laws which shall be necessary and proper for carrying into Execution the foregoing Powers [the enumerated powers of § 8], and all other Powers vested by this Constitution in the government of the United States, or in any Department or Officer thereof." It is long-settled that Congress may "exercise its best judgment in the selection of measures, to carry into execution the constitutional powers of the government," and "avail itself of experience, to exer-

cise its reasons, and to accommodate its legislation to circumstances. . . ."

The Court heeded this counsel in approving the modern administrative state. The Court's holding today that all legislative-type action must be enacted through the lawmaking process ignores that legislative authority is routinely delegated to the Executive branch, to the independent regulatory agencies, and to private individuals and groups.

"The rise of administrative bodies probably has been the most significant legal trend of the last century. . . . They have become a veritable fourth branch of the Government, which has deranged our three-branch legal theories."

This Court's decisions sanctioning such delegations make clear that Article I does not require all action with the effect of legislation to be passed as a law.

Theoretically, agencies and officials were asked only to "fill up the details," and the rule was that "Congress cannot delegate any part of its legislative power except under limitation of a prescribed standard. . . ." Chief Justice Taft elaborated the standard in *J.W. Hampton & Co. v. United States*. . . . "If Congress shall lay down by legislative act an intelligible principle to which the person or body authorized to fix such rates is directed to conform, such legislative action is not a forbidden delegation of legislative power." In practice, however, restrictions on the scope of the power that could be delegated diminished and all but disappeared. In only two instances did the Court find an unconstitutional delegation. . . ." In other cases, the "intelligible principle" through which agencies have attained enormous control over the economic affairs of the country was held to include such formulations as "just and reasonable," "public interest," "public convenience, interest, or necessity," and "unfair methods of competition. . . ."

The wisdom and the constitutionality of these broad delegations are matters that still have not been put to rest. But for present purposes, these cases establish that by virtue of congressional delegation, legislative power can be exercised by independent agencies and Executive departments without the passage of new legislation. For some time, the sheer amount of law—the substantive rules that regulate private conduct and direct the operation of government—made by the agencies has far outnumbered the lawmaking engaged in by Congress through the traditional process. There is no question but that agency rulemaking is lawmaking in any functional or realistic sense of the term. The Administrative Procedure Act, 5 U.S.C. § 551 (4) provides that a "rule" is an agency statement "designed to implement, interpret, or prescribe law or policy."

When agencies are authorized to prescribe law through substantive rulemaking, the administrator's regulation is not only due deference, but is accorded "legislative effect. . . ."

These regulations bind courts and officers of the federal government, may pre-empt state law . . . and grant rights to and impose obligations on the public. In sum, they have the force of law.

If Congress may delegate lawmaking power to independent and executive agencies, it is most difficult to understand Article I as forbidding Congress from also reserving a check on legislative power for itself. Absent the veto, the agencies receiving delegations of legislative or quasi-legislative power may issue regulations having the force of law without bicameral approval and without the President's signature. It is thus not apparent why the reservation of a veto over the exercise of that legislative power must be subject to a more exacting test. In both cases, it is enough that the initial statutory authorizations comply with the Article I requirements.

Nor are there strict limits on the agents that may receive such delegations of legislative authority so that it might be said that the legislature can delegate authority to others but not to itself. While most authority to issue rules and regulations is given to the executive branch and the independent regulatory agencies, statutory delegations to private persons have also passed this Court's scrutiny. In *Currin* v. *Wallace*, 306 U.S. 1 (1939), the statute provided that restrictions upon the production or marketing of agricultural commodities was to become effective only upon the favorable vote by a prescribed majority of the affected farmers. . . .

The *Rock Royal* decision upheld an act which gave producers of specified commodities the right to veto marketing orders issued by the Secretary of Agriculture. Assuming *Currin* and *Rock Royal Co-operative* remain sound law, the Court's decision today suggests that Congress may place a "veto" power over suspensions of deportation in private hands or in the hands of an independent agency, but is forbidden from reserving such authority for itself. Perhaps this odd result could be justified on other constitutional grounds, such as the separation of powers, but certainly it cannot be defended as consistent with the Court's view of the Article I presentment and bicameralism commands.

The Court's opinion in the present case comes closest to facing the reality of administrative lawmaking in considering the contention that the Attorney General's action in suspending deportation under § 244 is itself a legislative act. The Court posits that the Attorney General is acting in an Article II enforcement capacity under § 244. This characterization is at odds with *Mahler* v. *Eby* . . . where the power conferred on the Executive to deport aliens was considered a delegation of legislative power. The Court suggests, however, that the Attorney General acts in an Article II capacity because "[t]he courts when a case or controversy arises, can always ascertain whether the will of Congress has been obeyed . . . and can enforce adherence to statutory standards." . . . This assumption is simply wrong, as the Court itself points out: "We are aware of no decision . . . where a federal court has reviewed a decision of the Attorney General suspending deportation of an alien pursuant to the standards set out in § 244 (a)(1)." This is not surprising, given that no party to such action has either the motivation or the right to appeal from it. . . . It is perhaps on the erroneous premise that judicial review may check abuses of the § 244 power that the Court also submits that "The bicameral process is not necessary as a check on the Executive's administration of the laws because his administrative activity cannot reach beyond the limits of the statute that created it—a statute duly enacted pursuant to Art. I, §§ 1, 7." . . . On the other hand, the Court's reasoning does persuasively explain why a resolution of disapproval under § 244 (c)(2) need not again be subject to the bicameral process. Because it serves only to check the Attorney General's exercise of the suspension authority granted by § 244, the disapproval resolution—unlike the Attorney General's action—"cannot reach beyond the limits of the statute that created it—a statute duly enacted pursuant to Article I."

More fundamentally, even if the Court correctly characterizes the Attorney General's authority under § 244 as an Article II Executive power, the Court concedes that certain administrative agency action, such as rulemaking, "may resemble lawmaking" and recognizes that "[t]his Court has referred to agency activity as being 'quasi-legislative' in character. . . ." Such rules and adjudications by the agencies meet the Court's own definition of legislative action for they "alter the legal rights, duties, and relations of persons . . . outside the legislative branch," *ante*, at 32, and involve "determinations of policy," *ante*, at 34. Under the Court's analysis, the Executive Branch and the independent agencies may make rules with the effect of law while Congress, in whom the Framers confided the legislative power, Art. I, § 1, may not exercise a veto which precludes such rules from having operative force. If the effective functioning of a complex modern government requires the delegation of vast authority which, by virtue of its breadth, is legislative or "quasi-legislative" in character, I cannot accept that Article I—which is, after all, the source of the non-delegation doctrine—should forbid Congress from qualifying that grant with a legislative veto.

The Court also takes no account of perhaps the most relevant consideration: However resolutions of disapproval under § 244 (c) (2) are formally characterized, in reality, a departure from the status quo occurs only upon the concurrence of opinion among the House, Senate, and President. Reservations of legislative authority to be exercised by Congress should be upheld if the exercise of such reserved authority is consistent with the distribution of and limits upon legislative power that Article I provides.

As its history reveals, § 244 (c) (2) withstands this analysis. Until 1917, Congress had never established laws concerning the deportation of aliens. The Immigration Act of 1924 enlarged the categories of aliens subject to mandatory deportation, and substantially increased the likelihood of hardships to individuals by abolishing in most cases the previous time limitation of three years within which deportation proceedings had to be commenced. . . . Thousands of persons, who either had entered the country in more lenient times or had been smuggled in as children, or had overstayed their permits, faced the prospect of deportation. Enforcement of the Act grew more rigorous over the years with the deportation of thousands of aliens without regard to the mitigating circumstances of particular cases. . . . Congress provided relief in certain cases through the passage of private bills.

In 1933, when deportations reached their zenith, the Secretary of Labor temporarily suspended numerous deportations on grounds of hardship . . . and proposed legislation to allow certain deportable aliens to remain in the country. . . . The Labor Department bill was opposed, however, as "grant[ing] too much discretionary authority" . . . and it failed decisively. . . .

The following year, the administration proposed bills to authorize an inter-Departmental committee to grant permanent residence to deportable aliens who had lived in the United States for 10 years or who had close relatives here. S. 2969 and H. R. 8163, 74th Cong., 1st Sess. (1935). These bills were also attacked as an "abandonment of congressional control over the deportation of undesirable aliens" . . . and were not enacted. A similar fate awaited a bill introduced in the 75th Congress that would have authorized the Secretary to grant permanent residence to up to 8,000 deportable aliens. The measure passed the House, but did not come to a vote in the Senate. . . .

The succeeding Congress again attempted to find a legislative solution to the deportation problem.

The initial House bill required congressional action to cancel individual deportations . . . but the Senate amended the legislation to provide that deportable aliens should not be deported unless the Congress by Act or resolution rejected the recommendation of the Secretary . . . as reported with amendments by S. Rep. No. 1721, 76th Cong., 3d Sess. 2 (1940). The compromise solution, the immediate predecessor to § 244 (c), allowed the Attorney General to suspend the deportation of qualified aliens. Their deportation would be canceled and permanent residence granted if the House and Senate did not adopt a concurrent resolution of disapproval. . . . The Executive Branch played a major role in fashioning this compromise . . . and President Roosevelt approved the legislation, which became the Alien Registration Act of 1940. . . .

In 1947, the Department of Justice requested legislation authorizing the Attorney General to cancel deportations without congressional review. . . . The purpose of the proposal was to "save time and energy of everyone concerned. . . ." The Senate Judiciary Committee objected, stating that "affirmative action by the Congress in all suspension cases should be required before deportation proceedings may be canceled." . . . Congress not only rejected the Department's request for final authority but amended the Immigration Act to require that cancellation of deportation be approved by a concurrent resolution of the Congress. President Truman signed the bill without objection. . . .

Practice over the ensuing several years convinced Congress that the requirement of affirmative approval was "not workable . . . and would, in time, interfere with the legislative work of the House." . . .

In preparing the comprehensive immigration and Nationality Act of 1952, the Senate Judiciary Committee recommended that for certain classes of aliens the adjustment of status be subject to the disapproval of either House; but deportation of an alien "who is of the criminal, subversive, or immoral classes or who overstays his period of admission," would be cancelled only upon a concurrent resolution disapproving the deportation. . . .

Legislation reflecting this change was passed by both Houses, and enacted into law as part of the Immigration and Nationality Act of 1952 over President Truman's veto, which was not predicated on the presence of a legislative veto. . . . In subsequent years, the Congress refused further requests that the Attorney General be given final authority to grant discretionary relief for specified categories of aliens, and § 244 remained intact to the present.

Section 244 (A) (1) authorizes the Attorney General, in his discretion, to suspend the deportation of certain aliens who are otherwise deportable and upon Congress' approval, to adjust their status to that of aliens lawfully admitted for permanent residence. In order to be eligible for this relief, an alien must have been physically present in the United States for a continuous period of not less than seven years, must prove he is of good moral character, and must prove that he or his immediate family would suffer "extreme hardship" if he is deported. Judicial review of a denial of relief may be sought. Thus, the suspension proceeding "has two phases: a determination whether the statutory conditions have been met, which generally involves a question of law, and a determination whether relief shall be granted, which [ultimately] . . . is confided to the sound discretion of the Attorney General [and his delegates]." . . .

There is also a third phase to the process. Under § 244 (c) (1) the Attorney General must report all such suspensions, with a detailed statement of facts and reasons, to the Congress. Either House may then act, in that session or the next, to block the suspension of deportation by passing a resolution of disapproval. § 244 (c) (2). Upon Congressional approval of the suspension—by its silence—the alien's permanent status is adjusted to that of a lawful resident alien.

The history of the Immigration Act makes clear that § 244 (c) (2) did not alter the division of actual authority between Congress and the Executive. At all times, whether through private bills, or through affirmative concurrent resolutions, or through the present one-House veto, a permanent change in a deportable alien's status could be accomplished only with the agreement of the Attorney General, the House, and the Senate.

The central concern of the presentation and bicameralism requirements of Article I is that when a departure from the legal status quo is undertaken, it is done with the approval of the President and both Houses of Congress—or, in the event of a presidential veto, a two-thirds majority in both Houses. This interest is fully satisfied by the operation of § 244 (c) (2). The President's approval is found in the Attorney General's action in recommending to Congress that the deportation order for a given alien be suspended. The House and the Senate indicate their approval of the Executive's action by not passing a resolution of disapproval within the statutory period. Thus, a change in the legal status quo—the deportability of the alien—is consummated only with the approval of each of the three relevant actors. The disagreement of any one of the three maintains the alien's pre-existing status: the Executive may choose not to recommend suspension; the House and Senate may each veto the recommen-

dation. The effect on the rights and obligations of the affected individuals and upon the legislative system is precisely the same as if a private bill were introduced but failed to receive the necessary approval. "The President and the two Houses enjoy exactly the same say in what the law is to be as would have been true for each without the presence of the one-House veto, and nothing in the law is changed absent the concurrence of the President and a majority in each House."

This very construction of the Presentment Clauses which the Executive Branch now rejects was the basis upon which the Executive Branch defended the constitutionality of the Reorganization Act . . . which provides that the President's proposed reorganization plans take effect only if not vetoed by either House. When the Department of Justice advised the Senate on the constitutionality of congressional review in reorganization legislation in 1949, it stated: "In this procedure there is no question involved of the Congress taking legislative action beyond its initial passage of the Reorganization Act." . . . This also represents the position of the Attorney General more recently.

Thus understood, § 244 (c) (2) fully effectuates the purposes of the bicameralism and presentation requirements. I now briefly consider possible objections to the analysis.

First, it may be asserted that Chadha's status before legislative disapproval is one of nondeportation and that the exercise of the veto, unlike the failure of a private bill, works a change in the status quo. This position plainly ignores the statutory language. At no place in § 244 has Congress delegated to the Attorney General any final power to determine which aliens shall be allowed to remain in the United States. Congress has retained the ultimate power to pass on such changes in deportable status. By its own terms, § 244 (a) states that whatever power the Attorney General has been delegated to suspend deportation and adjust status is to be exercisable only "as hereinafter prescribed in this section." Subsection (c) is part of that section. A grant of "suspension" does not cancel the alien's deportation or adjust the alien's status to that of a permanent resident alien. A suspension order is merely a "deferment of deportation" . . . which can mature into a cancellation of deportation and adjustment of status only upon the approval of Congress—by way of silence—under § 244 (c) (2). Only then does the statute authorize the Attorney General to "cancel deportation proceedings" § 244 (c) (2), and "record the alien's lawful admission for permanent residence . . ." § 244 (d). The Immigration and Naturalization Service's action, on behalf of the Attorney General, "cannot become effective without ratification by Congress."

... Until that ratification occurs, the executive's action is simply a recommendation that Congress finalize the suspension—in itself, it works no legal change.

Second, it may be said that this approach leads to the incongruity that the two-House veto is more suspect than its one-House brother. Although the idea may be initially counter-intuitive, on close analysis, it is not at all unusual that the one-House veto is of more certain constitutionality than the two-House version. If the Attorney General's action is a proposal for legislation, then the disapproval of but a single House is all that is required to prevent its passage. Because approval is indicated by the failure to veto, the one-House veto satisfies the requirement of bicameral approval. The two-House version may present a different question. The concept that "neither branch of Congress, when acting separately, can lawfully exercise more power than is conferred by the Constitution on the whole body" ... is fully observed.

Third, it may be objected that Congress cannot indicate its approval of legislative change by inaction. In the Court of Appeals' view, inaction by Congress "could equally imply endorsement, acquiescence, passivity, indecision or indifference" ... and the Court appears to echo this concern. ... This objection appears more properly directed at the wisdom of the legislative veto than its constitutionality. The Constitution does not and cannot guarantee that legislators will carefully scrutinize legislation and deliberate before acting. In a democracy it is the electorate that holds the legislators accountable for the wisdom of their choices. It is hard to maintain that a private bill receives any greater individualized scrutiny than a resolution of disapproval under § 244 (c) (2). Certainly the legislative veto is no more susceptible to this attack than the Court's increasingly common practice of according weight to the failure of Congress to disturb an Executive or independent agency's action. ... Earlier this Term, the Court found it important that Congress failed to act on bills proposed to overturn the Internal Revenue Service's interpretation of the requirements for tax-exempt status under § 501 (c) (3) of the tax code. ... If Congress may be said to have ratified the Internal Revenue Service's interpretation without passing new legislation, Congress may also be said to approve a suspension of deportation by the Attorney General when it fails to exercise its veto authority. The requirements of Article I are not compromised by the Congressional scheme.

IV

The Court of Appeals struck § 244 (c) (2) as violative of the constitutional principle of separation of powers.

It is true that the purpose of separating the authority of government is to prevent unnecessary and dangerous concentration of power in one branch. For that reason, the Framers saw fit to divide and balance the powers of government so that each branch would be checked by the others. Virtually every part of our constitutional system bears the mark of this judgment.

But the history of the separation of powers doctrine is also a history of accommodation and practicality. Apprehensions of an overly powerful branch have not led to undue prophylactic measures that handicap the effective working of the national government as a whole. The Constitution does not contemplate total separation of the three branches of Government. ... "[A] hermetic sealing off of the three branches of Government from one another would preclude the establishment of a Nation capable of governing itself effectively. ..."

Our decisions reflect this judgment. As already noted, the Court, recognizing that modern government must address a formidable agenda of complex policy issues, countenanced the delegation of extensive legislative authority to executive and independent agencies. ... The separation of powers doctrine has heretofore led to the invalidation of government action only when the challenged action violated some express provision in the Constitution. In *Buckley* v. *Valeo* ... and *Myers* v. *United States* ... congressional action compromised the appointment power of the President. ... In *United States* v. *Klein* ... an Act of Congress was struck for encroaching upon judicial power, but the Court found that the Act also impinged upon the Executive's exclusive pardon power, Art. II, § 2. Because we must have a workable efficient government, this is as it should be.

This is the teaching of *Nixon* v. *Administrator of Gen. Servs* ... which, in rejecting a separation of powers objection to a law requiring that the Administrator take custody of certain presidential papers, set forth a framework for evaluating such claims:

"[I]n determining whether the Act disrupts the proper balance between the coordinate branches, the proper inquiry focuses on the extent to which it prevents the Executive Branch from accomplishing its constitutionally assigned functions. *United States* v. *Nixon*. ... Only where the potential for disruption is present must we then determine whether that impact is justified by an overriding need to promote objectives within the constitutional authority of Congress. ..."

Section 244 (c) (2) survives this test. The legislative veto provision does not "prevent the Executive Branch from accomplishing its constitutionally assigned functions." First, it is clear that the Executive Branch has no "constitutionally assigned" function of suspending the deportation of aliens. " 'Over no conceivable subject is the legislative power of Congress more complete than it is over' the admission of aliens." . . . Nor can it be said that the inherent function of the Executive Branch in executing the law is involved. *The Steel Seizure Case* resolved that the Article II mandate for the President to execute the law is a directive to enforce the law which Congress has written. . . . "The duty of the President to see that the laws be executed is a duty that does not go beyond the laws or require him to achieve more than Congress sees fit to leave within his power." . . . Here, § 244 grants the executive only a qualified suspension authority and it is only that authority which the President is constitutionally authorized to execute.

Moreover, the Court believes that the legislative veto we consider today is best characterized as an exercise of legislative or quasi-legislative authority. Under this characterization, the practice does not, even on the surface, constitute an infringement of executive or judicial prerogative. The Attorney General's suspension of deportation is equivalent to a proposal for legislation. The nature of the Attorney General's role as recommendatory is not altered because § 244 provides for congressional action through disapproval rather than by ratification. In comparison to private bills, which must be initiated in the Congress and which allow a Presidential veto to be overridden by a two-thirds majority in both Houses of Congress, § 244 augments rather than reduces the executive branch's authority. So understood, congressional review does not undermine, as the Court of Appeals thought, the "weight and dignity" that attends the decisions of the Executive Branch.

Nor does § 244 infringe on the judicial power, as JUSTICE POWELL would hold. Section 244 makes clear that Congress has reserved its own judgment as part of the statutory process. Congressional action does not substitute for judicial review of the Attorney General's decisions. The Act provides for judicial review of the refusal of the Attorney General to suspend a deportation and to transmit a recommendation to Congress. . . . But the courts have not been given the authority to review whether an alien should be given permanent status; review is limited to whether the Attorney General has properly applied the statutory standards for essentially denying the alien a recommendation that his deportable status be changed by the Congress. Moreover, there is no constitutional obligation to provide any judicial review whatever for a failure to suspend deportation. "The power of Congress, therefore, to expel, like the power to exclude aliens, or any specified class of aliens, from the country, may be exercised entirely through executive officers; or Congress may call in the aid of the judiciary to ascertain any contested facts on which an alien's right to be in the country has been made by Congress to depend." . . .

I do not suggest that all legislative vetoes are necessarily consistent with separation of powers principles. A legislative check on an inherently executive function, for example that of initiating prosecutions, poses an entirely different question. But the legislative veto device here—and in many other settings—is far from an instance of legislative tyranny over the Executive. It is a necessary check on the unavoidably expanding power of the agencies, both executive and independent, as they engage in exercising authority delegated by Congress.

V

I regret that I am in disagreement with my colleagues on the fundamental questions that this case presents. But even more I regret the destructive scope of the Court's holding. It reflects a profoundly different conception of the Constitution than that held by the Courts which sanctioned the modern administrative state. Today's decision strikes down in one fell swoop provisions in more laws enacted by Congress than the Court has cumulatively invalidated in its history. I fear it will now be more difficult "to insure that the fundamental policy decisions in our society will be made not by an appointed official but by the body immediately responsible to the people." . . . I must dissent. [Justice Rehnquist's dissent, which focused on the issue of severability, was omitted, as were Justice White's appendix listing all statutes employing the legislative veto and all footnotes].

The immediate reaction to the Chadha decision was mixed. Advocates of strong executive leadership wholeheartedly approved the Supreme Court's sweeping decision. Deputy Attorney General Edward C. Schmults of the Reagan administration's Justice Department testified before a House Judiciary subcommittee that 207 sections of 126 federal statutes were rendered unconstitutional by *INS* v. *Chadha*. Some congressional leaders urged immediate legislative action to ensure congressional authority and oversight of presidential and administrative actions. Deputy Attorney General Schmults argued that immediate congressional action was unnecessary. He cited the War Powers Resolution as an example, suggesting that the invalidation of one important section did not affect another key section of the resolution. Thus, while Chadha invalidated the section authorizing Congress to compel immediate withdrawal of U. S. military forces from foreign soil when hostilities were involved, because this could be done by two-chamber legislative veto without presidential approval, another key section could be deemed constitutionally valid. This section required withdrawal of U. S. troops from areas of foreign hostility after 60 days unless Congress passed legislation signed by the president to authorize the troops to remain.[13]

One presidential scholar, John P. Burke, has suggested that the Chadha decision's political implications are "great, perhaps rivaling the impact of the rulings against the New Deal in the 1930s."[14] Although dramatic executive-legislative confrontations are possible consequences of increased tensions between these branches, the less dramatic but possibly enduring impact of Chadha is in the area of legislative oversight of presidential and administrative actions. Congress may simply refrain from granting the president or his administrators many powers that it previously provided when it could invoke legislative veto power to curtail what it deemed as inappropriate actions. Congress itself may feel compelled to give greater attention to statutory detail and to enlarge its legitimate investigatory authority to redress the imbalance brought by the all-inclusive nature of the Chadha decision.

Conclusion

Paul Murphy's excellent constitutional history of the great transition in law and politics from 1918 through the chief justiceship of Earl Warren concluded with a perceptive evaluative chapter that emphasized the relative persistence of the doctrinal changes of the late 1930s, 1940s, 1950s, and 1960s. Murphy correctly noted that "no constitutional act between 1937 and 1969 regulating property was declared unconstitutional and very few state laws regulating industry or providing welfare programs were invalidated as interferences with contract rights or private property."[15] A 1969 *New York Times* article entitled "Warren Court Is Not Likely to Be Overruled"[16] was similarly cited. But since 1968, no new member of the Supreme Court has been chosen by a Democratic or liberal president. Procedural due process doctrines relating to criminal defendants have been modified considerably. Civil rights doctrines have been modified as well. While these conservative judicial changes have been widely discussed and evaluated, far less attention has been focused upon the revival of substantive due process and contract clause modes of curtailing federal and state governmental authority to regulate the economy.

Despite the reorientation of doctrinal emphasis that was introduced by the Nixon appointees in the 1970s, the Reagan administration and the advocates of the Far Right in Congress have made the Supreme Court a target of both specific doctrinal and general institutional attacks in the early 1980s.

The resignation of Associate Justice Potter Stewart provided Ronald Reagan an opportunity for a Supreme Court appointment only a few months after taking office as president, an opportunity that had eluded President Carter during his entire four-year term. Carter had compiled a largely unheralded but exemplary record of federal court of appeals and district court appointments. Because Carter had significantly broadened the judicial selection base by increasing the proportion of minority and female nominees on the federal courts, and because of his general interest in the Equal Rights Amendment, it was anticipated that if Carter won the 1980 presidential race, he would select a woman for a Supreme Court vacancy. Instead, in the summer of 1981, President Reagan surprised many by nominating Sandra Day O'Connor, an attorney, former Arizona state legislator, and current Arizona jurist. But despite high praise for his nomination of the first woman proposed for the Court, the recommendation drew severe criticism from antiabortion groups because of some of O'Connor's state legislative positions. After lengthy questioning before the Senate Judiciary Committee, O'Connor was approved by the committee 17–0 and went on to win full Senate approval. However, the antiabortion groups intensified their support for adoption of a court-curbing constitutional amendment designed to override *Roe* v. *Wade* and to limit judicial authority regarding abortion.

In October 1981, President Reagan's attorney general, William French Smith, opened a more broadly based attack on the Supreme Court in an address to the Federal Legal Council. Smith boldly invoked a direct political command, stating that

> We believe that the ground swell of conservatism, evidenced by the 1980 election, makes this an especially appropriate time to urge upon the courts more principled bases that would diminish judicial activism.

He cited three matters of "particular concern." First, he attacked the Court on the ground that it took issues that should not be decided by this tribunal or any court at all. This Smith termed "the erosion of restraint in consideration of justiciability." Second, Smith severely criticized the criteria employed by the Supreme Court to hold state or federal laws invalid under the national Constitution. Here he referred to "suspect classifications" in civil rights and civil liberties decisions, particularly with regard to the equal protection clause of the Fourteenth Amendment. Third, Smith leveled the charge that the Court made "extravagant" applications of enforcement remedies such as injunctions, judicial management of school systems, prison systems, or public housing programs.[17]

Liberals in the House and Senate proved totally unable, and in some instances unwilling, to limit the conservative thrust of President Reagan's domestic program in 1981. Consequently, by the beginning of 1982, the Supreme Court's elderly liberals were confronted by a growing conservative bloc. The Court as an institution was pressured by the Reagan administration, threatened by the Far Right, and largely abandoned by its former liberal allies in Congress. In the spring and summer of 1982, congressional liberals and moderates demonstrated more resolve in defending the Court by defeating or delaying Far Right efforts at limiting the authority of the Court regarding abortion and school prayers. But the attacks were by no means ended. The Far Right unhesitatingly carried the issue of Supreme Court activism and alleged secularism to both the hustings and the pulpit in the 1982 congressional elections. While suffering a setback, the Far Right and other conservative political forces unhesitatingly continued their efforts to change the Constitution in order to overturn Supreme Court decisions on abortion and prayers in the public schools. Since these efforts now draw the strong backing of President Ronald Reagan, the prospects for these anti-Court efforts may well be closely related to the outcome of the presidential election of 1984. Thus, the 1980s represent an era of unusual pressure upon the Supreme Court.

REFERENCES

1. Robert A. Diamond, ed., *Presidential Elections Since 1789* (Washington, D. C.: Congressional Quarterly, 1975), pp. 59, 98.
2. John R. Schmidhauser with Larry L. Berg, *The Supreme Court and Congress: Conflict and Interaction* (New York: Free Press, 1972), pp. 5–12.
3. Ibid.
4. For a full account of the impeachment attempt and its background, see James F. Simon, *Independent Journey: The Life of William O. Douglas* (New York: Harper and Row, 1980), pp. 391–411.
5. 418 U. S. 717 (1974).
6. Ibid.
7. 5 California 3rd 584; 487 Pacific 2nd 1241 (1971).
8. For a full discussion of the antecedents and issues of the case, see Allan P. Sindler, *Bakke, De Funis, and Minority Admissions: The Quest for Equal Opportunity* (New York: Longman, 1978).
9. Sindler, op. cit., p. 317.
10. 431 U. S. 1 (1977).
11. 438 U. S. 234 (1978).
12. 103 Supreme Court Reporter 2764 (1983).
13. Testimony cited in *Los Angeles Times*, July 19, 1983, Part 1, p. 10.
14. John P. Burke, "What a Veto-Free President Can Do," *Los Angeles Times*, July 24, 1983, Part IV, p. 5.
15. Paul L. Murphy, *The Constitution in Crisis Times: 1918–1969* (New York: Harper and Row, 1972), p. 459.
16. Ibid., pp. 483–484.
17. *Los Angeles Times*, Part I, October 30, 1981, p. 9.

11

The Supreme Court, Critical Elections, and the Transformation of Judicial Elites and Values in the United States

In each era of important political change in the United States, the political, social, and economic role of the Supreme Court has generated a great deal of interest and controversy. One fundamental question concerning the Supreme Court and critical elections is whether, in the description of Robert Jackson, the Court consistently acts as "a check of a preceding generation on the present one," a "check of conservative legal philosophy on a dynamic people," and the "check of a rejected regime on one in being."[1] Although it is not acknowledged as such, Robert Dahl's frequently cited essay on the Supreme Court as a national policymaker is, in certain respects, a direct intellectual counterpoint to Jackson's contentions. Where Jackson argued that the Court fulfilled a consistent role as an institutional dead hand of the past, Dahl contended that "except for short-lived transitional periods when the old alliance is disintegrating and the new one is struggling to take control of political institutions, the Supreme Court is inevitably a part of the dominant national alliance."[2]

The central institutional factor that both Jackson and Dahl had to assess is the constitutional provision guaranteeing life tenure on good behavior. Dahl concluded that "the policy views dominant on the Court are never long out of line with the policy views dominant among the lawmaking majorities of the United States."[3] He pointed out that presidents average a new Supreme Court appointment every 22 months. But as the court-packing controversy of the 1930s indicated, in specific historical eras, the overall averaging of such appointments has little direct bearing on contemporary institutional relationships. A president who cannot achieve any ideological changes because there are no Court vacancies is not likely to be consoled by the recitation of overall averages.

The relationship of critical elections to patterns of change in Supreme Court membership and doctrinal orientation involves several aspects of more general political and legal significance than the generalizations of Jackson and Dahl. These aspects can be combined and considered under three fundamental questions.

The first question deals with the characteristics and purposes of the appointing authority. Do presidents generally nominate prospective justices in order to establish and perpetuate their own policy preferences? Or, conversely, do presidents make judicial selections for political or nonpolitical policy preferences? Does the open expression or discussion of presidential judicial preferences stimulate senatorial opposition to presidential nominees? Are conflicts over such issues generally greater in periods when critical elections are imminent or taking place?

The second question concerns the Supreme Court itself. In the periods preceding each critical election, did the decisions of the Supreme Court deal with issues that were important in the election? Were such decisions contrary to the positions of the emergent electoral majority? Or were they irrelevant?

The third and closely related question also concerns the Court. Do Supreme Court members generally modify their doctrinal positions after critical elections? If so, do they turn toward the ideological and policy positions of the new electoral and policymaking majority, or do they turn even further away from these new positions?

All of these questions and the empirical evidence necessary to answer them fully provide either validation or factual rejection of Robert Dahl's contention that "the policy views dominant on the Court are never for long out of line with the policy views dominant among the lawmaking majorities of the United States."[4] The contradictory approach of Robert Jackson posits that the members of the Supreme Court may, in certain crucial periods of economic, political, and social change, comprise a highly influential and powerful rearguard of a political and legal generation that in most other segments of the nation, social as well as political, has been largely rejected and replaced by a new generation.

An elegant description of the conceptualization of the interplay of law and politics as the handiwork of successive political and legal generations was provided in 1881 by Oliver Wendell Holmes, Jr., in *The Common Law*, in which he observed

> . . . The life of the law has not been logic: it has been experience. The felt necessities of the time, the prevalent moral and political theories, intuitions of public policy, avowed or unconscious, even the prejudices which Judges share with their fellow-men, have had a good deal more than the syllogism in determining the rules by which men should be governed. The law embodies the story of a nation's development through many centuries, and it cannot be dealt with as if it contained only the axioms and corollaries of a book of mathematics. In order to know what it is, we must know what it has been, and what it tends to become. We must alternately consult history and existing theories of legislation. But the most difficult labor will be to understand the combination of the two into new products at every stage.[5]

The Federalist era

Each political and legal generation that has become dominant in the changing constitutional law of the Supreme Court of the United States shared certain fundamental assumptions about law and the political, social, and economic destiny of the nation. But it should be clearly understood that during any administration, not all of the contemporary lawyers and political leaders necessarily shared those assumptions. The characteristics of President George Washington's nominees for the Supreme Court illustrate this point. President Washington set the pattern for those subsequent presidents who insisted upon clear and consistent ideological and partisan standards for their appointees. All ten of his appointees to the Supreme Court were Federalists committed to developing a strong national government, to the maintenance of property rights, and to the supremacy of the new national government within the constitutional system. All had been committed to the successful revolutionary movement against Great Britain, but all were also opposed to any state legislative activity that they viewed as threatening to the gentry class and to stable property values. President Washington's selections also set the pattern of combining ideological and partisan considerations with a clearly defined concept of regional representation of the Supreme Court.

Washington was very conscious of the fact that he was establishing a totally new system, and he was determined to provide what he considered the proper tone and temper of the new national government. Most important, he wanted justices who shared his values concerning a strong and economically stable central government. There were other less orthodox leaders of that seminal political and legal generation who also had supported and shared in the dangers of the revolution against Great Britain and belonged to the same mercantile or plantation gentry class that the Federalist leaders comprised. But if they embraced the anti–Federalist cause, or spoke too urgently about states' rights, their stands were considered unsound. Washington himself was a bit more tolerant than the Federalist leaders in the Senate. John Rutledge departed from Federalist orthodoxy only once—over the soundness of the Jay Treaty of Peace with Great Britain. For his pains, he was denied Senate confirmation for the chief justiceship despite the fact that President Washington had supported him in nomination. Washington's first chief justice, John Jay, had contributed to the influential *Federalist Papers* and was second only to Alexander Hamilton in efforts to secure ratification of the new Constitution in New York. Associate Justice James Wilson of Pennsylvania had participated as a strong advocate of nationalism in the Philadelphia convention of 1787. Associate Justice John Blair of Virginia had supported both Washington and James Madison in behalf of a strong constitution in the same convention. Associate Justice William Cushing had strongly supported the Constitution as vice-president of the Massachusetts ratifying convention. Associate Justice James Iredell had served as state attorney general and had been a leading supporter of the new Constitution in North Carolina. Another early selectee (first for associate justice), John Rutledge of South Carolina, had played a key role in the Philadelphia convention. After Senate confirmation in 1791, Rutledge resigned to become the highest judicial officer of his state. He was rejected for the chief justiceship in 1795. Another Washington choice and supporter of the new Constitution in the Philadelphia convention, Associate Justice Thomas Johnson of Maryland, also resigned within a few months of his confirmation.

Johnson was subsequently replaced by Associate Justice William Paterson of New Jersey, who also had played an important role in the Philadelphia convention, in the New Jersey ratifying convention, and as one of two key senators (the other being Oliver Ellsworth) primarily responsible for the Judiciary Act of 1789. Associate Justice Samuel Chase of Maryland replaced John Blair, who resigned in 1795. Chase had not been an early supporter of the Constitution, but had become an aggressive Federalist soon after ratification. Finally, in 1796, President Washington made his last Court appointment, that of Chief Justice Oliver Ellsworth of Connecticut. Ellsworth had been a strong supporter of the Constitution in both the Philadelphia convention and the Connecticut ratifying convention and like Paterson was one of the major Senatorial architects of the Judiciary Act of 1789.

President John Adams made three Court appointments in his single term as president. All were strong Federalists. Associate Justice Bushrod Washington, George Washington's nephew, had served in the Virginia House of Delegates. Associate Justice Alfred Moore of North Carolina was a notable Federalist lawyer and judge. But the most important and most enduring of President Adam's Supreme Court appointments was the selection, after his defeat for re-election, of Secretary of State John Marshall of Virginia to succeed Oliver Ellsworth as chief justice of the United States. Marshall was an avowed Federalist thoroughly imbued with Hamiltonian notions of nationalism and the sanctity of property.

Although John Marshall was the chief judicial architect of broad constructionist interpretation and solicitous regard for the rights of property, his Federalist predecessors had clearly fulfilled the political and legal expectations of President Washington in these matters. Indeed, their nationalist and federalist partisanship had helped to arouse the opposition that led to the formation of the Jeffersonian Republican party. Before 1800, the Federalist justices aroused opposition by their highly partisan charges to grand juries while on circuit duty and by their extra-constitutional conception of federal common law jurisdiction in anticipation of the controversial Federalist Alien and Sedition Act. The invocation of the contract clause to protect vested property rights in *Van Horne's Lessee* v. *Dorrance* and the strong enunciation of federal supremacy in *Ware* v. *Hylton* anticipated the major doctrinal contributions of John Marshall after 1801. The Federalist Court's decision in *Chisholm* v. *Georgia* establishing the suability of a state on the basis of Article 3, Section 2 of the Constitution aroused overwhelming states' rights opposition. The result was the speedy nullification of this doctrine by the adoption of the Eleventh Amendment in 1798.

Prior to the first critical election in 1800, the justices appointed by Presidents George Washington and John Adams were totally supportive of the most fundamental of the constitutional principles identified with the Federalist party and their appointing authorities. Their agreement is evident even though the Court employed the institutional procedure of *seriatim* opinion writing. The Federalist justices also contributed to the intensification of partisan disagreements by clinging to doctrinal approaches subsequently repudiated or opposed by the new political party that defeated the Federalists in 1800. As members of the dominant political party in the era characterized as America's first party system, the Federalist justices had conformed to its most fundamental tenets. After the defeat of their party in 1800, they and their new Federalist chief justice had to decide whether they should stand firm in opposition to the ascendant Jeffersonian Republicans.

Conversely, on matters in which the dominant Jeffersonian Republican majority party was not divided, the Federalist Court majority backed down. *Marbury* v. *Madison* was a brilliant doctrinal sally by Chief Justice Marshall, but it failed to fulfill the practical goals of the Federalists who had not received their justice of the peace commissions. More important, in *Stuart* v. *Laird* the Federalist justices cryptically acquiesced in the unified Jeffersonian Republican statutory rejection of the Federalist Judiciary Act of 1801. Similarly, Federalists remaining on the Court in 1812 either rejected the concept of a Federal common law jurisdiction (which they had applied for partisan purposes before 1801) or abstained from participating in the decision in *United States* v. *Hudson and Goodwin*. Some Federalist justices finally modified their voting behavior in response to the critical election of 1800 and especially the possibility of impeachment dramatized by the successful action against District Judge John Pickering and the narrowly unsuccessful action against Associate Justice Samuel Chase. For example, Chase refrained from overt partisan activities after escaping impeachment. He voted against federal common law jurisdiction in the Hudson case although he had asserted such jurisdiction before 1801.

The evidence from the critical election of 1800 fails to support either Dahl's model or another broad generalization made by Robert Scigliano. Scigliano's conceptualization is based upon separation of powers attributes and upon some of the discussions in the Philadelphia convention of 1787 and in the *Federalist Papers*. He suggests that "the Constitution intended that the Supreme Court and the President would not be infrequently aligned against Congress. There is . . . a natural affinity between the judicial and executive powers."[6] Clearly there was no presidential alignment with the Federalist-dominated Supreme Court under the presidencies of Thomas Jefferson (whose deep antagonistic feelings about Chief Justice Marshall were reciprocated), James Madison, and James Monroe. John Quincy Adams dealt circumspectly with Chief Justice Marshall near the end of his presidential term.

Jeffersonian victories and Federalist judicial influence

After Thomas Jefferson took office, a number of factors combined to deny him an opportunity to appoint a working majority to the Supreme Court. Although he served two full presidential terms, his opportunities to make selections were limited. The old Federalists remained on the Court as long as they could. Thus, Jefferson had to wait several years for his first Supreme Court vacancy, which became available when Associate Justice Alfred Moore resigned because of poor health. During his second term, Jefferson had two additional opportunities, in 1806 when Associate Justice Paterson died, and in 1807 when Congress created a seventh Court seat to accommodate the judicial business of a new circuit comprising Kentucky, Tennessee, and Ohio. Two of Jefferson's Supreme Court appointees possessed impeccable Jeffersonian Republican credentials: William Johnson of South Carolina (1804) and Henry Brockholst Livingston of New York (1806). His third appointee, Thomas Todd of Kentucky (1807), was chosen largely on regional grounds.

Jefferson's friend and successor to the presidency, James Madison, had the opportunity to make Supreme Court appointments following the deaths of President Washington's last two appointees, Associate Justice William Cushing in 1810, and Associate Justice Samuel Chase in 1811. Madison's first nominee, Levi Lincoln, who had served as Jefferson's attorney general, was confirmed by the Senate but declined the nomination because of near blindness. Madison's second nominee, Alexander Wolcott of Connecticut, was rejected by the Senate 9 to 24, and his third nominee, John Quincy Adams, declined after unanimous Senate approval. After these abortive efforts at filling the Cushing vacancy, President Madison's primary objective was avoidance of further embarrassment. Thus, over Jefferson's objection, Madison nominated Joseph Story of Massachusetts. The weary Senate confirmed him in November of 1811. Story was nominally a Republican, described by Jefferson as a "pseudo-Republican," and a lobbyist for the Yazoo land investors[7] (a fact not widely known among his contemporaries). On the bench he became a doctrinal Federalist, consistently supporting John Marshall until the latter's death in 1835, and carrying on Marshall's doctrinal approaches until his own death in 1845. Madison filled Chase's vacancy with the comptroller general of Jefferson's and his own administration, Maryland Republican Gabriel Duvall. Duvall was more independent of Marshall; for example, he dissented in the Dartmouth College case. For the six remaining years of his presidency, James Madison had no Court vacancies to fill.

Madison's two-term successor, President James Monroe, filled only one vacancy, created by the death of Associate Justice Henry Brockholst Livingston in 1823. He chose a cabinet member, Secretary of the Navy Smith Thompson, a New York Republican with considerable judicial and political experience. Like Duvall, Thompson occasionally broke with Marshall. President John Quincy Adams, generally described as a National Republican, served one term in the presidency and was able to fill only one Supreme Court vacancy, although two occurred during his term. After the death of Associate Justice Thomas Todd in 1826, Adams nominated a nationalistic federal district judge from Kentucky, Robert Trimble. Trimble died before the end of Adams' presidency, but Adams was unable to fill the vacancy. When he attempted to appoint a former Whig senator and ally of Henry Clay, John J. Crittenden, the Senate voted 23 to 17 to postpone the appointment. A month later, in 1829, President Andrew Jackson took office, thus ushering in a new political era as a result of the critical election of 1828.

In assessing the impact of the first critical election, that of 1800, it is necessary to make a careful re-examination of notions about presidential goals in the selection of Supreme Court justices.

In his discussion of the "Satisfaction of Presidential Expectations," Scigliano cited instances in which presidential expectations were not fulfilled. A major example, he said, was the fact that "William Johnson (appointed by Jefferson) wrote a concurring opinion in *Gibbons* v. *Ogden* that went further than Marshall's majority opinion in claiming national control over commerce."[8] But the identification of presidential expectations is often far more complex than Scigliano's comments suggest. It is not at all clear that Johnson totally rejected Jefferson's position. As early as 1785, Jefferson had written to Monroe, "You see that my primary object in the formation of treaties is to take the commerce of the states out of the hands of the states, and to place it under the superintendence of Congress, so far as the imperfect provisions of our constitution will admit, and until the states shall by new compact make them more perfect."[9] Jefferson had left the presidency several years before *Gibbons* v. *Ogden* was handed down, and his partisanship in his private, out-of-office correspondence did not always coincide with the more conciliatory positions that he took as president. In addition, Jefferson often took pragmatic nationalistic positions while in office. His judicial appointments reflected that pragmatism as exemplified not only in his selection of William Johnson, but also in his promotion of Federalist William Cranch to the chief judgeship of the Circuit Court for the District of Columbia. Cranch was, in his own way, as strong a nationalist as John Marshall and served 20 years longer. Combining his years as judge (1801–1806) and chief judge (1806–1855), he served an astonishing 54 years. Cranch was the legal architect of the Kendall doctrine that proved so frustrating to Andrew Jackson's administration. In a word, Jefferson was as lax about ideological and partisan "purity" in his promotion of Cranch as was Madison in his nomination of Story.

In these and other instances, the presidents who led what Dahl would have called the "dominant" coalition after the first critical election of 1800 (and before the second critical election of 1828) had a number of nomination objectives among which ideological or doctrinal reliability was not always paramount. In addition, not all of these presidents were as antinationalistic as some commentators have assumed. Madison, for example, had written the Republican governor of Pennsylvania that he would be obliged to send federal troops to insure compliance with the Marshall Court's assertion of federal supremacy in the case of Judge Peters. Although President Monroe had taken a stand narrowly interpreting the scope of the commerce clause before *Gibbons* v. *Ogden*, he chose a nationalistically inclined Republican for his single Court vacancy, despite the objections of some senators in his own party.

One major consideration confronting Jefferson, Madison, Monroe, and Adams was the keen interest in Supreme Court nominations expressed by congressional coalitions, combined by mutual partisan considerations and leavened by regional and interest-group factors. Nowhere was this more clear than in the politics surrounding the alteration or creation of circuits.

In Thomas Jefferson's first term, the first enduring addition to the Supreme Court was made as part of a congressional statutory accommodation of the regional needs of three trans-Allegheny states for a separate circuit within the regular Federal judicial system. The Seventh Circuit, comprising Kentucky, Tennessee, and Ohio, was created by act of Congress on February 24, 1804. Its regional congressional sponsors wanted to influence the selection of the seventh justice.

Thus, the act provided that the new justice should "reside in the circuit." President Jefferson responded to the imperatives of regional accommodation by asking each member of the three states' congressional delegations for recommendations for the new associate justiceship. He chose Thomas Todd from among the top four recommended. It is clear that regional accommodation—especially Todd's legal expertise in the controversial and complex land law of the region—rather than ideological (Republican) orthodoxy was the paramount consideration in this appointment.[10]

Considerable circuit reorganization maneuvering occurred in Congress during James Monroe's second term. Associate Justice Joseph Story personally drafted a bill to reorganize the circuits and to relieve the justices of circuit-riding duties, but the effort bore no fruit. It is instructive that by this period (1824) Story did not send the draft to a Republican member of Congress but to Daniel Webster.[11] When John Quincy Adams succeeded President Monroe, the congressional pressure intensified. Strong congressional conflicts over proposals to reorganize and add to the circuits preceded Adams' selection of a successor to Associate Justice Thomas Todd in 1826. Congress was not able to unite on a specific judicial reorganization plan. Much of the legislative conflict centered upon the relationship of specific plans to the selection of judges from within the contemplated reorganized circuits. The inability to pass a bill limited the choice to the old circuit still comprising Kentucky, Tennessee, and Ohio. Like Jefferson's choice of Todd, John Quincy Adams' selection of Robert Trimble, a federal district judge of pronounced nationalistic tendencies, was largely determined by the intense regional politics of trans-Allegheny circuit reorganization rather than by clear presidential expectations of doctrinal orthodoxy. In Adams' case, however, Trimble's nationalistic bent was consistent with Adams' general approach.[12]

Adams' second attempt at filling a vacancy, after the death of Trimble in 1828, was even more directly linked with circuit enlargement. On February 12, 1829, Adams' congressional critics deferred both the issue of circuit reorganization (including addition of a new Supreme Court seat) and Adams' nomination of former Senator John Crittenden, to await Andrew Jackson's inauguration. Both the nomination and the Senate's deferral had direct doctrinal overtones as well as partisan objectives. Adams was correctly perceived as moving toward nationalistic and property-oriented positions associated with modified Federalism and the Whig program of Henry Clay. Chief Justice John Marshall himself wrote a strong letter endorsing Crittenden, which he addressed to Clay, who in turn presented it to President Adams.[13] In this instance the chief justice and the president were allied against a Senate majority but were defeated. Crittenden's nomination was deferred by a margin of 23 to 17 plus one abstention.

The Jacksonian period

Incoming President Andrew Jackson was thus assured a Supreme Court vacancy immediately upon taking office. Although some of his contemporaries and a number of modern scholars have described Jackson's impact upon Court selection as considerably less nationalistic than that of his predecessors, this doctrinal change was not immediately apparent. Jackson's first appointment, that of John McLean of Ohio, was clearly not doctrinally oriented. As postmaster general under President John Q. Adams, McLean had been suspected of covertly helping Jackson in the 1828 presidential contest. Jackson retained McLean as postmaster general, but Jackson's early patronage chief, Duff Green, found McLean uncooperative in removing postmasters for replacement by Jackson men. Some Jacksonians believed that McLean planned to keep his own followers in place for future political contests, possibly his own. Jackson offered him the associate justiceship vacated by Todd to remove him from the cabinet without arousing McLean's followers. As John Quincy Adams put it in his *Memoirs.* "McLean is made Judge of the Supreme Court to set him aside. He declined serving as the broom to sweep the post offices."[14] Prophetically, McLean had the support of a number of conservative attorneys.

When Bushrod Washington's seat became vacant in November 1829, President Jackson selected Henry Baldwin of Pennsylvania to fill the vacancy. Baldwin was a friend of Jackson's and a close political ally. But although he was a nominal Jacksonian Democrat, some more consistent Jacksonians viewed Baldwin as too close to Henry Clay on tariffs, favorable to the Bank of the United States, and close to John Marshall on constitutional issues. At the time of his selection, however, Baldwin was clearly identified with the anti–Calhoun wing of the party, and Jackson wanted to strengthen that wing. Baldwin was confirmed by a margin of 41–2 on January 6, 1830. The two negative votes were cast by the senators from South Carolina, where Calhoun's influence was strongest. Like McLean's, Baldwin's appointment was based on political considerations not directly related to doctrinal tendencies.

Jackson's third Supreme Court appointment also involved such nondoctrinal emphasis. When Jeffersonian Justice William Johnson died on August 4, 1830, Jackson had another important political conflict that overshadowed his doctrinal attitudes on corporations, national versus state authority, and the national bank. The split with the Calhoun wing had widened after the nullification controversy and passage of the Force Bill. To replace Johnson, President Jackson wanted a strong Unionist Democrat from the Sixth Circuit, which comprised Georgia and South Carolina. Georgia was controlled by Union Democrats and South Carolina by Calhoun's forces. Jackson chose James Wayne, a Georgia Union Democrat whose nationalistic and procorporation tendencies were close to those of the Whigs. Indeed, Wayne became identified as a Southern Whig after his appointment. Thus, Jackson's first three appointments were largely determined by direct political considerations rather than an effort to fulfill Jackson's overall doctrinal commitments.

Interestingly enough, while Jeffersonian and Jacksonian presidents manifested some degree of inconsistency about the doctrinal goals to be achieved in the appointing process, the Federalists and Whigs generally maintained a more tenacious sense of purpose. This commitment was nowhere more clear than among the Federalists and Whigs on the Supreme Court itself. There is evidence that the aged and ill William Cushing was persuaded to stay on the bench longer than he desired in the hope that the next election would bring about a favorable change in the appointing authority. Chief Justice John Marshall seriously considered resigning in 1831, but decided to wait until after the presidential election of 1832. (In fact, Marshall remained on the Court until his death in 1835.) The intensity of feeling among Federalists and Whigs over the prospects of Jacksonian control of the Court is illustrated by John Quincy Adams' comments about the possibility that Marshall would resign in 1831. He stated, "The terror is, that if he should be now withdrawn some shallow-pated wildcat like Philip P. Barbour, fit for nothing but to tear the Union to rags and tatters, would be appointed in his place."[15] The tenacity of Federalists in remaining on the Court was apparently clearly understood by Jeffersonian Republicans and Jacksonian Democrats. This was well summed up in a phrase attributed to Jefferson and quoted approvingly by Andrew Jackson: "Judges seldom die—and never resign."[16]

After his first three appointments, President Jackson began to insist upon a high degree of ideological and doctrinal consistency. When Associate Justice Gabriel Duvall resigned at age 82 on January 10, 1835, Jackson nominated Secretary of the Treasury Roger Brooke Taney for the associate justiceship. Taney was "sound" with respect to corporations, opposed to nullification and the bank, and generally supportive of states' rights. The advocates of the bank and the supporters of Calhoun, Webster, and Clay all opposed Taney's nomination for the seat, but hoped to accomplish his defeat by reorganizing the circuits. At the end of the Senate session of March 3, 1835, Daniel Webster successfully moved that Taney's nomination be postponed indefinitely. The motion was passed 24–21.

Ironically, Taney's apparently hopeless situation changed dramatically as a result of two unrelated events, the addition of more Jacksonian senators as a result of state legislative actions and the death of Chief Justice John Marshall (July 6, 1835). By the end of 1835, President Jackson had nominated Taney for the chief justiceship (to serve the Fourth Circuit comprising Maryland and Delaware) and Philip P. Barbour as associate justice (to serve in the Fifth Circuit, which included Virginia and North Carolina). Once again circuit reorganization was tied into the appointment process. On January 6, 1836, the Senate passed a circuit reorganization bill designed to lure senators with definite regional interests in gaining a new justiceship. The bill's sponsors intended to deny a seat to either Taney or Barbour. Placing Maryland and Virginia in the same circuit would eliminate one of the nominees. By creating two new circuits and one new justice for the trans-Allegheny states (while consolidating some older circuits), the reorganization initially attracted wide support and passed the Senate 38–1. Matters looked grim for one of the nominees. The Jacksonians in the House did not act, however. Then on March 15, 1836, Jacksonians in the Senate unexpectedly moved the confirmation of Roger Brooke Taney as chief justice. This vote carried 29–15. Immediately thereafter the confirmation of Philip P. Barbour was moved. Whig Senator Daniel Webster moved to stop proceedings until the circuit reorganization bill was passed, but his motion was defeated 26–16. Barbour was then confirmed 30–11. Barbour, like Taney, was a states' rights strict constructionist, but both had opposed Calhounian nullification and the Bank of the United States.

The surge of Jacksonian influence on the federal judiciary extended into the incoming Van Buren administration. After Martin Van Buren's election in 1836, the Congress approved, by act of March 3, 1837, a circuit reorganization act that created two new circuits, two new justices, and a reordering of trans-Allegheny circuits. The old Seventh Circuit now comprised Ohio, Indiana, Illinois, and Michigan. The new Eighth was composed of Kentucky, Tennessee, and Missouri. And the new Ninth embraced Alabama, Eastern Louisiana, Eastern Mississippi, and Arkansas. On the last day of his second term (March 3, 1837), President Jackson nominated John Catron of Tennessee for the new Eighth Circuit and William Smith of Alabama to the Ninth Circuit. Both men were confirmed with Van Buren's support after Jackson left office. The margins, on March 6, 1837, were 28–15 for Catron and 23–18 for Smith. Catron accepted the seat and Smith declined. President Van Buren then selected John McKinley, an Alabama Union Democrat. He was confirmed on September 25, 1837. Associate Justice Philip P. Barbour died a few days before President Van Buren would leave office after his defeat by William Henry Harrison. On February 26, 1841, President Van Buren nominated Peter V. Daniel of Virginia to the seat. After careful consideration of Daniel's ideological and political stands and commitments, Van Buren concluded that Daniel was "a Democrat *ab ovo* [who] is not in much danger of falling off the true spirit."[17] Daniel was a strict constructionist who had supported Jackson against nullification, the bank, and corporations. Henry Clay led the opposition to Daniel's nomination, but the Whigs, who left the Senate to prevent a quorum, were unable to stop action, and Daniels was confirmed 22–5.

President William Henry Harrison, a Whig, died in office before a Court vacancy occurred. His successor, Vice-President John Tyler, attempted to fill the seat that opened when Associate Justice Smith Thompson died on December 18, 1843. The Whigs in the Senate defeated Tyler's first nominee, John C. Spencer, 16–21, on January 31, 1844. His second nominee, Reuben Walworth of New York, was delayed. While Tyler maneuvered in the hope of gaining the judicial appointment, he had nominated Democrats in the effort to secure the Democratic presidential nomination. Both efforts ultimately failed, but before the next presidential election, yet another vacancy occurred when Associate Justice Henry Baldwin died on April 21, 1844. For this second vacancy, President Tyler nominated Edward King of Philadelphia. On June 14, 1844, however, both of his nominees were defeated in the Senate, Walworth by a margin of 27–20 (on a motion to table his nomination) and King by a vote of 29–18. The Whigs led the move to defeat Tyler because they believed that their presidential nominee, Henry Clay, would be elected. Instead, Jacksonian Democrat James Polk won the presidency. In the lame-duck session, Tyler withdrew Walworth's nomination and substituted that of Democrat Samuel Nelson, chief justice of the Supreme Court of New York. Nelson was confirmed without a recorded vote on February 14, 1845. Tyler's second substitute did not fare so well. He had replaced the King nomination with that of John M. Read of Pennsylvania, but the Senate refused to act on the nomination.

Incoming President James Polk had similar difficulty with the Senate despite an additional appointment because of Associate Justice Joseph Story's death on September 10, 1845. Although Polk was able to replace Story speedily with Maine

Democrat Levi Woodbury, in December 1845, he was less successful in attempting to fill the long-standing Pennsylvania vacancy. Polk's first nominee for the Baldwin vacancy (dating back to April 21, 1844) was George Washington Woodward of Pennsylvania, a Democrat of alleged nativist tendencies who was accused of trying to deny suffrage to all future immigrants. He was defeated 29–20, by 23 Whigs and 6 Democrats, on February 2, 1846. Finally, after the Baldwin seat had been vacant for more than two years, it was filled by Polk's second nominee, Robert C. Grier, a Pennsylvania Democrat and state Supreme Court judge, who was confirmed on August 4, 1846.

Although both Tyler and Polk had vowed that they would appoint no justice of the "school of Kent and Story," they had to outmaneuver senators who wished to influence or control the selection process, instead of concentrating on the judicial ideology of their appointees. Despite this, the Tyler and Polk selectees, Nelson, Woodbury, and Grier, were not as nationalistic as those justices closer to the Marshall-Story tradition, nor were they as devoted to states' rights or opposed to corporations as Daniel or Barbour.

The rising intensity of the regional conflict over slavery prior to the Civil War was reflected in greater attention to the ideology of Supreme Court nominees. Whig President Millard Fillmore, successor to President Zachary Taylor, provided a classic statement of presidential expectations when he filled the vacancy created by the death of Associate Justice Levi Woodbury on September 4, 1851. In a letter to Whig Senator Daniel Webster, Fillmore wrote that in filling the post, he would like to "obtain as long a lease, and as much moral and judicial power as possible, from the new appointment . . . [and] would therefore like to combine a vigorous constitution with high moral and intellectual qualifications, a good judicial mind, and such age as gives prospect of long service."[18] Fillmore and Webster felt that the able, 41-year-old, Massachusetts Whig attorney Benjamin Robbins Curtis fitted the requirements precisely. Curtis was nominated in September and confirmed in December 1851. Fillmore again attempted to ensure sound Whig principles in filling a second vacancy, created by the death of Associate Justice John McKinley on July 19, 1852. But Fillmore's nominees, Edward A. Bradford of Louisiana and George E. Badger of North Carolina, were rejected by the Senate—Bradford because the chamber failed to act, and Badger by a 26–25 vote to postpone confirmation until March 4, 1853, when Fillmore's Democratic successor would become president. Fillmore tried once again by nominating William C. Micou of Louisiana. Since the Senate refused to act, the seat was still vacant when Fillmore's term ended. Despite his difficulties and his generally undistinguished presidency, Fillmore's single judicial selection, that of Curtis, was an ideologically sound extension of the Whig principles that Fillmore sought to perpetuate.

Fillmore's successor to the presidency, Franklin Pierce of New Hampshire, was as inadequate as leader of the Jacksonian Democrats as Millard Fillmore had been of the Whigs. Yet like Fillmore, Pierce made an exceptionally sound ideological choice to fill the vacancy he inherited from his predecessor. Just as Fillmore had chosen an outstanding, comparatively young Whig attorney doctrinally close to the tradition of Marshall and Story, Pierce nominated an outstanding Alabama lawyer, 41 years of age, who opposed corporations and favored states' rights. Thus, John Archibald Campbell, confirmed in March 1853, was a direct partisan and ideological counterpoint to Benjamin R. Curtis.

The final judicial selection of the long but waning Jacksonian Democratic era was made by President James Buchanan. The vacancy came early in his term because of the bitter resignation of Associate Justice Curtis after the Dred Scott decision. His nominee was, like most of the Northern Democrats recently chosen for the Court, a "Northern man with Southern principles," a proslavery Jacksonian Democrat from Maine, Nathan Clifford. After a bitter Senate confrontation, his confirmation was achieved by the narrow margin of 26–23. Following the death of Associate Justice Peter V. Daniel on May 30, 1860, Buchanan nominated Jeremiah S. Black, an able Pennsylvania Democrat. The nomination came only a month before Buchanan would turn the presidency over to his Republican successor, Abraham Lincoln. Black was defeated by one vote, 25–26. The long, often tempestuous Jacksonian era came to an ignominious close when Buchanan's ineffective presidency ended.

A new Republican coalition

The years before the critical election of 1860 were highly controversial for the Court. With the exception of McLean, the Jacksonians, whether Northern or Southern, held proslavery positions in the years prior to the Civil War. The Dred Scott decision, which repudiated the ideology of the new Republican party led by Abraham Lincoln, put the majority of the Court on a virtual collision course with the victors of the 1860 election. Thus, this critical election might have led to a serious confrontation if three unanticipated vacancies had not eased the tension: the death of Associate Justice Peter V. Daniel in 1860, the death of Associate Justice John McLean on April 4, 1861, and the resignation of Associate Justice John Archibald Campbell to join the Confederacy in the same month. These vacancies averted an extremely serious crisis in relations between the largely elderly, proslavery Jacksonian Democratic Supreme Court majority and the Republican president and Congress. President Lincoln's appointees were all antislavery Republicans and unequivocal supporters of his efforts to save the Union. Noah H. Swayne of Ohio was confirmed on January 24, 1862 by a margin of 38–1; Samuel Freeman Miller of Iowa was confirmed in July 1862; and David Davis of Illinois was confirmed after an October recess appointment, in December 1862.

Like the Jacksonian Democrats and the Whigs, the Republicans used circuit reorganization and enlargement as a mode of influencing Supreme Court selections. Since the portions of the pre–Civil War circuits within the Confederacy were now dormant, the five old circuits in the southern region were reduced to three, the northern trans-Allegheny circuits were reorganized, and a new Ninth Circuit was created entirely west of the Mississippi River comprising Minnesota, Iowa, Kansas, and Missouri. Associate Justice Miller was chosen from this circuit.

In 1863 Congress created a Tenth Circuit, combining California and Oregon (and subsequently Nevada) and creating a new associate justiceship. President

Lincoln chose Stephen J. Field, a Union Democrat, brother of a strong Lincoln supporter, abolitionist, and eminent lawyer, David Dudley Field. Within three days of his nomination, Field was confirmed unanimously on March 10, 1863. In the fourth year of President Lincoln's first term, on October 12, 1864, Chief Justice Roger Brooke Taney died. His passing had been anticipated with an unseemly tinge of ghoulishness reflecting the deep hostility that the Radical Republicans felt for the Court that had supported slavery and had composed the inflamatory portions of the Dred Scott decision. Before Taney's death in 1864, Ben Wade, Radical Republican House member had written that

> When Judge Taney got sick after Lincoln's election (in 1860) I was scared for fear he would die before the inauguration and give Buchanan a chance to appoint his successor, and I prayed to God to spare his life until Buchanan should go out of office. Dammed if I did not overdo it. He's going to live out Lincoln's term.[19]

The Radical Republicans and Lincoln himself proved that they were very determined whenever they felt the Union or the war effort was threatened. They acted forcefully when the three proslavery circuit judges for the District of Columbia indicated that they would apply Chief Justice Taney's *habeas corpus* ruling in the Merryman case in issues that came to their court. With the approval of President Lincoln, the Congress abolished the Circuit Court for the District of Columbia, placed the three regular federal judges under house arrest in a D.C. hotel, and in 1863 created a new Supreme Court for the District of Columbia with an entirely new complement of Republican, antislavery judges.[20]

Following Lincoln's assassination, the Radical Republican Senators expressed their dislike for President Andrew Johnson by refusing to act upon his nomination of Attorney General Henry Stanberry of Ohio to fill the vacancy created by the death of Associate Justice John Catron on May 30, 1865. On July 25, 1866 Congress passed an act to reduce the size of the Supreme Court from ten to seven members as soon as the requisite number of vacancies occurred. The Supreme Court was under attack, including jurisdictional modification by this powerful and assertive Radical Republican Congress. But the Court did not, in any direct sense, align itself with President Andrew Johnson.

After President Ulysses S. Grant succeeded Johnson, the first reduction in the size of the Court took place as a result of the death of Associate Justice Wayne (on July 5, 1867). Congress began work to change the law and, on April 10, 1869, increased the size of the Court from seven to nine. Ironically, President Grant's nominee, Attorney General Ebenezer Rockwood Hoar of Massachusetts, was rejected on February 3, 1870 by a margin of 33–24, primarily because Hoar had alienated many Senators. During the long, drawn-out discussion of Hoar, Associate Justice Robert C. Grier resigned (in December 1869). To fill Grier's vacancy, Grant nominated Lincoln's former secretary of war, Edwin W. Stanton. The Senate promptly confirmed the elderly Stanton, 46–11, on December 20, 1869, but four days later Stanton died.

After Hoar's defeat in 1870, President Grant turned to two nominees who leaned toward the interests of emerging corporate business leaders, unlike Lincoln's appointees and Grant's earlier nominees, who had been concerned primarily with emancipating the slaves and providing a degree of equality for the blacks. The new political generation (for which Stephen J. Field might be considered an ideological harbinger) was to dominate constitutional law for the rest of the century. Grant's next two choices, William Strong of Pennsylvania and Joseph P. Bradley of New Jersey were clearly part of that new political generation in terms of their constitutional principles. Two additional vacancies occurred before Grant's second term ended. To fill the vacancy created by the resignation of Jacksonian Democratic Justice Samuel Nelson in 1872, Grant nominated Ward Hunt of New York. In May 1873, Chief Justice Salmon P. Chase died. After offering the post to one of the most corrupt members of the Senate, Roscoe Conkling of New York, who turned it down, Grant nominated Attorney General George H. Williams of Oregon, who was rejected by the Senate. He then nominated the even less acceptable Caleb Cushing. After withdrawing Cushing's nomination, he finally nominated Morrison Remick Waite of Ohio, then a relatively unknown Republican attorney.

Some scholars have speculated about Grant's inability to choose justices who reflected strong support for the purposes enunciated in the great post–Civil War Constitutional amendments, the Thirteenth, Fourteenth, and Fifteenth. Yet while the great transition in ideological commitment among Republican political leaders took place during the administration of Grant's successor, Rutherford B. Hayes, the fundamental shift had begun under Grant. The firmest commitment to the liberalization and equalization of the status of blacks was among the Radical Republicans in Congress. Grant and his administration were often identified with elements in the commercial and banking community and with the business-oriented leaders who subsequently emerged as the most influential forces in Republicanism after Hayes' presidency. Consequently, it is not at all clear that, after his earliest nominations, Grant sought justices who reflected the black emancipation and equalization ideology of the radical Republicans. Grant's lack of political skill and occasional gross failure to recognize minimal qualitative standards for Supreme Court justices (his efforts to secure Conkling and Williams) combined with Senatorial aggressiveness made any efforts by Grant to apply consistent ideological tests for his nominees problematical. But, in addition, it is not clear that Grant had any goals in mind other than partisan orthodoxy. Thus, unlike Lincoln, who had replaced Taney, the chief architect of the Dred Scott decision, with Salmon P. Chase, who had been called the "Attorney-General for Fugitive Slaves" in pre–Civil War Ohio politics, Grant chose not emancipators, but fairly consistent economic conservatives.

The last and most notable of the 19th century emancipators chosen for the Court was John Marshall Harlan of Kentucky. Harlan had originally taken pro-slavery positions, but later fought for the Union and took strong pro–Union positions in a bitterly divided state. He had become a Grant Republican and contributed to Hayes' narrowly successful Presidential campaign. It seems clear that Hayes' selection of Harlan, following the resignation of Associate Justice David Davis on March 7, 1877, was primarily a political reward and an attempt at regional balance rather than a clearcut ideological choice. Hayes' other selection, William Burnham Woods, an Ohio Republican but chosen from Alabama, was ideologically more consistent with President Hayes' own approach to legal and political issues. Although he was a carpetbagger, Woods was acceptable to Southerners and exemplified the new accommodationist approach that was based on Northern and Southern business interests instead of the emancipationist ethic of the radical Republicans. Woods had overwhelming support from Southern banking and commercial interests. Hayes' next nominee, Stanley Matthews, was an Ohio railroad attorney. The Senate refused to act on Matthew's nomination during the remainder of President Hayes' term, but after his successor, President James A. Garfield, renominated Matthews, the appointment was confirmed by the Senate by the narrow margin of 22–21 on May 12, 1881. Dubbed "Jay Gould's chief attorney in the middle west," Matthews carried the economic conservatism of his private practice to the Court. Thus, two of President Hayes' Court nominees accurately represented his economic conservatism and lack of enthusiasm for emancipation. Conversely, John Marshall Harlan embarked on a lonely doctrinal cause that distinguished him from all other appointees to the Court for the remainder of the 19th century.

After the assassination of President Garfield, his successor, Chester A. Arthur, appointed Horace Gray, a Republican and a distinguished conservative Massachusetts jurist, to replace Associate Justice Nathan Clifford, who had died July 25, 1881. Gray's confirmation was without opposition, in marked contrast to that of Matthews. From this meritorious appointment, which was free of either patronage or corporate influences (and reportedly made to fulfill the wishes of Arthur's assassinated predecessor), President Arthur turned for his next nomination to Roscoe Conkling, reputed to be one of the most corrupt, but powerful, political leaders in a rather unsavory era. The occasion for the second nomination was the resignation of Associate Justice Ward Hunt of New York, who was the beneficiary of a special act of Congress permitting him to retire on full pay even though he had not served the requisite ten years. He had been incapable of serving on the Court for five years before resigning. Conkling was promptly confirmed by the Senate 39–12, but, fortunately for the reputation of the Court, he declined. President Arthur next nominated Samuel Blatchford, also of New York. Before serving as a federal district judge and a federal circuit judge, Blatchford was a law partner of Lincoln's cabinet member William R. Seward. A consistent Republican, Blatchford had been heavily involved in corporate law practice with emphasis upon maritime and international law. Like others chosen in this era (Harlan excepted) he was an economic conservative.

The first post–Civil War Democratic President, Grover Cleveland, nominated a Southern Democrat, who had served the Confederacy, for the vacancy created by the death of Associate Justice William B. Woods on March 14, 1887. The nominee, Lucius Q. C. Lamar of Mississippi, was serving as Cleveland's secretary of interior. In spite of strong Republican opposition to a former Confederate, Lamar was confirmed 32–28 on January 16, 1888. As a senator and interior secretary, Lamar was considered friendly to railroad corporations. The two Republican Senators who voted for his confirmation were Senators Stewart of Nevada and Leland Stanford of California, both prominent in railroad activities. The death of Chief Justice Morrison R. Waite on March 23, 1888 provided Cleveland the choice of a new chief justice. This time he chose a politically active Northern Democrat, Melville Weston Fuller, a Chicago corporate attorney who had represented the Chicago, Burlington, and Quincy Railroad Company, Marshall Field, and the Armour Packing interests. Fuller received some Republican support in the Senate because he was recognized as an economic conservative.

After one term, President Cleveland was defeated by Benjamin Harrison, a Republican. Early in his presidency, Harrison filled a vacancy created by the death of Associate Justice Stanley Matthews on March 22, 1889. Except for the basic difference in party affiliation, Harrison's selection to replace Matthews followed the same pattern of economic conservatism that was characteristic of the Supreme Court appointments from President Grant's first (successful) nomination of William Strong in 1870 through William McKinley's single nomination of Joseph McKenna in 1898. The sole exception was President Hayes' nomination of John Marshall Harlan.

President Harrison's first appointee was David J. Brewer of Kansas, who was related to Stephen and Dudley Field. Brewer was confirmed on December 10, 1889 by a vote of 53–11. Following the death of Associate Justice Samuel Freeman Miller on October 14, 1890, President Harrison nominated Henry Billings Brown of Michigan. Brown was an active Republican and like most appointees of this era, an orthodox economic conservative whose legal work in private practice was corporate law with a specialization in admiralty law. He was confirmed by the Senate without serious opposition on December 28, 1890. President Harrison's third vacancy came when Associate Justice Joseph Bradley died on January 22, 1892. Harrison chose yet another economic conservative, George Shiras of Pennsylvania, a Republican who had represented railroad, banking, oil, coal, and iron corporations. Although he had never held public office, he was a cousin of by then deceased James G. Blaine. Despite some senatorial criticism of Shiras as a leading attorney for the Baltimore and Ohio Railroad Company, confirmation was achieved by July 26, 1892. Thus, yet another economic conservative was added to the Court. President Harrison's final appointment came after Grover Cleveland defeated him for reelection in 1892. Early in 1893, but before the end of the lame-duck session of Congress, Associate Justice Lucius Q. C. Lamar died (on January 24, 1893). Correctly assuming that Democrats in the Senate were likely to defeat a Republican nominee to save the seat for Grover Cleveland, President Harrison decided to choose a Southern Democrat who held conservative views. His nominee, Circuit Court Judge Howell E. Jackson of Tennessee, a former Whig, had served the Confederacy, the Tennessee legislature, and the U. S. Senate (to which he was elected with Republican support), as well as the federal circuit court. His economic conservatism was indistinguishable from that of Harrison's Republican nominees.

During the first year of his second term, Grover Cleveland had an opportunity to fill a vacancy arising from the death of Justice Samuel Blatchford (on July 7, 1893). But Cleveland's first two nominees, William B. Hornblower and Wheeler H. Peckham of New York, were both defeated in the Senate because of the opposition of fellow Democratic Senator David B. Hill (who had sought the presidential nomination captured by Grover Cleveland in 1892). President Cleveland finally succeeded by choosing a Southerner in the Senate, Edward D. White of Louisiana, who was approved by his fellow senators promptly and unanimously. When Associate Justice Howell E. Jackson died, President Cleveland made his peace with Senator Hill and gained his approval to appoint the New York attorney that Hill had sought initially, Rufus Peckham, the brother of the rejected Wheeler Peckham. Like his brother and like William Hornblower, Rufus Peckham was a corporate attorney, but he had also had extensive judicial experience. With the exception of Justice White, who was favorable to the income tax principle, Cleveland's appointees were as conservative as those of his Republican predecessors.

Republicans renewed in 1896

President William McKinley made only one Supreme Court nomination, the opportunity resulting from Associate Justice Stephen J. Field's resignation on October 12, 1897 to take effect on December 1, 1897. He chose his political ally and former fellow House Ways and Means Committee member, U. S. Attorney General Joseph McKenna from California. His choice was called "the weakest nomination for the Supreme Court in many years."[21] Senator Leland Stanford, the railroad magnate, who had backed the appointment of Field, was a key influence in the selection of McKenna. Despite severe criticism from many leaders of the Pacific coast bar, McKenna was confirmed on January 21, 1898.

President McKinley's appointment of Joseph McKenna marked the decline of a fairly consistent series of economic conservative selections beginning with Ulysses S. Grant's choice of Associate Justice Strong. The patterns of successive political and legal generations represented on the Supreme Court between the third critical election of 1860 and the fourth of 1896 were sharply delineated. The changes in judicial elites were permanent in that after 1860 no proslavery justices were chosen. For several decades, Republicans had a virtual monopoly on seats on the Court. Field and Jackson, the two Democratic exceptions, fulfilled the ideological needs of their appointing presidents. Field, in particular, was the judicial harbinger of the new economic conservatism that became the most conspicuous attribute of the Supreme Court during the last three decades of the 19th century.

The issues salient in the transformation of the Supreme Court during Abraham Lincoln's presidency had become secondary by the 1870s. The old emancipationist and equality oriented leaders of the Republican party and the Congress were soon replaced by leaders and legislators much more interested in corporate expansion and industrialization and generally less interested in the fate of the former slaves. The transition is exemplified by the fundamental differences in ideological orientation and organizational tactics of the radical Republicans of the 1860s and of Mark Hanna and his management of the Republican campaign of 1896. Because the shift in elite influence was from the older organizational and ideological type of leadership (adapted from the Jacksonian Democrats) to discreet party managers who often took their cues from corporate boardrooms, the transition was felt in the ranks of the Supreme Court more directly and more immediately than in the Congress. This transition, anticipated by Leland Stanford's special relationship with Stephen J. Field, was characterized by corporate interest in Supreme Court appointments from Grant through McKinley and was reinstated during Taft's presidency and through most, but not all, of the selections in the 1920s by Presidents Harding, Coolidge, and Hoover.

The major departures from the succession of economic conservative appointments occurred as a result of Progressive influence early in the 20th century during the presidencies of Theodore Roosevelt and Woodrow Wilson. Theodore Roosevelt's break with the tradition did not occur as a result of a critical election. In fact the critical election of 1896, which in part was fought over Supreme Court doctrinal policies and Populist remedies adopted by the Bryan forces, had been interpreted by its victor, President William McKinley, as a validation of the Supreme Court's economic conservatism. Not only had McKinley selected a weakly qualified conservative, McKenna, but before his death by assassination, he was prepared to choose Alfred Hemenway, an influential Boston corporate attorney, to fill a vacancy from the anticipated resignation of Associate Justice Horace Gray. After McKinley's death and Gray's actual resignation in 1902, President Theodore Roosevelt chose Oliver Wendall Holmes, Jr., Chief Justice of the Supreme Judicial Court of Massachusetts. Although Holmes was recognized as one of the most distinguished and able of contemporary jurists, President Roosevelt chose him because he believed that he would be independent of corporate influences, more sympathetic of the rights of working people, and nationalistic on the status of the colonies won in the Spanish-American War.

The resignation of Associate Justice George Shiras on February 23, 1903 provided Theodore Roosevelt's second vacancy. Regional as well as ideological considerations were influential. Roosevelt felt that William Rufus Day would enunciate a broad constructionist interpretation of Congress's power to regulate business by means of the Sherman Antitrust Act. But in fact, Day, an Ohio judge and long-time supporter of the deceased President McKinley, was on most issues an economic conservative. After the resignation of Associate Justice Henry Billings Brown on May 28, 1906, President Roosevelt made his second major effort to persuade William Howard Taft to accept a seat on the Court. When Taft was U.S. governor of the Philippines, Roosevelt had offered him a Supreme Court appointment, but Taft had chosen to remain in his post. In 1906 Taft was serving as Roosevelt's secretary of war. He again declined the Supreme Court seat, primarily because he expected the Republican party to nominate him for the presidency. Although Roosevelt considered Taft a political ally, Taft became a most consistent economic conservative. After a lengthy flirtation with the possibility of nominating a southern Democrat, Horace Lurton, President Roosevelt was dissuaded by Senator Henry Cabot Lodge. He subsequently nominated his attorney general, William H. Moody. Moody actually exemplified the ideological positions most cherished by Roosevelt. In short, for the three appointments President Theodore Roosevelt completed, two, Holmes and Moody, largely, but not slavishly, fulfilled his ideological expectations. Conversely, Day, primarily a product of Roosevelt's concern with regional considerations and some sense of obligation to the memory of McKinley, did not generally represent Roosevelt's expectations.

When William Howard Taft succeeded Theodore Roosevelt as president, he reinstated the conservative thrust established in McKinley's electoral victory in 1896. When Associate Justice Rufus Peckham died on October 24, 1909, Taft nominated a southern Democrat, Horace Lurton, whom he had recommended to Theodore Roosevelt on two separate occasions. Lurton was severely criticized by organized labor, but this opposition did not deter Taft, whose antilabor views had been manifested when he served as a federal circuit judge. Lurton, a conservative southern Democrat, was confirmed by the Senate on December 20, 1909. The death of Associate Justice David Brewer on March 28, 1910 gave Taft a second vacancy to fill. His military advisor and political confidante, Archie Butt, suggested that Republican Governor Charles Evans Hughes of New York might be a formidable rival for the Republican presidential nomination in 1912. Although Hughes was a corporate attorney with wide public service experience, he was not a thoroughgoing economic conservative. Presumably, Taft's ideological inclination for such a conservative was tempered by the prospect of getting rid of a potential rival.[22]

The death of Chief Justice Melville Weston Fuller on July 4, 1910 provided Taft's third vacancy. Taft ultimately chose to promote Associate Justice Edward D. White, although he had strongly intimated to Hughes that he would promote him to the chief justiceship if the vacancy occurred during his presidency. But when Archie Butt reminded him of this, Taft commented that "It does seem strange that the one place in the government which I would have liked to fill myself I am forced to give to another."[23] White, a conservative ex–Confederate, well reflected Taft's approach. After promoting White, the president had one vacancy created by the promotion and another resulting from the resignation, for health reasons, of Associate Justice Moody. His selection for Moody's seat was Willis Van Devanter, a very conservative federal circuit judge from Wyoming. Critics accused Van Devanter of being too close to the Union Pacific Railroad Company, which had been one of his clients. For the vacancy created by White's promotion, President Taft chose another southerner, Joseph Rucker Lamar of Georgia who, like Van Devanter, had represented railroad corporations. The death of Associate Justice John Marshall Harlan on October 14, 1911 brought President Taft's final opportunity to fill a vacancy. His selectee, Mahlon Pitney of New Jersey, was a prominent Republican who had served as Chancellor of the New Jersey judicial system. He was strongly backed by business interests and strongly opposed by organized labor, especially because of his state judicial rulings against peaceful picketing. The Senate confirmed Pitney by a margin of 50–26. Pitney also conformed to Taft's judicial ideology of strong economic conservatism accompanied by an antilabor perspective.

President William Howard Taft's judicial selections reinstated the conservative thrust of President McKinley's single selection and represented a delayed ideological fulfillment of the critical election of 1896, in which the conservatism of the Supreme Court had been a significant issue. The Progressive tenor of President Theodore Roosevelt's selections (actually two of the three appointments) proved to be temporary except for Holmes. The significance of Taft's appointments lay not only in the fundamental differences they reflected in contrast to Roosevelt's, but also in the pervasiveness of his influence for subsequent years. His successful nomination of Lurton, Hughes, Van Devanter, Lamar, and Pitney, and the promotion of White to the chief justiceship assured conservative economic dominance of the Supreme Court during an era in which Progressivism was popular. Thus, even though he was subsequently defeated in the three-way contest for the presidency among Bull Moose candidate Theodore Roosevelt, Democratic Woodrow Wilson, and himself, Taft's appointments to the Court blunted the thrust of Progressivism until the tide turned against the movement in the conservative reaction after World War I.

Interestingly enough, the first serious attempt to secure a Supreme Court nomination for a woman was made following Harlan's death. The president of the District of Columbia Woman Suffrage Association, Julia White Leavith, reminded President Taft that women were voting in six states comprising approximately one million voters. She recommended several female attorneys, all of whom had practiced before the Supreme Court for more than ten years.[24]

President Taft had been relatively successful in choosing judicial nominees who reflected his economic conservatism and antilabor tendencies, with Hughes providing occasional dissonance. Hughes was destined to resign to accept the Republican presidential nomination in 1916. One of Taft's nominees, Willis Van Devanter, remained on the Court until June 1937, distinguishing himself in conservative circles as an unyielding opponent of the New Deal. But Taft's other nominees, while ideologically sound and generally consistent with Taft's expectations, were old men when elevated to the Supreme Court. Consequently, with the exception of Van Devanter, none remained on the Court after 1922. But several remained long enough so that the election victory of Harding ensured the renewal of conservatives through the 1920s. President Woodrow Wilson's only appointments resulted from Hughes' resignation to run against him and the death of two Taft appointees, Associate Justices Horace Lurton on July 12, 1914, and Joseph R. Lamar on January 2, 1916.

President Wilson was as dedicated in his commitment to liberal justices as Taft was to economic conservatives. But surprisingly, Wilson's first appointee was an individual whose narrow conservatism became a constant on the Supreme Court until early 1941. James Clark McReynolds had achieved a reputation as a trust buster in the tobacco trust issue and had gained the backing of Colonel House, Wilson's influential "kitchen cabinet" advisor, who had promoted McReynolds' selection as attorney general. One persistent explanation is that Wilson "kicked McReynolds upstairs" because he was an uncooperative cabinet member. In any case, Wilson eventually recognized the appointment of McReynolds as a serious mistake, and one that he would not make again. When Associate Justice Lamar died in 1916, President Wilson made what conservatives viewed as one of the most controversial appointments in the modern history of the Court. He chose Louis D. Brandeis, a Boston attorney who had undertaken a wide variety of public interest causes against the monetary interests of large corporations. After a bitter fight in which six former presidents of the American Bar Association opposed Brandeis (William H. Taft among them), the Senate confirmed him by a margin of 47–22. Finally, when Charles Evans Hughes resigned on June 12, 1916, to enter the presidential race, President Wilson had another chance to make a liberal appointment. His choice was John H. Clarke of Ohio. Wilson had appointed Clarke a federal district judge in 1914. Although Clarke had had an extensive corporate law practice, he was basically a Progressive critic of corporate excesses whose judicial record on the Court fully justified the confidence expressed by President Wilson.

President Wilson's liberal influence on the Supreme Court was destined to be rather limited. His "mistake," Associate Justice McReynolds, virtually nullified, on a vote-to-vote basis, the positions taken by Wilson's greatest appointee, Associate Justice Brandeis. But McReynolds never matched the power, quality, and scope of Brandeis' opinions. Both had long careers on the bench, Brandeis serving until February 1939 and McReynolds remaining two years longer. Associate Justice Clarke resigned in 1922 to devote more than two decades to the then forlorn cause of American participation in the League of Nations.

The election of 1920 brought Warren G. Harding to the White House and with him a virtual stranglehold by economic conservatives on the Supreme Court. When Chief Justice Edward White died on May 19, 1921, President Harding nominated the man who had chosen White for promotion, former President William Howard Taft. Taft's major backers were from the ranks of large corporations, political conservatives, and southern Democrats. Progressives and organized labor opposed his nomination. Taft was confirmed in executive session of the Senate on June 30, 1921 in spite of opposition from Senators William Borah, Robert La Follette, Hiram Johnson, and Tom Watson. In 1922 President Harding was able to fill two more vacancies, these created by the resignations of Associate Justices Clarke and Day in September and November, respectively. For one post, Harding nominated his friend and political ally, former Senator George Sutherland of Utah, then president of the American Bar Association. Sutherland fulfilled perhaps even more ideally than Taft the conservative economic ideology sought by Harding. The former senator was confirmed on the day the Senate received his nomination, September 5, 1922. Harding's next choice was an extremely conservative Democrat, Minnesota railroad corporation attorney Pierce Butler. One of Butler's supporters was Chief Justice Taft. Progressive opposition was very strong, as was opposition from within Minnesota. The major criticisms were Butler's procorporation background, and his role as a regent of the University of Minnesota in dismissing liberal faculty members. On December 31, 1922, Associate Justice Mahlon Pitney resigned, providing President Harding with a fourth Supreme Court appointment. Harding's final nominee was Edward T. Sanford of Tennessee, a conservative Republican circuit court judge. Again Chief Justice Taft had strongly urged his selection. In addition to Taft's own elevation to the chief justiceship, the Harding appointees continued the trend of Taft's own presidential judicial selections. The result was a conservative judiciary with Holmes and Brandeis the only major exceptions.

President Calvin Coolidge completed Harding's term and one to which Coolidge himself was elected. But in contrast to Harding, who had made four appointments in only two years, Coolidge had only one vacancy to fill in five and one-half years. Although Coolidge was an economic conservative like Harding and Taft, when Justice McKenna resigned on January 5, 1925, the president's inclination to appoint a conservative was overshadowed by the need to handle the scandals inherited from Harding. Coolidge had chosen his personal friend and dean of the Columbia University Law School, Harlan Fiske Stone, as a reform attorney general. In 1925 Coolidge nominated Stone for the Court vacancy. Critics charged that Coolidge "kicked Stone upstairs" because of his vigorous prosecution of the aluminum trust. Whatever the explanation, Stone's appointment broke, momentarily, the succession of economic conservatives. More often than not, Stone's doctrinal affinity was with Holmes and Brandeis.

President Coolidge's successor, Herbert Hoover, had conservative inclinations, in the view of his senatorial critics, and his first Supreme Court selection seemed to confirm their deepest suspicions. The occasion was the resignation of the seriously ill chief justice, William Howard Taft, in February 1930. President Hoover's choice was Charles Evans Hughes, former associate justice, unsuccessful Republican presidential candidate in 1916, and very successful corporate attorney. Hughes' resignation from the Court in 1916 and his corporate ties became targets of intense opposition. Confirmation came only after prolonged debate, by a margin of 52–26, on February 13, 1930. Progressive Republicans and Democrats had led the opposition assault in the Senate and were thoroughly prepared to fight when President Hoover made his second nomination of a conservative. His nominee, John J. Parker of North Carolina, was a Republican and Federal circuit judge for the Fourth Circuit. Progressives viewed the Parker nomination as an attempt by Hoover to extend Republican influence to the South. Charged with anti–Negro bias in his race as Republican gubernatorial candidate in 1920 and antilabor bias in his judicial decisions, Judge Parker was rejected 41–39 on May 7, 1930. President Hoover was thus denied an economic conservative from the South. Two days after Parker's defeat, Hoover nominated Owen J. Roberts, a Philadelphia corporate attorney of conservative ideology, who was popular because of his successful role as special prosecutor in the Teapot Dome investigations. The Senate, worn out from the nomination fights over Hughes and Parker, confirmed Hoover's nominee unanimously, with little discussion. Thus, Hoover had succeeded in appointing a second conservative, who, like Hughes, came from the ranks of the small group of very successful corporate attorneys.

The third vacancy filled by President Hoover occurred as a result of the resignation of Associate Justice Oliver Wendell Holmes, Jr., on January 12, 1932. On February 15, after casting about for another conservative, President Hoover nominated a liberal Democrat, the second Jew and third New Yorker on the Court, the outstanding jurist Benjamin Nathan Cardozo. Senate approval, without debate, was unanimous on February 24, 1932. From the time of President Hoover's last appointment, that of Cardozo in March 1932, more than five years elapsed before another vacancy occurred on the Supreme Court.

Strong Senate opposition to Hoover's nominations of Hughes and Parker was one of the early warning signals of the tough political opposition that confronted President Hoover and his economically conservative administration. But the presidential election of 1932, unlike the critical election of 1896, did not turn the Supreme Court and its doctrinal tendencies into major campaign issues.

The New Deal and its aftermath

A serious confrontation of the emergent Democratic coalition of organized labor, big city political organizations, and the urban working population versus the Supreme Court had not developed before the critical election of 1932, perhaps in part because the main characteristics of the Democratic New Deal economic recovery program were not discussed in the political campaign. But the overwhelming dominance of Republican economic conservatives on the district courts and circuit courts, as well as the Supreme Court itself, made conflict virtually inevitable. Like the Federalist-dominated judiciary that confronted the victorious Jeffersonian Republicans in 1801, the conservative Republican jurists of the 1930s often treated economic control and property issues with the fervor of true believers. Their obstinacy was reinforced by their longevity and their determination to remain in office. Roosevelt administration leaders did not coin phrases as direct as the one attributed to Jefferson, "Judges seldom die—and never resign." But they did recognize clearly the interrelationship of tenure on good behavior, longevity, and determination to maintain doctrinal purity and judicial control.

Since passage of the act of April 10, 1869, federal justices and judges could retire at full salary at age 70 if they had served ten years. But ideological motivation often overshadowed monetary retirement considerations in periods of confrontation. The judges and justices, if in good health, can determine their own dates of termination. Indeed, in some instances jurists held on to their positions after their health had declined. Portions of two letters of Chief Justice William Howard Taft to his brother Horace illustrate the point vividly. On November 14, 1929, he wrote

> I am older and slower and less acute and more confused. However, as long as things continue as they are, and I am able to answer in my place, I must stay on the court in order to prevent the Bolsheviki from getting control. . . .

Again, on December 1, 1929, the chief justice wrote his brother:

> . . . The only hope we have of keeping a consistent declaration of constitutional law is for us to live as long as we can. . . . The truth is that Hoover is a Progressive just as Stone is and just as Brandeis is and just as Holmes is.[25]

Franklin Roosevelt's New Deal Attorney General Homer Cummings was keenly aware that justices and judges control vacancies because of tenure on good behavior. As he put it, "Because retirement is voluntary, the judges themselves, throughout the Federal System, exercise great control over the personnel of the various courts, since they may withhold their retirements until a President to their liking occupies the White House. The courts may thus 'pick' themselves."[26] When the log jam finally broke in 1937, changes came with great rapidity, beginning with Senator Hugo L. Black's selection in August of 1937, and seven appointments and one promotion later, ending with the confirmation of Wiley B. Rutledge in 1943. These relatively rapid changes resulted from resignations and retirements as well as deaths. But it is significant that none of the changes actually came before the "switch in time that saved nine," the modification of doctrinal positions, particularly by Chief Justice Hughes and Associate Justice

Roberts, which made passage of the Roosevelt "court-packing" bill impossible (if indeed it ever had a chance). The rapidly developing vacancies began with the retirement of Associate Justice Willis Van Devanter, who was replaced by Black in 1937. Then Associate Justice George Sutherland retired and was replaced by Stanley Reed in January 1938. Associate Justice Benjamin N. Cardozo died in July 1938 and was replaced by Harvard University law professor Felix Frankfurter in January 1939. Louis Brandeis' resignation in February 1939 created yet another vacancy, which was filled by William O. Douglas in April 1939. After the death of Pierce Butler in November 1939, Attorney General Frank Murphy was confirmed in January 1940. Only one month later, Associate Justice McReynolds resigned. He was replaced by James Byrnes of South Carolina in June 1941. Also in June 1941, Chief Justice Charles Evans Hughes resigned, and Associate Justice Harlan Fiske Stone was promoted to the chief justiceship. He, in turn, was succeeded by Robert H. Jackson, Roosevelt's attorney general, in July 1941. Finally, when Associate Justice James F. Byrnes resigned, he was replaced by the dean of the law school of the University of Iowa, Wiley B. Rutledge, in February 1943. As David Adamany correctly noted, the conservative retirements did not come until after the crisis had been resolved by the switch in the positions of Chief Justice Hughes and Associate Justice Roberts.[27]

During Harry S. Truman's presidency (1945–1953), four vacancies were filled, thus perpetuating New Deal/Fair Deal doctrinal ascendancy. When Justice Roberts retired in July 1945, President Truman chose a former Republican Senate colleague, Harold H. Burton, who was confirmed in September 1945. After Chief Justice Stone died in April 1946, President Truman chose Fred M. Vinson as chief justice. He was confirmed in June 1946. In July 1949, Associate Justice Murphy died; he was replaced by Tom C. Clark of Texas in August 1949. Truman's final selection came when Associate Justice Rutledge died in September 1949. As his replacement President Truman chose former Democratic Senator (and colleague) Sherman Minton of Indiana, who was confirmed in October 1949.

Dwight David Eisenhower's election to the presidency broke the two decades of Democratic dominance of that office and renewed the opportunity for Republicans to gain a majority on the federal bench. The death of Chief Justice Fred Vinson during Eisenhower's first year in office provided the greatest appointive prize immediately. Earl Warren of California was selected and confirmed unanimously on March 1, 1954. Although Eisenhower had not indicated his ideological preferences previously, he eventually made it clear that he was not happy with Warren's liberal doctrinal positions. The death of Associate Justice Jackson in October 1954 brought a second opportunity, which President Eisenhower filled with a conservative, John Marshall Harlan's grandson and namesake, who had had a very successful career as a New York corporate lawyer. Following the retirement of Associate Justice Sherman Minton in October 1956, President Eisenhower chose William Joseph Brennan, a Democratic New Jersey Supreme Court member of Roman Catholic faith and distinguished legal reputation. While the appointment was politically astute, it did not fulfill Eisenhower's doctrinal goals. In fact, Brennan's positions supported those of Chief Justice Warren, whom Eisenhower considered a great disappointment. President Eisenhower was far more pleased with the doctrinal contributions of his last two appointees. Charles E. Whittaker, a conservative midwestern corporate attorney, replaced Associate Justice Stanley Reed, who resigned in February 1957. Potter Stewart, a Republican member of the Ohio Supreme Court, was chosen after a Senate confirmation fight (70–17) following Associate Justice Harold Burton's resignation in October 1958. Thus, during Eisenhower's two terms as president, three of President Truman's appointees were replaced on the Court.

After President John F. Kennedy's narrow victory in 1960, his presidency lasted only until his tragic death in 1963. However, the resignations resulting from poor health of Associate Justices Whittaker and Frankfurter in April and August 1962, respectively, provided opportunities for Kennedy to replace supporters of judicial restraint with more liberal judicial activists. First chosen was President Kennedy's friend and assistant attorney general, Byron White, a rather guarded activist at first. In October of 1962 Kennedy chose labor attorney and current secretary of labor, Arthur Goldberg. Both were doctrinal fulfillments of their presidential nominator. In terms of judicial appointments, President Kennedy's successor, Lyndon Baines Johnson, was destined to fill only the same number of vacancies as his short-lived predecessor. When Arthur J. Goldberg resigned to take a key United Nations role, President Johnson chose his confidante (his enemies intoned "crony"), liberal corporate law firm member Abe Fortas. When Associate Justice Tom Clark resigned in June 1967, Johnson replaced him with the highly successful NAACP legal strategist and first black chosen for the Court, Thurgood Marshall. Johnson's appointees clearly reflected his judicial ideology. President Johnson's own early announcement that he would not run for reelection, the bitter and intense opposition of Senate conservatives, and the failure of nerve on the part of some Senate moderates combined to defeat Johnson's effort to promote Associate Justice Abe Fortas to the chief justiceship being vacated by the advance announcement of Chief Justice Earl Warren's resignation. When the Fortas promotion was defeated, technically on a 45–43 motion to end the conservative Senate filibuster on October 1, 1968, President Johnson's nomination of Texas federal judge Homer Thornberry to Fortas' associate justiceship fell with it.

Conservatism resurgent

As a result of these defeats and the subsequent resignation of Associate Justice Fortas in May 1969, President Richard Milhous Nixon immediately had two important vacancies to fill. For the greatest prize, he chose conservative Republican circuit judge Warren E. Burger of Minnesota. After two defeats while attempting to implement his "southern strategy," Nixon chose another Minnesota Republican and close friend of Burger, Eighth Circuit Judge Harry A. Blackmun. In 1971, President Nixon filled two more seats on the Court (these created by the retirements of Associate Justices Black and Harlan in September). Nixon chose two conservatives ostensibly as advocates of judicial restraint. But in reality both appointees, Assistant Attorney General William H. Rehnquist of Arizona and corporate attorney and former American Bar Association President Lewis Powell of Virginia, were conservative judicial activists who have fulfilled the ideological goals of President Nixon not only in the area of criminal justice, but in the reincarnation of economic conservative doctrines resembling some supposedly overturned permanently by the New Deal Court in the late 1930s and early 1940s.

After the tempestuous Watergate scandal, which threatened President Nixon with impeachment, he resigned and was immediately pardoned by his successor, President Gerald Ford. During his short presidency, Ford had one vacancy resulting from the retirement of Associate Justice William O. Douglas. Ford chose Seventh Circuit Judge John Paul Stevens in December 1975. Ford's successor, President Jimmy Carter, made no Supreme Court appointments. But, in turn, Carter's successor, President Ronald Reagan, had a vacancy to fill in his first year because of the resignation of Associate Justice Potter Stewart. Reagan succeeded in appointing a conservative without serious liberal Senate opposition by choosing a Republican woman, Arizona jurist Sandra Day O'Connor. So strong was the liberal acclaim for the first woman for the Court, that the Reagan administration and its nominee were not seriously scrutinized or challenged on her conservative ideology. To date, O'Connor fulfills Reagan's expectations.

Conclusion

In comparing the conditions surrounding all of the critical elections to the present, 1800 through 1932, it is clear that the circumstances involving the Supreme Court varied considerably. In two of the critical elections, the first in 1800 and the third in 1860, several key decisions and doctrines of the old Supreme Court majority directly contradicted the policy positions of the emerging political coalition destined to gain control of the presidency and the Congress for a significant length of time. In the fourth critical election, that of 1896, the conservative economic decisions and institutional role of the Supreme Court became salient issues, and major portions of the Populist party Court program were adapted as a significant part of the Democratic party platform. However, the political coalition attacking the Court was soundly defeated. Conversely, in the second and fifth critical elections, in 1828 and 1932, no such conflict developed *before* the elections, although one of the most serious institutional confrontations developed after 1932.

After the success of the Jeffersonian Republicans in the election of 1800, the Federalist justices did modify some of their positions, especially those that might have jeopardized the Court or the status of the Federalist justices themselves. On a great many other issues, the Court adamantly refused to change. Jeffersonian Republican disunity in the face of Federalist judicial unity and longevity gave Federalist principles a "long lease." Conversely, the serious and seemingly irreconcilable confrontation between the proslavery majority on the antebellum Supreme Court of the late 1850s and the Republican party led by Abraham Lincoln in 1860 was avoided in large part because of the deaths in office of some Jacksonian justices and the resignation of Justice John Archibald Campbell. In addition, some of the Jacksonian justices supported Lincoln's Civil War programs in doctrinal tests. The intense and bitter ideological conflict involving the Supreme Court prior to the critical election of 1896 was resolved in the election itself in favor of the Court's conservative political supporters.

The situations surrounding 1828 and 1932 are more complex. Both involved circumstances in which the Supreme Court and its majority positions did not challenge seriously or directly the new political coalition that would subsequently dominate the executive and legislative branches. But in both instances the Court did become pitted against such coalitions after the critical election. In the Jacksonian era, the contests were relatively short-lived because the Jacksonian Democrats were able to dominate the Court by replacements when the old Federalists died and by means of circuit reorganization that increased the number of members of the Court. Thus, the confrontation never reached the intensity of the New Deal crisis in the 1930s. Once again the contemporary pattern of longevity and delayed termination of judicial service had a direct bearing on the nature of the confrontation. During the controversy of the 1930s, the longevity and personal determination of conservative Republican justices intensified the crisis, which was probably inevitable because of the deep philosophical and public policy differences that divided the conservative Court majority and the New Deal Congress and president.

That the two factors—longevity and determination to remain on the Court to continue to influence doctrinal policy—are related to critical elections can be illustrated by means of a comparison of differential recruitment patterns. The clash of political generations is underscored in the contrasting patterns of judicial appointment opportunities available to successive presidents.

The combination of judicial longevity and partisan tenacity has not only thwarted emergent political coalitions after their victories in critical elections; it also has delayed, limited, and occasionally denied individual presidents the opportunity to select justices. President Jimmy Carter (1977–1981) served a full presidential term without a single vacancy to fill. Presidents William Henry Harrison (1841), Zachary Taylor (1849–1850), and Andrew Johnson (1865–1869) did not have full presidential terms, nor did they make any Supreme Court appointments. The pattern of vacancies available to presidents is generally controlled by health and partisan considerations. Charles Fairman is quite correct in recognizing that congressional adoption of a retirement statute for the regular federal judiciary eased the problems of justices with senility and other health problems. But the factor of individual motivation, generally partisan and doctrinal, often influenced the date of termination of judicial service of justices who were senile or incapacitated for other reasons.[28] The impact of these factors upon the appointment opportunities of all presidents, with special emphasis upon the critical elections of 1800, 1860, 1896, and 1932, is summarized in the tables in chapters 4, 5, 6, and 8. In order to dramatize the impact of older judicial political generations upon consecutive emerging political coalitions, each table emphasizes the length of time the new victorious electoral coalition had to wait before it gained an actual, rather than nominal, majority on the Supreme Court.

The critical elections of 1800, 1860, and 1932 provide the most important evidence of the impact of judicial longevity and partisan tenacity. The presidential elections of 1828 and 1896 are more ambiguous.

The circumstances surrounding the Court and the critical election of 1800 were unique. The political party totally committed to maintaining a one-party system was defeated in that election. But the two Federalist presidents were perhaps the most successful in choosing justices who uniformly fulfilled their doctrinal expectations, especially regarding national supremacy and the sanctity of property rights. Their political successors, the Jeffersonian Republicans, were not unified on these issues. Because of regional or other political considerations, Jeffersonian presidents occasionally chose nominees who did not fulfill their doctrinal expectations and who became identified with neo–Federalist and Whig doctrinal positions. The most notable examples were Todd and Story. President John Quincy Adams, generally described by historians as a National Republican, probably found Robert Trimble's doctrinal neo–Federalism compatible since Adams himself was moving toward the Whig position, which became his political mooring place for the rest of his long political career. The astonishing persistence of Federalist, neo–Federalist, and Whig doctrinal principles (all very similar) did not rest entirely upon the lack of consistency of appointment goals of Jeffersonian and Jacksonian presidents—although this inconsistency was an important factor later. The longevity and partisan tenacity of Federalist justices (and some judges) gave the Federalists a majority until the 1812 term. With Story and Todd on the Court, however, the actual ascendancy of Federalist doctrinal influences was maintained until 1837. This was possible because three of President Andrew Jackson's appointees, McLean, Baldwin, and Wayne, were also doctrinal Whigs. (McLean soon became a nominal Whig.) This influence, which was strengthened by Benjamin R. Curtis's service from 1851 to 1857, endured until the death of Justices McLean and Wayne in the era of Abraham Lincoln.

It should be noted also that not even the tenure of John Marshall, who served for 34 years, 1801 to 1835, surpassed that of William Cranch, nephew of Abigail Adams, who was assistant judge and chief judge of the Circuit Court for the District of Columbia for an astounding 54 years, 1801–1855. All of the key elements are combined in his tenure. His initial appointment by President John Adams in 1801 was part of the last-minute effort to present the incoming Jeffersonians with a solid Federalist judiciary. The appointment also smacked of gentry-class nepotism. Despite the fact that Cranch and his fellow Federalist assistant judge, James Marshall, brother of the chief justice, applied the Alien and Sedition Act to convict a pro–Jeffersonian publisher, President Thomas Jefferson inexplicably promoted Cranch to chief judge. The intensity of Cranch's judicial partisanship never weakened. In the 1830s he inflicted a serious judicial blow against Andrew Jackson's administration by developing the key doctrine adopted by a Supreme Court majority in the Amos Kendall case. Thus the Cranch appointment and promotion combined three elements. The first is longevity, over which a judge or justice has no direct control other than the maintenance of a healthful lifestyle. The second, partisan persistence, is a matter of choice by an incumbent jurist and for some involves not only doctrinal partisanship but the act, health permitting, of staying on the bench until a president of one's own party could choose a successor. The third factor is controlled by the appointing authority. In the selection of Cranch, President Jefferson did not chose a chief judge of his own doctrinal or partisan persuasion. Why he did not is something of a mystery.[29] The factor of presidential inconsistency in appointment objectives resulted in some astonishingly contradictory choices such as Hayes' selection of the first John

Marshall Harlan, Wilson's appointment of James Clark McReynolds, Hoover's nomination of Benjamin N. Cardozo, and Eisenhower's selections of Earl Warren and William J. Brennan, Jr.

Robert Carr has suggested, "There is a tradition nurtured by many historians and political scientists to the effect that try as presidents may to influence the Court and the development of constitutional law by naming certain men as justices, they have invariably been fooled. This tradition is a rather doubtful one."[30] The empirical evidence from the totality of presidential appointments substantiates Carr's judgment.

In comparison to the long-enduring influence of Federalist-Whig doctrinal principles (which in many respects became virtually incorporated into the fabric of American constitutional law), the Jacksonian Democratic influence was not destined to last very long after the party was replaced by the Republicans as the dominant political coalition in the critical election of 1860. The Civil War itself can be viewed in part as a vast and bloody referendum on the regional and proslavery doctrines of the Jacksonian Democratic Court majority, especially on the Dred Scott decision.[31] The critical election of 1860 brought about a fundamental shift in control of Congress and the presidency. But the act of seceding from the Union by the states comprising the Confederacy not only resulted in a bloody and bitter conflict, but made impossible the electoral success of the Jacksonian Democrats at the presidential level for many years thereafter. Thus, there was no opportunity even on an occasional basis for the renewal of justices of that persuasion for several decades. Simultaneously, the major doctrinal positions of the old Jacksonian Democratic party relating to slavery, states' rights, and the status of corporations were either permanently eliminated by constitutional amendments or seriously modified by such amendments and by wide-ranging statutory changes and judicial decisions. Thus, while the old Federalist-Whig judicial presence extended from 1789 to 1867 with the death of James M. Wayne, a doctrinal Whig, the Jacksonian judicial presence was much shorter. The Court majority that the Jacksonians achieved in 1837 came to an end in 1881 with the death of Nathan Clifford, who had hung on vainly awaiting the election of a Democratic president. However, the effective Jacksonian majority on the Court had ended by 1864, only four years after the last Jacksonian Democratic president, James Buchanan, left office. Unlike the influence of Federalist-Whig constitutional principles, those doctrines most clearly identified with the Jacksonian justices were eliminated or seriously modified soon after the Civil War.

The most enduring of the doctrinal influences on the Supreme Court of the United States were those related to economic conservatism with its emphasis upon the sanctity of property rights and the freedom of corporations to operate relatively free of state or national government control. In a number of important respects, the Federalist-Whig doctrinal contributions laid the framework for the post–Civil War version of such judicial conservatism. Perhaps the most important difference between the promulgators of the old doctrinal conservatism and the new was the emergence of justices with exceedingly close ties and often extended legal experience in corporate enterprises. To be sure, Joseph Story served as a director of a bank while serving on the Court. And Benjamin R. Curtis could accurately be called the first corporate lawyer appointed to the Supreme Court since he had represented large commercial corporations. Stephen J. Field came to the Court during Lincoln's first term as an intimate of railroad magnate and Senator Leland Stanford. But the relatively consistent selection of economically conservative justices, frequently with corporate law firm backgrounds, began during the presidency of Ulysses S. Grant. The critical election of 1896 reinstated conservative Republicans in the presidency and in Congress. William Jennings Bryan and his Populist-leaning supporters had no opportunity to select nonconservative alternatives. From the election of President Grant to the presidency of Theodore Roosevelt, the only significant exception to the selection of justices committed to conservative economic doctrines was President Hayes' choice of John Marshall Harlan in 1877.

President Hayes' selection of Harlan and President Wilson's choice of James C. McReynolds represented major exceptions to the general rule that both conservative and liberal presidents select justices whose doctrinal tendencies are similar to the ideology of the appointing authority. In a few instances these appointments were presidential mistakes. Theodore Roosevelt, a Progressive Republican, sought justices who would support antitrust regulation and moderate the antilabor doctrine of the sitting economic conservative justices. He succeeded in two of his three appointments, Oliver Wendell Holmes, Jr., and William Moody. But his other choice, William R. Day, an accommodation to the deceased McKinley's Ohio Republicans, was an old-style economic conservative. Democratic President Woodrow Wilson, similarly a Progressive, also achieved only two ideological successes out of three tries. To be sure, one of the successes was an intellectually spectacular one, his choice of Louis Brandeis, matching Theodore Roosevelt's selection of Oliver Wendell Holmes, Jr. But Wilson's nomination of James Clark McReynolds was probably the most spectacular ideological mistake of 20th century Supreme Court selection.

From 1921 to 1937 there were only two significant exceptions to a steady succession of economic conservative choices, Harlan F. Stone's nomination by President Coolidge and Benjamin N. Cardozo's by President Hoover. With the election of Franklin D. Roosevelt and a Democratic Congress in 1932, the stage was set for the bitter and intense confrontation between the conservatively dominated Court and the New Deal coalition.

President Roosevelt had no Supreme Court vacancies to fill until 1937. But after the doctrinal about-face by Chief Justice Hughes and Justice Roberts, most of the remaining Republican conservatives resigned, and two very elderly members died. Thus, in a startling turnabout, a Court dominated by conservative Republicans since 1877 became a New Deal Court only six years after Franklin Roosevelt took office in 1933. The addition of Black in 1937, Reed in 1938, Douglas and Frankfurter in 1939, along with liberal Republican Stone, marked a swift doctrinal reversal. It was not as swift, however, as the transition after a critical election that occurred during the Civil War. Because of deaths and important resignations including a defection to the Confederacy, the fundamental change came in less than four years, from Lincoln's inaugural in 1861 to Chief Justice Salmon P. Chase's appointment in 1864.

After the New Deal Democrats and their partisan successors gained control of the Supreme Court, some scholars assumed that the major doctrinal decisions of economic conservatism had been eliminated thoroughly and permanently. By the early 1940s, Roberts was the only conservative justice. President Truman also rejected economic conservatism in his appointments. As was the case after the critical election of 1828, emphasis shifted to doctrinal issues that had not been salient early in the new critical-election era. Just as on the eve of the Civil War Jacksonian Democratic justices had been confronted by major issues that were not central to the partisan and doctrinal battles of the period in which they were appointed, so did members of the New Deal/Fair Deal Court rapidly begin to confront issues that did not resemble the stubborn and bitter confrontations over the scope of national government authority in economic matters of the 1930s and early 1940s.

The additions of Chief Justice Warren and Justice Brennan continued and accentuated the shift toward greater judicial oversight of civil rights and state criminal justice systems. Again the belief spread that Supreme Court supervision of government-controlled economic matters and its strong protection of economic property rights were merely historic memories. From the presidency of Richard Nixon to that of Ronald Reagan, however, it has become apparent that economic conservatism has had a quiet but steady doctrinal revival, identified most closely with Justices Lewis Powell, William Rehnquist, Sandra O'Connor, and Chief Justice Burger. These strong critics of the alleged judicial activism by Court supporters of civil rights and criminal defendants' procedural rights have become the judicial activists of a new, more subtle version of economic conservatism and a social philosophy resembling the Social Darwinism of many earlier conservatives.

In terms of the fulfillment of presidential expectations, the historical evidence provides few substantial presidential failures, and most of these are attributable to significant intervening political pressures, with a few outright mistakes in judgment. These exceptions include Jefferson's choice of Thomas Todd, Madison's selection of Story, Jackson's choices of McLean, Baldwin, and Wayne, Tyler's nomination of Nelson, Hayes' selection of the first Harlan, Theodore Roosevelt's choice of Day, Wilson's of McReynolds, Coolidge's of Stone, Hoover's of Cardozo, and Eisenhower's selection of Warren and Brennan. Thus of 102 selections, only approximately 13 percent represented serious presidential failures in terms of doctrinal affinity.

When justices representing a judicial political generation are left isolated by the surge of a critical election, they may either conform to or seriously impede the victorious new political coalition, depending on the circumstances of the critical election and its aftermath. The most prolonged confrontation occurred after the first critical election. Old Federalists and their doctrinal allies or converts such as Joseph Story maintained Court control for about 12 years after the major and irreversible electoral defeat of their president and congressional cohorts. Their doctrinal influence extended beyond the Civil War and became woven into the fabric of American constitutional law, especially in those aspects related to nationalism and the safeguarding of property rights. The critical election of 1828 produced no direct doctrinal confrontation. In many respects the early differences between Jacksonians and Federalists and Whigs were often extensions of earlier conflicts, such as those related to the status of corporations and the scope of the commerce clause.

The third critical election, that of 1860, resulted in the most abrupt and comprehensive repudiation of an older judicial political generation. The Jacksonian Democratic majority had been superseded by 1864, and the most criticized of the doctrines associated with this older judicial generation were repudiated by the results of the Civil War, several postwar constitutional amendments, notably the Thirteenth, Fourteenth, and Fifteenth, and by numerous judicial decisions. Gerald Pomper preferred to describe the election of 1896 as a *converting* election because it resulted in a continuation in power of the generally dominant Republican coalition. If one accepts Pomper's designation, the election of 1828 must be classified as a converting election as well, because in 1828 as in 1896, most elements of a previously existing dominant coalition were continued with a somewhat different orientation. Supreme Court members did not feel constrained to modify their preelection doctrinal positions (except in isolated clashes such as the Kendall case in the Jacksonian era) because a direct challenge by the new dominant political coalition had not occurred. In contrast, after 1801 there was some minimal modification, such as abandonment of federal common law jurisdiction. After 1860 there was greater doctrinal accommodation to the new president's views by all the justices except Taney. After the bitter court-packing fight, which came as a result of conservative Republican judicial intransigence coupled with careless Democratic congressional statutory work, the famous modification of doctrinal positions by Hughes and Roberts helped ease a serious crisis. The Federalist justices after the election of 1800 were the least willing to modify their positions. After the election of 1860, the northern Jacksonian Democrats (and the Southerner, Wayne) were the most willing to alter their positions to accommodate the Lincoln administration.

The historical evidence contradicts Dahl's hypothesis about the relative unlikelihood of long-term intransigence on the Court successfully thwarting a new electoral coalition. The evidence is more supportive of the alternative position of Robert Jackson. The mere averaging of presidential appointment opportunities tells little about the intensity of the clash of adamantine judicial political generations. Furthermore, the modifications of doctrinal positions and justices' infrequent willingness to resign generally came, not because of a benign, periodic, and seemingly random appearance of a vacancy, but because the new political coalition moved or threatened to move politically and institutionally against the Court and occasionally against its members.

Scigliano's conception that there is an institutional affinity between the Supreme Court and the presidency against Congress finds virtually no support in the historical evidence. Clearly there was no basis for this hypothesis after the 1800 election and only marginally before the 1828 election (because of the indirect nomination exchange via Webster between John Quincy Adams and John Marshall). Before the Civil War, the only clear-cut example in which a president and the Court (or some elements of it) were aligned against elements of Congress occurred during James Buchanan's presidency in the covert communication of information about the Dred Scott decision. For the remainder of the period from 1789 through 1860, there were no major examples of coalitions of presidents and Supreme Court majorities against Congress. Despite constant conflict between president and Congress immediately after Lincoln's death, the Supreme Court did not align itself with President Andrew Johnson, nor did it risk any serious confrontation with this powerful, assertive Congress. Similarly, there were no major examples of such alleged institutional affinity during the rest of the 19th century or in the 20th century conflicts involving the Court.

In sum, in the numerous conflicts involving the Supreme Court after critical or converting elections, the salient factor has been the dissonance that results from the transformation of values under new administrations and resistance to change among the elderly members of the Court. The central constitutional factor is tenure on good behavior. A vital and necessary constitutional safeguard for judicial independence, this provision of Article 3, Section 1, helps to insure bold creativity on the bench. Thus, it is virtually inevitable that judicial independence and political and doctrinal conflict are integral parts of our tripartite constitutional system.

REFERENCES

1. Robert H. Jackson, *The Struggle for Judicial Supremacy,* op. cit., p. 315.
2. Robert A. Dahl, "Decision-Making in a Democracy: The Supreme Court as a National Policy-Maker," op. cit., p. 293.
3. Ibid., p. 294.
4. Ibid.
5. Oliver Wendell Holmes, Jr., *The Common Law,* ed. Mark DeWolfe Howe (Boston: Little, Brown, 1963), p. 5.
6. Robert Scigliano, *The Supreme Court and the Presidency* (New York: Free Press, 1971), p. 8.
7. Peter McGrath, *Yazoo: Law and Politics in the New Republic—the Case of Fletcher v. Peck* (New York: W. W. Norton, 1967), p. 39, 68, and 85.
8. Ibid., p. 127.
9. Dumas Malone, *Jefferson and the Rights of Man, Jefferson and His Time* (Boston: Little, Brown, 1951), p. 24.
10. Floyd E. McCaffree, *The Nomination and Confirmation of Justices of the Supreme Court of the United States, 1789–1949* (Ann Arbor, Mich.: Unpublished Doctoral Dissertation, University of Michigan, 1938), p. 148.
11. Letter of Story to Webster, January 4, 1824, cited in McCaffree, ibid. pp. 190–192.
12. Trimble's confirmation by a vote of 27–5 on May 9, 1826 represented a defeat for Senatorial courtesy. Senator Rowan of Kentucky (Trimble's home state) not only voted against confirmation, but also unsuccessfully sought to persuade his senatorial colleagues to reject the nominee.
13. For a full account, see McCaffree, op. cit., pp. 217–218.
14. Cited in McCaffree, op. cit., p. 238.
15. From John Quincy Adams, *Diary,* February 13, 1831, cited in McCaffree, op. cit., p. 251.
16. Andrew Jackson in a letter to Martin Van Buren, July 30, 1833, attributed the comment to Thomas Jefferson; quoted in McCaffree, op. cit., p. 264.
17. Quoted in McCaffree, op. cit., p. 296.
18. Cited in Warren, *2 The Supreme Court in United States History,* op. cit., p. 500.
19. Letter of Ben Wade to Clark Carr, quoted in Daniel S. McHargue, *Appointments to the Supreme Court of the United States: The Factors that Affected Appointments, 1789–1932* (Los Angeles: Unpublished doctoral dissertation, University of California, Los Angeles, 1949), p. 184.
20. John R. Schmidhauser, *Judges and Justices: The Federal Appellate Judiciary* (Boston: Little, Brown and Company, 1979), p. 240.

21. McHargue, op. cit., pp. 341–342.
22. Henry F. Pringle, *The Life and Times of William Howard Taft* (New York: Farrar and Rinehart, 1939) pp. 102–103 and 127–136.
23. Quoted in McHargue, op. cit., p. 378.
24. McHargue, op. cit., pp. 402–403.
25. Pringle, op. cit., p. 967.
26. Homer Cummings, *Progress of the President's Plan for Judicial Reform* (1937), p. 6.
27. David Adamany, "Legitimacy, Realining Elections, and the Supreme Court," *1973 Wisconsin Law Review*, p. 834.
28. For a full discussion of the evidence on these issues and of Fairman's "The Retirement of Federal Judges," *51 Harvard Law Review* (1939) see John R. Schmidhauser, "Age and Judicial Behavior—American Higher Appellate Judges" and, especially, "When and Why Justices Leave the Supreme Court," Chapters 9 and 10 in *The Politics of Age*, ed. Wilma Donahue and Clark Tibbets (Ann Arbor: University of Michigan Press, 1962).
29. Currently being investigated by the author.
30. Robert Carr, *The Supreme Court and Judicial Review* (New York: Farrar and Rinehart, 1942), p. 249.
31. Don E. Fehrenbacher, *The Dred Scott Case: Its Significance in American Law and Politics* (New York: Oxford University Press, 1978).

The Constitution of the United States of America

We the People of the United States, in Order to form a more perfect Union, establish Justice, insure domestic Tranquility, provide for the common defence, promote the general Welfare, and secure the Blessings of Liberty to ourselves and our Posterity, do ordain and establish this Constitution for the United States of America.

ARTICLE I

SECTION 1. All legislative Powers herein granted shall be vested in a Congress of the United States, which shall consist of a Senate and House of Representatives.

SECTION 2. The House of Representatives shall be composed of Members chosen every second Year by the People of the several States, and the Electors in each State shall have the Qualifications requisite for Electors of the most numerous Branch of the State Legislature.

No Person shall be a Representative who shall not have attained to the Age of twenty five Years, and been seven Years a Citizen of the United States, and who shall not, when elected, be an Inhabitant of that State in which he shall be chosen.

Representatives and direct Taxes shall be apportioned among the several States which may be included within this Union, according to their respective Numbers, which shall be determined by adding to the whole Number of free Persons, including those bound to Service for a Term of Years, and excluding Indians not taxed, three fifths of all other Persons. The actual Enumeration shall be made within three Years after the first Meeting of the Congress of the United States, and within every subsequent Term of ten Years, in such Manner as they shall by Law direct. The Number of Representatives shall not exceed one for every thirty Thousand, but each State shall have at Least one Representative; and until such enumeration shall be made, the state of New Hampshire shall be entitled to chuse three, Massachusetts eight, Rhode Island and Providence Plantations one, Connecticut five, New York six, New Jersey four, Pennsylvania eight, Delaware one, Maryland six, Virginia ten, North Carolina five, South Carolina five, and Georgia three.

When vacancies happen in the Representation from any State, the Executive Authority thereof shall issue Writs of Election to fill such Vacancies.

The House of Representatives shall chuse their Speaker and other Officers; and shall have the sole Power of Impeachment.

SECTION 3. The Senate of the United States shall be composed of two Senators from each State, chosen by the Legislature thereof, for six Years; and each Senator shall have one Vote.

Immediately after they shall be assembled in Consequence of the first Election, they shall be divided as equally as may be into three Classes. The Seats of the Senators of the first Class shall be vacated at the Expiration of the second Year, of the second Class at the Expiration of the fourth Year, and of the third Class at the Expiration of the sixth Year, so that one third may be chosen every second Year; and if Vacancies happen by Resignation, or otherwise, during the Recess of the Legislature of any state, the Executive thereof may make temporary Appointments until the next Meeting of the Legislature, which shall then fill such Vacancies.

No Person shall be a Senator who shall not have attained to the Age of thirty Years, and been nine Years a Citizen of the United States, and who shall not, when elected, be an Inhabitant of that State for which he shall be chosen.

The Vice President of the United States shall be President of the Senate, but shall have no Vote, unless they be equally divided.

The Senate shall chuse their other Officers, and also a President pro tempore, in the Absence of the Vice President, or when he shall exercise the Office of President of the United States.

The Senate shall have the sole Power to try all Impeachments. When sitting for that Purpose, they shall be on Oath or Affirmation. When the President of the United States is tried the Chief Justice shall preside: And no Person shall be convicted without the Concurrence of two thirds of the Members present.

Judgment in Cases of Impeachment shall not extend further than to removal from Office, and disqualification to hold and enjoy any Office of honor, Trust or Profit under the United States: but the Party convicted shall nevertheless be liable and subject to Indictment, Trial, Judgment and Punishment, according to Law.

SECTION 4.   The Times, Places and Manner of holding Elections for Senators and Representatives, shall be prescribed in each State by the Legislature thereof; but the Congress may at any time by Law make or alter such Regulations, except as to the Places of chusing Senators.

The Congress shall assemble at least once in every Year, and such Meeting shall be on the first Monday in December, unless they shall by Law appoint a different Day.

SECTION 5.   Each House shall be the judge of the Elections, Returns and Qualifications of its own Members, and a Majority of each shall constitute a Quorum to do Business; but a smaller Number may adjourn from day to day, and may be authorized to compel the Attendance of absent Members, in such Manner, and under such Penalties as each House may provide.

Each House may determine the Rules of its Proceedings, punish its Members for disorderly Behaviour, and, with the Concurrence of two thirds, expel a Member.

Each House shall keep a Journal of its Proceedings, and from time to time publish the same, excepting such Parts as may in their Judgment require Secrecy; and the Yeas and Nays of the Members of either House on any question shall, at the Desire of one fifth of those Present, be entered on the Journal.

Neither House, during the Session of Congress, shall, without the Consent of the other, adjourn for more than three days, nor to any other Place than that in which the two Houses shall be sitting.

SECTION 6.   The Senators and Representatives shall receive a Compensation for their Services, to be ascertained by Law, and paid out of the Treasury of the United States. They shall in all Cases, except Treason, Felony and Breach of the Peace, be privileged from Arrest during their Attendance at the Session of their respective Houses, and in going to and returning from the same; and for any Speech or Debate in either House, they shall not be questioned in any other Place.

No Senator or Representative shall, during the Time for which he was elected, be appointed to any civil Office under the Authority of the United States, which shall have been created, or the Emoluments whereof shall have been encreased during such time; and no Person holding any Office under the United States, shall be a Member of either House during his Continuance in Office.

SECTION 7.   All Bills for raising Revenue shall originate in the House of Representatives; but the Senate may propose or concur with amendments as on other Bills.

Every Bill which shall have passed the House of Representatives and the Senate, shall, before it become a Law, be presented to the President of the United States; If he approve he shall sign it, but if not he shall return it, with his Objections to that House in which it shall have originated, who shall enter the Objections at large on their Journal, and proceed to reconsider it. If after such Reconsideration two thirds of that House shall agree to pass the Bill, it shall be sent, together with the Objections, to the other House, by which it shall likewise be reconsidered, and if approved by two thirds of that House, it shall become a Law. But in all such Cases the Votes of both Houses shall be determined by Yeas and Nays, and the Names of the Persons voting for and against the Bill shall be entered on the Journal of each House respectively. If any Bill shall not be returned by the President within ten Days (Sunday excepted) after it shall have been presented to him, the Same shall be a Law, in like Manner as if he had signed it, unless the Congress by their Adjournment prevent its Return, in which Case it shall not be a Law.

Every Order, Resolution, or Vote to which the Concurrence of the Senate and House of Representatives may be necessary (except on a question of Adjournment) shall be presented to the President of the

United States; and before the Same shall take Effect, shall be approved by him, or being disapproved by him, shall be repassed by two thirds of the Senate and House of Representatives, according to the Rules and Limitations prescribed in the Case of a Bill.

SECTION 8. The Congress shall have Power To lay and collect Taxes, Duties, Imposts and Excises, to pay the Debts and provide for the common Defence and general Welfare of the United States; but all Duties, Imposts and Excises shall be uniform throughout the United States;

To borrow Money on the credit of the United States;

To regulate Commerce with foreign Nations, and among the several States, and with the Indian Tribes;

To establish an uniform Rule of Naturalization, and uniform Laws on the subject of Bankruptcies throughout the United States;

To coin Money, regulate the Value thereof, and of foreign Coin, and fix the Standard of Weights and Measures;

To provide for the Punishment of counterfeiting the Securities and current Coin of the United States;

To establish Post Offices and post Roads;

To promote the Progress of Science and useful Arts, by securing for limited Times to Authors and Inventors the exclusive Right to their respective Writings and Discoveries;

To constitute Tribunals inferior to the supreme Court;

To define and punish Piracies and Felonies committed on the high Seas, and Offences against the Law of Nations;

To declare War, grant Letters of Marque and Reprisal, and make Rules concerning Captures on Land and Water;

To raise and support Armies, but no Appropriation of Money to that Use shall be for a longer Term than two Years;

To provide and maintain a Navy;

To make Rules for the Government and Regulation of the land and naval Forces;

To provide for calling forth the Militia to execute the Laws of the Union, suppress Insurrections and repel Invasions;

To provide for organizing, arming, and disciplining, the Militia, and for governing such Part of them as may be employed in the Service of the United States, reserving to the States respectively, the Appointment of the Officers, and the Authority of training the Militia according to the discipline prescribed by Congress;

To exercise exclusive Legislation in all Cases whatsoever, over such District (not exceeding ten Miles square) as may, by Cession of particular States, and the Acceptance of Congress, become the Seat of the Government of the United States, and to exercise like Authority over all Places purchased by the Consent of the Legislature of the State in which the Same shall be, for the Erection of Forts, Magazines, Arsenals, dock-Yards, and other needful Buildings;—And

To make all Laws which shall be necessary and proper for carrying into Execution the foregoing Powers, and all other Powers vested by this Constitution in the Government of the United States, or in any Department or Officer thereof.

SECTION 9. The Migration or Importation of such Persons as any of the States now existing shall think proper to admit, shall not be prohibited by the Congress prior to the Year one thousand eight hundred and eight, but a Tax or duty may be imposed on such Importation, not exceeding ten dollars for each Person.

The Privilege of the Writ of Habeas Corpus shall not be suspended, unless when in Cases of Rebellion or Invasion the public Safety may require it.

No Bill of Attainder or ex post facto Law shall be passed.

No Capitation, or other direct, Tax shall be laid, unless in Proportion to the Census or Enumeration herein before directed to be taken.

No Tax or Duty shall be laid on Articles exported from any State.

No Preference shall be given by any Regulation of Commerce or Revenue to the Ports of one State over those of another; nor shall Vessels bound to, or from, one State, be obliged to enter, clear or pay Duties in another.

No Money shall be drawn from the Treasury, but in Consequence of Appropriations made by Law; and a regular Statement and Account of the Receipts and Expenditures of all public Money shall be published from time to time.

No Title of Nobility shall be granted by the United States: And no Person holding any Office of Profit or Trust under them, shall, without the Consent of the Congress, accept of any present, Emolument, Office, or Title, of any kind whatever, from any King, Prince or foreign State.

SECTION 10.   No State shall enter into any Treaty, Alliance, or Confederation; grant Letters of Marque and Reprisal; coin Money; emit Bills of Credit; make any Thing but gold and silver Coin a Tender in Payment of Debts; pass any Bill of Attainder, ex post facto Law, or Law impairing the Obligation of Contracts, or grant any Title of Nobility.

No State shall, without the Consent of the Congress, lay any Imposts or Duties on Imports or Exports, except what may be absolutely necessary for executing its inspection Laws: and the net Produce of all Duties and Imposts, laid by any State on Imports or Exports, shall be for the Use of the Treasury of the United States; and all such Laws shall be subject to the Revision and Controul of the Congress.

No State shall, without the consent of Congress, lay any Duty of Tonnage, keep Troops, or Ships of War in time of Peace, enter into any Agreement or Compact with another State, or with a foreign Power, or engage in War, unless actually invaded, or in such imminent Danger as will not admit of delay.

ARTICLE II

SECTION 1.   The executive Power shall be vested in a President of the United States of America. He shall hold his Office during the Term of four Years, and, together with the Vice President, chosen for the same Term, be elected, as follows

Each State shall appoint, in such Manner as the Legislature thereof may direct, a Number of Electors, equal to the whole Number of Senators and Representatives to which the State may be entitled in the Congress: but no Senator or Representative, or Person holding an Office of Trust or Profit under the United States, shall be appointed an Elector.

The Electors shall meet in their respective States, and vote by Ballot for two Persons, of whom one at least shall not be an Inhabitant of the same State with themselves. And they shall make a List of all the Persons voted for, and of the Number of Votes for each; which List they shall sign and certify, and transmit sealed to the Seat of the Government of the United States, directed to the President of the Senate. The President of the Senate shall, in the Presence of the Senate and House of Representatives, open all the Certificates, and the Votes shall then be counted. The Person having the greatest Number of Votes shall be the President, if such Number be a Majority of the whole Number of Electors appointed; and if there be more than one who have such Majority, and have an equal Number of Votes, then the House of Representatives shall immediately chuse by Ballot one of them for President; and if no Person have a Majority, then from the five highest on the List the said House shall in like Manner chuse the President. But in chusing the President, the Votes shall be taken by States, the Representation from each State having one Vote; a quorum for this Purpose shall consist of a Member or Members from two thirds of the States, and a Majority of all the States shall be necessary to a Choice. In every Case, after the Choice of the President, the Person having the greatest Number of Votes of the Electors shall be the Vice President. But if there should remain two or more who have equal Votes, the Senate shall chuse from them by Ballot the Vice President.

The Congress may determine the Time of chusing the Electors, and the Day on which they shall give their Votes; which Day shall be the same throughout the United States.

No Person except a natural born Citizen, or a Citizen of the United States, at the time of the Adoption of this Constitution, shall be eligible to the Office of President; neither shall any Person be eligible to that Office who shall not have attained to the Age of thirty five Years, and been fourteen Years a Resident within the United States.

In Case of the Removal of the President from Office, or of his Death, Resignation, or Inability to discharge the Powers and Duties of the said Office, the Same shall devolve on the Vice President, and the Congress may by Law provide for the Case of Removal, Death, Resignation or Inability, both of the President and Vice President, declaring what Officer shall then act as President, and such Officer shall act accordingly, until the Disability be removed, or a President shall be elected.

The President shall, at stated Times, receive for his Services, a Compensation, which shall neither be encreased nor diminished during the Period for which he shall have been elected, and he shall not receive within that Period any other Emolument from the United States, or any of them.

Before he enter on the Execution of his Office, he shall take the following Oath or Affirmation:—"I do solemnly swear (or affirm) that I will faithfully execute the Office of President of the United States, and will to the best of my Ability, preserve, protect and defend the Constitution of the United States."

SECTION 2. The President shall be Commander in Chief of the Army and Navy of the United States, and of the Militia of the several States, when called into the actual Service of the United States; he may require the Opinion, in writing, of the principal Officer in each of the executive Departments, upon any Subject relating to the Duties of their respective Offices, and he shall have Power to grant Reprieves and Pardons for Offences against the United States, except in Cases of Impeachment.

He shall have Power, by and with the Advice and Consent of the Senate, to make Treaties, provided two thirds of the Senators present concur; and he shall nominate, and by and with the Advice and Consent of the Senate, shall appoint Ambassadors, other public Ministers and Consuls, Judges of the supreme Court, and all other Officers of the United States, whose Appointments are not herein otherwise provided for, and which shall be established by Law; but the Congress may by Law vest the Appointment of such inferior Officers, as they think proper, in the President alone, in the Courts of Law, or in the Heads of Departments.

The President shall have Power to fill up all Vacancies that may happen during the Recess of the Senate, by granting Commissions which shall expire at the End of their next Session.

SECTION 3. He shall from time to time give to the Congress Information of the State of the Union, and recommend to their Consideration such Measures as he shall judge necessary and expedient; he may, on extraordinary Occasions, convene both Houses, or either of them, and in Case of Disagreement between them, with Respect to the Time of Adjournment, he may adjourn them to such Time as he shall think proper; he shall receive Ambassadors and other public Ministers; he shall take Care that the Laws be faithfully executed, and shall Commission all the Officers of the United States.

SECTION 4. The President, Vice President and all Civil Officers of the United States, shall be removed from Office on Impeachment for, and Conviction of, Treason, Bribery, or other high Crimes and Misdemeanors.

ARTICLE III

SECTION 1. The judicial Power of the United States, shall be vested in one supreme Court, and in such inferior Courts as the Congress may from time to time ordain and establish. The Judges, both of the supreme and inferior Courts, shall hold their Offices during good Behaviour, and shall, at stated Times, receive for their Services, a Compensation, which shall not be diminished during their Continuance in Office.

SECTION 2. The judicial Power shall extend to all Cases, in Law and Equity, arising under this Constitution, the Laws of the United States, and Treaties made, or which shall be made, under their Authority;—to all Cases affecting Ambassadors, other public Ministers and Consuls;—to all Cases of admiralty and maritime Jurisdiction;—to Controversies to which the United States shall be a Party;—to Controversies between two or more States;—between a State and Citizens of another State;—between Citizens of different States;—between Citizens of the same State claiming Lands under Grants of different States, and between a State, or the Citizens thereof, and foreign States, Citizens or Subjects.

In all Cases affecting Ambassadors, other public Ministers and Consuls, and those in which a State shall be Party, the Supreme Court shall have original Jurisdiction. In all the other Cases before mentioned, the supreme Court shall have appellate Jurisdiction, both as to Law and Fact, with such Exceptions, and under such Regulations as the Congress shall make.

The Trial of all Crimes, except in Cases of Impeachment, shall be by Jury; and such Trial shall be held in the State where the said Crimes shall have been committed; but when not committed within any State, the Trial shall be at such Place or Places as the Congress may by Law have directed.

SECTION 3. Treason against the United States, shall consist only in levying War against them, or in adhering to their Enemies, giving them Aid and Comfort. No Person shall be convicted of Treason unless on the Testimony of two Witnesses to the same overt Act, or on Confession in open Court.

The Congress shall have Power to declare the Punishment of Treason, but no Attainder of Treason shall work Corruption of Blood, or Forfeiture except during the Life of the Person attainted.

ARTICLE IV

SECTION 1. Full Faith and Credit shall be given in each State to the public Acts, Records, and judicial Proceedings of every other State. And the Congress may by general Laws prescribe the Manner in which such Acts, Records and Proceedings shall be proved, and the Effect thereof.

SECTION 2. The Citizens of each State shall be entitled to all Privileges and Immunities of Citizens in the several States.

A Person charged in any State with Treason, Felony, or other Crime, who shall flee from Justice, and be found in another State, shall on Demand of the executive Authority of the State from which he fled, be delivered up, to be removed to the State having Jurisdiction of the Crime.

No Person held to Service or Labour in one State, under the Laws thereof, escaping into another, shall, in Consequence of any Law or Regulation therein, be discharged from such Service or Labour, but shall be delivered up on Claim of the Party to whom such Service or Labour may be due.

SECTION 3. New States may be admitted by the Congress into this Union; but no new State shall be formed or erected within the Jurisdiction of any other State; nor any State be formed by the Junction of two or more States, or Parts of States, without the Consent of the Legislatures of the States concerned as well as of the Congress.

The Congress shall have Power to dispose of and make all needful Rules and Regulations respecting the Territory or other Property belonging to the United States; and nothing in this Constitution shall be so construed as to Prejudice any Claims of the United States, or of any particular State.

SECTION 4. The United States shall guarantee to every State in this Union a Republican Form of Government, and shall protect each of them against Invasion; and on Application of the Legislature, or of the Executive (when the Legislature cannot be convened) against domestic Violence.

ARTICLE V

The Congress, whenever two thirds of both Houses shall deem it necessary, shall propose Amendments to this Constitution, or, on the Application of the Legislatures of two thirds of the several States, shall call a Convention for proposing Amendments, which, in either Case, shall be valid to all Intents and Purposes, as Part of this Constitution, when ratified by the Legislatures of three fourths of the several States,

or by Conventions in three fourths thereof, as the one or the other Mode of Ratification may be proposed by the Congress; Provided that no Amendment which may be made prior to the Year One thousand eight hundred and eight shall in any Manner affect the first and fourth Clauses in the Ninth Section of the first Article; and that no State, without its Consent, shall be deprived of its equal Suffrage in the Senate.

ARTICLE VI

All Debts contracted and Engagements entered into, before the Adoption of this Constitution, shall be as valid against the United States under this Constitution, as under the Confederation.

This Constitution, and the Laws of the United States which shall be made in Pursuance thereof; and all Treaties made, or which shall be made, under the Authority of the United States, shall be the supreme Law of the Land; and the Judges in every State shall be bound thereby, any Thing in the Constitution or Laws of any State to the Contrary notwithstanding.

The Senators and Representatives before mentioned, and the Members of the several State Legislatures, and all executive and judicial Officers, both of the United States and of the several States, shall be bound by Oath or Affirmation, to support this Constitution; but no religious Test shall ever be required as a Qualification to any Office or public Trust under the United States.

ARTICLE VII

The Ratification of the Conventions of nine States, shall be sufficient for the Establishment of this Constitution between the States so ratifying the Same.

AMENDMENT I [1791]

Congress shall make no law respecting an establishment of religion, or prohibiting the free exercise thereof; or abridging the freedom of speech, or of the press; or the right of the people peaceably to assemble, and to petition the Government for a redress of grievances.

AMENDMENT II [1791]

A well regulated Militia, being necessary to the security of a free State, the right of the people to keep and bear Arms, shall not be infringed.

AMENDMENT III [1791]

No Soldier shall, in time of peace be quartered in any house, without the consent of the Owner, nor in time of war, but in a manner to be prescribed by law.

AMENDMENT IV [1791]

The right of the people to be secure in their persons, houses, papers, and effects, against unreasonable searches and seizures, shall not be violated, and no Warrants shall issue, but upon probable cause, supported by Oath or affirmation, and particularly describing the place to be searched, and the persons or things to be seized.

AMENDMENT V [1791]

No person shall be held to answer for a capital, or otherwise infamous crime, unless on a presentment or indictment of a Grand Jury, except in cases arising in the land or naval forces, or in the militia, when in actual service in time of War or public danger; nor shall any person be subject for the same offence to be twice put in jeopardy of life or limb; nor shall be compelled in any criminal case to be a witness against himself, nor be deprived of life, liberty, or property, without due process of law; nor shall private property be taken for public use, without just compensation.

AMENDMENT VI [1791]

In all criminal prosecutions, the accused shall enjoy the right to a speedy and public trial, by an impartial jury of the State and district wherein the crime shall have been committed, which district shall have been previously ascertained by law, and to be informed of the nature and cause of the accusation; to be confronted with the witnesses against him; to have compulsory process for obtaining Witnesses in his favor, and to have the Assistance of Counsel for his defence.

AMENDMENT VII [1791]

In Suits at common law, where the value in controversy shall exceed twenty dollars, the right of trial by jury shall be preserved, and no fact tried by a jury, shall be otherwise re-examined in any Court of the United States, than according to the rules of the common law.

AMENDMENT VIII [1791]

Excessive bail shall not be required, nor excessive fines imposed, nor cruel and unusual punishments inflicted.

AMENDMENT IX [1791]

The enumeration in the Constitution, of certain rights, shall not be construed to deny or disparage others retained by the people.

AMENDMENT X [1791]

The powers not delegated to the United States by the Constitution, nor prohibited by it to the States, are reserved to the States respectively, or to the people.

AMENDMENT XI [1798]

The Judicial power of the United States shall not be construed to extend to any suit in law or equity, commenced or prosecuted against one of the United States by Citizens of another State, or by Citizens or Subjects of any Foreign State.

AMENDMENT XII [1804]

The Electors shall meet in their respective states and vote by ballot for President and Vice-President, one of whom, at least, shall not be an inhabitant of the same state with themselves; they shall name in their ballots the person voted for as President, and in distinct ballots the person voted for as Vice-President, and they shall make distinct lists of all persons voted for as President, and of all persons voted for as Vice-President, and of the number of votes for each, which lists they shall sign and certify, and transmit sealed to the seat of the government of the United States, directed to the President of the Senate;—The President of the Senate shall, in the presence of the Senate and House of Representatives, open all the certificates and the votes shall then be counted;—The person having the greatest number of votes for President, shall be the President, if such number be a majority of the whole number of Electors appointed; and if no person have such majority, then from the persons having the highest numbers not exceeding three on the list of those voted for as President, the House of Representatives shall choose immediately, by ballot, the President. But in choosing the President, the votes shall be taken by states, the representation from each state having one vote; a quorum for this purpose shall consist of a member or members from two-thirds of the states, and a majority of all the states shall be necessary to a choice. And if the House of Representatives shall not choose a President whenever the right of choice shall devolve upon them, before the fourth day of March next following, then the Vice-President shall act as President, as in the case of the death or other constitutional disability of the President—The person having the greatest number of votes as Vice-President, shall be the Vice-President, if such number be a majority of the whole number of Electors appointed, and if no person have a majority, then from the two highest numbers on the list, the Senate shall choose the Vice-President; a quorum for the purpose shall consist of two-thirds of the whole number of Senators, and a majority of the whole number shall be necessary to a choice. But no person constitutionally ineligible to the office of President shall be eligible to that of Vice-President of the United States.

AMENDMENT XIII [1865]

SECTION 1.   Neither slavery nor involuntary servitude, except as a punishment for crime whereof the party shall have been duly convicted, shall exist within the United States, or any place subject to their jurisdiction.

SECTION 2.   Congress shall have power to enforce this article by appropriate legislation.

AMENDMENT XIV [1868]

SECTION 1.   All persons born or naturalized in the United States and subject to the jurisdiction thereof, are citizens of the United States and of the State wherein they reside. No State shall make or enforce any law which shall abridge the privileges or immunities of citizens of the United States; nor shall any State deprive any person of life, liberty, or property, without due process of law; nor deny to any person within its jurisdiction the equal protection of the laws.

SECTION 2.   Representatives shall be apportioned among the several States according to their respective numbers, counting the whole number of persons in each State, excluding Indians not taxed. But when the

right to vote at any election for the choice of electors for President and Vice President of the United States, Representatives in Congress, the Executive and Judicial officers of a State, or the members of the Legislature thereof, is denied to any of the male inhabitants of such State, being twenty-one years of age, and citizens of the United States, or in any way abridged, except for participation in rebellion, or other crime, the basis of representation therein shall be reduced in the proportion which the number of such male citizens shall bear to the whole number of male citizens twenty-one years of age in such State.

SECTION 3.   No person shall be a Senator or Representative in Congress, or elector of President and Vice President, or hold any office, civil or military, under the United States, or under any State, who, having previously taken an oath, as a member of Congress, or as an officer of the United States, or as a member of any State legislature, or as an executive or judicial officer of any State, to support the Constitution of the United States, shall have engaged in insurrection or rebellion against the same, or given aid or comfort to the enemies thereof. But Congress may by a vote of two-thirds of each House, remove such disability.

SECTION 4.   The validity of the public debt of the United States, authorized by law, including debts incurred for payment of pensions and bounties for services in suppressing insurrection or rebellion, shall not be questioned. But neither the United States nor any State shall assume or pay any debt or obligation incurred in aid of insurrection or rebellion against the United States, or any claim for the loss or emancipation of any slave; but all such debts, obligations and claims shall be held illegal and void.

SECTION 5.   The Congress shall have power to enforce, by appropriate legislation, the provisions of this article.

AMENDMENT XV [1870]

SECTION 1.   The right of citizens of the United States to vote shall not be denied or abridged by the United States or by any State on account of race, color, or previous condition of servitude.

SECTION 2.   The Congress shall have power to enforce this article by appropriate legislation.

AMENDMENT XVI [1913]

The Congress shall have power to lay and collect taxes on incomes, from whatever source derived, without apportionment among the several States, and without regard to any census or enumeration.

AMENDMENT XVII [1913]

The Senate of the United States shall be composed of two Senators from each State, elected by the people thereof, for six years; and each Senator shall have one vote. The electors in each State shall have the qualifications requisite for electors of the most numerous branch of the state legislatures.

When vacancies happen in the representation of any State in the Senate, the executive authority of such State shall issue writs of election to fill such vacancies: *Provided*, That the legislature of any State may empower the executive thereof to make temporary appointments until the people fill the vacancies by election as the legislature may direct.

This amendment shall not be so construed as to affect the election or term of any Senator chosen before it becomes valid as part of the Constitution.

AMENDMENT XVIII [1919]

SECTION 1. After one year from the ratification of this article the manufacture, sale, or transportation of intoxicating liquors within, the importation thereof into, or the exportation thereof from the United States and all territory subject to the jurisdiction thereof for beverage purposes is hereby prohibited.

SECTION 2. The Congress and the several States shall have concurrent power to enforce this article by appropriate legislation.

SECTION 3. This article shall be inoperative unless it shall have been ratified as an amendment to the Constitution by the legislatures of the several States, as provided in the Constitution, within seven years from the date of the submission hereof to the States by the Congress.

AMENDMENT XIX [1920]

The right of citizens of the United States to vote shall not be denied or abridged by the United States or by any State on account of sex.

Congress shall have power to enforce this article by appropriate legislation.

AMENDMENT XX [1933]

SECTION 1. The terms of the President and Vice President shall end at noon on the 20th day of January, and the terms of Senators and Representatives at noon on the 3d day of January, of the years in which such terms would have ended if this article had not been ratified; and the terms of their successors shall then begin.

SECTION 2. The Congress shall assemble at least once in every year, and such meeting shall begin at noon on the 3d day of January, unless they shall by law appoint a different day.

SECTION 3. If, at the time fixed for the beginning of the term of the President, the President elect shall have died, the Vice President elect shall become President. If a President shall not have been chosen before the time fixed for the beginning of his term, or if the President elect shall have failed to qualify, then the Vice President elect shall act as President until a President shall have qualified; and the Congress may by law provide for the case wherein neither a President elect nor a Vice President elect shall have qualified, declaring who shall then act as President, or the manner in which one who is to act shall be selected, and such person shall act accordingly until a President or Vice President shall have qualified.

SECTION 4. The Congress may by law provide for the case of the death of any of the persons from whom the House of Representatives may choose a President whenever the right of choice shall have devolved upon them, and for the case of the death of any of the persons from whom the Senate may choose a Vice President whenever the right of choice shall have devolved upon them.

SECTION 5. Sections 1 and 2 shall take effect on the 15th day of October following the ratification of this article.

SECTION 6. This article shall be inoperative unless it shall have been ratified as an amendment to the Constitution by the legislatures of three-fourths of the several States within seven years from the date of its submission.

AMENDMENT XXI [1933]

SECTION 1. The eighteenth article of amendment to the Constitution of the United States is hereby repealed.

SECTION 2. The transportation or importation into any State, Territory, or possession of the United States for delivery or use therein of intoxicating liquors, in violation of the laws thereof, is hereby prohibited.

SECTION 3. This article shall be inoperative unless it shall have been ratified as an amendment to the Constitution by conventions in the several States, as provided in the Constitution, within seven years from the date of the submission hereof to the States by the Congress.

AMENDMENT XXII [1951]

SECTION 1. No person shall be elected to the office of the President more than twice, and no person who has held the office of President, or acted as President, for more than two years of a term to which some other person was elected President shall be elected to the office of the President more than once. But this Article shall not apply to any person holding the office of President when this Article was proposed by the Congress, and shall not prevent any person who may be holding the office of President, or acting as President, during the term within which this Article becomes operative from holding the office of President or acting as President during the remainder of such term.

SECTION 2. This article shall be inoperative unless it shall have been ratified as an amendment to the Constitution by the legislatures of three-fourths of the several States within seven years from the date of its submission to the States by the Congress.

AMENDMENT XXIII [1961]

SECTION 1. The District constituting the seat of Government of the United States shall appoint in such manner as the Congress may direct:

A number of electors of President and Vice President equal to the whole number of Senators and Representatives in Congress to which the District would be entitled if it were a State, but in no event more than the least populous State; they shall be in addition to those appointed by the States, but they shall be considered, for the purposes of the election of President and Vice President, to be electors appointed by a State; and they shall meet in the District and perform such duties as provided by the twelfth article of amendment.

SECTION 2. The Congress shall have power to enforce this article by appropriate legislation.

AMENDMENT XXIV [1964]

SECTION 1. The right of citizens of the United States to vote in any primary or other election for President or Vice President, for electors for President or Vice President, or for Senator or Representative in Congress, shall not be denied or abridged by the United States or any State by reason of failure to pay any poll tax or other tax.

SECTION 2. The Congress shall have power to enforce this article by appropriate legislation.

AMENDMENT XXV [1967]

SECTION 1. In case of the removal of the President from office or of his death or resignation, the Vice President shall become President.

SECTION 2. Whenever there is a vacancy in the office of the Vice President, the President shall nominate a Vice President who shall take office upon confirmation by a majority vote of both Houses of Congress.

SECTION 3. Whenever the President transmits to the President pro tempore of the Senate and the Speaker of the House of Representatives his written declaration that he is unable to discharge the powers and duties of his office, and until he transmits to them a written declaration to the contrary, such powers and duties shall be discharged by the Vice President as Acting President.

SECTION 4. Whenever the Vice President and a majority of either the principal officers of the executive departments or of such other body as Congress may by law provide, transmit to the President pro tempore of the Senate and the Speaker of the House of Representatives their written declaration that the President is unable to discharge the powers and duties of his office, the Vice President shall immediately assume the powers and duties of the office as Acting President.

Thereafter, when the President transmits to the President pro tempore of the Senate and the Speaker of the House of Representatives his written declaration that no inability exists, he shall resume the powers and duties of his office unless the Vice President and a majority of either the principal officers of the executive department or of such other body as Congress may by law provide, transmit within four days to the President pro tempore of the Senate and the Speaker of the House of Representatives their written declaration that the President is unable to discharge the powers and duties of his office. Thereupon Congress shall decide the issue, assembling within forty-eight hours for that purpose if not in session. If the Congress, within twenty-one days after receipt of the latter written declaration, or, if Congress is not in session, within twenty-one days after Congress is required to assemble, determines by two-thirds vote of both Houses that the President is unable to discharge the powers and duties of his office, the Vice President shall continue to discharge the same as Acting President; otherwise, the President shall resume the powers and duties of his office.

AMENDMENT XXVI [1971]

SECTION 1.   The right of citizens of the United States, who are eighteen years of age or older, to vote shall not be denied or abridged by the United States or by any State on account of age.

SECTION 2.   The Congress shall have power to enforce this article by appropriate legislation.

AMENDMENT XXVII [Proposed]

SECTION 1.   Equality of rights under the law shall not be denied or abridged by the United States or by any State on account of sex.

SECTION 2.   The Congress shall have the power to enforce, by appropriate legislation, the provisions of this article.

SECTION 3.   This amendment shall take effect two years after the date of ratification.

[The 27th Amendment was first submitted to the states on March 22, 1972. In October 1978, the Congress extended the original seven years allotted for ratification to June 30, 1982. By that date, the Amendment still lacked ratification by three of the required 38 states.]

Bibliography

BOOKS

Adams, Henry (ed.). *Documents Relating to New England Federalism* (Boston: Little, Brown, 1877).

Adams, John Quincy. *Parties in the United States* (New York: Greenberg, 1941).

Ames, Herman V. (ed.). *State Documents on Federal Relations,* vol. 1 (1789–1809) (University of Pennsylvania, 1900).

Anderson, J. W. *Eisenhower, Brownell, and the Congress* (University Station: University of Alabama Press, 1964).

Barry, Richard. *Mr. Rutledge of South Carolina* (New York: Duell, Sloan, and Pearce, 1942).

Beveridge, Albert J. *The Life of John Marshall* (Boston, New York: Houghton, Mifflin, 1916).

Brant, Irving. *James Madison, Father of the Constitution, 1787–1800* (Indianapolis: Bobbs–Merrill, 1950).

Brown, Everett S. (ed.). *The Missouri Compromise and Presidential Politics, 1820–1825* (St. Louis: Missouri Historical Society, 1926).

Burnham, Walter Dean. *Critical Elections and the Main Springs of American Politics* (New York: W. W. Norton, 1970).

Carr, Robert. *The Supreme Court and Judicial Review* (New York: Farrar and Rinehart, 1942).

Cleveland, Grover. *Messages and Papers of the Presidents,* vol. 11 (Washington, D. C.: Government Printing Office, 1935).

Cortner, Richard C. *The Supreme Court and the Second Bill of Rights: The Fourteenth Amendment and the Nationalization of Civil Liberties* (Madison: University of Wisconsin Press, 1981).

Corwin, Edward Samuel. *John Marshall and the Constitution* (New Haven: Yale University Press, 1919).

———. *Court over Constitution* (Princeton: Princeton University Press, 1938).

Cralle, Richard (ed.). "Discourse on the Constitution and Government of the United States," *The Works of John C. Calhoun* 1 (Columbia: General Assembly of South Carolina, 1851).

Cunningham, Noble E., Jr. "The Election of 1800," in *The Coming to Power: Critical Presidential Elections in American History,* ed. Arthur M. Schlesinger, Jr. and Fred Israel (New York: Chelsea House, 1971).

Diamond, Robert A. (ed.). *Presidential Elections Since 1789* (Washington, D. C.: Congressional Quarterly, 1975).

Dionisopoulos, P. Allen. *Rebellion, Racism, and Representation: The Adam Clayton Powell Case and Its Antecedents* (Dekalb, Ill.: University of Northern Illinois Press, 1970).

Douglas, William O. *The Court Years, 1939–1975: The Autobiography of William O. Douglas* (New York: Random House, 1980).

Eisenstadt, S. N. *Revolution and the Transformation of Societies: A Comparative Study of Civilizations* (New York: Free Press, 1978).

Elliott, Jonathan. *Debates on the Adoption of the Federal Constitution*, vol. 3 (Philadelphia: J. B. Lippincott, 1901).

Ellis, Richard E. *The Jeffersonian Crisis: Courts and Politics in the Young Republic* (New York: Oxford University Press, 1971).

Fairman, Charles. *Mr. Justice Miller and the Supreme Court* (Cambridge: Harvard University Press, 1939).

Farrand, Max (ed.). *The Records of the Federal Convention of 1787* (New Haven: Yale University Press, 1911).

Fehrenbacher, Don E. *The Dred Scott Case: Its Significance in American Law and Politics* (New York: Oxford University Press, 1978).

Flanders, Henry. *The Lives and Times of the Chief Justices* (Philadelphia: J. B. Lippincott, 1858).

Ford, Paul L. (ed.). *Writings of Thomas Jefferson* (New York: G. P. Putnam & Sons, 1898).

Frankfurter, Felix. *The Commerce Clause Under Marshall, Taney and Waite* (Chapel Hill: University of North Carolina Press, 1937).

Gawalt, Gerald. *The Promise of Power* (Westport, Conn.: Greenwood Press, 1979).

Gilb, Corinne Lathrop. *Hidden Hierarchies* (New York: Harper and Row, 1966).

Goldman, Sheldon and Thomas Jahnige. *The Federal Courts as a Political System* (New York: Harper and Row, 1971).

Haines, Charles Grove. *The Role of the Supreme Court in American Government and Politics, 1789–1835* (Berkeley: University of California Press, 1944).

——— and Foster Sherwood. *The Role of the Supreme Court in American Government and Politics, 1835–1864* (Berkeley: University of California Press, 1957).

Hockett, Homer Carey. *The Constitutional History of the United States, 1776–1826*, vol. 1 (New York: Macmillan, 1939).

Holcombe, Arthur Norman. *Our More Perfect Union* (Cambridge: Harvard University Press, 1950).

Holmes, Oliver Wendell, Jr. *The Common Law*, ed. Mark DeWolfe Howe (Boston: Little, Brown, 1963).

Ickes, Harold. *Secret Diary*, vol. 1 (New York: Simon and Schuster, 1954).

Jackson, Robert. *The Struggle for Judicial Supremacy* (New York: Alfred Knopf, 1941).

Johnson, Allen (ed.). *Readings in American Constitutional History, 1776–1876* (Boston: Houghton, Mifflin, 1912).

Kelley, Alfred H. and Winfred A. Harbison. *The American Constitution: Its Origins and Development* (New York: W. W. Norton, 1976).

Koegel, Otto E. *Walter S. Carter, Collector of Young Masters or the Progenitor of Many Law Firms* (New York: Round Table Press, 1953).

Lodge, Henry Cabot (ed.). *The Federalist* (New York: G. P. Putnam's Sons, 1904).

Magrath, C. Peter. *Yazoo: Law and Politics in the New Republic* (Providence, R. I.: Brown University Press, 1966).

———. *Yazoo: Law and Politics in the New Republic—the Case of Fletcher v. Peck* (New York: W. W. Norton, 1967).

Malone, Dumas. *Jefferson and the Rights of Man, Jefferson and His Time* (Boston: Little, Brown, 1951).

McFarland, Carl. *Judicial Control of the Federal Trade Commission and the Interstate Commerce Commission* (Cambridge: Harvard University Press, 1933).

McLaughlin, Andrew C. *A Constitutional History of the United States* (New York: D. Appleton-Century Company, 1935).

McMaster, John Bach. *A History of the People of the United States* (New York: D. Appleton and Company).

Murphy, Paul L. *The Constitution in Crisis Times: 1918–1969* (New York: Harper and Row, 1972).

Oster, John E. *The Political and Economic Doctrines of John Marshall* (New York: Neale, 1914).

Pringle, Henry F. *The Life and Times of William Howard Taft* (New York: Farrar and Rinehart, 1939).

Roche, John. *Courts and Rights: The American Judiciary in Action* (New York: Random House, 1961).
Rose, Willie Lee. *Rehearsal for Reconstruction: The Port Royal Experiment* (New York: Vintage Books, 1967).

Schmidhauser, John R. *Judges and Justices: The Federal Appellate Judiciary* (Boston: Little, Brown, 1979).
————. *The Supreme Court as Final Arbiter in Federal State Relations, 1789–1957* (Chapel Hill: University of North Carolina Press, 1958).
————, with Larry L. Berg. *The Supreme Court and Congress: Conflict and Interaction* (New York: Free Press, 1972).
Scigliano, Robert. *The Supreme Court and the Presidency* (New York: Free Press, 1971).
Simon, James F. *Independent Journey: The Life of William O. Douglas* (New York: Harper and Row, 1980).
Sindler, Allan P. *Bakke, De Funis, and Minority Admissions: The Quest for Equal Opportunity* (New York: Longman, 1978).
Smigel, Erwin O. *The Wall Street Lawyer: Professional Organization Man?* (New York: Free Press, 1964).
Stanwood, Edward. *A History of Presidential Elections* (Boston: James R. Osgood and Company, 1884).
Story, Joseph. *Commentaries on the Constitution of the United States* (Boston: Little, Brown, 1858).
Swaine, Robert T. *The Cravath Firm and Its Predecessors, 1819–1964* (New York: Ad Press, 1964).
Swindler, William F. *Court and Constitution in the Twentieth Century: The Old Legality, 1889–1932* (Indianapolis: Bobbs–Merrill, 1969).
————. *Court and Constitution in the Twentieth Century: The New Legality, 1932–1968* (Indianapolis: Bobbs–Merrill, 1970).
Swisher, Carl Brent. *American Constitutional Development* (New York: Houghton, Mifflin Company, 1943).
————. *American Constitutional Development*, 2nd edition (Westport, Conn.: Greenwood Press, 1978).
————. *Roger B. Taney* (New York: Macmillan, 1935).

Thayer, James Bradley. *John Marshall* (Boston: Houghton, Mifflin, 1901).

Warren, Charles. *The Supreme Court and Sovereign States* (Princeton: Princeton University Press, 1924).
————. *The Supreme Court in United States History* (Boston: Little, Brown, 1937).
Willoughby, Westel W. *The Constitutional Law of the United States* (New York: Baker, Voorhis and Company, 1929).
————. *The Supreme Court of the United States, Its History and Influence in Our Constitutional System* (Baltimore: Johns Hopkins Press, 1890).
Wright, Benjamin F., Jr. *American Interpretations of Natural Law* (Cambridge: Harvard University Press, 1931).
————. *The Contract Clause of the Constitution* (Cambridge: Harvard University Press, 1938).
Wood, Gordon. *The Creation of the American Republic, 1776–1787* (New York: W. W. Norton, 1969).
Wood, Stephen B. *Constitutional Politics in the Progressive Era: Child Labor and the Law* (Chicago: University of Chicago Press, 1968).

ARTICLES

Adamany, David. "Legitimacy, Realigning Elections, and the Supreme Court," 1973 Wisconsin Law Review.
Allen, Francis A. "The Supreme Court, Federalism and State Systems of Criminal Justice," *University of Chicago Law School Record* 8 (Autumn 1958).
Anderson, Frank Malory. "The Enforcement of the Alien and Sedition Laws," in *Annual Report of the American Historical Association, 1912.*

Barrow, Thomas C. "The American Revolution as a Colonial War for Independence," *William and Mary Quarterly* 25 (1968).
Beck, Paul Allen. "Critical Elections and the Supreme Court: Putting the Cart after the Horse," *American Political Science Review* 70 (September 1976).

Bogart, Ernest L. "Taxation of the Second Bank of the United States by Ohio," *The American Historical Review* 18 (January 1912).

Burke, John P. "What a Veto-Free President Can Do," *Los Angeles Times,* July 24, 1983, Part 4, p. 5.

Caldeira, Gregory A., and Donald McCrone. "Of Time and Judicial Activism: A Study of the U. S. Supreme Court, 1800–1973," in *Supreme Court Activism and Restraint,* ed. Stephen Halpern and Charles Lamb (Lexington, Mass.: D. C. Heath, 1982).

Canon, Bradley, and Sidney Ulmer. "The Supreme Court and Critical Elections: A Dissent," *American Political Science Review* 70 (1976).

Casper, Jonathan D. "The Supreme Court and National Policy-Making," *American Political Science Review* 70 (1976).

Chamberlain, Daniel H. "Osborn v. The Bank of the United States," *Harvard Law Review* 1 (December 1887).

Coleman, William C. "The State as Defendant," *Harvard Law Review* 31 (December 1917).

Corwin, Edward S. "National Power and State Interposition," in *Selected Essays in Constitutional Law* 3 (Chicago: Foundation Press, 1938).

Cummings, Homer. "Progress of the President's Plan for Judicial Reform" (Washington: U. S. Government Printing Office, 1937).

Dahl, Robert A. "Decision-Making in a Democracy: The Supreme Court as a National Policy-Maker," *Journal of Public Law* 6 (1957).

Dodd, William E. "Chief Justice Marshall and Virginia, 1813–1821," *The American Historical Review* 12 (July 1907).

Douglas, William O. "The Dissent: A Safeguard of Democracy," *Journal of the American Judicature Society* 32 (December 1948).

Fairman, Charles. "The Retirement of Federal Judges," *Harvard Law Review* 31 (1939).

Farrand, Max. "The Judiciary Act of 1801," *The American Historical Review* 5 (July 1900).

Freidel, Frank. "The Election of 1932," in *The Coming to Power,* ed. Arthur M. Schlesinger and Fred Israel (New York: Chelsea House, 1971).

Funston, Richard. "The Supreme Court and Critical Elections," *American Political Science Review* 69 (1975).

Goldberg, Arthur J., Thomas E. Harris, and David E. Feller. "Brief for the Congress of Industrial Organizations as Amicus Curiae in *Gebhart* v. *Belton*," submitted to the Supreme Court of the United States, October Term, 1953.

Goodman, Paul. "The First American Party System," in *The American Party Systems: Stages of Political Development,* ed. W. N. Chambers and W. D. Burnham (New York: Oxford University Press, 1975).

Handberg, Roger, and Harold F. Hill, Jr. "Court Curbing, Court Reversals, and Judicial Review: The Supreme Court v. Congress," *Law and Society Review* 14 (1980).

King, Michael R., and Lester G. Seligman. "Critical Elections, Congressional Recruitment and Public Policy," in *Elite Recruitment in Democratic Politics: Comparative Studies Across Nations,* ed. Heinz Eulau and Moshe M. Czudnowski (New York: John Wiley, 1976).

Leuchtenberg, William E. "Franklin D. Roosevelt's Supreme 'Court-Packing' Plan," in *Essays on the New Deal,* ed. Harold M. Hollingsworth and William F. Holmes (Austin: University of Texas Press, 1969).

————. "The Origins of Franklin D. Roosevelt's 'Court-Packing' Plan," *The Supreme Court Review* (Chicago: University of Chicago Press, 1966).

McCaffree, Floyd E. *The Nomination and Confirmation of Justices of the Supreme Court of the United States, 1789–1949* (Ann Arbor, Mich.: Unpublished Doctoral Dissertation, University of Michigan, 1938).

McHargue, Daniel S. *Appointments to the Supreme Court of the United States: The Factors that Affected Appointments, 1789–1932* (Los Angeles: Unpublished Doctoral Dissertation, University of California, 1949).

Mendelson, Wallace. "Judicial Review and Party Politics," *Vanderbilt Law Review* 12 (1959).
Morrison, Elting. "The Election of 1860," in *The Coming to Power*, op. cit.

Nagel, Stuart S. "Curbing the Court: The Politics of Congressional Reaction" and "Curbing the Court: The Politics of Judicial Review," in *The Legal Process from a Behavioral Perspective* (Homewood, Ill.: Dorsey Press, 1969).
Nichols, Roy F., and Philip S. Klein. "The Election of 1856," in *The Coming to Power*, op. cit.
Niles, Hezekiah. *Niles Weekly Register*, XIV–XVI (Niles, Ohio, 1811).

Phillips, Ulrich B. "Georgia and State Rights," *Annual Report of the American History Association* 2 (1901).
Pomerantz, Sidney I. "The Election of 1876," in *The Coming to Power*, op. cit.
Prewitt, Kenneth, and William McAllister. "Changes in the American Executive Elite, 1930–1970," in *Elite Recruitment in Democratic Politics*, op. cit.

Remini, Robert V. "The Election of 1828," in *The Coming To Power*, op. cit.
Rezneck, Samuel. "The Depression of 1819–1822, a Social History," *The American Historical Review* 39 (October 1933).

Schmidhauser, John R. "Age and Judicial Behavior—American Higher Appellate Judges" and "When and Why Justices Leave the Supreme Court," Chapters 9 and 10 in *The Politics of Age*, ed. Wilma Donahue and Clark Tibbets (Ann Arbor: University of Michigan Press, 1962).
_____. "Judicial Behavior and the Sectional Crisis of 1837–1860," *Journal of Politics* 23 (1961).
_____. "'States' Rights' and the Origin of the Supreme Court's Power as Arbiter in Federal–State Relations," *Wayne State University Law Review* 4 (Spring 1958).

Tunnell, George. "The Legislative History of the Second Income Tax Law," *Journal of Political Economy* 3 (June 1895).

Warren, Charles. "The First Decade of the Supreme Court," *University of Chicago Law Review* 7.
_____. "Legislative and Judicial Attacks on the Supreme Court of the United States—a History of the 25th Section of the Judiciary Act," *American Law Review* 47 (1913).
_____. "New Light on the History of the Federal Judiciary Act of 1789," *Harvard Law Review* 37 (June 1940).
Westin, Alan. "The Supreme Court, The Populist Movement, and the Campaign of 1896," *Journal of Politics* 15 (February 1953).
Wickersham, George W. "Federal Control of Interstate Commerce," *Harvard Law Review* 23 (February 1910).

Index